CHILDREN

ELEVENTH EDITION

John W. Santrock

University of Texas at Dallas

Mc Graw Hill

*Connect
Learn
Succeed*™

The McGraw-Hill Companies

Connect
Learn
Succeed™

Published by McGraw-Hill, an imprint of The McGraw-Hill Companies, Inc., 1221 Avenue of the Americas, New York, NY 10020. Copyright © 2010, 2008, 2007, 2005, 2003, 2001, 1998. All rights reserved. No part of this publication may be reproduced or distributed in any form or by any means, or stored in a database or retrieval system, without the prior written consent of The McGraw-Hill Companies, Inc., including, but not limited to, in any network or other electronic storage or transmission, or broadcast for distance learning.

This book is printed on acid-free paper.

3 4 5 6 7 8 9 0 DOW/DOW 9 8 7 6 5 4 3 2 1

ISBN: 978-0-07-353200-4
MHID: 0-07-353200-2

Vice President Editorial: *Michael Ryan*
Executive Director: *Beth Mejia*
Publisher: *Michael Sugarman*
Executive Editor: *Krista Bettino*
Executive Marketing Manager: *James R. Headley*
Marketing Manager: *Yasuko Okada*
Marketing Specialist: *Rebecca Saidlower*
Director of Development: *Nancy Crochiere*
Developmental Editor: *Barbara A. Conover*
Editorial Coordinator: *Megan Stotts*
Production Editors: *Melissa Williams/Marilyn Rothenberger*
Manuscript Editor: *Beatrice Sussman*
Permissions Editor: *Marty Moga*
Interior Design: *Pam Verros*
Photo Research: *LouAnn Wilson*
Supplements Development Editor: *Sarah Colwell*
Senior Production Supervisor: *Tandra Jorgensen*
Composition: *9.5/12 Meridien by Aptara®, Inc.*
Printing: *RR Donnelley*

Credits: The credits section for this book begins on page 633 and is considered an extension of the copyright page.

Library of Congress Cataloging-in-Publication Data

Santrock, John W.
    Children / John W. Santrock. — 11th ed.
        p. cm.
    Includes biographical references and indexes
    ISBN: 978-0-07-353200-4; ISBN: 0-07-353200-2 (alk. paper)
    1. Child development. 2. Adolescence. I. Title.
HQ767.9.S268 2009
305.23—dc22

2009035320

The Internet addresses listed in the text were accurate at the time of publication. The inclusion of a Web site does not indicate an endorsement by the authors or McGraw-Hill, and McGraw-Hill does not guarantee the accuracy of the information presented at these sites.

With special appreciation to my grandchildren:
Jordan, Alex, and Luke

Jordan Bowles

Alex and Luke, the Bellucci Brothers

About the Author

John W. Santrock

John Santrock received his Ph.D. from the University of Minnesota in 1973. He taught at the University of Charleston and the University of Georgia before joining the program in psychology and human development at the University of Texas at Dallas, where he currently teaches a number of undergraduate courses and was given the university's Effective Teaching Award in 2006.

John has been a member of the editorial boards of *Child Development* and *Developmental Psychology*. His research on father custody is widely cited and used in expert witness testimony to promote flexibility and alternative considerations in custody disputes. John also has authored these exceptional McGraw-Hill texts: *Psychology* (seventh edition), *Adolescence* (thirteenth edition), *Life-Span Development* (twelfth edition), *Topical Life-Span Development* (fifth edition), *Educational Psychology* (fourth edition).

For many years, John was involved in tennis as a player, teaching professional, and coach of professional tennis players. He has been married for more than 40 years to his wife, Mary Jo, who is a Realtor. He has two daughters—Tracy, who also is a Realtor, and Jennifer, who is a medical sales specialist at Medtronic. He has one granddaughter, Jordan, age 18, and two grandsons, Alex, age 5, and Luke, age 3. Tracy recently completed the New York Marathon, and Jennifer was in the top 100 ranked players on the Women's Professional Tennis Tour. In the last decade, John also has spent time painting expressionist art.

John Santrock, teaching in his undergraduate course

Brief Contents

Contents

SECTION 2 BEGINNINGS 56

SECTION 3 INFANCY 140

SECTION 4 EARLY CHILDHOOD 250

CHAPTER 10
Socioemotional Development in Early Childhood 312

SECTION 5 MIDDLE AND LATE CHILDHOOD 350

CHAPTER 11
Physical Development in Middle and Late Childhood 352

SECTION 6 ADOLESCENCE 460

CHAPTER 16

Socioemotional Development in Adolescence 528

Expert Consultants

Children's development has become an enormous, complex field and no single author, or even several authors, can possibly keep up with all of the rapidly changing content in the many different areas of children's development. To solve this problem, author John Santrock sought the input of leading experts about content in many different areas of children's development. The experts provided detailed evaluations and recommendations in their area(s) of expertise. The biographies and photographs of the experts follow.

Martha Ann Bell

Dr. Bell is a leading expert in developmental cognitive neuroscience. She currently is a professor of psychology at Virginia Tech University. Dr. Bell obtained her Ph.D. in human development from the University of Maryland. Her research focuses on developmental changes in the brain's frontal lobe using both behavioral and electrophysiological methods. Dr. Bell's current work, funded by NIH/NICHD, centers on individual differences in the development of working memory and inhibitory control during infancy and early childhood. Dr. Bell is editor of *Infancy*, the official journal of the International Society on Infant Studies, and she is a Fellow of the American Psychological Association, Division 7 (Developmental). Her research has been published in journals such as *Developmental Psychobiology, Developmental Neuropsychology, Child Development*, and *Brain and Cognition*. Dr. Bell has contributed chapters to several edited books that highlight developmental neuroscience research, including most recently *Human Behavior, Learning, and the Developing Brain* and *Short- and Long-Term Memory in Infancy and Early Childhood*.

> *The content on the brain and its development in each section is outstanding. It is clear that Professor Santrock takes great care in writing this textbook because the work discussed is the most current in the field and the references are top-notch and very appropriate for this undergraduate text.*
>
> —DR. MARTHA ANN BELL

John Bates

Dr. Bates is one of the world's leading experts on infant temperament. He currently is a professor in psychology and brain sciences at Indiana University. Dr. Bates received his undergraduate degree in psychology at the University of Washington and his Ph.D. in clinical psychology at UCLA, with minors in developmental and social psychology. A major focus of his research is the development of behavior problems versus positive adjustment. Dr. Bates has especially been interested in the role of children's temperament characteristics, in combination with experiences, such as parenting. Most of his research has been longitudinal in nature, including one study from age 6 months to 17 years, another study from age 5 to age 25 (which includes analyses of temperament-environment interactions, and also gene-environment interactions), and yet another study from age 30 months to 42 months.

> *. . . the chapter (7) hits the most important topics in a generally interesting and easy-to-read way. It is both rooted in the "classic" history of the topic and conversant with the most recent research. This is impressive. . . . Nice work. Thanks for asking my opinion.*
>
> —DR. JOHN BATES

Stephanie Rowley

Dr. Rowley is a leading expert on the roles of ethnicity and parenting in children's development. She currently is a professor in development psychology and the combined program in education and psychology at the University of Michigan. Her research focuses on the influence of race- and gender-related attitudes and beliefs on the development of academic self-views. Dr. Rowley's research also emphasizes parents' roles in the development of these attitudes. Her recent projects examine the development of racial identity, race-related stereotypes, and racial socialization across the transition to middle school and the role of African American mothers' race-related experiences in predicting socialization strategies during the transition to first grade.

Paul Hastings

Dr. Hastings is a leading expert on children's socioemotional development. He currently is a professor in the Department of Psychology at the University of California—Davis and an adjunct professor at Concordia University in Montreal. Dr. Hastings obtained his Ph.D. in applied developmental psychology from the University of Toronto. His research interests are centered on the joint contributions of physiology and socialization to children's adaptive and maladaptive trajectories of socioemotional development. In particular, he studies young children's parasympathetic regulation of cardiac activity, or vagal tone, in relation to their experiences of maternal and paternal child rearing, to predict the development of emotion regulation, empathic concern for others, and social competence. He recently co-edited (with Joan Grusec) the *Handbook of Socialization*.

I reviewed Chapters 1, 7, 10, 13, 14, 15, and 16 of the latest edition of John Santrock's textbook, Children. *The chapters are uniformly excellent. His additions and alterations have only strengthened what was already an outstanding child development textbook. . . . He has made great effort to connect the science of child development research to real-world issues. The implications of research for child care, career choices, and social policy are insightful and informative. I am particularly impressed by the careful and balanced inclusion of diversity issues, including cultural, racial, ethnic, gender, and sexual diversity, into so many facets of developmental science. This will benefit our increasingly diverse student populations to see how their own experiences are beginning to be reflected in developmental science, and help all students to approach the topic of child development with broader and more open minds.*

—DR. PAUL HASTINGS

Barbara Alexander Pan

Dr. Pan is a leading expert on children's language development. She currently is an instructor research associate at the Harvard Graduate School of Education. Dr. Pan obtained her Ph.D. in developmental psychology from Boston University. Her research efforts over the last 15 years have focused on children's early language development, its link to other domains of development, and how it is related to later language and emergent literacy. She has been active in the national evaluation of Early Head Start, the federally funded intervention program for low-income families with children from birth to age 3. Dr. Pan is currently principal investigator on a federally funded grant on the early vocabulary development of Spanish-English bilingual toddlers. In both the Early Head Start project and her current research, she seeks to discover information that can improve the language development of at-risk children from low-income and minority families.

. . . the sections dealing with language development are accurate, representative of the field (though necessarily selective), and presented in a way that should be accessible to undergraduates.

—DR. BARBARA ALEXANDER PAN

Marika Ripke

Dr. Ripke is a leading expert on improving services for children and families, especially children in poverty. She obtained her Ph.D. in human development and family sciences from the University of Texas at Austin. Dr. Ripke currently works as a research scientist at the University of Hawaii's Center on the Family, where she directed the Hawaii Kids Count project and a project aimed at improving services to homeless populations in Hawaii. She has published several articles in professional journals such as *Child Development, New Directions for Youth Development,* and *Hülili: Multidisciplinary Research on Hawaiian Well-Being.* Dr. Ripke also recently co-edited (with Aletha Huston) a book entitled *Development Contexts in Middle Childhood.*

I found the chapters "Socioemotional Development in Infancy" [7], "Socioemotional Development in Early Childhood" [10], and "Socioemotional Development in Middle and Late Childhood" [13] to be comprehensive and well organized. The discussion questions are thought-provoking and a valuable addition.

—DR. MARIKA RIPKE

Janet DiPietro

Dr. DiPietro is one of the world's leading experts on prenatal development. She currently is the Associate Dean for Research at the Johns Hopkins School of Public Health and a professor in the Department of Population, Family and Reproductive Health. Dr. DiPietro is a development psychologist whose NIH-supported research focuses on the development of the human fetus. She is the author of numerous scientific articles on fetal development, including the manner in which fetal neurobehavioral development sets the stage for later child development as well as the role of prenatal maternal physiological and psychological factors in affecting both prenatal and postnatal child development.

> . . . I think the chapter (3) reads well and is engaging.
>
> —DR. JANET DIPIETRO

Lise Youngblade

Dr. Youngblade is a leading expert on adolescent development. She currently is a professor and department head in the Department of Human Development and Family Studies at Colorado State University. Dr. Youngblade is an applied developmental scientist whose areas of specialization include child and adolescent socioemotional development; access to health care for vulnerable youth, such as children with special health-care needs and adolescents; program evaluation; and analysis of developmental processes in applied contexts, such as low income and poverty, homelessness, child abuse, child care and maternal employment, and health care. Dr. Youngblade has published over 50 peer-reviewed papers and coauthored a book on the balance of maternal employment and children's well-being. Her work has been funded by various federal agencies such as the Maternal and Child Health Bureau, the Administration for Children and Families, the Agency for Healthcare Research and Quality, and the National Science Foundation. Youngblade is a past co-editor of the *Journal of Family Relations* and is currently on the editorial board of *Developmental Psychology*.

> . . . I really like John Santrock's books—I haven't taught an undergraduate course for several years now, but I have used his books previously, and reading these chapters reminded me of the fact that I liked them. Mainly, I find that students read his texts and find them accessible.
>
> —DR. LISE YOUNGBLADE

Preface

Children have a very special place in every society because they are every society's future. The study of development gives those who care for children many tools for improving the lives of children throughout the world and, therefore, contributing to a better future for humankind. This is an ambitious goal, but not an impossible one. As research in children's development has progressed and the information it offers is applied to family, educational, health, child care, and a variety of other contexts, it becomes clear that developmentalists can make a difference in children's lives.

In a broad sense, this text seeks to convey a clear understanding of what we know about children's development, how we arrived at this level of understanding, and how research in children's development can be applied in the various settings in which children develop. To achieve this goal, I have continued to emphasize and update *Children* in three main areas:

1. Research and content
2. Applications
3. Accessibility and interest

RESEARCH AND CONTENT

Six ways I have attempted to provide students with an understanding of research and content on children's development focus on (1) research coverage, (2) *Research in Children's Development* interludes, (3) expert consultants, (4) diversity, (5) nature and nurture, and (6) the brain.

Research Coverage

Above all, a text on children's development must include a solid research foundation. The eleventh edition of *Children* presents the latest, most contemporary research and has more than 1,200 citations from 2007, 2008, 2009, and 2010. Coverage has been extensively updated and expanded throughout the book.

Research in Children's Development Interludes

The *Research in Children's Development* interludes provide students with a more detailed look at research, either a single research study or a program of research studies focused on a topic related to the content in the chapter. One new *Research in Children's Development* interlude, "The Perspective Taking and Moral Motivation of Bullies, Bully-Victims, Victims, and Prosocial Children" (Gasser & Keller, 2009)," appears in Chapter 13, "Socioemotional Development in Middle and Late Childhood." Another new *Research in Children's Development* interlude in the eleventh edition

of the text is in Chapter 16 and focuses on Fast Track, a 10-year intervention that attempts to lower the risk of juvenile delinquency and other problems (Dodge & the Conduct Problems Prevention Research Group, 2007; Slough & others, 2008; Thomas & others, 2009). Also the *Research in Children's Development* interlude "Tiffany Field's Research on Massage Therapy" in Chapter 4 expands and updates the massage therapy research of Tiffany Field and her colleagues (Field, Diego, & Hernandez-Reif, 2008; Field & Diego, 2008), including new research Figure 4.5.

Expert Research Consultants

Children's development has become an enormous, complex field and no single author, or even several authors, can possibly be an expert in many different areas of children's development. To solve this problem, I sought the input of leading experts in many different research and applied areas of children's development. The experts provided me with detailed evaluations and recommendations for a chapter(s) in their area(s) of expertise. The expert research consultants for *Children*, eleventh edition, were:

Expert	*Chapters and Topics*
Martha Ann Bell *Virginia Tech*	Development of the brain throughout the book
John Bates *Indiana University*	Socioemotional development (Chapter 7)
Stephanie Rowley *University of Michigan*	Diversity and family processes throughout the book
Paul Hastings *Concordia University*	Topics of interest throughout the book
Barbara Alexander Pan *Harvard University*	Language development throughout the book
Marika Ripke *University of Hawaii at Manoa*	Socioemotional development throughout the book
Janet DiPietro *Johns Hopkins University*	Prenatal development (Chapter 3)
Lise Youngblade *Colorado State University*	Adolescence (Chapters 14, 15, and 16)

Diversity

Diversity is an extremely important aspect of children's development. Every effort was made to explore diversity issues in a sensitive manner in each chapter and to expand and update research content related to diversity. And each chapter has a *Diversity in Children's Development* interlude that focuses on a diversity topic related to the chapter's content. The *Diversity* interludes include "The Increased Diversity of Adopted Children and Adoptive Parents" (Chapter 2); "Early Childhood Education in Japan and Developing Countries" (Chapter 9); "Improving Resources of Schools and Families in Impoverished Areas" (new) (Chapter 13); and "Cross-Cultural Comparisons of Secondary Schools" (updated and expanded) (Chapter 15).

Nature and Nurture

I have extensively expanded and updated the discussion of nature and nurture in this new edition of *Children*. Following are some of the many new additions of material on nature and nurture:

- New discussion of gene-gene interaction (Chen & others, 2009; Jylhava & others, 2009) in Chapter 2

- Main new section and coverage of the concept of G × E, which involves the interaction of a specified measured variation in the DNA sequence and a specific measured aspect of the environment (Cheok & others, 2009; Diamond, 2009), including discussion of recent research studies of G × E (Caspers & others, 2009; Barry, Kochanska, & Philibert, 2009) in Chapter 2

- New final commentary on the interaction of heredity and environment that emphasizes development as a co-construction of biology, culture, and the individual in Chapter 2

- New main section, Nature, Nurture, and Perceptual Development, examining nativist and empiricist views of perception (Johnson & others, 2009 a, b, c; Slater & others, 2009) in Chapter 5

- New coverage of Baillargeon's (2008; Baillargeon & others, 2009) innate bias view as expressed in the principle of persistence in Chapter 6

- New section on the nature-nurture issue in infant cognitive development, including discussion of Elizabeth Spelke's core knowledge approach (Spelke & Kinzler, 2009) and Mark Johnson's (2008) criticism of Spelke's approach in Chapter 6

- New coverage of recent research linking autism spectrum disorders to genetic mutations on chromosome 16 in approximately 1 out of 100 cases of these disorders (Weiss & others, 2008) in Chapter 11

- New sections on nature-nurture and developmental changes and domain-specific giftedness in the discussion of children who are gifted in Chapter 12

The Brain

Research on the development of the brain is expanding at a rapid pace. Following is a description of some of the new material on the development of the brain in this new edition of *Children*:

- New information about the rapidly emerging fields of developmental cognitive neuroscience and developmental social neuroscience (Diamond, Casey, & Munakata, 2010) in Chapter 1

- Updated coverage of brain development in the prenatal period (Moulson & Nelson, 2008; Nelson, 2009) in Chapter 3

- Updated discussion of the development of the brain in infancy (Nelson, 2009) in Chapter 5

- New material on neurotransmitters and temperament (Pauli-Pott & others, 2009) in Chapter 7

- Main new section, Developmental Social Neuroscience and Attachment, including information about recent theory and views on the role of brain neuroanatomy, neurotransmitters, and hormones in the development of mother-infant attachment (Bales & Carter 2009; de Haan & Gunnar, 2009; Gonzalez, Atkinson, & Fleming, 2009) in Chapter 7

- New discussion of Mark Johnson and his colleagues' (2009) view on how the prefrontal cortex likely orchestrates the functioning of other neural regions during development in Chapter 11

- New research documenting a three-year delay in the thickening of the cerebral cortex in children with ADHD, including new Figure 11.7 in Chapter 11

- Description of the increasing research interest in the role that neurotransmitters such as serotonin might play in ADHD (Levy, 2009; Roessner & others, 2009) in Chapter 11

- New main section, The Neuroscience of Intelligence, including a discussion of the links between brain size and intelligence, recent research on a distributed network involving the frontal and parietal lobes and the neural network's link to intelligence (Colom & others, 2009), connection between a higher level of intelligence and a higher volume of gray matter in the brain (Luders & others, 2009), and new material on the role of neurological speed in intelligence in Chapter 12

- New coverage of recent research on changes in the brain in adolescence and resistance to peer pressure (Paus & others, 2008) in Chapter 14

- New description of how information about changes in the brain during adolescence reflect the rapidly emerging field of developmental social neuroscience (de Haan & Gunnar, 2009) in Chapter 14

- New discussion of social contexts, the brain's reward pathways, and adolescent decision making (Steinberg, 2008) in Chapter 15

APPLICATIONS

It is important not only to present the scientific foundation of children's development to students, but also to demonstrate that research has real-world applications, to include many applied examples of concepts, and to give students a sense that the field of children's development has personal meaning for them. Here are some of the ways I incorporated applications in the text:

- *How Would You . . . ? Questions.* New to this edition, these questions in the margins of each chapter highlight issues involving five main career areas of children's development: psychology, human development and family studies, education, health professions (such as nursing and pediatrics), and social work. The *How Would You . . . ?* questions ensure that this book orients students to the concepts that are important to their understanding of children's development. I have asked instructors specializing in these fields to contribute *How Would You . . . ?* questions for each chapter. Strategically placed in the margin next to relevant chapter content, these questions highlight essential ideas for students to take away from chapter content.

- *Applications of research in children's development to health, parenting, and education* receive special attention throughout the text. Following are just a few of these many applications: coverage of highly successful home nurse visiting program, the Nurse Family Partnership (Olds & others, 2007; Zielinski, Eckenrode, & Olds, 2009) in Chapter 3; discussion of recent research on maternal depression and its link to negative birth outcomes (Diego & others, 2009; Field & others, 2009) in Chapter 3; inclusion of recent information about changes in and effectiveness of various aspects of the WIC (Special Supplemental Nutrition Program for Women, Infants, and Children) program (Black & others, 2009; Olson & others, 2009a, b) in Chapter 5; much expanded and updated material on emergent literacy skills in young children (Forget-Dubois & others, 2009; Korat, 2009; Rodriguez & others, 2009) and discussion of NAEYC's (2009) extensively revised and updated guidelines for developmentally appropriate education in Chapter 9; extensive updating of research on overweight children with a special focus on weight reduction intervention (Wells & others, 2008), new information about the most effective treatment of ADHD (Fabiano, 2009; Svanborg & others, 2009), and significantly updated and expanded material on autism spectrum disorders (Anderson & others, 2009; Gong & others, 2009) in Chapter 11; new research on improving the lives of children who are gifted with an emphasis on the domain-specific aspects of giftedness (Keating, 2009; Matthews, 2009) in Chapter 12; much expanded and updated research on juvenile delinquency, including a recent parenting intervention that was effective in lowering delinquency (Forgatch & others, 2009) in Chapter 16; and new material on social policy and improving the lives of children in poverty and low-income circumstances in numerous chapters (Fiscella & Kitzman, 2009; McLoyd & others, 2009).

- *Caring for Children* interludes in every chapter that outline important ways to improve the lives of children. *Caring for Children* interludes for this edition include "Strategies for Parenting, Educating, and Interacting with Children Based on Erikson's Theory" (new) (Chapter 1); "From Waterbirth to Music Therapy" (Chapter 4); "Improving the Nutrition of Infants, and Young Children living in Low-Income Families" (Chapter 5); "Communicating with Children About Divorce" (Chapter 10); "Increasing Children's Self-Esteem" (Chapter 13); and "Strategies for Parenting Adolescents" (Chapter 16)

- Every chapter also has at least one *Careers in Children's Development* profile that describes an individual whose career relates to the chapter's content. Most of the *Careers* profiles include a photograph of the person at work. In addition, the Careers Appendix titled "Careers in Children's Development," which follows Chapter 1, describes a number of careers in the education/research, clinical/counseling, medical/nursing/physical development, and family/relationship categories.

- At the end of each chapter, two features—*Making a Difference* and *Resources for Improving Children's Lives*—provide valuable information about ways to improve children's lives.

- On the book's Web site, students can hone their decision-making skills by completing exercises related to children's health and well-being, parenting, and education.

CHAPTER-BY-CHAPTER CHANGES

I made a number of changes in all 16 chapters of *Children,* eleventh edition. Highlights of these changes follow.

CHAPTER 1
INTRODUCTION

- Significant updating of research and citations

- Revised definition of gender based on expert consultant Diane Halpern's input

- Updated poverty statistics for U.S. children (Federal Interagency Forum on Child and Family Statistics, 2008)

- New comparison of child poverty rates in the United States, Canada, and Sweden

- Updated coverage of improving family policy (Balsano, Theokas, & Bobek, 2009; Fiscella & Kitzman, 2009; Hildebrandt & Stevens, 2009)

- Updated information about the Minnesota Family Investment Program (2009), including coverage of a current study that is examining the influence of specific family services on families at high risk for engaging in child maltreatment

- Description of recent research revealing the cumulative effects of poverty on physiological indices of stress in children (Evans & Kim, 2007)

- Much expanded and updated coverage of connecting biological, cognitive, and socioemotional processes (Diamond, 2009; Diamond, Casey, & Munakata, 2010)

- New description of the rapidly emerging fields of developmental cognitive neuroscience and developmental social neuroscience to illustrate the interface of biological, cognitive, and socioemotional processes (Diamond, Casey, and Munakata, 2010; Johnson & others, 2009)

- New *Caring for Children* interlude, "Strategies for Parenting, Educating, and Interacting with Children Based on Erikson's Theory"

- New *How Would You . . . ?* inserts in margin to stimulate students to reflect on applications of a concept

CHAPTER 2
BIOLOGICAL BEGINNINGS

- Considerable rewriting and editing of content for improved clarification and student learning

- Extensive research and citation updating

- New Figure 2.3 of sperm penetrating an egg
- Description of recent research on the characteristics of boys with Klinefelter syndrome (Ross & others, 2008)
- Updated and expanded coverage of fragile X syndrome, including a new photograph of a boy with fragile X syndrome (Ono, Farzin, & Hagerman, 2008)
- Inclusion of recent research on cognitive deficits in boys with fragile X syndrome (Hooper & others, 2008)
- New coverage of the underutilization of the only drug (hydroxyurea) approved to treat sickle-cell anemia in adolescents and adults, and current research that is under way to determine if the drug is effective in treating babies
- Description of a recent research review on how genetic counseling clients interpret risk (Sivell & others, 2008)
- New section on the extensive recent research on the potential for using noninvasive prenatal diagnosis (NIPD) as an alternative to chorionic villus sampling and amniocentesis (Avent & others, 2008; Finning & Chitty, 2008)
- New Figure 2.8 showing a fetal fMRI
- New coverage of a recent national study on the influence of the woman's age on the success rate of in vitro fertilization, including new Figure 2.9
- Description of a recent research review on the self-esteem of adopted and nonadopted children, and transracial and same-race adoptees (Juffer & van Ijzendoorn, 2007)
- New material on the concept of gene-gene interaction (Chen & others, 2009; Jylhava & others, 2009)
- Description of epigenetic research on early rearing experiences and their alteration of gene expression with that expression being linked to later behavior (Pauli-Pott & others, 2009)
- Inclusion of information based on a recent research review of the main risk factors in the future health of babies born through assisted reproduction techniques (Basatemur & Sutcliffe, 2008)
- Updated and expanded discussion of heredity-environment interaction (Barry, Kochanska, & Philibert, 2008; Shen, 2009)
- New section and coverage of the concept of G × E, which involves the interaction of a specific measured variation in the DNA sequence and a specific measured aspect of the environment (Cheok & others, 2009; Diamond, 2009)
- Discussion of a recent G × E interaction study on the gene *5-HTTLPR* and how the long version of the gene likely serves a protective function in children's parental loss (Caspers & others, 2009)
- New description of recent research on secure attachment in infancy serving as a protective factor in the development of self-regulation in early childhood for children who have the long version of the *5-HTTLPR* gene (Barry, Kochanska, & Philibert, 2009)
- New coverage of the field of pharmacogenetics and how it reflects G × E (Berlin, Paul, & Vesell, 2009; Lima & others, 2009)

- New final paragraph on the interaction of heredity and environment interaction that emphasizes development as a co-construction of biology, culture, and the individual
- Multiple new *How Would You . . . ?* reflective questions for students related to different career disciplines

CHAPTER 3
PRENATAL DEVELOPMENT

- Extensive editing and updating of chapter based on recommendations by expert consultants Maria Hernandez-Reif and Janet DiPietro
- Considerable research and citation updating
- Updated coverage of brain development in the prenatal period (Moulson & Nelson, 2008, Nelson, 2009)
- New section, What Are Some Important Strategies That Enhance the Expectant Mother's Health and Prenatal Care?, emphasizing nutrition, exercise, and prenatal care
- Description of two recent research studies indicating that exercise in pregnancy is linked to a reduced risk of preterm birth (Hegaard & others, 2008; Juhl & others, 2008)
- Extensively revised and updated *Caring for Children* interlude, "Exercise Guidelines for Expectant Mothers," based on the recommendations of the American College of Obstetricians and Gynecologists (2008)
- New *Careers in Children's Development* profile, "Rachel Thompson, Obstetrician/Gynecologist"
- Coverage of a highly successful home nurse visiting program, the Nurse Family Partnership, conducted by David Olds and his colleagues (2007, Zielinski, Eckenrode, & Olds, 2009), that has produced positive outcomes for mothers and their children
- Discussion of recent research on a home visitation program that reduced the incidence of low birth weight infants (Lee & others, 2009)
- New description of what the field of behavioral teratology involves (DiPietro, 2008)
- Inclusion of information from a recent research review of aspirin and reproductive outcomes (James, Brancazio, & Price, 2008)
- Coverage of a recent study on caffeine intake during pregnancy and risk for miscarriage (Weng, Odouli, & Li, 2008)
- Change of label from FAS to FASD (fetal alcohol spectrum disorders) in keeping with recently developed terminology and expanded coverage of FASD (Olson, King, & Jirikowic, 2008)
- Description of recent research on impaired memory development in children with FASD (Pei & others, 2008)
- Inclusion of recent research on the extent of reduction in alcohol intake in non-Latino White and African American women when they become pregnant (Morris & others, 2008)
- Coverage of a recent review that concluded tobacco is a key contributor to intrauterine growth retardation (Romo, Carceller, & Tobajas, 2009)

- Description of recent research on maternal smoking during pregnancy and inattention/hyperactivity in children (Knopik, 2009; Obel & others, 2009; Pinkhardt & others, 2009)

- Coverage of recent research on the harmful effects of cocaine use during pregnancy on growth, language development, and attention (Accornero & others, 2007; Lewis & others, 2007; Richardson, Goldschmidt, & Willford, 2008)

- Description of a recent study linking prenatal cocaine exposure to an increased likelihood of being in special education and receiving support services (Levine & others, 2008)

- Inclusion of information about a recent study that revealed negative neonatal outcomes following exposure to metnamphetamine in the prenatal period (Smith & others, 2008)

- Description of a recent study on prenatal marijuana exposure and lower intelligence in childhood (Goldschmidt & others, 2008)

- Inclusion of recent research on continuous versus late methadone treatment during pregnancy and neonatal outcomes (Burns & others, 2007)

- Discussion of recent research on maternal lead exposure during pregnancy and infant mental development (Hu & others, 2007)

- Coverage of a recent analysis proposing that fetal programming from an overweight pregnant woman is likely linked to the offspring's being overweight in childhood and adolescence (McMillen & others, 2008)

- Updated and expanded material on the offspring of diabetic mothers (Gluck & others, 2009; Eriksson, 2009)

- Coverage of a recent study of a link between children who experienced gestational diabetes and adiposity at 3 years of age (Wright & others, 2009)

- Inclusion of recent research on a link between folic acid and a reduction in preterm birth (Bukowski & others, 2008)

- Updated research on fetal mercury exposure and developmental outcomes (Axelrad & others, 2007; Xue & others, 2007)

- Description of a recent research review on maternal stress during pregnancy and negative developmental outcomes in offspring (Talge & others, 2007)

- New discussion of two recent studies on maternal depression and its link to negative prenatal and birth outcomes (Diego & others, 2009; Field & others, 2009)

CHAPTER 4
BIRTH

- Extensive editing and updating of chapter based on recommendations by expert consultant Maria Hernandez-Reif

- Discussion of a recent research review of waterbirth (Cluett & Burns, 2009)

- Description of three recent studies that revealed positive outcomes for the use of acupuncture during labor and delivery

(Borup & others, 2009; Citcovitz & others, 2009; Gaudet & others, 2008)

- Updated coverage of trends in cesarean delivery (National Center for Health Statistics, 2007)

- Description of a recent national study comparing neonatal death rates of cesarean delivery with no labor complications to neonatal deaths rates involving planned vaginal delivery (MacDorman & others, 2008)

- Expanded and updated coverage of cesarean delivery, including when elective cesarean delivery is not recommended and recent research (Greene, 2009; Tita & others, 2009)

- Updated figures on the increasing number of preterm births in the United States (National Center for Health Statistics, 2009)

- Coverage of the factors involved in why poverty continues to contribute to preterm birth in the United States (Nagahawatte & Goldenberg, 2008)

- Considerably expanded and updated material on the consequences of preterm birth (Foster-Cohen & others, 2007; Johnson, 2007)

- Description of recent MRI study of brain deficiencies in children born very preterm (Narberhaus & others, 2008)

- Discussion of three recent studies indicating that low birth weight children have more difficulties in socializing and have different lifestyles as emerging adults and adults than their normal birth weight counterparts (Kajantie & others, 2008; Moster, Lie, & Markestad, 2008; Schmidt & others, 2008)

- Updated research about the use of progestin in reducing the risk of preterm birth (Fonseca & others, 2007; Rouse & others, 2007; Tita & Rouse, 2009)

- Coverage of a recent study that revealed a substantial reduction in preterm birth when women took folic acid for one year prior to delivering (Bukowski & others, 2008)

- New introduction to the section Nurturing Preterm Infants, emphasizing the importance of reducing the risk of low birth weight before it occurs (Lee & others, 2009)

- Discussion of a recent intervention study that improved the development of preterm infants for a number of outcomes (Newnham, Milgrom, & Skouteris, 2009)

- Coverage of two recent studies that found kangaroo care reduces pain responses in preterm infants (Akcan, Yigit, & Atici, 2009; Johnson & others, 2009)

- Description of two recent experimental studies revealing the benefits of kangaroo care (Gathwala, Singh, & Balhara, 2008; Suman, Udani, & Nanavati, 2008)

- Updated coverage of the *Research in Life-Span Development* interlude on Tiffany Field's massage therapy research, including recent research on the effects of massage therapy on preterm infants' stress behaviors with a new Figure 4.5 illustrating the results (Field & Diego, 2008; Field, Diego, & Hernandez-Reif, 2008; Hernandez-Reif, Diego, & Field, 2007)

- New coverage of the sleep deprivation experienced by postpartum women, including new Figure 4.6 (Gunderson & others, 2008; National Sleep Foundation, 2007)

- Expanded and updated description of postpartum mothers' patterns of interaction with their infants (Teti & Towe-Goodman, 2008)

- Coverage of a recent study of mothers' postpartum depression, preterm/full-term infants, and maternal synchrony (Feldman & Eidelman, 2007)

- Description of the unsettled issue of the optimal course of therapy for the depressed, breast feeding mother, and breast fed infant (Field, 2008)

- Discussion of a recent study on the percent of women with postpartum depression who seek help for their depression (McGarry & others, 2009)

- Inclusion of recent research on the beneficial roles of individualized peer-based telephone support and home-based interventions in reducing postpartum depression in women (Dennis & others, 2009; Leis & others, 2009)

- New *Careers in Children's Development* profile: "Diane Sanford, Clinical Psychologist and Postpartum Expert"

- Description of a recent study linking high levels of maternal depression in the postpartum period with infant colic and prolonged crying (Vik & others, 2009)

- Expanded and updated coverage of fathers' adjustment during the postpartum period (Dietz & others, 2009; Smith & Howard, 2008)

CHAPTER 5
PHYSICAL DEVELOPMENT IN INFANCY

- Extensive rewriting and editing of chapter for improved student understanding, including a number of changes based on input from expert consultant Maria Hernandez-Reif

- Updated coverage of the development of the brain (Nelson, 2009)

- New material on which individuals are most often the perpetrators of shaken baby syndrome (National Center on Shaken Baby Syndrome, 2009)

- Updated and expanded material on sleep patterns in infancy (Sadeh, 2008)

- Description of recent research on factors related to infant night waking (DeLeon & Karraker, 2007)

- Expanded discussion of REM sleep in infancy and question raised about whether we can know for sure whether infants dream

- Expanded coverage of developmental changes in infants' eating patterns (Black & Hurley, 2007; Black & Lozoff, 2008)

- Inclusion of material from a recent research review by the American Academy of Pediatrics indicating no link between breast feeding and children's allergies (Greer & others, 2008)

- Extensive updating, revision, and expansion of material on breast feeding based on a recent large-scale research review (Agency for Healthcare Research and Quality, 2007)

- Description of recent research linking longer breast feeding with a lower incidence of metabolic syndrome in midlife women (Ram & others, 2008)

- Discussion of an important issue related to the correlational nature of breast versus bottle feeding studies (Agency for Healthcare Research and Quality, 2007)

- New *Caring for Children* interlude, "Improving the Nutrition of Mothers, Infants, and Young Children in Low-Income Families"

- Recent information about changes in the WIC program for 2009 (Food & Nutrition Service, 2009)

- Inclusion of recent research on the changes and effectiveness of various aspects of the WIC program (Black & others, 2009; Heinig & others, 2009; Olson & others, 2009a, b)

- Description of recent research on infants' walking patterns and their occasional large steps (Badaly & Adolph, 2008)

- Updated coverage of cultural variation in infant motor development (Adolph & Joh, 2009)

- Updated information about the development of visual acuity in young infants (Aslin & Lathrop, 2008)

- New section on the perception of occluded objects

- New material on the age at which infants develop ability to perceive that occluded objects are complete (Slater, Field, & Hernandez-Reif, 2007)

- Discussion of Scott Johnson's (2009a, b, c) view on why infants are able to develop the ability to perceive occluded objects as complete

- New description of a recent study by Bennett Bertenthal and his colleagues (2007) on infants' predictive tracking of briefly occluded moving objects, including new Figure 5.22

- New main section, Nature, Nurture, and Perceptual Development, examining nativist and empiricist views of perception (Arterberry, 2008; Slater & others, 2009)

- Updated and expanded coverage of perceptual-motor coupling, including how infants develop new perceptual-motor couplings.

CHAPTER 6
COGNITIVE DEVELOPMENT IN INFANCY

- New discussion of Baillargeon's (2008; Baillargeon & others, 2009) innate bias view as expressed in the principle of persistence

- Recent revised interpretation of A-not-B error (Clearfield & others, 2006)

- Expanded analysis of object permanence, including Andrew Meltzoff's (2008; Moore & Meltzoff, 2008) criticisms of the violation of expectations method as an accurate measure of object permanence

- Updated and expanded evaluation of Piaget's view of infant cognitive development (Aslin, 2009; Woodward & Needham, 2009)

- New section on the nature-nurture issue in infant cognitive development

- New discussion of Elizabeth Spelke's (2000; Kinzler & Spelke, 2007; Spelke & Kinzler, 2009) core knowledge approach

- New coverage of the intriguing question of whether young infants have a sense of number

- Description of a recent study on the area of the brain activated when 3-month-old infants were observing changes in the number of objects compared with changes in the type of objects (Izard, Dehaene-Lambertz, & Dehaene, 2008)

- Inclusion of criticism of Spelke's core knowledge approach by Mark Johnson (2008)

- Expanded and updated conclusion regarding the focus and most difficult task infant researchers face in determining the influence of nature and nurture (Aslin, 2009)

- Expanded and updated coverage of attention, including developmental changes in orienting/investigative and sustained attention (Courage & Richards, 2008)

- Expanded and updated discussion of habituation and its importance in infant development (Slater, Field, & Hernandez-Reif, 2007)

- New Figure 6.7, indicating how long infants of different ages can remember information (Bauer, 2009)

- Updated and expanded information on Meltzoff's (2007) view of infant imitation

- Expanded and updated coverage of concept formation and categorization in infancy (Booth, 2006; Quinn, 2009)

- New description of the Bayley-III, including its two new scales—socioemotional and adaptive, that are assessed by questionnaires given to the infant's primary caregiver (Lennon & others, 2008)

- Coverage of two recent studies of severely malnourished children and their cognitive development (Kar, Rao, & Chandramouli, 2008; Nahar & others, 2008).

- Inclusion of two recent studies on the prediction of language skills at 24 months of age by joint attention as early as 10 to 11 months (Brooks & Meltzoff, 2008; Mundy & others, 2007)

- Description of recent research on the early development of intense interests in particular categories, including strong gender differences, including new Figure 6.11 (DeLoache, Simcock, & Macari, 2007)

- Expanded and updated coverage of predicting children's intelligence from assessment of habituation in early infancy (Domsch, Lohaus, & Thomas, 2009)

- Revised, updated, and expanded coverage of early language development based on leading experts Beverly Goldfield's and Barbara Pan's recommendations

- Movement of recognizing speech sounds before babbling in the section on early development of language in infancy

- New section on gestures to indicate their importance in early language development and expansion of this topic

- Expanded discussion of infant understanding of words before speaking first word

- Coverage of a recent study indicating the importance of maternal sensitivity in children's language development (Pungello & others, 2009)

- New material on shared book reading and its benefits for infants and toddlers (Raikes & others, 2006; Rodriguez, Hines, & Montiel, 2008)

 **CHAPTER 7
SOCIOEMOTIONAL DEVELOPMENT
IN INFANCY**

- Extensive rewriting of chapter for improved student understanding, including addition of numerous concrete examples of concepts and more descriptions of infants' behaviors and emotions

- Updated and expanded description of separation protest in infants (Kagan, 2008)

- Expanded and updated coverage of infant smiling, including new Figure 7.3 on showing the characteristics of an intense smile by a 6-month-old (Messinger, 2008)

- New discussion of anticipatory smiling in infancy and its link to social competence in early childhood (Parlade & others, 2009)

- New description of cultural variations in how parents handle infant emotions (Cole & Tan, 2007)

- Inclusion of new material on links between infant fear and guilt, empathy, and low aggression in childhood (Rothbart, 2007)

- New coverage of the importance of considering the multiple temperament dimensions of children rather than classifying them on a single dimension (Bates, 2008)

- New discussion of developmental changes in temperament characteristics and the importance of considering the individual differences that emerge from these developmental changes (Bates, 2008; Rothbart & Gartstein, 2008)

- Description of recent research on factors that benefited children with a difficult temperament (Bradley & Corwyn, 2008)

- Description of a recent study indicating an interaction between temperament style and the type of child care young children experience (Pluess & Belsky, 2009)

- New material on a possible link between the neurotransmitter serotonin and an inhibited temperament (Pauli-Pott & others, 2009)

- Expanded coverage of the role of locomotion in social orientation and motivation (Thompson, 2008b).

- Coverage of a recent meta-analysis of studies using the still-face paradigm and links between affect and secure attachment (Mesman, van IJzendoorn, & Bakersman-Kranenburg, 2009)

- Description of a recent study on links between joint attention in infancy and social competence at 30 months of age (Vaughn Van Hecke & others, 2007)

- New summary description of the increasing belief that infants are more socially sophisticated and insightful at earlier ages that previously envisioned (Thompson, 2008a, b; Tomasello, Carpenter, & Liszkowski, 2007)

- New commentary about how recent findings regarding infants' earlier social understanding may be linked to understanding goals and intentions in Bowlby's phase 3 of attachment rather than phase 4 (Thompson, 2008b)
- Discussion of a recent study of maternal sensitive parenting and infant attachment security (Finger & others, 2009)
- New commentary about the most consistent link between early attachment and subsequent development occurring for insecure disorganized babies (Bates, 2008)
- Description of recent research indicating a gene × environment interaction between disorganized attachment, the short version of the serotonin transporter gene—5-*HTTLPR*—and a low level of maternal responsiveness (Spangler & others, 2009)
- Important new section, Developmental Social Neuroscience and Attachment, including recent theory and views on the role of the brain neuroanatomy, neurotransmitters, and hormones in the development of mother-infant attachment (Bales & Carter, 2009; de Haan & Gunnar, 2009; Gonzalez, Atkinson, & Fleming, 2009)
- New Figure 7.9, showing the key brain structures that are likely involved in infant-mother attachment
- Much expanded discussion of fathers and mothers as caregivers
- New coverage of the Aka pygmy culture, where fathers are as involved in infant caregiving as much as mothers are
- Description of a recent study of multiple child-care arrangements and young children's behavioral outcomes (Morrissey, 2009)
- New coverage of John Gottman and his colleagues (2004) Bringing Home Baby project
- Description of recent research on parent-infant synchrony and children's self-regulation (Feldman, 2007)
- Coverage of a recent longitudinal study on infant attachment and cognitive development in the elementary school years (O'Connor & McCartney, 2007)
- New Figure 7.11 on the dramatic increase in the percentage of U.S. fathers staying at home full-time with their children and the results of a recent study of stay-at-home fathers (Rochlen & others, 2008)
- New Figure 7.12 on the primary care arrangements for children under 5 years of age with employed mothers (Clarke-Stewart & Miner, 2008)
- Updated and expanded coverage of family leave policies around the world related to childbirth in the *Diversity in Children's Development* interlude (Tolani & Brooks-Gunn, 2008)
- Inclusion of recent research on the positive outcomes that develop when low-income parents select higher-quality child care (McCartney & others, 2007)
- Expanded and updated material on the important role of sensitive parenting in child outcomes for children in child care (Friedman, Melhuish, & Hill, 2009)

CHAPTER 8
PHYSICAL DEVELOPMENT IN EARLY CHILDHOOD

- Inclusion of information about four recent studies focused on increasing young children's physical activity (Beets & Foley, 2008; Bower & others, 2008; Brown & others, 2009; Trost, Fees, & Dzewaltowski, 2008)
- Updating of the Denver Development Screening Test, which is now in its second edition
- Updated material on young children's art (Golomb, 2008)
- Expanded and updated description of young children's sleep patterns and adjustment (National Sleep Foundation, 2009)
- Inclusion of recent research on a link between inadequate sleep and injuries that require attention in preschool children (Koulouglioti, Cole, & Kitzman, 2008)
- Discussion of a recent study linking sleep problems from 3 to 8 years of age with the early onset of drug use and depression in adolescence (Wong, Brower, & Zucker, 2009)
- Description of a recent longitudinal study on characteristics linked to young children having bad dreams (Simard & others, 2008)
- Inclusion of recent research on bedtime sleep resistance and problem behaviors in children (Carvalho Bos & others, 2009)
- Description of recent research on short sleep duration and being overweight in childhood (Nixon & others, 2008; Patel & Hu, 2008)
- Inclusion of information from a recent national survey of young children's consumption of fat in their diet (Kranz, Lin, & Wagstaff, 2007)
- Inclusion of a recent study that found children's weight at 5 years of age was significantly related to their weight at 9 years of age (Gardner & others, 2009)
- Discussion of a recent study on developmental changes in the percentage of overweight children from 4 to 11 years of age, depending on whether they have lean or obese parents (Semmler & others, 2009)
- Coverage of a recent national study of trends in children's meals eaten outside the home and the percentage of children's meals that exceed the recommended amount of saturated fat and trans fat (Center for Science in the Public Interest, 2008)
- New discussion of the role of caregiver feeding behavior and styles in young children's eating behavior (Black & Hurley, 2007; Black & Lozoff, 2008)
- Coverage of a recent large-scale U.S. study on the percentage of children 2 to 19 years of age who have weight problems and the recent leveling off in overweight categories (Odgen, Carroll, & Flegal, 2008)
- Coverage of a recent study of ethnic variations in being overweight in 3-year-old children (Kimbro, Brooks-Gunn, & McLanahan, 2006)

CHAPTER 9
COGNITIVE DEVELOPMENT IN
EARLY CHILDHOOD

- Revised, improved Figure 9.1 on Piaget's three mountains task, providing students with a better understanding of the concept of egocentrism

- Expanded description of criticisms of Vygotsky (Gauvain, 2008)

- New coverage of advances in executive attention and sustained attention in early childhood (Rothbart & Gartstein, 2008)

- Discussion of a recent study that linked children's attention problems at 54 months of age with a lower level of social skills in peer relations in the first and third grades (NICHD Early Child Care Research Network, 2009)

- New description of exercises used in some European kindergartens to improve young children's attention (Mills & Mills, 2000; Posner & Rothbart, 2007)

- Much expanded and updated coverage of the young child's theory of mind with considerable input from leading expert Candice Mills

- Description of a recent study linking infant attention to 4-year-olds' theory of mind (Wellman & others, 2008)

- Coverage of a recent study linking young children's theory of mind competence with later metamemory skills (Lockl & Schneider, 2007)

- New discussion of reasons to question false-belief understanding as a pivotal point in the development of a theory of mind

- New Figures 9.11 and 9.12, showing stimuli used in theory of mind research

- New section, Theory of Mind and Autism (Harris, 2006; National Autism Association, 2008)

- Updated description of 3-year-olds' phonological advances (Menn & Stoel-Gammon, 2009)

- Expanded and updated coverage of young children's improvements in pragmatics (Aktar & Herold, 2008)

- Expanded discussion of emergent literacy skills in young children, including a recent study linking maternal education with emergent literacy skills (Korat, 2009)

- Coverage of a recent study of key factors in young children's early literacy experiences in low-income families (Rodriguez & others, 2009)

- Description of a recent longitudinal study linking early home environment with early language skills, which in turn predicted school readiness (Forget-Dubois & others, 2009)

- Coverage of a recent study of 4-year-olds that revealed peers' expressive language abilities were positive linked to the 4-year-olds' receptive and expressive language development (Mashburn & others, 2009)

- Movement of section on Young Children's Literacy to the topic of Language Development from Early Childhood Education because of the importance of both families and schools in young children's literacy

- Inclusion of NAEYC's extensively revised and updated guidelines for developmentally appropriate practice (NAEYC, 2009)

- Description of how not all developmentally appropriate programs show significant benefits for children and recent changes in the concept of developmentally appropriate education (Hyson, 2007)

- Updated material on Project Head Start including information about it being the largest federally funded program for U.S. children (Hagen & Lamb-Parker, 2008)

- Coverage of a recent large-scale longitudinal study of school readiness skills/characteristics and later academic achievement (Duncan & others, 2007)

CHAPTER 10
SOCIOEMOTIONAL DEVELOPMENT IN
EARLY CHILDHOOD

- Expanded explanation of why young children have unrealistically positive self-descriptions (Thompson, 2008)

- Description of recent research on the age at which young children take into account the relative frequency of errors informants make in deciding whether to trust the person (Pasquini & others, 2007)

- Reorganization of the discussion of emotional development into these categories based on expert Susan Denham's recommendation: Expressing emotions, understanding emotions, and regulating emotions

- Expanded discussion of advances in young children's understanding of emotions (Cole & others, 2009)

- Coverage of recent research on emotion-dismissing parents and children's poor emotion regulation (Lunkenheimer, Shields, & Cortina, 2007)

- New section on young children's development of a conscience (Kochanska & Aksan, 2007)

- Coverage of recent study linking an early mutually responsive orientation between parents and their infant, a decrease in power assertive discipline in early childhood, and an increase in the young child's internalization and self-regulation (Kochanska & others, 2008)

- Updated description of gender identity (Blakemore, Berenbaum, & Liben, 2009; Egan & Perry, 2001)

- Coverage of a recent study linking higher prenatal testosterone levels to increased male-typical play in 6- to 10-year-old boys and girls (Auyeung & others, 2009)

- New section, Further Thoughts on Parenting Styles, including material on caution in interpreting studies of parenting styles and children's development and the interest in "unpacking" components of parenting styles

- Discussion of the increasing number of recent research studies that have found negative developmental outcomes for children who have been physically punished by their parents (Bender & others, 2007; Mulvaney & Mebert, 2007)

- Updated child maltreatment statistics in the United States (U.S. Department of Health and Human Services, 2008)

- New material on adolescent outcomes of child abuse and neglect (Wekerle & others, 2009)

- New coverage of data indicating that child neglect occurs up to three times as often as child abuse (Benoit, Coolbear, & Crawford, 2008)

- New information about abnormal stress hormone levels in children who have been maltreated (Gunnar, Fisher, & the Early Experience, Stress, and Prevention Network, 2006), including new Figure 10.4

- New description of three main characteristics of sibling relationships (Dunn, 2007)

- Inclusion of recent research on mediating training for parents and positive sibling outcomes (Smith & Ross, 2007)

- Updated coverage of birth order based on a recent review (Paulhus, 2008)

- New description of a link between working mothers and a reduction in children's (especially girls') gender stereotyping (Goldberg & Lucas-Thompson, 2008)

- Added commentary about the problems that children from divorced families experience often stem from active marital conflict in the predivorce period

- New description of low-income families having less access to resources than higher-income families (Leon-Guererro, 2009; Philipsen, Johnson, & Brooks-Gunn, 2009)

- New section on the early development of friendships during the preschool years (Howes, 2009)

- New section, The Connected Worlds of Parent-Child and Peer Relations (Hartup, 2009; Ross & Howe, 2009)

- Description of a recent study on parenting behaviors that are linked to children's social competence and social acceptance (McDowell & Parke, 2009)

- New discussion of the important role that play has as a context for the development of language and communication skills (Coplan & Arbeau, 2009)

- Enhanced and updated discussion of why pretend play is an important aspect of early childhood development (Coplan & Arbeau, 2009)

- Expanded coverage of pretend play, including Catherine Garvey's and Angeline Lillard's views

- New recommended book on improving the lives of children: *Gender Development* by Judith Blakemore, Sheri Berenbaum, & Lynn Liben (2009)

CHAPTER 11
PHYSICAL DEVELOPMENT IN MIDDLE AND LATE CHILDHOOD

- New discussion of Mark Johnson and his colleagues (2009) view on how the prefrontal cortex likely orchestrates the functioning of other neural regions during development

- Coverage of a recent study that revealed a positive role of aerobic exercise fitness on 9-year-old girls' performance on a cognitive control task that required them to inhibit irrelevant responses to obtain correct solutions (Hillman & others, 2009)

- Coverage of recent research on the benefits of an intensive resistance training program on reducing children's body fat and increasing their muscle strength (Benson, Torode, & Fiatarone Singh, 2008)

- Inclusion of recent research indicating the amount of daily physical activity that is associated with lower odds of childhood obesity (Wittmeier, Mollard, & Kriellaars, 2008)

- Description of a recent study linking aerobic exercise to an increase in planning skills in overweight children (Davis & others, 2007)

- Updated material on the increase in overweight children in many countries around the world (Chan, 2008; Li & others, 2008)

- Description of a recent large-scale U.S. study showing a recent leveling off in child obesity (Ogden, Carroll, & Flegall, 2008).

- Coverage of a recent large-scale U.S. study indicating a higher percentage of being overweight or obese for African American and Latino children than non-Latino White children (Benson, Baer, & Kaelber, 2009)

- Description of a recent study linking high levels of watching TV with being overweight in childhood (Wells & others, 2008)

- Expanded and updated coverage of the developmental outcomes of children who are overweight

- Coverage of a recent study indicating a link between body mass index and waist circumference in childhood and metabolic syndrome in adulthood (Sun & others, 2008)

- Description of a recent study on how peers perceived obese children (Zeller, Reiter-Purtill, & Ramey, 2008)

- Inclusion of recent data regarding the incidence and treatment of childhood cancer in the United States (National Cancer Institute, 2008a, b)

- Description of a recent study of significant underdiagnosis of high blood pressure in 75 percent of affected children (Hansen, Gunn, & Kaelber, 2007)

- New discussion of a recent national study indicating an increase in the percentage of U.S. children and adolescents with elevated blood pressure (Ostchega & others, 2009)

- Inclusion of a recent study linking preterm birth and child care outside the home to childhood asthma (van Beijsterveldt & Moomsma, 2008)

- Coverage of a recent study in four developing countries linking caregiver depression with child injuries (Howe, Hutley, & Abramsky, 2006)

- Considerable editing of material on children with disabilities based on expert consultant Karen Harris's recommendations

- Updated description of the percentage of students with disabilities who receive special services (National Center for Education Statistics, 2008)

- Revised definition of learning disabilities to more closely approximate the U.S. government's definition

- Coverage of trends in the percentage of students with learning disabilities who receive special services (National Center for Education, 2008)

- New description of the variation that occurs across states and school systems in how learning disabilities are defined and diagnosed (Bender, 2008)

- New coverage of dysgraphia

- Description of a recent intensive 16-week instruction program that increased the reading skills of first-grade students with severe reading problems who had not responded adequately to reading instruction (Simos & others, 2007)

- Added description of how an ADHD diagnosis requires that the characteristics appear early in childhood and be debilitating for the child

- New description of how ADHD should not be diagnosed by school teams but rather by a specialist, such as a child psychiatrist (Bender, 2008)

- New material documenting a three-year delay in the thickening of the cerebral cortex in children with ADHD, including new Figure 11.7

- Description of the increasing research interest in the role that neurotransmitters such as serotonin might play in ADHD (Levy, 2009; Roessner & others, 2009)

- Updated coverage of new stimulant and nonstimulant drugs that are being evaluated in the treatment of ADHD (Faraone, 2007)

- New material on the important role the teacher plays in monitoring the effectiveness of an ADHD students' medication

- Description of a recent meta-analysis indicating that behavior management treatments are effective in reducing the effects of ADHD (Fabiano, 2009)

- Discussion of a recent experimental study that found atomoxetine combined with a psychoeducational treatment was effective in reducing children's ADHD symptoms (Svanborg & others, 2009)

- Significantly updated and expanded discussion of autism spectrum disorders (Anderson & others, 2009; Gong & others, 2009)

- New information about the recent increase in the estimate of the number of children with autistic spectrum disorders

- Expanded discussion of gender and autism, including Baron-Cohen's (2008) argument that autism reflects an extreme male brain

- New material on recent research using animated faces and emotions to improve autistic children's ability to recognize faces, including new Figure 11.8 (Baron-Cohen & others, 2007)

- New coverage of recent research linking autism spectrum disorders to genetic mutations on chromosome 16 in approximately 1 out of 100 cases of these disorders (Weiss & others, 2008)

- New Figure 11.9 showing the percentage of U.S. students with disabilities who spent time in the regular classroom in a recent school year (National Center for Education Statistics, 2007)

CHAPTER 12

COGNITIVE DEVELOPMENT IN MIDDLE AND LATE CHILDHOOD

- New coverage of how schools and teachers can increase children's creative thinking, including mounting concern that the No Child Left Behind legislation has harmed the development of students' creative thinking skills (Sternberg, Kaufman, & Grigorenko, 2008)

- Inclusion of new strategies teachers can use to encourage students' creativity by (1) building students' self-confidence, (2) encouraging students to take risks, and (3) guiding students to be persistent and delay gratification

- Description of recent research on more than 107,000 students in 41 countries linking family, economic, and cultural influences to science achievement (Chiu, 2007)

- Updated discussion of the Wechsler scales to include recently introduced composite indexes such as the Verbal Contribution Index, the Working Memory Index, and the Processing Speed Index

- Considerable editing and updating of the discussion of intelligence based on feedback from expert consultant Robert J. Sternberg

- New discussion of Sternberg's recent application of his triarchic theory of intelligence to the concept of wisdom, including an emphasis on teaching wisdom in schools (Sternberg, 2009d, e; Sternberg, Jarvin, & Grigorenko, 2009; Sternberg, Jarvin, & Reznitskaya, 2009)

- Expanded and updated coverage of evaluating general tests of intelligence and the concept of *g* in comparison to the concept of multiple intelligences, including Sternberg's (2007) most recent position on these topics

- New section, The Neuroscience of Intelligence

- Discussion of the link between overall brain size and intelligence

- Coverage of recent research on a distributed neural network that involves the frontal and parietal lobes and the neural network's link to intelligence (Colom, Jung, & Haier, 2007; Colom & others, 2009; Jung & Haier, 2007)

- Description of the link between a higher level of intelligence and a higher volume of gray matter in the brain (Colom, Jung, & Haier, 2006; Luders & others, 2009)

- New material on the role of neurological speed in intelligence

- New description of Sternberg and his colleagues (Sternberg & Grigrorenko, 2008; Zhang & Sternberg, 2009) that there are no culture-fair tests, only culture-reduced tests

- Expanded and updated coverage of gifted education, including recent concerns that the No Child Left Behind policy may be harming students who are gifted (Clark, 2008; Cloud, 2007)

- New sections discussing nature-nurture and developmental changes and domain-specific giftedness in the discussion of children who are gifted

- New discussion of John Colombo and his colleagues' (2004, 2009) research on attempting to predict from infancy which children will have high cognitive ability in the preschool years

- New material on developmental changes in giftedness in childhood and adolescence with increased emphasis on domain-specific giftedness (Keating, 2009; Matthews, 2009)

- Inclusion of commentary by Bill Gates about domain-specific giftedness

- Coverage of a recent research review on which cognitive processes used in one language transfer more easily to learning a second language (Bialystok, 2007)

- Expanded and updated discussion of research indicating more complex conclusions about whether there are sensitive periods in learning a second language (Thomas & Johnson, 2008)

- New conclusions section that reflects the increasing view of leading psychologists that aspects of both intrinsic and extrinsic motivation can benefit children's achievement (Cameron & Pierce, 2008; Schunk, 2008)

- Inclusion of information about a recent study illustrating the importance of mastery goals in students' effort in mathematics (Chouinrad, Karsenti, & Roy, 2007)

- New coverage that emphasizes how mastery and performance goals aren't always mutually exclusive and that for many children combining mastery and performance goals orientations benefit them (Anderman & Mueller, 2009; Schunk, Pintrich, & Meece, 2008)

- New material on observations of classrooms by Michael Pressley and his colleagues (Pressley, Mohan, Fingeret, & others, 2007; Pressley, Mohan, Raphael, & others, 2007) that illustrates the importance of the teacher's role in helping students to develop strategies that will improve their achievement

- Description of a recent observational study of teachers in 12 classrooms to determine the learning factors that are linked to teachers with high, average, and low expectations for students' success (Rubie-Davies, 2007)

- Discussion of recent study on teachers' and mothers' expectations and their link with children's achievement outcomes (Benner & Mistry, 2007)

- Coverage of a recent study indicating that teachers' positive expectations help to protect students from the influence of parents' negative expectations (Wood, Kaplan, & McLoyd, 2007)

- New description of the lack of resources to support learning in the homes of students from low-income families (Schunk, Pintrich, & Meece, 2008)

- New discussion of the recent results from the large-scale international assessment of fourth-grade students' math and science scores with a focus on how U.S. students compare to students in other countries (TIMMS, 2008)

CHAPTER 13
SOCIOEMOTIONAL DEVELOPMENT IN MIDDLE AND LATE CHILDHOOD

- Description of recent research on the costs of high self-esteem in aggressive children (Menon & others, 2007)

- Updated and expanded coverage of children's outcomes following a disaster (Kar, 2009)

- Revision of the description of Kohlberg's theory based on leading expert John Gibbs' feedback

- Coverage of a recent research review of cross-cultural studies of Kohlberg's moral judgment stages, including the role of perspective taking (Gibbs & others, 2007)

- Updated conclusions about whether gender differences in moral orientation are as strong as Gilligan suggests (Blakemore, Berenbaum, & Liben, 2009)

- Description of recent research on an increase in gender stereotyping from preschool through the fifth grade (Miller & others, 2008)

- New summary of sex differences in the brain, emphasizing caution in interpreting differences (Blakemore, Berenbaum, & Liben, 2009)

- New material on no gender differences in overall intelligence but differences in some cognitive areas (Blakemore, Berenbaum, & Liben, 2009; Galambos, Berenbaum, & McHale, 2009)

- Coverage of recent large-scale assessments of a gender difference in writing (National Assessment of Educational Progress, 2007) and lack of a difference in math (Hyde & others, 2008)

- Description of a recent research review on gender and visuospatial skills (Halpern & others, 2007)

- Inclusion of information about an increase in relational aggression in middle and late childhood (Dishion & Piehler, 2009)

- Description of a recent study linking parents' psychological control to a higher incidence of relational aggression in their children (Kuppens & others, 2009)

- Updating of discussion of relational aggression, including research that indicates relational aggression comprises a greater percentage of girls' total aggression than is the case for boys (Putallaz & others, 2007)

- Updated description of gender differences in emotion (Blakemore, Berenbaum, & Liben, 2009)

- Inclusion of a recent study of rejected children and classroom participation (Ladd, Herald-Brown, & Reiser, 2008)

- Updated and expanded discussion of bullying, including the roles of social contexts and the larger peer group (Salmivalli & Peets, 2009)

- New *Research in Children's Development* interlude, "The Perspective Taking and Moral Motivation of Bullies, Bully-Victims, Victims, and Prosocial Children" (Gasser & Keller, 2009)

- Coverage of recent research on links between bullying and negative developmental outcomes (Arsenault & others, 2008; Beaty & Alexeyev, 2008; Nylund & others, 2007)

- New description of two promising bullying intervention programs (Frey & others, 2005; Olweus, 2003)

- Inclusion of information about the increasing problem of cyberbullying (Hinduja & Patchin, 2009)

- Updated discussion of accountability and the No Child Left Behind legislation, including recent research on how many states actually have lowered rather than raised standards because of NCLB and NCLB's failure to meet its goal of reducing the ethnic achievement gap (Darling-Hammond, 2007)

- Coverage of a recent study on neighborhood disadvantage and child outcomes such as behavior problems and low verbal ability (Kohen & others, 2008)

- Description of a recent study linking chronic poverty to adverse cognitive development outcomes in children (Najman & others, 2009)

- New *Diversity in Children's Development* interlude, "The New Hope Intervention Program," including recent research by Aletha Huston and her colleagues (Huston & others, 2006) on intervening in impoverished families

- New coverage of Jonathan Kozol's (2005) *The Shame of the Nation*, including a photograph and description of an elementary school circumstance in Indianapolis

CHAPTER 14
PHYSICAL DEVELOPMENT IN ADOLESCENCE

- New *Images of Children's Development* opening story, "Latisha, Arnie, and Katie"

- Discussion of William Damon's (2008) recent book, *The Path to Purpose*, and how today's parents are instilling short-term solutions to tasks and problems in youth and not adequately communicating with adolescents about the importance of finding a purpose in life

- New discussion of the positive youth development that highlights the positive characteristics and developmental trajectories that are desirable for youth (Lerner & others, 2009)

- New discussion of precocious puberty (Blakemore, Berenbaum, & Liben, 2009)

- Inclusion of recent information that early-maturing girls are less likely to graduate from high school and more likely to cohabit and marry earlier (Cavanagh, 2009)

- New coverage of the importance of social norms in adolescent sexual behavior, including a recent study of perceptions of peers' sexual permissiveness and adolescents' sexual behavior (Potard, Courtois, & Rusch, 2008)

- Inclusion of information about a recent study on early-maturing girls who try cigarettes and alcohol without their parents' knowledge (Westling & others, 2008)

- Coverage of recent research on changes in the brain in adolescence and resistance to peer pressure (Paus & others, 2008)

- New description of how the information about changes in the adolescent brain reflects the rapidly emerging field of developmental social neuroscience (de Haan & Gunnar, 2009)

- Discussion of a recent study on adolescents' level of watching sexual content on popular TV shows and whether they are likely to become pregnant or father an out-of-wedlock baby (Chandra & others, 2008)

- Description of a recent national study on the percentage of U.S. high school students who were currently sexually active (Eaton & others, 2008)

- Inclusion of information about a recent longitudinal study linking attention problems and disruptive aggressive behavior at school entry to a constellation of problems in middle school, which in turn were related to early initiation of sexual activity (Schofield & others, 2008)

- Description of a recent research review on factors linked to having sexual intercourse earlier in adolescence (Zimmer-Gembeck & Helfand, 2008)

- Coverage of a recent study of middle school students indicating that better academic achievement was a protective factor in keeping boys and girls from engaging in early initiation of sexual intercourse (Laflin & others, 2008)

- Inclusion of a recent study of acculturation and the sexual behavior of Latino adolescents (McDonald, Manlove, & Ikramullah, 2009)

- Coverage of a recent study that revealed a link between maternal communication about sex and a reduction in risky sexual behavior by Latino adolescents (Trejos-Castillo & Vazonyi, 2009)

- Inclusion of a recent study of factors linked to inconsistent and consistent condom use in Latino youth (Brady & others, 2009)

- Discussion of a large-scale U.S. study on the increase in the use of a contraceptive during the last time high school students had sexual intercourse (Centers for Disease Control and Prevention, 2008a).

- Description of recent national data on the U.S. adolescent birth rate, indicating an increase in 2006, including new Figure 14.7 of trends (Child Trends, 2008)

- Discussion of the high fertility rate of Latina adolescents and comparison of their recent adolescent pregnancy and birth rates with those of other ethnic groups (Santelli, Abraido-Lanza, & Melnikas, 2009)

- New coverage of information comparing ethnic groups on the likelihood of having a second child in adolescence (Rosengard, 2009)

- Description of a national study documenting the high percentage of daughters of teenage mothers who become pregnant themselves, and other risk factors in the daughters' lives for becoming pregnant (Meade, Kershaw, & Ickovics, 2008)

- New section on risk factors in the development of adolescent sexual problems

- Coverage of recent research on a link between various risk factors and early sexual intercourse (Hyde & Price, 2007)

- Coverage of recent research reviews indicating that abstinence-only education is not effective in delaying sexual intercourse in adolescence and is not effective in reducing HIV risk behaviors (Kirby, Laris, & Rolleir, 2007; Underhill, Montgomery, & Operario, 2007)

- Discussion of a large-scale U.S. study on the increase in the use of a contraceptive during the last time high school students had sexual intercourse (Centers for Disease Control and Prevention, 2008a).

- Description of a recent study that revealed that adolescents who experienced comprehensive sex education reported fewer pregnancies than did adolescents who were given abstinence-only or no education (Kohler, Manhart, & Lafferty, 2008)

- Description of a recent study indicating the percent of overweight male and female adolescents who become obese adults (Wang & others, 2008)

- New material on the negative health and social outcomes of being overweight in adolescence (Pasch & others, 2008)

- Updated information about causes of adolescent deaths in the United States (National Vital Statistics Reports, 2008)

- Updating of the trends in the percentage of U.S. adolescents who ate fruits and vegetables on a regular basis (Eaton & others, 2008)

- Inclusion of a recent research review on family factors linked to whether or not adolescents eat fruits and vegetables (Pearson, Biddle, & Gorely, 2008)

- Discussion of a recent study on eating regular family meals and healthy eating patterns five years later (Burgess-Champoux & others, 2009)

- New description of a recent national study of U.S. 9- to 15-year-old boys' and girls' exercise patterns showing a significant decline in physical activity from 9 to 15 years of age, including new Figure 14.9 (Nader & others, 2008)

- Updated coverage of ethnicity by gender rates of exercise for U.S. adolescents (Eaton & others, 2008)

- Coverage of a recent national study showing that 13 years of age is when a decline in exercise occurs in many adolescents and factors that increase the likelihood that adolescents will engage in regular exercise (Kahan & others, 2008)

- Coverage of a recent study indicating a gender difference in adolescents in meeting U.S. guidelines for physical activity (Butcher & others, 2008)

- New coverage of the positive health benefits of regular exercise in adolescence (McMurray & others, 2008)

- Description of studies illustrating the importance of regular exercise in buffering stress and improving adolescents' mental health and well-being (Schmalz & others, 2007; Schneider, Dunton, & Cooper, 2008)

- Coverage of a recent national study of adolescent sleep patterns, including developmental changes from the ninth through the twelfth grade as well as new Figure 14.11 illustrating the changes (Eaton & others, 2008)

- Description of a recent study of Chinese adolescents' sleep patterns (Liu & others, 2008)

- Description of recent research on adolescents who eat dinner with their families and lower incidences of drug abuse (CASA, 2007)

- Description of recent research on how early educational success provides important protection against developing drug problems in adolescence (Bachman & others, 2008)

- Coverage of a recent study indicating that higher physical activity at 9 and 11 years of age predicted higher self-esteem at 11 and 13 years of age (Schmalz & others, 2007)

- Description of a recent study on factors linked to adolescents' negative body images (Ata, Ludden, & Lally, 2007)

- Updated results from the Monitoring the Future study regarding adolescent substance use and abuse (Johnston & others, 2009)

- Recent research on the increasing recognition of the importance of family functioning in anorexia nervosa and its treatment (Benninghoven & others, 2007; Bulik & others, 2007)

- Discussion of recent research on activities, resources, and relationships that are related to adolescents' health-enhancing behaviors (Youngblade & Curry, 2006)

- Coverage of recent research study on social capital and adolescent risk-taking behavior (Youngblade & others, 2006)

CHAPTER 15
COGNITIVE DEVELOPMENT IN ADOLESCENCE

- Expanded introduction to information processing and thinking in adolescence based on Deanna Kuhn's (2009) recent view on differences in childhood and adolescent cognitive development that emphasizes the importance of advances in executive functioning

- Much expanded and updated discussion of adolescent decision making, including recent research and views (Gerrard & others, 2008; Reyna & Rivers, 2008)

- Inclusion of new material about the importance of social contexts, especially peers and how their presence activates the brain's reward pathways, in adolescent decision making (Steinberg, 2008)

- Description of how graduated driver licensing (GDL) reduces adolescent crashes and fatalities (Keating, 2007)

- Inclusion of recent information about 40 of 50 states that now have mandates regarding character education (Nucci & Narváez, 2008)

- Coverage of the recent acceptance of using a care perspective as part of character education (Sherblom, 2008)

- Inclusion of a recent study of gender differences in service learning (Webster & Worrell, 2008)

- New section on cheating, including recent research and information about why students cheat and strategies for preventing cheating (Anderman & Murdock, 2007; Stephens, 2008)

- Updated and expanded coverage of links between cognitive changes and adolescents' religious and spiritual development (Good & Willoughby, 2008)

- Discussion of a recent study of changes in religiousness and attending religious services from 14 to 25 years of age, including new Figure 15.3 (Koening, McGue, & Iacono, 2008)

- Coverage of a recent study of Indonesian Muslim 13-year-olds' religious involvement and social competence (French & others, 2008)

- Updated coverage of college students' values, including a recent increase in developing a meaningful philosophy of life (Pryor & others, 2008)

- Description of William Damon's (2008) *The Path to Purpose* and its link to youths' development of values

- Inclusion of a recent study comparing discipline problems in sixth-graders in middle school versus sixth-graders in elementary schools (Cook & others, 2008)

- Updated statistics on school dropouts, including the substantial decrease in Latino dropouts since 2000 (National Center for Education Statistics, 2008)

- Coverage of a recent study indicating the importance of parents in reducing the likelihood adolescents will drop out of school (Englund, Egeland, & Collins, 2008)

- Expanded and updated description of the positive outcomes of the "I Have a Dream" Foundation including a recent evaluation of the Houston program (2009)

- Coverage of a longitudinal study of participation in organized school and community activities and success in emerging adulthood (Gardner, Roth, & Brooks-Gunn, 2008)

- Description of a longitudinal study of extracurricular activity participation by vulnerable youth in adolescence and educational outcomes in emerging adulthood (Peck & others, 2008)

- New coverage of recent information on timing of poverty in childhood and adolescence and its link to achievement and educational outcomes (McLoyd & others, 2009; Taylor & Graham, 2007)

- Discussion of a recent longitudinal study of the transition to high school of multiethnic urban adolescents (Benner & Graham, 2009)

- Expanded material on cross-cultural comparisons of secondary education in the *Diversity in Children's Development* interlude, "Cross-Cultural Comparisons of Secondary Schools," with observations of Chinese education

- Description of the recent initiative by the Bill and Melinda Gates Foundation (2008) to reduce the dropout rate in schools with high dropout rates by keeping high-risk students with the same teachers across the high school years

- Application of William Damon's (2008) ideas in the *Path to Purpose* to career development

- Coverage of a recent study on the key factors involved in students' career decision-making self-efficacy (Patel, Salahuddin, & O' Brien, 2008)

- New discussion of developmental changes in how school counselors advise middle school and high school students about careers (Baggerly, 2008)

- At the request of adopters and reviewers, deletion of section on work during adolescence to allow for a briefer chapter.

 CHAPTER 16
SOCIOEMOTIONAL DEVELOPMENT
IN ADOLESCENCE

- Coverage of a recent study on a link between relationship authenticity and an increase in self-esteem during adolescence (Impett & others, 2008)

- New discussion of William Damon's (2008) book, *The Path to Purpose,* and his views on why too many of today's youth are struggling to find a path to a positive identity

- Discussion of a recent study of the implications of ethnic identity exploration for developing a secure sense of one's ethnic identity, which in turn was linked to a positive attitude toward one's own group and other groups (Whitehead & others, 2009)

- Expanded and updated description of why college often stimulates a greater integration of identity at a higher level (Phinney, 2008)

- Description of a recent study on the bicultural identity of Mexican American and Asian American college students (Devos, 2006)

- Inclusion of recent research on ethnic identity in Navajo adolescents (Jones & Galliher, 2007)

- Description of a recent longitudinal study of ethnic identity resolution and proactive coping with discrimination (Umana-Taylor & others, 2008)

- Discussion of a recent longitudinal study of secure attachment in adolescence and outcomes in emerging adulthood (Allen & others, 2009)

- Discussion of recent research on age differences in resistance to peer influence (Steinberg & Monahan, 2007)

- New discussion of the talk-featured, gossip aspect of friendship in adolescence (Buhrmester & Chong, 2009)

- Description of recent research on girls and friendships with older boys (Poulin & Pedersen, 2007)

- Inclusion of material on the positive aspect of girls' friendships with achievement-oriented best friends and how this is linked to taking math courses in high school (Crosnoe & others, 2008)

- Coverage of recent research indicating the importance of friends' grade-point average in adolescent development (Cook, Deng, & Morgano, 2007)

- Expanded and updated material on which adolescents are most likely to conform to their peers (Prinstein, 2007; Prinstein & Dodge, 2008)

- New coverage of three stages in the development of romantic relationships in adolescence (Connolly & McIsaac, 2009)

- New material on the percentage of adolescents who are early and late bloomers in developing romantic relationships (Connolly & McIsaac, 2009)

- Coverage of a recent study of adolescents' romantic experience and links to various aspects of adjustment (Furman, Low, & Ho, 2009)

- Discussion of two recent studies of adolescent girls' romantic involvement and its link to co-rumination, depressive symptoms, and emotionally unavailable parents (Starr & Davila, 2008; Steinberg & Davila, 2008)

- Coverage of a 12-year longitudinal study of SES and ethnic group influences on adolescent and emerging adults' educational and occupational expectations that illustrates the importance of controlling for SES in studies of ethnic minority children and youth (Mello, 2009)

- Description of a recent study of adolescents' perceived racial discrimination and its link to the broader society's negative views of African Americans (Seaton, Yip, & Sellers, 2009)

- New section, Media and Technology, including material on the dramatic increase in media multitasking by children and youth and how if this is factored into media use figures, children and adolescents now use electronic media an average of eight hours per day (Roberts, Henriksen, & Foehr, 2009; Roberts & Foehr, 2008)

- Discussion of recent research on adolescent self-disclosure on the Internet and which gender benefits more from self-disclosing with friends on the Internet (Schouten, Valkenburg, & Peter, 2007; Valkenburg & Peter, 2009)

- Description of a recent survey of the significant threat minors encounter with both online and offline bullying (Palfrey & others, 2009)

- Description of a recent study of the sequence of using various electronic communication technologies by college females and males (Yang & Brown, 2009)

- Coverage of a recent study of pubertal timing and what adolescent boys do online (Skoog, Stattin, & Kerr, 2009)

- Expanded and updated coverage of the increase of adolescents' and emerging adults' reliance on digital mediation of their social environment (Roberts, Henriksen, & Foehr, 2009)

- Discussion of a recent study indicating that many parents do not monitor their adolescents' online activities (Rosen, Cheever, & Carrier, 2008)

- Coverage of a recent study linking parents' lack of knowledge of their young adolescents' whereabouts and the adolescents' engagement in delinquency later in adolescence (Lahey & others, 2008)

- Description of recent research on maternal monitoring and a lower incidence of delinquency in Latina adolescents (Loukas, Suizzo, & Prelow, 2007)

- Discussion of a recent study implicating harsh discipline at 8 to 10 years of age as a predictor of which adolescent delinquents would persist in criminal activity after age 21 (Farrington, Ttofi, & Coid, 2009)

- Coverage of a recent longitudinal experimental study involving a parenting intervention with divorced mothers and sons and a subsequent lower level of delinquency (Forgatch & others, 2009)

- Inclusion of recent research on the role of deviant peers in predicting delinquency in African American males (Bowman, Prelow, & Weaver, 2007).

- Coverage of recent estimates of the incidence of depression in adolescence (Graber & Sontag, 2009)

- Discussion of recent research on friendship, co-rumination, and depression in adolescence (Rose, Carlson, & Waller, 2007)

- Description of recent studies on protective factors linked with a lower incidence of depressed mood in adolescence (Costello & others, 2008)

- Discussion of a recent study on the role of worry, anxiety, and oversensivity in predicting depressive symptoms in adolescent girls (Chaplin, Gillham, & Seligman, 2009)

- New material on the role of pubertal status combined with stressful peer relations in contributing to depression in adolescent girls (Conley & Rudolph, 2009)

- Coverage of recent research that examined variations in therapies to reduce adolescent depression (TADS, 2007)

- New Figure 16.7 on the percentage of adolescents who say they have seriously considered suicide or attempted it unsuccessfully (Eaton & others, 2006)

- New discussion of the cultural contexts of suicide attempts, including new Figure 16.8 on ethnic variations in suicide attempts by U.S. adolescents (Goldston & others, 2008)

- Description of a recent study using data from the National Longitudinal Study of Adolescent Health that found a number of risks for suicidal behavior (Thompson, Kuruwita, & Foster, 2009)

- Coverage of a recent study on the influence of suicide attempts by members of an adolescent's social groups on the adolescent's probability of attempting suicide (de Leo & Heller, 2008)

- Description of a recent study that found a link between peer victimization and suicidal thoughts and attempts (Klomek & others, 2008)

- Inclusion of recent research linking thwarted belongingness and perception of being a burden to others with suicidal thoughts (Van Orden & others, 2008)

- Description of a recent study on preteen alcohol use and suicide attempts in adolescence (Swahn, Bossarte, & Sullivent, 2008)

- Extensively updated discussion of juvenile delinquency, including research on cognitive factors such as IQ, self-control, and sustained attention (Koolhof & others, 2007;

Loeber & others, 2007), physical abuse (Lansford & others, 2007), peer rejection and deviate friends (Vitaro, Pedersen, & Brengden, 2007)

- New *Research in Children's Development* interlude, "Fast Track," providing very recent information about an extensive intervention with high-risk kindergarten children and outcomes of the intervention in adolescence (Conduct Problems Prevention Research Group, 2007; Dodge, 2009; Dodge & the Conduct Problems Prevention Research Group, 2007)

ACKNOWLEDGMENTS

I very much appreciate the support and guidance provided to me by many people at McGraw-Hill. Beth Mejia, Editorial Director, has done a marvelous job of directing and monitoring the development and publication of this text. Mike Sugarman, Publisher, has brought a wealth of publishing knowledge and vision to bear on improving my texts. Krista Bettino, Executive Editor, deserves special mention for the superb work she has done as the new editor for this book. The Developmental Editor, Barbara Conover, has done an excellent job of editing the manuscript and handling the page-by-page changes to this new edition. Nancy Crochiere, Director of Development, has done a superb job of organizing and monitoring the many tasks necessary to move this book through the editorial process. Megan Stotts, Sarah DeHaas, and AJ Lafererra, Editorial Coordinators, have done a competent job of obtaining reviewers and handling many editorial chores. James Headley, Marketing Manager, has contributed in numerous positive ways to this book. Beatrice Sussman did a superb job as the book's copy editor. Marilyn Rothenberger did a terrific job in coordinating the book's production. LouAnn Wilson, Photo Researcher, did excellent work in tracking down elusive photographs for the book.

REVIEWERS

I owe a special gratitude to the reviewers who provided detailed feedback about the book.

Expert Consultants

I already listed the expert consultants earlier in the preface. Their photographs and biographies appear on pages xiv to xvi. The study of children's development has become an enormous, complex field and no single author, or even several authors, can be experts in many different areas of children's development. To solve this problem, I have sought the input of many leading experts in many areas of children's development. The experts provided me with detailed recommendations of new research and applications to include in every period of children's development. The panel of experts is literally a who's who in the field of children's development.

General Text Reviewers

I also owe a great deal of thanks to the instructors who teach children's development and who have provided feedback about

the book. Many of the changes in *Children*, eleventh edition, are based on their input. For their help and encouragement, I thank these individuals:

Eleventh Edition Reviewers

Kristine Anthis, *Southern Connecticut State University*
Albert Bramante, *Union County College*
Jo Ann Burnside, *Richard J Daley College*
Victoria Candelora, *Brevard Community College*
Ruth Doyle, *Casper College*
Karen Falcone, *San Joaquin Delta College*
Kate Fogarty, *University of Florida at Gainsville*
Dale Fryxell, *Chaminade University*
Hsin-Hui Lin, *University of Houston at Victoria*
Cynthia Rickert, *Dominican College*
Kourtney Vaillancourt, *New Mexico State University*

Reviewers of Previous Editions

I also remain indebted to the individuals who reviewed previous editions and whose recommendations have been carried forward into the present edition.

John A. Addleman, *Messiah College*
Linda Anderson, *Northwestern Michigan College*
Harry H. Avis, *Sierra College*
Diana Baumrind, *University of California–Berkeley*
Lori A. Beasley, *University of Central Oklahoma*
Patricia J. Bence, *Tompkins Cortland Community College*
Michael Bergmire, *Jefferson College*
Minhnoi Wroble Biglan, *Penn State, Beaver*
Belinda Blevins-Knabe, *University of Arkansas–Little Rock*
Ruth Brinkman, *St. Louis Community College, Florissant Valley*
Eileen Donahue Brittain, *City College of Harry S Truman*
Urie Bronfenbrenner, *Cornell University*
Phyllis Bronstein, *University of Vermont*
Dan W. Brunworth, *Kishwaukee College*
Carole Burke-Braxton, *Austin Community College*
Kate Byerwalter, *Grand Rapids Community*
Alison S. Carson, *Hofstra University*
Rosalind Charlesworth, *Weber State University*
Nancy Coghill, *University of Southwest Louisiana*
Malinda Jo Colwell, *Texas Tech University*
Jane Couperus, *Hampshire College*
Jennifer Cousins, *University of Houston*
Dixie R. Crase, *Memphis State University*
Kathleen Crowley-Long, *The College of Saint Rose*
Florence Denmark, *Pace University*
Sheridan DeWolf, *Grossmont Community College*
Swen H. Digranes, *Northeastern State University*
Ruth H. Doyle, *N.C.C., L.P.C., Casper College*
Laura Duvall, *Heartland Community College*
Celina V. Echols, *Southeastern Louisiana State University*
Beverly Edmondson, *Buena Vista University*
Timothy P. Eicher, *Dixie Community College*
Sarah Erikson, *University of New Mexico*

Jennifer Fager, *Western Michigan University*
Karen Falcone, *San Joaquin Delta College*
JoAnn Farver, *Oklahoma State University*
Greta Fein, *University of Maryland*
Tiffany Field, *University of Miami, Florida*
Johanna Filp, *Sonoma State University*
Cheryl Fortner-Wood, *Winthrop College*
Janet Fuller, *Mansfield University*
Sabine Gerhardt, *Akron University*
Thomas Gerry, *Columbia Greene Community College*
Sam Givhan, *Minnesota State University*
Art Gonchar, *University of La Verne*
Sandra Graham, *UCLA*
Susan Hale, *Holyoke Community College*
Barbara Springer Hammons, *Palomar College*
Cory Anne Hansen, *Arizona State University*
Barbara H. Harkness, *San Bernardino Valley College*
Algea Harrison, *Oakland University*
Susan Heidrich, *University of Wisconsin*
Ashleigh Hillier, *Ohio University*
Alice S. Hoenig, *Syracuse University*
Sally Hoppstetter, *Palo Alto College*
Jean W. Hunt, *University of Cumberlands*
Marylou Hyson, *National Association for the Education of Young Children*
Robert J. Ivy, *George Mason University*
Diane Carlson Jones, *Texas A&M University*
Ellen Junn, *Indiana University*
Marcia Karwas, *California State University–Monterey*
Melvyn B. King, *State College of New York at Cortland*
Kathleen Kleissler, *Kutztown University*
Dene G. Klinzing, *University of Delaware*
Ramona Knight, *Yuba College*
Claire B. Kopp, *UCLA*
Cally Beth Kostakis, *Rockland Community College*
Tara L. Kuther, *Western Connecticut State University*
Linda Lavine, *State University of New York–Cortland*
Sara Lawrence, *California State University–Northridge*
Campbell Leaper, *University of California–Santa Cruz*
Gloria Lopez, *Sacramento City College*
James Marcia, *Concordia University*
James E. Marcia, *Simon Fraser University*
Deborah N. Margolis, *Boston College*
Julie Ann McIntyre, *Russell Sage College*
Mary Ann McLaughlin, *Clarion University*
Chloe Merrill, *Weber State College*
Karla Miley, *Black Hawk College*
Jody Miller, *Los Angeles Pierce College*
Carrie L. Mori, *Boise State University*
Joyce Munsch, *California State University at Northridge*
Barbara J. Myers, *Virginia Commonwealth University*
Jeffrey Nagelbush, *Ferris State University*
Sonia Nieves, *Broward Community College*
Nel Noddings, *Stanford University*
Caroline Olko, *Nassau Community College*
Sandy Osborne, *Montana State University*

William H. Overman, *University of North Carolina at Wilmington*
Michelle Paludi, *Michelle Paludi & Affiliates*
Susan Peet, *Bowling Green State University*
Pete Peterson, *Johnson County Community College*
Pamela Schuetze Pizarro, *Buffalo State College*
Joe Price, *San Diego State University*
Linda Pugh, *Johns Hopkins University*
Charles L. Reid, *Essex County College*
Barbara Reynolds, *College of the Sequoias*
Richard Riggle, *Coe College*
Lynne Rompelman, *Concordia University, Wisconsin*
James A. Rysberg, *California State University–Chico*
Marcia Rysztak, *Lansing Community College*
David Sadker, *American University*
Peter C. Scales, *Search Institute*
Pamela Schuetze-Pizarro, *Buffalo State College*
Pamela A. Schulze, *University of Akron*
Diane Scott-Jones, *University of Illinois*
Clyde Shepherd, *Keene State College*
Carol S. Soule, *Appalachian State University*
Helen Swanson, *University of Wisconsin*
Dorothy D. Sweeney, *Bristol Community College*
Anita Thomas, *Northeastern Illinois University*
Ross Thompson, *University of California–Davis*
Ross A. Thompson, *University of Nebraska–Lincoln*
Paul Vonnahme, *New Mexico State University*
Naomi Wagner, *San Jose State University*
Richard L. Wagner, *Mount Senario College*
Patricia J. Wall, *Northern Arizona University*
Dorothy A. Wedge, *Fairmont State College*
Teion Wells, *Florida State University–Tallahassee*
Carla Graham Wells, *Odessa College*
Becky G. West, *Coahoma Community College*
Alida Westman, *Eastern Michigan University*
Allan Wigfield, *University of Maryland–College Park*
Marilyn E. Willis, *Indiana University of Pennsylvania*
Mary E. Wilson, *Northern Essex Community College*
Susan D. Witt, *University of Akron*
Bonnie Wright, *Gardner Webb University*
Sarah Young, *Longwood College*
William H. Zachry, *University of Tennessee–Martin*

SUPPLEMENTS

For the Instructor

The instructor side of the Online Learning Center at http://www.mhhe.com/santrockc11e contains the Instructor's Manual, Test Bank files, PowerPoint slides, Image Gallery, and other valuable material to help you design and enhance your course. Ask your local McGraw-Hill representative for your password.

Instructor's Manual *by Andrea Rosati, Elmira College* Each chapter of the *Instructor's Manual* is introduced by a Total Teaching Package Outline. This fully integrated tool helps instructors more easily locate and choose among the many resources available for the course by linking each element of the Instructor's Manual to a particular teaching topic within the chapter. These elements include chapter outline, suggested lecture topics, classroom activities and demonstrations, suggested student research projects, essay questions, critical thinking questions, and implications for guidance.

Test Bank and Computerized Test Bank   *by John Addleman, Messiah College* This comprehensive Test Bank includes more than 1,500 multiple-choice and approximately 75 essay questions. Organized by chapter, the questions are designed to test factual, applied, and conceptual understanding. All test questions are compatible with EZ Test, McGraw-Hill's Computerized Test Bank program.

Powerpoint Slides   *by L. Ann Butzin, Owens Community College* These presentations cover the key points of each chapter and include charts and graphs from the text. They can be used as is, or you may modify them to meet your specific needs.

CPS Questions   *by Alisha Janowsky, University of Central Florida* These questions, formatted for use with the interactive Classroom Performance System, are organized by chapter and designed to test factual, applied, and conceptual understanding. These test questions are also compatible with EZTest, McGraw-Hill's Computerized Test Bank program.

McGraw-Hill's Visual Asset Database for Lifespan Development ("VAD")   McGraw-Hill's Visual Assets Database for Lifespan Development (VAD 2.0) www.mhhe.com/vad is an on-line database of videos for use in the developmental psychology classroom, created specifically for instructors. You can customize classroom presentations by downloading the videos to your computer and showing the videos on their own or insert them into your course cartridge or PowerPoint presentations. All of the videos are available with or without captions. Ask your McGraw-Hill representative for access information.

Multimedia Courseware For Child Development   *Charlotte J. Patterson, University of Virginia* This video-based set of two CD-ROMS covers classic and contemporary experiments in child development. Respected researcher Charlotte J. Patterson selected the content and wrote accompanying modules that can be assigned to students. These modules include suggestions for additional projects as well as a testing component. Multimedia Courseware can be packaged with the text at a discount.

Annual Editions: Child Growth and Development 09/10   This reader is a collection of articles on topics related to the latest research and thinking in human development. Annual Editions are updated regularly and include useful features such as a topic guide, an annotated table of contents, unit overviews, and a topical index.

Taking Sides: Clashing Views in Childhood and Society   Current controversial issues are presented in a debate-style format designed to stimulate student interest and develop critical thinking skills. Each issue is thoughtfully framed with an issue summary, an issue introduction, and a postscript.

Cases in Child and Adolescent Development for Teachers   Containing more than 40 cases, *Case Studies in Child and Adolescent Development for Teachers* brings developmental issues to life. The reality-based cases address a variety of developmental issues, giving students an opportunity to think critically about the way development influences children every day.

For The Student:

Online Learning Center (OLC)   This companion Web site, at www.mhhe.com/santrockc11e offers a wide variety of student resources. **Multiple Choice, True/False,** and **Matching Tests** for each chapter reinforce key principles, terms, and ideas and cover all the major concepts discussed throughout the text. Entirely different from the test items in the Test Bank, the questions have been written to quiz students but also to help them learn. Key terms from the text are reproduced in a **Glossary of Key Terms** where they can be accessed in alphabetical order for easy reference and review. **Decision Making Scenarios** present students with the opportunity to apply the information in the chapter to realistic situations, and see what effects their decisions have.

Visual Tour for Students

This book provides you with important study tools to help you more effectively learn about children's development. Especially important is the learning goals system that is integrated throughout each chapter. In the visual walk-through of features, pay special attention to how the learning goals system works.

THE LEARNING GOALS SYSTEM

Using the learning goals system will help you to learn the material more easily. Key aspects of the learning goals system are the learning goals, chapter maps, Review and Reflect, and Reach Your Learning Goals sections, which are all linked together. At the beginning of each chapter, you will see a page that includes three to six learning goals that preview the chapter's main themes and underscore the most important ideas in the chapter. Then, at the beginning of each major section of a chapter, you will see a mini–chapter map that provides you with a visual organization of the key topics you are about to read in the section. At the end of each section is Review and Reflect, in which the learning goal for the section is restated, a series of review questions related to the mini–chapter map are asked, and a question that encourages you to think critically about a topic related to the section appears. At the end of the chapter, you will come to a section titled Reach Your Learning Goals. This includes an overall chapter map that visually organizes all of the main headings, a restatement of the chapter's learning goals, and a summary of the chapter's content that is directly linked to the chapter outline at the beginning of the chapter and the questions asked in the Review part of Review and Reflect within the chapter. The end-of-chapter Reach Your Learning Goals feature essentially answers the questions asked in the within-chapter Review sections.

CHAPTER LEARNING GOALS

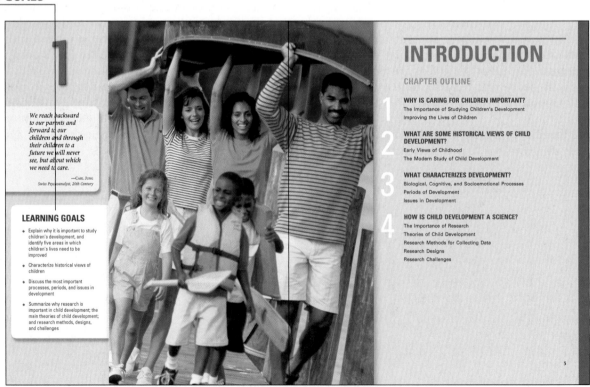

1

We reach backward to our parents and forward to our children and through their children to a future we will never see, but about which we need to care.

—CARL JUNG
Swiss Psychoanalyst, 20th Century

LEARNING GOALS

- Explain why it is important to study children's development, and identify five areas in which children's lives need to be improved

- Characterize historical views of children

- Discuss the most important processes, periods, and issues in development

- Summarize why research is important in child development; the main theories of child development; and research methods, designs, and challenges

INTRODUCTION

CHAPTER OUTLINE

WHY IS CARING FOR CHILDREN IMPORTANT?
The Importance of Studying Children's Development
Improving the Lives of Children

WHAT ARE SOME HISTORICAL VIEWS OF CHILD DEVELOPMENT?
Early Views of Childhood
The Modern Study of Child Development

WHAT CHARACTERIZES DEVELOPMENT?
Biological, Cognitive, and Socioemotional Processes
Periods of Development
Issues in Development

HOW IS CHILD DEVELOPMENT A SCIENCE?
The Importance of Research
Theories of Child Development
Research Methods for Collecting Data
Research Designs
Research Challenges

5

MINI–CHAPTER MAP

4 HOW DO HEREDITY AND ENVIRONMENT INTERACT? THE NATURE-NURTURE DEBATE

Behavior Genetics

Shared and Nonshared
Environmental Experiences

Conclusions About Heredity-
Environment Correlations

Heredity-Environment Correlations

The Epigenetic View and Gene ×
Environment (G × E) Interaction

In each section of this chapter so far, we have examined parts of the nature-nurture debate. We have seen how the environment exerts selective pressures on the characteristics of species over generations, examined how genes are passed from parents to children, and discussed how reproductive technologies and adoption influence

REVIEW AND REFLECT

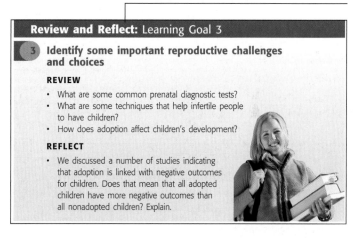

Review and Reflect: Learning Goal 3

3 **Identify some important reproductive challenges and choices**

REVIEW

• What are some common prenatal diagnostic tests?
• What are some techniques that help infertile people to have children?
• How does adoption affect children's development?

REFLECT

• We discussed a number of studies indicating that adoption is linked with negative outcomes for children. Does that mean that all adopted children have more negative outcomes than all nonadopted children? Explain.

REACH YOUR LEARNING GOALS

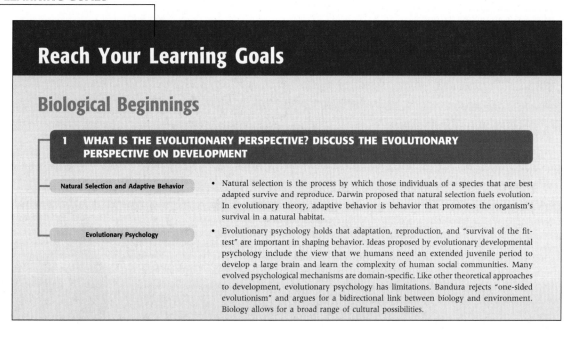

Reach Your Learning Goals

Biological Beginnings

1 WHAT IS THE EVOLUTIONARY PERSPECTIVE? DISCUSS THE EVOLUTIONARY PERSPECTIVE ON DEVELOPMENT

Natural Selection and Adaptive Behavior

• Natural selection is the process by which those individuals of a species that are best adapted survive and reproduce. Darwin proposed that natural selection fuels evolution. In evolutionary theory, adaptive behavior is behavior that promotes the organism's survival in a natural habitat.

Evolutionary Psychology

• Evolutionary psychology holds that adaptation, reproduction, and "survival of the fittest" are important in shaping behavior. Ideas proposed by evolutionary developmental psychology include the view that we humans need an extended juvenile period to develop a large brain and learn the complexity of human social communities. Many evolved psychological mechanisms are domain-specific. Like other theoretical approaches to development, evolutionary psychology has limitations. Bandura rejects "one-sided evolutionism" and argues for a bidirectional link between biology and environment. Biology allows for a broad range of cultural possibilities.

OTHER LEARNING SYSTEM FEATURES

RESEARCH IN CHILDREN'S DEVELOPMENT INTERLUDE

One *Research in Children's Development* interlude appears in every chapter. The research interludes describe a research study or program and are designed to acquaint you with how research on children's development is conducted.

Research in Children's Development

PHYSICAL ACTIVITY IN YOUNG CHILDREN ATTENDING PRESCHOOLS

One study examined the activity level of 281 3- to 5-year-olds in nine preschools (Pate & others, 2004). The preschool children wore accelerometers, a small activity monitor, for four to five hours a day. Height and weight assessments of the children were made to calculate their BMI.

Guidelines recommend that preschool children engage in two hours of physical activity per day, divided into one hour of structured activity and one hour of unstructured free play (National Association for Sport and Physical Education, 2002). In this study, the young children participated in an average of 7.7 minutes per hour of moderate to vigorous activity, usually in a block of time when they were outside. Over the course of eight hours of a preschool day, these children would get approximately one hour of moderate and vigorous physical activity—only about 50 percent of the amount recommended. The researchers concluded that young children are unlikely to engage in another hour per day of moderate and vigorous physical activity outside their eight hours spent in preschool and thus are not getting adequate opportunities for physical activity.

Gender and age differences characterized the preschool children's physical activity. Boys were more likely to engage in moderate or vigorous physical activity than girls. Four- and five-year-old children were more likely to be sedentary than three-year-old children.

The young children's physical activity also varied according to the particular preschool they attended. The extent they participated in moderate and vigorous physical activity ranged from 4.4 to 10.2 minutes per hour across the nine preschools. Thus, the policies and practices of particular preschools influence the extent to which children engage in physical activity. The researchers concluded that young children need more vigorous play and organized activities.

What are some guidelines for preschool children's exercise?

Caring for Children

PARENTING AND THE CHILD'S TEMPERAMENT

What are the implications of temperamental variations for parenting? Although answers to this question necessarily are speculative, these conclusions regarding the best parenting strategies to use in relation to children's temperament were reached by temperament experts Ann Sanson and Mary Rothbart (1995):

- *Attention to and respect for individuality.* Good parenting involves sensitivity to the child's individual characteristics. A goal might be accomplished in one way with one child and in another way with another child, depending on the child's temperament.
- *Structuring the child's environment.* Crowded, noisy environments can pose greater problems for some children (such as a "difficult child") than for others (such as an "easy child"). We might also expect that a fearful, withdrawing child would benefit from slower entry into new contexts.
- *The "difficult child" and packaged parenting programs.* Programs for parents often focus on dealing with children who have "difficult" temperaments. In some cases, "difficult child" refers to Thomas and Chess's description of a child who reacts negatively, cries frequently, engages in irregular daily routines, and is slow to accept change. In others, the concept might be used to describe a child who is irritable, displays anger frequently, does not follow directions well, or some

CARING FOR CHILDREN INTERLUDE

Every chapter has one *Caring for Children* interlude, which provides applied information about parenting, education, or health and well-being related to a topic in the chapter.

DIVERSITY IN CHILDREN'S DEVELOPMENT INTERLUDE

Once each chapter a *Diversity in Children's Development* interlude appears to provide information about diversity related to a chapter topic.

Diversity in Children's Development

CHILD-CARE POLICIES AROUND THE WORLD

Child-care policies around the world vary in eligibility criteria, leave duration, benefit level, and the extent to which parents take advantage of the policies (Tolani & Brooks-Gunn, 2008). There are five types of parental leave from employment (Kamerman, 1989, 2000a, b):

- *Maternity leave.* In some countries, the prebirth leave is compulsory as is a 6- to 10-week leave following birth.
- *Paternity leave.* This is usually much briefer than maternity leave. It may be especially important when a second child is born and the first child requires care.
- *Parental leave.* This gender-neutral leave usually follows a maternity leave and allows either women or men to share the leave policy or choose which of them will use it. In 1998, the European Union mandated a three-month parental leave.

Nature and Nurture The **nature-nurture issue** involves the debate about whether development is primarily influenced by nature or by nurture (Diamond, 2009; D'Onofrio, 2008). Nature refers to an organism's biological inheritance, nurture to its environmental experiences. Almost no one today argues that development can be explained by nature alone or by nurture alone. But some ("nature" proponents) claim that the more important influence on development is biological inheritance, and others ("nurture" proponents) claim that environmental experiences are the more important influence.

How Would You...?
As an educator, how would you apply your understanding of the developmental influences of nature and nurture to create appropriate classroom strategies for students who display learning or behavioral problems?

HOW WOULD YOU... ? QUESTIONS

These appear multiple times in the margins of each chapter and encourage students to apply concepts to career areas in human development and family studies, education, health professions (such as nursing and pediatrics), psychology, and social work.

KEY TERMS AND GLOSSARY

Key terms appear in boldface. Their definitions appear in the margin near where they are introduced.

experiment A carefully regulated procedure in which one or more of the factors believed to influence the behavior being studied are manipulated, while all other factors are held constant.

For example, suppose that you conducted a study to determine whether aerobic exercise by pregnant women changes the breathing and sleeping patterns of newborn babies. You might require one group of pregnant women to engage in a certain amount of exercise each week while another group of pregnant women does not exercise; thus, the amount of exercise is the independent variable. When the infants are born, you would observe and measure their breathing and sleeping patterns.

KEY TERMS

schemes 182	coordination of secondary	memory 194	semantics 203
assimilation 182	circular reactions 186	implicit memory 194	pragmatics 203
accommodation 184	tertiary circular reactions,	explicit memory 194	telegraphic speech 206
organization 184	novelty, and	deferred imitation 194	Broca's area 206
equilibration 184	curiosity 186	developmental quotient	Wernicke's area 206
sensorimotor stage 184	internalization of	(DQ) 198	aphasia 206
simple reflexes 185	schemes 186	Bayley Scales of Infant	language acquisition device
first habits and primary	object permanence 186	Development 198	(LAD) 206
circular reactions 185	A-not-B error 187	language 202	child-directed speech 209
primary circular	core knowledge	infinite generativity 202	
reaction 185	approach 190	phonology 202	
secondary circular	attention 192	morphology 202	
reactions 186	joint attention 193	syntax 203	

Key terms also are listed and page-referenced at the end of each chapter.

Key terms are alphabetically listed, defined, and page-referenced in a Glossary at the end of the book.

GLOSSARY

A

A-not-B error Also called AB error, this occurs when infants make the mistake of selecting the familiar hiding place (A) rather than the new hiding place (B) as they progress into substage 4 in Piaget's sensorimotor stage. 189

accommodation Piagetian concept of adjusting schemes to fit new information and experiences. 184

active (niche-picking) genotype-environment

animism The belief that inanimate objects have lifelike qualities and are capable of action. 283

anorexia nervosa An eating disorder that involves the relentless pursuit of thinness through starvation. 489

Apgar Scale A widely used method to assess the health of newborns at one and five minutes after birth. The Apgar Scale evaluates infants' heart rate, respiratory effort, muscle tone, body color, and reflex irritability. 125

aphasia A loss or impairment of language

characterized by problems with social interaction, with verbal and nonverbal communication, and with repetitive behaviors. 372

autistic disorder A severe autism spectrum disorder that has its onset in the first three years of life and includes deficiencies in social relationships, abnormalities in communication, and restricted, repetitive, and stereotyped patterns of behavior. 374

autonomous morality The second stage of moral development in Piaget's theory, displayed by older children (about 10 years of age and older).

Spinach: Divide into little piles. Rearrange again into new piles. After five or six maneuvers, sit back and say you are full.

—Delia Ephron
American Writer and Humorist, 20th Century

taste and appetite adults take for granted (Dovey & others, 2008). Caregivers should allow for the child's developing tastes in food. However, when young children eat too many sweets—candy bars, cola, and sweetened cereals, for example—they can spoil their appetite and then not want to eat more nutritious foods at mealtime. Thus, caregivers need to be firm in limiting the amount of sweets young children eat.

Most preschool children need to eat more often than the adults in the family because preschool children use up so much energy. It is a long time from breakfast to lunch and from lunch to dinner for the active young child. Thus, a midmorning and midafternoon snack are recommended. A good strategy is to avoid giving sweets to young children during these snack times (Skinner & others, 2004). Better choices include whole-grain bagels spread with creamy peanut butter, pureed fruit shakes, or tortillas with refried beans. Keep in mind that some foods are known choking hazards—avoid giving young children snack foods such as hard candy, nuts, any hard raw vegetable, or whole grapes.

QUOTATIONS

These appear occasionally in the margins to stimulate further thought about a topic.

CRITICAL-THINKING AND CONTENT QUESTIONS IN PHOTOGRAPH CAPTIONS

Most photographs have a caption that ends with a critical-thinking or knowledge question in italics to stimulate further thought about a topic.

Attachment does not emerge suddenly but rather develops in a series of phases, moving from a baby's general preference for human beings to a partnership with primary caregivers. Following are four such phases based on Bowlby's conceptualization of attachment (Schaffer, 1996):

- *Phase 1: From birth to 2 months.* Infants instinctively direct their attachment to human figures. Strangers, siblings, and parents are equally likely to elicit smiling or crying from the infant.
- *Phase 2: From 2 to 7 months.* Attachment becomes focused on one figure, usually the primary caregiver, as the baby gradually learns to distinguish familiar from unfamiliar people.
- *Phase 3: From 7 to 24 months.* Specific attachments develop. With increased locomotor skills, babies actively seek contact with regular caregivers, such as the mother or father.
- *Phase 4: From 24 months on.* Children become aware of others' feelings, goals, and plans and begin to take these into account in forming their own actions.

In Bowlby's model, what are four phases of attachment?

Researchers' recent findings that infants are more socially sophisticated and insightful than previously envisioned suggest that some of the characteristics of Bowlby's phase

---

Careers in Children's Development

Toosje Thyssen Van Beveren, Infant Assessment Specialist

Toosje Thyssen Van Beveren is a developmental psychologist at the University of Texas Medical Center in Dallas. She has a master's degree in child clinical psychology and a Ph.D. in human development. Currently, Van Beveren is involved in a 12-week program called New Connections, which is a comprehensive intervention for young children who were affected by substance abuse prenatally and for their caregivers.

In the New Connections program, Van Beveren assesses infants' developmental status and progress. She might refer the infants to a speech, physical, or occupational therapist and monitor the infants' services and progress. Van Beveren trains the program staff and encourages them to use the exercises she recommends. She also discusses the child's problems with the primary caregivers, suggests activities, and assists them in enrolling infants in appropriate programs.

During her graduate work at the University of Texas at Dallas, Van Beveren was author John Santrock's teaching assistant in his undergraduate course on life-span development for four years. As a teaching assistant, she attended classes, graded exams, counseled students, and occasionally gave lectures. Each semester,

Van Beveren returns to give a lecture on prenatal development and infancy. She also teaches part-time in the psychology department at UT–Dallas. In Van Beveren's words, "My days are busy and full. The work is often challenging. There are some disappointments but mostly the work is enormously gratifying."

Toosje Thyssen Van Beveren conducting an infant assessment.

CAREERS IN CHILDREN'S DEVELOPMENT PROFILES

Throughout the book, *Careers in Children's Development* profiles feature a person working in a children's development field related to the chapter's content.

KEY PEOPLE

The most important theorists and researchers in the chapter are listed and page-referenced at the end of each chapter.

KEY PEOPLE

Jean Piaget 182
Renée Baillargeon 187
Eleanor Gibson 189
Elizabeth Spelke 189
Andrew Meltzoff 190

Karen Wynn 190
Carolyn Rovee-
  Collier 192
Jean Mandler 194
Arnold Gesell 198

Nancy Bayley 198
Patricia Kuhl 204
Noam Chomsky 207
Roger Brown 207
Michael Tomasello 208

Betty Hart and Todd
  Risley 208
Janellen Huttenlocher 208
Naomi Baron 210

E-LEARNING TOOLS

E-LEARNING TOOLS

Connect to **www.mhhe.com/santrockc11** to research the answers and complete these exercises. In addition, you'll find a number of other resources and valuable study tools for Chapter 2, "Biological Beginnings," on this Web site.

Taking It to the Net

1. Ahmahl, a biochemistry major, is writing a psychology paper on the potential dilemmas that society and scientists may face as a result of decoding the human genome. What are some of the main issues or concerns that Ahmahl should address in his class paper?

2. Brandon and Katie are thrilled to learn that they are expecting their first child. They are curious about the genetic makeup of their unborn child and seek answers to a number of related questions. (a) What disorders might be identified through prenatal genetic testing, and (b) which tests, if any, Katie should undergo to help determine this information?

3. Greg and Courtney have three boys. They would love to have a girl. Courtney read that there is a clinic in Virginia where you can pick the sex of your child. How successful are such efforts? Would you want to have this choice available to you?

Health and Well-Being, Parenting, and Education

Build your decision-making skills by trying your hand at the health and well-being, parenting, and education exercises.

Video Clips

The Online Learning Center includes the following video for this chapter:

- *Interview with Adoptive Parents—3004*
  An interview with a couple that adopted a second child.

This feature appears at the end of each chapter and consists of three parts: *Taking It to the Net* Internet problem-solving exercises; *Health and Well-Being, Parenting, and Education* exercises, which provide an opportunity to practice decision-making skills related to real-world applications; and *Video Clips*, which are available online. By going to the Online Learning Center for this book, where you can complete these valuable and enjoyable exercises, you will find many learning activities to improve your knowledge and understanding of the chapter.

MAKING A DIFFERENCE

At the end of each chapter, this feature provides practical information that individuals can use to improve the lives of children.

MAKING A DIFFERENCE

Lessons for Life

Marian Wright Edelman is one of America's foremost crusaders in the quest for improving the lives of children. Here are some of the main strategies she advocates for improving not only children's lives but our own as well (Edelman, 1992, pp. xxi, 42, 60):

- *"Don't feel as if you are entitled to anything that you don't sweat and struggle for."* Take the initiative to create opportunities. Don't wait around for people to give you favors. A door never has to stay closed. Push on it until it opens.
- *"Don't be afraid of taking risks or of being criticized."* We all make mistakes. It is only through making mistakes that we learn how to do things right. "It doesn't matter how many times you fall down. What matters is how many times we get up." We need "more courageous shepherds and fewer sheep."
- *"Don't ever stop learning and improving your mind or you're going to get left behind."* College is a great investment, but don't think you can park your mind there and everything you need to know will somehow be magically poured into it. Be an active learner. Be curious and ask questions. Explore new horizons.
- *"Stand up for children."* According to Edelman, this is the most important mission in the world. Parenting and nurturing the next generation of children are our society's most important functions, and we need to take them more seriously than we have in the past.

RESOURCES FOR IMPROVING CHILDREN'S LIVES

At the end of each chapter, resources provide information about books, Web sites, and organizations relevant to the chapter's topics

RESOURCES FOR IMPROVING CHILDREN'S LIVES

Children's Defense Fund
25 E Street
Washington, DC 20001
800–424–9602
www.childrensdefense.org

The Children's Defense Fund exists to provide a strong and effective voice for children and adolescents who cannot vote, lobby, or speak for themselves. The Children's Defense Fund is especially interested in the needs of poor, minority, and handicapped children and adolescents. The fund provides information, technical assistance, and support to a network of state and local child and youth advocates. The Children's Defense Fund publishes a number of excellent books and pamphlets related to children's needs.

Handbook of Child Psychology
edited by William Damon and Richard Lerner (6th ed., Vols. 1–4, 2006)
New York: John Wiley

The *Handbook of Child Psychology* is the standard reference work for overviews of theory and research in this field. It has in-depth discussions of many topics that we explore in this book.

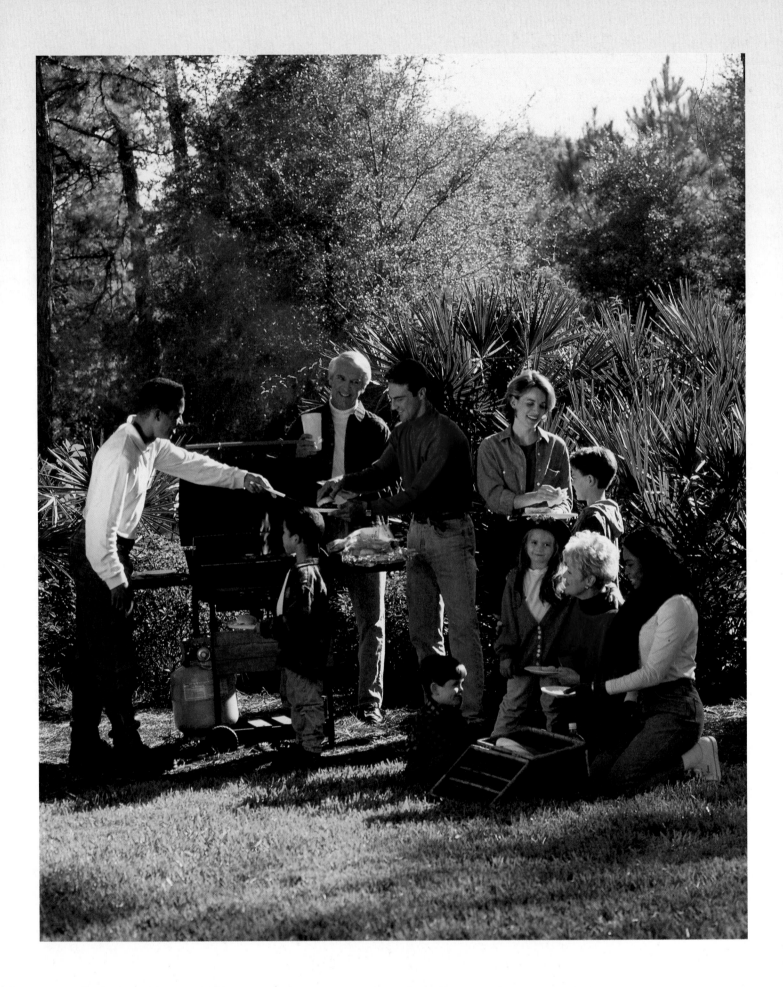

If I had my child to raise over again

If I had my child to raise over again,

I'd finger paint more, and point the finger less.

I'd do less correcting, and more connecting.

I'd take my eyes off my watch, and watch more with my eyes.

I would care to know less, and know to care more.

I'd take more hikes and fly more kites.

I'd stop playing serious, and seriously play.

I would run through more fields, and gaze at more stars.

I'd do more hugging, and less tugging.

I would be firm less often, and affirm much more.

I'd build self-esteem first, and the house later.

I'd teach less about the love of power,

And more about the power of love.

—Diane Loomans

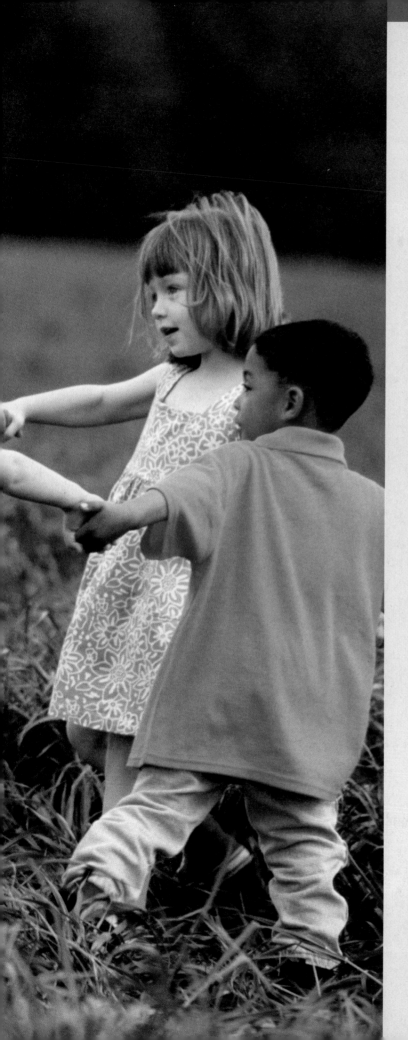

ONE

THE NATURE OF CHILDREN'S DEVELOPMENT

In every child who is born, under no matter what circumstances, and of no matter what parents, the potentiality of the human race is born again.

—JAMES AGEE
American Writer, 20th Century

Examining the shape of childhood allows us to understand it better. Every childhood is distinct, the first chapter of a new biography in the world. This book is about children's development, its universal features, its individual variations, its nature at the beginning of the twenty-first century. *Children* is about the rhythm and meaning of children's lives, about turning mystery into understanding, and about weaving together a portrait of who each of us was, is, and will be. In Section 1 you will read "Introduction" (Chapter 1).

1

> *We reach backward to our parents and forward to our children and through their children to a future we will never see, but about which we need to care.*
>
> —CARL JUNG
> *Swiss Psychoanalyst, 20th Century*

LEARNING GOALS

♦ Explain why it is important to study children's development, and identify five areas in which children's lives need to be improved

♦ Characterize historical views of children

♦ Discuss the most important processes, periods, and issues in development

♦ Summarize why research is important in child development; the main theories of child development; and research methods, designs, and challenges

INTRODUCTION

5

Images of Children's Development
The Stories of Ted Kaczynski and Alice Walker

Ted Kaczynski sprinted through high school, not bothering with his junior year and making only passing efforts at social contact. Off to Harvard at age 16, Kaczynski was a loner during his college years. One of his roommates at Harvard said that he avoided people by quickly shuffling by them and slamming the door behind him. After obtaining his Ph.D. in mathematics at the University of Michigan, Kaczynski became a professor at the University of California at Berkeley. His colleagues there remember him as hiding from social circumstances—no friends, no allies, no networking.

After several years at Berkeley, Kaczynski resigned and moved to a rural area of Montana where he lived as a hermit in a crude shack for 25 years. Town residents described him as a bearded eccentric. Kaczynski traced his own difficulties to growing up as a genius in a kid's body and sticking out like a sore thumb in his surroundings as a child. In 1996, he was arrested and charged as the notorious Unabomber, America's most wanted killer. Over the course of 17 years, Kaczynski had sent 16 mail bombs that left 23 people wounded or maimed and 3 people dead. In 1998, he pleaded guilty to the offenses and was sentenced to life in prison.

A decade before Kaczynski mailed his first bomb, Alice Walker spent her days battling racism in Mississippi. She had recently won her first writing fellowship, but rather than use the money to follow her dream of moving to Senegal, Africa, she put herself into the heart and heat of the civil rights movement. Walker had grown up knowing the brutal effects of poverty and racism. Born in 1944, she was the eighth child of Georgia sharecroppers who earned $300 a year. When Walker was 8, her brother accidentally shot her in the left eye with a BB gun. Because her parents had no car, it took them a week to get her to a hospital. By the time she received medical care, she was blind in that eye, and it had developed a disfiguring layer of scar tissue. Despite the counts against her, Walker overcame pain and anger and went on to win a Pulitzer Prize for her book *The Color Purple*. She became not only a novelist but also an essayist, a poet, a short-story writer, and a social activist.

Ted Kaczynski, about age 14.

Alice Walker, about age 8.

Ted Kaczynski, the convicted unabomber, traced his difficulties to growing up as a genius in a kid's body and not fitting in when he was a child.

Alice Walker *What might be some reasons that she overcame trauma in her childhood to develop in impressive ways?*

What leads one individual, so full of promise, to commit brutal acts of violence and another to turn poverty and trauma into a rich literary harvest? If you have ever wondered why people turn out the way they do, you have asked yourself the central question we will explore in this book.

PREVIEW

Why study children? Perhaps you are, or will be, a parent or teacher, and responsibility for children is, or will be, a part of your everyday life. The more you learn about children, the better you can guide them. Perhaps you hope to gain an understanding of your own history—as an infant, as a child, and as an adolescent. Perhaps you accidentally came across the course description and found it intriguing. Whatever your reasons, you will discover that the study of child development is provocative, intriguing, and informative. In this first chapter, we explore why caring for children is so important, describe historical changes in the study of children's development, examine the nature of development, and outline how science helps us to understand it.

---

1 WHY IS CARING FOR CHILDREN IMPORTANT?

The Importance of Studying Children's Development

Improving the Lives of Children

Caring for children is an important theme of this text. To think about why caring for children is such an important theme, we will explore why it is beneficial to study children's development and some areas in which children's lives need to be improved. Just what do we mean when we speak of an individual's development? **Development** is the pattern of change that begins at conception and continues through the life span. Most development involves growth, although it also includes decline.

The Importance of Studying Children's Development

How might you benefit from examining children's development? Perhaps you are, or will be, a parent or teacher and you want to learn about children so that you can become a better parent or educator. Perhaps you hope to gain some insight about your own history—as an infant, a child, and an adolescent. Or perhaps you think that the study of children's development might raise some provocative issues. Whatever your reasons for reading this book, you will discover that the study of children's development is intriguing and filled with information about who we are and how we came to be this way.

As we indicated earlier, most human development involves growth, but it also includes decline. For example, think about how your ability to speak and write your native language has grown since you were a young child. But your ability to achieve a high level of competence in learning to speak a new language has probably declined (Thomas & Johnson, 2008). In this book, we examine children's development from the point of conception through adolescence. You will see yourself as an infant, as a child, and as an adolescent—and be stimulated to think about how those years influenced you.

Children are the legacy we leave for the time we will not live to see.

—ARISTOTLE
Greek Philosopher, 4th Century B.C.

development The pattern of movement or change that begins at conception and continues through the human life span.

Improving the Lives of Children

If you were to pick up a newspaper or magazine in any U.S. town or city, you might see headlines like these: "Political Leanings May Be Written in the Genes," "Mother Accused of Tossing Children into Bay," "Gender Gap Widens," and "FDA Warns About ADHD Drug." Researchers are examining these and many other topics of contemporary concern. The roles that health and well-being, parenting, education, and sociocultural contexts play in children's development, as well as how social policy is related to these issues, are a special focus of this textbook.

Health and Well-Being   Does a pregnant woman endanger her fetus if she has a few beers a week? How does a poor diet affect a child's ability to learn? Are children exercising less today than in the past? What roles do parents and peers play in whether adolescents abuse drugs? Throughout this text we discuss many questions like these regarding health and well-being. Investigating these questions, and their answers, is an important goal for just about everyone.

Health professionals today recognize the power of lifestyles and psychological states in health and well-being (Insel & Roth, 2010; Hahn, Payne, & Lucas, 2009). In every chapter of this book, issues of health and well-being are integrated into our discussion.

Clinical psychologists are among the health professionals who help people improve their well-being. In this chapter's *Careers in Children's Development* profile, you can read about clinical psychologist Luis Vargas, who helps adolescents with problems. A Careers Appendix that follows Chapter 1 describes the education and training required to become a clinical psychologist and other careers in child development.

Parenting   Can two gay men raise a healthy family? Are children harmed if both parents work outside the home? Do adopted children fare as well as children raised by their biological parents? How damaging is divorce to children's development?

Careers in Children's Development

Luis Vargas, Clinical Child Psychologist

Luis Vargas is the director of the Clinical Child Psychology Internship Program and a professor in child and adolescent psychiatry at the University of New Mexico School of Medicine. Vargas obtained an undergraduate degree in psychology from Trinity University in Texas and a Ph.D. in clinical psychology at the University of Nebraska–Lincoln.

Vargas' work includes assessing and treating children, adolescents, and their families, especially when a child or adolescent has a serious mental disorder. He also trains mental health professionals to provide culturally responsive and developmentally appropriate mental health services. In addition, he is interested in cultural and assessment issues with children, adolescents, and their families. He co-authored (with Joan Koss-Chiono a medical anthropologist) *Working with Latino Youth: Culture, Context, and Development* (1999).

Vargas' clinical work is heavily influenced by contextual and ecological theories of development (which we discuss later in this chapter). His first undergraduate course in human development, and subsequent courses in development, contributed to his decision to pursue a career in clinical child psychology.

Luis Vargas (*left*) conducting a child therapy session.

We hear many questions like these related to pressures on the contemporary family (Hewitt-Taylor, 2009; Winslow & others, 2009). We examine these questions and others that provide a context for understanding factors that influence parents' lives and how effectively they rear their children. How parents, as well as other adults, can make a positive difference in children's lives is a major theme of this book.

You might be a parent someday or might already be one. You should take seriously the importance of rearing your children, because they are the future of our society. Good parenting takes considerable time. If you plan to become a parent, commit yourself day after day, week after week, month after month, and year after year to providing your children with a warm, supportive, safe, and stimulating environment that will make them feel secure and allow them to reach their full potential as human beings. The poster shown here, which states "Children learn to love when they are loved," reflects this theme.

Understanding the nature of children's development can help you become a better parent (Grusec, Almas, & Willoughby, 2008; Morawaska, Winter, & Sanders, 2009). Many parents learn parenting practices from their parents. Unfortunately, when parenting practices and child-care strategies are passed from one generation to the next, both desirable and undesirable ones are usually perpetuated. This book and your instructor's lectures in this course can help you become more knowledgeable about children's development and sort through which practices in your own upbringing you should continue with your own children and which you should abandon.

Children learn to love when they are loved

Education   There is widespread agreement that something needs to be done to improve the education of our nation's children (Ballantine & Hammock, 2009; Webb, Metha, & Jordan, 2010). A number of questions are involved in improving schools (Florence, 2010). For example, are they failing to teach children how to read and write and calculate adequately? Should there be more accountability in schools with accountability of student learning and teaching assessed by formal tests? Have schools become too soft and watered down? Should they make more demands on, and have higher expectations of, children? Should schooling involve less memorization and more attention to the development of children's ability to process information more efficiently? Should schools focus only on developing the child's knowledge and cognitive skills, or should they pay more attention to the whole child and consider the child's socioemotional and physical development as well? For example, should schools be dramatically changed so that they serve as a locus for a wide range of services, such as primary health care, child care, preschool education, parent education, recreation, and family counseling, as well as the traditional educational activities, such as learning in the classroom? Are U.S. schools teaching children to be immoral? In this text, we examine such questions about the state of education in the United States and consider recent research on solutions to educational problems.

Sociocultural Contexts and Diversity   Health and well-being, parenting, and education—like development itself—are all shaped by their sociocultural context (Shiraev & Levy, 2010; Taylor & Whittaker, 2009). The term **context** refers to the settings in which development occurs. These settings are influenced by historical, economic, social, and cultural factors. Four contexts that we pay special attention to in this text are culture, ethnicity, socioeconomic status, and gender.

Culture encompasses the behavior patterns, beliefs, and all other products of a specific group of people that are passed on from generation to generation. Culture results from the interaction of people over many years (Shiraev & Levy, 2010). A cultural group can be as large as the United States or as small as an isolated Appalachian town. Whatever its size, the group's culture influences the behavior of

context   The settings, influenced by historical, economic, social, and cultural factors, in which development occurs.

culture   The behavior patterns, beliefs, and all other products of a group that are passed on from generation to generation.

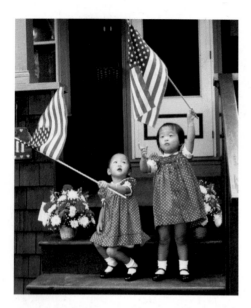

These two Korean-born children on the day they became U.S. citizens represent the dramatic increase in the percentage of ethnic minority children in the United States.

its members. **Cross-cultural studies** compare aspects of two or more cultures. The comparison provides information about the degree to which development is similar, or universal, across cultures, or is instead culture-specific (Hayashino & Chopra, 2009; Matsumoto & Juang, 2008).

Ethnicity (the word ethnic comes from the Greek word for "nation") is rooted in cultural heritage, nationality, race, religion, and language. African Americans, Latinos, Asian Americans, Native Americans, Polish Americans, and Italian Americans are a few examples of ethnic groups (Spring 2010). Diversity exists within each ethnic group (Hall, 2010; Liu & others, 2009). Contrary to stereotypes, not all African Americans live in low-income circumstances; not all Latinos are Catholics; not all Asian Americans are high school math whizzes.

Socioeconomic status (SES) refers to a person's position within society based on occupational, educational, and economic characteristics. Socioeconomic status implies certain inequalities. Generally, members of a society have (1) occupations that vary in prestige, and some individuals have more access than others to higher-status occupations; (2) different levels of educational attainment, and some individuals have more access than others to better education; (3) different economic resources; and (4) different levels of power to influence a community's institutions. These differences in the ability to control resources and to participate in society's rewards produce unequal opportunities (Healey, 2009; McLoyd & others, 2009).

Gender Gender is another key dimension of children's development (Helgeson, 2009). **Gender** refers to the characteristics of people as males and females. Few aspects of our development are more central to our identity and social relationships than gender (Best, 2010; Galambos, Berenbaum, & McHale, 2009). How you view yourself, your relationships with other people, your life, and your goals are shaped to a great extent by whether you are male or female and how your culture defines the proper roles of males and females (Eagly, 2009).

Each of these dimensions of the sociocultural context—culture, ethnicity, SES, and gender—helps mold how an individual develops through life, as discussions in later chapters demonstrate. We explore, for example, questions such as the following:

- Do infants around the world form attachments with their parents in the same way, or do these attachments differ from one culture to another?

- Does poverty influence the likelihood that young children will be provided with fewer educational opportunities than children growing up in more affluent families?

- Is there a parenting style that is universally effective, or does the effectiveness of different types of parenting depend on the ethnic group or culture?

- If adolescents from minority groups identify with their ethnic culture, is that likely to help or hinder their socioemotional development?

In the United States, the sociocultural context has become increasingly diverse in recent years. Its population includes an increasing percentage of children from ethnic minority families, especially Latino and Asian American, who recently have immigrated to the United States. For example, from 2000 to 2006, the non-Latino White school population increased 4 percent, while the Latino school population increased 21 percent (U.S. Census Bureau, 2007). This changing demographic tapestry promises not only the richness that diversity produces but also difficult challenges in extending the American dream to all individuals (Cushner, McClelland, & Stafford, 2009; Hall, 2010; Suarez-Orosco & Suarez-Orosco, 2010).

We discuss sociocultural contexts and diversity in each chapter. In addition, a *Diversity in Children's Development* interlude appears in every chapter. The first Diversity interlude, which focuses on gender, families, and children's development around the world, follows.

How Would You...?
As a psychologist, how would you explain the importance of examining sociocultural factors in developmental research?

cross-cultural studies Comparisons of one culture with one or more other cultures. These comparisons provide information about the degree to which children's development is similar, or universal, across cultures, and the degree to which it is culture-specific.

ethnicity A characteristic based on cultural heritage, nationality, race, religion, and language.

socioeconomic status (SES) An individual's position within society based on occupational, educational, and economic characteristics.

gender The characteristics of people as females or males.

Diversity in Children's Development

GENDER, FAMILIES, AND CHILDREN'S DEVELOPMENT

Around the world, the experiences of male and female children and adolescents continue to be quite different (Brown & Larson, 2002; UNICEF, 2009). Except in a few areas, such as Japan, the Philippines, and Western countries, males have far greater access to educational opportunities than females. In many countries, adolescent females have less freedom to pursue a variety of careers and engage in various leisure acts than males. Gender differences in sexual expression are widespread, especially in India, Southeast Asia, Latin America, and Arab countries—where there are far more restrictions on the sexual activity of adolescent females than of males. In certain areas around the world, these gender differences do appear to be narrowing over time. In some countries, educational and career opportunities for women are expanding, and in some parts of the world control over adolescent girls' romantic and sexual relationships is weakening. However, in many countries females still experience considerable discrimination, and much work is needed to bridge the gap between the rights of males and females.

In certain parts of the world, children grow up in closely knit families with extensive extended-kin networks "that provide a web of connections and reinforce a traditional way of life" (Brown & Larson, 2002, p. 6). For example, in Arab countries, adolescents are required to adopt strict codes of conduct and loyalty. However, in Western countries such as the United States, children and adolescents are growing up in much larger numbers in divorced families and stepfamilies. Parenting in Western countries is less authoritarian than in the past.

Some of the trends that are occurring in many countries around the world "include greater family mobility, migration to urban areas, family members working in distant cities or countries, smaller families, fewer extended-family households, and increases in mothers' employment" (Brown & Larson, 2002, p. 7). Unfortunately, many of these changes may reduce the ability of families to provide time and resources for children and adolescents.

Doly Akter, age 17, lives in a slum in Dhaka, Bangladesh, where sewers overflow, garbage rots in the streets, and children are undernourished. Nearly two-thirds of young women in Bangladesh get married before they are 18. Doly recently organized a club supported by UNICEF in which girls go door-to-door to monitor the hygiene habits of households in their neighborhood. The monitoring has led to improved hygiene and health in the families. Also, her group has managed to stop several child marriages by meeting with parents and convincing them that it is not in their daughter's best interests. When talking with parents in their neighborhoods, the girls in the club emphasize the importance of staying in school and how this will improve their daughter's future. Doly says that the girls in her UNICEF group are far more aware of their rights than their mothers ever were (UNICEF, 2007).

Source	Characteristic
Individual	Good intellectual functioning Appealing, sociable, easygoing disposition Self-confidence, high self-esteem Talents Faith
Family	Close relationship to caring parent figure Authoritative parenting: warmth, structure, high expectations Socioeconomic advantages Connections to extended supportive family networks
Extrafamilial context	Bonds to caring adults outside the family Connections to positive organizations Attending effective schools

FIGURE 1.1 Characteristics of Resilient Children and Their Contexts

Resilience, Social Policy, and Children's Development   Some children develop confidence in their abilities despite negative stereotypes about their gender or their ethnic group. And some children triumph over poverty or other adversities. They show *resilience* (Gutman, 2008). Think back to the chapter-opening story about Alice Walker. In spite of racism, poverty, her low socioeconomic status, and a disfiguring eye injury, she went on to become a successful author and champion for equality.

Are there certain characteristics that make children like Alice Walker resilient? Are there other characteristics that make children like Ted Kaczynski, who despite his intelligence and education became a killer? After analyzing research on this topic, Ann Masten and her colleagues (2001, 2006, 2007; Masten, Burt, & Coatsworth, 2006) concluded that a number of individual factors, such as good intellectual functioning, influence resiliency. In addition, as Figure 1.1 shows, their families and extrafamilial contexts tend to show certain features. For example, resilient children are likely to have a close relationship to a caring parent figure and bonds to caring adults outside the family.

Should governments also take action to improve the contexts of children's development and aid their resilience? **Social policy** is a government's course of action designed to promote the welfare of its citizens. The shape and scope of social policy related to children are tied to the political system. The values held by citizens and elected officials, the nation's economic strengths and weaknesses, and partisan politics all influence the policy agenda.

When concern about broad social issues is widespread, comprehensive social policies often result. Child labor laws were established in the early twentieth century to protect not only children but also jobs for adults; federal child-care funding during World War II was justified by the need for women laborers in factories; and Head Start and other War on Poverty programs in the 1960s were implemented to decrease intergenerational poverty.

Out of concern that policy makers are doing too little to protect the well-being of children, researchers increasingly are undertaking studies that they hope will lead to wise and effective decision making about social policy (Huston & Bentley, 2010). Children who grow up in poverty represent a special concern (Fiscella & Kitzman, 2009; Hildebrandt & Stevens, 2009). In 2006, approximately 17.4 percent of U.S. children were living in families below the poverty line (Federal Interagency Forum on Child and Family Statistics, 2008). This is an increase from

social policy A government's course of action designed to promote the welfare of its citizens.

Marian Wright Edelman, president of the Children's Defense Fund (shown here interacting with young children), has been a tireless advocate of children's rights and has been instrumental in calling attention to the needs of children. *What are some of these needs?*

2001 (16.2 percent) but a decrease from a peak of 22.7 percent in 1993. As indicated in Figure 1.2, one study found that a higher percentage of U.S. children in poor families than in middle-income families were exposed to family turmoil, separation from a parent, violence, crowding, excessive noise, and poor housing (Evans & English, 2002). A recent study also revealed that the more years children spent living in poverty, the more their physiological indices of stress were elevated (Evans & Kim, 2007).

The U.S. figure of 17.4 percent of children living in poverty is much higher than those from other industrialized nations. For example, Canada has a child poverty rate of 9 percent and Sweden has a rate of 2 percent.

In the United States, the national government, state governments, and city governments all play a role in influencing the well-being of children (Children's Defense Fund, 2009). When families fail or seriously endanger a child's well-being, governments often step in to help. At the national and state levels, policy makers have debated for decades whether helping poor parents ends up helping their children as well. Researchers are providing some answers by examining the effects of specific policies (Balsano, Theokas, & Bobek, 2009; Gupta, Thornton, & Huston, 2008).

For example, the Minnesota Family Investment Program (MFIP) was designed in the 1990s primarily to influence the behavior of adults—specifically, to move adults off the welfare rolls and into paid employment. A key element of the program was that it guaranteed that adults participating in the program would receive more income if they worked than if they did not. When the adults' income rose, how did that affect their children? A study of the effects of MFIP found that increases in the incomes of working poor parents were linked with benefits for their children (Gennetian & Miller, 2002). The children's achievement in school improved, and their behavior problems decreased. A current MFIP study is examining the influence of specific services on low-income families at risk for child maltreatment and other negative outcomes for children (Minnesota Family Investment Program, 2009).

Developmental psychologists and other researchers have examined the effects of many other government policies. They are seeking ways to help families living in poverty improve their well-being, and they have offered many suggestions for improving government policies (Johnson, Tarrant, & Brooks-Gunn, 2008; McLoyd & others, 2009).

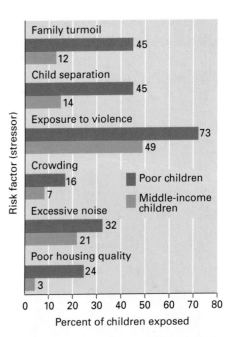

FIGURE 1.2 Exposure to Six Stressors Among Poor and Middle-Income Children. One study analyzed the exposure to six stressors among poor children and middle-income children (Evans & English, 2002). Poor children were much more likely to face each of these stressors.

How Would You...?
As a health-care professional, what types of social policies would you recommend to improve healthy development of young children?

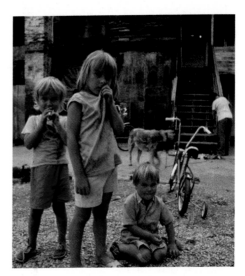

These children live in a slum area of a small Vermont town where the unemployment rate is very high because of a decline in industrial jobs. *What should be the government's role in improving the lives of these children?*

Review and Reflect: Learning Goal 1

1 **Explain why it is important to study children's development, and identify five areas in which children's lives need to be improved**

REVIEW
- Why is it important to study children's development?
- What are five aspects of children's development that need to be improved?

REFLECT
- Imagine what your development as a child would have been like in a culture that offered fewer or distinctively different choices than your own? How might your development have been different if your family was significantly richer or poorer than it was?

2 WHAT ARE SOME HISTORICAL VIEWS OF CHILD DEVELOPMENT?

Early Views of Childhood   The Modern Study of Child Development

Anywhere you turn today, the development of children captures public attention. Historically, though, interest in the development of children has been uneven.

Early Views of Childhood

Childhood has become such a distinct period that it is hard to imagine that it was not always thought of as markedly different from adulthood. However, in medieval Europe laws generally did not distinguish between child and adult offenses. After analyzing samples of art along with available publications, historian Philippe Ariès (1962) concluded that European societies prior to 1600 did not give any special status to children.

Were children actually treated as miniature adults with no special status in medieval Europe? Ariès primarily sampled aristocratic, idealized subjects, and this focus might have been misleading. Childhood probably was recognized as a distinct phase of life more than Ariès believed, but his analysis helped to highlight cultural differences in how children are viewed and treated.

Throughout history, philosophers have speculated at length about the nature of children and how they should be reared. The ancient Egyptians, Greeks, and Romans held rich conceptions of children's development. More recently in European history, three influential philosophical views portrayed children in terms of original sin, tabula rasa, and innate goodness:

This artistic impression shows how some children were viewed as miniature adults earlier in history. Many artists' renditions of children as miniature adults may have been too stereotypical.

- In the **original sin view,** especially advocated during the Middle Ages, children were perceived as being born into the world as evil beings. The goal of child rearing was to provide salvation, to remove sin from the child's life.

- Toward the end of the seventeenth century, the **tabula rasa view** was proposed by English philosopher John Locke. He argued that children are not innately bad but, instead, are like a "blank tablet." Locke maintained that childhood experiences are important in determining adult characteristics. He advised parents to spend time with their children and to help them become contributing members of society.

- In the eighteenth century, the **innate goodness view** was presented by Swiss-born French philosopher Jean-Jacques Rousseau. He stressed that children are inherently good. Because children are basically good, said Rousseau, they should be permitted to grow naturally, with little parental monitoring or constraint.

Today, the Western view of children holds that childhood is a highly eventful and unique period of life that lays an important foundation for the adult years and is markedly different from them. Most current approaches to childhood identify distinct periods in which children master specific skills and tasks that prepare them for adulthood. Childhood is no longer seen as an inconvenient waiting period during which adults must suffer the incompetencies of the young. Instead, we protect children from the stresses and responsibilities of adult work through strict child labor laws. We handle their crimes in a special system of juvenile justice. We also have provisions for helping children when families fail. In short, we now value childhood as a special time of growth and change, and we invest great resources in caring for and educating children.

original sin view Advocated during the Middle Ages, the belief that children were born into the world as evil beings and were basically bad.

tabula rasa view The idea, proposed by John Locke, that children are not innately bad but are like a "blank tablet."

innate goodness view The idea, presented by Swiss-born French philosopher Jean-Jacques Rousseau, that children are inherently good.

The Modern Study of Child Development

The modern era of studying children began with some important developments in the late 1800s (Cairns & Cairns, 2006). Since then, the study of child development has evolved into a sophisticated science with major theories, as well as elegant techniques and methods of study that help organize our thinking about children's development (Damon & Lerner, 2006). This new era began during the last quarter of the nineteenth century when a major shift took place—from a strictly philosophical approach to human psychology to an approach that includes systematic observation and experimentation.

Methods for a New Science   Most of the influential early psychologists were trained either in the natural sciences such as biology or medicine or in philosophy. The natural scientists valued experiments and reliable observations; after all, experiments and systematic observation had advanced knowledge in physics, chemistry, and biology. But these scientists were not at all sure that people, much less children or infants, could be studied in this way. Their hesitation was due, in part, to a lack of examples to follow in studying children. In addition, philosophers of the time debated, on both intellectual and ethical grounds, whether the methods of science were appropriate for studying people.

The deadlock was broken when some daring thinkers began to try new methods of studying infants, children, and adolescents. For example, a the end of the nineteenth century and the beginning of the twentieth century, French psychologist Alfred Binet invented many tasks to study attention and memory. He used them to study his own daughters, other normal children, children with mental retardation, extremely gifted children, and adults. Eventually, he collaborated in the development of the first modern test of intelligence (the Binet test). About the same time, G. Stanley Hall pioneered the use of questionnaires with large groups of children. In one investigation, Hall tested 400 children in the Boston schools to find out how much they "knew" about themselves and the world, asking them such questions as "Where are your ribs?"

Later, during the 1920s, many child development research centers were created and their professional staffs began to observe and chart a myriad of behaviors in infants and children. Research centers at the Universities of Minnesota, Iowa, California at Berkeley, Columbia, and Toronto became famous for their investigations of children's play, friendship patterns, fears, aggression and conflict, and sociability. This work became closely associated with the so-called child study movement, and a new organization, the Society for Research in Child Development, was formed about the same time.

Another ardent observer of children was Arnold Gesell. With his photographic dome (shown in Figure 1.3), Gesell (1928) could systematically observe children's behavior without interrupting them. He strove for precision in charting what a child is like at specific ages.

The direct study of children, in which investigators directly observe children's behavior, conduct experiments, and obtain information about children by questioning their parents and teachers, had an auspicious start in the work of these child study experts. The flow of information about children, based on direct study, has not slowed since that time.

Theories for a New Science   Gesell not only developed sophisticated strategies for studying children but also had provocative views on children's development. His views were strongly influenced by Charles Darwin's evolutionary theory. (Darwin had made the scientific study of children respectable when he developed a baby journal for recording systematic observations of children.) Gesell argued that certain characteristics of children simply "bloom" with age because of a biological, maturational blueprint.

Evolutionary theory also influenced G. Stanley Hall. Hall (1904) argued that child development follows a natural evolutionary course that can be revealed by child study. He theorized that child development unfolds in stages, with distinct motives and capabilities at each stage.

Stages are also a feature of Sigmund Freud's portrait of child development. According to Freud's (1917) psychoanalytic theory, children are rarely aware of the motives and reasons for their behavior, and the bulk of their mental life is unconscious.

> *A*h! What would the world be to us
> If the children were no more?
> We should dread the desert behind us
> Worse than the dark before.
>
> —HENRY WADSWORTH LONGFELLOW
> *American Poet, 19th Century*

FIGURE 1.3 Gesell's Photographic Dome
Cameras rode on metal tracks at the top of the dome and were moved as needed to record the child's activities.

Freud's ideas were compatible with Hall's, emphasizing conflict and biological influences on development, although Freud stressed that a child's experiences with parents in the first five years of life are important determinants of later personality development. Freud envisioned the child moving through a series of stages, filled with conflict between biological urges and societal demands. In the early part of the twentieth century, Freud's theory had a profound influence on the study of children's personality development and socialization.

A competing view that gained prominence during the 1920s and 1930s was John Watson's (1928) theory of behaviorism. Watson argued that children can be shaped into whatever society wishes by examining and changing the environment. He believed strongly in the systematic observation of children's behavior under controlled conditions. Watson had some provocative views about child rearing as well. He claimed that parents are too soft on children. "Quit cuddling and smiling at babies so much," he told parents.

Whereas John Watson was observing the environment's influence on children's behavior, and Sigmund Freud was probing the depths of the unconscious mind to discover clues about our early experiences with our parents, others were more concerned about the development of children's conscious thoughts—that is, the thoughts of which they are aware. James Mark Baldwin was a pioneer in the study of children's thought (Cairns & Cairns, 2006). He gave the term **genetic epistemology** to the study of how children's knowledge changes over the course of their development. (The term *genetic* at that time was a synonym for "developmental," and the term *epistemology* means "the nature or study of knowledge.")

Baldwin's ideas initially were proposed in the 1880s. Later, in the twentieth century, Swiss psychologist Jean Piaget adopted and elaborated on many of Baldwin's themes, keenly observing the development of his own children and devising clever experiments to investigate how children think. Piaget became a giant in developmental psychology. Some of you, perhaps, are already familiar with his view that children pass through a series of cognitive, or thought, stages from infancy through adolescence. According to Piaget, children think in a manner that is qualitatively different from that of adults.

This introduction to several theories of children's development has been brief, designed to give you a glimpse of some of the different ways children have been viewed as the study of child development unfolded. You will read more about theoretical perspectives later in this chapter and in subsequent chapters. These theories helped push forward the scientific study of child development. New knowledge about children—based on direct observation and testing—is accumulating at a breathtaking pace.

Review and Reflect: Learning Goal 2

 Characterize historical views of children

REVIEW

• What are three philosophical views of children?
• How can development of the modern study of children be described?

REFLECT

• Which of the three philosophical views of children—original sin, tabula rasa, and innate goodness—appeals to you? Why?

genetic epistemology The study of how children's knowledge changes over the course of their development.

3 WHAT CHARACTERIZES DEVELOPMENT?

Biological, Cognitive, and Socioemotional Processes

Periods of Development

Issues in Development

Each of us develops in certain ways like all other individuals, like some other individuals, and like no other individuals. Most of the time, our attention is directed to a person's uniqueness, but psychologists who study development are drawn to our shared characteristics as well as what makes us unique. As humans, we all have traveled some common paths. Each of us—Leonardo da Vinci, Joan of Arc, George Washington, Martin Luther King, Jr., and you—walked at about the age of 1, engaged in fantasy play as a young child, and became more independent as a youth. What shapes this common path of human development, and what are its milestones?

Biological, Cognitive, and Socioemotional Processes

The pattern of human development is created by the interplay of several processes—biological, cognitive, and socioemotional. **Biological processes** produce changes in an individual's body. Genes inherited from parents, the development of the brain, height and weight gains, motor skills, and the hormonal changes of puberty all reflect the role of biological processes in development.

Cognitive processes refer to changes in an individual's thought, intelligence, and language. The tasks of watching a mobile swinging above a crib, putting together a two-word sentence, memorizing a poem, solving a math problem, and imagining what it would be like to be a movie star all involve cognitive processes.

Socioemotional processes involve changes in an individual's relationships with other people, changes in emotions, and changes in personality. An infant's smile in response to her mother's touch, a child's attack on a playmate, another's development of assertiveness, and an adolescent's joy at the senior prom all reflect socioemotional development.

Biological, cognitive, and socioemotional processes are inextricably intertwined (Diamond, Casey, & Munakata, 2009, 2010). Consider a baby smiling in response to a parent's touch. This response depends on biological processes (the physical nature of touch and responsiveness to it), cognitive processes (the ability to understand intentional acts), and socioemotional processes (the act of smiling often reflects a positive emotional feeling, and smiling helps to connect us in positive ways with other human beings). Nowhere is the connection across biological, cognitive, and socioemotional processes more obvious than in two rapidly emerging fields:

- *Developmental cognitive neuroscience,* which explores links between development, cognitive processes, and the brain (Diamond, Casey, & Munakata, 2010)

PEANUTS © United Feature Syndicate, Inc.

biological processes Changes in an individual's body.

cognitive processes Changes in an individual's thought, intelligence, and language.

socioemotional processes Changes in an individual's relationships with other people, changes in emotions, and changes in personality.

FIGURE 1.4 Biological, Cognitive, and Socioemotional Processes Changes in development are the result of biological, cognitive, and socioemotional processes. These processes interact as individuals develop.

• *Developmental social neuroscience*, which examines connections between socioemotional processes, development, and the brain (de Haan & Gunnar, 2009; Johnson & others, 2009)

In many instances, biological, cognitive, and socioemotional processes are bidirectional. For example, biological processes can influence cognitive processes and vice versa. Thus, although usually we will study the different processes of development (biological, cognitive, and socioemotional) in separate locations, keep in mind that we are talking about the development of an integrated human child with a mind and body that are interdependent (see Figure 1.4). In many places throughout the book we will call attention to these connections.

Periods of Development

For the purposes of organization and understanding, a child's development is commonly described in terms of periods, which are given approximate age ranges. The most widely used classification of developmental periods describes a child's development in terms of the following sequence: the prenatal period, infancy, early childhood, middle and late childhood, and adolescence.

The **prenatal period** is the time from conception to birth, roughly a nine-month period. During this amazing time, a single cell grows into an organism, complete with a brain and behavioral capabilities.

Infancy is the developmental period that extends from birth to about 18 to 24 months of age. Infancy is a time of extreme dependence on adults. Many psychological activities are just beginning—the ability to speak, to coordinate sensations and physical actions, to think with symbols, and to imitate and learn from others.

Early childhood is the developmental period that extends from the end of infancy to about 5 to 6 years of age; sometimes this period is called the preschool years. During this time, young children learn to become more self-sufficient and to care for themselves; they develop school readiness skills (following instructions, identifying letters), and they spend many hours in play and with peers. First grade typically marks the end of this period.

Middle and late childhood is the developmental period that extends from about 6 to 11 years of age; sometimes this period is referred to as the elementary school years. Children master the fundamental skills of reading, writing, and arithmetic, and they are formally exposed to the larger world and its culture. Achievement becomes a more central theme of the child's world, and self-control increases.

Adolescence is the developmental period of transition from childhood to early adulthood, entered at approximately 10 to 12 years of age and ending at 18 to 22 years of age. Adolescence begins with rapid physical changes—dramatic gains in height and weight; changes in body contour; and the development of sexual characteristics such as enlargement of the breasts, development of pubic and facial hair, and deepening of the voice. The pursuit of independence and an identity are prominent features of this period of development. More and more time is spent outside the family. Thought becomes more abstract, idealistic, and logical.

Today, developmentalists do not suggest that change ends with adolescence (Baltes, 2009; Schaie, 2009). They describe development as a life-long process. However, the purpose of this text is to describe the changes in development that take place from conception through adolescence. All of these periods of development are produced by the interplay of biological, cognitive, and socioemotional processes (see Figure 1.5).

prenatal period The time from conception to birth.

infancy The developmental period that extends from birth to 18 to 24 months of age.

early childhood The developmental period that extends from the end of infancy to about 5 to 6 years of age; sometimes called the preschool years.

middle and late childhood The developmental period that extends from about 6 to 11 years of age; sometimes called the elementary school years.

adolescence The developmental period of transition from childhood to early adulthood, entered at approximately 10 to 12 years of age and ending at 18 to 22 years of age.

Periods of Development

| Prenatal period | Infancy | Early childhood | Middle and late childhood | Adolescence |

Biological processes

Cognitive processes

Socioemotional processes

Processes of Development

FIGURE 1.5 Processes and Periods of Development Development moves through the prenatal, infancy, early childhood, middle and late childhood, and adolescence periods. These periods of development are the result of biological, cognitive, and socioemotional processes. Development is the creation of increasingly complex forms.

Issues in Development

Many questions about children's development remain unanswered. For example, what exactly drives the biological, cognitive, and socioemotional processes of development, and how does what happens in infancy influence middle childhood or adolescence? Despite all of the knowledge that researchers have acquired, debate continues about the relative importance of factors that influence the developmental processes and about how the periods of development are related. The most important issues in the study of children's development include nature and nurture, continuity and discontinuity, and early and later experience.

Nature and Nurture   The **nature-nurture issue** involves the debate about whether development is primarily influenced by nature or by nurture (Diamond, 2009; D'Onofrio, 2008). Nature refers to an organism's biological inheritance, nurture to its environmental experiences. Almost no one today argues that development can be explained by nature alone or by nurture alone. But some ("nature" proponents) claim that the more important influence on development is biological inheritance, and others ("nurture" proponents) claim that environmental experiences are the more important influence.

According to the nature proponents, just as a sunflower grows in an orderly way—unless it is defeated by an unfriendly environment—so does a person. The range of environments can be vast, but evolutionary and genetic foundations produce commonalities in growth and development (Buss, 2008). We walk before we talk, speak one word before two words, grow rapidly in infancy and less so in early childhood, and experience a rush of sexual hormones in puberty. Extreme environments—those that are psychologically barren or hostile—can stunt development, but nature proponents emphasize the influence of tendencies that are genetically wired into humans (Balasubramanian, Koontz, & Reynolds, 2008).

How Would You...?
As an educator, how would you apply your understanding of the developmental influences of nature and nurture to create appropriate classroom strategies for students who display learning or behavioral problems?

nature-nurture issue   The issue regarding whether development is primarily influenced by nature or nurture. The "nature" proponents claim biological inheritance is the more important influence on development; the "nurture" proponents claim that environmental experiences are the more important.

By contrast, other psychologists emphasize the importance of nurture, or environmental experiences, to development. Experiences run the gamut from the individual's biological environment (nutrition, medical care, drugs, and physical accidents) to the social environment (family, peers, schools, community, media, and culture). For example, a child's diet can affect how tall the child grows and even how effectively the child can think and solve problems. Despite their genetic wiring, a child born and raised in a poor village in Bangladesh and a child in the suburbs of Denver are likely to have different skills, different ways of thinking about the world, and different ways of relating to people.

Continuity and Discontinuity Think about your own development for a moment. Did you become the person you are gradually, like the seedling that slowly, cumulatively grows into a giant oak? Or did you experience sudden, distinct changes, like the caterpillar that changes into a butterfly (see Figure 1.6)?

The **continuity-discontinuity issue** focuses on the extent to which development involves gradual, cumulative change (continuity) or distinct stages (discontinuity). For the most part, developmentalists who emphasize nurture usually describe development as a gradual, continuous process, like the seedling's growth into an oak. Those who emphasize nature often describe development as a series of distinct stages, like the change from caterpillar to butterfly.

Consider continuity first. As the oak grows from seedling to giant oak, it becomes more oak—its development is continuous. Similarly, a child's first word, though seemingly an abrupt, discontinuous event, is actually the result of weeks and months of growth and practice. Puberty, another seemingly abrupt, discontinuous occurrence, is actually a gradual process occurring over several years.

Viewed in terms of discontinuity, each person is described as passing through a sequence of stages in which change is qualitatively rather than quantitatively different. As the caterpillar changes to a butterfly, it is not more caterpillar, it is a different kind of organism—its development is discontinuous. Similarly, at some point a child moves from not being able to think abstractly about the world to being able to. This change is a qualitative, discontinuous change in development, not a quantitative, continuous change.

Continuity

Discontinuity

FIGURE 1.6 Continuity and Discontinuity in Development *Is our development like that of a seedling gradually growing into a giant oak? Or is it more like that of a caterpillar suddenly becoming a butterfly?*

Early and Later Experience The **early-later experience** issue focuses on the degree to which early experiences (especially in infancy) or later experiences are the key determinants of the child's development. That is, if infants experience harmful circumstances, can those experiences be overcome by later, positive ones? Or are the early experiences so critical—possibly because they are the infant's first, prototypical experiences—that they cannot be overridden by a later, better environment? To those who emphasize early experiences, life is an unbroken trail on which a psychological quality can be traced back to its origin (Kagan, 1992, 2000). In contrast, to those who emphasize later experiences, development is like a river, continually ebbing and flowing.

The early-later experience issue has a long history and continues to be hotly debated among developmentalists (Kagan, 2010; Thompson, 2009). The ancient Greek philosopher Plato was sure that infants who were rocked frequently become better athletes. Nineteenth-century New England ministers told parents in Sunday afternoon sermons that the way they handled their infants would determine their children's later character. Some developmentalists argue that, unless infants experience warm, nurturing care during the first year or so of life, their development will never quite be optimal (Koshanska, Philibert, & Barry, 2009).

In contrast, later-experience advocates argue that children are malleable throughout development and that later sensitive caregiving is just as important as earlier

continuity-discontinuity issue The issue regarding whether development involves gradual, cumulative change (continuity) or distinct stages (discontinuity).

early-later experience issue The issue of the degree to which early experiences (especially infancy) or later experiences are the key determinants of the child's development.

sensitive caregiving. A number of experts on life-span development stress that too little attention has been given to later experiences in development (Baltes, 2009; Schaie, 2009). They accept that early experiences are important contributors to development but no more important than later experiences. Jerome Kagan (2000, 2009) points out that even children who show the qualities of an inhibited temperament, which is linked to heredity, have the capacity to change their behavior. In his research, almost one-third of a group of children who had an inhibited temperament at 2 years of age were not unusually shy or fearful when they were 4 years of age (Kagan & Snidman, 1991).

People in Western cultures, especially those influenced by Freudian theory, have tended to support the idea that early experiences are more important than later experiences (Lamb & Sternberg, 1992). The majority of people in the world do not share this belief. For example, people in many Asian countries believe that experiences occurring after about 6 to 7 years of age are more important to development than are earlier experiences. This stance stems from the long-standing belief in Eastern cultures that children's reasoning skills begin to develop in important ways during middle childhood.

Evaluating the Developmental Issues   Most developmentalists recognize that it is unwise to take an extreme position on the issues of nature and nurture, continuity and discontinuity, and early and later experiences. Development is not all nature or all nurture, not all continuity or all discontinuity, and not all early or later experiences (D'Onofrio, 2008). Nature and nurture, continuity and discontinuity, and early and later experiences all play a part in development through the human life span. Along with this consensus, there is still spirited debate about how strongly development is influenced by each of these factors (Blakemore, Berenbaum, & Liben, 2009; Thompson, 2009). Are girls less likely to do well in math mostly because of inherited characteristics or because of society's expectations and because of how girls are raised? Can enriched experiences during adolescence remove deficits resulting from poverty, neglect, and poor schooling during childhood? The answers also have a bearing on social policy decisions about children and adolescents—and consequently on each of our lives.

What is the nature of the early and later experience issue?

Review and Reflect: Learning Goal 3

3   **Discuss the most important processes, periods, and issues in development**

REVIEW

- What are biological, cognitive, and socioemotional processes?
- What are the main periods of development?
- What are three important issues in development?

REFLECT

- Can you identify an early experience that you believe contributed in important ways to your development? Can you identify a recent or current (later) experience that you think had (is having) a strong influence on your development?

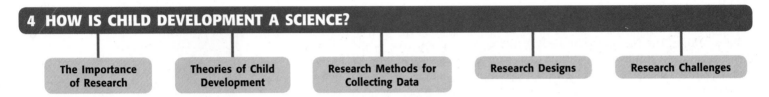

4 HOW IS CHILD DEVELOPMENT A SCIENCE?

| The Importance of Research | Theories of Child Development | Research Methods for Collecting Data | Research Designs | Research Challenges |

This section introduces the theories and methods that are the foundation of the science of child development. We consider why research is important in understanding children's development and examine the main theories of children's development, as well as the main methods and research designs that researchers use. At the end of the section, we explore some of the ethical challenges and biases that researchers must guard against to protect the integrity of their results and respect the rights of the participants in their studies.

The Importance of Research

Science refines everyday thinking.

—ALBERT EINSTEIN
German-born American Physicist, 20th Century

Some individuals have difficulty thinking of child development as a science like physics, chemistry, and biology. Can a discipline that studies how parents nurture children, how peers interact, what are the developmental changes in children's thinking, and whether watching TV hour after hour is linked with being overweight be equated with disciplines that study the molecular structure of a compound and how gravity works? Is child development really a science? The answer is yes. Science is defined not by what it investigates, but by how it investigates. Whether you're studying photosynthesis, butterflies, Saturn's moons, or children's development, it is the way you study that makes the approach scientific or not.

Scientific research is objective, systematic, and testable. It reduces the likelihood that information will be based on personal beliefs, opinions, and feelings (Beins, 2009; Smith & Davis, 2010). Scientific research is based on the **scientific method,** an approach that can be used to discover accurate information. It includes these steps: conceptualize the problem, collect data, draw conclusions, and revise research conclusions and theory.

The first step, *conceptualizing a problem*, involves identifying the problem. At a general level, this may not seem like a difficult task. However, researchers must go beyond a general description of the problem by isolating, analyzing, narrowing, and focusing more specifically on what they want to study. For example, a team of researchers decides to study ways to improve the achievement of children from impoverished backgrounds. Perhaps they choose to examine whether mentoring that involves sustained support, guidance, and concrete assistance can improve the children's academic performance. At this point, even more narrowing and focusing takes place. For instance, what specific strategies should the mentors use? How often will they see the children? How long will the mentoring program last? What aspects of the children's achievement will be assessed?

As part of the first step in formulating a problem to study, researchers often *draw on theories and develop a hypothesis*. A **theory** is an interrelated, coherent set of ideas that helps to explain and to make predictions. For example, a theory on mentoring might attempt to explain and predict why sustained support, guidance, and concrete experience make a difference in the lives of children from impoverished backgrounds. The theory might focus on children's opportunities to model the behavior and strategies of mentors, or it might focus on the effects of individual attention, which might be missing in the children's lives. A **hypothesis** is a specific testable assumption or prediction. A hypothesis is often written as an if-then statement. In our example, a sample hypothesis might be: If children from impoverished backgrounds are given individual attention by mentors, the children will spend more time studying and make higher grades. Testing a hypothesis can inform researchers whether or not a theory may be accurate.

How Would You...?
As a health-care professional, how would you apply the scientific method to examine developmental concerns such as adolescent pregnancy?

scientific method An approach that can be used to obtain accurate information. It includes these steps: (1) conceptualize the problem, (2) collect data, (3) draw conclusions, and (4) revise research conclusions and theory.

theory An interrelated, coherent set of ideas that helps to explain and make predictions.

hypothesis A specific assumption or prediction that can be tested to determine its accuracy.

The second step in the scientific method is to *collect information (data)*. In the study of mentoring, the researchers might decide to conduct the mentoring program for six months. Their data might consist of classroom observations, teachers' ratings, and achievement tests given to the mentored children before the mentoring began and at the end of six months of mentoring.

Once data have been collected, child development researchers use *statistical procedures* to understand the meaning of the data (Howell, 2010). Then they try to *draw conclusions*. In this third step, statistics help to determine whether or not the researchers' observations are due to chance.

After data have been collected and analyzed, researchers compare their findings with those of other researchers on the same topic. The final step in the scientific method is *revising research conclusions and theory*.

Theories of Child Development

A wide range of theories makes understanding children's development a challenging undertaking. Just when you think one theory has the most helpful explanation of children's development, another theory crops up and makes you rethink your earlier conclusion. To keep from getting frustrated, remember that child development is a complex, multifaceted topic. No single theory has been able to account for all aspects of child development. Each theory contributes an important piece to the child development puzzle. Although the theories sometimes disagree, much of their information is complementary rather than contradictory. Together they let us see the total landscape of development in all its richness.

We briefly explore five major theoretical perspectives on development: psychoanalytic, cognitive, behavioral and social cognitive, ethological, and ecological. As you will see, these theoretical approaches examine in varying degrees the three major processes involved in children's development: biological, cognitive, and socioemotional.

Psychoanalytic Theories   **Psychoanalytic theories** describe development as primarily unconscious (beyond awareness) and heavily colored by emotion. Psychoanalytic theorists emphasize that behavior is merely a surface characteristic and that a true understanding of development requires analyzing the symbolic meanings of behavior and the deep inner workings of the mind. Psychoanalytic theorists also stress that early experiences with parents extensively shape development. These characteristics are highlighted in the psychoanalytic theory of Sigmund Freud (1856–1939).

Freud's Theory   Freud (1917) proposed that personality has three structures: the id, the ego, and the superego. The *id* is the Freudian structure of personality that consists of instincts, which are an individual's reservoir of psychic energy. In Freud's view, the id is totally unconscious; it has no contact with reality. As children experience the demands and constraints of reality, a new structure of personality emerges—the *ego*. It deals with the demands of reality and is called the "executive branch" of personality because it uses reasoning to make decisions. The id and the ego have no morality—they do not take into account whether something is right or wrong. The *superego* is the Freudian structure of personality that is the moral branch of personality, the part that considers whether something is right or wrong. Think of the superego as what we often refer to as our "conscience."

As Freud listened to, probed, and analyzed his patients, he became convinced that their problems were the result of experiences early in life. He thought that as children grow up, their focus of pleasure and sexual impulses shifts from the mouth to the anus and eventually to the genitals. As a result, we go through five

Sigmund Freud, the pioneering architect of psychoanalytic theory. *What are some characteristics of Freud's theory?*

psychoanalytic theories   Describe development as primarily unconscious and heavily colored by emotion. Behavior is merely a surface characteristic, and the symbolic workings of the mind have to be analyzed to understand behavior. Early experiences with parents are emphasized.

Oral Stage

Infant's pleasure centers on the mouth.

Birth to 1½ Years

Anal Stage

Child's pleasure focuses on the anus.

1½ to 3 Years

Phallic Stage

Child's pleasure focuses on the genitals.

3 to 6 Years

Latency Stage

Child represses sexual interest and develops social and intellectual skills.

6 Years to Puberty

Genital Stage

A time of sexual reawakening; source of sexual pleasure becomes someone outside the family.

Puberty Onward

FIGURE 1.7 Freudian Stages

stages of psychosexual development: oral, anal, phallic, latency, and genital (see Figure 1.7). Our adult personality, Freud claimed, is determined by the way we resolve conflicts between sources of pleasure at each stage and the demands of reality.

Freud's theory has been significantly revised by a number of psychoanalytic theorists. Many contemporary psychoanalytic theorists maintain that Freud overemphasized sexual instincts; they place more emphasis on cultural experiences as determinants of an individual's development. Unconscious thought remains a central theme, but most contemporary psychoanalysts stress that conscious thought plays a greater role than Freud envisioned. Next, we outline the ideas of an important revisionist of Freud's ideas—Erik Erikson.

Erikson's Psychosocial Theory   Erik Erikson (1902–1994) recognized Freud's contributions but argued that Freud misjudged some important dimensions of human development. For one thing, Erikson (1950, 1968) said we develop in psychosocial stages rather than in psychosexual stages, as Freud maintained. According to Freud, the primary motivation for human behavior is sexual in nature; according to Erikson, it is social and reflects a desire to affiliate with other people. According to Freud, our basic personality is shaped in the first five years of life; according to Erikson, developmental change occurs throughout the life span. Thus, in terms of the early versus later experience issue described earlier in this chapter, Freud argued that early experience is far more important than later experiences, whereas Erikson emphasized the importance of both early and later experiences.

In **Erikson's theory,** eight stages of development unfold as we go through life (see Figure 1.8). At each stage, a unique developmental task confronts individuals with a crisis that must be resolved. According to Erikson, this crisis is not a catastrophe but a turning point marked by both increased vulnerability and enhanced potential. The more successfully an individual resolves the crises, the healthier his or her development will be.

Trust versus mistrust is Erikson's first psychosocial stage, which is experienced in the first year of life. Trust in infancy sets the stage for a life-long expectation that the world will be a good and pleasant place to live.

After gaining trust in their caregivers, infants begin to discover that their behavior is their own. They start to assert their sense of independence, or autonomy. If infants are restrained too much or punished too harshly, they are likely to develop a sense of shame and doubt. This is Erikson's second stage of development, *autonomy versus shame and doubt*, which occurs in late infancy and toddlerhood (1 to 3 years of age).

Initiative versus guilt, Erikson's third stage of development, occurs during the preschool years. As preschool children encounter a widening social world, they face new challenges that require active, purposeful behavior. Children are asked to assume responsibility for their bodies, their behavior, their toys, and their

Erikson's theory   Includes eight stages of human development. Each stage consists of a unique developmental task that confronts individuals with a crisis that must be resolved.

Erik Erikson with his wife, Joan, an artist. Erikson generated one of the most important developmental theories of the twentieth century. *Which stage of Erikson's theory are you in? Does Erikson's description of this stage characterize you?*

pets—and they take initiative. Feelings of guilt may arise, though, if the child is irresponsible and is made to feel too anxious.

Industry versus inferiority is Erikson's fourth developmental stage, occurring approximately in the elementary school years. Children's initiative brings them in contact with a wealth of new experiences. As they move into middle and late childhood, they direct their energy toward mastering knowledge and intellectual skills. At no other time is the child more enthusiastic about learning than at the end of early childhood's period of expansive imagination. The danger is that the child can develop a sense of inferiority—feeling incompetent and unproductive.

During the adolescent years, individuals are faced with finding out who they are, what they are all about, and where they are going in life. This is Erikson's fifth developmental stage, *identity versus identity confusion*. Adolescents are confronted with many new roles and adult statuses—vocational and romantic, for example. If they explore roles in a healthy manner and arrive at a positive path to follow in life, then they achieve a positive identity. If parents push an identity on adolescents, and if adolescents do not adequately explore many roles and define a positive future path, then identity confusion reigns.

Intimacy versus isolation is Erikson's sixth developmental stage, which individuals experience during the early adulthood years. At this time, individuals face the developmental task of forming intimate relationships. Erikson describes intimacy as finding oneself yet losing oneself in another. If the young adult forms healthy friendships and an intimate relationship with another, intimacy will be achieved; if not, isolation will result.

Generativity versus stagnation, Erikson's seventh developmental stage, occurs during middle adulthood. By generativity Erikson means primarily a concern for helping the younger generation to develop and lead useful lives. The feeling of having done nothing to help the next generation is stagnation.

Integrity versus despair is Erikson's eighth and final stage of development, which individuals experience in late adulthood. During this stage, a person reflects on the past. Through many different routes, the person may have developed a positive outlook in most or all of the previous stages of development. If so, the person's review of his or her life will reveal a life well spent, and the person will feel a sense of satisfaction—integrity will be achieved. If the person had resolved many of the earlier stages negatively, the retrospective glances likely will yield doubt or gloom—the despair Erikson described.

Each of Erikson's stages has a "positive" pole, such as trust, and a "negative" pole, such as mistrust. In the healthy solution to the crisis of each stage, the positive pole dominates, but Erikson maintained that some exposure or commitment to the negative side is sometimes inevitable. For example, learning to trust is an important outcome of Erikson's first stage, but you cannot trust all people under all circumstances and survive. We discuss Erikson's theory again in the chapters on socioemotional development. In the *Caring for Children* interlude, you can read about some effective strategies for improving the lives of children based on Erikson's view.

Erikson's stages	Developmental period
Integrity versus despair	Late adulthood (60s onward)
Generativity versus stagnation	Middle adulthood (40s, 50s)
Intimacy versus isolation	Early adulthood (20s, 30s)
Identity versus identity confusion	Adolescence (10 to 20 years)
Industry versus inferiority	Middle and late childhood (elementary school years, 6 years to puberty)
Initiative versus guilt	Early childhood (preschool years, 3 to 5 years)
Autonomy versus shame and doubt	Infancy (1 to 3 years)
Trust versus mistrust	Infancy (first year)

FIGURE 1.8 Erikson's Eight Life-Span Stages

Caring for Children

STRATEGIES FOR PARENTING, EDUCATING, AND INTERACTING WITH CHILDREN BASED ON ERIKSON'S THEORY

Parents, child-care specialists, teachers, counselors, youth workers, and other adults can adopt positive strategies for interacting with children based on Erikson's theory. These strategies include:

1. ***Nurture infants and develop their trust, then encourage and monitor toddlers' autonomy.*** Because infants depend on others for their needs, it is critical for caregivers to consistently provide positive, attentive care for infants. Infants who experience consistently positive care feel safe and secure, sensing that people are reliable and loving, which leads them to develop trust in the world. Caregivers who neglect or abuse infants are likely to have infants who develop a sense of mistrust in their world. Now that they have developed a sense of trust in their world, as infants move into the toddler years it is important that they are given the freedom to explore it. Toddlers whose caregivers are too restrictive or harsh are likely to develop shame and doubt, sensing that they can't adequately do things on their own. As toddlers gain more independence, caregivers need to monitor their exploration and curiosity because there are many things that can harm them, such as running into the street and touching a hot stove.

2. ***Encourage initiative in young children.*** Children should be given a great deal of freedom to explore their world. They should be allowed to choose some of the activities they engage in. If their requests for doing certain activities are reasonable, the requests should be honored. Children need to be provided exciting materials that will stimulate their imagination. Young children at this stage love to play. It not only benefits their socioemotional development but also is an important medium for their cognitive growth. Criticism should be kept to a minimum so that children will not develop high levels of guilt and anxiety. Young children are going to make lots of mistakes and have lots of spills. They need good models far more than harsh critics. Their activities and environment need structure for successes rather than failures by giving them developmentally appropriate tasks. For example, young children get frustrated when they have to sit for long periods of time and do academic paper-and-pencil tasks.

3. ***Promote industry in elementary school children.*** It was Erikson's hope that teachers could provide an atmosphere in which children become passionate about learning. In Erikson's words, teachers should mildly but firmly coerce children into the adventure of finding out that they can learn to accomplish things that they themselves would never have thought they could do. In elementary school, children thirst to know. Most arrive at elementary school steeped in curiosity and a motivation to master tasks. In Erikson's view, it is important for teachers to nourish this motivation for mastery and curiosity. Teachers need to challenge students, but not overwhelm them; be firm in requiring students to be productive, but not be overly critical; and especially be tolerant of honest mistakes and make sure that every student has opportunities for many successes.

4. ***Stimulate identity exploration in adolescence.*** It is important to recognize that the adolescent's identity is multidimensional. Aspects include vocational goals; intellectual achievement; and interests in hobbies, sports, music, and other areas. Adolescents can be asked to write essays about such dimensions, exploring who they are and what they want to do with their lives. They should be encouraged to think independently and to freely express their views, which stimulates their self-exploration. Adolescents can also be encouraged to listen to debates on

What are some applications of Erikson's theory for effective parenting from infancy through adolescence?

political and ideological issues, which stimulates them to examine different perspectives. Another good strategy is to encourage adolescents to talk with a school counselor about career options as well as other aspects of their identity. Teachers can have people from different careers come and talk with their students about their work regardless of grade level.

Evaluating the Psychoanalytic Theories The contributions of psychoanalytic theories include these ideas: (1) early experiences play an important part in development; (2) family relationships are a central aspect of development; (3) personality can be better understood if it is examined developmentally; (4) the mind is not all conscious—unconscious aspects of the mind need to be considered; and (5) in Erikson's theory, changes take place in adulthood as well as in childhood.

There are some criticisms of psychoanalytic theories. First, the main concepts of psychoanalytic theories have been difficult to test scientifically. Second, much of the data used to support psychoanalytic theories come from individuals' reconstruction of the past, often the distant past, and are of unknown accuracy. Third, the sexual underpinnings of development are given too much importance (especially in Freud's theory), and the unconscious mind is given too much credit for influencing development. In addition, psychoanalytic theories (especially in Freud's theory) present an image of humans that is too negative and are culture- and gender-biased, treating Western culture and males as the measure for evaluating everyone.

Cognitive Theories
Whereas psychoanalytic theories stress the importance of the unconscious, cognitive theories emphasize conscious thoughts. Three important cognitive theories are Piaget's cognitive developmental theory, Vygotsky's sociocultural cognitive theory, and information-processing theory.

Piaget's Cognitive Developmental Theory **Piaget's theory** states that children actively construct their understanding of the world and go through four stages of cognitive development. Two processes underlie the four stages of development in Piaget's theory: organization and adaptation. To make sense of our world, we organize our experiences. For example, we separate important ideas from less important ideas, and we connect one idea to another. In addition to organizing our observations and experiences, we *adapt*, adjusting to new environmental demands (Byrnes, 2008; Carpendale, Muller, & Bibok, 2008).

Piaget (1896–1980) also proposed that we go through four stages in understanding the world (see Figure 1.9). Each stage is age-related and consists of a distinct

How Would You...?
As a human development and family studies professional, how would you apply psychoanalytic theory to advise the foster family of a newly placed child who reports no history of abuse yet shows considerable violent behavior?

Piaget's theory States that children actively construct their understanding of the world and go through four stages of cognitive development.

FIGURE 1.9 Piaget's Four Stages of Cognitive Development

Sensorimotor Stage	**Preoperational Stage**	**Concrete Operational Stage**	**Formal Operational Stage**
The infant constructs an understanding of the world by coordinating sensory experiences with physical actions. An infant progresses from reflexive, instinctual action at birth to the beginning of symbolic thought toward the end of the stage.	The child begins to represent the world with words and images. These words and images reflect increased symbolic thinking and go beyond the connection of sensory information and physical action.	The child can now reason logically about concrete events and classify objects into different sets.	The adolescent reasons in more abstract, idealistic, and logical ways.
Birth to 2 Years of Age	*2 to 7 Years of Age*	*7 to 11 Years of Age*	*11 Years of Age Through Adulthood*

Jean Piaget, the famous Swiss developmental psychologist, changed the way we think about the development of children's minds. *What are some key ideas in Piaget's theory?*

There is considerable interest today in Lev Vygotsky's sociocultural cognitive theory of child development. *What were Vygotsky's basic ideas about children's development?*

way of thinking, a different way of understanding the world. Thus, according to Piaget (1954), the child's cognition is *qualitatively* different in one stage compared with another. What are Piaget's four stages of cognitive development like?

The *sensorimotor stage*, which lasts from birth to about 2 years of age, is the first Piagetian stage. In this stage, infants construct an understanding of the world by coordinating sensory experiences (such as seeing and hearing) with physical, motoric actions—hence the term *sensorimotor*.

The *preoperational stage*, which lasts from approximately 2 to 7 years of age, is Piaget's second stage. In this stage, children begin to go beyond simply connecting sensory information with physical action and represent the world with words, images, and drawings. However, according to Piaget, preschool children still lack the ability to perform what he calls operations, which are internalized mental actions that allow children to do mentally what they previously could only do physically. For example, if you imagine putting two sticks together to see whether they would be as long as another stick, without actually moving the sticks, you are performing a concrete operation.

The *concrete operational stage*, which lasts from approximately 7 to 11 years of age, is the third Piagetian stage. In this stage, children can perform operations that involve objects, and they can reason logically as long as reasoning can be applied to specific or concrete examples. For example, concrete operational thinkers understand that two rows of four nickels have the same number of nickels regardless of how far apart the nickels in the row are spaced. However, concrete operational thinkers cannot imagine the steps necessary to complete an algebraic equation, which is too abstract for thinking at this stage of development.

The *formal operational stage*, which appears between the ages of 11 and 15 and continues through adulthood, is Piaget's fourth and final stage. In this stage, individuals move beyond concrete experiences and think in abstract and more logical terms. As part of thinking more abstractly, adolescents develop images of ideal circumstances. They might think about what an ideal parent is like and compare their parents to this ideal standard. They begin to entertain possibilities for the future and are fascinated with what they can be. In solving problems, they become more systematic, developing hypotheses about why something is happening the way it is and then testing these hypotheses.

In sum, this brief introduction to Piaget's theory that children's cognitive development goes through four stages is provided here, along with other theories, to give you a broad understanding. Later in the text, when we study cognitive development in infancy, early childhood, middle and late childhood, and adolescence, we return to Piaget and examine his theory in more depth.

Vygotsky's Sociocultural Cognitive Theory Like Piaget, the Russian developmentalist Lev Vygotsky (1896–1934) said that children actively construct their knowledge. Unlike Piaget, Vygotsky (1962) did not propose that cognitive development occurs in stages, and he gave social interaction and culture far more important roles in cognitive development than Piaget did. **Vygotsky's theory** is a sociocultural cognitive theory that emphasizes how culture and social interaction guide cognitive development.

Vygotsky portrayed the child's development as inseparable from social and cultural activities (Gredler, 2008; Holzman, 2009). He argued that development of memory, attention, and reasoning involves learning to use the inventions of society, such as language, mathematical systems, and memory strategies. Thus in one culture, children might learn to count with the help of a computer; in another, they might learn by using beads. According to Vygotsky, children's social interaction with more-skilled adults and peers is indispensable to their cognitive development (Alvarez & del Rio, 2007). Through this interaction, they learn to use the tools that will help them adapt and be successful in their culture. For example, if you regularly help a child learn how to read, you not only advance a child's reading skills but also communicate to the child that reading is an important activity in his or her culture.

Vygotsky's theory has stimulated considerable interest in the view that knowledge is situated and collaborative (Bodrova & Leong, 2007; Gauvain, & Parke, 2010). In this view, knowledge is not generated from within the individual but rather is constructed through interaction with other people and objects in the culture, such as books. This suggests that knowledge can best be advanced through interaction with others in cooperative activities.

Vygotsky's theory, like Piaget's, remained virtually unknown to American psychologists until the 1960s, but eventually both became influential among educators as well as psychologists. We examine ideas about learning and teaching that are based on Vygotsky's theory when we study cognitive development in early childhood.

The Information–Processing Theory Early computers may be the best candidates for the title of "founding fathers" of information-processing theory. Although many factors stimulated the growth of this theory, none was more important than the computer. Psychologists began to wonder if the logical operations carried out by computers might tell us something about how the human mind works. They drew analogies between a computer's hardware and the brain and between computer software and cognition.

This line of thinking helped to generate **information-processing theory,** which emphasizes that individuals manipulate information, monitor it, and strategize about it. Unlike Piaget's theory, but like Vygotsky's theory, information-processing theory does not describe development as stage-like. Instead, according to this theory, individuals develop a gradually increasing capacity for processing information, which allows them to acquire increasingly complex knowledge and skills (Halford, 2008; Vallotton & Fischer, 2008).

Robert Siegler (2006), a leading expert on children's information processing, states that thinking is information processing. In other words, when individuals perceive, encode, represent, store, and retrieve information, they are thinking. Siegler emphasizes that an important aspect of development is learning good strategies for processing information. For example, becoming a better reader might involve learning to monitor the key themes of the material being read.

Evaluating the Cognitive Theories The primary contributions of cognitive theories are that (1) they present a positive view of development, emphasizing conscious thinking; (2) they emphasize the individual's active construction of understanding (especially Piaget's and Vygotsky's theories); (3) Piaget's and Vygotsky's theories underscore the importance of examining developmental changes in children's thinking; and (4) information-processing theory offers detailed descriptions of cognitive processes.

There are several criticisms of cognitive theories. First, Piaget's stages are not as uniform as he theorized. Piaget also underestimated the cognitive skills of infants and overestimated the cognitive skills of adolescents. Second, the cognitive theories do not give adequate attention to individual variations in cognitive development. Third, information-processing theory does not provide an adequate description of developmental changes in cognition. In addition, psychoanalytic theorists argue that the cognitive theories do not give enough credit to unconscious thought.

Behavioral and Social Cognitive Theories In the early twentieth century, as Freud was interpreting patients' unconscious minds through their early childhood experiences, Ivan Pavlov and John B. Watson were conducting detailed observations of behavior in controlled laboratory settings. Their work provided the foundations of

Vygotsky's theory A sociocultural cognitive theory that emphasizes how culture and social interaction guide cognitive development.

information-processing theory Emphasizes that individuals manipulate information, monitor it, and strategize about it. Central to this theory are the processes of memory and thinking.

behaviorism, which essentially holds that we can study scientifically only what can be directly observed and measured. Out of the behavioral tradition grew the belief that development is observable behavior that can be learned through experience with the environment (Chance, 2008; Klein, 2009). In terms of the continuity-discontinuity issue discussed earlier in this chapter, the behavioral and social cognitive theories emphasize continuity in development and argue that development does not occur in stage-like fashion. The three versions of the behavioral and social cognitive theories that we explore are Pavlov's classical conditioning, Skinner's operant conditioning, and Bandura's social cognitive theory.

Pavlov's Classical Conditioning   In the early 1900s, the Russian physiologist Ivan Pavlov (1927) knew that dogs innately salivate when they taste food. He became curious when he observed that dogs salivate to various sights and sounds before eating their food. For example, when an individual paired the ringing of a bell with the food, the bell ringing subsequently elicited salivation from the dogs when it was presented by itself. With this experiment, Pavlov discovered the principle of *classical conditioning*, in which a neutral stimulus (in our example, ringing a bell) acquires the ability to produce a response originally produced by another stimulus (in our example, food).

In the early twentieth century, John Watson demonstrated that classical conditioning occurs in human. He showed an infant named Albert a white rat to see if he was afraid of it. He was not. As Albert played with the rat, a loud noise was sounded behind his head. As you might imagine, the noise caused little Albert to cry. After several pairings of the loud noise and the white rat, Albert began to cry at the sight of the rat even when the noise was not sounded (Watson & Rayner, 1920). Albert had been classically conditioned to fear the rat. Similarly, many of our fears may result from classical conditioning: Fear of the dentist may be learned from a painful experience, fear of driving from being in an automobile accident, fear of heights from falling off a high chair when we were infants, and fear of dogs from being bitten.

B. F. Skinner was a tinkerer who liked to make new gadgets. The younger of his two daughters, Deborah, was raised in Skinner's enclosed Air-Crib, which he invented because he wanted to control her environment completely. The Air-Crib was sound-proofed and temperature-controlled. Debbie, shown here as a child with her parents, is currently a successful artist, is married, and lives in London. *What do you think about Skinner's Air-Crib?*

Skinner's Operant Conditioning   Classical conditioning may explain how we develop many involuntary responses such as fears, but B. F. Skinner argued that a second type of conditioning accounts for the development of other types of behavior. According to Skinner (1938), through *operant conditioning* the consequences of a behavior produce changes in the probability of the behavior's occurrence. A behavior followed by a rewarding stimulus is more likely to recur, whereas a behavior followed by a punishing stimulus is less likely to recur. For example, when a person smiles at a child after the child has done something, the child is more likely to engage in the activity than if the person gives the child a nasty look.

According to Skinner, such rewards and punishments shape development. For example, Skinner's approach argues that shy people learned to be shy as a result of experiences they had while growing up. It follows that modifications in an environment can help a shy person become more socially oriented. Also, for Skinner the key aspect of development is behavior, not thoughts and feelings. He emphasized that development consists of the pattern of behavioral changes that are brought about by rewards and punishments.

Bandura's Social Cognitive Theory   Some psychologists agree with the behaviorists' notion that development is learned and is influenced strongly by environmental interactions. However, unlike Skinner, they argue that cognition is also important in understanding development. **Social cognitive theory** holds that behavior, environment, and cognition are the key factors in development.

social cognitive theory   The view of psychologists who emphasize behavior, environment, and cognition as the key factors in development.

American psychologist Albert Bandura (1925–) is the leading architect of social cognitive theory. Bandura (2001, 2007, 2008, 2009) emphasizes that cognitive processes have important links with the environment and behavior. His early research program focused heavily on *observational learning* (also called *imitation*, or *modeling*), which is learning that occurs through observing what others do. For example, a young boy might observe his father yelling in anger and treating other people with hostility; with his peers, the young boy later acts very aggressively, showing the same characteristics as his father's behavior. A girl might adopt the dominant and sarcastic style of her teacher, saying to her younger brother, "You are so slow. How can you do this work so slowly?" Social cognitive theorists stress that people acquire a wide range of behaviors, thoughts, and feelings through observing others' behavior and that these observations form an important part of children's development.

What is cognitive about observational learning in Bandura's view? He proposes that people cognitively represent the behavior of others and then sometimes adopt this behavior themselves.

Bandura's (2001, 2007, 2008, 2009) most recent model of learning and development includes three elements: behavior, the person/cognition, and the environment. An individual's confidence that he or she can control his or her success is an example of a person factor; strategies are an example of a cognitive factor. As shown in Figure 1.10, behavior, person/cognitive, and environmental factors operate interactively. Behavior can influence person factors and vice versa. Cognitive activities can influence the environment, the environment can change the person's cognition, and so on.

Evaluating the Behavioral and Social Cognitive Theories   Contributions of the behavioral and social cognitive theories include (1) their emphasis on the importance of scientific research; (2) their focus on environmental determinants of behavior; (3) the identification and explanation of observational learning (by Bandura); and (4) the inclusion of person/cognitive factors (in social cognitive theory).

Criticisms of the behavioral and social cognitive theories include the objections that they give (1) too little emphasis on cognition (in Pavlov's and Skinner's theories); (2) too much emphasis on environmental determinants; (3) inadequate attention to developmental changes; and (4) inadequate consideration of human spontaneity and creativity.

Behavioral and social cognitive theories emphasize the importance of environmental experiences in human development. Next we turn our attention to a theory that underscores the importance of the biological foundations of development—ethological theory.

Ethological Theory   American developmental psychologists began to pay attention to the biological bases of development thanks to the work of European zoologists who pioneered the field of ethology. **Ethology** stresses that behavior is strongly influenced by biology, is tied to evolution, and is characterized by critical or sensitive periods. These are specific time frames during which, according to ethologists, the presence or absence of certain experiences has a long-lasting influence on individuals.

European zoologist Konrad Lorenz (1903–1989) helped bring ethology to prominence. In his best-known experiment, Lorenz (1965) studied the behavior of grey-lag geese, which will follow their mother as soon as they hatch.

In a remarkable set of experiments, Lorenz separated the eggs laid by one goose into two groups. One group he returned to the goose to be hatched by her. The other group was hatched in an incubator. The goslings in the first group performed as predicted. They followed their mother as soon as they hatched. However, those in the second group, which saw Lorenz when they first hatched, followed him everywhere, as though he were their mother. Lorenz marked the goslings and then

How Would You…?
As a social worker, how would you use Bandura's model of observational learning to discuss the impact of violent television programming on children's development?

Albert Bandura has been one of the leading architects of social cognitive theory. *What is the nature of his theory?*

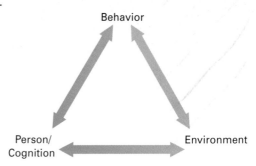

FIGURE 1.10 Bandura's Social Cognitive Model The arrows illustrate how relations between behavior, person/cognition, and environment are reciprocal rather than unidirectional.

ethology Stresses that behavior is strongly influenced by biology, is tied to evolution, and is characterized by critical or sensitive periods.

Konrad Lorenz, a pioneering student of animal behavior, is followed through the water by three imprinted greylag geese. Describe Lorenz's experiment with the geese. *Do you think his experiment would have the same results with human babies? Explain.*

placed both groups under a box. Mother goose and "mother" Lorenz stood aside as the box lifted. Each group of goslings went directly to its "mother." Lorenz called this process *imprinting*, the rapid, innate learning within a limited critical period of time that involves attachment to the first moving object seen.

Ethological research and theory at first had little or nothing to say about the nature of social relationships across the human life span, and the theory stimulated few studies with humans. Ethologists' view that normal development requires that certain behaviors emerge during a critical period, a fixed time period very early in development, seemed to be overdrawn.

However, John Bowlby (1969, 1989) illustrated an important application of ethological theory to human development. Bowlby argued that attachment to a caregiver over the first year of life has important consequences throughout the life span. In his view, if this attachment is positive and secure, the individual will likely develop positively in childhood and adulthood. If the attachment is negative and insecure, life-span development will likely not be optimal. Thus, in this view the first year of life is a sensitive period for the development of social relationships. In Chapter 7, "Socioemotional Development in Infancy," we explore the concept of infant attachment in much greater detail.

Contributions of ethological theory include (1) an increased focus on the biological and evolutionary basis of development; (2) use of careful observations in naturalistic settings; and (3) an emphasis on sensitive periods of development.

Criticisms of ethological theory include the following: (1) the concepts of critical and sensitive periods are perhaps too rigid; (2) the emphasis on biological foundations is too strong; (3) cognition receives inadequate attention; and (4) the theory is better at generating research with animals than with humans.

Another theory that emphasizes the biological aspects of human development— evolutionary psychology—is be presented in Chapter 2, "Biological Beginnings," along with views on the role of heredity in development.

Ecological Theory Ethological theory stresses biological factors, whereas ecological theory emphasizes environmental factors. One ecological theory that has important implications for understanding children's development was created by Urie Bronfenbrenner (1917–2005).

Bronfenbrenner's ecological theory (1986, 2000; Bronfenbrenner & Morris, 2006) holds that development reflects the influence of several environmental systems. The theory identifies five environmental systems (see Figure 1.11):

- *Microsystem*—the setting in which the individual lives. These contexts include the person's family, peers, school, neighborhood, and work. It is in the

Bronfenbrenner's ecological theory An environmental systems theory that focuses on five environmental systems: microsystem, mesosystem, exosystem, macrosystem, and chronosystem.

eclectic theoretical orientation An orientation that does not follow any one theoretical approach but rather selects from each theory whatever is considered the best in it.

microsystem that the most direct interactions with social agents take place—with parents, peers, and teachers, for example.

- *Mesosystem*—relations between microsystems or connections between contexts. Examples are the relation of family experiences to school experiences, school experiences to church experiences, and family experiences to peer experiences. For example, children whose parents have rejected them may have difficulty developing positive relations with teachers.

- *Exosystem*—links between a social setting in which the individual does not have an active role and the individual's immediate context. For example, a husband's or child's experience at home may be influenced by a mother's experiences at work. The mother might receive a promotion that requires more travel, which might increase conflict with the husband and change patterns of interaction with the child.

- *Macrosystem*—the culture in which individuals live. Remember from earlier in this chapter that culture refers to the behavior patterns, beliefs, and all other products of a group of people that are passed on from generation to generation. Remember also that cross-cultural studies—comparisons of one culture with one or more other cultures—provide information about the generality of development (Shiraev & Levy, 2010).

- *Chronosystem*—the patterning of environmental events and transitions over the life course, as well as sociohistorical circumstances (Schaie, 2007). For example, divorce is one transition. Researchers have found that the negative effects of divorce on children often peak in the first year after the divorce (Hetherington, 2006). By two years after the divorce, family interaction is less chaotic and more stable. As an example of sociohistorical circumstances, consider how the opportunities for women to pursue a career have increased during the last thirty years.

Bronfenbrenner (2000; Bronfenbrenner & Morris, 2006) has added biological influences to his theory and now describes it as a *bioecological* theory. Nonetheless, ecological, environmental contexts still predominate in Bronfenbrenner's theory.

The contributions of ecological theory include (1) a systematic examination of macro and micro dimensions of environmental systems; (2) attention to connections between environmental settings (mesosystem); and (3) consideration of sociohistorical influences on development (chronosystem).

Some criticisms of ecological theory include (1) too little attention to biological foundations of development, even with the added discussion of biological influences; and (2) inadequate attention to cognitive processes.

An Eclectic Theoretical Orientation   The theories that we have discussed were developed at different points in the twentieth century, as Figure 1.12 shows. No single theory described in this chapter can explain entirely the rich complexity of children's development, but each has contributed to our understanding of development. Psychoanalytic theory best explains the unconscious mind. Erikson's theory best describes the changes that occur in adult development. Piaget's, Vygotsky's, and the information-processing views provide the most complete description of cognitive development. The behavioral and social cognitive and ecological theories have been the most adept at examining the environmental determinants of development. The ethological theories have highlighted biology's role and the importance of sensitive periods in development.

In short, although theories are helpful guides, relying on a single theory to explain development is probably a mistake. This book instead takes an **eclectic theoretical orientation,** which does not follow any one theoretical approach but

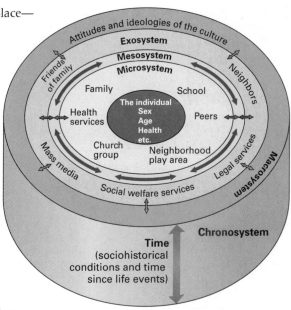

FIGURE 1.11 Bronfenbrenner's Ecological Theory of Development Bronfenbrenner's ecological theory consists of five environmental systems: microsystem, mesosystem, exosystem, macrosystem, and chronosystem.

How Would You...?
As an educator, how might you explain a student's chronic failure to complete homework from the mesosystem level? From the exosystem level?

Urie Bronfenbrenner developed ecological theory, a perspective that is receiving increased attention. *What is the nature of ecological theory?*

FIGURE 1.12 Time Line for Major Developmental Theories

rather selects from each theory whatever is considered its best features. In this way, you can view the study of development as it actually exists—with different theorists making different assumptions, stressing different empirical problems, and using different strategies to discover information. Figure 1.13 compares the main theoretical perspectives in terms of how they view important developmental issues in children's development.

Research Methods for Collecting Data

If they follow an eclectic orientation, how do scholars and researchers determine that one feature of a theory is somehow better than another? The scientific method discussed earlier in this chapter provides the guide. Recall that the steps in the

laboratory A controlled setting in which many of the complex factors of the "real world" are removed.

naturalistic observation Observing behavior in real-world settings.

THEORY	ISSUES	
	Continuity/discontinuity, early versus later experiences	**Biological and environmental factors**
Psychoanalytic	Discontinuity between stages—continuity between early experiences and later development; early experiences very important; later changes in development emphasized in Erikson's theory	Freud's biological determination interacting with early family experiences; Erikson's more balanced biological-cultural interaction perspective
Cognitive	Discontinuity between stages in Piaget's theory; continuity between early experiences and later development in Piaget's and Vygotsky's theories; no stages in Vygotsky's theory or information-processing theory	Piaget's emphasis on interaction and adaptation; environment provides the setting for cognitive structures to develop; information-processing view has not addressed this issue extensively but mainly emphasizes biological-environmental interaction
Behavioral and social cognitive	Continuity (no stages); experience at all points of development important	Environment viewed as the cause of behavior in both views
Ethological	Discontinuity but no stages; critical or sensitive periods emphasized; early experiences very important	Strong biological view
Ecological	Little attention to continuity/discontinuity; change emphasized more than stability	Strong environmental view

FIGURE 1.13 A Comparison of Theories and Issues in Children's Development

scientific method involve conceptualizing the problem, collecting data, drawing conclusions, and revising research conclusions and theories. Through scientific research,
the features of theories can be tested and refined.

Whether we are interested in studying attachment in infants, the cognitive skills
of children, or the peer relations of adolescents, we can choose from several ways
of collecting data. Here we outline the measures most often used, including their
advantages and disadvantages, beginning with observation.

Observation   Scientific observation requires an important set of skills (Jackson,
2008). Unless we are trained observers and practice our skills regularly, we might
not know what to look for, we might not remember what we saw, we might not
realize that what we are looking for is changing from one moment to the next, and
we might not communicate our observations effectively.

For observations to be effective, they have to be systematic. We have to have
some idea of what we are looking for. We have to know whom we are observing,
when and where we will observe, how the observations will be made, and how they
will be recorded.

*What are some important strategies in conduct-
ing observational research with children?*

Where should we make our observations? We have two choices: the laboratory
and the everyday world.

When we observe scientifically, we often need to control certain factors that
determine behavior but are not the focus of our inquiry (Salkind, 2009). For this
reason, some research in children's development is conducted in a **laboratory,** a
controlled setting with many of the complex factors of the "real world" removed.
For example, suppose you want to observe how children react when they see other
people act aggressively. If you observe children in their homes or schools, you have
no control over how much aggression the children observe, what kind of aggression
they see, which people they see acting aggressively, or how other people treat the
children. In contrast, if you observe the children in a laboratory, you can control
these and other factors and therefore have more confidence about how to interpret
your observations.

Laboratory research does have some drawbacks, however. First, it is almost
impossible to conduct research without the participants' knowing they are being
studied. Second, the laboratory setting is unnatural and therefore can cause the
participants to behave unnaturally. Third, people who are willing to come to a
university laboratory may not fairly represent groups from diverse cultural backgrounds. Fourth, people who are unfamiliar with university settings, and with
the idea of "helping science," may be intimidated by the laboratory setting. In
addition, some aspects of children's development are difficult, if not impossible,
to examine in the laboratory. Last, laboratory studies of certain types of stress
may even be unethical.

Naturalistic observation provides insights that we sometimes cannot achieve in
the laboratory. **Naturalistic observation** means observing behavior in real-world
settings, making no effort to manipulate or control the situation. Life-span researchers conduct naturalistic observations at sporting events, child-care centers, work
settings, malls, and other places people live in and frequent.

Naturalistic observation was used in one study that focused on conversations in
a children's science museum (Crowley & others, 2001). Parents were over three
times more likely to engage boys than girls in explanatory talk while visiting exhib-
its at the science museum, suggesting a gender bias that encourages boys more than
girls to be interested in science (see Figure 1.14). In another study, Mexican American
parents who had completed high school used more explanations with their children
when visiting a science museum than Mexican American parents who had not
completed high school (Tenenbaum & others, 2002).

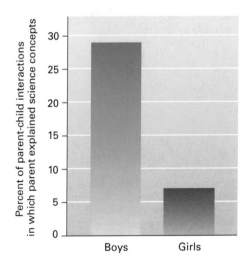

**FIGURE 1.14 Parent's Explanation of
Science to Sons and Daughters at a Science
Museum** In a naturalistic observation study at
a children's science museum, parents were over
three times more likely to explain science to
boys than girls (Crowley & others, 2001). The
gender difference occurred regardless of
whether the father, the mother, or both parents
were with the child, although the gender difference was greatest for father's science explanations to sons and daughters.

Survey and Interview   Sometimes the best and quickest way to get information
about people is to ask them for it. One technique is to *interview* them directly. A related

method is the *survey* (sometimes referred to as a questionnaire), which is especially useful when information from many people is needed (Gay, Mills, & Airasian, 2009). A standard set of questions is used to obtain peoples' self-reported attitudes or beliefs about a specific topic. In a good survey, the questions are clear and unbiased, allowing respondents to answer unambiguously.

Surveys and interviews can be used to study a wide range of topics from religious beliefs to sexual habits to attitudes about gun control to beliefs about how to improve schools. Surveys and interviews today are conducted in person, over the telephone, and over the Internet.

One problem with surveys and interviews is the tendency of participants to answer questions in a way that they think is socially acceptable or desirable rather than telling what they truly think or feel (Leedy & Ormrod, 2009). For example, on a survey or in an interview some individuals might say that they do not take drugs even though they do.

Standardized Test   A **standardized test** has uniform procedures for administration and scoring. Many standardized tests allow a person's performance to be compared with the performance of other individuals—thus they provide information about individual differences among people (Kingston, 2008). One example is the Stanford-Binet intelligence test, which is described in Chapter 12, "Cognitive Development in Middle and Late Childhood." Your score on the Stanford-Binet test tells you how your performance compares with that of thousands of other people who have taken the test (Bart & Peterson, 2008).

Standardized tests also have three key weaknesses. First, they do not always predict behavior in nontest situations. Second, standardized tests are based on the belief that a person's behavior is consistent and stable, yet personality and intelligence—two primary targets of standardized testing—can vary with the situation. For example, individuals may perform poorly on a standardized intelligence test in an office setting but score much higher at home, where they are less anxious. This criticism is especially relevant for members of minority groups, some of whom have been inaccurately classified as mentally retarded on the basis of their scores on intelligence tests. A third weakness of standardized tests is that many psychological tests developed in Western cultures might not be appropriate in other cultures (Matsumoto & Juang, 2008). The experiences of people in differing cultures may lead them to interpret and respond to questions differently.

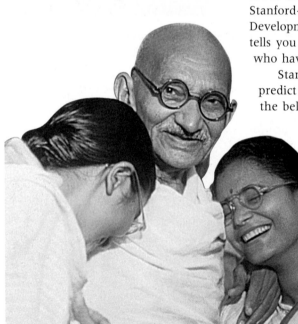

Mahatma Gandhi was the spiritual leader of India in the middle of the twentieth century. Erik Erikson conducted an extensive case study of Gandhi's life to determine what contributed to his identity development. *What are some limitations of the case study approach?*

standardized test   A test with uniform procedures for administration and scoring. Many standardized tests allow a person's performance to be compared with the performance of other individuals.

case study   An in-depth look at a single individual.

Case Study   A **case study** is an in-depth look at a single individual. Case studies are performed mainly by mental health professionals, when—for either practical or ethical reasons—the unique aspects of an individual's life cannot be duplicated and tested in other individuals. A case study provides information about one person's fears, hopes, fantasies, traumatic experiences, upbringing, family relationships, health, or anything that helps the psychologist understand the person's mind and behavior. In later chapters, we discuss vivid case studies, such as studies of Michael Rehbein, who had much of the left side of his brain removed at 7 years of age to end severe epileptic seizures.

Case histories provide dramatic, in-depth portrayals of people's lives, but remember that we must be cautious when generalizing from this information. The subject of a case study is unique, with a genetic makeup and personal history that no one else shares. In addition, case studies involve judgments of unknown reliability. Psychologists who conduct case studies rarely check to see if other psychologists agree with their observations.

Physiological Measures   Researchers are increasingly using *physiological measures* when they study children's development (Hofheimer & Lester, 2008; Nelson, 2009). For example, as puberty unfolds, the blood levels of certain hormones increase. To determine the nature of these hormonal changes, researchers take blood samples from willing adolescents (Susman & Dorn, 2009).

Another physiological measure that is increasingly being used is neuroimaging, especially *functional magnetic resonance imaging (fMRI)*, in which electromagnetic waves are used to construct images of a person's brain tissue and biochemical activity. We have much more to say about neuroimaging and other physiological measures at various points in this book.

A functional magnetic resonance image of a child's brain.

Research Designs

Suppose you want to find out whether the children of permissive parents are more likely than other children to be rude and unruly. The data-collection method that researchers choose often depends on the goal of their research. The goal may be simply to describe a phenomenon, or it may be to describe relationships between phenomena, or to determine the causes or effects of a phenomenon.

Perhaps you decide that you need to observe both permissive and strict parents with their children and compare them. How would you do that? In addition to a method for collecting data, you would need a research design. There are three main types of research design: descriptive, correlational, and experimental.

Descriptive Research   All of the data-collection methods that we have discussed can be used in **descriptive research,** which aims to observe and record behavior. For example, a researcher might observe the extent to which people are altruistic or aggressive toward each other. By itself, descriptive research cannot prove what causes some phenomenon, but it can reveal important information about people's behavior (Leady & Ormrod, 2010).

Correlational Research   Correlational research goes beyond describing phenomena to provide information that will help us to predict how people will behave. In **correlational research,** the goal is to describe the strength of the relationship between two or more events or characteristics. The more strongly the two events are correlated (or related or associated), the more effectively we can predict one event from the other (Kiess & Green, 2010).

For example, to study if children of permissive parents have less self-control than other children, you would need to carefully record observations of parents' permissiveness and their children's self-control. The data could then be analyzed statistically to yield a numerical measure, called a **correlation coefficient,** a number based on a statistical analysis that is used to describe the degree of association between two variables. The correlation coefficient ranges from −1.00 to +1.00. A negative number means an inverse relation. For example, researchers often find a negative correlation between permissive parenting and children's self-control. By contrast, they often find a positive correlation between parental monitoring of children and children's self-control.

The higher the correlation coefficient (whether positive or negative), the stronger the association between the two variables. A correlation of 0 means that there is no association between the variables. A correlation of −.40 is stronger than a correlation of +.20 because we disregard whether the correlation is positive or negative in determining the strength of the correlation.

descriptive research   A research design that has the purpose of observing and recording behavior.

correlational research   A research design whose goal is to describe the strength of the relationship between two or more events or characteristics.

correlation coefficient   A number based on statistical analysis that is used to describe the degree of association between two variables.

Observed correlation   **Possible explanations for this correlation**

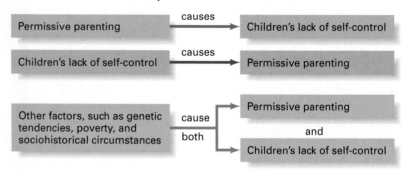

FIGURE 1.15 **Possible Explanations for Correlational Data** An observed correlation between two events cannot be used to conclude that one event caused the other. Some possibilities are that the second event caused the first event or that a third, unknown, event caused the correlation between the first two events.

A caution is in order, however. Correlation does not equal causation (Wiersman & Jurs, 2009). The correlational finding just mentioned does not mean that permissive parenting necessarily causes low self-control in children. It could mean that, but it also could mean that a child's lack of self-control caused the parents to simply throw up their arms in despair and give up trying to control the child. It also could mean that other factors, such as heredity or poverty, caused the correlation between permissive parenting and low self-control in children. Figure 1.15 illustrates these possible interpretations of correlational data.

Throughout this book, you will read about numerous correlational research studies. Keep in mind how easy it is to assume causality when two events or characteristics merely are correlated.

Experimental Research   To study causality, researchers turn to experimental research. An **experiment** is a carefully regulated procedure in which one or more factors believed to influence the behavior being studied are manipulated, while all other factors are held constant. If the behavior under study changes when a factor is manipulated, we say that the manipulated factor has caused the behavior to change. In other words, the experiment has demonstrated cause and effect. The cause is the factor that was manipulated. The effect is the behavior that changed because of the manipulation. Nonexperimental research methods (descriptive and correlational research) cannot establish cause and effect because they do not involve manipulating factors in a controlled way (Mitchell & Jolley, 2010).

Independent and Dependent Variables   Experiments include two types of changeable factors, or variables: independent and dependent. An *independent variable* is a manipulated, influential, experimental factor. It is a potential cause. The label independent is used because this variable can be manipulated independently of other factors to determine its effect. One experiment may include several independent variables.

A *dependent variable* is a factor that can change in an experiment, in response to changes in the independent variable. As researchers manipulate the independent variable, they measure the dependent variable for any resulting effect.

For example, suppose that you conducted a study to determine whether aerobic exercise by pregnant women changes the breathing and sleeping patterns of newborn babies. You might require one group of pregnant women to engage in a certain amount of exercise each week while another group of pregnant women does not exercise; thus, the amount of exercise is the independent variable. When the infants are born, you would observe and measure their breathing and sleeping patterns.

experiment   A carefully regulated procedure in which one or more of the factors believed to influence the behavior being studied are manipulated, while all other factors are held constant.

These patterns are the dependent variable, the factor that changes as the result of your manipulation.

Experimental and Control Groups   Experiments can involve one or more experimental groups and one or more control groups. An *experimental group* is a group whose experience is manipulated. A *control group* is a comparison group that is as much like the experimental group as possible and that is treated in every way like the experimental group except for the manipulated factor (independent variable). The control group serves as a baseline against which the effects of the manipulated condition can be compared.

Random assignment is an important principle for deciding whether each participant will be placed in the experimental group or in the control group. Random assignment means that researchers assign participants to experimental and control groups by chance. It reduces the likelihood that the experiment's results will be due to any preexisting differences between groups (Martin, 2008). In the example of the effects of aerobic exercise by pregnant women on the breathing and sleeping patterns of their newborns, you would randomly assign half of the pregnant women to engage in aerobic exercise over a period of weeks (the experimental group) and the other half to not exercise over the same number of weeks (the control group). Figure 1.16 illustrates the nature of experimental research.

Time Span of Research   Researchers in child development have a special concern with studies that focus on the relation of age to some other variable. To do this, they can study different individuals of different ages and compare them, or they can study the same individuals as they age over time.

Cross-Sectional Approach   The **cross-sectional approach** is a research strategy in which individuals of different ages are compared at one time. A typical cross-sectional study might include a group of 5-year-olds, 8-year-olds, and 11-year-olds. The groups can be compared with respect to a variety of dependent variables: IQ, memory, peer relations, attachment to parents, hormonal changes, and so on. All of these comparisons can be accomplished in a short time. In some studies, data are collected in a single day. Even in large-scale cross-sectional studies with hundreds of participants, data collection does not usually take longer than several months to complete.

The main advantage of the cross-sectional study is that researchers don't have to wait for children to grow older. Despite its efficiency, the cross-sectional approach has its drawbacks. It gives no information about how individual children change or about the stability of their characteristics. It can obscure the increases and decreases of development—the hills and valleys of growth and development.

Longitudinal Approach   The **longitudinal approach** is a research strategy in which the same individuals are studied over a period of time, usually several years or more. For example, if a study of self-esteem were conducted longitudinally, the same children might be assessed three times—at 5, 8, and 11 years of age. Some longitudinal studies take place over shorter time frames, even just a year or so.

Longitudinal studies provide a wealth of information about such important issues as stability and change in development and the importance of early experience for later development, but they are not without their problems (Ong & Fuller-Rowell, 2009). They are expensive and time-consuming. Also, the longer the study lasts, the more participants drop out. For example, children's families may move, get sick, lose interest, and so forth. Those who remain in the study may be dissimilar to those who drop out, biasing the results. Those individuals who remain in a longitudinal study over a number of years may be more compulsive and conformity-oriented or they might have more stable lives.

Independent variable

Dependent variable

FIGURE 1.16 Principles of Experimental Research   Imagine that you decide to conduct an experimental study of the effects of aerobic exercise by pregnant women on their newborns' breathing and sleeping patterns. You would randomly assign pregnant women to experimental and control groups. The experimental-group women would engage in aerobic exercise over a specified number of sessions and weeks. The control group would not. Then, when the infants are born, you would assess their breathing and sleeping patterns. If the breathing and sleeping patterns of newborns whose mothers were in the experimental group arc more positive than those of the control group, you would conclude that aerobic exercise caused the positive effects.

cross-sectional approach   A research strategy in which individuals of different ages are compared at one time.

longitudinal approach   A research strategy in which the same individuals are studied over a period of time, usually several years or more.

So far we have discussed many aspects of scientific research in child development. In the *Research in Children's Development* interlude, you can read about the research journals in which this research is published.

Research in Children's Development

RESEARCH JOURNALS

Regardless of whether you pursue a career in child development, psychology, or some related scientific field, you can benefit by learning about the journal process. As a student you might be required to look up original research in journals. As a parent, teacher, or nurse you might want to consult journals to obtain information that will help you understand and work more effectively with people. And as an inquiring person, you might look up information in journals after you have heard or read something that piqued your curiosity.

A journal publishes scholarly and academic information, usually in a specific domain—like physics, math, sociology, or, our current interest, child development. Scholars in these fields publish most of their research in journals, which are the source of core information in virtually every academic discipline.

An increasing number of journals publish information about child development. Among the leading journals in child development are *Developmental Psychology, Child Development, Developmental Psychopathology, Pediatrics, Pediatric Nursing, Infant Behavior and Development, Journal of Research on Adolescence, Human Development,* and many others. Also, a number of journals that do not focus solely on development include articles on various aspects of human development. These journals include *Journal of Educational Psychology, Sex Roles, Journal of Cross-Cultural Research, Journal of Marriage and the Family, Exceptional Children,* and *Journal of Consulting and Clinical Psychology.*

Every journal has a board of experts who evaluate articles submitted for publication. Each submitted paper is accepted or rejected on the basis of such factors as its contribution to the field, methodological excellence, and clarity of writing. Some of the most prestigious journals reject as many as 80 to 90 percent of the articles submitted.

Journal articles are usually written for other professionals in the specialized field of the journal's focus—therefore, they often contain technical language and terms specific to the discipline that are difficult for nonprofessionals to understand. Their organization often takes this course: abstract, introduction, method, results, discussion, and references.

The *abstract* is a brief summary that appears at the beginning of the article. The abstract lets readers quickly determine whether the article is relevant to their interests. The *introduction* introduces the problem or issue that is being studied. It includes a concise review of research relevant to the topic, theoretical ties, and one or more hypotheses to be tested. The *method* section consists of a clear description of the subjects evaluated in the study, the measures used, and the procedures that were followed. The method section should be sufficiently clear and detailed so that by reading it another researcher could repeat or replicate the study. The *results* section reports the analysis of the data collected. In most cases, the results section includes statistical analyses that are

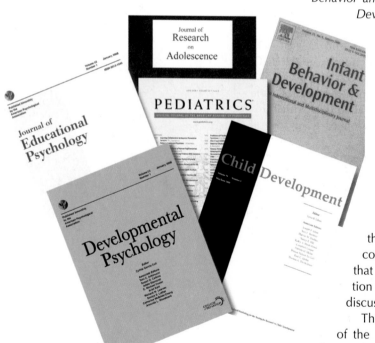

Research journals are the core of information in virtually every academic discipline. Those shown here are among the increasing number of research journals that publish information about child development. *What are the main parts of a research article that presents findings from original research?*

difficult for nonprofessionals to understand. The *discussion* section describes the author's conclusions, inferences, and interpretation of what was found. Statements are usually made about whether the hypotheses presented in the introduction were supported, limitations of the study, and suggestions for future research. The last part of the journal article, called *references*, includes bibliographic information for each source cited in the article. The references section is often a good source for finding other articles relevant to the topic that interests you.

Where do you find journals such as those we have described? Your college or university library likely has some of them, and some public libraries also carry journals. Online resources such as PsycINFO, which can facilitate the search for journal articles, are available to students on many campuses.

Research Challenges

The scientific foundation of research in child development helps to minimize the effect of research bias and maximize the objectivity of the results. Still, subtle challenges remain for each researcher to resolve. One is to ensure that research is conducted in an ethical way; another is to recognize, and try to overcome, deeply buried personal biases.

Conducting Ethical Research   The explosion in technology has forced society to grapple with looming ethical questions that were unimaginable only a few decades ago. The same line of research that enables previously sterile couples to have children might someday let prospective parents "call up and order" the characteristics they prefer in their children or tip the balance of males and females in the world. For example, should embryos left over from procedures for increasing fertility be saved or discarded? Should people with inheritable fatal diseases (such as Huntington disease) be discouraged from having children?

Researchers also face ethical questions both new and old. They have a responsibility to anticipate the personal problems their research might cause and to at least inform the participants of the possible fallout. Safeguarding the rights of research participants is a challenge because the potential harm is not always obvious (Graziano & Raulin, 2010).

Ethics in research may affect you personally if you ever serve as a participant in a study. In that event, you need to know your rights as a participant and the responsibilities of researchers to assure that these rights are safeguarded.

If you ever become a researcher in child development yourself, you will need an even deeper understanding of ethics. Even if you only carry out experimental projects in psychology courses, you must consider the rights of the participants in those projects.

Today, proposed research at colleges and universities must pass the scrutiny of a research ethics committee before the research can be initiated. In addition, the American Psychological Association (APA) has developed ethics guidelines for its members. The code of ethics instructs psychologists to protect their participants from mental and physical harm. The participants' best interests need to be kept foremost in the researcher's mind (Wiersman & Jurs, 2009). APA's guidelines address four important issues: informed consent, confidentiality, debriefing, and deception.

- *Informed consent.* All participants must know what their participation will involve and what risks might develop. For example, participants in a study on dating should be told beforehand that a questionnaire might stimulate thoughts about issues in their relationship that they have not considered. Participants also should be informed that in some instances a discussion of the issues might improve their relationship, but in others might worsen the relationship and even end it. Even after informed consent is given, participants must retain the right to withdraw from the study at any time and for any reason.

- *Confidentiality.* Researchers are responsible for keeping all of the data they gather on individuals completely confidential and, when possible, completely anonymous.

- *Debriefing.* After the study has been completed, participants should be informed of its purpose and the methods that were used. In most cases, the experimenter also can inform participants in a general manner beforehand about the purpose of the research without leading participants to behave in a way they think that the experimenter is expecting. When preliminary information about the study is likely to affect the results, participants can at least be debriefed after the study has been completed.

- *Deception.* This is an ethical issue that researchers debate extensively. In some circumstances, telling the participants beforehand what the research study is about substantially alters the participants' behavior and invalidates the researcher's data. In all cases, however, the psychologist must ensure that the deception will not harm the participants and that the participants will be told the complete nature of the study (debriefed) as soon as possible after the study is completed.

Minimizing Bias   Studies of children's development are most useful when they are conducted without bias or prejudice toward any specific group of people. Of special concern is bias based on gender and bias based on culture or ethnicity.

Gender Bias   For most of its existence, our society has had a strong gender bias, a preconceived notion about the abilities of males and females that prevented individuals from pursuing their own interests and achieving their potential (Matlin, 2008). Gender bias also has had a less obvious effect within the field of child development. For example, it is not unusual for conclusions to be drawn about females' attitudes and behaviors from research conducted with males as the only participants.

Furthermore, when researchers find gender differences, their reports sometimes magnify those differences (Denmark & others, 1988). For example, a researcher might report that 74 percent of the boys in a study had high achievement expectations versus only 67 percent of the girls and go on to talk about the differences in some detail. In reality, this might be a rather small difference. It also might disappear if the study were repeated, or the study might have methodological problems that don't allow such strong interpretations.

Pam Reid is a leading researcher who studies gender and ethnic bias in development. To read about Pam's interests, see the *Careers in Children's Development* profile.

Cultural and Ethnic Bias   The realization that research on children's development needs to include more children from diverse ethnic groups has especially been building (Graham, 2006; Kim & others, 2009; Parke & others, 2008). Historically, children from ethnic minority groups (African American, Latino, Asian American, and Native American) were excluded from most research in the United States and simply thought of as variations from the norm or average. If minority children were included in samples and their scores didn't fit the norm, they were viewed as confounds or "noise" in data and discounted. Given the fact that children from diverse ethnic groups were excluded from research on child development for so long, we might reasonably conclude that children's real lives are perhaps more varied than research data have indicated in the past.

Researchers also have tended to overgeneralize about ethnic groups (Healey, 2009; Liu & others, 2009). **Ethnic gloss** is the use of an ethnic label such as African American or Latino in a superficial way that portrays an ethnic group as being more

ethnic gloss The use of an ethnic label such as African American or Latino in a superficial way that portrays an ethnic group as being more homogeneous than it really is.

Careers in Children's Development

Pam Reid, Educational and Developmental Psychologist

When she was a child, Pam Reid liked to play with chemistry sets. Reid majored in chemistry during college and wanted to become a doctor. However, when some of her friends signed up for a psychology class as an elective, she also decided to take the course. She was intrigued by learning about how people think, behave, and develop—so much so that she changed her major to psychology. Reid went on to obtain her Ph.D. in psychology (American Psychological Association, 2003, p. 16).

For a number of years, Reid, was a professor of education and psychology at the University of Michigan, where she also was a research scientist at the Institute for Research on Women and Gender. Her main focus has been on how children and adolescents develop social skills with a special interest in the development of African American girls (Reid & Zalk, 2001). In 2004, Reid became provost and executive vice-president at Roosevelt University in Chicago, and in 2008 she became president of Saint Joseph College in Hartford, Connecticut.

Pam Reid (*center, back row*) with some of the graduate students she mentored at the University of Michigan.

homogeneous than it really is (Trimble, 1988). For example, a researcher might describe a research sample like this: "The participants were 60 Latinos." A more complete description of the Latino group might be something like this: "The 60 Latino participants were Mexican Americans from low-income neighborhoods in the southwestern area of Los Angeles. Thirty-six were from homes in which Spanish is the dominant language spoken, 24 from homes in which English is the main language

(a)

(b)

Look at these two photographs, (*a*) one of all non-Latino White boys, the other (*b*) of boys and girls from diverse ethnic backgrounds. Consider a topic in child development such as independence seeking, cultural values, parenting education, or health care. *If you were conducting research on this topic, might the results of the study be different depending on whether the participants in your study were the children in the photo on the left or the photo on the right?*

spoken. Thirty were born in the United States, 30 in Mexico. Twenty-eight described themselves as Mexican American, 14 as Mexican, 9 as American, 6 as Chicano, and 3 as Latino." Ethnic gloss can cause researchers to obtain samples of ethnic groups that are not representative of the group's diversity, which can lead to overgeneralization and stereotyping.

Research on ethnic minority children and their families has not been given adequate attention, especially in light of their significant rate of growth (Fuligni, Hughes, & Way, 2009; McLoyd & others, 2009). Until recently, ethnic minority families were combined in the category "minority," which masks important differences among ethnic groups as well as diversity within an ethnic group. At present and in the foreseeable future, the growth of minority families in the United States will be mainly due to the immigration of Latino and Asian families. Researchers need to take into account their acculturation level and the generational status of parents and children, and how these influence family processes and child outcomes (Kim & others, 2009). More attention also needs to be given to biculturalism because the complexity of diversity means that some children of color identify with two or more ethnic groups.

Review and Reflect: Learning Goal 4

 4 **Summarize why research is important in child development, the main theories of child development, and research methods, designs, and challenges**

REVIEW

- Why is research on child development important?
- What are the main theories of child development?
- What are the main research methods for collecting data about children's development?
- What types of research designs do child development researchers use?
- What are some research challenges in studying children's development?

REFLECT

- Imagine that you are conducting a research study on the sexual attitudes and behaviors of adolescents. What ethical safeguards should you use in conducting the study?

Reach Your Learning Goals

Introduction

1 WHY IS CARING FOR CHILDREN IMPORTANT? EXPLAIN WHY IT IS IMPORTANT TO STUDY CHILDREN'S DEVELOPMENT, AND IDENTIFY FIVE AREAS IN WHICH CHILDREN'S LIVES NEED TO BE IMPROVED

The Importance of Studying Children's Development

Improving the Lives of Children

- Studying children's development is important because it will help you to better understand your own childhood and provide you with strategies for being a competent parent or educator.

- Health and well-being are important areas in which children's lives can be improved. Today, many children in the United States and around the world need improved health care. We now recognize the importance of lifestyles and psychological states in promoting health and well-being. Parenting is an important influence on children's development. One-parent families, working parents, and child care are among the family issues that influence children's well-being. Education can also contribute to children's health and well-being. There is widespread concern that the education of children needs to be more effective, and there are many views in contemporary education about ways to improve schools. Sociocultural contexts are important influences on children's development. Culture, ethnicity, socioeconomic status, and gender are four key aspects of sociocultural contexts. Social policy is a national government's course of action designed to influence the welfare of its citizens. Researchers increasingly are conducting studies that are related to social policy.

2 WHAT ARE SOME HISTORICAL VIEWS OF CHILD DEVELOPMENT? CHARACTERIZE HISTORICAL VIEWS OF CHILDREN

Early Views of Childhood

- The history of interest in children is long and rich. Prior to the nineteenth century, philosophical views of childhood were prominent, including the notions of original sin (children are basically bad, born into the world as evil beings), tabula rasa (children are not innately bad or good but rather like a "blank tablet"), and innate goodness (children are inherently good). Today, we conceive of childhood as an important time of development.

The Modern Study of Child Development

- The modern era of studying children spans a little more than a century, an era in which the study of child development has become a sophisticated science. During the late 1800s, a major shift took place—from a strictly philosophical perspective to one that focuses on direct observation and experimentation. During the 1920s, a number of child development research centers were created. Early modern theorists included Arnold Gesell, who argued that certain characteristics of children simply "bloom" with age because of a biological, maturational blueprint; G. Stanley Hall, who theorized that child development follows an evolutionary course; Sigmund Freud, who thought that children were rarely aware of the motives and reasons for their behaviors; John Watson, who argued that children can be shaped into whatever society wishes by examining and changing the environment; James Mark Baldwin, who was a pioneer in the study of children's thought; and Jean Piaget, who proposed a sequence of cognitive stages that children pass through.

3   WHAT CHARACTERIZES DEVELOPMENT? DISCUSS THE MOST IMPORTANT PROCESSES, PERIODS, AND ISSUES IN DEVELOPMENT

Biological, Cognitive, and Socioemotional Processes

- Three key processes of development are biological, cognitive, and socioemotional. Biological processes (such as genetic inheritance) involve changes in an individual's physical nature. Cognitive processes (such as thinking) consist of changes in an individual's thought, intelligence, and language. Socioemotional processes (such as smiling) include changes in an individual's relationships with others, in emotions, and in personality.

Periods of Development

- Childhood's five main developmental periods are (1) prenatal—conception to birth, (2) infancy—birth to 18 to 24 months, (3) early childhood—end of infancy to about 5 to 6 years of age, (4) middle and late childhood—about 6 to 11 years of age, and (5) adolescence—begins at about 10 to 12 and ends at about 18 to 22 years of age.

Issues in Development

- The nature-nurture issue focuses on the extent to which development is mainly influenced by nature (biological inheritance) or nurture (environmental experience). Some developmentalists describe development as continuous (gradual, cumulative change); others describe it as discontinuous (a sequence of abrupt stages). The early-later experience issue focuses on whether early experiences (especially in infancy) are more important in development than later experiences. Most developmentalists recognize that extreme positions on the nature-nurture, continuity-discontinuity, and early-later experience issues are not supported by research. Despite this consensus, they continue to debate the degree to which each position influences children's development.

4   HOW IS CHILD DEVELOPMENT A SCIENCE? SUMMARIZE WHY RESEARCH IS IMPORTANT IN CHILD DEVELOPMENT, THE MAIN THEORIES OF CHILD DEVELOPMENT, AND RESEARCH METHODS, DESIGNS, AND CHALLENGES

The Importance of Research

- When we base information on personal experience, we aren't always objective. Research provides a vehicle for evaluating the accuracy of information. Scientific research is objective, systematic, and testable. Scientific research is based on the scientific method, which includes these steps: conceptualize the problem, collect data, draw conclusions, and revise research conclusions and theory.

Theories of Child Development

- Psychoanalytic theories describe development as primarily unconscious and as heavily colored by emotion. The two main psychoanalytic theories in developmental psychology are Freud's and Erikson's. Freud proposed that individuals go through five psychosexual stages—oral, anal, phallic, latency, and genital. Erikson's theory emphasizes eight psychosocial stages of development. The three main cognitive theories are Piaget's cognitive developmental theory, Vygotsky's sociocultural cognitive theory, and information-processing theory. Cognitive theories emphasize conscious thoughts. In Piaget's theory, children go through four cognitive stages: sensorimotor, preoperational, concrete operational, and formal operational. Vygotsky's sociocultural cognitive theory emphasizes how culture and social interaction guide cognitive development. The information-processing theory emphasizes that individuals manipulate information, monitor it, and strategize about it. Three versions of the behavioral and social cognitive approach are Pavlov's classical conditioning, Skinner's operant conditioning, and Bandura's social cognitive theory. Ethology stresses that behavior is strongly influenced by biology, is tied to evolution, and is characterized by critical or sensitive periods. Ecological theory is Bronfenbrenner's environmental systems view of development. It consists of five environmental systems: microsystem, mesosystem, exosystem, macrosystem, and chronosystem. An eclectic theoretical orientation

Research Methods for Collecting Data

Research Designs

Research Challenges

does not follow any one theoretical approach but rather selects from each theory whatever is considered the best in it.

- Research methods for collecting data about child development include observation (in a laboratory or a naturalistic setting), survey (questionnaire) or interview, standardized test, case study, and physiological measures.

- Descriptive research aims to observe and record behavior. In correlational research, the goal is to describe the strength of the relationship between two or more events or characteristics. Experimental research involves conducting an experiment, which can determine cause and effect. An independent variable is the manipulated, influential, experimental factor. A dependent variable is a factor that can change in an experiment, in response to changes in the independent variable. Experiments can involve one or more experimental groups and control groups. In random assignment, researchers assign participants to experimental and control groups by chance. When researchers decide about the time span of their research, they can conduct cross-sectional or longitudinal studies.

- Researchers' ethical responsibilities include seeking participants' informed consent, ensuring their confidentiality, debriefing them about the purpose and potential personal consequences of participating, and avoiding unnecessary deception of participants. Researchers need to guard against gender, cultural, and ethnic bias in research. Every effort should be made to make research equitable for both females and males. Individuals from varied ethnic backgrounds need to be included as participants in child research, and overgeneralization about diverse members within a group must be avoided.

KEY TERMS

development 7
context 9
culture 9
cross-cultural studies 10
ethnicity 10
socioeconomic status
  (SES) 10
gender 10
social policy 12
original sin view 14
tabula rasa view 14
innate goodness view 14
genetic epistemology 16
biological processes 17

cognitive processes 17
socioemotional
  processes 17
prenatal period 18
infancy 18
early childhood 18
middle and late
  childhood 18
adolescence 18
nature-nurture issue 19
continuity-discontinuity
  issue 20
early-later experience
  issue 20

scientific method 22
theory 22
hypothesis 22
psychoanalytic theories 23
Erikson's theory 24
Piaget's theory 27
Vygotsky's theory 28
information-processing
  theory 28
social cognitive theory 30
ethology 31
Bronfenbrenner's ecological
  theory 32

eclectic theoretical
  orientation 32
laboratory 34
naturalistic observation 34
standardized test 36
case study 36
descriptive research 37
correlational research 37
correlation coefficient 37
experiment 38
cross-sectional approach 39
longitudinal approach 39
ethnic gloss 42

KEY PEOPLE

Ann Masten 12
Philippe Ariès 14
John Locke 14
Jean-Jacques Rousseau 14
Alfred Binet 15
Arnold Gesell 15

G. Stanley Hall 15
Charles Darwin 15
Sigmund Freud 15
John Watson 16
James Mark Baldwin 16
Jean Piaget 16

Jerome Kagan 21
Sigmund Freud 23
Erik Erikson 24
Lev Vygotsky 28
Robert Siegler 29
Ivan Pavlov 30

B. F. Skinner 30
Albert Bandura 31
Konrad Lorenz 31
John Bowlby 32
Urie Bronfenbrenner 32

MAKING A DIFFERENCE

Lessons for Life

Marian Wright Edelman is one of America's foremost crusaders in the quest for improving the lives of children. Here are some of the main strategies she advocates for improving not only children's lives but our own as well (Edelman, 1992, pp. xxi, 42, 60):

- *"Don't feel as if you are entitled to anything that you don't sweat and struggle for."* Take the initiative to create opportunities. Don't wait around for people to give you favors. A door never has to stay closed. Push on it until it opens.

- *"Don't be afraid of taking risks or of being criticized."* We all make mistakes. It is only through making mistakes that we learn how to do things right. "It doesn't matter how many times you fall down. What matters is how many times we get up." We need "more courageous shepherds and fewer sheep."

- *"Don't ever stop learning and improving your mind or you're going to get left behind."* College is a great investment, but don't think you can park your mind there and everything you need to know will somehow be magically poured into it. Be an active learner. Be curious and ask questions. Explore new horizons.

- *"Stand up for children."* According to Edelman, this is the most important mission in the world. Parenting and nurturing the next generation of children are our society's most important functions, and we need to take them more seriously than we have in the past.

RESOURCES FOR IMPROVING CHILDREN'S LIVES

Children's Defense Fund
25 E Street
Washington, DC 20001
800–424–9602
www.childrensdefense.org

The Children's Defense Fund exists to provide a strong and effective voice for children and adolescents who cannot vote, lobby, or speak for themselves. The Children's Defense Fund is especially interested in the needs of poor, minority, and handicapped children and adolescents. The fund provides information, technical assistance, and support to a network of state and local child and youth advocates. The Children's Defense Fund publishes a number of excellent books and pamphlets related to children's needs.

Handbook of Child Psychology
edited by William Damon and Richard Lerner (6th ed., Vols. 1–4, 2006)
New York: John Wiley

The *Handbook of Child Psychology* is the standard reference work for overviews of theory and research in this field. It has in-depth discussions of many topics that we explore in this book.

E-LEARNING TOOLS

Connect to **www.mhhe.com/santrockc11** to research the answers and complete these exercises. In addition, you'll find a number of other resources and valuable study tools for Chapter 1, "Introduction," on this Web site.

Taking It to the Net

1. George is teaching fourth grade. He wants his students to learn about the difficulties and challenges of being a child in colonial America. What was life like for children in the early history of our country?

2. Janice thinks that better and stricter gun control laws will help decrease violent crime among children. Her husband, Elliott, disagrees. Janice found a March 2000 Department of Justice study that provides support for her argument. What facts in the report can she point to in order to convince Elliott?

3. For his political science class, Darren has to track federal funding appropriations in the most recent Congress for any issue of his choice. He has chosen children's issues. How did children and families fare in terms of congressional appropriations in the current Congress?

Health and Well-Being, Parenting, and Education

Build your decision-making skills by trying your hand at the health and well-being, parenting, and education exercises.

Video Clips

The Online Learning Center includes the following videos for this chapter:

- *Career in Child Development—905*
  Dr. Richard Lerner gives a humorous account of decision to major in psychology in college.

- *Career in Developmental Psychology—245*
  Dr. Marsha Weinraub, one of the leading researchers on the NICHD Early Child Care Study, describes how she became interested in developmental psychology.

- *Ethical Issues in Studying Infants—274*
  Renowned infant researcher Albert Yonas discusses the ethical issues he faces when studying infants.

- *Schools and Public Policy—931*
  Dr. Jacquelynne Eccles describes how her research on gender and school transitions has influenced public policy.

Appendix

Careers in Children's Development

Each of us wants to find a rewarding career and enjoy the work we do. The field of child development offers an amazing breadth of career options that can provide extremely satisfying work.

If you decide to pursue a career in child development, what career options are available to you? There are many. Colleges and university professors teach courses in areas of child development, education, family development, nursing, and medicine. Teachers impart knowledge, understanding, and skills to children and adolescents. Counselors, clinical psychologists, nurses, and physicians help parents and children of different ages to cope more effectively with their lives and well-being. Various professionals work with families to improve the quality and family functioning.

Although an advanced degree is not absolutely necessary in some areas of child development, you usually can expand your opportunities (and income) considerably by obtaining a graduate degree. Many careers in child development pay reasonably well. For example, psychologists earn well above the median salary in the United States. Also, by working in the field of child development you can guide people in improving their lives, understand yourself and others better, possibly advance the state of knowledge in the field, and have an enjoyable time while you are doing these things.

If you are considering a career in child development, would you prefer to work with infants? Children? Adolescents? Parents? As you go through this term, try to spend some time with children of different ages. Observe their behavior. Talk with them about their lives. Think about whether you would like to work with children of this age in your life's work.

Another important aspect of exploring careers is to talk with people who work in various jobs. For example, if you have some interest in becoming a school counselor, call a school, ask to speak with a counselor, and set up an appointment to discuss the counselor's career and work.

Something else that should benefit you is to work in one or more jobs related to your career interests while you are in college. Many colleges and universities have internships or work experiences for students who major in such fields as child development. In some instances, these jobs earn course credit or pay; in others, they are strictly on a volunteer basis. Take advantage of these opportunities. They can provide you with valuable experiences to help you decide if this is the right career for you—and they can help you get into graduate school, if you decide you want to go.

In the upcoming sections, we profile careers in four areas: education and research; clinical and counseling; medical, nursing, and physical development; and families and relationships. These are not the only career options in child development, but they should provide you with an idea of the range of opportunities available and information about some of the main career avenues you might pursue. In profiling these careers, we address the amount of education required, the nature of the training, and a description of the work.

EDUCATION AND RESEARCH

Numerous career opportunities in child development involve education or research. These range from a college professor to child-care director to school psychologist.

College/University Professor

Courses in child development are taught in many programs and schools in college and universities, including psychology, education, nursing, child and family studies, social work, and medicine. The work that college professors do includes teaching courses either at the undergraduate or graduate level (or both), conducting research in a specific area, advising students and/or directing their research, and serving on college or university committees. Some college instructors do not conduct research as part of their job but instead focus mainly on teaching. Research is most likely to be part of the job description at universities with master's and Ph.D. programs. A Ph.D. or master's degree almost always is required to teach in some area of child development in a college or university. Obtaining a doctoral degree usually takes four to six years of graduate work. A master's degree requires approximately two years of graduate work. The training involves taking graduate courses, learning to conduct research, and attending and presenting papers at professional meetings. Many graduate students work as teaching or research assistants for professors in an apprenticeship relationship that helps them to become competent teachers and researchers.

If you are interested in becoming a college or university professor, you might want to make an appointment with your instructor in this class on child development to learn more about his or her profession and work. To read about the work of one college professor, see the *Careers in Children's Development* profile.

Researcher

Some individuals in the field of child development work in research positions. In most instances, they have either a master's or Ph.D. in some area of child development. The researchers might work at a university, in some cases in a university professor's research program, in government at such agencies as the National Institute of Mental Health or in private industry. Individuals who have full-time research positions in child development generate innovative research ideas, plan studies,

Valerie Pang, Professor of Teacher Education

Valerie Pang is a professor of teacher education at San Diego State University and formerly was an elementary school teacher. Like Dr. Pang, many professors of teacher education have a doctorate and have experience in teaching at the elementary or secondary school level.

Pang earned a doctorate at the University of Washington. She has received a Multicultural Educator Award from the National Association of Multicultural Education for her work on culture and equity. She also was given the Distinguished Scholar Award from the American Educational Research Association's Committee on the Role and Status of Minorities in Education.

Pang (2005) believes that competent teachers need to:

- Recognize the power and complexity of cultural influences on students.

- Be sensitive to whether their expectations for students are culturally biased.

- Evaluate whether they are doing a good job of seeing life from the perspective of students who come from different cultures.

Valerie Pang is a professor in the School of Education of San Diego State University and formerly an elementary school teacher. Valerie believes it is important for teachers to create a caring classroom that affirms all students.

carry out the research by collecting data, analyzing the data, and then interpreting it. Then they will usually attempt to publish the research in a scientific journal. A researcher often works in a collaborative manner with other researchers on a project and may present the research at scientific meetings. One researcher might spend much of his or her time in laboratory; another researcher might work out in the field, such as in schools, hospitals, and so on.

Elementary School Teacher

The work of an elementary or secondary school teacher involves teaching in one or more subject areas, preparing the curriculum, giving tests, assigning grades, monitoring students' progress, conducting parent-teacher conferences, and attending in-service workshops. Becoming an elementary or secondary school teacher requires a minimum of an undergraduate degree. The training involves taking a wide range of courses with a major or concentration in education, as well as completing a supervised practice-teaching internship.

Exceptional Children (Special Education) Teacher

A teacher of exceptional children spends concentrated time with individual children who have a disability or are gifted. Among the children a teacher of exceptional children might work with are children with learning disabilities, ADHD (attention deficit hyperactivity disorder), mental retardation, or a physical disability such as cerebral palsy. Some of this work will usually be done outside of the student's regular classroom, some of it will be carried out when the student is in the regular classroom. The exceptional children teacher works closely with the student's regular classroom teacher and parents to create the best educational program for the student. Becoming a teacher of exceptional children requires a minimum of an undergraduate degree. The training consists of taking a wide range of courses in education and a concentration of courses in educating children with disabilities or children who are gifted. Teachers of exceptional children often continue their education after obtaining their undergraduate degree and attain a master's degree.

Early Childhood Educator

Early childhood educators work on college faculties and have a minimum of a master's degree in their field. In graduate school, they take courses in early childhood education and receive supervisory training in child-care or early childhood programs. Early childhood educators usually teach in community colleges that award an associate degree in early childhood education.

Preschool/Kindergarten Teacher

Preschool teachers teach mainly 4-year-old children, and kindergarten teachers primarily teach 5-year-old children.

They usually have an undergraduate degree in education, specializing in early childhood education. State certification to become a preschool or kindergarten teacher usually is required.

Family and Consumer Science Educator

Family and consumer science educators may specialize in early childhood education or instruct middle and high school students about such matters as nutrition, interpersonal relationships, human sexuality, parenting, and human development. Hundreds of colleges and universities throughout the United States offer two- and four-year degree programs in family and consumer science. These programs usually include an internship requirement. Additional education courses may be needed to obtain a teaching certificate. Some family and consumer educators go on to graduate school for further training, which provides a background for possible jobs in college teaching or research.

Educational Psychologist

An educational psychologist most often teaches in a college or university and conducts research in such areas of educational psychology as learning, motivation, classroom management, and assessment. Most educational psychologists have a doctorate in education, which takes four to six years of graduate work. They help to train students who will take various positions in education, including educational psychology, school psychology, and teaching.

School Psychologist

School psychologists focus on improving the psychological and intellectual well-being of elementary and secondary school students. They may work in a centralized office in a school district or in one or more schools. They give psychological tests, interview students and their parents, consult with teachers, and may provide counseling to students and their families.

School psychologists usually have a master's or doctoral degree in school psychology. In graduate school, they take courses in counseling, assessment, learning, and other areas of education and psychology.

CLINICAL AND COUNSELING

There are a wide variety of clinical and counseling jobs that are linked with child development. These range from child clinical psychologist to adolescent drug counselor.

Clinical Psychologist

Clinical psychologists seek to help people with psychological problems. They work in a variety of settings, including colleges and universities, clinics, medical schools, and private practice. Some clinical psychologists only conduct psychother-

apy, others do psychological assessment and psychotherapy, and some also do research. Clinical psychologists may specialize in a particular age group, such as children (child clinical psychologist).

Clinical psychologists have either a Ph.D. (which involves clinical and research training) or a Psy.D. degree (which involves only clinical training). This graduate training usually takes five to seven years and includes courses in clinical psychology and a one-year supervised internship in an accredited setting toward the end of the training. In most cases, they must pass a test to become licensed in a state and to call themselves clinical psychologists.

Psychiatrist

Like clinical psychologists, psychiatrists might specialize in working with children (child psychiatry) or adolescents (adolescent psychiatry). Psychiatrists might work in medical schools in teaching and research roles, in a medical clinic, or in private practice. In addition to administering drugs to help improve the lives of people with psychological problems, psychiatrists also may conduct psychotherapy. Psychiatrists obtain a medical degree and then do a residency in psychiatry. Medical school takes approximately four years, and the psychiatry residency another three to four years. Unlike psychologists (who do not go to medical school) in most states, psychiatrists can administer drugs to clients.

Counseling Psychologist

Counseling psychologists work in the same settings as clinical psychologists and may do psychotherapy, teach, or conduct research. In many instances, however, counseling psychologists do not work with individuals who have a severe mental disorder. A counseling psychologist might specialize in working with children, adolescents, and/or families.

Counseling psychologists go through much of the same training as clinical psychologists, although in a graduate program in counseling rather than clinical psychology. Counseling psychologists have either a master's degree or a doctoral degree. They also must go through a licensing procedure. One type of master's degree in counseling leads to the designation of licensed professional counselor.

School Counselor

School counselors help to identify students' abilities and interests, guide students in developing academic plans, and explore career options with students. They may help students cope with adjustment problems. They may work with students individually, in small groups, or even in a classroom. They often consult with parents, teachers, and school administrators when trying to help students with their problems.

High school counselors advise students on choosing a major, admissions requirements for college, taking entrance exams, applying for financial aid, and on appropriate vocational and technical training. Elementary school counselors are mainly involved in counseling students about social and personal problems. They may observe children in the classroom and at play as part of their work. School counselors usually have a master's degree in counseling.

Career Counselor

Career counselors help individuals to identify their best career options and guide them in applying for jobs. They may work in private industry or at a college/university. They usually interview individuals and give them vocational or psychological tests to help them provide students with information about careers that fit their interests and abilities. Sometimes they help individuals to create résumés or conduct mock interviews to help them feel comfortable in a job interview. They may create and promote job fairs or other recruiting events to help individuals obtain jobs.

Social Worker

Social workers often are involved in helping people with social or economic problems. They may investigate, evaluate, and attempt to rectify reported cases of abuse, neglect, endangerment, or domestic disputes. They can intervene in families if necessary and provide counseling and referral services to individuals and families.

Social workers have a minimum of an undergraduate degree from a school of social work that includes course work in various areas of sociology and psychology. Some social workers also have a master's or doctoral degree. They often work for publicly funded agencies at the city, state, or national level, although increasingly they work in the private sector in areas such as drug rehabilitation and family counseling.

In some cases, social workers specialize in a certain area, as is true of a medical social worker, who has a master's degree in social work (MSW). This involves graduate course work and supervised clinical experiences in medical settings. A medical social worker might coordinate a variety of support services to people with a severe or long-term disability. Family-care social workers often work with families who need support services.

Drug Counselor

Drug counselors provide counseling to individuals with drug abuse problems. They may work on an individual basis with a substance abuser or conduct group therapy sessions. They may work in private practice, with a state or federal government agency, with a company, or in a hospital setting. Some drug counselors specialize in working with adolescents or families. Most states provide a certification procedure for obtaining a license to practice drug counseling.

At a minimum, drug counselors go through an associate's or certificate program. Many have an undergraduate degree in substance-abuse counseling, and some have master's and doctoral degrees.

MEDICAL, NURSING, AND PHYSICAL DEVELOPMENT

This third main area of careers in child development includes a wide range of careers in the medical and nursing areas, as well as jobs pertaining to improving some aspect of the child's physical development.

Obstetrician/Gynecologist

An obstetrician/gynecologist prescribes prenatal and postnatal care and performs deliveries in maternity cases. The individual also treats diseases and injuries of the female reproductive system. Obstetricians may work in private practice, in a medical clinic, in a hospital, or in a medical school. Becoming an obstetrician/gynecologist requires a medical degree plus three to five years of residency in obstetrics/gynecology.

Pediatrician

A pediatrician monitors infants' and children's health, works to prevent disease or injury, helps children attain optimal health, and treats children with health problems. Pediatricians may work in private practice, in a medical clinic, in a hospital, or in a medical school. As medical doctors, they can administer drugs to children and may counsel parents and children on ways to improve the children's health. Many pediatricians on the faculty of medical schools also teach and conduct research on children's health and diseases. Pediatricians have attained a medical degree and completed a three- to five-year residency in pediatrics.

Neonatal Nurse

A neonatal nurse is involved in the delivery and care of the newborn infant. The neonatal nurse may work to improve the health and well-being of infants born under normal circumstances or be involved in the delivery of care to premature and critically ill neonates.

A minimum of an undergraduate degree in nursing with a specialization in the newborn is required. This training involves course work in nursing and the biological sciences, as well as supervisory clinical experiences.

Nurse-Midwife

A nurse-midwife formulates and provides comprehensive care to selected maternity patients, cares for the expectant mother as she prepares to give birth and guides her through the birth process, and cares for the postpartum patient. The nurse-midwife also may provide care to the newborn, counsel parents on the infant's development and parenting, and provide guidance about health practices. Becoming a nurse-midwife generally requires an undergraduate degree from a school of nursing. A nurse-midwife most often works in a hospital setting.

Careers in Children's Development

Katherine Duchen Smith, Nurse and Child-Care Health Consultant

Katherine Duchen Smith has a master's degree in nursing and works as a child-care health consultant. She lives in Ft. Collins, Colorado, and in 2004 was appointed as the public relations chair of the National Association of Pediatric Nurse Practitioners (NAPNAP), which has more than 6,000 members.

Smith provides health consultation and educational services to child-care centers, private schools, and hospitals. She also teaches in the Regis University Family Nurse Practitioner Program. Smith developed an interest in outreach and public-relations activities during her five-year term as a board member for the Fort Collins Poudre Valley Hospital System. Later, she became the organization's outreach consultant.

As child-care health consultants, nurses might provide telephone consultation and link children, families, or staff with primary care providers. In underserved areas, they might also be asked to administer immunizations, help chronically ill children access specialty care, or develop a comprehensive health promotion or injury prevention program for caregivers and families.

Katherine Duchen Smith (*left*), nurse and child-care health consultant, at a child-care center where she is a consultant.

Pediatric Nurse

Pediatric nurses have a degree in nursing that takes from two to five years to complete. Some also may obtain a master's or doctoral degree in pediatric nursing. Pediatric nurses take courses in biological sciences, nursing care, and pediatrics, usually in a school of nursing. They also undergo supervised clinical experiences in medical settings. They monitor infants' and children's health, work to prevent disease or injury, and help children attain optimal health. They may work in hospitals, schools of nursing, or with pediatricians in private practice or at a medical clinic. To read about the work of one pediatric nurse practitioner, see the *Careers in Children's Development* profile.

Audiologist

An audiologist has a minimum of an undergraduate degree in hearing science. This includes courses and supervisory training. Audiologists assess and identify the presence and severity of hearing loss, as well as problems in balance. Some audiologists also go on to obtain a master's and/or doctoral degree. They may work in a medical clinic, with a physician in private practice, in a hospital, or in a medical school.

Speech Therapist

Speech therapists are health-care professionals who are trained to identify, assess, and treat speech and language problems. They may work with physicians, psychologists, social workers, and other health-care professionals as a team to help individuals with physical or psychological problems that include speech and language problems. Speech pathologists have a minimum of an undergraduate degree in the speech and hearing science or communications disorders area. They may work in private practice, in hospitals and medical schools, and in government agencies with individuals of any age. Some specialize in working with children or with a particular type of speech disorder.

Genetic Counselor

Genetic counselors work as members of a health-care team, providing information and support to families who have members with birth defects or genetic disorders and to families who may be at risk for a variety of inherited conditions. They identify families at risk and provide supportive counseling. They serve as educators and resource people for other health-care professionals and the public. Almost half work in university medical centers, and another one-fourth work in private hospital settings.

Most genetic counselors enter the field after majoring in undergraduate school in such disciplines as biology, genetics, psychology, nursing, public health, and social work. They have specialized graduate degrees and experience in medical genetics and counseling.

FAMILIES AND RELATIONSHIPS

A number of careers are available for working with families and relationship problems. These range from being a child welfare worker to marriage and family therapist.

Child Welfare Worker

A child welfare worker is employed by the child protective services unit of each state. The child welfare worker protects the child's rights, evaluates any maltreatment the child might experience, and may have the child removed from the home if necessary. A child social worker has a minimum of an undergraduate degree in social work.

Child Life Specialist

Child life specialists work with children and their families when the child needs to be hospitalized. They monitor the child patient's activities, seek to reduce the child's stress, help the child cope effectively, and assist the child in enjoying the hospital experience as much as possible. Child life specialists may provide parent education and develop individualized treatment plans based on an assessment of the child's development, temperament, medical plan, and available social supports.

Child life specialists have an undergraduate degree. As undergraduates, they take courses in child development and education and usually take additional courses in a child life program.

Marriage and Family Therapist

Marriage and family therapists work on the principle that many individuals who have psychological problems benefit when psychotherapy is provided in the context of a marital or family relationship. Marriage and family therapists may provide marital therapy, couple therapy to individuals in a relationship who are not married, and family therapy to two or more members of a family.

Marriage and family therapists have a master's or doctoral degree. They go through a training program in graduate school similar to that of a clinical psychologist but with the focus on martial and family relationships. To practice marital and family therapy in most states, it is necessary to go through a licensing procedure.

TWO

BEGINNINGS

There are one hundred and ninety-three living species of monkeys and apes. One hundred and ninety-two of them are covered with hair. The exception is the naked ape, self-named **Homo sapiens.**

—DESMOND MORRIS
British Zoologist, 20th Century

The rhythm and meaning of life involve beginnings. Questions

are raised about how, from so simple a beginning, endless

forms develop, grow, and mature. What was this organism,

what is this organism, and what will this organism be? In

Section 2, you will read three chapters: "Biological Beginnings"

(Chapter 2), "Prenatal Development" (Chapter 3), and "Birth"

(Chapter 4).

2

*What endless
questions vex the
thought, of whence
and whither, when
and how.*

—SIR RICHARD BURTON
British Explorer, 19th Century

LEARNING GOALS

◆ Discuss the evolutionary
   perspective on development

◆ Describe what genes are and how
   they influence human development

◆ Identify some important reproductive
   challenges and choices

◆ Characterize some of the ways that
   heredity and environment interact
   to produce individual differences in
   development

BIOLOGICAL BEGINNINGS

CHAPTER OUTLINE

Images of Children's Development
The Story of the Jim and Jim Twins

Jim Lewis (*left*) and Jim Springer (*right*).

Jim Springer and Jim Lewis are identical twins. They were separated at 4 weeks of age and did not see each other again until they were 39 years old. Both worked as part-time deputy sheriffs, vacationed in Florida, drove Chevrolets, had dogs named Toy, and married and divorced women named Betty. One twin named his son James Allan, and the other named his son James Alan. Both liked math but not spelling, enjoyed carpentry and mechanical drawing, chewed their fingernails down to the nubs, had almost identical drinking and smoking habits, had hemorrhoids, put on 10 pounds at about the same point in development, first suffered headaches at the age of 18, and had similar sleep patterns.

Jim and Jim do have some differences. One wears his hair over his forehead, the other slicks it back and has sideburns. One expresses himself best orally; the other is more proficient in writing. But, for the most part, their profiles are remarkably similar.

Jim and Jim were part of the Minnesota Study of Twins Reared Apart, directed by Thomas Bouchard and his colleagues (Bouchard, 1995, 2008; Johnson & others, 2007). The study brings identical twins (identical genetically because they come from the same fertilized egg) and fraternal twins (who come from different fertilized eggs) from all over the world to Minneapolis to investigate their lives. There the twins complete personality and intelligence tests, and they provide detailed medical histories, including information about diet and smoking, exercise habits, chest X-rays, heart stress tests, and electroencephalograms (EEGs). The twins are asked more than 15,000 questions about their family and childhood, personal interests, vocational orientation, values, and aesthetic judgments.

Another pair of identical twins in the Minnesota study, Daphne and Barbara, are called the "giggle sisters" because, after being reunited, they were always making each other laugh. A thorough search of their adoptive families' histories revealed no gigglers. The giggle sisters ignored stress, avoided conflict and controversy whenever possible, and showed no interest in politics.

Two other identical twin sisters were separated at 6 weeks and reunited in their fifties. Both described hauntingly similar nightmares in which they had doorknobs and fishhooks in their mouths as they smothered to death. The nightmares began during early adolescence and stopped within the past 10 to 12 years. Both women were bed wetters until about 12 or 13 years of age, and their educational and marital histories are remarkably similar.

When genetically identical twins who were separated as infants show such striking similarities in their tastes and habits and choices, can we conclude that their genes must have caused the development of those tastes and habits and choices? Other possible causes need to be considered. The twins shared not only the same genes but also some experiences. Some of the separated twins lived together for several months prior to their adoption; some of the twins had been reunited prior to testing (in some cases, many years earlier); adoption agencies often place twins in similar homes; and even strangers who spend several hours together and start comparing their lives are likely to come up with some coincidental similarities (Joseph, 2006). The Minnesota study of identical twins points to both the importance of the genetic basis of human development and the need for further research on genetic and environmental factors.

PREVIEW

The examples of Jim and Jim, the giggle sisters, and the identical twins who had the same nightmares stimulate us to think about our genetic heritage and the biological foundations of our existence. Organisms are not like billiard balls, moved by simple, external forces to predictable positions on life's pool table. Environmental experiences and biological foundations work together to make us who we are. Our exploration of life's biological beginnings focuses on evolution, genetic foundations, challenges and choices regarding reproduction, and the interaction of heredity and environment.

1 WHAT IS THE EVOLUTIONARY PERSPECTIVE?

| Natural Selection and Adaptive Behavior | Evolutionary Psychology |

As our earliest ancestors left the forest to feed in the savannahs, and then to form hunting societies on the open plains, their minds and behaviors changed, and they eventually established humans as the dominant species on Earth. How did this evolution come about?

Natural Selection and Adaptive Behavior

Natural selection is the evolutionary process by which those individuals of a species that are best adapted are the ones that survive and reproduce. To understand what this means, let's return to the middle of the nineteenth century, when the British naturalist Charles Darwin was traveling around the world, observing many different species of animals in their natural surroundings. Darwin, who published his observations and thoughts in *On the Origin of Species* (1859), noted that most organisms reproduce at rates that would cause enormous increases in the population of most species and yet populations remain nearly constant. He reasoned that an intense, constant struggle for food, water, and resources must occur among the many young born each generation, because many of the young do not survive. Those that do survive, and reproduce, pass on their characteristics to the next generation. Darwin observed that these survivors are better *adapted* to their world than are the nonsurvivors (Johnson, & Losos, 2010). The best-adapted individuals survive to leave the most offspring. Over the course of many generations, organisms with the characteristics needed for survival make up an increased percentage of the population. Over many, many generations, this could produce a gradual modification of the whole population. If environmental conditions change, however, other characteristics might become favored by natural selection, moving the species in a different direction (Mader, 2010).

All organisms must adapt to particular places, climates, food sources, and ways of life. An eagle's claws are a physical adaptation that facilitates predation. *Adaptive behavior* is behavior that promotes an organism's survival in the natural habitat (Enger, Ross, & Bailey, 2009). For example, attachment between a caregiver and a baby ensures the infant's closeness to a caregiver for feeding and protection from danger, thus increasing the infant's chances of survival. Or consider pregnancy sickness, which is a tendency for women to become nauseous during pregnancy and avoid certain foods (Schmitt & Pilcher, 2004). Women with

How does the attachment of this Vietnamese baby to its mother reflect the evolutionary process of adaptive behavior?

pregnancy sickness tend to avoid foods that are higher in toxins, such as coffee, that may harm the fetus. Thus, pregnancy sickness may be an evolution-based adaptation that enhances the offspring's ability to survive.

Evolutionary Psychology

Although Darwin introduced the theory of evolution by natural selection in 1859, his ideas only recently have become a popular framework for explaining behavior. Psychology's newest approach, **evolutionary psychology,** emphasizes the importance of adaptation, reproduction, and "survival of the fittest" in shaping behavior. "Fit" in this sense refers to the ability to bear offspring that survive long enough to bear offspring of their own. In this view, natural selection favors behaviors that increase reproductive success: the ability to pass your genes to the next generation (Bjorklund, 2006, 2007).

David Buss (1995, 2004, 2008) has been especially influential in stimulating new interest in how evolution can explain human behavior. He argues that just as evolution shapes our physical features, such as body shape and height, it also pervasively influences our decision making, our degree of aggression, our fears, and our mating patterns. For example, assume that our ancestors were hunters and gatherers on the plains and that men did most of the hunting and women stayed close to home, gathering seeds and plants for food. If you have to travel some distance from your home in an effort to find and slay a fleeing animal, you need not only certain physical traits but also the ability for certain types of spatial thinking. Men born with these traits would be more likely than men without them to survive, to bring home lots of food, and to be considered attractive mates—and thus to reproduce and pass on these characteristics to their children. In other words, these traits would provide a reproductive advantage for males and, over many generations, men with good spatial thinking skills might become more numerous in the population. Critics point out that this scenario might or might not have actually happened.

Evolutionary Developmental Psychology Recently, interest has grown in using the concepts of evolutionary psychology to understand human development (Bjorklund, 2006, 2007). Following are some ideas proposed by evolutionary developmental psychologists (Bjorklund & Pellegrini, 2002).

An extended childhood period evolved because humans require time to develop a large brain and learn the complexity of human societies. Humans take longer to become reproductively mature than any other mammal (see Figure 2.1). During this extended childhood period, they develop a large brain and the experiences needed to become competent adults in a complex society.

Many evolved psychological mechanisms are domain-specific. That is, the mechanisms apply only to a specific aspect of a person's makeup. According to evolutionary psychology, information processing is one example. In this view, the mind is not a general-purpose device that can be applied equally to a vast array of problems. Instead, as our ancestors dealt with certain recurring problems such as hunting and finding shelter, specialized modules evolved that process information related to those problems—for example, a module for physical knowledge for tracking animals, a module for mathematical knowledge for trading, and a module for language.

Evolved mechanisms are not always adaptive in contemporary society. Some behaviors that were adaptive for our prehistoric ancestors may not serve us well today. For example, the food-scarce environment of our ancestors likely led to humans' propensity to gorge when food is available and to crave high-caloric foods, a trait that might lead to an epidemic of obesity when food is plentiful.

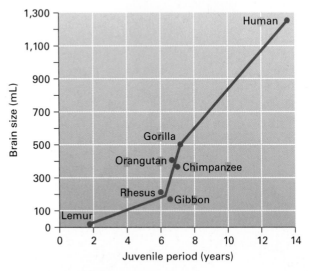

FIGURE 2.1 The Brain Sizes of Various Primates and Humans in Relation to the Length of the Juvenile Period

evolutionary psychology Branch of psychology that emphasizes the importance of adaptation, reproduction, and "survival of the fittest" in shaping behavior.

Evaluating Evolutionary Psychology   Although evolutionary psychology is getting increased attention, it remains just one theoretical approach. Like the theories described in Chapter 1, "Introduction," it has limitations, weaknesses, and critics. Albert Bandura (1998), whose social cognitive theory was described in Chapter 1, acknowledges the important influence of evolution on human adaptation. However, he rejects what he calls "one-sided evolutionism," which sees social behavior as the product of evolved biology. An alternative is a *bidirectional view*, in which environmental and biological conditions influence each other. In this view, evolutionary pressures created changes in biological structures that allowed the use of tools, which enabled our ancestors to manipulate the environment, constructing new environmental conditions. In turn, environmental innovations produced new selection pressures that led to the evolution of specialized biological systems for consciousness, thought, and language.

In other words, evolution gave us bodily structures and biological potentialities; it does not dictate behavior. People have used their biological capacities to produce diverse cultures—aggressive and pacific, egalitarian and autocratic. As American scientist Steven Jay Gould (1981) concluded, in most domains of human functioning, biology allows a broad range of cultural possibilities.

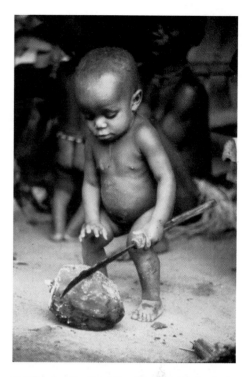

Children in all cultures are interested in the tools that adults in the cultures use. For example, this 11-month-old boy from the Efe culture in the Democratic Republic of the Congo in Africa is trying to cut a papaya with a sharp stick. *Might the infant's behavior be evolutionary-based or be due to both biological and environmental conditions?*

Review and Reflect: Learning Goal 1

 Discuss the evolutionary perspective on development

REVIEW

- How can natural selection and adaptive behavior be defined?
- What is evolutionary psychology? What are some basic ideas about human development proposed by evolutionary developmental psychologists? How can evolutionary psychology be evaluated?

REFLECT

- Which is more persuasive to you: the views of evolutionary psychologists or those of their critics? Why?

---

2 WHAT ARE THE GENETIC FOUNDATIONS OF DEVELOPMENT?

| The Collaborative Gene | Genes and Chromosomes | Genetic Principles | Chromosomal and Gene-Linked Abnormalities |

How are characteristics that suit a species for survival transmitted from one generation to the next? Darwin did not know because genes and the principles of genetics had not yet been discovered. Each of us carries a "genetic code" that we inherited from our parents. Because a fertilized egg carries this human code, a fertilized human egg cannot grow into an egret, eagle, or elephant.

The Collaborative Gene

Each of us began life as a single cell weighing about one twenty-millionth of an ounce! This tiny piece of matter housed our entire genetic code—instructions that orchestrated growth from that single cell to a person made of trillions of cells, each containing a

FIGURE 2.2 Cells, Chromosomes, DNA, and Genes (*Top*) The body contains trillions of cells. Each cell contains a central structure, the nucleus. (*Middle*) Chromosomes are threadlike structures located in the nucleus of the cell. Chromosomes are composed of DNA. (*Bottom*) DNA has the structure of a spiraled double chain. A gene is a segment of DNA.

chromosomes Threadlike structures made up of deoxyribonucleic acid, or DNA.

DNA A complex molecule with a double helix shape; contains genetic information.

genes Units of hereditary information composed of DNA. Genes direct cells to reproduce themselves and manufacture the proteins that maintain life.

replica of the original code. That code is carried by our genes (Johnson, & Losos, 2010). What are genes and what do they do? For the answer, we need to look into our cells.

The nucleus of each human cell contains **chromosomes,** which are threadlike structures made up of deoxyribonucleic acid, or DNA. **DNA** is a complex molecule that has a double helix shape, like a spiral staircase, and contains genetic information. **Genes,** the units of hereditary information, are short segments of DNA, as you can see in Figure 2.2. They direct cells to reproduce themselves and to assemble proteins. Proteins, in turn, are the building blocks of cells as well as the regulators that direct the body's processes (Mader, 2010; Hoefnagels, 2009).

Each gene has its own location, its own designated place on a particular chromosome. Today, there is a great deal of enthusiasm about efforts to discover the specific locations of genes that are linked to certain functions (Brooker, 2009; Plomin & others, 2009). An important step in this direction was accomplished in 2003 when the Human Genome Project and the Celera Corporation completed a preliminary map of the human *genome*—the complete set of developmental instructions for creating proteins that initiate the making of a human organism (Antonarakis, 2009).

One of the big surprises of the Human Genome Project was a report indicating that humans have only about 30,000 genes (U.S. Department of Energy, 2001). More recently, the number of human genes has been revised further downward to approximately 20,500 (Ensembl Human, 2008). Scientists had thought that humans had as many as 100,000 or more genes. They had also believed that each gene programmed just one protein. In fact, humans appear to have far more proteins than they have genes, so there cannot be a one-to-one correspondence between genes and proteins (Commoner, 2002). Each gene is not translated, in automaton-like fashion, into one and only one protein. A gene does not act independently, as developmental psychologist David Moore (2001) emphasized by titling his book *The Dependent Gene.*

Rather than being a group of independent genes, the human genome consists of many genes that collaborate both with each other and with nongenetic factors inside and outside the body. The collaboration operates at many points. For example, the cellular machinery mixes, matches, and links small pieces of DNA to reproduce the genes, and that machinery is influenced by what is going on around it.

A positive result from the Human Genome Project. Shortly after Andrew Gobea was born, his cells were genetically altered to prevent his immune system from failing.

Whether a gene is turned "on"—that is, working to assemble proteins—is also a matter of collaboration. The activity of genes (*genetic expression*) is affected by their environment (Gottlieb, 2007). For example, hormones that circulate in the blood make their way into the cell where they can turn genes "on" and "off." And the flow of hormones can be affected by environmental conditions, such as light, day length, nutrition, and behavior. Numerous studies have shown that external events outside the original cell and the person, as well as events inside the cell, can excite or inhibit gene expression (Gottlieb, 2007). For example, one recent study revealed that an increase in the concentration of stress hormones such as cortisol produced a fivefold increase in DNA damage (Flint & others, 2007).

Genes and Chromosomes

Genes are not only collaborative, they are enduring. How do the genes manage to get passed from generation to generation and end up in all of the trillion cells in

Calvin and Hobbes   by Bill Watterson

CALVIN AND HOBBES Copyright © 1991 Watterson. Distributed by UNIVERSAL PRESS SYNDICATE. Reprinted with permission. All rights reserved.

the body? Three processes explain the heart of the story: mitosis, meiosis, and fertilization.

Mitosis, Meiosis, and Fertilization   All cells in your body, except the sperm and egg, have 46 chromosomes arranged in 23 pairs. These cells reproduce by a process called **mitosis.** During mitosis, the cell's nucleus—including the chromosomes— duplicates itself and the cell divides. Two new cells are formed, each containing the same DNA as the original cell, arranged in the same 23 pairs of chromosomes.

However, a different type of cell division—**meiosis**—forms eggs and sperm (or *gametes*). During meiosis, a cell of the testes (in men) or ovaries (in women) duplicates its chromosomes but then divides *twice*, thus forming four cells, each of which has only half of the genetic material of the parent cell (Mader, 2010). By the end of meiosis, each egg or sperm has 23 *unpaired* chromosomes.

During **fertilization,** an egg and a sperm fuse to create a single cell, called a **zygote** (see Figure 2.3). In the zygote, the 23 unpaired chromosomes from the egg and the 23 unpaired chromosomes from the sperm combine to form one set of 23 paired chromosomes—one chromosome of each pair from the mother's egg and the other from the father's sperm. In this manner, each parent contributes half of the offspring's genetic material.

Figure 2.4 shows 23 paired chromosomes of a male and a female. The members of each pair of chromosomes are both similar and different: Each chromosome in the pair contains varying forms of the same genes, at the same location on the chromosome. A gene for hair color, for example, is located on both members of one pair of chromosomes, in the same location on each. However, one of those chromosomes might carry the gene for blond hair; the other chromosome in the pair might carry the gene for brown hair.

Do you notice any obvious differences between the chromosomes of the male and the chromosomes of the female in Figure 2.4? The difference lies in the 23rd pair. Ordinarily, in females this pair consists of two chromosomes called *X chromosomes;* in males the 23rd pair consists of an X and a *Y chromosome.* The presence of a Y chromosome is what makes an individual male.

Sources of Variability   Combining the genes of two parents in offspring increases genetic variability in the population, which is valuable for a species because it provides more characteristics for natural selection to operate on (Cowan & Talaro, 2009; Hyde, 2009). In fact, the human genetic process creates several important sources of variability.

First, the chromosomes in the zygote are not exact copies of those in mother's ovaries and the father's testes. During the formation of the sperm and egg in meiosis, the members of each pair of chromosomes are separated, but which chromosome in the pair goes to the gamete is a matter of chance. In addition, before the pairs separate, pieces of the two chromosomes in each pair are exchanged, creating a new

How Would You...?
As a psychologist, how would you explain to an enthusiast of the Human Genome Project that genes don't provide an exact blueprint for how children's development will unfold?

FIGURE 2.3 A Single Sperm Penetrating an Egg at the Point of Fertilization

mitosis Cellular reproduction in which the cell's nucleus duplicates itself with two new cells being formed, each containing the same DNA as the parent cell, arranged in the same 23 pairs of chromosomes.

meiosis A specialized form of cell division that occurs to form eggs and sperm (or gametes).

fertilization A stage in reproduction whereby an egg and a sperm fuse to create a single cell, called a zygote.

zygote A single cell formed through fertilization.

(a)

(b)

FIGURE 2.4 The Genetic Difference Between Males and Females Set (*a*) shows the chromosome structure of a male, and set (*b*) shows the chromosome structure of a female. The last pair of 23 pairs of chromosomes is in the bottom right box of each set. Notice that the Y chromosome of the male is smaller than the X chromosome of the female. To obtain this kind of chromosomal picture, a cell is removed from a person's body, usually from the inside of the mouth. The chromosomes are stained by chemical treatment, magnified extensively, and then photographed.

genotype A person's genetic heritage; the actual genetic material.

phenotype The way an individual's genotype is expressed in observed and measurable characteristics.

combination of genes on each chromosome. Thus, when chromosomes from the mother's egg and the father's sperm are brought together in the zygote, the result is a truly unique combination of genes (Starr, Evers, & Starr, 2010).

If each zygote is unique, how do identical twins like those discussed in the opening of the chapter exist? *Identical twins* (also called monozygotic twins) develop from a single zygote that splits into two genetically identical replicas, each of which becomes a person. *Fraternal twins* (called dizygotic twins) develop from separate eggs and separate sperm, making them genetically no more similar than ordinary siblings.

Another source of variability comes from DNA (Cummings, 2009). Chance, a mistake by cellular machinery, or damage from an environmental agent such as radiation may produce a *mutated gene,* which is a permanently altered segment of DNA (Enger, Ross, & Bailey, 2009).

Even when their genes are identical, however, people vary. The difference between genotypes and phenotypes helps us to understand this source of variability. All of a person's genetic material makes up his or her **genotype.** However, not all of the genetic material is apparent in our observed and measurable characteristics. A **phenotype** consists of observable characteristics. Phenotypes include physical characteristics (such as height, weight, and hair color) and psychological characteristics (such as personality and intelligence).

For each genotype, a range of phenotypes can be expressed, providing another source of variability (Gottlieb, 2007). An individual can inherit the genetic potential to grow very large, for example, but good nutrition, among other things, will be essential to achieving that potential. The giggle sisters introduced in the chapter opening might have inherited the same genetic potential to be very tall, but if Daphne had grown up malnourished, she might have ended up noticeably shorter than Barbara. This principle is so widely applicable it has a name: heredity-environment interaction (or gene-environment interaction).

Genetic Principles

What determines how a genotype is expressed to create a particular phenotype? Much is unknown about the answer to this question (Hartwell, 2008; Talaro, 2008). However, a number of genetic principles have been discovered, among them those of dominant-recessive genes, sex-linked genes, genetic imprinting, and polygenically determined characteristics.

Dominant–Recessive Genes Principle In some cases, one gene of a pair always exerts its effects; it is *dominant,* overriding the potential influence of the other gene, called the *recessive* gene. This is the *dominant-recessive genes principle.* A recessive gene exerts its influence only if the two genes of a pair are both recessive. If you inherit a recessive gene for a trait from each of your parents, you will show the trait. If you inherit a recessive gene from only one parent, you may never know you carry the gene. Brown hair, farsightedness, and dimples rule over blond hair, nearsightedness, and freckles in the world of dominant-recessive genes.

Can two brown-haired parents have a blond-haired child? Yes, they can. Suppose that each parent has a dominant gene for brown hair and a recessive gene for blond hair. Because dominant genes override recessive genes, the parents have brown hair, but both are carriers of blondness and pass on their recessive genes for blond hair. With no dominant gene to override them, the recessive genes can make the child's hair blond (see Figure 2.5).

Sex-Linked Genes Most mutated genes are recessive. When a mutated gene is carried on the X chromosome, the result is called *X-linked inheritance.* The implications for males may be very different from those for females (Peterson, Wang, & Willems, 2008). Remember that males have only one X chromosome. Thus, if there is an altered, disease-creating gene on the X chromosome, males have no "backup"

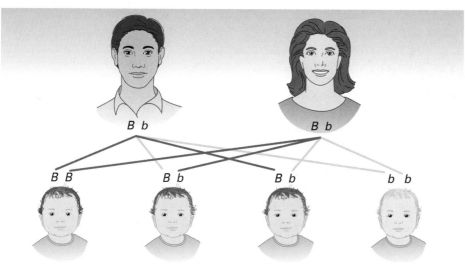

FIGURE 2.5 How Brown-Haired Parents Can Have a Blond-Haired Child In this example, both parents have brown hair, but each parent carries the recessive gene for blond hair. Therefore, the odds of their child having blond hair is one in four—the probability the child will receive a recessive gene (*b*) from each parent.

B = Gene for brown hair   *b* = Gene for blond hair

copy to counter the harmful gene and therefore may carry an X-linked disease. However, females have a second X chromosome, which is likely to be unchanged. As a result, they are not likely to have the X-linked disease. Thus, most individuals who have X-linked diseases are males. Females who have one changed copy of the X gene are known as "carriers," and they usually do not show any signs of the X-linked disease. Hemophilia and fragile X syndrome, which we discuss later in the chapter, are examples of X-linked inherited diseases (Balasubramanian, Koontz, & Reynolds, 2008).

Genetic Imprinting   *Genetic imprinting* occurs when genes have differing effects depending on whether they are inherited from the mother or the father (Horsthemke & Buiting, 2008; Wan & Bartolomei, 2008). A chemical process "silences" one member of the gene pair. For example, as a result of imprinting, only the maternally derived copy of a gene might be active, while the paternally derived copy of the same gene is silenced—or vice versa. Only a small percentage of human genes appears to undergo imprinting, but it is a normal and important aspect of development (Ginder, Gnanapragasam, & Mian, 2008; Hampton, 2008). When imprinting goes awry, development is disturbed, as in the case of Beckwith-Wiedemann syndrome, a growth disorder, and Wilms tumor, a type of cancer (Gropman & Adams, 2007).

Polygenic Inheritance   Genetic transmission is usually more complex than the simple examples we have examined thus far (Fry, 2009). Few characteristics reflect the influence of only a single gene or pair of genes. Most are determined by the interaction of many different genes; they are said to be *polygenically determined.* Even simple characteristics such as height, for example, reflect the interaction of many genes, as well as the influence of the environment.

The term *gene-gene interaction* is increasingly used to describe studies that focus on the interdependence of two or more genes in influencing characteristics, behavior, diseases, and development (Li & others, 2008). For example, recent studies have documented gene-gene interaction in cancer (Chen & others, 2009) and cardiovascular disease (Jylhava & others, 2009).

Chromosomal and Gene-Linked Abnormalities

Sometimes, abnormalities characterize the genetic process. Some of these abnormalities involve whole chromosomes that do not separate properly during meiosis. Other abnormalities are produced by harmful genes.

Name	Description	Treatment	Incidence
Down syndrome	An extra chromosome causes mild to severe retardation and physical abnormalities.	Surgery, early intervention, infant stimulation, and special learning programs	1 in 1,900 births at age 20 1 in 300 births at age 35 1 in 30 births at age 45
Klinefelter syndrome	An extra X chromosome causes physical abnormalities.	Hormone therapy can be effective	1 in 800 male births
Fragile X syndrome	An abnormality in the X chromosome can cause mental retardation, learning disabilities, or short attention span.	Special education, speech and language therapy	More common in males than in females
Turner syndrome	A missing X chromosome in females can cause mental retardation and sexual underdevelopment.	Hormone therapy in childhood and puberty	1 in 2,500 female births
XYY syndrome	An extra Y chromosome can cause above-average height.	No special treatment required	1 in 1,000 male births

FIGURE 2.6 Some Chromosomal Abnormalities *Note:* Treatment does not necessarily erase the problem but may improve the individual's adaptive behavior and quality of life.

These athletes, many of whom have Down syndrome, are participating in a Special Olympics competition. Notice the distinctive facial features of the individuals with Down syndrome, such as a round face and a flattened skull. *What causes Down syndrome?*

Down syndrome A chromosomally transmitted form of mental retardation, caused by the presence of an extra copy of chromosome 21.

Klinefelter syndrome A genetic disorder in which males have an extra X chromosome, making them XXY instead of XY.

fragile X syndrome A genetic disorder involving an abnormality in the X chromosome, which becomes constricted and often breaks.

Chromosomal Abnormalities   Sometimes, when a gamete is formed, the sperm and ovum do not have their normal set of 23 chromosomes. The most notable examples involve Down syndrome and abnormalities of the sex chromosomes (see Figure 2.6).

Down Syndrome   An individual with **Down syndrome** has a round face, a flattened skull, an extra fold of skin over the eyelids, a protruding tongue, short limbs, and retardation of motor and mental abilities. The syndrome is caused by the presence of an extra copy of chromosome 21 (Fidler, 2008). It is not known why the extra chromosome is present, but the health of the male sperm or female ovum may be involved.

Down syndrome appears approximately once in every 700 live births. Women between the ages of 16 and 34 are less likely to give birth to a child with Down syndrome than are younger or older women. African American children are rarely born with Down syndrome.

Sex-Linked Chromosomal Abnormalities   Recall that a newborn normally has either an X and a Y chromosome, or two X chromosomes. Human embryos must possess at least one X chromosome to be viable. The most common sex-linked chromosomal abnormalities involve the presence of an extra chromosome (either an X or Y) or the absence of one X chromosome in females.

Klinefelter syndrome is a genetic disorder in which males have an extra X chromosome, making them XXY instead of XY. Males with this disorder have undeveloped testes, and they usually have enlarged breasts and become tall (Bojesen & Gravholt, 2007). A recent study revealed significant impairment in language, academic, attentional, and motor abilities in boys with the syndrome (Ross & others, 2008). Klinefelter syndrome occurs approximately once in every 800 live male births.

Fragile X syndrome is a genetic disorder that results from an abnormality in the X chromosome, which becomes constricted and often breaks (Penagarikano, Mulle, & Warren, 2007). The physical appearance of children with fragile X syndrome often appears normal, although these children typically have prominent ears, a long face, a high-arched palate, and soft skin (Ono, Farzin, & Hagerman, 2008). Mental deficiency often is an outcome, but it may take the form of mental retardation, a learning disability, or a short attention span. A recent study revealed that boys with fragile X syndrome were characterized by cognitive deficits in inhibition, memory, and planning (Hooper & others, 2008). This disorder occurs more frequently in males than in females, possibly because the second X chromosome in females negates the effects of the other abnormal X chromosome (Kochi & others, 2007).

Turner syndrome is a chromosomal disorder in females in which either an X chromosome is missing, making the person XO instead of XX, or part of one X chromosome is deleted. Females with Turner syndrome are short in stature and have a webbed neck. They might be infertile and have difficulty in mathematics, but their verbal ability often is quite good (Murphy & Mazzocco, 2008). Turner syndrome occurs in approximately 1 of every 2,500 live female births.

The **XYY syndrome** is a chromosomal disorder in which the male has an extra Y chromosome (Isen & Baker, 2008). Early interest in this syndrome focused on the belief that the extra Y chromosome found in some males contributed to aggression and violence. However, researchers subsequently found that XYY males are no more likely to commit crimes than are XY males (Witkin & others, 1976).

A boy with fragile X syndrome.

Gene–Linked Abnormalities Abnormalities can be produced not only by an uneven number of chromosomes but also by harmful genes (Presson & Jenner, 2008). More than 7,000 such genetic disorders have been identified, although most of them are rare.

Phenylketonuria (PKU) is a genetic disorder in which the individual cannot properly metabolize phenylalanine, an amino acid. It results from a recessive gene and occurs about once in every 10,000 to 20,000 live births. Today, phenylketonuria is easily detected, and it is treated by a diet that prevents an excess accumulation of phenylalanine. If phenylketonuria is left untreated, however, excess phenylalanine builds up in the child, producing mental retardation and hyperactivity. Phenylketonuria accounts for approximately 1 percent of institutionalized individuals who are mentally retarded, and it occurs primarily in non-Latino Whites.

The story of phenylketonuria has important implications for the nature-nurture issue. Although phenylketonuria is a genetic disorder (nature), how or whether a gene's influence in phenylketonuria is played out depends on environmental influences because the disorder can be treated (nurture) (Ney & others, 2008). That is, the presence of a genetic defect *does not* inevitably lead to the development of the disorder *if* the individual develops in the right environment (one free of phenylalanine) (Cipriano, Rupar, & Zaric, 2007). This is one example of the important principle of heredity-environment interaction. Under one environmental condition (phenylalanine in the diet), mental retardation results, but when other nutrients replace phenylalanine, intelligence develops in the normal range. The same genotype has different outcomes depending on the environment (in this case, the nutritional environment).

Sickle-cell anemia, which occurs most often in African Americans, is a genetic disorder that impairs the body's red blood cells. Red blood cells carry oxygen to the body's cells and are usually shaped like a disk. In sickle-cell anemia, a recessive gene causes the red blood cell to become a hook-shaped "sickle" that cannot carry oxygen properly and dies quickly. As a result, the body's cells do not receive adequate oxygen, causing anemia and early death (King, DeBraun, & White, 2008). About 1 in 400 African American babies is affected by sickle-cell anemia. One in 10 African Americans is a carrier, as is 1 in 20 Latin Americans. A National Institutes of Health (2008) panel recently concluded that the only FDA-approved drug (hydroxyurea) to treat sickle-cell anemia in adolescents and adults is not widely used. Research is currently being conducted in a study named Baby HUG to determine if the drug works with babies.

Other diseases that result from genetic abnormalities include cystic fibrosis, diabetes, hemophilia, spina bifida, and Tay-Sachs disease (Dunn & others, 2008). Figure 2.7 provides further information about these diseases. Someday, scientists may identify why these and other genetic abnormalities occur and discover how to cure them.

Turner syndrome A chromosomal disorder in females in which either an X chromosome is missing, making the person XO instead of XX, or the second X chromosome is partially deleted.

XYY syndrome A chromosomal disorder in which males have an extra Y chromosome.

phenylketonuria (PKU) A genetic disorder in which the individual cannot properly metabolize phenylalanine, an amino acid. PKU is now easily detected—but if left untreated, results in mental retardation and hyperactivity.

sickle-cell anemia A genetic disorder that affects the red blood cells and occurs most often in people of African descent.

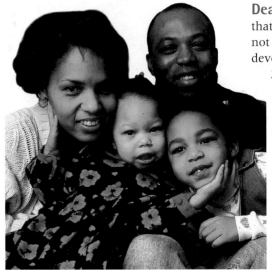

During a physical examination for a college football tryout, Jerry Hubbard, 32, learned that he carried the gene for sickle-cell anemia. Daughter Sara is healthy, but daughter Avery (in the print dress) has sickle-cell anemia. *If you were a genetic counselor, would you recommend that this family have more children? Explain.*

Dealing with Genetic Abnormalities Every individual carries DNA variations that might predispose the person to serious physical disease or mental disorder. But not all individuals who carry a genetic disorder display the disorder. Other genes or developmental events sometimes compensate for genetic abnormalities (Gottlieb, 2007). For example, recall the example of phenylketonuria from the previous section: Even though individuals might carry the genetic disorder of phenylketonuria, it is not expressed when phenylalanine is replaced by other nutrients in their diet.

Thus, genes are not destiny, but genes that are missing, nonfunctional, or mutated can be associated with disorders (Lenzi & Johnson, 2008). Identifying such genetic flaws could enable doctors to predict an individual's risks, recommend healthy practices, and prescribe the safest and most effective drugs (Blaine & others, 2008; Gaff, Williams, & McInerney, 2008). A decade or two from now, parents of a newborn baby may be able to leave the hospital with a full genome analysis of their offspring that reveals disease risks.

However, this knowledge might bring important costs as well as benefits. Who would have access to a person's genetic profile? An individual's ability to land and hold jobs or obtain insurance might be threatened if it is known that a person is considered at risk for some disease. For example, should an airline pilot or a neurosurgeon who is predisposed to develop a disorder that makes one's hands shake be required to leave that job early?

Genetic counselors, usually physicians or biologists who are well versed in the field of medical genetics, understand the kinds of problems just described, the odds of encountering them, and helpful strategies for offsetting some of their effects (Latimer, 2007). A recent research review found that many individuals who receive genetic counseling find it difficult to quantify risk and tend to overestimate risk (Sivell & others, 2008). To read about the career and work of a genetic counselor, see the *Careers in Children's Development* profile.

FIGURE 2.7 Some Gene-Linked Abnormalities

Name	Description	Treatment	Incidence
Cystic fibrosis	Glandular dysfunction that interferes with mucus production; breathing and digestion are hampered, resulting in a shortened life span.	Physical and oxygen therapy, synthetic enzymes, and antibiotics; most individuals live to middle age.	1 in 2,000 births
Diabetes	Body does not produce enough insulin, which causes abnormal metabolism of sugar.	Early onset can be fatal unless treated with insulin.	1 in 2,500 births
Hemophilia	Delayed blood clotting causes internal and external bleeding.	Blood transfusions/injections can reduce or prevent damage due to internal bleeding.	1 in 10,000 males
Phenylketonuria (PKU)	Metabolic disorder that, left untreated, causes mental retardation.	Special diet can result in average intelligence and normal life span.	1 in 10,000 to 20,000 births
Sickle-cell anemia	Blood disorder that limits the body's oxygen supply; it can cause joint swelling, as well as heart and kidney failure.	Penicillin, medication for pain, antibiotics, and blood transfusions.	1 in 400 African American children (lower among other groups)
Spina bifida	Neural tube disorder that causes brain and spine abnormalities.	Corrective surgery at birth, orthopedic devices, and physical/medical therapy.	2 in 1,000 births
Tay-Sachs disease	Deceleration of mental and physical development caused by an accumulation of lipids in the nervous system.	Medication and special diet are used, but death is likely by 5 years of age.	One in 30 American Jews is a carrier.

Careers in Children's Development

Holly Ishmael, Genetic Counselor

Holly Ishmael is a genetic counselor at Children's Mercy Hospital in Kansas City. She obtained an undergraduate degree in psychology and then a master's degree in genetic counseling from Sarah Lawrence College.

Genetic counselors, like Ishmael, work as members of a health-care team, providing information and support to families with birth defects or genetic disorders. They identify families at risk by analyzing inheritance patterns and explore options with the family. Some genetic counselors, like Ishmael, become specialists in prenatal and pediatric genetics; others might specialize in cancer genetics or psychiatric genetic disorders.

Ishmael says, "Genetic counseling is a perfect combination for people who want to do something science-oriented, but need human contact and don't want to spend all of their time in a lab or have their nose in a book" (Rizzo, 1999, p. 3).

Genetic counselors have specialized graduate degrees in the areas of medical genetics and counseling. They enter graduate school with undergraduate backgrounds from a variety of disci-

plines, including biology, genetics, psychology, public health, and social work. There are approximately thirty graduate genetic counseling programs in the United States. If you are interested in this profession, you can obtain further information from the National Society of Genetic Counselors at www.nsgc.org.

Holly Ishmael (*left*) in a genetic counseling session.

Review and Reflect: Learning Goal 2

2   **Describe what genes are and how they influence human development**

REVIEW

- What are genes?
- How are genes passed on from one generation to another?
- What basic principles describe how genes interact?
- What are some chromosomal and gene-linked abnormalities?

REFLECT

- What are some possible ethical issues regarding genetics and development that might arise in the future?

3   WHAT ARE SOME REPRODUCTIVE CHALLENGES AND CHOICES?

| Prenatal Diagnostic Tests | Infertility and Reproductive Technology | Adoption |

The facts and principles we have discussed regarding meiosis, genetics, and genetic abnormalities are a small part of the recent explosion of knowledge about human biology. This knowledge not only helps us understand human development but also

A 6-month-old infant poses with the ultrasound sonography record taken four months into the baby's prenatal development. *What is ultrasound sonography?*

opens up many new choices to prospective parents, choices that can also raise ethical questions.

Prenatal Diagnostic Tests

One choice open to prospective mothers is the extent to which they should undergo prenatal testing. A number of tests can indicate whether a fetus is developing normally; these include ultrasound sonography, fetal MRI, chorionic villus sampling, amniocentesis, maternal blood screening, and noninvasive prenatal diagnosis (NIPD). There has been a dramatic increase in research on the use of less invasive techniques, such as fetal MRI and NIPD, which pose lower risks to the fetus than more invasive techniques such as chorionic villus sampling and amniocentesis (Kent, 2008; Lenzi & Johnson, 2008).

Ultrasound Sonography An ultrasound test is often conducted seven weeks into a pregnancy and at various times later in pregnancy. *Ultrasound sonography* is a prenatal medical procedure in which high-frequency sound waves are directed into the pregnant woman's abdomen. The echo from the sounds is transformed into a visual representation of the fetus's inner structures. This technique can detect many structural abnormalities in the fetus, including microencephaly, a form of mental retardation involving an abnormally small brain; it can also determine the number of fetuses and give clues to the baby's sex (Gerards & others, 2008; Sonek, 2007). This test poses virtually no risk to the woman or the fetus.

Fetal MRI The development of brain-imaging techniques has led to increasing use of *fetal MRI* to diagnose fetal malformations (Garel, 2008; Huisman & Kellenberger, 2008) (see Figure 2.8). MRI stands for magnetic resonance imaging and uses a powerful magnet and radio images to generate detailed images of the body's organs and structure. Currently, ultrasound is still the first choice in fetal screening, but fetal MRI can provide more detailed images than ultrasound. In many instances, ultrasound will indicate a possible abnormality, and then fetal MRI will be used to obtain a clearer, more detailed image (Obenauer & Maestre, 2008). Among the fetal malformations that fetal MRI may be able to detect better than ultrasound sonography are certain central nervous system, chest, gastrointestinal, genital/urinary, and placental abnormalities (Fratelli & others, 2007).

Chorionic Villus Sampling At some point between 9.5 and 12.5 weeks of pregnancy, chorionic villus sampling may be used to detect genetic defects and chromosomal abnormalities, such as the ones discussed in the previous section (Csaba, Bush, & Saphier, 2006). Diagnosis takes approximately 10 days. *Chorionic villus sampling (CVS)* is a prenatal medical procedure in which a small sample of the placenta (the vascular organ that links the fetus to the mother's uterus) is removed. There is a small risk of limb deformity when CVS is used.

Amniocentesis Between the 14th and 20th weeks of pregnancy, amniocentesis may be performed. *Amniocentesis* is a prenatal medical procedure in which a sample of amniotic fluid is withdrawn by syringe and tested for chromosomal or metabolic disorders (Nagel & others, 2007). The amnionic fluid is found within the amnion, a thin sac in which the embryo is suspended. Ultrasound sonography is often used during amniocentesis so that the syringe can be placed precisely. The later amniocentesis is performed, the better its diagnostic potential. The earlier it is performed, the more useful it is in deciding how to handle a pregnancy. It may take two weeks for enough cells to

FIGURE 2.8 A Fetal MRI, Which Is Increasingly Being Used in Prenatal Diagnosis of Fetal Malformations

grow and amniocentesis test results to be obtained. Amniocentesis brings a small risk of miscarriage—about 1 woman in every 200 to 300 miscarries after amniocentesis.

Both amniocentesis and chorionic villus sampling provide valuable information about the presence of birth defects, but they also raise difficult issues for parents about whether an abortion should be obtained if birth defects are present (Quadrelli & others, 2007). Chorionic villus sampling allows a decision to be made sooner, at a time when abortion is safer and less traumatic. Although earlier reports indicated that chorionic villus sampling brings a slightly higher risk of pregnancy loss than amniocentesis, a recent U.S. study of more than 40,000 pregnancies found that loss rates for CVS decreased from 1998 to 2003, and that there is no longer a difference in pregnancy loss risk between CVS and amniocentesis (Caughey, Hopkins, & Norton, 2006).

How Would You...?
As a health professional, how would you discuss the benefits and risks of having prenatal diagnostic tests with a woman who has just found out that she is pregnant?

Maternal Blood Screening   During the 16th to 18th weeks of pregnancy, maternal blood screening may be performed. *Maternal blood screening* identifies pregnancies that have an elevated risk for birth defects such as spina bifida (a defect in the spinal cord) and Down syndrome (Palomaki & others, 2006). The current blood test is called the *triple screen* because it measures three substances in the mother's blood. After an abnormal triple screen result, the next step is usually an ultrasound examination. If an ultrasound does not explain the abnormal triple screen results, amniocentesis is typically used.

Noninvasive Prenatal Diagnosis (NIPD)   *Noninvasive prenatal diagnosis (NIPD)* is increasingly being explored as an alternative to such procedures as chorionic villus sampling and amniocentesis (Avent & others, 2008). At this point, NIPD has mainly focused on the isolation and examination of fetal cells circulating in the mother's blood and analysis of cell-free fetal DNA in maternal plasma (Finning & Chitty, 2008; Norbury & Norbury, 2008). Researchers already have used NIPD to successfully test for genes inherited from a father that cause cystic fibrosis and Huntington disease. They also are exploring the potential for using NIPD to diagnose Down syndrome and to identify a baby's sex as early as five weeks after conception (Avent & others, 2008; Hahn, Zhong, & Holzgreve, 2008). Being able to detect an offspring's sex and various diseases and defects so early raises ethical concerns about couples' motivation to terminate a pregnancy (Newsom, 2008; van den Heuvel & Marteau, 2008).

Technical challenges still characterize the use of NIPD, but its benefit in reducing risk makes it an attractive diagnostic candidate (van der Schoot, Hahn, & Chitty, 2008). The main technical challenge is to efficiently separate out the fetal cells, which comprise only about one of every million cells in a mother's blood.

A technician using a micro-needle to inject human sperm into a human egg cell as part of an in vitro fertilization procedure. The injected sperm fertilizes the egg, and the resulting zygote is then grown in the laboratory until it reaches an early stage of embryonic development. Then it is implanted in the uterus.

Infertility and Reproductive Technology

Recent advances in biological knowledge have also opened up many choices for infertile people. Approximately 10 to 15 percent of couples in the United States experience infertility, which is defined as the inability to conceive a child after 12 months of regular intercourse without contraception. The cause of infertility can rest with the woman or the man. The woman may not be ovulating (releasing eggs to be fertilized), she may be producing abnormal ova, her fallopian tubes by which ova normally reach the womb may be blocked, or she may have a disease that prevents implantation of the embryo into the uterus. The man may produce too few sperm, the sperm may lack motility (the ability to move adequately), or he may have a blocked passageway (Hesmet & Lo, 2006).

In the United States, more than 2 million couples seek help for infertility every year. In some cases of infertility, surgery may correct the cause; in others, hormone-based drugs may improve the probability of having a child. Of the 2 million couples

Singer Celine Dion became pregnant through in vitro fertilization and gave birth to her son Rene-Charles in 2001.

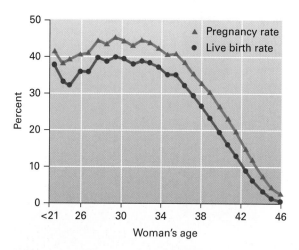

FIGURE 2.9 Success Rates of In Vitro Fertilization Vary According to the Woman's Age

who seek help for infertility every year, about 40,000 try high-tech assisted reproduction. By far the most common technique used is *in vitro fertilization (IVF)*, in which eggs and a sperm are combined in a laboratory dish. If any eggs are successfully fertilized, one or more of the resulting eggs are transferred into the woman's uterus. A national U.S. study in 2004 by the Centers for Disease Control and Prevention found the success rate of IVF depends on the mother's age (see Figure 2.9).

The creation of families by means of the new reproductive technologies raises important questions about the physical and psychological consequences for children (Gurgan & Demirol, 2007; Wagenaar & others, 2008a). One result of fertility treatments is an increase in multiple births (Jones, 2007; Reddy & others, 2007). Twenty-five to 30 percent of pregnancies achieved by fertility treatments—including in vitro fertilization—now result in multiple births. A recent research review concluded that the two main risk factors associated with assisted reproductive techniques are multiple pregnancies and low birth weight (Basatemur & Sutcliffe, 2008). Any multiple birth increases the likelihood that the babies will have life-threatening and costly problems, such as extremely low birth weight (Cheung, 2006).

Not nearly as many studies have examined the psychological outcomes of IVF as the physical outcomes. To read about a study that addresses these consequences, see the *Research in Children's Development* interlude that follows.

Research in Children's Development

IN VITRO FERTILIZATION AND DEVELOPMENTAL OUTCOMES IN ADOLESCENCE

A longitudinal study examined 34 in vitro fertilization families, 49 adoptive families, and 38 families with a naturally conceived child (Golombok, MacCallum, & Goodman, 2001). Each type of family included a similar portion of boys and girls. Also, the age of the young adolescents did not differ according to family type (mean age of 11 years, 11 months).

Children's socioemotional development was assessed by (1) interviewing the mother and obtaining detailed descriptions of any problems the child might have; (2) administering a Strengths and Difficulties questionnaire to the child's mother and teacher; and (3) administering the Social Adjustment Inventory for Children and Adolescents, which examines functioning in school, peer relationships, and self-esteem.

No significant differences between the children from the in vitro fertilization, adoptive, and naturally conceiving families were found. The results from the Social Adjustment Inventory for Children and Adolescents are shown in Figure 2.10. Two other studies also revealed no psychological differences between IVF babies and those not conceived by IVF (Hahn & Dipietro, 2001; Wagenaar & others, 2008a). And a recent review concluded that research indicates no difference in school outcomes and the social well-being of IVF children and those conceived naturally (Wagenaar & others, 2008b).

FIGURE 2.10 Socioemotional Development at Adolescence of Children in Three Family Types: In Vitro Fertilization, Naturally Conceived, and Adopted In this study, there were no significant differences in socioemotional development at the beginning of adolescence in terms of school functioning, peer relations, and self-esteem (Golombok, MacCallum, & Goodman, 2001). The mean scores shown for the different measures are all in the normal range of functioning.

Adoption

Although surgery and fertility drugs can sometimes solve the infertility problem, another choice is to adopt a child (Bernard & Dozier, 2008; Cohen & others, 2008). Adoption is the social and legal process by which a parent-child relationship is established between persons unrelated at birth. As we see next in the *Diversity in Children's Development* interlude, an increase in diversity has characterized the adoption of children in the United States in recent years.

Diversity in Children's Development

THE INCREASED DIVERSITY OF ADOPTED CHILDREN AND ADOPTIVE PARENTS

Several changes occurred during the last several decades of the twentieth century in the characteristics both of adopted children and of adoptive parents (Brodzinsky & Pinderhughes, 2002, pp. 280–282). Until the 1960s, most U.S. adopted children were healthy, European American infants, who were adopted within a few days or weeks after birth. However, in recent decades, an increasing number of unmarried U.S. mothers decided to keep their babies, and the number of unwanted births decreased as contraception became readily available and abortion was legalized. As a result, the number of healthy European American infants available for adoption dropped dramatically. Increasingly, U.S. couples adopted children who were not European Americans, children from other countries, and children in foster care whose characteristics—such as age, minority status, exposure to neglect or abuse, or physical or mental health problems—"were once thought to be barriers to adoption" (p. 281).

Changes also have characterized adoptive parents. Until the last several decades of the twentieth century, most adoptive parents had a middle or upper socioeconomic status and were "married, infertile, European American couples, usually in their 30s and 40s, and free of any disability. Adoption agencies *screened out* couples who did not have these characteristics" (p. 281). Today, however, many adoption agencies *screen in* as many applicants as possible and have no income requirements for adoptive parents. Many agencies now permit single adults, older adults, and gay and lesbian adults to adopt children (Matthews & Cramer, 2006; Ryan, Pearlmutter, & Groza, 2004).

Do these changes matter? They open opportunities for many children and many couples, but possible effects of changes in the characteristics of parents on the outcomes for children are still unknown. For example, in one study, adopted adolescents were more likely to have problems if the adoptive parents had low levels of education (Miller & others, 2000). In another study, international adoptees showed fewer behavior problems and were less likely to be using mental health services than domestic adoptees (Juffer & van IJzendoorn, 2005). More research is needed before definitive conclusions can be reached about the changing demographic characteristics of adoption.

The changes in adoption practices over the last several decades make it difficult to generalize about the average adopted child or average adoptive parent. As we see next, though, some researchers have provided useful comparisons between adopted children and nonadopted children and their families.

An increasing number of Hollywood celebrities are adopting children from developing countries. Actress Angelina Jolie adopted a baby girl, Zahara (*above*), in Ethiopia as well as two other children.

How do adopted children fare after they are adopted? Children who are adopted very early in their lives are more likely to have positive outcomes than children adopted later in life (Bernard & Dozier, 2008). In one study, the later adoption occurred, the more problems the adoptees had. Infant adoptees had the fewest adjustment difficulties; those adopted after they were 10 years of age had the most problems (Sharma, McGue, & Benson, 1996).

In general, adopted children and adolescents are more likely to experience psychological and school-related problems than nonadopted children (Bernard & Dozier, 2008; Rosnati, Montirosso, & Barni, 2008). For example, a recent meta-analysis (a statistical procedure that combines the results of a number of studies) revealed that adoptees were far more likely to be using mental health services than their non-adopted counterparts. (Juffer & van IJzendoorn, 2005). Adopted children also showed more behavior problems than nonadoptees, but this difference was small.

A recent large-scale study found that adopted children are more likely to have a learning disability than are nonadopted children (Altarac & Saroha, 2007).

Research that contrasts adopted and nonadopted adolescents has also found positive characteristics among the adopted adolescents. For example, in one study, although adopted adolescents were more likely than nonadopted adolescents to use illicit drugs and to engage in delinquent behavior, the adopted adolescents were also less likely to be withdrawn and engaged in more prosocial behavior, such as being altruistic, caring, and supportive of others (Sharma, McGue, & Benson, 1996).

In short, the vast majority of adopted children (including those adopted at older ages, transracially, and across national borders) adjust effectively, and their parents report considerable satisfaction with their decision to adopt (Brodzinsky & Pinderhughes, 2002). In one recent national study, there were no differences in the antisocial behavior of adopted and nonadopted young adults (Grotevant & others, 2006). A recent research review of 88 studies also revealed no difference in the self-esteem of adopted and nonadopted children, as well as no differences between transracial and same-race adoptees (Juffer & van IJzendoorn, 2007). Furthermore, adopted children fare much better than children in long-term foster care or in an institutional environment (Bernard & Dozier, 2008). To read more about adoption, see the *Caring for Children* interlude in which we discuss effective parenting strategies with adopted children.

Caring for Children

PARENTING ADOPTED CHILDREN

Many of the keys to effectively parenting adopted children are no different from those for effectively parenting biological children: Be supportive and caring, be involved and monitor the child's behavior and whereabouts, be a good communicator, and help the child to learn to develop self-control. However, parents of adopted children face some unique circumstances (Fontenot, 2007). They need to recognize the differences involved in adoptive family life, communicate about these differences, show respect for the birth family, and support the child's search for self and identity.

David Brodzinsky and Ellen Pinderhughes (2002, pp. 288–292) discussed how to handle some of the challenges that parents face when their adopted children are at different points in development:

- *Infancy.* Researchers have found few differences in the attachment that adopted and nonadopted infants form with their parents, but attachment can be compromised "when parents have difficulty in claiming the child as their own either because of unresolved fertility issues, lack of support from family and friends, and/or when their expectations about the child have not been met" (p. 288). Competent adoption agencies or counselors can help prospective adoptive parents develop realistic expectations.

- *Early childhood.* Because many children begin to ask where they came from when they are about 4 to 6 years old, this is a natural time to begin to talk in simple ways to children about their adoption status (Warshak, 2008). Some parents (although not as many as in the past) decide not to tell their children about the adoption. This secrecy may create psychological risks for the child if he or she later finds out about the adoption.

- *Middle and late childhood.* During the elementary school years, children begin to express "much more curiosity about their origins: *Where did I come from? What did my birthmother and birthfather look like? Why didn't they keep me? Where are they now? Can I meet them?*" (p. 290). As they grow older, children

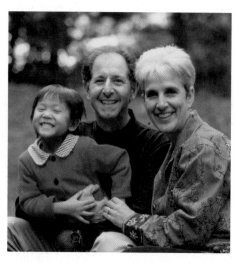

What are some strategies for parenting adopted children at different points in their development?

may become more ambivalent about being adopted and question their adoptive parents' explanations. It is important for adoptive parents to recognize that this ambivalence is normal. Also, problems may come from the desire of adoptive parents to make life too perfect for the adopted child and to present a perfect image of themselves to the child. The result too often is that adopted children feel that they cannot release any angry feelings and openly discuss problems (Warshak, 2008).

How Would You...?
As a human development and family studies professional, how would you advise adoptive parents about when and how to explain to their adopted child that he or she is adopted?

• *Adolescence.* Adolescents are likely to develop more abstract and logical thinking, to focus their attention on their bodies, and to search for an identity. These characteristics provide the foundation for adopted adolescents to reflect on their adoption status in more complex ways, to become "preoccupied with the lack of physical resemblance between themselves and others in the family" (p. 291), and to explore how the fact that they were adopted fits into their identity.

Adoptive parents "need to be aware of these many complexities and provide teenagers with the support they need to cope with these adoption-related tasks" (p. 292).

Review and Reflect: Learning Goal 3

 Identify some important reproductive challenges and choices

REVIEW

• What are some common prenatal diagnostic tests?
• What are some techniques that help infertile people to have children?
• How does adoption affect children's development?

REFLECT

• We discussed a number of studies indicating that adoption is linked with negative outcomes for children. Does that mean that all adopted children have more negative outcomes than all nonadopted children? Explain.

---

4 HOW DO HEREDITY AND ENVIRONMENT INTERACT? THE NATURE-NURTURE DEBATE

Behavior Genetics

Shared and Nonshared Environmental Experiences

Conclusions About Heredity-Environment Interaction

Heredity-Environment Correlations

The Epigenetic View and Gene × Environment (G × E) Interaction

In each section of this chapter so far, we have examined parts of the nature-nurture debate. We have seen how the environment exerts selective pressures on the characteristics of species over generations, examined how genes are passed from parents to children, and discussed how reproductive technologies and adoption influence the course of children's lives. But in all of these situations, heredity and environment interact to produce development. After all, Jim and Jim (and each of the other pairs of identical twins discussed in the opening of the chapter) have the same genotype, but they are not the same person; each is unique. What made them different? Whether we are studying how genes produce proteins, their influence on how tall a person is, or how PKU might affect an individual, we end up discussing heredity-environment interactions.

Is it possible to untangle the influence of heredity from that of environment and discover the role of each in producing individual differences in development? When heredity and environment interact, how does heredity influence the environment, and vice versa?

Behavior Genetics

Behavior genetics is the field that seeks to discover the influence of heredity and environment on individual differences in human traits and development (Kandler & others, 2009; Plomin & others, 2009). Note that behavior genetics does not determine the extent to which genetics or the environment affects an individual's traits. Instead, what behavior geneticists try to do is to figure out what is responsible for the differences among people—that is, to what extent do people differ because of differences in genes, environment, or a combination of these? To study the influence of heredity on behavior, behavior geneticists often use either twins or adoption situations (Goldsmith, 2008; Plomin & others, 2009).

In the most common **twin study,** the behavioral similarity of identical twins (who are genetically identical) is compared with the behavioral similarity of fraternal twins. Recall that although fraternal twins share the same womb, they are no more genetically alike than brothers or sisters. Thus, by comparing groups of identical and fraternal twins, behavior geneticists capitalize on the basic knowledge that identical twins are more similar genetically than are fraternal twins (Isen & others, 2009; Wood & others, 2008). For example, one study revealed that conduct problems were more prevalent in identical twins than fraternal twins; the researchers concluded that the study demonstrated an important role for heredity in conduct problems (Scourfield & others, 2004).

However, several issues complicate interpretation of twin studies (Vogler, 2006). For example, perhaps the environments of identical twins are more similar than the environments of fraternal twins. Adults might stress the similarities of identical twins more than those of fraternal twins, and identical twins might perceive themselves as a "set" and play together more than fraternal twins do. If so, the influence of the environment on the observed similarities between identical and fraternal twins might be very significant.

In an **adoption study,** investigators seek to discover whether the behavior and psychological characteristics of adopted children are more like those of their adoptive parents, who have provided a home environment, or more like those of their biological parents, who have contributed their heredity (Loehlin, Horn, & Ernst, 2007). Another form of the adoption study compares adopted and biological siblings.

Heredity–Environment Correlations

The difficulties that researchers encounter when they interpret the results of twin studies and adoption studies reflect the complexities of heredity-environment interaction. Some of these interactions are *heredity-environment correlations*, which means that individuals' genes may influence the types of environments to which they are exposed. In a sense, individuals "inherit" environments that may be related or linked to genetic "propensities" (Plomin, DeFries, & Fulker, 2007). Behavior geneticist Sandra Scarr (1993) described three ways that heredity and environment are correlated (see Figure 2.11):

- **Passive genotype-environment correlations** occur because biological parents, who are genetically related to the child, provide a rearing environment for the child. For example, the parents might have a genetic predisposition to be intelligent and read skillfully. Because they read well and enjoy reading,

Twin studies compare identical twins with fraternal twins. Identical twins develop from a single fertilized egg that splits into two genetically identical organisms. Fraternal twins develop from separate eggs, making them genetically no more similar than nontwin siblings. *What is the nature of the twin study method?*

behavior genetics The field that seeks to discover the influence of heredity and environment on individual differences in human traits and development.

twin study A study in which the behavioral similarity of identical twins is compared with the behavioral similarity of fraternal twins.

adoption study A study in which investigators seek to discover whether, in behavior and psychological characteristics, adopted children are more like their adoptive parents, who provided a home environment, or more like their biological parents, who contributed their heredity. Another form of the adoption study is to compare adopted and biological siblings.

passive genotype-environment correlations Correlations that exist when the biological parents, who are genetically related to the child, provide a rearing environment for the child.

Heredity-Environment Correlation	Description	Examples
Passive	Children inherit genetic tendencies from their parents and parents also provide an environment that matches their own genetic tendencies.	Musically inclined parents usually have musically inclined children and they are likely to provide an environment rich in music for their children.
Evocative	The child's genetic tendencies elicit stimulation from the environment that supports a particular trait. Thus genes evoke environmental support.	A happy, outgoing child elicits smiles and friendly responses from others.
Active (niche-picking)	Children actively seek out "niches" in their environment that reflect their own interests and talents and are thus in accord with their genotype.	Libraries, sports fields, and a store with musical instruments are examples of environmental niches children might seek out if they have intellectual interests in books, talent in sports, or musical talents, respectively.

FIGURE 2.11 Exploring Heredity-Environment Correlations

they provide their children with books to read. The likely outcome is that their children, given their own inherited predispositions from their parents and their book-filled environment, will become skilled readers.

- **Evocative genotype-environment correlations** occur because a child's characteristics elicit certain types of environments. For example, active, smiling children receive more social stimulation than passive, quiet children do. Cooperative, attentive children evoke more pleasant and instructional responses from the adults around them than uncooperative, distractible children do.

- **Active (niche-picking) genotype-environment correlations** occur when children seek out environments that they find compatible and stimulating. *Niche-picking* refers to finding a setting that is suited to one's abilities. Children select from their surrounding environment some aspect that they respond to, learn about, or ignore. Their active selections of environments are related to their particular genotype. For example, outgoing children tend to seek out social contexts in which to interact with people, whereas shy children don't. Children who are musically inclined are likely to select musical environments in which they can successfully perform their skills. How these "tendencies" come about is discussed shortly under the topic of the epigenetic view.

Scarr argues that the relative importance of the three genotype-environment correlations changes as children develop from infancy through adolescence. In infancy, much of the environment that children experience is provided by adults. Thus, passive genotype-environment correlations are more common in the lives of infants and young children than they are for older children and adolescents who can extend their experiences beyond the family's influence and create their environments to a greater degree.

Notice that this analysis gives the preeminent role in development to heredity—the analysis describes how heredity may influence the types of environments that children experience. Critics argue that the concept of heredity-environment correlation gives heredity too much of a one-sided influence in determining development because it does not consider the role of prior environmental influences in shaping the correlation itself (Gottlieb, Wahlsten, & Lickliter, 2006). Before considering this criticism and a different view of the heredity-environment linkage, let's take a closer look at how behavior geneticists analyze the environments involved in heredity.

Shared and Nonshared Environmental Experiences

Behavior geneticists have argued that to understand the environment's role in differences between people, we should distinguish between shared and nonshared

evocative genotype-environment correlations Correlations that exist when the child's characteristics elicit certain types of physical and social environments.

active (niche-picking) genotype-environment correlations Correlations that exist when children seek out environments they find compatible and stimulating.

Tennis stars Venus and Serena Williams. *What might be some shared and nonshared environmental experiences they had while they were growing up that contributed to their tennis stardom?*

FIGURE 2.12 Comparison of the Heredity-Environment Correlation and Epigenetic Views

shared environmental experiences Siblings' common experiences, such as their parents' personalities and intellectual orientation, the family's socioeconomic status, and the neighborhood in which they live.

nonshared environmental experiences The child's own unique experiences, both within the family and outside the family, that are not shared by another sibling. Thus, experiences occurring within the family can be part of the "nonshared environment."

epigenetic view Emphasizes that development is the result of an ongoing, bidirectional interchange between heredity and environment.

environments. That is, we should consider experiences that children share in common with other children living in the same home, and experiences that are not shared (Sartor & others, 2009; Wardle & others, 2008).

Shared environmental experiences are siblings' common experiences, such as their parents' personalities or intellectual orientation, the family's socioeconomic status, and the neighborhood in which they live. By contrast, **nonshared environmental experiences** are a child's unique experiences, both within the family and outside the family, that are not shared with a sibling. Even experiences occurring within the family can be part of the "nonshared environment." For example, parents often interact differently with each sibling, and siblings interact differently with parents (Hetherington, Reiss, & Plomin, 1994). Siblings often have different peer groups, different friends, and different teachers at school.

Behavior geneticist Robert Plomin (2004) has found that shared environment accounts for little of the variation in children's personality or interests. In other words, even though two children live under the same roof with the same parents, their personalities are often very different. Further, Plomin and his colleagues (2007) argue that heredity influences the nonshared environments of siblings through the heredity-environment correlations we described earlier. For example, a child who has inherited a genetic tendency to be athletic is likely to spend more time in environments related to sports; a child who has inherited a tendency to be musically inclined is more likely to spend time in environments related to music.

What are the implications of Plomin's interpretation of the role of shared and nonshared environments in development? In the *Nurture Assumption*, Judith Harris (1998) argued that what parents do does not make a difference in their children's and adolescents' behavior. Yell at them. Hug them. Read to them. Ignore them. Harris says it won't influence how they turn out. She argues that genes and peers are far more important than parents in children's and adolescents' development.

Genes and peers do matter, but Harris' descriptions of peer influences do not take into account the complexity of peer contexts and developmental trajectories (Hartup, 2009). In addition, Harris is wrong in saying that parents don't matter. For example, in the early child years parents play an important role in selecting children's peers and indirectly influencing children's development. Volumes of parenting literature with many research studies document the importance of parents in children's development (Parke & others, 2008; Schultz & others, 2009). We discuss parents' important roles throughout this book.

The Epigenetic View and Gene × Environment (G × E) Interaction

Critics argue that the concept of heredity-environment correlation gives heredity too much of a one-sided influence in determining development because it does not consider the role of prior environmental influences in shaping the correlation itself (Gottlieb, 2007). However, earlier in the chapter we discussed how genes are collaborative, not determining an individual's traits in an independent manner, but rather in an interactive manner with the environment.

The Epigenetic View In line with the concept of a collaborative gene, Gilbert Gottlieb (2007) emphasizes the **epigenetic view,** which states that development is the result of an ongoing, bidirectional interchange between heredity and the environment. Figure 2.12 compares the heredity-environment correlation and epigenetic views of development.

Let's look at an example that reflects the epigenetic view. A baby inherits genes from both parents at conception. During prenatal development, toxins, nutrition, and stress can influence some genes to stop functioning while others become stronger or weaker. During infancy, environmental experiences such as toxins, nutrition, stress, learning, and encouragement continue to modify the genetic activity and the activity of the nervous system that directly underlie behavior (Gottlieb, 2007). Heredity and environment operate together—or collaborate—to produce a person's intelligence, temperament, height, weight, ability to pitch a baseball, ability to read, and so on (Gottlieb, 2007; Rutter, 2007).

Gene × Environment (G × E) Interaction   An increasing number of studies are exploring how the interaction of heredity and environment influence development, including interactions that involve specific DNA sequences (Barry, Kochanska, & Philibert, 2008; Diamond, 2009; Pauli-Pott & others, 2009; Shen, 2009). One research study found that individuals who have a short version of a genotype labeled *5-HTTLPR* (a gene involving the neurotransmitter serotonin) only have an elevated risk of developing depression if they also have stressful lives (Caspi & others, 2003). Thus, the specific gene did not link directly to the development of depression, but rather interacted with environmental exposure to stress to predict whether individuals would develop depression; however, some studies have not replicated this finding (Risch 7 others, 2009). In a recent study, adults who experienced parental loss as young children were more likely to have unresolved attachment as adults only when they had the short version of the *5-HTTLPR* gene (Caspers & others, 2009). The long version of the serotonin transporter gene apparently provided some protection and ability to cope better with parental loss.

The type of research just described is referred to as **genetic × environment (G × E) interaction**—the interaction of a specific measured variation in the DNA and a specific measured aspect of the environment (Diamond, 2009; Moffitt, Caspi, & Rutter, 2006). The field of *pharmacogenetics* is the study of gene-environment interaction involving the individual's genotype and drug treatment (the environment factor)(Cheok & others, 2009). The goal of many pharmacogenetic studies is to discover if certain drugs are safer or more dangerous to use if the individual's genotype is known (Berlin, Paul, & Vesell, 2009; Lima & others, 2009).

Conclusions About Heredity-Environment Interaction

If a strong, fast, athletic girl wins a championship tennis match in her high school, is her success due to heredity or to environment? Of course, the answer is both.

The relative contributions of heredity and environment are not additive. That is, we can't say that such-and-such a percentage of nature and such-and-such a percentage of experience make us who we are. Nor is it accurate to say that full genetic expression happens once, around conception or birth, after which we carry our genetic legacy into the world to see how far it takes us. Genes produce proteins throughout the life span, in many different environments. Or they don't produce these proteins, depending in part on how harsh or nourishing those environments are.

The emerging view is that complex behaviors have some *genetic loading* that gives people a propensity for a particular developmental trajectory (Guo & others, 2009; Kagan, 2009; Plomin & others, 2009). However, the actual development requires more: an environment. And that environment is complex, just like the mixture of genes we inherit (Schultz & others, 2009; Thompson, 2009). Environmental influences range from the things we lump together under "nurture" (such as parenting, family dynamics, schooling, and neighborhood quality) to biological encounters (such as viruses, birth complications, and even biological events in cells).

Consider for a moment the cluster of genes associated with diabetes. The adolescent who carries this genetic mixture might experience a world of loving parents, nutritious meals, and regular medical intervention. Or the adolescent's world might include parental neglect, a diet high in sugar, and little help from competent physicians. In which of these environments are the adolescent's genes likely to result in diabetes?

How Would You...?
As a human development and family studies professional, how would you apply the epigenetic view to explain why one identical twin can develop alcoholism, while the other twin does not?

How Would You...?
As a health-care professional, how would you explain the heredity-environment interaction to new parents who are upset about discovering that their child has a treatable genetic defect?

gene × environment (G × E) interaction The interaction of a specific measured variation in the DNA and a specific measured aspect of the environment.

If heredity and environment interact to determine the course of development, is that all there is to answering the question of what causes development? Are children completely at the mercy of their genes and environment as they develop? Children's genetic heritage and environmental experiences are pervasive influences on their development. But children's development is not only the outcome of their heredity and the environment they experience. Children also can author a unique developmental path by changing the environment. As one psychologist recently concluded:

> In reality, we are both the creatures and creators of our worlds. We are . . . the products of our genes and environments. Nevertheless, . . . the stream of causation that shapes the future runs through our present choices. . . . Mind matters. . . . Our hopes, goals, and expectations influence our future. (Myers, 2010, p. 168)

Review and Reflect: Learning Goal 4

 4 Characterize some of the ways that heredity and environment interact to produce individual differences in development

REVIEW

- What is behavior genetics?
- What are three types of heredity-environment correlations?
- What is meant by the concepts of shared and nonshared environmental experiences?
- What is the epigenetic view of development? What characterizes gene × environment (G × E) interaction?
- What conclusions can be reached about heredity-environment interaction?

REFLECT

- Someone tells you that she has analyzed her genetic background and environmental experiences and reached the conclusion that environment definitely has had little influence on her intelligence. What would you say to this person about her ability to make this self-diagnosis?

Reach Your Learning Goals

Biological Beginnings

1   WHAT IS THE EVOLUTIONARY PERSPECTIVE? DISCUSS THE EVOLUTIONARY PERSPECTIVE ON DEVELOPMENT

Natural Selection and Adaptive Behavior

- Natural selection is the process by which those individuals of a species that are best adapted survive and reproduce. Darwin proposed that natural selection fuels evolution. In evolutionary theory, adaptive behavior is behavior that promotes the organism's survival in a natural habitat.

Evolutionary Psychology

- Evolutionary psychology holds that adaptation, reproduction, and "survival of the fittest" are important in shaping behavior. Ideas proposed by evolutionary developmental psychology include the view that we humans need an extended juvenile period to develop a large brain and learn the complexity of human social communities. Many evolved psychological mechanisms are domain-specific. Like other theoretical approaches to development, evolutionary psychology has limitations. Bandura rejects "one-sided evolutionism" and argues for a bidirectional link between biology and environment. Biology allows for a broad range of cultural possibilities.

2   WHAT ARE THE GENETIC FOUNDATIONS OF DEVELOPMENT? DESCRIBE WHAT GENES ARE AND HOW THEY INFLUENCE HUMAN DEVELOPMENT

The Collaborative Gene

- Short segments of DNA constitute genes, the units of hereditary information that direct cells to reproduce and manufacture proteins. Except in the sperm and egg, the nucleus of each human cell contains 46 chromosomes (arranged in 23 pairs), which are composed of DNA. Genes act collaboratively, not independently.

Genes and Chromosomes

- Genes are passed on to new cells when chromosomes are duplicated during the processes of mitosis and meiosis, which are two ways in which new cells are formed. When an egg and a sperm unite in the fertilization process, the resulting zygote contains the genes from the chromosomes in the father's sperm and the mother's egg. Despite this transmission of genes from generation to generation, variability is created in several ways, including the exchange of chromosomal segments during meiosis, mutations, and the distinction between a genotype and a phenotype.

Genetic Principles

- Genetic principles that describe how genes interact include those involving dominant-recessive genes, sex-linked genes, genetic imprinting, and polygenic inheritance.

Chromosomal and Gene-Linked Abnormalities

- Chromosomal abnormalities produce Down syndrome, which is caused by the presence of an extra copy of chromosome 21, as well as sex-linked chromosomal abnormalities such as Klinefelter syndrome, fragile X syndrome, Turner syndrome, and XYY syndrome. Gene-linked abnormalities involve harmful genes. Gene-linked disorders include phenylketonuria (PKU) and sickle-cell anemia. Genetic counseling offers couples information about their risk of having a child with inherited abnormalities.

3   WHAT ARE SOME REPRODUCTIVE CHALLENGES AND CHOICES? IDENTIFY SOME IMPORTANT REPRODUCTIVE CHALLENGES AND CHOICES

Prenatal Diagnostic Tests

- Amniocentesis, ultrasound sonography, fetal MRI, chorionic villus sampling, maternal blood screening, and noninvasive prenatal diagnosis (NIPD) are used to determine

Infertility and Reproductive Technology

whether a fetus is developing normally. There has been a dramatic increase in research on less invasive diagnosis, such as fetal MRI and NIPD.

- Approximately 10 to 15 percent of U.S. couples have infertility problems, some of which can be corrected through surgery or fertility drugs. An additional option includes in vitro fertilization.

Adoption

- Although adopted children and adolescents have more problems than their nonadopted counterparts, the vast majority of adopted children adapt effectively. When adoption occurs very early in development, the outcomes for the child are improved. Because of the dramatic changes that have occurred in adoption in recent decades, it is difficult to generalize about the average adopted child or average adoptive family.

4   HOW DO HEREDITY AND ENVIRONMENT INTERACT? THE NATURE-NURTURE DEBATE: CHARACTERIZE SOME OF THE WAYS THAT HEREDITY AND ENVIRONMENT INTERACT TO PRODUCE INDIVIDUAL DIFFERENCES IN DEVELOPMENT

Behavior Genetics

- Behavior genetics is seeks to discover the influence of heredity and environment on individual differences in the traits and development of humans. Methods used by behavior geneticists include twin studies and adoption studies.

Heredity-Environment Correlations

- In Scarr's heredity-environment correlations view, heredity directs the types of environments that children experience. She describes three genotype-environment correlations: passive, evocative, and active (niche-picking). Scarr maintains that the relative importance of these three genotype-environment correlations changes as children develop.

Shared and Nonshared Environmental Experiences

- Shared environmental experiences refer to siblings' common experiences, such as their parents' personalities and intellectual orientation, the family's socioeconomic status, and the neighborhood in which they live. Nonshared environmental experiences involve the child's unique experiences, both within a family and outside a family, that are not shared with a sibling. Many behavior geneticists argue that differences in the development of siblings are due to nonshared environmental experiences (and heredity) rather than shared environmental experiences.

The Epigenetic View and Gene × Environment (G × E) Interaction

- The epigenetic view emphasizes that development is the result of an ongoing, bidirectional interchange between heredity and environment. Gene × environment interaction involves the interaction of a specific measured variation in the DNA and a specific measured aspect of the environment. An increasing number of G × E studies are being conducted.

Conclusions About Heredity-Environment Interaction

- Complex behaviors have some genetic loading that gives people a propensity for a particular developmental trajectory. However, actual development also requires an environment, and that environment is complex. The interaction of heredity and environment is extensive. Much remains to be discovered about the specific ways that heredity and environment interact to influence development.

KEY TERMS

evolutionary psychology 62
chromosomes 64
DNA 64
genes 64
mitosis 65
meiosis 65
fertilization 65
zygote 65
genotype 66
phenotype 66

Down syndrome 68
Klinefelter syndrome 68
fragile X syndrome 68
Turner syndrome 69
XYY syndrome 69
phenylketonuria
   (PKU) 69
sickle-cell anemia 69
behavior genetics 78
twin study 78

adoption study 78
passive genotype-
   environment
   correlations 78
evocative genotype-
   environment
   correlations 79
active (niche-picking)
   genotype-environment
   correlations 79

shared environmental
   experiences 80
nonshared environmental
   experiences 80
epigenetic view 80
gene × environment (G × E)
   interaction 81

KEY PEOPLE

MAKING A DIFFERENCE

Some Prepregnancy Strategies

Even before a woman becomes pregnant, she can adopt some strategies that may make a difference in how healthy the pregnancy is and its developmental outcomes:

- *Become knowledgeable about prepregnancy planning and health-care providers.* The kinds of health-care providers who are qualified to provide care for pregnant women include an obstetrician/gynecologist, a family practitioner, a nurse practitioner, and a certified nurse-midwife.

- *Meet with a health professional before conception.* A good strategy is that both potential parents meet with a health professional prior

to conception to assess their health and review personal and family histories. During this meeting, the health professional will discuss nutrition and other aspects of health that might affect the baby.

- *Find a health-care provider who is competent.* The health-care provider should (1) take time to do a thorough family history; (2) not be patronizing; (3) be knowledgeable and stay current on prenatal testing; (4) be honest about risks, benefits, and side effects of any tests or treatments; and (5) inspire trust.

RESOURCES FOR IMPROVING CHILDREN'S LIVES

American Fertility Association
www.theafa.org

The American Fertility Association provides information about infertility and possible solutions to it.

How Healthy Is Your Family Tree?
by Carol Krause (1995)
New York: Simon & Schuster

In this book, you will learn how to create a family medical tree. Once you put together a family medical tree, a specialist or genetic counselor can help you understand it.

National Organization for Rare Disorders (NORD)
www.rarediseases.org

NORD supports awareness and education about rare birth defects and genetic disorders.

The Twins Foundation
www.twinsfoundation.com

For information about twins and multiple births, contact The Twins Foundation.

E-LEARNING TOOLS

Connect to **www.mhhe.com/santrockc11** to research the answers and complete these exercises. In addition, you'll find a number of other resources and valuable study tools for Chapter 2, "Biological Beginnings," on this Web site.

Taking It to the Net

1. Ahmahl, a biochemistry major, is writing a psychology paper on the potential dilemmas that society and scientists may face as a result of decoding the human genome. What are some of the main issues or concerns that Ahmahl should address in his class paper?

2. Brandon and Katie are thrilled to learn that they are expecting their first child. They are curious about the genetic makeup of their unborn child and seek answers to a number of related questions. (a) What disorders might be identified through prenatal genetic testing, and (b) which tests, if any, Katie should undergo to help determine this information?

3. Greg and Courtney have three boys. They would love to have a girl. Courtney read that there is a clinic in Virginia where you can pick the sex of your child. How successful are such efforts? Would you want to have this choice available to you?

Health and Well-Being, Parenting, and Education

Build your decision-making skills by trying your hand at the health and well-being, parenting, and education exercises.

Video Clips

The Online Learning Center includes the following video for this chapter:

- *Interview with Adoptive Parents—3004*
  An interview with a couple that adopted a second child.

3

The history of man for nine months preceding his birth would probably be far more interesting and contain events of greater moment than all three score and ten years that follow it.

—SAMUEL TAYLOR COLERIDGE
English Poet Essayist, 19th Century

LEARNING GOALS

♦ Discuss the three periods of prenatal development

♦ Summarize how nutrition, exercise, and prenatal care are important aspects of the expectant mother's pregnancy

♦ Describe potential hazards during prenatal development

PRENATAL DEVELOPMENT

CHAPTER OUTLINE

Images of Children's Development
The Story of Mr. Littles

Diana and Roger married when he was 38 and she was 34. Both worked full-time and were excited when Diana became pregnant. Two months later, Diana began to have some unusual pains and bleeding. Just two months into her pregnancy she had lost the baby. Diana thought deeply about why she was unable to carry the baby to full term. It was about the time she became pregnant that the federal government began to warn that eating certain types of fish with a high mercury content on a regular basis during pregnancy can cause a miscarriage. Although most early miscarriages are the result of embryonic defects, she eliminated these fish from her diet.

Six months later, Diana became pregnant again. She and Roger read about pregnancy, prenatal development, and birth, and signed up for birth preparation classes. Each Friday night for eight weeks they practiced simulated contractions. They talked about what kind of parents they wanted to be and discussed what changes in their lives the baby would make. When they found out that their offspring was going to be a boy, they gave him a name: "Mr. Littles."

This time, Diana's pregnancy went well, and Alex, also known as Mr. Littles, was born. During the birth, however, Diana's heart rate dropped precipitously and she was given a stimulant to raise it. Apparently the stimulant also increased Alex's heart rate and breathing to a dangerous point, and he had to be placed in a neonatal intensive care unit (NICU).

Several times a day, Diana and Roger visited Alex in the NICU. A number of babies in the NICU who had a very low birth weight had been in intensive care for weeks, and some of these babies were not doing well. Fortunately, Alex was in better health. After several days in the NICU, his parents were permitted to take home a very healthy Alex.

Alex, also known as "Mr. Littles."

PREVIEW

This chapter chronicles the truly remarkable changes that take place from conception to birth. Imagine . . . at one time you were suspended in a sea of fluid in your mother's womb. In this chapter, we explore the course of prenatal development, expectant parents' experiences, and some potential hazards to prenatal development.

1 WHAT IS THE COURSE OF PRENATAL DEVELOPMENT?

| The Germinal Period | The Embryonic Period | The Fetal Period | The Brain |

Imagine how Alex ("Mr. Littles") came to be. Out of thousands of eggs and millions of sperm, one egg and one sperm united to produce him. Had the union of sperm and egg come a day or even an hour earlier or later, he would have been very different—maybe even of the opposite sex. Conception occurs when a single sperm cell from the male unites with an ovum (egg) in the female's fallopian tube in a

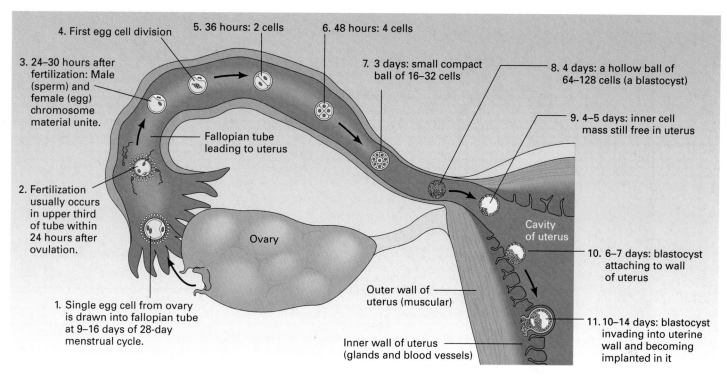

FIGURE 3.1 Significant Developments in the Germinal Period

process called fertilization. Over the next few months, the genetic code, discussed in Chapter 2, "Biological Beginnings," directs a series of changes in the fertilized egg, but many events and hazards will influence how that egg develops and becomes tiny Alex.

Typical prenatal development begins with fertilization and ends with birth, lasting 266 days (38 weeks) from conception. It can be divided into three periods: germinal, embryonic, and fetal.

The Germinal Period

The **germinal period** is the period of prenatal development that takes place in the first two weeks after conception. It includes the creation of the fertilized egg, called a zygote, cell division, and the attachment of the zygote to the uterine wall.

Rapid cell division by the zygote continues throughout the germinal period. (Recall from Chapter 2, "Biological Beginnings," that this cell division occurs through a process called *mitosis*.) By approximately one week after conception, the differentiation of these cells—their specialization for different tasks—has already begun. At this stage, the group of cells, now called the **blastocyst,** consists of an inner mass of cells that will eventually develop into the embryo and the **trophoblast,** an outer layer of cells that later provides nutrition and support for the embryo. *Implantation,* the attachment of the zygote to the uterine wall, takes place about 10 to 14 days after conception. Figure 3.1 illustrates some of the most significant developments during the germinal period.

The Embryonic Period

The **embryonic period** is the period of prenatal development that occurs from two to eight weeks after conception. During the embryonic period, the rate of cell differentiation intensifies, support systems for cells form, and organs appear.

germinal period The period of prenatal development that takes place in the first two weeks after conception. It includes the creation of the zygote, continued cell division, and the attachment of the zygote to the uterine wall.

blastocyst The inner mass of cells that develops during the germinal period. These cells later develop into the embryo.

trophoblast The outer layer of cells that develops in the germinal period. These cells later provide nutrition and support for the embryo.

embryonic period The period of prenatal development that occurs two to eight weeks after conception. During the embryonic period, the rate of cell differentiation intensifies, support systems for the cells form, and organs appear.

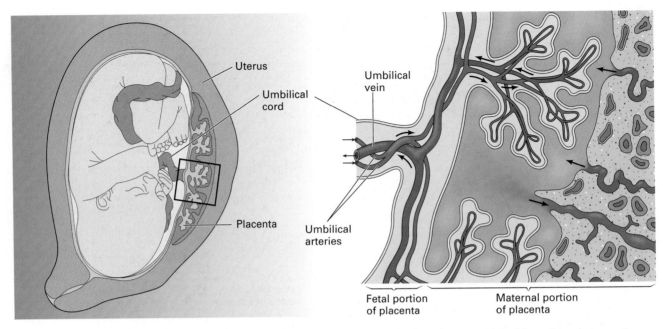

FIGURE 3.2 The Placenta and the Umbilical Cord Maternal blood flows through the uterine arteries to the spaces housing the placenta, and it returns through the uterine veins to the maternal circulation. Fetal blood flows through the umbilical arteries, which transport oxygen-poor blood into the capillaries of the placenta, and returns oxygen-rich blood to the fetal circulation through the umbilical vein. This exchange of materials occurs across the layer separating the maternal and fetal blood supplies, so the maternal blood never comes into contact with the fetal blood. *Note:* The area bounded by the square is enlarged in the right half of the illustration. Arrows indicate the direction of blood flow.

This period begins as the blastocyst attaches to the uterine wall. The mass of cells is now called an *embryo*, and three layers of cells form. The embryo's **endoderm** is the inner layer of cells, which will develop into the digestive and respiratory systems. The **mesoderm** is the middle layer, which will become the circulatory system, bones, muscles, excretory system, and reproductive system. The **ectoderm** is the outermost layer, which will become the nervous system and brain, sensory receptors (ears, nose, and eyes, for example), and skin parts (hair and nails, for example). Every body part eventually develops from these three layers. The endoderm primarily produces internal body parts, the mesoderm primarily produces parts that surround the internal areas, and the ectoderm primarily produces surface parts.

As the embryo's three layers form, life-support systems for the embryo develop rapidly. These life-support systems include the amnion, the umbilical cord (both of which develop from the fertilized egg, not the mother's body), and the placenta. The **amnion** is like a bag or an envelope and contains a clear fluid in which the developing embryo floats. The amniotic fluid provides an environment that is temperature and humidity controlled, as well as shockproof. The **umbilical cord** contains two arteries and one vein, and connects the baby to the placenta. The **placenta** consists of a disk-shaped group of tissues in which small blood vessels from the mother and the offspring intertwine but do not join.

Figure 3.2 illustrates the placenta, the umbilical cord, and the blood flow in the expectant mother and developing organism. Very small molecules—oxygen, water, salt, food from the mother's blood, as well as carbon dioxide and digestive wastes from the offspring's blood—pass back and forth between the mother and embryo or fetus (Fowden & others, 2008). Large molecules cannot pass through the placental wall; these include red blood cells and harmful substances, such as most bacteria, maternal wastes, and hormones. The complex mechanisms that govern the transfer

endoderm The inner layer of cells, which develops into digestive and respiratory systems.

mesoderm The middle layer of cells, which becomes the circulatory system, bones, muscles, excretory system, and reproductive system.

ectoderm The outermost layer of cells, which becomes the nervous system and brain, sensory receptors (ears, nose, and eyes, for example), and skin parts (hair and nails, for example).

amnion The life-support system that is a thin bag or envelope that contains a clear fluid in which the developing embryo floats.

umbilical cord Contains two arteries and one vein, and connects the baby to the placenta.

placenta Consists of a disk-shaped group of tissues in which small blood vessels from the mother and the offspring intertwine but don't join.

of substances across the placental barrier are still not entirely understood (Cetin & Alvino, 2009; Nanovskaya & others, 2008).

By the time most women know they are pregnant, the major organs have begun to form. **Organogenesis** is the name given to the process of organ formation during the first two months of prenatal development. While they are being formed, the organs are especially vulnerable to environmental changes (Mullis & Tonella, 2008). In the third week after conception, the neural tube that eventually becomes the spinal cord forms. At about 21 days, eyes begin to appear, and at 24 days the cells for the heart begin to differentiate. During the fourth week, the urogenital system becomes apparent, and arm and leg buds emerge. Four chambers of the heart take shape, and blood vessels appear. From the fifth to the eighth week, arms and legs differentiate further; at this time, the face starts to form but still is not very recognizable. The intestinal tract develops and the facial structures fuse. At eight weeks, the developing organism weighs about 1/30 ounce and is just over 1 inch long.

The Fetal Period

The **fetal period,** lasting about seven months, is the prenatal period between two months after conception and birth in typical pregnancies. Growth and development continue their dramatic course during this time.

Three months after conception, the fetus is about 3 inches long and weighs about 3 ounces. It has become active, moving its arms and legs, opening and closing its mouth, and moving its head. The face, forehead, eyelids, nose, and chin are distinguishable, as are the upper arms, lower arms, hands, and lower limbs. In most cases, the genitals can be identified as male or female. By the end of the fourth month of pregnancy, the fetus has grown to 6 inches in length and weighs 4 to 7 ounces. At this time, a growth spurt occurs in the body's lower parts. For the first time, the mother can feel arm and leg movements.

By the end of the fifth month, the fetus is about 12 inches long and weighs close to a pound. Structures of the skin have formed—toenails and fingernails, for example. The fetus is more active, showing a preference for a particular position in the womb. By the end of the sixth month, the fetus is about 14 inches long and has gained another half pound to a pound. The eyes and eyelids are completely formed, and a fine layer of hair covers the head. A grasping reflex is present and irregular breathing movements occur.

As early as six months of pregnancy (about 24 to 25 weeks after conception), the fetus for the first time has a chance of surviving outside the womb—that is, it is *viable*. Infants born between 24 and 37 weeks of pregnancy usually need help breathing because their lungs are not yet fully mature. By the end of the seventh month, the fetus is about 16 inches long and weighs about 3 pounds.

During the last two months of prenatal development, fatty tissues develop, and the functioning of various organ systems—heart and kidneys, for example—steps up. During the eighth and ninth months, the fetus grows longer and gains substantial weight—about another 4 pounds. At birth, the average American baby weighs 7½ pounds and is about 20 inches long.

Figure 3.3 gives an overview of the main events during prenatal development. Notice that instead of describing development in terms of germinal, embryonic, and fetal periods, Figure 3.3 divides prenatal development into equal periods of three months, called *trimesters*. Remember that the three trimesters are not the same as the three prenatal periods we have discussed. The germinal and embryonic periods occur in the first trimester. The fetal period begins toward the end of the first trimester and continues through the second and third trimesters. Viability (the chances of surviving outside the womb) occurs at the very end of the second trimester.

How Would You...?
As a human development and family studies professional, how would you characterize the greatest risks at each period of prenatal development?

organogenesis Process of organ formation that takes place during the first two months of prenatal development.

fetal period The prenatal period of development that begins two months after conception and lasts for seven months, on the average.

First trimester (first 3 months)

Prenatal growth	Conception to 4 weeks	8 weeks	12 weeks
	• Is less than 1/10 inch long • Beginning development of spinal cord, nervous system, gastrointestinal system, heart, and lungs • Amniotic sac envelopes the preliminary tissues of entire body • Is called a "zygote"	• Is just over 1 inch long • Face is forming with rudimentary eyes, ears, mouth, and tooth buds • Arms and legs are moving • Brain is forming • Fetal heartbeat is detectable with ultrasound • Is called an "embryo"	• Is about 3 inches long and weighs about 1 ounce • Can move arms, legs, fingers, and toes • Fingerprints are present • Can smile, frown, suck, and swallow • Sex is distinguishable • Can urinate • Is called a "fetus"

Second trimester (middle 3 months)

Prenatal growth	16 weeks	20 weeks	24 weeks
	• Is about 6 inches long and weighs about 4 to 7 ounces • Heartbeat is strong • Skin is thin, transparent • Downy hair (lanugo) covers body • Fingernails and toenails are forming • Has coordinated movements; is able to roll over in amniotic fluid	• Is 10 to 12 inches long and weighs 1/2 to 1 pound • Heartbeat is audible with ordinary stethoscope • Sucks thumb • Hiccups • Hair, eyelashes, eyebrows are present	• Is 11 to 14 inches long and weighs 1 to 1 1/2 pounds • Skin is wrinkled and covered with protective coating (vernix caseosa) • Eyes are open • Waste matter is collected in bowel • Has strong grip

Third trimester (last 3 months)

Prenatal growth	28 weeks	32 weeks	36 to 38 weeks
	• Is 14 to 17 inches long and weighs 2 1/2 to 3 pounds • Is adding body fat • Is very active • Rudimentary breathing movements are present	• Is 16 1/2 to 18 inches long and weighs 4 to 5 pounds • Has periods of sleep and wakefulness • Responds to sounds • May assume the birth position • Bones of head are soft and flexible • Iron is being stored in liver	• Is 19 to 20 inches long and weighs 6 to 7 1/2 pounds • Skin is less wrinkled • Vernix caseosa is thick • Lanugo is mostly gone • Is less active • Is gaining immunities from mother

FIGURE 3.3 The Three Trimesters of Prenatal Development Both the germinal and embryonic periods occur during the first trimester. The end of the first trimester as well as the second and third trimesters are part of the fetal period.

The Brain

One of the most remarkable aspects of the prenatal period is the development of the brain (Moulson & Nelson, 2008; Nelson, 2009). By the time babies are born, they have approximately 100 billion **neurons,** or nerve cells, which handle information processing at the cellular level in the brain. During prenatal development, neurons spend time moving to the right locations and are starting to become connected. The

neurons The term for nerve cells, which handle information processing at the cellular level.

basic architecture of the human brain is assembled during the first two trimesters of prenatal development. In typical development, the third trimester of prenatal development and the first two years of postnatal life are characterized by connectivity and functioning of neurons (Nelson, 2009).

As the human embryo develops inside its mother's womb, the nervous system begins forming as a long, hollow tube located on the embryo's back. This pear-shaped *neural tube*, which forms about 18 to 24 days after conception, develops out of the ectoderm. The tube closes at the top and bottom ends about 24 days after conception. Figure 3.4 shows that the nervous system still has a tubular appearance six weeks after conception.

Two birth defects related to a failure of the neural tube to close are anencephaly and spina bifida. The highest regions of the brain fail to develop when fetuses have anencephaly or when the head end of neural tube fails to close, and most die in the womb, during childbirth, or shortly after birth (Levene & Chervenak, 2009). Spina bifida results in varying degrees of paralysis of the lower limbs. Individuals with spina bifida usually need assistive devices such as crutches, braces, or wheelchairs. Pregnant women can help to prevent neural tube defects by taking adequate amounts of the B vitamin folic acid, a topic we further discuss later in the chapter (Bell & Oakley, 2009).

In a normal pregnancy, once the neural tube has closed, a massive proliferation of new immature neurons begins to take place about the fifth prenatal week and continues throughout the remainder of the prenatal period. The generation of new neurons is called **neurogenesis.** At the peak of neurogenesis, it is estimated that as many as 200,000 neurons are being generated every minute.

At approximately 6 to 24 weeks after conception, *neuronal migration* occurs (Nelson, 2009). This involves cells moving outward from their point of origin to their appropriate locations and creating the different levels, structures, and regions of the brain (Hepper, 2007). Once a cell has migrated to its target destination, it must mature and develop a more complex structure.

At about 23 prenatal weeks, connections between neurons begin to occur, a process that continues postnatally (Moulson & Nelson, 2008). We will have much more to consider about the structure of neurons, their connectivity, and the development of the infant brain in Chapter 5, "Physical Development in Infancy."

FIGURE 3.4 Early Formation of the Nervous System
The photograph shows the primitive, tubular appearance of the nervous system at six weeks in the human embryo.

These individuals are members of the Spina Bifida Association of Greater New Orleans. The association is made up of parents, family members, children, and adults with spina bifida, and health professionals who provide care for individuals born with spina bifida and their families.

Review and Reflect: Learning Goal 1

1 **Discuss the three periods of prenatal development**

REVIEW

- How can the germinal period be characterized?
- What takes place during the embryonic period?
- How can the fetal period be described?
- How does the brain develop in the prenatal period?

REFLECT

- What is the most important thing you learned in the section on exploring prenatal development that you did not previously know?

neurogenesis The formation of new neurons.

2 WHAT ARE SOME IMPORTANT STRATEGIES THAT ENHANCE THE EXPECTANT MOTHER'S HEALTH AND PRENATAL CARE?

The Expectant Mother's Nutrition, Weight Gain, and Exercise

Prenatal Care

How much do you know about prenatal development and maintaining a healthy pregnancy? How much weight gain on average should occur during pregnancy?

What can the expectant mother do that will improve the likelihood of being healthy herself and the likelihood her offspring will be healthy? Among the most important strategies she can adopt involve nutrition, exercise, and prenatal care.

The Expectant Mother's Nutrition, Weight Gain, and Exercise

The mother's nutrition can have a strong influence on the development of the fetus. Here we discuss the mother's nutritional needs and optimal nutrition during pregnancy, as well as the role of exercise in the expectant mother's health.

Nutrition and Weight Gain The best assurance of an adequate caloric intake during pregnancy is a satisfactory weight gain over time (Vyas & others, 2008). The optimal weight gain depends on the expectant mother's height, bone structure, and prepregnant nutritional state. However, maternal weight gains that average from 25 to 35 pounds are associated with the best reproductive outcomes.

An increasing number of pregnant women gain more than this recommended amount (Dixit & Girling, 2008; Langer, 2008a). Maternal obesity adversely impacts pregnancy outcomes through increased rates of hypertension, diabetes, respiratory complications, and infections in the mother (Galtier & others, 2008; Guelinckx & others, 2008). Also, pregnancies in obese women are characterized by a higher incidence of neural tube defects, preterm deliveries, and late fetal deaths (Siega-Ritz, Siega-Ritz, & Laraia, 2006). We further discuss obesity as a potential hazard to prenatal development later in the chapter.

The pattern of weight gain is also important. The ideal pattern of weight gain during pregnancy is 2 to 4.4 pounds during the first trimester, followed by an average gain of 1 pound per week during the last two trimesters. In the second trimester, most of the weight gain is due to increased blood volume; the enlargement of breasts, uterus, and associated tissue and fluid; and the deposit of maternal fat. In the third trimester, weight gain mainly involves the fetus, placenta, and amniotic fluid. A 25-pound weight gain during pregnancy is generally distributed in this way: 11 pounds: fetus, placenta, and amniotic fluid; 5 pounds: maternal stores; 4 pounds: increased blood volume; 3 pounds: tissue fluid; and 2 pounds: uterus and breasts.

During the second and third trimesters, inadequate gains of less than 2.2 pounds per month or excessive gains of more than

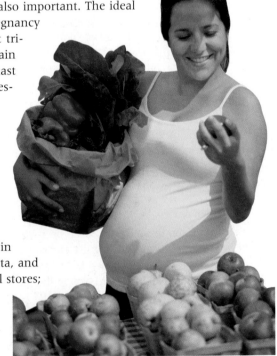

What are some guidelines for expectant mothers' eating patterns?

6.6 pounds per month should be evaluated and the need for nutritional counseling considered. Inadequate weight gain has been associated with low birth weight infants. Sudden sharp increases in weight of 3 to 5 pounds in a week may result from fluid retention and may require evaluation.

The recommended daily allowance (RDA) for all nutrients increases during pregnancy. The expectant mother should eat three meals a day, with nutritious snacks of fruits, cheese, milk, or other foods between meals if desired. More frequent, smaller meals also are recommended. Water is an essential nutrient. Four to six 8-ounce glasses of water and a total of 8 to 10 cups (64 to 80 ounces) of total fluid should be consumed daily. The need for protein, iron, vitamin D, folacin, calcium, phosphorus, and magnesium increases by 50 percent or more. Recommended increases for other nutrients range from 15 to 40 percent (see Figure 3.5). Researchers have recently found that women who take a multivitamin prior to pregnancy may be at a reduced risk for delivering a preterm infant (Vahratian & others, 2004).

Exercise   How much and what type of exercise is best during pregnancy depend to some degree on the course of the pregnancy, the expectant mother's fitness, and her customary activity level. Normal participation in exercise can continue throughout an uncomplicated pregnancy (Baraket, Ruiz, & Lucia, 2009; Hausenblas & others, 2008; Lu & Lu, 2008). In general, the skilled sportswoman is no longer discouraged from participating in sports she participated in prior to her pregnancy. However, pregnancy is not the appropriate time to begin strenuous activity.

Because of the increased emphasis on physical fitness in our society, more women routinely jog as part of a physical fitness program prior to pregnancy. There are few concerns about continuing to jog during the early part of pregnancy, but in the latter part of pregnancy there is some concern about the jarring effect of jogging on the breasts and abdomen. As pregnancy progresses, low-impact activities, such as walking, swimming, water aerobics, and bicycling, are safer and provide fitness as well as greater comfort, eliminating the bouncing associated with jogging (Cavalcante & others, 2009).

Exercise during pregnancy helps prevent constipation, conditions the body, and is associated with a more positive mental state (Rafla, Nair, & Kumar, 2008). However, it is important to remember not to overdo it. Pregnant women should always consult their physician before starting any exercise program (Olson & others, 2009).

Might the mother's exercise during pregnancy be related to the development of the fetus and the birth of the child? Few studies have been conducted on this topic, but several studies indicate that moderate exercise three to four times a week was linked to healthy weight gain in the fetus and a normal birth weight, whereas the risk of low birth weight increased for women who exercised intensely most days of the week and for women who exercised less than twice a week or not at all (Campbell & Mottols, 2001). Two recent studies confirmed that physical exercise during pregnancy is not linked to an increase in preterm birth (Hegaard & others, 2008; Juhl & others, 2008). In one of the studies, compared with sedentary pregnant women, women who engaged in light leisure time physical activity had a 24 percent reduced likelihood of preterm delivery and those who participated in moderate to heavy leisure time physical activity had a 66 percent reduced risk of preterm delivery (Hegaard & others, 2008).

We discuss some guidelines for exercise in the following *Caring for Children* interlude.

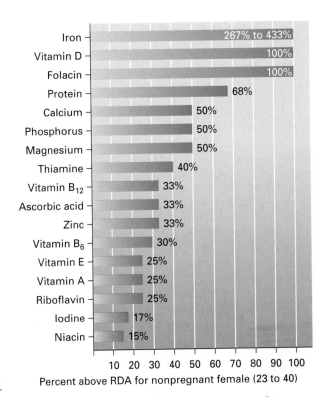

FIGURE 3.5 **Recommended Nutrient Increases for Expectant Mothers**

How might the woman's exercise in pregnancy benefit her and her offspring?

Caring for Children

EXERCISE GUIDELINES FOR EXPECTANT MOTHERS

Exercise during pregnancy is just as important in pregnancy as before or after pregnancy. The following guidelines for exercise are recommended for expectant mothers by the American College of Obstetricians and Gynecologists (2008, pp. 1–4):

- *Changes in the woman's body.* Some of the changes in the woman's body during pregnancy require adaptations in exercise. Joints and ligaments become more mobile during pregnancy. Avoiding jerky, bouncy, or high-impact motions can reduce the risk of injuring joints and ligaments. During pregnancy women carry extra weight, and the pregnant woman's center of gravity shifts, placing stress on joints and muscles, especially in the pelvis and lower back. Thus, maintaining balance while exercising during pregnancy is sometimes difficult and requires attention. The extra weight pregnant women carry makes their body work harder so it important not to exercise too strenuously.

- *Getting started.* Before starting an exercise program, pregnant women should talk with their doctor to ensure that they don't have an obstetric or health condition that might limit their activity. Women with the following conditions will be advised by their doctor not to exercise during pregnancy: risk factors for preterm labor, vaginal bleeding, and premature rupture of membranes.

What are some recommended guidelines for exercise during pregnancy?

- *Choosing safe exercises.* Most types of exercise are safe during pregnancy but some types involve positions and movements that may be uncomfortable, tiring, or harmful. For example, after the first trimester of pregnancy, women should not do exercises that require them to lie flat on their backs. Some sports are safe during pregnancy, even for beginners. Walking is a good exercise for anyone, swimming is excellent because it works so many muscles, cycling provides a good aerobic workout (because balance is affected by pregnancy, a stationary bicycle is recommended in later pregnancy); aerobic exercise is effective in keeping the heart and lungs strong; and strength training can strengthen muscles and help prevent some common aches and pains during pregnancy. Women who were runners or played racquet sports before becoming pregnant should talk with their doctor about exercising certain cautions if they plan to continue these activities during pregnancy. The following activities should be avoided during pregnancy: downhill snow skiing, contact sports, and scuba diving.

- *Establishing a routine.* Exercise is most practical during the first 24 weeks of pregnancy; during the last three months many exercises that were easy earlier in pregnancy are now often difficult. It is important to begin each exercise session with a 5- to 10-minute warm-up and end each session with a 5- to 10-minute cooldown. During the warm-up and cooldown, stretching exercises should be done. Pregnant women should not exercise to the point that they are exhausted. If during exercise, pregnant women experience any of the following they should stop exercising and call their doctor: vaginal bleeding, dizziness or feeling faint, increased shortness of breath, chest pain, headache, muscle weakness, calf pain or swelling, uterine contractions, decreased fetal movement, or fluid leaking from the vagina.

Prenatal Care

Although prenatal care varies enormously, it usually involves a defined schedule of visits for medical care, which typically includes screening for manageable conditions and treatable diseases that can affect the baby or the mother (Lu & Lu, 2008; Mennuti, 2008). In addition to medical care, prenatal programs often include comprehensive educational, social, and nutritional services.

The education provided in prenatal care varies during the course of pregnancy. Those in the early stages of pregnancy as well as couples who are anticipating a pregnancy may participate in early prenatal classes (Davidson, London, & Ladewig, 2008). In addition to providing information on dangers to the fetus, early prenatal classes often discuss the development of the embryo and the fetus; sexuality during pregnancy; choices about the birth setting and care providers; nutrition, rest, and exercise; common discomforts of pregnancy and relief measures; psychological changes in the expectant mother and her partner; and factors that increase the risk of preterm labor and possible symptoms of preterm labor. Early classes also may include information about the advantages and disadvantages of breast feeding and bottle feeding. (Fifty to eighty percent of expectant mothers decide how they will feed their infant prior to the sixth month of pregnancy.) During the second or third trimester of pregnancy, prenatal classes focus on preparing for the birth, infant care and feeding, choices about birth, and postpartum self-care.

Does prenatal care matter? Information about pregnancy, labor, delivery, and caring for the newborn can be especially valuable for first-time mothers (Flynn, Budd, & Modelski, 2008). Prenatal care is also very important for women in poverty because it links them with other social services (Hogan & others, 2007; Hueston, Geesey, & Diaz, 2008). The legacy of prenatal care continues after the birth because women who experience this type of care are more likely to get preventive care for their infants.

Research contrasting the experiences of mothers who had prenatal care and those who did not supports the importance of prenatal care (McFarlin, 2009). One study found that U.S. women who had no prenatal care were far more likely than their counterparts who received prenatal care to have infants who had low birth weight, increased mortality, and a number of other physical problems (Herbst & others, 2003). In other studies, low birth weight and preterm deliveries were common among U.S. mothers who received no prenatal care, and the absence of prenatal care increased the risk for preterm birth by almost threefold in both non-Latino White and African American women (Stringer & others, 2005).

Inadequate prenatal care may help explain a disturbing fact: Rates of infant mortality and low birth weight indicate that many other nations have healthier babies than the United States (Goldenberg & Culhane, 2007). In many countries that have a lower percentage of low birth weight infants than the United States, mothers receive either free or very low cost prenatal and postnatal care, and can receive paid maternity leave from work that ranges from 9 to 40 weeks. In Norway and the Netherlands, prenatal care is coordinated with a general practitioner, an obstetrician, and a midwife. To read about the work and career of a U.S. obstetrician/gynecologist see the *Careers in Children's Development* profile.

Why do some U.S. women receive inadequate prenatal care? Sometimes the reasons are tied to the health-care system, to provider practices, and to their own individual and social characteristics (Magriples & others, 2008). Women who do not want to be pregnant, who have negative attitudes about being pregnant, or who unintentionally become pregnant are more likely to delay prenatal care or to miss appointments. As we noted earlier, adolescent girls are less likely than adult women to obtain prenatal care. Within the United States, there are differences among ethnic groups both in the health of babies and in prenatal care (Wasserman, Bender, & Lee, 2007). In the 1980s, more than one-fifth of all non-Latino White mothers and

How Would You...?
As a human development and family studies professional, how would you justify the need for prenatal education classes for couples expecting a child?

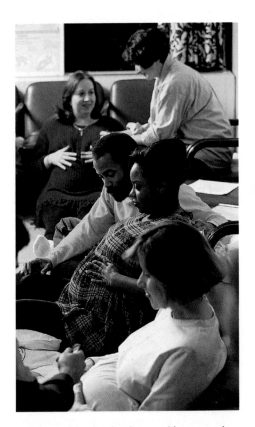

Partners or friends take classes with prospective mothers in many prenatal care programs. *What characterizes the content of prenatal care programs?*

Careers in Children's Development

Rachel Thompson, Obstetrician/ Gynecologist

Rachel Thompson is the senior member of Houston Women's Care Associates, which specializes in health care for women. She has one of Houston's most popular obstetrics/gynecology (OB/GYN) practices. Thompson's medical degree is from Baylor College of Medicine, where she also completed her internship and residency.

In addition to her clinical practice, Thompson also is a clinical instructor in the Department of Obstetrics and Gynecology at Baylor College of Medicine. Thompson says that one of the unique features of their health-care group is that the staff comprises only women who are full-time practitioners.

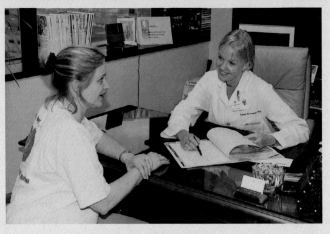

Rachel Thompson (*right*), talking with one of her patients at Houston Women's Care Associates.

one-third of all African American mothers did not receive prenatal care in the first trimester of their pregnancy, and 5 percent of White mothers and 10 percent of African American mothers received no prenatal care at all (Wegman, 1987).

The situation has been improving. From 1990 to 2004, the use of timely prenatal care increased for women from a variety of ethnic backgrounds in the United States, although non-Latino White women were still more likely to obtain prenatal care than African American and Latino women (Martin & others, 2005) (see Figure 3.6). The United States needs more comprehensive medical and educational services to improve the quality of prenatal care and to reduce the number of low birth weight and preterm infants (Lu & Lu, 2008).

An innovative program that is rapidly expanding in the United States and other countries is CenteringPregnancy (Massey, Rising, & Ickovics, 2006; Teate & others, 2009; Walker & Worrell, 2008). This relationship-centered program provides complete prenatal care in a group setting. CenteringPregnancy replaces traditional 15-minute physician visits with 90-minute peer group support settings, and self-examination led by a physician or certified nurse-midwife. Groups of up to 10 women (and often their partners) meet regularly beginning at 12 to 16 weeks of pregnancy. The sessions emphasize empowering women to play an active role in experiencing a positive pregnancy. A recent study revealed that Centering-Pregnancy groups made more prenatal visits, had higher breast feeding rates, and were more satisfied with their prenatal care than women in individual care (Klima & others, 2009).

Some prenatal programs for parents focus on home visitation (Lee & others, 2009). Research evaluations indicate that the most successful home visitation program is the Nurse Family Partnership created by David Olds and his colleagues (2004, 2007; Zielinski, Eckenrode, & Olds, 2009). The Nurse Family Partnership involves home visits by trained nurses beginning in the second or third trimester of prenatal development. The extensive program consists of approximately 50 home visits from the prenatal period through 2 years of age. The home visits focus on the mother's health, access to health care, parenting, and improvement of the mother's life by providing her guidance in education, work, and relationships. Research revealed that the Nurse Family Partnership has numerous positive

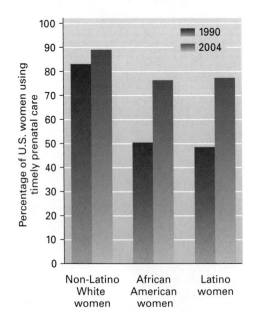

FIGURE 3.6 Percentage of U.S. Women Using Timely Prenatal Care: 1990 to 2004
From 1990 to 2004, the use of timely prenatal care increased by 7 percent (to 89.1) for non-Latino White women, by 25 percent (to 76.5) for African American women, and by 28 percent (to 77.4) for Latino women in the United States.

outcomes including fewer pregnancies, better work circumstances, and stability in relationship partners for the mother and improved academic success and social development for the child (Olds & others, 2004, 2007).

In another home visitation program, high-risk pregnant women and adolescents, many living in poverty conditions, were provided biweekly home visitation services that encouraged healthy prenatal behavior, social support, and links to medical and other community services (Lee & others, 2009). Compared with a control group of pregnant women and adolescents who did not receive the home visits, the home visitation group gave birth to fewer low birth weight infants.

Cultures around the world have differing views of pregnancy. In the *Diversity in Children's Development* interlude that follows, we explore these beliefs.

A CenteringPregnancy program. This rapidly increasing program alters routine prenatal care by bringing women out of exam rooms and into relationship-oriented groups.

Diversity in Children's Development

CULTURAL BELIEFS ABOUT PREGNANCY

All cultures have beliefs and practices that surround life's major events, and one such event is pregnancy. When a woman who immigrated to the United States becomes pregnant, the beliefs and practices of her native culture may be as important as, or more important than, those of the mainstream U.S. culture that now surrounds her. The conflict between cultural tradition and Western medicine may pose a risk for the pregnancy and a challenge for the health-care professional who wishes to give proper care while respecting the woman's values.

The American Public Health Association (2006) has identified a variety of cultural beliefs and practices that are observed among various immigrant groups, such as:

- *Food cravings.* Latin American, Asian, and some African cultures believe that it is important for a pregnant woman's food cravings to be satisfied because they are thought to be the cravings of the baby. If cravings are left unsatisfied, the baby might take on certain unpleasant personality and/or physical traits, perhaps characteristic of the food (Taylor, Ko, & Pan, 1999). As an example, in African cultures women often eat soil, chalk, or clay during pregnancy; this is believed to satisfy the baby's hunger as well as affirming soil as a symbol of female fertility (American Public Health Association, 2006).

- *"Hot-cold" theory of illness.* Many cultures in Latin America, Asia, and Africa characterize foods, medications, and illnesses as "hot" or "cold"; this has nothing to do with temperature or spiciness, but with traditional definitions and categories. Most of these cultures view pregnancy as a "hot" condition, although the Chinese view it as "cold" (Taylor, Ko, & Pan, 1999). As a result, a woman may resist taking a prescribed medication because of concern that it could create too much "heat" and cause a miscarriage; in Indian culture, iron-rich foods are also considered unacceptably "hot" for pregnant women (DeSantis, 1998).

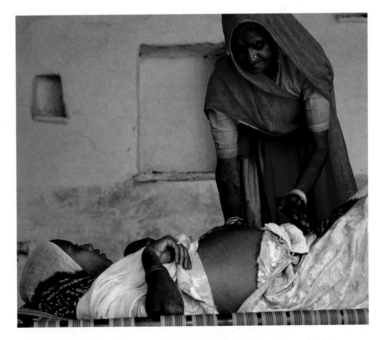

In India, a midwife checks on the size, position, and heartbeat of a fetus. Midwives deliver babies in many cultures around the world. *What are some cultural variations in prenatal care?*

(continued on next page)

- *Extended family.* In many immigrant cultures, the extended family is a vital support system, and health-care decisions are made based on the needs of the family over those of the individual. Western health-care providers need to be sensitive to this dynamic, which runs counter to today's practices of protecting patient confidentiality and autonomy.
- *Stoicism.* In many Asian cultures, stoicism is valued, as suffering is seen as part of life (Uba, 1992). Physicians are also viewed with great respect. As a result, a pregnant Asian woman may behave submissively and avoid voicing complaints to her health-care provider, but may privately fail to follow the provider's advice (Assanand & others, 1990).

Some cultures treat pregnancy simply as a natural occurrence; others see it as a medical condition (Walsh, 2006). How expectant mothers behave during pregnancy may depend in part on the prevalence of traditional home-care remedies and folk beliefs, the importance of indigenous healers, and the influence of health-care professionals in their culture. In various cultures women may consult herbalists and/or faith healers during pregnancy (Mbonye, Neema, & Magnussen, 2006).

Health-care workers should assess whether a woman's beliefs or practices pose a threat to her or the fetus. If they do, health-care professionals should consider a culturally sensitive way to handle the problem (Kenner, Sugrue, & Finkelman, 2007).

Review and Reflect: Learning Goal 2

 2 **Summarize how nutrition, exercise, and prenatal care are important aspects of the expectant mother's pregnancy**

REVIEW

- What are some recommendations for the expectant mother's nutrition, weight gain, and exercise?
- What are some important aspects of prenatal care?

REFLECT

- What are some beliefs about pregnancy and prenatal development in your culture?

---

3 WHAT ARE SOME POTENTIAL HAZARDS TO PRENATAL DEVELOPMENT?

| Some General Principles | | Psychoactive Drugs | | Environmental Hazards | | Other Parental Factors |

| Prescription and Nonprescription Drugs | Incompatible Blood Types | Maternal Diseases |

For Alex, the baby discussed at the opening of this chapter, the course of prenatal development went smoothly. His mother's womb protected him as he developed. Despite this protection, the environment can affect the embryo or fetus in many well-documented ways.

Some General Principles

A **teratogen** is any agent that can potentially cause a physical birth defect. (The word comes from the Greek word *tera* meaning "monster"). The field of study that investigates the causes of birth defects is called *teratology*. Some exposures to teratogens do not cause physical birth defects but can alter the developing brain and influence cognitive and behavioral functioning, in which case the field of study is called *behavioral teratology* (DiPietro, 2008).

Teratogens include drugs, incompatible blood types, environmental pollutants, infectious diseases, nutritional deficiencies, maternal stress, advanced maternal and paternal age, and environmental pollutants. In fact, thousands of babies are born deformed or mentally retarded every year as a result of events that occurred in the mother's life as early as one or two months *before* conception. As we further discuss teratogens, you will see that factors related to the father also can influence prenatal development.

So many teratogens exist that practically every fetus is exposed to at least some of them. For this reason, it is difficult to determine which teratogen causes which problem. In addition, it may take a long time for the effects of a teratogen to show up. Only about half of all potential effects appear at birth.

The time of exposure, dose, and genetic susceptibility to a particular teratogen influence both the severity of the damage to an embryo or fetus and the type of defect:

- *Time of Exposure.* Teratogens do more damage when they occur at some points in development than at others (Nava-Ocampo & Koren, 2007). Damage during the germinal period may even prevent implantation. In general, the embryonic period is more vulnerable than the fetal period.

- *Dose.* The dose effect is rather obvious—the greater the dose of an agent, such as a drug, the greater the effect.

- *Genetic Susceptibility.* The type or severity of abnormalities caused by a teratogen is linked to the genotype of the pregnant woman and the genotype of the embryo or fetus (Wakschlag & others, 2009; Wiebe & others, 2009). For example, how a mother metabolizes a particular drug can influence the degree to which the drug effects are transmitted to the embryo or fetus. Differences in placental membranes and placental transport also affect exposure. The extent to which an embryo or fetus is vulnerable to a teratogen may also depend on its genotype (Marinucci, & others, 2009).

Also, for unknown reasons, male fetuses are far more likely to be affected by teratogens than female fetuses (DiPietro, 2008).

Figure 3.7 summarizes additional information about the effects of time of exposure to a teratogen. The probability of a structural defect is greatest early in the embryonic period, when organs are being formed (Hill, 2007; Lu & Lu, 2008). Each body structure has its own critical period of formation. Recall from Chapter 1, "Introduction," that a *critical period* is a fixed time period very early in development during which certain experiences or events can have a long-lasting effect on development. The critical period for the nervous system (week 3) is earlier than that for arms and legs (weeks 4 and 5).

After organogenesis is complete, teratogens can no longer cause anatomical defects. Instead, exposure during the fetal period is more likely instead to stunt growth or to create problems in the way organs function. To examine some key teratogens and their effects, let's begin with drugs.

Prescription and Nonprescription Drugs

Many U.S. women are given prescriptions for drugs while they are pregnant—especially antibiotics, analgesics, and asthma medications. Prescription as well as nonprescription drugs, however, may have effects on the embryo or fetus that the women never imagined. (Weiner & Buhimschi, 2009).

teratogen From the Greek word *tera*, meaning "monster," any agent that can potentially cause a physical birth defect. The field of study that investigates the causes of birth defects is called teratology.

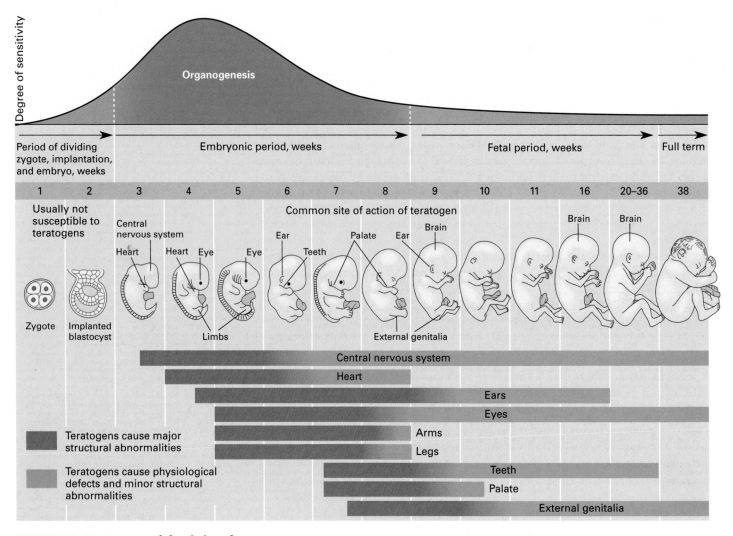

FIGURE 3.7 Teratogens and the Timing of Their Effects on Prenatal Development The danger of structural defects caused by teratogens is greatest early in embryonic development. The period of organogenesis (red color) lasts for about six weeks. Later assaults by teratogens (blue color) mainly occur in the fetal period and instead of causing structural damage are more likely to stunt growth or cause problems of organ function.

The damage that drugs can do was tragically highlighted in 1961, when many pregnant women took a popular sedative, thalidomide, to alleviate their morning sickness. In adults, the effects of thalidomide are typically not damaging; in embryos, however, they are devastating. Not all infants were affected in the same way. If the mother took thalidomide on day 26 (probably before she knew she was pregnant), an arm might not grow. If she took the drug two days later, the arm might not grow past the elbow. The thalidomide tragedy shocked the medical community and parents and taught a valuable lesson: Taking the wrong drug at the wrong time is enough to physically handicap the offspring for life (Brent, 2008).

Prescription drugs that can function as teratogens include antibiotics, such as streptomycin and tetracycline; some antidepressants; certain hormones, such as progestin and synthetic estrogen; and Accutane (isotretinoin), which often is prescribed for acne (Garcia-Bournissen & others, 2008; Schaefer, Meister, & Weber-Schoendorfer, 2009). Nonprescription drugs that can be harmful include diet pills and aspirin (Norgard & others, 2005). A recent research review indicated that low doses of aspirin pose no harm for the fetus but that high doses can contribute to maternal and fetal bleeding (James, Brancazio, & Price, 2008).

Psychoactive Drugs

Psychoactive drugs are drugs that act on the nervous system to alter states of consciousness, modify perceptions, and change moods. Examples include caffeine, alcohol, and nicotine, as well as illicit drugs such as cocaine, methamphetamine, marijuana, and heroin.

Caffeine   People often consume caffeine when they drink coffee, tea, or colas, or when they eat chocolate. A review of studies on caffeine consumption during pregnancy concluded that a small increase in the risks for spontaneous abortion and low birth weight occurs for pregnant women consuming more than 150 milligrams of caffeine (approximately two cups of brewed coffee or two to three 12-ounce cans of cola) per day (Fernandez & others, 1998). (Low birth weight is linked to a variety of health and developmental problems, which we will discuss later in the chapter.) A recent study revealed that pregnant women who consumed 200 or more milligrams of caffeine a day had an increased risk of miscarriage (Weng, Odouli, & Li, 2008). Taking into account such results, the U.S. Food and Drug Administration recommends that pregnant women either not consume caffeine or consume it only sparingly.

Alcohol   Heavy drinking by pregnant women can be devastating to the offspring (Borowski & Niebyl, 2008). **Fetal alcohol spectrum disorders (FASD)** are a cluster of abnormalities and problems that appear in the offspring of mothers who drink alcohol heavily during pregnancy (Olson, King, & Jirikowic, 2008). The abnormalities include facial deformities and defective limbs, face, and heart. Some children with FASD have these body malformations but others don't. Most children with FASD are characterized by learning problems, and many are below average in intelligence with some being mentally retarded (Caley & others, 2008; Cuzon & others, 2008). A recent study revealed that children with FASD have impaired memory development (Pei & others, 2008). And another recent study revealed that as young adults individuals diagnosed with FASD in infancy were characterized by intellectual disability, limited occupational options, and dependent living (Spohr, Willms, & Steinhausen, 2007). Although women who drink heavily during pregnancy are at a higher risk of having a child with FASD, not all pregnant heavy drinkers have children with FASD.

Drinking alcohol during pregnancy, however, can have serious effects on offspring even when they are not afflicted with FASD (Pollard, 2007; Sayal & others, 2007). Serious malformations, such as those produced by FASD, are not found in infants born to mothers who are moderate drinkers, but even moderate drinking can have a negative effect on the offspring.

What are some guidelines for alcohol use during pregnancy? The U.S. Surgeon General recommends that *no* alcohol be consumed during pregnancy. And research suggests that it may not be wise to consume alcohol at the time of conception. One study revealed that intakes of alcohol by both men and women during the weeks of conception increased the risk of early pregnancy loss (Henriksen & others, 2004). And a recent study revealed that although both non-Latino White women and African American women lowered their alcohol intake when they became pregnant, non-Latino White women lowered their alcohol intake more than African American women (Morris & others, 2008). In sum, it is recommended that pregnant women avoid drinking alcohol entirely.

Nicotine   Cigarette smoking by pregnant women can also adversely influence prenatal development, birth, and postnatal development (Cooper & Moley, 2008; Romo, Carceller, & Tobajas, 2009). Preterm births and low birth weights, fetal and neonatal deaths, and respiratory problems and sudden infant death syndrome (SIDS, also known as crib death) are all more common among the offspring of mothers who smoked during pregnancy (Henderson, 2008; Landau, 2008). A recent review concluded that tobacco (active maternal smoking and environmental smoke) is a key contributor to intrauterine (within the womb) growth retardation

Fetal alcohol spectrum disorders (FASD) are characterized by a number of physical abnormalities and learning problems. Notice the wide-set eyes, flat cheekbones, and thin upper lip in this child with FASD.

How Would You...?

As a social worker, how would you counsel a woman who continues to drink alcohol in the early weeks of pregnancy because she believes she can't harm the baby until it has developed further?

fetal alcohol spectrum disorders (FASD) A cluster of abnormalities and problems that appears in the offspring of mothers who drink alcohol heavily during pregnancy.

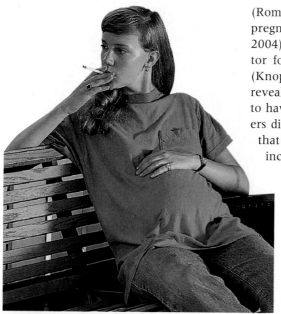

What are some links between expectant mothers' cigarette smoking and outcomes for their offspring?

(Romo, Carceller, & Tobajas, 2009). One study also linked heavy smoking during pregnancy to nicotine withdrawal symptoms in newborns (Godding & others, 2004). Maternal smoking during pregnancy also has been identified as a risk factor for the development of attention deficit hyperactivity disorder in offspring (Knopik, 2009; Pinkhardt & others, 2009). For example, a recent study also revealed that children whose mothers smoked during pregnancy were more likely to have a higher level of inattention and hyperactivity than children whose mothers did not smoke in pregnancy (Obel & others, 2009). Other research has found that prenatal exposure to cigarette smoking during pregnancy is related to an increased incidence of attention deficit hyperactivity disorder at 5 to 16 years of age (Thapar & others, 2003). A recent research review also indicated that environmental tobacco smoke was linked to an increased risk of low birth weight in offspring (Leonardi-Bee & others, 2008).

Intervention programs designed to help pregnant women stop smoking can reduce some of smoking's negative effects, especially by raising birth weights (Barron & others, 2007). A recent study revealed that women who quit smoking during pregnancy had offspring with higher birth weights than their counterparts who continued smoking (Jaddoe & others, 2008). To read further about the negative outcomes for smoking during pregnancy, see the *Research in Children's Development* interlude.

Research in Children's Development

EXPECTANT MOTHERS' CIGARETTE SMOKING AND CIGARETTE SMOKING BY THEIR ADOLESCENT OFFSPRING

Nicotine and other substances in cigarette smoke cross the placental barrier and pass from the expectant mother to the fetus, stimulating the fetal brain as early as the first trimester of pregnancy (Hellstrom-Lindahl & Nordberg, 2002). Researchers are exploring the possibility that this prenatal exposure of the brain to cigarette smoke may predispose individuals to be more vulnerable to addiction in adolescence.

One study examined whether expectant mothers' cigarette smoking and marijuana use were linked to an increased risk for substance use in adolescence by their offspring (Porath & Fried, 2005). One hundred fifty-two 16- to 21-year-olds were asked to complete a drug history questionnaire that included their past and current cigarette smoking. A urine sample was also obtained from the participants and analyzed for the presence of drugs. The adolescent participants' mothers had been asked about the extent of their cigarette smoking during their pregnancy several decades earlier as part of the Ottawa Prenatal Prospective Study.

The results indicated that adolescent offspring of mothers who reported that they smoked cigarettes during pregnancy were more than twice as likely to have initiated smoking during adolescence than their counterparts whose mothers reported not smoking during their pregnancy. These findings indicate that cigarette smoking by expectant mothers is a risk factor for later cigarette smoking by their adolescent offspring. Such results add to the strength of the evidence that supports drug use prevention and cessation among expectant mothers.

Cocaine   Does cocaine use during pregnancy harm the developing embryo and fetus? The most consistent finding is that cocaine exposure during prenatal development is associated with reduced birth weight, length, and head circumference (Smith

& others, 2001). Also, in other studies, prenatal cocaine exposure has been linked to lower arousal, less effective self-regulation, higher excitability, and lower quality of reflexes at 1 month of age (Lester & others, 2002); to impaired motor development in the second year of life (Richardson, Goldschmidt, & Willford, 2008); to slower growth rate through 10 years of age (Richardson, Goldsmith, & Larkby, 2008); to impaired language development and information processing (Beeghly & others, 2006; Lewis & others, 2007), including attention deficits in preschool children (Noland & others, 2005) and elementary school children (Accornero & others, 2007); to learning disabilities at age 7 (Morrow & others, 2006); and to increased likelihood of being in a special education program that involves support services (Levine & others, 2008).

This baby was exposed to cocaine prenatally. *What are some of the possible effects on development of being exposed to cocaine prenatally?*

Some researchers argue that these findings should be interpreted cautiously. Why? Because other factors in the lives of pregnant women who use cocaine (such as poverty, malnutrition, and other substance abuse) often cannot be ruled out as possible contributors to the problems found in their children (Hurt & others, 2005). For example, cocaine users are more likely than nonusers to smoke cigarettes, use marijuana, drink alcohol, and take amphetamines.

Despite these cautions, the weight of research evidence indicates that children born to mothers who use cocaine are likely to have neurological and cognitive deficits (Field, 2007; Mayer & Zhang, 2009; Richardson, Goldschmidt, & Larkby, 2008). Cocaine use by pregnant women is never recommended.

Methamphetamine

Methamphetamine, like cocaine, is a stimulant, speeding up an individual's nervous system. Babies born to mothers who use methamphetamine, or "meth," during pregnancy are at risk for a number of problems, including high infant mortality, low birth weight, and developmental and behavioral problems (Forrester & Merz, 2007). A recent study revealed that meth exposure during prenatal development was linked to decreased arousal, increased stress, and poor movement quality in newborns (Smith & others, 2008).

Meth use during pregnancy is increasing, and some experts conclude that meth use during pregnancy has become a greater problem in the United States than cocaine use (Elliott, 2004). A recent survey revealed that 5 percent of U.S. women used methamphetamine during their pregnancy (Arria & others, 2006).

Marijuana

An increasing number of studies find that marijuana use by pregnant women also has negative outcomes for offspring (Huizink & Mulder, 2006; Williams & Ross, 2007). A research review concluded that marijuana use by pregnant women is related to deficits in memory and information processing in their offspring (Kalant, 2004). For example, in a longitudinal study, prenatal marijuana exposure was related to learning and memory difficulties at age 11 (Richardson & others, 2002). A recent study also revealed that prenatal marijuana exposure was linked to lower intelligence in children (Goldschmidt & others, 2008). Another study revealed that prenatal marijuana exposure was related to depressive symptoms at 10 years of age (Gray & others, 2005). Further, a recent study indicated that prenatal exposure to marijuana was linked to marijuana use at 14 years of age (Day, Goldschmidt, & Thomas, 2006). In sum, marijuana use is not recommended for pregnant women.

Heroin

It is well documented that infants whose mothers are addicted to heroin show several behavioral difficulties at birth (Steinhausen, Blattmann, & Pfund, 2007). The difficulties include withdrawal symptoms, such as tremors, irritability, abnormal crying, disturbed sleep, and impaired motor control. Many still show behavioral problems at their first birthday, and attention deficits may appear later in development. The most common treatment for heroin addiction, methadone, is associated with very severe withdrawal symptoms in newborns (Binder & Vavrinkova, 2008). A recent study revealed that when compared to late methadone treatment

How Would You...?

As a social worker, how would you advise women in their childbearing years who frequently abuse drugs and other psychoactive substances?

(less than six months prior to birth), continuous methadone treatment during pregnancy was linked to improved neonatal outcomes (Burns & others, 2007).

Incompatible Blood Types

Incompatibility between the mother's and father's blood type poses another risk to prenatal development. Blood types are created by differences in the surface structure of red blood cells. One type of difference in the surface of red blood cells creates the familiar blood groups—A, B, O, and AB. A second difference creates what is called Rh-positive and Rh-negative blood. If a surface marker, called the *Rh factor*, is present in an individual's red blood cells, the person is said to be Rh-positive; if the Rh marker is not present, the person is said to be Rh-negative. If a pregnant woman is Rh-negative and her partner is Rh-positive, the fetus may be Rh-positive. If the fetus' blood is Rh-positive and the mother's is Rh-negative, the mother's immune system may produce antibodies that will attack the fetus. Such an assault can result in any number of problems, including miscarriage or stillbirth, anemia, jaundice, heart defects, brain damage, or death soon after birth (Moise, 2005).

Generally, the first Rh-positive baby of an Rh-negative mother is not at risk, but with each subsequent pregnancy the risk increases. A vaccine (RhoGAM) may be given to the mother within three days of the first child's birth to prevent her body from making antibodies that will attack any future Rh-positive fetuses in subsequent pregnancies. Also, babies affected by Rh incompatibility can be given blood transfusions before or right after birth (Flegal, 2007).

Environmental Hazards

Many aspects of our modern industrial world can endanger the embryo or fetus (O'Connor & Roy, 2008). Some specific hazards to the embryo or fetus that are worth a closer look include radiation, toxic wastes, and other chemical pollutants (Orecchia, Lucignani, & Tosi, 2008; Raabe & Muller, 2008).

Radiation can cause a gene mutation (an abrupt, permanent change in DNA). Chromosomal abnormalities are elevated among the offspring of fathers exposed to high levels of radiation in their occupations (Schrag & Dixon, 1985). X-ray radiation also can affect the developing embryo or fetus, especially in the first several weeks after conception, when women do not yet know they are pregnant (Urbano & Tait, 2004). Possible effects include microencephaly (an abnormally small brain), mental retardation, and leukemia. Women and their physicians should weigh the risk of an X-ray when an actual or potential pregnancy is involved (Menias & others, 2007). However, a routine diagnostic X-ray of a body area other than the abdomen, with the women's abdomen protected by a lead apron, is generally considered safe (Brent, 2009).

Environmental pollutants and toxic wastes are also sources of danger to unborn children. Among the dangerous pollutants are carbon monoxide, mercury, and lead, as well as certain fertilizers and pesticides. Exposure to lead can come from lead-based paint that flakes off the walls of a home or from leaded gasoline emitted by cars on a nearby busy highway. Early exposure to lead can affect children's mental development (Canfield & Jusko, 2008). For example, a recent study revealed that a moderately high maternal lead level in the first trimester of pregnancy was linked to lower scores on an index of mental development in infancy (Hu & others, 2007).

Maternal Diseases

Maternal diseases and infections can produce defects in offspring by crossing the placental barrier, or they can cause damage during birth. Rubella (German measles) is one disease that can cause prenatal defects. The greatest damage occurs if a mother contracts rubella in the third or fourth week of pregnancy, although infection during

An explosion at the Chernobyl nuclear power plant in the Ukraine produced radioactive contamination that spread to surrounding areas. Thousands of infants were born with health problems and deformities as a result of the nuclear contamination, including this boy whose arm did not form. *Other than radioactive contamination, what are some types of environmental hazards to prenatal development?*

the second month is also damaging (Kobayashi & others, 2005). A rubella outbreak in 1964–1965 resulted in 30,000 prenatal and neonatal (newborn) deaths, and more than 20,000 affected infants were born with malformations, including mental retardation, blindness, deafness, and heart problems. Elaborate preventive efforts ensure that rubella will never again have such disastrous effects. A vaccine that prevents German measles is now routinely administered to children, and women who plan to have children should have a blood test before they become pregnant to determine if they are immune to the disease (Dontigny & others, 2008).

Syphilis (a sexually transmitted infection) is more damaging later in prenatal development—four months or more after conception. Rather than affecting organogenesis, as rubella does, syphilis damages organs after they have formed. Damage includes eye lesions, which can cause blindness, and skin lesions. When syphilis is present at birth, problems can develop in the central nervous system and gastrointestinal tract (Johnson, Erbelding, & Ghanem, 2007). Most states require that pregnant women be given a blood test to detect the presence of syphilis.

Another infection that has received widespread attention recently is genital herpes. Newborns contract this virus when they are delivered through the birth canal of a mother with genital herpes (Hollier & Wendel, 2008; Shapiro-Mendoza & others, 2008). About one-third of babies delivered through an infected birth canal die; another one-fourth become brain damaged. If an active case of genital herpes is detected in a pregnant woman close to her delivery date, a cesarean section can be performed (in which the infant is delivered through an incision in the mother's abdomen) to keep the virus from infecting the newborn (Sellner & others, 2009).

AIDS is a sexually transmitted infection that is caused by the human immunodeficiency virus (HIV), which destroys the body's immune system. A mother can infect her offspring with HIV/AIDS in three ways: (1) during gestation across the placenta, (2) during delivery through contact with maternal blood or fluids, and (3) postpartum (after birth) through breast feeding. The transmission of AIDS through breast feeding is especially a problem in many developing countries (Lunney & others, 2008; UNICEF, 2009). Babies born to HIV-infected mothers can be (1) infected and symptomatic (show HIV symptoms), (2) infected but asymptomatic (not show HIV symptoms), or (3) not infected at all. An infant who is infected and asymptomatic may still develop HIV symptoms up until 15 months of age.

In the early 1990s, before preventive treatments were available, 1,000 to 2,000 infants were born with HIV infection each year in the United States. Since then, transmission of HIV from mothers to fetuses has been reduced dramatically (Anderson & Cu-Uvin, 2009; Goetghebuer & others, 2009). Only about one-third as many cases of newborns with HIV appear today as in the early 1990s. This decline is due to the increase in counseling and voluntary testing of pregnant women for HIV and to the use of zidovudine (AZT) by infected women during pregnancy and by the infant after birth. In many poor countries, however, treatment with AZT is limited, and HIV infection of infants remains a major problem (Guidozzi & Black, 2009).

The more widespread disease of diabetes, characterized by high levels of sugar in the blood, also affects offspring (Oostdam & others, 2009; Most & others, 2009; Simeoni & Barker, 2009). A recent large-scale study revealed that from 1999 to 2005 twice as many women and five times as many adolescents giving birth had diabetes (Lawrence & others, 2008). The increase in diabetes likely was fueled by the dramatic increase in being overweight or obese.

A research review indicated that when newborns have physical defects they are more likely to have diabetic mothers (Eriksson, 2009). Women who have gestational diabetes also may deliver very large infants (weighing 10 pounds or more), and the infants themselves are at risk for diabetes (Gluck & others, 2009). And a recent study revealed that children who were exposed to gestational diabetes (during prenatal development because their mothers were diabetic) had a higher level of adiposity (body fat content) at 3 years of age, and the adiposity was linked to higher systolic blood pressure in the children (Wright & others, 2009).

Other Parental Factors

So far we have discussed a number of drugs, environmental hazards, maternal diseases, and incompatible blood types that can harm the embryo or fetus. Here we explore other characteristics of the mother and father that can affect prenatal and child development, including nutrition, age, and emotional states and stress.

Maternal Diet and Nutrition   A developing embryo or fetus depends completely on its mother for nutrition, which comes from the mother's blood. The nutritional status of the embryo or fetus is determined by the mother's total caloric intake, and her intake of proteins, vitamins, and minerals. Children born to malnourished mothers are more likely than other children to be malformed.

Because the fetus depends entirely on its mother for nutrition, it is important for the pregnant woman to have good nutritional habits. In Kenya, this government clinic provides pregnant women with information about how their diet can influence the health of their fetus and offspring. *What might the information about diet be like?*

Being overweight before and during pregnancy can also put the embryo or fetus at risk, and an increasing number of pregnant women in the United States are overweight (Chu & others, 2009; Torloni & others, 2009). Researchers have found that obese women have a significant risk of fetal death (Nohr & others, 2005). Recent studies indicate that prepregnancy maternal obesity doubles the risk of stillbirth and neonatal death, and is linked with defects in the central nervous system of offspring (Anderson & others, 2005; Frederick & others, 2008). Further, a recent analysis proposed that overnutrition in fetal life (due to overeating on the part of the pregnant woman) results in a series of neuroendocrine changes that in turn program the development of fat cells and appetite regulation system (McMillen & others, 2008). In this analysis, it was predicted that such early fetal programming is likely linked to being overweight in childhood and adolescence.

One aspect of maternal nutrition that is important for normal prenatal development is folic acid, a B-complex vitamin (Goh & Koren, 2008). As we indicated earlier in the chapter, a lack of folic acid is linked with neural tube defects in offspring, such as spina bifida (Levene & Chervenak, 2009). A recent study of more than 34,000 pregnant women revealed that taking folic acid either alone or as part of a multivitamin for at least one year prior to conceiving was linked with a 70 percent lower risk of delivering from 20 to 28 weeks and a 50 percent lower risk of delivering between 28 to 32 weeks (Bukowski & others, 2008). Another study revealed that maternal use of folic acid and iron during the first month of pregnancy was associated with a lower risk of Down syndrome in offspring, although more studies are needed to confirm this connection (Czeizel & Puho, 2005). The U.S. Public Health Service recommends that pregnant women consume a minimum of 400 micrograms of folic acid per day (about twice the amount the average woman gets in one day). Orange juice and spinach are examples of foods rich in folic acid.

Eating fish is often recommended as part of a healthy diet, but pollution has made many fish a risky choice for pregnant women. Some fish contain high levels of mercury, which is released into the air both naturally and by industrial pollution. When mercury falls into the water, it can become toxic and accumulate in large fish, such as shark, swordfish, king mackerel, and some species of large tuna. Mercury is easily transferred across the placenta, and the embryo's developing brain and nervous system are highly sensitive to the metal. Researchers have found that prenatal mercury exposure is linked to adverse outcomes, including miscarriage, preterm birth, and lower intelligence (Axelrad & others, 2007; Xue & others, 2007). The U.S. Food and Drug Administration (2004) gave the following recommendations for women of childbearing age and young children: Don't eat shark, swordfish, king mackerel, or tilefish; eat up to 12 ounces (two average meals) a week of fish and shellfish that are lower in mercury, such as shrimp, canned light tuna, salmon, pollock, and catfish.

PCB-polluted fish also pose a risk to prenatal development. PCBs (polychlorinated biphenyls) are chemicals that were used in manufacturing until they were banned in the 1970s in the United States, but they are still present in landfills, sediments, and wildlife. One study that kept track of the extent to which pregnant women ate PCB-polluted fish from Lake Michigan examined their children as newborns, young children, and at 11 years of age (Jacobson & others, 1984; Jacobson & Jacobson, 2002, 2003). The women who had eaten more PCB-polluted fish were more likely to have smaller, preterm infants who were more apt to react slowly to stimuli. As preschool children, greater prenatal exposure to PCBs was linked with less effective short-term memory, and at age 11 with lower verbal intelligence and reading comprehension.

Maternal Age   When possible harmful effects on the fetus and infant are considered, two maternal ages are of special interest: adolescence and 35 and older (Malizia, Hacker, & Penzias, 2009). One recent study revealed that the rate of stillbirth was elevated for adolescent girls and women 35 years and older (Bateman & Simpson, 2006).

These adolescent mothers are participating in a program that is designed to improve their parenting skills. *What are some of the risks for infants born to adolescent mothers?*

The mortality rate of infants born to adolescent mothers is double that of infants born to mothers in their twenties. Although this high rate probably reflects the immaturity of the mother's reproductive system, poor nutrition, lack of prenatal care, and low socioeconomic status may also play a role (Smithbattle, 2007). Adequate prenatal care decreases the probability that a child born to an adolescent girl will have physical problems. However, adolescents are the least likely of women in all age groups to obtain prenatal assistance from clinics and health services.

Maternal age is also linked to the risk that a child will have Down syndrome (Allen & others, 2009). As discussed in Chapter 2, "Biological Beginnings," an individual with *Down syndrome* has distinctive facial characteristics, short limbs, and retardation of motor and mental abilities. Advanced maternal age confers a much greater risk of having a baby with Down syndrome. When the mother reaches 40 years of age, the probability is slightly more than 1 in 100 that a baby born to her will have Down syndrome, and by age 50 it is almost 1 in 10.

When mothers are 35 years and older, risks also increase for low birth weight, for preterm delivery, and for fetal death (Fretts, Zera, & Heffner, 2008; Mbugua Gitau, & others, 2009). One study found that low birth weight delivery increased 11 percent and preterm delivery increased 14 percent in women 35 years and older (Tough & others, 2002). In another study, fetal death was low for women 30 to 34 years of age but increased progressively for women 35 to 44 years of age (Canterino & others, 2004).

We still have much to learn about the role of the mother's age in pregnancy and childbirth (Montan, 2007). As women remain active, exercise regularly, and are careful about their nutrition, their reproductive systems may remain healthier at older ages than was thought possible in the past. For example, in one study, two-thirds of the pregnancies of women 45 years and older in Australia were free of complications (Callaway, Lust, & McIntrye, 2005).

How Would You...?
As a health-care professional, how would you advise a couple in their late thirties and early forties who are considering having a baby?

Emotional States and Stress   When a pregnant woman experiences intense fears, anxieties, and other emotions or negative mood states, physiological changes occur that may affect her fetus (Entringer & others, 2009). Maternal stress may increase the level of the stress hormone cortisol early in pregnancy (Latendresse, 2009). Elevated levels of cortisol in the fetus have been linked to premature delivery

How do pregnant women's emotional states and stress affect prenatal development and birth?

How Would You...?
As a health-care professional, how would you advise an expectant mother who is experiencing extreme psychological stress?

In one study, in China, the longer fathers smoked the greater the risk that their children would develop cancer (Ji & others, 1997). *What are some other paternal factors that can influence the development of the fetus and the child?*

in infants (Field, 2007). A recent study also revealed that a decline in stress during pregnancy was linked to a lower incidence of preterm birth (Glynn & others, 2008). A mother's stress may also influence the fetus indirectly by increasing the likelihood that the mother will engage in unhealthy behaviors, such as taking drugs and engaging in poor prenatal care.

High maternal anxiety and stress during pregnancy can have long-term consequences for the offspring (Davis & others, 2007). A recent research review indicated that pregnant women with high levels of stress are at increased risk for having a child with emotional or cognitive problems, attention deficit hyperactivity disorder (ADHD), and language delay (Talge & others, 2007).

Might maternal depression also have an adverse effect on prenatal development and birth? A recent study revealed maternal depression was linked to preterm birth and slower prenatal growth rates (Diego & others, 2009). In this study, mothers who were depressed had elevated cortisol levels, which likely contributed to the negative outcomes for the fetus and newborn. Another recent study found that depressed African American pregnant women had elevated levels of anxiety, anger, daily hassles, sleep disturbance, and cortisol (Field & others, 2009). This combination of negative maternal factors may contribute to the higher rate of preterm and low birth weight African American newborns.

Positive emotional states also appear to make a difference to the fetus. Pregnant women who are optimistic thinkers have less adverse outcomes than pregnant women who are pessimistic thinkers (Loebel & Yali, 1999). Optimists are more likely to believe that they have control over the outcomes of their pregnancies.

Paternal Factors   So far, we have discussed how characteristics of the mother—such as drug use, disease, diet and nutrition, age, and emotional states—can influence prenatal development and the development of the child. Might there also be some paternal risk factors? Indeed, there are several. Men's exposure to lead, radiation, certain pesticides, and petrochemicals may cause abnormalities in sperm that lead to miscarriage or diseases, such as childhood cancer (Cordier, 2008; Fear & others, 2007; Monge & others, 2007). When fathers have a diet low in vitamin C, their offspring have a higher risk of birth defects and cancer (Fraga & others, 1991). Also, it has been speculated that, when fathers take cocaine, it may attach itself to sperm and cause birth defects, but the evidence for this effect is not yet strong. In one study, long-term use of cocaine by men was related to low sperm count, low motility, and a higher number of abnormally formed sperm (Bracken & others, 1990). Cocaine-related infertility appears to be reversible if users stop taking the drug for at least one year.

The father's smoking during the mother's pregnancy also can cause problems for the offspring. In one investigation, the newborns of fathers who smoked around their wives during the pregnancy were 4 ounces lighter at birth for each pack of cigarettes smoked per day than were the newborns whose fathers did not smoke during their wives' pregnancy (Rubin & others, 1986). In another study, in China, the longer the fathers smoked, the stronger the risk that their children would develop cancer (Ji & others, 1997). In yet another study, heavy paternal smoking was associated with the risk of early pregnancy loss (Venners & others, 2004). All of these negative effects may be related to secondhand smoke.

The father's age also makes a difference (Maconochie & others, 2007; Yang & others, 2007). About 5 percent of children with Down syndrome have older fathers. The offspring of older fathers also face increased risk for other birth defects, including dwarfism and Marfan syndrome, which involves head and limb deformities.

There are also risks to offspring when both the mother and father are older (Dunson, Baird, & Colombo, 2004). In one study, the risk of an adverse pregnancy outcome, such as miscarriage, rose considerably when the woman was 35 years or older and the man was 40 years of age or older (de la Rocheborchard & Thonneau, 2002).

Much of our discussion so far in this chapter has focused on what can go wrong with prenatal development. Prospective parents should take steps to avoid the vulnerabilities to fetal development that we have described. But it is important to keep in mind that most of the time, prenatal development does not go awry and development occurs along the positive path that we described at the beginning of the chapter.

Review and Reflect: Learning Goal 3

 3 **Describe potential hazards during prenatal development**

REVIEW

- What is teratology? What are some general principles regarding teratogens?
- Which prescription and nonprescription drugs can influence prenatal development?
- How do different psychoactive drugs affect prenatal development?
- How do incompatible blood types influence prenatal development?
- What are some environmental hazards that can influence prenatal development?
- Which maternal diseases can affect prenatal development?
- What other parental factors can affect prenatal development?

REFLECT

- What can be done to convince women who are pregnant not to smoke or drink? Consider the role of health-care providers, the role of insurance companies, and specific programs targeted at women who are pregnant.

Reach Your Learning Goals

Prenatal Development

1 WHAT IS THE COURSE OF PRENATAL DEVELOPMENT? DISCUSS THE THREE PERIODS OF PRENATAL DEVELOPMENT

The Germinal Period

- The germinal period is from conception until about two weeks later. It includes the creation of a fertilized egg, which is called a zygote, and cell division. The period ends when the zygote attaches to the uterine wall in a process called implantation.

The Embryonic Period

- The embryonic period lasts from about two to eight weeks after conception. The embryo differentiates into three layers of cells (endoderm, mesoderm, and ectoderm), life-support systems develop, and organ systems form (organogenesis).

The Fetal Period

- The fetal period lasts from about two months after conception until nine months, or when the infant is born. Growth and development continue their dramatic course, and organ systems mature to the point at which life can be sustained outside the womb.

The Brain

- The growth of the brain during prenatal development is nothing short of remarkable. By the time babies are born, they have approximately 100 billion neurons, or nerve cells. Neurogenesis is the term that means the formation of new neurons. The nervous system begins with the formation of a neural tube at 18 to 24 days after conception. Proliferation and neuronal migration are two processes that characterize brain development in the prenatal period. The basic architecture of the brain is formed in the first two trimesters of prenatal development.

2 WHAT ARE SOME IMPORTANT STRATEGIES THAT ENHANCE THE EXPECTANT MOTHER'S HEALTH AND PRENATAL CARE? SUMMARIZE HOW NUTRITION, EXERCISE, AND PRENATAL CARE ARE IMPORTANT ASPECTS OF THE EXPECTANT MOTHER'S PREGNANCY

The Expectant Mother's Nutrition, Weight Gain, and Exercise

- The best assurance of adequate caloric intake during pregnancy is a satisfactory weight gain over time. Maternal weight gain that averages 25 to 35 pounds is often linked with the best reproductive outcomes. The RDA for all nutrients increases during pregnancy, and the need for such nutrients as vitamin D, folacin, and iron increases by more than 50 percent. If the expectant mother's health allows, exercise can benefit her well-being during pregnancy and may reduce the risk of having a preterm birth. How much and what type of exercise depends to some extent on the course of pregnancy, the expectant mother's fitness, and her customary activity level.

Prenatal Care

- Prenatal care varies extensively but usually involves medical care services with a defined schedule of visits and often includes educational, social, and nutritional services. Much needs to be done to improve prenatal care in the United States, especially for low-income families.

3 WHAT ARE SOME POTENTIAL HAZARDS TO PRENATAL DEVELOPMENT? DESCRIBE POTENTIAL HAZARDS DURING PRENATAL DEVELOPMENT

Some General Principles

- Teratology is the field that investigates the causes of birth defects. Any agent that can potentially cause birth defects is called a teratogen. The time of exposure, dose, and genetic susceptibility influence the severity of the damage to an unborn child and the type of defect that occurs.

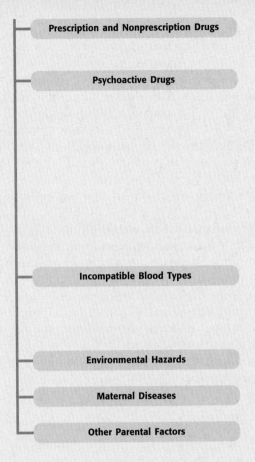

Prescription and Nonprescription Drugs

Psychoactive Drugs

Incompatible Blood Types

Environmental Hazards

Maternal Diseases

Other Parental Factors

- Prescription drugs that can be harmful include antibiotics, some antidepressants, and certain hormones. Nonprescription drugs that can be harmful include diet pills and aspirin.

- Legal psychoactive drugs that are potentially harmful to prenatal development include alcohol, nicotine, and caffeine. Fetal alcohol spectrum disorders (FASD) consist of a cluster of abnormalities that appear in offspring of mothers who drink heavily during pregnancy. Even when pregnant women drink moderately, negative effects on their offspring have been found. Cigarette smoking by pregnant women can have serious adverse effects on prenatal and child development (such as low birth weight and SIDS). Illegal psychoactive drugs that are potentially harmful to offspring include methamphetamine, which can produce high infant mortality, low birth weight, and developmental problems; marijuana, which can result in a child's impaired information processing; cocaine, which is associated with reduced birth weight, length, and head circumference; and heroin, which produces behaviorial problems at birth and may result in attention deficits later in development.

- Incompatibility of the mother's and the father's blood types can also be harmful to the fetus. A woman is at risk when she has a negative Rh factor and her partner has a positive Rh factor. If the fetus is Rh-positive, and the mother is Rh-negative, the mother's immune system may attack the fetus, resulting in problems such as miscarriage or brain damage.

- Environmental hazards include radiation, environmental pollutants, and toxic wastes.

- Syphilis, rubella (German measles), genital herpes, and AIDS are infectious diseases that can harm the fetus.

- Other parental factors include maternal diet and nutrition, age, emotional states and stress, and paternal factors. A developing fetus depends entirely on its mother for nutrition. One nutrient that is especially important very early in development is folic acid. A potential hazard to prenatal development occurs when the mother consumes fish with a high mercury content. Maternal age can negatively affect the offspring's development if the mother is an adolescent or over 35. High stress in the mother is linked with less than optimal prenatal and birth outcomes. Paternal factors that can adversely affect prenatal development include exposure to lead, radiation, certain pesticides, and petrochemicals, as well as smoking.

KEY TERMS

germinal period 89
blastocyst 89
trophoblast 89
embryonic period 89
endoderm 90

ectoderm 90
mesoderm 90
amnion 90
umbilical cord 90
placenta 90

organogenesis 91
fetal period 91
neuron 92
neurogenesis 93
teratogen 101

fetal alcohol spectrum
disorders (FASD) 103

KEY PEOPLE

David Olds 98

MAKING A DIFFERENCE

Maximizing Positive Prenatal Outcomes

What are some good strategies during pregnancy that are likely to maximize positive outcomes for prenatal development?

- *Eat nutritiously and monitor weight gain.* The recommended daily allowances for all nutrients increase during pregnancy. The pregnant woman should eat three balanced meals a day and nutritious snacks between meals if desired. Weight gains that average 25 to 35 pounds are associated with the best reproductive outcomes.

- *Engage in safe exercise.* How much and what type of exercise is best during pregnancy depends to some degree on the course of the pregnancy, the expectant mother's fitness, and her customary activity level. Normal participation in exercise can continue throughout an uncomplicated pregnancy. It is important to remember not to overdo exercise. Exercising for shorter intervals and decreasing the intensity of exercise as pregnancy proceeds are good strategies. Pregnant women should always consult a physician before starting an exercise program.

- *Don't drink alcohol or take other potentially harmful drugs.* An important strategy for pregnancy is to totally abstain from alcohol and other drugs, such as nicotine and cocaine. In this chapter, we considered the harmful effects that these drugs

can have on the developing fetus. Fathers also need to be aware of potentially harmful effects they can have on prenatal development.

- *Have a support system of family and friends.* The pregnant woman benefits from a support system of family members and friends. A positive relationship with a spouse helps keep stress levels down, as does a close relationship with one or more friends.

- *Reduce stress and stay calm.* Try to maintain an even, calm emotional state during pregnancy. High stress levels can harm the fetus. Pregnant women who are feeling a lot of anxiety can reduce their anxiety through a relaxation or stress management program.

- *Stay away from environmental hazards.* We saw in this chapter that some environmental hazards, such as pollutants and toxic wastes, can harm prenatal development. Be aware of these hazards and stay away from them.

- *Get excellent prenatal care.* The quality of prenatal care varies extensively. The education the mother receives about pregnancy, labor and delivery, and care of the newborn can be valuable, especially for first-time mothers.

- *Read a good book for expectant mothers.* An excellent one is *What to Expect When You're Expecting*, which is described here.

RESOURCES FOR IMPROVING CHILDREN'S LIVES

March of Dimes
www.marchofdimes.com

A major emphasis on the part of the March of Dimes is to promote healthy pregnancy. Their Web site includes extensive information about many aspects of pregnancy and prenatal development.

National Center for Education in Maternal and Child Health (NCEMCH)
www.ncemch.org

NCEMCH answers questions about pregnancy and childbirth, high-risk infants, and maternal and child health programs. It also publishes a free guide, *Maternal and Child Health Publications*.

Pregnancy.org
www.pregnancy.org

This extensive Web site provides up-to-date information about pregnancy and prenatal development.

What to Expect When You're Expecting
by Heidi Murkoff, Arlene Eisenberg, and Sandee Hathaway
(4th ed., 2008)
New York: Workman

This highly popular book on pregnancy and prenatal development provides detailed month-by-month descriptions of what pregnancy and prenatal growth are like.

Prenatal Care Tips

Pregnant women can call this federal government toll-free number for prenatal care advice and referral to local health-care providers: 800–311–2229.

E-LEARNING TOOLS

Connect to **www.mhhe.com/santrockc11e** to research the answers and complete these exercises. In addition, you'll find a number of other resources and valuable study tools for Chapter 3, "Prenatal Development," on this Web site.

Taking It to the Net

1. Mara's best friend, Aida, suffered a miscarriage after several years of trying to become pregnant. Before Mara goes to visit Aida, how can she find out more about the psychological

trauma that Aida may be experiencing as a result of the miscarriage?

2. Mai, age 28, has just learned that she is pregnant. She is proud of the fact that she weighs the same as she did in high school. She is terrified of getting fat and not being able to lose the weight after the baby is born. How can Mai eat properly to keep her and her baby healthy while minimizing unnecessary and unhealthy weight gain?

3. Sven and Diana have made an application with a foreign adoption agency to adopt a child from a former Soviet Union state. The agency told them the boy they have chosen may be suffering from a mild version of fetal alcohol spectrum disorders. How can Sven and Diana find out more about FASD before their application is approved?

Health and Well-Being, Parenting, and Education

Build your decision-making skills by trying your hand at the health and well-being, parenting, and education exercises.

Video Clips

The Online Learning Center includes the following videos for this chapter:

- *Childbirth Education Alternatives—1936*
  A childbirth educator describes the types of childbirth classes that are available to expectant parents and the benefits of childbirth education.

- *Teen Pregnancy and Families—553*
  Dr. Gunn describes the risk factors that are related to teen pregnancy. All involve the context (for example, poverty, ineffective schools) in which these young girls are raised.

4

> *We must respect this instant of birth, this fragile moment. The baby is between two worlds, on a threshold.*
>
> —FREDERICK LEBOYER
> *French Obstetrician, 20th Century*

LEARNING GOALS

- ◆ Discuss the stages, decisions involved, and transitions in birth

- ◆ Describe three measures of neonatal health and responsiveness

- ◆ Characterize the development of low birth weight and preterm infants

- ◆ Explain the physical and psychological aspects of the postpartum period

BIRTH

CHAPTER OUTLINE

Images of Children's Development
Tanner Roberts' Birth: A Fantastic Voyage

Tanner Roberts was born in a suite at St. Joseph's Medical Center in Burbank, California (Warrick, 1992, pp. E1, E11, E12). Let's examine what took place in the hours leading up to his birth. It is day 266 of his mother Cindy's pregnancy. She is in the frozen-food aisle of a convenience store and feels a sharp pain, starting in the small of her back and reaching around her middle, which causes her to gasp. For weeks, painless Braxton Hicks spasms (named for the gynecologist who discovered them) have been flexing her uterine muscles. But these practice contractions were not nearly as intense and painful as the one she just experienced. After six hours of irregular spasms, her uterus settles into a more predictable rhythm.

At 3 a.m., Cindy and her husband Tom are wide awake. They time Cindy's contractions with a stopwatch. The contractions are now only six minutes apart. It's time to call the hospital. A short time later, Tom and Cindy arrive at the hospital's labor-delivery suite. A nurse puts a webbed belt and fetal monitor around Cindy's middle to measure her labor. The monitor picks up the fetal heart rate. With each contraction of the uterine wall, Tanner's heartbeat jumps from its resting state of about 140 beats to 160 to 170 beats per minute. When the cervix is dilated to more than 4 centimeters, or almost half open, Cindy receives her first medication. As Demerol begins to drip into her veins, the pain of her contractions is less intense. Tanner's heart rate dips to 130 and then 120.

Contractions are now coming every three to four minutes, each one lasting about 25 seconds. The Demerol does not completely obliterate Cindy's pain. She hugs her husband as the nurse urges her to "relax those muscles. Breathe deep. Relax. You're almost there."

Each contraction briefly cuts off Tanner's source of oxygen, his mother's blood. However, in the minutes of rest between contractions, Cindy's deep breathing helps rush fresh blood to the baby's heart and brain.

At 8 a.m., Cindy's cervix is almost completely dilated and the obstetrician arrives. Using a tool made for the purpose, he reaches into the birth canal and tears the membranes of the amniotic sac, and about half a liter of clear fluid flows out. Contractions are now coming every two minutes, and each one is lasting a full minute.

By 9 a.m., the labor suite has been transformed into a delivery room. Tanner's body is compressed by his mother's contractions and pushes. As he nears his entrance into the world, the compressions help press the fluid from his lungs in preparation for his first breath. Squeezed tightly in the birth canal, the top of Tanner's head emerges. His face is puffy and scrunched. Although fiercely squinting because of the sudden light, Tanner's eyes are open. Tiny bubbles of clear mucus are on his lips. Before any more of his body emerges, the nurse cradles Tanner's head and suctions his nose and mouth. Tanner takes his first breath, a large gasp followed by whimpering, and then a loud cry. Tanner's body is wet but only slightly bloody as the doctor lifts him onto his mother's abdomen. The umbilical cord, still connecting Tanner with his mother, slows and stops pulsating. The obstetrician cuts it, severing Tanner's connection to his mother's womb. Now Tanner's blood flows not to his mother's body for nourishment— but to his own lungs, intestines, and other organs.

PREVIEW

As the story of Tanner Roberts' birth reveals, many changes take place during the birth of a baby. In this chapter, we further explore what happens during the birth process, measures of neonatal health and responsiveness, the development of preterm and low birth weight infants, and characteristics of the postpartum period.

1 WHAT HAPPENS DURING THE BIRTH PROCESS?

| Stages of the Birth Process | Childbirth Setting and Attendants | Methods of Childbirth | The Transition from Fetus to Newborn |

Nature writes the basic script for how birth occurs, but parents make important choices about conditions surrounding birth. We look first at the sequence of physical steps when a child is born.

Stages of the Birth Process

The birth process occurs in three stages. The first stage is the longest of the three stages. Uterine contractions are 15 to 20 minutes apart at the beginning and last up to a minute. These contractions cause the woman's cervix to stretch and open. As the first stage progresses, the contractions come closer together, appearing every two to five minutes. Their intensity increases. By the end of the first birth stage, contractions dilate the cervix to an opening of about 4 inches, so that the baby can move from the uterus to the birth canal. For a woman having her first child, the first stage lasts an average of 12 to 14 hours; for subsequent children, this stage may be shorter.

The second birth stage begins when the baby's head starts to move through the cervix and the birth canal. It terminates when the baby completely emerges from the mother's body. With each contraction, the mother bears down hard to push the baby out of her body. By the time the baby's head is out of the mother's body, the contractions come almost every minute and last for about a minute. This stage typically lasts approximately 45 minutes to an hour.

Afterbirth is the third stage, at which time the placenta, umbilical cord, and other membranes are detached and expelled. This final stage is the shortest of the three birth stages, lasting only minutes (see Figure 4.1).

Childbirth Setting and Attendants

In the United States, 99 percent of births take place in hospitals, a figure that has remained constant for several decades (Martin & others, 2005). Some women with

afterbirth The third stage of birth, when the placenta, umbilical cord, and other membranes are detached and expelled.

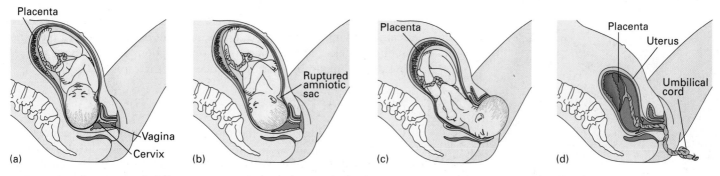

FIGURE 4.1 The Stages of Birth (*a*) First stage: cervix is dilating; (*b*) late first stage (transition stage): cervix is fully dilated, and the amniotic sac has ruptured, releasing amniotic fluid; (*c*) second stage: birth of the infant; (*d*) third stage: delivery of the placenta (afterbirth).

A woman in the African !Kung culture giving birth in a sitting position. Notice the help and support being given by another woman. *What are some cultural variations in childbirth?*

A doula assisting a birth. *What types of support do doulas provide?*

good medical histories and low risk for problems may choose a delivery at home or in a freestanding birth center, which is usually staffed by nurse-midwives. Births at home are far more common in many other countries—for example, in Holland, 35 percent of the babies are born at home. Some critics worry that the U.S. tendency to view birth through a medical lens may lead to unnecessary medical procedures (Hausman, 2005).

Who helps a mother during birth varies across cultures. In U.S. hospitals, it has become the norm for fathers or birth coaches to be with the mother throughout labor and delivery. In the East African Nigoni culture, men are completely excluded from the childbirth process. When a woman is ready to give birth, female relatives move into the woman's hut and the husband leaves, taking his belongings (clothes, tools, weapons, and so on) with him. He is not permitted to return until after the baby is born. In some cultures, childbirth is an open, community affair. For example, in the Pukapukan culture in the Pacific Islands, women give birth in a shelter that is open for villagers to observe.

Midwives Midwifery is the norm throughout most of the world (Fallon, Engel, & Boyle, 2009; Tiran, 2008; Wickham, 2009). In Holland, more than 40 percent of babies are delivered by midwives rather than doctors (Treffers & others, 1990). But in 2003, 91 percent of U.S. births were attended by physicians, and only 8 percent of women who delivered a baby were attended by a *midwife* (Martin & others, 2005). However, the 8 percent figure in 2003 represents a substantial increase from less than 1 percent of U.S. women attended by a midwife in 1975 (Martin & others, 2005). Ninety-five percent of the midwives who delivered babies in the United States in 2003 were certified nurse-midwives. Compared with physicians, certified nurse-midwives generally spend more time with patients during prenatal visits, place more emphasis on patient counseling and education, provide more emotional support, and are more likely to be with the patient one-on-one during the entire labor and delivery process, which may explain the more positive outcomes for babies delivered by certified nurse-midwives (Davis, 2005).

Doulas In many countries, a doula attends a childbearing woman. *Doula* is a Greek word that means "a woman who helps." A **doula** is a caregiver who provides continuous physical, emotional, and educational support for the mother before, during, and after childbirth. Doulas remain with the mother throughout labor, assessing and responding to her needs. Researchers have found positive effects when a doula is present at the birth of a child (Berghella, Baxter, & Chauhan, 2008; McComish & Visger, 2009). In a recent study, low-income pregnant women who were given doula support spent a shorter time in labor and their newborns had a higher health rating at one and five minutes after birth than their low-income counterparts who did not receive doula support (Campbell & others, 2006). Another recent study revealed that doula care was linked to improved childbirth outcomes, such as shorter labor, and a higher rate of breast feeding (Nommsen-Rivers & others, 2009).

In the United States, most doulas work as independent providers hired by the expectant mother. Doulas typically function as part of a "birthing team," serving as an adjunct to the midwife or the hospital's obstetric staff (Dundek, 2006). Managed care organizations are increasingly offering doula support as a part of regular obstetric care.

Methods of Childbirth

U.S. hospitals often allow the mother and her obstetrician a range of options regarding their method of delivery. Key choices involve the use of medication, whether to use any of a number of nonmedicated techniques to reduce pain, and when to resort to a cesarean delivery (Downe, 2008; Moleti, 2009).

Medication   Three basic kinds of drugs are used for labor: analgesics, anesthesia, and oxytocics. **Analgesics** are used to relieve pain. Analgesics include tranquilizers, barbiturates, and narcotics (such as Demerol).

Anesthesia is used in late first-stage labor and during expulsion of the baby to block sensation in an area of the body or to block consciousness. There is a trend toward not using general anesthesia, which blocks consciousness, in normal births because general anesthesia can be transmitted through the placenta to the fetus (Lieberman & others, 2005). An *epidural block* is regional anesthesia that numbs the woman's body from the waist down (Kukulu & Demirok, 2008). Even this drug, thought to be relatively safe, has come under recent criticism because it is associated with fever, extended labor, and increased risk for cesarean delivery (Birnbach & Ranasinghe, 2008).

Oxytocin is a synthetic hormone that is used to stimulate contractions; pitocin is the most widely used oxytocin (Ratcliffe, 2008). The benefits and risks of oxytocin as a part of childbirth continue to be debated (Mendelson, 2009; Wei & others, 2009). One recent large-scale Swedish study revealed that pregnant women who were given oxytocin during childbirth were more likely to have newborns with lower health ratings than pregnant women who were not given oxytocin during childbirth (Oscarsson & others, 2006).

Predicting how a drug will affect an individual woman and her fetus is difficult (Funai, Evans, & Lockwood, 2008; Smith, 2009). A particular drug might have only a minimal effect on one fetus yet have a much stronger effect on another. The drug's dosage also is a factor (Buhimschi & Weiner, 2009; Weiner & Buhimschi, 2009). Stronger doses of tranquilizers and narcotics given to decrease the mother's pain potentially have a more negative effect on the fetus than mild doses. It is important for the mother to assess her level of pain and have a voice in the decision of whether she should receive medication (Young, 2001).

Natural and Prepared Childbirth   For a brief time not long ago, the idea of avoiding all medication during childbirth gained favor in the United States. Instead, many women chose to reduce the pain of childbirth through techniques known as natural childbirth, and prepared childbirth became popular. Today, at least some medication is used in the typical childbirth, but elements of natural childbirth and prepared childbirth remain popular (Hogan & others, 2007; Hotelling, 2009).

Natural childbirth is the method that aims to reduce the mother's pain by decreasing her fear through education about childbirth and by teaching her to use breathing methods and relaxation techniques during delivery (Romano & Lothian, 2008). This approach was developed in 1914 by English obstetrician Grantley Dick-Read. Dick-Read believed that the doctor's relationship with the mother plays an important role in reducing her perception of pain and that the doctor should be present, providing reassurance, during her active labor prior to delivery.

French obstetrician Ferdinand Lamaze developed a method similar to natural childbirth that is known as **prepared childbirth,** or the Lamaze method. It includes a special breathing technique to control pushing in the final stages of labor, as well as more detailed education about anatomy and physiology than Dick-Read's approach provides. The Lamaze method has become very popular in the United States. The pregnant woman's partner usually serves as a coach, who attends childbirth classes with her and helps her with her breathing and relaxation during delivery.

Many other prepared childbirth techniques have been developed (Davidson, London, & Ladewig, 2008). They usually include elements of Dick-Read's natural childbirth or Lamaze's method, plus one or more other components. For instance, the Bradley method emphasizes the father's role as a labor coach (Signore, 2004). Virtually all of the prepared childbirth methods emphasize education, relaxation and breathing exercises, and support.

In sum, proponents of current prepared childbirth methods believe that when information and support are provided, women *know* how to give birth. To read about

doula   A caregiver who provides continuous physical, emotional, and educational support to the mother before, during, and after childbirth.

analgesics   Drugs used to alleviate pain, such as tranquilizers, barbiturates, and narcotics.

anesthesia   Drugs used in late first-stage labor and during expulsion of the baby to block sensation in an area of the body or to block consciousness.

oxytocin   A synthetic hormone that is used to stimulate contractions.

natural childbirth   Method developed in 1914 by English obstetrician Grantley Dick-Read; it attempts to reduce the mother's pain by decreasing her fear through education about childbirth and breathing methods and relaxation techniques during delivery.

prepared childbirth   Method developed by French obstetrician Ferdinand Lamaze; this childbirth strategy is similar to natural childbirth but includes a special breathing technique to control pushing in the final stages of labor and also a more detailed anatomy and physiology course.

Linda Pugh, Perinatal Nurse

Perinatal nurses work with childbearing women to support health and growth during the childbearing experience. Linda Pugh (Ph.D., R.N.C.) is a perinatal nurse on the faculty at the Johns Hopkins University School of Nursing. She is certified as an inpatient obstetric nurse and specializes in the care of women during labor and delivery. Pugh teaches nursing to both undergraduate and graduate students. In addition to educating professional nurses and conducting research, Pugh consults with hospitals and organizations about women's health issues.

Pugh's research interests include nursing interventions with low-income breast feeding women, discovering ways to prevent and ameliorate fatigue during childbearing, and using effective breathing exercises during labor.

Linda Pugh (*right*) with a mother and her newborn.

one nurse whose research focuses on fatigue during childbearing and breathing exercises during labor, see the *Careers in Children's Development* profile. And to read about the increased variety of techniques now being used to reduce stress and control pain during labor, see the *Caring for Children* interlude.

Caring for Children

FROM WATERBIRTH TO MUSIC THERAPY

The effort to reduce stress and control pain during labor has recently led to an increase in the use of some older and some newer nonmedicated techniques (Field, 2007; Golianu & others, 2007; Simkin & Bolding, 2004). These include waterbirth, massage, acupuncture, hypnosis, and music therapy.

Waterbirth

Waterbirth involves giving birth in a tub of warm water. Some women go through labor in the water and get out for delivery, others remain in the water for delivery. The rationale for waterbirth is that the baby has been in an amniotic sac for many months and that delivery in a similar environment is likely to be less stressful for the baby and the mother. Mothers get into the warm water when contractions become closer together and more intense. Getting into the water too soon can cause labor to slow or stop. Reviews of research have indicated mixed results for waterbirths (Cluett & Burns, 2009; Field, 2007; Thoni & Moroder, 2004). In a comparison of almost 6,000 landbirths and more than 3,500 waterbirths, waterbirths resulted in a lower incidence of episiotomies (an incision made to widen the vagina for delivery), fewer perineal lacerations (the perineum is a muscle between the vagina and the rectum), fewer vaginal tears, and a lower rate of newborn complications (Geissbuehler, Stein, & Eberhard, 2004). A recent research review concluded that water immersion during the first stage of labor reduces the use of epidural/spinal analgesia and that waterbirth does not increase adverse effects on the fetus/newborn or mother (Cluett & Burns, 2009). Critics of waterbirth indicate that in some cases drowning and infectious disease may result (Pinnette, Wax, & Wilson, 2004). Waterbirth has been practiced more often in European countries such as Switzerland and Sweden in recent decades than in the United States but is increasingly being included in U.S. birth plans.

Massage

Massage is increasingly used as a procedure prior to and during delivery (Field, 2007; Kimber & others, 2008). Researchers have found that massage can reduce pain and anxiety during labor (Chang, Chen, & Huang, 2006). A recent research review concluded that massage reduces the incidence of perineal trauma (damage to genitalia) following birth (Beckmann & Garrett, 2006).

Acupuncture

Acupuncture, the insertion of very fine needles into specific locations in the body, is used as a standard procedure to reduce the pain of childbirth in China, although it only recently has begun to be used in the United States for this purpose. Recent research studies indicate that acupuncture can have positive effects on labor and delivery. These studies have revealed that acupuncture is linked with less use of pharmacological and invasive methods and higher Apgar scores at five minutes after birth (Borup & others, 2009); improved comfort during delivery and fewer cesarean sections (Citkovitz & others, 2009); and reduction in time to delivery (Gaudet & others, 2008).

Hypnosis

Hypnosis, the induction of a psychological state of altered attention and awareness in which the individual is unusually responsive to suggestions, is also increasingly being used during childbirth (Mottershead, 2006). Some studies have indicated positive effects of hypnosis for reducing pain during childbirth (Barabasaz & Perez, 2007; VandeVusse & others, 2007). However, further research is needed to determine the risks and benefits of this procedure (Simpkin & Bolding, 2004).

Music Therapy

Music therapy during childbirth, which involves the use of music to reduce stress and manage pain, is increasingly used (Cepeda & others, 2006; Hunter, 2009; Tagore, 2009). Few research studies have been conducted to determine its effectiveness (Simpkin & Bolding, 2004).

What characterizes the use of waterbirth in delivering a baby?

Cesarean Delivery   Normally, the baby's head comes through the vagina first. But if the baby is in a **breech position,** the baby's buttocks are the first part to emerge from the vagina. In 1 of every 25 deliveries, the baby's head is still in the uterus when the rest of the body is out. Breech births can cause respiratory problems. As a result, if the baby is in a breech position, a surgical procedure known as a cesarean section, or a cesarean delivery, is usually preformed (Lee, El-Sayed, & Gould, 2008). In a **cesarean delivery,** the baby is removed from the mother's uterus through an incision made in her abdomen. Cesarean deliveries also are performed if the baby is lying crosswise in the uterus, if the baby's head is too large to pass through the mother's pelvis, if the baby develops complications, or if the mother is bleeding vaginally. Cesarean deliveries can be life-saving, but they do bring risks. Compared with vaginal deliveries, they involve a higher infection rate, longer hospital stays, and the greater expense and stress that accompany any surgery. A recent national study of all U.S. live births and infant deaths from 1999 to 2002 revealed that cesarean deliveries with no labor complications resulted in a neonatal death rate that was 2.4 times that of planned vaginal deliveries (MacDorman & others, 2008).

breech position The baby's position in the uterus that causes the buttocks to be the first part to emerge from the vagina.

cesarean delivery Delivery in which the baby is removed from the mother's uterus through an incision made in her abdomen. This also is sometimes referred to as a cesarean section.

Because of increased rates of respiratory complications, elective cesarean delivery is not recommended prior to 39 weeks of gestation unless there is an indication of fetal lung maturity (Greene, 2009). A recent study revealed that elective repeat cesarean delivery before 39 weeks of gestation is common and is linked with adverse respiratory outcomes (Tita & others, 2009).

The benefits and risks of cesarean sections continue to be debated (Jonsdottir & others, 2009; Walsh & Walsh, 2009). Some critics believe that too many babies are delivered by cesarean section in the United States (Chaillet & Dumont, 2007). More cesarean sections are performed in the United States than in any other country in the world. The cesarean delivery rate jumped 5 percent from 2002 to 2006 in the United States to 31 percent of all births, the highest level since these data began to be reported on birth certificates in 1989 (National Center for Health Statistics, 2007). Higher cesarean delivery rates may be due to a better ability to identify infants in distress during birth and the increase in overweight and obese pregnant women (Coleman & others, 2005). Also, some doctors may be overly cautious and recommend a cesarean delivery to defend against a potential lawsuit.

The Transition from Fetus to Newborn

Much of our discussion of birth so far has focused on the mother. Being born also involves considerable stress for the baby. During each contraction, when the placenta and umbilical cord are compressed as the uterine muscles draw together, the supply of oxygen to the fetus is decreased. If the delivery takes too long, the baby can develop *anoxia*, a condition in which the fetus or newborn has an insufficient supply of oxygen. Anoxia can cause brain damage (Smith, 2008).

The baby has considerable capacity to withstand the stress of birth. Large quantities of adrenaline and noradrenaline, hormones that protect the fetus in the event of oxygen deficiency, are secreted in stressful circumstances. These hormones increase the heart's pumping activity, speed up heart rate, channel blood flow to the brain, and raise the blood-sugar level. Never again in life will such large amounts of these hormones be secreted. This circumstance underscores how stressful it is to be born and also how well prepared and adapted the fetus is for birth (Van Beveren, 2008).

At the time of birth, the baby is covered with a protective skin grease called *vernix caseosa*. This vernix consists of fatty secretions and dead cells, thought to help protect the baby's skin against heat loss before and during birth.

What is the transition from fetus to newborn like?

Immediately after birth, the umbilical cord is cut and the baby is on its own. Before birth, oxygen came from the mother via the umbilical cord, but now the baby is self-sufficient and can breathe on its own. Now 25 million little air sacs in the lungs must be filled with air. These first breaths may be the hardest ones an individual takes.

Review and Reflect: Learning Goal 1

 Discuss the stages, decisions involved, and transitions in birth

REVIEW

- What are the three stages involved in the birth process?
- What characterizes the childbirth setting and attendants?
- What are the main methods of childbirth?
- What is the fetus/newborn transition like?

REFLECT

- Which childbirth strategy do you think is best for mothers to adopt? Why?

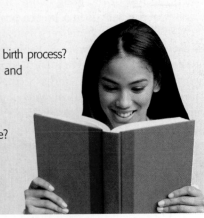

2 WHAT ARE SOME MEASURES OF NEONATAL HEALTH AND RESPONSIVENESS?

Almost immediately after birth, after the baby and mother have been introduced, a newborn is taken to be weighed, cleaned up, and tested for signs of developmental problems that might require urgent attention (Als & Butler, 2008). The **Apgar Scale** is widely used to assess the health of newborns at one and five minutes after birth. The Apgar Scale evaluates infants' heart rate, respiratory effort, muscle tone, body color, and reflex irritability. An obstetrician or a nurse does the evaluation and gives the newborn a score, or reading, of 0, 1, or 2 on each of these five health signs (see Figure 4.2). A total score of 7 to 10 indicates that the newborn's condition is good. A score of 5 indicates there may be developmental difficulties. A score of 3 or below signals an emergency and indicates that the baby might not survive.

The Apgar Scale is especially good at assessing the newborn's ability to respond to the stress of delivery and the new environment (Oberlander & others, 2008). It also identifies high-risk infants who need resuscitation. For a more thorough assessment of the newborn, however, the Brazelton Neonatal Behavioral Assessment Scale or the Neonatal Intensive Care Unit Network Neurobehavioral Scale may be used.

The **Brazelton Neonatal Behavioral Assessment Scale (NBAS)** is typically performed within 24 to 36 hours after birth. It is also used as a sensitive index of neurological competence up to one month after birth for typical infants and in many studies as a measure of infant development (Arditi & others, 2008; Mamtani, Patel, & Kulkarni, 2008). The NBAS assesses the newborn's neurological development, reflexes, and reactions to people and objects. Sixteen reflexes, such as sneezing, blinking, and rooting, are assessed, along with reactions to circumstances, such as the infant's reaction to a rattle. (We will have more to say about reflexes in Chapter 5, "Physical Development in Infancy," when we discuss motor development in infancy.)

A very low NBAS score can indicate brain damage, or stress to the brain that may heal in time. If an infant merely seems sluggish, parents are encouraged to give the infant attention and become more sensitive to the infant's needs. Parents are shown how the newborn can respond to people and how to stimulate such responses. These communications with parents can improve their interaction skills with both high-risk infants and healthy, responsive infants (Girling, 2006).

An "offspring" of the NBAS, the **Neonatal Intensive Care Unit Network Neurobehavioral Scale (NNNS)** provides a more comprehensive analysis of the newborn's behavior, neurological and stress responses, and regulatory capacities (Lester, Tronick, & Brazelton, 2004). Whereas the NBAS was developed to assess

Apgar Scale A widely used method to assess the health of newborns at one and five minutes after birth. The Apgar Scale evaluates infants' heart rate, respiratory effort, muscle tone, body color, and reflex irritability.

Brazelton Neonatal Behavioral Assessment Scale (NBAS) A test performed within 24 to 36 hours after birth to assess newborns' neurological development, reflexes, and reactions to people.

Neonatal Intensive Care Unit Network Neurobehavioral Scale (NNNS) An "offspring" of the NBAS, the NNNS provides a more comprehensive analysis of the newborn's behavior, neurological and stress responses, and regulatory capacities.

Score	0	1	2
Heart rate	Absent	Slow—less than 100 beats per minute	Fast—100 to 140 beats per minute
Respiratory effort	No breathing for more than one minute	Irregular and slow	Good breathing with normal crying
Muscle tone	Limp and flaccid	Weak, inactive, but some flexion of extremities	Strong, active motion
Body color	Blue and pale	Body pink, but extremities blue	Entire body pink
Reflex irritability	No response	Grimace	Coughing, sneezing, and crying

FIGURE 4.2 The Apgar Scale A newborn's score on the Apgar Scale indicates whether the baby has urgent medical problems. *What are some trends in the Apgar Scores of U.S. babies?*

normal, healthy, term infants, T. Berry Brazelton, along with Barry Lester and Edward Tronick, developed the NNNS to assess the "at-risk" infant. It is especially useful for evaluating preterm infants (although it may not be appropriate for those less than 30 weeks' gestational age) and substance-exposed infants (Boukydis & Lester, 2008; de Moares Barros & others, 2008; Paz & others, 2009).

Review and Reflect: Learning Goal 2

 2 **Describe three measures of neonatal health and responsiveness**

REVIEW

- How can the Apgar Scale, the Brazelton Neonatal Behavioral Assessment Scale, and the Neonatal Intensive Care Unit Network Neurobehavioral Scale be characterized?

REFLECT

- What information does the Brazelton assessment provide that the Apgar does not?

---

3 HOW DO LOW BIRTH WEIGHT AND PRETERM INFANTS DEVELOP?

Preterm and Small for Date Infants	Consequences of Preterm Birth and Low Birth Weight	Nurturing Preterm Infants

Different conditions that pose threats for newborns have been given different labels. We next examine these conditions and discuss interventions for improving outcomes of preterm infants.

Preterm and Small for Date Infants

Three related conditions pose threats to many newborns: having a low birth weight, being preterm, and being small for date. **Low birth weight infants** weigh less than 5½ pounds at birth. *Very low birth weight* newborns weigh under 3½ pounds, and *extremely low birth weight* newborns weigh under 2 pounds. **Preterm infants** are those born three weeks or more before the pregnancy has reached its full term—in other words, before the completion of 37 weeks of gestation (the time between fertilization and birth). **Small for date (small for gestational age) infants** are those whose birth weight is below normal when the length of the pregnancy is considered. They weigh less than 90 percent of what all babies of the same gestational age weigh. Small for date infants may be preterm or full term. One study found that small for date infants had more than a fourfold risk of death (Regev & others, 2003).

In 2006, 12.8 percent of U.S. infants were born preterm—a 36 percent increase since the 1980s (National Center for Health Statistics, 2008). The increase in preterm birth is likely due to such factors as the increasing number of births to women 35 years and older, increasing rates of multiple births, increased management of maternal and fetal conditions (for example, inducing labor preterm if medical technology indicates it will increase the likelihood of survival), increased substance abuse (tobacco, alcohol), and increased stress (Goldenberg & Culhane, 2007). Ethnic variations characterize preterm birth (Balchin & Steer, 2007; Sparks, 2009). For example, in 2006, the likelihood of being born preterm was 12.8 percent for all U.S.

A "kilogram kid," weighing less than 2.3 pounds at birth. *What are some possible outcomes for low birth weight infants?*

infants, but the rate was 18.5 percent for African American infants (National Center for Health Statistics, 2009).

Recently, there has been considerable interest generated in the role that progestin might play in reducing preterm births (Lamont & Jayasooriya, 2009; Rittenberg & others, 2009; Tita & Rouse, 2009). In one study, weekly injections of the hormone progesterone, which is naturally produced by the ovaries, lowered the rate of preterm births by one-third (Meis & Peaceman, 2003). Other studies provide further support for the use of progestin in the second trimester of pregnancy in reducing the risk of preterm delivery (Fonseca & others, 2007; Lamont & Jaggat, 2007). However, one recent study did not find a reduction in preterm labor when progestin was given to women who were pregnant with twins (Rouse & others, 2007). A recent survey indicated that the use of progestin to prevent preterm birth increased from 38 percent of maternal-fetal medicine specialists in 2003 to 67 percent in 2005 (Ness & others, 2006). Also, recall from Chapter 3, "Prenatal Development," that a recent study revealed that taking folic acid either alone or as part of a multivitamin for one year prior to conceiving was linked to a substantial reduction in preterm birth (Bukowski & others, 2008).

As we see next, in the *Diversity in Children's Development* interlude, the incidence and causes of low birth weight vary across countries.

Diversity in Children's Development

INCIDENCE AND CAUSES OF LOW BIRTH WEIGHT AROUND THE WORLD

Most, but not all, preterm babies are also low birth weight babies. The incidence of low birth weight varies considerably from country to country. In some countries, such as India and Sudan, where poverty is rampant and the health and nutrition of mothers are poor, the percentage of low birth weight babies reaches as high as 31 percent (see Figure 4.3). In the United States, there has been an increase in low birth weight infants in the last two decades. The U.S. low birth weight rate of 8.1 percent in 2004 is considerably higher than that of many other developed countries (Hoyert & others, 2006). For example, only 4 percent of the infants born in Sweden, Finland, Norway, and Korea are low birth weight, and only 5 percent of those born in New Zealand, Australia, and France are low birth weight.

The causes of low birth weight also vary (Mortensen & others, 2009). In the developing world, low birth weight stems mainly from the mother's poor health and nutrition (Christian, 2009). For example, diarrhea and malaria, which are common in developing countries, can impair fetal growth if the mother becomes affected while she is pregnant. In developed countries, cigarette smoking during pregnancy is the leading cause of low birth weight (Fertig, 2009; Nabet & others, 2007). In both developed and developing countries, adolescents who give birth when their bodies have not fully matured are at risk for having low birth weight babies (Malamitsi-Puchner & Boutsikou, 2006). In the United States, the increase in the number of low birth weight infants is due to such factors as the use of drugs, poor nutrition, multiple births, reproductive technologies, and improved technology and prenatal care, resulting in a higher survival rate of high-risk babies (Chen, Wen, Fleming, & others, 2007; Chen, Wen, Yang, & others, 2007). Nonetheless, poverty still is a major factor in preterm birth in the United States. Women living in poverty conditions are more likely to be obese, have diabetes and hypertension, smoke cigarettes and use illicit drugs, and be less likely to have regular prenatal care (Nagahawatte & Goldenberg, 2008).

FIGURE 4.3 Percentage of Infants Born with Low Birth Weight in Selected Countries

How Would You...?
As a social worker, how would you advise couples living in poverty who are considering having a child about reducing the risk of having a low birth weight child?

low birth weight infants Babies that weigh less than 5½ pounds at birth.

preterm infants Babies born three weeks or more before the pregnancy has reached its full term.

small for date (small for gestational age) infants Babies whose birth weight is below normal when the length of pregnancy is considered.

FIGURE 4.4 Percentage of Preterm and Full-Term Birth Infants Who Dropped Out of School

Consequences of Preterm Birth and Low Birth Weight

Although most preterm and low birth weight infants are healthy, as a group they have more health and developmental problems than normal birth weight infants (Datar & Jacknowitz, 2009; Morse & others, 2009; Petrini & others, 2009). For preterm birth, the terms *extremely preterm* and *very preterm* are increasingly used (Smith, 2008). *Extremely preterm infants* are those born at less than 28 weeks preterm, and *very preterm infants* are those born at less than 33 weeks of gestational age. Figure 4.4 shows the results of a recent Norwegian study indicating that the earlier preterm infants are born, the more likely they will drop out of school (Swamy, Ostbye, & Skjaerven, 2008). Another recent study found that extremely preterm infants were more likely to show pervasive delays in early language development (such as vocabulary size and quality of word use) than very preterm infants, who in turn showed more early language delays than full-term infants (Foster-Cohen & others, 2007). A recent research review also revealed that very preterm infants had lower IQ scores, less effective information-processing skills, and were more at risk for behavioral problems than full-term infants (Johnson, 2007).

The number and severity of these problems increase when infants are born very early and as their birth weight decreases (Hack & others, 2009; Woodward & others, 2009). Survival rates for infants who are born very early and very small have risen, but with this improved survival rate have come increases in rates of severe brain damage. The earlier the birth and the lower the birth weight, the greater the likelihood of brain injury. Approximately 7 percent of moderately low birth weight infants (3 pounds 5 ounces to 5 pounds 8 ounces) have brain injuries. This figure increases to 20 percent for the smallest newborns (1 pound 2 ounces to 3 pounds 5 ounces). A recent magnetic resonance imaging (MRI) study revealed that adolescents who had experienced very preterm birth were more likely to show reduced prefrontal lobe (where the most advanced cognitive functioning, such as reasoning, occurs) and corpus callosum (the fibers that connect the brain's two hemispheres) functioning than full-term adolescents (Narberhaus & others, 2008). Low birth weight infants are also more likely than normal birth weight infants to have lung or liver diseases (Streubel, Donohue, & Aucott, 2008).

At school age, children who were born low in birth weight are more likely than their normal birth weight counterparts to have a learning disability, attention deficit hyperactivity disorder, or breathing problems such as asthma (Greenough, 2007; Santo, Portuguez, & Nunes, 2009). A recent study found that extremely low birth weight children at 8 years of age had more symptoms of anxiety, attention deficit hyperactivity disorder, and autistic syndrome disorders than their normal weight counterparts (Hack & others, 2009). One study revealed that 17-year-olds who were born with low birth weight were 50 percent more likely than normal birth weight individuals to have reading and mathematics deficits (Breslau, Paneth, & Lucia, 2004). Approximately 50 percent of all low birth weight children are enrolled in special education programs.

An increasing number of studies indicate that low birth weight infants have more difficulty in socializing and have different lifestyles as emerging adults and adults. The results of three of these studies follow:

- As adults, extremely low birth weight infants were more likely to report that they were more inhibited and had a lower level of emotional well-being than normal birth weight infants were likely to report as adults (Schmidt & others, 2008).

- As emerging adults, low birth weight infants were more likely to still be living in their parents' home, less likely be cohabiting with an intimate partner, and less likely to be sexually active than their normal birth weight counterparts (Kajantie & others, 2008).

- As young adults, the more premature infants were when they were born, the less likely they were to get married (Moster, Lie, & Markestad, 2008).

Nurturing Preterm Infants

An important strategy when considering how to treat low birth weight and preterm births is to reduce the risk of low birth weight before it occurs. Recall from Chapter 3, "Prenatal Development," that a home visitation program for high-risk pregnant women and adolescents that encouraged healthy prenatal behavior, provided social support, and linked them to medical and other community services, decreased their risk of delivering a low birth weight baby (Lee & others, 2009).

Some effects of being born low in birth weight can be reduced or even reversed. Intensive enrichment programs that provide medical and educational services for both the parents and children can improve short-term outcomes for low birth weight children (Massaro & others, 2009; Melnyk & Feinstein, 2009; Minde & Zelkowitz, 2008). In a recent study, mothers of hospitalized preterm infants were randomly assigned to intervention and control groups (Newnham, Milgrom, & Skouteris, 2009). The intervention group was given seven sessions prior to infant discharge from the hospital and two sessions over the next three months. These sessions involved extensive information and training about practice in handling infants, observing infants (especially for cues regarding disorganization and stress), recognizing infant states and responding to infant cues, initiating activity, kangaroo care and massage (which will be discussed shortly), and mutual enjoyment through play. When the infants were 3 months of age, the intervention group had more positive mother-infant interaction, the infants cried less, slept better, and had better communication skills, and the mothers were less stressed than the control group.

At present, federal laws mandate that services for school-aged children must be expanded to include family-based care for infants born with severe disabilities. The availability of services for moderately low birth weight children who do not have severe physical problems varies, but most states do not provide these services.

Currently, the two most popular Neonatal Intensive Care Unit (NICU) interventions that involve parents are breast feeding and **kangaroo care,** treatment for preterm infants that involves skin-to-skin contact. Both of these interventions were uncommon until recently. Recent surveys indicated that kangaroo care is used from 82 to 97 percent by nurses in NICUs (Engler & others, 2002; Field & others, 2006). Also in one of these surveys, massage therapy was used in 37 percent of the NICUs (Field & others, 2006).

Let's further examine kangaroo care and massage therapy. In kangaroo care, the baby, wearing only a diaper, is held upright against the parent's bare chest, much as a baby kangaroo is carried by its mother. Kangaroo care is typically practiced for two to three hours per day, skin-to-skin over an extended time in early infancy (Arora, 2009; Johnson, 2007).

Why use kangaroo care with preterm infants? Preterm infants often have difficulty coordinating their breathing and heart rate, and the close physical contact with the parent provided by kangaroo care can help to stabilize the preterm infant's heartbeat, temperature, and breathing (Begum & others, 2008). Further, preterm infants who experience kangaroo care have longer periods of sleep, gain more weight, decrease their crying, have longer periods of alertness, and have earlier hospital discharge (Ludington-Hoe & others, 2006). One study compared 26 low birth weight infants who received kangaroo care with 27 low birth weight infants who received standard medical/nursing care (Ohgi & others, 2002). At both 6 and 12 months of age, the kangaroo care infants were more alert and responsive, were less irritable and fussy, and had a more positive mood. Another study found that preterm infants who received kangaroo care had better control of their arousal, more effectively attended to stimuli, and engaged in more sustained exploration during a toy session than a control group of preterm infants who did not receive kangaroo care (Feldman & others, 2002). Two recent studies found that kangaroo care decreased pain responses in preterm infants (Akcan, Yigit,

A new mother practicing kangaroo care. *What is kangaroo care?*

kangaroo care A way of holding a preterm infant so that there is skin-to-skin contact.

& Atici, 2009; Johnson & others, 2009). And two recent experimental studies revealed that low birth weight infants randomly assigned to kangaroo mother care compared with traditional mother care gained more weight, were less likely to experience hypothermia and hypoglycemia, and were more strongly attached to their mother (Gathwala, Singh, & Balhara, 2008; Suman, Udani, & Nanavati, 2008). Kangaroo care increasingly is being recommended for full-term infants as well (Ferber & Makhoul, 2008; Walters & others, 2008).

Many preterm infants experience less touch than full-term infants because they are isolated in temperature-controlled incubators (Chia, Selleck, & Gan, 2006). The research of Tiffany Field has led to a surge of interest in the role that massage might play in improving the developmental outcomes for preterm infants. To read about her research, see the following *Research in Children's Development* interlude.

How Would You...?
As a health-care professional, how would you advise hospital administrators about implementing kangaroo care or massage therapy in the neonatal intensive care unit?

Research in Children's Development

Shown here is Tiffany Field massaging a newborn infant. *What types of infants has massage therapy been shown to help?*

FIGURE 4.5 Effects of Massage Therapy on Stress Behavior in Newborns

TIFFANY FIELD'S RESEARCH ON MASSAGE THERAPY

Throughout history and in many cultures, caregivers have massaged infants. In Africa and Asia, infants are routinely massaged by parents or other family members for several months after birth. In the United States, interest in using touch and massage to improve the growth, health, and well-being of infants has been stimulated by the research of Tiffany Field (2001, 2003, 2007; Field & Diego, 2008; Field, Diego, & Hernandez-Reif, 2007, 2008; Field & others, 2006; Hernandez-Reif, Diego, & Field, 2007), director of the Touch Research Institute at the University of Miami School of Medicine.

In a recent study, preterm infants in a neonatal intensive care unit (NICU) were randomly assigned to a massage therapy group or a control group. For five consecutive days, the preterm infants in the massage group were given three 15-minute moderate-pressure massages (Hernandez-Reif, Diego, & Field, 2007). Behavioral observations of the following stress behaviors were made on the first and last days of the study: crying, grimacing, yawning, sneezing, jerky arm and leg movements, startles, and finger flaring. The various stress behaviors were summarized in a composite stress behavior index. As indicated in Figure 4.5, massage had a stress-reducing effect on the preterm infants, which is especially important because they encounter numerous stressors while they are hospitalized.

In another study, Field and her colleagues (2004) tested a more cost-effective massage strategy. They taught mothers how to massage their full-term infants rather than having health care professionals do the massage. Beginning from day one of the newborn's life to the end of the first month, once a day before bedtime the mothers massaged the babies using either light or moderate pressure. Infants who were massaged with moderate pressure gained more weight, performed better on the orientation scale of the Brazelton, were less excitable and less depressed, and were less agitated during sleep.

Field has demonstrated the benefits of massage therapy for infants who face a variety of problems. For example, preterm infants exposed to cocaine in utero who received massage therapy gained weight and improved their scores on developmental tests (Wheeden & others, 1993). Another study investigated 1- to 3-month-old infants born to depressed adolescent mothers (Field & others, 1996). The infants of depressed mothers who received massage therapy had lower stress—as well as improved emotionality, sociability, and soothability—compared with the nonmassaged infants of depressed mothers.

In a research review of massage therapy with preterm infants, Field and her colleagues (2004) concluded that the most consistent findings involve two positive results: (1) increased weight gain, and (2) discharge from the hospital from three to six days earlier.

Infants are not the only ones who may benefit from massage therapy (Field, 2007). In other studies, Field and her colleagues have demonstrated the benefits of massage therapy for women in reducing labor pain (Field, Hernandez-Rief, Taylor, & others, 1997), for children who have asthma (Field, Henteleff, & others, 1998), for autistic children's attentiveness (Field, Lasko, & others, 1997), and for adolescents who have attention deficit hyperactivity disorder (Field, Quintino, & others, 1998).

Review and Reflect: Learning Goal 3

 3 **Characterize the development of low birth weight and preterm infants**

REVIEW

- What is a low birth weight infant? How can preterm and small for date infants be distinguished?
- What are the long-term outcomes for low birth weight infants?
- What is known about the roles of kangaroo care and massage therapy with preterm infants?

REFLECT

- What can be done to reduce the United States' high rates of low birth weight babies?

4 WHAT HAPPENS DURING THE POSTPARTUM PERIOD?

| Physical Adjustments | Emotional and Psychological Adjustments | Bonding |

The weeks after childbirth present challenges for many new parents and their offspring. This is the **postpartum period,** the period after childbirth or delivery that lasts for about six weeks or until the mother's body has completed its adjustment and has returned to a nearly prepregnant state. It is a time when the woman adjusts, both physically and psychologically, to the process of childbearing.

The postpartum period involves a great deal of adjustment and adaptation. The baby has to be cared for. The mother has to recover from childbirth, to learn how to take care of the baby, and to learn to feel good about herself as a mother. The father needs to learn how to take care of his recovering partner, to learn how to take care of the baby, and to learn how to feel good about himself as a father. Many health professionals believe that the best way to meet these challenges is with a family-centered approach that uses the family's resources to support an early and smooth adjustment to the newborn by all family members. The adjustments needed are physical, emotional, and psychological.

Physical Adjustments

A woman's body makes numerous physical adjustments in the first days and weeks after childbirth (Smith, 2009). She may have a great deal of energy or feel

postpartum period The period after childbirth when the mother adjusts, both physically and psychologically, to the process of childbearing. This period lasts for about six weeks, or until her body has completed its adjustment and has returned to a near-prepregnant state.

FIGURE 4.6 Sleep Deprivation in Pregnant and Postpartum Women

"Baby blues"
Symptoms appear 2 to 3 days after delivery and subside within 1 to 2 weeks.

Postpartum depression
Symptoms linger for weeks or months and interfere with daily functioning.

No symptoms

FIGURE 4.7 "Baby Blues" and Postpartum Depression Among U.S. Women Some health professionals refer to the postpartum period as the "fourth trimester." Though the time span of the postpartum period does not necessarily cover three months, the term "fourth trimester" suggests continuity and the importance of the first several months after birth for the mother.

exhausted and let down. Most new mothers feel tired and need rest. Though these changes are normal, the fatigue can undermine the new mother's sense of well-being and confidence in her ability to cope with a new baby and a new family life (Runquist, 2007).

A concern is the loss of sleep that the primary caregiver experiences in the postpartum period (Gunderson & others, 2008; Hunter, Rychnovsky, & Yount, 2009). A recent analysis indicated that the primary caregiver loses as much as 700 hours of sleep in the first year following the baby's birth (Maas, 2008). In the 2007 Sleep in America Survey, a substantial percentage of women reported loss of sleep during pregnancy and in the postpartum period (National Sleep Foundation, 2007) (see Figure 4.6). The loss of sleep can contribute to stress, relationship conflict, and impaired decision making (Meerlo, Sgoifo, & Suchecki, 2008). Even after their newborn begins to sleep better through the night by the middle of the baby's first year, many mothers report waking up several times a night when their baby is asleep. Sleep experts say it takes several weeks to several months for parents' internal sleep clocks to adjust.

After delivery, a mother's body undergoes sudden and dramatic changes in hormone production. When the placenta is delivered, estrogen and progesterone levels drop steeply and remain low until the ovaries start producing hormones again. The woman will probably begin menstruating again in four to eight weeks if she is not breast feeding. If she is breast feeding, she might not menstruate for several months to a year or more, though ovulation usually occurs during this time. The first several menstrual periods following delivery might be heavier than usual, but periods soon return to normal.

Involution is the process by which the uterus returns to its prepregnant size five or six weeks after birth. Immediately following birth, the uterus weighs 2 to 3 pounds. By the end of five or six weeks, the uterus weighs 2 to 3½ ounces. Nursing the baby helps contract the uterus at a rapid rate.

If the woman regularly engaged in conditioning exercises during pregnancy, exercise will help her recover her former body contour and strength. With a caregiver's approval, the new mother can begin some exercises as soon as one hour after delivery. One study found that women who maintained or increased their exercise from prepregnancy to postpartum had better maternal well-being than women who engaged in no exercise or decreased their exercise from prepregnancy to postpartum (Blum, Beaudoin, & Caton-Lemos, 2005).

Relaxation techniques are also helpful during the postpartum period. Five minutes of slow breathing on a stressful day in the postpartum period can relax and refresh the new mother, and this will indirectly benefit the new baby.

Emotional and Psychological Adjustments

Emotional fluctuations are common for mothers in the postpartum period. For some women, emotional fluctuations decrease within several weeks after the delivery, but other women experience more long-lasting emotional swings.

As shown in Figure 4.7, about 70 percent of new mothers in the United States have what are called "baby blues." About two to three days after birth, they begin to feel depressed, anxious, and upset. These feelings may come and go for several weeks after the birth, often peaking about three to five days after birth.

For other women, emotional fluctuations persist and can produce feelings of anxiety, depression, and difficulty in coping with stress (Figueiredo & Costa, 2009; Phillips & others, 2009). Mothers who have such feelings, even when they are getting adequate rest, may benefit from professional help in dealing with their problems. Indications of a need for professional counseling about postpartum adaptation include excessive worrying, depression, extreme changes in appetite, crying spells, and inability to sleep.

Postpartum depression involves a major depressive episode that typically occurs about four weeks after delivery. In other words, women with postpartum depression have such strong feelings of sadness, anxiety, or despair that for at least a two-week period they have trouble coping with their daily tasks. Without treatment, postpartum depression may become worse and last for many months (Nolen-Hoeksema, 2010). And many women with postpartum treatment don't seek help. For example, one recent study found that 15 percent of the women reported postpartum depression symptoms but less than half sought help (McGarry & others, 2009). Estimates indicate that 10 to 14 percent of new mothers experience postpartum depression.

Hormonal changes that occur after childbirth are believed to play a role in postpartum depression (Fan & others, 2009; Taylor & others, 2009). Estrogen helps some women with postpartum depression, but estrogen also has some possible problematic side effects (Grigoriadis & Kennedy, 2002). Several antidepressant drugs are effective in treating postpartum depression and appear to be safe for breast feeding women (Logsdon, Wisner, & Hanusa, 2009). Psychotherapy, especially cognitive therapy, also is an effective treatment of postpartum depression for many women (Beck, 2006; Pearlstein & others, 2009). Also, engaging in regular exercise may help in treating postpartum depression (Daley, Macarthur, & Winter, 2007). A recent study revealed that individualized telephone-based peer support (by mothers) reduced postpartum depression in high-risk women (Dennis & others, 2009). A recent research review found that home-based interventions also were effective in reducing postpartum depression in women (Leis & others, 2009).

One concern about postpartum depression is that breast feeding is less common among postpartum depressed women. They may not breast feed because of their concern about potentially negative effects of antidepressants that can be transmitted to their young infant through breast milk (Einarson & Ito, 2007). Currently, little research has been conducted on whether the positive effects of breast feeding might outweigh the positive effects of antidepressants for both the mother and the infant (Field, 2008).

Can a mother's postpartum depression affect the way mothers interact with their infants? Researchers have found that depressed mothers interact less with their infants and are less likely to respond to their infants' effort to get attention (Teti & Towe-Goodman, 2008). A recent national survey indicated that mothers who were depressed were 1.5 times more likely to provide less healthy feeding and sleeping practices for their newborns (Paulson, Dauber, & Leiferman, 2006). Another recent study revealed that postpartum depression was more common in mothers who had preterm rather than full-term infants (Feldman & Eidelman, 2007). In this study, with both preterm and full-term infants, mothers with postpartum depression showed a low level of maternal-infant synchrony. Yet another recent study revealed that mothers with high levels of depression in the postpartum period were more likely to have infants with colic and prolonged crying than were mothers with low levels of depression (Vik & others, 2009). To read about an individual who specializes in helping women adjust in the postpartum period, see the *Careers in Children's Development* profile.

Fathers also undergo considerable adjustment in the postpartum period, even when they work away from home all day (Cox, 2006). Many fathers feel that the baby comes first and gets all of the mother's attention; some feel that they have been replaced by the baby.

The father's support and caring can play a role in whether the mother develops postpartum depression (Dietz & others, 2009; Gao, Chan, & Mao, 2009). A recent study revealed that higher support by fathers was related to a lower incidence of postpartum depression in women (Smith & Howard, 2008).

Some fathers develop postpartum depression, and it can be detrimental to the child's development (Schumacher, Zubaran, & White, 2008). A recent study revealed that paternal postpartum depression (independent of maternal postpartum depression) was linked to psychological disorders in their children seven years later (Ramchandani & others, 2008).

How Would You...?
As a human development and family studies professional, how would you talk with mothers and fathers about vulnerabilities in mental health and relationships in the postpartum period?

involution The process by which the uterus returns to its prepregnant size.

postpartum depression Involves a major depressive episode characterized by strong feelings of sadness, anxiety, or despair in new mothers, making it difficult for them to carry out daily tasks.

Careers in Children's Development

Diane Sanford, Clinical Psychologist and Postpartum Expert

Diane Sanford has a doctorate in clinical psychology, and for many years she had a private practice that focused on marital and family relationships. But after she began collaborating with a psychiatrist whose clients included women with postpartum depression, Dr. Sanford, along with a women's health nurse, founded Women's Healthcare Partnership in St. Louis, Missouri, which specializes in women's adjustment during the postpartum period. Subsequently, they added a marriage and family relationships counselor and a social worker to their staff, and then later hired nurse educators, a dietician, and a fitness expert as consultants.

Source: Clay, R. (2001)

Diane Sanford holding an infant of one of the mothers who comes to her for help in coping with postpartum issues.

The postpartum period is a time of considerable adjustment and adaptation for both the mother and the father. Fathers can provide an important support system for mothers, especially in helping mothers care for young infants. *What kinds of tasks might the father of a newborn do to support the mother?*

bonding A close connection, especially a physical bond between parents and their newborn in the period shortly after birth.

To help the father adjust, parents should set aside some special time to be together with each other. The father's postpartum reaction also likely will be improved if he has taken childbirth classes with the mother and is an active participant in caring for the baby.

Bonding

A special component of the parent-infant relationship is **bonding,** the formation of a connection, especially a physical bond between parents and the newborn in the period shortly after birth. Sometimes hospitals seem determined to deter bonding. Drugs given to the mother to make her delivery less painful can make the mother drowsy, interfering with her ability to respond to and stimulate the newborn. Mothers and newborns are often separated shortly after delivery, and preterm infants are isolated from their mothers even more than are full-term infants.

Do these practices do any harm? Some physicians believe that during the period shortly after birth, the parents and newborn need to form an emotional attachment as a foundation for optimal development in years to come (Kennell, 2006; Kennell & McGrath, 1999). Is there evidence that close contact between mothers in the first several days after birth is critical for optimal development later in life? Although some research supports this bonding hypothesis (Klaus & Kennell, 1976), a body of research challenges the significance of the first few days of life as a critical period (Bakeman & Brown, 1980; Rode & others, 1981). Indeed, the extreme form of the bonding hypothesis—that the newborn must have close contact with the mother in the first few days of life to develop optimally—simply is not true.

Nonetheless, the weakness of the bonding hypothesis should not be used as an excuse to keep motivated mothers from interacting with their newborns. Such contact brings pleasure to many mothers. In some mother-infant pairs—including preterm infants, adolescent mothers, and mothers from disadvantaged circumstances—early close contact may establish a climate for improved interaction after the mother and infant leave the hospital.

Many hospitals now offer a *rooming-in* arrangement, in which the baby remains in the mother's room most of the time during its hospital stay. However, if parents choose not to use this rooming-in arrangement, the weight of the research suggests that this decision will not harm the infant emotionally (Lamb, 1994).

Review and Reflect: Learning Goal 4

 4 Explain the physical and psychological aspects of the postpartum period

REVIEW

- What does the postpartum period involve? What physical adjustments does the woman's body make in this period?
- What emotional and psychological adjustments characterize the postpartum period?
- Is bonding critical for optimal development?

REFLECT

- If you are a female, what can you do to adjust effectively in the postpartum period? If you are a male, what can you do to help in the postpartum period?

A mother bonds with her infant moments after it is born. *How critical is bonding for the development of social competence later in childhood?*

Reach Your Learning Goals

Birth

1 WHAT HAPPENS DURING THE BIRTH PROCESS? DISCUSS THE STAGES, DECISIONS INVOLVED, AND TRANSITIONS IN BIRTH

Stages of the Birth Process

- The first stage of birth is the longest and lasts about 12 to 14 hours for a woman having her first child. The cervix dilates to about 4 inches. The second stage begins when the baby's head starts to move through the cervix and ends with the baby's complete emergence. The third stage is afterbirth.

Childbirth Setting and Attendants

- In the United States, the vast majority of births occur in hospitals and are attended by physicians. Many hospitals now have birthing centers. Some women who have good medical histories and who are at low risk for problem deliveries have babies at home. In many countries, such as Holland, much higher percentages of babies are born at home. Some births are attended by a midwife, and in many countries a doula attends.

Methods of Childbirth

- Among the methods of delivery are medicated, natural and prepared, and cesarean. The three basic kinds of drugs used in delivering a baby are analgesics, anesthesia, and oxytocics. Predicting how a particular drug will affect an individual pregnant woman and the fetus is difficult. Today the trend is toward using some medication during childbirth but keeping it to a minimum, if possible. Some believe that the U.S. cesarean rate is too high. The Lamaze method of childbirth is widely used in the United States.

The Transition from Fetus to Newborn

- In some cases, if the delivery takes too long, anoxia can occur. Anoxia involves an insufficient supply of oxygen in the fetus/newborn condition. Being born involves considerable stress, but the baby is well prepared and adapted to handle the stress. Large quantities of stress-related hormones (adrenaline and noradrenaline) are secreted during the fetus/newborn transition.

2 WHAT ARE SOME MEASURES OF NEONATAL HEALTH AND RESPONSIVENESS? DESCRIBE THREE MEASURES OF NEONATAL HEALTH AND RESPONSIVENESS

- For many years, the Apgar Scale has been used to assess the newborn's health. It is used one and five minutes after birth and assesses heart rate, respiratory effort, muscle tone, body color, and reflex irritability. The Brazelton Neonatal Behavioral Assessment Scale (NBAS) is performed within 24 to 36 hours after birth to examine the newborn's neurological development, reflexes, and reactions to people. Recently, the Neonatal Intensive Care Unit Network Neurobehavioral Scale (NNNS) was constructed; it provides a more comprehensive analysis of the newborn's behavior, neurological and stress responses, and regulatory capacities.

3 HOW DO LOW BIRTH WEIGHT AND PRETERM INFANTS DEVELOP? CHARACTERIZE THE DEVELOPMENT OF LOW BIRTH WEIGHT AND PRETERM INFANTS

Preterm and Small for Date Infants

- Low birth weight infants weigh less than 5½ pounds at birth. Low birth weight babies may be preterm (born three weeks or more before the pregnancy has reached full term) or small for date (also called small for gestational age, which refers to infants whose birth weight is below normal when the length of pregnancy is considered). Small for date infants may be preterm or full term.

| Consequences of Preterm Birth and Low Birth Weight | • Although most low birth weight babies are normal and healthy, as a group they have more health and developmental problems than full-term babies. The number and severity of the problems increase when infants are born very early and as their birth weight decreases. |

| Nurturing Preterm Infants | • Kangaroo care, a way of holding a preterm infant so that there is skin-to-skin contact, has positive effects on preterm infants. Massage therapy is increasingly being used with preterm infants and has positive outcomes. |

4 WHAT HAPPENS DURING THE POSTPARTUM PERIOD? EXPLAIN THE PHYSICAL AND PSYCHOLOGICAL ASPECTS OF THE POSTPARTUM PERIOD

| Physical Adjustments | • The postpartum period is the period after childbirth or delivery. It is a time when the woman adjusts, both physically and psychologically, to the process of childbearing. It lasts for about six weeks, or until the body has completed its adjustment. Physical adjustments include fatigue, involution, hormonal changes that include a dramatic drop in estrogen and progesterone, and exercises to recover former body contour and strength. |

| Emotional and Psychological Adjustments | • The mother's emotional fluctuations are common in the postpartum period. These fluctuations may be due to hormonal changes, fatigue, inexperience or lack of confidence in caring for a newborn, or the extensive demands involved in caring for a newborn. For some, these emotional fluctuations are minimal and disappear in a few weeks, but for others they can be more long-lasting. Postpartum depression involves such strong feelings of sadness, anxiety, or despair that new mothers have difficulty carrying out daily tasks. Postpartum depression affects approximately 10 percent of new mothers. The father also goes through a postpartum adjustment. He may feel that the baby now receives all his wife's attention. Being an active participant in caring for the baby helps the father's postpartum reaction. Both parents need to set aside special time to spend together. |

| Bonding | • Bonding refers to the occurrence of a connection, especially a physical bond, between parents and the newborn shortly after birth. Bonding has not been found to be critical in the development of a competent infant or child, although it may stimulate positive interaction between some mother-infant pairs. |

KEY TERMS

afterbirth 119
doula 120
analgesics 121
anesthesia 121
oxytocin 121
natural childbirth 121
prepared childbirth 121
breech position 123

cesarean delivery 123
Apgar Scale 125
Brazelton Neonatal
  Behavioral Assessment
  Scale (NBAS) 125
Neonatal Intensive Care Unit
  Network Neurobehavioral
  Scale (NNNS) 125

low birth weight
  infants 126
preterm infants 126
small for date (small for
  gestational age)
  infants 126
kangaroo care 129
postpartum period 131

involution 132
postpartum depression 132
bonding 134

KEY PEOPLE

Grantley Dick-Read 121

Ferdinand Lamaze 121

T. Berry Brazelton, Barry Lester, and Edward Tronick 125

Tiffany Field 130

MAKING A DIFFERENCE

Effective Birth Strategies

Here are some birth strategies that may benefit the baby and the mother:

- *Take a childbirth class.* These classes provide information about the childbirth experience.
- *Become knowledgeable about different childbirth techniques.* We considered a number of different childbirth techniques in this chapter, including Lamaze and use of doulas. Obtain more detailed information about such techniques by reading a good book, such as *Pregnancy, Childbirth, and the Newborn* by Penny Simkin, Janet Whalley, and Ann Keppler (2001).
- *Use positive intervention with at-risk infants.* Massage can improve the developmental outcome of at-risk infants. Intensive enrichment programs that include medical, educational, psychological,

occupational, and physical domains can benefit low birth weight infants. Intervention with low birth weight infants should involve an individualized plan.

- *Involve the family in the birth process.* If they are motivated to participate, the husband, partner, and siblings can benefit from being involved in the birth process. A mother, sister, or friend can also provide support.
- *Know about the adaptation required in the postpartum period.* The postpartum period involves considerable adaptation and adjustment by the mother and the father. The mother's adjustment is both physical and emotional. Exercise and relaxation techniques can benefit mothers in the postpartum period. So can an understanding, supportive husband.

RESOURCES FOR IMPROVING CHILDREN'S LIVES

Lamaze International
www.lamaze.com

Lamaze provides information about the Lamaze method and taking or teaching Lamaze classes.

The Doula Book

by Marshall Klaus, John Kennell, and Phyllis Klaus (2002)
New York: Perseus Books

Learn more about how valuable a doula can be in the childbirth process in this book.

Birth: Issues in Perinatal Care

This multidisciplinary journal on perinatal care is written for health professionals and contains articles on research and clinical practice, review articles, and commentary.

International Cesarean Awareness Network
www.icanon-line.org

This organization provides extensive information and advice about cesarean birth.

Postpartum Support International (PSI)
www.postpartum.net

PSI provides information about postpartum depression.

E-LEARNING TOOLS

Connect to **www.mhhe.com/santrockc11e** to research the answers and complete these exercises. In addition, you'll find a number of other resources and valuable study tools for Chapter 4, "Birth," on this Web site.

Taking It to the Net

1. Jessica and Eric have just given birth to their first child. Eric has noticed that since the birth three months ago, Jessica has seemed a bit withdrawn and sad. He remembers from their

Lamaze classes that there is a condition called postpartum depression. What can Eric do to help Jessica through this difficult time period?

2. The author of your text provides a summary of the most widely used birthing methods in the United States. What other birthing methods might a woman consider?

3. You have just given birth, and the nurse has informed you that tomorrow your baby will be assessed using the Brazelton Neonatal Behavioral Assessment Scale. What will your baby's experience be like during this assessment?

Health and Well-Being, Parenting, and Education

Build your decision-making skills by trying your hand at the health and well-being, parenting, and education exercises.

Video Clips

The Online Learning Center includes the following video for this chapter:

- *Midwifery—1524*
  A certified midwife discusses midwives and how they differ from obstetricians.

INFANCY

*Babies are such a nice
way to start people.*

—DON HEROLD
American Writer, 20th Century

As newborns, we were not empty-headed organisms. We had

some basic reflexes, among them crying, kicking, and

coughing. We slept a lot, and occasionally we smiled, although

the meaning of our first smiles was not entirely clear. We ate

and we grew. We crawled and then we walked, a journey of

a thousand miles beginning with a single step. Sometimes

we conformed; sometimes others conformed to us. Our

development was a continuous creation of more complex

forms. Our helpless kind demanded meeting the eyes of love.

We juggled the necessity of curbing our will with becoming

what we could will freely. Section 3 contains three chapters:

"Physical Development in Infancy" (Chapter 5), "Cognitive

Development in Infancy" (Chapter 6), and "Socioemotional

Development in Infancy" (Chapter 7).

5

> *A baby is the most complicated object made by unskilled labor.*
>
> —Anonymous

LEARNING GOALS

- ◆ Discuss physical growth and development in infancy

- ◆ Describe infants' motor development

- ◆ Explain sensory and perceptual development in infancy

PHYSICAL DEVELOPMENT IN INFANCY

CHAPTER OUTLINE

Images of Children's Development
The Stories of Latonya and Ramona: Breast and Bottle Feeding in Africa

Latonya is a newborn baby in Ghana. During her first days of life, she has been kept apart from her mother and bottle fed. Manufacturers of infant formula provide the hospital where she was born with free or subsidized milk powder. Her mother has been persuaded to bottle feed rather than breast feed her. When her mother bottle feeds Latonya, she overdilutes the milk formula with unclean water. Latonya's feeding bottles have not been sterilized. Latonya becomes very sick. She dies before her first birthday.

Ramona was born in Nigeria with a "baby-friendly" program. In this program, babies are not separated from their mothers when they are born, and the mothers are encouraged to breast feed them. The mothers are told of the perils that bottle feeding can bring because of unsafe water and unsterilized bottles. They also are informed about the advantages of breast milk, which include its nutritious and hygienic qualities, its ability to immunize babies against common illnesses, and its role in reducing the mother's risk of breast and ovarian cancer. Ramona's mother is breast feeding her. At 1 year of age, Ramona is very healthy.

For many years, maternity units in hospitals favored bottle feeding and did not give mothers adequate information about the benefits of breast feeding. In recent years, the World Health Organization and UNICEF have tried to reverse the trend toward bottle feeding of infants in many impoverished countries. They instituted the baby-friendly program in many of these countries . They also persuaded the International Association of Infant Formula Manufacturers to stop marketing their baby formulas to hospitals in countries where the governments support the baby-friendly initiatives. For the hospitals themselves, costs actually were reduced as infant formula, feeding bottles, and separate nurseries become unnecessary. For example, baby-friendly Jose Fabella Memorial Hospital in the Philippines reported saving 8 percent of its annual budget. Still, there are many places in the world where the baby-friendly initiatives have not been implemented (UNICEF, 2004).

The advantages of breast feeding in impoverished countries are substantial. However, these advantages must be balanced against the risk of passing HIV to the baby through breast milk if the mothers have the virus; the majority of mothers don't know that they are infected (Anderson & Cu-Uvin, 2009; Fadnes & others, 2009; Moorthy & others, 2009). In some areas of Africa, more than 30 percent of mothers have the HIV virus.

(*Top*) An HIV-infected mother breast feeding her baby in Nairobi, Africa. (*Bottom*) A Rhwandan mother bottle feeding her baby. *What are some concerns about breast versus bottle feeding in impoverished African countries?*

PREVIEW

It is very important for infants to get a healthy start. When they do, their first two years of life are likely to be a time of amazing development. In this chapter, we focus on the biological domain and the infant's physical development, exploring physical growth, motor development, and sensory and perceptual development.

1 HOW DO INFANTS GROW AND DEVELOP PHYSICALLY?

| Patterns of Growth | Height and Weight | The Brain | Sleep | Nutrition | Health |

Infants' physical development in the first two years of life is extensive. At birth, a newborn's head is quite large when compared to the rest of the body. They have little strength in their neck and cannot hold their head up. They have some basic reflexes. In the span of 12 months, infants become capable of sitting anywhere, standing, stooping, climbing, and usually walking. During the second year, growth decelerates, but rapid increases in such activities as running and climbing take place. Let's now examine in greater detail the sequence of physical development in infancy.

Patterns of Growth

An extraordinary proportion of the total body is occupied by the head during prenatal development and early infancy (see Figure 5.1). The **cephalocaudal pattern** is the sequence in which the earliest growth always occurs at the top—the head—with physical growth and differentiation of features gradually working their way down from top to bottom (for example, shoulders, middle trunk, and so on) (Pedroso, 2008). This same pattern occurs in the head area, because the top parts of the head—the eyes and brain—grow faster than the lower parts, such as the jaw.

Sensory and motor development generally proceed according to the cephalocaudal principle. For example, infants see objects before they can control their torso, and they can use their hands long before they can crawl or walk. However, development does not follow a rigid blueprint. One study found that infants reached for toys with their feet prior to reaching with their hands (Galloway & Thelen, 2004). On average, infants first touched the toy with their feet when they were 12 weeks old and with their hands when they were 16 weeks old.

cephalocaudal pattern The sequence in which the earliest growth always occurs at the top—the head—with physical growth and feature differentiation gradually working from top to bottom.

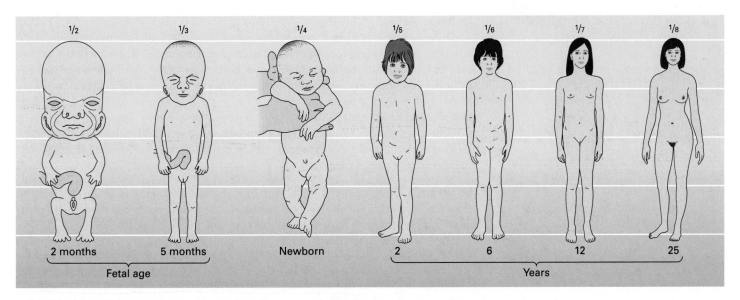

| 1/2 | 1/3 | | 1/4 | 1/5 | 1/6 | 1/7 | 1/8 |

| 2 months | 5 months | Newborn | 2 | 6 | 12 | 25 |

Fetal age   Years

FIGURE 5.1 Changes in Proportions of the Human Body During Growth As individuals develop from infancy through adulthood, one of the most noticeable physical changes is that the head becomes smaller in relation to the rest of the body. The fractions listed refer to head size as a proportion of total body length at different ages.

Growth also follows the **proximodistal pattern,** the sequence in which growth starts at the center of the body and moves toward the extremities. For example, infants control the muscles of their trunk and arms before they control their hands and fingers, and they use their whole hands before they can control several fingers.

Height and Weight

The average North American newborn is 20 inches long and weighs 7½ pounds. Ninety-five percent of full-term newborns are 18 to 22 inches long and weigh between 5½ and 10 pounds.

In the first several days of life, most newborns lose 5 to 7 percent of their body weight before they adjust to feeding by sucking, swallowing, and digesting. Then they grow rapidly, gaining an average of 5 to 6 ounces per week during the first month. They have doubled their birth weight by the age of 4 months and have nearly tripled it by their first birthday. Infants grow about 1 inch per month during the first year, reaching approximately 1½ times their birth length by their first birthday.

Growth slows considerably in the second year of life (Lampl, 2008). By 2 years of age, infants weigh approximately 26 to 32 pounds, having gained a quarter to half a pound per month during the second year; now they have reached about one-fifth of their adult weight. At 2 years of age, the average infant is 32 to 35 inches in height, which is nearly half of their adult height.

The Brain

We described the amazing growth of the brain from conception to birth in Chapter 3, "Prenatal Development." By the time it is born, the infant that began as a single cell is estimated to have a brain that contains approximately 100 billion nerve cells, or neurons. Extensive brain development continues after birth, through infancy and later (de Haan & Martinos, 2008; Nelson, 2009). Because the brain is still developing so rapidly in infancy, the infant's head should be protected from falls or other injuries and the baby should never be shaken. *Shaken baby syndrome,* which includes brain swelling and hemorrhaging, affects hundreds of babies in the United States each year (Altimer, 2008; Squire, 2008). A recent analysis found that fathers most often were the perpetrators of shaken baby syndrome, followed by child-care providers, and boyfriends of the victims' mothers (National Center on Shaken Baby Syndrome, 2008).

Studying the brain's development in infancy is not as easy as it might seem. Even the latest brain-imaging technologies (described in Chapter 1, "Introduction") cannot make out fine details in adult brains and cannot be used with babies (de Haan & Martinos, 2008). Positron-emission tomography (PET) scans pose a radiation risk to babies, and infants wriggle too much to capture accurate images using magnetic resonance imaging (MRI) (Marcus, Mulrine, & Wong, 1999). However, researchers are having success in using the electroencephalogram (EEG), which measures the brain's electrical activity, to learn more about the brain's development in infancy (Bell & Wolfe, 2007) (see Figure 5.2).

The Brain's Development
At birth, the newborn's brain is about 25 percent of its adult weight. By the second birthday, the brain is about 75 percent of its adult weight. However, the brain's areas do not mature uniformly.

Mapping the Brain Scientists analyze and categorize areas of the brain in numerous ways (Levene & Chervenak, 2009; Nelson, 2009). We are most concerned with the portion farthest from the spinal cord known as the *forebrain,* which includes the cerebral cortex and several structures beneath it. The *cerebral cortex* covers the forebrain like a wrinkled cap. It has two halves, or hemispheres (see Figure 5.3). Based on ridges and valleys in the cortex, scientists distinguish four main areas, called

How Would You...?
As a health-care professional, how would you talk with parents about shaken baby syndrome?

proximodistal pattern The sequence in which growth starts at the center of the body and moves toward the extremities.

lateralization Specialization of function in one hemisphere of the cerebral cortex or the other.

FIGURE 5.2 Measuring the Activity of an Infant's Brain By attaching up to 128 electrodes to a baby's scalp to measure the brain's activity, Charles Nelson and his colleagues (2006) have found that even newborns produce distinctive brain waves that reveal they can distinguish their mother's from another woman's, even while they are asleep. *Why is it so difficult to measure infants' brain activity?*

FIGURE 5.3 The Human Brain's Hemispheres The two hemispheres of the human brain are clearly seen in this photograph. It is a myth that the left hemisphere is the exclusive location of language and logical thinking or that the right hemisphere is the exclusive location of emotion and creative thinking.

lobes, in each hemisphere. Although the lobes usually work together, each has a somewhat different primary function (see Figure 5.4):

- *Frontal lobes,* which are involved in voluntary movement, thinking, personality, memory, emotion, sustained attention, and intentionality or purpose
- *Occipital lobes,* which function in vision
- *Temporal lobes,* which have an active role in hearing, language processing, and memory
- *Parietal lobes,* which play important roles in registering spatial location, attention, and motor control

To some extent, the type of information handled by neurons depends on whether they are in the left or right hemisphere of the cortex (Bortfield, Fava, & Boas, 2009). Speech and grammar, for example, depend on activity in the left hemisphere in most people; humor and the use of metaphors depend on activity in the right hemisphere (Imada & others, 2007). This specialization of function in one hemisphere of the cerebral cortex or the other is called **lateralization.** However, most neuroscientists agree that complex functions such as reading or performing music involve both hemispheres. Labeling people as "left-brained" because they are logical thinkers and "right-brained" because they are creative thinkers does not correspond to the way the brain's hemispheres work (Stroobant, Buijus, & Vingerhoets, 2009). Complex thinking in normal people is the outcome of communication between both hemispheres of the brain (Liegeois & others, 2008).

At birth, the hemispheres of the cerebral cortex already have started to specialize: Newborns show greater electrical brain activity in the left hemisphere than the right hemisphere when they are listening to speech sounds (Hahn, 1987). How are the areas of the brain different in the newborn and

Frontal   Parietal

Occipital

Temporal

FIGURE 5.4 The Brain's Four Lobes Shown here are the locations of the brain's four lobes: frontal, occipital, temporal, and parietal.

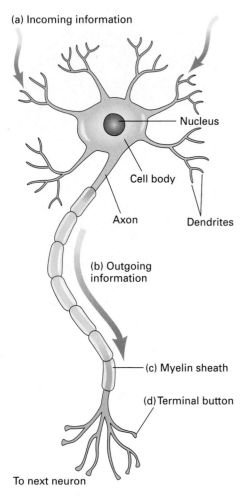

(a) Incoming information

Nucleus

Cell body

Axon

Dendrites

(b) Outgoing information

(c) Myelin sheath

(d) Terminal button

To next neuron

FIGURE 5.5 The Neuron (*a*) The dendrites of the cell body receive information from other neurons, muscles, or glands through the axon. (*b*) Axons transmit information away from the cell body. (*c*) A myelin sheath covers most axons and speeds information transmission. (*d*) As the axon ends, it branches out into terminal buttons.

the infant from those in an adult, and why do the differences matter? Important differences have been documented at both the cellular and the structural level.

Changes in Neurons   Within the brain, the type of nerve cells called neurons send electrical and chemical signals, communicating with each other. As we discussed in Chapter 3, "Prenatal Developments," *a neuron* is a nerve cell that handles information processing (see Figure 5.5). Extending from the neuron's cell body are two types of fibers known as axons and dendrites. Generally, the axon carries signals away from the cell body and dendrites carry signals toward it. A *myelin sheath*, which is a layer of fat cells, encases many axons (see Figure 5.5). The myelin sheath insulates axons and helps electrical signals travel faster down the axon (Dubois & others, 2008; Fair & Schlaggar, 2008). Myelination also may be involved in providing energy to neurons and in communication (Haynes & others, 2006). At the end of the axon are terminal buttons, which release chemicals called *neurotransmitters* into *synapses,* tiny gaps between neurons' fibers. Chemical interactions in synapses connect axons and dendrites, allowing information to pass from neuron to neuron. Think of the synapse as a river that blocks a road. A grocery truck arrives at one bank of the river, crosses by ferry, and continues its journey to market. Similarly, a message in the brain is "ferried" across the synapse by a neurotransmitter, which pours out information contained in chemicals when it reaches the other side of the river.

Neurons change in two very significant ways during the first years of life. First, *myelination,* the process of encasing axons with fat cells, begins prenatally and continues after birth, even into adolescence (Paus, 2009). Second, connectivity among neurons increases, creating new neural pathways, as Figure 5.6 illustrates. New dendrites grow, connections among dendrites increase, and synaptic connections between axons and dendrites proliferate. Whereas myelination speeds up neural transmissions, the expansion of dendritic connections facilitates the spreading of neural pathways in infant development.

Researchers have discovered an intriguing aspect of synaptic connections. Nearly twice as many of these connections are made as will ever be used (Huttenlocher & Dabholkar, 1997). The connections that are used become strengthened and survive, while the unused ones are replaced by other pathways or disappear (Fair & Schlaggar, 2008). In the language of neuroscience, these connections will be "pruned" (Moulson & Nelson, 2008). For example, the more that babies engage in physical activity or use language, the more those pathways will be strengthened.

Changes in Regions of the Brain   Figure 5.7 vividly illustrates the dramatic growth and later pruning of synapses in the visual, auditory, and prefrontal cortex (Huttenlocher & Dabholkar, 1997). Notice that "blooming and pruning" vary considerably by brain

FIGURE 5.6 The Development of Dendritic Spreading Note the increase in connectedness between neurons over the course of the first two years of life. Copyright © 1939, 1975 by the President and Fellows of Harvard College.

At birth   1 month   3 months   15 months   24 months

region. For example, the peak of synaptic overproduction in the visual cortex occurs at about the fourth postnatal month, followed by a gradual retraction until the middle to end of the preschool years (Huttenlocher & Dabholkar, 1997). In areas of the brain involved in hearing and language, a similar, though somewhat later, course is detected. However, in the *prefrontal cortex,* the area of the brain where higher-level thinking and self-regulation occur, the peak of overproduction occurs at just over 3 years of age; it is not until middle to late adolescence that the adult density of synapses is achieved. Both heredity and environment are thought to influence the timing and course of synaptic overproduction and subsequent retraction.

Meanwhile, the pace of myelination also varies in different areas of the brain (Dubois & others, 2008). Myelination for visual pathways occurs rapidly after birth and is completed in the first six months. Auditory myelination is not completed until 4 or 5 years of age.

In general, some areas of the brain, such as the primary motor areas, develop earlier than others, such as the primary sensory areas. The frontal lobes are immature in the newborn. However, as neurons in the frontal lobes become myelinated and interconnected during the first year of life, infants develop an ability to regulate their physiological states, such as sleep, and gain more control over their reflexes. Cognitive skills that require deliberate thinking do not emerge until later in the first year (Bell & Fox, 1992; Bell & Morasch, 2007). Indeed, the prefrontal region of the frontal lobe has the most prolonged development of any brain region, with changes detectable at least into emerging adulthood (Steinberg, 2009).

Early Experience and the Brain Children who grow up in a deprived environment may have depressed brain activity (Nelson, Zeanah, & Fox, 2007; Reeb & others, 2009). As shown in Figure 5.8, a child who grew up in the unresponsive

FIGURE 5.7 Synaptic Density in the Human Brain from Infancy to Adulthood The graph shows the dramatic increase and then pruning in synaptic density for three regions of the brain: visual cortex, auditory cortex, and prefrontal cortex. Synaptic density is believed to be an important indication of the extent of connectivity between neurons.

(a)

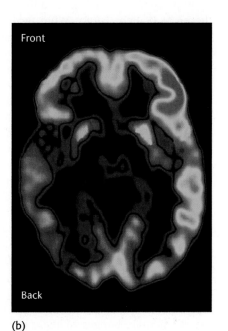

(b)

FIGURE 5.8 Early Deprivation and Brain Activity These two photographs are PET (positron-emission tomography) scans—which use radioactive tracers to image and analyze blood flow and metabolic activity in the body's organs. These scans show the brains of (*a*) a normal child and (*b*) an institutionalized Romanian orphan who experienced substantial deprivation since birth. In PET scans, the highest to lowest brain activity is reflected in the colors of red, yellow, green, blue, and black, respectively. As can be seen, red and yellow show up to a much greater degree in the PET scan of the normal child than the deprived Romanian orphan.

and unstimulating environment of a Romanian orphanage showed considerably depressed brain activity compared with a normal child.

Are the effects of deprived environments irreversible? There is reason to think the answer is no. The brain demonstrates both flexibility and resilience. Consider 14-year-old Michael Rehbein. At age 7, he began to experience uncontrollable seizures—as many as 400 a day. Doctors said the only solution was to remove the left hemisphere of his brain where the seizures were occurring. Recovery was slow, but his right hemisphere began to reorganize and take over functions that normally occur in the brain's left hemisphere, including speech (see Figure 5.9).

Neuroscientists believe that what wires the brain—or rewires it, in the case of Michael Rehbein—is repeated experience. Each time a baby tries to touch an attractive object or gazes intently at a face, tiny bursts of electricity shoot through the brain, knitting together neurons into circuits. The results are some of the behavioral milestones we discuss in this chapter.

In sum, the infant's brain depends on experiences to determine how connections are made (Dalton & Bergenn, 2007). Before birth, it appears that genes mainly direct basic wiring patterns. Neurons grow and travel to distant places awaiting further instructions. After birth, the inflowing stream of sights, sounds, smells, touches, language, and eye contact help shape the brain's neural connections (Nelson, 2009).

Sleep

When we were infants, sleep consumed more of our time than it does now (Miano & others, 2009). The typical newborn sleeps approximately 18 hours a day, but newborns vary a lot in how much they sleep (Sadeh, 2008). The range is from about 10 hours to about 21 hours.

Infants also vary in their preferred times for sleeping and their patterns of sleep. Although the total amount of time spent sleeping remains somewhat consistent, an infant may change from sleeping seven or eight hours several times a day to sleeping for only a few hours three or four times a day. By about 1 month of age, many American infants have begun to sleep longer at night. By 6 months of age, they usually have moved closer to adultlike sleep patterns, spending the most time sleeping at night and the most time awake during the day (Sadeh, 2008).

The most common infant sleep-related problem reported by parents is night waking (The Hospital for Sick Children & others, 2010). Surveys indicate that 20 to 30 percent of infants have difficulty going to sleep at night and sleeping through the night (Sadeh, 2008). What factors are involved in infant night waking? Infant night-waking problems have consistently been linked to excessive parental involvement in sleep-related interactions with their infant (Sadeh, 2008). Also, a recent study of 9-month-old infants revealed that more time awake at night was linked to intrinsic factors such as daytime crying and fussing, and extrinsic factors such as distress when separated from the mother, breast feeding, and sleeping with parents in their bed (DeLeon & Karraker, 2007).

Cultural variations influence infant sleeping patterns. For example, in the Kipsigis culture in Kenya, infants sleep with their mothers at night and are permitted to nurse on demand (Super & Harkness, 1997). During the day, they are strapped to their mothers' backs, accompanying them on daily rounds of chores and social activities. As a result, the Kipsigis infants do not sleep through the night until much later than American infants do. During the first eight months of postnatal life, Kipsigis infants rarely sleep longer than three hours at a stretch, even at night. This sleep pattern contrasts with that of American infants, many of whom begin to sleep up to eight hours a night by 8 months of age.

REM Sleep In *REM sleep*, the eyes flutter beneath closed lids; in *non-REM sleep*, this type of eye movement does not occur and sleep is more quiet. Figure 5.10 shows developmental changes in the average number of total hours spent in REM and

(a)

(b)

FIGURE 5.9 Plasticity in the Brain's Hemispheres (*a*) Michael Rehbein at 14 years of age. (*b*) Michael's right hemisphere (*right*) has reorganized to take over the language functions normally carried out by corresponding areas in the left hemisphere of an intact brain (*left*). However, the right hemisphere is not as efficient as the left, and more areas of the brain are recruited to process speech.

Sleep that knits up the raveled sleave Of care . . . Balm of hurt minds, nature's Second course. Chief nourisher in life's feast.

—William Shakespeare
English Playwright, 17th Century

non-REM sleep. By the time they reach adulthood, individuals spend about one-fifth of their night in REM sleep, and REM sleep usually appears about one hour after non-REM sleep. However, about half of an infant's sleep is REM sleep, and infants often begin their sleep cycle with REM sleep rather than non-REM sleep (Sadeh, 2008). A much greater amount of time is taken up by REM sleep in infancy than at any other point in the life span. By the time infants reach 3 months of age, the percentage of time they spend in REM sleep falls to about 40 percent, and REM sleep no longer begins their sleep cycle.

Why do infants spend so much time in REM sleep? Researchers are not certain. The large amount of REM sleep may provide infants with added self-stimulation, since they spend less time awake than do older children. REM sleep also might promote the brain's development in infancy (Graven, 2006).

When adults are awakened during REM sleep, they frequently report that they have been dreaming, but when they are awakened during non-REM sleep they are much less likely to report they have been dreaming (Cartwright & others, 2006). Because infants spend more time than adults in REM sleep, can we conclude that they dream a lot? We don't know whether infants dream or not, because they don't have any way of reporting dreams.

FIGURE 5.10 Developmental Changes in REM and Non-REM Sleep.

Shared Sleeping   Sleeping arrangements for newborns vary from culture to culture. For example, sharing a bed with a mother is a common practice in many cultures, such as Guatamala and China, whereas in others, such as the United States and Great Britain, newborns sleep in a crib, either in the same room as the parents or in a separate room. In some cultures, infants sleep with the mother until they are weaned, after which they sleep with siblings until middle and late childhood (Walker, 2006). Whatever the sleeping arrangements, it is recommended that the infant's bedding provide firm support and that cribs have side rails.

Shared sleeping, or co-sleeping, is a controversial issue among experts (Sadeh, 2008). According to some child experts, shared sleeping brings several benefits: It promotes breast feeding and a quicker response to the baby's cries, and it allows the mother to detect potentially dangerous breathing pauses in the baby (Pelayo & others, 2006). However, shared sleeping remains a controversial issue, with some experts recommending it, others arguing against it (Mitchell, 2007; Sadeh, 2008). The American Academy of Pediatrics Task Force on Infant Positioning and SIDS (AAPTFIPS) (2000) discourages shared sleeping. The Task Force concluded that bed sharing increases the risk that the sleeping mother will roll over onto her baby or increase the risk of sudden infant death syndrome (SIDS). Recent studies have found that bed sharing is linked with a greater incidence of SIDS, especially when parents smoke (Alm, Lagercrantz, & Wennergren, 2006; Bajanowski & others, 2007). Also, shared sleeping is likely to place the infant at risk more if the caregivers are impaired by alcohol or are overly tired (Baddock & others, 2007). And recent studies indicate that African American mothers and their infants are more likely to bed share than non-Latino White mothers (Fu & others, 2008; Hauck & others, 2008).

SIDS   **Sudden infant death syndrome (SIDS)** is a condition that occurs when infants stop breathing, usually during the night, and die suddenly without an apparent cause. SIDS remains the highest cause of infant death in the United States with nearly 3,000 deaths annually attributed to it. Risk of SIDS is highest at 2 to 4 months of age (NICHD, 2008).

sudden infant death syndrome (SIDS)   A condition that occurs when an infant stops breathing, usually during the night, and suddenly dies without an apparent cause.

Is this a good sleep position for infants? Why or why not?

How Would You...?
As a health-care professional, how would you advise parents about preventing SIDS?

Since 1992, The American Academy of Pediatrics (AAP) has recommended that infants be placed to sleep on their backs to reduce the risk of SIDS, and the frequency of prone sleeping among U.S. infants has dropped dramatically (AAPTFIPS, 2000). Researchers have found that SIDS does indeed decrease when infants sleep on their backs rather than on their stomachs or sides (Dwyer & Ponsonby, 2009; McMullen, Lipke, & LeMura, 2009). Among the reasons given that prone sleeping is a high risk factor for SIDS are impairment of the infant's arousal from sleep and the restriction of the infant's ability to swallow effectively (Keens & Gemmill, 2008; Mitchell, 2009). A recent study revealed that at 3 months, 26 percent of U.S. mothers did not use the recommended supine position for their infants' nighttime sleep (Hauck & others, 2008).

In addition to sleeping in a prone position, researchers have found that the following are risk factors for SIDS:

- Low birth weight infants are 5 to 10 times more likely to die of SIDS than are their normal-weight counterparts (Horne & others, 2002).

- Infants whose siblings have died of SIDS are two to four times as likely to die of it (Lenoir, Mallet, & Calenda, 2000).

- Six percent of infants with *sleep apnea,* a temporary cessation of breathing in which the airway is completely blocked, usually for 10 seconds or longer, die of SIDS (McNamara & Sullivan, 2000).

- African American and Eskimo infants are four to six times as likely as all others to die of SIDS (Ige & Shelton, 2004).

- SIDS is more common in lower socioeconomic groups (Mitchell & others, 2000).

- SIDS is more common in infants who are passively exposed to cigarette smoke (Shea & Steiner, 2008).

- SIDS is more common if infants sleep in soft bedding (McGarvey & others, 2006).

- SIDS is less likely to occur in infants who use a pacifier when they go to sleep (Li & others, 2006).

- SIDS is less common when infants sleep in a bedroom with a fan. A recent study revealed that infants who sleep in a bedroom with a fan have a 70 percent lower risk of SIDS (Coleman-Phox, Odouli, & Li, 2008).

- SIDS occurs more often in infants with abnormal brain stem functioning involving the neurotransmitter serotonin (Kinney & others, 2009).

Nutrition

From birth to 1 year of age, human infants nearly triple their weight and increase their length by 50 percent. What do they need to sustain this growth, and what characterizes their eating behavior?

Nutritional Needs and Eating Behavior   Individual differences among infants in terms of their nutrient reserves, body composition, growth rates, and activity patterns make defining actual nutrient needs difficult (Burns & others, 2009; Wardlaw & Smith, 2009). However, because parents need guidelines, nutritionists recommend that infants consume approximately 50 calories per day for each pound they weigh—more than twice an adult's requirement per pound.

A number of developmental changes involving eating characterize the infant's first year (Black & Hurley, 2007). As infants' motor skills improve, they change from using suck-and-swallow movements with breast milk or formula to chew-and-swallow movements with semisolid and then more complex foods. As their fine motor control improves in the first year, they transition from being fed by others toward self-feeding. "By the end of the first year of life, children can sit independently, can chew and swallow a range of textures, are learning to feed themselves, and are making the transition to the family diet and meal patterns" (Black & Hurley, 2007, p. 1). At this point, infants need to have a diet that includes a variety of foods—especially fruits and vegetables.

Caregivers play very important roles in infants' early development of eating patterns (Black & others, 2009). Caregivers who are not sensitive to developmental changes in infants' nutritional needs, neglectful caregivers, and conditions of poverty can contribute to the development of eating problems in infants (Black & Lozoff, 2008).

A national study of more than 3,000 randomly selected 4- to 24-month-olds documented that many U.S. parents aren't feeding their babies enough fruits and vegetables but are feeding them too much junk food (Fox & others, 2004). Up to one-third of the babies ate no vegetables and fruit but frequently ate french fries, and almost half of the 7- to 8-month-old babies were fed desserts, sweets, or sweetened drinks. By 15 months, french fries were the most common vegetable the babies ate.

Such poor dietary patterns early in development can result in more infants being overweight. One analysis revealed that in 1980, 3.4 percent of U.S. babies less than 6 months old were overweight, a percentage that increased to 5.9 percent in 2001 (Kim & others, 2006). As shown in Figure 5.11, as younger infants become older infants, an even greater percentage are overweight. Also in this study, in addition to the 5.9 percent of infants less than 6 months old who were overweight in 2001, another 11 percent were categorized as at risk for being overweight. In this study, infants were categorized as overweight if they were above the 95th percentile for their age and gender on a weight-for-height index; they were labeled at risk for being overweight if they were between the 85th and 95th percentile.

In addition to eating too many french fries, sweetened drinks, and desserts, are there other factors that might explain this increase in overweight U.S. infants? A mother's weight gain during pregnancy and a mother's own high weight before pregnancy may be factors (Wardlaw & Smith, 2009). One important factor likely is whether an infant is breast fed or bottle fed. Breast fed infants have lower rates of weight gain than bottle fed infants by school age, and it is estimated that breast feeding reduces the risk of obesity by approximately 20 percent (Li & others, 2007).

Breast versus Bottle Feeding   For the first four to six months of life, human milk or an alternative formula is the baby's source of nutrients and energy. For years, debate has focused on whether breast feeding is better for the infant than bottle feeding. The growing consensus is that breast feeding is better for the baby's health (Lawrence, 2008; Thorley, 2009). Since the 1970s, breast feeding by U.S. mothers has soared (see Figure 5.12). In 2004, more than two-thirds of U.S. mothers breast fed their newborns, and more than a third breast fed their 6-month-olds. The American Academy of Pediatrics (AAP) and the American Dietetic Association strongly endorse breast feeding throughout the infant's first year (AAP Working Group on Breastfeeding, 1997; James & Dobson, 2005).

What are some of the benefits of breast feeding? The following conclusions have been reached based on the current state of research:

Benefits for the Child

- *Gastrointestinal infections.* Breast fed infants have fewer gastrointestinal infections (Newburg & Walker, 2007).

- *Lower respiratory tract infections.* Breast fed infants have fewer lower respiratory tract infections (Ip & others, 2007).

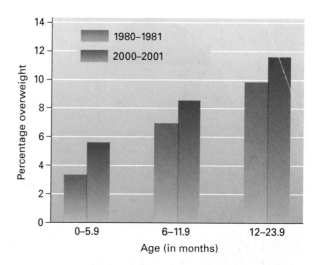

FIGURE 5.11 Percentage of Overweight U.S. Infants in 1980–1981 and 2000–2001
Note: Infants above the 95th percentile for their age and gender on a weight-for-height index were categorized as overweight.

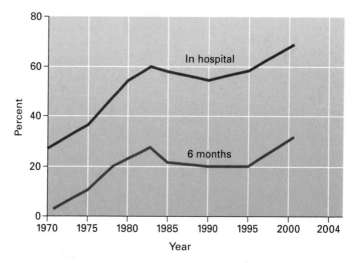

FIGURE 5.12 Trends in Breast Feeding in the United States: 1970–2001

Human milk or an alternative formula is a baby's source of nutrients for the first four to six months. The growing consensus is that breast feeding is better for the baby's health, although controversy still swirls about the issue of breast feeding versus bottle feeding. *Why is breast feeding strongly recommended by pediatricians?*

- *Allergies.* A recent research review by the American Academy of Pediatrics indicated that there is no evidence that breast feeding reduces the risk of allergies in children (Greer & others, 2008). The research review also concluded that modest evidence exists for feeding hypoallergenic formulas to susceptible babies if they are not solely breast fed.

- *Asthma.* The recent research review by the American Academy of Pediatrics concluded that exclusive breast feeding for three months protects against wheezing in babies, but whether it prevents asthma in older children is unclear (Greer & others, 2008).

- *Otitis media.* Breast fed infants are less likely to develop this middle ear infection (Rovers, de Kok, & Schilder, 2006).

- *Atopic dermatitis.* Breast fed babies are less likely to have this chronic inflammation of the skin (Snijders & others, 2007). The recent research review by the American Academy of Pediatrics also concluded that for infants with a family history of allergies, breast feeding exclusively for at least four months is linked to a lower risk of skin rashes (Greer & others, 2008).

  - *Overweight and obesity.* Consistent evidence indicates that breast fed infants are less likely to become overweight or obese in childhood, adolescence, and adulthood (Moschonis, Grammatikaki, & Manios, 2008).

  - *Diabetes.* Breast fed infants are less likely to develop type 1 diabetes in childhood (Ping & Hagopian, 2006) and type 2 diabetes in adulthood (Villegas & others, 2008).

- *SIDS.* Breast fed infants are less likely to experience SIDS (Alm, Lagercrantz, & Wennergren 2006).

In a large-scale research review, no conclusive evidence for the benefits of breast feeding was found for children's cognitive development and cardiovascular system (Agency for Healthcare Research and Quality, 2007).

Benefits for the Mother

- *Breast cancer.* Consistent evidence indicates a lower incidence of breast cancer in women who breast feed their infants (Shema & others, 2007).

- *Ovarian cancer.* Evidence also reveals a reduction in ovarian cancer in women who breast feed their infants (Jordan & others, 2008).

- *Type 2 diabetes.* Some evidence suggests a small reduction in type 2 diabetes in women who breast feed their infants (Ip & others, 2007).

How Would You...?
As a health-care professional, how would you advise mothers about whether to breast feed or bottle feed their infants?

In a large-scale research review, no conclusive evidence could be found for the maternal benefits of breast feeding on return to prepregnancy weight, osteoporosis, and postpartum depression (Agency for Healthcare Research and Quality, 2007). However, a recent study revealed that women who breast fed their infants had a lower incidence of metabolic syndrome (a disorder characterized by obesity, hypertension, and insulin resistance) in midlife (Ram & others, 2008).

Which women are least likely to breast feed? They include mothers who work full-time outside the home, mothers under age 25, mothers without a high school education, African American mothers, and mothers in low-income circumstances (Merewood & others, 2007). In one study of low-income mothers in Georgia, interventions (such as counseling focused on the benefits of breast feeding and the free loan of a breast pump) increased the incidence of breast feeding (Ahluwalia & others, 2000). Increasingly, mothers who return to work in the infant's first year of life use a breast pump to extract breast milk that can be stored for later feeding of the infant when the mother is not present.

The AAP Work Group on Breastfeeding (AAPWGB) strongly endorses breast feeding throughout the first year of life (AAPWGB, 1997). Are there circumstances when mothers should not breast feed? Yes, a mother should not breast feed (1) when the mother is infected with HIV or some other infectious disease that can be transmitted through her milk, (2) if she has active tuberculosis, or (3) if she is taking any drug that may not be safe for the infant (Berlin, Paul, & Vesell, 2009; Buhimschi & Weiner, 2009).

Some women cannot breast feed their infants because of physical difficulties; others feel guilty if they terminate breast feeding early (Walshaw & Owens, 2006). Mothers may also worry that they are depriving their infants of important emotional and psychological benefits if they bottle feed rather than breast feed. Some researchers have found, however, that there are no psychological differences between breast fed and bottle fed infants (Ferguson, Harwood, & Shannon, 1987; Young, 1990).

A further issue in interpreting the benefits of breast feeding was underscored in a recent large-scale research review (Agency for Healthcare Research and Quality, 2007). While highlighting a number of breast feeding benefits for children and mothers, the report issued a caution about breast feeding research: None of the findings imply causality. Breast versus bottle feeding studies are correlational, not experimental, and women who breast feed are wealthier, older, more educated, and likely more health-conscious than their bottle-feeding counterparts, characteristics that could explain why breast fed children are healthier.

Malnutrition in Infancy   Many infants around the world are malnourished (Edmond & others, 2008). Early weaning of infants from breast milk to inadequate sources of nutrients, such as unsuitable and unsanitary cow's milk formula, can cause protein deficiency and malnutrition in infants (Kramer, 2003). Something that looks like milk but is not, usually a form of tapioca or rice, is also often substituted for breast milk. In many of the world's developing countries, mothers used to breast feed their infants for at least two years. To become more modern, they stopped breast feeding much earlier and replaced it with bottle feeding. Comparisons of breast fed and bottle fed infants in such countries as Afghanistan, Haiti, Ghana, and Chile document that the mortality rate of bottle fed infants is as much as five times that of breast fed infants (Grant, 1997). However, as we saw in the *Images of Children's Development* opening story, a concern in developing countries is the increasing number of women who are HIV-positive and the fear that they will transmit this virus to their offspring (Fadnes & others, 2009; Moorthy & others, 2009). Breast feeding is more optimal for mothers and infants in developing countries, except for mothers who have or are suspected of having HIV/AIDS.

Two life-threatening conditions that can result from malnutrition are marasmus and kwashiorkor. **Marasmus** is caused by a severe protein-calorie deficiency and results in a wasting away of body tissues in the infant's first year. The infant becomes grossly underweight and his or her muscles atrophy. **Kwashiorkor,** caused by severe protein deficiency, usually appears between 1 and 3 years of age. Children with kwashiorkor sometimes appear to be well fed even though they are not because the disease can cause the child's abdomen and feet to swell with water (Ahrens & others, 2008). Kwashiorkor causes a child's vital organs to collect the nutrients that are present and deprive other parts of the body of them. The child's hair also becomes thin, brittle, and colorless, and the child's behavior often becomes listless.

Even if not fatal, severe and lengthy malnutrition is detrimental to physical, cognitive, and social development (Fanjiang & Kleinman, 2007). In a longitudinal study over two decades in rural Guatemala, Ernesto Pollitt and his colleagues (1993) found that early nutritional supplements in the form of protein and increased calories can have positive long-term effects on cognitive development. The researchers also found that the relation of nutrition to cognitive performance is moderated both by the time period during which the supplement is given and by socioeconomic status. Although there still was a positive nutritional influence when supplementation began after 2 years of age, the effect on cognitive development was less powerful. Also, the children in the lowest socioeconomic groups benefited more than did the children in higher socioeconomic groups.

This Honduran child has kwashiorkor. Notice the telltale sign of kwashiorkor—a greatly expanded abdomen without the appearance of such expansion in other body areas, such as arms and legs. *What are some other characteristics of kwashiorkor?*

How Would You...?
As a social worker, how would you counsel parents living in poverty about the importance of healthy nutrition for their infant?

marasmus   A wasting away of body tissues in the infant's first year, caused by severe protein-calorie deficiency.

kwashiorkor   A condition caused by a severe deficiency in protein in which the child's abdomen and feet become swollen with water; usually appears between 1 to 3 years of age.

Another study linked the diets of rural Guatemalan infants with their social development at the time they entered elementary school (Barrett, Radke-Yarrow, & Klein, 1982). Children whose mothers had been given nutritious supplements during pregnancy, and who themselves had been given more nutritious, high-calorie foods in their first two years of life, were more active, more involved, more helpful with their peers, less anxious, and happier than their counterparts who had not been given nutritional supplements. To read further about providing nutritional supplements to improve infants' and young children's nutrition, see the *Caring for Children* interlude.

Caring for Children

IMPROVING THE NUTRITION OF INFANTS AND YOUNG CHILDREN LIVING IN LOW-INCOME FAMILIES

Poor nutrition is a special concern in the lives of infants from low-income families. To address this problem in the United States, the WIC (Women, Infants, and Children) program provides federal grants to states for healthy supplemental foods, health-care referrals, and nutrition education for women from low-income families beginning in pregnancy, and to infants and young children up to 5 years of age who are at nutritional risk (Food & Nutrition Service, 2009; WIC New York, 2009). WIC serves approximately 7,500,000 participants in the United States. In 2009, WIC made changes in the program to promote breast feeding and provide more nutritious food (Food & Nutrition Service, 2009; WIC New York, 2009):

- *Increase breast feeding.* WIC staff are being trained in lactation counseling and in most programs, peer counseling services are available to pregnant women and new mothers.
- *Provide food that is lower in fat content.* Only 1 percent or skim milk is available for children 2 years of age and older and women; low-fat cheese and tofu are options.
- *Distribute food that is higher in fiber and that includes more vegetables and fruits.* Vouchers provided to low-income families encourage the consumption of whole-grain cereals and breads, as well as more vegetables and fruits.
- *Have food available that is more culturally appropriate.* For example, brown rice or whole-grain tortillas can be substituted for whole-grain breads; calcium-set tofu or calcium-fortified soy milk can be substituted for cow's milk.

An increasing research initiative is exploring ways to improve the WIC program and assess its influence on mothers, infants, and young children's nutrition and health (Black & others, 2009; Hannan & others, 2009; Heinig & others, 2009; Olson & others, 2009a). A recent study revealed that a WIC program that introduced peer counseling services for pregnant women increased breast feeding initiation by 27 percent (Olson & others, 2009b). Another recent study found that entry in the first trimester of pregnancy to the WIC program in Rhode Island reduced maternal cigarette smoking (Brodsky, Viner-Brown, & Handler, 2008). Yet another study indicated that participating in WIC was linked with a lower risk for being overweight in young Mexican American children (Melgar-Quinonez & Kaiser, 2004).

Adequate early nutrition is an important aspect of healthy development (Schiff, 2009). In addition to sound nutrition, children need a nurturant, supportive environment (Floyd, Mimms, & Yelding, 2008). One individual who has stood out as an

Careers in Children's Development

T. Berry Brazelton, Pediatrician

T. Berry Brazelton is America's best-known pediatrician as a result of his numerous books, television appearances, and newspaper and magazine articles about parenting and children's health. He takes a family-centered approach to child development issues and communicates with parents in easy-to-understand ways.

Dr. Brazelton founded the Child Development Unit at Boston Children's Hospital and created the Brazelton Neonatal Behavioral Assessment Scale, a widely used measure of the newborn's health and well-being (which you read about in Chapter 4, "Birth"). He also has conducted a number of research studies on infants and children and has been president of the Society for Research in Child Development, a leading research organization.

T. Berry Brazelton, pediatrician, with a young child.

advocate of caring for children is T. Berry Brazelton, who is featured in the *Careers in Children's Development* profile.

Health

Among the important aspects of infant health are immunization and accident prevention. Immunization has greatly improved children's health.

Immunization One of the most dramatic advances in infant health has been the decline of infectious disease over the last four decades because of widespread immunization for preventable diseases. Although many presently available immunizations can be given at any age, the recommended schedule is to begin in infancy (Russ, Regalado, & Halfon, 2008). The recommended age for various immunizations is presented in Figure 5.13.

Accident Prevention Accidents are a major cause of death in infancy, especially from 6 to 12 months of age (Andrews, Brouilette, & Brouilette, 2008; Wolraich & others, 2008). Infants need to be closely monitored as their locomotor and manipulative skills develop along with a strong curiosity to explore their environment (Wilson & Hockenberry, 2008). Aspiration of foreign objects, suffocation, falls, poisoning, burns, and motor vehicles are among the most common accidents in infancy (Betz & Snowden, 2008; Burns & others, 2009).

Asphyxiation by foreign material in the respiratory tract is the leading cause of fatal injury in infants under 1 year of age (Baren & others, 2008). Toys need to be carefully inspected for potential danger and some foods, such as whole grapes, nuts, and hard candy, can be choking hazards.

Burns can result from scalding water, excessive sunburn, and electrical wires, sockets, and space heaters. One of the best burn safety devices is a smoke detector.

Age	Immunization
Birth	Hepatitis B
2 months	Diphtheria, tetanus, pertussis Polio Influenza Pneumococcal
4 months	Hepatitis B Diphtheria, tetanus, pertussis Polio Influenza Pneumococcal
6 months	Diphtheria, tetanus, pertussis Influenza Pneumococcal
1 year	Influenza Pneumococcal
15 months	Measles, mumps, rubella Influenza Varicella
18 months	Hepatitis B Diphtheria, tetanus, pertussis Polio
4 to 6 years	Diphtheria, tetanus, pertussis Polio Measles, mumps, rubella
11 to 12 years	Measles, mumps, rubella
14 to 16 years	Tetanus, diphtheria

FIGURE 5.13 Recommended Immunization Schedule of Infants and Children

Automobile accidents are the leading cause of accidents in children over 1 year of age. The major danger for the infant is improper restraint within a motor vehicle (Martin & others, 2007). All infants, newborns included, should be secured in special infant car seats in the backseat of a car rather than being held on an adult's lap or placed in the seat of the car.

Accidents can harm infants in other ways (Alario & Birnkrant, 2008; Schwebel, 2008). For example, sharp, jagged objects can cause skin wounds and long, pointed objects can be poked in the eye. Thus, a fork should not be given for self-feeding until the infant has mastered a spoon, which typically happens by 18 months of age. Another often unrecognized danger to infants is attacks by siblings and pets, especially dogs and cats.

Review and Reflect: Learning Goal 1

1 **Discuss physical growth and development in infancy**

REVIEW

- What are cephalocaudal and proximodistal patterns?
- What changes in height and weight take place in infancy?
- What are some key features of the brain and its development in infancy?
- What changes occur in sleep during infancy?
- What are infants' nutritional needs and eating patterns?
- What characterizes immunization and accident prevention in infancy?

REFLECT

- What three pieces of advice about the infant's physical development would you want to give a friend who has just had a baby? Why those three?

2 HOW DO INFANTS DEVELOP MOTOR SKILLS?

| The Dynamic Systems View | Reflexes | Gross Motor Skills | Fine Motor Skills |

As a newborn, Ramona, whom we met in the chapter opening, could suck, fling her arms, and tightly grip a finger placed in her tiny hand. Within just two years, she would be toddling around on her own, opening doors and jars as she explored her little world. Are her accomplishments inevitable? How do infants develop their motor skills, and which skills do they develop when?

The Dynamic Systems View

Developmentalist Arnold Gesell (1934) thought his painstaking observations had revealed how people develop their motor skills. He had discovered that infants and children develop rolling, sitting, standing, and other motor skills in a fixed order and within specific time frames. These observations, said Gesell, show that motor development comes about through the unfolding of a genetic plan, or *maturation*.

Later studies, however, demonstrated that the sequence of developmental milestones is not as fixed as Gesell indicated and not due as much to heredity as Gesell argued (Adolph, 2008; Adolph & Joh, 2009; Adolph, Karasik, & Tamis-LeMonda, 2010). In the last two decades, the study of motor development experienced a renaissance as psychologists developed new insights about *how* motor skills develop (Thelen & Smith, 1998, 2006). One increasingly influential theory is dynamic systems theory, proposed by Esther Thelen.

According to **dynamic systems theory,** infants assemble motor skills for perceiving and acting. Notice that perception and action are coupled according to this theory (Thelen & Smith, 2006). To develop motor skills, infants must perceive something in the environment that motivates them to act and use their perceptions to fine-tune their movements. Motor skills represent solutions to the infant's goals (Clearfield & others, 2009).

How is a motor skill developed according to this theory? When infants are motivated to do something, they might create a new motor behavior. The new behavior is the result of many converging factors: the development of the nervous system, the body's physical properties and its possibilities for movement, the goal the child is motivated to reach, and the environmental support for the skill (Bertenthal, 2008; von Hofsten, 2008). For example, babies learn to walk only when maturation of the nervous system allows them to control certain leg muscles, when their legs have grown enough to support their weight, and when they want to move.

Esther Thelen is shown conducting an experiment to discover how infants learn to control their arms to reach and grasp for objects. A computer device is used to monitor the infant's arm movements and to track muscle patterns. Thelen's research is conducted from a dynamic systems perspective. *What is the nature of this perspective?*

Mastering a motor skill requires the infant's active efforts to coordinate several components of the skill. Infants explore and select possible solutions to the demands of a new task; they assemble adaptive patterns by modifying their current movement patterns. The first step occurs when the infant is motivated by a new challenge—such as the desire to cross a room—and gets into the "ballpark" of the task demands by taking a couple of stumbling steps. Then, the infant "tunes" these movements to make them smoother and more effective. The tuning is achieved through repeated cycles of action and perception of the consequences of that action. According to the dynamic systems view, even universal milestones, such as crawling, reaching, and walking, are learned through this process of adaptation: infants modulate their movement patterns to fit a new task by exploring and selecting possible configurations (Adolph, Karasik, & Tamis-LeMonda, 2010; Spencer & others, 2009; Thelen & Smith, 2006).

To see how dynamic systems theory explains motor behavior, imagine that you offer a new toy to a baby named Gabriel (Thelen & others, 1993). There is no exact program that can tell Gabriel ahead of time how to move his arm and hand and fingers to grasp the toy. Gabriel must adapt to his goal—grasping the toy—and the context. From his sitting position, he must make split-second adjustments to extend his arm, holding his body steady so that his arm and torso don't plow into the toy. Muscles in his arm and shoulder contract and stretch in a host of combinations, exerting a variety of forces. He improvises a way to reach out with one arm and wrap his fingers around the toy.

Thus, according to dynamic systems theory, motor development is not a passive process in which genes dictate the unfolding of a sequence of skills over time. Rather, the infant actively puts together a skill to achieve a goal within the constraints set by the infant's body and environment. Nature and nurture, the infant and the environment, are all working together as part of an ever-changing system.

As we examine the course of motor development, we will describe how dynamic systems theory applies to some specific skills. First, though, let's examine how the story of motor development begins with reflexes.

Reflexes

The newborn is not completely helpless. Among other things, it has some basic reflexes (Pedroso, 2008). For example, the newborn automatically holds its breath and contracts

dynamic systems theory The perspective on motor development that seeks to explain how motor skills are assembled for perceiving and acting.

its throat to keep water out. **Reflexes** are built-in reactions to stimuli; they govern the newborn's movements, which are automatic and beyond the newborn's control. Reflexes are genetically carried survival mechanisms. They allow infants to respond adaptively to their environment before they have had the opportunity to learn.

The rooting and sucking reflexes are important examples. Both have survival value for newborn mammals, which must find a mother's breast to obtain nourishment. The **rooting reflex** occurs when the infant's cheek is stroked or the side of the mouth is touched. In response, the infant turns its head toward the side that was touched in an apparent effort to find something to suck. The **sucking reflex** occurs when a newborn automatically sucks an object placed in its mouth. This reflex enables newborns to get nourishment before they have associated a nipple with food and also serves as a self-soothing or self-regulating mechanism.

Another example is the **Moro reflex,** which occurs in response to a sudden, intense noise or movement (see Figure 5.14). When startled, the newborn arches its back, throws back its head, and flings out its arms and legs. Then the newborn rapidly

FIGURE 5.14 Infant Reflexes This chart describes some of the infant's reflexes.

Babinski reflex

Grasping reflex

Moro reflex

Reflex	Stimulation	Infant's Response	Developmental Pattern
Blinking	Flash of light, puff of air	Closes both eyes	Permanent
Babinski	Sole of foot stroked	Fans out toes, twists foot in	Disappears after 9 months to 1 year
Grasping	Palms touched	Grasps tightly	Weakens after 3 months, disappears after 1 year
Moro (startle)	Sudden stimulation, such as hearing loud noise or being dropped	Startles, arches back, throws head back, flings out arms and legs and then rapidly closes them to center of body	Disappears after 3 to 4 months
Rooting	Cheek stroked or side of mouth touched	Turns head, opens mouth, begins sucking	Disappears after 3 to 4 months
Stepping	Infant held above surface and feet lowered to touch surface	Moves feet as if to walk	Disappears after 3 to 4 months
Sucking	Object touching mouth	Sucks automatically	Disappears after 3 to 4 months
Swimming	Infant put face down in water	Makes coordinated swimming movements	Disappears after 6 to 7 months
Tonic neck	Infant placed on back	Forms fists with both hands and usually turns head to the right (sometimes called the "fencer's pose" because the infant looks like it is assuming a fencer's position)	Disappears after 2 months

closes its arms and legs. The Moro reflex is believed to be a way of grabbing for support while falling; it would have had survival value for our primate ancestors.

Some reflexes—coughing, sneezing, blinking, shivering, and yawning, for example—persist throughout life. They are as important for the adult as they are for the infant. Other reflexes, though, disappear several months following birth, as the infant's brain matures, and voluntary control over many behaviors develops. The rooting and Moro reflexes, for example, tend to disappear when the infant is 3 to 4 months old. The **Babinski reflex,** in which infants fan out their toes and twist their foot inward when the sole of their foot is stroked, disappears after 9 months to 1 year of age.

The movements of some reflexes eventually become incorporated into more complex, voluntary actions. One important example is the **grasping reflex,** which occurs when something touches the infant's palms (see Figure 5.14). The infant responds by grasping tightly. By the end of the third month, the grasping reflex diminishes, and the infant shows a more voluntary grasp. As its motor development becomes smoother, the infant will grasp objects, carefully manipulate them, and explore their qualities.

Although reflexes are automatic and inborn, differences in reflexive behavior are soon apparent. For example, the sucking capabilities of newborns vary considerably. Some newborns are efficient at forceful sucking and obtaining milk; others are not as adept and get tired before they are full. Most infants take several weeks to establish a sucking style that is coordinated with the way the mother is holding the infant, the way milk is coming out of the bottle or breast, and the infant's temperament (Blass, 2008).

Pediatrician T. Berry Brazelton (1956) observed how infants' sucking changed as they grew older. Over 85 percent of the infants engaged in considerable sucking behavior unrelated to feeding. They sucked their finger, their fists, and pacifiers. By the age of 1 year, most had stopped the sucking behavior, but as many as 40 percent of children continue to suck their thumbs after they have started school (Kessen Haith, & Salapatek, 1970). Most developmentalists do not attach a great deal of significance to this behavior.

Gross Motor Skills

Ask any parents about their baby, and sooner or later you are likely to hear about one or more motor milestones, such as "Cassandra just learned to crawl," "Jesse is finally sitting alone," or "Angela took her first step last week." Parents proudly announce such milestones as their children transform themselves from babies unable to lift their heads to toddlers who grab things off the grocery store shelf, chase a cat, and participate actively in the family's social life (Thelen, 2000). These milestones are examples of **gross motor skills,** which are skills that involve large-muscle activities, such as moving one's arms and walking.

The Development of Posture
How do gross motor skills develop? As a foundation, these skills require postural control (Adolph & Joh, 2009). For example, to track moving objects, you must be able to control your head in order to stabilize your gaze; before you can walk, you must be able to balance on one leg.

Posture is more than just holding still and straight. Posture is a dynamic process that is linked with sensory information in the skin, joints, and muscles, which tell us where we are in space; in vestibular organs in the inner ear that regulate balance and equilibrium; and in vision and hearing (Thelen & Smith, 2006).

Newborn infants cannot voluntarily control their posture. Within a few weeks, though, they can hold their heads erect, and soon they can lift their heads while prone. By 2 months of age, babies can sit while supported on a lap or an infant seat, but they cannot sit independently until they are 6 or 7 months of age. Standing also develops gradually during the first year of life. By about 8 to 9 months of age,

reflexes Built-in reactions to stimuli that govern the newborn's movements, which are automatic and beyond the newborn's control.

rooting reflex A newborn's built-in reaction that occurs when the infant's cheek is stroked or the side of the mouth is touched. In response, the infant turns its head toward the side that was touched in an apparent effort to find something to suck.

sucking reflex A newborn's built-in reaction to automatically suck an object placed in its mouth. The sucking reflex enables the infant to get nourishment before he or she has associated a nipple with food and also serves as a self-soothing or self-regulating mechanism.

Moro reflex A neonatal startle response that occurs in reaction to a sudden, intense noise or movement. When startled, the newborn arches its back, throws its head back, and flings out its arms and legs. Then the newborn rapidly closes its arms and legs to the center of the body.

Babinski reflex A reflex in which infants fan out their toes and twist their foot inward when the sole of their foot is stroked.

grasping reflex A neonatal reflex that occurs when something touches the infant's palms. The infant responds by grasping tightly.

gross motor skills Motor skills that involve large-muscle activities, such as walking.

infants usually learn to pull themselves up and hold on to a chair, and they often can stand alone by about 10 to 12 months of age.

What are some developmental changes in posture during infancy?

Learning to Walk Locomotion and postural control are closely linked, especially in walking upright (Adolph, 2008; Adolph & Joh, 2009). To walk upright, babies must be able both to balance on one leg as they swing the other forward and to shift the weight from one leg to the other.

Even young infants can make the alternating leg movements they need for walking. The neural pathways that control leg alternation are in place from a very early age, possibly even at birth or before. Infants engage in frequent alternating kicking movements throughout the first six months of life when they are lying on their backs. Also when 1- to 2-month-olds are given support with their feet in contact with a motorized treadmill, they show well-coordinated, alternating steps. Despite these early abilities, most infants do not learn to walk until about the time of their first birthday.

If infants can produce forward stepping movements so early, why does it take them so long to learn to walk? The key skills in learning to walk appear to be stabilizing balance on one leg long enough to swing the other forward and shifting the weight without falling. These are difficult biomechanical problems to solve, and it takes infants about a year to do it.

When infants learn to walk, they typically take small steps because of their limited balance control and strength. However, a recent study revealed that infants occasionally take a few large steps that even exceed their leg length and these large steps indicate increased balance and strength (Badaly & Adolph, 2008).

In learning to locomote, infants learn what kinds of places and surfaces are safe for locomotion (Adolph & Joh, 2009; Gill, Adolph, & Vereijken, 2009). Karen Adolph (1997) investigated how experienced and inexperienced crawling infants and walking infants go down steep slopes (see Figure 5.15). Newly crawling infants, who averaged about 8½ months in age, rather indiscriminately went down the steep slopes, often falling in the process (with their mothers next to the slope to catch them). After weeks of practice, the crawling babies became more adept at judging which slopes were too steep to crawl down and which ones they could navigate safely. New walkers also could not judge the safety of the slopes, but experienced walkers accurately matched their skills with the steepness of the slopes. They rarely fell downhill, either refusing to go down the steep slopes or going down backward in a cautious manner. Experienced walkers perceptually assessed the situation—looking, swaying, touching, and thinking before they moved down the slope. With experience, both the crawlers and the walkers learned to avoid the risky slopes where they would fall, integrating perceptual information with the development of

FIGURE 5.15 The Role of Experience in Crawling and Walking Infants' Judgments of Whether to Go Down a Slope Karen Adolph (1997) found that locomotor experience rather than age was the primary predictor of adaptive responding on slopes of varying steepness. Newly crawling and walking infants could not judge the safety of the various slopes. With experience, they learned to avoid slopes where they would fall. When expert crawlers began to walk, they again made mistakes and fell, even though they had judged the same slope accurately when crawling. Adolph referred to this as the *specificity of learning* because it does not transfer across crawling and walking.

Newly crawling infant

Experienced walker

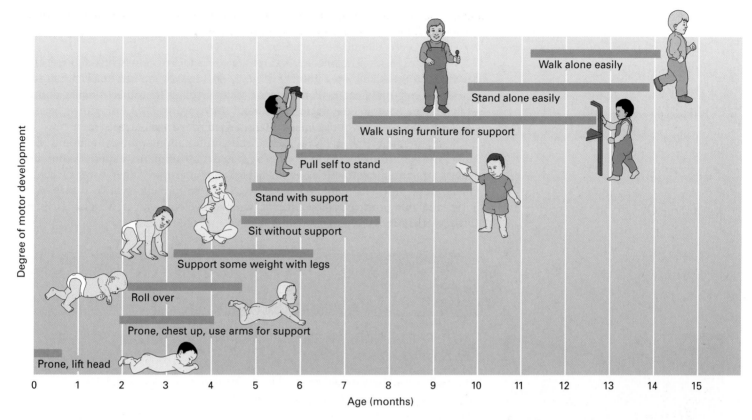

FIGURE 5.16 Milestones in Gross Motor Development

a new motor behavior. Practice is especially important in learning to walk (Adolph & Joh, 2009). Infants and toddlers accumulate an immense number of experiences with balance and locomotion. For example, the average toddler traverses almost 40 football fields a day and has 15 falls per hour (Adolph, 2009). From the perspective of Karen Adolph and her colleagues (2003, p. 495):

> Thousands of daily walking steps, each step slightly different from the last because of variations in the terrain and the continually varying bio-mechanical constraints on the body, may help infants to identify the relevant combination of strength and balance required to improve their walking skills.

The First Year: Motor Development Milestones and Variations   Figure 5.16 summarizes important accomplishments in gross motor skills during the first year, culminating in the ability to walk easily. The timing of these milestones, especially the later ones, may vary by as much as two to four months, and experiences can modify the onset of these accomplishments. For example, since 1992, when pediatricians began recommending that parents place their babies on their backs when they sleep, fewer babies crawled and those who did crawled later (Davis & others, 1998). Also, some infants do not follow the standard sequence of motor accomplishments (Eaton, 2008). For example, many American infants never crawl on their belly or on their hands and knees. They may discover an idiosyncratic form of locomotion before walking, such as rolling, or they might never locomote until they get upright (Adolph & Joh, 2009). In the African Mali tribe, most infants do not crawl (Bril, 1999).

According to Karen Adolph and Sarah Berger (2005), "the old-fashioned view that growth and motor development reflect merely the age-related output of maturation is, at best, incomplete. Rather, infants acquire new skills with the help of their caregivers in a real-world environment of objects, surfaces, and planes."

Development in the Second Year   The motor accomplishments of the first year bring increasing independence, allowing infants to explore their environment more extensively and to initiate interaction with others more readily. In the second year

How Would You...?
As a psychologist, how would you advise parents who are concerned that their infant is one or two months behind the average gross motor milestones?

A baby is an angel whose wings decrease as his legs increase.

—FRENCH PROVERB

of life, toddlers become more motorically skilled and mobile. Motor activity during the second year is vital to the child's competent development and few restrictions, except for safety, should be placed on their adventures.

By 13 to 18 months, toddlers can pull a toy attached to a string and use their hands and legs to climb up a number of steps. By 18 to 24 months, toddlers can walk quickly or run stiffly for a short distance, balance on their feet in a squat position while playing with objects on the floor, walk backward without losing their balance, stand and kick a ball without falling, stand and throw a ball, and jump in place.

Can parents give their babies a head start on becoming physically fit and physically talented through structured exercise classes? Most infancy experts recommend against structured exercise classes for babies. But there are other ways of guiding infants' motor development. Caregivers in some cultures do handle babies vigorously, and this practice might advance motor development, as we discuss in the *Diversity in Children's Development* interlude.

Diversity in Children's Development

CULTURAL VARIATIONS IN GUIDING INFANTS' MOTOR DEVELOPMENT

Mothers in developing countries tend to stimulate their infants' motor skills more than mothers in more modern countries (Hopkins, 1991). In many African, Indian, and Caribbean cultures, mothers massage and stretch their infants during daily baths (Adolph, Karasik, & Tamis-LeMonda, 2010). Jamaican and Mali mothers regularly massage their infants and stretch their arms and legs (Adolph, Karasik, & Tamis-LeMonda, 2010). Mothers in the Gusii culture of Kenya also encourage vigorous movement in their babies (Hopkins & Westra, 1988).

Do these cultural variations make a difference in the infant's motor development? When caregivers provide babies with physical guidance by physically handling them in special ways (such as stroking, massaging, or stretching) or by giving them opportunities for exercise, the infants often reach motor milestones earlier than infants whose caregivers have not provided these activities (Adolph, Karasik, & Tamis-LeMonda, 2010). For example, Jamaican mothers expect their infants to sit and walk alone two to three months earlier than English mothers do (Hopkins & Westra, 1990).

Nonetheless, even when infants' motor activity is restricted, many infants still reach the milestones of motor development at a normal age. For example, Algonquin infants in Quebec, Canada, spend much of their first year strapped to a cradle board. Despite their inactivity, these infants still sit up, crawl, and walk within an age range similar to that of infants in cultures who have had much greater opportunity for activity.

(Top) In the Algonquin culture in Quebec, Canada, babies are strapped to a cradle board for much of their infancy. *(Bottom)* In Jamaica, mothers massage and stretch their infants' arms and legs. *To what extent do cultural variations in the activity infants engage in influence the time at which they reach motor milestones?*

fine motor skills Motor skills that involve finely tuned movements, such as finger dexterity.

Fine Motor Skills

Whereas gross motor skills involve large muscle activity, **fine motor skills** involve finely tuned movements. Grasping a toy, using a spoon, buttoning a shirt, or accomplishing anything that requires finger dexterity demonstrates fine motor skills. Infants have hardly any control over fine motor skills at birth, but newborns do have many components of what will become finely coordinated arm, hand, and finger movements.

The onset of reaching and grasping marks a significant achievement in infants' ability to interact with their surroundings (van Hof, van der Kamp, & Savelsbergh, 2008; von Hofsten, 2008). During the first two years of life, infants refine how they reach and grasp (Barrett & Needham, 2008; Barrett, Traupman, & Needham, 2008;

Needham, 2009). Initially, infants reach by moving their shoulders and elbows crudely, swinging toward an object. Later, when infants reach for an object they move their wrists, rotate their hands, and coordinate their thumb and forefinger. Infants do not have to see their own hands in order to reach for an object (Clifton & others, 1993). Cues from muscles, tendons, and joints—not sight of the limb—guide reaching by 4-month-old infants.

Infants refine their ability to grasp objects by developing two types of grasps. Initially, infants grip with the whole hand, which is called the *palmer grasp*. Later, toward the end of the first year, infants also grasp small objects with their thumb and forefinger, which is called the *pincer grip*. Their grasping system is very flexible. They vary their grip on an object depending on its size, shape, and texture, as well as the size of their own hands relative to the object's size. Infants grip small objects with their thumb and forefinger (and sometimes their middle finger too), whereas they grip large objects with all of the fingers of one hand or both hands.

Perceptual-motor coupling is necessary for the infant to coordinate grasping. Which perceptual system the infant is most likely to use in coordinating grasping varies with age. Four-month-old infants rely greatly on touch to determine how they will grip an object; 8-month-olds are more likely to use vision as a guide (Newell & others, 1989). This developmental change is efficient because vision lets infants preshape their hands as they reach for an object.

Experience plays a role in reaching and grasping. In one study, 3-month-old infants participated in play sessions wearing "sticky mittens"—"mittens with palms that stuck to the edges of toys and allowed the infants to pick up the toys" (Needham, Barrett, & Peterman, 2002, p. 279) (see Figure 5.17). Infants who participated in sessions with the mittens grasped and manipulated objects earlier in their development than a control group of infants who did not receive the "mitten" experience. The experienced infants looked at the objects longer, swatted at them more during visual contact, and were more likely to mouth the objects.

Just as infants need to exercise their gross motor skills, they also need to exercise their fine motor skills (Barrett, Davis, & Needham, 2007; Needham, 2009). Especially when they can manage a pincer grip, infants delight in picking up small objects. Many develop the pincer grip and begin to crawl at about the same time, and infants at this time pick up virtually everything in sight, especially on the floor, and put the objects in their mouth. Thus, parents need to be vigilant in regularly monitoring what objects are within the infant's reach.

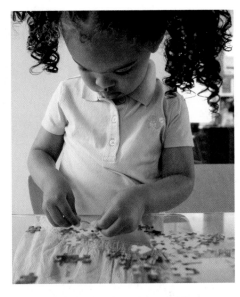

A young girl using a pincer grip to pick up puzzle pieces.

FIGURE 5.17 Infants' Use of "Sticky Mittens" to Explore Objects Amy Needham and her colleagues (2002) found that "Sticky Mittens" enhanced young infants' object exploration skills.

Review and Reflect: Learning Goal 2

2 Describe infants' motor development

REVIEW

- What is dynamic systems theory?
- What are some reflexes that infants have?
- How do gross motor skills develop in infancy?
- How do fine motor skills develop in infancy?

REFLECT

- Which view of infant motor development do you prefer—the traditional maturational view or the dynamic systems view? Why?

3 HOW CAN INFANTS' SENSORY AND PERCEPTUAL DEVELOPMENT BE CHARACTERIZED?

How do sensations and perceptions develop? Can newborns see? If so, what can they perceive? What about the other senses—hearing, smell, taste, and touch? What are they like in newborns, and how do they develop? Can infants put together information from two modalities, such as sight and sound? These are among the intriguing questions that we will explore in this section.

What Are Sensation and Perception?

How does a newborn know that her mother's skin is soft rather than rough? How does a 5-year-old know what color his hair is? Infants and children "know" these things as a result of information that comes through the senses. Without vision, hearing, touch, taste, and smell, we would be isolated from the world; we would live in dark silence, a tasteless, colorless, feelingless void.

Sensation occurs when information interacts with sensory *receptors*—the eyes, ears, tongue, nostrils, and skin. The sensation of hearing occurs when waves of pulsating air are collected by the outer ear and transmitted through the bones of the inner ear to the auditory nerve. The sensation of vision occurs as rays of light contact the eyes, become focused on the retina, and are transmitted by the optic nerve to the visual centers of the brain.

Perception is the interpretation of what is sensed. The air waves that contact the ears might be interpreted as noise or as musical sounds, for example. The physical energy transmitted to the retina of the eye might be interpreted as a particular color, pattern, or shape, depending on how it is perceived.

The Ecological View

For the past several decades, much of the research on perceptual development in infancy has been guided by the ecological view of Eleanor and James J. Gibson (E. Gibson, 1969, 1989, 2001; J. Gibson, 1966, 1979). They argue that we do not have to take bits and pieces of data from sensations and build up representations of the world in our minds. Instead, our perceptual system can select from the rich information that the environment itself provides.

According to the Gibsons' **ecological view,** we directly perceive information that exists in the world around us. Thus, perception brings us into contact with the environment in order to interact with and adapt to it. Perception is designed for action. Perception gives people such information as when to duck, when to turn their bodies through a narrow passageway, and when to put their hands up to catch something.

In the Gibsons' view, objects have **affordances,** which are opportunities for interaction offered by objects that fit within our capabilities to perform activities. A pot may afford you something to cook with, and it may afford a toddler something to bang. Adults typically know when a chair is appropriate for sitting, when a surface is safe for walking, or when an object is within reach. We directly and accurately perceive these affordances by sensing information from the environment—the light or sound reflecting from the surfaces of the world—and from our own bodies through muscle receptors, joint receptors, and skin receptors, for example.

> *T*he experiences of the first three years of life are almost entirely lost to us, and when we attempt to enter into a small child's world, we come as foreigners who have forgotten the landscape and no longer speak the native tongue.
>
> —SELMA FRAIBERG
> ***Developmentalist and Child Advocate, 20th Century***

How would you use the Gibsons' ecological theory of perception and the concept of affordance to explain the role that perception is playing in this toddler's activity?

Studying the infant's perception has not been an easy task. The *Research in Children's Development* interlude describes some of the ingenious ways researchers study the infant's perception.

Research in Children's Development

STUDYING THE NEWBORN'S PERCEPTION

The creature has poor motor coordination and can move itself only with great difficulty. Although it cries when uncomfortable, it uses few other vocalizations. In fact, it sleeps most of the time, about 16 to 17 hours a day. You are curious about this creature and want to know more about what it can do. You think to yourself, "I wonder if it can see. How could I find out?"

You obviously have a communication problem with the creature. You must devise a way that will allow the creature to "tell" you that it can see. While examining the creature one day, you make an interesting discovery. When you move an object horizontally in front of the creature, its eyes follow the object's movement.

The creature's head movement suggests that it has at least some vision. In case you haven't already guessed, the creature you have been reading about is the human infant, and the role you played is that of a researcher interested in devising techniques to learn about the infant's visual perception. After years of work, scientists have developed research methods and tools sophisticated enough to examine the subtle abilities of infants and to interpret their complex actions (Bendersky & Sullivan, 2007).

Visual Preference Method
Robert Fantz (1963) was a pioneer in this effort. Fantz made an important discovery that advanced the ability of researchers to investigate infants' visual perception: Infants look at different things for different lengths of time. Fantz placed infants in a "looking chamber," which had two visual displays on the ceiling above the infant's head. An experimenter viewed the infant's eyes by looking through a peephole. If the infant was fixating on one of the displays, the experimenter could see the display's reflection in the infant's eyes. This arrangement allowed the experimenter to determine how long the infant looked at each display. Fantz (1963) found that infants only 2 days old look longer at patterned stimuli, such as faces and concentric circles, than at red, white, or yellow discs. Infants 2 to 3 weeks old preferred to look at patterns—a face, a piece of printed matter, or a bull's-eye—longer than at red, yellow, or white discs (see Figure 5.18). Fantz's research method—studying whether infants can distinguish one stimulus from another by measuring the length of time they attend to different stimuli—is referred to as the **visual preference method.**

Habituation and Dishabituation
Another way that researchers have studied infant perception is to present a stimulus (such as a sight or a sound) a number of times. If there is a decrease in the infant's response to the stimulus after several presentations, it indicates that the infant is no longer interested in looking at the stimulus. If the researcher now presents a new stimulus, the infant's response will recover—indicating the infant could discriminate between the old and new stimulus (Snyder & Torrence, 2008).

Habituation is the name given to decreased responsiveness to a stimulus after repeated presentations of the stimulus. **Dishabituation** is the recovery of a habituated response after a change in stimulation. Newborn infants can habituate to repeated sights, sounds, smells, or touches (Rovee-Collier, 2004). Among the measures researchers use in habituation studies are sucking behavior (sucking stops when the young infant

(continued on next page)

sensation The product of the interaction between information and the sensory receptors—the eyes, ears, tongue, nostrils, and skin.

perception The interpretation of what is sensed.

ecological view The view that perception functions to bring organisms in contact with the environment and to increase adaptation.

affordances Opportunities for interaction offered by objects that fit within our capabilities to perform functional activities.

visual preference method A method used to determine whether infants can distinguish one stimulus from another by measuring the length of time they attend to different stimuli.

habituation Decreased responsiveness to a stimulus after repeated presentations of the stimulus.

dishabituation Recovery of a habituated response after a change in stimulation.

FIGURE 5.18 Fantz's Experiment on Infants' Visual Perception (a) Infants 2 to 3 weeks old preferred to look at some stimuli more than others. In Fantz's experiment, infants preferred to look at patterns rather than at color or brightness. For example, they looked longer at a face, a piece of printed matter, or a bull's-eye than at red, yellow, or white discs. (b) Fantz used a "looking chamber" to study infants' perception of stimuli.

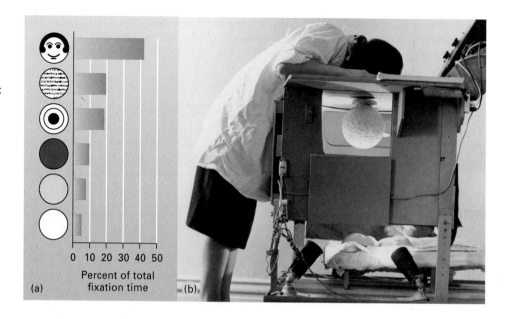

(a) Percent of total fixation time

(b)

attends to a novel object), heart and respiration rates, and the length of time the infant looks at an object. Figure 5.19 shows the results of one study of habituation and dishabituation with newborns (Slater, Morison, & Somers, 1988).

High-Amplitude Sucking

To assess an infant's attention to sound, researchers often use a method called *high-amplitude sucking.* In this method, infants are given a nonnutritive nipple to suck, and the nipple is connected to "a sound generating system. Each suck causes a noise to be generated and the infant learns quickly that sucking brings about this noise. At first, babies suck frequently, so the noise occurs often. Then, gradually, they lose interest in hearing repetitions of the same noise and begin to suck less frequently. At this point, the experimenter changes the sound that is being generated. If the babies renew vigorous sucking, we infer that they have discriminated the sound change and are sucking more because they want to hear the interesting new sound" (Menn & Stoel-Gammon, 2009, p. 67).

The Orienting Response and Tracking

A technique that can be used to determine if an infant can see or hear is the *orienting response,* which involves turning one's head toward a sight or sound. Another technique, *tracking,* consists of eye movements that follow (*track*) a moving object and can

FIGURE 5.19 Habituation and Dishabituation In the first part of one study, 7-hour-old newborns were shown the stimulus in (a). As indicated, the newborns looked at it an average of 41 seconds when it was first presented to them (Slater, Morison, & Somers, 1988). Over seven more presentations of the stimulus, they looked at it less and less. In the second part of the study, infants were presented with both the familiar stimulus to which they had just become habituated to (a) and a new stimulus—shown in (b), which was rotated 90 degrees. The newborns looked at the new stimulus three times as much as the familiar stimulus.

Habituation

(a) Trial

Dishabituation

(b) Percent time looking

be used to evaluate an infant's early visual ability or to determine an infant's reaction to a noise (Bendersky & Sullivan, 2007).

Equipment

Technology can facilitate the use of most methods for investigating the infant's perceptual abilities. Videotape equipment allows researchers to investigate elusive behaviors. High-speed computers make it possible to perform complex data analysis in minutes. Other equipment records respiration, heart rate, body movement, visual fixation, and sucking behavior, which provide clues to what the infant is perceiving. For example, some researchers use equipment that detects whether a change in infants' respiration follows a change in the pitch of a sound. If so, it suggests that the infants heard the pitch change. Thus, scientists have become ingenious at assessing the development of infants, discovering ways to "interview" them even though they cannot yet talk.

Visual Perception

What do newborns see? How does visual perception develop in infancy?

Visual Acuity and Human Faces   Psychologist William James (1890/1950) called the newborn's perceptual world a "blooming, buzzing confusion." More than a century later, we can safely say that he was wrong. Even the newborn perceives a world with some order. That world, however, is far different from the one perceived by the toddler or the adult.

Just how well can infants see? At birth, the nerves and muscles and lens of the eye are still developing. As a result, newborns cannot see small things that are far away. Estimates of the newborn's visual acuity varies from 20/240 to 20/640 on the well-known Snellen chart used for eye examinations, which means that a newborn can see at 20 feet what a normal adult can see at 240 to 640 feet. In other words, an object 20 feet away is only as clear to the newborn as it would be if it were 640 feet away from an adult with normal vision (20/20). By 6 months of age, though, *on average* vision is 20/40 (Aslin & Lathrop, 2008).

Infants show an interest in human faces soon after birth (Quinn & others, 2009; Slater, Field, & Hernandez-Rief, 2007). Figure 5.20 shows a computer estimation of what a picture of a face looks like to an infant at different ages from a distance of about 6 inches. Infants spend more time looking at their mother's face than a stranger's face as early as 12 hours after being born (Bushnell, 2003). By 3 months of age, infants match voices to faces, distinguish between male and female faces, and discriminate between faces of their own ethnic group and those of other ethnic groups (Kelly & others, 2005, 2007, 2009; Pascalis & Kelly, 2008).

Even very young infants soon change the way they gather information from the visual world, including human faces (Aslin & Lathrop, 2008). By using a special

FIGURE 5.20 Visual Acuity During the First Months of Life The four photographs represent a computer estimation of what a picture of a face looks like to a 1-month-old, 2-month-old, 3-month-old, and 1-year-old (which approximates that of an adult).

FIGURE 5.21 How 1- and 2-Month-Old Infants Scan the Human Face

mirror arrangement, researchers projected an image of human faces in front of infants' eyes so that the infants' eye movements could be photographed (Maurer & Salapatek, 1976). As Figure 5.21 shows, the 2-month-old scans much more of the face than the 1-month-old, and the 2-month-old spends more time examining the internal details of the face. Thus, the 2-month-old gains more information about the world than the 1-month-old.

Color Vision The infant's color vision also improves (Aslin & Lathrop, 2008). By 8 weeks, and possibly by even 4 weeks, infants can discriminate some colors (Kelly, Borchert, & Teller, 1997). By 4 months of age, they have color preferences that mirror adults' in some cases, preferring saturated colors such as royal blue over pale blue, for example (Bornstein, 1975). In part, these changes in vision reflect maturation. Experience, however, is also necessary for color vision to develop normally (Sugita, 2004).

Perceptual Constancy Some perceptual accomplishments are especially intriguing because they indicate that the infant's perception goes beyond the information provided by the senses (Arterberry, 2008). This is the case in *perceptual constancy*, in which sensory stimulation is changing but perception of the physical world remains constant. If infants did not develop perceptual constancy, each time they saw an object at a different distance or in a different orientation, they would perceive it as a different object. Thus, the development of perceptual constancy allows infants to perceive their world as stable. Two types of perceptual constancy are size constancy and shape constancy.

Size constancy is the recognition that an object remains the same even though the retinal image of the object changes as you move toward or away from the object. The farther away from us an object is, the smaller its image is on our eyes. Thus, the size of an object on the retina is not sufficient to tell us its actual size. For example, you perceive a bicycle standing right in front of you as smaller than the car parked across the street, even though the bicycle casts a larger image on your eyes than the car does. When you move away from the bicycle, you do not perceive it to be shrinking even though its image on your retinas shrinks; you perceive its size as constant.

But what about babies? Do they have size constancy? Researchers have found that babies as young as 3 months of age show size constancy (Bower, 1966; Day & McKenzie, 1973). However, at 3 months of age, this ability is not full-blown. It continues to develop until 10 or 11 years of age (Kellman & Banks, 1998).

Shape constancy is the recognition that an object remains the same shape even though its orientation to us changes. Look around the room you are in right now. You likely see objects of varying shapes, such as tables and chairs. If you get up and walk around the room, you will see these objects from different sides and angles. Even though your retinal image of the objects changes as you walk and look, you will still perceive the objects as the same shape.

Do babies have shape constancy? As with size constancy, researchers have found that babies as young as 3 months of age have shape constancy (Bower, 1966; Day & McKenzie, 1973). Three-month-old infants, however, do not have shape constancy for irregularly shaped objects, such as tilted planes (Cook & Birch, 1984).

Perception of Occluded Objects Look around the context where you are now. You likely see that some objects are partly occluded by other objects that are in front of them—possibly a desk behind a chair, some books behind a computer, or a car parked behind a tree. Do infants perceive an object as complete when it is occluded by an object in front of it?

In the first two months of postnatal development, infants don't perceive occluded objects as complete, instead perceiving only what is visible (Johnson, 2009a). Beginning

size constancy The recognition that an object remains the same even though the retinal image of the object changes as you move toward or away from the object.

shape constancy The recognition that an object's shape remains the same even though its orientation to us changes.

at about 2 months of age, infants develop the ability to perceive that occluded objects are whole (Slater, Field, & Hernandez-Reif, 2007). How does perceptual completion develop? In Scott Johnson's (2004, 2009a, b, c; Johnson & others, 2000) research, learning, experience, and self-directed exploration via eye movements play key roles in the development of perceptual completion in young infants.

Many of the objects in the world that are occluded appear and disappear behind closer objects, as when you are walking down the street and see cars appear and disappear behind buildings as they move or you move. Can infants predictively track briefly occluded moving objects? They develop the ability to track briefly occluded moving objects at about 3 to 5 months of age (Bertenthal, 2008). A recent study explored the ability of 5- to 9-month-old infants' ability to track moving objects that disappeared gradually behind an occluded partition, disappeared abruptly, or imploded (shrank quickly in size) (Bertenthal, Longo, & Kenny, 2007). In this study, the infants were more likely to accurately predict the moving object when it disappeared gradually rather than abruptly or imploding.

Depth Perception Decades ago, the inspiration for what would become a classic experiment came to Eleanor Gibson as she was eating a picnic lunch on the edge of the Grand Canyon. She wondered whether an infant looking over the canyon's rim would perceive the dangerous drop-off and back up. She also was worried that her own two young children would play too close to the canyon's edge and fall off. Might even infants perceive depth?

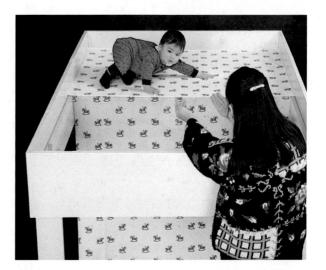

FIGURE 5.22 Examining Infants' Depth Perception on the Visual Cliff Eleanor Gibson and Richard Walk (1960) found that most infants would not crawl out on the glass, which indicated that they had depth perception.

To investigate this question, Eleanor Gibson and Richard Walk (1960) constructed a miniature cliff with a drop-off covered by glass in their laboratory. They placed infants on the edge of this visual cliff and had their mothers coax them to crawl onto the glass (see Figure 5.22). Most infants would not crawl out on the glass, choosing instead to remain on the shallow side, an indication that they could perceive depth.

The 6- to 12-month-old infants in the visual cliff experiment had extensive visual experience. Do younger infants without this experience still perceive depth? Since younger infants do not crawl, this question is difficult to answer. Two- to 4-month-old infants show differences in heart rate when they are placed directly on the deep side of the visual cliff instead of on the shallow side (Campos, Langer, & Krowitz, 1970). However, these differences might mean that young infants respond to differences in some visual characteristics of the deep and shallow cliffs, with no actual knowledge of depth. Although researchers do not know exactly how early in life infants can perceive depth, we do know that infants develop the ability to use binocular cues to depth by about 3 to 4 months of age.

Other Senses

Other sensory systems besides vision also develop during infancy. We explore development in hearing, touch and pain, smell, and taste.

Hearing During the last two months of pregnancy, as the fetus nestles in its mother's womb, it can hear sounds such as the mother's voice, music, and so on (Kisilevsky & others, 2009; Morokuma & others, 2008). Two psychologists wanted to find out if a fetus that heard Dr. Seuss' classic story *The Cat in the Hat* while still in the mother's womb would prefer hearing the story after birth (DeCasper & Spence, 1986). During the last months of pregnancy, sixteen women read *The Cat in the Hat* to their fetuses. Then, shortly after the infants were born, the mothers read either *The Cat in the Hat* or a story with a different rhyme and pace, *The King, the Mice and the Cheese* (which was not read to them during prenatal development). The infants sucked on a nipple

(a)

(b)

FIGURE 5.23 Hearing in the Womb
(a) Pregnant mothers read *The Cat in the Hat* to their fetuses during the last few months of pregnancy. (b) When they were born, the babies preferred listening to a recording of their mother's voice—as evidenced by their rate of sucking on the nipple—rather than another story, *The King, the Mice, and the Cheese.*

in a different way when the mothers read the two stories, suggesting that the infants recognized the pattern and tone of *The Cat in the Hat* (see Figure 5.23). This study illustrates not only that a fetus can hear but also that it has a remarkable ability to learn even before birth. The fetus can also recognize the mother's voice, as a recent study demonstrated (Kisilevsky & others, 2003). Sixty term fetuses (mean gestational age, 38.4 weeks) were exposed to a tape recording either of their mother or of a female stranger reading a passage. The sounds of the tape were delivered through a loudspeaker held just above the mother's abdomen. Fetal heart rate increased in response to the mother's voice but decreased in response to the stranger's voice.

What kind of changes in hearing take place during infancy? They involve perception of a sound's loudness, pitch, and localization:

- *Loudness.* Immediately after birth, infants cannot hear soft sounds quite as well as adults can; a stimulus must be louder to be heard by a newborn than by an adult (Trehub & others, 1991). For example, an adult can hear a whisper from about 4 to 5 feet away, but a newborn requires that sounds be closer to a normal conversational level to be heard at that distance.

- *Pitch.* Infants are also less sensitive to the pitch of a sound than adults are. *Pitch* is the perception of the frequency of a sound. A soprano voice sounds high pitched, a bass voice low pitched. Infants are less sensitive to low- pitched sounds and are more likely to hear high-pitched sounds (Aslin, Jusczyk, & Pisoni, 1998). By 2 years of age, infants have considerably improved their ability to distinguish sounds with different pitches.

- *Localization.* Even newborns can determine the general location from where a sound is coming—but by 6 months of age, they are more proficient at *localizing* sounds or detecting their origins. Their ability to localize sounds continues to improve in the second year (Saffran, Werker, & Warner, 2006).

Touch and Pain   Do newborns respond to touch? Can they feel pain?

Newborns do respond to touch. A touch to the cheek produces a turning of the head; a touch to the lips produces sucking movements.

Newborns can also feel pain (Field & Hernandez-Reif, 2008; Gunnar & Quevado, 2007). If and when you have a son and consider whether he should be circumcised, the issue of an infant's pain perception probably will become important to you. Circumcision is usually performed on young boys about the third day after birth. Will your young son experience pain if he is circumcised when he is three days old? An investigation by Megan Gunnar and her colleagues (1987) found that newborn infant males cried intensely during circumcision. The circumcised infants also display amazing resiliency. Within several minutes after the surgery, they can nurse and interact in a normal manner with their mothers. And, if allowed to, the newly circumcised newborn drifts into a deep sleep, which seems to serve as a coping mechanism.

For many years, doctors performed operations on newborns without anesthesia. This practice was accepted because of the dangers of anesthesia and because of the supposition that newborns do not feel pain. As researchers demonstrated that newborns can feel pain, the practice of operating on newborns without anesthesia is being challenged. Anesthesia now is used in some circumcisions (Taddio, 2008).

The important ability to connect information about vision with information about touch is evident during infancy. Coordination of vision and touch has been well documented in 6-month-olds (Rose, 1990) and in one study was demonstrated in 2- to 3-month-olds (Streri, 1987).

Smell   Newborns can differentiate odors (Doty & Shah, 2008). The expressions on their faces seem to indicate that they like the way vanilla and strawberry smell but do not like the way rotten eggs and fish smell (Steiner, 1979). In one investigation, 6-day-old infants who were breast fed showed a clear preference for smelling their mother's breast pad rather than a clean breast pad (MacFarlane, 1975) (see Figure 5.24). However, when they were 2 days old, they did not show this preference, an indication that they require several days of experience to recognize this odor.

Taste Sensitivity to taste might be present even before birth (Doty & Shah, 2008). When saccharin was added to the amniotic fluid of a near-term fetus, swallowing increased (Windle, 1940). In one study, even at only 2 hours of age, babies made different facial expressions when they tasted sweet, sour, and bitter solutions (Rosenstein & Oster, 1988) (see Figure 5.25). At about 4 months of age, infants begin to prefer salty tastes, which as newborns they had found to be aversive (Doty & Shah, 2008).

Intermodal Perception

Imagine yourself playing basketball or tennis. You are experiencing many visual inputs: the ball coming and going, other players moving around, and so on. However, you are experiencing many auditory inputs as well: the sound of the ball bouncing or being hit, the grunts and groans, and so on. There is good correspondence between much of the visual and auditory information: When you see the ball bounce, you hear a bouncing sound; when a player stretches to hit a ball, you hear a groan. When you look at and listen to what is going on, you do not experience just the sounds or just the sights; you put all these things together. You experience a unitary episode. This is **intermodal perception,** which involves integrating information from two or more sensory modalities, such as vision and hearing.

Early, exploratory forms of intermodal perception exist even in newborns (Bahrick & Hollich, 2008; Sann & Streri, 2007). For example, newborns turn their eyes and their head toward the sound of a voice or rattle when the sound is maintained for several seconds (Clifton & others, 1981), but the newborn can localize a sound and look at an object only in a crude way (Bechtold, Bushnell, & Salapatek, 1979). These early forms of intermodal perception become sharpened with experience in the first year of life (Hollich, Newman, & Jusczyk, 2005). In one study, infants as young as 3½ months old looked more at their mother when they also heard her voice and longer at their father when they also heard his voice (Spelke & Owsley, 1979). Thus even young infants can coordinate visual-auditory information involving people.

Can young infants put vision and sound together as precisely as adults do? In the first six months, infants have difficulty connecting sensory input from different modes, but in the second half of the first year they show an increased ability to make this connection mentally.

FIGURE 5.24 Newborns' Preference for the Smell of Their Mother's Breast Pad In the experiment by MacFarlane (1975), 6-day-old infants preferred to smell their mother's breast pad over a clean one that had never been used, but 2-day-old infants did not show this preference, indicating that this odor preference requires several days of experience to develop.

intermodal perception The ability to relate and integrate information from two or more sensory modalities, such as vision and hearing.

FIGURE 5.25 Newborns' Facial Responses to Basic Tastes Facial expressions elicited by (a) a sweet solution, (b) a sour solution, and (c) a bitter solution.

Thus, babies are born into the world with some innate abilities to perceive relations among sensory modalities, but their intermodal abilities improve considerably through experience (Banks, 2005). As with all aspects of development, in perceptual development, nature and nurture interact and cooperate (Banks, 2005).

Nature, Nurture, and Perceptual Development

Now that we have discussed many aspects of perceptual development, let's further explore one of developmental psychology's key issues as it relates to perceptual development: the nature-nurture issue. There has been a longstanding interest in how strongly infants' perception is influenced by nature or nurture (Aslin, 2009; Johnson, 2009a, b, c; Slater & others, 2009). In the field of perceptual development, nature proponents are referred to as *nativists* and those who emphasize learning and experience are called *empiricists*.

In the nativist view, the ability to perceive the world in a competent, organized way is inborn or innate. At the beginning of our discussion of perceptual development, we examined the ecological view of the Gibsons because it has played such a pivotal role in guiding research in perceptual development. This view leans toward a nativist explanation of perceptual development because it holds that perception is direct and has evolved over time to allow the detection of size and shape constancy, a three-dimensional world, intermodal perception, and so on early in infancy. However, the view is not entirely nativist because the Gibsons emphasized that perceptual development involves distinctive features that are detected at different ages (Slater & others, 2009).

The Gibsons' ecological view is quite different from Piaget's constructivist view, which reflects an empiricist approach to explaining perceptual development. According to Piaget, much of perceptual development in infancy must await the development of a sequence of cognitive stages for infants to construct more complex perceptual tasks. Thus, Piaget feels that the ability to perceive size and shape constancy, a three-dimensional world, intermodal perception, and so on develops later in infancy than the Gibsons envision.

Today, it is clear that an extreme empiricist position on perceptual development is unwarranted. Much of early perception develops from innate (nature) foundations, and the basic foundation of many perceptual abilities can be detected in newborns, whereas others unfold maturationally (Arterberry, 2008; Kellman & Arterberry, 2006). However, as infants develop, environmental experiences (nurture) refine or calibrate many perceptual functions, and they may be the driving force behind some functions. The accumulation of experience with and knowledge about their perceptual world contributes to infants' ability to perceive coherent perceptions of people and things (Slater & others, 2009). Thus, a full portrait of perceptual development includes the influence of nature, nurture, and a developing sensitivity to information (Arterberry, 2008; Werker, Maurer, & Yoshida, 2010).

*T*he infant is by no means as helpless as it looks and is quite capable of some very complex and important actions.

—HERB PICK
Contemporary Developmental Psychologist, University of Minnesota

Perceptual–Motor Coupling

As we come to the end of this chapter, we return to the important theme of perceptual-motor coupling. The distinction between perceiving and doing has been a time-honored tradition in psychology. However, a number of experts on perceptual and motor development question whether this distinction makes sense (Adolph & Joh, 2009; Bertenthal, 2008; Thelen & Smith, 2006). The main thrust of research in Esther Thelen's dynamic systems approach is to explore how people assemble motor behaviors for perceiving and acting. The main theme of the ecological approach of Eleanor and James J. Gibson is to discover how perception guides action. Action can guide perception, and perception can guide action. Only by moving one's eyes, head, hands, and arms and by moving from one location to another can an individual fully experience his or her environment and learn how to adapt to it. Perception and action are coupled.

Babies, for example, continually coordinate their movements with perceptual information to learn how to maintain balance, reach for objects in space, and move across various surfaces and terrains (Bertenthal, 2008; Corbetta & Snapp-Childs, 2009). They are motivated to move by what they perceive. Consider the sight of an attractive toy across the room. In this situation, infants must perceive the current state of their bodies and learn how to use their limbs to reach the toy. Although their movements at first are awkward and uncoordinated, babies soon learn to select patterns that are appropriate for reaching their goals.

Equally important is the other part of the perception-action coupling. That is, action educates perception (Adolph, 2008). For example, watching an object while exploring it manually helps infants to discriminate its texture, size, and hardness. Locomoting in the environment teaches babies about how objects and people look from different perspectives, or whether surfaces will support their weight. Individuals perceive in order to move and move in order to perceive. Perceptual and motor development do not occur in isolation from each other but instead are coupled.

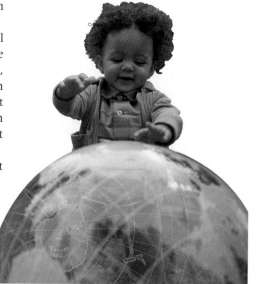

How are perception and action coupled in infants' development?

Review and Reflect: Learning Goal 3

 Explain sensory and perceptual development in infancy

REVIEW

- What are sensation and perception?
- What is the ecological view of perception?
- How does visual perception develop in infancy?
- How do hearing, touch and pain, smell, and taste develop in infancy?
- What is intermodal perception?
- What is the nativist view of perception? What is the empiricist view?
- How is perceptual-motor development coupled?

REFLECT

- How much sensory stimulation should caregivers provide for infants? A little? A lot? Could an infant be given too much sensory stimulation? Explain.

Reach Your Learning Goals

Physical Development in Infancy

1 HOW DO INFANTS GROW AND DEVELOP PHYSICALLY? DISCUSS PHYSICAL GROWTH AND DEVELOPMENT IN INFANCY

Patterns of Growth

- The cephalocaudal pattern is the sequence in which growth proceeds from top to bottom. The proximodistal pattern is the sequence in which growth starts at the center of the body and moves toward the extremities.

Height and Weight

- The average North American newborn is 20 inches long and weighs 7½ pounds. Infants grow about 1 inch per month in the first year and nearly triple their weight by their first birthday. The rate of growth slows in the second year.

The Brain

- One of the most dramatic changes in the brain in the first two years of life is dendritic spreading, which increases the connections between neurons. Myelination, which speeds the conduction of nerve impulses, continues through infancy and even into adolescence. The cerebral cortex has two hemispheres (left and right). Lateralization refers to specialization of function in one hemisphere or the other. Early experiences play an important role in brain development. Neural connections are formed early in an infant's life. Before birth, genes mainly direct neurons to different locations. After birth, the inflowing stream of sights, sounds, smells, touches, language, and eye contact help shape the brain's neural connections, as does stimulation from caregivers and others.

Sleep

- Newborns usually sleep about 18 hours a day. By 6 months of age, many American infants approach adultlike sleeping patterns. REM sleep—during which dreaming occurs—is present more in early infancy than in childhood and adulthood. Sleeping arrangements for infants vary across cultures. In America, infants are more likely to sleep alone than in many other cultures. Some experts believe shared sleeping can lead to sudden infant death syndrome (SIDS), a condition that occurs when a sleeping infant suddenly stops breathing and dies without an apparent cause.

Nutrition

- A number of developmental changes characterize infants' nutritional needs and eating behavior in infancy. Caregivers play important roles in infants' development of healthy eating patterns. The growing consensus is that in most instances breast feeding is superior to bottle feeding for both the infant and the mother, although the correlational nature of studies must be considered. Severe infant malnutrition is still prevalent in many parts of the world. A special concern in impoverished countries is early weaning from breast milk and the misuse and hygiene problems associated with bottle feeding in these countries.

Health

- Widespread immunization of infants has led to a significant decline in infectious diseases. Accidents are a major cause of death in infancy. These accidents include the aspiration of foreign objects, suffocation, falls, and automobile accidents.

2 HOW DO INFANTS DEVELOP MOTOR SKILLS? DESCRIBE INFANTS' MOTOR DEVELOPMENT

The Dynamic Systems View

- Thelen's dynamic systems theory seeks to explain how motor skills are assembled for perceiving and acting. Perception and action are coupled. According to this theory, motor skills are the result of many converging factors, such as the development of the nervous system, the body's physical properties and its movement possibilities, the goal the child is motivated to reach, and environmental support for the skill. In the dynamic systems view, motor development is far more complex than the result of a genetic blueprint.

176

| Reflexes | • Reflexes—built-in reactions to stimuli—govern the newborn's behavior. They include the sucking, rooting, Babinski, and Moro reflexes. The rooting and Moro reflexes disappear after three to four months. Permanent reflexes include coughing and blinking. For infants, sucking is an especially important reflex because it provides a means of obtaining nutrition. |

Reflexes

- Reflexes—built-in reactions to stimuli—govern the newborn's behavior. They include the sucking, rooting, Babinski, and Moro reflexes. The rooting and Moro reflexes disappear after three to four months. Permanent reflexes include coughing and blinking. For infants, sucking is an especially important reflex because it provides a means of obtaining nutrition.

Gross Motor Skills

- Gross motor skills involve large-muscle activities. Key skills developed during infancy include control of posture and walking. Although infants usually learn to walk by their first birthday, the neural pathways that allow walking begin to form earlier. The time at which infants reach milestones in the development of gross motor skills may vary by as much as two to four months, especially for milestones in late infancy.

Fine Motor Skills

- Fine motor skills involve finely tuned movements. The onset of reaching and grasping marks a significant accomplishment, and this becomes more refined during the first two years of life.

3 HOW CAN INFANTS' SENSORY AND PERCEPTUAL DEVELOPMENT BE CHARACTERIZED? EXPLAIN SENSORY AND PERCEPTUAL DEVELOPMENT IN INFANCY

What Are Sensation and Perception?

- Sensation occurs when information interacts with sensory receptors. Perception is the interpretation of sensation.

The Ecological View

- Created by the Gibsons, the ecological view states that we directly perceive information that exists in the world around us. Perception brings people in contact with the environment to interact with and adapt to it. Affordances provide opportunities for interaction offered by objects that fit within our capabilities to perform activities.

Visual Perception

- Researchers have developed a number of methods to assess the infant's perception, including the visual preference method (which Fantz used to determine young infants' interest in looking at patterned over nonpatterned displays), habituation and dishabituation, and tracking. The infant's visual acuity increases dramatically in the first year of life. Infants' color vision improves as they develop. Young infants systematically scan human faces. By 3 months of age, infants show size and shape constancy. At approximately 2 months of age, infants develop the ability to perceive that occluded objects are complete. In Gibson and Walk's classic study, infants as young as 6 months of age had depth perception.

Other Senses

- The fetus can hear several weeks prior to birth. Immediately after birth, newborns can hear, but their sensory threshold is higher than that of adults. Developmental changes in the perception of loudness, pitch, and localization of sound occur during infancy. Newborns can respond to touch and feel pain. Newborns can differentiate odors, and sensitivity to taste may be present before birth.

Intermodal Perception

- Early, exploratory forms of intermodal perception—the ability to relate and integrate information from two or more sensory modalities—are present in newborns and become sharpened over the first year of life.

Nature, Nurture, and Perceptual Development

- In perception, nature advocates are referred to as nativists and nurture proponents are called empiricists. The Gibsons' ecological view that has guided much of perceptual development research leans toward a nativist approach but still allows for developmental changes in distinctive features. Piaget's constructivist view leans toward an empiricist approach emphasizing that many perceptual accomplishments must await the development of cognitive stages in infancy. A strong empiricist approach is unwarranted. A full account of perceptual development includes the roles of nature, nurture, and the developing sensitivity to information.

Perceptual-Motor Coupling

- Perception and action are often not isolated but rather are coupled. Individuals perceive in order to move and move in order to perceive.

KEY TERMS

cephalocaudal pattern 145
proximodistal pattern 146
lateralization 147
sudden infant death
   syndrome (SIDS) 151
marasmus 155
kwashiorkor 155

dynamic systems theory 159
reflexes 161
rooting reflex 161
sucking reflex 161
Moro reflex 161
Babinski reflex 161
grasping reflex 161

gross motor skills 161
fine motor skills 164
sensation 166
perception 166
ecological view 166
affordances 166
visual preference method 167

habituation 167
dishabituation 167
size constancy 170
shape constancy 170
intermodal perception 173

KEY PEOPLE

Ernesto Pollitt 155
T. Berry Brazelton 161

Esther Thelen 159
Karen Adolph 162

Eleanor and James J. Gibson 166
Robert Fantz 167

William James 169
Richard Walk 171

MAKING A DIFFERENCE

Supporting the Infant's Physical Development

What are some good strategies for helping the infant develop in physically competent ways?

- *Be flexible about the infant's sleep patterns.* Don't try to put the infant on a rigid sleep schedule. By about 4 months of age, most infants have moved closer to adultlike sleep patterns.

- *Provide the infant with good nutrition.* Make sure the infant has adequate energy and nutrient intake. Provide this in a loving and supportive environment. Don't put an infant on a diet. Weaning should be gradual, not abrupt.

- *Breast feed the infant, if possible.* Breast feeding provides more ideal nutrition than bottle feeding. If because of work demands the mother cannot breast feed the infant, she should consider "pumping."

- *Give the infant extensive opportunities to explore safe environments.* Infants don't need exercise classes. What they should be provided are many opportunities to actively explore safe environments. Infants should not be constricted to small, confined environments for any length of time.

- *Don't push the infant's physical development or get uptight about physical norms.* In American culture, we tend to want our child to grow faster than other children. Remember that there is wide individual variation in normal physical development. Just because an infant is not at the top of a physical chart doesn't mean parents should start pushing the infant's physical skills. Infants develop at different paces. Respect and nurture the infant's individuality.

RESOURCES FOR IMPROVING CHILDREN'S LIVES

The Amazing Infant
by Tiffany Field (2007)
Malden, MA: Blackwell

The Amazing Infant is an outstanding book on infant development, written by one of the world's leading researchers on infant development. The book accurately captures the flavor of the young infant as an active learner and one far more competent than once was believed.

Solve Your Child's Sleep Problems
by Richard Ferber (2006)
New York: Simon & Schuster

Solve Your Child's Sleep Problems helps parents recognize when their infant or child has a sleep problem and tells them what to do about it.

E-LEARNING TOOLS

Connect to **www.mhhe.com/santrockc11e** to research the answers and complete these exercises. In addition, you'll find a number of other resources and valuable study tools for Chapter 5, "Physical Development in Infancy," on this Web site.

Taking It to the Net

1. Min-lee and Chung-jung are first-time parents. Min-lee insists that their 2-month-old daughter, Yu-Hsuan, can tell the difference between her mother's face and father's face,

voice, and touch. Chung-jung says that is ridiculous. Who is correct?

2. Mary's mother, Robin, has just arrived from out of town and has seen her 3-month-old grandson, Troy, for the first time. Robin exclaims, "What are you feeding this roly-poly hunk? He looks overweight to me." Mary is shocked. She didn't think a baby could be overweight. Should she cut back on Troy's feedings?

3. Isabelle, who has had three children, volunteers to babysit for her friend Nick's 5-month-old boy so that Nick can go on a job interview. As Isabelle is undressing Alexandre, she thinks it's odd that he doesn't seem to be able to turn over in his crib. When she cradles him in her arm to bathe him, he feels "floppy" and appears to lack muscle strength. Is Alexandre evidencing any motor development delays?

Health and Well-Being, Parenting, and Education

Build your decision-making skills by trying your hand at the health and well-being, parenting, and education exercises.

Video Clips

The Online Learning Center includes the following videos for this chapter:

* *Babinski Reflex at 2 Weeks—261*
  The distinct Babinski reflex is demonstrated on this 2-week-old boy.

* *Startle Reflex at 2 Weeks—263*
  Here we see the newborn startle reflex as a 2-week-old boy reacts to a sudden bang of a tambourine.

* *Crying at 10 Weeks—697*
  Here a 10-week-old baby boy cries and waves his arms and legs around as his mother attempts to soothe him.

* *Auditory Tracking at 4 Months—178*
  A 4-month-old girl demonstrates auditory perception when she looks up at her mother, after hearing her mother call her name.

6

I wish I could travel down by the road that crosses the baby's mind where reason makes kites of her laws and flies them.

—RABINDRANATH TAGORE
Bengali Poet, Essayist, 20th Century

LEARNING GOALS

- ◆ Summarize and evaluate Piaget's theory of infant development

- ◆ Describe how infants learn, remember, and conceptualize

- ◆ Discuss infant assessment measures and the prediction of intelligence

- ◆ Characterize early environmental influences on cognitive development

- ◆ Describe the nature of language and how it develops in infancy

COGNITIVE DEVELOPMENT IN INFANCY

CHAPTER OUTLINE

Images of Children's Development
The Stories of Laurent, Lucienne, and Jacqueline

Jean Piaget, the famous Swiss psychologist, was a meticulous observer of his three children: Laurent, Lucienne, and Jacqueline. His books on cognitive development are filled with these observations. Here are a few of Piaget's observations of his children in infancy (Piaget, 1952):

- At 21 days of age, "Laurent found his thumb after three attempts: prolonged sucking begins each time. But, once he has been placed on his back, he does not know how to coordinate the movement of the arms with that of the mouth and his hands draw back even when his lips are seeking them" (p. 27).

- "During the third month, thumb sucking becomes less important to Laurent because of new visual and auditory interests. But, when he cries, his thumb goes to the rescue."

- Toward the end of Lucienne's fourth month, while she is lying in her crib, Piaget hangs a doll above her feet. Lucienne thrusts her feet at the doll and makes it move. "Afterward, she looks at her motionless foot for a second, then recommences. There is no visual control of her foot, for the movements are the same when Lucienne only looks at the doll or when I place the doll over her head. On the other hand, the tactile control of the foot is apparent: after the first shakes, Lucienne makes slow foot movements as though to grasp and explore" (p. 159).

- At 11 months, "Jacqueline is seated and shakes a little bell. She then pauses abruptly in order to delicately place the bell in front of her right foot; then she kicks hard. Unable to recapture it, she grasps a ball which she then places at the same spot in order to give it another kick" (p. 225).

- At 1 year, 2 months, "Jacqueline holds in her hands an object which is new to her: a round, flat box which she turns all over, shakes, [and] rubs against the bassinet. . . . She lets it go and tries to pick it up. But she only succeeds in touching it with her index finger, without grasping it. She nevertheless makes an attempt and presses on the edge. The box then tilts up and falls again" (p. 273). Jacqueline shows an interest in this result and studies the fallen box.

- At 1 year, 8 months, "Jacqueline arrives at a closed door with a blade of grass in each hand. She stretches out her right hand toward the [door] knob but sees that she cannot turn it without letting go of the grass. She puts the grass on the floor, opens the door, picks up the grass again, and enters. But when she wants to leave the room, things become complicated. She puts the grass on the floor and grasps the doorknob. But then she perceives that in pulling the door toward her she will simultaneously chase away the grass which she placed between the door and the threshold. She therefore picks it up in order to put it outside the door's zone of movement" (p. 339).

For Piaget, these observations reflect important changes in the infant's cognitive development. Piaget believed that infants go through six substages as they progress in less than two short years from Laurent's thumb sucking to Jacqueline's problem solving.

schemes In Piaget's theory, actions or mental representations that organize knowledge.

assimilation Piagetian concept of the incorporation of new information into existing schemes.

study of infant cognition have been fueled by an interest in what new-borns and infants know, by continued fascination about innate and learned factors in the infant's cognitive development, and by controversies about whether infants construct their knowledge (Piaget's view) or know their world more directly. In this chapter, we study not only Piaget's theory of infant development but also learning, remembering, and conceptualizing by infants; individual differences; and language development.

1 WHAT IS PIAGET'S THEORY OF INFANT DEVELOPMENT?

Cognitive Processes   **The Sensorimotor Stage**   **Evaluating Piaget's Sensorimotor Stage**

Poet Nora Perry asks, "Who knows the thoughts of a child?" As much as anyone, Piaget knew. Through careful observations of his own three children—Laurent, Lucienne, and Jacqueline—and observations of and interviews with other children, Piaget changed perceptions of the way children think about the world.

Piaget's theory is a general, unifying story of how biology and experience sculpt cognitive development. Piaget thought that, just as our physical bodies have structures that enable us to adapt to the world, we build mental structures that help us to adapt to the world. *Adaptation* involves adjusting to new environmental demands. Piaget stressed that children actively construct their own cognitive worlds; information is not just poured into their minds from the environment. He sought to discover how children at different points in their development think about the world and how systematic changes in their thinking occur.

We are born capable of learning.

—JEAN JACQUES ROUSSEAU
Swiss-Born French Philosopher, 18th Century

Cognitive Processes

What processes do children use as they construct their knowledge of the world? Piaget developed several concepts to answer this question; especially important are schemes, assimilation, accommodation, organization, equilibrium, and equilibration.

Schemes   As the infant or child seeks to construct an understanding of the world, said Piaget (1954), the developing brain creates **schemes.** These are actions or mental representations that organize knowledge. In Piaget's theory, behavioral schemes (physical activities) characterize infancy and mental schemes (cognitive activities) develop in childhood (Lamb, Bornstein, & Teti, 2002). A baby's schemes are structured by simple actions that can be performed on objects, such as sucking, looking, and grasping. Older children have schemes that include strategies and plans for solving problems. For example, in the descriptions at the opening of this chapter, Laurent displayed a scheme for sucking; Jacqueline displayed a problem-solving scheme when she was able to open the door without losing her blade of grass. By the time we have reached adulthood, we have constructed an enormous number of diverse schemes, ranging from knowing how to drive a car to balancing a budget to understanding the concept of fairness.

Assimilation and Accommodation   To explain how children use and adapt their schemes, Piaget offered two concepts: assimilation and accommodation. **Assimilation** occurs when children use their existing schemes to deal with new

In Piaget's view, what is a scheme? What schemes might this young infant be displaying?

How might assimilation and accommodation be involved in infants' sucking?

information or experiences. **Accommodation** occurs when children adjust their schemes to take new information and experiences into account.

Think about a toddler who has learned the word *car* to identify the family's car. The toddler might call all moving vehicles on roads "cars," including motorcycles and trucks; the child has assimilated these objects to his or her existing scheme. But the child soon learns that motorcycles and trucks are not cars and fine-tunes the category to exclude motorcycles and trucks, thus accommodating the scheme.

Assimilation and accommodation operate even in very young infants. Newborns reflexively suck everything that touches their lips; they assimilate all sorts of objects into their sucking scheme. By sucking different objects, they learn about their taste, texture, shape, and so on. After several months of experience, though, they construct their understanding of the world differently. Some objects, such as fingers and the mother's breast, can be sucked, and others, such as fuzzy blankets, should not be sucked. In other words, they accommodate their sucking scheme.

Organization   To make sense out of their world, said Piaget, children cognitively organize their experiences. **Organization** in Piaget's theory is the grouping of isolated behaviors and thoughts into a higher-order system. Continual refinement of this organization is an inherent part of development. A boy who has only a vague idea about how to use a hammer may also have a vague idea about how to use other tools. After learning how to use each one, he relates these uses, organizing his knowledge.

Equilibration and Stages of Development   Assimilation and accommodation always take the child to a higher ground, according to Piaget. In trying to understand the world, the child inevitably experiences cognitive conflict, or *disequilibrium*. That is, the child is constantly faced with counterexamples to his or her existing schemes and with inconsistencies. For example, if a child believes that pouring water from a short and wide container into a tall and narrow container changes the amount of water, then the child might be puzzled by where the "extra" water came from and whether there is actually more water to drink. The puzzle creates disequilibrium; for Piaget, an internal search for equilibrium creates motivation for change. The child assimilates and accommodates, adjusting old schemes, developing new schemes, and organizing and reorganizing the old and new schemes. Eventually, the organization is fundamentally different from the old organization; it is a new way of thinking.

In short, according to Piaget, children constantly assimilate and accommodate as they seek *equilibrium*. There is considerable movement between states of cognitive equilibrium and disequilibrium as assimilation and accommodation work in concert to produce cognitive change. **Equilibration** is the name Piaget gave to this mechanism by which children shift from one stage of thought to the next.

The result of these processes, according to Piaget, is that individuals go through four stages of development. A different way of understanding the world makes one stage more advanced than another. Cognition is *qualitatively* different in one stage compared with another. In other words, the way children reason at one stage is different from the way they reason at another stage. In this chapter, our focus is on Piaget's stage of infant cognitive development. In later chapters, when we study cognitive development in early, middle, and late childhood, and adolescence, we explore the last three Piagetian stages.

The Sensorimotor Stage

The **sensorimotor stage** lasts from birth to about 2 years of age. In this stage, infants construct an understanding of the world by coordinating sensory experiences (such as seeing and hearing) with physical, motoric actions—hence the term

accommodation Piagetian concept of adjusting schemes to fit new information and experiences.

organization Piaget's concept of grouping isolated behaviors and thoughts into a higher-order system, a more smoothly functioning cognitive system.

equilibration A mechanism that Piaget proposed to explain how children shift from one stage of thought to the next.

sensorimotor stage The first of Piaget's stages, which lasts from birth to about 2 years of age; infants construct an understanding of the world by coordinating sensory experiences with motoric actions.

Substage	Age	Description	Example
1 Simple reflexes	Birth to 1 month	Coordination of sensation and action through reflexive behaviors.	Rooting, sucking, and grasping reflexes; newborns suck reflexively when their lips are touched.
2 First habits and primary circular reactions	1 to 4 months	Coordination of sensation and two types of schemes: habits (reflex) and primary circular reactions (reproduction of an event that initially occurred by chance). Main focus is still on the infant's body.	Repeating a body sensation first experienced by chance (sucking thumb, for example); then infants might accommodate actions by sucking their thumb differently than they suck on a nipple.
3 Secondary circular reactions	4 to 8 months	Infants become more object-oriented, moving beyond self-preoccupation; repeat actions that bring interesting or pleasurable results.	An infant coos to make a person stay near; as the person starts to leave, the infant coos again.
4 Coordination of secondary circular reactions	8 to 12 months	Coordination of vision and touch—hand-eye coordination; coordination of schemes and intentionality.	Infant manipulates a stick in order to bring an attractive toy within reach.
5 Tertiary circular reactions, novelty, and curiosity	12 to 18 months	Infants become intrigued by the many properties of objects and by the many things they can make happen to objects; they experiment with new behavior.	A block can be made to fall, spin, hit another object, and slide across the ground.
6 Internalization of schemes	18 to 24 months	Infants develop the ability to use primitive symbols and form enduring mental representations.	An infant who has never thrown a temper tantrum before sees a playmate throw a tantrum; the infant retains a memory of the event, then throws one himself the next day.

FIGURE 6.1 Piaget's Six Substages of Sensorimotor Development

"sensorimotor." At the beginning of this stage, newborns have little more than reflexes with which to work. At the end of the sensorimotor stage, 2-year-olds can produce complex sensorimotor patterns and use primitive symbols. We first summarize Piaget's descriptions of how infants develop. Later we consider criticisms of his view.

Substages Piaget divided the sensorimotor stage into six substages: (1) simple reflexes; (2) first habits and primary circular reactions; (3) secondary circular reactions; (4) coordination of secondary circular reactions; (5) tertiary circular reactions, novelty, and curiosity; and (6) internalization of schemes (see Figure 6.1).

Simple reflexes, the first sensorimotor substage, corresponds to the first month after birth. In this substage, sensation and action are coordinated primarily through reflexive behaviors, such as rooting and sucking. Soon the infant produces behaviors that resemble reflexes in the absence of the usual stimulus for the reflex. For example, a newborn will suck a nipple or bottle only when it is placed directly in the baby's mouth or touched to the lips. Even in the first month of life, the infant is initiating action and actively structuring experiences.

First habits and primary circular reactions is the second sensorimotor substage, which develops between 1 and 4 months of age. In this substage, the infant coordinates sensation and two types of schemes: habits and primary circular reactions. A *habit* is a scheme based on a reflex that has become completely separated from its eliciting stimulus. For example, infants in substage 1 suck when bottles are put to their lips or when they see a bottle. Infants in substage 2 might suck even when no bottle is present. A *circular reaction* is a repetitive action.

A **primary circular reaction** is a scheme based on the attempt to reproduce an event that initially occurred by chance. For example, suppose an infant accidentally sucks his fingers when they are placed near his mouth. Later, he searches for

simple reflexes Piaget's first sensorimotor substage, which corresponds to the first month after birth. In this substage, sensation and action are coordinated primarily through reflexive behaviors.

first habits and primary circular reactions Piaget's second sensorimotor substage, which develops between 1 and 4 months of age. In this substage, the infant coordinates sensation and two types of schemes: habits and primary circular reactions.

primary circular reaction A scheme based on the attempt to reproduce an event that initially occurred by chance.

This 17-month-old is in Piaget's stage of tertiary circular reactions, novelty, and curiosity. *What might the infant do to suggest that she is in this stage?*

secondary circular reactions Piaget's third sensorimotor substage, which develops between 4 and 8 months of age. In this substage, the infant becomes more object-oriented, moving beyond preoccupation with the self.

coordination of secondary circular reactions Piaget's fourth sensorimotor substage, which develops between 8 and 12 months of age. Actions become more outwardly directed, and infants coordinate schemes and act with intentionality.

tertiary circular reactions, novelty, and curiosity Piaget's fifth sensorimotor substage, which develops between 12 and 18 months of age. In this substage, infants become intrigued by the many properties of objects and by the many things that they can make happen to objects.

internalization of schemes Piaget's sixth and final sensorimotor substage, which develops between 18 and 24 months of age. In this substage, the infant develops the ability to use primitive symbols.

object permanence Piagetian term for understanding that objects continue to exist, even when they cannot directly be seen, heard, or touched.

his fingers to suck them again, but the fingers do not cooperate because the infant cannot coordinate visual and manual actions.

Habits and circular reactions are stereotyped—that is, the infant repeats them the same way each time. During this substage, the infant's own body remains the infant's center of attention. There is no outward pull by environmental events.

Secondary circular reactions is the third sensorimotor substage, which develops between 4 and 8 months of age. In this substage, the infant becomes more object-oriented, moving beyond preoccupation with the self. The infant's schemes are not intentional or goal-directed, but they are repeated because of their consequences. By chance, an infant might shake a rattle. The infant repeats this action for the sake of its fascination. This is a *secondary circular reaction:* an action repeated because of its consequences. The infant also imitates some simple actions, such as the baby talk or burbling of adults, and some physical gestures. However, the baby imitates only actions that he or she is already able to produce.

Coordination of secondary circular reactions is Piaget's fourth sensorimotor substage, which develops between 8 and 12 months of age. To progress into this substage, the infant must coordinate vision and touch, hand and eye. Actions become more outwardly directed. Significant changes during this substage involve the coordination of schemes and intentionality. Infants readily combine and recombine previously learned schemes in a coordinated way. They might look at an object and grasp it simultaneously, or they might visually inspect a toy, such as a rattle, and finger it simultaneously, exploring it tactilely. Actions are even more outwardly directed than before. Related to this coordination is the second achievement—the presence of intentionality. For example, infants might manipulate a stick in order to bring a desired toy within reach or they might knock over one block to reach and play with another one. Similarly, when 11-month-old Jacqueline, as described in the chapter opening, placed the ball in front of her and kicked it, she was demonstrating intentionality.

Tertiary circular reactions, novelty, and curiosity is Piaget's fifth sensorimotor substage, which develops between 12 and 18 months of age. In this substage, infants become intrigued by the many properties of objects and by the many things that they can make happen to objects. A block can be made to fall, spin, hit another object, and slide across the ground. *Tertiary circular reactions* are schemes in which the infant purposely explores new possibilities with objects, continually doing new things to them and exploring the results. Piaget says that this stage marks the starting point for human curiosity and interest in novelty.

Internalization of schemes is Piaget's sixth and final sensorimotor substage, which develops between 18 and 24 months of age. In this substage, the infant develops the ability to use primitive symbols. For Piaget, a *symbol* is an internalized sensory image or word that represents an event. Primitive symbols permit the infant to think about concrete events without directly acting them out or perceiving them. Moreover, symbols allow the infant to manipulate and transform the represented events in simple ways. In a favorite Piagetian example, Piaget's young daughter saw a matchbox being opened and closed. Later, she mimicked the event by opening and closing her mouth. This was an obvious expression of her image of the event.

Object Permanence
Imagine how chaotic and unpredictable your life would be if you could not distinguish between yourself and your world. This is what the life of a newborn must be like, according to Piaget. There is no differentiation between the self and world; objects have no separate, permanent existence.

By the end of the sensorimotor period, objects are both separate from the self and permanent. **Object permanence** is the understanding that objects continue to exist even when they cannot be seen, heard, or touched. Acquiring the sense of object permanence is one of the infant's most important accomplishments, according to Piaget.

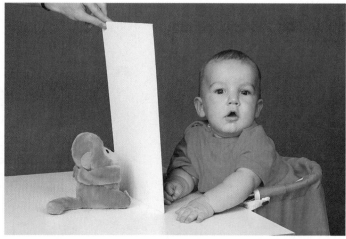

FIGURE 6.2 Object Permanence Piaget argued that object permanence is one of infancy's landmark cognitive accomplishments. For this 5-month-old boy, "out of sight" is literally out of mind. The infant looks at the toy monkey (*left*), but, when his view of the toy is blocked (*right*), he does not search for it. Several months later, he will search for the hidden toy monkey, reflecting the presence of object permanence.

How could anyone know whether an infant had a sense of object permanence or not? The principal way that object permanence is studied is by watching an infant's reaction when an interesting object disappears (see Figure 6.2). If infants search for the object, it is assumed that they believe it continues to exist.

Object permanence is just one of the basic concepts about the physical world developed by babies. To Piaget, children, even infants, are much like little scientists, examining the world to see how it works. The *Research in Children's Development* interlude that follows describes some of the ways in which adult scientists try to discover what these "baby scientists" are finding out about the world.

Research in Children's Development

OBJECT PERMANENCE AND CAUSALITY

Two accomplishments of infants that Piaget examined were the development of object permanence and the child's understanding of causality. Let's examine two research studies that address these topics.

In both studies, Renée Baillargeon and her colleagues used a research method that involves *violation of expectations*. In this method, infants see an event happen as it normally would. Then, the event is changed, often in a way that creates a physically impossible event. That infants look longer at the changed event indicates they are surprised by it. In other words, the infant's reaction is interpreted to indicate that the infant had certain expectations about the world that were violated.

In one study focused on object permanence, researchers showed infants a toy car that moved down an inclined track, disappeared behind a screen, and then reemerged at the other end, still on the track (Baillargeon & DeVos, 1991) (see Figure 6.3a). After this sequence was repeated several times, something different occurred: A toy mouse was placed *behind* the tracks but was hidden by the screen while the car rolled by (see Figure 6.3b). This was the "possible" event. Then, the researchers created an "impossible event": The toy mouse was placed *on* the tracks but was secretly removed after the screen was lowered so that the car seemed to go through the mouse (see Figure 6.3c). In this study, infants as young as 3½ months of age looked longer at the impossible event than at the possible event, an indication that they were surprised by it. Their surprise suggested that they remembered not only the existence of the toy mouse (object permanence) but also its location.

(continued on next page)

(a) Practice (No toy mouse)

(b) Possible event (Toy mouse behind the track)

(c) Impossible event (Toy mouse on the track)

FIGURE 6.3 Using the Violation of Expectations Method to Study Object Permanence in Infants If infants looked longer at (c) than at (b), researchers reasoned that the impossible event in (c) violated the infants' expectations and that they remembered that the toy mouse existed.

Another study focused on the infant's understanding of causality (Kotovsky & Baillargeon, 1994). In this research, a cylinder rolls down a ramp and hits a toy bug at the bottom of the ramp. By 5½ and 6½ months of age, after infants have seen how far the bug will be pushed by a medium-sized cylinder, their reactions indicate that they understand that the bug will roll farther if it is hit by a large cylinder than if it is hit by a small cylinder. Thus, by the middle of the first year of life, these infants understand that the size of a moving object determines how far it will move a stationary object that it collides with.

In Baillargeon's (2008; Baillargeon & others, 2009) view, infants have a preadapted, innate bias called the *principle of persistence* that explains their assumption that objects don't change their properties—including how solid they are, their location, their color, and their form—unless some external factor (a person moves the object, for example) obviously intervenes. Shortly, we revisit the extent to which nature and nurture are at work in the changes that take place in the infant's cognitive development.

The research findings discussed in this interlude and other research indicate that infants develop object permanence and causal reasoning much earlier than Piaget proposed (Baillargeon & others, 2009; Luo, Kaufman, & Baillargeon, 2009). Indeed, as you will see in the next section, a major theme of infant cognitive development today is that infants are more cognitively competent than Piaget envisioned.

Evaluating Piaget's Sensorimotor Stage

Piaget opened up a new way of looking at infants with his view that their main task is to coordinate their sensory impressions with their motor activity. However, the infant's cognitive world is not as neatly packaged as Piaget portrayed it, and some of Piaget's explanations for the cause of change are debated. In the past several decades, sophisticated experimental techniques have been devised to study infants, and there have been a large number of research studies on infant development. Much of the new research suggests that Piaget's view of sensorimotor development needs to be modified (Baillargeon & others, 2009; Quinn & Bhatt, 2009; Spelke & Kinzler, 2009; Woodward & Needham, 2009).

The A-not-B Error One modification concerns Piaget's claim that certain processes are crucial in transitions from one stage to the next. The data do not always support his explanations. For example, in Piaget's theory, an important feature in the progression into substage 4, *coordination of secondary circular reactions*, is an infant's inclination to search for a hidden object in a familiar location rather than to look for the object in a new location. Thus, if a toy is hidden twice, initially at location A and subsequently at location B, 8- to 12-month-old infants search correctly at location A initially. But when the toy is subsequently hidden at location B, they make the mistake of continuing to search for it at location A. **A-not-B error** (also called AB̄ error) is the term used to describe this common mistake. Older infants are less likely to make the A-not-B error because their concept of object permanence is more complete.

Researchers have found, however, that the A-not-B error does not show up consistently (Sophian, 1985). The evidence indicates that A-not-B errors are sensitive to the delay between hiding the object at B and the infant's attempt to find it (Diamond, 1985). Thus, the A-not-B error might be due to a failure in memory. Another explanation is that infants tend to repeat a previous motor behavior (Clearfield & others, 2006; Smith, 1999).

Perceptual Development and Expectation A number of theorists, such as Eleanor Gibson (2001) and Elizabeth Spelke (1991; Kinzler & Spelke, 2007; Spelke & Kinzler, 2009), maintain that infants' perceptual abilities are highly developed very early in development. Spelke argues that young infants interpret the world as having predictable occurrences. For example, in Chapter 5, "Physical Development in Infancy," we discussed research that demonstrated the presence of intermodal perception—the ability to coordinate information from two or more sensory modalities, such as vision and hearing—by 3½ months of age, much earlier than Piaget would have predicted (Spelke & Owsley, 1979).

Research also suggests that infants develop the ability to understand how the world works at a very early age (Baillargeon & others, 2009; Gopnik & Schultz, 2007; Johnson, 2009a, b, c). For example, by the time they are 3 months of age, infants develop expectations about future events. Marshall Haith and his colleagues (Canfield & Haith, 1991; Haith, Hazen, & Goodman, 1988) presented pictures to infants in either a regular alternating sequence (such as left, right, left, right) or an unpredictable sequence (such as right, right, left, right). When the sequence was predictable, the 3-month-old infants began to anticipate the location of the picture, looking at the side on which it was expected to appear. However, younger infants did not develop expectations about where a picture would be presented.

What kinds of expectations do infants form? Are we born expecting the world to obey basic physical laws, such as gravity, or when do we learn about how the world works? Experiments by Elizabeth Spelke (1991, 2000; Spelke & Hespos, 2001) have addressed these questions. She placed babies before a puppet stage and showed them a series of actions that are unexpected if you know how the physical world works—for example, one ball seemed to roll through a solid barrier, another seemed to leap between two platforms, and a third appeared to hang in midair (Spelke, 1979). Spelke measured and compared the babies' looking times for unexpected and expected actions. She concluded that, by 4 months of age, even though infants do not yet have the ability to talk about objects, move around objects, manipulate objects, or even see objects with high resolution, they expect objects to be solid and continuous. However, at 4 months of age, infants do not expect an object to obey gravitational constraints (Spelke & others, 1992). Similarly, research by Renée Baillargeon (1995, 2004) documents that infants as young as 3 to 4 months expect objects to be *substantial* (in the sense that other objects cannot move through them) and *permanent* (in the sense that objects continue to exist when they are hidden).

Infants know that objects are substantial and permanent at an earlier age than Piaget envisioned.

—RENÉE BAILLARGEON
Contemporary Psychologist, University of Illinois

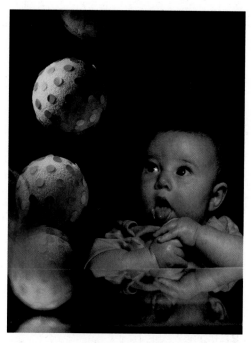

A 4-month-old in Elizabeth Spelke's infant perception laboratory is tested to determine if she knows that an object in motion will not stop in midair. Spelke concluded that at 4 months babies don't expect objects like these balls to obey gravitational constraints, but that they do expect objects to be solid and continuous. Research by Spelke, Renee Baillargeon, and others suggest that infants develop an ability to understand how the world works earlier than Piaget envisioned. However, critics such as Andrew Meltzoff fault their research and conclude there is still controversy about how early some infant cognitive accomplishments occur.

A-not-B error Also called AB̄ error, this occurs when infants make the mistake of selecting the familiar hiding place (A) rather than the new hiding place (B̄) as they progress into substage 4 in Piaget's sensorimotor stage.

In sum, researchers such as Baillargeon and Spelke conclude that infants see objects as bounded, unitary, solid, and separate from their background, possibly at birth or shortly thereafter, but definitely by 3 to 4 months of age, much earlier than Piaget envisioned. Young infants still have much to learn about objects, but the world appears both stable and orderly to them.

However, some critics, such as Andrew Meltzoff (2008; Moore & Meltzoff, 2008), argue that Spelke's and Baillargeon's research relies on how long infants look at unexpected events and thus assess infants' *perceptual expectations* about where and when objects will reappear rather than tapping their *knowledge* about where the objects are when they are out of sight. Meltzoff points out that whether infants act on their perception is an important aspect of assessing object permanence and states that it does not appear that young infants can act on the information. Thus, Meltzoff (2008) concludes that whether longer looking time is a valid measure of object permanence and how early infants develop object permanence remain controversial.

By 6 to 8 months, infants have learned to perceive gravity and support—that an object hanging on the end of a table should fall, that ball bearings will travel farther when rolled down a longer rather than a shorter ramp, and that cup handles will not fall when attached to a cup (Slater, Field, & Hernandez-Reif, 2007). As infants develop, their experiences and actions on objects help them to understand physical laws (Bremner, 2007).

The Nature–Nurture Issue   In considering the big issue of whether nature or nurture plays the more important role in infant development, Elizabeth Spelke (Spelke, 2000; Spelke & Kinzler, 2007, 2009) comes down clearly on the side of nature. Spelke endorses a **core knowledge approach,** which states that infants are born with domain-specific innate knowledge systems. Among these domain-specific knowledge systems are those involving space, number sense, object permanence, and language (which we discuss later in this chapter). Strongly influenced by evolution, the core knowledge domains are theorized to be prewired to allow infants to make sense of their world. After all, Spelke concludes, how could infants possibly grasp the complex world in which they live if they didn't come into the world equipped with core sets of knowledge? In this approach, the innate core knowledge domains form a foundation around which more mature cognitive functioning and learning develop. The core knowledge approach argues that Piaget greatly underestimated the cognitive abilities of infants, especially young infants.

An intriguing domain of core knowledge that has been investigated in young infants is whether they have a sense of number. Spelke concludes that they do. Using the violations of expectations method discussed in the *Research in Children's Development* interlude, Karen Wynn (1992) conducted an early experiment on infants' sense of numbers. Five-month-old infants were shown one or two Mickey Mouse dolls on a puppet stage. Then the experimenter hid the doll(s) behind a screen and visibly removed or added one. Next, when the screen was lifted, the infants looked longer when they saw the incorrect number of dolls. Spelke and her colleagues (Hyde & Spelke, 2009; Lipton & Spelke, 2004; Spelke & Kinsler, 2007; Xu, Spelke, & Goddard, 2005) have found that infants can distinguish between different numbers of objects, actions, and sounds. Efforts to find further support for infants' sense of number are extending to assessments of brain activity. For example, a recent study of 3-month-olds observing changes either in the identity of objects or the number of objects revealed that changes in the type of objects activated a region of the brain's temporal lobe, whereas changes in the number of objects activated an additional region of the parietal lobe (Izard, Dehaene-Lambertz, & Dehaene, 2008). In older children and adults, number sense activates the same region of the parietal lobe activated in the 3-month-old infants in this study.

core knowledge approach View that infants are born with domain-specific innate knowledge systems.

Of course, not everyone agrees with Spelke's conclusions about young infants' math skills (Cohen, 2002). One criticism is that infants in the number experiments are merely responding to changes in the display that violated their expectations.

In criticizing the core knowledge approach, British developmental psychologist Mark Johnson (2008) says that the infants Spelke assesses in her research already have accumulated hundreds, and in some cases even thousands, of hours of experience in grasping what the world is about, which gives considerable room for the environment's role in the development of infant cognition (Highfield, 2008). According to Johnson (2008), infants likely come into the world with "soft biases to perceive and attend to different aspects of the environment, and to learn about the world in particular ways." Although debate about the cause and course of infant cognitive development continues, most developmentalists today agree that Piaget underestimated the early cognitive accomplishments of infants and that both nature and nurture are involved in infants' cognitive development.

What revisions in Piaget's theory of sensorimotor development do contemporary researchers conclude need to be made? What characterizes the nature-nurture controversy in infant cognitive development?

Conclusions In sum, many researchers conclude that Piaget wasn't specific enough about how infants learn about their world and that infants, especially young infants, are more competent than Piaget thought (Baillargeon & others, 2009; Diamond, Casey, & Munakata, 2010; Johnson, 2009a, b, c; Spelke & Kinzler, 2009). As they have examined the specific ways that infants learn, the field of infant cognition has become very specialized. There are many researchers working on different questions, with no general theory emerging that can connect all of the different findings (Nelson, 1999). Their theories often are local theories, focused on specific research questions, rather than grand theories like Piaget's (Kuhn, 1998). If there is a unifying theme, it is that investigators in infant development seek to understand more precisely how developmental changes in cognition take place and the big issue of nature and nurture (Aslin, 2009; Woodward & Needham, 2009). As they seek to answer more precisely the contributions of nature and nurture to infant development, researchers face the difficult task of determining whether the course of acquiring information, which is very rapid in some domains, is best accounted for by an innate set of biases (that is, core knowledge), or by the extensive input of environmental experiences to which the infant is exposed (Aslin, 2009).

Review and Reflect: Learning Goal 1

1 **Summarize and evaluate Piaget's theory of infant development**

REVIEW

- What cognitive processes are important in Piaget's theory?
- What are some characteristics of Piaget's stage of sensorimotor development?
- What are some contributions and criticisms of Piaget's sensorimotor stage?

REFLECT

- What are some implications of Piaget's theory of infant development for parenting?

Conditioning   Attention   Memory   Imitation   Concept Formation and Categorization

When Piaget hung a doll above 4-month-old Lucienne's feet, as described in the chapter opening, would she remember the doll? If Piaget had rewarded her for moving the doll with her foot, would the reward have affected Lucienne's behavior? If he had showed her how to shake the doll's hand, could she have imitated him? If he had showed her a different doll, could she have formed the concept of a "doll"?

Questions like these might be examined by researchers taking the behavioral and social cognitive or information processing approaches introduced in Chapter 1, "Introduction." In contrast to Piaget's theory, these approaches do not describe infant development in terms of stages. Instead, they document gradual changes in the infant's ability to understand and process information about the world. In this section, we explore what researchers using these approaches can tell us about how infants learn, remember, and conceptualize.

Conditioning

In Chapter 1, "Introduction," we described Pavlov's classical conditioning (in which, as a result of pairing, a new stimulus comes to elicit a response previously given to another stimulus) and Skinner's operant conditioning (in which the consequences of a behavior produce changes in the probability of the behavior's occurrence). Infants can learn through both types of conditioning. For example, if an infant's behavior is followed by a rewarding stimulus, the behavior is likely to recur.

Operant conditioning has been especially helpful to researchers in their efforts to determine what infants perceive (Watanabe & Taga, 2006). For example, infants will suck faster on a nipple when the sucking behavior is followed by a visual display, music, or a human voice (Rovee-Collier, 1987, 2007).

Carolyn Rovee-Collier (1987) also demonstrated how infants can retain information from the experience of being conditioned. She placed a 2½-month-old baby in a crib under an elaborate mobile (see Figure 6.4). She then tied one end of a ribbon to the baby's ankle and the other end to the mobile. Subsequently, she observed that the baby kicked and made the mobile move. The movement of the mobile was the reinforcing stimulus (which increased the baby's kicking behavior) in this experiment. Weeks later, the baby was returned to the crib, but its foot was not tied to the mobile. The baby kicked, which suggests it had retained the information that if it kicked a leg, the mobile would move.

Attention

Attention, the focusing of mental resources on select information, improves cognitive processing on many tasks. Even newborns can detect a contour and fix their attention on it. Older infants scan patterns more thoroughly. By 4 months, infants can selectively attend to an object. In adults, when individuals orient their attention to an object or event, the parietal lobes in the cerebral cortex are involved (Posner, 2003). It is likely that the parietal lobes are active when infants orient their attention, although research has not yet documented this. (Figure 5.4 p. 147, illustrates the location of the parietal lobes in the brain.)

Attention in the first year of life is dominated by an *orienting/investigative process* (Posner & Rothbart, 2007). This process involves directing attention to potentially important locations in the environment (that is, *where*) and recognizing objects and

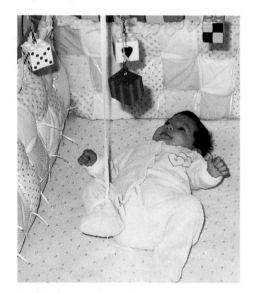

FIGURE 6.4 Conditioning and Memory in Infants In Rovee-Collier's experiment, operant conditioning was used to demonstrate that infants as young as 2½ months of age can retain information from the experience of being conditioned. *What did infants recall in Rovee-Collier's experiment?*

attention The focusing of mental resources on select information.

their features (such as color and form) (that is, *what*) (Courage & Richards, 2008). From 3 to 9 months of age, infants can deploy their attention more flexibly and quickly. Another important type of attention is *sustained attention,* also referred to as *focused attention* (Courage & Richards, 2008). New stimuli typically elicit an orienting response followed by sustained attention. It is sustained attention that allows infants to learn about and remember characteristics of a stimulus as it becomes familiar. Researchers have found that infants as young as 3 months of age engage in 5 to 10 seconds of sustained attention. From this age through the second year, the length of sustained attention increases (Courage & Richards, 2008).

Habituation and Dishabituation Closely linked with attention are the processes of habituation and dishabituation, which we discussed in Chapter 5, "Physical Development in Infancy." If you say the same word or show the same toy to a baby several times in a row, the baby usually pays less attention to it each time. This is *habituation*—decreased responsiveness to a stimulus after repeated presentations of the stimulus. *Dishabituation* is the increase in responsiveness after a change in stimulation. Chapter 5 described some of the measures that researchers use to study whether habituation is occurring, such as sucking behavior (sucking stops when an infant attends to a novel object), heart rates, and the length of time the infant looks at an object.

Infants' attention is strongly governed by novelty and habituation (Courage & Richards, 2008; Snyder & Torrence, 2008). When an object becomes familiar, attention becomes shorter, making infants more vulnerable to distraction (Oakes, Kannass, & Shaddy, 2002). One study found that 10-month-olds were more distractible than 26-month-olds (Ruff & Capozzoli, 2003). Another study revealed that infants who were labeled "short lookers" because of the brief time they focused attention had better memory at 1 year of age than those labeled "long lookers," who had more sustained attention (Courage, Howe, & Squires, 2004).

Researchers study habituation to determine the extent to which infants can see, hear, smell, taste, and experience touch (Colombo & Mitchell, 2009; Slater, Field, & Hernandez-Reif, 2007). Studies of habituation can also indicate whether infants recognize something they have previously experienced. Habituation provides a measure of an infant's maturity and well-being. Infants who have brain damage do not habituate well.

Knowing about habituation and dishabituation can help parents interact effectively with infants. Infants respond to changes in stimulation. Wise parents sense when an infant shows an interest and realize that they may have to repeat something many times for the infant to process information. But if the stimulation is repeated often, the infant stops responding to the parent. In parent-infant interaction, it is important for parents to do novel things and to repeat them often until the infant stops responding. The parent stops or changes behaviors when the infant redirects his or her attention (Rosenblith, 1992).

Joint Attention Another aspect of attention that is an important part of infant development is **joint attention,** in which individuals focus on the same object or event. Joint attention requires (1) an ability to track another's behavior, such as following someone's gaze; (2) one person directing another's attention; and (3) reciprocal interaction (Butterworth, 2004). Early in infancy, joint attention usually involves a caregiver pointing or using words to direct an infant's attention. Emerging forms of joint attention occur at about 7 to 8 months, but it is not until toward the end of the first year that joint attention skills are frequently observed (Heimann & others, 2006; Meltzoff & Brooks, 2006). In a study conducted by Rechele Brooks and Andrew

This young infant's attention is riveted on the blue toy frog that has just been placed in front of him. The young infant's attention to the toy frog will be strongly regulated by the processes of habituation and dishabituation. *What characterizes these processes?*

How Would You. . . ?
As a human development and family studies professional, what strategies would likely help parents improve an infant's development of attention?

joint attention Occurs when individuals focus on the same object or event, and an ability to track another's behavior is present; one individual directs another's attention, and reciprocal interaction is present.

FIGURE 6.5 Gaze Following in Infancy
Researcher Rechele Brooks shifts her eyes from the infant to a toy in the foreground (*a*). The infant then follows her eye movement to the toy (*b*). Brooks and colleague Andrew Meltzoff (2005) found that infants begin to engage in this kind of behavior called "gaze following" at 10 to 11 months of age. *Why might gaze following be an important accomplishment for an infant?*

(a)   (b)

A mother and her infant daughter engaging in joint attention. *What about this photograph tells you that joint attention is occurring? Why is joint attention an important aspect of infant development?*

memory A central feature of cognitive development, involving the retention of information over time.

implicit memory Memory without conscious recollection; involves skills and routine procedures that are automatically performed.

explicit memory Conscious memory of facts and experiences.

deferred imitation Imitation that occurs after a delay of hours or days.

Meltzoff (2005), at 10 to 11 months of age infants first began engaging in "gaze following," looking where another person has just looked (see Figure 6.5). And by their first birthday, infants have begun to direct adults' attention to objects that capture their interest (Heimann & others, 2006).

Joint attention plays important roles in many aspects of infant development and considerably increases infants' ability to learn from other people (Striano, Reid, & Hoehl, 2006). Nowhere is this more apparent than in observations of interchanges between caregivers and infants as infants are learning language (Poulin-Dubois & Graham, 2007). When caregivers and infants frequently engage in joint attention, infants say their first word earlier and develop a larger vocabulary (Carpenter, Nagell, & Tomasello, 1998; Flom & Pick, 2003). Later in the chapter in our discussion of language, we further discuss joint attention as an early predictor of language development in older infants and toddlers (Brooks & Meltzoff, 2008; Meltzoff & Brooks, 2009).

Memory

Memory involves the retention of information over time. Attention plays an important role in memory as part of a process called *encoding*, which is the process by which information gets into memory. What can infants remember, when?

Some researchers such as Rovee-Collier (2008) have concluded that infants as young as 2 to 6 months of age can remember some experiences through 1½ to 2 years of age. However, critics such as Jean Mandler (2004), a leading expert on infant cognition, argue that the infants in Rovee-Collier's experiments are displaying only implicit memory. **Implicit memory** refers to memory without conscious recollection—memories of skills and routine procedures that are performed automatically. In contrast, **explicit memory** refers to the conscious memory of facts and experiences.

When people think about memory, they are usually referring to explicit memory. Most researchers find that babies do not show explicit memory until the second half of the first year (Bauer, 2007, 2009; Bauer & others, 2003; Mandler & McDonough, 1993). Then, explicit memory improves substantially during the second year of life (Bauer, 2007, 2009; Carver & Bauer, 2001). In one longitudinal study, infants were assessed several times during their second year (Bauer & others, 2000). Older infants showed more accurate memory and required fewer prompts to demonstrate their memory than younger infants.

Researchers have found that infants of different ages can remember information for various lengths of time (Bauer, 2009). Researchers have documented that 6-month-olds can remember information for 24 hours, but by 20 months of age infants can remember information they encountered 12 months earlier.

What changes in the brain are linked to infants' memory development? From about 6 to 12 months of age, the maturation of the hippocampus and the surrounding cerebral cortex, especially the frontal lobes, makes the emergence of explicit memory possible (Nelson, 2009; Nelson, Thomas, & de Haan, 2006) (see Figure 6.6). Explicit memory continues to improve in the second year, as these brain structures further mature and connections between them increase. Less is known about the areas of the brain involved in implicit memory in infancy.

Let's examine another aspect of memory. Do you remember your third birthday party? Probably not. Most adults can remember little if anything from the first three years of their life. This is called *infantile,* or *childhood, amnesia.* The few reported adult memories of life at age 2 or 3 are at best very sketchy (Newcombe, 2008). Elementary school children also do not remember much of their early child years (Lie & Newcombe, 1999).

What is the cause of infantile amnesia? One reason older children and adults have difficulty recalling events from their infant and early child years is that during these early years the prefrontal lobes of the brain are immature; this area of the brain is believed to play an important role in storing memories for events (Boyer & Diamond, 1992).

In sum, most of young infants' conscious memories appear to be rather fragile and short-lived, although their implicit memory of perceptual-motor actions can be substantial (Bauer, 2007, 2009; Mandler, 2004). By the end of the second year, long-term memory is more substantial and reliable (Bauer, 2007, 2009).

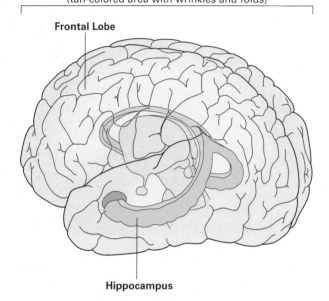

Cerebral Cortex
(tan-colored area with wrinkles and folds)

Frontal Lobe

Hippocampus

FIGURE 6.6 Key Brain Structures Involved in Memory Development in Infancy

Imitation

Can infants imitate someone else's emotional expressions? If an adult smiles, will the baby follow with a smile? If an adult protrudes her lower lip, wrinkles her forehead, and frowns, will the baby show a sad face?

Infant development researcher Andrew Meltzoff (2004, 2005, 2007; Meltzoff & Moore, 1999) has conducted numerous studies of infants' imitative abilities. He sees infants' imitative abilities as biologically based, because infants can imitate a facial expression within the first few days after birth. He also emphasizes that the infant's imitative abilities do not resemble a hardwired response but rather involve flexibility and adaptability. In Meltzoff's observations of infants across the first 72 hours of life, the infants gradually displayed more complete imitation of an adult's facial expression, such as protruding the tongue or opening the mouth wide (see Figure 6.7).

Meltzoff (2007; Meltzoff & Williamson, 2008) concludes that infants don't blindly imitate everything they see and often make creative errors. He also argues that beginning at birth there is an interplay between learning by observing and learning by doing (Piaget emphasized learning by doing).

Not all experts on infant development accept Meltzoff's conclusions that newborns are capable of imitation. Some say that these babies were engaging in little more than automatic responses to a stimulus.

Meltzoff (2005) also has studied **deferred imitation,** which occurs after a time delay of hours or days. Piaget held that deferred imitation doesn't occur until about 18 months of age. Meltzoff's research suggested that it occurs much earlier. In one study, Meltzoff (1988) demonstrated that 9-month-old infants could imitate actions—such as pushing a recessed button in a box, which produced a beeping sound—that they had seen performed 24 hours earlier. Also, in a recent study, engagement in deferred imitation at 9 months of age was a strong predictor of more extensive production of communicative gestures at 14 months of age (Heimann & others, 2006). Two of the most common infant gestures are (1) extending the

FIGURE 6.7 Infant Imitation Infant development researcher Andrew Meltzoff protrudes his tongue in an attempt to get the infant to imitate his behavior. *How do Meltzoff's findings about imitation compare with Piaget's descriptions of infants' abilities?*

FIGURE 6.8 Categorization in 9- to 11-Month-Olds These are the stimuli used in the study that indicated 9- to 11-month-old infants categorize as different (birds and planes) (Mandler & McDonough, 1993).

How Would You. . . ?
As an educator, how would you talk with parents about the importance of their infant developing concepts?

arm to show caregiver something the infant is holding, and (2) pointing with the arm and index finger extended at some interesting object or event.

Concept Formation and Categorization

Along with attention, memory, and imitation, concepts are key aspects of infants' cognitive development (Cohen, 2009; Mandler, 2009; Quinn, 2009; Oakes & others, 2009). To understand what concepts are, we first have to define categories—*categories* group objects, events, and characteristics on the basis of common properties. *Concepts* are ideas about what categories represent, or, said another way, the sort of thing we think category members are. Concepts and categories help us to simplify and summarize information (Oakes, 2008). Without concepts, you would see each object and event as unique; you would not be able to make any generalizations.

Do infants have concepts? Yes, they do, although we do not know just how early concept formation begins (Mandler, 2009; Oakes & Rakison, 2009).

Using habituation experiments like those described earlier in the chapter, some researchers have found that infants as young as 3 months of age can group together objects with similar appearances (Quinn, 2009). This research capitalizes on the knowledge that infants are more likely to look at a novel object than a familiar object. For example, in a characteristic study, young infants are shown a series of photographs of different types of cats in pairs (Quinn & Eimas, 1996). As they are shown more pictures of cats, they habituate to the animals, looking at them less and less. Then, when they are shown a photograph of a cat paired with a photograph of a dog, they take a longer look at the dog, indicating an ability to group together objects characterized by similar properties.

Jean Mandler (2004, 2009) argues that these early categorizations are best described as *perceptual categorization*. That is, the categorizations are based on similar perceptual features of objects, such as size, color, and movement, as well as parts of objects, such as legs for animals. Mandler (2004) concludes that it is not until about 7 to 9 months of age that infants form *conceptual* categories rather than just making perceptual discriminations between different categories. In one study of 9- to 11-month-olds, infants classified birds as animals and airplanes as vehicles even though the objects were perceptually similar—airplanes and birds with their wings spread (Mandler & McDonough, 1993) (see Figure 6.8).

Further advances in categorization occur in the second year of life (Booth, 2006). Many infants' "first concepts are broad and global in nature, such as 'animal' or 'indoor thing.' Gradually, over the first two years these broad concepts become more differentiated into concepts such as 'land animal,' then 'dog,' or to 'furniture,' then 'chair'" (Mandler, 2006, p. 1). Also in the second year, infants often categorize objects on the basis of their shape (Landau, Smith, & Jones, 1998).

Do some very young children develop an intense, passionate interest in a particular category of objects or activities? A recent study of 11-month-old to 6-year-old children confirmed that they do (DeLoache, Simcock, & Macari, 2007). A striking finding was the large gender difference in categories with an intense interest in particular categories stronger for boys than for girls. Categorization of boys' intense interests focused on vehicles, trains, machines, dinosaurs, and balls; girls' intense interests were more likely to involve dress-ups and books/reading (see Figure 6.9). When your author's grandson Alex was 18 to 24 months old, he already had developed an intense, passionate interest in the category of vehicles. He categorized vehicles into such subcategories as cars, trucks, earthmoving equipment, and buses.

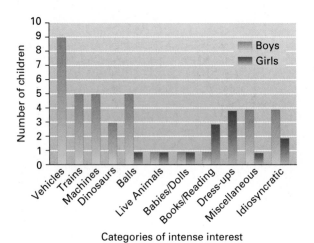

FIGURE 6.9 Categorization of Boys' and Girls' Intense Interests

In addition to common classifications of cars into police cars, jeeps, taxis, and such, and trucks into fire trucks, dump trucks, and the like, his categorical knowledge of earthmoving equipment included bulldozers and excavators, and he categorized buses into school buses, London buses, and funky Malta buses (retro buses on the island of Malta). Later, at 2 to 3 years of age, Alex developed an intense, passionate interest in categorizing dinosaurs.

In sum, the infant's advances in processing information—through attention, memory, imitation, and concept formation—is much richer, more gradual, and less stage-like and occurs earlier than was envisioned by earlier theorists, such as Piaget (Diamond, Casey, & Munakata, 2010; Johnson, 2009a, b, c; Quinn & others, 2009; Woodward & Needham, 2009). As leading infant researcher Jean Mandler (2004) concluded, "The human infant shows a remarkable degree of learning power and complexity in what is being learned and in the way it is represented" (p. 304).

> *Infants are creating concepts and organizing their world into conceptual domains that will form the backbone of their thought throughout life.*
>
> —**JEAN MANDLER**
> *Contemporary Psychologist, University of California–San Diego*

The author's grandson Alex at 2 years of age showing his intense, passionate interest in the category of vehicles while playing with a London taxi and a funky Malta bus.

Review and Reflect: Learning Goal 2

2 **Describe how infants learn, remember, and conceptualize**

REVIEW

- How do infants learn through conditioning?
- What is attention? What characterizes attention in infants?
- What is memory?
- To what extent can infants remember?
- How is imitation involved in infant learning?
- When do infants develop concepts, and how does concept formation change during infancy?

REFLECT

- If a friend told you that she remembers being abused by her parents when she was 2 years old, would you believe her? Explain your answer.

---

3 HOW ARE INDIVIDUAL DIFFERENCES IN INFANCY ASSESSED, AND DO THESE ASSESSMENTS PREDICT INTELLIGENCE?

Measures of Infant Development   Predicting Intelligence

So far in this chapter, we have discussed how the cognitive development of infants generally progresses. We have emphasized what is typical of the largest number of infants or the average infant, but the results obtained for *most* infants do not apply to *all* infants. It is advantageous to know whether an infant is developing at a slow, normal, or advanced pace during the course of infancy. If an infant advances at an especially slow rate, then some form of enrichment may be necessary. If an infant develops at an advanced pace, parents may be advised to provide toys that stimulate cognitive growth in slightly older infants. How is an infant's cognitive development assessed?

Careers in Children's Development

Toosje Thyssen Van Beveren, Infant Assessment Specialist

Toosje Thyssen Van Beveren is a developmental psychologist at the University of Texas Medical Center in Dallas. She has a master's degree in child clinical psychology and a Ph.D. in human development. Currently, Van Beveren is involved in a 12-week program called New Connections, which is a comprehensive intervention for young children who were affected by substance abuse prenatally and for their caregivers.

In the New Connections program, Van Beveren assesses infants' developmental status and progress. She might refer the infants to a speech, physical, or occupational therapist and monitor the infants' services and progress. Van Beveren trains the program staff and encourages them to use the exercises she recommends. She also discusses the child's problems with the primary caregivers, suggests activities, and assists them in enrolling infants in appropriate programs.

During her graduate work at the University of Texas at Dallas, Van Beveren was author John Santrock's teaching assistant in his undergraduate course on life-span development for four years. As a teaching assistant, she attended classes, graded exams, counseled students, and occasionally gave lectures. Each semester,

Van Beveren returns to give a lecture on prenatal development and infancy. She also teaches part-time in the psychology department at UT–Dallas. In Van Beveren's words, "My days are busy and full. The work is often challenging. There are some disappointments but mostly the work is enormously gratifying."

Toosje Thyssen Van Beveren conducting an infant assessment.

Measures of Infant Development

Individual differences in infant cognitive development have been studied primarily through the use of developmental scales or infant intelligence tests. For example, in Chapter 4, "Birth," we discussed the Brazelton Neonatal Behavioral Assessment Scale (NBAS) and the Neonatal Intensive Care Unit Network Neurobehavioral Scale (NNNS), which are used to evaluate newborns. To read about the work of one infant assessment specialist, see the *Careers in Children's Development* profile.

The most important early contributor to the testing of infants was Arnold Gesell (1934). He developed a measure that helped to sort out potentially normal babies from abnormal ones. This was especially useful to adoption agencies, which had large numbers of babies awaiting placement. Gesell's examination was used widely for many years and still is frequently employed by pediatricians to distinguish normal and abnormal infants. The current version of the Gesell test has four categories of behavior: motor, language, adaptive, and personal-social. The **developmental quotient (DQ)** combines subscores in these categories to provide an overall score.

The widely used **Bayley Scales of Infant Development** were developed by Nancy Bayley (1969) in order to assess infant behavior and predict later development. The current version, the Bayley Scales of Infant and Toddler Development—Third Edition (Bayley-III), has five scales: cognitive, language, motor, socio-emotional, and adaptive (Bayley, 2005). The first three scales are administered directly to the infant, the latter two are questionnaires given to the caregiver. The Bayley-III also is more appropriate for use in clinical settings than the two previous editions (Lennon & others, 2008).

Items in the Bayley Scales of Infant and Toddler Development—Third Edition.

How should a 6-month-old perform on the Bayley cognitive scale? The 6-month-old infant should be able to vocalize pleasure and displeasure, persistently search for objects that are just out of immediate reach, and approach a mirror that is placed in front of the infant by the examiner. By 12 months of age, the infant should be able to inhibit behavior when commanded to do so, imitate words the examiner says (such as *Mama*), and respond to simple requests (such as "Take a drink").

The explosion of interest in infant development has produced many new measures, especially tasks that evaluate the ways infants process information (Rose, Feldman, & Wallace, 1992). The Fagan Test of Infant Intelligence is increasingly being used (Fagan, 1992). This test focuses on the infant's ability to process information in such ways as encoding the attributes of objects, detecting similarities and differences between objects, forming mental representations, and retrieving these representations. For example, it uses the amount of time babies look at a new object compared with the amount of time they spend looking at a familiar object to estimate their intelligence.

Predicting Intelligence

The infant-testing movement grew out of the tradition of IQ testing. However, IQ tests of older children pay more attention to verbal ability. Tests for infants contain far more items related to perceptual-motor development and include measures of social interaction.

Overall scores on such tests as the Gesell and the Bayley scales do not correlate highly with IQ scores obtained later in childhood. This is not surprising because the components tested in infancy are not the same as the components tested by IQ tests.

Unlike the Gesell and Bayley scales, the Fagan test is correlated with measures of intelligence in older children. In fact, evidence is accumulating that measures of habituation and dishabituation are linked to intelligence in childhood and adolescence (Fagan, Holland, & Wheeler, 2007; Kavsek, 2004). One recent study revealed that habituation at 3 or 6 months of age was linked to verbal skills and intelligence assessed at 32 months of age (Domsch, Lohaus, & Thomas, 2009). It is important, however, not to go too far and think that connections between cognitive development in early infancy and later cognitive development are so strong that no discontinuity takes place. Some important changes in cognitive development occur after infancy, changes that we describe in later chapters.

Review and Reflect: Learning Goal 3

3 **Discuss infant assessment measures and the prediction of intelligence**

REVIEW

- What are some measures of individual differences in infancy?
- Do tests of infants predict intelligence later in life?

REFLECT

- Parents have their 1-year-old infant assessed with a developmental scale, and the infant does very well on it. How confident should they be that the infant is going to be a genius when he or she grows up?

developmental quotient (DQ) An overall score that combines subscores in motor, language, adaptive, and personal-social domains in the Gesell assessment of infants.

Bayley Scales of Infant Development Scales developed by Nancy Bayley that are widely used in the assessment of infant development. The current version, the Bayley Scales of Infant and Toddler Development—Third Edition (Bayley-III), has five components: a cognitive scale, a language scale, a motor scale, a socio-emotional scale, and an adaptive scale.

4 WHAT ARE SOME EARLY ENVIRONMENTAL INFLUENCES ON COGNITIVE DEVELOPMENT?

Nutrition   **Poverty**

So far, we have discussed a number of approaches to infants' cognitive development, but an important aspect of this development remains to be examined. What are some early environmental experiences that might influence this cognitive development? Two areas in which researchers have investigated this question are nutrition and poverty.

Nutrition

When we think about how nutrition affects development, we usually think of physical development, such as skeletal growth, body shape, and susceptibility to disease. However, malnutrition also can restrict an infant's cognitive development (Grantham-McGregor, Ani, & Fernald, 2001; Nahar & others, 2008).

In one study, two groups of extremely malnourished 1-year-old South African infants were examined (Bayley, 1970). The children in one group were given adequate nourishment during the next six years. No intervention took place in the lives of the other group of children. After the seventh year, the poorly nourished group of children performed worse on intelligence tests than did the adequately nourished group.

In another study, George Gutherie and his co-workers (1976) evaluated a group of severely underweight, malnourished infants in a rural area of the Philippines. They found that a combination of malnutrition, infection, and inadequate social stimulation from caregivers was associated with very low scores on the Bayley Scales of Infant Development.

A poverty area in the Philippine Islands, where many infants are malnourished. *How does malnutrition influence children's cognitive development?*

A recent study of Indian children further documented the negative influence of chronic malnutrition on children's development. Children who had a history of chronic malnutrition performed more poorly on tests of attention and memory than their counterparts who were not malnourished (Kar, Rao, & Chandramouli, 2008). Another recent study of severely malnourished Bangladesh children revealed that standard nutritional care combined with a psychosocial intervention (group meetings with mothers and play sessions with infants, as well as six months of home visits) reduced the negative effects of malnutrition on 6- to 24-month-olds' cognitive development, assessed with the Bayley Scales of Infant and Toddler Development (Nahar & others, 2008).

Poverty

Researchers are increasingly interested in manipulating the early environment in children's lives when they are living in poverty, with the hope that the changes will have a positive effect on their cognitive development (Powell, 2006; Ramey, Ramey, & Lanzi, 2006). Two ways this can be carried out are (1) to change parents' adaptive and responsive functioning, and (2) to provide competent educational child care.

The emphasis on children at risk for low intelligence is on prevention rather than on remediation. Many low-income parents have difficulty providing an intellectually stimulating environment for their children. Programs that educate parents to be more sensitive caregivers and train them to be better teachers, as well as support services such as high-quality Head Start programs, can make a difference in a child's intellectual development. The current trend is to conduct two-generation poverty interventions by working to improve the quality of life and

How Would You...?
As a social worker, how would you work with families in poverty to support their children's cognitive development?

skills of parents, as well as providing the child with an enriched environment (McLoyd, 1998).

The Abecedarian Intervention program at the University of North Carolina at Chapel Hill is conducted by Craig Ramey and his associates (Ramey & Campbell, 1984; Ramey, Ramey, & Lanzi, 1998, 2006). They randomly assigned 111 young children from low-income, poorly educated families to an intervention group, which experienced full-time, year-round child care along with medical and social work services, or to a control group, which got medical and social benefits but no child care. The child-care program included gamelike learning activities aimed at improving language, motor, social, and cognitive skills. The success of the program in improving IQ was evident by the time the children were 3 years old, when the children in the experimental group showed normal IQs averaging 101, a 17-point advantage over the control group. Follow-up results suggested that the effects were long-lasting. More than a decade later, at age 15, children from the intervention group still maintained an IQ advantage of 5 points over the control-group children (97.7 to 92.6) (Ramey, Ramey, & Lanzi, 2001). They also did better on standardized tests of reading and math and were less likely to be held back a year in school (see Figure 6.10). Also the greatest IQ gains were by the children whose mothers had especially low IQs—below 70. At age 15, these children showed a 10-point IQ advantage over a group of children whose mothers had IQs below 70 but did not experience the child-care intervention.

Early intervention programs for infants in poverty conditions vary. Some are center-based, like the North Carolina program just described; others are home-based. Some are brief interventions; others are long-term. Some are time-intensive (such as all-day educational child care); others are less intensive (such as one-hour-a-day or once-a-week sessions). In general, researchers have found that early intervention programs for infants living in poverty have the most positive developmental outcomes when (1) the program is long-lasting; (2) the program is time-intensive; (3) the program provides direct educational benefits, often in educational contexts, and does not rely on parental training alone; and (4) the program is comprehensive and multidimensional, including educational, health, and counseling services for parents, in addition to working directly with infants. We further explore intervention in the lives of children in poverty by discussing Project Head Start in Chapter 9, "Cognitive Development in Early Childhood."

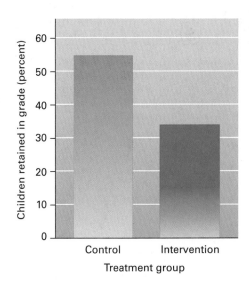

FIGURE 6.10 Early Intervention and Retention in School When the children in the Abecedarian program were 15 years of age, those who experienced the preschool intervention were less likely to have been retained in a grade than the children in the control group.

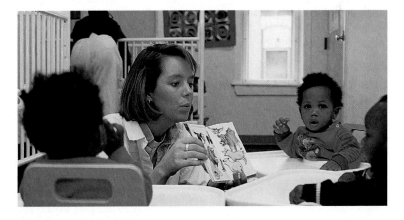

What are the characteristics of effective early intervention programs for infants in poverty conditions?

Review and Reflect: Learning Goal 4

 Characterize early environmental influences on cognitive development

REVIEW

- How is nutrition linked with infants' cognitive development?
- What role does poverty play in infants' cognitive development?

REFLECT

- If you were going to conduct an intervention to improve the cognitive skills of infants living in poverty, what would the intervention involve? Write down a minimum of five components in the intervention.

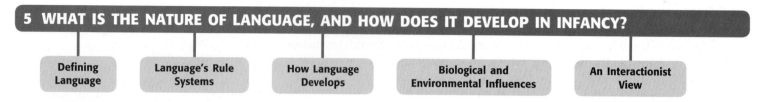

In 1799, a nude boy was observed running through the woods in France. The boy was captured when he was 11 years old. He was called the Wild Boy of Aveyron and was believed to have lived in the woods alone for six years (Lane, 1976). When found, he made no effort to communicate. He never learned to communicate effectively. A modern-day wild child named Genie was discovered in Los Angeles in 1970. Sadly, despite intensive intervention, Genie has never acquired more than a primitive form of language. Both cases—the Wild Boy of Aveyron and Genie—raise questions about the biological and environmental determinants of language, topics that we also examine later in the chapter. First, though, we need to define language.

Defining Language

Language is a form of communication—whether spoken, written, or signed—that is based on a system of symbols. Language consists of the words used by a community and the rules for varying and combining them.

Think how important language is in our everyday lives. We need language to speak with others, listen to others, read, and write. Our language enables us to describe past events in detail and to plan for the future. Language lets us pass down information from one generation to the next and create a rich cultural heritage.

All human languages have some common characteristics (Berko Gleason, 2009). These include infinite generativity and organizational rules. **Infinite generativity** is the ability to produce an endless number of meaningful sentences using a finite set of words and rules. Rules describe the way language works. Let's explore what these rules involve.

Language's Rule Systems

When nineteenth-century American writer Ralph Waldo Emerson said, "The world was built in order and the atoms march in tune," he must have had language in mind. Language is highly ordered and organized. The organization involves five systems of rules: phonology, morphology, syntax, semantics, and pragmatics.

Phonology   Every language is made up of basic sounds. **Phonology** is the sound system of the language, including the sounds that are used and how they may be combined (Menn & Stoel-Gammon, 2009; Panneton, McIlreavy & Bhullar, 2008). For example, English has the initial consonant cluster *spr* as in *spring*, but no words begin with the cluster *rsp*.

Phonology provides a basis for constructing a large and expandable set of words out of two or three dozen phonemes. A *phoneme* is the basic unit of sound in a language; it is the smallest unit of sound that affects meaning. For example, in English the sound represented by the letter *p*, as in the words *pot* and *spot*, is a phoneme. The /p/ sound is slightly different in the two words, but this variation is not distinguished in English, and therefore the /p/ sound is a single phoneme. In some languages, such as Hindi, the variations of the /p/ sound represent separate phonemes.

Morphology   **Morphology** refers to the units of meaning involved in word formation. A *morpheme* is a minimal unit of meaning; it is a word or a part of a word that cannot be broken into smaller meaningful parts. Every word in the English language is made up of one or more morphemes. Some words consist of a single

language A form of communication, whether spoken, written, or signed, that is based on a system of symbols.

infinite generativity The ability to produce an endless number of meaningful sentences using a finite set of words and rules.

phonology The sound system of the language, including the sounds that are used and how they may be combined.

morphology Units of meaning involved in word formation.

morpheme (for example, *help*), whereas others are made up of more than one morpheme (for example, *helper* has two morphemes, *help* + *er*, with the morpheme *-er* meaning "one who," in this case "one who helps"). Thus, not all morphemes are words by themselves; for example, *pre-*, *-tion*, and *-ing* are morphemes.

Just as the rules that govern phonology describe the sound sequences that can occur in a language, the rules of morphology describe the way meaningful units (morphemes) can be combined in words (Lieven, 2008; Tager-Flusberg & Zukowski, 2009). Morphemes have many jobs in grammar, such as marking tense (for example, she walks versus she walked) and number (she walks versus they walk).

Syntax   **Syntax** involves the way words are combined to form acceptable phrases and sentences (Tager-Flusberg & Zukowski, 2009). If someone says to you, "Bob slugged Tom" or "Bob was slugged by Tom," you know who did the slugging and who was slugged in each case because you have a syntactic understanding of these sentence structures. You also understand that the sentence, "You didn't stay, did you?" is a grammatical sentence but that "You didn't stay, didn't you?" is unacceptable and ambiguous.

If you learn another language, English syntax will not get you very far. For example, in English an adjective usually precedes a noun (as in *blue sky*), whereas in Spanish the adjective usually follows the noun (*cielo azul*). Despite the differences in their syntactic structures, however, syntactic systems in all the world's languages have some common ground (Naigles & Swensen, 2007). For example, no language we know of permits sentences like the following one:

The mouse the cat the farmer chased killed ate the cheese.

It appears that language users cannot process subjects and objects arranged in too complex a fashion in a sentence.

Semantics   **Semantics** refers to the meaning of words and sentences (Li, 2009). Every word has a set of semantic features, which are required attributes related to meaning. *Girl* and *women*, for example, share many semantic features but they differ semantically in regard to age.

Words have semantic restrictions on how they can be used in sentences (Bhagwat & Casasola, 2008; Pan & Uccelli, 2009). The sentence *The bicycle talked the boy into buying a candy bar* is syntactically correct but semantically incorrect. The sentence violates our semantic knowledge that bicycles don't talk.

Pragmatics   A final set of language rules involves **pragmatics,** the appropriate use of language in different contexts. Pragmatics covers a lot of territory (Akhtar & Herold, 2008; Bryant, 2009). When you take turns speaking in a discussion or use a question to convey a command ("Why is it so noisy in here?" "What is this, Grand Central Station?"), you are demonstrating knowledge of pragmatics. You also apply the pragmatics of English when you use polite language in appropriate situations (for example, when talking to one's teacher) or tell stories that are interesting, jokes that are funny, and lies that convince. In each of these cases, you are demonstrating that you understand the rules of your culture for adjusting language to suit the context.

At this point, we have discussed five important rule systems involved in language. An overview of these rule systems is presented in Figure 6.11.

How Language Develops

According to an ancient historian, in the thirteenth century Emperor Frederick II of Germany had a cruel idea. He wanted to know what language children would speak if no one talked to them. He selected several newborns and threatened their caregivers with death if they ever talked to the infants. Frederick never found out

syntax The ways words are combined to form acceptable phrases and sentences.

semantics The meaning of words and sentences.

pragmatics The appropriate use of language in different contexts.

Rule System	Description	Examples
Phonology	The sound system of a language. A phoneme is the smallest sound unit in a language.	The word *chat* has three phonemes or sounds: /ch/ /a/ /t/. An example of phonological rule in the English language is while the phoneme /r/ can follow the phonemes /t/ or /d/ in an English consonant cluster (such as *track* or *drab*), the phoneme /l/ cannot follow these letters.
Morphology	The system of meaningful units involved in word formation.	The smallest sound units that have a meaning are called morphemes, or meaning units. The word *girl* is one morpheme, or meaning unit; it cannot be broken down any further and still have meaning. When the suffix *s* is added, the word becomes *girls* and has two morphemes because the *s* changed the meaning of the word, indicating that there is more than one girl.
Syntax	The system that involves the way words are combined to form acceptable phrases and sentences.	Word order is very important in determining meaning in the English language. For example, the sentence, "Sebastian pushed the bike" has a different meaning than "The bike pushed Sebastian."
Semantics	The system that involves the meaning of words and sentences.	Knowing the meaning of individual words—that is, vocabulary. For example, semantics includes knowing the meaning of such words as *orange*, *transportation*, and *intelligent*.
Pragmatics	The system of using appropriate conversation and knowledge of how to effectively use language in context.	An example is using polite language in appropriate situations, such as being mannerly when talking with one's teacher. Taking turns in a conversation involves pragmatics.

FIGURE 6.11 The Rule Systems of Language

what language the children spoke because they all died. Today, we are still curious about infants' development of language, although our experiments and observations are, to say the least, far more humane than the evil Frederick's.

Whatever language they learn, infants all over the world follow a similar path in language development. What are some key milestones in this development?

Recognizing Language Sounds   Long before they begin to learn words, infants can make fine distinctions among the sounds of the language (Panneton, McIlreavy, & Bhullar, 2008). In Patricia Kuhl's (1993, 2000, 2007, 2009) research, phonemes from languages all over the world are piped through a speaker for infants to hear (see Figure 6.12). A box with a toy bear in it is placed where the infant can see it. A string of identical syllables is played, then the syllables are changed (for example, *ba ba ba ba*, and then *pa pa pa pa*). If the infant turns its head when the syllables change, the box lights up and the bear dances and drums, and the infant is rewarded for noticing the change.

Kuhl's (2007, 2009) research has demonstrated that from birth up to about 6 months of age, infants are "citizens of the world": they recognize when sounds change most of the time no matter what language the syllables come from. But over

FIGURE 6.12 From Universal Linguist to Language-Specific Listener A baby is shown in Patricia Kuhl's research laboratory. In this research, babies listen to tape-recorded voices that repeat syllables. When the sounds of the syllables change, the babies quickly learn to look at the bear. Using this technique, Kuhl has demonstrated that babies are universal linguists until about 6 months of age, but in the next six months become language-specific listeners. *Does Kuhl's research give support to the view that either "nature" or "nurture" is the source of language acquisition?*

the next six months, infants get even better at perceiving the changes in sounds from their "own" language, the one their parents speak, and they gradually lose the ability to recognize differences that are not important in their own language.

Infants must fish out individual words from the nonstop stream of sound that makes up ordinary speech (Jusczyk, 2000). To do so, they must find the boundaries between words, a task that is very difficult for infants because adults don't pause between words when they speak (Newman, 2008). Still, infants begin to detect word boundaries by 8 months of age. For example, in one study, 8-month-old infants listened to recorded stories that contained unusual words, such as *hornbill* and *python* (Jusczyk & Hohne, 1997). Two weeks later, the researchers tested the infants with two lists of words, one made up of words in the stories, the other of new, unusual words that did not appear in the stories. The infants listened to the familiar words for a second longer, on average, than to new words.

Babbling and Other Vocalizations   Long before infants speak recognizable words, they produce a number of vocalizations (Menn & Stoel-Gammon, 2009; Sachs, 2009). The functions of these early vocalizations are to practice making sounds, to communicate, and to attract attention. Babies' sounds go through this sequence during the first year:

- *Crying.* Babies cry even at birth. Crying can signal distress, but as we will discuss in Chapter 7, "Socioemotional Development in Infancy," different types of cries signal different things.
- *Cooing.* Babies first coo at about 1 to 2 months. These gurgling sounds are made in the back of the throat and usually express pleasure during interaction with the caregiver.
- *Babbling.* In the middle of the first year babies babble—that is, they produce strings of consonant-vowel combinations, such as "ba, ba, ba, ba."

Gestures   Infants start using gestures, such as showing and pointing, at about 8 to 12 months of age. They may wave bye-bye, nod to mean "yes," show an empty cup to want more milk, and point to a dog to draw attention to it. Some early gestures are symbolic, as when an infant smacks her lips to indicate food/drink. Pointing is considered by language experts as an important index of the social aspects of language and it follows this developmental sequence: From pointing without checking on adult gaze to pointing while looking back and forth between an object and the adult. Lack of pointing is a significant indicator of problems in the infant's communication system. For example, failure to engage in pointing characterizes many autistic children.

First Words   Children understand their first words earlier than they speak them. As early as 5 months of age, infants recognize their name when someone says it. On the average, infants understand about 50 words at about 13 months, but they can't say this many words until about 18 months (Menyuk, Liebergott, & Schultz, 1995). Thus, in infancy *receptive vocabulary* (words the child understands) considerably exceeds *spoken vocabulary* (words the child uses).

A child's first words include those that name important people (*dada*), familiar animals (*kitty*), vehicles (*car*), toys (*ball*), food (*milk*), body parts (*eye*), clothes (*hat*), household items (*clock*), and greeting terms (*bye*). These were the first words of babies 50 years ago. They are the first words of babies today. Children often express various intentions with their single words, so that "cookie" might mean, "That's a cookie" or "I want a cookie."

The infant's spoken vocabulary rapidly increases once the first word is spoken (Fenson & others, 2007). The average 18-month-old can speak about 50 words, but

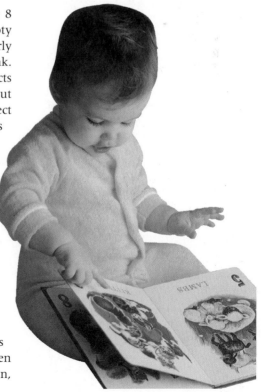

What characterizes the infant's early word learning?

FIGURE 6.13 Variation in Language Milestones

How Would You...?
As a psychologist, how would you advise parents whose 18-month-old has not yet spoken his first word?

Around the world, most young children learn to speak in two-word utterances, at about 18 to 24 months of age. *What are some examples of these two-word utterances?*

telegraphic speech The use of content words without grammatical markers such as articles, auxiliary verbs, and other connectives.

Broca's area An area in the brain's left frontal lobe involved in speech production.

Wernicke's area An area of the brain's left hemisphere that is involved in language comprehension.

aphasia A loss or impairment of language processing caused by brain damage in Broca's area or Wernicke's area.

language acquisition device (LAD) Chomsky's term that describes a biological endowment that enables the child to detect the features and rules of language, including phonology, syntax, and semantics.

by the age of 2 years can speak about 200 words. This rapid increase in vocabulary that begins at approximately 18 months is called the *vocabulary spurt* (Bloom, Lifter, & Broughton, 1985).

Like the timing of a child's first word, the timing of the vocabulary spurt varies (Lieven, 2008). Figure 6.13 shows the range for these two language milestones in 14 children. On average, these children said their first word at 13 months and had a vocabulary spurt at 19 months. However, the ages for the first word of individual children varied from 10 to 17 months and for their vocabulary spurt from 13 to 25 months.

Children sometimes overextend or underextend the meanings of the words they use (Pan & Uccelli, 2009; Woodward & Markman, 1998). *Overextension* is the tendency to apply a word to objects that are inappropriate for the word's meaning. For example, children at first may say *"dada"* not only for "father" but also for other men, strangers, or boys. With time, overextensions decrease and eventually disappear. *Underextension* is the tendency to apply a word too narrowly; it occurs when children fail to use a word to name a relevant event or object. For example, a child might use the word *boy* to describe a 5-year-old neighbor but not apply the word to a male infant or to a 9-year-old male.

Two-Word Utterances   By the time children are 18 to 24 months of age, they usually utter two-word utterances. To convey meaning with just two words, the child relies heavily on gesture, tone, and context. The wealth of meaning children can communicate with a two-word utterance includes the following (Slobin, 1972):

- Identification: "See doggie."
- Location: "Book there."
- Repetition: "More milk."
- Nonexistence: "All gone."
- Negation: "Not wolf."
- Possession: "My candy."
- Attribution: "Big car."
- Agent-action: "Mama walk."
- Action-direct object: "Hit you."
- Action-indirect object: "Give Papa."
- Action-instrument: "Cut knife."
- Question: "Where ball?"

These examples are from children whose first language is English, German, Russian, Finnish, Turkish, or Samoan.

Notice that the two-word utterances omit many parts of speech and are remarkably succinct. In fact, in every language, a child's first combinations of words have this economical quality; they are telegraphic. **Telegraphic speech** is the use of content words without grammatical markers such as articles, auxiliary verbs, and other connectives. Telegraphic speech is not limited to two words. "Mommy give ice cream" and "Mommy give Tommy ice cream" also are examples of telegraphic speech.

Biological and Environmental Influences

We have discussed a number of language milestones in infancy; Figure 6.14 summarizes the approximate time at which infants typically reach these milestones. But what makes this amazing development possible? Everyone who uses language in some way "knows" its rules and has the ability to create an infinite number of words and sentences. Where does this knowledge come from? Is it the product of biology? Is language learned and influenced by experiences?

Biological Influences   The ability to speak and understand language requires a certain vocal apparatus as well as a nervous system with certain capabilities. The nervous system and vocal apparatus of humanity's predecessors changed over hundreds of thousands or millions of years. With advances in the nervous system and vocal structures, *Homo sapiens* went beyond the grunting and shrieking of other animals to develop speech. Although estimates vary, many experts believe that humans acquired language about 100,000 years ago, which in evolutionary time, represents a very recent acquisition. It gave humans an enormous edge over other animals and increased the chances of human survival.

Some language scholars view the remarkable similarities in how children acquire language all over the world as strong evidence that language has a biological basis. There is evidence that particular regions of the brain are predisposed to be used for language (Bortfield, Fava, & Boas, 2009; Fridriksson & others, 2009). Two regions involved in language were first discovered in studies of brain-damaged individuals: **Broca's area,** an area in the left frontal lobe of the brain involved in producing words, and **Wernicke's area,** a region of the brain's left hemisphere involved in language comprehension (see Figure 6.15). Damage to either of these areas produces types of **aphasia,** which is a loss or impairment of language processing. Individuals with damage to Broca's area have difficulty producing words correctly; individuals with damage to Wernicke's area have poor comprehension and often produce incomprehensible speech.

Linguist Noam Chomsky (1957) proposed that humans are biologically prewired to learn language at a certain time and in a certain way. He said that children are born into the world with a **language acquisition device (LAD),** a biological endowment that enables the child to detect certain features and rules of language, including phonology, syntax, and semantics. Children are prepared by nature with the ability to detect the sounds of language, for example, and follow rules such as how to form plurals and ask questions.

Chomsky's LAD is a theoretical construct, not a physical part of the brain. Is there evidence for the existence of a LAD? Supporters of the LAD concept cite the uniformity of language milestones across languages and cultures, evidence that children create language even in the absence of well-formed input, and biological substrates of language. But, as we will see, critics argue that even if infants have something like a LAD, it cannot explain the whole story of language acquisition.

Environmental Influences   Decades ago, behaviorists opposed Chomsky's hypothesis and argued that language represents nothing more than chains of responses acquired through reinforcement (Skinner, 1957). A baby happens to babble "Ma-ma"; Mama rewards the baby with hugs and smiles; the baby says "Mama" more and more. Bit by bit, said the behaviorists, the baby's language is built up. According to behaviorists, language is a complex learned skill, much like playing the piano or dancing.

There are several problems with the behaviorist view of language learning. First, it does not explain how people create novel sentences—sentences that people have never heard or spoken before. Second, children learn the syntax of their native language even if they are not reinforced for doing so. Social psychologist and psycholinguist Roger Brown (1973) spent long hours observing parents and their young children. He found that parents did not directly or explicitly reward or correct the syntax of most children's utterances. That is, parents did not say "good," "correct," "right," "wrong," and so on. Also, parents did not offer direct corrections such as "You should say two shoes, not two shoe." However, as we will see shortly, many parents do expand on their young children's grammatically incorrect utterances and recast many of those that have grammatical errors.

The behavioral view is no longer considered a viable explanation of how children acquire language. But a great deal of research describes ways in which children's environmental experiences influence their language skills (Goldstein &

Typical Age	Language Milestones
Birth	Crying
2 to 4 months	Cooing begins
5 months	Understands first word
6 months	Babbling begins
7 to 11 months	Changes from universal linguist to language-specific listener
8 to 12 months	Uses gestures, such as showing and pointing Comprehension of words appears
13 months	First word spoken
18 months	Vocabulary spurt starts
18 to 24 months	Uses two-word utterances Rapid expansion of understanding of words

FIGURE 6.14 Some Language Milestones in Infancy Despite great variations in the language input they receive, infants around the world follow a similar path in learning to speak.

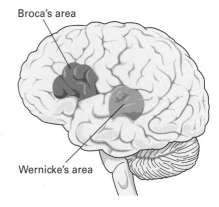

FIGURE 6.15 Broca's Area and Wernicke's Area Broca's area is located in the frontal lobe of the brain's left hemisphere, and it is involved in the control of speech. Wernicke's area is a portion of the left hemisphere's temporal lobe that is involved in understanding language. *How does the role of these areas of the brain relate to lateralization, which was discussed in Chapter 5?*

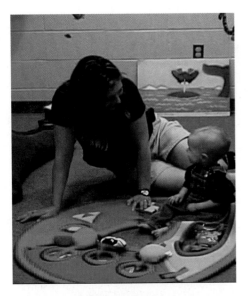

FIGURE 6.16 Social Interaction and Babbling One study focused on two groups of mothers and their 8-month-old infants (Goldstein, King, & West, 2003). One group of mothers was instructed to smile and touch their infants immediately after the babies cooed and babbled; the other group was also told to smile and touch their infants but in a random manner, unconnected to sounds the infants made. The infants whose mothers immediately responded in positive ways to their babbling subsequently made more complex, speechlike sounds, such as "da" and "gu." The research setting for this study, which underscores how important caregivers are in the early development of language, is shown above.

Schwade, 2008). Many language experts argue that a child's experiences, the particular language to be learned, and the context in which learning takes place can strongly influence language acquisition (Berko Gleason, 2009; Goldfield & Snow, 2009).

Language is not learned in a social vacuum. Most children are bathed in language from a very early age (Brooks & Meltzoff, 2008; Kuhl, 2009). The Wild Boy of Aveyron who never learned to communicate effectively had lived in social isolation for years. The support and involvement of caregivers and teachers greatly facilitate a child's language learning (Snow & Yang, 2006). For example, one study found that when mothers immediately smiled and touched their 8-month-old infants after they babbled, the infants subsequently made more complex speechlike sounds than when mothers responded to their infants in a random manner (Goldstein, King, & West, 2003) (see Figure 6.16).

Michael Tomasello (2003, 2006) stresses that young children are intensely interested in their social world and that early in their development they can understand the intentions of other people. His *interaction view* of language emphasizes that children learn language in specific contexts. For example, when a toddler and a father are jointly focused on a book, the father might say, "See the birdie." In this case, even a toddler understands that the father intends to name something and knows to look in the direction of the pointing. Through this kind of joint attention, early in their development children are able to use their social skills to acquire language (Tomasello & Carpenter, 2007; Tomasello, Carpenter, & Liszkowski, 2007). For example, one recent study revealed that joint visual attention behavior at 10 to 11 months of age (before children spoke their first words) was linked to vocabulary growth at 14, 18, and 24 months of age (Brooks & Meltzoff, 2008). Another recent study revealed that joint attention at 12 and 18 months predicted language skills at 24 months of age (Mundy & others, 2007).

In particular, researchers have found that the child's vocabulary development is linked to the family's socioeconomic status and the type of talk that parents direct to their children (Pan & Uccelli, 2009). To read about these links, see the *Diversity in Children's Development* interlude that follows.

Diversity in Children's Development

*T*he linguistics problems children have to solve are always embedded in personal and interpersonal contexts.

—LOIS BLOOM
Contemporary Psychologist, Columbia University

LANGUAGE ENVIRONMENT, POVERTY, AND LANGUAGE DEVELOPMENT

What characteristics of a family make a difference to a child's language development? Socioeconomic status has been linked with how much parents talk to their children and with young children's vocabulary (Pan & Uccelli, 2009; Raizada & others, 2008). Betty Hart and Todd Risley (1995) observed the language environments of children whose parents were professionals and children whose parents were on welfare. Compared with the professional parents, the parents on welfare talked much less to their young children, talked less about past events, and provided less elaboration. As indicated in Figure 6.17, the children of the professional parents had a much larger vocabulary at 36 months of age than the children of the welfare parents.

Other research has linked how much mothers speak to their infants and the infants' vocabularies. For example, in one study by Janellen Huttenlocher and her colleagues (1991), infants whose mothers spoke more often to them had markedly higher vocabularies. By the second birthday, vocabulary differences were substantial.

(a)

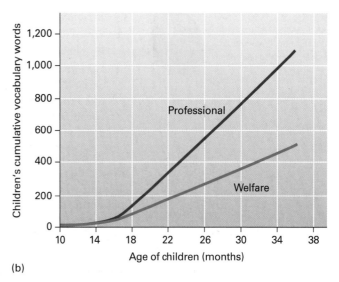

(b)

FIGURE 6.17 Language Input in Professional and Welfare Families and Young Children's Vocabulary Development (*a*) In this study (Hart & Risely, 1995), parents from professional families talked with their young children more than parents from welfare families. (*b*) All of the children learned to talk, but children from professional families developed vocabularies that were twice as large as those from welfare families. Thus, by the time children go to preschool, they already have experienced considerable differences in language input in their families and developed different levels of vocabulary that are linked to their socioeconomic context. *Does this study indicate that poverty caused deficiencies in vocabulary development?*

However, a study of 1- to 3-year-old children living in low-income families found that the sheer amount of maternal talk was not the best predictor of a child's vocabulary growth (Pan & others, 2005). Rather, it was maternal language and literacy skills, and mothers' use of diverse vocabulary that best predicted children's vocabulary development. Also, mothers who frequently used pointing gestures had children with a greater vocabulary. Pointing usually occurs in concert with speech and it may enhance the meaning of mothers' verbal input to their children.

A recent study revealed that maternal sensitivity (responds warmly to the child's bids and anticipates her child's emotional needs, for example), regardless of socioeconomic status and ethnicity, was positively linked with growth in young children's receptive and expressive language development from 18 to 36 months of age (Pungello & others, 2009). In this study, negative intrusive parenting (physically restraining the child or dominating interaction with the child with unnecessary verbal direction, for example) was related to a slower rate of growth of receptive language.

These research studies and others (NICHD Early Child Care Research Network, 2005) demonstrate the important effect that early speech input and poverty can have on the development of a child's language skills.

One intriguing component of the young child's linguistic environment is **child-directed speech,** language spoken in a higher pitch than normal with simple words and sentences (Bonhannon & Bonvillian, 2009; Clark, 2009). It is hard to use child-directed speech when not in the presence of a baby. As soon as we start talking to a baby, though, most of us shift into child-directed speech. Much of this is automatic and something most parents are not aware they are doing. Even 4-year-olds speak in simpler ways to 2-year-olds than to their 4-year-old friends. Child-directed speech has the important function of capturing the infant's attention and maintaining communication (Jaswal & Fernald, 2007).

Adults often use strategies other than child-directed speech to enhance the child's acquisition of language, including recasting, expanding, and labeling:

- *Recasting* is rephrasing something the child has said, perhaps turning it into a question or restating the child's immature utterance in the form of a fully grammatical sentence. For example, if the child says, "The dog was barking," the adult can respond by asking, "When was the dog barking?" Effective recasting lets the child indicate an interest and then elaborates on that interest.

child-directed speech Language spoken in a higher pitch than normal with simple words and sentences.

How Would You...?

As a human development and family studies professional, how would you encourage parents to talk with their infants and toddlers?

- *Expanding* is restating, in a linguistically sophisticated form, what a child has said. For example, a child says, "Doggie eat," and the parent replies, "Yes, the doggie is eating."
- *Labeling* is identifying the names of objects. Young children are forever being asked to identify the names of objects. Roger Brown (1958) called this "the original word game" and claimed that much of a child's early vocabulary is motivated by this adult pressure to identify the words associated with objects.

Parents use these strategies naturally and in meaningful conversations. Parents do not need to use a particular method to teach their children to talk, even for children who are slow in learning language. Children usually benefit when parents follow the child's lead, talking about things the child is interested in at the moment, and when parents provide information in ways that children can process effectively (Pan, 2008). If children are not ready to take in some information, they are likely to tell you (perhaps by turning away). Thus, giving the child more information is not always better.

Infants, toddlers, and young children benefit when adults read books to and with them (shared reading) (DeLoache & Ganea, 2009; Rodriguez, Hines, & Montiel, 2008; Westerlund & Lagerberg, 2008). In one study, a majority of U.S. mothers in low-income families reported that they were reading to their infants and toddlers with some regularity (Raikes & others, 2006). In this study, non-Latino White, more highly educated mothers who were parenting a firstborn child were more likely to read books to their infants and toddlers than were African American and Latino mothers who were parenting later-born children. Reading daily to children at 14 to 24 months of age was positively related to the children's language and cognitive development at 36 months of age.

Remember, the encouragement of language development, not drill and practice, is the key. Language development is not a simple matter of imitation and reinforcement. To read further about ways that parents can facilitate children's language development, see the applications in the *Caring for Children* interlude.

Caring for Children

HOW PARENTS CAN FACILITATE INFANTS' AND TODDLERS' LANGUAGE DEVELOPMENT

In *Growing Up with Language*, linguist Naomi Baron (1992) provided ideas to help parents facilitate their child's language development. A summary of her ideas follows:

Infants

- *Be an active conversational partner.* Initiate conversation with the infant. If the infant is in a day-long child-care program, ensure that the baby receives adequate language stimulation from adults.
- *Talk as if the infant understands what you are saying.* Parents can generate self-fulfilling prophecies by addressing their young children as if they understand what is being said. The process may take four to five years, but children gradually rise to match the language model presented to them.
- *Use a language style with which you feel comfortable.* Don't worry about how you sound to other adults when you talk with your child. Your affect, not your content, is more important when talking with an infant. Use whatever type of talk with which you feel comfortable.

Toddlers

- *Continue to be an active conversational partner.* Engaging toddlers in conversation, even one-sided conversation, is the most important thing a parent can do to nourish a child linguistically.

- *Remember to listen.* Since toddlers' speech is often slow and laborious, parents are often tempted to supply words and thoughts for them. Be patient and let toddlers express themselves, no matter how painstaking the process is or how great a hurry you are in.

- *Use a language style with which you are comfortable, but consider ways of expanding your child's language abilities and horizons.* For example, using long sentences need not be problematic. Use rhymes. Ask questions that encourage answers other than "Yes" and "No." Actively repeat, expand, and recast the child's utterances. Introduce new topics. And use humor in your conversation.

- *Adjust to your child's idiosyncrasies instead of working against them.* Many toddlers have difficulty pronouncing words and making themselves understood. Whenever possible, make toddlers feel that they are being understood.

- *Avoid sexual stereotypes.* Don't let the toddler's sex determine your amount or style of conversation. Many American mothers are more linguistically supportive of girls than of boys, and many fathers talk less with their children than mothers do. Cognitively enriching initiatives from both mothers and fathers benefit both boys and girls.

- *Resist making normative comparisons.* Be aware of the ages at which your child reaches specific milestones (such as the first word, first 50 words), but do not measure this development rigidly against that of other children. Such social comparisons can bring about unnecessary anxiety.

It is a good idea for parents to begin talking to their babies at the start. The best language teaching occurs when the talking is begun before the infant becomes capable of its first intelligible speech. *What are some other guidelines for parents to follow in helping their infants and toddlers develop their language?*

An Interactionist View

If language acquisition depended only on biology, then the Wild Boy of Aveyron and Genie (discussed earlier in the chapter) should have talked without difficulty. A child's experiences influence language acquisition. But we have seen that language does have strong biological foundations (Goldin-Meadow, 2008). No matter how much you converse with a dog, it won't learn to talk. In contrast, children are biologically prepared to learn language. Children all over the world acquire language milestones at about the same time and in about the same order.

Environmental influences are also very important in development competence in language (Berko Gleason, 2009; Goldfield & Snow, 2009). Children whose parents provide them with a rich verbal environment show many positive benefits. Parents who pay attention to what their children are trying to say, expand their children's utterances, read to them, and label things in the environment, are providing valuable benefits for them (Berko Gleason, 2009).

An interactionist view emphasizes that both biology and experience contribute to language development. How much of the language is biologically determined and how much depends on interaction with others is a subject of debate among linguists and psychologists (Lieven & Stoll, 2010). However, all agree that both biological capacity and relevant experience are necessary (Berko Gleason, 2009; Lieven, 2008).

Review and Reflect: Learning Goal 5

 Describe the nature of language and how it develops in infancy

REVIEW

- What is language?
- What are language's rule systems?
- How does language develop in infancy?
- What are some biological and environmental influences on language?
- To what extent do biological and environmental influences interact to produce language development?

REFLECT

- Would it be a good idea for parents to hold large flash cards of words in front of their infant to help the infant learn language? Why or why not? What do you think Piaget would say about this activity?

Reach Your Learning Goals

Cognitive Development in Infancy

1 WHAT IS PIAGET'S THEORY OF INFANT DEVELOPMENT? SUMMARIZE AND EVALUATE PIAGET'S THEORY OF INFANT DEVELOPMENT

Cognitive Processes

- In Piaget's theory, children construct their own cognitive worlds, building mental structures to adapt to their world. Schemes are actions or mental representations that organize knowledge. Behavioral schemes (physical activities) characterize infancy, whereas mental schemes (cognitive activities) develop in childhood. Assimilation occurs when children incorporate new information into existing schemes; accommodation refers to children's adjustment of their schemes in the face of new information. Through organization, children group isolated behaviors into a higher-order, more smoothly functioning cognitive system. Equilibration is a mechanism Piaget proposed to explain how children shift from one stage of thought to the next. As children experience cognitive conflict in trying to understand the world, they use assimilation and accommodation to obtain equilibrium. The result is a new stage of thought. According to Piaget, there are four qualitatively different stages of thought.

The Sensorimotor Stage

- In sensorimotor thought, the first of Piaget's four stages, the infant organizes and coordinates sensory experiences with physical movements. The stage lasts from birth to about 2 years of age. The sensorimotor stage has six substages: simple reflexes; first habits and primary circular reactions; secondary circular reactions; coordination of secondary circular reactions; tertiary circular reactions, novelty, and curiosity; and internalization of schemes. One key accomplishment of this stage is object permanence, the ability to understand that objects continue to exist even though the infant is no longer observing them. Another aspect involves infants' understanding of cause and effect.

Evaluating Piaget's Sensorimotor Stage

- Piaget opened up a whole new way of looking at infant development in terms of coordinating sensory input with motoric actions. In the past decades, revisions of Piaget's view have been proposed based on research. For example, researchers have found that a stable and differentiated perceptual world is established earlier than Piaget envisioned, and infants begin to develop concepts as well. The nature-nurture issue in regard to infant cognitive development continues to be debated. Spelke endorses a core knowledge approach, which states that infants are born with domain-specific innate knowledge systems. Critics argue that Spelke has not given adequate attention to early experiences that infants have.

2 HOW DO INFANTS LEARN, REMEMBER, AND CONCEPTUALIZE? DESCRIBE HOW INFANTS LEARN, REMEMBER, AND CONCEPTUALIZE

Conditioning

- Both classical and operant conditioning occur in infants. Operant conditioning techniques have especially been useful to researchers in demonstrating infants' perception and retention of information about perceptual-motor actions.

Attention

- Attention is the focusing of mental resources on select information, and in infancy attention is closely linked with habituation. In the first year, much of attention is of the orienting/investigate type, but sustained attention also becomes important. Habituation is the repeated presentation of the same stimulus, causing reduced attention to the stimulus. If a different stimulus is presented, and the infant pays increased attention to it, dishabituation is occurring. Joint attention plays an important role in infant development, especially in the infant's acquisition of language.

- Memory is the retention of information over time. Infants as young as 2 to 6 months of age can retain information about some experiences. However, many experts argue that what we commonly think of as memory (consciously remembering the past, or explicit memory) does not occur until the second half of the first year of life. By the end of the second year, explicit memory continues to improve. The hippocampus and frontal lobes of the brain are involved in development of explicit memory in infancy. The phenomenon of not being able to remember events that occurred before the age of 2 or 3—known as infantile, or childhood, amnesia—may be due to the immaturity of the prefrontal lobes of the brain at that age.

- Meltzoff has shown that newborns can match their behaviors (such as protruding their tongue) to a model. His research also shows that deferred imitation occurs as early as 9 months of age.

- Mandler argues that it is not until about 7 to 9 months of age that infants form conceptual categories, although we do not know precisely when concept formation begins. Infants' first concepts are broad. Over the first two years of life, these broad concepts gradually become more differentiated. Many infants and young children develop an intense interest in a particular category(ies).

3   HOW ARE INDIVIDUAL DIFFERENCES IN INFANCY ASSESSED, AND DO THESE ASSESSMENTS PREDICT INTELLIGENCE? DISCUSS INFANT ASSESSMENT MEASURES AND THE PREDICTION OF INTELLIGENCE

Measures of Infant Development

- Developmental scales for infants grew out of the tradition of IQ testing of older children. These scales are less verbal than IQ tests. Gesell's test is still widely used by pediatricians to distinguish normal and abnormal infants; it provides a developmental quotient (DQ). The Bayley scales, developed by Nancy Bayley, continue to be widely used today to assess infant development. The current version, the Bayley-III, consists of cognitive, language, motor, socio-emotional, and adaptive scales. Increasingly used, the Fagan Test of Infant Intelligence assesses how effectively the infant processes information.

Predicting Intelligence

- Global scores on the Gesell and Bayley scales are not good predictors of childhood intelligence. However, measures of information processing such as speed of habituation and degree of dishabituation do correlate with intelligence later in childhood. There is both continuity and discontinuity between infant cognitive development and cognitive development later in childhood.

4   WHAT ARE SOME EARLY ENVIRONMENTAL INFLUENCES ON COGNITIVE DEVELOPMENT? CHARACTERIZE EARLY ENVIRONMENTAL INFLUENCES ON COGNITIVE DEVELOPMENT

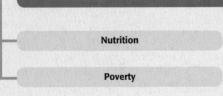

- Nutritional supplements given to malnourished infants improve their cognitive development.

- Early intervention programs that target infants living in poverty are often more effective when they are (1) long-lasting, (2) time-intensive, (3) able to provide educational benefits directly to children, and (4) comprehensive and multidimensional.

5   WHAT IS THE NATURE OF LANGUAGE, AND HOW DOES IT DEVELOP IN INFANCY? DESCRIBE THE NATURE OF LANGUAGE AND HOW IT DEVELOPS IN INFANCY

Defining Language

- Language is a form of communication, whether spoken, written, or signed, that is based on a system of symbols. Language consists of all the words used by a community and the rules for varying and combining them. It is marked by infinite generativity.

Language's Rule Systems

- Phonology is the sound system of the language, including the sounds that are used and how they may be combined. Morphology refers to the units of meaning involved in word formation. Syntax is the way words are combined to form acceptable phrases and sentences. Semantics involves the meaning of words and sentences. Pragmatics is the appropriate use of language in different contexts.

How Language Develops

- Among the milestones in infant language development are crying (birth), cooing (1 to 2 months), babbling (6 months), making the transition from universal linguist to language-specific listener (7 to 11 months), using gestures (8 to 12 months), comprehension of words (8 to 12 months), first word spoken (13 months), vocabulary spurt (18 months), rapid expansion of understanding words (18 to 24 months), and two-word utterances (18 to 24 months).

Biological and Environmental Influences

- In evolution, language clearly gave humans an enormous advantage over other animals and increased their chance of survival. Broca's area and Wernicke's are important locations for language processing in the brain's left hemisphere. Chomsky argues that children are born with the ability to detect basic features and rules of language. In other words, they are biologically prepared to learn language with a prewired language acquisition device (LAD). The behavioral view—that children acquire language as a result of reinforcement—has not been supported. Adults help children acquire language through child-directed speech, recasting, expanding, and labeling. Environmental influences are demonstrated by differences in the language development of children as a consequence of being exposed to different language environments in the home. Parents should talk extensively with an infant, especially about what the baby is attending to.

An Interactionist View

- Today, most language researchers believe that children everywhere arrive in the world with special social and linguistic capacities that make language acquisition possible. How much of the language is biologically determined, and how much depends on interaction with others is a subject of debate among linguists and psychologists. However, all agree that both biological capacity and relevant experience are necessary.

KEY TERMS

schemes 182
assimilation 182
accommodation 184
organization 184
equilibration 184
sensorimotor stage 184
simple reflexes 185
first habits and primary
    circular reactions 185
primary circular
    reaction 185
secondary circular
    reactions 186

coordination of secondary
    circular reactions 186
tertiary circular reactions,
    novelty, and
    curiosity 186
internalization of
    schemes 186
object permanence 186
A-not-B error 189
core knowledge
    approach 190
attention 192
joint attention 193

memory 194
implicit memory 194
explicit memory 194
deferred imitation 194
developmental quotient
    (DQ) 198
Bayley Scales of Infant
    Development 198
language 202
infinite generativity 202
phonology 202
morphology 202
syntax 203

semantics 203
pragmatics 203
telegraphic speech 206
Broca's area 206
Wernicke's area 206
aphasia 206
language acquisition device
    (LAD) 206
child-directed speech 209

KEY PEOPLE

Jean Piaget 182
Renée Baillargeon 187
Eleanor Gibson 189
Elizabeth Spelke 189
Andrew Meltzoff 190

Karen Wynn 190
Carolyn Rovee-
  Collier 192
Jean Mandler 194
Arnold Gesell 198

Nancy Bayley 198
Patricia Kuhl 204
Noam Chomsky 207
Roger Brown 207
Michael Tomasello 208

Betty Hart and Todd
  Risley 208
Janellen Huttenlocher 208
Naomi Baron 210

MAKING A DIFFERENCE

Nourishing the Infant's Cognitive Development

What are some good strategies for helping infants develop in cognitively competent ways?

- *Provide the infant with many play opportunities in a rich and varied environment.* Give the infant extensive opportunities to experience objects of different sizes, shapes, textures, and colors. Recognize that play with objects stimulates the infant's cognitive development.

- *Actively communicate with the infant.* Don't let the infant spend long bouts of waking hours in social isolation. Infants need caregivers who actively communicate with them. This active communication with adults is necessary for the infant's competent cognitive development.

- *Don't try to overaccelerate the infant's cognitive development.* Most experts stress that infants cognitively benefit when they learn concepts naturally. The experts emphasize that restricting infants to a passive role and showing them flash cards to accelerate their cognitive development are not good strategies.

RESOURCES FOR IMPROVING CHILDREN'S LIVES

Growing Up with Language
by Naomi Baron (1992)
Reading, MA: Addison Wesley

Baron focuses on three representative children and their families. She explores how children put their first words together, struggle to understand meaning, and use language as a creative tool. She shows parents how they play a key role in their child's language development.

How Babies Talk
by Roberta Golinkoff and Kathy Hirsh-Pasek (2000)
New York: Plume

Targeted for parents, this book by leading experts details the fascinating world of infant language. Included are activities parents

can use with their infants and indicators of delayed language that can alert parents to possible language problems.

The Development of Language
by Jean Berko Gleason and Nan Ratner (2009, 7th ed.)
Boston: Allyn & Bacon

A number of leading experts provide up-to-date discussion of many aspects of language development, including the development of language, language rule systems, and communication in infancy.

E-LEARNING TOOLS

Connect to **www.mhhe.com/santrockc11e** to research the answers and complete these exercises. In addition, you'll find a number of other resources and valuable study tools for Chapter 6, "Cognitive Development in Infancy," on this Web site.

Taking It to the Net

1. Anthony is surveying *Time* magazine's list of top 100 people of the twentieth century. He notices that Jean Piaget made the list. Why?

2. Marco is 16 months old. He is cooing and babbling, but he has not yet uttered his first word. His father, Tony, is concerned that Marco is delayed in his language development. Should Tony be concerned? What developments in language can be expected for infants and toddlers? How might Tony identify whether Marco has a problem?

3. Poverty has serious negative consequences for children's cognitive development. Is it possible to buffer the effects of poverty through early intervention? If so, what benefits might be linked to early intervention?

Health and Well-Being, Parenting, and Education

Build your decision-making skills by trying your hand at the health and well-being, parenting, and education exercises.

Video Clips

The Online Learning Center includes the following videos for this chapter:

- *Babbling at 7.5 months—1264*
- *Brain Development and Cognition—659*

Renowned brain researcher Charles Nelson describes findings from his research.

- *Language Ability at Age 2—2699*
  While engaging in a pretend tea party with her mother, 2-year-old Abby demonstrates advancing language ability.
- *Motherese with a 4-Year-Old—2150*
  A mother displays the unique ways that many parents speak to their infants.

7

We never know the love of our parents until we have become parents.

—HENRY WARD BEECHER
American Writer, 19th Century

LEARNING GOALS

- ◆ Discuss emotional and personality development in infancy

- ◆ Describe the development of social orientation/understanding and attachment in infancy

- ◆ Explain how social contexts influence the infant's development

SOCIOEMOTIONAL DEVELOPMENT IN INFANCY

CHAPTER OUTLINE

1

HOW DO EMOTIONS AND PERSONALITY DEVELOP IN INFANCY?

Emotional Development

Temperament

Personality Development

2

HOW DO SOCIAL ORIENTATION/UNDERSTANDING AND ATTACHMENT DEVELOP IN INFANCY?

Social Orientation/Understanding

Attachment and Its Development

Individual Differences in Attachment

Caregiving Styles and Attachment

Developmental Social Neuroscience and Attachment

3

HOW DO SOCIAL CONTEXTS INFLUENCE SOCIOEMOTIONAL DEVELOPMENT IN INFANCY?

The Family

Child Care

Images of Children's Development
The Story of Darius' Fathering

Many fathers are spending more time with their infants today than in the past.

An increasing number of fathers are staying home to care for their children (Cohen, 2009; Rochlen & others, 2008). Consider 17-month-old Darius. On weekdays, Darius's father, a writer, cares for him during the day while his mother works full-time as a landscape architect. Darius's father is doing a great job of caring for him. He keeps Darius nearby while he is writing and spends lots of time talking to him and playing with him. From their interactions, it is clear that they genuinely enjoy each other.

Last month, Darius began spending one day a week at a child-care center. His parents carefully selected the center after observing a number of centers and interviewing teachers and center directors. His parents placed him in the center one day a week because they wanted Darius to get some experience with peers and to give his father some time out from his caregiving.

Darius's father looks to the future and imagines the Little League games Darius will play in and the many other activities he can enjoy with Darius. Remembering how little time his own father spent with him, he is dedicated to making sure that Darius has an involved, nurturing experience with his father.

When Darius's mother comes home in the evening, she spends considerable time with him. Darius shows a positive attachment to both his mother and his father.

> **PREVIEW**
>
> In Chapters 5 and 6, you read about how the infant perceives, learns, and remembers. Infants also are socioemotional beings, capable of displaying emotions and initiating social interaction with people close to them. The main topics that we explore in this chapter are emotional and personality development, social understanding and attachment, and the social contexts of the family and child care.

1 HOW DO EMOTIONS AND PERSONALITY DEVELOP IN INFANCY?

Emotional Development	Temperament	Personality Development

Anyone who has been around infants for even a brief time detects that they are emotional beings. Not only do infants express emotions, but they also vary in their temperament. Some are shy and others are outgoing, for example. In this section, we explore these and other aspects of emotional and personality development in infants.

Emotional Development

Imagine your life without emotion. Emotion is the color and music of life, as well as the tie that binds people together. How do psychologists define and classify emotions, and why are they important to development? How do emotions develop during the first two years of life?

What Are Emotions?   For our purposes, we will define **emotion** as feeling, or affect, that occurs when a person is in a state or an interaction that is important to him or her, especially to his or her well-being (Campos, 2005). Psychologists classify the broad range of emotions in many ways, but almost all classifications designate an emotion as either positive or negative (Barrett & others, 2007; Izard, 2009). Positive emotions include enthusiasm, joy, and love. Negative emotions include anxiety, anger, guilt, and sadness.

Biological and Environmental Influences   Emotions are influenced both by biological foundations and by a person's experience. Biology's importance to emotion is also apparent in the changes in a baby's emotional capacities (Bell & Wolfe, 2007; de Hann & Matheson, 2009). Certain regions of the brain that develop early in life play a role in distress, excitement, and rage, and even infants display these emotions (Buss & Goldsmith, 2007; Payne & Bachevalier, 2009). But, as we discuss later in the chapter, infants only gradually develop the ability to regulate their emotions, and this ability seems tied to the gradual maturation of frontal regions of the cerebral cortex (discussed in Chapter 5, "Physical Development in Infancy") that can exert control over other areas of the brain (Thompson, Meyer, & Jochem, 2008).

These biological factors, however, are only part of the story of emotion. Emotions serve important functions in our relationships (Thompson, 2009a, b). As we discuss later in this section, emotions are the first language with which parents and infants communicate. Emotion-linked interchanges, as when Darius cries and his father sensitively responds, provide the foundation for the infant's developing attachment to the parent.

Social relationships, in turn, provide the setting for the development of a rich variety of emotions (Brownell & Kopp, 2007; Thompson, 2009a, b). When toddlers hear their parents quarreling, they often react with distress and inhibit their play. Well-functioning families make each other laugh and may develop a light mood to defuse conflicts. Biological evolution has endowed human beings to be *emotional*, but embeddedness in relationships and culture with others provides diversity in emotional experiences (Thompson & Virmani, 2010). For example, researchers have found that East Asian infants display less frequent and less positive and negative emotions than non-Latino White infants (Camras & others, 1998; Cole & Tan, 2007). Throughout childhood, East Asian parents encourage their children to show emotional reserve rather than to be emotionally expressive (Camras & others, 1998; Cole & Tan, 2007). Further, Japanese parents try to prevent children from experiencing negative emotions, whereas non-Latino White mothers more frequently respond after their children become distressed and then help them cope (Cole & Tan, 2007; Rothbaum & Trommsdorff, 2007).

Early Emotions   Leading expert on infant emotional development, Michael Lewis (2007, 2008), distinguishes between primary emotions and self-conscious emotions. **Primary emotions** are emotions that are present in humans and animals; these emotions appear in the first six months of the human infant's development. Primary emotions include surprise, interest, joy, anger, sadness, fear, and disgust (see Figure 7.1 for infants' facial expressions of some of these early emotions). In Lewis's classification,

*Blossoms are scattered by the wind
And the wind cares nothing, but
The blossoms of the heart
No wind can touch.*

—Youshida Kenko
Buddhist Monk, 14th Century

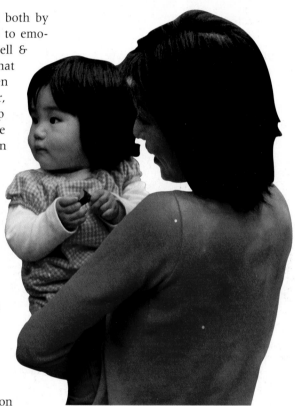

How do Japanese mothers handle their infants' and children's emotional development differently than non-Latino White mothers?

emotion Feeling, or affect, that occurs when a person is in a state or interaction that is important to him or her. Emotion can be characterized as positive (enthusiasm, joy, love, for example) or negative (anxiety, guilt, or sadness, for example).

primary emotions Emotions that are present in humans and other animals, and emerge early in life; examples are joy, anger, sadness, fear, and disgust.

FIGURE 7.1 Expression of Different Emotions in Infants

FIGURE 7.2 Research Setting for Sybil Hart's Attempt to Assess the Early Development of Jealousy An infant becomes distressed when his mother gives attention to a lifelike baby doll. *What are some possible interpretations of the infant's distress?*

What are some different types of cries?

self-conscious emotions require self-awareness that involves consciousness and a sense of "me." Self-conscious emotions include jealousy, empathy, embarrassment, pride, shame, and guilt, most of these occurring for the first time at some point in the second half of the first year through the second year. Some experts on emotion call self-conscious emotions such as embarrassment, shame, guilt, and pride *other-conscious emotions* because they involve the emotional reactions of others when they are generated (Saarni & others, 2006). For example, approval from parents is linked to toddlers beginning to show pride when they successfully complete a task

Researchers such as Joseph Campos (2005) and Michael Lewis (2007) debate how early in the infant and toddler years the emotions that we have described first appear and their sequence. As an indication of the controversy regarding when certain emotions first are displayed by infants, consider jealousy. Some researchers argue that jealousy does not emerge until approximately 18 months of age (Lewis, 2007), whereas others emphasize that it is displayed much earlier (Draghi-Lorenz, 2007). Consider a study of 6-month-old infants in which mothers gave attention either to a life-like baby doll (hugging or gently rocking it, for example) or to a book (Hart & Carrington, 2002). When mothers directed their attention to the doll, the infants were more likely to display negative emotions, such as anger and sadness, which may have indicated their jealousy (see Figure 7.2). On the other hand, their expressions of anger and sadness may have reflected frustration in not being able to have the novel doll to play with. Debate about the onset of an emotion such as jealousy illustrates the complexity and difficulty in indexing early emotions.

Emotional Expression and Social Relationships Emotional expressions are involved in infants' first relationships. The ability of infants to communicate emotions permits coordinated interactions with their caregivers and the beginning of an emotional bond between them (Thomann & Carter, 2008; Thompson, 2008a). Not only do parents change their emotional expressions in response to infants' emotional expressions, but infants also modify their emotional expressions in response to their parents' emotional expressions. In other words, these interactions are mutually regulated (Bridgett & others, 2009). Because of this coordination, the interactions are described as *reciprocal*, or *synchronous*, when all is going well. Sensitive, responsive parents help their infants grow emotionally, whether the infants respond in distressed or happy ways (Gunnar & Quevado, 2007; Thompson & Newton, 2009).

Cries and smiles are two emotional expressions that infants display when interacting with parents. These are babies' first forms of emotional communication.

Crying Crying is the most important mechanism newborns have for communicating with their world. The first cry verifies that the baby's lungs have filled with air. Cries also may provide information about the health of the newborn's central nervous system.

Babies have at least three types of cries:

• **Basic cry.** A rhythmic pattern that usually consists of a cry, followed by a briefer silence, then a shorter whistle that is somewhat higher in pitch than the main cry, then another brief rest before the next cry. Some infancy experts believe that hunger is one of the conditions that incite the basic cry.

- **Anger cry.** A variation of the basic cry in which more excess air is forced through the vocal cords.
- **Pain cry.** A sudden long, initial loud cry followed by breath holding; no preliminary moaning is present. The pain cry is stimulated by a high-intensity stimulus.

Most adults can determine whether an infant's cries signify anger or pain. Parents can distinguish the cries of their own baby better than those of another baby.

Smiling   Two types of smiling can be distinguished in infants:

- **Reflexive smile.** A smile that does not occur in response to external stimuli and appears during the first month after birth, usually during sleep.
- **Social smile.** A smile that occurs in response to an external stimulus, typically a face in the case of the young infant. Social smiling occurs as early as four to six weeks after birth, usually when the infant is gazing at a parent (Messinger, 2008).

Daniel Messinger (2008) recently described the developmental course of infant smiling. From two to six months after birth, infants' social smiling increases considerably, both in self-initiated smiles and smiles in response to others' smiles. At age 6 to 12 months, smiles that couple what is called the Duchenne marker (eye constriction) and mouth opening occur in the midst of highly enjoyable interactions and play with parents (see Figure 7.3). In the second year, smiling continues to occur in such positive circumstances with parents, and in many cases an increase in smiling occurs when interacting with peers. Also in the second year, toddlers become increasingly aware of the social meaning of smiles, especially in their relationship with parents.

Infants also engage in *anticipatory smiling,* in which they communicate preexisting positive emotion by smiling at an object and then turning their smile toward an adult. A recent study revealed that anticipatory smiling at 9 months of age was linked to parents' rating of the child's social competence at 2½ years of age (Parlade & others, 2009).

Fear   One of a baby's earliest emotions is fear, which typically first appears at about 6 months of age and peaks at about 18 months. However, abused and neglected infants can show fear as early as 3 months (Campos, 2005). Researchers have found that infant fear is linked to guilt, empathy, and low aggression at 6 to 7 years of age (Rothbart, 2007).

The most frequent expression of an infant's fear involves **stranger anxiety,** in which an infant shows a fear and wariness of strangers. Stranger anxiety usually emerges gradually. It first appears at about 6 months of age in the form of wary reactions. By age 9 months, the fear of strangers is often more intense, reaching a peak toward the end of the first year of life, then decreasing thereafter (Scher & Harel, 2008).

Not all infants show distress when they encounter a stranger. Besides individual variations, whether an infant shows stranger anxiety also depends on the social context and the characteristics of the stranger (Kagan, 2008).

Infants show less stranger anxiety when they are in familiar settings. For example, in one study, 10-month-olds showed little stranger anxiety when they met a stranger in their own home but much greater fear when they encountered a stranger in a research laboratory (Sroufe, Waters, & Matas, 1974). Thus, it appears that, when infants feel secure, they are less likely to show stranger anxiety.

Who the stranger is and how the stranger behaves also influence stranger anxiety in infants. Infants are less fearful of child strangers than of adult strangers. They also are less fearful of friendly, outgoing, smiling strangers than of passive, unsmiling strangers (Bretherton, Stolberg, & Kreye, 1981).

FIGURE 7.3 A 6-Month-Old's Strong Smile
This strong smile reflects the Duchenne marker (eye constriction) and mouth opening.

How Would You...?
As a human development and family studies professional, how would you respond to the parents of a 13-month-old baby who are concerned because their son has suddenly started crying every morning when they drop him off at child care—despite the fact that he has been going to the same child care for over six months?

self-conscious emotions Emotions that require self-awareness, especially consciousness and a sense of "me"; examples include jealousy, empathy, and embarrassment.

basic cry A rhythmic pattern usually consisting of a cry, a briefer silence, a shorter inspiratory whistle that is higher pitched than the main cry, and then a brief rest before the next cry.

anger cry A cry similar to the basic cry, with more excess air forced through the vocal cords.

pain cry A sudden appearance of a long, initial loud cry without preliminary moaning, followed by breath holding.

reflexive smile A smile that does not occur in response to external stimuli. It happens during the month after birth, usually during sleep.

social smile A smile in response to an external stimulus, which, early in development, typically is a face.

stranger anxiety An infant's fear and wariness of strangers; it tends to appear in the second half of the first year of life.

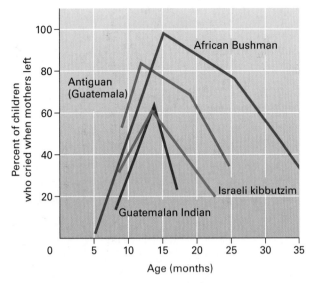

FIGURE 7.4 Separation Anxiety in Four Cultures Note that separation protest peaked at about the same time in all four cultures in this study (13 to 15 months of age) (Kagan, Kearsley, & Zelazo, 1978). However, a higher percentage (100 percent) of infants in an African Bushman culture engaged in separation protest compared to only about 60 percent of infants in Guatemalan Indian and Israeli kibbutzim cultures. *What might explain the fact that separation protest peaks at about the same time in these cultures?* Copyright © 1978 by the President and Fellows of Harvard College.

Should a baby be given attention and soothed, or does this spoil the infant? Should the infant's age, the type of cry, and the circumstances be considered?

How Would You...?

As a social worker, how would you advise a parent who is frustrated with her 18-month-old child because she tends to whine and cry excessively compared to her 3-year-old sibling?

In addition to stranger anxiety, infants experience fear of being separated from their caregivers. The result is **separation protest**—crying when the caregiver leaves. Separation protest is initially displayed by infants at approximately 7 to 8 months and peaks at about 15 months (Kagan, 2008). One study revealed that separation protest peaked at about 13 to 15 months in four different cultures (Kagan, Kearsley, & Zelazo, 1978). As indicated in Figure 7.4, the percentage of infants who engaged in separation protest varied across cultures, but the infants reached a peak of protest at about the same age—just before the middle of the second year of life.

Emotional Regulation and Coping   During the first year of life, the infant gradually develops an ability to inhibit, or minimize, the intensity and duration of emotional reactions (Calkins, 2007; Kopp, 2008). From early in infancy, babies put their thumbs in their mouths to soothe themselves. But, at first, infants mainly depend on caregivers to help them soothe their emotions, as when a caregiver rocks an infant to sleep, sings lullabies to the infant, gently strokes the infant, and so on.

Later in infancy, when they become aroused, infants sometimes redirect their attention or distract themselves in order to reduce their arousal. By 2 years of age, toddlers can use language to define their feeling states and the context that is upsetting them (Kopp, 2008). A toddler might say, "Feel bad. Dog scare." This type of communication may help caregivers to help the child in regulating emotion.

Contexts can influence emotional regulation (Thompson, 2009a, b). Infants are often affected by fatigue, hunger, time of day, which people are around them, and where they are. Infants must learn to adapt to different contexts that require emotional regulation. Further, new demands appear as the infant becomes older and parents modify their expectations. For example, a parent may take it in stride if a 6-month-old infant screams in a restaurant but may react very differently if a 1½-year-old starts screaming.

To soothe or not to soothe—should a crying baby be given attention and soothed, or does this spoil the infant? Many years ago, the behaviorist John Watson (1928) argued that parents spend too much time responding to infant crying. As a consequence, he said, parents reward crying and increase its incidence. More recently, behaviorist Jacob Gewirtz (1977) found that a caregiver's quick, soothing response to crying increased crying. In contrast, infancy experts Mary Ainsworth (1979) and John Bowlby (1989) stress that you can't respond too much to infant crying in the first year of life. They believe that a quick, comforting response to the infant's cries is an important ingredient in the development of a strong bond between the infant and caregiver. In one of Ainsworth's studies, infants whose mothers responded quickly when they cried at 3 months of age cried less later in the first year of life (Bell & Ainsworth, 1972).

Controversy still characterizes the question of whether or how parents should respond to an infant's cries (Lewis & Ramsay, 1999). However, developmentalists increasingly argue that an infant cannot be spoiled in the first year of life, which suggests that parents should soothe a crying infant. This reaction should help infants develop a sense of trust and secure attachment to the caregiver.

Temperament

Do you get upset a lot? Does it take much to get you angry, or to make you laugh? Even at birth, babies seem to have different emotional styles. One infant is cheerful and happy much of the time; another baby seems to cry constantly. These tendencies reflect **temperament,** which is an individual's behavioral style and characteristic way of emotionally responding.

Describing and Classifying Temperament   How would you describe your temperament or the temperament of a friend? Researchers have described and classified the temperament of individuals in different ways. Here we will examine three of those ways.

Chess and Thomas' Classification   Psychiatrists Alexander Chess and Stella Thomas (Chess & Thomas, 1977; Thomas & Chess, 1991) identified three basic types, or clusters, of temperament:

- **Easy child.** This child is generally in a positive mood, quickly establishes regular routines in infancy, and adapts easily to new experiences.
- **Difficult child.** This child reacts negatively and cries frequently, engages in irregular daily routines, and is slow to accept change.
- **Slow-to-warm-up child.** This child has a low activity level, is somewhat negative, and displays a low intensity of mood.

In their longitudinal investigation, Chess and Thomas found that 40 percent of the children they studied could be classified as easy, 10 percent as difficult, and 15 percent as slow to warm up. Notice that 35 percent did not fit any of the three patterns. Researchers have found that these three basic clusters of temperament are moderately stable across the childhood years. A recent study revealed that young children with a difficult temperament showed more problems when they experienced low-quality child care and fewer problems when they experienced high-quality child care than young children with an easy temperament (Pluess & Belsky, 2009).

Kagan's Behavioral Inhibition   Another way of classifying temperament focuses on the differences between a shy, subdued, timid child and a sociable, extraverted, bold child (Asendorph, 2008). Jerome Kagan (2002, 2008, 2010) regards shyness with strangers (peers or adults) as one feature of a broad temperament category called *inhibition to the unfamiliar*. Inhibited children react to many aspects of unfamiliarity with initial avoidance, distress, or subdued affect, beginning about 7 to 9 months of age.

Kagan has found that inhibition shows considerable stability from infancy through early childhood. One study classified toddlers into extremely inhibited, extremely uninhibited, and intermediate groups (Pfeifer & others, 2002). Follow-up assessments occurred at 4 and 7 years of age. Continuity was demonstrated for both inhibition and lack of inhibition, although a substantial number of the inhibited children moved into the intermediate groups at 7 years of age.

Rothbart and Bates' Classification   New classifications of temperament continue to be forged. Mary Rothbart and John Bates (2006) argue that three broad dimensions best represent what researchers have found to characterize the structure of temperament: extraversion/surgency, negative affectivity, and effortful control (self-regulation):

- *Extraversion/surgency*, which includes "positive anticipation, impulsivity, activity level, and sensation seeking" (Rothbart, 2004, p. 495). Kagan's uninhibited children fit into this category.

"Oh, he's cute, all right, but he's got the temperament of a car alarm."

separation protest An infant's distressed reaction when the caregiver leaves.

temperament An individual's behavioral style and characteristic way of emotionally responding.

easy child A child who is generally in a positive mood, who quickly establishes regular routines in infancy, and who adapts easily to new experiences.

difficult child A child who tends to react negatively and cry frequently, who engages in irregular daily routines, and who is slow to accept new experiences.

slow-to-warm-up child A child who has a low activity level, is somewhat negative, and displays a low intensity of mood.

- *Negative affectivity,* which includes "fear, frustration, sadness, and discomfort" (Rothbart, 2004, p. 495). These children are easily distressed; they may fret and cry often. Kagan's inhibited children fit this category.

- *Effortful control (self-regulation),* which includes "attentional focusing and shifting, inhibitory control, perceptual sensitivity, and low-intensity pleasure" (Rothbart, 2004, p. 495). Infants who are high on effortful control show an ability to keep their arousal from getting too high and have strategies for soothing themselves. By contrast, children low on effortful control are often unable to control their arousal; they become easily agitated and intensely emotional.

In Rothbart's (2004, p. 497) view, "early theoretical models of temperament stressed the way we are moved by our positive and negative emotions or level of arousal, with our actions driven by these tendencies." The more recent emphasis on effortful control, however, advocates that individuals can engage in a more cognitive, flexible approach to stressful circumstances.

An important point about temperament classifications such as Chess and Thomas's and Rothbart and Bates's is that children should not be pigeonholed as having only one temperament dimension, such as "difficult" or "negative affectivity." A good strategy when classifying a child's temperament is to think of temperament as consisting of multiple dimensions (Bates, 2008). For example, one child might be extraverted, show little emotional negativity, and have good self-regulation. Another child might be introverted, show little emotional negativity, and have a low level of self-regulation.

Rothbart and Maria Gartstein (2008, p. 323) recently described the following developmental changes in temperament during infancy. During early infancy, smiling and laughter are emerging as part of the positive affectivity dimension of temperament. Also, by 2 months of age, infants show anger and frustration when their actions don't produce an interesting outcome. During this time, infants often are susceptible to distress and overstimulation. From 4 to 12 months of age, fear and irritability become more differentiated, with inhibition (fear) increasingly linked to new and unpredictable experiences. Not all temperament characteristics are in place by the first birthday. Positive emotionality becomes more stable later in infancy and the characteristics of extraversion/surgency can be determined in the toddler period. Improved attention skills in the toddler and preschool years are related to an increase in effortful control, which serves as a foundation for improved self-regulation.

The developmental changes just described reflect normative capabilities of children, not individual differences in children. The development of these capabilities, such as effortful control, allow individual differences to emerge (Bates, 2008). For example, although maturation of the brain's prefrontal lobes must occur for any child's attention to improve and the child to achieve effortful control, some children develop effortful control, others do not. And it is these individual differences in children that are at the heart of what temperament is (Bates, 2008).

Biological Foundations and Experience

How does a child acquire a certain temperament? Kagan (2002, 2008, 2010) argues that children inherit a physiology that biases them to have a particular type of temperament. However, through experience they may learn to modify their temperament to some extent. For example, children may inherit a physiology that biases them to be fearful and inhibited, but they learn to reduce their fear and inhibition to some degree.

What are some ways that developmentalists have classified infants' temperaments? Which classification makes the most sense to you, based on your observations of infants?

Biological Influences   Physiological characteristics have been linked with different temperaments (Schmidt & Jetha, 2009). In particular, an inhibited temperament is associated with a unique physiological pattern that includes high and stable heart rate, high level of the hormone cortisol, and high activity in the right frontal lobe of the brain (Kagan, 2008). This pattern may be tied to the excitability of the amygdala, a structure of the brain that plays an important role in fear and inhibition. An inhibited temperament or negative affectivity may also be linked to low levels of the neurotransmitter serotonin, which may increase an individual's vulnerability to fear and frustration (Pauli-Pott & others, 2009).

What is heredity's role in the biological foundations of temperament? Twin and adoption studies suggest that heredity has a moderate influence on differences in temperament within a group of people (Goldsmith, 2010; Plomin & others, 2009). The contemporary view is that temperament is a biologically based but evolving aspect of behavior; it evolves as the child's experiences are incorporated into a network of self-perceptions and behavioral preferences that characterize the child's personality (Thompson & Goodvin, 2005).

Gender, Culture, and Temperament   Gender may be an important factor shaping the context that influences the fate of temperament (Blakemore, Berenbaum, & Liben, 2009). Parents might react differently to an infant's temperament depending on whether the baby is a boy or a girl. For example, in one study, mothers were more responsive to the crying of irritable girls than to the crying of irritable boys (Crockenberg, 1986).

Similarly, the reaction to an infant's temperament may depend in part on culture (Cole & Tan, 2007; Garstein & others, 2009). For example, an active temperament might be valued in some cultures (such as the United States) but not in other cultures (such as China). Indeed, children's temperament can vary across cultures (Putnam, Sanson, & Rothbart, 2002). Behavioral inhibition is more highly valued in China than in North America, and researchers have found that Chinese children are more inhibited than Canadian children (Chen & others, 1998). The cultural differences in temperament were linked to parent attitude and behaviors. Canadian mothers of inhibited 2-year-olds were less accepting of their infants' inhibited temperament, whereas Chinese mothers were more accepting.

In short, many aspects of a child's environment can encourage or discourage the persistence of temperament characteristics. One useful way of thinking about these relationships applies the concept of goodness of fit, which we examine next.

An infant's temperament can vary across cultures. *What do parents need to know about a child's temperament?*

Goodness of Fit and Parenting

Goodness of fit refers to the match between a child's temperament and the environmental demands the child must cope with (Schoppe-Sullivan & others, 2007). Suppose Jason is an active toddler who is made to sit still for long periods of time and Jack is a slow-to-warm-up toddler who is abruptly pushed into new situations on a regular basis. Both Jason and Jack face a lack of fit between their temperament and environmental demands. Lack of fit can produce adjustment problems (Rothbart & Bates, 2006).

Some temperament characteristics pose more parenting challenges than others, at least in modern Western societies (Bates & Pettit, 2007; Rothbart & Bates, 2006). When children are prone to distress, as exhibited by frequent crying and irritability, their parents may eventually respond by ignoring the child's distress or trying to force the child to "behave." In one research study, though, extra support and training for mothers of distress-prone infants improved the quality of mother-infant interaction (van den Boom, 1989). The training led the mothers to alter their demands on the child, improving the fit between the child and the environment.

Many parents don't become believers in temperament's importance until the birth of their second child. They viewed their first child's behavior as a result of how they treated the child. But then they find that some strategies that worked with their first child are not as effective with the second child. Some problems

How Would You...?
As a social worker, how would you apply information about an infant's temperament to maximize the goodness of fit in a clinical setting?

goodness of fit Refers to the match between a child's temperament and the environmental demands with which the child must cope.

experienced with the first child (such as those involved in feeding, sleeping, and coping with strangers) do not exist with the second child, but new problems arise. Such experiences strongly suggest that children differ from each other very early in life, and that these differences have important implications for parent-child interaction (Kwak & others, 1999; Rothbart & Putnam, 2002). To read further about some positive strategies for parenting that take into account the child's temperament, see the *Caring for Children* interlude.

Caring for Children

PARENTING AND THE CHILD'S TEMPERAMENT

What are the implications of temperamental variations for parenting? Although answers to this question necessarily are speculative, these conclusions regarding the best parenting strategies to use in relation to children's temperament were reached by temperament experts Ann Sanson and Mary Rothbart (1995):

- *Attention to and respect for individuality.* Good parenting involves sensitivity to the child's individual characteristics. A goal might be accomplished in one way with one child and in another way with another child, depending on the child's temperament.
- *Structuring the child's environment.* Crowded, noisy environments can pose greater problems for some children (such as a "difficult child") than for others (such as an "easy child"). We might also expect that a fearful, withdrawing child would benefit from slower entry into new contexts.
- *The "difficult child" and packaged parenting programs.* Programs for parents often focus on dealing with children who have "difficult" temperaments. In some cases, "difficult child" refers to Thomas and Chess's description of a child who reacts negatively, cries frequently, engages in irregular daily routines, and is slow to accept change. In others, the concept might be used to describe a child who is irritable, displays anger frequently, does not follow directions well, or some other negative characteristic. Acknowledging that some children are harder than others to parent is often helpful, and advice on how to handle particular difficult characteristics can be useful. However, whether a particular characteristic is difficult depends on its fit with the environment. To label a child "difficult" has the danger of becoming a self-fulfilling prophecy. If a child is identified as "difficult," people may treat the child in a way that actually elicits "difficult" behavior. One recent study did find that having access to experiences that encourage coping and build self-regulatory skills was beneficial to children with a difficult temperament (Bradley & Corwyn, 2008).

Too often, we pigeonhole children into categories without examining the context (Rothbart & Bates, 2006; Saarni, 2002). Nonetheless, caregivers need to take children's temperament into account. Research does not yet allow for many highly specific recommendations, but, in general, caregivers should (1) be sensitive to the individual characteristics of the child, (2) be flexible in responding to these characteristics, and (3) avoid applying negative labels to the child.

Personality Development

Emotions and temperament form key aspects of *personality,* the enduring personal characteristics of individuals. Let's now examine characteristics that often are thought of as central to personality development during infancy: trust and the development of self and independence.

Trust   According to Erik Erikson (1968), the first year of life is characterized by the trust versus mistrust stage of development. Following a life of regularity, warmth, and protection in the mother's womb, the infant faces a world that is less secure. Erikson proposed that infants learn trust when they are cared for in a consistent, warm manner. If the infant is not well fed and kept warm on a consistent basis, a sense of mistrust is likely to develop.

Trust versus mistrust is not resolved once and for all in the first year of life. It arises again at each successive stage of development, a pathway that can have positive or negative outcomes. For example, children who leave infancy with a sense of trust can still have their sense of mistrust activated at a later stage, perhaps if their parents are separated or divorced under conflicting circumstances.

The Developing Sense of Self   Real or imagined, the sense of self is a strong motivating force in life. When does the individual begin to sense a separate existence from others?

According to leading expert Ross Thompson (2007), studying the self in infancy is difficult mainly because infants cannot tell us how they experience themselves. Infants cannot verbally express their views of the self. They also cannot understand complex instructions from researchers.

One ingenious strategy to test infants' visual self-recognition is the use of a mirror technique, in which an infant's mother first puts a dot of rouge on the infant's nose. Then an observer watches to see how often the infant touches its nose. Next, the infant is placed in front of a mirror, and observers detect whether nose touching increases. Why does this matter? The idea is that increased nose touching indicates that the infant recognizes the self in the mirror and is trying to touch or rub off the rouge because the rouge violates the infant's view of the self. Increased touching indicates that the infant realizes that it is the self in the mirror but that something is not right since the real self does not have a dot of rouge on it.

Figure 7.5 displays the results of two investigations that used the mirror technique. The researchers found that before they were 1 year old, infants did not recognize themselves in the mirror (Amsterdam, 1968; Lewis & Brooks-Gunn, 1979). Signs of self-recognition began to appear among some infants when they were 15 to 18 months old. By the time they were 2 years old, most children recognized themselves in the mirror. In sum, infants begin to develop a self-understanding called self-recognition at approximately 18 months of age (Hart & Karmel, 1996; Lewis, 2005).

Late in the second year and early in the third year, toddlers show other emerging forms of self-awareness that reflect a sense of "me" (Laible & Thompson, 2007). For example, they refer to themselves such as by saying "me big"; they label their internal experiences such as emotions; they monitor themselves as when a toddler says, "do it myself"; and they say that things are theirs (Bates, 1990; Fasig, 2000).

Independence   Not only does the infant develop a sense of self in the second year of life, but independence also becomes a more central theme in the infant's life (Keller, 2007; Mangelsdorf & Wong, 2008). The theories of Margaret Mahler and Erik Erikson have important implications for both self-development and independence. Mahler (1979) argues that the child goes through a separation and then an individuation process. *Separation* involves the infant's movement away from the mother. *Individuation* involves the development of self.

Erikson (1968), like Mahler, stressed that independence is an important issue in the second year of life. Erikson describes the second stage of development

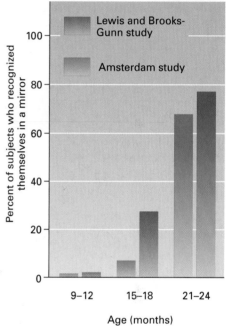

FIGURE 7.5 The Development of Self-Recognition in Infancy The graph shows the findings of two studies in which infants less than 1 year of age did not recognize themselves in the mirror. A slight increase in the percentage of infant self-recognition occurred around 15 to 18 months of age. By 2 years of age, a majority of children recognized themselves. *Why do researchers study whether infants recognize themselves in a mirror?*

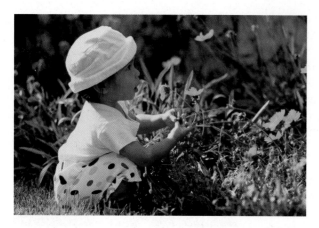

Erikson argued that autonomy versus shame and doubt is the key developmental theme of the toddler years. *What are some good strategies for parents to use with their toddlers?*

as the stage of autonomy versus shame and doubt. Autonomy builds as the infant's mental and motor abilities develop. At this point in development, not only can infants walk, but they can also climb, open and close, drop, push and pull, and hold and let go. Infants feel pride in these new accomplishments and want to do everything themselves, whether the activity is flushing a toilet, pulling the wrapping off a package, or deciding what to eat. It is important for parents to recognize the motivation of toddlers to do what they are capable of doing at their own pace. Then they can learn to control their muscles and their impulses themselves. But when caregivers are impatient and do for toddlers what they are capable of doing themselves, shame and doubt develop. Every parent has rushed a child from time to time. It is only when parents consistently overprotect toddlers or criticize accidents (wetting, soiling, spilling, or breaking, for example) that children develop an excessive sense of shame and doubt about their ability to control themselves and their world. As we discuss in later chapters, Erikson argued that the stage of autonomy versus shame and doubt has important implications for the individual's future development.

How Would You...?
As a human development and family studies professional, how would you work with a parent who shows signs of being overly protective or critical to the point of impairing their toddler's autonomy?

Review and Reflect: Learning Goal 1

1 Discuss emotional and personality development in infancy

REVIEW
- What is the nature of an infant's emotions, and how do they change?
- What is temperament, and how does it develop in infancy?
- What are some important aspects of personality in infancy, and how do they develop?

REFLECT
- How would you describe your temperament? Does it fit one of Chess and Thomas' three styles—easy, slow to warm up, or difficult? If you have siblings, is your temperament similar or different from theirs?

2 HOW DO SOCIAL ORIENTATION/UNDERSTANDING AND ATTACHMENT DEVELOP IN INFANCY?

| Social Orientation/ Understanding | Attachment and Its Development | Individual Differences in Attachment | Caregiving Styles and Attachment | Developmental Social Neuroscience and Attachment |

So far, we have discussed how emotions and emotional competence change as children develop. We have also examined the role of emotional style; in effect, we have seen how emotions set the tone of our experiences in life. But emotions also write the lyrics because they are at the core of our relationships with others.

Social Orientation/Understanding

As socioemotional beings, infants show a strong interest in the social world and are motivated to orient to it and understand it. In earlier chapters, we described many of the biological and cognitive foundations that contribute to the infant's development of social orientation and understanding. We will call attention to relevant biological and cognitive factors as we explore social orientation; locomotion; intention, goal-directed behavior, and cooperation; and social referencing. Discussing biological, cognitive, and social processes together reminds us of an important aspect of development that was pointed out in Chapter 1, "Introduction": These processes are intricately intertwined (Diamond, 2009; Diamond, Casey, & Munakata, 2010).

Social Orientation   From early in their development, infants are captivated by the social world. As we discussed in our coverage of infant perception in Chapter 5, "Physical Development in Infancy," young infants stare intently at faces and are attuned to the sounds of human voices, especially their caregiver's (Ramsay-Rennels & Langlois, 2007). Later, they become adept at interpreting the meaning of facial expressions.

Face-to-face play often begins to characterize caregiver-infant interactions when the infant is about 2 to 3 months of age. The focused social interaction of face-to-face play may include vocalizations, touch, and gestures (Leppanen & others, 2007; Moore & others, 2009). Such play is part of many mothers' motivation to create a positive emotional state in their infants (Thompson, 2009a).

In part because of such positive social interchanges between caregivers and infants, by 2 to 3 months of age, infants respond differently to people than they do to objects, showing more positive emotion to people than to inanimate objects, such as puppets (Legerstee, 1997). At this age, most infants expect people to react positively when the infants initiate a behavior, such as a smile or a vocalization. This finding has been discovered using a method called the *still-face paradigm,* in which the caregiver alternates between engaging in face-to-face interaction with the infant and remaining still and unresponsive. As early as 2 to 3 months of age, infants show more withdrawal, negative emotions, and self-directed behavior when their caregivers are still and unresponsive (Adamson & Frick, 2003). The frequency of face-to-face play decreases after 7 months of age as infants become more mobile (Thompson, 2006). A recent meta-analysis revealed that infants' higher positive affect and lower negative affect as displayed during the still-face paradigm were linked to secure attachment at 1 year of age (Mesman, van IJzendoorn, & Bakersman-Kranenburg, 2009).

Infants also learn about the social world through contexts other than face-to-face play with a caregiver (Thompson, 2008a; Thompson & Newton, 2009). Even though infants as young as 6 months of age show an interest in each other, their interaction with peers increases considerably in the last half of the second year. Between 18 and 24 months of age, children markedly increase their imitative and reciprocal play, such as imitating nonverbal actions like jumping and running (Eckerman & Whitehead, 1999). One recent study involved presenting 1- and 2-year-olds with a simple cooperative task that consisted of pulling a lever to get an attractive toy (Brownell, Ramani, & Zerwas, 2006) (see Figure 7.6). Any coordinated actions of the 1-year-olds appeared to be more coincidental than cooperative, whereas the 2-year-olds' behavior was characterized as more active cooperation to reach a goal. As increasing numbers of U.S. infants experience child care outside the home, they are spending more time

A mother and her baby engaging in face-to-face play. *At what age does face-to-face play usually begin, and when does it typically start decreasing in frequency?*

FIGURE 7.6 The Cooperation Task The cooperation task consisted of two handles on a box, atop which was an animated musical toy, surreptitiously activated by remote control when both handles were pulled. The handles were placed far enough apart that one child could not pull both handles. The experimenter demonstrated the task, saying, "Watch! If you pull the handles, the doggie will sing" (Brownell, Ramani, & Zerwas, 2006).

in social play with other peers (Field, 2007). Later in the chapter, we further discuss child care.

Locomotion   Recall from earlier in the chapter how important independence is for infants, especially in the second year of life. As infants develop the ability to crawl, walk, and run, they are able to explore and expand their social world. These newly developed, self-produced locomotor skills allow the infant to independently initiate social interchanges on a more frequent basis (Laible & Thompson, 2007; Thompson, 2006). Remember from Chapter 5, "Physical Development in Infancy," that the development of these gross motor skills is the result of a number of factors including the development of the nervous system, the goal the infant is motivated to reach, and environmental support for the skill (Adolph, 2008; Adolph & Joh, 2009).

Locomotion is also important for its motivational implications (Thompson, 2008b). Once infants have the ability to move in goal-directed pursuits, the reward from these pursuits leads to further efforts to explore and develop skills.

Intention, Goal-Directed Behavior, and Cooperation   Perceiving people as engaging in intentional and goal-directed behavior is an important social cognitive accomplishment, and this initially occurs toward the end of the first year (Laible & Thompson, 2007). Joint attention and gaze following help the infant to understand that other people have intentions (Meltzoff & Brooks, 2009; Moll & others, 2008).

Recall from Chapter 6, "Cognitive Development in Infancy," that joint attention occurs when the caregiver and infant focus on the same object or event. We know that emerging aspects of joint attention occur at about 7 to 8 months, but at about 10 to 11 months of age joint attention intensifies and infants begin to follow the caregiver's gaze. By their first birthday, infants have begun to direct the caregiver's attention to objects that capture their interest (Heimann & others, 2006).

In the study on cooperating to reach a goal that was discussed earlier, 1- and 2-year-olds also were assessed as to two social understanding tasks: observation of children's behavior in a joint attention task, and the parents' perceptions of the language the children use about the self and others (Brownell, Ramani, & Zerwas, 2006). Those with more advanced social understanding were more likely to cooperate. To cooperate, the children had to connect their own intentions with the peer's intentions and put this understanding to use in interacting with the peer to reach a goal. Further, a recent study revealed that initiating and responding to joint attention at 12 months of age were linked to being socially competent (for example, not being aggressive or defiant, showing empathy, and engaging in sustained attention) at 30 months of age (Vaughan Van Hecke & others, 2007).

Social Referencing   Another important social cognitive accomplishment in infancy is developing the ability to "read" the emotions of other people. **Social referencing** is the term used to describe "reading" emotional cues in others to help determine how to act in a particular situation. The development of social referencing helps infants to interpret ambiguous situations more accurately, as when they encounter a stranger and need to know whether to fear the person (de Rosnay & others, 2006; Thompson, 2006). By the end of the first year, a mother's facial expression—either smiling or fearful—influences whether an infant will explore an unfamiliar environment.

Infants become better at social referencing in the second year of life. At this age, they tend to "check" with their mother before they act; they look at her to see if she is happy, angry, or fearful. For example, in one study, 14- to

What is social referencing? What are some developmental changes in social referencing?

social referencing   "Reading" emotional cues in others to help determine how to act in a particular situation.

22-month-old infants were more likely to look at their mother's face as a source of information for how to act in a situation than were 6- to 9-month-old infants (Walden, 1991).

Infants' Social Sophistication and Insight In sum, researchers are discovering that infants are more socially sophisticated and insightful at younger ages than previously envisioned (Hamlin, Hallinan, & Woodward, 2008; Thompson, 2008a, b, 2009a). Such sophistication and insight are reflected in infants' perceptions of others' actions as intentionally motivated and goal-directed (Brune & Woodward, 2007) and their motivation to share and participate in that intentionality by their first birthday (Tomasello, Carpenter, & Liszkowski, 2007). The more advanced social cognitive skills of infants could be expected to influence their understanding and awareness of attachment to a caregiver.

Attachment and Its Development

A small curly-haired girl named Danielle, age 11 months, begins to whimper. After a few seconds, she begins to wail. Soon her mother comes into the room, and Danielle's crying ceases. Quickly, Danielle crawls over to where her mother is seated and reaches out to be held. Danielle has just demonstrated attachment to her mother. **Attachment** is a close emotional bond between two people.

There is no shortage of theories about infant attachment. Three theorists discussed in Chapter 1, "Introduction"—Freud, Erikson, and Bowlby—proposed influential views.

Freud emphasized that infants become attached to the person or object that provides oral satisfaction. For most infants, this is the mother, since she is most likely to feed the infant. Is feeding as important as Freud thought? A classic study by Harry Harlow (1958) reveals that the answer is no (see Figure 7.7).

Harlow removed infant monkeys from their mothers at birth; for six months they were reared by surrogate (substitute) "mothers." One surrogate mother was made of wire, the other of cloth. Half of the infant monkeys were fed by the wire mother, half by the cloth mother. Periodically, the amount of time the infant monkeys spent with either the wire or the cloth mother was computed. Regardless of which mother fed them, the infant monkeys spent far more time with the cloth mother. Even if the wire mother, but not the cloth mother, provided nourishment, the infant monkeys spent more time with the cloth mother. And, when Harlow frightened the monkeys, those "raised" by the cloth mother ran to the mother and clung to it; those raised by the wire mother did not. Whether the mother provided comfort seemed to determine whether the monkeys associated the mother with security. This study clearly demonstrated that feeding is not the crucial element in the attachment process and that contact comfort is important.

Physical comfort also plays a role in Erik Erikson's (1968) view of the infant's development. Recall Erikson's proposal that the first year of life represents the stage of trust versus mistrust. Physical comfort and sensitive care, according to Erikson (1968), are key to establishing a basic trust in infants. The infant's sense of trust, in turn, is the foundation for attachment and sets the stage for a lifelong expectation that the world will be a good and pleasant place to be.

The ethological perspective of British psychiatrist John Bowlby (1969, 1989) also stresses the importance of attachment in the first year of life and the responsiveness of the caregiver. Bowlby maintains that both infants and their primary caregivers are biologically predisposed to form attachments. He argues that the newborn is biologically equipped to elicit attachment behavior. The baby cries, clings, coos, and smiles. Later, the infant crawls, walks, and follows the mother. The immediate result is to keep the primary caregiver nearby; the long-term effect is to increase the infant's chances of survival (Thompson, 2006).

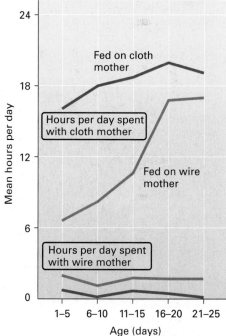

FIGURE 7.7 Contact Time with Wire and Cloth Surrogate Mothers Regardless of whether the infant monkeys were fed by a wire or a cloth mother, they overwhelmingly preferred to spend contact time with the cloth mother. *How do these results compare with what Freud's theory and Erikson's theory would predict about human infants?*

attachment A close emotional bond between two people.

In Bowlby's model, what are four phases of attachment?

What is the nature of secure and insecure attachment? How are caregiving styles related to attachment classification?

Strange Situation An observational measure of infant attachment that requires the infant to move through a series of introductions, separations, and reunions with the caregiver and an adult stranger in a prescribed order.

securely attached babies Babies that use the caregiver as a secure base from which to explore the environment.

Attachment does not emerge suddenly but rather develops in a series of phases, moving from a baby's general preference for human beings to a partnership with primary caregivers. Following are four such phases based on Bowlby's conceptualization of attachment (Schaffer, 1996):

- *Phase 1: From birth to 2 months.* Infants instinctively direct their attachment to human figures. Strangers, siblings, and parents are equally likely to elicit smiling or crying from the infant.
- *Phase 2: From 2 to 7 months.* Attachment becomes focused on one figure, usually the primary caregiver, as the baby gradually learns to distinguish familiar from unfamiliar people.
- *Phase 3: From 7 to 24 months.* Specific attachments develop. With increased locomotor skills, babies actively seek contact with regular caregivers, such as the mother or father.
- *Phase 4: From 24 months on.* Children become aware of others' feelings, goals, and plans and begin to take these into account in forming their own actions.

Researchers' recent findings that infants are more socially sophisticated and insightful than previously envisioned suggest that some of the characteristics of Bowlby's phase 4, such as understanding the goals and intentions of the attachment figure, appear to be developing in phase 3 as attachment security is taking shape (Thompson, 2008b).

Bowlby argued that infants develop an *internal working model* of attachment, a simple mental model of the caregiver, their relationship, and the self as deserving of nurturant care. The infant's internal working model of attachment with the caregiver influences the infant's and, later, the child's subsequent responses to other people (Bretherton & Munholland, 2008; Posada, 2008). The internal model of attachment also has played a pivotal role in the discovery of links between attachment and subsequent emotional understanding, conscious development, and self-concept (Thompson, 2006).

In sum, attachment emerges from the social cognitive advances that allow infants to develop expectations for the caregiver's behavior and to determine the affective quality of their relationship (Laible & Thompson, 2007; Thompson, 2008a). These social cognitive advances include recognizing the caregiver's face, voice, and other features, as well as developing an internal working model of expecting the caregiver to provide pleasure in social interaction and relief from distress.

Individual Differences in Attachment

Although attachment to a caregiver intensifies midway through the first year, isn't it likely that the quality of babies' attachment experiences varies? Mary Ainsworth (1979) thought so. Ainsworth created the **Strange Situation,** an observational measure of infant attachment in which the infant experiences a series of introductions, separations, and reunions with the caregiver and an adult stranger in a prescribed order. In using the Strange Situation, researchers hope that their observations will provide information about the infant's motivation to be near the caregiver and the degree to which the caregiver's presence provides the infant with security and confidence.

Based on how babies respond in the Strange Situation, they are described as being securely attached or insecurely attached (in one of three ways) to the caregiver:

- **Securely attached babies** use the caregiver as a secure base from which to explore the environment. When in the presence of their caregiver, securely attached infants explore the room and examine toys that have been placed in it. When the caregiver departs, securely attached infants might mildly protest, and when the caregiver returns these infants reestablish positive interaction with her, perhaps by smiling or climbing on her lap. Subsequently, they often resume playing with the toys in the room.

- **Insecure avoidant babies** show insecurity by avoiding the caregiver. In the Strange Situation, these babies engage in little interaction with the caregiver, are not distressed when she leaves the room, usually do not reestablish contact with her on her return, and may even turn their back on her. If contact is established, the infant usually leans away or looks away.

- **Insecure resistant babies** often cling to the caregiver and then resist her by fighting against the closeness, perhaps by kicking or pushing away. In the Strange Situation, these babies often cling anxiously to the caregiver and don't explore the playroom. When the caregiver leaves, they often cry loudly and push away if she tries to comfort them on her return.

- **Insecure disorganized babies** are disorganized and disoriented. In the Strange Situation, these babies might appear dazed, confused, and fearful. To be classified as disorganized, babies must show strong patterns of avoidance and resistance or display certain specified behaviors, such as extreme fearfulness around the caregiver.

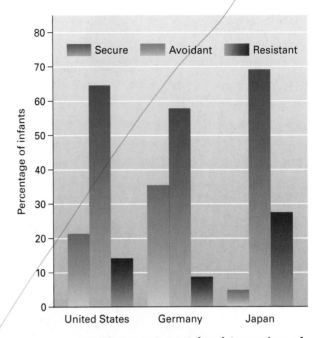

FIGURE 7.8 Cross-Cultural Comparison of Attachment In one study, infant attachment in three countries—the United States, Germany, and Japan—was measured in the Ainsworth Strange Situation (van IJzendoorn & Kroonenberg, 1988). The dominant attachment pattern in all three countries was secure attachment. However, German infants were more avoidant and Japanese infants were less avoidant and more resistant than U.S. infants. *What are some explanations for differences in how German, Japanese, and U.S. infants respond to the Strange Situation?*

Evaluating the Strange Situation   Does the Strange Situation capture important differences among infants? As a measure of attachment, it may be culturally biased. For example, German and Japanese babies often show patterns of attachment different from those of American infants. As illustrated in Figure 7.8, German infants are more likely to show an avoidant attachment pattern and Japanese infants are less likely to display this pattern than U.S. infants (van IJzendoorn & Kroonenberg, 1988). The avoidant pattern in German babies likely occurs because their caregivers encourage them to be independent (Grossmann & others, 1985). Also as shown in Figure 7.8, Japanese babies are more likely than American babies to be categorized as resistant. This pattern may have more to do with the Strange Situation as a measure of attachment than with attachment insecurity itself. Japanese mothers rarely let anyone unfamiliar with their babies care for them. Thus, the Strange Situation might create considerably more stress for Japanese infants than for American infants, who are more accustomed to separation from their mothers (Miyake, Chen, & Campos, 1985). Even though there are cultural variations in attachment classification, the most frequent classification in every culture studied so far is secure attachment (Thompson, 2006; van IJzendoorn & Kroonenberg, 1988).

Some critics stress that behavior in the Strange Situation—like other laboratory assessments—might not indicate what infants do in a natural environment. But researchers have found that infants' behaviors in the Strange Situation are closely related to how they behave at home in response to separation and reunion with their mothers (Pederson & Moran, 1996). Thus, many infant researchers believe the Strange Situation continues to show merit as a measure of infant attachment.

Interpreting Differences in Attachment   Do individual differences in attachment matter? Ainsworth argues that secure attachment in the first year of life provides an important foundation for psychological development later in life. The securely attached infant moves freely away from the mother but keeps track of where she is through periodic glances. The securely attached infant responds positively to being picked up by others and, when put back down, freely moves away to play. An insecurely attached infant, by contrast, avoids the mother or is ambivalent toward her, fears strangers, and is upset by minor, everyday separations.

If early attachment to a caregiver is important, it should relate to a child's social behavior later in development. For some children, early attachments seem

insecure avoidant babies Babies that show insecurity by avoiding the caregiver.

insecure resistant babies Babies that often cling to the caregiver, then resist her by fighting against the closeness, perhaps by kicking or pushing away.

insecure disorganized babies Babies that show insecurity by being disorganized and disoriented.

to foreshadow later functioning (Cassidy, 2008). In the extensive longitudinal study conducted by Alan Sroufe and his colleagues (2005), early secure attachment (assessed by the Strange Situation at 12 and 18 months) was linked with positive emotional health, high self-esteem, self-confidence, and socially competent interaction with peers, teachers, camp counselors, and romantic partners through adolescence.

For some children, though, there is less continuity (Thompson & Goodvin, 2005). Not all research reveals the power of infant attachment to predict subsequent development (Bates, 2008). In one longitudinal study, attachment classification in infancy did not predict attachment classification at 18 years of age (Lewis, Feiring, & Rosenthal, 2000). In this study, the best predictor of an insecure attachment classification at 18 was the occurrence of parental divorce in the intervening years. Consistently positive caregiving over a number of years is likely an important factor in connecting early attachment and the child's functioning later in development. Indeed, researchers have found that early secure attachment *and* subsequent experiences, especially maternal care and life stresses, are linked with children's later behavior and adjustment (Belsky & Pasco Fearon, 2002; Thompson, 2006).

Some developmentalists conclude that too much emphasis has been placed on the attachment bond in infancy (Newcombe, 2007). Jerome Kagan (1987), for example, believes that infants are highly resilient and adaptive; he argues that they are evolutionarily equipped to stay on a positive developmental course, even in the face of wide variations in parenting. Kagan and others stress that genetic characteristics and temperament play more important roles in a child's social competence than the attachment theorists, such as Bowlby and Ainsworth, are willing to acknowledge (Bakermans-Kranenburg & others, 2007; Chaudhuri & Williams, 1999). For example, if some infants inherit a low tolerance for stress, this, rather than an insecure attachment bond, may be responsible for an inability to get along with peers. A recent study found links between disorganized attachment in infancy, a specific gene, and level of maternal responsiveness. In this study, a disorganized attachment style developed in infancy only when infants had the short version of the serotonin transporter gene—*5-HTTLPR* (Spangler & others, 2009). Infants were not characterized by this attachment style when they had the long version of the gene (Spangler & others 2009). Further, this gene-environment interaction occurred only when mothers showed a low level of responsiveness toward their infants.

Another criticism of attachment theory is that it ignores the diversity of socializing agents and contexts that exists in an infant's world. A culture's value system can influence the nature of attachment (van IJzendoorn & Sagi-Schwartz, 2008). In some cultures, infants show attachments to many people. Among the Hausa (who live in Nigeria), both grandmothers and siblings provide a significant amount of care for infants (Harkness & Super, 1995). Infants in agricultural societies tend to form attachments to older siblings, who are assigned a major responsibility for younger siblings' care. Researchers recognize the importance of competent, nurturant caregivers in an infant's development (Thompson, 2009a, b, c). At issue, though, is whether or not secure attachment, especially to a single caregiver, is critical (Lamb, 2005; Thompson, 2006).

Despite such criticisms, there is ample evidence that security of attachment is important to development (Posada, 2008; Thompson, 2008a). Secure attachment in infancy is important because it reflects a positive parent-infant relationship and provides the foundation that supports healthy socioemotional development in the years that follow.

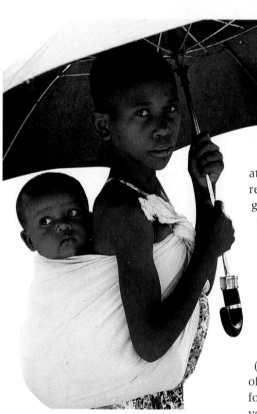

In the Hausa culture, siblings and grandmothers provide a significant amount of care for infants. *How might these variations in care affect attachment?*

Caregiving Styles and Attachment

Is the style of caregiving linked with the quality of the infant's attachment? Securely attached babies have caregivers who are sensitive to their signals and are consistently available to respond to their infants' needs (Cassidy, 2008; Juffer, Bakermans-Kranenburg, & van IJzendoorn, 2007). These caregivers often let their babies have an active part in determining the onset and pacing of interaction in the first year of life. A recent study revealed that maternal sensitive responding was linked to infant attachment security (Finger & others, 2009).

How do the caregivers of insecurely attached babies interact with them? Caregivers of avoidant babies tend to be unavailable or rejecting (Bakermans-Kranenburg & others, 2007). They often don't respond to their babies' signals and have little physical contact with them. When they do interact with their babies, they may behave in an angry and irritable way. Caregivers of resistant babies tend to be inconsistent; sometimes they respond to their babies' needs, and sometimes they don't. In general, they tend not to be very affectionate with their babies and show little synchrony when interacting with them. Caregivers of disorganized babies often neglect or physically abuse them (Benoit, Coolbear, & Crawford, 2008). In some cases, these caregivers are depressed or have other pathologies (Thompson, 2008b).

Developmental Social Neuroscience and Attachment

In Chapter 1, "Introduction," we described the emerging field of developmental social neuroscience, which examines connections between socioemotional processes, development, and the brain. Attachment is one of the main areas in which theory and research on developmental social neuroscience has focused. These connections of attachment and the brain involve the neuroanatomy of the brain, neurotransmitters, and hormones.

Theory and research on the role of the brain's regions in mother-infant attachment is just emerging (de Haan & Gunnar, 2009). A recent theoretical view proposed that the prefrontal cortex likely has an important role in maternal attachment behavior, as do the subcortical (areas of the brain lower than the cortex) regions of the amygdala (which is strongly involved in emotion) and the hypothalamus (Gonzalez, Atkinson, & Fleming, 2009). An ongoing fMRI longitudinal study is exploring the possibility that different attachment patterns can be distinguished by different patterns of brain activity (Strathearn, 2007).

Research on the role of hormones and neurotransmitters in attachment has emphasized the importance of the neuropeptide hormones of oxytocin and vasopression in the formation of the maternal-infant bond (Bales & Carter, 2009). Oxytocin, a mammalian hormone that also acts as a neurotransmitter in the brain, is released during breast feeding and by contact and warmth. Oxytocin is especially thought to be a likely candidate in the formation of infant-mother attachment (Bales & Carter, 2009).

The influence of these neuropeptides on the neurotransmitter dopamine in the nucleus accumbens (a collection of neurons in the forebrain that are involved in pleasure) likely is important in motivating approach to the attachment object (de Haan & Gunnar, 2009). Figure 7.9 shows the regions of the brain we have described that are likely important in infant-mother attachment.

In sum, it is likely that a number of brain regions, neurotransmitters, and hormones are involved in the development of infant-mother attachment. Key candidates for influencing this attachment are connections between the prefrontal cortex, amygdala, and hypothalamus; the neuropeptides oxytocin and vasopression; and the activity of the neurotransmitter dopamine in the nucleus accumbens.

How Would You...?
As a health-care professional, how would you use an infant's attachment style and/or a parent's caregiving style to determine if an infant may be at risk for neglect or abuse?

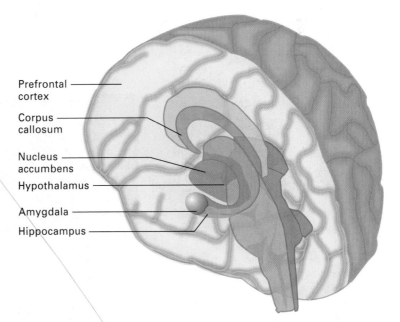

Prefrontal cortex
Corpus callosum
Nucleus accumbens
Hypothalamus
Amygdala
Hippocampus

FIGURE 7.9 Regions of the Brain Proposed as Likely Important in Infant-Mother Attachment *Note:* This illustration shows the brain's left hemisphere. The corpus callosum is the large bundle of axons that connect the brain's two hemispheres.

Review and Reflect: Learning Goal 2

2 **Describe the development of social orientation/ understanding and attachment in infancy**

REVIEW

• How do social orientation/understanding develop in infancy?
• What is attachment, and how is it conceptualized?
• What are some individual variations in attachment? What are some criticisms of attachment theory?
• How are caregiving styles related to attachment?
• What characterizes the study of developmental social neuroscience and attachment?

REFLECT

• How might the infant's temperament be related to the way in which attachment is classified? Look at the temperament categories we described and reflect on how these might be more likely to show up in infants in some attachment categories than others.

3 HOW DO SOCIAL CONTEXTS INFLUENCE SOCIOEMOTIONAL DEVELOPMENT IN INFANCY?

The Family   **Child Care**

Now that we have explored the infant's emotional and personality development and attachment, let's examine the social contexts in which these occur. We begin by studying a number of aspects of the family and then turn to a social context in which infants increasingly spend time—child care.

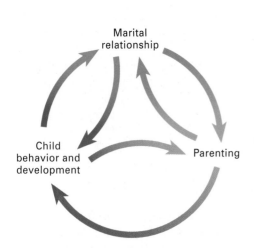

FIGURE 7.10 Interaction Between Children and Their Parents: Direct and Indirect Effects

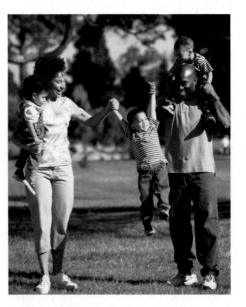

Children socialize parents just as parents socialize children.

The Family

The family can be thought of as a constellation of subsystems—a complex whole made up of interrelated, interacting parts—defined in terms of generation, gender, and role. Each family member participates in several subsystems (Fiese & Winter, 2008; Parke & others, 2008). The father and child represent one subsystem, the mother and father another, the mother-father-child represent yet another, and so on.

These subsystems have reciprocal influences on each other (Belsky, 2009a), as Figure 7.10 highlights. For example, Jay Belsky (1981) emphasizes that marital relations, parenting, and infant behavior and development can have both direct and indirect effects on each other. An example of a direct effect is the influence of the parents' behavior on the child. An indirect effect is how the relationship between the spouses mediates the way a parent acts toward the child (Hsu, 2004). For example, marital conflict might reduce the efficiency of parenting, in which case marital conflict would indirectly affect the child's behavior. The simple fact that two people are becoming parents may have profound effects of their relationship.

The Transition to Parenthood   When people become parents through pregnancy, adoption, or stepparenting, they face disequilibrium and must adapt. Parents want to develop a strong attachment with their infant, but they still want to maintain strong attachments to their spouse and friends, and possibly continue their careers. Parents ask themselves how this new being will change their lives. A baby places new restrictions on partners; no longer will they be able to rush out to a movie on a moment's notice, and money may not be readily available for vacations and other luxuries. Dual-career parents ask, "Will it harm the baby to place her in child care? Will we be able to find responsible baby-sitters?"

In a longitudinal investigation of couples from late pregnancy until 3½ years after the baby was born, couples enjoyed more positive marital relations before the baby was born than after (Cowan & Cowan, 2000; Cowan & others, 2005). Still, almost one-third showed an increase in marital satisfaction. Some couples said that the baby had both brought them closer together and moved them farther apart; being parents enhanced their sense of themselves and gave them a new, more stable identity as a couple. Babies opened men up to a concern with intimate relationships, and the demands of juggling work and family roles stimulated women to manage family tasks more efficiently and pay attention to their own personal growth.

The Bringing Home Baby project is a workshop for new parents that emphasizes strengthening the couples' relationship, understanding and becoming acquainted with the baby, resolving conflict, and developing parenting skills. Evaluations of the project revealed that parents who participated improved in their ability to work together as parents, fathers were more involved with their baby and sensitive to the baby's behavior, mothers had a lower incidence of postpartum depression symptoms, and their babies showed better overall development than participants in a control group (Gottman, Shapiro, & Parthemer, 2004; Shapiro & Gottman, 2005).

Reciprocal Socialization   For many years, socialization between parents and children was viewed as a one-way process: Children were considered to be the products of their parents' socialization techniques. However, parent-child interaction is reciprocal (Fiese & Winter, 2008; Thompson & Newton, 2009). **Reciprocal socialization** is socialization that is bidirectional. That is, children socialize parents just as parents socialize children. For example, the interaction of mothers and their infants is like a dance or a dialogue in which successive actions of the partners are closely coordinated. This coordinated dance or dialogue can assume the form of mutual synchrony in which each person's behavior depends on the partner's previous behavior. Or it can be reciprocal in the sense that actions of the partners are matched, as when one partner imitates the other or when there is mutual smiling.

What kinds of adaptations do new parents need to make?

Caregivers often play games such as peek-a-boo and pat-a-cake. *How is scaffolding involved in these games?*

When reciprocal socialization has been studied in infancy, mutual gaze, or eye contact, plays an important role in early social interaction. In one investigation, the mother and infant engaged in a variety of behaviors while they looked at each other. By contrast, when they looked away from each other, the rate of such behaviors

reciprocal socialization Socialization that is bidirectional; children socialize parents, just as parents socialize children.

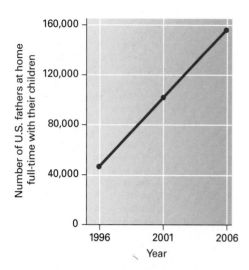

FIGURE 7.11 The Increase in the Number of U.S. Fathers Staying at Home Full Time with Their Children

How Would You...?
As an educator, how would you explain the value of games and the role of scaffolding in the development of infants and toddlers?

How do most fathers and mothers interact differently with infants?

scaffolding Parents time interactions so that infants experience turn-taking with the parents.

dropped considerably (Stern & others, 1977). In sum, the behaviors of mothers and infants involve substantial interconnection, mutual regulation, and synchronization (Moreno, Posada, & Goldyn, 2006). A recent study revealed that *parent-infant synchrony*—the temporal coordination of social behavior—played an important role in children's development (Feldman, 2007). In this study, parent-infant synchrony at 3 and 9 months of age was positively linked to children's self-regulation from 2 to 6 years of age.

An important form of reciprocal socialization is **scaffolding,** in which parents time interactions in such a way that the infant experiences turn-taking with the parents. Scaffolding involves parental behavior that supports children's efforts, allowing them to be more skillful than they would be if they were to rely only on their own abilities (Field, 2007). In using scaffolding, caregivers provide a positive, reciprocal framework in which they and their children interact. For example, in the game peek-a-boo, the mother initially covers the baby. Then she removes the cover and registers "surprise" at the infant's reappearance. As infants become more skilled at peek-a-boo, pat-a-cake, and so on, there are other caregiver games that exemplify scaffolding and turn-taking sequences. Engaging in turn-taking and games like peek-a-boo reflect the development of joint attention by the caregiver and infant, which we discussed in Chapter 6, "Cognitive Development in Infancy" (Tomasello & Carpenter, 2007).

Maternal and Paternal Caregiving An increasing number of U.S. fathers stay home full-time with their children (Wong & Rochlen, 2008). As indicated in Figure 7.11, there was a 300-plus percent increase in stay-at-home fathers in the United States from 1996 to 2006. A large portion of the full-time fathers have career-focused wives who provide the main family income. A recent study revealed that the stay-at-home fathers were as satisfied with their marriage as traditional parents, although they indicated that they missed their daily life in the workplace (Rochlen & others, 2008). In this study, the stay-at-home fathers reported that they tended to be ostracized when they took their children to playgrounds and often were excluded from parent groups.

Can fathers take care of infants as competently as mothers can? Observations of fathers and their infants suggest that fathers have the ability to act as sensitively and responsively as mothers with their infants (Parke, 2004; Parke & Buriel, 2006). Consider the Aka pygmy culture in Africa, where fathers spend as much time interacting with their infants as do the mothers (Hewlett, 1991, 2000). Remember, however, that although fathers can be active, nurturant, involved caregivers with their infants as Aka pygmy fathers are, in many cultures many fathers have not chosen to follow this pattern (Lamb & Lewis, 2005).

Do fathers behave differently toward infants than mothers do? Maternal interactions usually center on child-care activities—feeding, changing diapers, bathing. Paternal interactions are more likely to include play (Parke, 2004; Parke & Buriel, 2006). Fathers engage in more rough-and-tumble play. They bounce infants, throw them up in the air, tickle them, and so on (Lamb, 2000). Mothers do play with infants, but their play is less physical and arousing than that of fathers.

In one study, fathers were interviewed about their caregiving responsibilities when their children were 6, 15, 24, and 36 months of age (NICHD Early Child Care Research Network, 2000). Some of the fathers were videotaped while playing with their children at 6 and 36 months. Fathers were more involved in caregiving—bathing, feeding, dressing the child, taking the child to child care, and so on—when they worked fewer hours and mothers worked more hours, when mothers and fathers were younger, when mothers reported greater marital intimacy, and when the children were boys.

Child Care

Many U.S. children today experience multiple caregivers. Most do not have a parent staying home to care for them; instead, the children have some type of care provided by others—"child care." Many parents worry that child care will reduce their infants' emotional attachment to them, retard the infants' cognitive development, fail to teach them how to control anger, and allow them to be unduly influenced by their peers. How extensive is child care? Are the worries of these parents justified?

Parental Leave   Today far more young children are in child care than at any other time in history. About 2 million children in the United States currently receive formal, licensed child care, and uncounted millions of children are cared for by unlicensed baby-sitters. As described in the *Diversity in Children's Development* interlude, many countries provide far more extensive parental leave policies than the United States.

How Would You...?
As a social worker, how would you use your knowledge of parental leave policies in various countries to advise an immigrant family about parental leave and child-care options in the United States?

Diversity in Children's Development

CHILD-CARE POLICIES AROUND THE WORLD

Child-care policies around the world vary in eligibility criteria, leave duration, benefit level, and the extent to which parents take advantage of the policies (Tolani & Brooks-Gunn, 2008). There are five types of parental leave from employment (Kamerman, 1989, 2000a, b):

- *Maternity leave.* In some countries, the prebirth leave is compulsory as is a 6- to 10-week leave following birth.
- *Paternity leave.* This is usually much briefer than maternity leave. It may be especially important when a second child is born and the first child requires care.
- *Parental leave.* This gender-neutral leave usually follows a maternity leave and allows either women or men to share the leave policy or choose which of them will use it. In 1998, the European Union mandated a three-month parental leave.
- *Child-rearing leave.* In some countries, this is a supplement to a maternity leave or a variation on a parental leave. A child-rearing leave is usually longer than a maternity leave and is typically paid at a much lower level.
- *Family leave.* This covers reasons other than the birth of a new baby and can allow time off from employment to care for an ill child or other family members, time to accompany a child to school for the first time, or time to visit a child's school.

Europe led the way in creating new standards of parental leave: The European Union (EU) mandated a paid 14-week maternity leave in 1992. In most European countries today, working parents on leave receive from 70 percent of the worker's prior wage to the full wage, and paid leave averages about 16 weeks (Tolani & Brooks-Gunn, 2008). The United States currently allows up to 12 weeks of unpaid leave for caring for a newborn.

Most countries restrict eligible benefits to women employed for a minimum time prior to childbirth. In Denmark, even unemployed mothers are eligible for extended pay related to childbirth. In Germany, child-rearing leave is available to almost all parents. The Nordic countries (Denmark, Norway, and Sweden) have extensive gender-equity family leave policies for childbirth that emphasize the contributions of both women and men (Tolani & Brooks-Gunn, 2008). For example, in Sweden, parents can take an 18-month job-protected parental leave with benefits allowed to be shared by parents and applied to full-time or part-time work.

How are child-care policies in many European countries, such as Sweden, different from those in the United States?

Careers in Children's Development

Rashmi Nakhre, Child-Care Director

Rashmi Nakhre has two master's degrees—one in psychology, the other in child development—and is director of the Hattie Daniels Day Care Center in Wilson, North Carolina. At a "Celebrating a Century of Women" ceremony, Nakhre received the Distinguished Women of North Carolina Award for 1999–2000.

Dr. Nakhre first worked at the child-care center soon after she arrived in the United States 25 years ago. She says that she took the job initially because she needed the money but "ended up falling in love with my job." Dr. Nakhre has turned the Wilson, North Carolina, child-care center into a model for other centers. The Hattie Daniels center almost closed several years after she began working there because of financial difficulties. Dr. Nakhre played a major role in raising funds not only to keep it open but to improve it. The center provides quality child care for the children of many Latino migrant workers.

Rashmi Nakhre, child-care director, working with some of the children at her center.

Variations in Child Care   Child care in the United States has become a major national concern (Belsky, 2009; Tolani & Brooks-Gunn, 2008). Many factors influence the effects of child care, including the age of the child, the type of child care, and the quality of the program.

The type of child care varies extensively. Child care is provided in large centers with elaborate facilities and in private homes. Some child-care centers are commercial operations; others are nonprofit centers run by churches, civic groups, and employers. Some child-care providers are professionals; others are mothers who want to earn extra money. Figure 7.12 presents the primary care arrangement for children under 5 years of age with employed mothers (Clarke-Stewart & Miner, 2008).

In the United States, approximately 15 percent of children 5 years of age and younger attend more than one child-care arrangement. A recent study of 2- and 3-year-old children revealed that an increase in the number of child-care arrangements the children experienced was linked to an increase in behavioral problems and a decrease in prosocial behavior (Morrissey, 2009).

Child-care quality makes a difference. What constitutes a high-quality child-care program for infants? In high-quality child care (Clarke-Stewart & Miner, 2008, p. 273):

> caregivers encourage the children to be actively engaged in a variety of activities, have frequent, positive interactions that include smiling, touching, holding, and speaking at the child's eye level, respond properly to the child's questions or requests, and encourage children to talk about their experiences, feelings, and ideas.

High-quality child care also involves providing children with a safe environment, access to age-appropriate toys and participation in age-appropriate activities, and a low caregiver-child ratio that allows caregivers to spend considerable time with children on an individual basis.

Children are more likely to experience poor-quality child care if they come from families with few resources (psychological, social, and economic) (Cabrera, Hutchens, & Peters, 2006). One study found that extensive child care was harmful to low-income children only when the care was of low quality (Votruba-Drzal & others, 2004). Even if the child was in child care more than 45 hours a week, high-quality

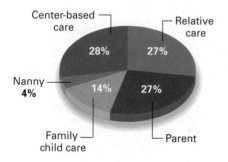

FIGURE 7.12 Primary Care Arrangements in the United States for Children Under 5 Years of Age with Employed Mothers

care was linked with fewer internalizing problems (anxiety, for example) and externalizing problems (aggressive and destructive behaviors, for example). A recent study revealed that children from low-income families benefited in terms of school readiness and language development when their parents selected higher-quality child care (McCartney & others, 2007).

To read about one individual who provides quality child care to individuals from impoverished backgrounds, see the *Careers in Children's Development* profile. In the *Research in Children's Development* interlude, you can read about an ongoing national study of child care and its effects.

How Would You...?
As an educator, how would you design the ideal child-care program to promote optimal infant development?

Research in Children's Development

A NATIONAL LONGITUDINAL STUDY OF CHILD CARE

In 1991, the National Institute of Child Health and Human Development (NICHD) began a comprehensive, longitudinal study of child-care experiences. Data were collected on a diverse sample of almost 1,400 children and their families at 10 locations across the United States over a period of seven years. Researchers used multiple methods (trained observers, interviews, questionnaires, and testing), and they measured many facets of children's development, including physical health, cognitive development, and socioemotional development. Following are some of the results of what is now referred to as the NICHD Study of Early Child Care and Youth Development, or NICHD SECCYD (NICHD Early Child Care Research Network, 2001, 2002, 2003, 2004, 2005, 2006).

- *Patterns of use.* Many families placed their infants in child care very soon after the child's birth, and there was considerable instability in the child-care arrangements. By 4 months of age, nearly three-fourths of the infants had entered some form of nonmaternal child care. Almost half of the infants were cared for by a relative when they first entered care; only 12 percent were enrolled in child-care centers. Socioeconomic factors were linked to the amount and type of care. For example, mothers with higher incomes and families that were more dependent on the mother's income placed their infants in child care at an earlier age. Mothers who believed that maternal employment has positive effects on children were more likely than other mothers to place their infant in nonmaternal care for more hours. Low-income families were more likely than more affluent families to use child care, but infants from low-income families who were in child care averaged as many hours as other income groups. In the preschool years, mothers who were single, those with more education, and families with higher incomes used more hours of center care than other families. Minority families and mothers with less education used more hours of care by relatives.

- *Quality of care.* Evaluations of quality of care were based on such characteristics as group size, child–adult ratio, physical environment, caregiver characteristics (such as formal education, specialized training, and child-care experience), and caregiver behavior (such as sensitivity to children). An alarming conclusion is that a majority of the child care in the first three years of life was of unacceptable low quality. Positive caregiving by nonparents in child-care settings was infrequent—only

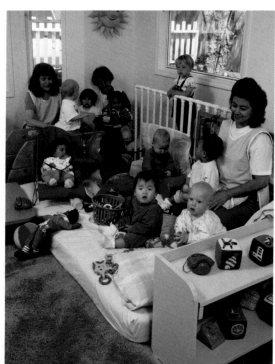

What are some important findings from the national longitudinal study of child care conducted by the National Institute of Child Health and Human Development?

(continued on next page)

12 percent of the children studied experienced positive nonparental child care (such as positive talk, lack of detachment and flat affect, and language stimulation)! Further, infants from low-income families experienced lower quality of child care than infants from higher-income families. When quality of caregivers' care was high, children performed better on cognitive and language tasks, were more cooperative with their mothers during play, showed more positive and skilled interaction with peers, and had fewer behavior problems. Caregiver training and good child-staff ratios were linked with higher cognitive and social competence when children were 54 months of age. Using data collected as part of the NICHD early-child care longitudinal study, a recent analysis indicated that higher-quality early child care, especially at 27 months of age, was linked to children's higher vocabulary scores in the fifth grade (Belsky & others, 2007).

Higher-quality child care was also related to higher-quality mother-child interaction among the families that used nonmaternal care. Further, poor-quality care was related to an increase of insecure attachment to the mother among infants who were 15 months of age, but only when the mother was low in sensitivity and responsiveness. However, child-care quality was not linked to attachment security at 36 months of age.

- *Amount of child care.* The quantity of child care predicted some child outcomes. When children spent extensive amounts of time in child care beginning in infancy, they experienced less sensitive interactions with their mother, showed more behavior problems, and had higher rates of illness (Vandell, 2004). Many of these comparisons involved children in child care for less than 30 hours a week versus those in child care for more than 45 hours a week. In general, though, when children spent 30 hours or more per week in child care, their development was less than optimal (Ramey, 2005).

- *Family and parenting influences.* The influence of families and parenting was not weakened by extensive child care. Parents played a significant role in helping children to regulate their emotions. Especially important parenting influences were being sensitive to children's needs, being involved with children, and cognitively stimulating them. Indeed, parental sensitivity has been the most consistent predictor of a secure attachment, with child-care experiences being relevant in many cases only when mothers engage in insensitive parenting (Friedman, Melhuish, & Hill, 2009).

What are some strategies parents can follow in regard to child care? Child-care expert Kathleen McCartney (2003, p.4) offered this advice:

- *Recognize that the quality of your parenting is a key factor in your child's development.*

- *Make decisions that will improve the likelihood you will be good parents.* "For some this will mean working full-time"—for personal fulfillment, income, or both. "For others, this will mean working part-time or not working outside the home."

- *Monitor your child's development.* "Parents should observe for themselves whether their children seem to be having behavior problems." They need to talk with child-care providers and their pediatrician about their child's behavior.

- *Take some time to find the best child care.* Observe different child-care facilities and be certain that you like what you see. "Quality child care costs money, and not all parents can afford the child care they want. However, state subsidies, and other programs like Head Start, are available for families in need."

How Would You...?
As a psychologist, what factors would you encourage parents to consider in deciding whether to place their infant in child care so that both parents can return to work?

Review and Reflect: Learning Goal 3

 Explain how social contexts influence the infant's development

REVIEW

- What are some important family processes in infant development?
- How does child care influence infant development?

REFLECT

- Imagine that a friend of yours is getting ready to put her baby in child care. What advice would you give to her? Do you think she should stay home with the baby? Why or why not? What type of child care would you recommend?

Reach Your Learning Goals

Socioemotional Development in Infancy

---

1 HOW DO EMOTIONS AND PERSONALITY DEVELOP IN INFANCY? DISCUSS EMOTIONAL AND PERSONALITY DEVELOPMENT IN INFANCY

Emotional Development

- Emotion is feeling, or affect, that occurs when a person is in a state or an interaction that is important to them. Emotion can be classified as either positive (for example, joy) or negative (for example, anger). Psychologists hold that emotions, especially facial expressions of emotions, have a biological foundation. Biological evolution endowed humans to be emotional, but embeddedness in culture and relationships provides diversity in emotional experiences. Emotions play key roles in parent-child relationships. Infants display a number of emotions early in their development, although researchers debate the onset and sequence of these emotions. Lewis distinguishes between primary emotions and self-conscious emotions. Crying is the most important mechanism newborns have for communicating with their world. Babies have at least three types of cries—basic, anger, and pain cries. Controversy swirls about whether babies should be soothed when they cry, although increasingly experts recommend immediately responding in a caring way in the first year. Social smiling occurs as early as 2 months of age and then increases considerably from 2 to 6 months. Two fears that infants develop are stranger anxiety and separation from a caregiver (which is reflected in separation protest). As infants develop, it is important for them to engage in emotional regulation.

Temperament

- Temperament is an individual's behavioral style and characteristic way of emotionally responding. Chess and Thomas classified infants as (1) easy, (2) difficult, or (3) slow to warm up. Kagan proposed that inhibition to the unfamiliar is an important temperament category. Rothbart and Bates' view of temperament emphasizes this classification: (1) extraversion/surgency, (2) negative affectivity, and (3) effortful control (self-regulation). Physiological characteristics are associated with different temperaments. Children inherit a physiology that biases them to have a particular type of temperament, but through experience they learn to modify their temperament style to some degree. Goodness of fit refers to the match between a child's temperament and the environmental demands the child must cope with. Goodness of fit can be an important aspect of a child's adjustment. Although research evidence is sketchy at this point in time, some general recommendations are that caregivers should (1) be sensitive to the individual characteristics of the child, (2) be flexible in responding to these characteristics, and (3) avoid negative labeling of the child.

Personality Development

- Erikson argued that an infant's first year is characterized by the stage of trust versus mistrust. Some infants develop signs of self-recognition at about 15 to 18 months of age. Independence becomes a central theme in the second year of life. Mahler argues that the infant separates himself or herself from the mother and then develops individuation. Erikson stressed that the second year of life is characterized by the stage of autonomy versus shame and doubt.

---

2 HOW DO SOCIAL ORIENTATION/UNDERSTANDING AND ATTACHMENT DEVELOP IN INFANCY? DESCRIBE THE DEVELOPMENT OF SOCIAL ORIENTATION/UNDERSTANDING AND ATTACHMENT IN INFANCY

Social Orientation/Understanding

- Infants show a strong interest in the social world and are motivated to understand it. Infants orient to the social world early in their development. Face-to-face play with a caregiver begins to occur at 2 to 3 months of age. Newly developed self-produced

Attachment and Its Development

locomotion skills significantly expand the infant's ability to initiate social interchanges and explore their social world more independently. Perceiving people as engaging in intentional and goal-directed behavior is an important social cognitive accomplishment, and this initially occurs toward the end of the first year. Social referencing increases in the second year of life.

- Attachment is a close emotional bond between two people. In infancy, contact comfort and trust are important in the development of attachment. Bowlby's ethological theory stresses that the caregiver and the infant are biologically predisposed to form an attachment. Attachment develops in four phases during infancy.

Individual Differences in Attachment

- Securely attached babies use the caregiver, usually the mother, as a secure base from which to explore the environment. Three types of insecure attachment are avoidant, resistant, and disorganized. Ainsworth created the Strange Situation, an observational measure of attachment. Ainsworth argues that secure attachment in the first year of life provides an important foundation for psychological development later in life. The strength of the link between early attachment and later development has varied somewhat across studies. Some critics argue that attachment theorists have not given adequate attention to genetics and temperament. Other critics stress that they have not adequately taken into account the diversity of social agents and contexts. Cultural variations in attachment have been found, but in all cultures studied to date secure attachment is the most common classification.

Caregiving Styles and Attachment

- Caregivers of secure babies are sensitive to the babies' signals and are consistently available to meet their needs. Caregivers of avoidant babies tend to be unavailable or rejecting. Caregivers of resistant babies tend to be inconsistently available to their babies and usually are not very affectionate. Caregivers of disorganized babies often neglect or physically abuse their babies.

Developmental Social Neuroscience and Attachment

- Increased interest is occurring in the role of the brain in the development of attachment. The hormone oxytocin is a key candidate for influencing the development of maternal-infant attachment.

---

3 HOW DO SOCIAL CONTEXTS INFLUENCE SOCIOEMOTIONAL DEVELOPMENT IN INFANCY? EXPLAIN HOW SOCIAL CONTEXTS INFLUENCE THE INFANT'S DEVELOPMENT

The Family

- The transition to parenthood requires considerable adaptation and adjustment on the part of parents. Children socialize parents just as parents socialize children. Mutual regulation and scaffolding are important aspects of reciprocal socialization. Belsky's model describes direct and indirect effects. The mother's primary role when interacting with the infant is caregiving; the father's is playful interaction.

Child Care

- More U.S. children are in child care now than at any earlier point in history. The quality of child care is uneven, and child care remains a controversial topic. Quality child care can be achieved and seems to have few adverse effects on children. In the NICHD child-care study, infants from low-income families were more likely to receive the lowest quality of care. Also, higher quality of child care was linked with fewer child problems.

KEY TERMS

KEY PEOPLE

MAKING A DIFFERENCE

Nurturing the Infant's Socioemotional Development

What are the best ways to help the infant develop socioemotional competencies?

- *Develop a secure attachment with the infant.* Infants need the warmth and support of one or more caregivers. The caregiver(s) should be sensitive to the infant's signals and respond nurturantly.

- *Be sure that both the mother and the father nurture the infant.* Infants develop best when both the mother and the father provide warm, nurturant support. Fathers need to seriously evaluate their responsibility in rearing a competent infant.

- *Select competent child care.* If the infant will be placed in child care, spend time evaluating different options. Be sure the infant–caregiver ratio is low. Also assess whether the adults enjoy and are knowledgeable about interacting with infants. Determine if the facility is safe and provides stimulating activities.

- *Understand and respect the infant's temperament.* Be sensitive to the characteristics of each child. It may be necessary to provide extra support for distress-prone infants, for example. Avoid negative labeling of the infant.

- *Adapt to developmental changes in the infant.* An 18-month-old toddler is very different from a 6-month-old infant. Be knowledgeable about how infants develop and adapt to the changing infant. Let toddlers explore a wider but safe environment.

- *Be physically and mentally healthy.* Infants' socioemotional development benefits when their caregivers are physically and mentally healthy. For example, a depressed parent may not sensitively respond to the infant's signals.

- *Read a good book on infant development.* Any of T. Berry Brazelton's books is a good start. One is *Touchpoints*. Two other good books by other authors are *Infancy* by Tiffany Field and *Baby Steps* by Claire Kopp.

RESOURCES FOR IMPROVING CHILDREN'S LIVES

The Happiest Baby on the Block
by Harvey Karp (2002).
New York: Bantam

An outstanding book on ways to calm a crying baby.

Touchpoints: Birth to Three
by T. Berry Brazelton and Joshua Sparrow (2006)
Cambridge, MA: Da Capo Press

Covering the period from birth through age 3, Brazelton and Sparrow focus on the concerns and questions parents have about the child's feelings, behavior, and development.

E-LEARNING TOOLS

Connect to **www.mhhe.com/santrockc11e** to research the answers and complete these exercises. In addition, you'll find a number of other resources and valuable study tools for Chapter 7, "Socioemotional Development in Infancy," on this Web site.

Taking It to the Net

1. Catherine is conducting a class for new parents at a local clinic. What advice should Catherine give the parents about how parenting practices can affect a child's inborn temperament?

2. Peter and Rachel are adopting a 3-month-old infant. What are some practical things they can do to help ensure that their child develops a healthy attachment bond with them, in spite of not being with them in the first few months of life?

3. Veronica is anxious about choosing the best child-care center for her child. What are the main things she should consider as she visits the facilities on her list?

Health and Well-Being, Parenting, and Education

Build your decision-making skills by trying your hand at the health and well-being, parenting, and education exercises.

Video Clips

The Online Learning Center includes the following videos for this chapter:

- *Sex-Typed Play at Age 1*
  A 1-year-old girl is shown in a room surrounded by an assortment of toys. She only shows interest in the Barbie dolls, which she examines carefully from every angle.

- *Attachment Theory—300*
  Renowned attachment researcher L. Alan Sroufe defines attachment theory and how it relates to children's social and emotional development. He states that attachment theory led to a revolution in developmental psychology. He uses examples from his own research to illustrate the significance of attachment relationships.

- *Daycare Environment at 3 Years—225*
  In this clip, we see 3-year-old Josh outside during preschool. With the guidance of his teacher, he is making a necklace out of cereal, which they discuss as he works.

FOUR

EARLY CHILDHOOD

You are troubled at seeing him spend his early years doing nothing. What! Is it nothing to be happy? Is it nothing to skip, to play, to run about all day long? Never in his life will he be so busy as now.

—JEAN-JACQUES ROUSSEAU
Swiss-Born French Philosopher,
18th Century

In early childhood, our greatest untold poem was being only 4 years old. We skipped and ran and played all the sun long, never in our lives so busy, busy being something we had not quite grasped yet. Who knew our thoughts, which we worked up into small mythologies all our own? Our thoughts and images and drawings took wings. The blossoms of our heart, no wind could touch. Our small world widened as we discovered new refuges and new people. When we said, "I," we meant something totally unique, not to be confused with any other. Section 4 consists of three chapters: "Physical Development in Early Childhood" (Chapter 8), "Cognitive Development in Early Childhood" (Chapter 9), and "Socioemotional Development in Early Childhood" (Chapter 10).

8

*The greatest person
ever known
Is one all poets have
outgrown;
The poetry, innate and
untold,
Of being only four
years old.*

—CHRISTOPHER MORLEY
American Novelist, 20th Century

LEARNING GOALS

- Discuss growth and change in the young child's body and brain

- Describe changes in motor development in early childhood

- Characterize the health of young children

PHYSICAL DEVELOPMENT IN EARLY CHILDHOOD

CHAPTER OUTLINE

Images of Children's Development
The Story of Teresa Amabile and Her Art

Teresa Amabile remembers that, when she was in kindergarten, she rushed in every day, excited and enthusiastic about getting to the easel and painting with bright colors and big brushes. Children in Teresa's class had free access to a clay table with all kinds of art materials on it. Teresa remembers going home every day and telling her mother she wanted to draw and paint. Teresa's kindergarten experience, unfortunately, was the high point of her enthusiasm for art classes in school.

A description of Teresa's further childhood experiences with art and creativity follows (Goleman, Kaufman, & Ray, 1993, p. 60):

> The next year she entered a strict, traditional school, and things began to change. As she tells it, "Instead of having free access to art materials every day, art became just another subject, something you had for an hour and a half every Friday afternoon."
>
> Week after week, all through elementary school, it was the same art class. And a very restricted, even demoralizing one at that.

The children were not given any help in developing their skills. Also, the teacher graded the children on the art they produced, adding evaluation pressure to the situation. Teresa was aware at that time that her motivation for doing artwork was being completely destroyed. In her words, "I no longer wanted to go home at the end of the day and take out my art materials and draw or paint."

In spite of the negative instruction imposed upon her in art classes, Teresa Amabile continued her education and eventually obtained a Ph.D. in psychology. In part, because of her positive experiences in kindergarten, she became one of the leading researchers on creativity. Her hope is that more elementary schools will not crush children's enthusiasm for creativity, the way hers did. So many young children, like Teresa, are excited about exploring and creating, but by the time they reach the third or fourth grade, many don't like school, let alone have any sense of pleasure in their own creativity.

PREVIEW

As twentieth-century Welsh poet Dylan Thomas artfully observed, young children do "run all the sun long." And as their physical development advances, young children's small worlds widen. We begin this chapter by examining how young children's bodies grow and change. Then we discuss the development of young children's motor skills and conclude by exploring important aspects of their health.

1 HOW DOES A YOUNG CHILD'S BODY AND BRAIN GROW AND CHANGE?

Height and Weight   The Brain

growth hormone deficiency The absence or deficiency of growth hormone produced by the pituitary gland to stimulate the body to grow.

In this section, we examine the height and weight changes for boys and girls in early childhood along with individual growth patterns. In addition, we look at how the brain and nervous system continue to develop, and how young children's cognitive abilities expand.

Height and Weight

Remember from Chapter 5, "Physical Development in Infancy," that the infant's growth in the first year is rapid. During the infant's second year, the growth rate begins to slow down, and the growth rate continues to slow in early childhood. Otherwise, we would be a species of giants. The average child grows 2½ inches in height and gains between 5 and 7 pounds a year during early childhood. As the preschool child grows older, the percentage of increase in height and weight decreases with each additional year (Darrah, Senthilselvan, & Magill-Evans, 2009). Figure 8.1 shows the average height and weight of children as they age from 2 to 6 years (Centers for Disease Control and Prevention, 2000). Girls are only slightly smaller and lighter than boys during these years, a difference that continues until puberty. During the preschool years, both boys and girls slim down as the trunks of their bodies lengthen. Although their heads are still somewhat large for their bodies, by the end of the preschool years most children have lost their top-heavy look. Body fat also shows a slow, steady decline during the preschool years. The chubby baby often looks much leaner by the end of early childhood. Girls have more fatty tissue than boys, and boys have more muscle tissue.

Growth patterns vary individually. Think back to your elementary school years. This was probably the first time you noticed that some children were taller than you, some shorter; some were stronger, some weaker. Much of the variation is due to heredity, but environmental experiences are involved to some extent. A review of the height and weight of children around the world concluded that the two most important contributors to height differences are ethnic origin and nutrition (Meredith, 1978). The urban, middle-socioeconomic-status, and firstborn children were taller than rural, lower-socioeconomic status, and later-born children. The children whose mothers smoked during pregnancy were half an inch shorter than the children whose mothers did not smoke during pregnancy. In the United States, African American children are taller than non-Latino White children.

Why are some children unusually short? The primary contributing influences are congenital factors (genetic or prenatal problems), growth hormone deficiency, a physical problem that develops in childhood, maternal smoking during pregnancy, or an emotional difficulty (Cooper & others, 2008). Chronically sick children are shorter than their rarely sick counterparts. Children who have been physically abused or neglected may not secrete adequate growth hormone, the lack of which can restrict their physical growth.

Growth hormone deficiency is the absence or deficiency of growth hormone produced by the pituitary gland to stimulate the body to grow. Growth hormone deficiency may occur during infancy or later in childhood (Oswiecimska & others, 2008). As many as 10,000 to 15,000 U.S. children may have growth hormone deficiency (Stanford University Medical Center, 2008). Without treatment, most children with growth hormone deficiency will not reach a height of five feet. Treatment involves regular injections of growth hormone and usually lasts several years (Rosenfeld & Bakker, 2008). Some children receive daily injections, others several times a week. Twice as many boys as girls are treated with growth hormone (Lee & Howell, 2006).

There has been a significant increase in treating short children with growth hormone therapy (Hindmarsh & Dattani, 2006). Some medical experts have expressed concern that many young children who are being treated with growth hormone therapy are merely short but don't have a growth hormone deficiency (Dunkel, 2006). In such cases, parents often perceive that there is a handicap in being short, especially in boys.

Few studies have been conducted on the psychological and social outcomes of having a short stature in childhood. Most of those that have been carried out find little or no difference in the psychological and social functioning of short children and children who are average in height or tall (Sandberg & Colsman, 2005).

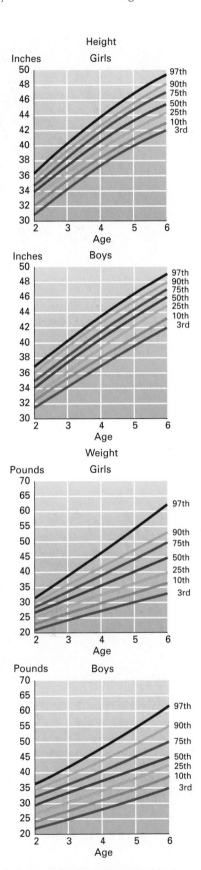

FIGURE 8.1 Height and Weight Changes from 2 Through 6 Years of Age These graphs show the percentiles of height and weight for boys and girls from 2 through 6 years of age in the United States.

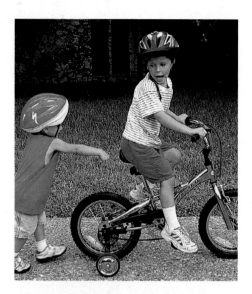

The bodies of 5-year-olds and 2-year-olds are different. Notice that the 5-year-old not only is taller and weighs more but also has a longer trunk and legs than the 2-year-old. *Can you think of some other physical differences between 2- and 5-year-olds?*

FIGURE 8.2 Growth Curves for the Head and Brain and for Height and Weight The more rapid growth of the brain and head can easily be seen. Height and weight advance more gradually over the first two decades of life.

myelination The process in which the nerve cells are covered and insulated with a layer of fat cells, which increases the speed at which information travels through the nervous system.

The Brain

One of the most important physical developments during early childhood is the continuing development of the brain and nervous system (Moulson & Nelson, 2008; Nelson, 2009). Although the brain continues to grow in early childhood, it does not grow as rapidly as in infancy. By the time children reach 3 years of age, the brain is three-quarters of its adult size. By age 6, the brain has reached about 95 percent of its adult volume (Lenroot & Giedd, 2006). Thus, the brain of a 5-year-old is nearly the size it will be when the child reaches adulthood, but as we see in later chapters, the development that occurs inside the brain continues through the remaining childhood and adolescent years.

The brain and the head grow more rapidly than any other part of the body. The top parts of the head, the eyes, and the brain grow faster than the lower portions, such as the jaw. Figure 8.2 reveals how the growth curve for the head and brain advances more rapidly than the growth curve for height and weight. At 5 years of age, when the brain has attained approximately 90 percent of its adult weight, the 5-year-old's total body weight is only about one-third of what it will be when the child reaches adulthood.

Neuronal Changes In Chapters 3, "Prenatal Development," and 5 "Physical Development in Infancy," we discussed the brain's development during the prenatal and infancy periods. Changes in neurons in early childhood involve connections between neurons and myelination, just as they did in infancy (de Haan & Martinos, 2008). Communication in the brain is characterized by the transmission of information between neurons, or nerve cells. Some of the brain's increase in size during early childhood is due to the increase in the number and size of nerve endings and receptors, which allows more effective communication to occur.

Neurons communicate with each other through *neurotransmitters* (chemical substances) that carry information across gaps (called *synapses*) between the neurons. One neurotransmitter that has been shown to increase substantially in the 3- to 6-year age period is *dopamine* (Diamond, 2001). We return to a discussion of dopamine later in this section.

Some of the brain's increase in size also is due to the increase in **myelination,** in which nerve cells are covered and insulated with a layer of fat cells (see Figure 8.3). This has the effect of increasing the speed and efficiency of information traveling through the nervous system (Fair & Schlaggar, 2008). Myelination is important in the development of a number of children's abilities (Fornari & others, 2007). For example, myelination in the areas of the brain related to hand-eye coordination is not complete until about 4 years of age. One fMRI study of children (mean age: 4 years) found that children with developmental delay of motor and cognitive milestones had significantly reduced levels of myelination (Pujol & others, 2004). Myelination in the areas of the brain related to focusing attention is not complete until the end of the middle or late childhood.

Structural Changes Until recently, scientists lacked adequate technology to detect sensitive changes and view detailed maps of the developing human brain. However, sophisticated brain-scanning techniques, such as magnetic resonance imaging (MRI), now allow us to better detect these changes (Toga, Thompson, & Sowell, 2006). With high-resolution MRI, scientists have evolved spatially complex, four-dimensional growth pattern maps of the developing brain, allowing the brain to be monitored with greater sensitivity than ever before. Using these techniques, scientists have discovered that children's brains undergo dramatic anatomical changes between the ages of 3 and 15 (Thompson & others, 2000). By repeatedly obtaining brain scans of the same children for up to four years, they found that the children's brains experience rapid, distinct spurts of growth. The amount of brain material in some areas can nearly double within as little as a year, followed by a drastic loss of tissue as unneeded cells are purged and the brain continues to reorganize itself. The scientists found that the overall size of the brain did not show dramatic growth in the 3- to 15-year age range. However, what did dramatically change were local patterns within the brain.

Researchers have found that in children from 3 to 6 years of age, the most rapid growth takes place in the frontal lobe areas involved in planning and organizing new actions, and in maintaining attention to tasks. They have discovered that from age 6 through puberty, the most rapid growth takes place in the temporal and parietal lobes, especially areas that play major roles in language and spatial relations.

The Brain and Cognitive Development   The substantial increases in memory and rapid learning that characterize infants and young children are related to cell loss, synaptic growth, and myelination. Somewhat amazingly, neuroscientists have found that the density of synapses peaks at 4 years of age (Moulson & Nelson, 2008). Some leading cognitive scientists argue that the true episodic memory (memory for the when and where of life's happenings, such as remembering what one had for breakfast this morning) and self-awareness do not develop until about this time (4 years of age) (Craik, 2006). However, recall from Chapters 6, "Cognitive Development in Infancy," and 7, "Socioemotional Development in Infancy," that some infant development researchers conclude that episodic memory and self-awareness emerge in infancy (Bauer, 2009).

These aspects of the brain's maturation, combined with opportunities to experience a widening world, contribute to children's emerging cognitive abilities. Consider a child who is learning to read and is asked by a teacher to read aloud to the class. Input from the child's eyes is transmitted to the child's brain, then passed through many brain systems, which translate (process) the patterns of black and white into codes for letters, words, and associations. The output occurs in the form of messages to the child's lips and tongue. The child's own gift of speech is possible because brain systems are organized in ways that permit language processing.

The brain is organized according to many neural circuits, which are neural networks composed of many neurons with certain functions. One neural circuit is thought to have an important function in the development of attention and working memory (a type of short-term memory that is like a mental workbench in performing many cognitive tasks) (Kramer & Goldman-Rakic, 2001). This neural circuit involves the *prefrontal cortex*, and the neurotransmitter dopamine may be a key aspect of information transmission in the prefrontal cortex and this neural circuit (Diamond, 2001) (see Figure 8.4). The maturation of the prefrontal cortex is important in the development of a number of cognitive and socioemotional skills, including attention, memory, and self-regulation (Durston & Casey, 2006).

In sum, scientists are beginning to chart connections between children's cognitive development in areas such as attention and memory, brain regions

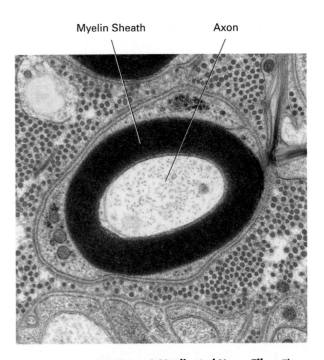

FIGURE 8.3 A Myelinated Nerve Fiber The myelin sheath, shown in brown, encases the axon (white). This image was produced by an electron microscope that magnified the nerve fiber 12,000 times. *What role does myelination play in the brain's development and children's cognition?*

FIGURE 8.4 The Prefrontal Cortex The prefrontal cortex, the highest level in the brain, shows extensive development from 3 to 6 years of age and, as will be seen in later chapters, continues to grow through the remainder of childhood and adolescence. The prefrontal cortex plays important roles in attention, memory, and self-regulation. The image on the left shows a side view of the location of the prefrontal cortex. The image on the right (frontal view) is a composite of more than 100 fMRI images of the prefrontal cortex that were taken to assess individuals' speed of processing information under different conditions.

such as the prefrontal cortex, and the transmission of information at the level of the neuron such as the neurotransmitter dopamine (de Haan & Martinos, 2008; Moulson & Nelson, 2008). As advancements in technology allow scientists to "look inside" the brain to observe its activity, we will likely see an increased precision in our understanding of the brain's functioning in various aspects of cognitive development (Diamond, Casey, & Munakata, 2010).

Review and Reflect: Learning Goal 1

1 **Discuss growth and change in the young child's body and brain**

REVIEW

- What changes in height and weight characterize early childhood?
- How does the brain change in young children?

REFLECT

- Think back to when you were a young child. How would you characterize your body growth? Was your growth about the same as most children your age or was it different?

---

2 HOW DO YOUNG CHILDREN'S MOTOR SKILLS DEVELOP?

| Gross and Fine Motor Skills | Young Children's Artistic Drawings | Handedness |

Running as fast as you can, falling down, getting right back up and running just as fast as you can . . . building towers with blocks . . . scribbling, scribbling, and scribbling some more . . . cutting paper with scissors . . . During your preschool years, you probably developed the ability to perform all of these activities.

Gross and Fine Motor Skills

Considerable progress is made in both gross and fine motor skills during early childhood. Young children develop a sense of mastery through increased proficiency in gross motor skills such as walking and running. Improvement in fine motor skills—such as being able to turn the pages of a book, one at a time—also contributes to the child's sense of mastery in the second year. First, let's explore changes in gross motor skills.

Gross Motor Skills   The preschool child no longer has to make an effort simply to stay upright and to move around. As children move their legs with more confidence and carry themselves more purposefully, moving around in the environment becomes more automatic.

At 3 years of age, children enjoy simple movements, such as hopping, jumping, and running back and forth, just for the sheer delight of performing these activities. They take considerable

37 to 48 Months	49 to 60 Months	61 to 72 Months
Throws ball underhanded (4 feet)	Bounces and catches ball	Throws ball (44 feet, boys; 25 feet, girls)
Pedals tricycle 10 feet	Runs 10 feet and stops	Carries a 16-pound object
Catches large ball	Pushes/pulls a wagon/doll buggy	Kicks rolling ball
Completes forward somersault (aided)	Kicks 10-inch ball toward target	Skips alternating feet
Jumps to floor from 12 inches	Carries 12-pound object	Roller skates
Hops three hops with both feet	Catches ball	Skips rope
Steps on footprint pattern	Bounces ball under control	Rolls ball to hit object
Catches bounced ball	Hops on one foot four hops	Rides bike with training wheels

FIGURE 8.5 The Development of Gross Motor Skills in Early Childhood The skills are listed in the approximate order of difficulty within each age period.

pride in showing how they can run across a room and jump all of 6 inches. The run-and-jump will win no Olympic gold medals, but for the 3-year-old the activity is a source of considerable pride and accomplishment.

At 4 years of age, children are still enjoying the same kind of activities, but they have become more adventurous. They scramble over low jungle gyms as they display their athletic prowess. Although they have been able to climb stairs with one foot on each step for some time, they are just beginning to be able to come down the same way. They still often revert to putting two feet on each step.

At 5 years of age, children are even more adventuresome than when they were at 4. It is not unusual for self-assured 5-year-olds to perform hair-raising stunts on practically any climbing object. Five-year-olds run hard and enjoy races with each other and their parents. A summary of development in gross motor skills during early childhood is shown in Figure 8.5.

You probably have arrived at one important conclusion about preschool children: They are very, very active. Indeed, 3-year-old children have the highest activity level of any age in the entire human life span. They fidget when they watch television. They fidget when they sit at the dinner table. Even when they sleep, they move around quite a bit. Because of their activity level and the development of large muscles, especially in the arms and legs, preschool children need daily exercise (Timmons, Naylor, & Pfeiffer, 2007). The following four studies address the importance of physical activity in young children:

How Would You...?
As a health-care professional, how would you advise parents who want to get their talented 4-year-old child in a soccer league for preschool children?

- Observations of 3- to 5-year-old children during outdoor play at preschools revealed that the preschool children were mainly sedentary even when participating in outdoor play (Brown & others, 2009). In this study, throughout the day the preschoolers were sedentary 89 percent of the time, engaged in light activity 8 percent of the time, and participated in moderate to vigorous physical activity only 3 percent of the time.

- Preschool children's physical activity was enhanced by family members' engaging in sports together and by parents' perception that it was safe for their children to play outside (Beets & Foley, 2008).

- Preschool children's physical activity varied greatly across different child-care centers (Bower & others, 2008). Active opportunities, presence of fixed and portable play equipment, and physical activity training were linked to preschool children's higher physical activity in the centers.

- Incorporation of a "move and learn" physical activity curriculum increased the activity level of 3- to 5-year-old children in a half-day preschool program (Trost, Fees, & Dzewaltowski, 2008).

Designing and implementing a developmentally appropriate movement curriculum (one that's appropriate for the child's age and the child individually) facilitates the development of children's gross motor skills. To read further about supporting young children's motor development, see the *Caring for Children* interlude.

Caring for Children

SUPPORTING YOUNG CHILDREN'S MOTOR DEVELOPMENT

If you observe young children, you will see that they spend a great deal of time engaging in such motor activities as running, jumping, throwing, and catching. These activities can form the basis of advanced, sports-related skills. For children to progress to effective, coordinated, and controlled motor performance, interaction with, and instruction from, supportive adults can be beneficial.

How can early childhood educators support young children's motor development? When planning physical instruction for young children, it is important to keep in mind that their attention span is rather short, so instruction should be brief and to the point. Young children need to practice skills in order to learn them, so instruction should be followed with ample time for practice (Thompson, 2006).

Fitness is an important dimension of people's lives, and it is beneficial to develop a positive attitude toward it early. Preschoolers need vigorous activities for short periods of time. They can be encouraged to rest or change to a quieter activity as needed.

Movement, even within the classroom, can improve a child's stamina. Such movement activities might be as basic as practicing locomotor skills or as complex as navigating an obstacle course. A number of locomotor skills (such as walking, running, jumping, sliding, skipping, and leaping) can be practiced forward and backward. And it is important to keep practice fun, allowing children to enjoy movement for the sheer pleasure of it (Sutterby & Frost, 2006).

There can be long-term negative effects for children who fail to develop basic motor skills (Edwards & Sarwark, 2005). These children will not be as able to join in group games or participate in sports during their school years and in adulthood. However, the positive development of motor skills has benefits besides participation in games and sports. Engaging in motor skills fulfills young children's needs and desires for movement, and exercise builds muscles, strengthens the heart, and enhances aerobic capacity.

What are some effective strategies for supporting young children's motor development?

Fine Motor Skills At 3 years of age, children show a more mature ability to place and handle things than when they were infants. Although for some time they have had the ability to pick up the tiniest objects between their thumb and forefinger, they are still somewhat clumsy at it. Three-year-olds can build surprisingly high block towers, each block placed with intense concentration but often not in a completely straight line. When 3-year-olds play with a simple jigsaw puzzle, they are rather rough in placing the pieces. Even when they recognize the location a piece fits into, they are not very precise in positioning the piece. They often try to force the piece in the location or pat it vigorously.

By 4 years of age, children's fine motor coordination has improved substantially and is more precise. Sometimes 4-year-old children have trouble building high towers with blocks because in their desire to place each of the blocks perfectly, they may upset those already stacked. By age 5, children's fine motor coordination has

37 to 48 Months	49 to 60 Months	61 to 72 Months
Approximates a circle in drawing	Strings and laces shoelace	Folds paper into halves and quarters
Cuts paper	Cuts following a line	Traces around hand
Pastes using pointer finger	Strings 10 beads	Draws rectangle, circle, square, and triangle
Builds three-block bridge	Copies figure X	Cuts interior piece from paper
Builds eight-block tower	Opens and places clothespins (one-handed)	Uses crayons appropriately
Draws 0 and +	Builds a five-block bridge	Makes clay object with two small parts
Dresses and undresses doll	Pours from various containers	Reproduces letters
Pours from pitcher without spilling	Prints first name	Copies two short words

FIGURE 8.6 The Development of Fine Motor Skills in Early Childhood *Note:* The skills are listed in the approximate order of difficulty within each age period.

improved. Hand, arm, and body all move together under better command of the eye. Mere towers no longer interest the 5-year-old, who now wants to build a house or a church, complete with steeple, though adults may still need to be told what each finished project is meant to be. A summary of the development of fine motor skills in early childhood is shown in Figure 8.6.

How do developmentalists measure children's motor development? The **Denver Developmental Screening Test II** is a simple, inexpensive, fast method of diagnosing developmental delay in children from birth through 6 years of age. The test is individually administered and includes separate assessments of gross and fine motor skills, as well as language and personal-social ability (Schatz & others, 2008). Among the gross motor skills this test measures are the child's ability to sit, walk, long jump, pedal a tricycle, throw a ball overhand, catch a bounced ball, hop on one foot, and balance on one foot. Fine motor skills measured by the test include the child's ability to stack cubes, reach for objects, and draw a person.

Young Children's Artistic Drawings

In the story that opened the chapter, you read about Teresa Amabile's artistic skills and interest during kindergarten. The story revealed how these skills were restricted once she went to elementary school. Indeed, many young children show a special interest in drawing, just as Teresa did.

The unintended irregularities of children's drawings suggest spontaneity, freedom, and directness (Golomb, 2008). They may use lavish colors that come close, but perhaps won't match the reality of their subjects. Form and clarity give way to bold lines flowing freely on the page. It is not the end product that matters so much, but the joy of creating, the fun of mixing colors, experimenting with different mediums, and getting messy in the process.

Young children often use the same formula for drawing different things. Though modified in small ways, one basic form can cover a range of objects. When children begin to draw animals, they portray them in the same way they portray humans: standing upright with a smiling face, legs, and arms. Pointed ears may be a clue to adults about the nature of the particular beast. As children become more sophisticated, their drawing of a cat will look more catlike to an adult. It may be resting on all four paws, tail in the air, and fur gleaming.

Not all children embrace art with equal enthusiasm, and the same child may want to draw one day but have no interest in it the next day. For most children, however, art is an important vehicle for conveying feelings and ideas that are not easily expressed in words (Thompson, 2006). Drawing and constructing also provide children with a hands-on opportunity to use their problem-solving skills to develop

"You moved."
© The New Yorker Collection 1987 Lee Lorenz from cartoonbank.com. All Rights Reserved.

Denver Development Screening Test II A test used to diagnose developmental delay in children from birth to 6 years of age; includes separate assessments of gross and fine motor skills, language, and personal-social ability.

(a)
Age 2
20 basic scribbles

(b)
Age 2 to 3
Placement stage

(c)
Age 3
Shape stage

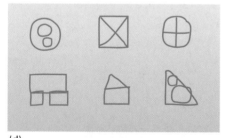

(d)
Age 3 to 4
Design stage

(e)
Age 4 to 5
Pictorial stage

FIGURE 8.7 The Stages of Young Children's Artistic Drawings

creative ways to represent scale, space, and motion. Parents can provide a context for artistic exploration by giving children a work space where they are not overly concerned about messiness or damage. They can make supplies available, have a bulletin board display space for the child's art, and support and encourage the child's art activity. When viewing children's art, many parents take special delight in hearing about the creative process. Questions such as "Can you tell me about this?" and "What were you thinking about when you made this?" encourage children and help parents to see the world through their children's eyes.

Developmental Changes and Stages   The development of fine motor skills in the preschool years allows children to become budding artists. There are dramatic changes in how children depict what they see. Art provides unique insights into children's perceptual worlds—what they are attending to, how space and distance are viewed, how they experience patterns and forms (Dorn, Madeja, & Sabol, 2004). Rhoda Kellogg is a creative teacher of preschool children who has observed and guided young children's artistic efforts for many decades. She has assembled an impressive array of tens of thousands of drawings produced by more than 2,000 preschool children. Adults who are unfamiliar with young children's art often view the productions of this age group as meaningless scribbles. However, Kellogg (1970) documented that young children's artistic productions are orderly, meaningful, and structured.

By their second birthday, children can scribble. Scribbles represent the earliest form of drawing. Every form of graphic art, no matter how complex, contains the lines found in children's artwork, which Kellogg calls the 20 basic scribbles. These include vertical, horizontal, diagonal, circular, curving, waving or zigzag lines and dots. As young children progress from scribbling to picture making, they go through four distinguishable stages: placement, shape, design, and pictorial (see Figure 8.7).

Following young children's scribbles is the **placement stage,** Kellogg's term for 2- to 3-year-olds' drawings, drawn on a page in placement patterns. One example of these patterns is the spaced border pattern shown in Figure 8.7b. The **shape stage** is Kellogg's term for 3-year-olds' drawings consisting of diagrams in different shapes (see Figure 8.7c). Young children draw six basic shapes: circles, squares or rectangles, triangles, crosses, Xs, and forms. The **design stage** is Kellogg's term for 3- to 4-year-olds' drawings in which young children mix two basic shapes into a more complex design (see Figure 8.7d). This stage occurs rather quickly after the shape stage. The **pictorial stage** is Kellogg's term for 4- to 5-year-olds' drawings that consist of objects that adults can recognize (see Figure 8.7e).

Child Art in Context   Claire Golomb (2002, 2008) has studied and conducted research on children's art for a number of decades. Golomb especially criticizes views of young children's art that describe it as primitive and a reflection of conceptual immaturity. She argues that children, like all novices, tend to use forms economically, and their comments indicate that their simplified version works. Rather than reflecting conceptual immaturity, Golomb views children's art as inventive problem solving.

Golomb maintains that developmental changes in the way children draw are not strictly age-related but also depend on talent, motivation, familial support, and cultural values. Thus, her view contrasts with Kellogg's universal stage approach in which all children go through the same sequence in developing art skills, which we just discussed. In Golomb's view, child art flourishes in sociocultural contexts where tools are made available and where this activity is valued. In Chapter 9, "Cognitive Development in Early Childhood," we look further at young children's art, paying special attention to the role of cognitive development in their art.

Handedness

For centuries, left-handers have suffered unfair discrimination in a world designed for right-handers. Even the devil himself has been portrayed as a left-hander. For many years, teachers forced all children to write with their right hand, even if they had a left-hand tendency. Today, most U.S. teachers let children write with the hand they favor (Wenze & Wenze, 2004). However, in some cultures, such as the Republic of Malawi in southern Africa, adults still strongly encourage all children to use their right hand rather than their left hand (Zverev, 2006).

Origin and Development of Handedness   What is the origin of hand preference? Genetic inheritance likely is strong (Doyen & others, 2008). In one study, the handedness of adopted children was not related to the handedness of their adoptive parents but was related to the handedness of their biological parents (Carter-Saltzman, 1980).

Right-handedness is dominant in all cultures (it appears approximately in a ratio of 90 percent right-handers and 10 percent left-handers), and it appears before the impact of culture. For example, in one study ultrasound observations of fetal thumb sucking showed that 9 of 10 fetuses were more likely to be sucking their right hand's thumb (Hepper, Shahidullah, & White, 1990).

Thus, although adults often don't notice a child's hand preference until the toddler or early childhood years, researchers have found that hand preference occurs earlier, possibly even in the womb as we just discussed (Stroganova & others, 2004). Newborns also show a preference for one side of their body over the other. In one study, 65 percent of the infants turned their head to the right when they were lying on their back in the crib (Michel, 1981). Fifteen percent preferred to face toward the left. These preferences for the right or left were linked with handedness later in development.

At about 7 months of age, infants prefer grabbing with one hand or the other and this too is related to later handedness (Ramsay, 1980). By 2 years of age, about 10 percent of children prefer to use their left hand. Many preschool children, though, use both hands, with a clear hand preference not completely distinguished until later in development.

Handedness, the Brain, and Language   A contemporary interest is the role of the brain in handedness (Miller & others, 2006; Wang & others, 2007). Approximately 95 percent of right-handed individuals process speech primarily in the brain's left hemisphere (Springer & Deutsch, 1985). However, left-handed individuals show more variation. More than half of left-handers process speech in their left hemisphere, just like right-handers. However, about one-fourth of left-handers process speech in their right hemisphere and another one-fourth process speech equally in both hemispheres (Knecht & others, 2000). Are there differences in the language development of left- and right-handers? The most consistent finding is that left-handers are more likely to have reading problems (Geschwind & Behan, 1984; Natsopoulos & others, 1998).

Handedness and Other Abilities   Although there is a tendency for left-handers to have more reading problems than right-handers, left-handers are more common among mathematicians, musicians, architects, and artists. Michelangelo, Leonardo da Vinci, and Picasso were all lefties (Schachter & Ransil, 1996). Architects and artists who are left-handed benefit from the tendency of left-handers to have unusually good visuospatial skills and to be able to imagine spatial layouts (Holtzen, 2000). Also, in one study of more than 100,000 students taking the Scholastic Aptitude Test (SAT), 20 percent of the top-scoring group was left-handed, twice the rate of left-handedness found in the general population (10 percent) (Bower, 1985).

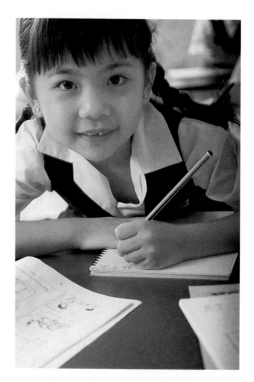

Today, most teachers let children write with the hand they favor. *What are the main reasons children become left- or right-handed?*

placement stage Kellogg's term for 2- to 3-year-olds' drawings that are drawn on a page in placement patterns.

shape stage Kellogg's term for 3-year-olds' drawings consisting of diagrams in different shapes.

design stage Kellogg's term for 3- to 4-year-olds' drawings that mix two basic shapes into more complex designs.

pictorial stage Kellogg's term for 4- to 5-year-olds' drawings depicting objects that adults can recognize.

Review and Reflect: Learning Goal 2

2 **Describe changes in motor development in early childhood**

REVIEW

- How do gross and fine motor skills change in early childhood?
- How can young children's artistic drawings be characterized?
- What is the nature of handedness?

REFLECT

- Assume that you are the director of a preschool program, and the parents ask you to develop a program to teach the children how to participate in sports. Think through how you would explain to parents why most 3-year-olds are not ready for participation in sports programs. Include in your answer information about 3-year-olds' limited motor skills, as well as the importance of learning basic motor skills first and having unrealistic expectations for young children's development of sports skills.

3 WHAT ARE SOME IMPORTANT ASPECTS OF YOUNG CHILDREN'S HEALTH?

| Sleep and Sleep Problems | Nutrition | Health, Safety, and Illness |

So far, we have discussed young children's body growth and change, as well as their development of motor skills. In this section, we explore another aspect of young children's physical development—health. To learn more about young children's health, we focus on their sleep, nutrition, safety, and illness.

Sleep and Sleep Problems

Experts recommend that young children get 11 to 13 hours of a sleep each night (National Sleep Foundation, 2009). Most young children sleep through the night and have one daytime nap (Davis, Parker, & Montgomery, 2004). Not only is the amount of sleep children get important, but so is uninterrupted sleep. Also, it sometimes is difficult to get young children to go to sleep as they drag out their bedtime routine (Hoban, 2004). One study revealed that disruption in 4- to 5-year-old children's sleep (variability in amount of sleep, variability in bedtime, and lateness in going to bed) was linked to less than optimal adjustment in preschool (Bates & others, 2002). And a recent study found that bedtime resistance was associated with conduct problems or hyperactivity in children (Carvalho Bos & others, 2009).

Helping the child slow down before bedtime often contributes to less resistance in going to bed. Reading the child a story, playing quietly with the child in the bath, and letting the child sit on the caregiver's lap while listening to music are quieting activities (Burke, Kuhn, & Peterson, 2004).

Transitional Objects Many young children want to take a soft, cuddly object, such as a favorite blanket, teddy bear, or other stuffed animal, to bed with them. **Transitional objects** are those that children repeatedly use as bedtime companions.

transitional objects Objects that children repeatedly use as bedtime companions. These usually are soft and cuddly and probably mark the child's transition from being dependent to being more independent.

They usually are soft and cuddly, and most developmentalists view them as representing a transition from being a dependent person to being a more independent one. Therefore, using transitional objects at bedtime is normal behavior for young children (Steer & Lehman, 2000). In one study, children who relied on transitional objects at age 4 showed the same level of emotional adjustment at ages 11 and 16 as children who had not relied on transitional objects (Newson, Newson, & Mahalski, 1982).

Sleep Problems Children can experience a number of sleep problems (Nevsimalova, 2009, Sadeh, 2008). One estimate indicates that more than 40 percent of children experience a sleep problem at some point in their development (Boyle & Cropley, 2004). In one study, there was a connection between children's behavioral problems and sleep problems (Smedje, Broman, & Hetta, 2001). First, children who were hyperactive during the day also were likely to toss and turn a lot during their sleep. They also were more likely to sleepwalk than children who were not hyperactive. Second, children with conduct problems (for example, fighting) were more likely to resist going to bed at night. Third, children with emotional problems were more likely to have night terrors and difficulty falling asleep. In addition, children with peer problems had a shorter sleep time. Also, researchers have found children who have sleep problems are more likely to show depression and anxiety than children who do not have sleep problems (Mehl & others, 2006). A recent study revealed that preschool children who did not get adequate sleep were more likely to experience injuries that required medical attention (Kouloaglioti, Cole, & Kitzman, 2008). Yet another recent study revealed that children who had sleep problems from 3 to 8 years of age were more likely to develop adolescent problems, such as early onset of drug use and depression (Wong, Brower, & Zucker, 2009). And recent research indicates that short sleep duration in children is linked with being overweight (Nixon & others, 2008; Patel & Hu, 2008).

Let's now explore these sleep problems in children: nightmares, night terrors, sleepwalking, and sleep talking. **Nightmares** are frightening dreams that awaken the sleeper, more often toward the morning than just after the child has gone to bed at night. Caregivers should not worry about young children having occasional nightmares because almost every child has them. If children have nightmares persistently, it may indicate that they are feeling too much stress during their waking hours. One study found that children who experience nightmares have higher levels of anxiety than those who do not have nightmares (Mindell & Barrett, 2002). And a recent study revealed that preschool children who tended to have bad dreams were characterized by a difficult temperament at 5 months of age and anxiousness at 17 months of age (Simard & others, 2008).

Night terrors are characterized by a sudden arousal from sleep and an intense fear, usually accompanied by a number of physiological reactions, such as rapid heart rate and breathing, loud screams, heavy perspiration, and physical movement (Bruni & others, 2008). In most instances, the child has little or no memory of what happened during the night terror (Mason & Pack, 2006). Night terrors are less common than nightmares and occur more often in deep sleep than do nightmares. Many children who experience night terrors return to sleep rather quickly after the night terror. Caregivers tend to be especially worried when children have night terrors, although they are usually not a serious problem (Mason & Pack, 2006).

Children usually outgrow night terrors. Although benzodiazepines (diazepam, for example) occasionally may be prescribed to be given to children at bedtime to help reduce night terrors, medication usually is not recommended (National Institutes of Health, 2007). In most cases, the only treatment needed is to reassure and comfort the child (Lam & Mason, 2007).

How Would You...?
As a human development and family studies professional, how would you advise parents of a young child who is resisting going to bed at night?

nightmares Frightening dreams that awaken the sleeper.

night terrors Characterized by sudden arousal from sleep, intense fear, and usually physiological reactions such as rapid heart rate and breathing, loud screams, heavy perspiration, and physical movement.

FIGURE 8.8 Recommended Energy Intakes for Children Ages 1 Through 10

Age	Weight (kg)	Height (cm)	Energy needs (calories)	Calorie ranges
1 to 3	13	90	1,300	900 to 1,800
4 to 6	20	112	1,700	1,300 to 2,300
7 to 10	28	132	2,400	1,650 to 3,300

Somnambulism (sleepwalking) occurs during the deepest stage of sleep. Approximately 15 percent of children sleepwalk at least once, and from 1 to 5 percent do it regularly. Most children outgrow the problem without professional intervention (Laberge & others, 2000). Except for the danger of accidents while children are walking around asleep in the dark, there is nothing abnormal about sleepwalking. It is safe to awaken sleepwalking children, and it is a good idea to do so because they might harm themselves. If children sleepwalk regularly, parents need to make the bedroom and house as safe from harm as possible and also to consult a physician to treat the child with medication (Remulla & Guilleminault, 2004).

Sleep talkers are soundly asleep as they speak, although occasionally they make fairly coherent statements for a brief period of time. Most of the time, though, you can't understand what children are saying during sleep talking. There is nothing abnormal about sleep talking, and there is no reason to try to stop it from occurring.

Nutrition

Four-year-old Bobby is on a steady diet of double cheeseburgers, french fries, and chocolate milk shakes. Between meals, he gobbles up candy bars and marshmallows. He hates green vegetables. Bobby, a preschooler, already has developed poor nutritional habits. What are a preschool child's energy needs? What is a preschooler's eating behavior like?

Energy Needs   Feeding and eating habits are important aspects of development during early childhood (Manios & others, 2008). What children eat affects their skeletal growth, body shape, and susceptibility to disease (Hahn, Payne, & Lucas, 2009). The preschool child requires up to 1,800 calories per day. Figure 8.8 shows the increasing energy needs of children as they move from infancy through the childhood years. Energy needs of individual children of the same age, sex, and size vary. However, an increasing number of children have an energy intake that exceeds what they need (Mendoza & others, 2006). A recent recommendation by the World Health Organization is that on average for children 7 years of age and younger, boys should have an 18 percent, and girls a 20 percent, reduction in energy intake (Butte, 2006).

Diet, Eating Behavior, and Parental Feeding Styles   A national study found that from the late 1970s through the late 1990s, key dietary shifts took place in U.S. children: greater away-from-home consumption; large increases in total energy from salty snacks, soft drinks, and pizza; and large decreases in energy from low- and medium-fat milk and medium- and high-fat beef and pork (Nielsen, Siega-Riz, & Popkin, 2002). In this study, children's total energy intake increased from the late 1970s to late 1990s. These dietary changes occurred for children as young as 2 years of age through the adult years.

A recent national study revealed that 45 percent of children's meals exceed recommendations for saturated and trans fat, which can raise cholesterol levels and increase the risk of heart disease (Center for Science in the Public Interest, 2008). Also this study found that one-third of children's daily caloric intake comes from

somnambulism Sleep walking; occurs in the deepest stage of sleep.

restaurants, twice the percentage consumed away from home in the 1980s. Further, 93 percent of almost 1,500 possible choices at 13 major fast-food chains exceeded 430 calories—one-third of what the National Institute of Medicine recommends that 4- to 8-year-old children consume in a day. Nearly every combination of children's meals at KFC, Taco Bell, Sonic, Jack in the Box, and Chick-fil-A were too high in calories.

Young children's eating behavior is strongly influenced by their caregivers' behavior (Black & Hurley, 2007). Young children's eating behavior improves when caregivers eat with children on a predictable schedule, model eating healthy food, make mealtimes pleasant occasions, and engage in certain feeding styles. Distractions from television, family arguments, and competing activities should be minimized so children can focus on eating. A sensitive/responsive caregiver feeding style, in which the caregiver is nurturant, provides clear information about what is expected, and appropriately responds to children's cues, is recommended (Black & Hurley, 2007). Forceful and restrictive caregiver behaviors are not recommended. For example, a restrictive feeding style is linked to children being overweight (Black & Lozoff, 2008).

Another problem is that many parents do not recognize that their children are overweight. One recent study of parents with 2- to 17-year-old children found that few parents of overweight children perceived their children to be too heavy and were not worried about the children's weight (Eckstein & others, 2006).

What are some positive strategies parents can adopt regarding their young children's eating behavior?

Fat and Sugar Consumption   Although some health-conscious parents may be providing too little fat in their infants' and children's diets, other parents are raising their children on diets in which the percentage of fat is far too high (Schiff, 2009). In a national survey, 4- to 18-year-olds often consumed the high-fat varieties of milk, yogurt, cheese, ice cream, and dairy-based toppings (Kranz, Lin, & Wagstaff, 2007).

Our changing lifestyles, in which we often eat on the run and pick up fast-food meals, contribute to the increased fat levels in children's diets. Most fast-food meals are high in protein, especially meat and dairy products. But the average American child does not need to be concerned about getting enough protein. What must be of concern is the vast number of young children who are being weaned on fast foods that are not only high in protein but also high in fat. Eating habits become ingrained very early in life; unfortunately, it is during the preschool years that many people get their first taste of fast food. The American Heart Association recommends that the daily limit for calories from fat should be approximately 35 percent.

The concern is not only about excessive fat in children's diets but also about excessive sugar (Briefel & others, 2004). Consider Robert, age 3, who loves chocolate. His mother lets him have three chocolate candy bars a day. He also drinks an average of four cans of caffeinated cola a day, and he eats sugar-coated cereal each morning at breakfast. The average American child consumes almost 2 pounds of sugar per week (Riddle & Prinz, 1984). One study found that children from low-income families were more likely to have added sugar consumption than their counterparts from higher-income families (Kranz & Siega-Riz, 2002).

How does sugar consumption influence the health and behavior of young children? The association of sugar consumption with children's health problems—dental cavities and obesity, for example—has been widely documented (Declerck & others, 2008).

In sum, although there is individual variation in appropriate nutrition for children, their diets should be well balanced and should include fats, carbohydrates, protein, vitamins, and minerals (Wardlaw & Smith, 2009). An occasional candy bar does not hurt, but a steady diet of hamburgers, french fries, milk shakes, and candy bars should be avoided.

"Fussy Eaters," Sweets, and Snacks   Many young children get labeled as "fussy" or "difficult eaters" when they are only trying to exercise the same rights to personal

How Would You...?
As a health-care professional, how would you work with parents to increase the nutritional value of meals and snacks they provide to their young children?

*S*pinach: Divide into little piles. Rearrange again into new piles. After five or six maneuvers, sit back and say you are full.

—**DELIA EPHRON**
American Writer and Humorist, 20th Century

*T*his would be a better world for children if parents had to eat the spinach.

—**GROUCHO MARX**
American Comedian, 20th Century

What are some trends in the eating habits and weight of young children?

taste and appetite adults take for granted (Dovey & others, 2008). Caregivers should allow for the child's developing tastes in food. However, when young children eat too many sweets—candy bars, cola, and sweetened cereals, for example—they can spoil their appetite and then not want to eat more nutritious foods at mealtime. Thus, caregivers need to be firm in limiting the amount of sweets young children eat.

Most preschool children need to eat more often than the adults in the family because preschool children use up so much energy. It is a long time from breakfast to lunch and from lunch to dinner for the active young child. Thus, a midmorning and midafternoon snack are recommended. A good strategy is to avoid giving sweets to young children during these snack times (Skinner & others, 2004). Better choices include whole-grain bagels spread with creamy peanut butter, pureed fruit shakes, or tortillas with refried beans. Keep in mind that some foods are known choking hazards—avoid giving young children snack foods such as hard candy, nuts, any hard raw vegetable, or whole grapes.

Overweight Young Children Being overweight has become a serious health problem in early childhood (Bolling & Daniel, 2008). The Centers for Disease Control and Prevention (2009) has a category of obesity for adults but does not have an obesity category for children and adolescents because of the stigma the label may bring. Rather they have categories for being overweight or at risk for being overweight in childhood and adolescence. These categories are determined by body mass index (BMI), which is computed by a formula that takes into account height and weight. Only children and adolescents at or above the 95th percentile of BMI are included in the overweight category, and those at or above the 85th percentile are included in the at risk for being overweight category.

The percentage of young children who are overweight or at risk for being in the United States has increased dramatically in recent decades and the percentage is likely to grow unless changes occur in children's lifestyles (Benson, Baer, & Kaelber, 2009; Ebbeling & Ludwig, 2008). A recent study revealed that in 2003 to 2006, 11 percent of U.S. 2- to 19-year-olds were obese, 16 percent were overweight, and 38 percent were at risk for being overweight (Ogden, Carroll, & Flegal, 2008). The good news from this large-scale study is that the percentages in these categories have started to level off rather than increase, as they had been doing in the last several decades.

The risk for overweight young children of continuing to be overweight when they become older was documented in another recent study (Nader & others, 2006). The body mass index of more than 1,000 children was obtained from their health records at seven different times from 2 to 12 years of age. Eighty percent of the children who were at risk for being overweight at 3 years of age were also at risk for being overweight or were overweight at 12 years of age. Forty percent of the children who were in the 50th BMI percentile or above at 3 years of age were at risk for being overweight or were overweight at 12 years of age. Another study found that children's weight at 5 years of age was significantly linked to their weight at 9 years of age (Gardner & others, 2009). And another study revealed that the prevalence of being overweight remained stable from 4 to 11 years of age for children with lean parents but more than doubled across this time frame for children with obese parents (17 percent to 45 percent) (Semmler & others, 2009). A recent study of 3-year-old children in low-income, urban families revealed that young Latino children were twice as likely to be overweight as African American and non-Latino White young children (Kimbro, Brooks-Gunn, & McLanahan, 2006).

One recent comparison of 34 countries revealed that the United States had the second highest rate of childhood obesity (Janssen & others, 2005). Childhood obesity contributes to a number of health problems (Williams & Strobino, 2008). For example, physicians are now seeing type 2 (adult-onset) diabetes (a condition directly linked with obesity and a low level of fitness) in children as young as 5 years of age (Jones, 2008).

Being overweight also is linked to young children's psychological makeup. In one study, the relation between weight status and self-esteem in 5-year-old girls was examined (Davison & Birth, 2001). The girls who were overweight had lower body self-esteem than those who were not overweight. Thus, as early as 5 years of age, being overweight is linked with lower self-esteem.

Prevention of obesity in children includes helping children and parents see food as a way to satisfy hunger and nutritional needs, not as proof of love or as a reward for good behavior (Nowicka & Flodmark, 2008). Snack foods should be low in fat, in simple sugars, and in salt, as well as high in fiber. Routine physical activity should be a daily occurrence (Dowda & others, 2009; Robbins, Powers, & Burgess, 2008).

In sum, the child's life should be centered around activities, not meals (Robbins, Powers, & Burgess, 2008). To read further about a research study focused on the importance of activities in young children's lives, see the *Research in Children's Development* interlude.

Research in Children's Development

PHYSICAL ACTIVITY IN YOUNG CHILDREN ATTENDING PRESCHOOLS

One study examined the activity level of 281 3- to 5-year-olds in nine preschools (Pate & others, 2004). The preschool children wore accelerometers, a small activity monitor, for four to five hours a day. Height and weight assessments of the children were made to calculate their BMI.

Guidelines recommend that preschool children engage in two hours of physical activity per day, divided into one hour of structured activity and one hour of unstructured free play (National Association for Sport and Physical Education, 2002). In this study, the young children participated in an average of 7.7 minutes per hour of moderate to vigorous activity, usually in a block of time when they were outside. Over the course of eight hours of a preschool day, these children would get approximately one hour of moderate and vigorous physical activity—only about 50 percent of the amount recommended. The researchers concluded that young children are unlikely to engage in another hour per day of moderate and vigorous physical activity outside their eight hours spent in preschool and thus are not getting adequate opportunities for physical activity.

Gender and age differences characterized the preschool children's physical activity. Boys were more likely to engage in moderate or vigorous physical activity than girls. Four- and five-year-old children were more likely to be sedentary than three-year-old children.

The young children's physical activity also varied according to the particular preschool they attended. The extent they participated in moderate and vigorous physical activity ranged from 4.4 to 10.2 minutes per hour across the nine preschools. Thus, the policies and practices of particular preschools influence the extent to which children engage in physical activity. The researchers concluded that young children need more vigorous play and organized activities.

What are some guidelines for preschool children's exercise?

Malnutrition in Young Children from Low-Income Families One of the most common nutritional problems in early childhood is iron deficiency anemia, which results in chronic fatigue (Bartle, 2007). This problem results from the failure to eat adequate amounts of quality meats and dark green vegetables. Young children from low-income families are most likely to develop iron deficiency anemia (Lonnerdal & Kelleher, 2007). A recent study revealed that preschool children with iron deficiency anemia were slower to display positive affect and touch novel toys for the first time than their nonanemic counterparts (Lozoff & others, 2007).

A recent study revealed that young children who had lower intakes of fresh fruit and vegetables cooked in olive oil, and higher intakes of canned fruit and vegetables, and processed salad dressing were more likely to come from lower-income, less-educated families than higher-income, more educated families (Sausenthaler & others, 2007). In part, to address this problem in the United States, the Special Supplemental Nutrition Program for Women, Infants, and Children (WIC) serves approximately 7,500,000 participants in the United States. Positive influences on young children's nutrition and health have been found for participants in WIC (Herman & others, 2008). For example, one study found that participating in WIC was linked with a lower risk for being overweight in young Mexican American children (Melgar-Quinonez & Kaiser, 2004). Another study revealed that WIC children who were anemic improved the most when they did not eat snacks and dried fruits (Swanson & others, 2007).

Some researchers argue that malnutrition is directly linked to cognitive deficits because of negative effects on brain development (Liu & others, 2003). However, an increasing number of researchers conclude that the links between child under-nutrition, physical growth, and cognitive development are more complex (Marcon, 2003). For example, nutritional influences can be viewed in the context of socioe-motional factors that often coincide with undernutrition. Thus, children who vary considerably from the norm in physical growth also differ on other biological and socioemotional factors that might influence cognitive development. For example, children who are underfed often are also less supervised, less stimulated, and less educated than children who are well nourished. As we discussed earlier, poverty is an especially strong risk factor that interacts with children's nutritional status to affect physical and cognitive development (Black & others, 2008).

Malnutrition may be linked to other aspects of development in addition to cog-nitive deficits. One longitudinal study found that U.S. children who were malnour-ished at 3 years of age showed more aggressive and hyperactive behavior at age 8, had more externalizing problems at age 11, and evidenced more excessive motor behavior at age 17 (Liu & others, 2004).

Health, Safety, and Illness

The story of children's health in the past 50 years is a shift away from fighting infectious diseases toward prevention and outpatient care. In recent decades, vac-cines have nearly eradicated disabling bacterial meningitis and have greatly reduced the incidence of measles, rubella, mumps, and chicken pox. In the effort to make a child's world safer, one of the main strategies is to prevent childhood injuries.

Preventing Childhood Injuries   Young children's active and exploratory nature, coupled with being unaware of danger in many instances, often puts them in situ-ations in which they are at risk for injuries. Most of young children's cuts, bumps, and bruises are minor, but some accidental injuries can produce serious injuries or even death (Schwebel, 2008).

In the United States, motor vehicle accidents are the leading cause of death in young children, followed by cancer and cardiovascular disease (National Vital Statistics Reports, 2004) (see Figure 8.9). In addition to motor vehicle accidents, other accidental deaths in children involve drowning, falls, burns, and poisoning (Bessey & others, 2006).

Notice in Figure 8.9 that the seventh leading cause of death in young children in the United States involves firearms. In one cross-cultural comparison, the rate of

How Would You...?
As a social worker, how would you attempt to help parents living in poverty to provide more nutritious meals for their young children?

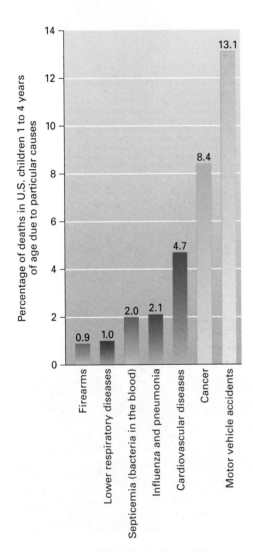

FIGURE 8.9 Main Causes of Death in Children 1 Through 4 Years of Age These figures show the percentage of deaths in U.S. children 1 to 4 years of age due to particular causes in 2002 (National Vital Statistics Reports, 2004).

firearm-related death among children less than 15 years of age in 26 industrialized countries was the highest in the United States (American Academy of Pediatrics, 2001). Among those industrialized countries with no firearm-related deaths in children were Japan, Singapore, and the Netherlands.

Many of young children's injuries can be prevented (Snowdon & others, 2008). Among the preventive measures are regularly restraining children in automobiles, reducing access to firearms, and making homes and playgrounds safer (Lee & others, 2008).

Influences on children's safety include the acquisition and practice of individual skills and safety behaviors, family and home influences, school and peer influences, and the community's actions. Notice that these influences reflect Bronfenbrenner's ecological model of development that we described in Chapter 1, "Introduction." Figure 8.10 shows how these ecological contexts can influence children's safety, security, and injury prevention (Sleet & Mercy, 2003). We have more to say about contextual influences on young children's health shortly.

Reducing access to firearms is a wise strategy (Guralnick, 2007). In 12 states that passed laws requiring that firearms be made inaccessible to children, unintentional shooting deaths of children fell almost 25 percent. In one recent study, many parents in homes with firearms reported that their children never handled the firearms, but interviews with their children contradicted the parents' perceptions (Baxley & Miller, 2006).

Deaths in young children due to automobile accidents have declined considerably in the United States since the invention of the seat belt. All U.S. states and the District of Columbia have laws that require young children to be restrained in the back seats of cars, either in specially designed seats or by seat belts. In many instances, when young children are killed today in automobile accidents, they are unrestrained. Although many parents today use car seats or "booster seats" for their children, most don't install the seats properly. If the seat is not installed correctly, children are at risk for serious injury or death in automobile accidents (Elliott & others, 2006). Nearly all local police departments will assist parents in installing their children's car seats safely. This service is provided free of charge.

Most fatal non-vehicle-related deaths in young children occur in or around the home. Young children have drowned in bathtubs and swimming pools, been burned in fires and explosions, experienced falls from heights, and drunk or eaten poisonous substances.

Playgrounds also can be a source of children's injuries (Morrongiello & Matheis, 2007). One of the major problems is that playground equipment is often not constructed over impact-absorbing surfaces, such as wood chips or sand.

Contexts of Young Children's Health

Among the contexts involved in young children's health are poverty and ethnicity, home and child care, environmental tobacco smoke, and exposure to lead. In addition, we discuss the state of illness and health in the world's children.

Poverty and Ethnicity   A special concern focuses on the health of young children living in poverty (Ruel & others, 2008). Low income is linked with poor health in young children (Larson & others, 2008). Many health problems of young children in poverty begin before birth when their mothers receive inadequate, if any, health care, which can produce a low birth weight child and other complications that can still

Individual

Development of social skills and ability to regulate emotions

Involvement in activities that promote positive attachment and prosocial skills

Acquisition of early academic skills and knowledge

Impulse control (such as not darting out into a street to retrieve a ball)

Frequent use of personal protection (such as bike helmets and safety seats)

Family/Home

High awareness and knowledge of child management and parenting skills

Caregiver participation in the child's education and social activities

Frequent parent protective behaviors (such as use of child safety seats)

Presence of home safety equipment (such as smoke alarms and cabinet locks)

School/Peers

Promotion of home/school partnerships

Availability of enrichment programs, especially for low-income families

Absence of playground hazards

Management support for safety and injury prevention

Injury prevention and safety promotion policies and programs

Community

Availability of positive activities for children and their parents

Active surveillance of environmental hazards

Effective prevention policies in place (such as pool fencing)

Commitment to emergency medical services for children and trauma care

Emphasis on safety themes

FIGURE 8.10 Characteristics That Enhance Young Children's Safety In each context of a child's life, steps can be taken to create conditions that enhance the child's safety and reduce the likelihood of injury. *How are the contexts listed in the figure related to Bronfenbrenner's theory (described in Chapter 1)?*

affect the child years later (Dubay & others, 2001). Children living in poverty may experience unsanitary conditions, live in crowded housing, and be inadequately supervised (Neumann, Gewa, & Bwibo, 2004). Children in poverty are more likely to be exposed to lead poisoning than children growing up in higher socioeconomic conditions (Morrissey-Ross, 2000). The families of many children in poverty do not have adequate medical insurance, and thus the children often receive less adequate medical care compared with children living in higher socioeconomic conditions (Olson, Tang, & Newacheck, 2005).

Ethnicity is also linked to children's health. For example, one study found that even when socioeconomic status was controlled, Latino, African American, and Asian American children were less likely to have a usual health-care source, health professional, doctor visit, and dental visit in the past year (Shi & Stevens, 2005). Another study revealed that children whose parents had limited English proficiency were three times more likely to have fair or poor health status than their English-proficient counterparts (Flores, Abreu, & Tomany-Korman, 2005).

Safety at Home and in Child Care   Caregivers—whether parents at home or teachers and supervisors in child care—play an important role in the health of young children (Boles & Roberts, 2008; Schwebel, 2008). For example, by controlling the speed of the vehicles they drive, by decreasing or eliminating their drinking—especially before driving—and by not smoking around children, caregivers enhance the likelihood that children will be healthy (Tinsley, 2003).

Young children may lack the intellectual skills—including reading ability—to discriminate between safe and unsafe household substances. And they may lack the impulse control to keep from running out into a busy street while chasing a ball. In these and many other situations, competent adult supervision and monitoring of young children are important to prevent injuries. In communicating with young children, caregivers need to make the information they give to children cognitively simple. And an important strategy is that parents guide children in learning how to control and regulate their own health behavior.

Parents also influence how children cope with medical treatment (Tinsley & others, 2002). Much of this research focuses on how parents influence children's fear and coping during inpatient and outpatient pediatric medical visits (Melamed, Roth, & Fogel, 2001). Researchers have found that parents who use distraction, are less agitated, and are more reassuring have children who display lower levels of distress in these medical settings (Stephens, Barkey, & Hall, 1999).

A special concern involves the selection of the best parenting strategies with a chronically ill child. Health researcher Barbara Melamed (2002, p. 341) provided these recommendations:

- *"Balance the illness with other family needs."*
- *"Maintain clear family boundaries."* During an illness crisis, extended family members may help with chores or caring for healthy children in the family.
- *"Develop communication competence."* Think about the best ways to talk to the physicians involved, and communicate effectively about the illness to others.
- *"Attribute positive meanings to the situation."* Demonstrate how the family can be resilient in this difficult circumstance.
- *"Engage in active coping efforts."* Seek positive problem-solving solutions in dealing with stressful aspects of the child's illness.

Parents also should invest effort in finding a competent health-care provider for their children (Hickson & Clayton, 2002, p. 456). This "includes consulting sources of information and asking questions likely to provide useful information about practice characteristics that may affect the parent-doctor relationship. Parents, for example, might seek information concerning a physician's willingness to answer questions and involve parents in decision making or at least to outline options. Parents might

How Would You... ?
As a health-care professional, how would you advise parents of young children to improve the safety of their home?

Careers in Children's Development

Barbara Deloin, Pediatric Nurse

Barbara Deloin is a pediatric nurse in Denver, Colorado. She practices nursing in the Pediatric Oral Feeding Clinic and is involved in research as part of an irritable infant study for the Children's Hospital in Denver. She also is on the faculty of nursing at the Colorado Health Sciences Center. Deloin previously worked in San Diego where she was coordinator of the Child Health Program for the County of San Diego.

Her research interests focus on children with special health-care needs, especially high-risk infants and children, and promoting positive parent-child experiences. She was elected president of the National Association of Pediatric Nurse Associates and Practitioners for the 2000–2001 term.

Barbara Deloin, conducting a pediatric evaluation.

also inquire about the physician's style of practice and philosophies about treatment, behavior management, nutrition, and other general health maintenance practices." To read about Barbara Deloin, a pediatric nurse who promotes positive parent-child experiences and positive links of families to the health-care system, see the *Careers in Children's Development* profile.

Environmental Tobacco Smoke Estimates indicate that approximately 22 percent of children and adolescents in the United States are exposed to tobacco smoke in the home. An increasing number of studies reach the conclusion that children are at risk for health problems when they live in homes in which a parent smokes (Bolte, Fromme, & the GME Study Group, 2009; Johansson, Ludvigsson, & Hermansson, 2008). If the mother smoked, her children were twice as likely to develop respiratory problems (Etzel, 1988). In one study, young children whose fathers smoked at home were more likely to have upper respiratory tract infections than those whose fathers did not smoke at home (Shiva & others, 2004). Children exposed to tobacco smoke in the home are more likely to develop wheezing symptoms and asthma than children in nonsmoking homes (Chang, 2009; Hermann, King, & Weitzman, 2008).

Environmental tobacco smoke also affects the amount of vitamin C in children and adolescents. In one study, when parents smoked at home their 4- to 18-year-old children and adolescents had significantly lower levels of vitamin C in their blood than their counterparts in nonsmoking homes (Strauss, 2001). The more parents smoked, the less vitamin C the children and adolescents had. Children exposed to environmental smoke should be encouraged to eat foods rich in vitamin C or be given this vitamin as a supplement (Preston & others, 2003).

How Would You...?
As a health-care professional, how would you talk with parents about the impact of secondhand smoke on children's health to encourage parents to stop smoking?

Exposure to Lead There is a special concern about lead poisoning in young children (Canfield & Jusko, 2008). Approximately 3 million children under 6 years of age are estimated to be at risk for lead poisoning, which might harm their development (Ahamed & others, 2005). As we mentioned earlier, children in poverty are at greater risk for lead poisoning than children living in higher socioeconomic conditions (Moralez, Gutierrez, & Escarce, 2005). Lead can get into children's bloodstreams through food or water that is contaminated by lead, from putting lead-contaminated fingers in their mouths, or from inhaling dust from lead-based paint (Wigle & others, 2007). The negative effects of high lead levels in children's blood include lower intelligence, lower achievement, attention deficit hyperactivity disorder, and elevated blood pressure (Bellinger, 2008; Canfield & Jusko, 2008). One study found that 5-year-old children exposed to lead performed more poorly on tests of memory and problem solving (Canfield, Gendle, & Cory-Slechta, 2004). And a recent fMRI study of adults who had extensive exposure to lead from birth through early childhood showed deficits in areas of the brain, such as Wernicke's area and the frontal cortex adjacent to Broca's area, that are associated with language function (Weihong & others, 2006). Because of such negative outcomes, the Centers for Disease Control and Prevention recommends that children be screened for the presence of lead contamination in their blood.

To read further about children's illness and health, see the *Diversity in Children's Development* interlude.

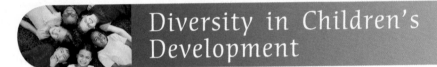

Diversity in Children's Development

THE STATE OF ILLNESS AND HEALTH IN THE WORLD'S CHILDREN

Each year UNICEF produces a report entitled *The State of the World's Children*. In a recent report, UNICEF (2008) emphasized the importance of information about the under-5 mortality rate of a nation. UNICEF concluded that the under-5 mortality rate is the result of a wide range of factors, including the nutritional health and health knowledge of mothers, the level of immunization, dehydration, availability of maternal and child health services, income and food availability in the family, availability of clean water and safe sanitation, and the overall safety of the child's environment.

UNICEF reports annual data on the rank of nations' under-5 mortality rate. In 2006, 38 nations had a lower under-5 mortality rate than the United States with Singapore, Sweden, Iceland, San Marino, and Liechtenstein having the lowest rate of all nations (UNICEF, 2008). The relatively high under-5 mortality rate of the United States compared with other developed nations is due to such factors as poverty and inadequate health care. The devastating effects on the health of young children occur in countries where poverty rates are high (UNICEF, 2009). The poor are the majority in nearly one of every five nations in the world. They often experience lives of hunger, malnutrition, illness, inadequate access to health care, unsafe water, and a lack of protection from harm (Bhutta & others, 2008).

A leading cause of childhood death in impoverished countries is dehydration caused by diarrhea. In 1980, diarrhea was responsible for over 4.6 million childhood deaths. Oral rehydration therapy (ORT) was introduced in 1979 and quickly became the foundation for controlling diarrheal diseases. ORT now is given to the majority of children in impoverished countries suffering with diarrhea, which has decreased the number of deaths due to dehydration caused by diarrhea.

Acute respiratory infections, such as pneumonia, also have killed many children under the age of 5. Many of these children's lives could have been saved with antibiotics administered by a community health worker. Undernutrition also is a contributing factor to many deaths of children under the age of 5 in impoverished countries (Amuna & Zotor, 2008).

In the last decade, there has been a dramatic increase in the number of young children who have died because of HIV/AIDS transmitted to them by their parents (UNICEF, 2008). Deaths in young children due to HIV/AIDS especially occur in countries with high rates of poverty and low levels of education (Boeving & Forsyth, 2008). For example, the uneducated are four times more likely to believe that there is no way

Many children in impoverished countries die before reaching the age of 5 from dehydration and malnutrition brought about by diarrhea. *What are some of the other main causes of death in young children around the world?*

to avoid AIDS and three times more likely to be unaware that the virus can be transmitted from mother to child (UNICEF, 2008).

Many of the deaths of young children around the world can be prevented by a reduction in poverty and improvements in nutrition, sanitation, education, and health services (Bhutta & others, 2009; Black & others, 2008).

Review and Reflect: Learning Goal 3

 Characterize the health of young children

REVIEW

- What is the nature of sleep and sleep problems in young children?
- What are young children's energy needs? What characterizes young children's eating behavior?
- How can the nature of children's injuries be summarized? How do contexts influence children's health?

REFLECT

- If you become a parent of a young child, what precautions will you take to improve your child's health?

Reach Your Learning Goals

Physical Development in Early Childhood

1 HOW DOES A YOUNG CHILD'S BODY AND BRAIN GROW AND CHANGE? DISCUSS GROWTH AND CHANGE IN THE YOUNG CHILD'S BODY AND BRAIN

Height and Weight

- The average child grows 2½ inches in height and gains between 5 and 7 pounds a year during early childhood. Growth patterns vary individually, though. Some children are unusually short because of congenital factors, growth hormone deficiency, a physical problem that develops in childhood, maternal smoking during pregnancy, or an emotional difficulty.

The Brain

- By age 6, the brain has reached about 95 percent of its adult volume. Some of the increase is due to increases in the number and size of nerve endings and receptors. One neurotransmitter that increases in concentration from 3 to 6 years of age is dopamine. Researchers have found that changes in local patterns in the brain occur from 3 to 15 years of age. From 3 to 6 years of age, the most rapid growth occurs in the frontal lobes. From age 6 through puberty, the most substantial growth takes place in the temporal and parietal lobes. Increasing brain maturation contributes to changes in cognitive abilities. One link involves the prefrontal cortex, dopamine, and improved attention and working memory.

2 HOW DO YOUNG CHILDREN'S MOTOR SKILLS DEVELOP? DESCRIBE CHANGES IN MOTOR DEVELOPMENT IN EARLY CHILDHOOD

Gross and Fine Motor Skills

- Gross motor skills increase dramatically in early childhood. Children become increasingly adventuresome as their gross motor skills improve. It is important for early childhood educators to design and implement developmentally appropriate activities for young children's gross motor skills. Three types of these activities are fundamental movement, daily fitness, and perceptual-motor. Fine motor skills also improve substantially during early childhood. The Denver Developmental Screening Test II is a simple, inexpensive method of diagnosing developmental delay and includes separate assessments of gross and fine motor skills.

Young Children's Artistic Drawings

- The development of fine motor skills allows young children to become budding artists. Scribbling begins at 2 years of age, followed by four stages of drawing, culminating in the pictorial stage at 4 to 5 years of age. Golomb argues that it is important to explore the sociocultural contexts of children's art and that such factors as talent, motivation, familial support, and cultural values influence the development of children's art.

Handedness

- In today's world, the strategy is to let children use the hand they favor. Handedness likely has a strong genetic link. About 90 percent of children are right-handed and 10 percent are left-handed. Left-handers are more likely to process speech in the right hemisphere of the brain than right-handers, and left-handers tend to have more reading problems. Left-handers often show up in higher than expected numbers as mathematicians, musicians, architects, and artists. Left-handers tend to have unusually good visuospatial skills.

WHAT ARE SOME IMPORTANT ASPECTS OF YOUNG CHILDREN'S HEALTH? CHARACTERIZE THE HEALTH OF YOUNG CHILDREN

Sleep and Sleep Problems

- Most young children sleep through the night and have one daytime nap. Helping the young child slow down before bedtime often leads to less resistance in going to bed. Many young children take transitional objects to bed with them; these objects represent a bridge between dependence and independence. Among the sleep problems that can develop in young children are nightmares, night terrors, and somnambulism (sleepwalking), and sleep talking.

Nutrition

- Energy needs increase as children go through the early childhood years. The preschool child requires up to 1,800 calories daily. National assessments indicate that a large majority of young children in the United States do not have a healthy diet and that over the last two decades their eating habits have worsened. Too many parents are rearing young children on diets that are high in fat and sugar. Children's diets should contain well-balanced proportions of fats, carbohydrates, protein, vitamins, and minerals. Parents should keep children's eating completely separate from discipline, and a child's life should revolve around activities, not meals. A special concern is the poor nutrition of young children from impoverished families.

Health, Safety, and Illness

- In the United States, motor vehicle accidents are the cause of the most deaths in young children. Firearm deaths are especially high in young children in the United States in comparison with other countries. Among the strategies for preventing childhood injuries are restraining children in automobiles, reducing access to firearms, and making the home and playground safer. Among the contexts involved in children's health are poverty and ethnicity, home and child care, environmental tobacco smoke, and exposure to lead. The most devastating effects on the health of young children occur in countries with high poverty rates. Among the problems that low-income families face in these countries around the world are hunger, malnutrition, illness, inadequate access to health care, unsafe water, and a lack of protection from harm. In recent decades, the trend in children's illness and health is toward prevention as vaccines have been developed to reduce the number of diseases children have. Parents play an important role in young children's health. They influence their children's health by the way they behave in regard to children's illness symptoms. Parents can use a number of positive strategies in coping with the stress of having a chronically ill child. Parents need to invest effort in selecting a competent health-care provider for their children.

KEY TERMS

growth hormone
  deficiency 254
myelination 256
Denver Developmental
  Screening Test II 261

placement
  stage 262
shape stage 262
design stage 262

pictorial stage 262
transitional
  objects 264
nightmares 265

night terrors 265
somnambulism 266

KEY PEOPLE

Teresa Amabile 254   Rhoda Kellogg 262   Claire Golomb 262

MAKING A DIFFERENCE

Supporting Young Children's Physical Development

What are some good strategies for supporting young children's physical development?

- *Give young children plenty of opportunities to be active and explore their world*. Young children are extremely active and should not be constrained for long periods of time. Competent teachers plan daily fitness activities for young children. Preschool-aged children are too young for organized sports.

- *Make sure that young children's motor activities are fun and appropriate for their age*. Young children should enjoy the motor activities they participate in. Also, don't try to push young children into activities more appropriate for older children. For example, don't try to train a 3-year-old to ride a bicycle or have a 4-year-old take tennis lessons.

- *Give young children ample opportunities to engage in art*. Don't constrain young children's drawing. Let them freely create their drawings.

- *Provide young children with good nutrition*. Know how many calories preschool children need to meet their energy needs, which are greater than in infancy. Too many young children are raised on fast foods. Monitor the amount of fat and sugar in young children's diet. Nutritious midmorning and midafternoon snacks are recommended in addition to breakfast, lunch, and dinner. Make sure that young children get adequate iron, vitamins, and protein.

- *Make sure that young children have regular medical checkups*. These are especially important for children living in impoverished conditions, who are less likely to get such checkups.

- *Be a positive health role model for young children*. When you have young children with you, control the speed of the vehicle you are driving. Don't smoke in their presence. Eat healthy foods. Just by being in your presence, young children will imitate many of your behaviors.

- *Make sure that where children play is safe*. Walk through the areas where children play and check for any potential hazards.

RESOURCES FOR IMPROVING CHILDREN'S LIVES

Child Art in Context
by Claire Golomb (2002)
Washington, DC: American Psychological Association

One of the world's leading experts on children's art reviews the latest research and presents her contextual theory of children's art. Includes many children's drawings to illustrate points related to the theory.

American Academy of Pediatrics
www.aap.org

This Web site provides extensive information about strategies for improving children's health.

How Children Learn to Be Healthy
by Barbara Tinsley (2003)
New York: Cambridge University Press

A leading expert explores the ways in which health behavior develops in children, especially focusing on the roles of parents, schools, and the media in influencing children's health.

E-LEARNING TOOLS

Connect to **www.mhhe.com/santrockc11e** to research the answers and complete these exercises. In addition, you'll find a number of other resources and valuable study tools for Chapter 8, "Physical Development in Early Childhood," on this Web site.

Taking It to the Net

1. Rachel, a preschool teacher, notices that Mariah did not bring a snack to preschool today. "Mariah, did you forget your snack?" Rachel asks. "No," says Mariah. "Mommy didn't have anything to give me." Mariah's response worries Rachel and causes her to wonder whether Mariah is receiving adequate nutrition. What are some of the consequences of nutritional deficiency in childhood? What kinds of things might alleviate this problem?

2. Greg and Keith like to take their daughter, Emily, to the local playground. Some of the equipment is old, and both Greg and Keith are concerned about whether the equipment is

safe. How common are playground injuries among preschoolers? What are some of the safety standards for playground equipment?

3. Dana's part-time job involves helping in a community center's after-school program for inner-city elementary school children. Many of the children eat too much junk food, have low energy levels, and are overweight. She wants to institute an exercise program as part of each day's activities. What are some things that Dana should keep in mind?

Health and Well-Being, Parenting, and Education

Build your decision-making skills by trying your hand at the health and well-being, parenting, and education exercises.

9

The mind is an enchanting thing.

—MARIANNE MOORE
American Poet, 20th Century

LEARNING GOALS

◆ Describe three views of the cognitive changes that occur in early childhood

◆ Summarize how language develops in early childhood

◆ Evaluate different approaches to early childhood education

COGNITIVE DEVELOPMENT IN EARLY CHILDHOOD

CHAPTER OUTLINE

1

WHAT ARE THREE VIEWS OF THE COGNITIVE CHANGES THAT OCCUR IN EARLY CHILDHOOD?

Piaget's Preoperational Stage

Vygotsky's Theory

Information Processing

2

HOW DO YOUNG CHILDREN DEVELOP LANGUAGE?

Understanding Phonology and Morphology

Changes in Syntax and Semantics

Advances in Pragmatics

Young Children's Literacy

3

WHAT ARE SOME IMPORTANT FEATURES OF YOUNG CHILDREN'S EDUCATION?

Variations in Early Childhood Education

Educating Young Children Who Are Disadvantaged

Controversies in Early Childhood Education

Images of Children's Development
The Story of Reggio Emilia's Children

The Reggio Emilia approach is an educational program for young children that was developed in the northern Italian city of Reggio Emilia. Children of single parents and children with disabilities have priority in admission; other children are admitted according to a scale of needs. Parents pay on a sliding scale based on income.

The children are encouraged to learn by investigating and exploring topics that interest them. A wide range of stimulating media and materials is available for children to use as they learn music, movement, drawing, painting, sculpting, collages, puppets and disguises, and photography, for example (Schroeder-Yu, 2008; Strong-Wilson & Ellis, 2007).

In this program, children often explore topics in a group, which fosters a sense of community, respect for diversity, and a collaborative approach to problem solving (Hyson, Copple, & Jones, 2006). Two co-teachers are present to serve as guides for children. The Reggio Emilia teachers consider a project as an adventure, which can start from an adult's suggestion, from a child's idea, or from an event, such as a snowfall or another unexpected happening. Every project is based on what the children say and do. The teachers allow children enough time to think and craft a project.

At the core of the Reggio Emilia approach is the image of children who are competent and have rights, especially the right to outstanding care and education. Parent participation is considered essential, and cooperation is a major theme in the schools. Many early childhood education experts believe the Reggio Emilia approach provides a supportive, stimulating context in which children are motivated to explore their world in a competent and confident manner (New, 2007).

A Reggio Emilia classroom in which young children explore topics that interest them.

> ### PREVIEW
>
> Children make a number of significant cognitive advances in early childhood. In the opening section, we explore the cognitive changes described by the major cognitive theories. Then we examine the dramatic changes in young children's language, and conclude by discussing a wide range of topics on early childhood education.

1 WHAT ARE THREE VIEWS OF THE COGNITIVE CHANGES THAT OCCUR IN EARLY CHILDHOOD?

| Piaget's Preoperational Stage | Vygotsky's Theory | Information Processing |

The cognitive world of the preschool child is creative, free, and fanciful. Preschool children's imaginations work overtime, and their mental grasp of the world improves. Our coverage of cognitive development in early childhood focuses on three theories: Piaget's, Vygotsky's, and information processing.

Piaget's Preoperational Stage

Remember from Chapter 6, "Cognitive Development in Infancy," that during Piaget's first stage of development, the sensorimotor stage, the infant progresses in the ability to organize and coordinate sensations and perceptions with physical movements and actions. The **preoperational stage,** which lasts from approximately 2 to 7 years of age, is the second Piagetian stage. In this stage, children begin to represent the world with words, images, and drawings. They form stable concepts and begin to reason. At the same time, the young child's cognitive world is dominated by egocentrism and magical beliefs.

Because Piaget called this stage "preoperational," it might sound like an unimportant waiting period. Not so. However, the label *preoperational* emphasizes that the child does not yet perform **operations,** which are reversible mental actions; they allow children to do mentally what before they could do only physically. Mentally adding and subtracting numbers are examples of operations. *Preoperational thought* is the beginning of the ability to reconstruct in thought what has been established in behavior. It can be divided into two substages: the symbolic function substage and the intuitive thought substage.

The Symbolic Function Substage

The **symbolic function substage** is the first substage of preoperational thought, occurring roughly between the ages of 2 and 4. In this substage, the young child gains the ability to mentally represent an object that is not present. This ability vastly expands the child's mental world (Carlson & Zelazo, 2008). Young children use scribble designs to represent people, houses, cars, clouds, and so on; they begin to use language and engage in pretend play. However, although young children make distinct progress during this substage, their thought still has important limitations, two of which are egocentrism and animism.

Egocentrism is the inability to distinguish between one's own perspective and someone else's perspective. Piaget and Barbel Inhelder (1969) initially studied young children's egocentrism by devising the three mountains task (see Figure 9.1). The child walks around the model of the mountains and becomes familiar with what the mountains look like from different perspectives and can see that there are different objects on the mountains. The child is then seated on one side of the table on which the mountains are placed. The experimenter moves a doll to different locations around the table, at each location asking the child to select from a series of photos the one photo that most accurately reflects the view that the doll is seeing. Children in the preoperational stage often pick their own view rather than the doll's view. Preschool children frequently show the ability to take another's perspective on some tasks but not others.

Animism, another limitation of preoperational thought, is the belief that inanimate objects have lifelike qualities and are capable of action. A young child

preoperational stage Piaget's second stage, lasting from 2 to 7 years of age, during which time children begin to represent the world with words, images, and drawings. In this stage, they also form stable concepts and begin to reason. At the same time, their cognitive world is dominated by egocentrism and magical beliefs.

operations In Piaget's theory, reversible mental actions that allow children to do mentally what they formerly did physically.

symbolic function substage Piaget's first substage of preoperational thought, in which the child gains the ability to mentally represent an object that is not present (occurs roughly between 2 and 4 years of age).

egocentrism Piaget's concept that describes the inability to distinguish between one's own perspective and someone else's perspective.

animism The belief that inanimate objects have lifelike qualities and are capable of action.

Model of Mountains

C

D · B

A
Child seated here

Photo 1
(View from A)

Photo 2
(View from B)

Photo 3
(View from C)

Photo 4
(View from D)

FIGURE 9.1 The Three Mountains Task The mountain model on the far left shows the child's perspective from view A, where he or she is sitting. The four squares represent photos showing the mountains from four different viewpoints of the model—A, B, C, and D. The experimenter asks the child to identify the photo in which the mountains look as they would from position B. To identify the photo correctly, the child has to take the perspective of a person sitting at spot B. Invariably, a child who thinks in a preoperational way cannot perform this task. When asked what a view of the mountains looks like from position B, the child selects Photo 1, taken from location A (the child's own view at the time) instead of Photo 2, the correct view.

(a)

(b)

FIGURE 9.2 The Symbolic Drawings of Young Children (*a*) A 3½-year-old's symbolic drawing. Halfway into his drawing, the 3½-year-old artist said it was a "pelican kissing a seal." (*b*) This 11-year-old's drawing is neater and more realistic but also less inventive.

"I still don't have all the answers, but I'm beginning to ask the right questions."
© The New Yorker Collection, 1989, Lee Lorenz from cartoonbank.com. All Rights Reserved.

might show animism by saying, "That tree pushed the leaf off, and it fell down" or "The sidewalk made me mad; it made me fall down." A young child who uses animism fails to distinguish the appropriate occasions for using human and non-human perspectives.

Possibly because young children are not very concerned about reality, their drawings are fanciful and inventive. Suns are blue, skies are yellow, and cars float on clouds in their symbolic, imaginative world. One 3½-year-old looked at a scribble he had just drawn and described it as a pelican kissing a seal (see Figure 9.2a). The symbolism is simple but strong, like abstractions found in some modern art. Twentieth-century Spanish artist Pablo Picasso commented, "I used to draw like Raphael but it has taken me a lifetime to draw like young children." In the elementary school years, a child's drawings become more realistic, neat, and precise (see Figure 9.2b). Suns are yellow, skies are blue, and cars travel on roads (Winner, 1986).

The Intuitive Thought Substage

The **intuitive thought substage** is the second substage of preoperational thought, occurring between approximately 4 and 7 years of age. In this substage, children begin to use primitive reasoning and want to know the answers to all sorts of questions. Consider 4-year-old Tommy, who is at the beginning of the intuitive thought substage. Although he is starting to develop his own ideas about the world he lives in, his ideas are still simple, and he is not very good at thinking things out. He has difficulty understanding events that he knows are taking place but that he cannot see. His fantasized thoughts bear little resemblance to reality. He cannot yet answer the question "What if?" in any reliable way. For example, he has only a vague idea of what would happen if a car were to hit him. He also has difficulty negotiating traffic because he cannot do the mental calculations necessary to estimate whether an approaching car will hit him when he crosses the road.

By the age of 5 children have just about exhausted the adults around them with "why" questions. The child's questions signal the emergence of interest in reasoning and in figuring out why things are the way they are. Following are some samples of the questions children ask during the questioning period of 4 to 6 years of age (Elkind, 1976):

> What makes you grow up?
>
> Who was the mother when everybody was a baby?
>
> Why do leaves fall?
>
> Why does the sun shine?

Piaget called this substage *intuitive* because young children seem so sure about their knowledge and understanding yet are unaware of how they know what they know. That is, they know something but know it without the use of rational thinking.

Centration and the Limits of Preoperational Thought

One limitation of preoperational thought is **centration,** a centering of attention on one characteristic to the exclusion of all others. Centration is most clearly evidenced in young children's lack of **conservation,** the awareness that altering an object's or a substance's appearance does not change its basic properties. For example, to adults, it is obvious that a certain amount of liquid stays the same, regardless of a container's shape. But this is not at all obvious to young children. Instead, they are struck by the height of the liquid in the container; they focus on that characteristic to the exclusion of others.

The situation that Piaget devised to study conservation is his most famous task. In the conservation task, children are presented with two

(a)   A   B   C

(b)   A   B   C

FIGURE 9.3 Piaget's Conservation Task
The beaker test is a well-known Piagetian test to determine whether a child can think operationally—that is, can mentally reverse actions and show conservation of the substance. (*a*) Two identical beakers are presented to the child. Then the experimenter pours the liquid from B into C, which is taller and thinner than A or B. (*b*) The child is asked if these beakers (A and C) have the same amount of liquid. The preoperational child says "no." When asked to point to the beaker that has more liquid, the preoperational child points to the tall, thin beaker.

identical beakers, each filled to the same level with liquid (see Figure 9.3). They are asked if these beakers have the same amount of liquid, and they usually say yes. Next, the liquid from one beaker is poured into a third beaker, which is taller and thinner than the first two. Then, the children are asked if the amount of liquid in the tall, thin beaker is equal to that which remains in one of the original beakers. Children who are less than 7 or 8 years old usually say no and justify their answers in terms of the differing height or width of the beakers. Older children usually answer yes and justify their answers appropriately ("If you poured the water back, the amount would still be the same").

In Piaget's theory, failing the conservation-of-liquid task is a sign that children are at the preoperational stage of cognitive development. The failure demonstrates not only centration but also an inability to mentally reverse actions. For example, in the conservation of matter example shown in Figure 9.4, preoperational children say that the longer shape has more clay because they assume that "longer is more." Preoperational children cannot mentally reverse the clay-rolling process to see that the amount of clay is the same in both the shorter ball shape and the longer stick shape.

intuitive thought substage Piaget's second substage of preoperational thought, in which children begin to use primitive reasoning and want to know the answers to all sorts of questions (occurs between about 4 and 7 years of age).

centration The focusing of attention on one characteristic to the exclusion of all others.

conservation The concept that an object's or substance's basic properties stay the same even though its appearance has been altered.

Type of conservation	Initial presentation	Manipulation	Preoperational child's answer
Number	Two identical rows of objects are shown to the child, who agrees they have the same number.	One row is lengthened and the child is asked whether one row now has more objects.	Yes, the longer row.
Matter	Two identical balls of clay are shown to the child. The child agrees that they are equal.	The experimenter changes the shape of one of the balls and asks the child whether they still contain equal amounts of clay.	No, the longer one has more.
Length	Two sticks are aligned in front of the child. The child agrees that they are the same length.	The experimenter moves one stick to the right, then asks the child if they are equal in length.	No, the one on the top is longer.

FIGURE 9.4 Some Dimensions of Conservation: Number, Matter, and Length

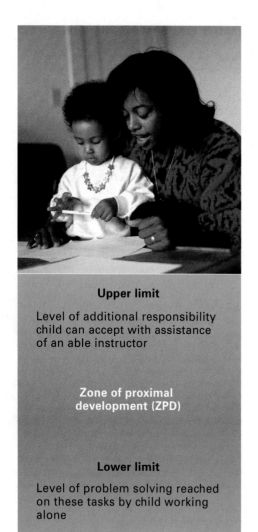

Upper limit

Level of additional responsibility child can accept with assistance of an able instructor

Zone of proximal development (ZPD)

Lower limit

Level of problem solving reached on these tasks by child working alone

FIGURE 9.5 Vygotsky's Zone of Proximal Development Vygotsky's zone of proximal development has a lower limit and an upper limit. Tasks in the ZPD are too difficult for the child to perform alone. They require assistance from an adult or a more-skilled child. As children experience the verbal instruction or demonstration, they organize the information in their existing mental structures, so they can eventually perform the skill or task alone.

zone of proximal development (ZPD) Vygotsky's term for the range of tasks that are too difficult for children to achieve alone and what they can achieve with the guidance and assistance of adults or more-skilled children.

scaffolding In cognitive development, Vygotsky used this term to describe the changing level of support over the course of a teaching session, with the more-skilled person adjusting guidance to fit the child's current performance level.

In addition to failing to conserve volume, preoperational children also fail to conserve number, matter, length, and area. However, children often vary in their performance on different conservation tasks. Thus, a child might be able to conserve volume but not number.

Some developmentalists disagree with Piaget's estimate of when children's conservation skills emerge (Byrnes, 2008). For example, Rochel Gelman (1969) showed that when the child's attention to relevant aspects of the conservation task is improved, the child is more likely to conserve. Gelman has also demonstrated that attentional training on one dimension, such as number, improves the preschool child's performance on another dimension, such as mass. Thus, Gelman argues that conservation appears earlier than Piaget thought and that attention is especially important in explaining conservation.

Vygotsky's Theory

Piaget's theory is a major developmental theory. Another developmental theory that focuses on children's cognition is Lev Vygotsky's theory. Like Piaget, Vygotsky (1896–1934) emphasized that children actively construct their knowledge and understanding. In Piaget's theory, children develop ways of thinking and understanding by their actions and interactions with the physical world. In Vygotsky's theory, children are more often described as social creatures than in Piaget's theory. They develop their ways of thinking and understanding primarily through social interaction (Gauvain, 2008; Gauvain & Parke, 2010). Their cognitive development depends on the tools provided by society, and their minds are shaped by the cultural context in which they live (Gredler, 2008; Holzman, 2009).

We briefly considered Vygotsky's theory in Chapter 1, "Introduction." Here we take a closer look at his ideas about how children learn and his view of the role of language in cognitive development.

The Zone of Proximal Development Vygotsky's (1962) belief in the importance of social influences, especially instruction, on children's cognitive development is reflected in his concept of the zone of proximal development. **Zone of proximal development (ZPD)** is Vygotsky's term for the range of tasks that are too difficult for the child to master alone but that can be learned with guidance and assistance of adults or more-skilled children. Thus, the lower limit of the ZPD is the level of skill reached by the child working independently. The upper limit is the level of additional responsibility the child can accept with the assistance of an able instructor (see Figure 9.5). The ZPD captures the child's cognitive skills that are in the process of maturing and can be accomplished only with the assistance of a more-skilled person (Alvarez & del Rio, 2007; Gauvain & Perez, 2007). Vygotsky (1962) called these the "buds" or "flowers" of development, to distinguish them from the "fruits" of development, which the child already can accomplish independently.

Scaffolding Closely linked to the idea of the ZPD is the concept of scaffolding. **Scaffolding** means changing the level of support. Over the course of a teaching session, a more-skilled person (a teacher or an advanced peer) adjusts the amount of guidance to fit the child's current performance (Daniels, 2007). When the student is learning a new task, the more-skilled person may use direct instruction. As the student's competence increases, the person gives less guidance.

Language and Thought According to Vygotsky, children use speech not only for social communication but also to help in solving problems. Vygotsky (1962) further argued that young children use language to plan, guide, and monitor their behavior. This use of language for self-regulation is called *private speech*. For Piaget, private speech is egocentric and immature—but for Vygotsky, it is an important tool of thought during the early childhood years (John-Steiner, 2007).

Vygotsky said that language and thought initially develop independently of each other and then merge. He emphasized that all mental functions have external, or social, origins. Children must use language to communicate with others before they can focus inward on their own thoughts. Children also must communicate externally and use language for a long period of time before they can make the transition from external to internal speech. This transition period occurs between 3 and 7 years of age and involves talking to oneself. After a while, the self-talk becomes second nature to children, and they can act without verbalizing. At this point, children have internalized their egocentric speech in the form of *inner speech*, which becomes their thoughts.

Vygotsky maintained that children who use a lot of private speech are more socially competent than those who don't. He argued that private speech represents an early transition in becoming more socially communicative. For Vygotsky, when young children talk to themselves, they are using language to govern their behavior and guide themselves. For example, a child working on a puzzle might say to herself, "Which pieces should I put together first? I'll try those green ones first. Now I need some blue ones. No, that blue one doesn't fit there. I'll try it over here."

Piaget argued that self-talk is egocentric and reflects immaturity. However, researchers have found support for Vygotsky's view that private speech plays a positive role in children's development (Winsler, Carlton, & Barry, 2000). Researchers have found that children use private speech more when tasks are difficult, after they have made an error, and when they are not sure how to proceed (Berk, 1994). They also have revealed that children who use private speech are more attentive and improve their performance more than children who do not use private speech (Berk & Spuhl, 1995).

Lev Vygotsky (1896–1934), shown here with his daughter, stressed that children's cognitive development is advanced through social interaction with more-skilled individuals embedded in a sociocultural backdrop. *How is Vygotsky's theory different from Piaget's?*

Teaching Strategies Vygotsky's theory has been embraced by many teachers and has been successfully applied to education (Daniels, 2007). Here are some ways Vygotsky's theory can be incorporated in classrooms:

1. *Assess the child's ZPD.* Like Piaget, Vygotsky did not hold that formal, standardized tests are the best way to assess children's learning. Rather, Vygotsky argued that assessment should focus on determining the child's zone of proximal development. The skilled helper presents the child with tasks of varying difficulty to determine the best level at which to begin instruction.

2. *Use the child's ZPD in teaching.* Teaching should begin toward the zone's upper limit, so that the child can reach the goal with help and move to a higher level of skill and knowledge. Offer just enough assistance. You might ask, "What can I do to help you?" Or simply observe the child's intentions and attempts and provide support when needed. When the child hesitates, offer encouragement. And encourage the child to practice the skill. You may watch and appreciate the child's practice or offer support when the child forgets what to do.

3. *Use more-skilled peers as teachers.* Remember that it is not just adults who are important in helping children learn. Children also benefit from the support and guidance of more-skilled children (John-Steiner, 2007).

4. *Monitor and encourage children's use of private speech.* Be aware of the developmental change from externally talking to oneself when solving a problem during the preschool years to privately talking to oneself in the early elementary school years. In the elementary school years, encourage children to internalize and self-regulate their talk to themselves.

5. *Place instruction in a meaningful context.* Educators today are moving away from abstract presentations of material, and instead provide students with

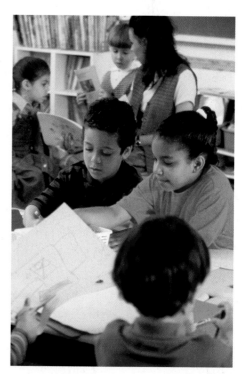

How can Vygotsky's ideas be applied to educating children?

opportunities to experience learning in real-world settings. For example, instead of just memorizing math formulas, students work on math problems with real-world implications.

6. *Transform the classroom with Vygotskian ideas.* What does a Vygotskian classroom look like? The Kamehameha Elementary Education Program (KEEP) is based on Vygotsky's theory (Tharp, 1994). The ZPD is the key element of instruction in this program. Children might read a story and then interpret its meaning. Many of the learning activities take place in small groups. All children spend at least 20 minutes each morning in a setting called "Center One." In this context, scaffolding is used to improve children's literacy skills. The instructor asks questions, responds to students' queries, and builds on the ideas that students generate. Thousands of children from low-income families have attended KEEP public schools—in Hawaii, on an Arizona Navajo reservation, and in Los Angeles. Compared with a control group of non-KEEP children, the KEEP children participated more actively in classroom discussion, were more attentive in class, and had higher reading achievement (Tharp & Gallimore, 1988).

The *Caring for Children* interlude further explores the implications of Vygotsky's theory for children's education.

Caring for Children

TOOLS OF THE MIND

Tools of the Mind is an early childhood education curriculum that emphasizes children's development of self-regulation and the cognitive foundations of literacy (Hyson, Copple, & Jones, 2006). The curriculum was created by Elena Bodrova and Deborah Leong (2007) and has been implemented in more than 200 classrooms. Most of the children in the Tools of the Mind programs are at risk because of their living circumstances, which in many instances involve poverty and other difficult conditions such as being homeless and having parents with drug problems.

Tools of the Mind is grounded in Vygotsky's (1962) theory with special attention given to cultural tools and developing self-regulation, the zone of proximal development, scaffolding, private speech, shared activity, and play as important activity. In a Tools of the Mind classroom, dramatic play has a central role. Teachers guide children in creating themes that are based on the children's interests, such as treasure hunt, store, hospital, and restaurant. Teachers also incorporate field trips, visitor presentations, videos, and books in the development of children's play. They also help children develop a play plan, which increases the maturity of their play. Play plans describe what the children expect to do in the play period, including the imaginary context, roles, and props to be used. The play plans increase the quality of their play and self-regulation.

Scaffolding writing is another important theme in the Tools of the Mind classroom. Teachers guide children in planning their own message by drawing a line to stand for each word the child says. Children then repeat the message, pointing to each line as they say the word. Then, the child writes on the lines, trying to represent each word with some letters or symbols. Figure 9.6 shows how the scaffolding writing process improved a 5-year-old child's writing over the course of two months.

Research assessments of children's writing in Tools of the Mind classrooms revealed that they have more advanced writing skills than children in other early childhood

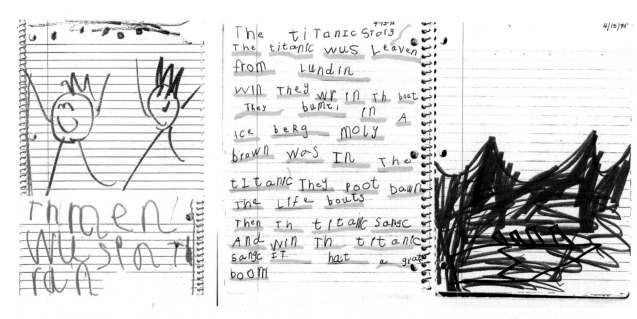

(a) Five-year-old Aaron's independent journal writing prior to the scaffolded writing technique.

(b) Aaron's journal two months after using the scaffolded writing technique. He is now making the lines for himself and had no interaction with the story until he had completed it (a total of four pages of writing). The number of sentences and words per sentence continues to increase. He has become a prolific writer in a short period of time.

FIGURE 9.6 Writing Progress of a 5-Year-Old Boy Over Two Months Using the Scaffolding Writing Process in Tools of the Mind

programs (Bodrova & Leong, 2007) (see Figure 9.6). For example, they write more complex messages, use more words, spell more accurately, show better letter recognition, and have a better understanding of the concept of a sentence.

Evaluating Vygotsky's Theory Even though their theories were proposed at about the same time, most of the world learned about Vygotsky's theory later than they learned about Piaget's theory, so Vygotsky's theory has not yet been evaluated as thoroughly. Vygotsky's view of the importance of sociocultural influences on children's development fits with the current belief that it is important to evaluate the contextual factors in learning (Gauvain & Parke, 2010; Holzman, 2009).

In moving from Piaget to Vygotsky, the conceptual shift is from the individual to collaboration, social interaction, and sociocultural activity (Halford, 2008). The endpoint of cognitive development for Piaget is formal operational thought. For Vygotsky, the endpoint can differ depending on which skills are considered to be the most important in a particular culture. For Piaget, children construct knowledge by transforming, organizing, and reorganizing previous knowledge. For Vygotsky, children construct knowledge through social interaction (Rogoff & others, 2007). The implication of Piaget's theory for teaching is that children need support to explore their world and discover knowledge. The main implication of Vygotsky's theory for teaching is that students need many opportunities to learn with the

social constructivist approach An approach that emphasizes the social contexts of learning and the fact that knowledge is mutually built and constructed; Vygotsky's theory is a social constructivist approach.

	Vygotsky	Piaget
Sociocultural context	Strong emphasis	Little emphasis
Constructivism	Social constructivist	Cognitive constructivist
Stages	No general stages of development proposed	Strong emphasis on stages (sensorimotor, preoperational, concrete operational, and formal operational)
Key processes	Zone of proximal development, language, dialogue, tools of the culture	Schema, assimilation, accommodation, operations, conservation, classification, hypothetical-deductive reasoning
Role of language	A major role; language plays a powerful role in shaping thought	Language has a minimal role; cognition primarily directs language
View on education	Education plays a central role, helping children learn the tools of the culture.	Education merely refines the child's cognitive skills that have already emerged.
Teaching implications	Teacher is a facilitator and guide, not a director; establish many opportunities for children to learn with the teacher and more-skilled peers	Also views teacher as a facilitator and guide, not a director; provide support for children to explore their world and discover knowledge

FIGURE 9.7 Comparison of Vygotsky's and Piaget's Theories

What are some advances in children's attention in early childhood?

teacher and more-skilled peers. In both Piaget's and Vygotsky's theories, teachers serve as facilitators and guides, rather than as directors and molders of learning. Figure 9.7 compares Vygotsky's and Piaget's theories.

Criticisms of Vygotsky's theory also have surfaced (Karpov, 2006). Some critics point out that Vygotsky was not specific enough about age-related changes (Gauvain, 2008). Another criticism claims that Vygotsky did not adequately describe how changes in socioemotional capabilities contribute to cognitive development (Gauvain, 2008). Yet another criticism is that he overemphasized the role of language in thinking. Also, his emphasis on collaboration and guidance has potential pitfalls. Might facilitators be too helpful in some cases, as when a parent becomes too overbearing and controlling? Further, some children might become lazy and expect help when they might have done something on their own.

Information Processing

Piaget's and Vygotsky's theories provided important ideas about how young children think and how their thinking changes. More recently, the information-processing approach has generated research that illuminates how children process information during the preschool years. What are the limitations and advances in the young child's ability to pay attention to the environment, to remember, to develop strategies and solve problems, and to understand their own mental processes and those of others?

Attention   Recall from Chapter 6, "Cognitive Development in Infancy," that *attention* was defined as the focusing of mental resources on select information. The child's ability to pay attention improves significantly during the preschool years

(Posner & Rothbart, 2007). Toddlers wander around, shift attention from one activity to another, and seem to spend little time focused on any one object or event. By comparison, the preschool child might be observed watching television for a half hour. One study videotaped young children in their homes (Anderson & others, 1985). In 99 families who were observed for 4,672 hours, visual attention to television dramatically increased during the preschool years.

Young children especially make advances in two aspects of attention—executive attention and sustained attention (Courage & Richards, 2008; Rothbart & Gartstein, 2008). **Executive attention** involves action planning, allocating attention to goals, error detection and compensation, monitoring progress on tasks, and dealing with novel or difficult circumstances. **Sustained attention** is focused and extended engagement with an object, task, event, or other aspect of the environment.

Mary Rothbart and Maria Gartstein (2008, p. 332) recently described why advances in executive and sustained attention are so important in early childhood:

> The development of the . . . executive attention system supports the rapid increases in effortful control in the toddler and preschool years. Increases in attention are due, in part, to advances in comprehension and language development. As children are better able to understand their environment, this increased appreciation of their surroundings helps them to sustain attention for longer periods of time.

In at least two ways, however, the preschool child's control of attention is still deficient:

- *Salient versus relevant dimensions.* Preschool children are likely to pay attention to stimuli that stand out, or are *salient,* even when those stimuli are not relevant to solving a problem or performing a task. For example, if a flashy, attractive clown presents the directions for solving a problem, preschool children are likely to pay more attention to the clown than to the directions. After the age of 6 or 7, children attend more efficiently to the dimensions of the task that are relevant, such as the directions for solving a problem. This change reflects a shift to cognitive control of attention, so that children act less impulsively and reflect more.

- *Planfulness.* Although in general young children's planning improves as part of advances in executive attention, when experimenters ask children to judge whether two complex pictures are the same, preschool children tend to use a haphazard comparison strategy, not examining all of the details before making a judgment. By comparison, elementary-school-age children are more likely to systematically compare the details across the pictures, one detail at a time (Vurpillot, 1968) (see Figure 9.8).

In Central European countries, such as Hungary, kindergarten children participate in exercises designed to improve their attention (Mills & Mills, 2000; Posner & Rothbart, 2007). For example, in one eye-contact exercise, the teacher sits in the center of a circle of children, and each child is required to catch the teacher's eye before being permitted to leave the group. In other exercises created to improve attention, teachers have children participate in stop-go activities during which they have to listen for a specific signal, such as a drumbeat or an exact number of rhythmic beats, before stopping the activity.

Preschool children's ability to control and sustain their attention is related to school readiness (Posner & Rothbart, 2007). For example, a study of more than 1,000 children revealed that their ability to sustain their attention at 54 months of age was linked to their school readiness (which included achievement and language skills) (NICHD Early Child Care Research Network, 2005). And in a recent study, children whose parents and teachers rated them higher on a scale of having attention problems at 54 months of age had a lower level of social skills in peer relations in the first and third grades than their counterparts who were rated lower on the

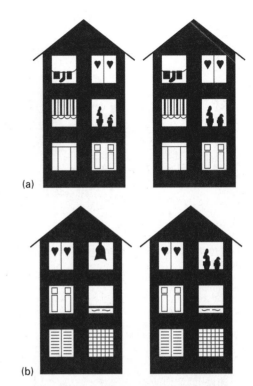

(a)

(b)

FIGURE 9.8 The Planfulness of Attention
In one study, children were given pairs of houses to examine, like the ones shown here (Vurpillot, 1968). For three pairs of houses, what was in the windows was identical (a). For the other three pairs, the windows had different items in them (b). By filming the reflection in the children's eyes, it could be determined what they were looking at, how long they looked, and the sequence of their eye movements. Children under 6 examined only a fragmentary portion of each display and made their judgments on the basis of insufficient information. By contrast, older children scanned the windows in more detailed ways and were more accurate in their judgments of which windows were identical.

executive attention Involves action planning, allocating attention to goals, error detection and compensation, monitoring progress on tasks, and dealing with novel or difficult circumstances.

sustained attention Focused and extended engagement with an object, task, event, or other aspect of the environment.

"Can we hurry up and get to the test? My short-term memory is better than my long-term memory."
Copyright © 1999. Reprinted courtesy of Bunny Hoest and Parade Magazine.

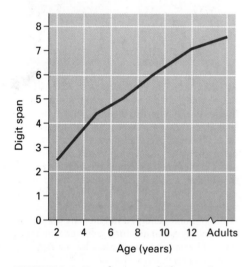

FIGURE 9.9 Developmental Changes in Memory Span In one study, from 2 years of age to 7 years of age children's memory span increased about 3 digits to 5 digits (Dempster, 1981). By 12 years of age, memory span had increased on average only another 1½ digits, to 7 digits. *What factors might contribute to the increase in memory span during childhood?*

short-term memory The memory component in which individuals retain information for up to 30 seconds, assuming there is no rehearsal.

attention problems scale at 54 months of age (NICHD Early Child Care Research Network, 2009).

Memory *Memory*—the retention of information over time—is a central process in children's cognitive development. In Chapter 6, "Cognitive Development in Infancy," we saw that many of an infant's memories are fragile and, for the most part, short-lived—except for the memory of perceptual-motor actions, which can be substantial (Mandler, 2004). Thus, we saw that to understand the infant's capacity to remember we need to distinguish *implicit memory* from *explicit memory*. Explicit memory itself, however, comes in many forms. One distinction occurs between relatively permanent, or *long-term memory*, and *short-term memory*.

Short-Term Memory In **short-term memory,** individuals retain information for up to 30 seconds if there is no rehearsal of the information. Using rehearsal (repeating information after it has been presented), we can keep information in short-term memory for a much longer period. One method of assessing short-term memory is the memory-span task. You hear a short list of stimuli—usually digits—presented at a rapid pace (one per second, for example). Then you are asked to repeat the digits.

Research with the memory-span task suggests that short-term memory increases during early childhood. For example, in one investigation, memory span increased from about 2 digits in 2- to 3-year-old children to about 5 digits in 7-year-old children, yet between 7 and 13 years of age memory span increased only by 1½ digits (Dempster, 1981) (see Figure 9.9). Keep in mind, though, that memory span varies from one individual to another.

Why does memory span change with age? Rehearsal of information is important; older children rehearse the digits more than younger children. Speed and efficiency of processing information are important, too, especially the speed with which memory items can be identified (Schneider, 2004).

The speed-of-processing explanation highlights a key point in the information-processing perspective: The speed with which a child processes information is an important aspect of the child's cognitive abilities, and there is abundant evidence that the speed with which many cognitive tasks are completed improves dramatically across the childhood years (Kail, 2007).

How Accurate Are Young Children's Long-Term Memories? While the toddlers' short-term memory span increases during the early childhood years, their memory also becomes more accurate. Young children can remember a great deal of information if they are given appropriate cues and prompts. Increasingly, young children are even being allowed to testify in court, especially if they are the only witnesses to abuse, a crime, and so forth. Several factors can influence the accuracy of a young child's memory (Bruck & Ceci, 1999):

- *There are age differences in children's susceptibility to suggestion.* Preschoolers are the most suggestible age group in comparison with older children and adults (Crossman, Scullin, & Melnyk, 2004). For example, preschool children are more susceptible to believing misleading or incorrect information given after an event (Ghetti & Alexander, 2004). Despite these age differences, there is still concern about the reaction of older children when they are subjected to suggestive interviews (Ceci & others, 2007).

- *There are individual differences in susceptibility.* Some preschoolers are highly resistant to interviewers' suggestions, whereas others immediately succumb to the slightest suggestion (Pipe, 2008). A recent study revealed that preschool children's ability to produce a high-quality narrative was linked to their resistance to suggestion (Kulkofsky & Klemfuss, 2008).

- *Interviewing techniques can produce substantial distortions in children's reports about highly salient events.* Children are suggestible not just about peripheral details but also about the central aspects of an event (Bruck, Ceci, & Hembrooke, 1998). In some cases, children's false reports can be tinged with sexual connotations. In laboratory studies, young children have made false claims about "silly events" that involved body contact (such as "Did the nurse lick your knee?" or "Did she blow in your ear?"). A significant number of preschool children have falsely reported that someone touched their private parts, kissed them, and hugged them, when these events clearly did not happen in the research. Nonetheless, young children are capable of recalling much that is relevant about an event (Fivush, 1993). When young children do accurately recall information about an event, the interviewer often has a neutral tone, there is limited use of misleading questions, and there is an absence of any motivation for the child to make a false report (Bruck & Ceci, 1999).

To read further about false memories in children, see the *Research in Children's Development* interlude.

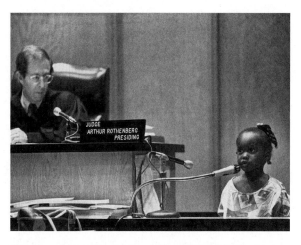

Four-year-old Jennifer Royal was the only eyewitness to one of her playmates being shot to death. She was allowed to testify in open court and the clarity of her statements helped to convict the gunman. *What are some issues involved in whether young children should be allowed to testify in court?*

Research in Children's Development

SUGGESTING FALSE EVENTS TO CHILDREN

As described in Bruck and Ceci (1999, pp. 429–430), a study by Deborah Poole and D. Stephen Lindsay revealed how parents can subtly influence their young children's memory for events. Preschool children participated in four activities (such as lifting cans with pulleys) with "Mr. Science" in a university laboratory (Poole & Lindsay, 1995). Four months later, the children's parents were mailed a storybook with a description of their child's visit to see Mr. Science. The storybook described two of the activities in which the child had participated, but it also described two in which the child had not participated. Each description ended with this fabrication of what happened when it was time to leave the laboratory: "Mr. Science wiped (child's name) hands and face with a wet-wipe. The cloth got close to (child's name) mouth and tasted real yucky."

Parents read the descriptions to their children three times. Later, the children told the experimenter that they had participated in the activities that actually had only been mentioned in the descriptions read by their parents. For example, when asked whether Mr. Science had put anything yucky in their mouth, more than half of the young children said that he had. Subsequently, when asked whether Mr. Science put something in their mouth or their parent just read this to them in a story, 71 percent of the young children said that it really happened.

This study shows how subtle suggestions can influence children's inaccurate reporting of nonevents. If such inaccurate reports are pursued in follow-up questioning by an interviewer who suspected that something sexual occurred, the result could be a sexual interpretation. This study also revealed the difficulty preschool children have in identifying the source of a suggestion (called *source-monitoring errors*). Children in this study confused their parent's reading the suggestion to them with their experience of the suggestion.

In sum, whether a young child's eyewitness testimony is accurate or not may depend on a number of factors such as the type, number, and intensity of the suggestive techniques the child has experienced. It appears that the reliability of young children's reports has as much to do with the skills and motivation of the interviewer as with any natural limitations on young children's memory (Ceci & others, 2007).

According to leading experts who study children's suggestibility, research indicates that three changes need to be implemented (Bruck, Ceci, & Principe, 2006). First, interviewers should be required to electronically preserve their interviews with children. Second, a research-validated interview schedule with children needs to be developed. Third, programs need to be created to teach interviewers how to use interviewing protocols.

Strategies and Problem Solving   In Chapter 1, "Introduction," we mentioned that information-processing theory emphasizes the importance of using good strategies. **Strategies** consist of deliberate mental activities to improve the processing of information. For example, rehearsing information and organizing it are two typical strategies that older children and adults use to remember more effectively. For the most part, young children do not use rehearsal and organization to remember.

During early childhood, the relatively stimulus-driven toddler is transformed into a child capable of flexible, goal-directed problem solving (Carlson & Zelazo, 2008). For example, 3- to 4-year-olds cannot understand that a single stimulus can be described in incompatible ways from two different perspectives (Perner & others, 2002). Consider a problem in which children must sort stimuli using the rule of *color*. In the course of the color sorting, a child may describe a red rabbit as "a *red one*" to solve the problem. However, in a subsequent task, the child may need to discover a rule that describes the rabbit as just "a *rabbit*" to solve the problem. If 3- to 4-year-olds fail to understand that it is possible to provide multiple descriptions of the same stimulus, they persist in describing the stimulus as "a red rabbit." Researchers have found that at about 4 years of age, children acquire the concept of perspectives, which allows them to appreciate that a single stimulus can be described in two different ways (Frye, 1999).

Some developmental psychologists use their training in areas such as cognitive development to pursue careers in applied areas. To read about the work of Helen Schwe, an individual who followed this path, see the *Careers in Children's Development* profile.

The Child's Theory of Mind   Even young children are curious about the nature of the human mind (Gelman, 2009). They have a **theory of mind**, which refers to awareness of one's own mental processes and the mental processes of others. Studies of theory of mind view the child as "a thinker who is trying to explain, predict, and understand people's thoughts, feelings, and utterances" (Harris, 2006, p. 847). Researchers are increasingly discovering that children's theory of mind is linked to cognitive processes (Wellman & others, 2008). For example, a recent study revealed that infants' attention to intentional actions was linked to 4-year-old's theory of mind. And another recent study found that theory of mind competence at age 3 is related to a higher level of metamemory at age 5 (Lockl & Schneider, 2007).

Developmental Changes   Children's theory of mind changes as they develop through childhood (Doherty, 2008; Flavell, 2004; Gelman, 2009). Some changes occur quite early in development, as we see next.

From 18 months to 3 years of age, children begin to understand three mental states:

- *Perceptions.* By 2 years of age, children recognize that another person will see what's in front of her own eyes instead of what's in front of the child's eyes (Lempers, Flavell, & Flavell, 1977), and by 3 years of age, they realize

strategies Deliberate mental activities to improve the processing of information.

theory of mind A concept that refers to awareness of one's own mental processes and the mental processes of others.

Careers in Children's Development

Helen Schwe, Developmental Psychologist and Toy Designer

Helen Schwe obtained a Ph.D. from Stanford University in developmental psychology, but she now spends her days talking with computer engineers and designing "smart" toys for children. Smart toys are designed to improve children's problem-solving and symbolic thinking skills.

When she was a graduate student, Schwe worked part-time for Hasbro toys, testing its children's software on preschoolers. Her first job after graduate school was with Zowie entertainment, which was subsequently bought by LEGO. According to Helen, "Even in a toy's most primitive stage of development, . . . you see children's creativity in responding to challenges, their satisfaction when a problem is solved or simply their delight when they are having fun" (p. 50). In addition to conducting experiments and focus groups at different stages of a toy's development, Schwe also assesses the age-appropriateness of a toy. Most of her current work focuses on 3- to 5-year-old children.

(Source: Schlegel, 2000, pp. 50–51)

Helen Schwe, a developmental psychologist, with some of the "smart" toys she designed.

---

that looking leads to knowing what's inside a container (Pratt & Bryant, 1990).

- *Emotions.* The child can distinguish between positive (for example, happy) and negative (sad, for example) emotions. A child might say, "Tommy feels bad."

- *Desires.* All humans have some sort of desires. But when do children begin to recognize that someone else's desires may differ from their own? Toddlers recognize that if people want something, they will try to get it. For instance, a child might say, "I want my mommy."

Two- to three-year-olds understand the way that desires are related to actions and to simple emotions. For example, they understand that people will search for what they want and that if they obtain it, they are likely to feel happy, but if they don't they will keep searching for it and are likely to feel sad or angry (Wellman & Woolley, 1990). Children also refer to desires earlier and more frequently than they refer to cognitive states such as thinking and knowing (Bartsch & Wellman, 1995).

One of the landmark developments in understanding others' desires is recognizing that someone else may have different desires from one's own (Astington & Dack, 2008). Eighteen-month-olds understand that their own food preferences may not match the preferences of others: They will give an adult the food to which she says "Yummy!" even if the food is something that the infants detest (Repacholi & Gopnik, 1997). As they get older, they can verbalize that they themselves do not like something but an adult might (Flavell & others, 1992).

Between the ages of 3 to 5, children come to understand that the mind can represent objects and events accurately or inaccurately. The realization that people can have *false beliefs*—beliefs that are not true—develops in a majority of children by the time they are 5 years old (Wellman, Cross, & Watson, 2001) (see Figure 9.10).

FIGURE 9.10 Developmental Changes in False-Belief Performance False-belief performance dramatically increases from 2½ years of age through the middle of the elementary school years. In a summary of the results of many studies, 2½-year-olds gave incorrect responses about 80 percent of the time (Wellman, Cross, & Watson, 2001). At 3 years, 8 months, they were correct about 50 percent of the time, and after that, gave increasingly correct responses.

Sally   Anne

FIGURE 9.11 The Sally and Anne False-Belief Task In the false-belief task, the skit above in which Sally has a basket and Anne has a box is shown to children. Sally places a toy in her basket and then leaves. While Sally is gone and can't watch, Anne removes the toy from Sally's basket and places it in her box. Sally then comes back and the children are asked where they think Sally will look for her toy. Children are said to "pass" the false-belief task if they understand that Sally looks in her basket first before realizing the toy isn't there.

FIGURE 9.12 Ambiguous Line Drawing

This point is often described as a pivotal one in understanding the mind—recognizing that beliefs are not just mapped directly into the mind from the surrounding world, but also that different people can have different, and sometimes incorrect, beliefs (Gelman, 2009; Liu & others, 2008). In a classic false-belief task, young children were shown a Band-Aids box and asked what was inside (Jenkins & Astington, 1996). To the children's surprise, the box actually contained pencils. When asked what a child who had never seen the box would think was inside, 3-year-olds typically responded, "Pencils." However, the 4- and 5-year-olds, grinning at the anticipation of the false beliefs of other children who had not seen what was inside the box, were more likely to say "Band-Aids."

In a similar task, children are told a story about Sally and Anne: Sally places a toy in a basket and then leaves the room (see Figure 9.11). In her absence, Anne takes the toy from the basket and places it in a box. Children are asked where Sally will look for the toy when she returns. The major finding is that 3-year-olds tend to fail false-belief tasks, saying that Sally will look in the box (even though Sally could not know that the toy has moved to this new location). Four-year-olds and older children tend to pass the task, correctly saying that Sally will have a "false belief"—she will think the object is in the basket, even though that belief is now false. The conclusion from these studies is that children younger than 4 years old do not understand that it is possible to have a false belief.

It is only beyond the preschool years—at approximately 5 to 7 years of age—that children have a deepening appreciation of the mind itself rather than just an understanding of mental states. For example, they begin to recognize that people's behaviors do not necessarily reflect their thoughts and feelings (Flavell, Green, & Flavell, 1993). Not until middle and late childhood do children see the mind as an active constructor of knowledge or processing center (Flavell, Green, & Flavell, 1998) and move from understanding that beliefs can be false to realizing that the same event can be open to multiple interpretations (Carpendale & Chandler, 1996). For example, in one study, children saw an ambiguous line drawing (for example, a drawing that could be viewed as either a duck or a rabbit); one puppet told the child she believed the drawing was a duck, while another puppet told the child he believed the drawing was a rabbit (see Figure 9.12). Before the age of 7, children said that there was one right answer, and it was not okay for both puppets to have different opinions.

Five- and six-year olds understand that human sources may have different experiences, but they still think there is an objective truth (Kuhn, Cheney, & Weinstock, 2000). They reason that if others have misinformation or misunderstand something, they must be inaccurately perceiving reality. By age 7, children are able to recognize that reality is not directly knowable, that knowledge is subjective, and that people may have different interpretations of the same event due to differing interpretive processes.

Although most research on children's theory of mind focuses on children around or before their preschool years, at 7 years of age and beyond there are important developments in the ability to understand the beliefs and thoughts of others. While understanding that people may have different interpretations is important, it is also important to recognize that some interpretations and beliefs may still be evaluated on the basis of the merits of arguments and evidence (Kuhn, Cheney, & Weinstock, 2000). In early adolescence, children begin to understand that people can have ambivalent feelings (Harter, 2006). They start to recognize that the same person can feel both happy and sad about the same event. They also engage in more recursive thinking: thinking about what other people are thinking about.

Individual Differences As in other developmental research, there are individual differences in when children reach certain milestones in their theory of mind. For example, preschoolers who have more siblings perform better on theory of mind tasks than preschoolers with fewer siblings, especially if they have older siblings (McAlister & Peterson, 2007). Children who as 2-year-olds talk with their parents about feelings frequently show better performance on theory of mind tasks (Ruffman, Slade, & Crowe, 2002), as do children who frequently engage in pretend play (Harris, 2000). Children who are deaf but have hearing parents perform more poorly on theory of mind tasks than deaf children raised by deaf parents, presumably because they have fewer opportunities to engage in communication with their parents about mental states (Courtin, 2000).

Executive function, which describes several functions (such as inhibition and planning) that are important for flexible, future-oriented behavior, also may be connected to theory of mind development (Astington & Dack, 2008; Doherty, 2008). For example, in one executive function task, children are asked to say the word *night* when they see a picture of a sun, and the word *day* when they see a picture of a moon and stars. Children who perform better at executive function tasks seem also to have a better understanding of theory of mind (Sabbagh & others, 2006).

Theory of Mind and Autism Another individual difference in understanding the mind involves autism (Doherty, 2008). Approximately 2 to 6 of 1,000 children are estimated to have some sort of autism disorder (National Institute of Mental Health, 2004). Autism can usually be diagnosed by the age of 3 years, and sometimes earlier. Children with autism show a number of behaviors different from children their age, including deficits in social interaction and communication as well as repetitive behaviors or interests (National Autism Association, 2008). It now is accepted that autism is linked to genetic and brain abnormalities (Iacoboni & Dapretto, 2006).

Children and adults with autism have difficulty in social interactions, often described as huge deficits in theory of mind (Peterson & others, 2009). These deficits are generally greater than deficits in children the same mental age with mental retardation (Baron-Cohen, 1995). Researchers have found that autistic children have difficulty in developing a theory of mind, especially in understanding others' beliefs and emotions (Harris, 2006). Although children with autism tend to do poorly on reasoning in false-belief tasks (Peterson, 2005), they can perform much better on reasoning tasks requiring an understanding of physical causality.

However, it is important to consider individual variations in autistic children and particular aspects of theory of mind (Harris, 2006). Autistic children are not a homogeneous group, and some have less severe social and communication problems than others. Thus, it is not surprising that children who have less severe forms of autism do better than those who have more severe forms of the disorder on some theory of mind tasks. For example, higher-functioning autistic children show reasonable progress in understanding others' desires (Harris, 2006). A further important consideration in thinking about autism and theory of mind is that autistic children's difficulty in understanding others' beliefs and emotions might be due not solely to theory of mind deficits but to other aspects of cognition, such as problems in focusing attention or some general intellectual impairment (Renner, Grofer Klinger, & Klinger, 2006). Some recent theories of autism suggest that weaknesses in executive functioning may relate to the problems those with autism have on theory of mind tasks. Other theories have pointed out that typically developing individuals process information by extracting the big picture, whereas those with autism process information in a very detailed, obsessive way. It may be that in autism, a number of different but related deficits lead to the social cognitive deficits (Rajendran & Mitchell, 2007).

The boy sitting on the sofa is autistic. *What are some characteristics of autistic children? What are some deficits in autistic children's theory of mind?*

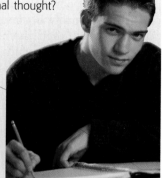

Review and Reflect: Learning Goal 1

1 **Describe three views of the cognitive changes that occur in early childhood**

REVIEW

- What characterizes Piaget's stage of preoperational thought?
- What does Vygotsky's theory suggest about how preschool children construct knowledge?
- What are some important ways in which information processing changes during early childhood? What characterizes children's theory of mind?

REFLECT

- Should children be taught concepts such as conservation? Explain.

2 HOW DO YOUNG CHILDREN DEVELOP LANGUAGE?

| Understanding Phonology and Morphology | Changes in Syntax and Semantics | Advances in Pragmatics | Young Children's Literacy |

Toddlers move rather quickly from producing two-word utterances to creating three-, four-, and five-word combinations. Between 2 and 3 years of age, they begin the transition from saying simple sentences that express a single proposition to saying complex sentences.

As young children learn the special features of their own language, there are extensive regularities in how they acquire that particular language (Berko Gleason, 2009). For example, all children learn the prepositions *on* and *in* before other prepositions. Children learning other languages, such as Russian or Chinese, also acquire the particular features of those languages in a consistent order.

Understanding Phonology and Morphology

During the preschool years, most children gradually become more sensitive to the sounds of spoken words and become increasingly capable of producing all the sounds of their language (National Research Council, 1999). By the time children are 3 years of age, they can produce all the vowel sounds and most of the consonant sounds (Menn & Stoel-Gammon, 2009).

Young children can even produce complex consonant clusters such as *str-* and *-mpt-*. They notice rhymes, enjoy poems, make up silly names for things by substituting one sound for another (such as *bubblegum, bubblebum, bubbleyum*), and clap along with each syllable in a phrase.

By the time children move beyond two-word utterances, they demonstrate a knowledge of morphology rules (Tager Flusberg & Zukowski, 2009). Children begin using the plural and possessive forms of nouns (such as *dogs* and *dog's*). They put appropriate endings on verbs (such as *-s* when the subject is third-person singular and *-ed* for the past tense). They use prepositions (such as *in* and *on*), articles (such as *a* and *the*), and various forms of the verb *to be* (such as "I *was* going to the store"). Some of the best evidence for changes in children's use of morphological rules occurs in their overgeneralization of the rules, as when a preschool child say "foots" instead of "feet," or "goed" instead of "went."

In a classic experiment that was designed to study children's knowledge of morphological rules, such as how to make a plural, Jean Berko (1958) presented preschool children and first-grade children with cards such as the one shown in Figure 9.13. Children were asked to look at the card while the experimenter read aloud the words on the card. Then the children were asked to supply the missing word. This task might sound easy, but Berko was interested in the children's ability to apply the appropriate morphological rule—in this case, to say "wugs" with the *z* sound that indicates the plural.

Although the children's answers were not perfect, they were much better than chance. What makes Berko's study impressive is that most of the words were made up for the experiment. Thus, the children could not base their responses on remembering past instances of hearing the words. That they could make the plurals or past tenses of words they had never heard before was proof that they knew the morphological rules.

Changes in Syntax and Semantics

Preschool children also learn and apply rules of syntax (Lieven, 2008; Tager Flusberg & Zukowski, 2009). They show a growing mastery of complex rules for how words should be ordered.

Consider *wh-* questions, such as "Where is Daddy going?" or "What is that boy doing?" To ask these questions properly, the child must know two important differences between *wh-* questions and affirmative statements (for instance, "Daddy is going to work" and "That boy is waiting on the school bus"). First, a *wh-* word must be added at the beginning of the sentence. Second, the auxiliary verb must be inverted—that is, exchanged with the subject of the sentence. Young children learn quite early where to put the *wh-* word, but they take much longer to learn the auxiliary-inversion rule. Thus, preschool children might ask, "Where Daddy is going?" and "What that boy is doing?"

Gains in semantics also characterize early childhood. Vocabulary development is dramatic (Lieven, 2008; Pan & Uccelli, 2009). Some experts have concluded that between 18 months and 6 years of age, young children learn about one new word every waking hour (Gelman & Kalish, 2006)! By the time they enter first grade, it is estimated that children know about 14,000 words (Clark, 1993).

Advances in Pragmatics

Changes in pragmatics also characterize young children's language development (Aktar & Herold, 2008; Bryant, 2009). A 6-year-old is simply a much better conversationalist than a 2-year-old is (Lieven, 2008). What are some of the improvements in pragmatics during the preschool years?

Young children begin to engage in extended discourse (Aktar & Herold, 2008, p. 581). For example, they learn culturally specific rules of conversation and politeness, and become sensitive to the need to adapt their speech in different settings. Their developing linguistic skills and increasing ability to take the perspective of others contribute to their generation of more competent narratives.

As children get older, they become increasingly able to talk about things that are not here (grandma's house, for example) and not now (what happened to them yesterday or might happen tomorrow, for example). A preschool child can tell you what she wants for lunch tomorrow, something that would not have been possible at the two-word stage of language development.

Around 4 to 5 years of age, children learn to change their speech style to suit the situation. For example, even 4-year-old children speak differently to a 2-year-old than to a same-aged peer; they use shorter sentences with the 2-year-old. They also speak differently to an adult than to a same-aged peer, using more polite and formal language with the adult (Shatz & Gelman, 1973).

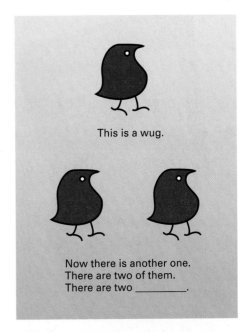

This is a wug.

Now there is another one. There are two of them. There are two _____.

FIGURE 9.13 Stimuli in Berko's Study of Young Children's Understanding of Morphological Rules In Jean Berko's (1958) study, young children were presented cards, such as this one with a "wug" on it. Then the children were asked to supply the missing word; in supplying the missing word, they had to say it correctly too. "Wugs" is the correct response here.

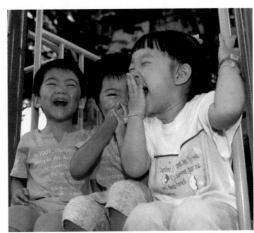

What are some advances in pragmatics that characterize children's development in early childhood?

Peers also can play an important role in aspects of language other than pragmatics. A recent study of more than 1,800 4-year-olds revealed that peers' expressive language abilities (transmitting language to others) were positively linked with young children's expressive and receptive (what a child hears and reads) language development (Mashburn & others, 2009).

Young Children's Literacy

The concern about the ability of U.S. children to read and write has led to a careful examination of preschool and kindergarten children's experiences, with the hope that a positive orientation toward reading and writing can be developed early in life (Morrow, 2009; Otto, 2010). Parents and teachers need to provide young children a supportive environment for them to develop literacy skills (Kim, 2009). Children should be active participants and be immersed in a wide range of interesting listening, talking, writing, and reading experiences. A recent study revealed that children whose mothers had more education had more advanced emergent literacy skills than children whose mothers had less education (Korat, 2009). Another recent study found that literacy experiences (such as how often the child was read to), the quality of the mother's engagement with her child (such as attempts to cognitively stimulate the child), and provision of learning materials (such as age-appropriate learning materials and books) were important home literacy experiences in low-income families that were linked to the children's language development in positive ways (Rodriguez & others, 2009).

The following three longitudinal studies indicate the importance of early language skills and children's school readiness:

- Phonological awareness, letter name and sound knowledge, and naming speed in kindergarten were linked to reading success in the first and second grade (Schattschneider & others, 2004).

- Children's early home environment influenced their early language skills, which in turn predicted their readiness for school (Forget-Dubois & others 2009).

- The number of letters children knew in kindergarten was highly correlated (.52) with their reading achievement in high school (Stevenson & Newman, 1986).

The advances in language that take place in early childhood lay the foundation for later development in the elementary school years, which we discuss in Chapter 13, "Socioemotional Development in Middle and Late Childhood."

Review and Reflect: Learning Goal 2

 Summarize how language develops in early childhood

REVIEW

- How do phonology and morphology change during early childhood?
- What characterizes young children's understanding of syntax and semantics in early childhood?
- What advances in pragmatics occur in early childhood?
- What are some effective ways to guide young children's literacy?

REFLECT

- How are nature and nurture likely to be involved in the dramatic increase in a young child's spoken vocabulary?

3 WHAT ARE SOME IMPORTANT FEATURES OF YOUNG CHILDREN'S EDUCATION?

| Variations in Early Childhood Education | Educating Young Children Who Are Disadvantaged | Controversies in Early Childhood Education |

To the teachers at a Reggio Emilia program (described in the chapter opening), preschool children are active learners, exploring the world with their peers, constructing their knowledge of the world in collaboration with their community, aided but not directed by the teachers. In many ways, the Reggio Emilia approach applies ideas consistent with the views of Piaget and Vygotsky discussed in this chapter. Does it matter to the children? How do other early education programs treat children, and how do the children fare? Our exploration of early childhood education focuses on variations in programs, education for children who are disadvantaged, and some controversies in early childhood education.

Variations in Early Childhood Education

Attending preschool is rapidly becoming the norm for U.S. children (Feeney & others, 2010). Thirty-eight states have publically funded preschool programs for 3- and 4-year-old children (King & Kepner, 2008). Many other 3- and 4-year-old children attend private preschool programs.

There are many variations in the way young children are educated (Henniger, 2009; Marion, 2010). The foundation of early childhood education has been the child-centered kindergarten.

The Child-Centered Kindergarten Nurturing is a key aspect of the **child-centered kindergarten,** which emphasizes the education of the whole child and concern for his or her physical, cognitive, and socioemotional development (Marion, 2010). Instruction is organized around the child's needs, interests, and learning styles. Emphasis is on the process of learning, rather than what is learned (Hendrick & Weissman, 2010; Morrison, 2009). The child-centered kindergarten honors three principles: Each child follows a unique developmental pattern; young children learn best through firsthand experiences with people and materials; and play is extremely important in the child's total development. *Experimenting, exploring, discovering, trying out, restructuring, speaking,* and *listening* are frequent activities in excellent kindergarten programs. Such programs are closely attuned to the developmental status of 4- and 5-year-old children.

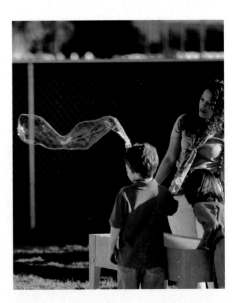

What are some characteristics of the child-centered kindergarten?

The Montessori Approach Montessori schools are patterned after the educational philosophy of Maria Montessori (1870–1952), an Italian physician-turned-educator, who crafted a revolutionary approach to young children's education at the beginning of the twentieth century. Her work began in Rome with a group of children who were mentally retarded. She was successful in teaching them to read, write, and pass examinations designed for normal children. Some time later, she turned her attention to poor children from the slums of Rome and had similar success in teaching them. Her approach has since been adopted extensively in private nursery schools in the United States.

The **Montessori approach** is a philosophy of education in which children are given considerable freedom and spontaneity in choosing activities. They are allowed to move from one activity to another as they desire. The teacher acts as a facilitator rather than a director. The teacher shows the child how to perform intellectual activities, demonstrates interesting ways to explore curriculum materials, and offers help when the child requests it (Drake, 2009; Lillard, 2009). "By encouraging children to make decisions from an early age, Montessori programs seek to develop

child-centered kindergarten Education that involves the whole child by considering the child's physical, cognitive, and socioemotional development and the child's needs, interests, and learning styles.

Montessori approach An educational philosophy in which children are given considerable freedom and spontaneity in choosing activities and specially designed curriculum materials.

Larry Page and Sergey Brin, founders of the highly successful Internet search engine, Google, recently said that their early years at Montessori schools were a major factor in their success (International Montessori Council, 2006). During an interview with Barbara Walters, they said they learned how to be self-directed and self-starters at Montessori (ABC News, 2005). They commented that Montessori experiences encouraged them to think for themselves and allowed them the freedom to develop their own interests.

What characterizes developmentally appropriate education?

developmentally appropriate practice
Education that focuses on the typical developmental patterns of children (age appropriateness) as well as the uniqueness of each child (individual appropriateness). Such practice contrasts with *developmentally inappropriate practice,* which ignores the concrete, hands-on approach to learning. Direct teaching largely through abstract paper-and-pencil activities presented to large groups of young children is believed to be developmentally inappropriate.

Project Head Start Compensatory education designed to provide children from low-income families the opportunity to acquire the skills and experiences important for school success.

self-regulated problem solvers who can make choices and manage their time effectively" (Hyson, Copple, & Jones, 2006, p. 14). The number of Montessori schools in the United States has expanded dramatically in recent years, from one school in 1959 to 355 schools in 1970 to approximately 4,000 in 2005 (Whitescarver, 2006).

Some developmentalists favor the Montessori approach, but others believe that it neglects children's social development (Chattin-McNichols, 1992). For example, while Montessori fosters independence and the development of cognitive skills, it deemphasizes verbal interaction between the teacher and child and peer interaction. Montessori's critics also argue that it restricts imaginative play and that its heavy reliance on self-corrective materials may not adequately allow for creativity and for a variety of learning styles (Goffin & Wilson, 2001).

Developmentally Appropriate and Inappropriate Education   Many educators and psychologists conclude that preschool and young elementary school children learn best through active, hands-on teaching methods such as games and dramatic play. They know that children develop at varying rates and that schools need to allow for these individual differences. They also argue that schools should focus on improving children's socioemotional development, as well as their cognitive development (Henniger, 2009; Morrison, 2009). Educators refer to this type of schooling as **developmentally appropriate practice,** which is based on knowledge of the typical development of children within an age span (age appropriateness) as well as the uniqueness of the child (individual appropriateness). In contrast, developmentally inappropriate practice for young children relies on abstract paper-and-pencil activities presented to large groups. Figure 9.14 provides examples of the National Association for the Education of Young Children's (NAEYC) guidelines for developmentally appropriate practices (NAEYC, 2009).

One study compared 182 children from five developmentally appropriate kindergarten classrooms (with hands-on activities and integrated curriculum tailored to meet age group, cultural, and individual learning styles) and five developmentally inappropriate kindergarten classrooms (which had an academic, direct instruction emphasis with extensive use of workbooks/worksheets, seatwork, and rote drill/practice activities) in a Louisiana school system (Hart & others, 2003). Children from the two types of classrooms did not differ in pre-kindergarten readiness, and the classrooms were balanced in terms of sex and socioeconomic status. Teacher ratings of child behavior and scores on the California Achievement Test were obtained through the third grade. Children taught in developmentally inappropriate classrooms had slower growth in vocabulary, math application, and math computation.

However, not all studies show significant positive benefits for developmentally appropriate education (Hyson, 2007). Among the reasons it is difficult to generalize about research on developmentally appropriate education are that individual programs often vary and that developmentally appropriate education is an evolving concept. Recent changes in the concept have given more attention to sociocultural factors and the teacher's active involvement and implementation of systematic intentions, as well as how strong academic skills should be emphasized and how they should be taught.

Educating Young Children Who Are Disadvantaged

For many years, U.S. children from low-income families did not receive any education before they entered the first grade. Often, they began first grade already several steps behind their classmates in their readiness to learn. In the summer of 1965, the federal government began an effort to break the cycle of poverty and poor education for young children in the United States through **Project Head Start.** It is a compensatory program designed to provide children from low-income families

Core Considerations in Developmentally Appropriate Practice

1. **Knowledge to consider in making decisions.**
   In all aspects of working with children, early childhood practitioners need to consider these three areas of knowledge; (a) what is known about child development and learning, especially age-related characteristics; (b) what is known about each child as an individual; and (c) what is known about the social and cultural contexts in which children live.

2. **Challenging and achievable goals.**
   Keeping in mind desired goals and what is known about the children as a group and individually, teachers plan experiences to promote children's learning and development.

Principles of Child Development and Learning That Inform Practice

1. All the domains of development and learning—physical, cognitive, and social—are important, and they are linked.

2. Many aspects of children's learning and development follow well-documented sequences, with later abilities, skills, and knowledge building on those already acquired.

3. Development and learning proceed at varying rates from child to child, and at uneven rates across different areas of a child's individual functioning.

4. Development and learning result from the interaction of biology and experience.

5. Early experiences have strong effects—both cumulative and delayed—on children's development and learning; optimal periods exist for certain types of development and learning.

6. Development proceeds toward greater complexity, self-regulation, and symbolic or representational capacities.

7. Children develop best when they have secure, consistent relationships with responsive adults and opportunities for positive peer relations.

8. Development and learning occur in and are influenced by multiple social and cultural contexts.

9. Always mentally active in seeking to understand the world around them, children learn in a variety of ways; a wide range of teaching strategies can be effective in guiding children's learning.

10. Play is an important context for developing self-regulation and for promoting language, cognition, and competence.

11. Development and learning advance when children are challenged to achieve at a level just beyond their current mastery and when they are given opportunities to practice newly acquired skills.

12. Children's experiences shape their motivation and approaches to learning, such as persistence, initiative, and flexibility; in turn, these characteristics influence their learning and development.

Guidelines for Developmentally Appropriate Practice

1. **Creating a caring community of learners.**
   Each member of the community should be valued by the others; relationships are an important context through which children learn; practitioners ensure that members of the community feel psychologically safe.

2. **Teaching to enhance development and learning.**
   The teacher takes responsibility for stimulating, directing, and supporting children's learning by providing the experiences that each child needs.

3. **Planning curriculum to achieve important goals.**
   The curriculum is planned to help children achieve goals that are developmentally appropriate and educationally significant.

4. **Assessing children's development and learning.**
   In developmentally appropriate practice, assessments are linked to the program's goals for children.

5. **Establishing reciprocal relationships with families.**
   A positive partnership between teachers and families benefits children's learning and development.

FIGURE 9.14 Recommendations by NAEYC for Developmentally Appropriate Practice in Early Childhood Programs Serving Children from Birth Through Age 8
Source: NAEYC (2009). Developmentally appropriate practice in early childhood programs serving children from birth through age 8. Washington, DC: Author.

the opportunity to acquire the skills and experiences important for success in school. After almost half a century, Head Start continues to be the largest federally funded program for U.S. children, with almost 1 million U.S. children enrolled annually (Hagen & Lamb-Parker, 2008). In 2007, 3 percent of Head Start children were 5 years old, 51 percent were 4 years old, 36 percent were 3 years old, and 10 percent were under 3 years of age (Administration for Children and Families, 2008).

Early Head Start was established in 1995 to serve children from birth to 3 years of age. In 2007, half of all new funds appropriated for Head Start programs were used for the expansion of Early Head Start. Researchers have found positive effects for Early Head Start (Hoffman & Ewen, 2007).

Head Start programs are not all created equal. One estimate is that 40 percent of the 1,400 Head Start programs are of questionable quality (Zigler & Styfco, 1994). More attention needs to be given to developing Head Start programs that are consistently high quality. One individual who is strongly motivated to make Head Start a valuable

Careers in Children's Development

Yolanda Garcia, Director of Children's Services/Head Start

Yolanda Garcia has worked in the field of early childhood education and family support for three decades. She has been the director of the Children's Services Department for the Santa Clara, California, County Office of Education since 1980. As director, she is responsible for managing child development programs for 2,500 3- to 5-year-old children in 127 classrooms. Her training includes two master's degrees, one in public policy and child welfare from the University of Chicago and another in educational administration from San Jose State University.

Garcia has served on many national advisory committees that have resulted in improvements in the staffing of Head Start programs. Most notably, she served on the Head Start Quality Committee that recommended the development of Early Head Start and revised performance standards for Head Start programs. Garcia currently is a member of the American Academy of Science Committee on the Integration of Science and Early Childhood Education.

Yolanda Garcia, Director of Children's Services/Head Start, working with some Head Start children in Santa Clara, California.

learning experience for young children from disadvantaged backgrounds is Yolanda Garcia. To read about her work, see the *Careers in Children's Development* Profile.

Evaluations support the positive influence of quality early childhood programs on both the cognitive and social worlds of disadvantaged young children (Hagen & Lamb-Parker, 2008; Ryan, Fauth, & Brooks-Gunn, 2006). One high-quality early childhood education program (although not a Head Start program) is the Perry Preschool program in Ypsilanti, Michigan, a 2-year preschool program that includes weekly home visits from program personnel. In analyses of the long-term effects of the program, adults who had been in the Perry Preschool program were compared with a control group of adults from the same background who did not receive the enriched early childhood education (Schweinhart & others, 2005; Weikart, 1993). Those who had been in the Perry Preschool program had fewer teen pregnancies and better high school graduation rates, and at age 40 more were in the workforce, owned their own homes, had a saving account, and had fewer arrests.

Controversies in Early Childhood Education

Four controversies in early childhood education involve (1) the curriculum, (2) universal preschool education, (3) whether preschool matters, and (4) school readiness.

What Should the Curriculum Emphasis Be in Early Childhood Education?
Regarding the curriculum controversy, on one side are those who advocate a child-centered, constructivist approach much like that emphasized by the NAEYC along the lines of developmentally appropriate practice. On the other side are those who advocate an academic, direct instruction approach.

In reality, many high-quality early childhood education programs include both academic and constructivist approaches. Many education experts like Lilian Katz (1999), though, worry about academic approaches that place too much pressure on young children to achieve and don't provide any opportunities to actively construct knowledge. Competent early childhood programs also should focus on cognitive development *and* socioemotional development, not exclusively on cognitive development (NAEYC, 2002).

Should All Children Be Provided Preschool Education?

Another early childhood education controversy focuses on whether preschool education should be instituted for all U.S. 4-year-old children. Edward Zigler and his colleagues (2006) recently argued that the United States should have universal preschool education. They emphasize that quality preschools prepare children for school readiness and academic success. Zigler and his colleagues (2006) cite research that shows quality preschool programs increase the likelihood that once children go to elementary and secondary school they will be less likely to be retained in a grade or drop out of school. They also point to analyses indicating that universal preschool would bring considerable cost savings on the order of billions of dollars because of a diminished need for remedial services (Karoly & Bigelow, 2005).

What is the curriculum controversy in early childhood education?

Critics of universal preschool education argue that the gains attributed to preschool and kindergarten education are often overstated. They especially stress that research has not proven that nondisadvantaged children improve as a result of attending a preschool. Thus, the critics say it is more important to improve preschool education for young children who are disadvantaged than to fund preschool education for all 4-year-old children. Some critics, especially homeschooling advocates, emphasize that young children should be educated by their parents, not by schools. Thus, controversy continues to characterize whether universal preschool education should be implemented.

Does Preschool Matter?

Is preschool a good thing for all children? According to developmental psychologist David Elkind (1988), parents who are exceptionally competent and dedicated, and who have both the time and the energy, can provide the basic ingredients of early childhood education in their home. If parents have the competence and resources to provide young children with a variety of learning experiences and exposure to other children and adults (possibly through neighborhood play groups), along with opportunities for extensive play, then home schooling may sufficiently educate young children. However, if parents do not have the commitment, the time, the energy, and the resources to provide young children with an environment that approximates a good early childhood program, then it *does* matter whether a child attends preschool.

What Is Required for School Readiness?

Educational reform has prompted considerable concern about children's readiness to enter kindergarten and first grade (Halle & others, 2007; Morrison & Hindman, 2008). National studies suggest that 40 percent of kindergartners are not ready for first grade (Kauffman, Early Education Exchange, 2002).

The National Association for the Education of Young Children (NAEYC, 1990) stresses that government officials and educators who promote universal school readiness should commit to:

- Addressing the inequities in early life experiences, such as poverty, so that all children have access to the opportunities that promote success in school
- Recognizing and supporting individual differences in children
- Establishing reasonable and appropriate expectations for children's capabilities on school entry

Inadequate health care and economic difficulties place many children at risk for academic failure before they enter school (Naude, Pretorius, & Vijoen, 2003). Thus, it is important to provide families with access to the services and support necessary to prepare children to succeed in school (Booth & Crouter, 2007). These services include basic health care, economic support, basic nutrition, adequate housing, family support services, and high-quality early childhood education programs.

Craig and Sharon Ramey (1999, 2004) reviewed scientific research on school readiness and concluded that the following six caregiver activities are necessary in the infant and early childhood years to ensure that children are ready for elementary school (Ramey & Ramey, 1999, p. 145):

1. Encourage exploration.
2. Mentor in basic skills.
3. Celebrate developmental advances.
4. Research and extend new skills.
5. Protect from inappropriate disapproval, teasing, and punishment.
6. Guide and limit behavior.

A child's attention is an important aspect of school-entry readiness.

A recent longitudinal study using six data sets examined various factors that might be linked to school readiness and the extent they predicted later achievement in reading and math (Duncan & others, 2007). Across all six data sets, the strongest predictors of later achievement were school-entry-level math, reading, and attention skills. However, school-entry-level socioemotional behaviors, such as internalizing and externalizing problems, and social skills showed little connection to later academic achievement.

An increasing number of U.S. parents are delaying the entry of their children into the first grade with the hope that the additional year will provide their child with a competitive advantage. Borrowing the term from college athletics (in which an athlete is held out of competition for a year in hope that greater maturity and experience will produce improved performance), this strategy has been referred to as "academic redshirting." On the whole, the evidence about the short-term and long-term effects of redshirting are inconclusive (ERIC/EECE, 2002; West, Denton, & Germino-Hausken, 2000). When benefits of redshirting appear, they typically are short-lived and may in the long term be disadvantageous (Graue & DiPerna, 2000).

A related issue involves whether a child who is not doing well in kindergarten should be held back for a second year of kindergarten rather than entering the first grade. Researchers have found that this is generally not a good strategy; it resulted in lower academic achievement and self-esteem (Carlton & Winsler, 1999; Hong & Raudenbush, 2005).

In some developed countries, such as Japan, as well as in many developing countries, the goals of early childhood education are quite different from those of American programs. To read about the differences, see the *Diversity in Children's Development* interlude.

Diversity in Children's Development

EARLY CHILDHOOD EDUCATION IN JAPAN AND DEVELOPING COUNTRIES

As in America, there is diversity in Japanese early childhood education. Some Japanese kindergartens have specific aims, such as early musical training or the practice of Montessori strategies. In large cities, some kindergartens are attached to universities that have elementary and secondary schools. In most Japanese preschools, however, little emphasis is put on academic instruction.

In one study, 300 Japanese and 210 American preschool teachers, child development specialists, and parents were asked about various aspects of early childhood education (Tobin, Wu, & Davidson, 1989). Only 2 percent of the Japanese respondents listed "to give children a good start academically" as one of their top three reasons for a society to have preschools. In contrast, over half the American respondents chose this as one of their top three choices. Japanese schools do not teach reading, writing, and mathematics but rather skills like persistence, concentration, and the ability to function as a member of a group. The vast majority of young Japanese children are taught to read at home by their parents.

In the comparison of Japanese and American parents, more than 60 percent of the Japanese parents said that the purpose of preschool is to give children experience at being a member of the group compared with only 20 percent of the U.S. parents (Tobin, Wu, & Davidson, 1989) (see Figure 9.15). Lessons in living and working together grow naturally out of the Japanese culture. In many Japanese kindergartens, children wear the same uniforms, including caps, which are of different colors to indicate the classrooms to which they belong. They have identical sets of equipment, kept in identical drawers and shelves. This system is not intended to turn the young children into robots, as some Americans have observed, but to impress on them that other people, just like themselves, have needs and desires that are equally important (Hendry, 1995).

Japan is a highly advanced industrialized country. What about developing countries—how do they compare to the United States in educating young children? The wide range of programs and emphasis on the education of the whole child—physically, cognitively, and socioemotionally—that characterizes U.S. early childhood does not exist in many developing countries (Roopnarine & Metingdogan, 2006). Economic pressures and parents' belief that education should be academically rigorous have produced teacher-centered rather than child-centered early childhood education programs in most developing countries. Among the countries in which this type of early childhood education has been observed are Jamaica, China, Thailand, Kenya, and Turkey. In these countries, young children are usually given few choices and are educated in highly structured settings. Emphasis is on learning academic skills through rote memory and recitation (Lin, Johnson, & Johnson, 2003). Programs in Mexico, Singapore, Korea, and Hong Kong have been observed to be closer to those in the United States in their emphasis on curriculum flexibility and play-based methods (Cisneros-Cohernour & others, 2000).

What characterizes early childhood education in Japan?

A kindergarten class in Kingston, Jamaica. What characterizes kindergarten in many developing countries like Jamaica?

Review and Reflect: Learning Goal 3

 Evaluate different approaches to early childhood education

REVIEW

- What are some variations in early childhood education?
- What are the main efforts to educate young children who are disadvantaged?
- What are four controversies about early childhood education?

REFLECT

- Might preschool be more beneficial to children from middle-income than from low-income families? Why?

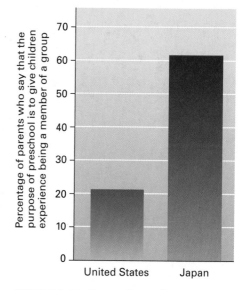

FIGURE 9.15 Comparison of Japanese and U.S. Parents' Views on the Purpose of Preschool

Reach Your Learning Goals

Cognitive Development in Early Childhood

1 WHAT ARE THREE VIEWS OF THE COGNITIVE CHANGES THAT OCCUR IN EARLY CHILDHOOD? DESCRIBE THREE VIEWS OF THE COGNITIVE CHANGES THAT OCCUR IN EARLY CHILDHOOD

Piaget's Preoperational Stage

- According to Piaget, in the preoperational stage, which lasts from about 2 to 7 years of age, children cannot yet perform operations, which are reversible mental actions, but they begin to represent the world with words, images, and drawings, to form stable concepts, and to reason. During the symbolic function substage, which occurs between 2 and 4 years of age, children begin to mentally represent an object that is not present; their thought is limited by egocentrism and animism. During the intuitive thought substage, which stretches from about 4 to 7 years of age, children begin to reason and to bombard adults with questions. Thought at this substage is called intuitive because children seem so sure about their knowledge yet are unaware of how they know what they know. Centration and a lack of conservation also characterize the preoperational stage.

Vygotsky's Theory

- Vygotsky's theory represents a social constructivist approach to development. According to Vygotsky, children construct knowledge through social interaction, and they use language not only to communicate with others but also to plan, guide, and monitor their own behavior and to help them solve problems. His theory suggests that adults should access and use the child's zone of proximal development (ZPD), which is the range of tasks that are too difficult for children to master alone but that can be learned with the guidance and assistance of adults or more-skilled children. The theory also suggests that adults and peers should teach through scaffolding, which involves changing the level of support over the course of a teaching session, with the more-skilled person adjusting guidance to fit the student's current performance level.

Information Processing

- The child's ability to attend to stimuli dramatically improves during early childhood. Advances in executive attention and sustained attention are especially important in early childhood, but the young child still attends to the salient rather than the relevant features of a task. Significant improvement in short-term memory occurs during early childhood. With good prompts, young children's long-term memories can be accurate, although young children can be led into developing false memories. Young children usually don't use strategies to remember, but they can learn rather simple problem-solving strategies. Theory of mind is the awareness of one's own mental processes and the mental processes of others. Children begin to understand mental states involving perceptions, desires, and emotions from 18 months to 3 years of age; by 5 years of age a majority realize that people can have false beliefs. It is only beyond the pre-school years that children have a deepening appreciation of the mind itself rather than just understanding mental states. Autistic children have difficulty in developing a theory of mind.

2 HOW DO YOUNG CHILDREN DEVELOP LANGUAGE? SUMMARIZE HOW LANGUAGE DEVELOPS IN EARLY CHILDHOOD

Understanding Phonology and Morphology

- Young children increase their grasp of language's rule systems. In terms of phonology, most young children become more sensitive to the sounds of spoken language. Berko's classic experiment demonstrated that young children understand morphological rules.

Changes in Syntax and Semantics	• Preschool children learn and apply rules of syntax and how words should be ordered. In terms of semantics, vocabulary development increases dramatically during early childhood.
Advances in Pragmatics	• Young children's conversational skills improve, they increase their sensitivity to the needs of others in conversation, and they learn to change their speech style to suit the situation.
Young Children's Literacy	• There has been increased interest in young children's literacy. Young children need to develop positive images of reading and writing skills through a supportive environment. Children should be active participants and be immersed in a wide range of interesting and enjoyable listening, talking, writing, and reading experiences.

3 WHAT ARE SOME IMPORTANT FEATURES OF YOUNG CHILDREN'S EDUCATION? EVALUATE DIFFERENT APPROACHES TO EARLY CHILDHOOD EDUCATION

Variations in Early Childhood Education	• The child-centered kindergarten emphasizes the education of the whole child, with particular attention to individual variation, the process of learning, and the importance of play in development. The Montessori approach allows children to choose from a range of activities while teachers serve as facilitators. Developmentally appropriate practice focuses on the typical patterns of children (age appropriateness) and the uniqueness of each child (individual appropriateness). Such practice contrasts with developmentally inappropriate practice, which ignores the concrete, hands-on approach to learning.
Educating Young Children Who Are Disadvantaged	• The U.S. government has tried to break the poverty cycle with programs such as Head Start. Model programs have been shown to have positive effects on children who live in poverty.
Controversies in Early Childhood Education	• Controversy characterizes early childhood education curricula. On the one side are the child-centered, constructivist advocates; on the other are those who advocate a direct instruction, academic approach. Another controversy involves whether universal preschool education should be implemented for all U.S. 4-year-olds. Yet another controversy focuses on whether preschool education matters. Some parents can educate young children as effectively as a school does; however, most parents do not have the skills, time, and commitment to do so. A fourth controversy focuses on school readiness, including such topics as academic redshirting and whether some children should be held back for a second year in kindergarten. School readiness skills in math, reading, and attention are especially important in predicting later academic achievement.

KEY TERMS

KEY PEOPLE

MAKING A DIFFERENCE

Nourish the Young Child's Cognitive Development

What are some good strategies for helping young children develop their cognitive competencies?

- *Provide opportunities for the young child's development of symbolic thought.* Give the child ample opportunities to scribble and draw. Provide the child opportunities to engage in make-believe play. Don't criticize the young child's art and play. Let the child's imagination flourish.

- *Encourage exploration.* Let the child select many of the activities he or she wants to explore. Don't have the child do rigid paper-and-pencil exercises that involve rote learning. The young child should not be spending lots of time passively sitting, watching, and listening.

- *Be an active language partner with the young child.* Encourage the young child to speak in entire sentences instead of using single words. Be a good listener. Ask the child lots of questions. Don't spend time correcting the child's grammar; simply model

correct grammar yourself when you talk with the child. Don't correct the young child's writing. Spend time selecting age-appropriate books for the young child. Read books with the young child.

- *Become sensitive to the child's zone of proximal development.* Monitor the child's level of cognitive functioning. Know what tasks the child can competently perform alone and those that are too difficult, even with your help. Guide and assist the child in the proper performance of skills and use of tools in the child's zone of proximal development. Warmly support the young child's practice of these skills.

- *Evaluate the quality of the child's early childhood education program.* Make sure the early childhood program the child attends involves developmentally appropriate education. The program should be age appropriate and individual appropriate for the child. It should not be a high-intensity, academic-at-all-costs program. Don't pressure the child to achieve at this age.

RESOURCES FOR IMPROVING CHILDREN'S LIVES

National Association for the Education of Young Children (NAEYC)
800–424–2460
www.naeyc.com

NAEYC is an important professional organization and advocacy group for young children and has developed guidelines for a number of dimensions of early childhood education. It publishes the excellent journal *Young Children*.

Motivated Minds: Raising Children to Love Learning
by Deborah Stipek and Kathy Seal (2001)
Hudson, OH: Owl Books

An excellent book for parents who want to guide their children's learning in a positive direction.

E-LEARNING TOOLS

Connect to **www.mhhe.com/santrockc11e** to research the answers and complete these exercises. In addition, you'll find a number of other resources and valuable study tools for Chapter 9, "Cognitive Development in Early Childhood," on this Web site.

Taking It to the Net

1. Judith and Louis have a 3-year-old son, Mitchell. Many of their friends are enrolling their children in preschool. Judith and Louis do not think they can afford to enroll Mitchell in a preschool program, although both of them think that the benefits

of preschool might justify the cost. Are there significant benefits associated with preschool programs? Are there particular types of preschools that seem more beneficial for children? If Mitchell does not attend a preschool program, what can they do at home to further their child's development?

2. Todd is working in a child-care center after school. He notices that there is a wide range in the children's use of language, even within age groups. Are there any guidelines that Todd can obtain that could help determine if a child is delayed in language development?

3. You are visiting a number of preschools to help your friend determine which program might be most appropriate for her 4-year-old child. You have heard that the National Association for the Education of Young Children is a great resource for both educators and parents. What kinds of tools can you find on the NAEYC Web site to assist you and your friend as you search the programs in your area?

Health and Well-Being, Parenting, and Education

Build your decision-making skills by trying your hand at the health and well-being, parenting, and education exercises.

Video Clips

The Online Learning Center includes the following videos for this chapter:

- *Categorizing Animals and Food at Age 3—7780*
  Here we watch a 3-year-old demonstrate his ability to categorize animals and food. In the second demonstration, when presented with pictures of a zebra, turtle, bird, and kite, he makes a distinction between animals and birds.

- *Categorizing Pictures at Age 4—7155*
  A 4-year-old is presented with pictures of a lion, bear, zebra, and wagon and asked which one is different from the others. He insists, "They're all different!" The interviewer probes him, but he is more interested in adding and subtracting pictures, which he does very well. Another set of pictures is presented to him, and again he says that all are different.

- *Understanding Conservation (Liquid) at Age 4—2168*
  A girl proves she has an understanding of the concept of conservation when presented with Piaget's classic liquid test. This clip provides a good example of the age variation in the emergence of conservation.

- *Memory Ability at Age 4—1606*
  Here a 4-year-old girl is presented with a sequence of numbers and asked to repeat them. She recalls the numbers successfully and then smiles at her accomplishment.

10

*Let us play, for it is yet day
And we cannot go to sleep;
Besides, in the sky the little birds fly
And the hills are all covered with sheep.*

—WILLIAM BLAKE
English Poet, 19th Century

LEARNING GOALS

◆ Discuss emotional and personality development in early childhood

◆ Explain how families can influence young children's development

◆ Describe the roles of peers, play, and television in young children's development

SOCIOEMOTIONAL DEVELOPMENT IN EARLY CHILDHOOD

CHAPTER OUTLINE

Images of Children's Development
Craig Lesley's Complicated Early Emotional and Social Life

In his memoir *Burning Fence: A Western Memoir of Fatherhood,* award-winning novelist Craig Lesley describes one memory from his early childhood:

> Lifting me high above his head, my father placed me in the crotch of the Bing cherry tree growing beside my mother's parents' house in The Dalles. A little frightened at the dizzying height, I pressed my palms into the tree's rough, peeling bark. My father stood close, reassuring. I could see his olive skin, dazzling smile, and sharp-creased army uniform.
>
> "Rudell, don't let him fall." My mother watched, her arms held out halfway, as if to catch me. . . .
>
> The cherries were ripe and robins flittered through the green leaves, pecking at the Bings. Tipping my head back I could see blue sky beyond the extended branches.
>
> "That's enough. Bring him down now." My mother's arms reached out farther.
>
> Laughing, my father grabbed me under the arms, twirled me around, and plunked me into the grass. I wobbled a little. Imprinted on my palms was the pattern of the tree bark, and I brushed off the little bark pieces on my dungarees.
>
> In a moment, my grandmother gave me a small glass of lemonade. . . .
>
> This first childhood memory of my father remains etched in my mind. . . .
>
> When I grew older, I realized that my father had never lifted me into the cherry tree. After Rudell left, I never saw him until I was fifteen. My grandfather had put me in the tree. Still, the memory of my father lifting me into the tree persists. Even today, I remain half-convinced by the details, the press of bark against my palms, the taste of lemonade, the texture of my father's serge uniform. Apparently, my mind has cross-wired the photographs of my handsome father in his army uniform with the logical reality that my grandfather set me in the crotch of the tree.
>
> Why can I remember the event so vividly? I guess because I wanted so much for my father to be there. I have no easy answers. (Lesley, 2005, pp. 8–10)

Like millions of other children, Lesley experienced a family torn by divorce; he would also experience abuse by a stepfather. When his father left, Lesley was an infant, but even as a preschooler, he felt his father's absence. Once he planned to win a gift for his father so that his grandmother "could take it to him and then he'd come to see me" (Lesley, 2005, p. 16). In just a few years, the infant had become a child with a complicated emotional and social life.

PREVIEW
In early childhood, children's emotional lives and personalities develop in significant ways and their small worlds widen. In addition to the continuing influence of family relationships, peers take on a more significant role in children's development and play fills the days of many young children's lives.

1 WHAT CHARACTERIZES YOUNG CHILDREN'S EMOTIONAL AND PERSONALITY DEVELOPMENT?

The Self	Emotional Development	Moral Development	Gender

Many changes characterize young children's socioemotional development in early childhood. Their developing minds and social experiences produce remarkable advances in the development of their self, emotional maturity, moral understanding, and gender awareness.

The Self

We learned in Chapter 7, "Socioemotional Development in Infancy," that during the second year of life children make considerable progress in self-recognition. In the early childhood years, young children develop in many ways that enable them to enhance their self-understanding.

Initiative Versus Guilt   In Chapter 1, "Introduction," you read about Erik Erikson's (1968) eight developmental stages that are encountered during certain time periods in the human life span. As you learned in the chapter, Erikson's first stage, trust versus mistrust, describes what he considers to be the main developmental task of infancy. Erikson's psychosocial stage associated with early childhood is *initiative versus guilt.* By now, children have become convinced that they are persons of their own; during early childhood, they begin to discover what kind of person they will become. They identify intensely with their parents, who most of the time appear to them to be powerful and beautiful, although often unreasonable, disagreeable, and sometimes even dangerous. During early childhood, children use their perceptual, motor, cognitive, and language skills to make things happen. They have a surplus of energy that permits them to forget failures quickly and to approach new areas that seem desirable—even if dangerous—with undiminished zest and some increased sense of direction. On their own *initiative,* then, children at this stage exuberantly move out into a wider social world.

The great governor of initiative is *guilt.* Young children's initiative and enthusiasm may bring them not only rewards but also guilt, which lowers self-esteem.

Self-Understanding and Understanding Others   Recent research studies have revealed that young children are more psychologically aware—of themselves and others—than used to be thought (Laible & Thompson, 2007; Mueller & others, 2008). This increased psychological awareness reflects young children's expanding psychological sophistication.

Self-Understanding   In Erikson's portrait of early childhood, the young child clearly has begun to develop **self-understanding,** which is the representation of self, the substance and content of self-conceptions (Harter, 2006). Though not the whole of personal identity, self-understanding provides its rational underpinnings. Mainly through interviews, researchers have probed children's conceptions of many aspects of self-understanding.

As we saw in Chapter 7, "Socioemotional Development in Infancy," early self-understanding involves self-recognition. In early childhood, young children think that the self can be described by many material characteristics, such as size, shape, and color. They distinguish themselves from others through many physical and material attributes. Says 4-year-old Sandra, "I'm different from Jennifer because I have brown hair and she has blond hair." Says 4-year-old Ralph, "I am different from Hank because I am taller and I am different from my sister because I have a bicycle." Physical activities are also a central component of the self in early childhood (Keller, Ford, & Meacham, 1978). For example, preschool children often

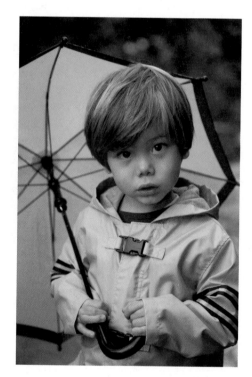

What characterizes self-understanding in young children?

self-understanding The child's cognitive representation of self, the substance and content of the child's self-conceptions.

describe themselves in terms of activities such as play. In sum, in early childhood, children often provide self-descriptions that involve body attributes, material possessions, and physical activities.

Although young children mainly describe themselves in terms of concrete, observable features and action tendencies, at about 4 to 5 years of age, as they hear others use psychological trait and emotion terms, they begin to include these in their own self-descriptions (Marsh, Ellis, & Craven, 2002; Thompson, 2006). Thus, in a self-description, a 4-year-old might say, "I'm not scared. I'm always happy."

Young children's self-descriptions are typically unrealistically positive, as reflected in the comment of the 4-year-old above who says he is always happy, which he is not (Harter, 2006). This optimism occurs because they don't yet distinguish between their desired competence and their actual competence, tend to confuse ability and effort (thinking that differences in ability can be changed as easily as can differences in effort), don't engage in spontaneous social comparison of their abilities with those of others, and tend to compare their present abilities with what they could do at an earlier age (by which they usually look quite good). Perhaps as adults we should all be so optimistic about our abilities! (Thompson, 2008).

Understanding Others   Children also make advances in their understanding of others in early childhood (Bibok, Carpendale, & Lewis, 2008; Thompson, 2009a). As we saw in Chapter 9, "Cognitive Development in Early Childhood," young children's theory of mind includes understanding that other people have emotions and desires. And, at about 4 to 5 years of age, children not only start describing themselves in terms of psychological traits but they also begin to perceive others in terms of psychological traits. Thus, a 4-year-old might say, "My teacher is nice."

Something important for children to develop is an understanding that people don't always give accurate reports of their beliefs (Gee & Heyman, 2007). Researchers have found that even 4-year-olds understand that people may make statements that aren't true to obtain what they want or to avoid trouble (Lee & others, 2002). For example, one recent study revealed that 4- and 5-year-olds were increasingly skeptical of another child's claim to be sick when the children were informed that the child was motivated to avoid having to go to camp (Gee & Heyman, 2007). Another recent study found that at 3 years of age, children mistrusted people who made a single error but it wasn't until 4 years of age that, when deciding whom to trust, children took into account the relative frequency of errors informants made (Pasquini & others, 2007).

Individual differences characterize young children's social understanding (Thomspon, 2009a). Some young children are better than others at understanding what people are feeling and what they desire, for example. To some degree, these individual differences are linked to conversations caregivers have with young children about other people's feelings and desires, and children's opportunities to observe others talking about people's feelings and desires. For example, a mother might say to a 3-year-old, "Next time you should think about Raphael's feelings before you hit him."

Young children are more psychologically aware of themselves and others than used to be thought. Some children are better than others at understanding people's feelings and desires— and, to some degree, these individual differences are influenced by conversations caregivers have with young children about feelings and desires.

Emotional Development

The young child's growing awareness of self is linked to the ability to feel an expanding range of emotions. Young children, like adults, experience many emotions during the course of a day. Their emotional development in early childhood allows them to try to make sense of other people's emotional reactions and to begin to control their own emotions.

Expressing Emotions   Recall from Chapter 7, "Socioemotional Development in Infancy," that even young infants experience emotions such as joy and fear, but to experience *self-conscious emotions,* children must be able to refer to themselves and be aware of themselves as distinct from others (Lewis, 2008). Pride, shame, embarrassment, and guilt are examples of self-conscious emotions. Self-conscious emotions do not appear to develop until self-awareness appears around 18 months of age.

During the early childhood years, emotions such as pride and guilt become more common. They are especially influenced by parents' responses to children's behavior. For example, a young child may experience shame when a parent says, "You should feel bad about biting your sister."

Understanding Emotions

Among the most important changes in emotional development in early childhood is an increased understanding of emotion. During early childhood, young children increasingly understand that certain situations are likely to evoke particular emotions, facial expressions indicate specific emotions, emotions affect behavior, and emotions can be used to influence others' emotions (Cole & others, 2009).

Between 2 and 4 years of age, children considerably increase the number of terms they use to describe emotions. During this time, they are also learning about the causes and consequences of feelings (Denham, Bassett, & Wyatt, 2007).

When they are 4 to 5 years of age, children show an increased ability to reflect on emotions. They also begin to understand that the same event can elicit different feelings in different people. Moreover, they show a growing awareness that they need to manage their emotions to meet social standards. And by 5 years of age, most children can accurately determine emotions that are produced by challenging circumstances and describe strategies they might call on to cope with everyday stress (Cole & others, 2009).

Regulating Emotions

As we saw in Chapter 7, "Socioemotional Development in Infancy," emotion regulation is an important aspect of development. Emotion regulation especially plays a key role in children's ability to manage the demands and conflicts they face in interacting with others (Thompson, 2009a, b).

Emotion–Coaching and Emotion–Dismissing Parents   Parents can play an important role in helping young children regulate their emotions. Depending on how they talk with their children about emotion, parents can be described as taking an *emotion-coaching* or an *emotion-dismissing* approach (Gottman, 2009). The distinction between these approaches is most evident in the way the parent deals with the child's negative emotions (anger, frustration, sadness, and so on). *Emotion-coaching parents* monitor their children's emotions, view their children's negative emotions as opportunities for teaching, assist them in labeling emotions, and coach them in how to deal effectively with emotions. In contrast, *emotion-dismissing parents* view their role as to deny, ignore, or change negative emotions. Researchers have observed that emotion-coaching parents interact with their children in a less rejecting manner, use more scaffolding and praise, and are more nurturant than are emotion-dismissing parents (Gottman & DeClaire, 1997). Moreover, the children of emotion-coaching parents were better at soothing themselves when they got upset, more effective in regulating their negative affect, focused their attention better, and had fewer behavior problems than the children of emotion-dismissing parents. A recent study revealed that having emotion-dismissing parents is linked with children's poor emotion regulation (Lunkenheimer, Shields, & Cortina, 2007).

Regulation of Emotion and Peer Relations   Emotions play a strong role in determining the success of a child's peer relationships (Howes, 2009).

A young child expressing the emotion of shame, which occurs when a child evaluates his or her actions as not living up to standards. A child experiencing shame wishes to hide or disappear. *Why is shame called a self-conscious emotion?*

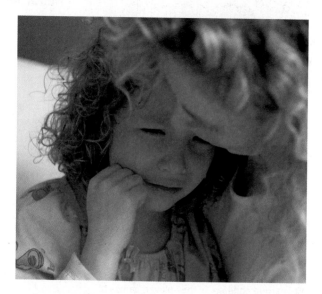

An emotion-coaching parent. *What are some differences in emotion-coaching and emotion-dismissing parents?*

Specifically, the ability to modulate one's emotions is an important skill that benefits children in their relationships with peers (Thompson, Meyer, & Jochem, 2008). Moody and emotionally negative children are more likely to experience rejection by their peers, whereas emotionally positive children are more popular (Stocker & Dunn, 1990). A recent study revealed that 4-year-olds recognized and generated strategies for controlling their anger more than did 3-year-olds (Cole & others, 2009).

Moral Development

Unlike a crying infant, a screaming 5-year-old is likely to be thought responsible for making a fuss. The parents may worry about whether the 5-year-old is a "bad" child. Although there are some who view children as innately good, many developmentalists maintain that just as parents help their children become good readers, musicians, or athletes, parents must nurture goodness and help their children develop morally. **Moral development** involves the development of thoughts, feelings, and behaviors regarding rules and conventions about what people should do in their interactions with other people. Major developmental theories have focused on different aspects of moral development.

Moral Feelings Feelings of anxiety and guilt are central to the account of moral development provided by Sigmund Freud's psychoanalytic theory (initially described in Chapter 1, "Introduction"). According to Freud, to reduce anxiety, avoid punishment, and maintain parental affection, children identify with parents, internalizing their standards of right and wrong, and thus form the *superego*, the moral element of personality.

Freud's ideas are not backed by research, but guilt certainly can motivate moral behavior. Other emotions, however, also contribute to the child's moral development, including positive feelings. One important example is *empathy*, which is responding to another person's feelings with an emotion that echoes the other's feelings (Eisenberg, Fabes, & Spinrad, 2006).

Infants have the capacity for some purely empathic responses, but empathy often requires the ability to discern another's inner psychological states, or what is called *perspective taking*. Learning how to identify a wide range of emotional states in others and to anticipate what kinds of action will improve another person's emotional state help to advance children's moral development (Thompson, 2009c).

Moral Reasoning Interest in how children think about moral issues was stimulated by Jean Piaget (1932), who extensively observed and interviewed children from the ages of 4 through 12. Piaget watched children play marbles to learn how they thought about and used the game's rules. He also asked children about ethical issues—theft, lies, punishment, and justice, for example. Piaget concluded that children go through two distinct stages in how they think about morality.

- From 4 to 7 years of age, children display **heteronomous morality,** the first stage of moral development in Piaget's theory. Children think of justice and rules as unchangeable properties of the world, removed from the control of people.
- From 7 to 10 years of age, children are in a transition, showing some features of the first stage of moral reasoning and some features of the second stage, autonomous morality.
- From about 10 years of age and older, children show **autonomous morality.** They become aware that rules and laws are created by people, and, in judging an action, they consider the actor's intentions as well as the consequences.

Because young children are heteronomous moralists, they judge the rightness or goodness of behavior by considering its consequences, not the intentions of the

*W*hat is moral is what you feel good after and what is immoral is what you feel bad after.

—ERNEST HEMINGWAY
American Author, 20th Century

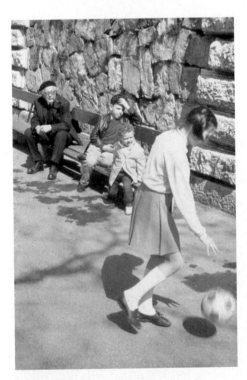

Piaget extensively observed and interviewed 4- to 12-year-old children as they played games to learn how they used and thought about the games' rules.

actor. For example, to the heteronomous moralist, breaking twelve cups accidentally is worse than breaking one cup intentionally. As children develop into moral autonomists, intentions become more important than consequences.

The heteronomous thinker also believes that rules are unchangeable and are handed down by all-powerful authorities. When Piaget suggested to young children that they use new rules in a game of marbles, they resisted. By contrast, older children—moral autonomists—accept change and recognize that rules are merely convenient conventions, subject to change.

The heteronomous thinker also believes in **immanent justice,** the concept that if a rule is broken, punishment will be meted out immediately. The young child believes that a violation is connected automatically to its punishment. Thus, young children often look around worriedly after doing something wrong, expecting inevitable punishment. Immanent justice also implies that if something unfortunate happens to someone, the person must have transgressed earlier. Older children are moral autonomists—that is, they recognize that punishment occurs only if someone witnesses the wrongdoing and that, even then, punishment is not inevitable.

How do these changes in moral reasoning occur? Piaget argued that, as children develop, they become more sophisticated in thinking about social matters, especially about the possibilities and conditions of cooperation. Piaget argued that this social understanding comes about through the mutual give-and-take of peer relations. In the peer group, where others have power and status similar to the child's, plans are negotiated and coordinated, and disagreements are reasoned about and eventually settled. Parent-child relations, in which parents have the power and children do not, are less likely to advance moral reasoning, because rules are often handed down in an authoritarian way.

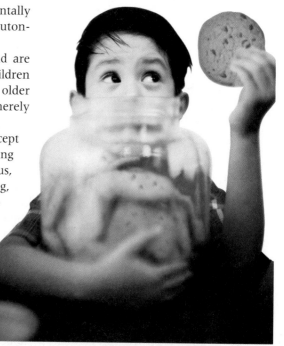

How is this child's moral thinking likely to be different about stealing a cookie depending on whether he is in Piaget's heteronomous or autonomous stage?

Moral Behavior The behavioral and social cognitive approach, initially described in Chapter 1, "Introduction," focuses on moral behavior rather than on moral reasoning (Bugental & Grusec, 2006). It holds that the processes of reinforcement, punishment, and imitation explain the development of moral behavior. When children are rewarded for behavior that is consistent with laws and social conventions, they are likely to repeat that behavior. When models who behave morally are provided, children are likely to adopt their actions. And, when children are punished for immoral behavior, those behaviors are likely to be reduced or eliminated. However, because punishment may have adverse side effects, as we discuss later in this chapter, it needs to be used judiciously and cautiously.

If a 4-year-old boy has been rewarded by his mother for telling the truth when he breaks a glass at home, does that mean that he is likely to tell the truth to his preschool teacher when he knocks over a vase and breaks it? Not necessarily; the situation influences behavior. More than half a century ago, a comprehensive study of thousands of children in many situations—at home, at school, and at church, for example—found that the totally honest child was virtually nonexistent; so was the child who cheated in all situations (Hartshorne & May, 1928–1930). Behavioral and social cognitive researchers emphasize that what children do in one situation is often only weakly related to what they do in other situations. A child might cheat in class but not in a game; a child might steal a piece of candy when alone but not steal it when others are present.

Social cognitive theorists also believe that the ability to resist temptation is closely tied to the development of self-control (Mischel, 2004). To achieve this self-control, children must learn to delay gratification. According to social cognitive theorists, cognitive factors are important in the child's development of self-control (Bandura, 2008, 2009).

Conscience **Conscience** refers to an internal regulation of standards of right and wrong that involves an integration of all three components of moral development

moral development Development that involves thoughts, feelings, and behaviors regarding rules and conventions about what people should do in their interactions with other people.

heteronomous morality The first stage of moral development in Piaget's theory, occurring from approximately 4 to 7 years of age. Justice and rules are conceived of as unchangeable properties of the world, removed from the control of people.

autonomous morality The second stage of moral development in Piaget's theory, displayed by older children (about 10 years of age and older). The child becomes aware that rules and laws are created by people and that, in judging an action, one should consider the actor's intentions as well as the consequences.

immanent justice The concept that, if a rule is broken, punishment will be meted out immediately.

conscience An internal regulation of standards of right and wrong that involves an integration of moral thought, feeling, and behavior.

we have described so far—moral thought, feeling, and behavior (Kochanska & Aksan, 2007). Reflecting the presence of a conscience in young children, researchers have found that young children are aware of right and wrong, have the capacity to show empathy toward others, experience guilt, indicate discomfort following a transgression, and are sensitive to violating rules (Kochanska & Aksan, 2007).

A major interest in young children's conscience focuses on the children's relationship with their caregivers (Thompson, 2009c). Especially important in this regard is the emergence of the young children's willingness to embrace the values of their parents that flows from a positive, close relationship (Kochanska & Aksan, 2007). For example, children who are securely attached are more likely to internalize their parents' values and rules (Thompson, 2009c). In the next section, we further examine the important role of parents in young children's development, with much of this discussion providing more detailed information about how parents influence the development of a child's conscience.

How does parenting contribute to young children's moral development?

Parenting and Young Children's Moral Development Both Piaget and Lawrence Kohlberg held that parents do not provide unique or essential inputs to children's moral development. Parents, in their view, are responsible for providing role-taking opportunities, cognitive conflict, and rules, but peers play the primary role in moral development. Research reveals that both parents and peers contribute to children's moral maturity (Hastings, Utendale, & Sullivan, 2007).

In Ross Thompson's (2006, 2009c) view, young children are moral apprentices, striving to understand what is moral. They can be assisted in this quest by the "sensitive guidance of adult mentors in the home who provide lessons about morality in everyday experiences" (Thompson, Meyer, & McGinley, 2006, p. 290). Among the most important aspects of the relationship between parents and children that contribute to children's moral development are relational quality, parental discipline, proactive strategies, and conversational dialogue.

Parent-child relationships introduce children to the mutual obligations of close relationships (Kochanska & others, 2008; Thompson, Meyer, & Jochem, 2008). Parents' obligations include engaging in positive caregiving and guiding children to become competent human beings. Children's obligations include responding appropriately to parents' initiatives and maintaining a positive relationship with parents. Also, secure attachment may play an important role in children's moral development. A secure attachment can place the child on a positive path for internalizing parents' socializing goals and family values (Kochanska & others, 2004). And a recent study revealed that an early mutually responsive orientation between parents and their infant and a decrease in parents' use of power assertion in disciplining a young child were linked to an increase in the child's internalization and self-regulation (Kochanska & others, 2008).

An important parenting strategy is to proactively avert potential misbehavior by children before it takes place (Thompson, Meyer, & McGinley, 2006). With younger children, being proactive means using diversion, such as distracting their attention or moving them to alternative activities. With older children, being proactive may involve talking with them about values that the parents deem important. Transmitting these values can help older children and adolescents to resist the temptations that inevitably emerge in such contexts as peer relations and the media that can be outside the scope of direct parental monitoring.

Conversations related to moral development can benefit children whether they occur as part of a discipline encounter or outside the encounter in the everyday stream of parent-child interaction (Thompson, Meyer, & McGinley, 2006). The conversations can be planned or spontaneous and can focus on topics such as past events (for example, a child's prior misbehavior or positive moral conduct), shared future events (for example, going somewhere that may involve a temptation and requires positive moral behavior), and immediate events (for example, talking with the child about a sibling's tantrums).

Gender

Recall from Chapter 1, "Introduction," that *gender* refers to the characteristics of people as males and females. **Gender identity** involves a sense of one's own gender, including knowledge, understanding, and acceptance of being male or female (Egan & Perry, 2001). One aspect of gender identity involves knowing whether you are a girl or boy, which most children can do by about 2½ years of age (Blakemore, Berenbaum, & Liben, 2009). **Gender roles** are sets of expectations that prescribe how females or males should think, act, and feel. During the preschool years, most children increasingly act in ways that match their culture's gender roles. **Gender typing** refers to acquisition of a traditional masculine or feminine role. For example, fighting is more characteristic of a traditional masculine role and crying is more characteristic of a traditional feminine role. A recent study revealed that sex-typed behavior (boys playing with cars and girls with jewelry, for example) increased during the preschool years, and children engaging in the most sex-typed behavior during the preschool years were still doing so at 8 years of age (Golombok & others, 2008).

How is gender influenced by biology? By children's social experiences? By cognitive factors?

Biological Influences   Biology clearly plays a role in gender development. Among the possible biological influences are chromosomes, hormones, and evolution.

Chromosomes and Hormones   Biologists have learned a great deal about how sex differences develop. Recall that humans normally have 46 chromosomes arranged in pairs (see Chapter 2, "Biological Beginnings,"). The 23rd pair consists of a combination of X and Y chromosomes, usually two X chromosomes in a female and an X and a Y in a male. In the first few weeks of gestation, however, female and male embryos look alike.

Males start to differ from females when genes on the Y chromosome in the male embryo trigger the development of testes rather than ovaries; the testes secrete copious amounts of the class of hormones known as androgens, which lead to the development of male sex organs. Low levels of androgens in the female embryo allow the normal development of female sex organs.

Thus, hormones play a key role in the development of sex differences (Lippa, 2005). The two main classes of sex hormones are estrogens and androgens, which are secreted by the *gonads* (ovaries in females, testes in males). *Estrogens,* such as estradiol, influence the development of female physical sex characteristics. *Androgens,* such as testosterone, promote the development of male physical sex characteristics. Sex hormones also can influence children's socioemotional development. A recent study revealed that higher fetal testosterone level measured from amniotic fluid was linked to increased male-typical play in 6- to 10-year-old boys and girls (Auyeung & others, 2009).

The Evolutionary Psychology View   How might physical differences between the sexes give rise to psychological differences between males and females? Evolutionary psychology (introduced in Chapter 2, "Biological Beginnings,") offers one answer. According to evolutionary psychology, adaptation during human evolution produced psychological differences between males and females (Buss, 2008). Because of their differing roles in reproduction, males and females faced differing pressures when the human species was evolving. In particular, because having multiple sexual liaisons improves the likelihood that males will pass on their genes, natural selection favored males who adopted short-term mating strategies. These are strategies that allow a male to win the competition with other males for sexual access to females.

gender identity The sense of one's own gender, including knowledge, understanding, and acceptance of being male or female.

gender role A set of expectations that prescribes how females or males should think, act, and feel.

gender typing Acquisition of a traditional masculine or feminine role.

Therefore, say evolutionary psychologists, males evolved dispositions that favor violence, competition, and risk taking.

In contrast, according to evolutionary psychologists, females' contributions to the gene pool were improved when they secured resources that ensured that their offspring would survive; this outcome was promoted by obtaining long-term mates who could provide their offspring with resources and protections (Geher & Miller, 2007). As a consequence, natural selection favored females who devoted effort to parenting and chose successful, ambitious mates who could provide their offspring with resources and protection.

Critics of evolutionary psychology argue that its hypotheses are backed by speculations about prehistory, not evidence, and that in any event people are not locked into behavior that was adaptive in the evolutionary past. Critics also claim that the evolutionary view pays little attention to cultural and individual variations in gender differences (Matlin, 2008).

Social Influences   Many social scientists do not locate the cause of psychological gender differences in biological dispositions. Rather, they argue that these differences are due to social experiences. Explanations for how gender differences come about through experience include both social and cognitive theories.

Social Theories of Gender   Three main social theories of gender have been proposed—social role theory, psychoanalytic theory, and social cognitive theory. Alice Eagly (2001, 2009) proposed **social role theory,** which states that gender differences result from the contrasting roles of women and men. In most cultures around the world, women have less power and status than men, and they control fewer resources (UNICEF, 2009). Compared with men, women perform more domestic work, spend fewer hours in paid employment, receive lower pay, and are more thinly represented in the highest levels of organizations. In Eagly's view, as women adapted to roles with less power and less status in society, they showed more cooperative, less dominant profiles than men. Thus, the social hierarchy and division of labor are important causes of gender differences in power, assertiveness, and nurture.

The **psychoanalytic theory of gender** stems from Freud's view that the preschool child develops a sexual attraction to the opposite-sex parent. This is the process known as the Oedipus complex (for boys) or Electra complex (for girls). At 5 or 6 years of age, the child renounces this attraction because of anxious feelings. Subsequently, the child identifies with the same-sex parent, unconsciously adopting the same-sex parent's characteristics. However, developmentalists have observed that gender development does not proceed as Freud proposed (Blakemore, Berenbaum, & Liben, 2009). Children become gender-typed much earlier than 5 or 6 years of age, and they become masculine or feminine even when the same-sex parent is not present in the family.

The social cognitive approach discussed in Chapter 2, "Biological Beginnings," provides an alternative explanation of how children develop gender-typed behavior. According to the **social cognitive theory of gender,** children's gender development occurs through observing and imitating what other people say and do, and through being rewarded and punished for gender-appropriate and gender-inappropriate behavior (Bussey & Bandura, 1999). From birth onward, males and females are treated differently. When infants and toddlers show gender differences, adults tend to reward them. Parents often use rewards and punishments to teach their daughters to be feminine ("Karen, you are being a good girl when you play gently with your doll") and their sons to be masculine ("Keith, a boy as big as you is not supposed to cry"). Parents, however, are only one of many sources through which children learn gender roles (Blakemore, Berenbaum, & Liben, 2009). Culture, schools, peers, the media, and other family members also provide gender-role models. For example, children also learn about gender from observing other adults in the neighborhood and on television

social role theory A theory that gender differences result from the contrasting roles of men and women.

psychoanalytic theory of gender A theory deriving from Freud's view that the preschool child develops a sexual attraction to the opposite-sex parent, by approximately 5 or 6 years of age renounces this attraction because of anxious feelings, and subsequently identifies with the same-sex parent, unconsciously adopting the same-sex parent's characteristics.

social cognitive theory of gender A theory that emphasizes that children's gender development occurs through the observation and imitation of gender behavior and through the rewards and punishments children experience for gender-appropriate and gender-inappropriate behavior.

(Bugental & Grusec, 2006). As children get older, peers become increasingly important. Let's take a closer look at the influence of parents and peers.

Parental Influences Parents, by action and by example, influence their children's gender development (Gore, 2009). Both mothers and fathers are psychologically important to their children's gender development (Grusec & Davidov, 2007). Cultures around the world, however, tend to give mothers and fathers different roles (Kagitcibasi, 2007). A research review provided these conclusions (Bronstein, 2006):

- *Mothers' socialization strategies.* In many cultures mothers, socialize their daughters to be more obedient and responsible than their sons. They also place more restrictions on daughters' autonomy.

- *Fathers' socialization strategies.* Fathers show more attention to sons than to daughters, engage in more activities with sons, and put forth more effort to promote sons' intellectual development.

Thus, despite increased awareness in the United States and other Western nations of the negative outcomes of gender stereotyping, many parents continue to foster behaviors and perceptions that reflect traditional gender-role norms (Bronstein, 2006).

Peer Influences Parents provide the earliest discrimination of gender roles, but before long, peers join the process of responding to and modeling masculine and feminine behavior. In fact, peers become so important to gender development that the playground has been called "gender school" (Luria & Herzog, 1985).

Peers extensively reward and punish gender behavior (Leaper & Friedman, 2007). For example, when children play in ways that the culture says are sex-appropriate, their peers tend to reward them. But peers often reject children who act in a manner that is considered more characteristic of the other gender (Matlin, 2008). A little girl who brings a doll to the park may find herself surrounded by new friends; a little boy might be jeered. However, there is greater pressure for boys to conform to a traditional male role than for girls to conform to a traditional female role (Fagot, Rodgers, & Leinbach, 2000). For example, a preschool girl who wants to wear boys' clothing receives considerably more approval than a boy who wants to wear a dress. The very term "tomboy" implies broad social acceptance of girls' adopting traditional male behaviors.

Gender molds important aspects of peer relations. It influences the composition of children's groups, the size of groups, and interactions within a group (Maccoby, 1998, 2002):

- *Gender composition of children's groups.* Around the age of 3, children already show a preference to spend time with same-sex playmates. From 4 to 12 years of age, this preference for playing in same-sex groups increases, and during the elementary school years children spend a large majority of their free time with children of their own sex (see Figure 10.1).

- *Group size.* From about 5 years of age onward, boys are more likely to associate together in larger clusters than girls are. Boys are also more likely to participate in organized group games than girls are. In one study, same-sex groups of six children were permitted to use play materials in any way they wished (Benenson, Apostolaris, & Parnass, 1997). Girls were more likely than boys to play in dyads or triads, whereas boys were more likely to interact in larger groups and seek to attain a group goal.

- *Interaction in same-sex groups.* Boys are more likely than girls to engage in rough-and-tumble play, competition, conflict, ego displays, risk taking, and seeking dominance. By contrast, girls are more likely to engage in "collaborative discourse," in which they talk and act in a more reciprocal manner.

First imagine that this is a photograph of a baby girl. *What expectations would you have for her?* Then imagine that this is a photograph of a baby boy. *What expectations would you have for him?*

How would you...?
As a human development and family studies professional, how would you describe the ways in which parents influence their children's notions of gender roles?

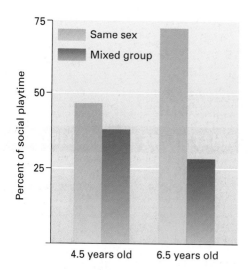

FIGURE 10.1 Developmental Changes in Percentage of Time Spent in Same-Sex and Mixed-Group Settings Observations of children show that they are more likely to play in same-sex than mixed-sex groups. This tendency increases between 4 and 6 years of age.

Cognitive Influences   Observation, imitation, rewards and punishment—these are the mechanisms by which gender develops according to social cognitive theory. Interactions between the child and the social environment are the main keys to gender development in this view. Some critics who adopt a cognitive approach argue that this explanation pays too little attention to the child's own mind and understanding, and portrays the child as passively acquiring gender roles (Martin & Ruble, 2004).

One influential cognitive theory is **gender schema theory,** which states that gender typing emerges as children gradually develop gender schemas of what is gender-appropriate and gender-inappropriate in their culture (Blakemore, Berenbaum, & Liben, 2009; Zosuls, Lurye, & Ruble, 2008). A *schema* is a cognitive structure, a network of associations that guide an individual's perceptions. A *gender schema* organizes the world in terms of female and male. Children are internally motivated to perceive the world and to act in accordance with their developing schemas. Bit by bit, children pick up what is gender-appropriate and gender-inappropriate in their culture, and develop gender schemas that shape how they perceive the world and what they remember. Children are motivated to act in ways that conform with these gender schemas. Thus, gender schemas fuel gender typing.

Review and Reflect: Learning Goal 1

1   **Discuss emotional and personality development in early childhood**

REVIEW

- What changes in the self occur during early childhood?
- What changes take place in emotional development in early childhood?
- What are some key aspects of moral development in young children?
- How does gender develop in young children?

REFLECT

- Which theory of gender development do you find most persuasive? What might an eclectic theoretical view of gender development be like? (You might want to review the discussion of an eclectic theoretical orientation in Chapter 1, "Introduction.")

---

2   WHAT ROLES DO FAMILIES PLAY IN YOUNG CHILDREN'S DEVELOPMENT?

| Parenting | Child Maltreatment | Sibling Relationships and Birth Order | The Changing Family in a Changing Social World |

gender schema theory   The theory that gender typing emerges as children gradually develop gender schemas of what is considered gender-appropriate and gender-inappropriate in their culture.

Attachment to a caregiver is a key social relationship during infancy, but we saw in Chapter 7, "Socioemotional Development in Infancy," that some experts maintain that secure attachment and the infant years have been overdramatized as determinants of children's development. Social and emotional development is also shaped by other relationships and by temperament, contexts, and social experiences in the early childhood years and later. In this section, we discuss social relationships of early childhood beyond attachment. We explore the different types of parenting, child maltreatment, sibling relationships, and variations in family structures.

Calvin and Hobbes

CALVIN AND HOBBES © 1993 Watterson. Reprinted with permission of UNIVERSAL PRESS SYNDICATE. All rights reserved.

Parenting

A few years ago, there was considerable interest in Mozart CDs that were marketed with the promise that playing them would enrich infants' and young children's brains. Some of the parents who bought them probably thought, "I don't have enough time to spend with my children, so I'll just play these intellectual CDs and then they won't need me as much." Similarly, one-minute bedtime stories are being marketed for parents to read to their children (Walsh, 2000). There are one-minute bedtime bear books, puppy books, and so on. Parents who buy them know it is good for them to read with their children, but they don't want to spend a lot of time doing it. Behind the popularity of these products is an unfortunate theme that suggests that parenting can be done quickly, with little or no inconvenience (Sroufe, 2000).

What is wrong with these quick-fix approaches to parenting? Good parenting takes time and effort (Chen, 2009a, b). You can't do it in a minute here and a minute there. You can't do it with CDs.

Of course, it's not just the quantity of time parents spend with children that is important for children's development—the quality of the parenting is clearly important (Benzies, Keown, & Magill-Evans, 2009; Gross & others, 2009). To understand variations in parenting, let's consider the styles parents use when they interact with their children, how they discipline their children, and coparenting.

Baumrind's Parenting Styles   Diana Baumrind (1971) holds that parents should be neither punitive nor aloof. Rather, they should develop rules for their children and be affectionate with them. She has described four types of parenting styles:

- **Authoritarian parenting** is a restrictive, punitive style in which parents exhort the child to follow their directions and respect their work and effort. The authoritarian parent places firm limits and controls on the child and allows little verbal exchange. For example, an authoritarian parent might say, "You do it my way or else." Authoritarian parents also might spank the child frequently, enforce rules rigidly but not explain them, and show rage toward the child. Children of authoritarian parents are often unhappy, fearful, and anxious about comparing themselves with others; fail to initiate activity; and have weak communication skills. Sons of authoritarian parents may behave aggressively (Hart & others, 2003).

- **Authoritative parenting** encourages children to be independent but still places limits and controls on their actions. Extensive verbal give-and-take is allowed, and parents are warm and nurturant toward the child. An authoritative parent might put his arm around the child in a comforting way and say, "You know you should not have done that. Let's talk about how you can handle the situation better next time." Authoritative parents show pleasure and support in response to children's constructive behavior. They also expect mature, independent, and age-appropriate behavior by children. Children

> *Parenting is a very important profession, but no test of fitness for it is ever imposed in the interest of children.*
>
> **—George Bernard Shaw**
> *Irish Playwright, 20th Century*

How Would You...?
As a human development and family studies professional, how would you characterize the parenting style that prevails within your own family?

authoritarian parenting A restrictive punitive style in which parents exhort the child to follow their directions and to respect work and effort. The authoritarian parent places firm limits and controls on the child and allows little verbal exchange. Authoritarian parenting is associated with children's social incompetence.

authoritative parenting A parenting style in which parents encourage their children to be independent but still place limits and controls on their actions. Extensive verbal give-and-take is allowed, and parents are warm and nurturant toward the child. Authoritative parenting is associated with children's social competence.

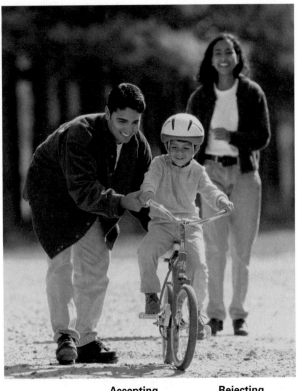

	Accepting, responsive	Rejecting, unresponsive
Demanding, controlling	Authoritative	Authoritarian
Undemanding, uncontrolling	Indulgent	Neglectful

FIGURE 10.2 Classification of Parenting Styles The four types of parenting styles (authoritative, authoritarian, indulgent, and neglectful) involve the dimensions of acceptance and responsiveness, on the one hand, and demand and control on the other. For example, authoritative parenting involves being both accepting/responsive and demanding/controlling.

How Would You...?
As a psychologist, how would you use the research on parenting styles to design a parent education class that teaches effective skills for interacting with young children?

neglectful parenting A style of parenting in which the parent is very uninvolved in the child's life; it is associated with children's social incompetence, especially a lack of self-control.

indulgent parenting A style of parenting in which parents are highly involved with their children but place few demands or controls on them. Indulgent parenting is associated with children's social incompetence, especially a lack of self-control.

whose parents are authoritative are often cheerful, self-controlled and self-reliant, and achievement-oriented; they tend to maintain friendly relations with peers, cooperate with adults, and cope well with stress.

- **Neglectful parenting** is a style in which the parent is very uninvolved in the child's life. Children whose parents are neglectful develop the sense that other aspects of the parents' lives are more important than they are. These children tend to be socially incompetent. Many have poor self-control and don't handle independence well. They frequently have low self-esteem, are immature, and may be alienated from the family. In adolescence, they may show patterns of truancy and delinquency.

- **Indulgent parenting** is a style in which parents are highly involved with their children but place few demands or controls on them. Such parents let their children do what they want. The result is that the children never learn to control their own behavior and always expect to get their way. Some parents deliberately rear their children in this way because they believe the combination of warm involvement and few restraints will produce a creative, confident child. However, children whose parents are indulgent rarely learn respect for others and have difficulty controlling their behavior. They might be domineering, egocentric, noncompliant, and have difficulties in peer relations.

These four classifications of parenting involve combinations of acceptance and responsiveness on the one hand and demand and control on the other (Maccoby & Martin, 1983). How these dimensions combine to produce authoritarian, authoritative, neglectful, and indulgent parenting is shown in Figure 10.2. Especially for non-Latino White children, authoritative parenting is linked with more positive child outcomes than the other three parenting styles (Bornstein & Zlotnik, 2008).

Parenting Styles in Context Researchers have found that in some ethnic groups, aspects of the authoritarian style may be associated with more positive child outcomes than Baumrind predicts (Parke & Buriel, 2006). Elements of the authoritarian style may take on different meanings and have different effects depending on the context.

For example, Asian-American parents often continue aspects of traditional Asian child-rearing practices that have sometimes been described as authoritarian. The parents exert considerable control over their children's lives. However, Ruth Chao (2005, 2007; Chao & Tseng, 2002) argues that the style of parenting used by many Asian American parents is distinct from the domineering control of the authoritarian style. Instead, Chao argues that the control reflects concern and involvement in their children's lives and is best conceptualized as a type of training. The high academic achievement of Asian American children may be a consequence of their "training" parents (Stevenson & Zusho, 2002).

An emphasis on requiring respect and obedience is also associated with the authoritarian style, but in Latino child rearing this focus may be positive rather than punitive. Rather than suppressing the child's development, it may encourage the development of a different type of self. Latino child-rearing practices encourage the development of a self and identity that is embedded in the family and requires respect and obedience (Harwood & others, 2002). Furthermore, many Latino families have several generations living together and helping each other (Zinn & Wells, 2000). In these circumstances, emphasizing respect and obedience by children may be part of maintaining a harmonious home and may be important in the formation of the child's identity.

Even physical punishment, another characteristic of the authoritarian style, may have varying effects in different contexts. African American parents are more likely than non-Latino White parents to use physical punishment (Deater-Deckard & Dodge, 1997). However, the use of physical punishment has been linked with increased externalized child problems (such as acting out and high levels of aggression) in non-Latino White families but not in African American families. One explanation of this finding points to the need for African American parents to enforce rules in the dangerous environments in which they are more likely to live (Harrison-Hale, McLoyd, & Smedley, 2004). In this context, requiring obedience to parental authority may be an adaptive strategy to keep children from engaging in antisocial behavior that can have serious consequences for the victim or the perpetrator. As we see next, though, overall, the use of physical punishment in disciplining children raises many concerns.

Further Thoughts on Parenting Styles   Several caveats about parenting styles are in order. First, the parenting styles do not capture the important themes of reciprocal socialization and synchrony (Laursen & Collins, 2009). Keep in mind that children socialize parents, just as parents socialize children (Kuczynski & Parkin, 2007). Second, many parents use a combination of techniques rather than a single technique, although one technique may be dominant. Although consistent parenting is usually recommended, the wise parent may sense the importance of being more permissive in certain situations, more authoritarian in others, and yet more authoritative in others. Also, some critics argue that the concept of parenting style is too broad and that more research needs to be conducted to "unpack" parenting styles by studying various components that comprise the styles (Maccoby, 2007). For example, is parental monitoring more important than warmth in predicting child and adolescent outcomes?

Punishment   For centuries, corporal (physical) punishment, such as spanking, has been considered a necessary and even desirable method of disciplining children. Use of corporal punishment is legal in every state in America. A national survey of U.S. parents with 3- and 4-year-old children found that 26 percent of parents reported spanking their children frequently and 67 percent of the parents reported yelling at their children frequently (Regalado & others, 2004). A cross-cultural comparison found that individuals in the United States were among those with the most favorable attitudes toward corporal punishment and were the most likely to remember it being used by their parents (Curran & others, 2001) (see Figure 10.3).

An increasing number of studies have examined the outcomes of physically punishing children, although those that have been conducted are correlational. Clearly, it would be highly unethical to randomly assign parents to either spank or not spank their children in an experimental study. Recall that cause and effect cannot be determined in a correlational study. In one correlational study, spanking by parents was linked with children's antisocial behavior, including cheating, telling lies, being mean to others, bullying, getting into fights, and being disobedient (Strauss, Sugarman, & Giles-Sims, 1997).

A research review concluded that corporal punishment by parents is associated with higher levels of immediate compliance and aggression by the children (Gershoff, 2002). The review also found that corporal punishment is associated with lower levels of moral internalization and mental health (Gershoff, 2002). One study revealed that children whose parents hit or slapped them in the prior two weeks showed more emotional and adjustment problems than children who had not been hit or slapped by parents in the same time frame (Aucoin, Frick, & Bodin, 2006). A recent study also found a link between the use of physical punishment by parents and children's negative behavioral adjustment at 36 months and in the first grade (Mulvaney & Mebert, 2007). Another recent study also discovered that a history of harsh physical discipline was

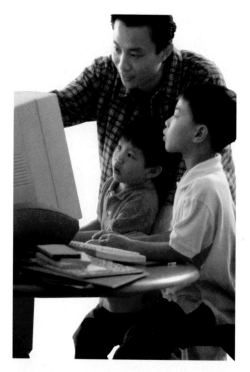

According to Ruth Chao, what type of parenting style do many Asian American parents use?

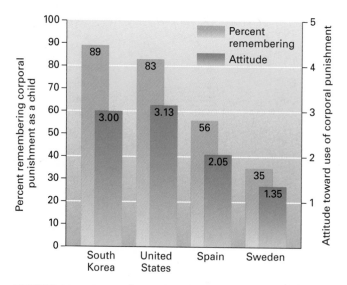

FIGURE 10.3 Corporal Punishment in Different Countries A 5-point scale was used to assess attitudes toward corporal punishment with scores closer to 1 indicating an attitude against its use and scores closer to 5 suggesting an attitude favoring its use. *Why are studies of corporal punishment correlational studies, and how does that affect their usefulness?*

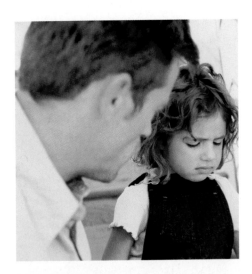

How do most child psychologists recommend handling a child's misbehavior?

How Would You...?
As a human development and family studies professional, how would you advise parents about why they should not spank their children and what alternatives to spanking would you recommend?

linked to adolescent depression and externalized problems, such as juvenile delinquency (Bender & others, 2007).

Some critics, though, argue that the research evidence is not yet sound enough to warrant a blanket injunction against corporal punishment, especially mild corporal punishment (Kazdin & Benjet, 2003).

What are some reasons for avoiding spanking or similar punishments? The reasons include the following:

- When adults punish a child by yelling, screaming, or spanking, they are presenting children with out-of-control models for handling stressful situations. Children may imitate this aggressive, out-of-control behavior (Sim & Ong, 2005).

- Punishment can instill fear, rage, or avoidance. For example, spanking the child may cause the child to avoid being around the parent and to fear the parent.

- Punishment tells children what not to do rather than what to do. Children should be given feedback, such as "Why don't you try this?"

- Punishment can be abusive. Parents might unintentionally become so aroused when they are punishing the child that they become abusive (Durrant, 2008).

Most child psychologists recommend handling misbehavior by reasoning with the child, especially explaining the consequences of the child's actions for others. *Time out*, in which the child is removed from a setting that offers positive reinforcement for bad behavior, can also be effective. For example, when the child has misbehaved, a parent might take away TV viewing for a specified time.

In Chapter 7, "Socioemotional Development in Infancy," we described the family as a system and discussed possible links between marital relationships and parenting practices. To read about a family systems study involving marital conflict and the use of physical punishment, see the *Research in Children's Development* interlude.

Research in Children's Development

MARITAL CONFLICT, INDIVIDUAL HOSTILITY, AND THE USE OF PHYSICAL PUNISHMENT

A longitudinal study assessed couples as they made the transition to becoming parents to investigate possible links between marital conflict, individual adult hostility, and the use of physical punishment with young children (Kanoy & others, 2003). Before the birth of the first child, the level of marital conflict was observed in a marital problem-solving discussion; answers to questionnaires regarding individual characteristics were also obtained. Thus, these characteristics of the couples were not influenced by characteristics of the child. When the children were 2 and 5 years old, the couples were interviewed about the frequency and intensity of their physical punishment of the children. At both ages, the parents' level of marital conflict was again observed in a marital problem-solving discussion.

The researchers found that both hostility and marital conflict were linked with the use of physical punishment. Individuals with high rates of hostility on the prenatal measures used more frequent and more severe physical punishment with their children. The same was evident for marital conflict—when marital conflict was high, both mothers and fathers were more likely to use physical punishment in disciplining their young children.

If parents who have a greater likelihood of using physical punishment can be identified in prenatal classes, these families could be encouraged to use other forms of discipline before they get into a pattern of physically punishing their children.

Careers in Children's Development

Darla Botkin, Marriage and Family Therapist

Darla Botkin is a marriage and family therapist who teaches, conducts research, and engages in marriage and family therapy. She is on the faculty of the University of Kentucky. Botkin obtained a bachelor's degree in elementary education with a concentration in special education and then went on to receive a master's degree in early childhood education. She spent the next six years working with children and their families in a variety of settings, including child care, elementary school, and Head Start. These experiences led Botkin to recognize the interdependence of the developmental settings that children and their parents experience (such as home, school, and work). She returned to graduate school and obtained a Ph.D. in family studies from the University of Tennessee. She then became a faculty member in the Family Studies program at the University of Kentucky. Completing further coursework and clinical training in marriage and family therapy, she became certified as a marriage and family therapist.

Botkin's current interests include working with young children in family therapy, gender and ethnic issues in family therapy, and the role of spirituality in family wellness.

Darla Botkin (*left*), conducting a family therapy session.

Coparenting The relationship between marital conflict and the use of punishment highlights the importance of *coparenting,* which is the support that parents provide one another in jointly raising a child (Parke & others, 2008). Poor coordination between parents, undermining of the other parent, lack of cooperation and warmth, and disconnection by one parent are conditions that place children at risk for problems (McHale, 2007; McHale & Sullivan, 2008; Schoppe-Sullivan & others, 2007). A recent study revealed that coparenting predicted young children's effortful control above and beyond maternal and paternal parenting (Karreman & others, 2008).

Parents who do not spend enough time with their children or who have problems in child rearing can benefit from counseling and therapy. To read about the work of marriage and family counselor Darla Botkin, see the *Careers in Children's Development* Profile.

Child Maltreatment

Unfortunately, punishment sometimes leads to the abuse of infants and children (Kennedy, 2009; Miller-Perrin, Perrin, & Kocur, 2009). In 2006, approximately 905,000 U.S. children were found to be victims of child abuse (U.S. Department of Health and Human Services, 2008). Eighty-four percent of these children were abused by a parent or parents. Laws in many states now require physicians and teachers to report suspected cases of child abuse, yet many cases go unreported, especially those of battered infants.

Whereas the public and many professionals use the term *child abuse* to refer to both abuse and neglect, developmentalists increasingly use the term *child maltreatment* (Cicchetti & others, 2009). This term does not have quite the emotional impact of the term *abuse* and acknowledges that maltreatment includes diverse conditions.

> *Child maltreatment involves grossly inadequate and destructive aspects of parenting.*
>
> —**DANTE CICCHETTI**
> *Contemporary Developmental Psychologist, University of Minnesota.*

How Would You...?
As a health-care professional, how would you work with parents during infant and child checkups to prevent child maltreatment?

Types of Child Maltreatment   The four main types of child maltreatment are physical abuse, child neglect, sexual abuse, and emotional abuse (National Clearinghouse on Child Abuse and Neglect, 2004):

- *Physical abuse* is characterized by the infliction of physical injury as result of punching, beating, kicking, biting, burning, shaking, or otherwise physically harming a child. The parent or other person may not have intended to hurt the child; the injury may have resulted from excessive physical punishment.

- *Child neglect* is characterized by failure to provide for the child's basic needs. Neglect can be physical (abandonment, for example), educational (allowing chronic truancy, for example), or emotional (marked inattention to the child's needs, for example). Child neglect is by far the most common form of child maltreatment. In every country where relevant data have been collected, neglect occurs up to three times more often than abuse (Benoit, Coolbear, & Crawford, 2008).

- *Sexual abuse* includes fondling a child's genitals, intercourse, incest, rape, sodomy, exhibitionism, and commercial exploitation through prostitution or the production of pornographic materials (Johnson, 2008).

- *Emotional abuse (psychological/verbal abuse/mental injury)* includes acts or omissions by parents or other caregivers that have caused, or could cause, serious behavioral, cognitive, or emotional problems (Wekerle & others, 2009).

Although any of these forms of child maltreatment may be found separately, they often occur in combination. Emotional abuse is almost always present when other forms are identified.

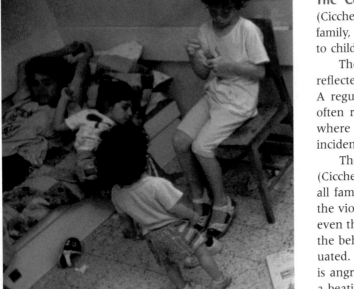

Children at a shelter for domestic violence in Tel Aviv, Israel.

The Context of Abuse   No single factor causes child maltreatment (Cicchetti & others, 2009). A combination of factors, including the culture, family, and developmental characteristics of the child, likely contributes to child maltreatment (Appleton & Stanley, 2009; Prinz & others, 2009).

The extensive violence that takes place in American culture is reflected in the occurrence of violence in the family (Durrant, 2008). A regular diet of violence appears on television screens, and parents often resort to power assertion as a disciplinary technique. In China, where physical punishment is rarely used to discipline children, the incidence of child abuse is reported to be very low.

The family itself is obviously a key part of the context of abuse (Cicchetti & others, 2009; Macmillan & others 2009). The interactions of all family members need to be considered, regardless of who performs the violent acts against the child (Cicchetti & Toth, 2006). For example, even though the father may be the one who physically abuses the child, the behavior of the mother, the child, and siblings also should be evaluated. A mother who conveniently goes shopping whenever the father is angry with the child, or siblings who tease the child for "deserving" a beating, may contribute to the abuse.

Were parents who abuse children abused by their own parents? About one-third of parents who were abused themselves when they were young go on to abuse their own children (Cicchetti & Toth, 2006). Thus, some, but not a majority, of parents are involved in an intergenerational transmission of abuse (Dixon, Browne, & Hamilton-Giachritsis, 2005). Mothers who break out of the intergenerational transmission of abuse often report having had at least one warm, caring adult in their background; have a close, positive marital relationship; and have received therapy (Egeland, Jacobvitz, & Sroufe, 1988).

How Would You...?
As an educator, how would you explain the potential impact of maltreatment in the home on a child's schooling?

Developmental Consequences of Abuse   Among the consequences of child maltreatment in childhood and adolescence are poor emotion regulation, attachment problems, problems in peer relations, difficulty in adapting to school, and other psychological problems such as depression and delinquency. As shown in Figure 10.4, maltreated young children in foster care were more likely to show abnormal stress hormone levels than middle-socioeconomic-status (middle-SES) young children living with their birth family (Gunnar, Fisher, & the Early Experience, Stress, and Prevention Network, 2006). In this study, the abnormal stress hormone levels were mainly present in the foster children who were neglected, best described as "institutional neglect" (Fisher, 2005). Abuse also may have this effect on young children (Gunnar, Fisher, & the Early Experience, Stress, and Prevention Network, 2006). Adolescents who experienced abuse or neglect as children are more likely than adolescents who were not maltreated as children to engage in violent romantic relationships, delinquency, sexual risk taking, and substance abuse (Wekerle & others, 2009). Later, during the adult years, individuals who were maltreated as children often have difficulty in establishing and maintaining healthy intimate relationships (Dozier, Stovall-McClough, & Albus, 2009). As adults, maltreated children are also at higher risk for violent behavior toward other adults—especially dating partners and marital partners—as well as for substance abuse, anxiety, and depression (Maas, Herrenkohl, & Sousa, 2008; Miller-Perrin, Perrin, & Kocur, 2009).

What can be done to prevent or reduce the incidence of child maltreatment? In one study of maltreating mothers and their 1-year-olds, two treatments were effective in reducing child maltreatment: (1) home visitation that emphasized improved parenting, coping with stress, and increasing support for the mother; and (2) parent-infant psychotherapy that focused on improving maternal-infant attachment (Cicchetti, Toth, and Rogosch, 2005).

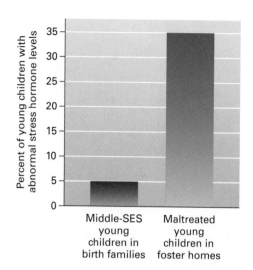

FIGURE 10.4 Abnormal Stress Hormone Levels in Young Children in Different Types of Rearing Conditions

Sibling Relationships and Birth Order

How do developmentalists characterize sibling relationships? How extensively does birth order influence behavior?

Sibling Relationships   Approximately 80 percent of American children have one or more siblings—that is, sisters and brothers (Dunn, 2007). Any of you who have grown up with siblings probably have a rich memory of aggressive, hostile interchanges. Siblings in the presence of each other when they are 2 to 4 years of age, on average, have a conflict once every 10 minutes and then the conflicts go down somewhat from 5 to 7 years of age (Kramer, 2006). What do parents do when they encounter siblings having a verbal or physical confrontation? One study revealed that they do one of three things: (1) intervene and try to help them resolve the conflict, (2) admonish or threaten them, or (3) do nothing at all (Kramer & Perozynski, 1999). Of interest is that in families with two siblings 2 to 5 years of age, the most frequent parental reaction is do nothing at all.

Laurie Kramer (2006), who had conducted a number of research studies on siblings, says that not intervening and letting sibling conflict escalate are not good strategies. She developed a program titled, "More Fun with Sisters and Brothers," which teaches 4- to 8-year-old siblings social skills for developing positive interactions (Kramer & Radey, 1997). Among the social skills taught in the program are how to appropriately initiate play, how to accept and refuse invitations to play, how to take another's perspective, how to deal with angry feelings, and how to manage conflict. A recent study of 5- to 10-year-old siblings and their parents found that training parents to mediate sibling disputes increased children's understanding of conflicts and reduced sibling conflict (Smith & Ross, 2007).

However, conflict is only one of the many dimensions of sibling relations (Steelman & Koch, 2009). Sibling relations include helping, sharing, teaching, fighting, and playing—and siblings can act as emotional supports, rivals, and communication partners (Howe & Recchia, 2008).

What characterizes children's sibling relationships?

The one-child family is becoming much more common in China because of the strong motivation to limit the population growth in the People's Republic of China. The policy is still relatively new, and its effects on children have not been fully examined. *In general, though, what have researchers found the only child to be like?*

Judy Dunn (2007), a leading expert on sibling relationships, recently described three important characteristics of sibling relationships:

- *Emotional quality of the relationship.* Both intensive positive and negative emotions are often expressed by siblings toward each other. Many children have mixed feelings toward their siblings.

- *Familiarity and intimacy of the relationship.* Siblings typically know each other very well and this intimacy suggests that they can either provide support or tease and undermine each other, depending on the situation.

- *Variation in sibling relationships.* Some siblings describe their relationships more positively than others. Thus, there is considerable variation in sibling relationships. Above we saw that many siblings have mixed feelings about each other, but some children mainly describe their sibling in warm, affectionate ways, whereas others primarily talk about how irritating and mean a sibling is.

Birth Order   Whether a child has older or younger siblings has been linked to development of certain personality characteristics. For example, a recent review concluded that "firstborns are the most intelligent, achieving, and conscientious, while later-borns are the most rebellious, liberal, and agreeable" (Paulhus, 2008, p. 210). Compared with later-born children, firstborn children have also been described as more adult-oriented, helpful, conforming, and self-controlled. However, when such birth order differences are reported, they often are small.

What might account for even small differences related to birth order? Proposed explanations usually point to variations in interactions with parents and siblings associated with being in a particular position in the family. This is especially true in the case of the firstborn child (Teti, 2001). The oldest child is the only one who does not have to share parental love and affection with other siblings—until another sibling comes along. An infant requires more attention than an older child; thus, the firstborn sibling receives less attention after the newborn arrives. Does this result in conflict between parents and the firstborn? In one research study, mothers became more negative, coercive, and restraining and played less with the firstborn following the birth of a second child (Dunn & Kendrick, 1982).

What is the only child like? The popular conception is that the only child is a "spoiled brat," with such undesirable characteristics as dependency, lack of self-control, and self-centered behavior. But researchers present a more positive portrayal of the only child. Only children often are achievement-oriented and display a desirable personality, especially in comparison with later-borns and children from large families (Falbo & Poston, 1993).

So far, our discussion suggests that birth order might be a strong predictor of behavior. However, an increasing number of family researchers stress that when all of the factors that influence behavior are considered, birth order itself shows limited ability to predict behavior. Think about some of the other important factors in children's lives that influence their behavior beyond birth order. They include heredity, models of competency or incompetency that parents present to children on a daily basis, peer influences, school influences, socioeconomic factors, sociohistorical factors, and cultural variations. When someone says firstborns are always like this but last-borns are always like that, the person is making overly simplistic statements that do not adequately take into account the complexity of influences on a child's development.

The Changing Family in a Changing Social World

Beyond variations in the number of siblings, the families that children experience differ in many important ways. The number of children growing up in single-parent

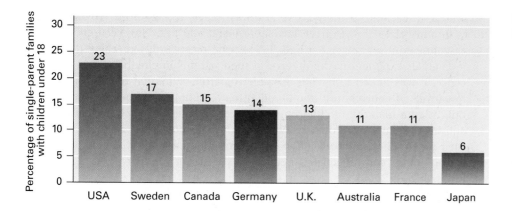

FIGURE 10.5 Single-Parent Families in Different Countries

families is staggering. As shown in Figure 10.5, the United States has one of the highest percentages of single-parent families in the world. Among two-parent families, there are those in which both parents work, or that have divorced parents who have remarried, or that have gay or lesbian parents. Differences in culture and SES also influence families. How do these variations in families affect children?

Working Parents   More than one of every two U.S. mothers with a child under the age of 5 is in the labor force; more than two of every three with a child from 6 to 17 years of age is. Maternal employment is a part of modern life, but its effects are still debated.

Work can produce positive and negative effects on parenting (Han, 2009). Recent research indicates that what matters for children's development is the nature of parents' work rather than whether one or both parents work outside the home (Clarke-Stewart, 2006; Goldberg & Lucas-Thompson, 2008). Ann Crouter (2006) described how parents bring their experiences at work into their homes. She concluded that parents who have poor working conditions, such as long hours, overtime work, stressful work, and lack of autonomy at work, are likely to be more irritable home and engage in less effective parenting than their counterparts who have better work conditions in their jobs. A consistent finding is that the children (especially girls) of working mothers engage in less gender stereotyping and have more egalitarian views of gender (Goldberg & Lucas-Thompson, 2008).

Children in Divorced Families   Divorce rates changed dramatically in the United States and many countries around the world in the late twentieth century (Amato & Irving, 2006). The U.S. divorce rate increased enormously in the 1960s and 1970s but has declined since the 1980s. However, the divorce rate in the United States is still much higher than in most other countries.

It is estimated that 40 percent of children born to married parents in the United States will experience their parents' divorce (Hetherington & Stanley-Hagan, 2002). Let's examine some important questions about children in divorced families:

- *Are children better adjusted in intact, never-divorced families than in divorced families?* Most researchers agree that children from divorced families show poorer adjustment than their counterparts in nondivorced families (Hetherington, 2006; Lansford, 2009; Wallerstein, 2008) (see Figure 10.6). Those who have experienced multiple divorces are at greater risk. Children in divorced families are more likely than children in nondivorced families to have academic problems, to show externalized problems (such as acting out and delinquency) and internalized problems (such as anxiety and depression), to be less socially responsible, to have less competent intimate relationships, to drop out of

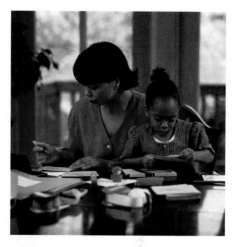

How does work affect parenting?

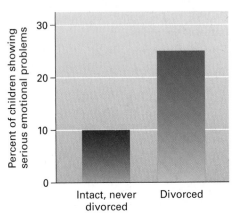

FIGURE 10.6 Divorce and Children's Emotional Problems In Hetherington's research, 25 percent of children from divorced families showed serious emotional problems compared with only 10 percent of children from intact, never-divorced families. However, keep in mind that a substantial majority (75 percent) of the children from divorced families did not show serious emotional problems.

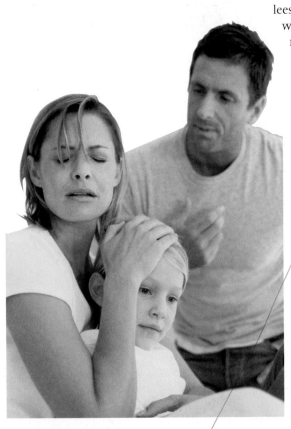

What concerns are involved in whether parents should stay together for the sake of the children or become divorced?

school, to become sexually active at an early age, to take drugs, to associate with antisocial peers, to have low self-esteem, and to be less securely attached as young adults (Conger & Chao, 1996). One recent study revealed that when individuals experienced the divorce of their parents in childhood and adolescence, it was linked to having unstable romantic or marital relationships and low levels of education in adulthood (Amato, 2006). Nonetheless, keep in mind that a majority of children in divorced families do not have significant adjustment problems (Ahrons, 2007). One study found that 20 years after their parents had divorced when they were children, approximately 80 percent of adults concluded that their parents' decision to divorce was a wise one (Ahrons, 2004).

- *Should parents stay together for the sake of the children?* Whether parents should stay in an unhappy or conflicted marriage for the sake of their children is one of the most commonly asked questions about divorce (Deutsch & Pruett, 2009; Hetherington, 2006; Ziol-Guest, 2009). If the stresses and disruptions in family relationships associated with an unhappy, conflictual marriage that erode the well-being of children are reduced by the move to a divorced, single-parent family, divorce can be advantageous. However, if the diminished resources and increased risks associated with divorce also are accompanied by inept parenting and sustained or increased conflict, not only between the divorced couple but also among the parents, children, and siblings, the best choice for the children would be for an unhappy marriage to be retained (Hetherington & Stanley-Hagan, 2002). It is difficult to determine how these "ifs" will play out when parents either remain together in an acrimonious marriage or become divorced.

    Note that marital conflict may have negative consequences for children in the context of marriage or divorce (Cox & others, 2008; Cummings & Merrilees, 2009). A longitudinal study revealed that conflict in nondivorced families was associated with emotional problems in children (Amato, 2006). Indeed, many of the problems children from divorced homes experience begin during the predivorce period, a time when parents are often in active conflict with one another. Thus, when children from divorced homes show problems, the problems may be due not only to the divorce, but also to the marital conflict that led to it (Thompson, 2008).

- *How much do family processes matter in divorced families?* Family processes matter a great deal (Lansford, 2009; Pruett & Barker, 2009a, b). When divorced parents' relationship with each other is harmonious and when they use authoritative parenting, the adjustment of children improves (Hetherington, 2006). A number of researchers have shown that a disequilibrium, which includes diminished parenting skills, occurs in the year following the divorce—but by two years after the divorce, restabilization has occurred and parenting skills have improved (Hetherington, 1989).

- *What factors influence an individual child's vulnerability to suffering negative consequences as a result of living in a divorced family?* Among the factors involved in the child's risk and vulnerability are the child's adjustment prior to the divorce, as well as the child's personality and temperament, gender, and custody situation (Hetherington, 2006). Children whose parents later divorce show poorer adjustment before the breakup (Amato & Booth, 1996; Lansford, 2009). Children who are socially mature and responsible, who show few behavioral problems, and who have an easy temperament are better able to cope with their parents' divorce. Children with a difficult temperament often have problems in coping with their parents' divorce (Hetherington, 2000).

Earlier studies reported gender differences in response to divorce, with divorce being more negative for girls than for boys in mother-custody families. However, more recent studies have shown that gender differences are less pronounced and consistent than was previously believed. Some of the inconsistency may be due to the increase in father custody, joint custody, and increased involvement of noncustodial fathers, especially in their sons' lives (Palmer, 2004). An analysis of studies found that children in joint-custody families were better adjusted than children in sole-custody families (Bauserman, 2002). Some studies have shown that boys adjust better in father-custody families, girls in mother-custody families, whereas other studies have not (Maccoby & Mnookin, 1992; Santrock & Warshak, 1979).

- *What role does socioeconomic status play in the lives of children in divorced families?* Custodial mothers experience the loss of about one-fourth to one-half of their predivorce income, in comparison with a loss of only one-tenth by custodial fathers (Emery, 1994). This income loss for divorced mothers is accompanied by increased workloads, high rates of job instability, and residential moves to less desirable neighborhoods with inferior schools (Sayer, 2006).

In sum, many factors are involved in determining how divorce influences a child's development (Wallerstein, 2008). To read about some strategies for helping children cope with the divorce of their parents, see the *Caring for Children* interlude.

> *As marriage has become a more optional, less permanent institution in contemporary America, children and adolescents are encountering stresses and adaptive challenges associated with their parents' marital transitions.*
>
> —E. MAVIS HETHERINGTON
> *Contemporary Psychologist, University of Virginia*

Caring for Children

COMMUNICATING WITH CHILDREN ABOUT DIVORCE

Ellen Galinsky and Judy David (1988) developed a number of guidelines for communicating with children about divorce:

- ***Explain the separation.*** As soon as daily activities in the home make it obvious that one parent is leaving, tell the children. If possible, both parents should be present when children are told about the separation to come. The reasons for the separation are very difficult for young children to understand. No matter what parents tell children, children can find reasons to argue against the separation. It is extremely important for parents to tell the children who will take care of them and to describe the specific arrangements for seeing the other parent.

- ***Explain that the separation is not the child's fault.*** Young children often believe their parents' separation or divorce is their own fault. Therefore, it is important to tell children that they are not the cause of the separation. Parents need to repeat this a number of times.

- ***Explain that it may take time to feel better.*** Tell young children that it's normal not to feel good about what is happening and that many other children feel this way when their parents become separated. It is also okay for divorced parents to share some of their emotions with children, by saying something like "I'm having a hard time since the separation just like you, but I know it's going to get better after a while." Such statements are best kept brief and should not criticize the other parent.

- ***Keep the door open for further discussion.*** Tell your children to come to you any time they want to talk about the separation. It is healthy for children to express their pent-up emotions in discussions with their parents and to learn that the parents are willing to listen to their feelings and fears.

(continued on next page)

How would you...?
As a human development and family studies professional, how would you apply the guidelines on communicating about divorce to help parents discuss the death of a family member with their children?

- *Provide as much continuity as possible.* The less children's worlds are disrupted by the separation, the easier their transition to a single-parent family will be. This means maintaining the rules already in place as much as possible. Children need parents who care enough not to only give them warmth and nurturance but also to set reasonable limits.

- *Provide support for your children and yourself.* Parents are as important to children after a divorce or separation as they were as before the divorce or separation. Divorced parents need to provide children with as much support as possible. Parents function best when other people are available to give them support as adults and as parents. Divorced parents can find people who provide practical help and with whom they can talk about their problems. For example, many individuals going through a divorce report that they benefit enormously from having a support system of friends they can turn to discuss their situation.

Gay Male and Lesbian Parents Increasingly, gay male and lesbian couples are creating families that include children. Approximately 20 percent of lesbians and 10 percent of gay men are parents (Patterson, 2009). There may be more than 1 million gay and lesbian parents in the United States today.

Like heterosexual couples, gay male and lesbian parents vary greatly. They may be single or they may have same-gender partners. Many lesbian mothers and gay fathers are noncustodial parents because they lost custody of their children to heterosexual spouses after a divorce.

Most children of gay and lesbian parents were born in a heterosexual relationship that ended in a divorce: In most cases, it was probably a relationship in which one or both parents only later identified themselves as gay male or lesbian. In other cases, lesbians and gay men became parents as a result of donor insemination and surrogates, or through adoption.

Parenthood among lesbians and gay men is controversial. Opponents claim that being raised by gay male or lesbian parents harms the child's development. But researchers have found few differences between children growing up with lesbian mothers or gay fathers on the one hand, and children growing up with heterosexual parents on the other (Patterson, 2009). For example, children growing up in gay or lesbian families are just as popular with their peers, and no differences are found in the adjustment and mental health of children living in these families when they are compared with children in heterosexual families (Hyde, 2007; Wainright & Patterson, 2008). Contrary to the once-popular expectation that being raised by a gay or lesbian parent would result in the child growing up to be gay or lesbian, in fact the overwhelming majority of children from gay or lesbian families have a heterosexual orientation (Tasker & Golombok, 1997).

Cultural, Ethnic, and Socioeconomic Variations Parenting can be influenced by culture, ethnicity, and socioeconomic status. Recall from Bronfenbrenner's ecological theory (Chapter 1, "Introduction") that a number of social contexts influence the child's development. In Bronfenbrenner's theory, culture, ethnicity, and socioeconomic status are classified as part of the macrosystem because they represent broader, societal contexts.

Cross-Cultural Studies Different cultures often give different answers to such basic questions as what the father's role in the family should be, what support systems are available to families, and how children should be disciplined (Fiese & Winter, 2008). There are important cross-cultural variations in parenting (Kagitcibasi, 2007). In some cultures (such as Arab countries), authoritarian parenting is widespread.

What are the research findings regarding the development and psychological well-being of children raised by gay male and lesbian couples?

Cultural change, brought about by such factors as increasingly frequent international travel, the Internet and electronic communications, and economic globalization, is coming to families in many countries around the world. There are trends toward greater family mobility, migration to urban areas, separation as some family members work in cities or countries far from their homes, smaller families, fewer extended-family households, and increases in maternal employment (Brown & Larson, 2002). These trends can change the resources that are available to children. For example, when several generations no longer live close by, children may lose support and guidance from grandparents, aunts, and uncles. On the positive side, smaller families may produce more openness and communication between parents and children.

Ethnicity Families within different ethnic groups in the United States differ in their typical size, structure, composition, reliance on kinship networks, and levels of income and education (Liu & others, 2009). Large and extended families are more common among minority groups than among the White majority. For example, 19 percent of Latino families have three or more children, compared with 14 percent of African American and 10 percent of White families. African American and Latino children interact more with grandparents, aunts, uncles, cousins, and more-distant relatives than do White children.

Single-parent families are more common among African Americans and Latinos than among White Americans (Brown & Lesane-Brown, 2009). In comparison with two-parent households, single parents often have more limited resources of time, money, and energy (Barajas, Phillipsen, & Brooks-Gunn, 2008; Wilson, 2008). Ethnic minority parents also are less educated and more likely to live in low-income circumstances than their White counterparts. Still, many impoverished ethnic minority families manage to find ways to raise competent children (Hattery & Smith, 2007).

Of course, individual families vary, and how ethnic minority families deal with stress depends on many factors (Galindo & Durham, 2009; Wong, Kinzie, & Kinzie, 2009). Whether the parents are native-born or immigrants, how long the family has been in this country, and what their socioeconomic status and national origin all make a difference (Parke & others, 2008). The characteristics of the family's social context also influence its adaptation. What are the attitudes toward the family's ethnic group within its neighborhood or city? Can the family's children attend good schools? Are there community groups that welcome people from the family's ethnic group? Do members of the family's ethnic group form community groups of their own? To read further about ethnic minority parenting, see the *Diversity in Children's Development* interlude.

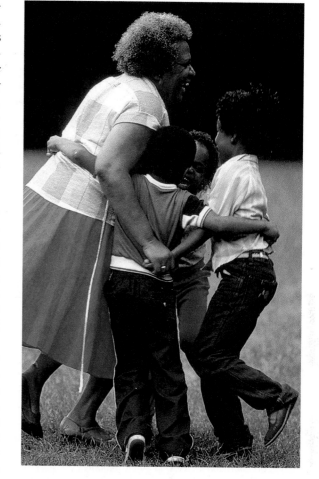

What are some characteristics of families within different ethnic groups?

Diversity in Children's Development

ACCULTURATION AND ETHNIC MINORITY PARENTING

Ethnic minority children and their parents undergo varying degrees of *acculturation*, which refers to cultural changes that occur when one culture comes in contact with another (Bornstein & Cote, 2010). Asian American parents, for example, may feel pressed to modify the traditional training style of parental control discussed earlier as they encounter the more permissive parenting typical of the dominant culture.

(continued on next page)

The level of family acculturation can affect parenting style by influencing expectations for children's development, parent-child interactions, and the role of the extended family (Ishii-Kuntz, 2004). For example, in one study, the level of acculturation and maternal education were the strongest predictors of maternal-infant interaction patterns in Latino families (Perez-Febles, 1992).

The family's level of acculturation also influences important decisions about child care and early childhood education (Bradley & McKelvey, 2007). For example,

> An African American mother might prefer to leave her children with extended family while she is at work because the kinship network is seen as a natural way to cope with maternal absence. This well-intentioned, culturally appropriate decision might, however, put the child at an educational and social disadvantage relative to other children of similar age who have the benefit of important preschool experiences that may ease the transition into early school years. (Garcia Coll & Pachter, 2002, p. 8)

Less acculturated and more acculturated family members may disagree about the appropriateness of various caregiving practices, possibly creating conflict or confusion.

The opportunities for acculturation that young children experience depend mainly on their parents and extended family. If they send the children to a child-care center, school, church, or other community setting, the children are likely to learn about the values and behaviors of the dominant culture, and they may be expected to adapt to that culture's norms. Thus, Latino children raised in a traditional family in which the family's good is considered more important than the individual's interests may attend a preschool in which children are rewarded for asserting themselves. Chinese American children whose traditional parents value behavioral inhibition (as discussed in Chapter 6, "Cognitive Development in Infancy") may be rewarded outside the home for being active and emotionally expressive. Over time, the differences in the level of acculturation experienced by children and by their parents and extended family may grow.

How is acculturation involved in ethnic minority parenting?

(Source: Garcia Coll & Pachter, 2002, pp. 7–8)

Socioeconomic Status Low-income families have less access to resources than higher-income families (Leon-Guererro, 2009; Philipsen, Johnson, & Brooks-Gunn, 2009). The differential in access to resources includes nutrition, health care, protection from danger, and enriching educational and socialization opportunities, such as tutoring and lessons in various activities. These differences are compounded in low-income families characterized by long-term poverty (Brandon, 2009; McLoyd & others, 2009).

In America and most Western cultures, differences have been found in child rearing among different SES groups (Hoff, Laursen, & Tardif, 2002, p. 246):

- "Lower-SES parents (1) are more concerned that their children conform to society's expectations, (2) create a home atmosphere in which it is clear that parents have authority over children," (3) use physical punishment more in disciplining their children, and (4) are more directive and less conversational with their children.

- "Higher-SES parents (1) are more concerned with developing children's initiative" and delay of gratification, "(2) create a home atmosphere in which children are more nearly equal participants and in which rules are discussed as opposed to being laid down" in an authoritarian manner, (3) are less likely to use physical punishment, and (4) "are less directive and more conversational" with their children.

Parents in different socioeconomic groups also tend to think differently about education (Huston & Ripke, 2006). Middle- and upper-income parents more often

How Would You...?
As an educator, how would you work with low-socioeconomic-status families to increase parental involvement in their children's educational activities?

think of education as something that should be mutually encouraged by parents and teachers. By contrast, low-income parents are more likely to view education as the teacher's job. Thus, increased school-family linkages can especially benefit students from low-income families.

Review and Reflect: Learning Goal 2

 Explain how families can influence young children's development

REVIEW

- What aspects of parenting are linked with young children's development?
- What are the types and consequences of child maltreatment?
- How are sibling relationships and birth order related to young children's development?
- How is children's development affected by having two wage-earning parents, having divorced parents, and being part of a particular cultural, ethnic, and socioeconomic group?

REFLECT

- Which style or styles of parenting did your mother and father use in rearing you? What effects do you think their parenting styles have had on your development?

---

3 HOW ARE PEER RELATIONS, PLAY, AND TELEVISION INVOLVED IN YOUNG CHILDREN'S DEVELOPMENT?

| Peer Relations | Play | Television |

The family is an important social context for children's development. However, children's development also is strongly influenced by what goes on in other social contexts, such as in peer groups, in play, or in watching television.

Peer Relations

As children grow older, they spend an increasing amount of time with their *peers*—children of about the same age or maturity level.

What are the functions of a child's peer group? One of its most important functions is to provide a source of information and comparison about the world outside the family. Children receive feedback about their abilities from their peer group. Children evaluate what they do in terms of whether it is better than, as good as, or worse than what other children do. It is hard to make these judgments at home because siblings are usually older or younger.

Good peer relations can be necessary for normal socioemotional development (Hartup, 2009; Ladd, 2009). Special concerns focus on children who are withdrawn and aggressive (Crick & others, 2009; Rubin, Bowker, & Kennedy, 2009). Withdrawn children who are rejected by peers or are victimized and feel lonely are at risk for depression. Children who are aggressive with their peers are at risk of developing

What are some characteristics of peer relations in early childhood?

a number of problems, including delinquency and dropping out of school (Prinstein & others, 2009).

Developmental Changes   Recall from our discussion of gender that by about the age of 3, children already prefer to spend time with same-sex rather than opposite-sex playmates, and this preference increases in early childhood. During these same years, the frequency of peer interaction, both positive and negative, picks up considerably (Coplan & Arbeau, 2009). Many preschool children spend considerable time in peer interaction conversing with playmates about such matters as "negotiating roles and rules in play, arguing, and agreeing" (Rubin, Bukowski, & Parker, 2006). And during early childhood, children's interactions with peers become more coordinated and involve longer turns and sequences (Coplan & Arbeau, 2009).

Friends   In early childhood, children distinguish between friends and nonfriends (Howes, 2009). For most young children, a friend is someone to play with. Young preschool children are more likely than older children to have friends who are of different gender and ethnicity (Howes, 2009).

The Connected Worlds of Parent-Child and Peer Relations   Parents may influence their children's peer relations in many ways, both direct and indirect (Booth-LaForce & Kerns, 2009; Ross & Howe, 2009). Parents affect their children's peer relations through their interactions with their children, how they manage their children's lives, and the opportunities they provide their children. A recent study revealed that warmth, advice giving, and provision of opportunities by mothers and fathers were linked to children's social competence (high prosocial behavior, low aggression), and subsequently to social acceptance (being well liked by peers and teachers) one year later (McDowell & Parke, 2009).

Basic lifestyle decisions by parents—their choices of neighborhoods, churches, schools, and their own friends—largely determine the pool from which their children select possible friends. These choices in turn affect which children their children meet, their purpose in interacting, and eventually which children become their friends.

Researchers also have found that children's peer relations are linked to attachment security and parents' marital quality (Booth-Laforce & Kerns, 2009; Ross & Howe, 2009). Early attachments to caregivers provide a connection to children's peer relations not only by creating a secure base for children to explore social relationships beyond the family but also by conveying a working model of relationships (Hartup, 2009).

Do these results indicate that children's peer relations always are wedded to parent-child relationships? Although parent-child relationships influence children's subsequent peer relations, children also learn other modes of relating through their relationships with peers. For example, rough-and-tumble play occurs mainly with other children, not in parent-child interaction. In times of stress, children often turn to parents, not peers, for support. In parent-child relationships, children learn how to relate to authority figures. With their peers, children are likely to interact on a much more equal basis and to learn a mode of relating based on mutual influence. We will have much more to say about peer relations in Chapter 13, "Socioemotional Development in Middle and Late Childhood."

Play

An extensive amount of peer interaction during childhood involves play, but social play is only one type of play. *Play* is a pleasurable activity that is engaged in for its own sake, and its functions and forms vary.

Play's Functions   Play is essential to the young child's health. Theorists have focused on different aspects of play and highlighted a long list of functions (Coplan & Arbeau, 2009).

According to Freud and Erikson, play helps the child master anxieties and conflicts. Because tensions are relieved in play, the child can cope with life's problems. Play permits the child to work off excess physical energy and to release pent-up tensions. Therapists use *play therapy* both to allow the child to work off frustrations and to analyze the child's conflicts and ways of coping with them (Malchiodi, 2008; Sanders, 2008). Children may feel less threatened and be more likely to express their true feelings in the context of play.

Play also is an important context for cognitive development (Coplan & Arbeau, 2009). Piaget (1962) maintained that play advances children's cognitive development. At the same time, he said that children's cognitive development *constrains* the way they play. Play permits children to practice their competencies and acquired skills in a relaxed, pleasurable way. Piaget thought that cognitive structures need to be exercised, and play provides the perfect setting for this exercise. For example, children who have just learned to add or multiply begin to play with numbers in different ways as they perfect these operations, laughing as they do so.

Vygotsky (1962) also considered play to be an excellent setting for cognitive development. He was especially interested in the symbolic and make-believe aspects of play, as when a child substitutes a stick for a horse and rides the stick as if it were a horse. For young children, the imaginary situation is real. Parents should encourage such imaginary play, because it advances the child's cognitive development, especially creative thought.

Daniel Berlyne (1960) described play as exciting and pleasurable in itself because it satisfies our exploratory drive. This drive involves curiosity and a desire for information about something new or unusual. Play is a means whereby children can safely explore and seek out new information. Play encourages exploratory behavior by offering children the possibilities of novelty, complexity, uncertainty, surprise, and incongruity.

More recently, play has been described as an important context for the development of language and communication skills (Coplan & Arbeau, 2009). Language and communication skills may be enhanced through discussions and negotiations regarding roles and rules in play as young children practice various words and phrases. These types of social interactions during play can benefit young children's literacy skills (Coplan & Arbeau, 2009). And, as we saw in Chapter 9, "Cognitive Development in Early Childhood," play is a central focus of the child-centered kindergarten and thought to be an essential aspect of early childhood education (Feeney & others, 2010).

Types of Play The contemporary perspective on play emphasizes both the cognitive and the social aspects of play (Sumaroka & Bornstein, 2008). Among the most widely studied types of children's play today are sensorimotor and practice play, pretense/symbolic play, social play, constructive play, and games (Bergen, 1988).

Sensorimotor and Practice Play **Sensorimotor play** is behavior by infants to derive pleasure from exercising their sensorimotor schemes. The development of sensorimotor play follows Piaget's description of sensorimotor thought, which we discussed in Chapter 6, "Cognitive Development in Infancy." Infants initially engage in exploratory and playful visual and motor transactions in the second quarter of the first year of life. For example, at 9 months of age, infants begin to select novel objects for exploration and play, especially responsive objects, such as toys that make noise or bounce. At 12 months of age, infants enjoy making things work and exploring cause and effect.

Practice play involves the repetition of behavior when new skills are being learned or when physical or mental mastery and coordination of skills are required for games or sports. Sensorimotor play, which often involves practice play, is primarily confined to infancy, whereas practice play can be engaged in throughout life.

And that park grew up with me; that small world widened as I learned its secrets and boundaries, as I discovered new refuges in its woods and jungles: hidden homes and lairs for the multitudes of imagination, for cowboys and Indians. . . . I used to dawdle on half holidays along the bent and Devon-facing seashore, hoping for gold watches or the skull of a sheep or a message in a bottle to be washed up with the tide.

—Dylan Thomas
Welsh Poet, 20th Century

sensorimotor play Behavior engaged in by infants to derive pleasure from exercising their existing sensorimotor schemas.

practice play Play that involves repetition of behavior when new skills are being learned or when physical or mental mastery and coordination of skills are required for games or sports.

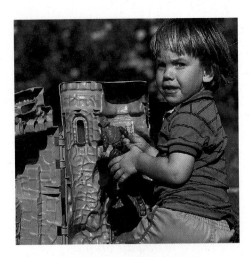

A preschool "superhero" at play.

During the preschool years, children often engage in practice play. Although practice play declines in the elementary school years, practice play activities such as running, jumping, sliding, twirling, and throwing balls or other objects are frequently observed on the playgrounds at elementary schools.

Pretense/Symbolic Play **Pretense/symbolic play** occurs when the child transforms the physical environment into a symbol. Between 9 and 30 months of age, children increase their use of objects in symbolic play. They learn to transform objects—substituting them for other objects and acting toward them as if they were these other objects (Kavanaugh, 2006). For example, a preschool child treats a table as if it were a car and says, "I'm fixing the car," as he grabs a leg of the table.

Many experts on play consider the preschool years the "golden age" of symbolic/pretense play that is dramatic or sociodramatic in nature (Fein, 1986). This type of make-believe play often appears at about 18 months of age and reaches a peak at 4 to 5 years of age, then gradually declines.

Some child psychologists conclude that pretend play is an important aspect of young children's development and often reflects advances in their cognitive development, especially as an indication of symbolic understanding. For example, Catherine Garvey (2000) and Angeline Lillard (2006) emphasize that hidden in young children's pretend play narratives are remarkable capacities for role-taking, balancing of social roles, metacognition (thinking about thinking), testing of the reality-pretense distinction, and numerous nonegocentric capacities that reveal the remarkable cognitive skills of young children. In one recent analysis, the development of children's ability to share their pretend play with peers was proposed as a major accomplishment in early childhood (Coplan & Arbeau, 2009).

Social Play **Social play** is play that involves interaction with peers. Social play increases dramatically during the preschool years. For many children, social play is the main context for social interactions with peers (Coplan & Arbeau, 2009). Many years ago, Mildred Parten (1932) developed an elaborate classification of children's play. Based on observations of children in free play at nursery school, Parten proposed the following types of play:

- *Unoccupied play* is not play as it is commonly understood. The child may stand in one spot or perform random movements that do not seem to have a goal. In most nursery schools, unoccupied play is less frequent than other forms of play.

- *Solitary play* happens when the child plays alone and independently of others. The child seems engrossed in the activity and does not care much about anything else that is happening. Two- and three-year-olds engage more frequently in solitary play than older preschoolers do.

- *Onlooker play* takes place when the child watches other children play. The child may talk with other children and ask questions but does not enter into their play behavior. The child's active interest in other children's play distinguishes onlooker play from unoccupied play.

- *Parallel play* occurs when the child plays separately from others but with toys like those the others are using or in a manner that mimics their play. The older children are, the less frequently they engage in this type of play. However, even older preschool children engage in parallel play quite often.

- *Associative play* involves social interaction with little or no organization. In this type of play, children seem to be more interested in each other than in the tasks they are performing. Borrowing or lending toys and following or leading one another in line are examples of associative play.

- *Cooperative play* consists of social interaction in a group with a sense of group identity and organized activity. Children's formal games, competition aimed at

pretense/symbolic play Play in which the child transforms the physical environment into a symbol.

social play Play that involves social interactions with peers.

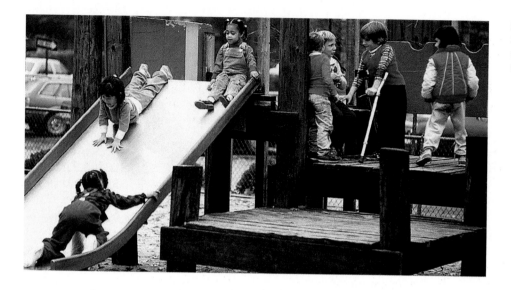

Mildred Parten classified play into six categories. *Study this photograph. Which of Parten's categories are reflected in the behavior of the children?*

winning, and groups formed by a teacher for doing things together are examples of cooperative play. Cooperative play is the prototype for the games of middle childhood. Little cooperative play is seen in the preschool years.

Constructive Play **Constructive play** combines sensorimotor/practice play with symbolic representation. Constructive play occurs when children engage in the self-regulated creation of a product or a solution. Constructive play increases in the preschool years as symbolic play increases and sensorimotor play decreases. Constructive play is also a frequent form of play in the elementary school years, both in and out of the classroom.

Games **Games** are activities that are engaged in for pleasure and that have rules. Often they involve competition. Preschool children may begin to participate in social games that involve simple rules of reciprocity and turn-taking. However, games take on a much stronger role in the lives of elementary school children. After age 12, playground and neighborhood games decline in popularity (Bergen, 1988).

Television

Few developments in society in the second half of the twentieth century had a greater impact on children than television (Bickham, 2009; Roberts, Henriksen, & Foehr, 2009). Although it is only one of the many types of mass media that affect children's behavior, television is the most influential. The persuasive capabilities of television are staggering (Scharrer & Demers, 2009).

Many children spend more time in front of the television set than they do with their parents. Just how much television do young children watch? Surveys vary, with the figures ranging from an average of two to four hours a day (Kaiser Family Foundation, 2006). Compared with their counterparts in other developed countries, children in the United States watch television for considerably longer periods (see Figure 10.7). Television can have a negative influence on children by making them passive learners, distracting them from doing homework, teaching them stereotypes, providing them with violent models of aggression, and presenting them with unrealistic views of the world (Dubow, Huesmann, & Greenwood, 2007; Murray, 2007). However, television can have a positive influence on children's development by presenting motivating educational programs, increasing their information about the world beyond their immediate environment, and providing models of prosocial behavior (Wilson, 2008).

How Would You…?
As an educator, how would you integrate play in the learning process?

"Mrs. Horton, could you stop by school today?"
© Martha Campbell. Reprinted with Permission.

constructive play Play that combines sensorimotor/practice play with symbolic representation. Constructive play occurs when children engage in self-regulated creation or construction of a product or a solution.

games Activities engaged in for pleasure that include rules and often competition with one or more individuals.

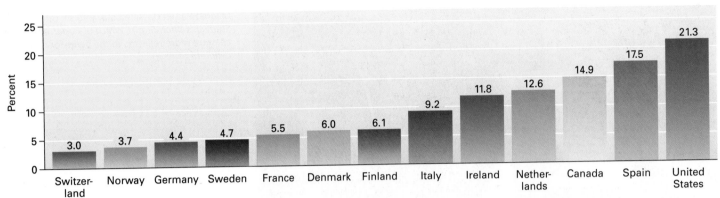

FIGURE 10.7 Percentage of 9-Year-Old Children Who Report Watching More Than Five Hours of Television per Weekday

Effects of Television on Children's Aggression The extent to which children are exposed to violence and aggression on television raises special concern (Roberts, Henriksen, & Foehr, 2009). For example, Saturday morning cartoon shows average more than 25 violent acts per hour. In one experiment, preschool children were randomly assigned to one of two groups: One group watched television shows taken directly from violent Saturday morning cartoons on 11 days; the second group watched television cartoon shows with all of the violence removed (Steur, Applefield, & Smith, 1971). The children were then observed during play at their preschool. The preschool children who had seen the TV cartoon shows with violence kicked, choked, and pushed their playmates more than did the preschool children who watched nonviolent TV cartoon shows. Because the children were randomly assigned to the two conditions (TV cartoons with violence versus nonviolent TV cartoons), we can conclude that exposure to TV violence *caused* the increased aggression in the children in this investigation.

Other research has found links between watching television violence as a child and acting aggressively years later (Parke & others, 2008). For example, in one study, exposure to media violence at 6 to 10 years of age was linked with young adult aggressive behavior (Huesmann & others, 2003). In another study, long-term exposure to television violence was significantly related to the likelihood of aggression in 1,565 12- to 17-year-old boys (Belson, 1978). Boys who watched the most aggression on television were the most likely to commit a violent crime, swear, be aggressive in sports, threaten violence toward another boy, write slogans on walls, or break windows. These studies are *correlational,* so we can conclude from them that television violence is *associated with* aggressive behavior.

In addition to television violence, there is increased concern about children who play violent video games, especially those that are highly realistic (Escobar-Chaves, & Anderson, 2008). Children can become so deeply immersed in some electronic games that they experience an altered state of consciousness in which rational thought is suspended and arousing aggressive scripts are learned (Roberts, Henriksen, & Foehr, 2004). The direct rewards that players receive ("winning points") for their actions may also enhance the influence of video games.

Correlational studies indicate that children who extensively play violent electronic games are more aggressive than their counterparts who spend less time playing the games or do not play them at all (Cohen, 1995). Experiments have not yet been conducted to demonstrate increased aggression subsequent to playing violent video games, although a recent analysis of research studies concluded that playing violent video games is linked to aggression in both males and females (Escobar-Chaves & Anderson, 2008).

How is television violence linked to children's aggression?

Effects of Television on Children's Prosocial Behavior   Television also can teach children that it is better to behave in positive, prosocial ways than in negative, antisocial ways (Bryant, 2007). In an early study, Aimee Leifer (1973) selected episodes from the television show *Sesame Street* that reflected positive social interchanges in which children were taught how to use their social skills. For example, in one interchange, two men were fighting over the amount of space available to them; they gradually began to cooperate and to share the space. Children who watched these episodes copied these behaviors, and in later social situations they applied the prosocial lessons they had learned.

Television, Cognitive Development, and Achievement   In general, television has not been shown to influence children's creativity but is negatively related to their mental ability (Comstock & Scharrer, 2006). Watching television is also linked with reductions in school achievement (Comstock & Scharrer, 2006). However, some types of television—such as educational programming for young children—may enhance achievement. For example, in one longitudinal study, viewing educational programs such as *Sesame Street* and *Mr. Rogers' Neighborhood* as preschoolers was associated with a host of desirable characteristics in adolescence: getting higher grades, reading more books, placing a higher value on achievement, being more creative, and acting less aggressively (Anderson & others, 2001) (see Figure 10.8). These associations were more consistent for boys than girls.

How would you...?
As a human development and family studies professional, how would you talk with parents about strategies for improving television viewing by their children?

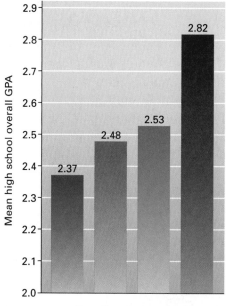

Quartiles of educational viewing at age 5

FIGURE 10.8 Educational TV Viewing and High School Grade-Point Average for Boys   When boys watched more educational television (especially *Sesame Street*) as preschoolers, they had higher grade point averages in high school (Anderson & others, 2001). The graph displays the boys' early TV viewing patterns in quartiles and the means of their grade-point averages. The bar on the left is for the lowest 25 percent of boys who viewed educational TV programs, the next bar the next 25 percent, and so on, with the bar on the right for the 25 percent of the boys who watched the most educational TV shows as preschoolers.

 Review and Reflect: Learning Goal 3

3   Describe the roles of peers, play, and television in young children's development

REVIEW

- How do peers affect young children's development?
- What are some theories and types of play?
- How does television influence children's development?

REFLECT

- What guidelines would you recommend to parents to help them to make television a more positive influence on their children's development? Consider factors such as the child's age, the child's activities other than TV, the parents' patterns of interaction with the children, and types of TV shows.

Reach Your Learning Goals

Socioemotional Development in Early Childhood

1 WHAT CHARACTERIZES YOUNG CHILDREN'S EMOTIONAL AND PERSONALITY DEVELOPMENT? DISCUSS EMOTIONAL AND PERSONALITY DEVELOPMENT IN EARLY CHILDHOOD

The Self

- In Erikson's theory, early childhood is a period when development involves resolving the conflict of initiative versus guilt. The toddler's rudimentary self-understanding develops into the preschooler's representation of the self in terms of body attributes, material possessions, and physical activities. At about 4 to 5 years of age, children also begin to use traitlike self-descriptions. Young children display more sophisticated self-understanding and understanding of others than previously thought.

Emotional Development

- Young children's range of emotions expands during early childhood as they increasingly experience self-conscious emotions such as pride, shame, and guilt. Between 2 and 4 years of age, use an increasing number of terms to describe emotion and learn more about the causes and consequences of feelings. At 4 to 5 years of age, children show an increased ability to reflect on emotions and understand that a single event can elicit different emotions in different people. They also show a growing awareness of the need to manage emotions to meet social standards. Emotion-coaching parents have children who engage in more effective self-regulation of their emotions than do emotion-dismissing parents. Emotional regulation plays an important role in successful peer relations.

Moral Development

- Moral development involves thoughts, feelings, and behaviors regarding rules and regulations about what people should do in their interactions with others. Freud's psychoanalytic theory emphasizes the importance of feelings in the development of the superego, the moral branch of personality. Positive emotions, such as empathy, also contribute to the child's moral development. Piaget analyzed moral reasoning and concluded that children from 4 to 7 years of age display heteronomous morality, judging behavior by its consequences. According to behavioral and social cognitive theorists, moral behavior develops as a result of reinforcement, punishment and imitation, and there is considerable situational variability in moral behavior. Conscience refers to an internal regulation of standards of right and wrong that involves an integration of moral thought, feeling, and behavior. Young children's conscience emerges out of relationships with parents. Parents influence young children's moral development by developing quality parent-child relationships, by being proactive in helping children avert misbehavior, and by engaging children in conversational dialogue about moral issues.

Gender

- Gender refers to the characteristics of people as males or females. Gender identity involves a sense of one's own gender, including knowledge, understanding, and acceptance of being male or female. A gender role is a set of expectations that prescribes how females or males should think, act, and feel. Gender typing refers to the acquisition of a traditional masculine or feminine role. Biological influences on gender development include chromosomes and hormones. However, biology is not the complete destiny in gender development; children's socialization experiences matter a great deal. Social role theory, psychoanalytic theory, and social cognitive theory emphasize various aspects of social experiences in the development of gender characteristics. Parents influence children's gender development, and peers are especially adept at rewarding gender-appropriate behavior. Gender schema theory emphasizes that gender typing emerges as children develop schemas of their culture's gender-appropriate and gender-inappropriate behaviors.

2 WHAT ROLES DO FAMILIES PLAY IN YOUNG CHILDREN'S DEVELOPMENT? EXPLAIN HOW FAMILIES CAN INFLUENCE YOUNG CHILDREN'S DEVELOPMENT

Parenting

- Authoritarian, authoritative, neglectful, and indulgent are four main parenting styles. Authoritative parenting is the most widely used style around the world and is the style most often associated with children's social competence. However, ethnic variations in parenting styles suggest that in Asian American families, some aspects of control may benefit children. Some criticisms of parenting styles have been made such as their failure to capture the themes of reciprocal socialization and synchrony. Physical punishment is widely used by U.S. parents, but there are a number of reasons why it is not a good choice. Coparenting has positive effects on children's development.

Child Maltreatment

- Child maltreatment may take the form of physical abuse, child neglect, sexual abuse, and emotional abuse. Child maltreatment places the child at risk for academic, emotional, and social problems. Adults who suffered child maltreatment are also vulnerable to a range of problems.

Sibling Relationships and Birth Order

- Siblings interact with each other in positive and negative ways. Birth order is related in certain ways to child characteristics, but by itself it is not a good predictor of behavior.

The Changing Family in a Changing Social World

- In general, having both parents employed full-time outside the home has not been shown to have negative effects on children. However, the nature of parents' work can affect their parenting quality. Divorce can have negative effects on children's adjustment, but so can an acrimonious relationship between parents who stay together for their children's sake. If divorced parents develop a harmonious relationship and practice authoritative parenting, children's adjustment improves. Researchers have found few differences between children growing up in gay or lesbian families and children growing up in heterosexual families. Cultures vary on a number of issues regarding families. African American and Latino children are more likely than White American children to live in single-parent families and larger families and to have extended-family connections. Low-income families have less access to resources than higher-income families. Lower-SES parents create a home atmosphere that involves more authority and physical punishment with children than higher-SES parents. Higher-SES parents are more concerned about developing children's initiative and delay of gratification.

3 HOW ARE PEER RELATIONS, PLAY, AND TELEVISION INVOLVED IN YOUNG CHILDREN'S DEVELOPMENT? DESCRIBE THE ROLES OF PEERS, PLAY, AND TELEVISION IN YOUNG CHILDREN'S DEVELOPMENT

Peer Relations

- Peers are powerful socialization agents. Peers provide a source of information and comparison about the world outside the family.

Play

- Play's functions include affiliation with peers, tension release, advances in cognitive development, exploration, and provision of a safe haven. The contemporary perspective on play emphasizes both the cognitive and the social aspects of play. Among the most widely studied types of children's play are sensorimotor play, practice play, pretense/symbolic play, social play, constructive play, and games. Parten created an elaborate classification of social play.

> Television

- Television can have both negative influences (such as turning children into passive learners and presenting them with aggressive models) and positive influences (such as providing models of prosocial behavior) on children's development. TV violence is not the only cause of children's aggression, but it can induce aggression. Prosocial behavior on TV can teach children positive behavior.

KEY TERMS

self-understanding 315
moral development 319
heteronomous morality 319
autonomous morality 319
immanent justice 319
conscience 319
gender identity 321

gender role 321
gender typing 321
social role theory 322
psychoanalytic theory of
    gender 322
social cognitive theory of
    gender 322

gender schema theory 324
authoritarian parenting 325
authoritative parenting 325
neglectful parenting 326
indulgent parenting 326
sensorimotor play 341
practice play 341

pretense/symbolic play 342
social play 342
constructive play 343
games 343

KEY PEOPLE

Erik Erikson 315
Sigmund Freud 318
Jean Piaget 318
Lawrence Kohlberg 320

Ross Thompson 320
Diana Baumrind 325
Ruth Chao 326
Laurie Kramer 331

Judy Dunn 332
Ann Crouter 333
Lev Vygotsky 341
Daniel Berlyne 341

Catherine Garvey 342
Angeline Lillard 342
Mildred Parten 342

MAKING A DIFFERENCE

Guiding Young Children's Socioemotional Development

How can young children's socioemotional skills be nourished? These strategies can help:

- *Look for situations to help children with their emotions.* Parents, teachers, and other adults can help children understand and handle their emotions in socially acceptable ways.

- *Present positive moral models for the child and use emotional situations to promote moral development.* Children benefit when they are around people who engage in prosocial rather than antisocial behavior. Encourage children to show empathy and learn to deal with their emotions.

- *Be an authoritative parent.* Children's self-control and social competence benefit when both parents are authoritative—that is, when they are neither punitive and overcontrolling nor permissive. Authoritative parents are nurturant, engage the child in verbal give-and-take, monitor the child, and use non-punitive control.

- *Adapt to the child's developmental changes.* Parents should use less physical manipulation and more reasoning or withholding of

special privileges in disciplining a 5-year-old, as opposed to disciplining a 2-year-old.

- *Communicate effectively with children in a divorced family.* Good strategies are to explain the separation and say it is not the child's fault, assure the child that it may take time to feel better, keep the door open for further discussion, provide as much continuity as possible, and supply a support system for the child.

- *Provide the child with opportunities for peer interaction.* Children learn a great deal from the mutual give-and-take of peer relations. Make sure the child gets considerable time to play with peers rather than watching TV or attending an academic early childhood program for the entire day.

- *Provide the child with many opportunities for play.* Positive play experiences can play important roles in the young child's socioemotional development.

- *Monitor the child's TV viewing.* Keep exposure to TV violence to a minimum. Develop a set of guidelines for the child's TV viewing.

RESOURCES FOR IMPROVING CHILDREN'S LIVES

The Emotional Development of Young Children
by Marylou Hyson (2004)
New York: Teachers College Press

An excellent book by a leading expert on early childhood that provides a good overview of young children's emotional development and many applications to children's emotional development in preschool and kindergarten.

For Better or For Worse: Divorce Reconsidered
by E. Mavis Hetherington and John Kelly (2002)
New York: W. W. Norton

E. Mavis Hetherington, a leading researcher, provides excellent descriptions of how divorce affects children and parents.

Gender Development
by Judith Blakemore, Sheri Berenbaum, and Lynn Liben (2009)
Clifton, NJ: Psychology Press

Very up-to-date coverage of many facets of children's gender development by leading experts.

E-LEARNING TOOLS

Connect to **www.mhhe.com/santrockc11e** to research the answers and complete these exercises. In addition, you'll find a number of other resources and valuable study tools for Chapter 10, "Socioemotional Development in Early Childhood," on this Web site.

Taking It to the Net

1. A social worker spoke to a psychology class about how children with serious developmental delays and disabilities are more prone to being abused by their parents than are children without disabilities. What are the general risk factors for abuse for all children, and how are they compounded for children with disabilities?

2. Karen is concerned about how to best help her daughter, Teresa, whose husband has abandoned her and their 5-year-old son. What are some of the challenges that Teresa may have to face, and how can her mother help her through this difficult time?

3. Jonathan and Diedre want to shield their children from the violence on television, but they are not sure how to go about it—other than by not allowing any television viewing at all. What recommendations does the APA have for parents?

4. Frieda is the middle child in a family with five siblings. She is interested in what sibling researchers have to say about the effect of birth order on sibling relationships. How does being a middle child contribute to the dynamics between Frieda and her brothers and sisters?

5. Rita's child development teacher wants each student to depict some aspect of child development from infancy to age 6 as a chronological time line represented by descriptions or illustrations. Rita has chosen the development of the self. What behaviors at 6, 12, and 18 months, and 2, 3, 4, 5, and 6 years

of age represent milestones in self-awareness, self-concept, self-understanding, and self-esteem?

Health and Well-Being, Parenting, and Education

Build your decision-making skills by trying your hand at the health and well-being, parenting, and education exercises.

Video Clips

The Online Learning Center includes the following videos for this chapter:

- *Lacking Gender Consistency at Age 4—508*
  A boy named Sal is asked to identify the gender of a male doll placed in front of him. After amusing himself by completely rotating the doll's head around, he explains that the doll is a male because of his hair. But when the interviewer puts a skirt on the doll, Sal demonstrates that he lacks an understanding of gender constancy when he explains that the doll is now a girl.

- *Early Gender Beliefs at Age 4—25*
  When presented with a male doll, a 4-year-old boy enthusiastically identifies the doll as a boy because "It doesn't have long hair!" When the interviewer puts a skirt on the doll, Bradley believes the doll changes into a girl because "It has a dress!"

- *Describing Friends at Age 5—99*
  Tara states that she has two special friends. She explains that these friends are special because they play together.

- *If My Son Wore a Dress—3001*
  A good example of how parents contribute to the gender socialization of children. Here, a couple with young children describe how they would feel if their son wanted to wear a dress.

SECTION
FIVE

MIDDLE AND LATE CHILDHOOD

Every forward step we take we leave some phantom of ourselves behind.

—JOHN LANCASTER SPALDING
American Educator, 19th Century

In middle and late childhood, children are on a different plane, belonging to a generation and feeling all their own. It is the wisdom of the human life span that at no time are children more ready to learn than during the period of expansive imagination at the end of early childhood. Children develop a sense of wanting to make things—and not just to make them, but to make them well and even perfectly. They seek to know and to understand. They are remarkable for their intelligence and for their curiosity. Their parents continue to be important influences in their lives, but their growth also is shaped by peers and friends. They don't think much about the future or about the past, but they enjoy the present moment. Section 5 consists of three chapters. "Physical Development in Middle and Late Childhood" (Chapter 11), "Cognitive Development in Middle and Late Childhood" (Chapter 12), and "Socioemotional Development in Middle and Late Childhood" (Chapter 13).

11

Blessed be childhood, which brings something of heaven into the midst of our rough earthliness.

—Henri Frédéric Amiel
Swiss Poet, Philosopher, 19th Century

LEARNING GOALS

◆ Discuss changes in body growth, the brain, and motor development in middle and late childhood

◆ Characterize children's health in middle and late childhood

◆ Summarize information about children with disabilities

PHYSICAL DEVELOPMENT IN MIDDLE AND LATE CHILDHOOD

CHAPTER OUTLINE

Images of Children's Development
The Story of Angie and Her Weight

The following comments are by Angie, an elementary-school-age girl:

> When I was eight years old, I weighed 125 pounds. My clothes were the size that large teenage girls wear. I hated my body and my classmates teased me all the time. I was so overweight and out of shape that when I took a P.E. class my face would get red and I had trouble breathing. I was jealous of the kids who played sports and weren't overweight like I was.
>
> I'm nine years old now and I've lost 30 pounds. I'm much happier and proud of myself. How did I lose the weight? My mom said she had finally decided enough was enough. She took me to a pediatrician who specializes in helping children lose weight and keep it off. The pediatrician counseled my mom about my eating and exercise habits, then had us join a group that he had created for overweight children and their parents. My mom and I go to the group once a week and we've now been participating in the program for six months. I no longer eat fast food meals and my mom is cooking more healthy meals. Now that I've lost weight, exercise is not as hard for me and I don't get teased by the kids at school. My mom's pretty happy too because she's lost 15 pounds herself since we've been in the counseling program.

Not all overweight children are as successful as Angie at reducing their weight. Indeed, being overweight in childhood has become a major national concern in the United States. Later in the chapter, we explore in detail being overweight in childhood, including its causes and outcomes.

PREVIEW

Considerable progress in children's physical development continues to take place in the middle and late childhood years. They grow taller, heavier, and stronger. They become more adept at using their physical skills. We begin the chapter by exploring the changes that characterize body growth and motor skills, then examine the central issues in children's health, and conclude by discussing children with disabilities and their education.

1 WHAT CHANGES TAKE PLACE IN BODY GROWTH, THE BRAIN, AND MOTOR DEVELOPMENT?

Skeletal and Muscular Systems	The Brain	Motor Development

The period of middle and late childhood involves slow, consistent growth. This is a period of calm before the rapid growth spurt of adolescence. Among the important aspects of body growth and proportion in this developmental period are those involving skeletal and muscular systems, the brain, and motor development.

Skeletal and Muscular Systems

During the elementary school years, children grow an average of 2 to 3 inches a year until, at the age of 11, the average girl is 4 feet, 9 inches tall, and the average boy is 4 feet, 7¾ inches tall. During the middle and late childhood years, children gain about 5 to 7 pounds a year. The weight increase is due mainly to increases in the size of the skeletal and muscular systems, as well as the size of some body organs. Muscle mass and strength gradually increase as "baby fat" decreases. The loose movements and knock-knees of early childhood give way to improved muscle tone. The

FIGURE 11.1 Changes in Height and Weight in Middle and Late Childhood

Height (inches)

Age	Female percentiles			Male percentiles		
	25th	50th	75th	25th	50th	75th
6	43.75	45.00	46.50	44.25	45.75	47.00
7	46.00	47.50	49.00	46.25	48.00	49.25
8	48.00	49.75	51.50	48.50	50.00	51.50
9	50.25	53.00	53.75	50.50	52.00	53.50
10	52.50	54.50	56.25	52.50	54.25	55.75
11	55.00	57.00	58.75	54.50	55.75	57.25

Weight (pounds)

Age	Female percentiles			Male percentiles		
6	39.25	43.00	47.25	42.00	45.50	49.50
7	43.50	48.50	53.25	46.25	50.25	55.00
8	49.00	54.75	61.50	51.00	55.75	61.50
9	55.75	62.75	71.50	56.00	62.00	69.25
10	63.25	71.75	82.75	62.00	69.25	78.50
11	71.75	81.25	94.25	69.00	77.75	89.00

Note: The percentile tells how the child compares with other children of the same age. The 50th percentile tells us that half of the children of a particular age are taller (heavier) or shorter (lighter). The 25th percentile tells us that 25 percent of the children of that age are shorter (lighter) and 75 percent are taller (heavier).

increase in muscular strength is due both to heredity and to exercise. Children also double their strength capabilities during these years. Because of their greater number of muscle cells, boys are usually stronger than girls. A summary of the changes in height and weight in middle and late childhood appears in Figure 11.1.

Proportional changes are among the most pronounced physical changes in middle and late childhood (Kliegman & others, 2007). Head circumference, waist circumference, and leg length decrease in relation to body height (Hockenberry & Wilson, 2009). A less noticeable physical change is that bones continue to ossify (harden) during middle and late childhood.

The Brain

The development of brain-imaging techniques, such as magnetic resonance imaging (MRI), has led to an increase in research on changes in the brain during middle and late childhood, and on how these brain changes are linked to improvements in cognitive development (Diamond, Casey, & Munakata, 2010). One such change involves increased myelination, which improves the speed of processing information and communication in the higher regions of the brain, such as the cerebral cortex. The increase in myelination during middle and late childhood is linked to more effective processing of information on cognitive tasks (Marsh & others, 2006). Recall from our discussion in Chapter 8, "Physical Development in Early Childhood," that myelination is the process of encasing axons with fat cells.

Total brain volume stabilizes by the end of middle and late childhood, but significant changes in various structures and regions of the brain continue to occur. In particular, the brain pathways and circuitry involving the prefrontal cortex, the highest level in the brain, continue to increase (Durston & Casey, 2006). These advances in the prefrontal cortex are linked to children's improved attention, reasoning, and cognitive control (Crone & others, 2009). (See Figure 8.4, p. 257 for the location of the prefrontal cortex in the brain.)

Leading developmental cognitive neuroscientist Mark Johnson and his colleagues (2009) recently proposed that the prefrontal cortex likely orchestrates the functions of many other brain regions during development. As part of this neural leadership and organizational role, the prefrontal cortex may provide an advantage to neural networks and connections that include the prefrontal cortex. In their view, the prefrontal cortex coordinates the best neural connections for solving a problem at hand.

Changes also occur in the thickness of the cerebral cortex (cortical thickness) in middle and late childhood (Toga, Thompson, & Sowell, 2006). One study used brain scans to assess cortical thickness in 5- to 11-year-old children (Sowell & others, 2004). Cortical thickening across a two-year time period was observed in the temporal and frontal lobe areas that function in language, which may account for improvements in language abilities such as reading.

As children develop, activation of some brain areas increases, while that of others decreases (Diamond, Casey, & Munakata, 2010; Nelson, 2009). One shift in activation that occurs as children develop is from diffuse, larger areas to more focal, smaller areas. This shift is characterized by synaptic pruning, in which areas of the brain not being used lose synaptic connections and those being used show an increase in connections. In a recent study, researchers found less diffusion and more focal activation in the prefrontal cortex from 7 to 30 years of age (Durston & others, 2006). The activation change was accompanied by increased efficiency in cognitive performance, especially in *cognitive control*, which involves flexible and effective control in a number of areas. These areas include controlling attention, reducing interfering thoughts, inhibiting motor actions, and being flexible in switching between competing choices (Munakata, 2006).

Motor Development

During middle and late childhood, children's motor development becomes much smoother and more coordinated than it was in early childhood. For example, only one child in a thousand can hit a tennis ball over the net at the age of 3, yet by the age of 10 or 11 most children can learn to play the sport. Running, climbing, skipping rope, swimming, bicycle riding, and skating are just a few of the many physical skills elementary school children can master. And, when mastered, these skills are a source of great pleasure and accomplishment for children. In gross motor skills involving large muscle activity, boys usually outperform girls.

As children move through the elementary school years, they gain greater control over their bodies and can sit for longer periods of time. However, elementary school children are far from being physically mature, and they need to be active. Elementary school children become more fatigued by long periods of sitting than by running, jumping, or bicycling. Physical action is essential for children to refine their developing skills, such as batting a ball, skipping rope, or balancing on a beam. An important principle of practice for elementary school children, therefore, is that they should be engaged in *active,* rather than passive, activities.

Increased myelination of the nervous system is reflected in the improvement of fine motor skills during middle and late childhood. Children use their hands more adroitly as tools. Six-year-olds can hammer, paste, tie shoes, and fasten clothes. By 7 years of age, children's hands have become steadier. At this age, children prefer a pencil to a crayon for printing, reversal of letters is less common, and printing becomes smaller. At 8 to 10 years of age, children can use their hands independently with more ease and precision. Fine motor coordination develops to the point at which children use cursive writing rather than printing. Letter size becomes smaller and more even. At 10 to 12 years of age, children begin to show manipulative skills similar to the abilities of adults. They can now master the complex, intricate, and rapid movements needed to produce fine-quality crafts or to play a difficult piece on a musical instrument. Girls usually outperform boys in fine motor skills. A summary of changes in motor skills in middle and late childhood appears in Figure 11.2. Note that some children perform these skills earlier or later than other children.

Age	Motor Skills
6	Children can skip. Children can throw with proper weight shift and step. Girls and boys can vertically jump 7 inches. Girls can do a standing long jump of 33 inches, boys 36 inches. Children can cut and paste. Children enjoy making simple figures in clay.
7	Children can balance on one foot without looking. Children can walk 2-inch-wide balance beams. Children can hop and jump accurately into small squares. Children can participate in jumping jack exercise. Girls can throw a ball 25 feet, boys 45 feet. Girls can vertically jump 8 inches, boys 9 inches. Girls can do a standing long jump of 41 inches, boys 43 inches.
8	Children can engage in alternate rhythmic hopping in different patterns. Girls can throw a ball 34 feet, boys 59 feet. Girls can vertically jump 9 inches, boys 10 inches. Girls can perform a standing long jump of 50 inches, boys 55 inches. Children's grip strength increases. Children can use common tools, such as a hammer.
9	Girls can throw a ball 41 feet, boys 71 feet. Girls can vertically jump 10 inches, boys 11 inches. Girls can perform a standing long jump of 53 inches, boys 57 inches. Children's perceptual-motor coordination becomes smoother.
10	Children can judge and intercept pathways of small balls thrown from a distance. Girls can throw a small ball 49 feet, boys 94 feet. Girls can vertically jump 10 inches, boys 11 inches.

FIGURE 11.2 Changes in Motor Skills During Middle and Late Childhood

Review and Reflect: Learning Goal 1

1 Discuss changes in body growth, the brain, and motor development in middle and late childhood

REVIEW

- How do skeletal and muscular systems change in middle and late childhood?
- What characterizes changes in the brain during middle and late childhood?
- How do children's gross and fine motor skills change in middle and late childhood?

REFLECT

- Look at Figure 11.2. On which of the motor skills were you especially competent? Not competent? Do you think your motor skills as a child were primarily influenced by your heredity or your environment? Explain.

2 WHAT ARE THE CENTRAL ISSUES IN CHILDREN'S HEALTH?

| Nutrition | Exercise and Sports | Overweight Children | Diseases | Accidents and Injuries |

Although we have become a health-conscious nation, many children as well as adults do not practice good health habits. Too much junk food and too much couch-potato behavior describe the habits of all too many children. We begin our exploration of children's health with nutrition and exercise, then turn to a number of health problems that can emerge.

Nutrition

In the middle and late childhood years, children's average body weight doubles. Children exert considerable energy as they engage in many different motor activities. To support their growth and active lives, children need to consume more food than they did in early childhood. From 1 to 3 years of age, infants and toddlers should consume about 1,300 calories per day. At 4 to 6 years of age, young children should take in around 1,700 calories per day. From 7 to 10 years of age, children should consume about 2,400 calories per day; however, depending on the child's size, the range of recommended calories for 7- to 10-year-olds is 1,650 to 3,300 per day.

Within these calorie ranges, it is important to impress on children the value of a balanced diet to promote their growth (Schiff, 2009). Children usually eat as their families eat, so the quality of their diet often depends largely on their family's pattern of eating. Most children acquire a taste for an increasing variety of food in middle and late childhood. However, with the increased availability of fast-food restaurants and media inducements, too many children fill up on food that has "empty calories" that do not promote effective growth. Many of these empty-calorie foods have a high content of sugar, starch, and excess fat (Wardlaw & Hampl, 2007).

Both parents and teachers can help children learn to eat better. In this vein, they can help children learn about the Food Guide Pyramid and what a healthy diet entails (Wardlaw & Smith, 2009).

FIGURE 11.3 Percentage of Children Involved in Daily Physical Education Programs in the United States from 1969 to 1999 There has been a dramatic drop in the percentage of children participating in daily physical education programs in the United States from 80 percent in 1969 to only 20 percent in 1999.

We are underexercised as a nation. We look instead of play. We ride instead of walk. Our existence deprives us of the minimum of physical activity essential for healthy living.

—JOHN F. KENNEDY
American President, 20th Century

Children should begin their day by eating a healthy breakfast; according to nutritionists, breakfast should make up about one-fourth of the day's calories. A nutritious breakfast helps children have more energy and be more alert in the morning hours of school (James & Ashwill, 2007). In one study of low-income elementary-school-age children, those who participated in a school breakfast program improved their standardized achievement test scores more, and had fewer absences, than the children who qualified for the program but did not participate (Meyers & others, 1989).

Exercise and Sports

How much exercise do children get? What are children's sports like? These topics and more are explored in the following section of this chapter.

Exercise American children are not getting enough exercise (Fahey, Insel, & Roth, 2009; Rink, 2009). In one historical comparison, the percentage of children involved in daily P.E. programs in schools decreased from 80 percent in 1969 to 20 percent in 1999 (Health Management Resources, 2001) (see Figure 11.3). Educators and policy makers in numerous other countries around the world, including China, Finland, and Great Britain, have become very concerned about the sedentary lifestyles of many children in their countries (Fogelholm, 2008; Liu & others, 2008).

Television watching is linked with low activity and obesity in children (Wells & others, 2008). A related concern is the dramatic increase in computer use by children. Researchers have found that the total time that children and adolescents spend in front of a television or computer screen places them at risk for reduced activity and being overweight (Lajunen & others, 2007). One study revealed that children who watched two or more hours of TV a day were less likely to participate in organized physical activities and less likely to have two or more servings of fruit a day than their counterparts who watched less than two hours of TV a day (Salmon, Campbell, & Crawford, 2006). A longitudinal study also found that a higher incidence of watching TV in childhood and adolescence was linked with being overweight, being less physically fit, and having higher cholesterol levels at 26 years of age (Hancox, Milne, & Poulton, 2004).

Some of the blame also falls on the nation's schools, many of which fail to provide daily physical education classes (Floriani & Kennedy, 2008; Rink, 2009). Many children's school weeks do not include adequate physical education classes, and the majority of children do not exercise vigorously even when they are in such classes (Kovar & others, 2007; Rink, 2009). Furthermore, most children's parents are poor role models for vigorous physical exercise (Lou, Ganley, & Flynn, 2002).

An increasing number of studies document the important of exercise in children's physical and cognitive development:

- A high-intensity resistance training program decreased children's body fat and increased their muscle strength (Benson, Torode, & Fiatarone Singh, 2008).
- Forty-five minutes of moderate physical activity and 15 minutes of vigorous physical activity daily were related to decreased odds that the children were overweight (Wittmeier, Mollard, & Kriellaars, 2008).
- Aerobic exercise was linked to increases in an important cognitive activity—planning—in overweight 9-year-old children (Davis & others, 2007).
- Nine-year-old girls who were more physically fit (as measured on a field test of aerobic capacity) showed better cognitive performance on a cognitive control task that involved inhibiting task-irrelevant information to obtain correct solutions than 9-year-old girls who were less physically fit (Hillman & others, 2009).

In addition to the school, the family plays an important role in a child's exercise program (Beets & Foley, 2008; Corbin & others, 2008). One study revealed that 9- to 13-year-olds were more likely to engage in physical activity during their free time when the children felt safe, had a number of places to be active, and had parents who participated in physical activities with them (Heitzler & others, 2006). Indeed, a wise strategy is that parents take up activities involving vigorous physical exercise that parents and children can enjoy together. Running, swimming, cycling, and hiking are especially recommended.

What are some good strategies for increasing children's exercise?

Sports Despite the growing concern about lack of exercise, more and more children become involved in sports every year. Both in public schools and in community agencies, children's sports programs have changed the shape of many children's lives.

Participation in sports can have both positive and negative consequences for children. Sports can provide exercise, opportunities to learn how to compete, increased self-esteem, and a setting for developing peer relations and friendships (Hoffman & others, 2005). One study revealed that participation in sports for three hours or more per week beyond regular physical education classes was related to increased physical fitness and lower fat mass in 9-year-old boys (Ara & others, 2004).

Sports also can have negative outcomes for children: the pressure to achieve and win, physical injuries, a distraction from academic work, and unrealistic expectations for success as an athlete (Lovell & Fazio, 2008; Metzl, 2008). Few people challenge the value of sports for children when they are conducted as part of a school physical education or intramural program. However, some critics question the appropriateness of highly competitive, win-oriented sports teams in schools and communities, intense participation in sports at an early age, and the physical strain placed on children's bodies that can result in overuse injuries (Browne & Lam, 2006). It is important to keep in mind that learning the basic skills of a sport, rather than narrowly focusing on winning, develops a child's self-confidence, coordination, and strength (Mood, Musker, & Rink, 2007).

In the *Caring for Children* interlude that follows, you can read about some positive strategies for parents to follow regarding their children's sports participation.

Caring for Children

PARENTS AND CHILDREN'S SPORTS

Most sports psychologists stress that it is important for parents to show an interest in their children's sports participation. Most children want their parents to watch them perform in sports. In fact, many children whose parents do not come to watch them play in sporting events feel that their parents do not adequately support them. However, some children become extremely nervous when their parents watch them perform, or they are embarrassed when their parents cheer too loudly or make a fuss. If children request that their parents not watch them perform, parents should respect their children's wishes (Schreiber, 1990).

Parents should compliment their children for their sports performance. In the course of a game, there are dozens of circumstances when the child has done something positive, and parents should stress a child's good performance, even if the child has limited abilities. Parents can tell their children how much the children hustled in the game and how enthusiastically they played (Dweck, 2006). Even if the child strikes out in a baseball game, a parent can say, "That was a nice swing."

(continued on next page)

One of the hardest things for parents to do is to watch their children practicing or performing at a sport without helping them, to let their children make mistakes without interfering. Naturally, parents want to provide their children with support and encouragement, but there is a point at which parental involvement becomes overinvolvement. I have coached a number of young tennis players and have seen many parents who handled well their roles as a nurturant, considerate parent—but I have observed others who became too involved in their children's sport. Some parents were aware of their tendency to become too involved and backed off from pushing their children too intensely. However, some were not aware of their intrusiveness and did not back off. The worst parent had a daughter who, at the age of 9, was already nationally ranked and showed great promise. Her father went to every lesson, every practice session, every tournament. Her tennis began to consume his life. At one tournament, he stormed onto the court during one of her matches and accused his daughter's 10-year-old opponent of cheating, embarrassing his daughter and himself. I called him the next day, told him I no longer could coach his daughter because of his behavior, and recommended that he seek counseling or not go to any more of her matches.

If parents do not become too involved, they can help their children build their physical skills and help them emotionally—discussing with them to deal with a difficult coach, how to cope with a tough loss, and how to put in perspective a poorly played game, and how to apply the things learned from sports to life in general (Dweck, 2006). Parents need to carefully monitor their children as they participate in sports for signs of developing stress. If the problems appear to be beyond the intuitive skills of a volunteer coach or parent, consultation with a counselor or clinician may be needed. Also, a parent needs to be sensitive to whether the sport in which the child is participating is the best one for the child and whether the child can handle its competitive pressures.

Some guidelines provided by the Women's Sports Foundation in its booklet *Parents' Guide to Girls' Sports* can benefit both parents and coaches of all children in sports:

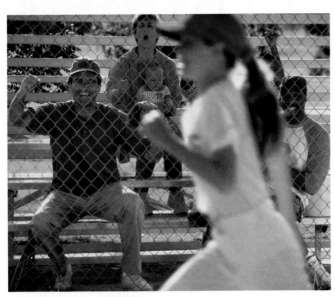

What are positive strategies for parents to adopt regarding their children's participation in sports?

The Dos

- Make sports fun; the more children enjoy sports, the more they will want to play.
- Remember that it is okay for children to make mistakes; it means they are trying.
- Allow children to ask questions about the sport and discuss the sport in a calm, supportive manner.
- Show respect for the child's sports participation.
- Be positive and convince the child that he or she is making a good effort.
- Be a positive role model for the child in sports.

The Don'ts

- Don't yell or scream at the child.
- Never condemn the child for poor play or continue to bring up failures long after they happen.
- Don't point out the child's errors in front of others.
- Don't expect the child to learn something immediately.
- Don't expect the child to become a pro.
- Never ridicule or make fun of the child.
- Never compare the child to siblings or to more talented children.
- Don't make sports all work and no fun.

Now let's turn our attention to additional children's health issues. For most children, middle and late childhood is a time of excellent health. Disease and death are less prevalent in this period than in other periods of childhood and adolescence. However, some children do have health problems, such as obesity, cancer, diabetes, cardiovascular disease, asthma, and injuries due to accidents.

Overweight Children

Being overweight is an increasing health problem in the United States and elsewhere (Frisco, 2009; Li & others, 2009). Recall from Chapter 8, "Physical Development in Early Childhood," that being overweight is defined in terms of body mass index (BMI), which is computed by a formula that takes into account height and weight. Also, children at or above the 95th percentile of BMI are included in the overweight category, whereas children at or above the 85th percentile are described as at risk for being overweight (Centers for Disease Control and Prevention, 2009).

Over the last three decades, the percentage of U.S. children who are at risk for being overweight has doubled from 15 percent in the 1970s to almost 30 percent today, and the percentage of children who are overweight has tripled during this time frame (Paxson & others, 2006). And it is not just in the United States that children are becoming more overweight. Recent surveys and policy prescriptions in Australia, mainland China, Hong Kong, and other countries indicate that more and more children in many countries around the world are becoming overweight (Chan, 2008; Li & others, 2008).

Recently, however, the increase in child obesity in the United States has begun to level off. A large-scale U.S. study using the criteria for obesity just stated revealed that child obesity increased from 7 percent to 11 percent from 1980 to 1994 but was essentially the same from 2002 (16 percent) to 2006 (17 percent), not a statistically significant increase (Odgen, Carroll, & Flegal, 2008).

Still, the levels of child obesity, overweight, and risk for being overweight are far too high (Frisco, 2009). Note that girls are more likely than boys to be overweight, and this gender difference occurs in many countries (Sweeting, 2008). In a recent large-scale U.S. study, African American and Latino children were more likely to be overweight or obese than non-Latino White children (Benson, Baer, & Kaelber, 2009).

Chapter 8, "Physical Development in Early Childhood," cited research that found being overweight at 3 years of age was a risk factor for being overweight at 12 years of age (Nader & others, 2006). In that study, it also was revealed that 80 percent of the children who were overweight at any time during the elementary school years remained overweight at 12 years of age. Researchers have found that being overweight as a child is a risk factor for being obese as an adult (Janssen & others, 2005). For example, a longitudinal study revealed that girls who were overweight in childhood were 11 to 30 times more likely to be obese in adulthood than girls who were not overweight in childhood (Thompson & others, 2007). And a recent study found that children with high body mass index and waist circumference are at risk for metabolic syndrome (a constellation of factors including obesity, high blood pressure, and type 2 diabetes that place individuals at risk for developing cardiovascular disease) in adulthood (Sun & others, 2008).

Girls are more likely than boys to be overweight (Sweeting, 2008). Overweight children with cardiovascular problems are more likely to come from low-socioeconomic-status families than higher-status ones (Longo-Mbenza, Lukoki, & M'Buyambia-Kabangu, 2007). Being overweight is less common in African American than in non-Latino White children during childhood, but this trend reverses during adolescence.

What Factors Are Linked with Being Overweight in Childhood? Heredity and environmental contexts are related to being overweight in childhood. Recent genetic analysis indicates that heredity is an important factor in children becoming overweight (Wardle & others, 2008). Overweight parents tend to have overweight children, even if they are not living in the same household (Wardlaw & Hampl, 2007). One study found that the greatest risk factor for being overweight at 9 years of age was having a parent who is overweight (Agras & others, 2004). Characteristics such as body type, height, body fat composition, and metabolism are inherited from parents (Walley, Blakemore, & Froguel, 2006).

Environmental factors that influence whether children become overweight or not include the greater availability of food (especially food high in fat content), energy-saving devices, declining physical activity, a lack of parental monitoring of children's eating habits, the context in which a child eats, and heavy TV watching (Byrd-Williams & others, 2008; Shoup & others, 2008). The American culture provides ample encouragement of overeating in children. Food is everywhere children go and is easily accessed—in vending machines, fast-food restaurants, and so on (Rosenheck, 2008). Also, the portion size that children eat in meals in the United States has grown. And a recent study revealed a link between higher levels of watching TV with being overweight in childhood (Wells & others, 2008).

Parents play an important role in children's eating habits and the likelihood they will become overweight or not (Wofford, 2008). One study revealed that Latino parents who monitored what their children ate had children who ate healthier foods and exercised more than their counterparts whose eating habits were not as closely monitored (Arredondo & others, 2006). In another study, the context in which fourth- to sixth-grade children ate was linked with what they ate and their tendency to be overweight (Cullen, 2001). Children who ate with their families were more likely to eat lower-fat foods (such as low-fat milk and salad dressing, lean meats, and vegetables) and drank fewer sodas than children who ate alone. Overweight children ate 50 percent of their meals in front of a TV, compared with only 35 percent of normal-weight children.

Consequences of Being Overweight in Childhood

The increase in overweight children in recent decades is cause for great concern because being overweight raises the risk for many medical and psychological problems (Oude & others, 2009; Pott & others, 2009). Overweight children are at risk for developing pulmonary problems, such as sleep apnea (which involves upper-airway obstruction), and hip problems (Tauman & Gozal, 2006). Diabetes, hypertension (high blood pressure), and elevated blood cholesterol levels also are common in children who are overweight (Viikari & others, 2009). Once considered rare, hypertension in children has become increasingly common in overweight children (Jafar, 2009). Overweight children with cardiovascular problems are more likely to come from low-socioeconomic-status families than higher-status ones (Longo-Mbenza, Jukoki, & M'Buyambia-Kabangu, 2007). Social and psychological consequences of being overweight in childhood include low self-esteem, depression, and some exclusion of obese children from peer groups (Datar & Sturm, 2004; Gibson & others, 2008). A recent study revealed that obese children were perceived as less attractive, more tired, and more socially withdrawn than nonobese peers (Zeller, Reiter-Purtill, & Ramey, 2008).

Treatment of Children Who Are Overweight

Many experts recommend a program that involves a combination of diet, exercise, and behavior modification to help children lose weight (Wittmeier, Mollard, & Kriellaars, 2008). One study found that overweight children spent 51 percent more time in sedentary activity than children who were not overweight (Yu & others, 2002). Thus, exercise is an extremely important component of a successful weight-loss program for overweight children (Benson, Torode, & Fiatarone Singh, 2008). Exercise increases the child's lean body mass, which increases the child's resting metabolic rate. These changes result in more calories being burned in the resting state.

Children's activity levels are influenced not only by heredity but also by their motivation to engage in energetic activities, as well as by caregivers who model an active lifestyle or provide children with opportunities to be active (Lindsay & others, 2006). In a typical behavior modification program, children are taught to monitor their own behavior, keeping a food diary while attempting to lose weight. The diary should record not only the type and amount of food eaten but also when, with whom, and where it was eaten. That is, do children eat in front of the TV, by themselves, or because they are angry or depressed? A diary identifies behaviors that need to be changed.

In keeping a diary, children, with the help of their parents, can calculate and keep track of the number of calories they consume. Moderate-calorie diets are more successful over the long term than are those involving extreme deprivation of calories. Educating children to modify their eating habits and learn to make wise food choices can help in weight control.

Intervention programs with overweight children are frequently conducted through schools and often focus on teaching children and parents about developing a healthy diet, exercising more, and reducing TV viewing time (Shaya & others, 2008). A promising strategy is to provide students with healthier foods to eat at school. Several states now have laws that require healthier foods to be sold in vending machines at schools. In one intervention, reducing soft drink consumption at schools was linked with a subsequent reduction in the number of 7- to 11-year-old children who were overweight (James & others, 2004). Schools also can play an important role by implementing programs that increase the amount of time children exercise.

Parents play an important role in preventing children from becoming overweight (Slawta & Deneui, 2009). They can encourage healthy eating habits in children by "increasing the number of family meals eaten together, making healthful foods available, and reducing the availability of sugar-sweetened beverages and sodas" (Lindsay & others, 2006, p. 173). They also can help reduce the likelihood their children will become overweight by reducing children's TV time, getting children involved in sports and other physical activities, and being healthy, physically active models themselves (Salmon, Campbell, & Crawford, 2006). As we learned in Angie's story, a combination of behavioral modification, parental involvement, and a structured program can effectively help overweight children (Robbins, Powers, & Burgess, 2008).

How Would You...?

As a health-care professional, how would you use your knowledge of overweight risk factors to design a workshop for parents and children about healthy lifestyle choices?

What can parents do to prevent their children from being overweight or obese?

Diseases

Four childhood diseases can especially be harmful to children's development. They are (1) cancer, (2) diabetes, (3) cardiovascular disease, and (4) asthma.

Cancer   Cancer is the second leading cause of death in U.S. children 5 to 14 years of age. One in every 330 children in the United States develops cancer before the age of 19. The incidence of cancer in children has slightly increased in recent years (National Cancer Institute, 2008a).

Child cancers mainly attack the white blood cells (leukemia), brain, bone, lymph system, muscles, kidneys, and nervous system. All are characterized by an uncontrolled proliferation of abnormal cells (Hijiya & others, 2007). As indicated in Figure 11.4, the most common cancer in children is leukemia, a cancer in which bone marrow manufactures an abundance of abnormal white blood cells, which crowd out normal cells, making the child susceptible to bruising and infection (Chang, 2009; Stanulla & Schrappe, 2009).

When cancer strikes children, it behaves differently than it does when it attacks adults. Children frequently have a more advanced stage of cancer when they are first diagnosed. When cancer is first diagnosed in adults, it has spread to distant parts of the body in only about 20 percent of the cases; however, that figure rises to 80 percent in children. Most adult cancers result from lifestyle factors, such as smoking, diet, occupation, and exposure to other cancer-causing agents. By contrast, little is

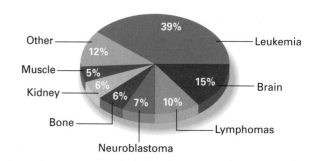

Other — 12%
Muscle — 5%
Kidney — 6%
Bone — 6%
Neuroblastoma — 7%
Lymphomas — 10%
Brain — 15%
Leukemia — 39%

FIGURE 11.4 Types of Cancer in Children Cancers in children have a profile different from that of cancers in adults, which attack mainly the lungs colon, breast, prostate, and pancreas.

known about the causes of childhood cancers. Researchers are searching for possible genetic links to childhood cancers (Kennedy & D'Andrea, 2006).

Because of advancements in cancer treatment, children with cancer are surviving longer (National Cancer Institute, 2008b). For example, in the 1960s, less than 5 percent of children with an acute form of leukemia survived for more than five years; today, approximately 25 percent of these children survive for five years or more.

Diabetes Diabetes is one of the most common chronic diseases in children and adolescents. In type 1 diabetes, the body produces little or no insulin (the hormone that regulates the body's blood sugar level). **Type 1 diabetes** is an autoimmune disease in which the body's immune system destroys insulin-producing cells. In **type 2 diabetes,** the most common type of diabetes, the body is able to produce insulin, but it may not be enough or the body cells may be unable to use it. Risk factors for type 2 diabetes include being overweight and/or physically inactive, having relatives with this disease, or belonging to certain ethnic groups (Jones, 2008; Song & Hardisty, 2008). Native Americans, African Americans, Latinos, and Asian Americans are at greater risk for developing diabetes.

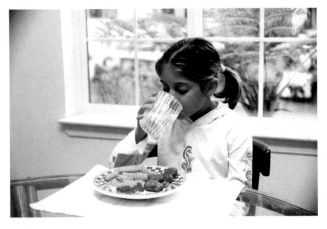

What are some concerns about children's cardiovascular health and obesity?

Cardiovascular Disease Cardiovascular disease is uncommon in children. Nonetheless, environmental experiences and behavior in the childhood years can sow the seeds for cardiovascular disease in adulthood. Many elementary-school-aged children already possess one or more of the risk factors for cardiovascular disease, such as hypertension and obesity (Beilin & Huang, 2008; Urbina, 2008). A recent national study found that an increasing percentage of U.S. children and adolescents had elevated blood pressure from 1988 to 2006 (Ostchega & others, 2009). In this study, children who were obese were more likely to have elevated blood pressure. A recent study revealed that high blood pressure goes undiagnosed in 75 percent of children with the disease (Hansen, Gunn, & Kaelber, 2007). Another study found that high blood pressure was most likely to be present in Latino children (25 percent) and least characteristic of Asian American children (14 percent) (Sorof & others, 2004). To read further about research on children's cardiovascular health, see the *Research in Children's Development* interlude.

Research in Children's Development

HEART SMART

One large-scale investigation designed to improve children's cardiovascular health is the Bogalusa Heart Study, also called Heart Smart. It involves an ongoing evaluation of 8,000 boys and girls in Bogalusa, Louisiana (Berenson, 2005; Chen, Srinivasan, & Berenson, 2008; Freedman & others, 2008; Frontini & others, 2008). Heart Smart intervention takes place in schools. Since 95 percent of children and adolescents aged 5 to 18 are in school, school is an efficient context in which to educate individuals about health. Special attention is given to teachers, who serve as role models. Teachers who value the role of health in life and who engage in health-enhancing behavior present children and adolescents with positive models for health. Teacher in-service education is conducted by an interdisciplinary team of specialists, including physicians, psychologists, nutritionists, physical educators, and exercise physiologists. The school's staff is introduced to heart health education, the nature of cardiovascular disease, and risk factors for heart disease. Coping behavior, exercise behavior, and eating behavior are discussed with the staff, and a Heart Smart curriculum is explained.

type 1 diabetes An autoimmune disease, in which the body's immune system destroys insulin-producing cells.

type 2 diabetes The most common type of diabetes, in which the body is able to produce insulin, but it may not be enough or the body cells may be unable to use it.

The Heart Smart curriculum for grade 5 includes strategies for improvement of cardiovascular health, eating behavior, and exercise. The physical education component of Heart Smart involves two to four class periods each week to incorporate a "Superkids-Superfit" exercise program. The physical education instructor teaches skills required by the school system plus aerobic activities aimed at cardiovascular conditioning, including jogging, racewalking, interval workouts, rope skipping, circuit training, aerobic dance, and games. Classes begin and end with five minutes of walking and stretching.

The school lunch program serves as an intervention site, where sodium, fat, and sugar levels are decreased. Children and adolescents are given reasons why they should eat healthy foods, such as a tuna sandwich, and why they should not eat unhealthy foods, such as a hot dog with chili. The school lunch program includes a salad bar, where children and adolescents can serve themselves. The amount and type of snack foods sold on the school premises are monitored.

High-risk children—those with elevated blood pressure, cholesterol, and high weight—are identified as part of Heart Smart (Freedman & others, 2008). A multidisciplinary team of physicians, nutritionists, nurses, and behavioral counselors works with the high-risk boys and girls and their parents through group-oriented activities and individual-based family counseling. High-risk boys and girls and their parents receive diet, exercise, and relaxation prescriptions in an intensive 12-session program, followed by long-term monthly evaluations.

Extensive assessment is a part of this ongoing program. Short-term and long-term changes in children's knowledge about cardiovascular disease and changes in their behavior are assessed.

Following are some results from the Bogalusa Heart Study:

- More than half of the children exceeded the recommended intake of salt, fat, cholesterol, and sugar (Nicklas & others, 1995).
- Consumption of sweetened beverages, sweets (desserts, candy), and total consumption of low-quality food were associated with being overweight in childhood (Nicklas & others, 2003).
- Adiposity (having excess body weight) beginning in childhood was related to cardiovascular problems in adulthood (Freedman & others, 2008; Li & others, 2004).
- Higher body mass index (BMI) in childhood was linked to the likelihood of developing metabolic syndrome (a cluster of characteristics that include excessive fat around the abdomen, high blood pressure, and diabetes) in adulthood (Freedman & others, 2005).

Asthma **Asthma** is a chronic lung disease that involves episodes of airflow obstruction. Symptoms of an asthma attack include shortness of breath, wheezing, or tightness in the chest. The incidence of asthma has risen steadily in recent decades, possibly because of increased air pollution (Robinson & Van Asperen, 2009; Zhao & others, 2008). Asthma is the most common chronic disease in U.S. children, being present in 7 to 12 percent of them (Liu, 2002). Asthma is the primary reason for absences from school, and it is responsible for a number of pediatric admissions to emergency rooms and hospitals (Horner & Bacharier, 2009; Sotir & others, 2006).

The exact causes of asthma are not known, but it is believed that the disease results from hypersensitivity to environmental substances, which trigger an allergic reaction (Heguy & others, 2008). A recent research review concluded that the following are asthma risk factors: being male, having one or both parents with asthma, and/or having allergy sensitivity, stress early in life, infections, obesity, and exposure to environmental tobacco smoke, indoor allergens, and outdoor pollutants (Feleszko & others, 2006). A recent study also revealed that preterm birth

asthma A chronic lung disease that involves episodes of airflow obstruction.

Careers in Children's Development

Sharon McLeod, Child Life Specialist

Sharon McLeod is a child life specialist who is clinical director of the Child Life and Recreational Therapy Department at the Children's Hospital Medical Center in Cincinnati.

Under McLeod's direction, the goals of the Child Life Department are to promote children's optimal growth and development, reduce the stress of health-care experiences, and provide support to child patients and their families. These goals are accomplished through therapeutic play and developmentally appropriate activities, educating and psychologically preparing children for medical procedures, and serving as a resource for parents and others professionals regarding children's development and health-care issues.

McLeod says that human growth and development provides the foundation for her profession of child life specialist. She also describes her best times as a student when she conducted fieldwork, had an internship, and experienced hands-on theories and concepts she learned in her courses.

Sharon McLeod, child life specialist, working with a child at Children's Hospital Medical Center in Cincinnati.

and child care outside the home were linked to childhood asthma (van Beijsterveldt & Boomsma, 2008).

Corticosteroids, which generally are inhaled, are the most effective anti-inflammatory drugs for treating asthmatic children (Zuidgeest & others, 2009). Often, parents have kept asthmatic children from exercising because they fear exercise will provoke an asthma attack. However, today it is believed that children with asthma should be encouraged to exercise, provided their asthma is under control, and participation should be evaluated on an individual basis (Basaran & others, 2006). Some asthmatic children lose their symptoms in adolescence and adulthood (Vonk & others, 2004).

One individual who helps children cope with their health-care experiences is child life specialist Sharon McLeod. To read about her work, see the *Careers in Children's Development* profile.

Accidents and Injuries

Injuries are the leading cause of death during middle and late childhood, and the most common cause of severe injury and death in this period is motor vehicle accidents, either as a pedestrian or as a passenger (Wilson & Hockenberry, 2008). The use of safety-belt restraint greatly reduces the severity of motor vehicle injuries. Other serious injuries involve bicycles, skateboards, roller skates, and other sports equipment.

Most accidents occur in or near the child's home or school. The most effective prevention strategy is to educate the child about proper use of equipment and the hazards of risk taking (Betz & Sowden, 2008). Safety helmets, protective eye and mouth shields, and protective padding are recommended for children who engage in active sports (Briem & others, 2004).

As we saw in Chapter 8, "Physical Development in Early Childhood," caregivers play a key role in preventing childhood injuries. A recent study in four developing countries (Ethiopia, Peru, Vietnam, and India) revealed that depression in caregivers was consistently linked to children's risk of injury for all types of injury assessed (burns, serious falls, broken bones, and near-fatal injury) (Howe, Huttly, & Abramsky, 2006).

How Would You...?
As a health-care professional, how would you work with school-age children to reduce their chances of injury due to accidents?

Review and Reflect: Learning Goal 2

2 **Characterize children's health in middle and late childhood**

REVIEW

- What are key aspects of children's nutrition in middle and late childhood?
- What roles do exercise and sports play in children's development?
- What is the nature of being overweight in childhood?
- What four diseases are especially harmful to children?
- What is the most common cause of severe injury and death in childhood?

REFLECT

- How good were your eating habits as a child? How much did you exercise in middle and late childhood? Are your eating and exercise habits today similar to or different from your eating and exercise habits as a child? Why are they similar or different?

---

3 WHAT ARE THE PREVALENT DISABILITIES IN CHILDREN?

| Who Are Children with Disabilities? | The Range of Disabilities | Educational Issues |

Our discussion of children's health has focused on nutrition and exercise. In addition, we have discussed some of the most common health problems, such as obesity, cancer, diabetes, cardiovascular disease, and asthma. In this section, we turn our attention to children with disabilities and the issues involved in their education.

Who Are Children with Disabilities?

Approximately 14 percent of all children from 3 to 21 years of age in the United States receive special education or related services (National Center for Education Statistics, 2008). Figure 11.5 shows the four largest groups of students with a disability who were served by federal programs in the 2006–2007 school year (National Center for Education Statistics, 2008). As indicated in Figure 11.5, students with a learning disability were by far the largest group of students with a disability to be given special education, followed by children with speech or language impairments, mental retardation, and emotional disturbance.

Educators now prefer to speak of "children with disabilities" rather than "handicapped children" to emphasize the person, not the disability (Hallahan, Kauffman, & Pullen, 2009). The term "handicapping conditions" is still used to describe impediments to the learning and functioning of individuals with a disability that have been imposed by society. For example, that children who use a wheelchair do not have access to a bathroom, transportation, and so on, this is referred to as a handicap situation.

The Range of Disabilities

In this section, we examine learning disabilities, attention deficit hyperactivity disorder, speech disorders, sensory disorders, physical disorders, emotional and behavioral disorders, and autism. In Chapter 12, "Cognitive Development in Middle and Late Childhood," we will study mental retardation.

Disability	Percentage of All Children in U.S. Public Schools
Learning disabilities	5.6
Speech and language impairments	3.0
Mental retardation	1.1
Emotional disturbance	0.9

FIGURE 11.5 The Four Highest Percentages of Students with a Disability Served by a Federal Program as a Percentage of All Students Enrolled in U.S. Public Schools (National Center for Education Statistics, 2008)

Learning Disabilities Bobby's second-grade teacher complains that his spelling is awful. Eight-year-old Tim says reading is really hard for him, and often the words don't make much sense. Alisha has good oral language skills but has considerable difficulty in computing correct answers to arithmetic problems. Each of these students has a learning disability.

Characteristics and Identification The U.S. government created a definition of learning disabilities in 1997 and then reauthorized the definition with a few minor changes in 2004. Following is a description of the government's definition of what determines whether a child should be classified as having a learning disability. A child with a **learning disability** has difficulty in learning that involves understanding or using spoken or written language, and the difficulty can appear in listening, thinking, reading, writing, or spelling. A learning disability also may involve difficulty in doing mathematics. To be classified as a learning disability, the learning problem is not primarily the result of visual, hearing, or motor disabilities; mental retardation; of emotional disorders; or of environmental, cultural, or economic disadvantage.

From the mid-1970s through the early 1990s, there was a dramatic increase in the percentage of U.S. students receiving special education services (from 1.8 percent in 1976–1977 to 12.2 percent in 1994–1995), although in the twenty-first century there has been a slight decrease in this percentage (6.1 percent in 2000 to 5.6 percent in 2006–2007) (National Center for Education Statistics, 2008). Some experts say that the dramatic increase reflected poor diagnostic practices and overidentification. They argue that teachers sometimes are too quick to label children with the slightest learning problem as having a learning disability, instead of recognizing that the problem may rest in their ineffective teaching. Other experts say the increase in the number of children being labeled with a "learning disability" is justified (Bender, 2008; Hallahan, Kaufmann, & Pullen, 2009).

About three times as many boys as girls are classified as having a learning disability. Among the explanations for this gender difference are a greater biological vulnerability among boys and *referral bias* (that is, boys are more likely to be referred by teachers for treatment because of their behavior) (Liederman, Kantrowitz, & Flannery, 2005).

Most learning disabilities are lifelong. Compared with children without a learning disability, children with a learning disability are more likely to show poor academic performance, high dropout rates, and poor employment and postsecondary education records (Berninger, 2006). Children with a learning disability who are taught in the regular classroom without extensive support rarely achieve the level of competence of even children who are low-achieving and do not have a disability (Hocutt, 1996). Still, despite the problems they encounter, many children with a learning disability grow up to lead normal lives and engage in productive work. For example, actress Whoopi Goldberg and investment company owner Charles Schwab have learning disabilities.

Diagnosing whether a child has a learning disability is often a difficult task (Bender, 2008; Fritschmann & Solari, 2008). Because federal guidelines are just that—guidelines—it is up to each state, or in some cases school systems within a state, to determine how to define and implement diagnosis of learning disabilities. The same child might be diagnosed as having a learning disability in one school system and receive services but not be diagnosed and not receive services in another school system. In such cases, parents sometimes will move either to obtain or to avoid the diagnosis.

Initial identification of a possible learning disability usually is made by the classroom teacher. If a learning disability is suspected, the teacher calls on specialists. An interdisciplinary team of professionals is best suited to verify whether a student has a learning disability. Individual psychological evaluations (of intelligence) and educational assessments (such as current level of achievement) are required (Hallahan, Kauffman, & Pullen, 2009). In addition, tests of visual-motor skills, language, and memory may be used.

How Would You...?
As an educator, how would you explain the nature of learning disabilities to a parent whose child has recently been diagnosed with a learning disability?

learning disability Disability in which a child has difficulty in learning that involves understanding or using spoken or written language, and the difficulty can appear in listening, thinking, reading, writing, or spelling. A learning disability also may involve difficulty in doing mathematics. To be classified as a learning disability, the learning problem is not primarily the result of visual, hearing, or motor disabilities; mental retardation; emotional disorders; or due to environmental, cultural, or economic disadvantage.

Reading, Writing, and Math Difficulties The most common academic areas in which children with a learning disability have problems are reading, writing, and math (Bursuck & Damer, 2007). A problem with reading affects approximately 80 percent of children with a learning disability (Shaywitz, Gruen, & Shaywitz, 2007). Such children have difficulty with phonological skills, which involve being able to understand how sounds and letters match up to make words, and also can have problems in comprehension. **Dyslexia** is a category reserved for individuals with a severe impairment in their ability to read and spell (Mathes & Fletcher, 2008; Reid & others, 2009).

Dysgraphia is a learning disability that involves difficulty in handwriting (Adi-Japha & others, 2007). Children with dysgraphia may write very slowly, their writing products may be virtually illegible, and they may make numerous spelling errors because of their inability to match up sounds and letters.

Dyscalculia, also known as developmental arithmetic disorder, is a learning disability that involves difficulty in math computation (Rubinsten & Henik, 2009). It is estimated to characterize 2 to 6 percent of U.S. elementary school children (National Center for Learning Disabilities, 2006). Researchers have found that children with difficulties in math computation often have cognitive and neuropsychological deficits, including problems with working memory, visual perception, and visuospatial abilities (Shalev, 2004). A child may have both a reading and a math disability, and there are cognitive deficits that characterize both types of disabilities, such as poor working memory (Siegel, 2003).

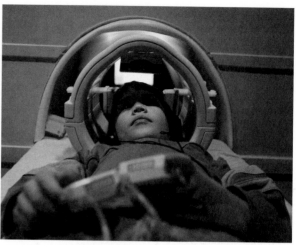

FIGURE 11.6 Brain Scans and Learning Disabilities An increasing number of studies are using MRI brain scans to examine the brain pathways involved in learning disabilities. Shown here is 9-year-old Patrick Price, who has dyslexia. Patrick is going through an MRI scanner disguised by drapes to look like a child-friendly castle. Inside the scanner, children must lie virtually motionless as words and symbols flash on a screen, and they are asked to identify them by clicking different buttons.

Causes and Intervention Strategies The precise causes of learning disabilities have not yet been determined. However, some possible causes have been proposed. Learning disabilities tend to run in families with one parent having a disability such as dyslexia or dyscalculia, although the specific genetic transmission of learning disabilities is not known (Astrom, Wadsworth, & DeFries, 2007). Also, some learning disabilities are likely caused by problems during prenatal development or delivery. For example, a number of studies have found that learning disabilities are more prevalent in low birth weight infants (Litt & others, 2005).

Researchers also use brain-imaging techniques, such as magnetic resonance imaging, to reveal any regions of the brain that might be involved in learning disabilities (Shaywitz, Morris, & Shaywitz, 2008) (see Figure 11.6). This research indicates that it is unlikely learning disabilities reside in a single, specific brain location. More likely, learning disabilities are due to problems in integrating information from multiple brain regions or to subtle problems in brain structure and function (National Institutes of Health, 1993).

Many interventions have focused on improving the child's reading ability (Bender, 2008). Intensive instruction over a period of time by a competent teacher can help many children (Berninger, 2006). For example, a recent brain-imaging study of 15 children with severe reading difficulties who had not shown adequate progress in response to reading instruction in the first grade were given an intensive eight weeks of instruction in phonological decoding skills and then another intensive eight weeks of word recognition skills (Simos & others, 2007). Significant improvement in a majority of the children's reading skills and changes in brain regions involved in reading occurred as a result of the intensive instruction.

Attention Deficit Hyperactivity Disorder

Matthew has attention deficit hyperactivity disorder, and the outward signs are fairly typical. He has trouble attending to the teacher's instructions and is easily distracted. He can't sit still for more than a few minutes at a time, and his handwriting is messy. His mother describes him as very fidgety.

dyslexia A category of learning disabilities involving a severe impairment in the ability to read and spell.

dysgraphia A learning disability that involves difficulty in handwriting.

dyscalculia Also known as developmental arithmetic disorder; a learning disability that involves difficulty in math computation.

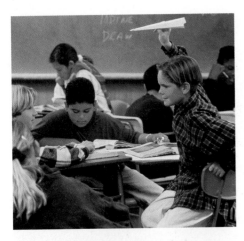

Many children with ADHD show impulsive behavior, such as this child who is jumping out of his seat and throwing a paper airplane at other children. *How would you handle this situation if you were a teacher and this were to happen in your classroom?*

How Would You...?
As a health-care professional, how would you respond to these statements by a parent? "I do not believe that ADHD is a real disorder. Children are supposed to be active."

attention deficit hyperactivity disorder (ADHD) A disability in which children consistently show one or more of the following characteristics: (1) inattention, (2) hyperactivity, and (3) impulsivity.

Characteristics Attention deficit hyperactivity disorder **(ADHD)** is a disability in which children consistently show one or more of these characteristics over a period of time: (1) inattention, (2) hyperactivity, and (3) impulsivity. For an ADHD diagnosis, onset of these characteristics early in childhood is required, and the characteristics must be debilitating for the child.

Inattentive children have difficulty focusing on any one thing and may get bored with a task after only a few minutes. One study found that problems in sustaining attention were the most common type of attentional problem in children with ADHD (Tsal, Shalev, & Mevorach, 2005). Hyperactive children show high levels of physical activity, almost always seeming to be in motion. Impulsive children have difficulty curbing their reactions and don't do a good job of thinking before they act. Depending on the characteristics that children with ADHD display, they can be diagnosed as (1) ADHD with predominantly inattention, (2) ADHD with predominantly hyperactivity/impulsivity, or (3) ADHD with both inattention and hyperactivity/impulsivity.

Diagnosis and Developmental Status The number of children diagnosed and treated for ADHD has increased substantially, by some estimates doubling in the 1990s (Stein, 2004). A recent national survey found that 7 percent of U.S. children 3 to 17 years of age had ADHD (Bloom & Dey, 2006). The disorder occurs as much as four to nine times more in boys than in girls. There is controversy about the increased diagnosis of ADHD, however (Parens & Johnston, 2009; Stolzer, 2009). Some experts attribute the increase mainly to heightened awareness of the disorder. Others are concerned that many children are being diagnosed without undergoing extensive professional evaluation based on input from multiple sources.

Unlike learning disabilities, ADHD is not supposed to be diagnosed by school teams because ADHD is a disorder that appears, with specific diagnostic criteria, in the American Psychiatric Association's *DSM-IV* classification of psychiatric disorders (Bender, 2008). Although some school teams may diagnose a child as having ADHD, this is incorrectly done and can lead to legal problems for schools and teachers. One reason that is given as to why a school team should not do the diagnosis for ADHD is that ADHD is difficult to differentiate from other childhood disorders, and accurate diagnosis requires the evaluation by a specialist in the disorder, such as a child psychiatrist.

Although signs of ADHD are often present in the preschool years, children with ADHD are not usually classified until the elementary school years (Zentall, 2006). The increased academic and social demands of formal schooling, as well as stricter standards for behavioral control, often illuminate the problems of the child with ADHD (Daley, 2006). Elementary school teachers typically report that this type of child has difficulty in working independently, completing seatwork, and organizing work. Restlessness and distractibility also are often noted. These problems are more likely to be observed in repetitive or difficult tasks, or tasks the child perceives to be boring (such as completing worksheets or doing homework).

It used to be thought that children with ADHD showed improvement during adolescence, but now it appears this often is not the case. Estimates suggest symptoms of ADHD decrease in only about one-third of adolescents. Increasingly, it is being recognized that these problems may continue into adulthood (Miller, Nigg, & Faraone, 2007).

Causes and Treatment Definitive causes of ADHD have not been found. However, a number of causes have been proposed (Stolzer, 2009). Some children likely inherit a tendency to develop ADHD from their parents (Pennington & others, 2009). Other children likely develop ADHD because of damage to their brain during prenatal or postnatal development (Thompson, Moore, & Symons, 2007). Among early possible contributors to ADHD are cigarette and alcohol exposure during prenatal development and low birth weight (Knopik, 2009).

As with learning disabilities, the development of brain-imaging techniques is leading to a better understanding of the brain's role in ADHD (Shaw & others, 2007).

A recent study revealed that peak thickness of the cerebral cortex occurred three years later (10.5 years) in children with ADHD than children without ADHD (peak at 7.5 years) (Shaw & others, 2007). The delay was more prominent in the prefrontal regions of the brain that are especially important in attention and planning (see Figure 11.7). Researchers also are exploring the roles that various neurotransmitters, such as serotonin, might play in ADHD (Levy, 2009; Roessner & others, 2009).

Stimulant medication such as Ritalin (methylphenidate) or Adderall (amphetamine and dextroamphetamine) is effective in improving the attention of many children with ADHD, but it usually does not improve their attention to the same level as children who do not have ADHD (Brams, Mao, & Doyle, 2009; Pliszka, 2007). A recent meta-analysis concluded that behavior management treatments are effective in reducing the effects of ADHD (Fabiano & others, 2009). Researchers have often found that a combination of medication (such as Ritalin) and behavior management improves the behavior of children with ADHD better than medication alone or behavior management alone, although not in all cases (Parens & Johnston, 2009). Other drugs, such as the stimulant called mixed amphetamine salts extended release (MAS XR) and the nonstimulant Strattera (atomoxetine), are currently being studied in the treatment of children with ADHD, and early findings involving these drugs are promising (Faraone, 2007). A recent experimental study revealed that atomoxetine combined with a psychoeducational treatment was more effective than a placebo drug alone or psychoeducational treatment alone in reducing ADHD symptoms (Svanborg & others, 2009).

Teachers play an important role in monitoring whether ADHD medication has been prescribed at the right dosage level. For example, it is not unusual for a student on ADHD medication to complete academic tasks in the morning, but in the afternoon, when the dosage has worn off, to be inattentive or hyperactive.

Critics argue that many physicians are too quick to prescribe stimulants for children with milder forms of ADHD (Marcovitch, 2004). Also, in 2006, the U.S. government issued a warning about the cardiovascular risks of stimulant medication used to treat ADHD.

Speech Disorders

Speech disorders include articulation disorders, voice disorders, and fluency disorders (Ratner, 2009). **Articulation disorders** are problems in pronouncing sounds correctly. A child's articulation at 6 to 7 years is still not always error-free, but it should be by age 8. A child with an articulation problem may find communication with peers and the teacher difficult or embarrassing. As a result, the child may avoid asking questions, participating in discussions, or communicating with peers. Articulation problems can usually be improved or resolved with speech therapy, though it may take months or years.

Voice disorders are reflected in speech that is hoarse, harsh, too loud, too high-pitched, or too low-pitched. Children with a cleft palate often have a voice disorder that makes their speech difficult to understand. If a student speaks in a way that is consistently difficult to understand, the child should be referred to a speech therapist.

Fluency disorders often involve what is commonly called "stuttering." Stuttering occurs when a child's speech has a spasmodic hesitation, prolongation, or repetition. The anxiety many children feel because they stutter can make their stuttering worse. Speech therapy is recommended.

One individual who helps children with their speech problems is Sharla Peltier. To read about her work, see the *Careers in Children's Development* profile.

Sensory Disorders

Sensory disorders include visual and hearing impairments. Sometimes these impairments are described as part of a larger category called "communication disorders," along with speech and language disorders.

Visual Impairments Some children may have mild vision problems that have not been corrected. If children frequently squint, hold books close to their face when they read,

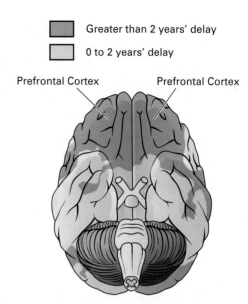

■ Greater than 2 years' delay

□ 0 to 2 years' delay

Prefrontal Cortex   Prefrontal Cortex

FIGURE 11.7 Regions of the Brain in Which Children with ADHD Had a Delayed Peak in the Thickness *Note:* The greatest delays occurred in the prefrontal cortex.

articulation disorders Problems in pronouncing sounds correctly.

voice disorders Disorders reflected in speech that is hoarse, harsh, too loud, too high-pitched, or too low-pitched.

fluency disorders Various disorders that involve what is commonly called "stuttering."

Careers in Children's Development

Sharla Peltier, Speech Pathologist

A speech pathologist is a health professional who works with individuals who have a communication disorder. Sharla Peltier is a speech pathologist in Manitoulin, Ontario, Canada. Peltier works with Native American children in the First Nations Schools. She conducts screening for speech/language and hearing problems and assesses infants as young as 6 months of age as well as school-age children. She works closely with community health nurses to identify hearing problems.

Diagnosing problems is only about half of what Peltier does in her work. She especially enjoys treating speech/language and hearing problems. She conducts parent training sessions to help parents understand and help with their children's language problem. As part of this training, she guides parents in improving their communication skills with their children.

Speech therapist Sharla Peltier, helping a young child improve her language and communication skills.

---

low vision Visual acuity between 20/70 and 20/2000.

educationally blind Unable to use one's vision in learning and must use hearing and touch to learn.

oral approaches Educational approaches to help hearing-impaired children; they include lip reading, speech reading, and whatever hearing the child has.

manual approaches Educational approaches to help hearing-impaired children; they include sign language and finger spelling.

orthopedic impairments Restrictions in movement abilities due to muscle, bone, or joint problems.

cerebral palsy A disorder that involves a lack of muscular coordination, shaking, and unclear speech.

emotional and behavioral disorders Serious, persistent problems that involve relationships, aggression, depression, fears associated with personal or school matters, as well as other inappropriate socioemotional characteristics.

autism spectrum disorders (ASDs) Also called pervasive developmental disorders; disorders that range from the severe disorder labeled autistic disorder to the milder disorder called Asperger syndrome. Children with these disorders are characterized by problems with social interaction, with verbal and nonverbal communication, and with repetitive behaviors.

rub their eyes often, say that things look blurred, or mention that words move about on the page, they should be referred to appropriate professionals to have their vision checked. In many cases, they need only corrective lenses. However, a small portion of children (about 1 in 1,000) have more serious visual problems and are classified as visually impaired. This includes children with low vision and blind children.

Children with **low vision** have visual acuity of between 20/70 and 20/2000 (on the Snellen scale, in which 20/20 is normal) with corrective lens. Children with low vision can read with the aid of large-print books or a magnifying glass. Children who are **educationally blind** cannot use their vision in learning and must use their hearing and touch to learn. Approximately 1 in every 3,000 children is educationally blind. Almost half of these children were born blind, and another one-third lost their vision in the first year of life. Many children who are educationally blind have normal intelligence and function very well academically with appropriate supports and learning aids.

An important task when working with a visually impaired child is to determine the modality (such as touch or hearing) through which the child learns best. Preferential seating in the front of the class is also helpful.

Hearing Impairments   A hearing impairment can make learning difficult for children. Children who are born deaf or experience a significant hearing loss in the first several years of life may not develop normal speech and language (Friend, 2008). Some children in middle and late childhood have hearing impairments that have not yet been detected. If children turn one ear toward the speaker, frequently ask to have something repeated, don't follow directions, or frequently complain of earaches, colds, and allergies, their hearing needs to be evaluated by a specialist, such as an audiologist (Patterson & Wright, 1990).

Many hearing-impaired children receive supplementary instruction beyond that of the regular classroom. Educational approaches to help children with hearing impairments learn fall into two categories: oral and manual (Hoskin & Herman, 2001).

- **Oral approaches** include using lip reading, speech reading (relies on visual cues to teach reading), and whatever hearing the child has.

- **Manual approaches** involve sign language and finger spelling. Sign language is a system of hand movements that symbolize words. Finger spelling consists of "spelling out" each word by placing the hand in different positions.

A total communication approach that includes both oral and manual approaches is increasingly being used with children who are hearing impaired (Hallahan, Kauffman, & Pullen, 2009).

Today many hearing-impaired children are educated in the regular classroom. With appropriate accommodations such as preferential seating and the assistance of hearing aids, cochlear implants, and other amplification devices, hearing-impaired children can be educated effectively (Ching & others, 2006).

Physical Disorders   Physical disorders that children may have include orthopedic impairments, such as cerebral palsy. Many children with physical disorders require special education, as well as related services. The related services may include transportation, physical therapy, school health services, and psychological services.

Orthopedic impairments involve restricted movement or lack of control over movement due to muscle, bone, or joint problems. The severity of problems ranges widely. Orthopedic impairments can be caused by prenatal or perinatal problems, or they can be due to disease or accident during the childhood years. With the help of adaptive devices and medical technology, many children with orthopedic impairments function well in the classroom (Hallahan, Kauffman, & Pullen, 2009).

Cerebral palsy is a disorder that involves a lack of muscular coordination, shaking, and unclear speech. The most common cause of cerebral palsy is lack of oxygen at birth. In the most common type of cerebral palsy, which is called *spastic*, children's muscles are stiff and difficult to move. The rigid muscles often pull the limbs into contorted positions. In a less common type, *ataxia*, children's muscles are rigid one moment and floppy the next moment, making movements clumsy and jerky.

Computers especially help children with cerebral palsy learn. If they have the coordination to use the keyboard, they can do their written work on the computer. A pen with a light can be added to a computer and used by the child as a pointer. Children with cerebral palsy have unclear speech. For these children, speech and voice synthesizers, communication boards, talking notes, and page turners can improve their communication.

Emotional and Behavioral Disorders   Most children have minor emotional difficulties sometime during their school years. A small percentage have problems so serious and persistent that they are classified as having an emotional or a behavioral disorder (Gargiulo, 2009; Kauffman & Landrum, 2009). **Emotional and behavioral disorders** consist of serious, persistent problems that involve relationships, aggression, depression, fears associated with personal or school matters, as well as other inappropriate socioemotional characteristics. Approximately 8 percent of children who have a disability and require an individualized education plan fall into this classification. Boys are three times as likely as girls to have these disorders. We further discuss aggression in Chapter 13, "Socioemotional Development in Middle and Late Childhood," and depression in Chapter 16, "Socioemotional Development in Adolescence."

Autism Spectrum Disorders   **Autism spectrum disorders (ASDs),** also called pervasive developmental disorders, range from the severe disorder labeled *autistic disorder* to the milder disorder called *Asperger syndrome*. Autism spectrum disorders are characterized by problems in social interaction, problems in verbal and nonverbal communication, and repetitive behaviors (Goldman & others,

Many students with physical disabilities such as cerebral palsy cannot use a conventional keyboard and mouse. Many can use alternative keyboards effectively.

What are some characteristics of children with an emotional or behavioral disorder?

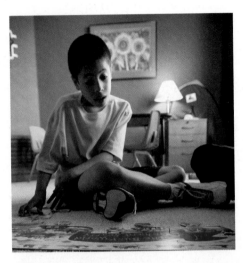

What characterizes autism spectrum disorders?

2009; Hall, 2009). Children with these disorders may also show atypical responses to sensory experiences (National Institute of Mental Health, 2008). Autism spectrum disorders can often be detected in children as early as 1 to 3 years of age.

Recent estimates of autism spectrum disorders indicate that they are increasing in occurrence or are increasingly being detected and labeled (Neal, 2009). Once thought to affect only 1 in 2,500 individuals, today's estimates suggest that they occur in about 1 in 150 individuals (Centers for Disease Control and Prevention, 2007).

Autistic disorder is a severe developmental autism spectrum disorder that has its onset in the first three years of life and includes deficiencies in social relationships, abnormalities in communication, and restricted, repetitive, and stereotyped patterns of behavior. Estimates indicate that approximately 2 to 5 of every 10,000 young children in the United States have autistic disorder. Boys are about four times more likely to have an autistic disorder than girls.

Asperger syndrome is a relatively mild autism spectrum disorder in which the child has relatively good verbal language, milder nonverbal language problems, and a restricted range of interests and relationships (Bennett & others, 2007). Children with Asperger syndrome often engage in obsessive repetitive routines and preoccupations with a particular subject (South, Ozofnoff, & McMahon, 2005). For example, a child may be obsessed with baseball scores or railroad timetables.

What causes the autism spectrum disorders? The current consensus is that autism is a brain dysfunction with abnormalities in brain structure and neurotransmitters (Anderson & others, 2009; Gilbert & others, 2009). Genetic factors likely play a role in the development of the autism spectrum disorders (Nishiyama & others, 2009). A recent study revealed that mutations—missing or duplicated pieces of DNA on chromosome 16—can raise a child's risk of developing autism 100-fold (Weiss & others, 2008). Estimates are that approximately 1 million U.S. children have an autistic disorder, so about 10,000 of them have this genetic mutation. There is no evidence that family socialization causes autism (Rutter & Schopler, 1987). Mental retardation is present in some children with autism; others show average or above-average intelligence (McCarthy, 2007).

Boys are four times as likely to have autism spectrum disorders as girls are (Gong & others, 2009). Expanding on autism's male-linkage, Simon Baron-Cohen (2008) recently argued that autism reflects an extreme male brain, especially indicative of males' less effective ability to show empathy and read facial expressions and gestures than girls are. In an attempt to improve these skills in 4- to 8-year-old autistic boys, Baron-Cohen and his colleagues (2007) produced a number of animations on a DVD that place faces with different emotions on toy train and tractor characters in a boy's bedroom. After watching the animations 15 minutes every weekday for one month, the autistic children's ability to recognize real faces in a different context equaled that of children without autism. A recent research review concluded that when these behavior modifications are intensely provided and used early in the autistic child's life, they are more effective (Howlin, Magiati, & Charman, 2009).

Many children with autism benefit from a well-structured classroom, individualized instruction, and small-group instruction (Pueschel & others, 1995). As with children who are mentally retarded, behavior modification techniques are sometimes effective in helping autistic children learn (Hall, 2009).

Educational Issues

The legal requirement that schools serve all children with a disability is fairly recent. Beginning in the mid-1960s to the mid-1970s, legislators, the federal courts, and the U.S. Congress laid down special educational rights for children with disabilities. Prior to that time, most children with a disability were either refused enrollment or inadequately served by schools. In 1975, **Public Law 94-142,** the Education for All Handicapped Children Act, required that all students with disabilities be given a free,

autistic disorder A severe autism spectrum disorder that has its onset in the first three years of life and includes deficiencies in social relationships, abnormalities in communication, and restricted, repetitive, and stereotyped patterns of behavior.

Asperger syndrome A relatively mild autism spectrum disorder in which the child has relatively good verbal language, milder nonverbal language problems, and a restricted range of interests and relationships.

Public Law 94-142 The Education for All Handicapped Children Act, created in 1975, which requires that all children with disabilities be given a free, appropriate public education and which provides the funding to help with the costs of implementing this education.

appropriate public education and be provided the funding to help implement this education.

In 1990, Public Law 94-142 was recast as the **Individuals with Disabilities Education Act (IDEA).** IDEA was amended in 1997 and then reauthorized in 2004 and renamed the Individuals with Disabilities Education Improvement Act. IDEA spells out broad mandates for services to all children with disabilities (Friend, 2008; Gargiulo, 2009). These include evaluation and eligibility determination, appropriate education and an individualized education plan (IEP), and education in the least restrictive environment (LRE) (Taylor, Smiley, & Richards, 2009).

A major aspect of the 2004 reauthorization of IDEA involved aligning it with the government's No Child Left Behind (NCLB) legislation, which was designed to improve the educational achievement of all students, including those with disabilities. Both IDEA and NCLB mandate that most students with disabilities be included in general assessments of educational progress. This alignment includes requiring most students with disabilities "to take standard tests of academic achievement and to achieve at a level equal to that of students without disabilities. Whether this expectation is reasonable is an open question" (Hallahan & Kauffman, 2006, pp. 28–29). Alternate assessments for students with disabilities and funding to help states improve instruction, assessment, and accountability for educating students with disabilities are included in the 2004 reauthorization of IDEA.

Increasingly, children with disabilities are being taught in the regular classroom, as is this child with mild mental retardation.

Evaluation and Eligibility Determination

Children who are thought to have a disability are evaluated to determine their eligibility for services under IDEA. Schools are prohibited from planning special education programs in advance and offering them on a space-available basis.

Children must be evaluated before a school can begin providing special services (Werts, Culatta, & Tompkins, 2007). Parents should be involved in the evaluation process. Reevaluation is required at least every three years (sometimes every year), when requested by parents, or when conditions suggest that a reevaluation is needed. A parent who disagrees with the school's evaluation can obtain an independent evaluation, which the school is required to consider in providing special education services. If the evaluation finds that the child has a disability and requires special services, the school must provide them to the child.

The IDEA has many specific provisions that relate to the parents of a child with a disability (Carter, Prater, & Dyches, 2009). These include requirements that schools send notices to parents of proposed actions, of attendance at meetings regarding the child's placement or individualized education plan, and of the right to appeal school decisions to an impartial evaluator.

Appropriate Education and the Individualized Education Plan (IEP)

The IDEA requires that students with disabilities have an **individualized education plan (IEP),** a written statement that spells out a program tailored specifically for the student with a disability (Lewis & Doorlag, 2006). In general, the IEP should be (1) related to the child's learning capacity, (2) specially constructed to meet the child's individual needs and not merely a copy of what is offered to other children, and (3) designed to provide educational benefits.

Amendments were made to the IDEA in 1997. Two of these involve positive behavioral support and functional behavioral assessment (U.S. Office of Education, 2000). *Positive behavioral support* focuses on culturally appropriate interventions to attain important behavioral changes in children. *Functional behavioral assessment* involves determining the consequences (what purpose the behavior serves), antecedents (what triggers the behavior), and setting events (in which contexts the behavior occurs).

Under IDEA, the child with a disability must be educated in the **least restrictive environment (LRE),** a setting as similar as possible to the one in which children who do not have a disability are educated. And schools must make an effort to educate children with a disability in the regular classroom. The term

Individuals with Disabilities Education Act (IDEA) The IDEA spells out broad mandates for services to all children with disabilities (IDEA is a renaming of Public Law 94-142); these include evaluation and eligibility determination, appropriate education and the individualized education plan (IEP), and education in the least restrictive environment (LRE).

individualized education plan (IEP) A written statement that spells out a program tailored to a child with a disability. The plan should be (1) related to the child's learning capacity, (2) specially constructed to meet the child's individual needs and not merely a copy of what is offered to other children, and (3) designed to provide educational benefits.

least restrictive environment (LRE) The concept that a child with a disability must be educated in a setting that is as similar as possible to the one in which children who do not have a disability are educated.

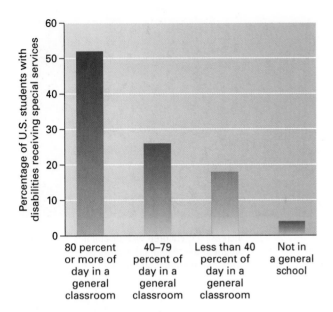

FIGURE 11.8 **Percentage of U.S. Students with Disabilities 6 to 21 Years of Age Receiving Special Services in the General Classroom (Data for 2004–2005 School Year; National Center for Education Statistics, 2007)**

inclusion means educating a child with special educational needs full-time in the regular classroom (Hick & Thomas, 2009). Figure 11.8 indicates that for the 2004–2005 school year, slightly more than 50 percent of U.S. students with a disability spent more than 80 percent of their school day in a general classroom.

Not long ago, it was considered appropriate to educate children with disabilities outside the regular classroom. However, today, schools must make every effort to provide inclusion for children with disabilities (Smith & others, 2008). These efforts can be very costly financially and very time consuming in terms of faculty effort.

The principle of least restrictive environment compels schools to examine possible modifications of the regular classroom before moving the child with a disability to a more restrictive placement (Turnbull, Turnbull, & Tompkins, 2007). Also, regular classroom teachers often need specialized training to help some children with a disability, and state educational agencies are required to provide such training (Vaughn, Bos, & Schumm, 2007).

Many of the legal changes regarding children with disabilities have been extremely positive (Carter, Prater, & Dyches, 2009; Turnbull, Huerta, & Stowe, 2009). Compared with several decades ago, far more children today are receiving competent, specialized services. For many children, inclusion in the regular classroom, with modifications or supplemental services, is appropriate (Friend, 2008). However, some leading experts on special education argue that the effort to use inclusion to educate children with disabilities has become too extreme in some cases. For example, James Kauffman and his colleagues (Kauffman & Hallahan, 2005; Kauffman, McGee, & Brigham, 2004) state that inclusion too often has meant making accommodations in the regular classroom that do not always benefit children with disabilities. They advocate a more individualized approach that does not always involve full inclusion but rather options such as special education outside the regular classroom. Kauffman and his colleagues (2004, p. 620) acknowledge that children with disabilities "*do* need the services of specially trained professionals to achieve their full potential. They *do* sometimes need altered curricula or adaptations to make their learning possible." However, "we sell students with disabilities short when we pretend that they are not different from typical students. We make the same error when we pretend that they must *not* be expected to put forth extra effort if they are to learn to do some things—or learn to do something in a different way." Like general education, an important aspect of special education should be to challenge students with disabilities "to become all they can be."

One concern about special education involves disproportionate representation of students from minority backgrounds in special education programs and classes (Artiles & others, 2005). The *Diversity in Children's Development* interlude addresses this issue.

Diversity in Children's Development

DISPROPORTIONATE REPRESENTATION OF MINORITY STUDENTS IN SPECIAL EDUCATION

The U.S. Office of Education (2000) has three concerns about the overrepresentation of minority students in special education programs and classes:

- Students may be unserved or receive services that do not meet their needs.
- Students may be misclassified or inappropriately labeled.
- Placement in special education classes may be a form of discrimination.

inclusion Educating a child with special education needs full-time in the regular classroom.

African American students are overrepresented in special education—15 percent of the U.S. student population is African American, but 20 percent of special education students are African American. In some disabilities, the discrepancies are even greater. For example, African American students represent 32 percent of the students in programs for mild mental retardation, 29 percent in programs for moderate mental retardation, and 24 percent in programs for serious emotional disturbance.

However, it is not just a simple matter of overrepresentation of certain minority groups in special education. Latino children may be underidentified in the categories of mental retardation and emotional disturbance.

More appropriate inclusion of minority students in special education is a complex problem and requires the creation of a successful school experience for all students. Recommendations for reducing disproportionate representation in special education include (Burnette, 1998):

- Reviewing school practices to identify and address factors that might contribute to having school difficulties
- Forming policy-making groups that include community members and promote partnerships with service agencies and cultural organizations
- Helping families get social, medical, mental health, and other support services
- Training more teachers from minority backgrounds and providing all teachers with more extensive course work and training in educating children with disabilities and in understanding diversity issues

Review and Reflect: Learning Goal 3

 3 **Summarize information about children with disabilities**

REVIEW

- Who are children with disabilities?
- What are some characteristics of the range of children's disabilities?
- What are some important issues in the education of children with disabilities?

REFLECT

- Think back to your own schooling and how students with learning disabilities were or were not diagnosed. Were you aware of such individuals in your classes? Were they given special attention by teachers and/or specialists? You may know one or more individuals with a learning disability. Interview them about their school experiences. Ask them what they think could have been done better to help them with their disability.

Reach Your Learning Goals

Physical Development in Middle and Late Childhood

1 WHAT CHANGES TAKE PLACE IN BODY GROWTH, THE BRAIN, AND MOTOR DEVELOPMENT? DISCUSS CHANGES IN BODY GROWTH, THE BRAIN, AND MOTOR DEVELOPMENT IN MIDDLE AND LATE CHILDHOOD

Skeletal and Muscular Systems

- The period of middle and late childhood involves slow, consistent growth. During this period, children grow an average of 2 to 3 inches a year. Muscle mass and strength gradually increase. Among the most pronounced changes are decreases in head circumference, waist circumference, and leg length in relation to body height.

The Brain

- Changes in the brain continue to occur in middle and late childhood, and these changes, such as increased myelination, are linked to improvements in cognitive functioning. In particular, there is an increase in pathways involving the prefrontal cortex—changes that are related to improved attention, reasoning, and cognitive control. During middle and late childhood, less diffusion and more focal activation occur in the prefrontal cortex, changes that are associated with an increase in cognitive control.

Motor Development

- During the middle and late childhood years, motor development becomes much smoother and more coordinated. Children gain greater control over their bodies and can sit and attend for longer periods of time. However, their lives should be activity-oriented and very active. Gross motor skills are expanded, and children refine such skills as hitting a tennis ball, skipping rope, or balancing on a beam. Increased myelination of the nervous system is reflected in improved fine motor skills, such as developing improved handwriting and playing a difficult piece on a musical instrument. Boys are usually better at gross motor skills, girls at fine motor skills.

2 WHAT ARE THE CENTRAL ISSUES IN CHILDREN'S HEALTH? CHARACTERIZE CHILDREN'S HEALTH IN MIDDLE AND LATE CHILDHOOD

Nutrition

- In the middle and late childhood years, weight doubles, and considerable energy is expended in motor activities. To support their growth, children need to consume more calories than when they were younger. A balanced diet is important. A special concern is that too many children fill up on "empty calories" that are high in sugar, starch, and excess fat. A healthy breakfast promotes higher energy and better alertness in school.

Exercise and Sports

- Every indication suggests that children in the United States are not getting enough exercise. Television viewing, parents who are poor role models for exercise, and inadequate physical education classes in schools are among the culprits. Children's participation in sports can have positive or negative consequences, however.

Overweight Children

- Although the increase of child obesity in the United States has begun to level off, over the last three decades the percentage of U.S. children who are overweight has tripled. An increasing number of children in many countries, such as Mainland China and Australia, are overweight. Being overweight in middle and late childhood substantially increases the risk of being overweight in adolescence and adulthood. Factors linked with being overweight in childhood include heredity and environmental contexts. Being overweight in childhood is related to a number of problems. Diet, exercise, and behavior modification are recommended in helping children to lose weight.

Diseases

- Cancer is the second leading cause of death in children (after accidents). Childhood cancers have a different profile from that of adult cancers. Diabetes is also a common disease in childhood. Cardiovascular disease is uncommon in children, but the precursors to adult cardiovascular disease are often already apparent in children. Asthma is the most common chronic disease in U.S. children.

Accidents and Injuries

- The most common cause of severe injury and death in childhood is motor vehicle accidents.

3 WHAT ARE THE PREVALENT DISABILITIES IN CHILDREN? SUMMARIZE INFORMATION ABOUT CHILDREN WITH DISABILITIES

Who Are Children with Disabilities?

- Approximately 14 percent of children from 3 to 21 years of age in the United States receive special education or related services. Students with a learning disability are by far the largest group of students with a disability that is provided special education. Substantial percentages also are represented by children with speech or language impairments, mental retardation, and emotional disturbance. The term "children with disabilities" is now recommended rather than "handicapped children." This is intended to focus the emphasis more on the child than on the disability.

The Range of Disabilities

- Children's disabilities cover a wide range and include learning disabilities, ADHD, speech disorders, sensory disorders, physical disorders, emotional and behavioral disorders, and autism spectrum disorders. A child with a learning disability has difficulty in learning that involves understanding or using spoken or written language and the difficulty can appear in listening, thinking, reading, writing, and spelling. A learning disability also may involve difficulty in doing mathematics. To be classified as a learning disability, the learning problem is not primarily the result of visual, hearing, or motor disabilities; mental retardation; emotional disorders; or due to environmental, cultural, or economic disadvantage.

  Diagnosing whether a child has a learning disability is difficult. About three times as many boys as girls have a learning disability. The most common academic problem for children with a learning disability is reading. Dyslexia is a severe impairment in the ability to read and spell. Dysgraphia is a learning disability that involves having difficulty in handwriting. Dyscalculia is a learning disability that involves difficulties in math computation. Controversy surrounds the "learning disability" category. Many interventions targeted for learning disabilities focus on improving the child's reading ability and include such strategies as improving decoding skills.

  Attention deficit hyperactivity disorder (ADHD) is a disability in which children consistently show problems in one or more of these areas: inattention, hyperactivity, and impulsivity. For an ADHD diagnosis, the characteristics must appear early in childhood and be debilitating for the child. Although signs of ADHD may be present in early childhood, diagnosis of ADHD often doesn't occur until the elementary school years. Many experts recommend a combination of academic, behavioral, and medical interventions to help students with ADHD learn and adapt.

  Speech disorders include articulation disorders, voice disorders, and fluency disorders. Sensory disorders include visual and hearing impairments. Physical disorders that children may have include orthopedic impairments and cerebral palsy. Emotional and behavioral disorders consist of serious, persistent problems that involve relationships, aggression, depression, fears associated with personal or school matters, as well as other inappropriate socioemotional characteristics.

  Autistic disorder is a severe developmental autism spectrum disorder with an onset in the first three years of life, and it involves abnormalities in social relationships and communication. It also is characterized by repetitive behaviors. The current consensus is that autism spectrum disorders involve an organic brain dysfunction. Autism spectrum disorders (ASDs) range from autistic disorder to the milder Asperger syndrome.

- Beginning in the 1960s and 1970s, the educational rights for children with disabilities were laid down. In 1975, Public Law 94-142 required all children to be given a free, appropriate public education. In 1990, Public Law 94-142 was renamed and called the Individuals with Disabilities Education Act (IDEA). Children who are thought to have a disability are evaluated to determine their eligibility for services. An individualized education plan (IEP) is a written plan that spells out a program tailored to the child with a disability. The concept of a least restrictive environment (LRE) is contained in the IDEA. The term inclusion means educating children with disabilities full time in the general classroom. The trend is toward greater use of using inclusion.

KEY TERMS

type 1 diabetes 364
type 2 diabetes 364
asthma 365
learning disability 368
dyslexia 369
dysgraphia 369
dyscalculia 369
attention deficit
   hyperactivity disorder
   (ADHD) 370

articulation disorders 371
voice disorders 371
fluency disorders 371
low vision 372
educationally blind 372
oral approaches 372
manual approaches 372
orthopedic
   impairments 372
cerebral palsy 372

emotional and behavioral
   disorders 372
autism spectrum disorders
   (ASDs) 372
autistic disorder 374
Asperger syndrome 374
Public Law 94-142 374
Individuals with Disabilities
   Education Act
   (IDEA) 375

individualized education
   plan (IEP) 375
least restrictive
   environment (LRE) 375
inclusion 376

KEY PEOPLE

Mark Johnson 355

Simon Baron-Cohen 374

James Kauffman 376

MAKING A DIFFERENCE

Nurturing Children's Physical Development and Health

What are some good strategies for supporting children's physical development and health in the middle and late childhood years?

- *Elementary school children should participate mainly in active rather than passive activities.* Goals should especially include reducing TV watching and increasing participation in such activities as swimming, skating, and bicycling.

- *Parents should monitor children's eating behavior.* Children need more calories now than when they were younger. However, a special concern is the increasing number of obese children. They need to have a medical checkup, to revise their diet, and to participate in a regular exercise program.

- *Elementary schools need to develop more and better physical education programs.* Only about one of every three elementary school children participates in a physical education program. Many of those who do aren't exercising much during the program.

- *Parents need to engage in physical activities that they can enjoy together with their children.* These activities include running, bicycling, hiking, and swimming.

- *Parents should try to make their children's experiences in sports positive ones.* They should stress the benefits of sports rather than displaying a win-at-all-costs philosophy.

- *Parents should help children avoid accidents and injuries.* They should educate their children about the hazards of risk taking and the improper use of equipment.

RESOURCES FOR IMPROVING CHILDREN'S LIVES

Children's HeartLink
www.childrensheartlink.org

This organization provides treatment for needy children with heart disease and support for rheumatic fever prevention programs. It also supports the education of foreign medical professionals and provides technical advice and medical equipment and supplies.

The Council for Exceptional Children (CEC)
www.cec.sped.org

The CEC maintains an information center on the education of children and adolescents with disabilities and publishes materials on a wide variety of topics.

Learning Disabilities Association of America (LDA)
www.ldaamerica/org

The LDA provides education and support for parents of children with learning disabilities, interested professionals, and others. More than 500 chapters are in operation nationwide, offering information services, pamphlets, and book recommendations.

E-LEARNING TOOLS

Connect to **www.mhhe.com/santrockc11e** to research the answers and complete these exercises. In addition, you'll find a number of other resources and valuable study tools for Chapter 11, "Physical Development in Middle and Late Childhood," on this Web site.

Taking It to the Net

1. Christina's daughter, Carmella, is having a difficult time in school. Her teacher says Carmella is unable to stay focused on her schoolwork, and she often gets into trouble for speaking out of turn and for getting out of her seat. The teacher recommends to Christina that her daughter be tested for ADHD. Christina has some reservations; she recently saw a television show about the overdiagnosis of ADHD. Is ADHD overdiagnosed in children? What are some of the controversies surrounding the ADHD diagnosis? What signs and symptoms characterize ADHD?

2. Morgan, a first-grader, has not been doing well in school. His father, John, doesn't think his poor performance has to do with his intelligence, because Morgan seems to be a fast learner. He does, however, suspect that Morgan might have problems with his vision. What kinds of visual impairments are common among school-age children? What accommodations can be made to improve Morgan's school performance?

3. Monika is a first-year physical education teacher at an elementary school. When she began her job, she was dismayed when she saw how sedentary most of her students were. Are her observations common? What levels of physical fitness do we commonly see in school-age children? How can children benefit from engaging in a physical fitness program?

Health and Well-Being, Parenting, and Education

Build your decision-making skills by trying your hand at the health and well-being, parenting, and education exercises.

Video Clips

The Online Learning Center includes the following videos for this chapter:

- *Copying Shapes at Age 7—1125*
  More advanced fine motor skills in middle childhood are demonstrated by this 7-year-old. With careful attention he copies a square, a triangle, and a circle.

- *Obesity—1714*
  Rebecca Roach, Registered Dietician, discusses reasons for the high rate of obesity in children today.

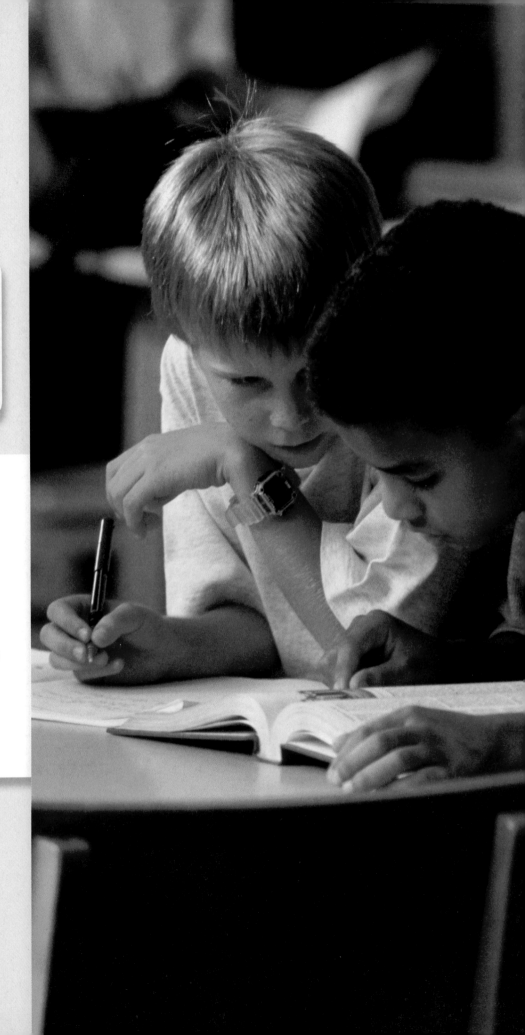

12

The thirst to know and understand . . .
These are the goods in life's rich hand.

—Sir William Watson
British Poet, 20th Century

LEARNING GOALS

◆ Discuss Piaget's stage of concrete operational thought and apply Piaget's theory to education

◆ Describe changes in information processing in middle and late childhood

◆ Characterize children's intelligence

◆ Summarize language development in middle and late childhood

◆ Explain the development of achievement in children

COGNITIVE DEVELOPMENT IN MIDDLE AND LATE CHILDHOOD

CHAPTER OUTLINE

383

Images of Children's Development
Marva Collins, Challenging Children to Achieve

On the first day of school, second-grade Chicago teacher Marva Collins tells her students, many of whom are repeating the second grade,

> "I know most of you can't spell your name. You don't know the alphabet, you don't know how to read . . . I promise you that you will. None of you has ever failed. School may have failed you. Well, goodbye to failure, children. Welcome to success. You will read hard books in here and understand what you read. You will write every day. . . . But you must help me to help you. If you don't give anything, don't expect anything. Success is not coming to you, you must come to it." (Dweck, 2006, pp. 188–189)

Her second-grade students usually have to start off with the lowest level of reader available, but by the end of the school year most of the students are reading at the fifth-grade level.

Collins takes inner-city children living in low-income, often poverty, circumstances, and challenges them to be all they can be. She won't accept failure by her students and teaches students to be responsible for their behavior every day of their lives. Collins tells students that being excellent at something is not a one-time thing but a habit, that determination and persistence are what move the world, and that thinking others will make you successful is a sure way to fail.

Marva Collins, challenging a child to achieve.

PREVIEW

We just saw that challenging children to succeed who had been taught to fail is an important theme of Marva Collins' teaching. Later in the chapter, we explore many aspects of achievement. First, we will examine three main aspects of cognitive changes—Piaget's cognitive developmental theory, information processing, and intelligence—that characterize middle and late childhood. Then, following our coverage of language changes, we explore children's achievement.

1 WHAT IS PIAGET'S THEORY OF COGNITIVE DEVELOPMENT IN MIDDLE AND LATE CHILDHOOD?

| Concrete Operational Thought | Evaluating Piaget's Concrete Operational Stage | Applications to Education |

According to Piaget (1952), the preschool child's thought is preoperational. Preschool children can form stable concepts, and they have begun to reason, but their thinking is flawed by egocentrism and magical belief systems. As we discussed in Chapter 9, "Cognitive Development in Early Childhood," however, Piaget may have underestimated the cognitive skills of preschool children. Some researchers argue that under the right conditions, young children may display abilities that are characteristic of Piaget's next stage of cognitive development, the stage of concrete operational thought (Gelman, 1969). Here we cover the characteristics of concrete operational thought, an evaluation of Piaget's portrait of this stage, and applications of Piaget's ideas to education.

Concrete Operational Thought

Piaget proposed that the *concrete operational stage* lasts from approximately 7 to 11 years of age. In this stage, children can perform concrete operations, and they can reason logically as long as they can apply their reasoning to specific or concrete examples. Remember that *operations* are mental actions that are reversible, and *concrete operations* are operations that are applied to real, concrete objects.

The conservation tasks described in Chapter 9, "Cognitive Development in Early Childhood," indicate whether children are capable of concrete operations. For example, recall that in one task involving conservation of matter, the child is presented with two identical balls of clay. The experimenter rolls one ball into a long, thin shape; the other remains in its original ball shape. The child is then asked if there is more clay in the ball or in the long, thin piece of clay. By the time children reach the age of 7 or 8, most answer that the amount of clay is the same. To answer this problem correctly, children have to imagine rolling the elongated clay back into a ball. This type of imagination involves a reversible mental action applied to a real, concrete object. Concrete operations allow the child to consider several characteristics rather than to focus on a single property of an object. In the clay example, the preoperational child is likely to focus on height *or* width. The concrete operational child coordinates information about both dimensions.

What other abilities are characteristic of children who have reached the concrete operational stage? One important skill is the ability to classify or divide things into different sets or subsets and to consider their interrelationships. Consider the family tree of four generations that is shown in Figure 12.1 (Furth & Wachs, 1975). This family tree suggests that the grandfather (A) has three children (B, C, and D), each of whom has two children (E through J), and that one of these children (J) has three children (K, L, and M). A child who comprehends the classification system can move up and down a level, across a level, and up and down and across within the system. The concrete operational child understands that person J can at the same time be father, brother, and grandson, for example.

Children who have reached the concrete operational stage are also capable of **seriation,** which is the ability to order stimuli along a quantitative dimension (such as length). To see if students can serialize, a teacher might haphazardly place eight sticks of different lengths on a table. The teacher then asks the students to order the sticks by length. Many young children end up with two or three small groups of "big" sticks or "little" sticks, rather than a correct ordering of all eight sticks. Another mistaken strategy they use is to evenly line up the tops of the sticks but ignore the bottoms. The concrete operational thinker simultaneously understands that each stick must be longer than the one that precedes it and shorter than the one that follows it.

Another aspect of reasoning about the relations between classes is **transitivity,** which is the ability to logically combine relations to understand certain conclusions. In this case, consider three sticks (A, B, and C) of differing lengths. A is the longest, B is intermediate in length, and C is the shortest. Does the child understand that if A is longer than B and B is longer than C, then A is longer than C? In Piaget's theory, concrete operational thinkers do; preoperational thinkers do not.

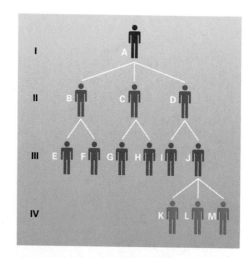

FIGURE 12.1 Classification: An Important Ability in Concrete Operational Thought A family tree of four generations (*I to IV*): The preoperational child has trouble classifying the members of the four generations; the concrete operational child can classify the members vertically, horizontally, and obliquely (up and down and across). For example, the concrete operational child understands that a family member can be a son, a brother, and a father, all at the same time.

Evaluating Piaget's Concrete Operational Stage

Has Piaget's portrait of the concrete operational child stood the test of research? According to Piaget, various aspects of a stage should emerge at the same time. In fact,

seriation The concrete operation that involves ordering stimuli along a quantitative dimension (such as length).

transitivity The ability to logically combine relations to understand certain conclusions.

An outstanding teacher and education in the logic of science and mathematics are important cultural experiences that promote the development of operational thought. *Might Piaget have underestimated the roles of culture and schooling in children's cognitive development?*

however, some concrete operational abilities do not appear in synchrony. For example, children do not learn to conserve at the same time they learn to cross-classify.

Furthermore, education and culture exert stronger influences on children's development than Piaget maintained (Cole, 2006). Some pre-operational children can be trained to reason at a concrete operational stage. And the age at which children acquire conservation skills is related to how much practice their culture provides in these skills. Among Wolof children in the West African nation of Senegal, for example, only 50 percent of the 10- to 13-year-olds understood the principle of conservation (Greenfield, 1966). Comparable studies among cultures in central Australia, New Guinea (an island north of Australia), the Amazon jungle region of Brazil, and rural Sardinia (an island off the coast of Italy) yielded similar results (Dasen, 1977).

Thus, although Piaget was a giant in the field of developmental psychology, his conclusions about the concrete operational stage have been challenged. In Chapter 15, "Cognitive Development in Adolescence," after examining the final stage in his theory of cognitive development, we evaluate Piaget's contributions and the criticisms of his theory.

Neo-Piagetians argue that Piaget got some things right but that his theory needs considerable revision. They place greater emphasis on how children use attention, memory, and strategies to process information (Case & Mueller, 2001; Morra & others, 2007). According to neo-Piagetians, a more accurate portrayal of children's thinking requires attention to children's strategies, the speed at which children process information, the particular task involved, and the division of problems into smaller, more precise steps. These are issues addressed by the information-processing approach, and we discuss some of them later in this chapter.

Another alternative to concrete operational thought comes from Vygotsky. As we discussed in Chapter 9, "Cognitive Development in Early Childhood," Vygotsky, like Piaget, held that children construct their knowledge of the world. But Vygotsky did not propose stages of cognitive development, and he emphasized the importance of social interaction, the social contexts of learning, and the young child's use of language to plan, guide, and monitor behavior (Gauvain, 2008; Holzman, 2009).

Applications to Education

Although Piaget was not an educator, he provided a sound conceptual framework for viewing learning and education. Following are some ideas in Piaget's theory that can be applied to teaching children (Elkind, 1976; Heuwinkel, 1996):

1. *Take a constructivist approach.* Piaget emphasized that children learn best when they are active and seek solutions for themselves. Piaget opposed teaching methods that treat children as passive receptacles. The educational implication of Piaget's view is that, in all subjects, students learn best by making discoveries, reflecting on them, and discussing them, rather than by blindly imitating the teacher or by doing things by rote.

2. *Facilitate, rather than direct, learning.* Effective teachers design situations that allow students to learn by doing. These situations promote students' thinking and discovery. Teachers listen, watch, and question students, to help them gain better understanding. Don't just examine what students think and the product of their learning. Rather, carefully observe them and find out how they think. Ask relevant questions to stimulate their thinking, and ask them to explain their answers.

neo-Piagetians Developmentalists who have elaborated on Piaget's theory, giving more emphasis to information processing, strategies, and precise cognitive steps.

3. *Consider the child's knowledge and level of thinking.* Students do not come to class with empty minds. They have many ideas about the physical and natural world. They have concepts of space, time, quantity, and causality. These ideas differ from the ideas of adults. Teachers need to interpret what a student is saying and respond in a way that is not too far from the student's level. Also, Piaget suggested that it is important to examine children's mistakes in thinking, not just what they get correct, to help guide them to a higher level of understanding.

4. *Use ongoing assessment.* Individually constructed meanings cannot be measured by standardized tests. To evaluate progress, you can use math and language portfolios (which contain work in progress as well as finished products), individual conferences in which students discuss their thinking strategies, and students' written and verbal explanations of their reasoning.

5. *Promote the student's intellectual health.* When Piaget came to lecture in the United States, he was asked, "What can I do to get my child to a higher cognitive stage sooner?" He was asked this question so often here compared with other countries that he called it "the American question." For Piaget, children's learning should occur naturally. Children should not be pushed and pressured into achieving too much too early in their development, before they are ready.

6. *Turn the classroom into a setting of exploration and discovery.* What do actual classrooms look like when the teachers adopt Piaget's views? Several first- and second-grade math classrooms provide some examples (Kamii, 1985, 1989). The teachers emphasize students' own exploration and discovery. The classrooms are less structured than what we think of as a typical classroom. Workbooks and predetermined assignments are not used. Rather, the teachers observe the students' interests and natural participation in activities to determine the course of learning. For example, a math lesson might be constructed around counting the day's lunch money or dividing supplies among students. Often, games are used to stimulate mathematical thinking. For example, a version of dominoes teaches children about even-numbered combinations; a variation on tic-tac-toe replaces *X*s and *O*s with numbers. Teachers encourage peer interaction during the lessons and games because students' different viewpoints can contribute to advances in thinking.

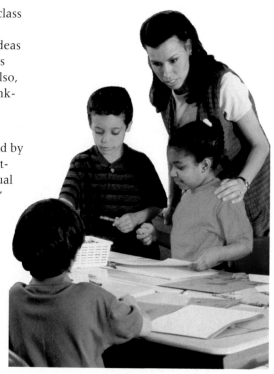

What are some educational strategies that can be derived from Piaget's theory?

Educators have also applied Vygotsky's ideas (Alvarez & del Rio, 2007; Daniels, 2007). His theory suggests that teachers should encourage elementary school children to internalize and regulate their talk to themselves. They should provide students with opportunities to experience learning in real-world settings—for example, instead of memorizing math formulas, students should work on math problems with real-world implications. In Chapter 9, "Cognitive Development in Early Childhood," we described other ways in which teachers have applied Vygotsky's ideas.

What does a Vygotskian classroom look like? The Kamehameha Elementary Education Program (KEEP) is based on Vygotsky's theory (Tharp, 1994). Many of the learning activities take place in small groups. The key element in this program is use of the zone of proximal development (the range of tasks that are too difficult for the child to master alone but that can be learned with guidance and assistance from more-skilled peers and adults). Children might read a story and then interpret its meaning. Scaffolding is used to improve children's literary skills. The instructor asks questions, responds to students' queries, and builds on the ideas that students generate. Thousands of children from low-income families have attended KEEP public schools—in Hawaii, on an Arizona Navajo Native American reservation, and in Los Angeles. Compared with a control group of non-KEEP children, the KEEP children participated more actively in classroom discussion, were more attentive in class, and had higher reading achievement (Tharp & Gallimore, 1988).

Review and Reflect: Learning Goal 1

1 **Discuss Piaget's stage of concrete operational thought, and apply Piaget's theory to education**

REVIEW
- How can concrete operational thought be characterized?
- How can Piaget's concrete operational stage be evaluated?
- How can Piaget's theory be applied to education?

REFLECT
- Imagine that you have become an elementary school teacher. Based on Piaget's theory, in what important ways is your thinking likely to differ from that of the children in your classroom? What adjustments in thinking might you need to make when you communicate with the children?

---

2 WHAT IS THE NATURE OF CHILDREN'S INFORMATION PROCESSING?

Memory   **Thinking**   **Metacognition**

During middle and late childhood, most children dramatically improve their ability to sustain and control attention. As we discussed in Chapter 9, "Cognitive Development in Early Childhood," they pay more attention to task-relevant stimuli such as teacher instructions than to salient stimuli such as the colors in the teacher's attire. Other changes in information processing during middle and late childhood involve memory, thinking, and metacognition. In the following pages, we examine each of these areas.

Memory

long-term memory A relatively permanent type of memory that holds huge amounts of information for a long period of time.

elaboration An important strategy that involves engaging in more extensive processing of information.

fuzzy trace theory A theory stating that memory is best understood by considering two types of memory representations: (1) verbatim memory trace and (2) gist. In this theory, older children's better memory is attributed to the fuzzy traces created by extracting the gist of information.

In Chapter 9, "Cognitive Development in Early Childhood," we concluded that short-term memory increases considerably during early childhood but after the age of 7 does not show as much increase. **Long-term memory,** a relatively permanent and unlimited type of memory, increases with age during middle and late childhood. In part, improvements in memory reflect children's increased knowledge and their increased use of strategies to retain information (Schraw, 2006).

Knowledge and Expertise   Much of the research on the role of knowledge in memory has compared experts and novices (Ericsson & others, 2006). *Experts* have acquired extensive knowledge about a particular content area; this knowledge influences what they notice and how they organize, represent, and interpret information. These skills in turn affect their ability to remember, reason, and solve problems.

When individuals have expertise about a particular subject, their memory also tends to be good regarding material related to that subject.

For example, one study found that 10- and 11-year-olds who were experienced chess players ("experts") were able to remember more information about chess pieces than college students who were not chess players ("novices") (Chi, 1978). In contrast, when the college students were presented with other stimuli, they were able to remember them better than the children were. Thus, the children's expertise in chess gave them superior memories, but only in chess.

There are developmental changes in expertise. Older children usually have more expertise about a subject than younger children do, which can contribute to their better memory for the subject.

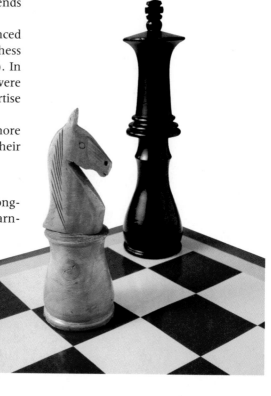

Strategies If we know anything at all about long-term memory, it is that long-term memory depends on the learning activities individuals engage in when learning and remembering information (Block & Pressley, 2007). Recall from Chapter 9, "Cognitive Development in Early Childhood," that *strategies* consist of deliberate mental activities to improve the processing of information. They do not occur automatically but require effort and work. Strategies, which are also called *control processes*, are under the learner's conscious control and can be used to improve memory. Two important strategies are creating mental images and elaborating on information (Murray, 2007).

Mental imagery can help even young schoolchildren to remember pictures. However, for remembering verbal information, mental imagery works better for older children than for younger children (Schneider, 2004). In one study, 20 sentences were presented to first- through sixth-grade children to remember—such as "The angry bird shouted at the white dog" and "The policeman painted the circus tent on a windy day" (Pressley & others, 1987). Children were randomly assigned either to an imagery condition, in which they were told to make a picture in their head for each sentence, or to a control condition, in which they were told just to try hard. The instructions to form images helped older elementary school children (fifth-graders) but did not help the younger elementary school children (second-graders) (see Figure 12.2).

Elaboration is an important strategy that involves engaging in more extensive processing of information. When individuals engage in elaboration, their memory benefits. Thinking of examples and referencing one's self are good ways to elaborate information. Thinking about personal associations with information makes the information more meaningful and helps children to remember it. For example, if the word *win* is on a list of words a child is asked to remember, the child might think of the last time he won a bicycle race with a friend.

The use of elaboration changes developmentally (Pressley & Harris, 2006). Adolescents are more likely to use elaboration spontaneously than are children. Elementary school children can be taught to use elaboration strategies on a learning task, but they will be less likely than adolescents to use the strategies on other learning tasks in the future. Nonetheless, verbal elaboration can be an effective strategy for processing information even for young elementary school children.

Fuzzy Trace Theory Might something other than knowledge and strategies be responsible for the improvement in memory during the elementary school years? Charles Brainerd and Valerie Reyna (1993; Reyna, 2004; Reyna & Brainerd, 1995) argue that fuzzy traces account for much of this improvement. Their **fuzzy trace theory** states that memory is best understood by considering two types of memory representations: (1) verbatim memory trace, and (2) gist. The *verbatim memory trace* consists of the precise details of the information, whereas *gist* refers to the central idea of the information. When gist is used, fuzzy traces are built up. Although

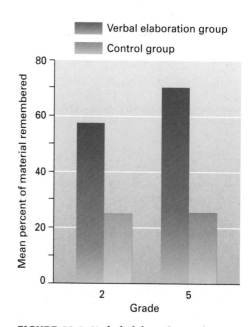

FIGURE 12.2 Verbal Elaboration and Memory Both second- and fifth-grade children remembered words better when they constructed a meaningful sentence for the word (verbal elaboration group) than when they merely heard the word and its definition (control group). The verbal elaboration worked better for the fifth-graders than for the second-graders.

individuals of all ages extract gist, young children tend to store and retrieve verbatim traces. At some point during the early elementary school years, children begin to use gist more and, according to the theory, its use contributes to the improved memory and reasoning of older children because fuzzy traces are more enduring and less likely to be forgotten than verbatim traces.

Thinking

Three important aspects of thinking are being able to think critically, creatively, and scientifically.

Critical Thinking   Currently, there is considerable interest in critical thinking among psychologists and educators (Sternberg, Roediger, & Halpern, 2007). **Critical thinking** involves thinking reflectively and productively, as well as evaluating evidence. In this book, the second part of the Review and Reflect sections of each chapter challenge you to think critically about a topic or an issue related to the discussion.

According to Ellen Langer (2005), **mindfulness**—being alert, mentally present, and cognitively flexible while going through life's everyday activities and tasks—is an important aspect of thinking critically. Mindful children and adults maintain an active awareness of the circumstances in their life and are motivated to find the best solutions to tasks. Mindful individuals create new ideas, are open to new information, and operate from a single perspective. By contrast, mindless individuals are entrapped in old ideas, engage in automatic behavior, and operate from a single perspective.

Jacqueline and Martin Brooks (2001) lament that few schools really teach students to think critically and develop a deep understanding of concepts. Deep understanding occurs when students are stimulated to rethink previously held ideas. In Brooks and Brooks' view, schools spend too much time getting students to give a single correct answer in an imitative way, rather than encouraging them to expand their thinking by coming up with new ideas and rethinking earlier conclusions. They observe that too often teachers ask students to recite, define, describe, state, and list, rather than to analyze, infer, connect, synthesize, criticize, create, evaluate, think, and rethink. Many successful students complete their assignments, do well on tests, and get good grades, yet they don't ever learn to think critically and deeply. They think superficially, staying on the surface of problems rather than stretching their minds and becoming deeply engaged in meaningful thinking.

Creative Thinking   Cognitively competent children think not only critically, but also creatively (Rickards, Moger, & Runco, 2009). **Creative thinking** is the ability to think in novel and unusual ways and to come up with unique solutions to problems. Thus, intelligence and creativity are not the same thing. This difference was recognized by J. P. Guilford (1967), who distinguished between **convergent thinking,** which produces one correct answer and characterizes the kind of thinking that is required on conventional tests of intelligence, and **divergent thinking,** which produces many different answers to the same question and characterizes creativity. For example, a typical item on a conventional intelligence test is "How many quarters will you get in return for 60 dimes?" In contrast, the following question has many possible answers: "What image comes to mind when you hear the phrase 'sitting alone in a dark room' or 'some unique uses for a paper clip'?"

An important teaching goal is to help students become more creative (Sternberg, 2009a; Sternberg, Kaufman, & Grigorkenko, 2008). Teachers need to recognize that students will show more creativity in some domains than in others (Rickards, Moger, & Runco, 2007). A student who shows creative thinking skills in mathematics may not exhibit these skills in art, for example.

I *think, therefore I am.*

—RENE DESCARTES
French Philosopher and
Mathematician, 17th Century

S. GROSS

"For God's sake, think! Why is he being so nice to you?"
Copyright © The New Yorker Collection 1998 Sam Gross from cartoonbank.com. All Rights Reserved.

critical thinking The ability to think reflectively and productively, as well as to evaluate the evidence.

mindfulness Being alert, mentally present, and cognitively flexible while going through life's everyday activities and tasks.

creative thinking The ability to think in novel and unusual ways and to come up with unique solutions to problems.

convergent thinking Thinking that produces one correct answer and is characteristic of the kind of thinking tested by standardized intelligence tests.

divergent thinking Thinking that produces many different answers to the same question and is characteristic of creativity.

The design of schools and classrooms may influence the creativity of students. School environments that encourage independent work, are stimulating but not distracting, and make resources readily available are likely to encourage students' creativity (Hasirci & Demirkan, 2003). There is mounting concern that the U.S. government's No Child Left Behind legislation has harmed the development of students' creative thinking by focusing attention on memorization of materials to do well on standardized tests (Burke-Adams, 2007; Kaufman & Sternberg, 2007).

An important goal is to help children become more creative. The following *Caring for Children* interlude examines some recommendations for ways to accomplish this goal.

What do you mean, "What is it?" It's the spontaneous, unfettered expression of a young mind not yet bound by the restraints of narrative or pictorial representation.
Science Cartoons Plus. Used with permission.

Caring for Children

STRATEGIES FOR INCREASING CHILDREN'S CREATIVE THINKING

Some strategies for increasing children's creative thinking include:

- *Encourage brainstorming.* **Brainstorming** is a technique in which people are encouraged to come up with creative ideas in a group, play off each other's ideas, and say practically whatever comes to mind that seems relevant to a particular issue. Participants are usually told to hold off from criticizing others' ideas at least until the end of the brainstorming session.

- *Provide environments that stimulate creativity.* Some environments nourish creativity, others inhibit it. Parents and teachers who encourage creativity often rely on children's natural curiosity. They provide exercises and activities that stimulate children to find insightful solutions to problems, rather than ask a lot of questions that require rote answers. Teachers also encourage creativity by taking students on field trips to locations where creativity is valued. Howard Gardner (1993) emphasizes that science, discovery, and children's museums offer rich opportunities to stimulate creativity.

- *Don't overcontrol students.* Teresa Amabile (1993) says that telling children exactly how to do things leaves them feeling that originality is a mistake and exploration is a waste of time. If, instead of dictating which activities they should engage in, you let children select their interests and you support their inclinations, you will be less likely to destroy their natural curiosity.

- *Encourage internal motivation.* Excessive use of prizes, such as gold stars, money, or toys, can stifle creativity by undermining the intrinsic pleasure students derive from creative activities. Creative children's motivation is the satisfaction generated by the work itself. Competition for prizes and formal evaluations often undermine intrinsic motivation and creativity (Amabile & Hennesey, 1992). However, this strategy should not rule out material rewards altogether.

- *Build children's confidence.* To expand children's creativity, encourage children to believe in their own ability to create something innovative and worthwhile. Building children's confidence in their creative skills aligns with Bandura's (2008, 2009) concept of *self-efficacy*, the belief that one can master a situation and produce positive outcomes.

(continued on next page)

How Would You...?
As a psychologist, how would you talk with teachers and parents about ways to improve children's creative thinking?

What are some good strategies for guiding children in thinking more creatively?

brainstorming A technique in which individuals are encouraged to come up with creative ideas in a group, play off each other's ideas, and say practically whatever comes to mind.

- *Guide children to be persistent and delay gratification.* Most highly successful creative products take years to develop. Most creative individuals work on ideas and projects for months and years without being rewarded for their efforts (Sternberg & Williams, 1996). Children don't become experts at sports, music, or art overnight. It usually takes many years of working at something to become an expert at it; so it is with being a creative thinker who produces a unique, worthwhile product.

- *Encourage children to take intellectual risks.* Creative individuals take intellectual risks and seek to discover or invent something never before discovered or invented (Sternberg & Williams, 1996). They risk spending extensive time on an idea or project that may not work. Creative people are not afraid of failing or getting something wrong (Sternberg, 2009a).

- *Introduce children to creative people.* Teachers can invite creative people to their classrooms and ask them to describe what helps them become creative or to demonstrate their creative skills. A writer, poet, musician, scientist, and many others can bring their props and productions to the class, turning it into a theater for stimulating students' creativity.

Scientific Thinking   Like scientists, children ask fundamental questions about reality and seek answers to problems that seem utterly trivial or unanswerable to other people (such as, "Why is the sky blue?"). Do children generate hypotheses, perform experiments, and reach conclusions about their data in ways resembling those of scientists?

Scientific reasoning often is aimed at identifying causal relations. Like scientists, children place a great deal of emphasis on causal mechanisms. Their understanding of how events are caused weighs more heavily in their causal inferences than even such strong influences as whether the cause happened immediately before the effect.

There also are important differences between the reasoning of children and the reasoning of scientists. Children are more influenced by happenstance events than by an overall pattern, and children tend to maintain their old theories regardless of the evidence (Kuhn, Schauble, & Garcia-Mila, 1992). Children might go through mental gymnastics in trying to reconcile seemingly contradictory new information with their existing beliefs. For example, after learning about the solar system, children sometimes conclude that there are two Earths, the seemingly flat world in which they live and the round ball floating in space that their teacher described.

Children also have difficulty designing experiments that can distinguish among alternative causes. Instead, they tend to bias the experiments in favor of whatever hypothesis they began with. Sometimes they see the results as supporting their original hypothesis even when the results directly contradict it (Schauble & others, 1996). Thus, although there are important similarities between children and scientists in their basic curiosity and in the kinds of questions they ask, there are also important differences in the degree to which they can separate theory and evidence and in their ability to design conclusive experiments (Lehrer & Schauble, 2006).

Too often, the skills scientists use—such as careful observation, graphing, self-regulatory thinking, and knowing when and how to apply one's knowledge to solve problems—are not routinely taught in schools (Bass, Contant, & Carin, 2009). Children have many concepts

Luis Recalde holds up a seaweed specimen in one of the hands-on, high-interest learning contexts he creates for students. Recalde, a fourth- and fifth-grade science teacher in New Haven, Connecticut, uses every opportunity to make science fascinating for students to learn. To help students get a better sense of what it is like to be a scientist, he brings lab coats to the classroom for students to wear. He often gives up his vacation time to help students with science projects.

that are incompatible with science and reality. Good teachers perceive and understand a child's underlying scientific concepts, and then use the concepts as a scaffold for learning (Magnusson & Palinscar, 2005). Effective science teaching helps children distinguish between fruitful errors and misconceptions and detect plainly wrong ideas that need to be replaced by more accurate conceptions.

Many science teachers help their students construct knowledge of science through discovery and hands-on laboratory investigations (Victor, Kellough, & Tai, 2008). Constructivist teaching emphasizes that children have to build their own scientific knowledge and understanding. Keep in mind, though, that it is important that students not be left completely on their own to construct scientific knowledge independent of *science content*. Students' inquiry should be guided (Moyer, Hackett, & Everett, 2007). It is important for teachers at a minimum to initially scaffold students' science learning, extensively monitor their progress, and ensure that they are learning science content. Thus, in pursuing science investigations, students need to learn inquiry skills *and* science content (Gallagher, 2007).

How might family, economic, and cultural experiences be linked to children's science achievement? A recent study of more than 107,000 students in 41 countries examined this question (Chiu, 2007). Students had higher science achievement scores when they lived in two-parent families, experienced more family involvement, lived with fewer siblings, their schools had more resources, they lived in wealthier countries, or they lived in countries with more equal distribution of household income.

Metacognition

One expert in children's thinking, Deanna Kuhn (1999), argues that to help students become better thinkers, schools should pay more attention to helping students develop skills that entail knowing about their own (and others') knowing. In other words, schools should do more to develop **metacognition,** which is cognition about cognition, or knowing about knowing (Flavell, 2004).

The majority of developmental studies classified as "metacognitive" have focused on *metamemory*, or knowledge about memory. This includes general knowledge about memory, such as knowing that recognition tests are easier than recall tests. It also encompasses knowledge about one's own memory, such as a student's ability to monitor whether she has studied enough for a test that is coming up next week.

Young children do have some general knowledge about memory. By 5 or 6 years of age, children usually already know that familiar items are easier to learn than unfamiliar ones, that short lists are easier than long ones, that recognition is easier than recall, and that forgetting is more likely to occur over time (Lyon & Flavell, 1993). However, in other ways young children's metamemory is limited. They don't understand that related items are easier to remember than unrelated ones and that remembering the gist of a story is easier than remembering information verbatim (Kreutzer, Leonard, & Flavell, 1975). By the fifth grade, however, students understand that gist recall is easier than verbatim recall.

Young children also have only limited knowledge about their own memory. They have an inflated opinion of their memory abilities. For example, in one study a majority of young children predicted that they would be able to recall all 10 items on a list of 10 items. When tested for this, none of the young children managed this feat (Flavell, Friedrichs, & Hoyt, 1970). As they move through the elementary school years, children give more realistic evaluations of their memory skills (Schneider & Pressley, 1997).

Cognitive developmentalist John Flavell (*left*) is a pioneer in providing insights about children's thinking. Among his many contributions are establishing the field of metacognition and conducting numerous studies in this area, including metamemory and theory of mind studies.

metacognition Cognition about cognition, or knowing about knowing.

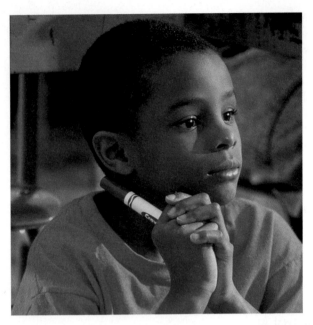

What are some developmental changes in metacognition?

In addition to metamemory, metacognition includes knowledge about strategies. In the view of Michael Pressley (2003), the key to education is helping students learn a rich repertoire of strategies that result in solutions to problems. Good thinkers routinely use strategies and effective planning to solve problems. Good thinkers also know when and where to use strategies. Understanding when and where to use strategies often results from monitoring the learning situation (Pressley & McCormick, 2007).

Pressley and his colleagues (Pressley & others, 2001, 2003, 2004; Pressley, Mohan, Fingeret, & others, 2007; Pressley, Mohan, Raphael, & Fingeret, 2007) have spent considerable time in recent years observing strategy instruction by teachers and strategy use by students in elementary and secondary school classrooms. They conclude that strategy instruction is far less complete and intense than what students need in order to learn how to use strategies effectively. They argue that education needs to be restructured so that students are provided with more opportunities to become competent strategic learners.

How Would You...?
As an educator, how would you advise teachers and parents about ways to improve their child's metacognitive skills?

Review and Reflect: Learning Goal 2

2 **Describe changes in information processing in middle and late childhood**

REVIEW

• What characterizes children's memory in middle and late childhood?
• What is involved in thinking critically, thinking creatively, and thinking scientifically?
• What is metacognition?

REFLECT

• When you were in elementary school, did classroom instruction prepare you adequately for critical thinking tasks? If you were a parent of an 8-year-old, what would you do to guide the child to think more critically and creatively?

---

3 HOW CAN CHILDREN'S INTELLIGENCE BE DESCRIBED?

| Intelligence and Its Assessment | Types of Intelligence | The Neuroscience of Intelligence | Interpreting Differences in IQ Scores | Extremes of Intelligence |

Twentieth-century English novelist Aldous Huxley said that children are remarkable for their curiosity and intelligence. What did Huxley mean when he used the word *intelligence?* How can intelligence be assessed?

Intelligence and Its Assessment

Just what is meant by the concept of "intelligence"? Some experts describe intelligence as problem-solving skills. Others describe it as the ability to adapt to and learn from life's everyday experiences. Combining these ideas, we can arrive at a definition of **intelligence** as problem-solving skills and the ability to learn from and adapt to life's everyday experiences.

Interest in intelligence has often focused on individual differences and assessment. **Individual differences** are the stable, consistent ways in which people are different from each other. We can talk about individual differences in personality or any other domain, but it is in the domain of intelligence that the most attention has been directed at individual differences. For example, an intelligence test purports to inform us about whether a student can reason better than others who have taken the test. Let's go back in history and see what the first intelligence test was like.

The Binet Tests   In 1904, the French Ministry of Education asked psychologist Alfred Binet to devise a method of identifying children who were unable to learn in school. School officials wanted to reduce crowding by placing students who did not benefit from regular classroom teaching in special schools. Binet and his student Theophile Simon developed an intelligence test to meet this request. The test, called the 1905 Scale, consisted of 30 questions on topics ranging from the ability to touch one's ear to the ability to draw designs from memory and define abstract concepts.

Binet developed the concept of **mental age (MA),** an individual's level of mental development relative to others. Not much later, in 1912, William Stern created the concept of **intelligence quotient (IQ),** a person's mental age divided by chronological age (CA), multiplied by 100. That is: $IQ = MA/CA \times 100$. If mental age is the same as chronological age, then the person's IQ is 100. If mental age is above chronological age, then IQ is more than 100. If mental age is below chronological age, then IQ is less than 100.

The Binet test has been revised many times to incorporate advances in the understanding of intelligence and intelligence tests. These revisions are called the *Stanford-Binet tests* (the revisions have been done at Stanford University). By administering the test to large numbers of people of different ages (from preschool through late adulthood) from different backgrounds, researchers have found that scores on the Stanford-Binet approximate a normal distribution (see Figure 12.3). A **normal distribution** is symmetrical, with a majority of the scores falling in the middle of the possible range of scores and few scores appearing toward the extremes of the range.

The Wechsler Scales   Another set of tests widely used to assess students' intelligence is called the Wechsler scales, developed by psychologist David Wechsler. They include the Wechsler Preschool and Primary Scale of Intelligence—Third Edition (WPPSI-III) to test children from the ages of 2 years 6 months to 7 years 3 months of age; the Wechsler Intelligence Scale for Children—Fourth Edition (WISC-IV) for children and adolescents 6 to 16 years of age; and the Wechsler Adult Intelligence Scale—Third Edition (WAIS-III).

intelligence Problem-solving skills and the ability to learn from and adapt to the experiences of everyday life.

individual differences The stable, consistent ways in which people are different from each other.

mental age (MA) Binet's measure of an individual's level of mental development, compared with that of others.

intelligence quotient (IQ) A person's mental age divided by chronological age, multiplied by 100.

normal distribution A symmetrical distribution with most scores falling in the middle of the possible range of scores and few scores appearing toward the extremes of the range.

FIGURE 12.3 The Normal Curve and Stanford-Binet IQ Scores

Verbal Subscales

Similarities

A child must think logically and abstractly to answer a number of questions about how things might be similar.

Example: "In what way are a lion and a tiger alike?"

Comprehension

This subscale is designed to measure an individual's judgment and common sense.

Example: "What is the advantage of keeping money in a bank?"

Nonverbal Subscales

Block Design

A child must assemble a set of multicolored blocks to match designs that the examiner shows. Visual-motor coordination, perceptual organization, and the ability to visualize spatially are assessed.

Example: "Use the four blocks on the left to make the pattern on the right."

FIGURE 12.4 Sample Subscales of the Wechsler Intelligence Scale for Children— Fourth Edition (WISC-IV) The Wechsler includes 11 subscales, 6 verbal and 5 nonverbal. Three of the subscales are shown here. Simulated items similar to those found in the *Wechsler Intelligence Scale for Children—Fourth Edition.* Copyright © 2003 by Harcourt Assessment, Inc. Reproduced by permission. All rights reserved. "Wechsler Intelligence Scale for Children" and "WISC" are trademarks of Harcourt Assessment, Inc. registered in the United States of America and/or other jurisdictions.

triarchic theory of intelligence Sternberg's theory that intelligence consists of analytical intelligence, creative intelligence, and practical intelligence.

The Wechsler scales not only provide an overall IQ score and scores on a number of subtests but also yield several composite indexes (for example, the Verbal Comprehension Index, the Working Memory Index, and the Processing Speed Index). The subtest and composite scores allow the examiner to quickly determine the areas in which a child is strong or weak. Three of the Wechsler subscales are shown in Figure 12.4.

Types of Intelligence

Is it more appropriate to think of a child's intelligence as a general ability or as a number of specific abilities? Robert Sternberg and Howard Gardner have proposed influential theories oriented to this second viewpoint.

Sternberg's Triarchic Theory   Robert J. Sternberg (1986, 2004, 2007, 2008, 2009b, c) developed the **triarchic theory of intelligence,** which states that intelligence comes in three forms:

- *Analytical intelligence*, referring to the ability to analyze, judge, evaluate, compare, and contrast
- *Creative intelligence*, consisting of the ability to create, design, invent, originate, and imagine
- *Practical intelligence*, involving the ability to use, apply, implement, and put ideas into practice

Sternberg (2002; Sternberg, Jarvin, & Grigorenko, 2009) says that children with different triarchic patterns "look different" in school. Students with high analytic ability tend to be favored in conventional schooling. They often do well under direct instruction, in which the teacher lectures and gives students objective tests. They often are considered to be "smart" students who get good grades, show up in high-level tracks, do well on traditional tests of intelligence and the SAT, and later get admitted to competitive colleges.

In contrast, children who are high in creative intelligence often are not on the top rung of their class. Many teachers have specific expectations about how assignments should be done, and creatively intelligent students may not conform to those expectations. Instead of giving conformist answers, they give unique answers, for which they might get reprimanded or marked down. No teacher wants to discourage creativity, but Sternberg stresses that too often a teacher's desire to improve students' knowledge suppresses creative thinking.

Like children high in creative intelligence, children who are intelligent practically often do not relate well to the demands of school. However, many of these children do well outside the classroom's walls. They may have excellent social skills and good common sense. As adults, some become successful managers, entrepreneurs, or politicians in spite of having undistinguished school records.

Recently, Sternberg (2009d, e) has applied his triarchic theory of intelligence to the concept of *wisdom*. In his view, academic intelligence is a necessary but in many cases insufficient requirement for wisdom. Practical knowledge about the realities of life

Robert J. Sternberg, who developed the triarchic theory of intelligence.

also is needed for wisdom. For Sternberg, balance between self-interest, the interests of others, and contexts produces a common good. Thus, wise individuals don't just look out for themselves—they also need to consider others' needs and perspectives, as well as the particular context involved. Sternberg assesses wisdom by presenting problems to individuals that require solutions which highlight various intrapersonal, interpersonal, and contextual interests. He also emphasizes that such aspects of wisdom should be taught in schools (Sternberg, 2009d, e; Sternberg, Jarvin, & Reznitskaya, 2009).

Gardner's Eight Frames of Mind   Howard Gardner (1983, 1993, 2002) suggests that there are eight types of intelligence, or "frames of mind." These are described here, with examples of the types of vocations in which they are reflected as strengths (Campbell, Campbell, & Dickinson, 2004):

- *Verbal:* the ability to think in words and use language to express meaning (occupations: authors, journalists, speakers)
- *Mathematical:* the ability to carry out mathematical operations (occupations: scientists, engineers, accountants)
- *Spatial:* the ability to think three-dimensionally (occupations: architects, artists, sailors)
- *Bodily-kinesthetic:* the ability to manipulate objects and be physically adept (occupations: surgeons, craftspeople, dancers, athletes)
- *Musical:* a sensitivity to pitch, melody, rhythm, and tone (occupations: composers, musicians, sensitive listeners)
- *Interpersonal:* the ability to understand and interact effectively with others (occupations: successful teachers, mental health professionals)
- *Intrapersonal:* the ability to understand oneself (occupations: theologians, psychologists)
- *Naturalist:* the ability to observe patterns in nature and understand natural and human-made systems (occupations: farmers, botanists, ecologists, landscapers)

According to Gardner, everyone has all of these intelligences to varying degrees. As a result, we prefer to learn and process information in different ways. People learn best when they can do so in a way that uses their stronger intelligences.

Evaluating the Multiple-Intelligence Approaches   Sternberg's and Gardner's approaches have much to offer. They have stimulated teachers to think more broadly about what makes up children's competencies. And they have motivated educators to develop programs that instruct students in multiple domains. These approaches have also contributed to interest in assessing intelligence and classroom learning in innovative ways, such as by evaluating student portfolios (Moran & Gardner, 2006, 2007).

Still, doubts about multiple-intelligences approaches persist. A number of psychologists think that the multiple-intelligence views have taken the concept of specific intelligences too far (Johnson & others, 2004). Some argue that a research base to support the three intelligences of Sternberg or the eight intelligences of Gardner has not yet emerged. One expert on intelligence, Nathan Brody (2007), observes that people who excel at one type of intellectual task are likely to excel in others. Thus, individuals who do well at memorizing lists of digits are also likely to be good at solving verbal problems and spatial layout problems. If musical skill reflects a distinct type of intelligence, ask other critics, why not label the skills of outstanding chess players, prizefighters, painters, and poets as types of intelligence?

The argument between those who support the concept of general intelligence and those who advocate the multiple-intelligences view is ongoing (Brody, 2007; Jensen, 2008; Sternberg, 2008). Sternberg (2009b, c) actually accepts that there is a general intelligence for the kinds of analytical tasks that traditional IQ tests assess but thinks that the range of tasks those tests measure is far too narrow.

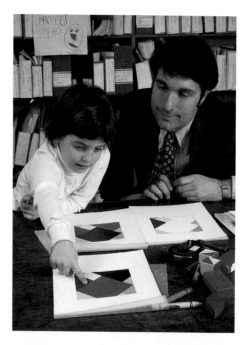

Howard Gardner, here working with a young child, developed the view that intelligence comes in the forms of these eight kinds of skills: verbal, mathematical, spatial, bodily-kinesthetic, musical, intrapersonal, interpersonal, and naturalist.

How Would You...?
As a psychologist, how would you use Gardner's theory of multiple intelligences to respond to children who are distressed by their below-average score on a traditional intelligence test?

Culture and Intelligence Differences in conceptions of intelligence occur not only among psychologists but also among cultures. What is viewed as intelligent in one culture may not be thought of as intelligent in another (Cole, 2006). For example, people in Western cultures tend to view intelligence in terms of reasoning and thinking skills, whereas people in Eastern cultures see intelligence as a way for members of a community to engage successfully in social roles (Nisbett, 2003). One study found that Taiwanese Chinese conceptions of intelligence emphasize understanding and relating to others, including when to show and when not to show one's intelligence (Yang & Sternberg, 1997).

The Neuroscience of Intelligence

In the current era of extensive research on the brain, interest in the neuroscience underpinnings of intelligence has increased (Glascher & others, 2009; Haier, 2009; Neubauer & Fink, 2009; Shenkin & others, 2009). Among the questions about the brain's role in intelligence being explored are these: Is having a big brain linked to higher intelligence? Is intelligence located in certain brain regions? Is how fast the brain processes information linked to intelligence?

Are individuals with a big brain more intelligent than those with a smaller brain? Recent studies using MRI scans to assess total brain volume indicate a moderate correlation (about +.3 to +.4) between brain size and intelligence (Carey, 2007; Luders & others, 2009; Witelson, Beresh, & Kigar, 2006).

Might intelligence be linked to specific regions of the brain? Early consensus was that the frontal lobes are the likely location of intelligence. However, researchers recently have found that intelligence is distributed more widely across brain regions (Haier, 2009; Haier & others, 2009; Karama & others, 2009; Luders & others, 2009). The most prominent finding from brain-imaging studies is that a distributed neural network involving the frontal and parietal lobes is related to higher intelligence (Colom, Jung, & Haier, 2007; Colom & others, 2009; Jung & Haier, 2007) (see Figure 12.5). Albert Einstein's total brain size was average, but a region of his brain's parietal lobe that is very active in processing math and spatial information was 15 percent larger than average (Witelson, Kigar, & Harvey, 1999). Other brain regions that have been linked to higher intelligence (although at a lower level of significance than the frontal/parietal lobe network) include the temporal and occipital lobes, as well as the cerebellum (Luders & others, 2009).

Neuroscientists also are intrigued by the roles that the brain's gray matter (the neuron's cell body) and white matter (axons and dendrites) might play in intelligence (Luders & others, 2009). The most consistent findings indicate that higher intelligence is linked to a higher volume of gray matter (Colom, Jung, & Haier, 2006; Luders & others, 2009). To a lesser degree, some studies also have found a connection between higher intelligence and a higher volume of white matter (Narr & others, 2007).

Examining the neuroscience of intelligence has also led to study of the role that neurological speed might play in intelligence (Waiter & others, 2009). Research results have not been consistent for this possible link, although one recent study did find that speed of neurological functioning was faster for intellectually gifted children than children with average intelligence (Liu & others, 2007).

As the technology to study the brain's functioning continues in coming decades, we are likely to see more specific conclusions about the brain's role in intelligence. As this research proceeds, keep in mind that both heredity and environment likely contribute to links between the brain and intelligence, including the connections we discussed between brain size and intelligence.

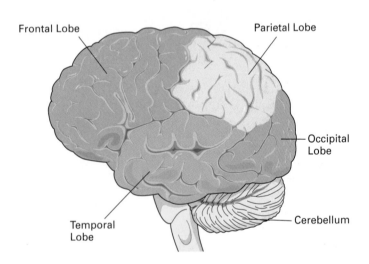

FIGURE 12.5 Intelligence and the Brain Researchers recently have found that a higher level of intelligence is linked to a distributed neural network in the frontal and parietal lobes. To a lesser extent than the frontal/parietal network, the temporal and occipital lobes, as well as the cerebellum, also have been found to have links to intelligence. The current consensus is that intelligence is likely to be distributed across brain regions rather than being localized in a specific region, such as the frontal lobes.

Interpreting Differences in IQ Scores

The IQ scores that result from tests such as the Stanford-Binet and Wechsler scales provide information about children's mental abilities. However, interpreting what performance on an intelligence test means is debated (Sternberg, 2009a, b; Plomin, De Fries, & Fulker, 2007).

The Influence of Genetics   How strong is the effect of genetics on intelligence? The concept of heritability attempts to tease apart the effects of heredity and environment in a population. **Heritability** is the fraction of the variance in a population that is attributed to genetics. The heritability index is computed using correlational techniques, which we first discussed in Chapter 1, "Introduction." Thus, 1.00 is the highest degree of heritability that is hypothetically possible, and correlations of .70 and above suggest a strong genetic influence. A committee of respected researchers convened by the American Psychological Association concluded that by late adolescence, the heritability of intelligence is about .75, which reflects a strong genetic influence (Neisser & others, 1996).

Most research on heredity and environment does not include environments that differ radically. Thus, it is not surprising that many genetic studies show environment to be a fairly weak influence on intelligence (Fraser, 1995).

The heritability index has several flaws. It is only as good as the data entered into its analysis and the interpretations made from it (Sternberg, Kaufman, & Grigorenko, 2008). The data are virtually all from traditional IQ tests, which some experts think are not always the best indicator of intelligence (Sternberg, 2008). Also, the heritability index assumes that we can treat genetic and environmental influences as factors that can be separated, with each part contributing a distinct amount of influence. As we discussed in Chapter 2, "Biological Beginnings," genes and the environment interact: Genes always exist in an environment, and the environment shapes their activity.

One strategy for examining the role of heredity in intelligence is to compare the IQs of identical and fraternal twins, which we initially discussed in Chapter 2, "Biological Beginnings." Recall that identical twins have exactly the same genetic makeup but fraternal twins do not. If intelligence is genetically determined, say some investigators, the IQs of identical twins should be more similar than the intelligence of fraternal twins. A research review of many studies found that the difference in the average correlation of intelligence between identical and fraternal twins was .15, a relatively low correlation (Grigorenko, 2000) (see Figure 12.6).

Today, most researchers agree that genetics and environment interact to influence intelligence (Gottlieb, 2007; Sternberg, 2009a, b). For most people, this means that modifications in environment can change their IQ scores considerably. Although genetic endowment may always influence a person's intellectual ability, the environmental influences and opportunities we provide children and adults do make a difference (Campbell, 2007; Sternberg, 2009a, b).

Environmental Influences   In one study, researchers went into homes and observed how extensively parents from welfare and middle-income professional families talked and communicated with their young children (Hart & Risley, 1995). They found that the middle-income professional parents were much more likely to communicate with their young children than the welfare parents were. How much the parents communicated with their children in the first three years of their lives was correlated with the children's Stanford-Binet IQ scores at age 3. The more parents communicated with their children, the higher the children's IQs were.

Schooling also influences intelligence (Gustafsson, 2007). The biggest effects have been found when large groups of children have been deprived of formal education

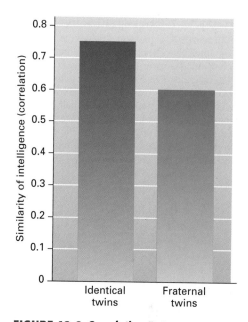

FIGURE 12.6 Correlation Between Intelligence Test Scores and Twin Status The graph represents a summary of research findings that have compared the intelligence test scores of identical and fraternal twins. An approximate .15 difference has been found, with a higher correlation (.75) for identical twins and a lower correlation (.60) for fraternal twins.

heritability The fraction of variance in a population that is attributed to genetics and is computed using correlational techniques.

FIGURE 12.7 Increasing IQ Scores from 1932 to 1997 As measured by the Stanford-Binet intelligence test, American children seem to be getting smarter. Scores of a group tested in 1932 fell along a bell-shaped curve with half below 100 and half above. Studies show that if children took that same test today, half would score above 120 on the 1932 scale. Very few of them would score in the "intellectually deficient" end, on the left side, and about one-fourth would rank in the "very superior" range.

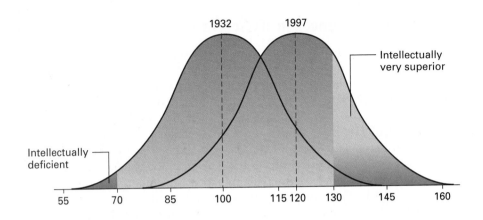

for an extended period, resulting in lower intelligence (Ceci & Gilstrap, 2000). Another possible effect of education can be seen in rapidly increasing IQ test scores around the world (Flynn, 1999, 2007). IQ scores have been increasing so fast that a high percentage of people regarded as having average intelligence at the turn of the century would be considered below average in intelligence today (see Figure 12.7). If a representative sample of people today took the Stanford-Binet test version used in 1932, about 25 percent would be defined as having very superior intelligence, a label usually accorded to fewer than 3 percent of the population. Because the increase has taken place in a relatively short time, it can't be due to heredity, but rather may be due to increasing levels of education attained by a much greater percentage of the world's population, or to other environmental factors such as the explosion of information to which people are exposed. The worldwide increase in intelligence test scores that has occurred over a short time frame has been called the *Flynn effect* after the researcher who discovered it, James Flynn.

Researchers are increasingly concerned about improving the early environment of children who are at risk for impoverished intelligence (Barajas, Philipsen, & Brooks-Gunn, 2008). For various reasons, many low-income parents have difficulty providing an intellectually stimulating environment for their children. Programs that educate parents to be more sensitive caregivers and better teachers, as well as support services such as quality child-care programs, can make a difference in a child's intellectual development (Coltrane & others, 2008). Thus the efforts to counteract a deprived early environment's effect on intelligence emphasize prevention rather than remediation.

A review of the research on early interventions concluded that (1) high-quality-child-care center-based interventions are associated with increases in children's intelligence and school achievement; (2) the interventions are most successful with poor children and children whose parents have little education; (3) the positive benefits continue through adolescence, but are not as strong as in early childhood or the beginning of elementary school; and (4) the programs that continue into middle and late childhood have the best long-term results (Brooks-Gunn, 2003).

Revisiting the Nature–Nurture Issue   In sum, there is a consensus among psychologists that both heredity and environment influence intelligence. This consensus reflects the nature-nurture issue that was highlighted in Chapter 1, "Introduction." Recall that the nature-nurture issue focuses on the extent to which development is influenced by nature (heredity) and nurture (environment). Although psychologists agree that intelligence is the product of both nature and nurture, there is still disagreement about how strongly each influences intelligence.

Group Differences   On the average, African American schoolchildren in the United States score 10 to 15 points lower on standardized intelligence tests than White

American schoolchildren do (Brody, 2000). Children from Latino families also score lower than White children. These are average scores, however; there is significant overlap in the distribution of scores. About 15 to 25 percent of African American schoolchildren score higher than half of White schoolchildren do, and many White schoolchildren score lower than most African American schoolchildren.

As African Americans have gained social, economic, and educational opportunities, the gap between African Americans and Whites on standardized intelligence tests has begun to narrow (Ogbu & Stern, 2001). This gap especially narrows in college, where African American and White students often experience more similar environments than in the elementary and high school years (Myerson & others, 1998). Also, when children from disadvantaged African American families are adopted into more advantaged middle-socioeconomic-status families, their scores on intelligence tests more closely resemble national averages for middle-socioeconomic-status children than for lower-socioeconomic-status children (Scarr & Weinberg, 1983).

Creating Culture–Fair Tests   **Culture-fair tests** are tests of intelligence that are intended to be free of cultural bias. Two types of culture-fair tests have been devised. The first includes items that are familiar to children from all socioeconomic and ethnic backgrounds, or items that at least are familiar to the children taking the test. For example, a child might be asked how a bird and a dog are different, on the assumption that all children have been exposed to birds and dogs. The second type of culture-fair test has no verbal questions.

Why is it so hard to create culture-fair tests? Most tests tend to reflect what the dominant culture thinks is important (Greenfield, Suzuki, & Rothstein-Fisch, 2006). Time limits on tests will bias the test against groups not concerned with time. If languages differ, the same words might have different meanings for different language groups. Even pictures can produce bias because some cultures have less experience with drawings and photographs than others (Anastasi & Urbina, 1997). Within the same culture, different subgroups could have different attitudes, values, and motivation, and these could affect their performance on intelligence tests. Items that ask why buildings should be made of brick are biased against children who have little or no experience with brick houses. Questions about railroads, furnaces, snow, distances between cities, and so on can be biased against groups who have less experience than others with these contexts. Recall, too, that cultures define what intelligent is differently. Because of such difficulties in creating culture-fair tests, Robert Sternberg and his colleagues (Sternberg & Grigorenko, 2008; Zhang & Sternberg, 2009) conclude that there are no culture-fair tests, only *culture-reduced tests*.

Using Intelligence Tests   Psychological tests are tools. Like all tools, their effectiveness depends on the knowledge, skill, and integrity of the user. A hammer can be used to build a beautiful kitchen cabinet, or it can be used as a weapon of assault. Like a hammer, psychological tests can be used for positive purposes, or they can be badly abused. Here are some cautions about IQ that can help you avoid the pitfalls of using information about a child's intelligence in negative ways:

- *Avoid stereotyping and preconceived expectations.* A special concern is that the scores on an IQ test easily can lead to stereotypes and preconceived expectations about students. Sweeping generalizations are too often made on the basis of an IQ score. An IQ test should always be considered a measure of current performance. It is not a measure of fixed potential. Maturational changes and enriched environmental experiences can advance a student's intelligence.

- *Know that IQ is not a sole indicator of competence.* Another concern about IQ tests occurs when they are used as the main or sole assessment of competence. A

"You can't build a hut, you don't know how to find edible roots and you know nothing about predicting the weather. In other words, you do terribly on our I.Q. test."
Copyright © 1992 by Sidney Harris. Reprinted with permission.

How Would You...?
As a social worker, how would you explain the role and purpose of intelligence test scores to a parent whose child is preparing to take a standardized intelligence test?

culture-fair tests Tests of intelligence that are designed to be free of cultural bias.

A child with Down Syndrome. *What causes a child to develop Down syndrome?*

high IQ is not the ultimate human value. As we have seen in this chapter, it is important to consider students' intellectual competence not only in such areas as verbal skills but also in their creative and practical skills.

- *Use caution in interpreting an overall IQ score.* In evaluating a child's intelligence, it is wiser to think of intelligence as consisting of a number of domains. Keep in mind the different types of intelligence described by Sternberg and Gardner. Remember that, by considering the different domains of intelligence, you can find that every child has at least one or more strengths.

Extremes of Intelligence

Intelligence tests have been used to discover indications of mental retardation or intellectual giftedness, the extremes of intelligence. At times, intelligence tests have been misused for this purpose. Keeping in mind the theme that an intelligence test should not be used as the sole indicator of mental retardation or giftedness, we will explore the nature of these intellectual extremes.

Mental Retardation   **Mental retardation** is a condition of limited mental ability in which an individual has a low IQ, usually below 70 on a traditional intelligence test, and has difficulty adapting to everyday life. About 5 million Americans fit this definition of mental retardation.

There are several classifications of mental retardation. About 89 percent of the mentally retarded fall into the mild category, with IQs of 55 to 70; most of them are able to live independently as adults and work at a variety of jobs. About 6 percent are classified as moderately retarded, with IQs of 40 to 54; these people can attain a second-grade level of skills and may be able to support themselves as adults through some types of labor. About 3.5 percent of the mentally retarded are in the severe category, with IQs of 25 to 39; these individuals learn to talk and accomplish very simple tasks but require extensive supervision. Less than 1 percent have IQs below 25; they fall into the profoundly mentally retarded classification and need constant supervision.

Mental retardation can have an organic cause, or it can be social and cultural in origin:

- **Organic retardation** is mental retardation that is caused by a genetic disorder or by brain damage; the word *organic* refers to the tissues or organs of the body and indicate physical damage. Most people who suffer from organic retardation have IQs that range between 0 and 50. However, children with Down syndrome have an average IQ of approximately 50. As discussed in Chapter 2, "Biological Beginnings," Down syndrome is caused by an extra copy of chromosome 21.

- **Cultural-familial retardation** is a mental deficit in which no evidence of organic brain damage can be found; individuals' IQs generally range from 50 to 70. Psychologists suspect that such mental deficits result from the normal variation that distributes people along the range of intelligence scores combined with growing up in a below-average intellectual environment.

Giftedness   There have always been people whose abilities and accomplishments outshine others'—the whiz kid in class, the star athlete, the natural musician. People who are **gifted** have above-average intelligence (an IQ of 130 or higher) and/or superior talent for something. When it comes to programs for the gifted, most school systems select children who have intellectual superiority and academic aptitude, whereas children who are talented in the visual and performing arts (arts, drama,

mental retardation A condition of limited mental ability in which an individual has a low IQ, usually below 70 on a traditional test of intelligence, and has difficulty adapting to everyday life.

organic retardation Mental retardation that involves some physical damage and is caused by a genetic disorder or brain damage.

cultural-familial retardation Retardation that is characterized by no evidence of organic brain damage, but the individual's IQ generally is between 50 and 70.

gifted Having above-average intelligence (an IQ of 130 or higher) and/or superior talent for something.

dance), athletics, or other special aptitudes tend to be overlooked (Clark, 2008; Karnes & Stephens, 2008).

Characteristics   What are the characteristics of children who are gifted? Despite speculation that giftedness is linked with having a mental disorder, no relation between giftedness and mental disorder has been found. Similarly, the idea that gifted children are maladjusted is a myth, as Lewis Terman (1925) found when he conducted an extensive study of 1,500 children whose Stanford-Binet IQs averaged 150. The children in Terman's study were socially well adjusted, and many went on to become successful doctors, lawyers, professors, and scientists. Studies support the conclusion that gifted people tend to be more mature than others, have fewer emotional problems than others, and grow up in a positive family climate (Davidson, 2000).

Ellen Winner (1996) described three criteria that characterize gifted children, whether in art, music, or academic domains:

1. *Precocity.* Gifted children are precocious. They begin to master an area earlier than their peers. Learning in their domain is more effortless for them than for ordinary children. In most instances, these gifted children are precocious because they have an inborn high ability in a particular domain or domains.

2. *Marching to their own drummer.* Gifted children learn in a qualitatively different way than ordinary children. One way that they march to a different drummer is that they need minimal help, or scaffolding, from adults to learn. In many instances, they resist any kind of explicit instruction. They often make discoveries on their own and solve problems in unique ways.

3. *A passion to master.* Gifted children are driven to understand the domain in which they have high ability. They display an intense, obsessive interest and an ability to focus. They motivate themselves, says Winner, and do not need to be "pushed" by their parents.

To read about one individual who is making a difference in programs for children who are gifted, see the *Careers in Children's Development* profile.

Careers in Children's Development

Sterling Jones, Supervisor of Gifted and Talented Education

Sterling Jones is program supervisor for gifted and talented children in the Detroit Public School System. Jones has been working for more than three decades with children who are gifted. He believes that students' mastery of skills mainly depends on the amount of time devoted to instruction and the length of time allowed for learning. Thus, he believes that many basic strategies for challenging children who are gifted to develop their skills can be applied to a wider range of students than once believed. He has rewritten several pamphlets for use by teachers and parents, including *How to Help Your Child Succeed* and *Gifted and Talented Education for Everyone*.

Jones has undergraduate and graduate degrees from Wayne State University and taught English for a number of years before becoming involved in the program for gifted children. He also has written materials on African Americans, such as *Voices from the Black Experience*, that are used in the Detroit schools.

Sterling Jones with some of the children in the gifted program in the Detroit Public School System.

Nature–Nurture Issue   Is giftedness a product of heredity or environment? Likely both (Sternberg, 2009f). Individuals who are gifted recall that they had signs of high ability in a particular area at a very young age, prior to or at the beginning of formal training (Howe & others, 1995). This suggests the importance of innate ability in giftedness. However, researchers have also found that individuals with world-class status in the arts, mathematics, science, and sports all report strong family support and years of training and practice (Bloom, 1985). Deliberate practice is an important characteristic of individuals who become experts in a particular domain.

Developmental Changes and Domain-Specific Giftedness   Can we predict from infancy who will be gifted as children, adolescents, and adults? John Colombo and his colleagues (2004, 2009) have found that measures of infant attention and habituation are not good predictors of high cognitive ability later in development. However, they have discovered a link between assessment with the Home Observation for Measure of the Environment at 18 months of age and high cognitive ability in the preschool years. The best predictor at 18 months of high cognitive ability in the preschool years was the provision of materials and a variety of experiences in the home. These findings illustrate the importance of the cognitive environment provided by parents in the development of children's giftedness.

Individuals who are highly gifted are typically not gifted in many domains, and research on giftedness is increasingly focused on domain-specific developmental trajectories (Liben, 2009; Matthews, 2009; Matthews, Subotnik, & Horowitz, 2009; Winner, 2009). During the childhood years, the domain(s) in which individuals are gifted usually emerges. Thus, at some point in the childhood years, the child who is to become a gifted artist or the child who is to become a gifted mathematician begins to show expertise in that domain. Regarding domain-specific giftedness, software genius Bill Gates (1998), the founder of Microsoft and one of the world's richest persons, commented that sometimes you have to be careful when you are good at something and resist the urge to think that you will be good at everything. Gates says that because he has been so successful at software development, people expect him to be brilliant about other domains about which he is far from being a genius.

A young Bill Gates, founder of Microsoft and now one of the world's richest persons. Like many highly gifted students, Gates was not especially fond of school. He hacked a computer security system when he was 13, and as a high school student, he was allowed to take some college math classes. He dropped out of Harvard University and began developing a plan for what was to become Microsoft Corporation. *What are some ways that schools can enrich the education of such highly talented students as Gates to make it a more challenging, interesting, and meaningful experience?*

Identifying an individual's domain-specific talent and providing the person individually appropriate and optional educational opportunities should be accomplished at the very latest by adolescence (Keating, 2009). During adolescence, individuals who are talented become less reliant on parental support and increasingly pursue their own interests.

Some children who are gifted become gifted adults, but many gifted children do not become gifted and highly creative adults. In Terman's research on children with superior IQs, the children typically became experts in a well-established domain, such as medicine, law, or business. However, they did not become major creators (Winner, 2000). That is, they did not create a new domain or revolutionize an old domain.

One reason that some gifted children do not become gifted adults is that they often have been pushed too hard by overzealous parents and teachers. As a result, they lose their intrinsic (internal) motivation (Winner, 2006). Another reason that gifted children may not become gifted adults is because the criteria for giftedness change—as an adult, an individual has to actually do something special to be labeled gifted.

Education   An increasing number of experts argue that the education of children who are gifted in the United States requires a significant overhaul (Horowitz, 2009; Webb & others, 2007). Here, too, some educators conclude that the inadequate education of children who are gifted has been compounded by the federal government's No Child Left Behind policy that seeks to raise the achievement level of students who are not doing well in school at the expense of enriching the education of children who are gifted (Clark, 2008; Cloud, 2007).

Ellen Winner (1996, 2006) argues that too often children who are gifted are socially isolated and underchallenged in the classroom. It is not unusual for them to be ostracized and labeled "nerds" or "geeks." A child who is truly gifted often is the only such child in the room who does not have the opportunity to learn with students of like ability. Many eminent adults report that school was a negative experience for them, that they were bored and sometimes knew more than their teachers (Bloom, 1985). Winner believes that American education will benefit when standards are raised for all children. When some children are still underchallenged, she recommends that they be allowed to attend advanced classes in their domain of exceptional ability—for example, that some especially precocious middle school students take college classes in their area of expertise. Bill Gates, founder of Microsoft, took college math classes and hacked a computer security system at 13; Yo-Yo Ma, famous cellist, graduated from high school at 15 and attended Juilliard School of Music in New York City.

How Would You...?
As an educator, how would you structure educational programs for children who are gifted that would challenge and expand their unique cognitive abilities?

Review and Reflect: Learning Goal 3

 3 **Characterize children's intelligence**

REVIEW

- What is intelligence? How can the Binet tests and the Wechsler scales be characterized?
- What are some different views of multiple intelligences? How can the multiple-intelligences approach be evaluated?
- What is involved in the neuroscience of intelligence?
- What are some issues in interpreting differences in IQ scores? Explain them.
- What is the nature of children's mental retardation? How can children's giftedness be described?

REFLECT

- A CD-ROM, *Children's IQ and Achievement Test,* now lets parents test their child's IQ. What problems might arise when parents give their own children an IQ test?

---

4 WHAT CHANGES IN LANGUAGE DEVELOPMENT OCCUR IN MIDDLE AND LATE CHILDHOOD?

| Vocabulary, Grammar, and Metalinguistic Awareness | Reading | Bilingualism and Second-Language Learning |

Knowledge of vocabulary words is a part of virtually all intelligence tests, and this as well as other aspects of language development are important aspects of children's intelligence. As they enter school, children gain new skills that make it possible for them to learn to read and write—these include increasingly using language to talk about things that are not physically present, learning what a word is, and learning how to recognize and talk about sounds (Berko Gleason, 2003). They have to learn the *alphabetic principle,* that the letters of the alphabet represent sounds of the language. As children develop during middle and late childhood, changes in their vocabulary and grammar also take place.

Vocabulary, Grammar, and Metalinguistic Awareness

During middle and late childhood, changes occur in the way children organize their mental vocabulary. When asked to say the first word that comes to mind when they hear a word, young children typically provide a word that often follows the word in a sentence. For example, when asked to respond to "dog" the young child may say "barks," or to the word "eat" say "lunch." At about 7 years of age, children begin to respond with a word that is the same part of speech as the stimulus word. For example, children may now respond to the word "dog" with "cat" or "horse." To "eat," they now might say "drink." These responses are evidence that children now have begun to categorize their vocabulary by parts of speech (Berko Gleason, 2003).

The process of categorizing becomes easier as children increase their vocabulary. Children's vocabulary grows from an average of about 14,000 words at 6 years of age to an average of about 40,000 words by 11 years of age.

Children make similar advances in grammar (Chang, Dell, & Bock, 2006; Lust, 2007). During the elementary school years, children's improvement in logical reasoning and analytical skills helps them understand such constructions as the appropriate use of comparatives (*shorter, deeper*) and subjunctives ("If you were president . . ."). During the elementary school years, children become increasingly able to understand and use complex grammar, such as the following sentence: *The boy who kissed his mother wore a hat.* They also learn to use language in a more connected way, producing connected discourse. They become able to relate sentences to one another to produce descriptions, definitions, and narratives that make sense. Children must be able to do these things orally before they can be expected to deal with them in written assignments.

These advances in vocabulary and grammar during the elementary school years are accompanied by the development of **metalinguistic awareness,** which is knowledge about language, such as knowing what a preposition is or the ability to discuss the sounds of a language. Metalinguistic awareness allows children "to think about their language, understand what words are, and even define them" (Berko Gleason, 2005, p. 4). It improves considerably during the elementary school years (Pan & Uccelli, 2009). Defining words becomes a regular part of classroom discourse, and children increase their knowledge of syntax as they study and talk about the components of sentences such as subjects and verbs (Meltzi & Ely, 2009).

Children also make progress in understanding how to use language in culturally appropriate ways—*pragmatics.* By the time they enter adolescence, most children know the rules for the use of language in everyday contexts—that is, what is appropriate to say and what is inappropriate to say.

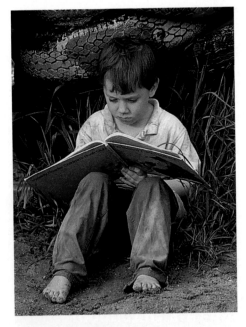

What are the main approaches to teaching children how to read?

metalinguistic awareness Refers to knowledge about language, such as knowing what a preposition is or the ability to discuss the sounds of a language.

Reading

Before learning to read, children learn to use language to talk about things that are not present; they learn what a word is; and they learn how to recognize sounds and talk about them (Berko Gleason, 2003). If they develop a large vocabulary, their path to reading is eased. Children who begin elementary school with a small vocabulary are at risk when it comes to learning to read (Berko Gleason, 2003).

Vocabulary development plays an important role in reading comprehension (Berninger, 2006). For example, one study revealed that a good vocabulary was linked with reading comprehension in second-grade students (Berninger & Abbott, 2005). Having a good vocabulary helps readers access word meaning effortlessly.

How should children be taught to read? Currently, debate focuses on the whole-language approach versus the phonics approach (Bear & others, 2010; Reutzel & Cooter, 2008).

The **whole-language approach** stresses that reading instruction should parallel children's natural language learning. In some whole-language classes beginning readers are taught to recognize whole words or even entire sentences, and to use the context of what they are reading to guess at the meaning of words. Reading materials that support the whole-language approach are whole and meaningful—that is, children are given material in its complete form, such as stories and poems, so that they learn to understand language's communicative function. Reading is connected with listening and writing skills. Although there are variations in whole-language programs, most share the premise that reading should be integrated with other skills and subjects, such as science and social studies, and that it should focus on real-world material. Thus, a class might read newspapers, magazines, or books, and then write about and discuss them.

In contrast, the **phonics approach** emphasizes that reading instruction should teach basic rules for translating written symbols into sounds. Early phonics-centered reading instruction should involve simplified materials. Only after children have learned correspondence rules that relate spoken phonemes to the alphabet letters that are used to represent them should they be given complex reading materials, such as books and poems.

Which approach is better? Children can benefit from both approaches, but instruction in phonics needs to be emphasized, especially in kindergarten and the first grade (Combs, 2010; Fox, 2010; Mayer, 2008; Tompkins, 2010). A recent study revealed that in a school in which students showed high achievement in reading both phonics and whole language were emphasized (Pressley, Mohan, Raphael, & others, 2007). In this study, intensive instruction in phonics improved the reading achievement of students with weak reading skills, whereas more holistic instruction was linked with higher achievement for students with stronger reading skills. An increasing number of experts in the field of reading now conclude that direct instruction in phonological training is a key aspect of learning to read (Meltzi & Ely, 2009).

Rich Mayer (2008) recently described three cognitive processes involved in being able to read a printed word: (1) *being aware of sound units in words*, which consists of recognizing phonemes; (2) *decoding words*, which involves converting printed words into sounds; and (3) *accessing word meaning*, which consists of finding a mental representation of a word's meaning.

This teacher is helping a student sound out words. Researchers have found that phonics instruction is a key aspect of teaching students to read, especially beginning readers and students with weak reading skills.

Bilingualism and Second-Language Learning

Are there sensitive periods in learning a second language? That is, if individuals want to learn a second language, how important is the age at which they begin to learn it? For many years, it was claimed that if individuals did not learn a second language before puberty, they would never reach native-language learners' proficiency in the second language (Johnson & Newport, 1991). However, recent research indicates a more complex conclusion: Sensitive periods likely vary across different language systems (Thomas & Johnson, 2008). Thus, for late language learners, such as adolescents and adults, new vocabulary is easier to learn than new sounds or new grammar (Neville, 2006; Werker & Tees, 2005). For example, children's ability to pronounce words with a nativelike accent in a second language typically decreases with age, with an especially sharp drop occurring after the age of about 10 to 12. Also, adults tend to learn a second language faster than children, but their final level of second-language attainment is not as high as children's. And the way children and adults learn a second language differs somewhat. Compared with adults,

whole-language approach An approach to reading instruction based on the idea that instruction should parallel children's natural language learning. Reading materials should be whole and meaningful.

phonics approach The idea that reading instruction should teach basic rules for translating written symbols into sounds.

children are less sensitive to feedback, less likely to use explicit strategies, and are more likely to learn a second language from a large amount of input (Thomas & Johnson, 2008).

Some aspects of children's ability to learn a second language are transferred more easily to the second language than others (Pena & Bedore, 2009). A recent research review indicated that in learning to read, phonological awareness is rooted in general cognitive processes and thus transfers easily across languages; however, decoding is more language-specific and needs to be relearned with each language (Bialystok, 2007).

Students in the United States are far behind their counterparts in many developed countries in learning a second language. For example, in Russia, schools have 10 grades, called *forms*, which roughly correspond to the 12 grades in American schools. Russian children begin school at age 7 and begin learning English in the third form. Because of this emphasis on teaching English, most Russian citizens under the age of 40 today are able to speak at least some English. The United States is the only technologically advanced Western nation that does not have a national foreign language requirement at the high school level, even for students in rigorous academic programs.

American students who do not learn a second language may be missing more than the chance to acquire a skill (Combs, 2010; Tompkins, 2010). *Bilingualism*—the ability to speak two languages—has a positive effect on children's cognitive development (Gibbons & Ng, 2004). Children who are fluent in two languages perform better than their single-language counterparts on tests of control of attention, concept formation, analytical reasoning, cognitive flexibility, and cognitive complexity (Bialystok, 1999, 2001). They also are more conscious of the structure of spoken and written language and better at noticing errors of grammar and meaning, skills that benefit their reading ability (Bialystok, 1993, 1997).

In the United States, many immigrant children go from being monolingual in their home language to being bilingual in that language and in English, only to end up monolingual speakers of English. This *subtractive bilingualism* can have negative effects on children, who often become ashamed of their home language.

A current controversy related to bilingualism involves bilingual education. To read about this controversy, see the *Diversity in Children's Development* interlude.

Diversity in Children's Development

BILINGUAL EDUCATION

A current controversy related to bilingualism involves the millions of U.S. children who come from homes in which English is not the primary language (Diaz-Rico, 2008; Jabr, 2010). What is the best way to teach these children?

For the last two decades, the preferred strategy has been *bilingual education*, which teaches academic subjects to immigrant children in their native language while slowly teaching English (Herrera, Perez, & Escamilla, 2010). Advocates of bilingual education programs argue that if children who do not know English are taught only in English, they will fall behind in academic subjects. How, they ask, can 7-year-olds learn arithmetic or history taught only in English when they do not speak the language?

Some critics of bilingual programs argue that too often it is thought that immigrant children need only one year of bilingual education. However, in general it takes immigrant children approximately three to five years to develop speaking proficiency and seven years to develop reading proficiency in English (Hakuta, Butler, & Witt,

2001). Also, immigrant children vary in their ability to learn English (Diaz-Rico, 2008; Echevarria, Voght, & Short, 2010). Children who come from lower socioeconomic backgrounds have more difficulty than those from higher socioeconomic backgrounds (Hakuta, 2001). Thus, especially for immigrant children from low socioeconomic backgrounds, more years of bilingual education may be needed than they currently are receiving.

Critics who oppose bilingual education argue that as a result of these programs, the children of immigrants are not learning English, which puts them at a permanent disadvantage in U.S. society. California, Arizona, and Massachusetts have significantly reduced the number of bilingual education programs. Some states continue to endorse bilingual education.

What have researchers found regarding outcomes of bilingual education programs? Drawing conclusions about the effectiveness of bilingual education programs is difficult because of variations across programs in the number of years they are in effect, type of instruction, qualities of schooling other than bilingual education, teachers, children, and other factors. Further, no effectively conducted experiments that compare bilingual education with English-only education in the United States have been conducted

A first- and second-grade bilingual English-Cantonese teacher instructing students in Chinese in Oakland, California. *What is the nature of bilingual education?*

(Snow & Yang, 2006). Some experts have concluded that the quality of instruction is more important in determining outcomes than the language in which it is delivered (Lesaux & Siegel, 2003).

Research does support bilingual education in that (1) children have difficulty learning a subject when it is taught in a language they do not understand; and (2) when both languages are integrated in the classroom, children learn the second language more readily and participate more actively (Hakuta, 2000, 2001, 2005). However, many of the research results report only modest rather than strong support for bilingual education, and some supporters of bilingual education now acknowledge that English-only instruction can produce positive outcomes for English-language learners (Lesaux & Siegel, 2003).

Review and Reflect: Learning Goal 4

 4 **Summarize language development in middle and late childhood**

REVIEW

- What are some changes in vocabulary, grammar, and metalinguistic awareness in the middle and late childhood years?
- What controversy characterizes how to teach children to read?
- What is bilingual education? What issues are involved in bilingual education?

REFLECT

- What are some of the key considerations in using a balanced approach to teaching reading?

5 WHAT CHARACTERIZES CHILDREN'S ACHIEVEMENT?

Extrinsic and Intrinsic Motivation	Mastery Motivation and Mindset	Self-Efficacy	Goal Setting, Planning, and Self-Regulation	Social Relationships and Contexts

We are a species motivated to do well at what we attempt, to gain mastery over the world in which we live, to explore unknown environments with enthusiasm and curiosity, and to achieve the heights of success. In this section, we explore some of the many different ways children effectively achieve their potential during middle and late childhood.

Extrinsic and Intrinsic Motivation

Extrinsic motivation involves external incentives such as rewards and punishments. The humanistic and cognitive approaches stress the importance of intrinsic motivation in achievement. **Intrinsic motivation** is based on internal factors such as self-determination, curiosity, challenge, and effort. Some individuals study hard because they want to make good grades or avoid parental disapproval (extrinsic motivation). Others study hard because they are internally motivated to achieve high standards in their work (intrinsic motivation).

One view of intrinsic motivation emphasizes self-determination (Ryan & Deci, 2001). In this view, children want to believe that they are doing something because of their own will, not because of external success or rewards.

An overwhelming conclusion of motivation research is that teachers should encourage students to become intrinsically motivated. Similarly, teachers should create learning environments that promote students' cognitive engagement and self-responsibility for learning (Meece & Eccles, 2010; Patell, Cooper, & Robinson, 2008). That said, the real world includes both intrinsic and extrinsic motivation, and too often intrinsic and extrinsic motivation have been pitted against each other as polar opposites. In many aspects of students' lives, both intrinsic and extrinsic motivation are at work (Cameron & Pierce, 2008). Further, both intrinsic and extrinsic motivation can operate simultaneously. Thus, a student may work hard in a course because she enjoys the content and likes learning about it (intrinsic) and to earn a good grade (extrinsic) (Schunk, 2008). Keep in mind, though, that many psychologists recommend that extrinsic motivation by itself is not a good strategy.

These students were given an opportunity to write and perform their own play. These kinds of self-determining opportunities can enhance students' motivation to achieve.

extrinsic motivation Involves external incentives such as rewards and punishments.

intrinsic motivation Involves internal factors such as self-determination, curiosity, challenge, and effort.

Calvin and Hobbes   by Bill Watterson

WHO WOULD LIKE TO SUMMARIZE WHAT WE JUST READ? CALVIN, HOW ABOUT YOU?

SORRY! I'M HERE AGAINST MY WILL. I REFUSE TO COOPERATE.

THEY CAN TRANSPORT MY *BODY* TO SCHOOL, BUT THEY CAN'T CHAIN MY *SPIRIT!* MY SPIRIT ROAMS FREE! WALLS CAN'T CONFINE IT! LAWS CAN'T RESTRAIN IT! AUTHORITY HAS NO POWER OVER IT!

CALVIN, IF YOU'D PUT HALF THE ENERGY OF YOUR PROTESTS INTO YOUR SCHOOLWORK...

YOU CAN TRY TO LEAVE A MESSAGE, BUT MY SPIRIT SCREENS ITS CALLS.

Mastery Motivation and Mindset

Becoming cognitively engaged and self-motivated to improve are reflected in children with a mastery motivation. These children also have a growth mindset that they can produce positive outcomes if they put forth the effort.

Mastery Motivation   Developmental psychologists Valanne Henderson and Carol Dweck (1990) have found that children often show two distinct responses to difficult or challenging circumstances. Individuals who display **mastery motivation** are task-oriented; instead of focusing on their ability, they concentrate on learning strategies and the process of achievement rather than the outcome. Those with a **helpless orientation** seem trapped by the experience of difficulty, and they attribute their difficulty to lack of ability. They frequently say such things as "I'm not very good at this," even though they might earlier have demonstrated their ability through many successes. And, once they view their behavior as failure, they often feel anxious, and their performance worsens even further.

In contrast, mastery-oriented children often instruct themselves to pay attention, to think carefully, and to remember strategies that have worked for them in previous situations. They frequently report feeling challenged and excited by difficult tasks, rather than being threatened by them (Anderman & Mueller, 2010). A recent study revealed that the mastery goals in mathematics of seventh- to eleventh-grade students were linked to how much effort they put forth (Chouinard, Karsenti, & Roy, 2007).

Another issue in motivation involves whether to adopt a mastery or a performance orientation. Children with a **performance orientation** are focused on achievement outcomes, believing that winning is what matters most, and happiness results from winning. Does this mean that mastery-oriented individuals do not like to win and that performance-oriented individuals are not motivated to experience the self-efficacy that comes from being able to take credit for one's accomplishments? No. A matter of emphasis or degree is involved, though. For mastery-oriented individuals, winning isn't everything; for performance-oriented individuals, skill development and self-efficacy take a backseat to winning. One recent study of fifth- and seventh-grade students found that girls were more likely than boys to have mastery rather than performance goals in their approach to math achievement (Kenny-Benson & others, 2006).

A final point needs to be made about mastery and performance goals: They are not always mutually exclusive. Students can be both mastery- and performance-oriented, and researchers have found that mastery goals combined with performance goals often benefit students' success (Anderman & Mueller, 2010; Schunk, Pintrich, & Meece, 2008).

Mindset   Carol Dweck's (2006) most recent analysis of motivation for achievement stresses the importance of children developing a **mindset,** which she defines as the cognitive view individuals develop for themselves. She concludes that individuals have one of two mindsets: (1) a *fixed mindset,* in which they believe that their qualities are carved in stone and cannot change; or (2) a *growth mindset,* in which they believe their qualities can change and improve through their effort. A fixed mindset is similar to a helpless orientation, a growth mindset in much like having mastery motivation.

In her book *Mindset,* Dweck (2006) argued that individuals' mindsets influence whether they will be optimistic or pessimistic, shape their goals and how hard they will strive to reach those goals, and affect many aspects of their lives, including achievement and success in school and sports. Dweck says that mindsets begin to be shaped in childhood as children interact with parents, teachers, and coaches, who themselves have either a fixed mindset or a growth mindset. Recall from the

> ... *K*eep the growth mindset in your thoughts. Then, when you bump up against obstacles, you can turn to it ... showing you a path into the future.
>
> —CAROL DWECK
> *Contemporary Psychologist, Stanford University*

mastery motivation An orientation in which one is task-oriented; instead of focusing on one's ability, the person is concerned with learning strategies and the achievement process.

helpless orientation An orientation in which one seems trapped by the experience of difficulty and attributes one's difficulty to a lack of ability.

performance orientation An orientation in which one focuses on achievement outcomes; winning is what matters most, and happiness is thought to result from winning.

mindset The cognitive view, either fixed or growth, that individuals develop for themselves.

chapter opening how successful Marva Collins was in guiding her students to develop more positive mindsets and consequently improve their achievement.

Self-Efficacy

They can because they think they can.

—VIRGIL
Roman Poet, 1st Century B.C.

Like having a growth mindset, **self-efficacy,** the belief that one can master a situation and produce favorable outcomes, is an important cognitive view for children to develop (Walsh, 2008). Albert Bandura (1997, 2004, 2007, 2008, 2010), whose social cognitive theory we discussed in Chapter 1, "Introduction," emphasizes that self-efficacy is a critical factor in whether or not students achieve. Self-efficacy has much in common with mastery motivation and intrinsic motivation. Self-efficacy is the belief that "I can"; helplessness is the belief that "I cannot" (Stipek, 2002). Students with high self-efficacy endorse such statements as "I know that I will be able to learn the material in this class" and "I expect to be able to do well at this activity."

Dale Schunk (2008) has applied the concept of self-efficacy to many aspects of students' achievement. In his view, self-efficacy influences a student's choice of activities. Students with low self-efficacy for learning may avoid many learning tasks, especially those that are challenging. By contrast, high-self-efficacy counterparts eagerly work at learning tasks. High-self-efficacy students are more likely to expend effort and persist longer at a learning task than low-self-efficacy students.

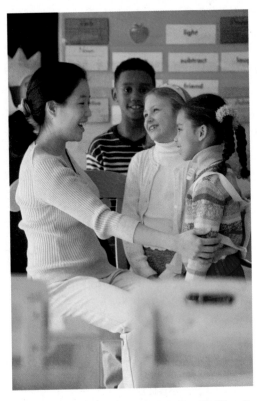

What characterizes students with high self-efficacy?

How Would You...?
As an educator, how would you encourage enhanced self-efficacy in a student who says, "I can't do this work!"?

Goal Setting, Planning, and Self-Regulation

Goal setting, planning, and self-monitoring are important aspects of achievement (Anderman & Mueller, 2010; Meece & Eccles, 2010). Researchers have found that self-efficacy and achievement improve when individuals set goals that are specific, proximal, and challenging (Bandura, 2001). A nonspecific, fuzzy goal is "I want to be successful." A more concrete, specific goal is "I want to do well on my spelling test this week."

Individuals can set both long-term (distal) and short-term (proximal) goals. It is okay for individuals to set some long-term goals, such as "I want to graduate from high school" or "I want to go to college," but they also need to create short-term goals, which are steps along the way. "Getting an A on the next math test" is an example of a short-term, proximal goal. So is "Doing all of my homework by 4 p.m. Sunday." David McNally (1990), author of *Even Eagles Need a Push,* advises that when individuals set goals and plan, they should be reminded to live their lives one day at a time. Have them make their commitments in bite-size chunks. A house is built one brick at a time, a cathedral one stone at a time. The artist paints one stroke at a time. The student should also work in small increments.

Another good strategy is for individuals to set challenging goals. A challenging goal is a commitment to self-improvement. Strong interest and involvement in activities are sparked by challenges. Goals that are easy to reach generate little interest or effort. However, goals should be optimally matched to the individual's skill level. If goals are unrealistically high, the result will be repeated failures that lower the individual's self-efficacy.

It is not enough just to get individuals to set goals. It also is important to encourage them to plan how they will reach their goals. Being a good planner means managing time effectively, setting priorities, and being organized. Younger children will likely need help from parents or teachers with goal setting, planning, and organizational skills.

Individuals not only should plan their next week's activities but also should monitor how well they are sticking to their plan. Once engaged in a task, they need to monitor their progress, judge how well they are doing on the task, and evaluate the outcomes to regulate what they do in the future (Schunk, 2008).

self-efficacy The belief that one can master a situation and produce favorable outcomes.

Social Relationships and Contexts

Children's relationships with parents, peers, friends, teachers, mentors, and others can profoundly affect their achievement. So can the social contexts of ethnicity and culture.

Parents Parents' child-rearing practices are linked to children's achievement (Eccles, 2007). Here are some positive parenting practices that result in improved motivation and achievement: knowing enough about the child to provide the right amount of challenge and the right amount of support; providing a positive emotional climate, which motivates children to internalize their parents' values and goals; and modeling motivated achievement behavior, such as working hard and persisting with effort at challenging tasks.

In addition to general child-rearing practices, parents provide various activities or resources at home that may influence students' interest and motivation to pursue various activities over time (Meece & Eccles, 2010). For example, reading to one's preschool children and providing reading materials in the home are positively related to students' later reading achievement and motivation (Wigfield & Asher, 1984).

Peers Students who are more accepted by their peers and who have good social skills often do better in school and have positive academic achievement motivation (Wentzel & Looney, 2007). In contrast, rejected students, especially those who are highly aggressive, are at risk for a number of achievement problems, including getting low grades and dropping out of school (Dodge, Coie, & Lynam, 2006).

Teachers Teachers play an important role in students' achievement (Patrick, Ryan, & Kaplan, 2007). When researchers have observed classrooms, they have found that effective, engaging teachers provide support for students to make good progress but also encourage them to become self-regulated achievers (Pressley, Mohan, Fingeret, & others, 2007; Pressley, Mohan, Raphael, & others, 2007). The encouragement takes place in a very positive environment, one in which students are constantly being motivated to try hard and to develop self-efficacy.

Teachers' expectations influence students' motivation and performance (Pressley, Mohan, Fingeret, & others, 2007; Pressley, Mohan, Raphael, & others, 2007). In a recent observational study of twelve classrooms, teachers with high expectations spent more time providing a framework for students' learning, asked higher-level questions, and were more effective in managing students' behavior than teachers with average and low expectations (Ruby-Davies, 2007).

In thinking about teachers' expectations, it also is important to examine these expectations in concert with parents' expectations. For example, a recent study revealed that mothers' and teachers' high expectations had a positive effect on urban youths' achievement outcomes, and further that mothers' high achievement expectations for their youth had a buffering effect in the face of low teacher expectations (Benner & Mistry, 2007). Another recent study revealed that teachers' high expectations can help to buffer the negative effect of parent's low expectations for students' achievement (Wood, Kaplan, & McLoyd, 2007).

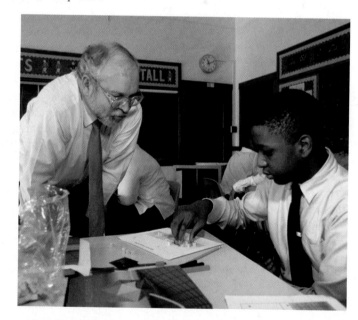

A student and teacher at Langston Hughes Elementary School in Chicago, a school whose teachers have high expectations for students. *How do teachers' expectations influence students' achievement?*

How Would You...?
As an educator, how would you describe the importance of teachers in children's achievement?

Ethnicity The diversity that exists among ethnic minority children is evident in their achievement (Hudley, 2009; Lee & Wong, 2009). In addition to recognizing

UCLA educational psychologist Sandra Graham is shown talking with adolescent boys about motivation. She has conducted a number of studies which reveal that middle-socioeconomic-status African American students—like their White counterparts—have high achievement expectations and attribute success to internal factors such as effort rather than external factors such as luck.

the diversity that exists within every cultural group in terms of their achievement, it also is important to distinguish between difference and deficiency (Banks, 2010). Too often, the achievements of ethnic minority students—especially African Americans, Latinos, and Native Americans—have been interpreted as *deficits* by middle-socioeconomic-status White standards, when they simply are *culturally different and distinct* (Jones, 1994). An especially important factor in the lower achievement of students from low-income families is lack of adequate resources, such an up-to-date computer in the home or even a computer at all, to support students' learning (Schunk, Pintrich, & Meece, 2008).

Sandra Graham (1986, 1990) has conducted a number of studies that reveal not only the stronger influence of socioeconomic status than ethnic differences in achievement but also the importance of studying ethnic minority student motivation in the context of general motivational theory. Her inquiries fall within the framework of attribution theory and focus on the causes that African American students give for their achievement orientation, such as why they succeed or fail. She is struck by how consistently middle-income African American students do not fit the stereotype of being unmotivated. Like their White middle-income counterparts, they have high achievement expectations and understand that failure is usually due to a lack of effort, rather than bad luck.

A special challenge for many ethnic minority students, especially those living in poverty, is dealing with racial prejudice, conflict between the values of their group and those of the majority group, and a lack of high-achieving adults in their cultural group who can serve as positive role models.

It also is important to consider the nature of the schools that primarily serve ethnic minority students (Garcia Coll, Szalacha, & Palacios, 2005). More than one-third of all African American and almost one-third of all Latino students attend schools in the 47 largest city school districts in the United States, compared with only 5 percent of all White and 22 percent of all Asian American students. Many of these ethnic minority students come from low-income families (more than half are eligible for free or reduced-cost lunches). These inner-city schools are less likely than other schools to serve more advantaged populations or to offer high-quality academic support services, advanced courses, and courses that challenge students' active thinking skills. Even students who are motivated to learn and achieve may find it difficult to perform effectively in such contexts.

Cross-Cultural Comparisons   In the past three decades, the poor performance of American children in math and science has become well publicized. In a recent large-scale comparison of math and science achievement in fourth-grade students in 2007, the average U.S. fourth-grade math score was higher than 23 of the 35 countries and lower than 8 countries (all in Asia and Europe) (TIMMS, 2008). Fourth-graders from Hong Kong had the highest math score. The average fourth-grade U.S. math score did improve slightly (11 points) from the same assessment in 1995, but some Asian countries improved their scores considerably more—the Hong Kong score was 50 points higher and the Slovenia score 40 points higher in 2007 than in 1995, for example.

In 2007, the fourth-grade U.S. science score was higher than those in 25 countries and lower than those in 4 countries (all in Asia). However, the average U.S. fourth-grade science score decreased 3 points from 1995 to 2007, while the science scores for some countries increased dramatically—63 points in Singapore, 56 points in Latvia, and 55 points in Iran, for example. In the *Research in Children's Development* interlude, you can read about Harold Stevenson's efforts to find out why American students fare so poorly in mathematics.

Research in Children's Development

CHILDREN'S MATH ACHIEVEMENT IN THE UNITED STATES, CHINA, TAIWAN, AND JAPAN

Harold Stevenson's (1995, 2000; Stevenson, Hofer, & Randel, 1999; Stevenson & others, 1990) research explores reasons for the poor performance of American students. Stevenson and his colleagues have completed five cross-cultural comparisons of students in the United States, China, Taiwan, and Japan. In these studies, Asian students consistently outperform American students. And, the longer the students are in school, the wider the gap becomes between Asian and American students—the lowest difference is in the first grade, the highest in the eleventh grade (the highest grade studied).

To learn more about the reasons for these large cross-cultural differences, Stevenson and his colleagues spent thousands of hours observing in classrooms, as well as interviewing and surveying teachers, students, and parents. They found that the Asian teachers spent more of their time teaching math than did the American teachers. For example, more than one-fourth of total classroom time in the first grade was spent on math instruction in Japan, compared with only one-tenth of the time in the U.S. first-grade classrooms. Also, the Asian students were in school an average of 240 days a year, compared with 178 days in the United States.

In addition to the substantially greater time spent on math instruction in the Asian schools than the American schools, differences were found between the Asian and American parents. The American parents had much lower expectations for their children's education and achievement than did the Asian parents. Also, the American parents were more likely to believe that their children's math achievement was due to innate ability; the Asian parents were more likely to say that their children's math achievement was the consequence of effort and training (see Figure 12.8). The Asian students were more likely to do math homework than were the American students, and the Asian parents were far more likely to help their children with their math homework than were the American parents (Chen & Stevenson, 1989).

FIGURE 12.8 Mothers' Beliefs About the Factors Responsible for Children's Math Achievement in Three Countries In one study, mothers in Japan and Taiwan were more likely to believe that their children's math achievement was due to effort rather than innate ability, whereas U.S. mothers were more likely to believe their children's math achievement was due to innate ability (Stevenson, Lee, & Stigler, 1986). If parents believe that their children's math achievement is due to innate ability and their children are not doing well in math, the implication is that they are less likely to think their children will benefit from putting forth more effort.

Asian grade schools intersperse studying with frequent periods of activities. This approach helps children maintain their attention and likely makes learning more enjoyable. Shown here are Japanese fourth-graders making wearable masks. *What are some differences in the way children in many Asian countries are taught compared with children in the United States?*

Review and Reflect: Learning Goal 5

5 **Explain the development of achievement in children**

REVIEW

- How does extrinsic motivation differ from intrinsic motivation?
- How does mastery motivation differ from helpless and performance orientations? What is mindset, and how does it influence children's achievement?
- What is self-efficacy, and how is it involved in achievement?
- What functions do goal setting, planning, and self-monitoring play in achievement?
- How are social relationships and contexts involved in children's achievement?

REFLECT

- Think about several of your own past schoolmates who showed low motivation in school. Why do you think they behaved that way? What teaching strategies might have helped them?

Reach Your Learning Goals

Cognitive Development in Middle and Late Childhood

1 WHAT IS PIAGET'S THEORY OF COGNITIVE DEVELOPMENT IN MIDDLE AND LATE CHILDHOOD? DISCUSS PIAGET'S STAGE OF CONCRETE OPERATIONAL THOUGHT, AND APPLY PIAGET'S THEORY TO EDUCATION

Concrete Operational Thought

- Concrete operational thought involves operations, conservation, classification, seriation, and transitivity. Thought is not as abstract as it is later in development.

Evaluating Piaget's Concrete Operational Stage

- Critics argue that elements of a stage do not appear at the same time, and that education and culture have more influence on development than Piaget predicted. Neo-Piagetians place more emphasis on how children process information, strategies, speed of information processing, and the division of cognitive problems into more precise steps.

Applications to Education

- Application of Piaget's ideas to education especially involves a constructivist approach that focuses on the teacher as a guide rather than a director and turns the classroom into a setting of exploration and discovery.

2 WHAT IS THE NATURE OF CHILDREN'S INFORMATION PROCESSING? DESCRIBE CHANGES IN INFORMATION PROCESSING IN MIDDLE AND LATE CHILDHOOD

Memory

- Long-term memory increases in middle and late childhood. Knowledge and expertise influence memory. Strategies such as imagery and elaboration can be used by children to improve their memory. Fuzzy trace theory has been proposed to explain developmental changes in memory.

Thinking

- Critical thinking involves thinking reflectively and productively, as well as evaluating the evidence. Mindfulness is an important aspect of critical thinking. A special concern is the lack of emphasis on critical thinking in many schools. Creative thinking is the ability to think in novel and unusual ways and to come up with unique solutions to problems. Guilford distinguished between convergent and divergent thinking. A number of strategies, including brainstorming, can be used to encourage children's creative thinking. Children think like scientists in some ways, but in other ways they don't.

Metacognition

- Metacognition is knowing about knowing, or cognition about cognition. Most metacognitive studies have focused on metamemory. Pressley views the key to education as helping students learn a rich repertoire of strategies.

3 HOW CAN CHILDREN'S INTELLIGENCE BE DESCRIBED? CHARACTERIZE CHILDREN'S INTELLIGENCE

Intelligence and Its Assessment

- Intelligence consists of problem-solving skills and the ability to adapt to and learn from life's everyday experiences. Interest in intelligence often focuses on individual differences and assessment. Widely used intelligence tests today include the Stanford-Binet tests and Wechsler scales. Results on these tests may be reported in terms of an overall IQ or in terms of performance on specific areas of the tests.

Types of Intelligence

- Sternberg proposed that intelligence comes in three main forms: analytical, creative, and practical. Gardner proposes that there are eight types of intelligence: verbal, math, spatial, bodily-kinesthetic, interpersonal skills, intrapersonal skills, musical skills, and naturalist skills. The multiple-intelligence approaches have expanded our conception of intelligence, but critics argue that the research base for these approaches is not well established.

The Neuroscience of Intelligence

- There has been a substantial increase in interest in discovering links between the brain and intelligence that has been stimulated by advances in brain imaging. A moderate correlation has been found between overall brain size and intelligence. Recent research has revealed a link between a distributed neural network in the frontal and parietal lobes and intelligence. Research on a connection between neural processing speed and intelligence has produced inconsistent findings.

Interpreting Differences in IQ Scores

- IQ scores are influenced by both genetics and characteristics of the environment. Studies of heritability indicate that genetics has a strong influence on the variance in IQ scores within a population, but environmental changes can alter the IQ scores of most people considerably. Parenting, home environments, schools, and intervention programs can influence these scores. Intelligence test scores have risen considerably around the world in recent decades—called the Flynn effect—and this rise supports the role of environment in intelligence. Group differences in IQ scores may reflect many influences, including cultural bias. Tests may be biased against certain groups because they are not familiar with a standard form of English, with the content that is being tested, or with the testing situation. Tests are likely to reflect the values and experience of the dominant culture.

Extremes of Intelligence

- Mental retardation involves low IQ and problems in adapting to everyday life. One classification of mental retardation distinguishes organic and cultural-familial retardation. A child who is gifted has above-average intelligence and/or superior talent for something. Terman contributed to our understanding that gifted children are not more maladjusted than nongifted children. Three characteristics of gifted children are precocity, individuality, and a passion to master a domain. Critics argue that gifted children have been miseducated.

4 WHAT CHANGES IN LANGUAGE DEVELOPMENT OCCUR IN MIDDLE AND LATE CHILDHOOD? SUMMARIZE LANGUAGE DEVELOPMENT IN MIDDLE AND LATE CHILDHOOD

Vocabulary, Grammar, and Metalinguistic Awareness

- In middle and late childhood, children become more analytical and logical in their approach to words and grammar. In terms of grammar, children now better understand comparatives and subjunctives. They become increasingly able to use complex grammar and produce narratives that make sense. Improvements in metalinguistic awareness—knowledge about language—are evident during the elementary school years as children increasingly define words, increase their knowledge of syntax, and understand better how to use language in culturally appropriate ways.

Reading

- A current debate in reading focuses on the phonics approach versus the whole-language approach. The phonics approach advocates phonetics instruction and giving children simplified materials. The whole-language approach stresses that reading instruction should parallel children's natural language learning and recommends giving children whole-language materials, such as books and newspapers. An increasing number of experts now conclude that although both approaches can benefit children, direct instruction in phonics is a key aspect of learning to read.

Bilingualism and Second-Language Learning

- Bilingual education aims to teach academic subjects to immigrant children in their native language while gradually adding English instruction. Researchers have found that bilingualism does not interfere with performance in either language. Success in learning a second language is greater in childhood than in adolescence.

5   WHAT CHARACTERIZES CHILDREN'S ACHIEVEMENT? EXPLAIN THE DEVELOPMENT OF ACHIEVEMENT IN CHILDREN

Extrinsic and Intrinsic Motivation

- Extrinsic motivation involves external incentives such as rewards and punishments. Intrinsic motivation is based on internal factors such as self-determination, curiosity, challenge, and effort. Giving children some choice and providing opportunities for personal responsibility increase intrinsic motivation.

Mastery Motivation and Mindset

- Individuals with a mastery motivation focus on the task rather than ability and use solution-oriented strategies. Mastery motivation is preferred over a helpless orientation (in which individuals seem trapped by the experience of difficulty and attribute their difficulty to lack of ability) or a performance orientation (being concerned with achievement outcomes—winning is what matters). Mindset is the cognitive view, either fixed or growth, that individuals develop for themselves. Dweck argues that a key aspect of children's development is to guide them in developing a growth mindset.

Self-Efficacy

- Self-efficacy is the belief that one can master a situation and produce positive outcomes. Bandura stresses that self-efficacy is a critical factor in whether children will achieve.

Goal Setting, Planning, and Self-Regulation

- Setting specific, proximal (short-term), and challenging goals benefits children's self-efficacy and achievement. Being a good planner means managing time effectively, setting priorities, and being organized. Self-monitoring is a key aspect of self-regulation and benefits children's learning.

Social Relationships and Contexts

- Among the social relationships and contexts that are linked to children's achievement are parenting practices, peer relationships, relationships with teachers, ethnicity, and culture. American children are more achievement-oriented than children in many countries but are less achievement-oriented than many children in Asian countries such as China, Taiwan, and Japan.

KEY TERMS

seriation 385
transitivity 385
neo-Piagetians 386
long-term memory 388
elaboration 388
fuzzy trace theory 388
critical thinking 390
mindfulness 390
creative thinking 390
convergent thinking 390

divergent thinking 390
brainstorming 391
metacognition 393
intelligence 395
individual differences 395
mental age (MA) 395
intelligence quotient (IQ) 395
normal distribution 395
triarchic theory of
   intelligence 396

heritability 399
culture-fair tests 401
mental retardation 402
organic
   retardation 402
cultural-familial
   retardation 402
gifted 402
metalinguistic
   awareness 406

whole-language
   approach 407
phonics approach 407
extrinsic motivation 410
intrinsic motivation 410
mastery motivation 411
helpless orientation 411
performance orientation 411
mindset 411
self-efficacy 412

KEY PEOPLE

Jean Piaget 384
Charles Brainerd and Valerie
   Reyna 389
Ellen Langer 390
Jacqueline and Martin
   Brooks 390
J. P. Guilford 390

Teresa Amabile 391
Deanna Kuhn 393
Michael Pressley 394
Alfred Binet 395
Theophile Simon 395
William Stern 395
David Wechsler 395

Robert J. Sternberg 396
Howard Gardner 397
Nathan Brody 397
Lewis Terman 403
Ellen Winner 403
John Colombo 404
Rich Mayer 407

Valanne Henderson and Carol
   Dweck 411
Albert Bandura 412
Dale Schunk 412
Sandra Graham 414
Harold Stevenson 414

MAKING A DIFFERENCE

Supporting Children's Cognitive Development

What are the best strategies for helping elementary school children develop their cognitive skills?

- *Facilitate rather than direct children's learning.* Design situations that let children learn by doing and that actively promote their thinking and discovery. Listen, watch, and question children to help them attain a better understanding.

- *Provide opportunities for children to think critically.* Encourage children to think reflectively, rather than automatically accepting everything as correct. Ask children questions about similarities and differences in things. Ask them questions of clarification, such as "What is the main point?" and "Why?" Ask children to justify their opinion. Ask them "what if" questions.

- *Be a good cognitive role model.* Model thinking and self-reflection for the child to see and hear. When children are around people who think critically and reflectively, they incorporate these cognitive styles into their own thinking repertoire.

- *Encourage collaboration with other children.* Children learn not only from adults but from other children as well. Cross-age teaching, in which older children who are competent thinkers interact with younger children, can be especially helpful. Collaborative problem solving teaches children how to work cooperatively with others.

- *Stimulate children's creative thinking.* Encourage children to take risks in their thinking. Don't overcontrol by telling children precisely what to do; let their originality come through. Don't set up grandiose expectations; it can hurt creativity. Encourage the child to think freely and come up with as many different ways of doing something as possible.

RESOURCES FOR IMPROVING CHILDREN'S LIVES

ERIC Database
www.eric.ed.gov

ERIC provides wide-ranging references to many educational topics, including educational practices, parent-school relations, and community programs.

National Association for Gifted Children (NAGC)
www.nagc.org

The NAGC is an association of academics, educators, and librarians. Its goal is to improve the education of gifted children. It publishes periodic reports on the education of gifted children and the journal *Gifted Children Quarterly*.

The New York Times Parent's Guide to the Best Books for Children
by Eden Lipson (2000, 3rd ed.)
New York: Crown

This revised and updated third edition includes book recommendations for children of all ages. More than 1,700 titles are evaluated.

Mindset
by Carol Dweck (2006)
New York: Random House

An outstanding book that emphasizes how critical it is for parents, teachers, and other adults to guide children in developing a growth rather than a fixed mindset.

E-LEARNING TOOLS

Connect to **www.mhhe.com/santrockc11e** to research the answers and complete these exercises. In addition, you'll find a number of other resources and valuable study tools for Chapter 12, "Cognitive Development in Middle and Late Childhood," on this Web site.

Taking It to the Net

1. Carla is the top student in mathematics. Mario displays exceptional talent in art class. Warren is very social and popular with his peers. What do these three students show us about different types of intelligence? How might traditional theories of intelligence miss the unique talents of these students?

2. Tae is the only Asian American student in his class. His teacher, Mr. Mantenga, does not have much experience working with Asian American students. He is under the impression that Tae is very gifted, particularly in math and in the sciences. Mr. Mantenga tries to challenge Tae with more difficult work. Is Mr. Mantenga helping Tae, or might he be basing his impressions of Tae on stereotypes? What would be helpful for Mr. Mantenga to know about Asian American children?

3. A group of parents have called a special PTA meeting to discuss the math curriculum at their children's elementary school. Apparently, students are using computers and calculators and working in groups on math "projects." The parents are alarmed that their children don't seem to be learning old-fashioned arithmetic. What happened to multiplication tables and long division?

4. Motabi is from the Congo. He is arguing with his developmental psychology classmates about the meaning of intelligence. Motabi insists that different cultures construct their own paradigms of intelligence and that intelligence in the Congo is a very different concept from intelligence in Illinois. Is there any evidence to support Motabi's argument?

Health and Well-Being, Parenting, and Education

Build your decision-making skills by trying your hand at the health and well-being, parenting, and education exercises.

Video Clips

The Online Learning Center includes the following videos for this chapter:

- *Memory Ability at Age 7—1130*
  A boy's memory is tested by presenting him with numbers to recall.

- *Sex Differences and School—928*
  Why are there achievement differences between boys and girls? The research is unclear, according to Dr. Eccles. She states that most likely it is a two-way interaction between biological and cultural factors.

13

*Children are busy
becoming something
they have not quite
grasped yet, something
which keeps changing.*

—ALASTAIR REID
American Poet, 20th Century

LEARNING GOALS

◆ Discuss emotional and personality
development in middle and late
childhood

◆ Describe changes in parenting
and families in middle and late
childhood

◆ Identify changes in peer
relationships in middle and late
childhood

◆ Characterize contemporary
approaches to student learning and
sociocultural diversity in schools

SOCIOEMOTIONAL DEVELOPMENT IN MIDDLE AND LATE CHILDHOOD

CHAPTER OUTLINE

423

Images of Children's Development

Stories from the South Bronx and Pax, a Make-Believe Planet

At P.S. 30 in the South Bronx, Mr. Bedrock teaches fifth grade. One student in his class, Serafina, recently lost her mother to AIDS. When author Jonathan Kozol visited the class, he was told that two other children had taken the role of "allies in the child's struggle for emotional survival" (Kozol, 2005, p. 291).

Textbooks are in short supply for the class, and the social studies text is so out of date it claims that Ronald Reagan is the country's president. But Mr. Bedrock told Kozol that it's a "wonderful" class this year. About their teacher, 56-year-old Mr. Bedrock, one student said, "'He's getting old, . . . but we love him anyway'" (p. 292). Kozol found the students orderly, interested, and engaged.

By late childhood, most children, like these students at P.S. 30, have developed friendships, learned to interact with adults other than their parents, and developed ideas about fairness and other moral concepts.

What are some of the challenges faced by children growing up in the South Bronx?

Can children understand such concepts as discrimination, economic inequality, affirmative action, and comparable worth? Probably not, if you ask them about those terms. But Phyllis Katz (1987) found that children can understand situations that involve those concepts. Katz (1987) asked elementary-school-age children to pretend that they had taken a long ride on a spaceship to a make-believe planet called Pax. Once there, the children find problematic situations. For example, citizens of Pax who had dotted noses couldn't get jobs. Instead the jobs went to the people with striped noses. "What would you do in this situation?" Katz asked the children.

She asked them for their opinions about various situations on this faraway planet. For example, what should a teacher do when two students were tied for a prize or when they had been fighting. The elementary school children often came up with interesting solutions to problems. For example, all but two children believed that teachers should earn as much as janitors—the holdouts said teachers should make less because they stay in one room or because cleaning toilets is more disgusting and therefore deserves higher wages. All but one thought that not giving a job to a qualified applicant who had different physical characteristics (a dotted rather than a striped nose) was unfair. War was mentioned as the biggest problem on Earth, although children were not certain whether it was presently occurring. Overall, the types of rules the children believed a society should abide by were quite sensible—almost all included the need for equitable sharing of resources and work and prohibitions against aggression.

PREVIEW

The years of middle and late childhood bring many changes to children's social and emotional lives. The development of their self-conceptions,

emotions, moral reasoning, and gendered behavior is significant. Transformations in their relationships with parents and peers also occur, and schooling takes on a more academic flavor.

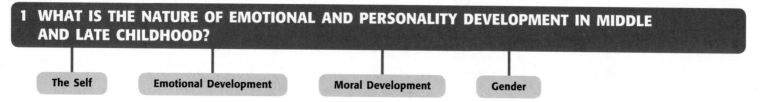

1 WHAT IS THE NATURE OF EMOTIONAL AND PERSONALITY DEVELOPMENT IN MIDDLE AND LATE CHILDHOOD?

| The Self | Emotional Development | Moral Development | Gender |

In this section, we explore how the self continues to develop during middle and late childhood and the emotional changes that take place during these years. We also discuss children's moral development and many aspects of the role that gender plays in their development in middle and late childhood.

The Self

What is the nature of the child's self-understanding, understanding of others, and self-esteem during the elementary school years? What role does self-regulation play in children's achievement?

The Development of Self–Understanding   In middle and late childhood, especially from 8 to 11 years of age, children increasingly describe themselves with psychological characteristics and traits in contrast to the more concrete self-descriptions of younger children. Older children are more likely to describe themselves as "popular, nice, helpful, mean, smart, and dumb" (Harter, 2006, p. 526).

In addition, during the elementary school years, children become more likely to recognize social aspects of the self (Harter, 2006). These include references to social groups in their self-descriptions, such as referring to themselves as Girl Scouts, as Catholics, or as someone who has two close friends (Livesly & Bromley, 1973).

Children's self-understanding in the elementary school years also includes increasing reference to social comparison (Harter, 2006). At this point in development, children are more likely to distinguish themselves from others in comparative rather than in absolute terms. That is, elementary-school-age children are no longer as likely to think about what they do or do not do, but are more likely to think about what they can do in comparison with others.

Consider a series of studies in which Diane Ruble (1983) investigated children's use of social comparison in their self-evaluations. Children were given a difficult task and then offered feedback on their performance, as well as information about the performances of other children their age. The children were then asked for self-evaluations. Children younger than 7 made virtually no reference to the information about other children's performances. However, many children older than 7 included socially comparative information in their self-descriptions.

In sum, in middle and late childhood, self-description increasingly involves psychological and social characteristics, including social comparison.

Understanding Others   In Chapter 10, "Socioemotional Development in Early Childhood," we described the advances and limitations of young children's understanding of others. In middle and late childhood, children show an increase in **perspective taking,** the ability to assume other people's perspectives and understand their thoughts and feelings. In Robert Selman's (1980) view, at about 6 to

*K*now yourself.

—SOCRATES
Greek Philosopher, 5th Century B.C.

How Would You...?
As a psychologist, how would you explain the role of social comparison for the development of a child's sense of self?

perspective taking The ability to assume other people's perspectives and understand their thoughts and feelings

What are some changes in children's understanding of others in middle and late childhood?

8 years of age, children begin to understand that others may have a perspective because some people have more access to information. Then, he says, in the next several years, children become aware that each individual is aware of the other's perspective and that putting one's self in the other's place is a way of judging the other person's intentions, purposes, and actions.

Perspective taking is especially thought to be important in whether children develop prosocial or antisocial attitudes and behavior. In terms of prosocial behavior, taking another's perspective improves children's likelihood of understanding and sympathizing with others when they are distressed or in need.

In middle and late childhood, children also become more skeptical of others' claims. In Chapter 10, "Socioemotional Development in Early Childhood," we indicated that even 4-year-old children show some skepticism of others' claims. In middle and late childhood, children become increasingly skeptical of some sources of information about psychological traits. For example, in one study, 10- to 11-year-olds were more likely to reject other children's self-reports that they were *smart* and *honest* than were 6- to 7-year-olds (Heyman & Legare, 2005). The more psychologically sophisticated 10- to 11-year-olds also showed a better understanding that others' self-reports may involve socially desirable tendencies than did the 6- to 7-year-olds. In a recent cross-cultural comparison of 6- to 11-year-olds from the United States and China, older children showed increased skepticism of others' self-reports concerning value-laden traits, such as *honest*, *smart*, and *nice*, but did not show increased skepticism about less value-laden characteristics such as *outgoing*, *likes salty food*, and *likes the color red* (Heyman, Fu, & Lee, 2007). Older Chinese children were more likely to expect others to show modesty when talking about themselves than were their U.S. counterparts.

Self-Esteem and Self-Concept

High self-esteem and a positive self-concept are important characteristics of children's well-being (Harter, 2006). Investigators sometimes use the terms self-esteem and self-concept interchangeably or do not precisely define them, but there is a meaningful difference between them. **Self-esteem** refers to global evaluations of the self; it is also called self-worth or self-image. For example, a child may perceive that she is not merely a person but a good person. **Self-concept** refers to domain-specific evaluations of the self. Children can make self-evaluations in many domains of their lives—academic, athletic, appearance, and so on. In sum, self-esteem refers to global self-evaluations, self-concept to domain-specific evaluations.

For most children, high self-esteem and a positive self-concept are important aspects of their well-being (Kaplan, 2009). However, for some children, self-esteem reflects perceptions that do not always match reality (Krueger, Vohs, & Baumeister, 2008). A child's self-esteem might reflect a belief about whether he or she is intelligent and attractive, for example, but that belief is not necessarily accurate. Thus, high self-esteem may refer to accurate, justified perceptions of one's worth as a person and one's successes and accomplishments but it can also refer to an arrogant, grandiose, unwarranted sense of superiority over others. In the same manner, low self-esteem may reflect either an accurate perception of one's shortcomings or a distorted, even pathological insecurity and inferiority.

Variations in self-esteem have been linked with many aspects of children's development. However, much of the research is *correlational* rather than *experimental*. Recall from Chapter 1, "Introduction," that correlation does not equal causation. Thus, if a correlational study finds an association between children's low self-esteem and low academic achievement, low academic achievement could cause the low self-esteem as much as low self-esteem causes low academic achievement.

self-esteem The global evaluative dimension of the self. Self-esteem is also referred to as self-worth or self-image.

self-concept Domain-specific evaluations of the self.

In fact, there are only moderate correlations between school performance and self-esteem, and these correlations do not suggest that high self-esteem produces better school performance (Baumeister & others, 2003). Efforts to increase students' self-esteem have not always led to improved school performance (Davies & Brember, 1999).

Children with high self-esteem have greater initiative, but this can produce positive or negative outcomes (Baumeister & others, 2003). High-self-esteem children are prone to both prosocial and antisocial actions. A recent study revealed that over time aggressive children with high self-esteem increasingly valued the rewards that aggression can bring and belittled their victims (Menon & others, 2007).

In addition, a current concern is that too many of today's children grow up receiving praise for mediocre or even poor performance and as a consequence have inflated self-esteem (Graham, 2005; Stipek, 2005). They may have difficulty handling competition and criticism. This theme is vividly captured by the title of a book, *Dumbing Down Our Kids: Why American Children Feel Good About Themselves But Can't Read, Write, or Add* (Sykes, 1995).

What are some good strategies for effectively increasing children's self-esteem? See the *Caring for Children* interlude for some answers to this question.

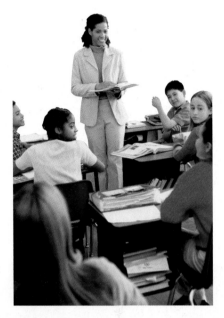

What are some issues involved in understanding children's self-esteem in school?

Caring for Children

How Would You...?
As an educator, how would you work with children to develop a healthy self-concept concerning their academic ability?

INCREASING CHILDREN'S SELF-ESTEEM

Four ways children's self-esteem can be improved include identifying the causes of low self-esteem, providing emotional support and social approval, helping children achieve, and helping children cope (Bednar, Wells, & Peterson, 1995; Harter, 2006):

- *Identify the causes of low self-esteem.* Intervention should target the causes of low self-esteem. Children have the highest self-esteem when they perform competently in domains that are important to them. Therefore, children should be encouraged to identify and value areas of competence. These areas might include academic skills, athletic skills, physical attractiveness, and social acceptance.

- *Provide emotional support and social approval.* Some children with low self-esteem come from conflicted families or conditions in which they experienced abuse or neglect—situations in which support was not available. In some cases, alternative sources of support can be arranged either informally through the encouragement of a teacher, a coach, or another significant adult, or more formally, through programs such as Big Brothers and Big Sisters.

- *Help children achieve.* Achievement also can improve children's self-esteem. For example, the straightforward teaching of real skills to children often results in increased achievement and, thus, in enhanced self-esteem. Children develop higher self-esteem because they know the important tasks that will achieve their goals, and they have performed them or similar behaviors in the past.

- *Help children cope.* Self-esteem is often increased when children face a problem and try to cope with it, rather than avoid it. If coping rather than avoidance prevails, children often face problems realistically, honestly, and nondefensively. This produces favorable self-evaluative thoughts, which lead to the self-generated approval that raises self-esteem.

How can parents help children develop higher self-esteem?

Self-Regulation   One of the most important aspects of the self in middle and late childhood is the increased capacity for self-regulation. This increased capacity is characterized by deliberate efforts to manage one's behavior, emotions, and thoughts that lead to increased social competence and achievement (Thompson, Meyer, & Jochem, 2008).

The increased capacity in self-regulation is linked to developmental advances in the brain's prefrontal cortex, which was discussed in Chapter 9, "Cognitive Development in Early Childhood." Recall our discussion there of the increased focal activation in the prefrontal cortex that is linked to improved cognitive control, which includes self-regulation (Durston & others, 2006).

Industry Versus Inferiority   In Chapter 1, "Introduction," we discussed Erik Erikson's (1968) eight stages of human development. His fourth stage, industry versus inferiority, appears during middle and late childhood. The term *industry* expresses a dominant theme of this period: Children become interested in how

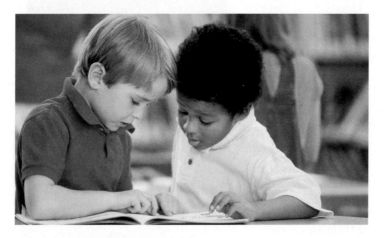

things are made and how they work. When children are encouraged in their efforts to make, build, and work—whether building a model airplane, constructing a tree house, fixing a bicycle, solving an addition problem, or cooking—their sense of industry increases. However, parents who see their children's efforts at making things as "mischief" or "making a mess" encourage children's development of a sense of inferiority.

Children's social worlds beyond their families also contribute to a sense of industry. School becomes especially important in this regard. Consider children who are slightly below average in intelligence. They are too bright to be in special classes but not bright enough to be in gifted classes. Failing frequently in their academic efforts, they develop a sense of inferiority. By contrast, consider children whose sense of industry is disparaged at home. A series of sensitive and committed teachers may revitalize their sense of industry (Elkind, 1970).

What characterizes Erikson's stage of industry versus inferiority?

Emotional Development

In Chapter 10, "Socioemotional Development in Early Childhood," we saw that preschoolers become more adept at talking about their own and others' emotions. They also show a growing awareness of the need to control and manage their emotions to meet social standards. In middle and late childhood, children further develop their understanding and self-regulation of emotion (Thompson, 2009a).

Developmental Changes   Developmental changes in emotions during the middle and late childhood years include the following (Denham, Bassett, & Wyatt, 2007; Kuebli, 1994; Thompson, 2009a):

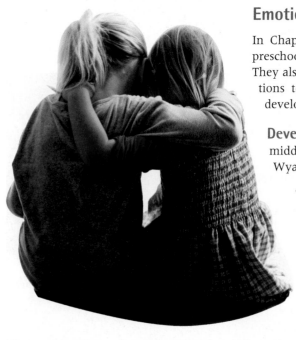

- *Improved emotional understanding.* For example, children in elementary school develop an increased ability to understand such complex emotions as pride and shame. These emotions become less tied to the reactions of other people; they become more self-generated and integrated with a sense of personal responsibility.

  - *Increased understanding that more than one emotion can be experienced in a particular situation.* A third-grader, for example, may realize that achieving something might involve both anxiety and joy.

  - *Increased tendency to be aware of the events leading to emotional reactions.* A fourth-grader may become aware that her sadness today is influenced by her friend's moving to another town last week.

What are some changes in emotion during the middle and late childhood years?

- *Ability to suppress or conceal negative emotional reactions.* When one of his classmates irritates him, a fifth-grader has learned to tone down his anger better than he used to.

- *The use of self-initiated strategies for redirecting feelings.* In the elementary school years, children become more reflective about their emotional lives and increasingly use strategies to control their emotions. They become more effective at cognitively managing their emotions, such as soothing themselves after an upset.

- *A capacity for genuine empathy.* For example, a fourth-grader feels sympathy for a distressed person and experiences vicariously the sadness the distressed person is feeling.

Coping with Stress   An important aspect of children's emotional lives is learning how to cope with stress (Coplan & Arbeau, 2008; Findlay, Coplan, & Bowker, 2009). As children get older, they more accurately appraise a stressful situation and determine how much control they have over it. Older children generate more coping alternatives to stressful conditions and use more cognitive coping strategies (Saarni & others, 2006). They are better than younger children at intentionally shifting their thoughts to something that is less stressful; and at reframing, or changing one's perception of a stressful situation. For example, a younger child may be very disappointed that a teacher did not say hello when the child arrived in the classroom. An older child may reframe the situation and think, "My teacher may have been busy with other things and just forgot to say hello."

By 10 years of age, most children are able to use these cognitive strategies to cope with stress (Saarni, 1999). However, in families that have not been supportive and are characterized by turmoil or trauma, children may be so overwhelmed by stress that they do not use such strategies (Klingman, 2006).

Disasters can especially harm children's development and produce adjustment problems. Among the outcomes for children who experience disasters are acute stress reactions, depression, panic disorder, and post-traumatic stress disorder (Kar, 2009). Proportions of children developing these problems following a disaster depend on such factors as the nature and severity of the disaster, as well as the support available to the children. The terrorist attacks on the World Trade Center in New York City and the Pentagon in Washington, D.C., on September 11, 2001, and Hurricanes Katrina and Rita in August/September 2005 raised special concerns about how to help children cope with such stressful events (Osofsky, 2007). Researchers have offered some recommendations for parents, teachers, and other adults caring for children (Gurwitch & others, 2001, pp. 4–11):

- Reassure children (numerous times, if necessary) of their safety and security.

- Allow children to retell events and be patient in listening to them.

- Encourage children to talk about any disturbing or confusing feelings, reassuring them that such feelings are normal after a stressful event.

- Protect children from reexposure to frightening situations and reminders of the trauma—for example, by limiting discussion of the event in front of the children.

- Help children make sense of what happened, keeping in mind that children may misunderstand what took place. For example, young children "may blame themselves, believe things happened that did not happen, believe that terrorists are in the school, and so on"(p. 10).

- "Gently help children develop a realistic understanding of the event" (p. 10).

Traumatic events may cause individuals to think about the moral aspects of life. Hopelessness and despair may short-circuit moral development when a child is confronted by the violence of war zones and impoverished inner cities (Nader, 2001). Let's further explore children's moral development.

What are some effective strategies to help children cope with traumatic events, such as the terrorist attacks on the United States on 9/11/2001 and Hurricane Katrina in August 2005?

How Would You...?
As a social worker, how would you counsel a child who has been exposed to a traumatic event?

Lawrence Kohlberg, the architect of a provocative cognitive developmental theory of moral development. *What is the nature of his theory?*

Moral Development

Remember from Chapter 10, "Socioemotional Development in Early Childhood," our description of Piaget's view of moral development. Piaget proposed that younger children are characterized by *heteronomous morality* but that, by 10 years of age, they have moved into a higher stage called *autonomous morality*. According to Piaget, older children consider the intentions of the individual, believe that rules are subject to change, and are aware that punishment does not always follow wrongdoing.

A second major perspective on moral development was proposed by Lawrence Kohlberg (1958, 1986). Piaget's cognitive stages of development serve as the underpinnings for Kohlberg's theory, but Kohlberg suggested that there are six stages of moral development. These stages, he argued, are universal. Development from one stage to another, said Kohlberg, is fostered by opportunities to take the perspective of others and to experience conflict between one's current stage of moral thinking and the reasoning of someone at a higher stage.

Kohlberg arrived at his view after 20 years of using a unique interview with children. In the interview, children are presented with a series of stories in which characters face moral dilemmas. The following is the most popular Kohlberg dilemma:

> In Europe a woman was near death from a special kind of cancer. There was one drug that the doctors thought might save her. It was a form of radium that a druggist in the same town had recently discovered. The drug was expensive to make, but the druggist was charging ten times what the drug cost him to make. He paid $200 for the radium and charged $2,000 for a small dose of the drug. The sick woman's husband, Heinz, went to everyone he knew to borrow the money, but he could only get together $1,000 which is half of what it cost. He told the druggist that his wife was dying and asked him to sell it cheaper or let him pay later. But the druggist said, "No, I discovered the drug, and I am going to make money from it." So Heinz got desperate and broke into the man's store to steal the drug for his wife. (Kohlberg, 1969, p. 379)

This story is one of eleven that Kohlberg devised to investigate the nature of moral thought. After reading the story, the interviewee answers a series of questions about the moral dilemma. Should Heinz have stolen the drug? Was stealing it right or wrong? Why? Is it a husband's duty to steal the drug for his wife if he can get it no other way? Would a good husband steal? Did the druggist have the right to charge that much when there was no law setting a limit on the price? Why or why not?

The Kohlberg Stages   Based on the answers interviewees gave for this and other moral dilemmas, Kohlberg described three levels of moral thinking, each of which is characterized by two stages (see Figure 13.1). A key concept in understanding progression through the levels and stages is that their morality becomes more internal or mature. That is, their reasons for their moral decisions or values begin to go beyond the external or superficial reasons they gave when they were younger. Let's further examine Kohlberg's stages.

Preconventional reasoning is the lowest level of moral reasoning, said Kohlberg. At this level, good and bad are interpreted in terms of external rewards and punishments.

- *Stage 1.* **Heteronomous morality** is the first stage in preconventional reasoning. At this stage, moral thinking is tied to punishment. For example, children think that they must obey because they fear punishment for disobedience.

- *Stage 2.* **Individualism, instrumental purpose, and exchange** is the second stage of preconventional reasoning. At this stage, individuals reason that pursuing their own interests is the right thing to do, but they let others

preconventional reasoning The lowest level in Kohlberg's theory of moral development. The individual's concept of good and bad is interpreted primarily by external rewards and punishment.

heteronomous morality Kohlberg's first stage in preconventional reasoning in which moral thinking is tied to punishment.

individualism, instrumental purpose, and exchange The second Kohlberg stage in preconventional reasoning. At this stage, individuals pursue their own interests but also let others do the same.

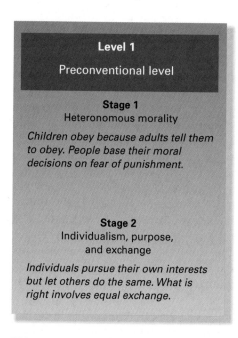

Level 1

Preconventional level

Stage 1
Heteronomous morality

Children obey because adults tell them to obey. People base their moral decisions on fear of punishment.

Stage 2
Individualism, purpose, and exchange

Individuals pursue their own interests but let others do the same. What is right involves equal exchange.

Level 2

Conventional level

Stage 3
Mutual interpersonal expectations, relationships, and interpersonal conformity

Individuals value trust, caring, and loyalty to others as a basis for moral judgments.

Stage 4
Social systems morality

Moral judgments are based on understanding of the social order, law, justice, and duty.

Level 3

Postconventional level

Stage 5
Social contract or utility and individual rights

Individuals reason that values, rights, and principles undergird or transcend the law.

Stage 6
Universal ethical principles

The person has developed moral judgments that are based on universal human rights. When faced with a dilemma between law and conscience, a personal, individualized conscience is followed.

FIGURE 13.1 Kohlberg's Three Levels and Six Stages of Moral Development

do the same. Thus, they think that what is right involves an equal exchange. They reason that if they are nice to others, others will be nice to them in return.

Conventional reasoning is the second, or intermediate, level in Kohlberg's theory of moral development. At this level, individuals apply certain standards, but they are the standards set by others, such as parents or the government.

- *Stage 3.* **Mutual interpersonal expectations, relationships, and interpersonal conformity** is Kohlberg's third stage of moral development. At this stage, individuals value trust, caring, and loyalty to others as a basis of moral judgments. Children and adolescents often adopt their parents' moral standards at this stage, seeking to be thought of by their parents as a "good girl" or a "good boy."

- *Stage 4.* **Social systems morality** is the fourth stage in Kohlberg's theory of moral development. At this stage, moral judgments are based on understanding the social order, law, justice, and duty. For example, adolescents may reason that in order for a community to work effectively, it needs to be protected by laws that are adhered to by its members.

Postconventional reasoning is the highest level in Kohlberg's theory of moral development. At this level, the individual recognizes alternative moral courses, explores the options, and then decides on a personal moral code.

- *Stage 5.* **Social contract or utility and individual rights** is the fifth Kohlberg stage. At this stage, individuals reason that values, rights, and principles undergird or transcend the law. A person evaluates the validity of actual laws, and social systems can be examined in terms of the degree to which they preserve and protect fundamental human rights and values.

- *Stage 6.* **Universal ethical principles** is the sixth and highest stage in Kohlberg's theory of moral development. At this stage, the person has developed a moral standard based on universal human rights. When faced with a conflict between law and conscience, the person reasons that conscience should be followed, even though the decision might bring risk.

How Would You...?
As a human development and family studies professional, how would you explain the progression of moral reasoning skills that develop during the elementary school years?

conventional reasoning The second, or intermediate, level in Kohlberg's theory of moral development. At this level, individuals abide by certain standards, but they are the standards of others such as parents or the government.

mutual interpersonal expectations, relationships, and interpersonal conformity Kohlberg's third stage of moral development. At this stage, individuals value trust, caring, and loyalty to others as a basis of moral judgments.

social systems morality The fourth stage in Kohlberg's theory of moral development. Moral judgments are based on understanding the social order, law, justice, and duty.

postconventional reasoning The highest level in Kohlberg's theory of moral development. At this level, the individual recognizes alternative moral courses, explores the options, and then decides on a personal moral code.

social contract or utility and individual rights The fifth Kohlberg stage. At this stage, individuals reason that values, rights, and principles undergird or transcend the law.

universal ethical principles The sixth and highest stage in Kohlberg's theory of moral development. Individuals develop a moral standard based on universal human rights.

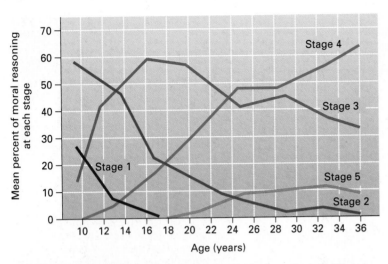

FIGURE 13.2 Age and the Percentage of Individuals at Each Kohlberg Stage In one longitudinal study of males from 10 to 36 years of age, at age 10 most moral reasoning was at stage 2 (Colby & others, 1983). At 16 to 18 years of age, stage 3 became the most frequent type of moral reasoning, and it was not until the mid-twenties that stage 4 became the most frequent. Stage 5 did not appear until 20 to 22 years of age and it never characterized more than 10 percent of the individuals. In this study, the moral stages appeared somewhat later than Kohlberg envisioned, and stage 6 was absent.

Kohlberg held that these levels and stages occur in a sequence and are age-related: Before age 9, most children use level 1, preconventional reasoning based on external rewards and punishments, when they consider moral choices. By early adolescence, their moral reasoning is increasingly based on the application of standards set by others. Most adolescents reason at stage 3, with some signs of stages 2 and 4. By early adulthood, a small number of individuals reason in postconventional ways.

What evidence supports this description of development? A 20-year longitudinal investigation found that use of stages 1 and 2 decreased with age (Colby & others, 1983) (see Figure 13.2). Stage 4, which did not appear at all in the moral reasoning of 10-year-olds, was reflected in the moral thinking of 62 percent of the 36-year-olds. Stage 5 did not appear until age 20 to 22 and never characterized more than 10 percent of the individuals.

Thus, the moral stages appeared somewhat later than Kohlberg initially envisioned, and reasoning at the higher stages, especially stage 6, was rare. Although stage 6 has been removed from the Kohlberg moral judgment scoring manual, it still is considered to be theoretically important in the Kohlberg scheme of moral development.

Influences on the Kohlberg Stages   What factors influence movement through Kohlberg' stages? Although moral reasoning at each stage presupposes a certain level of cognitive development, Kohlberg argued that advances in children's cognitive development did not ensure development of moral reasoning. Instead, moral reasoning also reflects children's experiences in dealing with moral questions and moral conflict.

Several investigators have tried to advance individuals' levels of moral development by having a model present arguments that reflect moral thinking one stage above the individuals' established levels. This approach applies the concepts of equilibrium and conflict that Piaget used to explain cognitive development. By presenting arguments slightly beyond the children' level of moral reasoning, the researchers created a disequilibrium that motivated the children to restructure their moral thought. The upshot of studies using this approach is that virtually any plus-stage discussion, for any length of time, seems to promote more advanced moral reasoning (Walker, 1982).

Kohlberg emphasized that peer interaction and perspective taking are critical aspects of the social stimulation that challenges children to change their moral reasoning. Whereas adults characteristically impose rules and regulations on children, the give-and-take among peers gives children an opportunity to take the perspective of another person and to generate rules democratically. Kohlberg stressed that in principle, encounters with any peers can produce perspective-taking opportunities that may advance a child's moral reasoning. A recent research review of cross-cultural studies involving Kohlberg's theory revealed strong support for a link between perspective-taking skills and more advanced moral judgments (Gibbs & others, 2007).

Kohlberg's Critics   Kohlberg's theory has provoked debate, research, and criticism (Gibbs, 2009; Narváez & Lapsley, 2009). Key criticisms involve the link between moral thought and moral behavior, the roles of culture and the family in moral development, and the significance of concern for others.

Moral Thought and Moral Behavior Kohlberg's theory has been criticized for placing too much emphasis on moral thought and not enough emphasis on moral behavior (Walker, 2004). Moral reasons can sometimes be a shelter for immoral behavior. Corrupt CEOs and politicians endorse the loftiest of moral virtues in public before their own behavior is exposed. Whatever the latest public scandal, you will probably find that the culprits displayed virtuous thoughts but engaged in immoral behavior. No one wants a nation of cheaters and thieves who can reason at the postconventional level. The cheaters and thieves may know what is right yet still do what is wrong. Heinous actions can be cloaked in a mantle of moral virtue.

The mantle of virtue is not necessarily a ruse; it is often taken on sincerely. Social cognitive theorist Albert Bandura (1999, 2002) argues that people usually do not engage in harmful conduct until they have justified the morality of their actions to themselves. Immoral conduct is made personally and socially acceptable by portraying it as serving socially worthy or moral purposes or even as doing God's will. Bandura provides the examples of Islamic extremists who mount jihad (holy war) against what they see as a tyrannical, decadent people seeking to enslave the Islamic world, and antiabortion activists who bomb abortion clinics or murder doctors in order to discourage abortions.

Culture and Moral Reasoning Kohlberg emphasized that his stages of moral reasoning are universal, but some critics claim his theory is culturally biased (Miller, 2007). Both Kohlberg and his critics may be partially correct. One review of 45 studies in 27 cultures around the world, mostly non-European, provided support for the universality of Kohlberg's first four stages (Snarey, 1987). Individuals in diverse cultures developed through these four stages in sequence as Kohlberg predicted. More recent research revealed support for the qualitative shift from stage 2 to stage 3 across cultures (Gibbs & others, 2007). Stages 5 and 6, however, have not been found in all cultures (Gibbs & others, 2007; Snarey, 1987). Furthermore, Kohlberg's scoring system does not recognize the higher-level moral reasoning of certain cultures and thus that moral reasoning is more culture-specific that Kohlberg envisioned (Snarey, 1987).

In sum, although Kohlberg's approach does capture much of the moral reasoning voiced in various cultures around the world, his approach misses or misconstrues some important moral concepts in particular cultures (Gibbs, 2009; Miller, 2007).

Families and Moral Development Kohlberg argued that family processes are essentially unimportant in children's moral development. As noted earlier, he argued that parent-child relationships usually provide children with little opportunity for give-and-take or perspective taking. Rather, Kohlberg said that such opportunities are more likely to be provided by children's peer relations.

Did Kohlberg underestimate the contribution of family relationships to moral development? A number of developmentalists emphasize that *inductive discipline*, which uses reasoning and focuses children's attention on the consequences of their actions for others, positively influences moral development (Hoffman, 1970). They also stress that parents' moral values influence children's developing moral thoughts (Laible & Thompson, 2007). Nonetheless, most developmentalists agree with Kohlberg, and Piaget, that peers play an important role in the development of moral reasoning.

Gender and the Care Perspective The most publicized criticism of Kohlberg's theory has come from Carol Gilligan (1982, 1992, 1996), who argues that Kohlberg's theory reflects a gender bias. According to Gilligan, Kohlberg's theory is based on a male norm that puts abstract principles above relationships and concern for

This 14-year-old boy in Nepal is thought to be the sixth holiest Buddhist in the world. In one study of 20 adolescent male Buddhist monks in Nepal, the issue of justice, a basic theme in Kohlberg's theory, was not a central focus in the monks' moral views (Huebner & Garrod, 1993). Also, the monks' concerns about prevention of suffering and the importance of compassion are not captured in Kohlberg's theory.

Carol Gilligan is shown with some of the students she has interviewed about the importance of relationships in a female's development. *What is Gilligan's view of moral development?*

others and sees the individual as standing alone and independently making moral decisions. It puts justice at the heart of morality. In contrast to Kohlberg's **justice perspective,** which focuses on the rights of the individual, Gilligan argues for a **care perspective,** which is a moral perspective that views people in terms of their connectedness with others and emphasizes interpersonal communication, relationships with others, and concern for others. According to Gilligan, Kohlberg greatly underplayed the care perspective, perhaps because he was a male, because most of his research was with males rather than females, and because he used male responses as a model for his theory.

In extensive interviews with girls from 6 to 18 years of age, Gilligan and her colleagues found that girls consistently interpret moral dilemmas in terms of human relationships and base these interpretations on listening and watching other people (Gilligan, 1992; Gilligan & others, 2003). However, a meta-analysis (a statistical analysis that combines the results of many different studies) casts doubt on Gilligan's claim of substantial gender differences in moral judgment (Jaffe & Hyde, 2000). A recent review concluded that girls' moral orientations are "somewhat more likely to focus on care for others than on abstract principles of justice, but they can use both moral orientations when needed (as can boys . . .)" (Blakemore, Berenbaum, & Liben, 2009, p. 132).

Social Conventional Reasoning Some theorists and researchers argue that Kohlberg did not adequately distinguish between moral reasoning and social conventional reasoning (Turiel, 2006). **Social conventional reasoning** focuses on conventional rules that have been established by social consensus in order to control behavior and maintain the social system. The rules themselves are arbitrary, such as using a fork at meals and raising your hand in class before speaking.

In contrast, moral reasoning focuses on ethical issues and rules of morality. Unlike conventional rules, moral rules are not arbitrary. They are obligatory, widely accepted, and somewhat impersonal (Smetana, 2006). Rules pertaining to lying, cheating, stealing, and physically harming another person are moral rules because violation of these rules affronts ethical standards that exist apart from social consensus and convention. Moral judgments involve concepts of justice, whereas social conventional judgments are concepts of social organization.

Prosocial Behavior Whereas Kohlberg's and Gilligan's theories have focused primarily on the development of moral reasoning, the study of prosocial moral behavior has placed more emphasis on the behavioral aspects of moral development (Hastings, Utendale, & Sullivan, 2007). Children engage in both immoral antisocial acts such as lying and cheating and prosocial moral behavior such as showing empathy or acting altruistically (Carlo, 2006). Even during the preschool years children may care for others or comfort others in distress, but prosocial behavior occurs more often in adolescence than in childhood (Eisenberg & Morris, 2004).

William Damon (1988) described how sharing develops. During their first years, when children share, it is usually not for reasons of empathy but for the fun of the social play ritual or out of imitation. Then, at about 4 years of age, a combination of empathic awareness and adult encouragement produces a sense of obligation on the part of the child to share with others. Most 4-year-olds are not selfless saints, however. Children believe they have an obligation to share but do not necessarily think they should be as generous to others as they are to themselves.

Children's sharing comes to reflect a more complex sense of what is just and right during middle and late childhood. By the start of the elementary school years, children begin to express objective ideas about fairness (Eisenberg, Fabes, & Spinrad, 2006). It is common to hear 6-year-old children use the word *fair* as synonymous with *equal* or *same.* By the mid to late elementary school years, children believe that

justice perspective A moral perspective that focuses on the rights of the individual; individuals independently make moral decisions.

care perspective The moral perspective of Carol Gilligan, which views people in terms of their connectedness with others and emphasizes interpersonal communication, relationships with others, and concern for others.

social conventional reasoning Thoughts about social consensus and convention established in order to control behavior and maintain the social system.

equity instead sometimes means that people with special merit or special needs deserve special treatment.

Missing from the factors that guide children's sharing is one that many adults might expect to be the most influential: the motivation to obey adult authority figures. Surprisingly, a number of studies have shown that adult authority has only a small influence on children's sharing (Eisenberg, 1982). Parental advice and prodding certainly foster standards of sharing, but the give-and-take of peer requests and arguments provides the most immediate stimulation of sharing.

Moral Personality   Beyond the development of moral reasoning and specific moral feelings and prosocial behaviors, do children also develop a pattern of moral characteristics that is distinctively their own? In other words, do children develop a *moral personality,* and if so, what are its components? Researchers have focused attention on three possible components: (1) moral identity, (2) moral character, and (3) moral exemplars:

How does children's sharing change from the preschool to the elementary school years?

- *Moral identity.* Individuals have a moral identity when moral notions and moral commitments are central to their lives. They construct the self with reference to moral categories. Violating their moral commitment would place the integrity of their self at risk (Narváez & Lapsley, 2009).

- *Moral character.* A person with moral character has the willpower, desires, and integrity to stand up to pressure, overcome distractions and disappointments, and behave morally (Walker & Frimer, 2009a, b). A person of good moral character displays moral virtues such as "honesty, truthfulness, and trustworthiness, as well as those of care, compassion, thoughtfulness, and considerateness. Other salient traits revolve around virtues of dependability, loyalty, and conscientiousness" (Walker, 2002, p. 74).

- *Moral exemplars.* Moral exemplars are people who have lived exemplary moral lives. Their moral personality, identity, character, and set of virtues reflect moral excellence and commitment.

In sum, moral development is a multifaceted, complex concept. Included in this complexity are thoughts, feelings, behaviors, and personality.

Gender

Gilligan's claim that Kohlberg's theory of moral development reflects gender bias reminds us of the pervasive influence of gender on development. Long before elementary school, boys and girls show preferences for different toys and activities. As we discussed in Chapter 10, "Socioemotional Development in Early Childhood," preschool children display a gender identity and gender-typed behavior that reflects biological, cognitive, and social influences. Here we will examine gender stereotypes, gender similarities and differences, and gender-role classification.

Gender Stereotypes   According to the old ditty, boys are made of "frogs and snails" and girls are made of "sugar and spice and all that is nice." In the past, a well-adjusted boy was supposed to be independent, aggressive, and powerful. A well-adjusted girl was supposed to be dependent, nurturant, and uninterested in power. The masculine characteristics were considered to be healthy and good by society; the feminine characteristics were considered undesirable. These notions reflect **gender stereotypes,** which are broad categories that reflect general impressions and beliefs about females and males.

Recent research has found that gender stereotypes are, to a great extent, still present in today's world, both in the lives of children and adults (Hyde, 2007a, b; Blakemore, Berenbaum, & Liben, 2009). A recent study revealed that children's gender stereotyping increased from preschool through the fifth grade (Miller &

*W*hat are little boys made of?
Frogs and snails
And puppy dogs' tails.
What are little girls made of?
Sugar and spice
And all that's nice.

—J. O. HALLIWELL
English Author, 19th Century

gender stereotypes Broad categories that reflect our impressions and beliefs about females and males.

others, 2008). In this study, preschoolers tended to stereotype dolls and appearance as characteristic of girls' interests and toys and behaviors (such as action heroes and hitting) as the province of boys. During middle and late childhood, children expanded the range and extent of their gender stereotyping in such areas as occupations, sports, and school tasks. Researchers also have found that boys' gender stereotypes are more rigid than girls' (Ruble, Martin, & Berenbaum, 2006).

A recent study of 3- to 10-year-old U.S. children revealed that girls and older children used a higher percentage of gender stereotypes (Miller & others, 2009). In this study, appearance stereotypes were more prevalent on the part of girls, whereas activity (sports, for example) and trait (aggressive, for example) stereotyping was more commonly engaged in by boys.

Gender Similarities and Differences   What is the reality behind gender stereotypes? Let's examine some of the similarities and differences between the sexes, keeping in mind that (1) the differences are averages—not all females versus all males; (2) even when differences are reported, there is considerable overlap between the sexes; and (3) the differences may be due primarily to biological factors, sociocultural factors, or both. First, we examine physical similarities and differences, and then we will turn to cognitive and socioemotional similarities and differences.

Physical Development   Women have about twice the body fat of men, most concentrated around breasts and hips. In males, fat is more likely to go to the abdomen. On the average, males grow to be 10 percent taller than females. Other physical differences are less obvious. From conception on, females have a longer life expectancy than males, and females are less likely than males to develop physical or mental disorders. Males have twice the risk of coronary disease as females.

Differences in hormones contribute to many physical differences between the sexes (Blakemore, Berenbaum, & Liben, 2009). Recall that androgens such as testosterone are male sex hormones and estrogens are female sex hormones, although both males and females produce androgens and estrogens. Male hormones promote the growth of long bones; female hormones stop such growth at puberty. Estrogen strengthens the immune system, making females more resistant to infection, for example. Female hormones also signal the liver to produce more "good" cholesterol, which makes females' blood vessels more elastic than males'. In contrast, testosterone triggers the production of low-density lipoprotein, which clogs blood vessels. Higher levels of stress hormones cause faster clotting in males, but also higher blood pressure than in females.

Does gender matter when it comes to brain structure and function? Human brains are much alike, whether the brain belongs to a male or a female (Halpern, 2006; Halpern & others, 2007). However, researchers have found some differences in the brains of males and females (Hofer & others, 2007a, b). Among the differences that have been discovered are:

- Female brains are smaller than male brains but female brains have more folds; the larger folds (called convolutions) allow more surface brain tissue within the skulls of females than males (Luders & others, 2004).

- One part of the hypothalamus responsible for sexual behavior is larger in men than women (Swaab & others, 2001).

- An area of the parietal lobe that functions in visuospatial skills is larger in males than females (Frederikse & others, 2000).

- The areas of the brain involved in emotional expression show more metabolic activity in females than males (Gur & others, 1995).

Although some differences in brain structure and function have been found, many of these differences are either small or research is inconsistent regarding the differences. Also, when sex differences in the brain have been revealed, in many cases they have not been directly linked to psychological differences (Blakemore, Berenbaum, & Liben, 2009). Although research on sex differences in the brain is still in its infancy, it is likely that there are far more similarities than differences in the brains of females and males.

Cognitive Development   No gender differences in general intelligence have been revealed, but some gender differences have been found in some cognitive areas (Blakemore, Berenbaum, & Liben, 2009; Galambos, Berenbaum, & McHale, 2009). Research has shown that in general girls and women have slightly better verbal skills than boys and men, although in some verbal skills areas the differences are substantial (Blakemore, Berenbaum, & Liben, 2009). For example, in recent national assessments, girls were significantly better than boys in reading and writing (National Assessment of Educational Progress, 2005, 2007).

Are there gender differences in math? In the National Assessment of Educational Progress in the United States, fourth- and eighth-grade males continued to slightly outperform females in math through 2007 (National Assessment of Educational Progress, 2005, 2007). However, not all recent studies have shown differences. A recent very large-scale study of more than 7 million U.S. students in grades 2 through 11 revealed no differences in math scores for boys and girls (Hyde & others, 2008).

One area of math that has been examined for possible gender differences is visuospatial skills, which include being able to rotate objects mentally and determine what they would look like when rotated. These types of skills are important in courses such as plane and solid geometry and geography. A recent research review revealed that boys have better visuospatial skills than girls (Halpern & others, 2007). For example, despite equal participation in the National Geography Bee, in most years all 10 finalists were boys (Liben, 1995). However, some experts argue that the gender difference in visuospatial skills is small (Hyde, 2007a, b).

Socioemotional Development   Four areas of socioemotional development in which gender similarities and differences have been studied extensively are aggression, communication in relationships, emotion, and prosocial behavior.

One of the most consistent gender differences is that boys are more physically aggressive than girls are (Baillargeon & others, 2007; Brendgen, 2009). The difference occurs in all cultures and appears very early in children's development (White, 2001). The physical aggression difference is especially pronounced when children are provoked. Both biological and environmental factors have been proposed to account for gender differences in aggression. Biological factors include heredity and hormones. Environmental factors include cultural expectations, adult and peer models, and social agents that reward aggression in boys and punish aggression in girls.

Although boys are consistently more physically aggressive than girls, might girls show as much or more verbal aggression, such as yelling, than boys? When verbal aggression is examined, gender differences often disappear; sometimes, though, verbal aggression is more pronounced in girls (Eagly & Steffen, 1986).

Recently, increased interest has been shown in *relational aggression,* which involves harming someone by manipulating a relationship (Crick & others, 2009; Salmivalli & Peets, 2009). Relational aggression includes such behaviors as trying to make others dislike a certain

"So according to the stereotype, you can put two and two together, but I can read the handwriting on the wall."
Copyright © 1994 Joel Pett. All rights reserved.
Reprinted by permission.

How Would You...?
As a psychologist, how would you discuss gender similarities and differences with a parent or teacher who is concerned about a child's academic progress and social skills?

What gender differences characterize aggression?

individual by spreading malicious rumors about the person (Underwood, 2004). Relational aggression increases in middle and late childhood (Dishion & Piehler, 2009). Researchers have found mixed results regarding gender and relational aggression, with some studies showing girls engaging in more relational aggression and others revealing no differences between boys and girls (Young, Boye, & Nelson, 2006). One consistency in findings is that relational aggression comprises a greater percentage of girls' overall aggression than is the case for boys (Putallaz & others, 2007). A recent study found links between parenting and children's relational aggression (Kuppens & others 2009). In this study, parents' psychological control was linked to a higher incidence of relational aggression in their children.

Are there gender differences in communication in relationships? Sociolinguist Deborah Tannen (1990) distinguishes between rapport talk and report talk:

- **Rapport talk** is the language of conversation and a way of establishing connections and negotiating relationships. Females enjoy rapport talk and conversation that is relationship-oriented more than males do.

- **Report talk** is talk that gives information. Public speaking is an example of report talk. Males hold center stage through report talk with such verbal performances as storytelling, joking, and lecturing with information.

Deborah Tannen. *What is her view of gender differences in communication in relationships? How has her view been criticized?*

Tannen says that boys and girls grow up in different worlds of talk—parents, siblings, peers, teachers, and others talk to boys and girls differently. The play of boys and girls is also different. Boys tend to play in large groups that are hierarchically structured, and their groups usually have a leader who tells the others what to do and how to do it. Boys' games have winners and losers and often are the subject of arguments. And boys often boast of their skill and argue about who is best at what. In contrast, girls are more likely to play in small groups or pairs, and at the center of a girl's world is often a best friend. In girls' friendships and peer groups, intimacy is pervasive. Turn-taking is more characteristic of girls' games than of boys' games. And much of the time, girls simply like to sit and talk with each other, concerned more about being liked by others than jockeying for status in some obvious way.

In sum, Tannen, like other gender experts such as Carol Gilligan, whose ideas you read about earlier in this chapter, concludes that girls are more relationship-oriented than boys—and that this relationship orientation should be prized as a skill in our culture more than it currently is. In support of Tannen's view, researchers have found that adolescent girls engage in more self-disclosure (communication of intimate details about themselves) in close relationships and are better at actively listening in a conversation than boys (Leaper & Friedman, 2007).

However, Tannen's view has been criticized as being overly simplified and her critics point out that communication between males and females is more complex than Tannen suggests (Edwards & Hamilton, 2004). Further, some researchers have found similarities in males' and females' relationship communication strategies. In one study, in their talk men and women described and responded to relationship problems in ways that were more similar than different (MacGeorge, 2004).

Further modification of Tannen's view is suggested by a recent *meta-analytic* review of gender differences in talkativeness (general communicative competence), affiliative speech (language used to establish or maintain connections with others, such as showing support or expanding on a person's prior remarks), and self-assertive speech (language used to influence others, such as directive statements or disagreements) (Leaper & Smith, 2004). A *meta-analysis* is a statistical analysis that combines the results of many different studies. This review confirms the criticism that Tannen overemphasizes the size of the gender difference in communication. Gender differences did occur, but they were small, with girls only slightly more talkative and engaging in more affiliative speech than boys, and boys being more likely to use self-assertive speech. Perhaps the most important

rapport talk The language of conversation and a way of establishing connections and negotiating relationships; more characteristic of females than of males.

report talk Talk that conveys information; more characteristic of males than females.

message from this review is that gender differences in communication often depended on the context:

- *Group size.* The gender difference in talkativeness (girls being more competent in communicating) occurred more in large groups than in dyads (two people).
- *Speaking with peers or adults.* No average differences in talk with peers occurred, but girls talked more with adults than did boys.
- *Familiarity.* The gender difference in self-assertive speech (boys using it more) was more likely to occur when talking with strangers than with familiar individuals.
- *Age.* The gender difference in affiliative speech was largest in adolescence. This may be due to adolescent girls' increased interest in socioemotional behavior traditionally prescribed for females.

Are there gender differences in emotion? Girls are more likely to express their emotions openly and intensely than are boys, especially in displaying sadness and fear (Blakemore, Berenbaum, & Liben, 2009). Girls also are better at reading others' emotions and more likely to show empathy than are boys (Blakemore, Berenbaum, & Liben, 2009). Males usually show less self-regulation of emotion than females, and this low self-control can translate into behavioral problems (Eisenberg, Spinrad, & Smith, 2004).

Are there gender differences in prosocial behavior? Across childhood and adolescence, females engage in more prosocial behavior (Eisenberg & others, 2009). The biggest gender difference occurs for kind and considerate behavior, with a smaller difference in sharing.

Gender-Role Classification   Not long ago, it was accepted that boys should grow up to be masculine and girls to be feminine. In the 1970s, however, as both females and males became dissatisfied with the burdens imposed by their stereotypic roles, alternatives to femininity and masculinity were proposed. Instead of describing masculinity and femininity as a continuum in which more of one means less of the other, it was proposed that individuals could have both masculine and feminine traits.

This thinking led to the development of the concept of **androgyny,** the presence of positive masculine and feminine characteristics in the same person (Bem, 1977; Spence & Helmreich, 1978). The androgynous boy might be assertive (masculine) and nurturant (feminine). The androgynous girl might be powerful (masculine) and sensitive to others' feelings (feminine). Measures have been developed to assess androgyny (see Figure 13.3).

androgyny The presence of positive masculine and feminine characteristics in the same individual.

The following items are from the Bem Sex-Role Inventory (BSRI). When taking the BSRI, a person is asked to indicate on a 7-point scale how well each of the 60 characteristics describes herself or himself. The scale ranges from 1 (never or almost never true) to 7 (always or almost always true).

FIGURE 13.3 The Bem Sex-Role Inventory

Examples of masculine items	Examples of feminine items
Defends open beliefs	Does not use harsh language
Forceful	Affectionate
Willing to take risks	Loves children
Dominant	Understanding
Aggressive	Gentle

Scoring: The items are scored on independent dimensions of masculinity and femininity as well as androgyny and undifferentiated classifications.

Gender experts such as Sandra Bem argue that androgynous individuals are more flexible, competent, and mentally healthy than their masculine or feminine counterparts. To some degree, though, which gender-role classification is best depends on the context involved. For example, in close relationships, feminine and androgynous orientations might be more desirable. One study found that girls and individuals high in femininity showed a stronger interest in caring than did boys and individuals high in masculinity (Karniol, Grosz, & Schorr, 2003). However, masculine and androgynous orientations might be more desirable in traditional academic and work settings because of the achievement demands in these contexts.

Despite talk about the "sensitive male," William Pollack (1999) argues that little has been done to change traditional ways of raising boys. He says that the "boy code" tells boys that they should show little if any emotion and should act tough. Boys learn the boy code in many contexts—sandboxes, playgrounds, schoolrooms, camps, hangouts. The result, according to Pollack, is a "national crisis of boyhood." Pollack and others suggest that boys would benefit from being socialized to express their anxieties and concerns and to better regulate their aggression.

Gender in Context Both the concept of androgeny and gender stereotypes describe people in terms of personality traits such as "aggressive" or "caring." However, which traits people display may vary with the situation (Blakemore, Berenbaum, & Liben, 2009; Leaper & Friedman, 2007). Thus, the nature and extent of gender differences may depend on the context.

Consider helping behavior. The stereotype is that females are better than males at helping. But it depends on the situation. Females are more likely than males to volunteer their time to help children with personal problems and to engage in caregiving behavior. However, in situations in which males feel a sense of competence or in situations that involve danger, males are more likely than females to help (Eagly & Crowley, 1986). For example, a male is more likely than a female to stop and help a person stranded by the roadside with a flat tire. Indeed, one study documented that males are more likely to help when the context is masculine in nature (MacGeorge, 2003).

"She is emotional; he is not"—that is the master emotional stereotype. However, like differences in helping behavior, emotional differences in males and females depend on the particular emotion involved and the context in which it is displayed (Shields, 1991). Males are more likely to show anger toward strangers, especially male strangers, when they feel they have been challenged. Males also are more likely to turn their anger into aggressive action. Emotional differences between females and males often show up in contexts that highlight social roles and relationships. For example, females are more likely to discuss emotions in terms of relationships, and they are more likely to express fear and sadness.

The importance of considering gender in context is nowhere more apparent than when we examine what is culturally prescribed behavior for females and males in different countries around the world (Chuang & Tamis-Lemonda, 2009; Lamb & Bougher, 2009; Pinto & Coltrane, 2009). Although there has been greater acceptance of androgyny and similarities in male and female behavior in the United States, in many countries gender roles have remained gender-specific. For example, in many Middle Eastern countries, the division of labor between males and females is dramatic. Males are socialized and schooled to work in the public sphere, females in the private world of home and child rearing. For example, in many Middle Eastern countries, the dominant view is that the man's duty is to provide for his family and the woman's is to care for her family and household. China and India also have been male-dominant cultures. Although women have made some strides in China and India, especially in urban areas, the male role is still dominant. Most males in China and India do not accept androgynous behavior and gender equity.

In China, females and males are usually socialized to behave, feel, and think differently. The old patriarchal traditions of male supremacy have not been completely uprooted. Chinese women still make considerably less money than Chinese men do, and, in rural China (such as here in the Lixian Village of Sichuan) male supremacy still governs many women's lives.

Review and Reflect: Learning Goal 1

1 **Discuss emotional and personality development in middle and late childhood**

REVIEW

- What changes take place in the self during the middle and late childhood years?
- How does emotion change during middle and late childhood?
- What is Kohlberg's theory of moral development, and how has it been criticized? How does prosocial behavior develop?
- What are gender stereotypes, and what are some important gender differences?

REFLECT

- A young man who had been sentenced to serve 10 years for selling a small amount of marijuana walked away from a prison camp six months after he was sent there. He is now in his fifties and has been a model citizen. Should he be sent back to prison? Why or why not? At which Kohlberg stage should your response be placed?

2 WHAT ARE SOME CHANGES IN PARENTING AND FAMILIES IN MIDDLE AND LATE CHILDHOOD?

| Developmental Changes in Parent–Child Relationships | Parents as Managers | Stepfamilies |

Our discussion of parenting and families in this section focuses on how parent-child interactions typically change in middle and late childhood, the importance of parents being effective managers of children's lives, and how elementary school children are affected by living with stepparents.

Developmental Changes in Parent–Child Relationships

As children move into the middle and late childhood years, parents spend considerably less time with them. In one study, parents spent less than half as much time with their children aged 5 to 12 in caregiving, instruction, reading, talking, and playing as when the children were younger (Hill & Stafford, 1980). Although parents spend less time with their children in middle and late childhood than in early childhood, parents continue to be extremely important in their children's lives. In a recent analysis of the contributions of parents in middle and late childhood, the following conclusion was reached: "Parents serve as gatekeepers and provide scaffolding as children assume more responsibility for themselves and . . . regulate their own lives" (Huston & Ripke, 2006, p. 422).

Parents especially play an important role in supporting and stimulating children's academic achievement in middle and late childhood (Gupta, Thornton, & Huston, 2008; Huston & Ripke, 2006). The value parents place on education can mean the difference in whether children do well in school. Parents not only influence children's in-school achievement, but they also make decisions about

What are some changes in the focus of parent-child relationships in middle and late childhood?

children's out-of-school activities. Whether children participate in such activities as sports, music, and other activities is heavily influenced by the extent to which parents sign up children for such activities or encourage their participation (Simpkins & others, 2006).

Elementary school children tend to receive less physical discipline than they did as preschoolers. Instead of spanking or coercive holding, their parents are more likely to use deprivation of privileges, appeals to the child's self-esteem, comments designed to increase the child's sense of guilt, and statements that the child is responsible for his or her actions.

During middle and late childhood, some control is transferred from parent to child. The process is gradual, and it produces *coregulation* rather than control by either the child or the parent alone. Parents continue to exercise general supervision and control, while children are allowed to engage in moment-to-moment self-regulation. The major shift to autonomy does not occur until about the age of 12 or later. A key developmental task as children move toward autonomy is learning to relate to adults outside the family on a regular basis—adults who interact with the child much differently than parents, such as teachers.

Parents as Managers

Parents can play important roles as managers of children's opportunities, as monitors of their behavior, and as social initiators and arrangers (Parke & Buriel, 2006). Mothers are more likely than fathers to engage in a managerial role in parenting.

Researchers have found that family management practices are positively related to students' grades and self-responsibility, and negatively to school-related problems (Eccles, 2007; Taylor & Lopez, 2005). Among the most important family management practices in this regard are maintaining a structured and organized family environment, such as establishing routines for homework, chores, meals, bedtime, and so on, and effectively monitoring the child's behavior. A recent research review of family functioning in African American students' academic achievement found that when African American parents monitored their son's academic achievement by ensuring that homework was completed, restricted time spent on nonproductive distractions (such as video games and TV), and participated in a consistent, positive dialogue with teachers and school officials, their son's academic achievement benefited (Mandara, 2006).

Stepfamilies

Not only has divorce become commonplace in the United States, so has getting remarried (Hetherington, 2006). It takes time for parents to marry, have children, get divorced, and then remarry. Consequently, there are far more elementary and secondary school children than infant or preschool children living in stepfamilies.

The number of remarriages involving children has grown steadily in recent years. Also, divorces occur at a 10 percent higher rate in remarriages than in first marriages (Cherlin & Furstenberg, 1994). About half of all children whose parents divorce will have a stepparent within four years of the separation.

Remarried parents face some unique tasks. The couple must define and strengthen their marriage and at the same time renegotiate the biological parent-child relationships and establish stepparent-stepchild and stepsibling relationships (Coleman, Ganong, & Fine, 2004). The complex histories and multiple relationships make adjustment in a stepfamily difficult (Hetherington & Stanley-Hagan, 2002). Only one-third of stepfamily couples stay remarried.

In some cases, the stepfamily may have been preceded by the death of a spouse. However, by far the largest number of stepfamilies are preceded by divorce rather than death (Pasley & Moorefield, 2004). Three common types of stepfamily structure are (1) stepfather, (2) stepmother, and (3) blended or complex. In stepfather families, the mother typically had custody of the children and remarried, introducing a stepfather into her children's lives. In stepmother families, the father usually had custody and remarried, introducing a stepmother into his children's lives. In a blended or complex stepfamily, both parents bring children from previous marriages to live in the newly formed stepfamily.

In E. Mavis Hetherington's (2006) most recent longitudinal analyses, children and adolescents who had been in a simple stepfamily (stepfather or stepmother) for a number of years were adjusting better than in the early years of the remarried family and were functioning well in comparison to children and adolescents in conflicted nondivorced families and children and adolescents in complex (blended) stepfamilies. More than 75 percent of the adolescents in long-established simple stepfamilies described their relationships with their stepparents as "close" or "very close." Hetherington (2006) concluded that in long-established simple stepfamilies adolescents seem to eventually benefit from the presence of a stepparent and the resources provided by the stepparent.

Children often have better relationships with their custodial parents (mothers in stepfather families, fathers in stepmother families) than with simple stepparents (Santrock, Sitterle, & Warshak, 1988). Also, children in simple families (stepmother, stepfather) often show better adjustment than their counterparts in complex (blended) families (Hetherington & Kelly, 2002).

As in divorced families, children in stepfamilies show more adjustment problems than children in nondivorced families (Hetherington & Kelly, 2002). The adjustment problems are similar to those found among children of divorced parents—academic problems and lower self-esteem, for example (Anderson & others, 1999). However, it is important to recognize that a majority of children in stepfamilies do not have problems. In one analysis, 25 percent of children from stepfamilies showed adjustment problems compared with 10 percent in intact, never-divorced families (Hetherington & Kelly, 2002).

Adolescence is an especially difficult time for the formation of a stepfamily (Anderson & others, 1999). Problems may occur because becoming part of a stepfamily exacerbates normal adolescent concerns about identity, sexuality, and autonomy.

How does living in a stepfamily influence a child's development?

How Would You...?
As a human development and family studies professional, how would you advise divorced parents on strategies to ease their children's adjustment to remarriage?

Review and Reflect: Learning Goal 2

2 **Describe changes in parenting and families in middle and late childhood**

REVIEW

- What changes characterize parent-child relationships in middle and late childhood?
- How can parents be effective managers of children's lives?
- How does being in a stepfamily influence children's development?

REFLECT

- What was your relationship with your parents like when you were in elementary school? How do you think it influenced your development?

3 WHAT CHANGES CHARACTERIZE PEER RELATIONSHIPS IN MIDDLE AND LATE CHILDHOOD?

| Developmental Changes | Peer Status | Social Cognition | Bullying | Friends |

Having positive relationships with peers is especially important in middle and late childhood. Engaging in positive interactions with peers, resolving conflicts with peers in nonaggressive ways, and have quality friendships in middle and late childhood not only have positive outcomes at this time in children's lives, but also are linked to more positive relationship outcomes in adolescence and adulthood (Huston & Ripke, 2006). For example, in one longitudinal study, being popular with peers and engaging in low levels of aggression at 8 years of age were related to higher levels of occupational status at 48 years of age (Huesmann & others, 2006). Another study found that peer competence (a composite measure that included social contact with peers, popularity with peers, friendship, and social skills) in middle and late childhood was linked to having better relationships with co-workers in early adulthood (Collins & van Dulmen, 2006).

Developmental Changes

As children enter the elementary school years, reciprocity becomes especially important in peer interchanges. Researchers estimate that the percentage of time spent in social interaction with peers increases from approximately 10 percent at 2 years of age to more than 30 percent in middle and late childhood (Rubin, Bukowski, & Parker, 2006). In one early study, a typical day in elementary school included approximately 300 episodes with peers (Barker & Wright, 1951). As children move through middle and late childhood, the size of their peer group increases, and peer interaction is less closely supervised by adults (Rubin, Bukowski, & Parker, 2006). Until about 12 years of age, children's preference for same-sex peer groups increases.

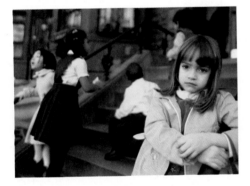

What are some statuses that children have with their peers?

Peer Status

Which children are likely to be popular with their peers and which ones are disliked? Developmentalists address these and similar questions by examining *sociometric status*, a term that describes the extent to which children are liked or disliked by their peer group (Cillessen, 2009; LaFontana & Cillessen, 2009). Sociometric status is typically assessed by asking children to rate how much they like or dislike each of their classmates. Or it may be assessed by asking children to nominate the children they like the most and those they like the least.

Developmentalists have distinguished five peer statuses (Wentzel & Asher, 1995):

- **Popular children** are frequently nominated as a best friend and are rarely disliked by the peers.
- **Average children** receive an average number of both positive and negative nominations from their peers.
- **Neglected children** are infrequently nominated as a best friend but are not disliked by their peers.
- **Rejected children** are infrequently nominated as someone's best friend and are actively disliked by their peers
- **Controversial children** are frequently nominated both as someone's best friend and as being disliked.

popular children Children who are frequently nominated as a best friend and are rarely disliked by their peers.

average children Children who receive an average number of both positive and negative nominations from peers.

neglected children Children who are infrequently nominated as a best friend but are not disliked by their peers.

rejected children Children who are infrequently nominated as a best friend and are actively disliked by their peers.

controversial children Children who are frequently nominated both as someone's best friend and as being disliked.

Popular children have a number of social skills that contribute to their being well liked (Asher & McDonald, 2009). They give out reinforcements, listen carefully, maintain open lines of communication with peers, are happy, control their negative emotions, act like themselves, show enthusiasm and concern for others, and are self-confident without being conceited (Hartup, 1983; Rubin, Bukowski, & Parker, 1998).

Neglected children engage in low rates of interaction with their peers and are often described as shy by peers. The goal of many training programs for neglected children is to help them attract attention from their peers in positive ways and to hold that attention by asking questions, by listening in a warm and friendly way, and by saying things about themselves that relate to the peers' interests. They also are taught to enter groups more effectively.

Rejected children often have more serious adjustment problems than those who are neglected (Dishion & Piehler, 2009; Prinstein & others, 2009). One study found that in kindergarten, children who were rejected by their peers were less likely to engage in classroom participation, more likely to express a desire to avoid school, and more likely to report being lonely than children who were accepted by their peers (Buhs & Ladd, 2001). The combination of being rejected by peers and being aggressive forecasts problems (Dishion & Piehler, 2009). Another study evaluated 112 fifth-grade boys over a period of seven years until the end of high school (Kupersmidt & Coie, 1990). The best predictor of whether rejected children would engage in delinquent behavior or drop out of school later during adolescence was aggression toward peers in elementary school. A recent study revealed that over the course of elementary school, during periods of peer rejection children were less likely to engage in classroom participation but during times when they were not rejected, participated more in class (Ladd, Herald-Brown, & Reiser, 2008).

John Coie (2004, pp. 252-253) provided three reasons why aggressive peer-rejected boys have problems in social relationships:

- "First, the rejected, aggressive boys are more impulsive and have problems sustaining attention. As a result, they are more likely to be disruptive of ongoing activities in the classroom and in focused group play.

- Second, rejected, aggressive boys are more emotionally reactive. They are aroused to anger more easily and probably have more difficulty calming down once aroused. Because of this they are more prone to become angry at peers and attack them verbally and physically. . .

- Third, rejected children have fewer social skills in making friends and maintaining positive relationships with peers."

Not all rejected children are aggressive (Bukowski, Brendgen, & Vitaro, 2007). Although aggression and its related characteristics of impulsiveness and disruptiveness underlie rejection about half the time, approximately 10 to 20 percent of rejected children are shy.

How can rejected children be trained to interact more effectively with their peers? Rejected children may be taught to more accurately assess whether the intentions of their peers are negative (Bierman, 2004). They may be asked to engage in role playing or to discuss hypothetical situations involving negative encounters with peers, such as when a peer cuts into a line ahead of them. In some programs, children are shown videotapes of appropriate peer interaction and asked to draw lessons from what they have seen (Ladd, Buhs, & Troop, 2004).

One social-skills intervention program was successful in increasing social acceptance and self-esteem and decreasing depression and anxiety in peer-rejected children (DeRosier, & Marcus, 2005). Students participated in the program once a week (50 to 60 minutes) for eight weeks. The program included instruction in how to manage emotions, how to improve prosocial skills, how to become better communicators, and how to compromise and negotiate.

How Would You...?
As a social worker, how would you help a neglected child become more involved in peer activities?

Social Cognition

A boy accidentally trips and knocks another boy's soft drink out of his hand. That boy misconstrues the encounter as hostile, and his interpretation leads him to retaliate aggressively against the boy who tripped. Through repeated encounters of this kind, the aggressive boy's classmates come to perceive him as habitually acting in inappropriate ways.

This example demonstrates the importance of *social cognition*—thoughts about social matters, such as the aggressive boy's interpretation of an encounter as hostile and his classmates' perception of his behavior as inappropriate (Prinstein & others, 2009). Children's social cognition about their peers becomes increasingly important for understanding peer relationships in middle and late childhood. Of special interest are the ways in which children process information about peer relations and their social knowledge (Dodge, Coie, & Lynam, 2006; Gibbons, Pomery, & Gerrard, 2008).

Kenneth Dodge (1983) argues that children go through five steps in processing information about their social world. They decode social cues, interpret, search for a response, select an optimal response, and enact. Dodge has found that aggressive boys are more likely to perceive another child's actions as hostile when the child's intention is ambiguous. And, when aggressive boys search for cues to determine a peer's intention, they respond more rapidly, less efficiently, and less reflectively than do nonaggressive children. These are among the social cognitive factors believed to be involved in children's conflicts.

Social knowledge also is involved in children's ability to get along with peers. They need to know what goals to pursue in poorly defined or ambiguous situations, how to initiate and maintain a social bond, and what scripts to follow to get other children to be their friends. For example, as part of the script for getting friends, it helps to know that saying nice things, regardless of what the peer does or says, will make the peer like the child more.

Bullying

Significant numbers of students are victimized by bullies (Faris, 2009; Kaiser & Rasminsky, 2009; Swearer, Espelage, & Napolitano, 2009). In a national survey of more than 15,000 sixth- through tenth-grade students, nearly one of every three students said that they had experienced occasional or frequent involvement as a victim or perpetrator in bullying (Nansel & others, 2001). In this study, *bullying* was defined as verbal or physical behavior intended to disturb someone less powerful. As shown in Figure 13.4, being belittled about looks or speech was the most frequent type of bullying. A recent study revealed that bullying decreased as students went from the fall of the sixth grade (20 percent were bullied extensively) through the spring of the eighth grade (6 percent were bullied extensively) (Nylund & others, 2007). Boys are more likely to be bullies than girls, but gender differences regarding victims of boys is less clear (Salmivalli & Peets, 2009).

Who is likely to be bullied? In the study just described, boys and younger middle school students were most likely to be affected (Nansel & others, 2001). Children who said they were bullied reported more loneliness and difficulty in making friends, whereas those who did the bullying were more likely to have low grades and to smoke and drink alcohol. Researchers have found that anxious, socially withdrawn, and aggressive children are often the victims of bullying (Hanish & Guerra, 2004). Anxious and socially withdrawn children may be victimized because they are nonthreatening and unlikely to retaliate if bullied, whereas aggressive children may be the targets of bullying because their behavior is irritating to bullies (Rubin, Bukowski, & Parker, 2006).

Social contexts also influence bullying. Recent research indicates that 70 to 80 percent of victims and their bullies are in the same school classroom (Salmivalli & Peets, 2009). Classmates often are aware of bullying incidents and in many cases

How Would You...?
As a psychologist, how would you characterize differences in the social cognition of aggressive children compared to children who behave in less hostile ways?

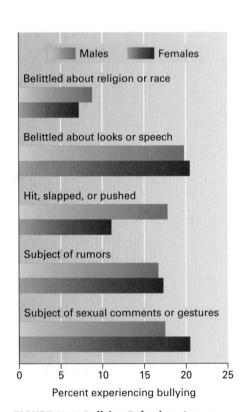

FIGURE 13.4 Bullying Behaviors Among U.S. Youth This graph shows the type of bullying most often experienced by U.S. youth. The percentages reflect the extent to which bullied students said that they had experienced a particular type of bullying. In terms of gender, note that when they were bullied, boys were more likely to be hit, slapped, or pushed than girls were.

witness bullying. The larger social context of the peer group plays an important role in bullying (Salmivalli & Peets, 2009). In many cases, bullies torment victims to gain higher status in the peer group, and bullies need others to witness their power displays.

What are the outcomes of bullying? Bullies and victims are characterized by a number of negative developmental outcomes (Arsenault & others, 2008; Beaty & Alexeyev, 2008). A recent study indicated that bullies and their victims in adolescence were more likely to experience depression and engage in suicidal ideation and attempt suicide than their counterparts who were not involved in bullying (Brunstein Klomek & others, 2007). Another recent study revealed that bullies, victims, or those who were both bullies and victims had more health problems (such as headaches, dizziness, sleep problems, and anxiety) than their counterparts who were not involved in bullying (Srabstein & others, 2006). To read further about bullying, see the *Research in Children's Development* interlude.

What are some characteristics of bullying? What are some strategies to reduce bullying?

Research in Children's Development

THE PERSPECTIVE TAKING AND MORAL MOTIVATION OF BULLIES, BULLY-VICTIMS, VICTIMS, AND PROSOCIAL CHILDREN

A recent study explored the roles that perspective taking and moral motivation play in the lives of bullies, bully-victims, victims, and prosocial children (Gasser & Keller, 2009):

- *Bullies* are highly aggressive toward other children but are not victims of bullying.
- *Bully-victims* are not only highly aggressive toward other children but also are the recipients of other children's bullying.
- *Victims* are passive, nonaggressive respondents to bullying.
- *Prosocial children* engage in such positive behaviors as sharing, helping, comforting, and empathizing.

Teacher and peer ratings in 34 classrooms were used to classify 212 7- to 8-year-old boys and girls into the aforementioned four categories. On a 5-point scale (from never to several times a week), teachers rated (1) how often the child bullied others and (2) how often the child was bullied. The ratings focused on three types of bullying and being victimized: physically, verbally, and excluding others. On a 4-point scale (from not applicable to very clearly applicable), teachers also rated children's prosocial behavior on three items: "willingly shares with others," "comforts others if necessary," and "empathizes with others." Peer ratings assessed children's nominations of which children in the classroom acted as bullies, were victimized by bullies, and engaged in prosocial behavior. Combining the teacher and peer ratings after eliminating those that did not agree on which children were bullies, victims, or prosocial children, the final sample consisted of 49 bullies, 80 bully-victims, 33 victims, and 50 prosocial children.

Children's perspective-taking skills were assessed using theory of mind tasks, and moral motivation was examined by interviewing children about aspects of right and wrong in stories about children's transgressions. In one theory of mind task, children were tested to see if they understood that people may have false beliefs about another individual. In another theory of mind task, children were assessed to determine if they understood that people sometimes hide their emotions by showing a different emotion than they really feel. A moral interview also was conducted in which children were told four moral transgression stories (with content about being unwilling to share with a classmate, stealing sweets from a classmate, hiding a victim's shoes, and verbally

(continued on next page)

bullying a victim) and then asked to judge whether the acts were right or wrong and how the participants in the stories likely felt.

The results of the study indicated that only bully-victims—but not bullies—were deficient in perspective taking. Further analysis revealed that both aggressive groups of children—bullies and bully-victims—had a deficiency in moral motivation. The analyses were consistent with a portrait of bullies as socially competent and knowledgeable in terms of perspective-taking skills and being able to effectively interact with peers. However, bullies use this social knowledge for their own manipulative purposes. The analysis also confirmed the picture of the bully as being morally insensitive.

An increasing number of prevention/intervention programs are being developed to reduce bullying (Bowes & others, 2008; Breakstone, Dreiblatt, & Dreiblatt, 2009). How can bullying be reduced? A recent research review revealed mixed results for school-based intervention (Vreeman & Carroll, 2007). School-based interventions vary greatly, ranging from involving the whole school in an antibullying campaign to individualized social-skills training. Following are two of the most promising bullying intervention programs and where you can obtain information about them:

How Would You...?
As an educator, how would you design and implement a bullying-reduction program at your school?

- *Olweus Bullying Prevention.* Created by Dan Olweus, this program focuses on 6- to 15-year-olds, with the goal of decreasing opportunities and rewards for bullying. School staff are instructed in ways to improve peer relations and make schools safer. When properly implemented, the program reduces bullying by 30 to 70 percent (Ericson, 2001; Olweus, 2003). Information on how to implement the program can be obtained from the Center for the Prevention of Violence at the University of Colorado: www.colorado.edu/cspv/blueprints.

- *Steps to Respect.* This bullying program consists of three steps: (1) establishing a school-wide approach, such as creating antibullying policies and determining consequences for bullying; (2) training staff and parents to deal with bullying; and (3) teaching students to recognize, not tolerate, and handle bullying. In this third step, teachers provide skills training, such as how to be assertive, and information about bullying to students in grades 3 through 6. The skills training by teachers occurs over a 12- to 14-week period. A recent study found that Steps to Respect was successful in reducing bullying and argumentativeness in third- through sixth-grade students (Frey & others, 2005). For more information about Steps to Respect, consult this Web site: www.cfchildren.org/.

There is increasing concern about *cyberbullying*, which involves a child being threatened, harassed, or humiliated by another child on the Internet (Hinduja & Patchin, 2009; Smith & others, 2008). Information about preventing cyberbullying can be found at www.stopcyberbullying.org/.

Friends

Like adult friendships, children's friendships are typically characterized by similarity. Throughout childhood, friends are more similar than dissimilar in terms of age, sex, race, and many other factors. Friends often have similar attitudes toward school, similar educational aspirations, and closely aligned achievement orientations.

Why are children's friendships important? Willard Hartup (1983, 1996, 2008; Hartup & Abecassis, 2004) has studied peer relations and friendship for more than three decades. He recently concluded that friends can be cognitive and emotional resources from childhood through old age. Friends can foster self-esteem and a sense of well-being.

More specifically, children's friendships can serve six functions (Gottman & Parker, 1987):

- *Companionship.* Friendship provides children with a familiar partner and playmate, someone who is willing to spend time with them and join in collaborative activities.

- *Stimulation.* Friendship provides children with interesting information, excitement, and amusement.

- *Physical support.* Friendship provides time, resources, and assistance.

- *Ego support.* Friendship provides the expectation of support, encouragement, and feedback, which helps children maintain an impression of themselves as competent, attractive, and worthwhile individuals.

- *Social comparison.* Friendship provides information about where the child stands vis-à-vis others and whether the child is doing okay.

- *Affection and intimacy.* Friendship provides children with a warm, close, trusting relationship with another individual. **Intimacy in friendships** is characterized by self-disclosure and the sharing of private thoughts. Research reveals that intimate friendships may not appear until early adolescence (Berndt & Perry, 1990).

What are the functions of children's friendships?

Although having friends can be a developmental advantage, not all friendships are alike. People differ in the company they keep—that is, who their friends are. Developmental advantages occur when children have friends who are socially skilled and supportive. However, it is not developmentally advantageous to have coercive and conflict-ridden friendships (Rubin, Bukowski, & Parker, 2006).

The importance of friendship was underscored in a two-year longitudinal study (Wentzel, Barry, & Caldwell, 2004). Sixth-grade students who did not have a friend engaged in less prosocial behavior (cooperation, sharing, helping others), had lower grades, and were more emotionally distressed (displaying depression, low well-being) than their counterparts who had one or more friends. Two years later, in the eighth grade, the students who did not have a friend in the sixth grade were still more emotionally distressed.

Review and Reflect: Learning Goal 3

 Identify changes in peer relationships in middle and late childhood

REVIEW

- What developmental changes characterize peer relations in middle and late childhood?
- How does children's peer status influence their development?
- How is social cognition involved in children's peer relations?
- What is the nature of bullying?
- What are children's friendships like?

REFLECT

- If you were a school principal, what would you do to reduce bullying in your school?

intimacy in friendships Self-disclosure and the sharing of private thoughts.

4 WHAT ARE SOME IMPORTANT ASPECTS OF SCHOOLS?

Contemporary Approaches to Student Learning

Socioeconomic Status and Ethnicity

For most children, entering the first grade signals new obligations. They develop new relationships and develop new standards by which to judge themselves. School provides children with a rich source of new ideas to shape their sense of self. They will spend many years in schools as members of small societies in which there are tasks to be accomplished, people to be socialized and socialized by, and rules that define and limit behavior, feelings, and attitudes. By the time students graduate from high school, they have spent 12,000 hours in the classroom.

Contemporary Approaches to Student Learning

Controversy swirls about the best way to teach children and how to hold schools and teachers accountable for whether children are learning (Armstrong, Henson, & Savage, 2009; Parkay & Stanford, 2010).

Constructivist and Direct Instruction Approaches   The **constructivist approach** is a learner-centered approach that emphasizes the importance of individuals actively constructing their knowledge and understanding with guidance from the teacher. In the constructivist view, teachers should not attempt to simply pour information into children's minds. Rather, children should be encouraged to explore their world, discover knowledge, reflect, and think critically with careful monitoring and meaningful guidance from the teacher (Holzman, 2009). The constructivist belief is that for too long in American education children have been required to sit still, be passive learners, and rotely memorize irrelevant as well as relevant information (Maxim, 2010).

Today, constructivism may include an emphasis on collaboration—children working with each other in their efforts to know and understand (Holzman, 2009). A teacher with a constructivist instructional philosophy would not have children memorize information rotely but would give them opportunities to meaningfully construct the knowledge and understand the material while guiding their learning (Maxim, 2010).

By contrast, the **direct instruction approach** is a structured, teacher-centered approach that is characterized by teacher direction and control, high teacher expectations for students' progress, maximum time spent by students on academic tasks, and efforts by the teacher to keep negative affect to a minimum. An important goal in the direct-instruction approach is maximizing student learning time.

Advocates of the constructivist approach argue that the direct instruction approach turns children into passive learners and does not adequately challenge them to think in critical and creative ways (Abruscato & DeRosa, 2010; Eby, Herrell, & Jordan, 2009). The direct instruction enthusiasts say that the constructivist approaches do not give enough attention to the content of a discipline, such as history or science. They also hold that the constructivist approaches are too relativistic and vague.

Some experts in educational psychology argue that many effective teachers use both a constructivist *and* a direct instruction approach rather than either exclusively (Bransford & others, 2006). Further, some circumstances may call more for a constructivist approach, others for a direction instruction approach. For example, experts increasingly recommend an

Is this classroom more likely constructivist or direct instruction? Explain.

explicit, intellectually engaging direct instruction approach when teaching students with a reading or a writing disability (Berninger, 2006).

Accountability   Since the 1990s, the U.S. public and governments at every level have demanded increased accountability from schools. One result was the spread of state-mandated tests to measure just what students had or had not learned (Gronlund & Waugh, 2009; Yell & Drasgow, 2009). Many states identified objectives for students in their state and created tests to measure whether students were meeting those objectives. This approach became national policy in 2002 when the No Child Left Behind (NCLB) legislation was signed into law.

Advocates argue that statewide standardized testing will have a number of positive effects. These include improved student performance; more time teaching the subjects that are tested; high expectations for all students; identification of poorly performing schools, teachers, and administrators; and improved confidence in schools as test scores rise.

Critics argue that the NCLB legislation is doing more harm than good (Connors, 2007; Noddings, 2007). One criticism stresses that using a single test as the sole indicator of students' progress and competence presents a very narrow view of students' skills (Lewis, 2007). This criticism is similar to the one leveled at IQ tests, which we discussed in Chapter 12, "Cognitive Development in Middle and Late Childhood." To assess student progress and achievement, many psychologists and educators emphasize that a number of measures should be used, including tests, quizzes, projects, portfolios, classroom observations, and so on. Also, the tests used as part of NCLB don't measure creativity, motivation, persistence, flexible thinking, and social skills (Ercikan, 2006). Critics point out that teachers end up spending far too much class time "teaching to the test" by drilling students and having them memorize isolated facts at the expense of teaching that focuses on thinking skills, which students need for success in life (Pressley, 2007). Also, recall from Chapter 12 that some individuals are concerned that in the era of No Child Left Behind policy there is a neglect of students who are gifted in the effort to raise the achievement level of students who are not doing well (Clark, 2008; Cloud, 2007).

Consider also that one goal of NCLB is to close the ethnic achievement gap that characterizes lower achievement by African American and Latino students and higher achievement by Asian American and non-Latino White students. However, leading expert Linda Darling-Hammond (2007) recently concluded that NCLB has failed to reach this goal. She criticizes NCLB for inappropriate assessment of English-language learners and students with special needs, strong incentives to exclude low-achieving students from school to achieve test score targets, and the continued shortage of highly qualified teachers in high-need schools.

What characterizes the U.S. government's No Child Left Behind legislation? What are some criticisms of No Child Left Behind?

Despite such criticisms, the U.S. Department of Education is committed to implementing No Child Left Behind, and schools are making accommodations to meet the requirement of this law. Indeed, most educators support the importance of high expectations and high standards of excellence for students and teachers. At issue, however, is whether the tests and procedures mandated by NCLB are the best ones for achieving these high standards (Yell & Drasgow, 2009).

Socioeconomic Status and Ethnicity

Children from low-income, ethnic minority backgrounds often have more difficulties in school than do their middle-socioeconomic-status, non-Latino White counterparts. Why? Critics argue that schools have not done a good job of educating low-income, ethnic minority students to overcome the barriers to their achievement (Gollnick &

constructivist approach A learner-centered approach that emphasizes the importance of individuals actively constructing their knowledge and understanding with guidance from the teacher.

direct instruction approach A structured, teacher-centered approach that is characterized by teacher direction and control, mastery of academic skills, high expectations for students' progress, maximum time spent on learning tasks, and efforts to keep negative affect to a minimum.

Jill Nakamura, teaching in her first-grade classroom. Jill Nakamura teaches at a school located in a high-poverty area. She visits students at home early in the school year in an effort to connect with them and develop a partnership with their parents. "She holds a daily after school club for students reading below grade level . . . ; those who don't want to attend must call parents to tell them." In one school year (2004), she raised the percentage of students reading at or above grade level from 29 percent to 76 percent (Wong Briggs, 2004, p. 6D).

Chinn, 2009; Taylor & Whittaker, 2009). Let's further explore the roles of socioeconomic status and ethnicity in schools.

The Education of Students from Low-Income Backgrounds

Many children in poverty face problems that present barriers to their learning (Ballentine & Hammock, 2009; Burrington & Browning, 2009; McLoyd & others, 2009). They might have parents who don't set high educational standards for them, who are incapable of reading to them, or who don't have enough money to pay for educational materials and experiences, such as books and trips to zoos and museums. They might be malnourished or live in areas where crime and violence are a way of life. A recent study revealed that neighborhood disadvantage (involving such characteristics as low neighborhood income and high unemployment) was linked to less consistent, less stimulating, and more punitive parenting, and ultimately to negative child outcomes such as behavioral problems and low verbal ability (Kohen & others, 2008). Another recent study revealed that the longer children experienced poverty the more detrimental the poverty was to their cognitive development (Najman & others, 2009).

Compared with schools in higher-income areas, schools in low-income areas are more likely to have more students with low achievement test scores, low graduation rates, and small percentages of students going to college; they are more likely to have young teachers with less experience; and they are more likely to encourage rote learning (Spring, 2008). Too few schools in low-income neighborhoods provide students with environments that are conducive to learning (Leventhal, Dupere, & Brooks-Gunn, 2009; Nelson & Lee, 2009). Many of the schools' buildings and classrooms are old and crumbling. These are the types of undesirable conditions Jonathan Kozol (2005) observed in many inner-city schools, including the South Bronx in New York City, as described at the beginning of the chapter. To read about ways to improve the schools and families of children living in poverty, see the *Diversity in Children's Development* interlude.

Diversity in Children's Development

THE NEW HOPE INTERVENTION PROGRAM

In sum, as we have just discussed, far too many schools in low-income neighborhoods provide students with environments that are not conducive to effective learning (Ballentine & Hammock, 2009; Hutson, 2008).

Might intervention with families of children living in poverty improve children's school performance? In a recent experimental study, Aletha Huston and her colleagues (2006; Gupta, Thornton, & Huston, 2007) evaluated the effects of New Hope, a program designed to increase parental employment and reduce family poverty, on adolescent development. They randomly assigned families with 6- to 10-year-old children living in poverty to the New Hope program and a control group. New Hope offered adults living in poverty who were employed 30 or more hours a week benefits that were designed to increase family income (a wage supplement that ensured that net income increased as parents earned more) and provide work supports through subsidized child care (for any child under age 13) and health insurance. Management services were provided to New Hope participants to assist them in job searches and other needs. The New Hope program was available to the experimental group families for three years (until the children were 9 to 13 years old). Five years after the program began and two years after it had ended, the program's effects on the children were examined when they were 11 to 16 years old. Compared with adolescents in the control group, New Hope adolescents were more competent at reading, had better school performance, were less likely to be in special education classes, had more positive social skills, and were more likely to be in formal after-school arrangements. New Hope parents reported better psychological well-being and a greater sense of self-efficacy in managing their adolescents than control parents did.

Ethnicity in Schools More than one-third of all African American and almost one-third of all Latino students attend schools in the 47 largest city school districts in the United States, compared with only 5 percent of all non-Latino White and 22 percent of all Asian American students. Many of these inner-city schools are still informally segregated, are grossly underfunded and, do not provide adequate opportunities for children to learn effectively. Thus, the effects of SES and the effects of ethnic minority status are often intertwined (Liu & others, 2009; Tewari & Alvarez, 2009).

Even outside inner-city schools, school segregation remains a factor in U.S. education (Nieto & Bode, 2008). Almost one-third of all African American and Latino students attend schools in which 90 percent or more of the students are from minority groups (Banks, 2008).

The school experiences of students from different ethnic groups vary considerably (Healey, 2009; McLoyd & others, 2009; Rowley, Kurtz-Costas, & Cooper, 2010). African American and Latino students are much less likely than non-Latino White or Asian American students to be enrolled in academic, college preparatory programs and are much more likely to be enrolled in remedial and special education programs. Asian American students are far more likely than other ethnic minority groups to take advanced math and science courses in high school. African American students are twice as likely as Latinos, Native Americans, or Whites to be suspended from school.

Following are some effective strategies for improving relationships among ethnically diverse students:

In *The Shame of the Nation,* Jonathan Kozol (2005) criticized the inadequate quality and lack of resources in many U.S. schools, especially those in the poverty areas of inner cities, that have high concentrations of ethnic minority children. Kozol praises teachers like Angela Lively (*above*), who keeps a box of shoes in her Indianapolis classroom for students in need.

How Would You...?
As an educator, how would you attempt to improve the quality of schools with high concentrations of ethnic minority children?

- *Turn the class into a jigsaw classroom.* When Elliot Aronson was a professor at the University of Texas at Austin, the school system contacted him for ideas on how to reduce the increasing racial tension in classrooms. Aronson (1986) developed the concept of "jigsaw classroom," in which students from different cultural backgrounds are placed in a cooperative group in which they have to construct different parts of a project to reach a common goal. Aronson used the term *jigsaw* because he saw the technique to be like a group of students cooperating to put different pieces together to complete a jigsaw puzzle. How might this work? Team sports, drama productions, and music performances are examples of contexts in which students participate cooperatively to reach a common goal; however, the jigsaw technique also lends itself to group science projects, history reports, and other learning experiences with a variety of subject matter.

- *Encourage students to have positive personal contact with diverse other students.* Mere contact does not do the job of improving relationships with diverse others. For example, busing ethnic minority students to predominantly non-Latino

What are some features of a jigsaw classroom?

White schools, or vice versa, has not reduced prejudice or improved interethnic relations. What matters is what happens after children get to school. Especially beneficial in improving interethnic relations is sharing one's worries, successes, failures, coping strategies, interests, and other personal information with people of other ethnicities. When this happens, people tend to look at others as individuals rather than as members of a homogeneous group.

• *Reduce bias.* Teachers can reduce bias by displaying images of children from diverse ethnic and cultural groups, selecting play materials and classroom activities that encourage cultural understanding, helping students resist stereotyping, and working with parents to reduce children's exposure to bias and prejudice at home.

• *View the school and community as a team.* James Comer (1988, 2004, 2006) advocates a community, team approach as the best way to educate children. Three important aspects of the Comer Project for Change are (1) a governance and management team that develops a comprehensive school plan, assessment strategy, and staff development plan; (2) a mental health or school support team; and (3) a parents' program. Comer believes that the entire school community should have a cooperative rather than an adversarial attitude. The Comer program is currently operating in more than 600 schools in 26 states. Read further about James Comer's work in the *Careers in Children's Development* profile.

• *Be a competent cultural mediator.* Teachers can play a powerful role as cultural mediators by being sensitive to biased content in materials and classroom interactions, learning more about different ethnic groups, being sensitive to children's ethnic attitudes, viewing students of color positively, and thinking of positive ways to get parents of color more involved as partners with teachers in educating children.

Careers in Children's Development

James Comer, Child Psychiatrist

James Comer grew up in a low-income neighborhood in East Chicago, Indiana, and credits his parents with leaving no doubt about the importance of education. He obtained a BA degree from Indiana University. He went on to obtain a medical degree from Howard University College of Medicine, a Master of Public Health degree from the University of Michigan School of Public Health, and psychiatry training at the Yale University School of Medicine's Child Study Center. He currently is the Maurice Falk Professor of Child Psychiatry at the Yale University Child Study Center and an associate dean at the Yale University Medical School. During his years at Yale, Comer has concentrated his career on promoting a focus on child development as a way of improving schools. His efforts in support of healthy development of young people are known internationally.

Comer is, perhaps, best known for the founding of the School Development Program in 1968, which promotes the collaboration of parents, educators, and community to improve social, emotional, and academic outcomes for children.

James Comer (*left*) is shown with some of the inner-city African American children who attend a school that became a better learning environment because of Comer's intervention.

Review and Reflect: Learning Goal 4

4   **Characterize contemporary approaches to student learning and sociocultural diversity in schools**

REVIEW

- What are two major contemporary issues in educating children?
- How do socioeconomic status and ethnicity influence schooling?

REFLECT

- Should the United States be worried about the low performance of its students in mathematics and science in comparison to Asian students? Are Americans' expectations for students too low?

Reach Your Learning Goals

Socioemotional Development in Middle and Late Childhood

1 WHAT IS THE NATURE OF EMOTIONAL AND PERSONALITY DEVELOPMENT IN MIDDLE AND LATE CHILDHOOD? DISCUSS EMOTIONAL AND PERSONALITY DEVELOPMENT IN MIDDLE AND LATE CHILDHOOD

The Self

- In middle and late childhood, self-understanding increasingly involves social and psychological characteristics, including social comparison. Children increase their perspective taking in middle and late childhood, and their social understanding shows increasing psychological sophistication as well. Self-concept refers to domain-specific evaluations of the self. Self-esteem refers to global evaluations of the self and is also referred to as self-worth or self-image. Self-esteem is only moderately related to school performance but is more strongly linked to initiative. Four ways to increase self-esteem are to (1) identify the causes of low self-esteem, (2) provide emotional support and social approval, (3) help children achieve, and (4) help children cope. Erikson's fourth stage of development, industry versus inferiority, characterizes the middle and late childhood years.

Emotional Development

- Developmental changes in emotion include increasing one's understanding of complex emotions such as pride and shame, detecting that more than one emotion can be experienced in a particular situation, taking into account the circumstances that led up to an emotional reaction, improving the ability to suppress or conceal negative emotions, and using self-initiated strategies to redirect feelings. As children get older, they use a greater variety of coping strategies and more cognitive strategies.

Moral Development

- Kohlberg argued that moral development consists of three levels—preconventional, conventional, and postconventional—and six stages (two at each level). Kohlberg maintained that these stages were age-related. Influences on movement through the stages include cognitive development, imitation and cognitive conflict, peer relations, and perspective taking. Criticisms of Kohlberg's theory have been made, especially by Gilligan, who advocates a stronger care perspective. Other criticisms focus on the inadequacy of moral reasoning to predict moral behavior, culture and family influences, and the distinction between moral reasoning and social conventional reasoning. Prosocial behavior involves positive moral behaviors such as sharing. Most sharing in the first three years is not done for empathy, but at about 4 years of age empathy contributes to sharing. By the start of the elementary school years, children express objective ideas about fairness. Recently, there has been a surge of interest in moral personality.

Gender

- Gender stereotypes are broad categories that reflect impressions and beliefs about males and females. A number of physical differences exist between males and females. In terms of cognitive skills, girls have better reading and writing skills than do boys. Some experts argue that cognitive differences between males and females have been exaggerated. In terms of socioemotional differences, males are more physically aggressive than females. Tannen argues that females prefer rapport talk and males prefer report talk, but recent research indicates that Tannen's view is overly simplified. Females regulate their emotions better and engage in more prosocial behavior than males. Gender-role classification focuses on how masculine, feminine, or androgynous individuals are. Androgyny means having both positive feminine and masculine characteristics. It is important to think about gender in terms of context.

2 WHAT ARE SOME CHANGES IN PARENTING AND FAMILIES IN MIDDLE AND LATE CHILDHOOD? DESCRIBE CHANGES IN PARENTING AND FAMILIES IN MIDDLE AND LATE CHILDHOOD

Developmental Changes in Parent-Child Relationships

- Parents spend less time with children during middle and late childhood than in early childhood. Parents especially play an important role in supporting and stimulating children's academic achievement. Discipline changes and control are more coregulatory.

Parents as Managers

- Parents have important roles as managers of children's opportunities, as monitors of their behavior, and as social initiators and arrangers. Mothers are more likely to function in these parental management roles than fathers.

Stepfamilies

- As in divorced families, children living in stepparent families have more adjustment problems than their counterparts in nondivorced families. However, a majority of children in stepfamilies do not have adjustment problems. Children in complex (blended) stepfamilies have more problems than children in simple stepfamilies or nondivorced families.

3 WHAT CHANGES CHARACTERIZE PEER RELATIONSHIPS IN MIDDLE AND LATE CHILDHOOD? IDENTIFY CHANGES IN PEER RELATIONSHIPS IN MIDDLE AND LATE CHILDHOOD

Developmental Changes

- Among the developmental changes in peer relations in middle and late childhood are increased preference for same-sex groups, an increase in time spent in peer interaction and the size of the peer group, and less supervision of the peer group by adults.

Peer Status

- Popular children are frequently nominated as a best friend and are rarely disliked by their peers. Average children receive an average number of both positive and negative nominations from their peers. Neglected children are infrequently nominated as a best friend but are not disliked by their peers. Rejected children are infrequently nominated as a best friend and are actively disliked by their peers. Controversial children are frequently nominated both as a best friend and as being disliked by peers. Rejected children are especially at risk for a number of problems.

Social Cognition

- Social information-processing skills and social knowledge are two important dimensions of social cognition in peer relations.

Bullying

- Significant numbers of children are bullied, and this can result in short-term and long-term negative effects for both the victims and the bullies.

Friends

- Like adult friends, children who are friends tend to be similar to each other. Children's friendships serve six functions: companionship, stimulation, physical support, ego support, social comparison, and intimacy/affection.

4 WHAT ARE SOME IMPORTANT ASPECTS OF SCHOOLS? CHARACTERIZE CONTEMPORARY APPROACHES TO STUDENT LEARNING AND SOCIOCULTURAL DIVERSITY IN SCHOOLS

Contemporary Approaches to Student Learning

- Contemporary approaches to student learning include the constructivist approach (a learner-centered approach) and the direct instruction approach (a teacher-centered approach). In the United States, standardized testing of elementary schools students has been mandated nationally in 2002 by the No Child Left Behind federal legislation. Numerous criticisms of NCLB have been made.

Socioeconomic Status and Ethnicity

- Children in poverty face many barriers to learning at school as well as at home. The effects of SES and ethnicity on schools are intertwined, as many U.S. schools are segregated. Low expectations for ethnic minority children represent one of the barriers to their learning.

KEY TERMS

perspective taking 425
self-esteem 426
self-concept 426
preconventional
    reasoning 430
heteronomous morality 430
individualism, instrumental
    purpose, and
    exchange 430
conventional reasoning 431

mutual interpersonal
    expectations,
    relationships, and
    interpersonal
    conformity 431
social systems morality 431
postconventional
    reasoning 431
social contract or utility and
    individual rights 431

universal ethical
    principles 431
justice perspective 434
care perspective 434
social conventional
    reasoning 434
gender stereotypes 435
rapport talk 438
report talk 438
androgyny 439

popular children 444
average children 444
neglected children 444
rejected children 444
controversial children 444
intimacy in friendships 449
constructivist
    approach 451
direct instruction
    approach 451

KEY PEOPLE

Jonathan Kozol 424
Diane Ruble 425
Erik Erikson 428
Lawrence Kohlberg 430
Carol Gilligan 433

William Damon 434
Deborah Tannen 438
Sandra Bem 440
William Pollack 440
E. Mavis Hetherington 443

John Coie 445
Kenneth Dodge 446
Dan Olweus 448
Willard Hartup 448
Linda Darling-Hammond 451

Aletha Huston 452
Elliot Aronson 453
James Comer 454

MAKING A DIFFERENCE

Guiding Children's Socioemotional Development

What are some good strategies for nourishing children's socioemotional skills?

- *Improve children's self-esteem.* This can be accomplished by identifying the causes of the child's low self-esteem, providing emotional support and social approval, and helping the child achieve.

- *Help children understand their emotions and cope with stress.* When children are experiencing considerable stress, try to remove at least one stressor from their lives. Also help the child learn effective coping strategies.

- *Nurture children's moral development.* Parents can improve their children's morality by being warm and supportive rather than punitive, using reasoning when disciplining, providing opportunities for children to learn about others' perspectives and feelings, involving children in family decision making, and modeling prosocial moral behavior.

- *Adapt to developmental changes in children.* Because parents typically spend less time with children in middle and late childhood, it is important to strengthen children's self-control. As in early

childhood, authoritative parenting should continue to be the choice, rather than authoritarian or permissive parenting.

- *Improve children's peer and friendship skills.* Peer and friendship relations become increasingly important to elementary school children. Adults can talk with children about the importance of being nice, engaging in prosocial behavior, and providing support in getting peers and friends to like them. Parents also can communicate to children that being aggressive, self-centered, and inconsiderate of others harms peer and friendship relations.

- *Create schools that support children's socioemotional development.* Not only do good teachers know how to challenge and stimulate children's cognitive development, but they also know how to make children feel good about themselves. Too much of elementary school education involves negative feedback. We need more classrooms in which children are excited about learning. This learning should be designed to increase children's self-esteem, not wreck their emotional well-being. Parents need to encourage and support their children's educational accomplishments but not set unrealistic achievement expectations.

RESOURCES FOR IMPROVING CHILDREN'S LIVES

Raising Black Children
by James P. Comer and Alvin E. Poussaint (1992)
New York: Plume

Raising Black Children is an excellent book for African American parents. It includes wise suggestions that are not in most child-rearing books (almost all others are written for middle-class White parents and do not deal with special problems faced by ethnic minority parents or parents from low-income backgrounds).

National Stepfamily Resource Center
www.stepfamilies.info

This center provides a clearinghouse and support network for stepparents, remarried parents, and their children.

E-LEARNING TOOLS

Connect to **www.mhhe.com/santrockc11e** to research the answers and complete these exercises. In addition, you'll find a number of other resources and valuable study tools for Chapter 13, "Socioemotional Development in Middle and Late Childhood," on this Web site.

Taking It to the Net

1. Frank is researching the latest information on bullying after his younger brother told him of his recent experiences with bullies at his junior high school. What information is available on the prevalence of bullying, the makeup of the children who bully, and why is this type of behavior is increasing?

2. Ellen is taking a class in gender psychology. She wants to test the theory of androgyny among her peers in her large geology lecture. She has heard that there is an online version of the test and thinks people will feel more comfortable taking it online. What conclusions can Ellen draw on the androgyny theory after taking this test?

Health and Well-Being, Parenting, and Education

Build your decision-making skills by trying your hand at the health and well-being, parenting, and education exercises.

Video Clips

The Online Learning Center includes the following videos for this chapter:

- *Best Friends at Age 7—1120*
  John describes that he plays with his best friend and that they listen to music together.

- *Describing Friendships at Age 8—1656*
  A boy describes his two best friends and what they like to do together. When asked if he has any girlfriends, he quickly responds, "No." But then he adds that his sisters are his friends.

- *Self-Perception at 10 Years and 8 Years of Age—1669*
  Two Mexican-origin siblings, Laura and Jared, are asked to describe themselves. Laura responds that she works hard, tries her best, and talks too much. Jared, however, responds only that he does not talk that much.

- *Describing Best Friends at Age 11—1722*
  An 11-year-old girl talks about her best friends and how they helped her through "sad times."

ADOLESCENCE

In no order of things is adolescence the simple time of life.

—JEAN ERSKINE STEWART
American Writer, 20th Century

Adolescents try on one face after another, seeking to find a

face of their own. Their generation of young people is the

fragile cable by which the best and the worst of their parents'

generation is transmitted to the present. In the end, there are

only two lasting bequests parents can leave youth—one being

roots, the other wings. Section 6 contains three chapters:

"Physical Development in Adolescence" (Chapter 14),

"Cognitive Development in Adolescence" (Chapter 15), and

"Socioemotional Development in Adolescence" (Chapter 16).

14

In youth, we clothe ourselves with rainbows, and go brave as the zodiac.

—RALPH WALDO EMERSON
American Poet, 19th Century

LEARNING GOALS

◆ Discuss views and developmental transitions that involve adolescence

◆ Describe puberty's characteristics, developmental changes, psychological dimensions, and the development of the brain

◆ Characterize adolescent sexuality

◆ Summarize adolescents' health and eating disorders

PHYSICAL DEVELOPMENT IN ADOLESCENCE

CHAPTER OUTLINE

Images of Children's Development
Latisha, Arnie, and Katie

Fifteen-year-old Latisha developed a drinking problem, and recently she was kicked off the cheerleading squad for missing practice so often—but that didn't stop her drinking. She and her friends began skipping school regularly so they could drink.

Fourteen-year-old Arnie is a juvenile delinquent. Last week he stole a TV set, struck his mother and bloodied her face, broke out some streetlights in the neighborhood, and threatened a boy with a wrench and hammer.

Twelve-year-old Katie Bell, more than just about anything else, wanted a playground in her town. She knew that the other kids also wanted one so she put together a group that generated funding ideas for the playground. They presented their ideas to the town council. Her group got more youth involved, and they raised money by selling candy and sandwiches door-to-door. The playground became a reality, a place where, as Katie says, "People have picnics and make friends." Katie's advice: "You won't get anywhere if you don't try."

Adolescents like Latisha and Arnie are the ones we hear about the most. But there are many adolescents like Katie who contribute in positive ways to their community and competently make the transition through adolescence. Indeed, for most adolescents, adolescence is not a time of rebellion, crisis, pathology, and deviance. A far more accurate vision of adolescence is that it is a time of evaluation, decision making, commitment, and carving out a place in the world. Most of the problems of today's youth are not with the youth themselves. What adolescents need is access to a range of legitimate opportunities and to long-term support from adults who care deeply about them.

Katie Bell (*front*) and some of her volunteers.

PREVIEW

Adolescence is an important juncture in the lives of many individuals, a time when many health habits—good or bad—are formed and ingrained. In this chapter, we explore what adolescence is, examine its physical and psychological changes, discuss adolescent sexuality, and then describe several adolescent problems and health.

1 WHAT IS THE NATURE OF ADOLESCENCE?

Positive and Negative Views of Adolescence

Developmental Transitions

As in development during childhood, genetic, biological, environmental, and social factors interact in adolescent development. During their first decade of life, adolescents experienced thousands of hours of interactions with parents, peers, and teachers, but now they face dramatic biological changes, new experiences, and new developmental tasks. Relationships with parents take a different form, moments with peers become more intimate, and dating occurs for the first time, as do sexual exploration and possibly intercourse. The adolescent's thoughts are more abstract and idealistic. Biological changes trigger a heightened interest in body image. Adolescence has both continuity and discontinuity with childhood.

Positive and Negative Views of Adolescence

There is a long history of worrying about how adolescents will turn out. In 1904, G. Stanley Hall proposed the "storm-and-stress" view that adolescence is a turbulent time charged with conflict and mood swings. However, when Daniel Offer and his colleagues (1988) studied the self-images of adolescents in the United States, Australia, Bangladesh, Hungary, Israel, Italy, Japan, Taiwan, Turkey, and West Germany, at least 73 percent of the adolescents displayed a healthy self-image. Although there were differences among them, the adolescents were happy most of the time, they enjoyed life, they perceived themselves as able to exercise self-control, they valued work and school, they expressed confidence about their sexual selves, they expressed positive feelings toward their families, and they felt they had the capability to cope with life's stresses—not exactly a storm-and-stress portrayal of adolescence.

However, in matters of taste and manners, the young people of every generation have seemed radical, unnerving, and different from adults—different in how they look, in how they behave, in the music they enjoy, in their hairstyles, and in the clothing they choose. It is an enormous error, though, to confuse adolescents' enthusiasm for trying on new identities and enjoying moderate amounts of outrageous behavior with hostility toward parental and societal standards. Acting out and boundary testing are time-honored ways in which adolescents move toward accepting, rather than rejecting, parental values.

What has been called *positive youth development (PYD)* in adolescence reflects the positive psychology approach. Positive youth development emphasizes the strengths of youth and the positive qualities and developmental trajectories that are desired for youth. Positive youth development has especially been promoted by Jacqueline Lerner and her colleagues (2009), who recently described the "Five Cs" of PYD:

- *Competence*, which involves having a positive perception of one's actions in domain-specific areas—social, academic, physical, career, and so on
- *Confidence*, which consists of having an overall positive sense of self-worth and self-efficacy (a sense that one can master a situation and produce positive outcomes)

Growing up has never been easy. However, adolescence is not best viewed as a time of rebellion, crisis, pathology, and deviance. A far more accurate vision of adolescence describes it as a time of evaluation, of decision making, of commitment, and of carving out a place in the world. Most of the problems of today's youth are not with the youth themselves. What adolescents need is access to a range of legitimate opportunities and to long-term support from adults who deeply care about them. *What might be some examples of such support and caring?*

- *Connection,* which is characterized by having positive relationships with others, including family, peers, teachers, and individuals in the community
- *Character,* which is comprised of having respect for societal rules, an understanding of right and wrong, and integrity
- *Caring/compassion,* which encompasses showing emotional concern for others, especially those in distress

Lerner and her colleagues (2009) conclude that to develop these five positive characteristics, youth need access to positive social contexts—such as youth development programs and organized youth activities—and competent people—such as caring teachers, community leaders, and mentors.

Most adolescents negotiate the lengthy path to adult maturity successfully, but too large a group does not. Ethnic, cultural, gender, socioeconomic, age, and lifestyle differences influence the actual life trajectory of every adolescent (Fuligni, Hughes, & Way, 2009; McLoyd & others, 2009). Different portrayals of adolescence emerge, depending on the particular group of adolescents being described. Today's adolescents are exposed to a complex menu of lifestyle options through technology, and many face the temptations of drug use and sexual activity at increasingly young ages. Too many adolescents are not provided with adequate opportunities and support to become competent adults (Balsano, Theokas, & Bobek, 2009; Lerner, Roeser, & Phelps, 2009).

One concern about the current generation of adolescents was recently voiced in *The Path to Purpose* by leading expert on adolescence William Damon (2008). Damon argues that many American adults have become effective at finding short-term solutions to various tasks and problems to get through their lives, and they are instilling the same immediate gratification, shortsighted thinking in their children and adolescents. In Damon's view, while these short-term solutions (such as getting homework done, getting a good grade on a test tomorrow, and making a team) are often necessary adaptations to a situation, they can distract adolescents from thinking about their life purpose, such as "What kind of person do I want to be? What do I want to do with my life? Why should I try to be successful?" Damon further emphasizes that parents can help to remedy this problem by giving them options and guiding them through choices, as well as talking with them about paths, themes, and issues in their own lives that they find meaningful and communicating how they have coped with setbacks and dilemmas. We expand on Damon's concept of the path to purpose later in the text in our discussion of values and religion in Chapter 15, "Cognitive Development in Adolescence," and identity development in Chapter 16, "Socioemotional Development in Adolescence."

Developmental Transitions

Developmental transitions are often important junctures in people's lives. Such transitions include moving from the prenatal period to birth and infancy, from infancy to early childhood, and from early childhood to middle and late childhood. For adolescents, two important transitions are from childhood to adolescence and from adolescence to adulthood. Let's explore these transitions.

Childhood to Adolescence   The transition from childhood to adolescence involves a number of biological, cognitive, and socioemotional changes. Among the biological changes are the growth spurt, hormonal changes, and sexual maturation that come with puberty. In early adolescence, changes take place in the brain that allow for more advanced thinking. Also at this time, adolescents begin to stay up later and sleep later in the morning.

Among the cognitive changes that occur during the transition from childhood to adolescence are increases in abstract, idealistic, and logical thinking. As they make this transition, adolescents begin to think in more egocentric ways, often sensing that they are onstage, unique, and invulnerable. In response to these changes, parents place more responsibility for decision making on the young adolescents' shoulders.

Among the socioemotional changes adolescents undergo are a quest for independence, conflict with parents, and a desire to spend more time with peers. Conversations with friends become more intimate and include more self-disclosure. As children enter adolescence, they attend schools that are larger and more impersonal than their neighborhood grade schools. Achievement becomes a more serious business, and academic challenges increase. At this time, increased sexual maturation produces a much greater interest in romantic relationships. Young adolescents also experience greater mood swings than they did when they were children.

In sum, the transition from childhood to adolescence is complex and multidimensional, involving change in many different aspects of an individual's life (Crosnoe & Trinitapoli, 2008). Negotiating this transition successfully requires considerable adaptation and thoughtful, sensitive support from caring adults.

What are some physical, cognitive, and socioemotional changes involved in the transition from childhood to adolescence? What characterizes emerging adulthood?

Adolescence to Adulthood: Emerging Adulthood   Another important transition occurs from adolescence to adulthood (Arnett, 2007). It has been said that adolescence begins in biology and ends in culture. That is, the transition from childhood to adolescence begins with the onset of pubertal maturation, whereas the transition from adolescence to adulthood is determined by cultural standards and experiences. Around the world, youth are increasingly expected to delay their entry into adulthood, in large part because the information society in which we now live requires that they obtain more education than their parents' generation (Hamilton & Hamilton, 2006). Thus, the transition between adolescence and adulthood can be a long one as adolescents develop more effective skills to become full members of society.

Recently, the transition from adolescence to adulthood has been referred to as **emerging adulthood** (Arnett, 2000, 2006, 2007). The age range for emerging adulthood is approximately 18 to 25 years of age. Experimentation and exploration characterize the emerging adult. At this point in their development, many individuals are still exploring which career path they want to follow, what they want their identity to be, and which lifestyle they want to adopt (for example, single, cohabiting, or married).

Jeffrey Arnett (2006) recently concluded that five key features characterize emerging adulthood:

- *Exploring identity, especially in love and work.* Emerging adulthood is the time during which key changes in identity take place for many individuals.

- *Experiencing instability.* Residential changes peak during early adulthood, a time during which there also is often instability in love, work, and education.

- *Being self-focused.* According to Arnett (2006, p. 10), emerging adults "are self-focused in the sense that they have little in the way of social obligations, little in the way of duties and commitments to others, which leaves with a great deal of autonomy in running their own lives."

- *Feeling in-between.* Many emerging adults don't consider themselves adolescents or full-fledged adults.

- *Experiencing the age of possibilities, a time when individuals have an opportunity to transform their lives.* Arnett (2006) describes two ways in which emerging adulthood is the age of possibilities. First, many emerging adults are optimistic about their future. Second, for emerging adults who have experienced difficult times while growing up, emerging adulthood presents an opportunity to direct their lives in a more positive direction (Masten, Obradovic, & Burt, 2006).

emerging adulthood Occurring from approximately 18 to 25 years of age, this transitional period between adolescence and adulthood is characterized by experimentation and exploration.

Review and Reflect: Learning Goal 1

1   **Discuss views and developmental transitions that involve adolescence**

REVIEW

- What are some positive and negative views of adolescence?
- What are two key developmental transitions involving adolescence?

REFLECT

- You likely experienced some instances of stereotyping as an adolescent. What are some examples of the circumstances in which you feel that you were stereotyped as an adolescent?

---

2 WHAT ARE THE PHYSICAL AND PSYCHOLOGICAL ASPECTS OF PUBERTY?

Sexual Maturation, Height, and Weight	Hormonal Changes	Timing and Variations in Puberty	Psychological Dimensions of Puberty	The Brain

One father remarked that the problem with his teenage son was not that he grew, but that he did not know when to stop growing. As we will see, there is considerable variation in the timing of the adolescent growth spurt. In addition to pubertal changes, other physical changes we explore involve sexuality and the brain.

Puberty is not the same as adolescence. For most of us, puberty ends long before adolescence does, although puberty is the most important marker of the beginning of adolescence. **Puberty** is a period of rapid physical maturation involving hormonal and bodily changes that occur primarily during early adolescence. Puberty is not a single, sudden event. We know whether a young boy or girl is going through puberty, but pinpointing puberty's beginning and end is difficult. Among the most noticeable changes are signs of sexual maturation and increases in height and weight.

Sexual Maturation, Height, and Weight

Think back to the onset of your puberty. Of all the striking changes that were taking place in your body, what was the first to occur? Researchers have found that male pubertal characteristics typically develop in this order: increase in penis and testicle size, appearance of straight pubic hair, minor voice change, first ejaculation (which usually occurs through masturbation or a wet dream), appearance of curly pubic hair, onset of maximum growth in height and weight, growth of hair in armpits, more detectable voice changes, and, finally, growth of facial hair.

What is the order of appearance of physical changes in females? First, either the breasts enlarge or pubic hair appears. Later, hair appears in the armpits. As these changes occur, the female grows in height and her hips become wider than her shoulders. **Menarche**—a girl's first menstruation—comes rather late in the pubertal cycle. Initially, her menstrual cycles may be highly irregular. For the first several years, she may not ovulate every menstrual cycle; some girls do not ovulate at all until a year or two after menstruation begins. No voice changes comparable to those in

puberty A period of rapid physical maturation involving hormonal and bodily changes that occur primarily in early adolescence.

menarche A girl's first menstrual period.

hormones Powerful chemical substances secreted by the endocrine glands and carried through the body by the bloodstream.

hypothalamus A structure in the brain that monitors eating and sex.

pituitary gland An important endocrine gland that controls growth and regulates other glands.

pubertal males occur in pubertal females. By the end of puberty, the female's breasts have become more fully rounded.

Marked weight gains coincide with the onset of puberty. During early adolescence, girls tend to outweigh boys, but by about age 14 boys begin to surpass girls. Similarly, at the beginning of the adolescent period, girls tend to be as tall as or taller than boys of their age, but by the end of the middle school years most boys have caught up or, in many cases, surpassed girls in height.

As indicated in Figure 14.1, the growth spurt occurs approximately two years earlier for girls than for boys. The mean age at the beginning of the growth spurt in girls is 9; for boys, it is 11. The peak rate of pubertal change occurs at 11½ years for girls and 13½ years for boys. During their growth spurt, girls increase in height about 3½ inches per year, boys about 4 inches. Boys and girls who are shorter or taller than their peers before adolescence are likely to remain so during adolescence; however, as much as 30 percent of an individual's height in late adolescence is unexplained by his or her height in the elementary school years.

Hormonal Changes

Behind the first whisker in boys and the widening of hips in girls is a flood of **hormones,** powerful chemical substances secreted by the endocrine glands and carried through the body by the bloodstream. The endocrine system's role in puberty involves the interaction of the hypothalamus, the pituitary gland, and the gonads (see Figure 14.2). The **hypothalamus** is a structure in the brain that is involved with eating and sex. The **pituitary gland** is an important endocrine gland that

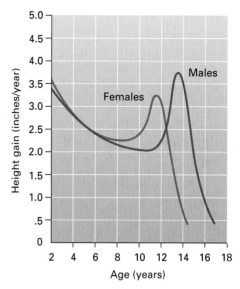

FIGURE 14.1 Pubertal Growth Spurt On the average, the peak of the growth spurt during puberty occurs two years earlier for girls (11½) than for boys (13½). *How are hormones related to the growth spurt and to the difference between the average height of adolescent boys and girls?*

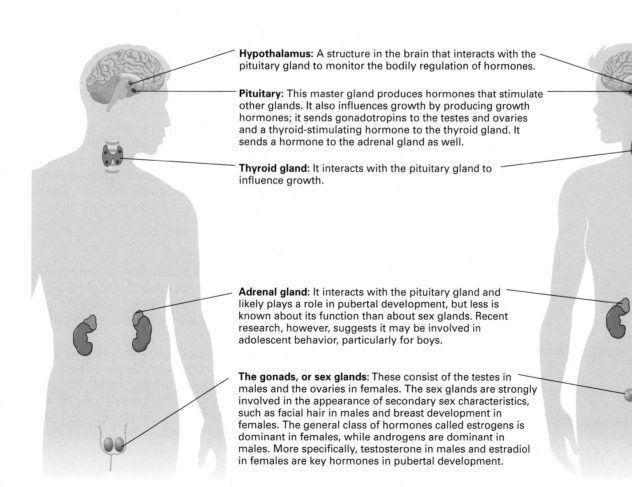

FIGURE 14.2 The Major Endocrine Glands Involved in Pubertal Change

controls growth and regulates other glands; among these, the **gonads**—the testes in males, the ovaries in females—are particularly important in giving rise to pubertal changes in the body.

How do the gonads, or sex glands, work? The pituitary sends a signal via **gonadotropins**—hormones that stimulate the testes or ovaries—to the appropriate gland to manufacture hormones. These hormones give rise to such changes as the production of sperm in males and menstruation and the release of eggs from the ovaries in females. The pituitary gland, through interaction with the hypothalamus, detects when the optimal level of hormones is reached and responds and maintains it with additional gonadotropin secretion.

Not only does the pituitary gland release gonadotropins that stimulate the testes and ovaries, but through interaction with the hypothalamus the pituitary gland also secretes hormones that either directly lead to growth and skeletal maturation or that produce growth effects through interaction with the thyroid gland, located at the base of the throat.

The concentrations of certain hormones increase dramatically during adolescence (Herbison & others, 2008; Susman & Dorn, 2009). **Testosterone** is a hormone associated in boys with the development of genitals, an increase in height, and a change in voice. **Estradiol** is a type of estrogen; in girls it is associated with breast, uterine, and skeletal development. In one study, testosterone levels increased eighteenfold in boys but only twofold in girls during puberty; estradiol increased eightfold in girls but only twofold in boys (Nottelmann & others, 1987). Thus, both testosterone and estradiol are present in the hormonal makeup of both boys and girls, but testosterone dominates in male pubertal development, estradiol in female pubertal development (Richmond & Rogol, 2007).

The same influx of hormones that grows hair on a male's chest and increases the fatty tissue in a female's breasts may also contribute to psychological development in adolescence (DeRose & Brooks-Gunn, 2008). In one study of boys and girls ranging in age from 9 to 14, a higher concentration of testosterone was present in boys who rated themselves as more socially competent (Nottelmann & others, 1987). However, hormonal effects by themselves do not account for adolescent development (Graber, 2008). For example, in one study, social factors were much better predictors of young adolescent girls' depression and anger than hormonal factors (Brooks-Gunn & Warren, 1989). Behavior and moods also can affect hormones. Stress, eating patterns, exercise, sexual activity, tension, and depression can activate or suppress various aspects of the hormonal system (Sontag & others, 2008). In sum, the hormone-behavior link is complex (Susman & Dorn, 2009).

Timing and Variations in Puberty

In the United States—where children mature up to a year earlier than children in European countries—the average age of menarche has declined significantly since the mid-nineteenth century. Fortunately, however, we are unlikely to see pubescent toddlers, since what has happened in the past century is likely the result of improved nutrition and health.

Why do the changes of puberty occur when they do, and how can variations in their timing be explained? The basic genetic program for puberty is wired into the species (Gajdos, Hirschhorn, & Palmert, 2009; McAnarney, 2008). However, nutrition, health, and other environmental factors also affect puberty's timing and makeup (Hermann-Giddens, 2007; Ji & Chen, 2008).

For most boys, the pubertal sequence may begin as early as age 10 or as late as 13½, and may end as early as age 13 or as late as 17. Thus the normal range is wide enough that, given two boys of the same chronological age, one might complete the pubertal sequence before the other one has begun it. For girls, menarche is considered within the normal range if it appears between the ages of 9 and 15.

gonads The sex glands—the testes in males, the ovaries in females.

gonadotropins Hormones that stimulate the testes or ovaries.

testosterone A hormone associated in boys with the development of genitals, an increase in height, and a change in voice.

estradiol A hormone associated in girls with breast, uterine, and skeletal development.

Precocious puberty is the term used to describe the very early onset and rapid progression of puberty. Judith Blakemore and her colleagues (2009) recently described the following characteristics of precocious puberty. Precocious puberty is usually diagnosed when the onset of puberty happens before 8 years of age in girls and before 9 years of age in boys. Precocious puberty occurs about 10 times more often in girls than in boys. Precocious puberty usually is treated by medically suppressing gonadotropic secretions, which temporarily halts pubertal change. This treatment is usually given because children who experience precocious puberty are eventually likely to have short stature, early sexual capability, and the potential for engaging in age-inappropriate behavior (Blakemore, Berenbaum, & Liben, 2009).

Psychological Dimensions of Puberty

A host of psychological changes accompanies pubertal development. These changes involve body image and early and late maturation.

Body Image One psychological aspect of physical change in puberty is certain: Adolescents are preoccupied with their bodies and develop images of what their bodies are like (Allen & others, 2008; Mueller, 2009). Preoccupation with body image is strong throughout adolescence, but it is especially acute during early adolescence, a time when adolescents are more dissatisfied with their bodies than in late adolescence (Graber & Brooks-Gunn, 2002).

Gender differences characterize adolescents' perceptions of their bodies. In general, girls are less happy with their bodies and have more negative body images than boys throughout puberty (Bearman & others, 2006). As pubertal change proceeds, girls often become more dissatisfied with their bodies, probably because their body fat increases. In contrast, boys become more satisfied as they move through puberty, probably because their muscle mass increases (Bearman & others, 2006).

Adolescents show a strong preoccupation with their changing bodies and develop images of what their bodies are like. *Why might adolescent males have more positive body images than adolescent females?*

Early and Late Maturation Some of you entered puberty early, others late, and still others on time. Adolescents who mature earlier or later than their peers perceive themselves differently (Costello & others, 2007). In the Berkeley Longitudinal Study some years ago, early-maturing boys perceived themselves more positively and had more successful peer relations than did their late-maturing counterparts (Jones, 1965). When the late-maturing boys were in their thirties, however, they had developed a stronger sense of identity than the early-maturing boys had (Peskin, 1967). This may have occurred because the late-maturing boys had more time to explore life's options, or because the early-maturing boys continued to focus on their advantageous physical status instead of on career development and achievement. More recent research confirms, though, that at least during adolescence it is advantageous to be an early-maturing rather than a late-maturing boy (Graber, Brooks-Gunn, & Warren, 2006).

For girls, early and late maturation have been linked with body image. In the sixth grade, early-maturing girls show greater satisfaction with their figures than do late-maturing girls, but by the tenth grade late-maturing girls are more satisfied (Simmons & Blyth, 1987) (see Figure 14.3). One possible reason for this developmental change is that in late adolescence early-maturing girls are shorter and stockier, whereas late-maturing girls are taller and thinner. Thus, late-maturing girls in late adolescence have bodies that more closely approximate the current American ideal of feminine beauty—tall and thin.

How does early and late maturation influence adolescent development?

precocious puberty The very early onset and rapid progression of puberty.

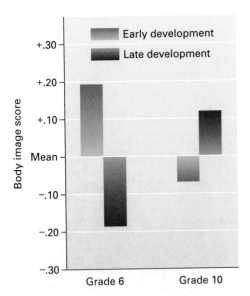

FIGURE 14.3 Early- and Late-Maturing Adolescent Girls' Perceptions of Body Image in Early and Late Adolescence

How would you...?

As a social worker, how would you design a community program to identify and assist early-maturing adolescent girls who are at risk for delinquency and early sexual behaviors?

Corpus callosum
These nerve fibers connect the brain's two hemispheres; they thicken in adolescence to process information more effectively.

Prefrontal cortex
This "judgment" region reins in intense emotions but doesn't finish developing until at least emerging adulthood.

Amygdala
The seat of emotions such as anger; this area develops quickly before other regions that help to control it.

FIGURE 14.4 Change in the Adolescent Brain

An increasing number of researchers have found that early maturation increases girls' vulnerability to a number of problems (Biehl, Natsuaki, & Ge, 2007; Mendle, Turkheimer, & Emery, 2007). Early-maturing girls are more likely to smoke, drink, be depressed, have an eating disorder, struggle for earlier independence from their parents, and have older friends; and their bodies are likely to elicit responses from males that lead to earlier dating and earlier sexual experiences (Wiesner & Ittel, 2002). For example, a recent study revealed that early-maturing girls were more likely to try cigarettes and alcohol without their parents' knowledge (Westling & others, 2008). And early maturing girls are less likely to graduate from high school; they also cohabit and marry earlier (Cavanagh, 2009).

The Brain

Along with the rest of the body, the brain is changing during adolescence, but the study of adolescent brain development is in its infancy. As advances in technology take place, significant strides will also likely be made in charting developmental changes in the adolescent brain (Giedd, 2008; Paus, 2009; Steinberg, 2009). What do we know now?

Using fMRI brain scans, scientists have recently discovered that adolescents' brains undergo significant structural changes. The **corpus callosum,** where fibers connect the brain's left and right hemispheres, thickens in adolescence, and this change improves adolescents' ability to process information (Giedd, 2008). We discussed advances in the development of the *prefrontal cortex*—the highest level of the frontal lobes involved in reasoning, decision making, and self-control—in Chapters 8, "Physical Development in Early Childhood," and 11 "Physical Development in Middle and Late Childhood." However, the prefrontal cortex does not finish maturing until the emerging adult years, approximately 18 to 25 years of age, or later, but the **amygdala**—the seat of emotions such as anger—matures earlier than the prefrontal cortex (Giedd, 2008; Lenroot & others, 2009). Figure 14.4 shows the locations of the corpus callosum, prefrontal cortex, and amygdala.

Many of the changes in the adolescent brain that we have described involve the rapidly emerging field of *social developmental neuroscience,* which involves connections between development, the brain, and socioemotional processes (de Haan & Gunnar, 2009). For example, consider leading researcher Charles Nelson's (2003) view that although adolescents are capable of very strong emotions their prefrontal cortex has not adequately developed to the point at which they can control these passions. It is as if their brain does not have the brakes to slow down their emotions. Or consider this interpretation of the development of emotion and cognition in adolescents: "early activation of strong 'turbo-charged' feelings with a relatively un-skilled set of 'driving skills' or cognitive abilities to modulate strong emotions and motivations" (Dahl, 2004, p. 18).

Of course, a major issue is which comes first, biological changes in the brain or experiences that stimulate these changes (Lerner, Boyd, & Du, 2008). Consider a recent study in which the prefrontal cortex thickened and more brain connections formed when adolescents resisted peer pressure (Paus & others, 2008). Scientists have yet to determine whether the brain changes come first or whether the brain changes are the result of experiences with peers, parents, and others. Once again, we encounter the nature-nurture issue that is so prominent in examining development through the life span.

Are there implications of what we now know about changes in the adolescent's brain in regard to taking drugs and the legal system?

According to leading expert Jay Giedd (2007, pp. 1–2D), "Biology doesn't make teens rebellious or have purple hair or take drugs. It does not mean you are going to do drugs, but it gives you more of a chance to do that." Also, can the recent brain research we have just discussed be used to argue that because the adolescent's brain, especially the higher-level prefrontal cortex, is still developing, adolescents should not be given a death penalty for committing a heinous crime? Leading expert Elizabeth Sowell (2004) says that scientists cannot just do brain scans on adolescents and decide if they should be tried as adults. In 2005, the death penalty for adolescents (under the age of 18) was prohibited by the U.S. Supreme Court, but it still continues to be debated (Ash, 2006).

Lee Malvo, was 17 years old, when he and John Muhammad, an adult, went on a sniper spree in 2002, terrorizing the Washington, D.C., area and killing 10 people. A 2005 U.S. Supreme Court ruling stated that individuals who are 18 years of age and under, like Malvo, cannot be given the death penalty. *Are there implications for what scientists are learning about the adolescent's brain for legal decisions, such as the death penalty?*

Review and Reflect: Learning Goal 2

 Describe puberty's characteristics, developmental changes, psychological dimensions, and the development of the brain

REVIEW

- What is puberty? What characterizes sexual maturation and the pubertal growth spurt?
- What are some hormonal changes in puberty?
- How has the timing of puberty changed, and what are some variations in puberty?
- What are some psychological dimensions of pubertal change?
- What developmental changes occur in the brain during adolescence?

REFLECT

- Did you experience puberty early, late, or on time? How do you think the timing of your puberty influenced your development?

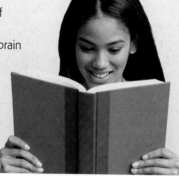

3 WHAT ARE THE DIMENSIONS OF ADOLESCENT SEXUALITY?

Developing a Sexual Identity	Timing and Trends in Adolescent Sexual Behavior	Sexual Risk Taking in Adolescence

Not only are adolescents characterized by substantial changes in physical growth and the development of the brain, but adolescence also is a bridge between the asexual child and the sexual adult (Kelly, 2008; Strong & others, 2008). Adolescence is a time of sexual exploration and experimentation, of sexual fantasies and realities, of incorporating sexuality into one's identity. Adolescents have an almost insatiable curiosity about sexuality. They are concerned about whether they are sexually attractive, how to do sex, and what the future holds for their sexual lives. Although most adolescents experience times of vulnerability and confusion, the majority will eventually develop a mature sexual identity.

Every society gives some attention to adolescent sexuality. In some societies, adults resolutely protect adolescent females from males by chaperoning them, while other societies promote very early marriage. Then there are societies that allow some sexual experimentation.

corpus callosum The location where fibers connect the brain's left and right hemispheres.

amygdala The seat of emotions, such as anger.

Sex is virtually everywhere in the American culture and is used to sell just about everything. *What evidence is cited in the text to indicate that messages from the media influence adolescents' attitudes or behavior?*

Sexual arousal emerges as a new phenomenon in adolescence and it is important to view sexuality as a normal aspect of adolescent development.

—SHIRLEY FELDMAN
*Contemporary Psychologist,
Stanford University*

In the United States, the sexual culture is widely available to adolescents. In addition to any advice adolescents get from parents, they learn a great deal about sex from television, videos, magazines, the lyrics of popular music, and the Internet (Epstein & Ward, 2008). A recent study revealed that adolescents who watched a high level of sexual content on popular TV shows were more than twice as likely to become pregnant or father an out-of-wedlock baby as adolescents than their adolescent counterparts who watched a low level of sexual content (Chandra & others, 2008).

Developing a Sexual Identity

Mastering emerging sexual feelings and forming a sense of sexual identity are multifaceted and lengthy processes. They involve learning to manage sexual feelings (such as sexual arousal and attraction), developing new forms of intimacy, and learning the skills to regulate sexual behavior to avoid undesirable consequences. Developing a sexual identity also involves more than just sexual behavior. Sexual identities emerge in the context of physical factors, social factors, and cultural factors, with most societies placing constraints on the sexual behavior of adolescents. As adolescent's sexual identity is influenced by *social norms* related to sex—the extent to which adolescents perceive that their peers are having sex, using protection, and so on. These social norms have important influences on adolescents' sexual behavior. For example, a recent study revealed that when adolescents perceived that their peers were sexually permissive, the adolescents had a higher rate of initiating sexual intercourse and engaging in risky sexual practices (Potard, Courtois, & Rusch, 2008).

An adolescent's sexual identity involves activities, interests, styles of behavior, and an indication of sexual orientation (whether an individual has same-sex or other-sex attractions) (Buzwell & Rosenthal, 1996). For example, some adolescents have a high anxiety level about sex, others a low level. Some adolescents are strongly aroused sexually, others less so. Some adolescents are very active sexually, others not at all. Some adolescents are sexually inactive in response to their strong religious upbringing; others go to church regularly, yet their religious training does not inhibit their sexual activity.

It is commonly believed that most gay males and lesbians quietly struggle with same-sex attractions in childhood, do not engage in heterosexual dating, and gradually recognize that they are a gay male or a lesbian in mid to late adolescence (Savin-Willliams & Diamond, 2004). Many youth do follow this developmental pathway, but others do not (Diamond & Savin-Williams, 2009). For example, many youth have no recollection of early same-sex attractions and experience a more abrupt sense of their same-sex attraction in late adolescence (Savin-Williams, 2006). Researchers also have found that the majority of adolescents with same-sex attractions also experience some degree of other-sex attractions (Savin-Williams, 2006). Even though some adolescents who are attracted to individuals of their same sex fall in love with these individuals, others claim that their same-sex attractions are purely physical (Diamond & Savin-Williams, 2009; Savin-Williams, 2006, 2008).

In sum, gay male and lesbian youth have diverse patterns of initial attraction, often have bisexual attractions, and may have physical or emotional attraction to same-sex individuals but do not always fall in love with them (Diamond, 2008; Diamond & Savin-Williams, 2009).

Timing and Trends in Adolescent Sexual Behavior

The timing of sexual initiation varies by country as well as by gender and other socioeconomic characteristics (Eaton & others, 2008). In one cross-cultural study, among females, the proportion having first intercourse by age 17 ranged from 72 percent in Mali to 47 percent in the United States and 45 percent in Tanzania (Singh & others, 2000). The percentage of males who had their first intercourse by age 17 ranged from 76 percent in Jamaica to 64 percent in the United States and 63 percent in Brazil. Within the United States, male, African American, and inner-city adolescents report being the most sexually active, whereas Asian American adolescents have the most restrictive sexual timetable (Feldman, Turner, & Araujo, 1999).

A recent study examined the role that acculturation might play in Latino adolescents' sexual behavior (McDonald, Manlove, & Ikramullah, 2009). Fewer first-generation Latino adolescents engaged in sexual intercourse before 18 years of age, and fewer first- and second-generation Latino adolescents used contraceptives consistently at 17 years of age, than third-generation Latino adolescents. Thus, as acculturation proceeded, the sexual behavior of the Latino adolescents began to more closely resemble that of non-Latino White adolescents—earlier sexual initiation and increased condom use.

What is the current profile of sexual activity of U.S. adolescents? In a recent U.S. national survey, 63 percent of twelfth-graders (64 percent of males, 62 percent of females) reported that they had experienced sexual intercourse compared with 34 percent of ninth-graders (39 percent of males, 29 percent of females (MMWR, 2006) (see Figure 14.5). By age 20, 77 percent of U.S. youth have engaged in sexual intercourse (Dworkin & Santelli, 2007). A recent national study indicated that 35 percent of U.S. high school students were currently sexually active (Eaton & others, 2008).

There has been a dramatic increase in oral sex during adolescence (Brewster & Tillman, 2008). In a national survey, 55 percent of U.S. 15- to 19-year-old boys and 54 percent of girls said they had engaged in oral sex (National Center for Health Statistics, 2002). In the survey, more than 20 percent of the adolescents who had not had sexual intercourse had engaged in oral sex. A recent study found that adolescents who engaged in oral sex were older, had engaged in heavy drinking in the past month, perceived their peers to be sexually active, and thought their friends would approve of their sexual activity more than adolescents who had not engaged in oral sex (Bersamin & others, 2006).

Sexual Risk Taking in Adolescence

A number of risk factors are related to the development of adolescent sexual problems. We examine these risk factors as well as contraceptive use, sexually transmitted infections, and adolescent pregnancy.

Most adolescents become sexually active at some point during adolescence, but many adolescents are at risk for sexual and other problems when they have sexual intercourse before 16 years of age. Adolescents who have sex before they are 16 years old are often ineffective users of contraceptives, which puts them at risk for adolescent pregnancy and sexually transmitted infections. One study found that use of alcohol and other drugs, as well as low academic achievement, were linked with the initiation of sexual

What developmental pathways characterize attraction to same-sex individuals?

How Would You...?
As a psychologist, how would you describe the cultural and ethnic differences in the timing of an adolescent's first sexual experience?

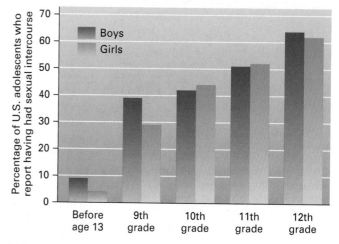

FIGURE 14.5 Timing of Sexual Intercourse in U.S. Adolescents

What are some risk factors for developing sexual problems in adolescence?

intercourse in early adolescence (Santelli & others, 2004). In a longitudinal study from 10 to 12 years of age to 25 years of age, early sexual intercourse and affiliation with deviant peers were linked to substance use disorders in emerging adulthood (Cornelius & others, 2006).

In addition to having sex in early adolescence, other risk factors for sexual problems in adolescence include contextual factors such as socioeconomic status (SES), as well as family/parenting and peer factors (Aronowitz, Rennells, & Todd, 2006). The percentage of sexually active young adolescents is higher in low-income areas of inner cities (Silver & Bauman, 2006). Further, having older sexually active siblings or pregnant/parenting teenage sisters places adolescents at an elevated risk of adolescent pregnancy (Miller, Benson, & Galbraith, 2001). A recent study also revealed that not feeling close to their parents, having low self-esteem, and watching television extensively were linked to adolescents being sexually active at 15 years of age (Hyde & Price, 2007). And a recent research review found that earlier onset of sexual intercourse was linked to living with people other than two biological parents and a lower level of parental monitoring (Zimmer-Gembeck & Helfand, 2008). In another study, maternal communication about sex (the extent mothers talked with their adolescents about having sexual intercourse and the negative things that could happen if he got someone pregnant/she got pregnant, for example) was linked with less risky sexual behavior by Latino adolescents (Trejos-Castillo & Vazonyi, 2009). Also, a recent study of middle school students revealed that better academic achievement was a protective factor in keeping boys and girls from engaging in early initiation of sexual intercourse (Laflin, Wang, & Barry, 2008).

Cognitive factors are increasingly implicated in sexual risk taking in adolescence (Fantasia, 2008). Two such factors are attention problems and self-regulation (the ability to control one's emotions and behavior). One longitudinal study revealed that attention problems and high rates of aggressive disruptive behavior at school entry increased the risk of multiple problem behaviors (school maladjustment, antisocial behavior, and substance use) in middle school, which in turn was linked to early initiation of sexual activity (Schofield & others, 2008). Another longitudinal study found that weak self-regulation at 8 to 9 years of age and risk proneness (tendency to seek sensation and make poor decisions) at 12 to 13 years of age set the stage for sexual risk taking at 16 to 17 years of age (Crockett, Raffaelli, & Shen, 2006). Also, in this study, substance abuse and negative peer pressure tended to also reflect risk proneness and poor self-regulation along the developmental pathway to risky sexual behavior.

Contraceptive Use   Sexual activity carries with it considerable risks if appropriate safeguards are not taken (Strong & others, 2008). Youth encounter two kinds of risks: unintended unwanted pregnancy and sexually transmitted infections. Both of these risks can be reduced significantly if contraception is used consistently.

The good news is that adolescents are increasing their use of contraceptives (Holcombe & others, 2008). For example, a recent large-scale study revealed a substantial increase in the use of a contraceptive (61.5 percent in 2007 compared with 46.2 percent in 1991) by U.S. high school students during the last time they had sexual intercourse (among students who were sexually active) (Centers for Disease Control and Prevention, 2008a).

Although adolescent contraceptive use is increasing, many sexually active adolescents still do not use contraceptives, or they use them inconsistently (Parkes & others, 2009; Sterling & Sadler, 2009). Also, there was a 2 percent decrease in condom use reported by adolescents from 2005 to 2007 (Centers for Disease Control and Prevention, 2008a; Holcombe & others, 2008). Sexually active younger adolescents are less likely than older adolescents to take contraceptive precautions. Younger adolescents are more likely to use a condom or withdrawal, whereas older adolescents are more likely to use the pill or a diaphragm. A recent study also revealed that adolescents with friends who did not use condoms were more likely to not use condoms themselves later during intercourse (Henry & others, 2007).

Psychologists are exploring ways to encourage adolescents to make less risky sexual decisions. Here an adolescent participates in an interactive video session developed by Julie Downs and her colleagues at the Department of Social and Decision Making Sciences at Carnegie Mellon University. The videos help adolescents evaluate their responses and decisions in high-risk sexual contexts.

And a recent study of 16- to 22-year-old Latino youth found that females' use of hormonal contraceptives, ambivalence about avoiding pregnancy, being in a sexual relationship longer, and more trust in a partner were linked to inconsistent condom use and more incidences of engaging in unprotected sexual intercourse (Brady & others, 2009). In this study, consistent condom use was related to the perception that one's main partner had potentially been unfaithful.

Sexually Transmitted Infections   Some forms of contraception, such as birth control pills or implants, do not protect against sexually transmitted infections, or STIs. **Sexually transmitted infections (STIs)** are diseases that are contracted primarily through sexual contact. This contact is not limited to vaginal intercourse but includes oral-genital and anal-genital contact as well. STIs are an increasing health problem. Approximately 25 percent of sexually active adolescents are estimated to become infected with an STI each year (Alan Guttmacher Institute, 1998). Among the main STIs adolescents can get are bacterial infections (such as gonorrhea, syphilis, and chlamydia), and STIs caused by viruses—genital herpes, genital warts, and **AIDS** (acquired immune deficiency syndrome). Figure 14.6 describes these sexually transmitted infections.

No single STI has had a greater impact on sexual behavior, or created more fear, in the last two decades than AIDS. AIDS is caused by a virus, the human immunodeficiency virus (HIV), which destroys the body's immune system. Following

How would you...?
As a social worker, how would you design an educational campaign to increase adolescents' effective use of contraception?

sexually transmitted infections (STIs)
Diseases that are contracted primarily through sexual contact. This contact is not limited to vaginal intercourse but includes oral-genital contact and anal-genital contact as well.

AIDS AIDS, or acquired immune deficiency syndrome, is caused by a virus, the human immunodeficiency virus (HIV), which destroys the body's immune system.

STI	Description/cause	Incidence	Treatment
Gonorrhea	Commonly called the "drip" or "clap." Caused by the bacterium *Neisseria gonorrhoeae*. Spread by contact between infected moist membranes (genital, oral-genital, or anal-genital) of two individuals. Characterized by discharge from penis or vagina and painful urination. Can lead to infertility.	500,000 cases annually in U.S.	Penicillin, other antibiotics
Syphilis	Caused by the bacterium *Treponema pallidum*. Characterized by the appearance of a sore where syphilis entered the body. The sore can be on the external genitals, vagina, or anus. Later, a skin rash breaks out on palms of hands and bottom of feet. If not treated, can eventually lead to paralysis or even death.	100,000 cases annually in U.S.	Penicillin
Chlamydia	A common STI named for the bacterium *Chlamydia trachomatis*, an organism that spreads by sexual contact and infects the genital organs of both sexes. A special concern is that females with chlamydia may become infertile. It is recommended that adolescent and young adult females have an annual screening for this STI.	About 3 million people in U.S. annually; estimates are that 10 percent of adolescent girls have this STI.	Antibiotics
Genital herpes	Caused by a family of viruses with different strains. Involves an eruption of sores and blisters. Spread by sexual contact.	One of five U.S. adolescents and adults	No known cure but antiviral medications can shorten outbreaks
AIDS	Caused by a virus, the human immunodeficiency virus (HIV) that destroys the body's immune system. Semen and blood are the main vehicles of transmission. Common symptoms include fevers, night sweats, weight loss, chronic fatigue, and swollen lymph nodes.	More than 6,000 13- to 19-year-olds in the U.S.; epidemic incidence in sub-Saharan adolescent girls	New treatments have slowed the progression from HIV to AIDS; no cure
Genital warts	Caused by the human papillomavirus, which does not always produce symptoms. Usually appear as small, hard painless bumps in the vaginal area, or around the anus. Very contagious. Certain high-risk types of this virus cause cervical cancer and other genital cancers. In 2007, the Centers for Disease Control and Prevention recommended that all 11- and 12-year-old girls be given the vaccine, Gardasil, which helps to fight off HPV and cervical cancer.	About 5.5 million new cases annually; considered the most common STI in the U.S.	A topical drug, freezing, or surgery.

FIGURE 14.6 Sexually Transmitted Infections

A 13-year-old boy pushes his friends around in his barrow during his break from his work as a barrow boy in a community in sub-Saharan Africa. He became the breadwinner in the family because both of his parents died of AIDS.

exposure to HIV, an individual is vulnerable to germs that a normal immune system could destroy.

In 2006, 15 percent of all individuals who had been diagnosed with HIV/AIDS in the United States were 13 to 24 years of age (Centers for Disease Control and Prevention, 2008b). Worldwide, the greatest concern about AIDS is in sub-Saharan Africa, where it has reached epidemic proportions (Singh & others, 2004; UNICEF, 2009). Adolescent girls in many African countries are especially vulnerable to infection with the HIV virus by adult men. Approximately six times as many adolescent girls as boys have AIDS in these countries. In Kenya, 25 percent of the 15- to 19-year-old girls are HIV-positive, compared with only 4 percent of this age group of boys. In Botswana, more than 30 percent of the adolescent girls who are pregnant are infected with the HIV virus. In some sub-Saharan countries, less than 20 percent of women and 40 percent of 15- to 19-year-olds reported that they used a condom the last time they had sexual intercourse (Singh & others, 2004).

There continues to be great concern about AIDS in many parts of the world, not just sub-Saharan Africa. In the United States, prevention is especially targeted at groups that show the highest incidence of AIDS. These include drug users, individuals with other STIs, young gay males, individuals living in low-income circumstances, Latinos, and African Americans (Centers for Disease Control and Prevention, 2008b).

Adolescent Pregnancy   In cross-cultural comparisons, the United States continues to have one of the highest adolescent pregnancy and childbearing rates in the industrialized world, despite a considerable decline in the 1990s (Cooksey, 2009). The U.S. adolescent pregnancy rate is eight times as high as that in the Netherlands. Although U.S. adolescents are no more sexually active than their counterparts in the Netherlands, their adolescent pregnancy rate is dramatically higher.

Despite the negative comparisons of the United States with many other developed countries, in the 1990s and through 2004, there were encouraging trends in U.S. adolescent pregnancy rates. In 2004, births to adolescent girls fell to a record low (Child Trends, 2006). The rate of births to adolescent girls has dropped 30 percent since 1991. Fear of sexually transmitted infections, especially AIDS; school/community health classes; and a greater hope for the future are the likely reasons for the recent decrease in U.S. adolescent pregnancy rates (Joyner, 2009). However, as shown in Figure 14.7, the U.S. adolescent birth rate increased in 2006 (Child Trends, 2008). Latina adolescents are more likely than African American and non-Latina White

FIGURE 14.7 Trends in High School Dropout Rates. From 1972 through 2006, the school dropout rate for Latinos remained very high (22 percent of 16- to 24-year-olds in 2005). The African American dropout rate was still higher (10 percent) than the White non-Latino rate (6 percent) in 2006. (*Source:* National Center for Education Statistics, 2008a).

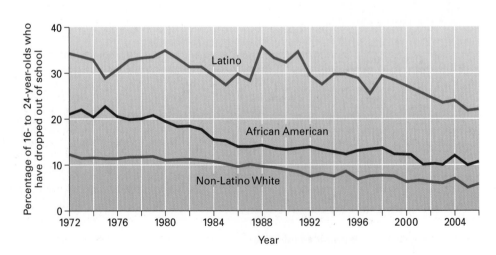

adolescents to become pregnant (Child Trends, 2008; Santelli, Abraido-Lanza, & Melnikas, 2009). Latino and African American adolescent girls who have a child are also more likely to have a second child than are non-Latino White adolescent girls (Rosengard, 2009).

Why are U.S. adolescent pregnancy rates so high? We discuss possible answers to this question in the following *Diversity in Children's Development* interlude.

Diversity in Children's Development

CROSS-CULTURAL COMPARISONS OF ADOLESCENT PREGNANCY

Three reasons as to why U.S. adolescent pregnancy rates are so high can be found in cross-cultural studies (Boonstra, 2002, pp. 9–10):

- *"Childbearing regarded as adult activity."* European countries, as well as Canada, give a strong consensus that childbearing belongs in adulthood "when young people have completed their education, have become employed and independent from their parents and are living in stable relationships. . . . In the United States, this attitude is much less strong and much more variable across groups and areas of the country."

- *"Clear messages about sexual behavior.* While adults in other countries strongly encourage teens to wait until they have established themselves before having children, they are generally more accepting than American adults of teens having sex. In France and Sweden, in particular, teen sexual expression is seen as normal and positive, but there is also widespread expectation that sexual intercourse will take place within committed relationships. In fact, relationships among U.S. teens tend to be more sporadic and of shorter duration. Equally strong is the expectation that young people who are having sex will take actions to protect themselves and their partners from pregnancy and sexually transmitted infections," which is much stronger in Europe than in the United States. "In keeping with this view, . . . schools in Great Britain, France, Sweden, and most of Canada" have sex education programs that provide more comprehensive information about prevention than U.S. schools. In addition, these countries use the media more often in "government-sponsored campaigns for promoting responsible sexual behavior."

- *"Access to family-planning services.* In countries that are more accepting of teenage sexual relationships, teenagers also have easier access to reproductive health services. In Canada, France, Great Britain, and Sweden, contraceptive services are integrated into other types of primary health care and are available free or at low cost for all teenagers. Generally, teens [in these countries] know where to obtain information and services and receive confidential and nonjudgmental care. . . . In the United States, where attitudes about teenage sexual relationships are more conflicted, teens have a harder time obtaining contraceptive services. Many do not have health insurance or cannot get birth control as part of their basic health care."

Adolescent pregnancy creates health risks for both the baby and the mother. Infants born to adolescent mothers are more likely to have low birth weights—a prominent factor in infant mortality—as well as neurological problems and childhood illness (Chedraui, 2008). Adolescent mothers often drop out of school. Although many adolescent mothers resume their education later in life, they

Careers in Children's Development

Lynn Blankenship, Family and Consumer Science Educator

Lynn Blankenship is a family and consumer science educator. She has an undergraduate degree in this area from University of Arizona. She has taught for more than 20 years, the last 14 at Tucson High Magnet School.

Blankenship was awarded the Tucson Federation of Teachers Educator of the Year Award for 1999–2000 and the Arizona Teacher of the Year in 1999.

Blankenship especially enjoys teaching life skills to adolescents. One of her favorite activities is having students care for an automated baby that imitates the needs of real babies. She says that this program has a profound impact on students because the baby must be cared for around the clock for the duration of the assignment. Blankenship also coordinates real-world work

experiences and training for students in several child-care facilities in the Tucson area.

Lynn Blankenship (*center*), teaching life skills to students.

How Would You...?
As an educator, how would you incorporate sex education throughout the curriculum to encourage adolescents' healthy, responsible sexual development?

generally never catch up economically with women who postpone childbearing until their twenties. One longitudinal study found that the children of women who had their first birth during their teens had lower achievement test scores and more behavioral problems than did children whose mothers had their first birth as adults (Hofferth & Reid, 2002).

Though the consequences of America's high adolescent pregnancy rate are cause for great concern, it often is not pregnancy alone that leads to negative consequences for an adolescent mother and her offspring (Oxford & others, 2006). Adolescent mothers are more likely to come from low-SES backgrounds (Crosby & Holtgrave, 2006). Many adolescent mothers also were not good students before they became pregnant. However, not every adolescent female who bears a child lives a life of poverty and low achievement. Thus, although adolescent pregnancy is a high-risk circumstance, and adolescents who do not become pregnant generally fare better than those who do, some adolescent mothers do well in school and have positive outcomes (Leadbeater & Way, 2001).

Serious, extensive efforts are needed to help pregnant adolescents and young mothers enhance their educational and occupational opportunities. Adolescent mothers also need help in obtaining competent child care and in planning for the future (Jumping-Eagle & others, 2008).

A special concern is that daughters of teenage mothers are at risk for teenage childbearing, thus perpetuating an intergenerational cycle. A recent study using data from the National Longitudinal Survey of Youth revealed that daughters of teenage mothers were 66 percent more likely to become teenage mothers themselves (Meade, Kershaw, & Ickovics, 2008). In this study, risks that increased the likelihood the daughters of the teenage mothers would become pregnant included low parental monitoring and poverty.

All adolescents can benefit from age-appropriate family-life education (Garwick & others, 2008; Key & others, 2008). Family and consumer science educators teach life skills, such as effective decision making, to adolescents. To read about the work of one family and consumer science educator, see the *Careers in Children's Development* profile. And to learn more about ways to reduce adolescent pregnancy, see the *Caring for Children* interlude.

What are some consequences of adolescent pregnancy? What are some strategies for reducing adolescent pregnancy?

Caring for Children

REDUCING ADOLESCENT PREGNANCY

One strategy for reducing adolescent pregnancy, called the Teen Outreach Program (TOP), focuses on engaging adolescents in volunteer community service and stimulates discussions that help adolescents appreciate the lessons they learn through volunteerism. In one study, 695 adolescents in grades 9 to 12 were randomly assigned to either a Teen Outreach group or a control group (Allen & others, 1997). They were assessed both at program entry and at program exit nine months later. The rate of pregnancy was substantially lower for the Teen Outreach adolescents. These adolescents also had a lower rate of school failure and academic suspension.

Girls, Inc., has four programs that are intended to increase adolescent girls' motivation to avoid pregnancy until they are mature enough to make responsible decisions about motherhood (Roth & others, 1998). Growing Together, a series of five two-hour workshops for mothers and adolescents, and Will Power/Won't Power, a series of six two-hour sessions that focus on assertiveness training, are for 12- to 14-year-old girls. For older adolescent girls, Taking Care of Business provides nine sessions that emphasize career planning as well as information about sexuality, reproduction, and contraception. Health Bridge coordinates health and education services— girls can participate in this program as one of their club activities. Girls who participated in these programs were less likely to get pregnant than girls who did not participate (Girls, Inc., 1991).

Currently, a major controversy in sex education is whether schools should have an abstinence-only program or a program that emphasizes contraceptive knowledge (Cabezon & others, 2005). Two recent research reviews found that abstinence-only programs do not delay the initiation of sexual intercourse and do not reduce HIV risk behaviors (Kirby, Laris, & Rolleri, 2007; Underhill, Montgomery, & Operario, 2007). Further, a recent study revealed that adolescents who experienced comprehensive sex education were less likely to report adolescent pregnancies than those who were given abstinence-only sex education or no education (Kohler, Manhart, & Lafferty, 2008).

A number of leading experts on adolescent sexuality now conclude that sex education programs that emphasize contraceptive knowledge do not increase the incidence

These are not adolescent mothers, but rather adolescents who are participating in the Teen Outreach Program (TOP), which engages adolescents in volunteer community service. These adolescent girls are serving as volunteers in a child-care center for crack babies. Researchers have found that such volunteer experiences can reduce the rate of adolescent pregnancy.

(continued on next page)

of sexual intercourse and are more likely to reduce the risk of adolescent pregnancy and sexually transmitted infections than abstinence-only programs (Constantine, 2008; Eisenberg & others, 2008; Hentz & Fields, 2009; Hyde & DeLamater, 2008).

Review and Reflect: Learning Goal 3

3 **Characterize adolescent sexuality**

REVIEW

- How do adolescents develop a sexual identity?
- What characterizes timing and trends in adolescent sexual behavior?
- What is the nature of sexual risk taking in adolescence?

REFLECT

- Caroline contracted genital herpes from her boyfriend, whom she had been dating for the last three years. After breaking off the relationship and spending more time on her own, she began dating Blake. Should Caroline tell Blake about her sexually transmitted infection? If so, how and when?

---

4 HOW CAN ADOLESCENTS' HEALTH AND HEALTH-ENHANCING ASSETS BE CHARACTERIZED?

Adolescent Health	Leading Causes of Death in Adolescence	Substance Use and Abuse	Eating Problems and Disorders	Risk Factors, Developmental Assets, and Social Capital

To improve adolescent health, adults should aim (1) to increase adolescents' *health-enhancing behaviors*, such as eating nutritiously, exercising, wearing seat belts, and getting adequate sleep; and (2) to reduce adolescents' *health-compromising behaviors*, such as drug abuse, violence, unprotected sexual intercourse, and dangerous driving.

Adolescent Health

Adolescence is a critical juncture in the adoption of behaviors that are relevant to health (Nyaronga & Wickrama, 2009; Ozer & Irwin, 2009; Park & others, 2008). Many of the behaviors that are linked to poor health habits and early death in adults begin during adolescence. Conversely, the early formation of healthy behavior patterns, such as regular exercise and a preference for foods low in fat and cholesterol not only has immediate health benefits but helps in adulthood to delay or prevent disability and mortality from heart disease, stroke, diabetes, and cancer (Insel & Roth, 2008).

Nutrition and Exercise   Concerns are growing about adolescents' nutrition and exercise (Knopfli & others, 2008; Sabiston & Crocker, 2008). The percentage of overweight U.S. 12- to 19-year-olds increased from 11 to 17 percent from the early 1990s through 2004 (Eaton & others, 2008). The negative outcomes of being overweight in adolescence were revealed in a recent study that found 62 percent of the male and 73 percent of the female adolescents in the 85th to 94th percentile of body mass index (BMI) became obese adults (Wang & others, 2008).

In this study, of those who were at the 95th percentile and higher for BMI, 80 percent of the male and 92 percent of the female adolescents became obese adults.

Other research indicates increases in being overweight during adolescence in European countries (Irwin, 2004). In a comparison of adolescents in 28 countries, U.S. adolescents ate more junk food and fewer fruits and vegetables than adolescents in most other countries (World Health Organization, 2000). The National Youth Risk Survey found that U.S. high school students decreased their intake of fruits and vegetables from 1999 through 2007 (Eaton & others, 2008) (see Figure 14.8). A recent research review found that these two family factors were linked to increased fruit and vegetable consumption by adolescents: availability of fruits and vegetables in the home and consumption of fruits and vegetables by parents (Pearson, Biddle, & Gorely, 2008). And a recent study revealed that eating regular family meals during early adolescence was linked to healthy eating habits five years later (Burgess-Champoux & others, 2009). Thus, parents play an important role in adolescents' nutrition through the food choices they make available to adolescents and serving as models for healthy or unhealthy nutrition.

In Chapter 11, "Physical Development in Middle and Late Childhood," the numerous negative developmental outcomes for being overweight in childhood were described. As in childhood, being overweight in adolescence also is linked to many negative health outcomes, including high blood pressure, hip problems, pulmonary problems, and type 2 diabetes (Urbina, 2008). Being overweight in adolescence also is related to lower self-esteem, depression, and more problems in peer relations (Pasch & others, 2008).

There also is major concern about the low level of exercise by U.S. adolescents. In a cross-cultural study, just two-thirds of U.S. adolescents exercised at least twice a week, compared with 80 percent or more of adolescents in Ireland, Austria, Germany, and the Slovak Republic (World Health Organization, 2000).

Researchers have found that individuals become less active as they reach and progress through adolescence (Butcher & others, 2008; Hills, King, & Armstrong, 2007). A recent national study of U.S. 9- to 15-year-olds revealed that almost all 9- and 11-year-olds met the federal government's moderate to vigorous exercise recommendations per day (a minimum of 60 minutes a day), but only 31 percent of 15-year-olds met the recommendations on weekdays, and on weekends only 17 percent met the recommendations (Nader & others, 2008). The recent national study also found that adolescent boys were more likely to engage in moderate to vigorous exercise than girls. Figure 14.9 shows the average amount of exercise of U.S. boys and girls from 9 to 15 years of age on weekdays and weekends. Another recent national study of U.S. adolescents revealed that physical activity increased until 13 years of age in boys and girls but then declined through 18 years of age (Kahn & others, 2008). In this study, adolescents were more likely to engage in regular exercise when they perceived it was important to present a

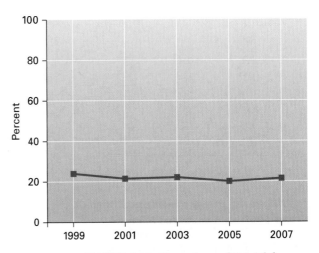

FIGURE 14.8 Percentage of U.S. High School Students Who Ate Fruits and Vegetables Five or More Times a Day, 1999 to 2007 *Note:* This graph shows the percentage of high school students over time who had eaten fruits and vegetables (100% fruit juice, fruit, green salad, potatoes—excluding french fries, fried potatoes, or potato chips—carrots, or other vegetables) five or more times a day during the preceding seven days (Eaton & others, 2008).

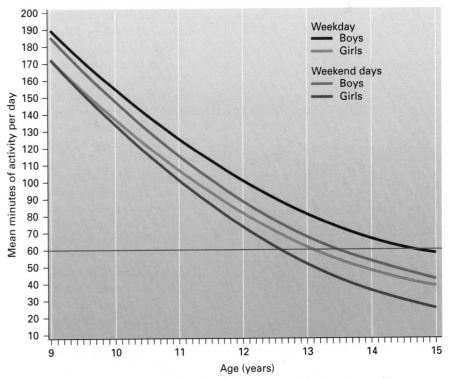

FIGURE 14.9 Average Amount of Moderate to Vigorous Exercise Engaged in By U.S. 9- to 15-Year-Olds on Weekdays and Weekends *Note:* The federal government recommends 60 minutes of moderate to vigorous physical activity per day.

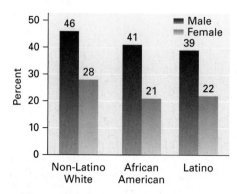

FIGURE 14.10 Exercise Rates of U.S. High School Students: Gender and Ethnicity
Note: Data are for high school students who were physically active doing any kind of physical activity that increased their heart rate and made them breathe hard some of the time for a total of at least 60 minutes a day on five or more of the seven days preceding the survey.

How would you...?
As a health-care professional, how would you explain the benefits of physical fitness in adolescence to adolescents, parents, and teachers?

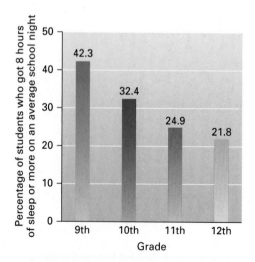

FIGURE 14.11 Developmental Changes in U.S. Adolescents' Sleep Patterns on an Average School Night

positive body image to their friends and when exercise was important to their parents. Yet another recent study documented that physical activity declined from 12 to 17 years of age in U.S. adolescents (Duncan & others, 2007). In this study, having physically active friends was linked to higher physical activity levels for adolescents.

Ethnic differences in exercise participation rates of U.S. adolescents also occur, and these rates vary by gender. As indicated in Figure 14.10, in the National Youth Risk Survey, non-Latino White boys exercised the most, African American girls the least (Eaton & others, 2008).

Exercise is linked to a number of positive physical outcomes (Dugan, 2008; Lumpkin, 2008). Regular exercise has a positive effect on adolescents' weight status. A recent study revealed that regular exercise from 9 to 16 years of age was associated with regular weight in girls (McMurray & others, 2008). Other positive outcomes of exercise in adolescence are reduced triglyceride levels, lower blood pressure, and a lower incidence of type 2 diabetes (Butcher & others, 2008). And another recent study revealed that physical fitness in adolescence was linked to physical fitness in adulthood (Mikkelsson & others, 2006).

An exciting possibility is that physical exercise might act as a buffer against the stress adolescents experience and improve their mental health and life satisfaction (Butcher & others, 2008; Sabiston & Crocker, 2008). Consider these studies that support this possibility:

- A nine-month physical activity intervention with sedentary adolescent girls improved their self-image (Schneider, Dunton, & Cooper, 2008).

- Higher physical activity at 9 and 11 years of age predicted higher self-esteem at 11 and 13 years of age (Schmalz & others, 2007).

- High school seniors who exercised frequently had higher grade-point averages, used drugs less frequently, were less depressed, and got along better with their parents than those who rarely exercised (Field, Diego, & Sanders, 2001).

Sleep Patterns Might changing sleep patterns in adolescence contribute to adolescents' health-compromising behaviors? Recently there has been a surge of interest in adolescent sleep patterns (Carskadon, 2006; Dahl, 2006; Liu & others, 2008; Loessl & others, 2008; Moore & Meltzer, 2008; Tarokh & Carskadon, 2008).

In a recent national survey of youth, only 31 percent of U.S. adolescents got eight or more hours of sleep on an average school night (Eaton & others, 2008). In this study, the percentage of adolescents getting this much sleep on an average school night decreased as they got older (see Figure 14.11).

Another recent study also found that adolescents are not getting adequate sleep. The National Sleep Foundation (2006) conducted a U.S. survey of 1,602 caregivers and their 11- to 17-year-olds. Forty-five percent of the adolescents got inadequate sleep on school nights (less than eight hours). Older adolescents (ninth- to twelfth-graders) got markedly less sleep on school nights than younger adolescents (sixth- to eighth-graders)—62 percent of the older adolescents got inadequate sleep compared with 21 percent of the younger adolescents. Adolescents who got inadequate sleep (eight hours or less) on school nights were more likely to feel more tired or sleepy, more cranky and irritable, fall asleep in school, be in a depressed mood, and drink caffeinated beverages than their counterparts who got optimal sleep (nine or more hours). In a recent study of more than 600 13- to 18-year-old boys and girls, 54 percent said they regularly got less than six to eight hours of sleep a night on school nights (Chen, Wang, & Jeng, 2006). In this study, getting less than six to eight hours of sleep per night during adolescence was linked to lower levels of exercise, less effective stress management, and adopting an unhealthy diet. In another recent study of 750 14- to 15-year-olds, getting less sleep at night was linked to higher levels of anxiety, depression, and fatigue the next day (Fuligni & Hardway, 2006).

Many adolescents, especially older adolescents, stay up later at night and sleep longer in the morning than they did when they were children. For example, a recent study of Chinese adolescents found that tenth-graders went to bed later and awoke earlier than seventh-graders, resulting in one hour less of sleep for the tenth-graders (Liu & others, 2008). These findings have implications for the hours during which adolescents learn most effectively in school (Moore & Meltzer, 2008).

Mary Carskadon and her colleagues (2002, 2004, 2006; Jenni & Carskadon, 2007; Tarokh & Carskadon, 2008) have conducted a number of research studies on adolescent sleep patterns. They found that when given the opportunity adolescents will sleep an average of nine hours and 25 minutes a night. Most get considerably less than nine hours of sleep, especially during the week. This shortfall creates a sleep deficit, which adolescents often attempt to make up on the weekend. The researchers also found that older adolescents tend to be more sleepy during the day than younger adolescents. They theorized that this sleepiness was not due to academic work or social pressures. Rather, their research suggests that adolescents' biological clocks undergo a shift as they get older, delaying their period of wakefulness by about one hour. A delay in the nightly release of the sleep-inducing hormone **melatonin,** which is produced in the brain's pineal gland, seems to underlie this shift. Melatonin is secreted at about 9:30 p.m. in younger adolescents and approximately an hour later in older adolescents.

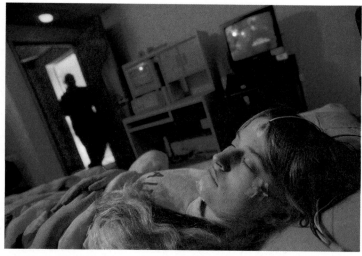

In Mary Carskadon's sleep laboratory at Brown University, an adolescent girl's brain activity is being monitored. Carskadon says that in the morning, sleep-deprived adolescents' "brains are telling them it's night time . . . and the rest of the world is saying it's time to go to school."

Carskadon has suggested that early school starting times may cause grogginess, inattention in class, and poor performance on tests. Based on her research, school officials in Edina, Minnesota, decided to start classes at 8:30 a.m. rather than the usual 7:25 a.m. Since then there have been fewer referrals for discipline problems, and the number of students who report being ill or depressed has decreased. The school system reports that test scores have improved for high school students, but not for middle school students. This finding supports Carskadon's suspicion that early start times are likely to be more stressful for older than for younger adolescents.

How Would You...?
As an educator, how would you use developmental research to convince your school board to change the starting time of high school?

Leading Causes of Death in Adolescence

The three leading causes of death in adolescence and emerging adulthood are accidents, homicide, and suicide (National Vital Statistics Reports, 2008). Almost half of all deaths from 15 to 24 years of age are due to unintentional injuries, approximately three-fourths of them involving motor vehicle accidents. Risky driving habits, such as speeding, tailgating, and driving under the influence of alcohol or other drugs, may be more important contributors to these accidents than lack of driving experience. In about 50 percent of motor vehicle fatalities involving adolescents, the driver has a blood alcohol level of 0.10 percent—twice the level needed to be designated as "under the influence" in some states. A high rate of intoxication is also found in adolescents who die as pedestrians, or while using recreational vehicles.

Homicide also is another leading cause of death in adolescence and emerging adulthood, especially among African American males, who are three times more likely to be killed by guns than by natural causes. Suicide is the third leading cause of death in adolescence and emerging adulthood. Since the 1950s, the adolescent and emerging adult suicide rate has tripled, although it has declined in recent years (Ash, 2008). We discuss suicide further in Chapter 16, "Socioemotional Development in Adolescence."

Substance Use and Abuse

Among the significant problems that can develop in adolescence are substance use and abuse (Chassin, Hussong, & Beltran, 2009; Hoffman, 2009; Patrick, Abar, & Maggs, 2009). We discuss these problems here, then, in Chapter 16, "Socioemotional Development in Adolescence," explore the adolescent problems of juvenile delinquency, depression, and suicide.

melatonin A sleep-inducing hormone that is produced in the brain's pineal gland.

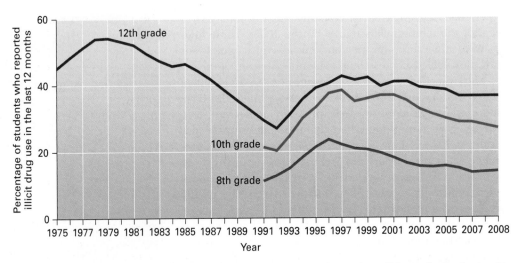

FIGURE 14.12 Trends in Drug Use by U.S. Eighth-, Tenth-, and Twelfth-Grade Students This graph shows the percentage of U.S. eighth-, tenth-, and twelfth-grade students who reported having taken an illicit drug in the last 12 months from 1991 to 2008, for eighth- and tenth-graders, and from 1975 to 2008 for twelfth-graders (Johnston & others, 2009).

Each year since 1975, Lloyd Johnston and his colleagues at the Institute of Social Research at the University of Michigan have monitored the drug use of America's high school seniors in a wide range of public and private high schools. Since 1991, they also have surveyed drug use by eighth- and tenth-graders. In 2007, the University of Michigan study, called the Monitoring the Future Study, surveyed 50,000 students in nearly 400 secondary schools.

According to this study, the proportions of eighth-, tenth-, and twelfth-grade U.S. students who used any illicit drug declined in the late 1990s and first years of the twenty-first century (Johnston & others, 2009) (see Figure 14.12). Nonetheless, even with the recent decline in use, the United States still has one of the highest rates of adolescent drug use of any industrialized nation. For example, one study revealed that a higher percentage of U.S. adolescents have used an illicit drug than adolescents in most European countries (Hibell & others, 2004).

How extensive is alcohol use by U.S. adolescents? Sizeable declines in adolescent alcohol use have occurred in recent years (Johnston & others, 2009). The percentage of U.S. eighth-graders saying that they had any alcohol to drink in the past 30 days fell from a 1996 high of 26 percent to 16 percent in 2008. The 30-day prevalence fell among tenth-graders from 39 percent in 2001 to 29 percent in 2008 and among high school seniors from 72 percent in 1980 to 43 percent in 2008. Binge drinking (defined in the University of Michigan surveys as having five or more drinks in a row in the last two weeks) by high school seniors declined from 41 percent in 1980 to 28 percent in 2008. Binge drinking by eighth- and tenth-graders also has dropped in recent years. A consistent sex difference occurs in binge drinking, with males engaging in this more than females.

Cigarette smoking among U.S. adolescents peaked in 1996 and 1997 and has gradually declined since then (Johnston & others, 2009). Following peak use in 1996, smoking rates for U.S. eighth-graders have fallen by 50 percent. In 2008, the percentages of adolescents who said they smoked cigarettes in the last 30 days were 20 percent (twelfth grade), 12 percent (tenth grade), and 7 percent (eighth grade).

Cigarette smoking (in which the active drug is nicotine) is one of the most serious yet preventable health problems. Smoking is likely to begin in grades 7 through 9, although sizable portions of youth are still establishing regular smoking habits during high school and college. Risk

What are some trends in alcohol use by U.S. adolescents?

factors for becoming a regular smoker in adolescence include having a friend who smokes, a weak academic orientation, and low parental support (Tucker, Ellickson, & Klein, 2003).

An alarming recent trend is use of prescription painkillers by adolescents (Forrester, 2007). A 2004 survey revealed that 18 percent of U.S. adolescents had used Vicodin (acetaminophen and hydrocodone) and 10 percent had used OxyContin (oxycodone) at some point in their lifetime (Partnership for a Drug-Free America, 2005). These drugs fall into the general class of drugs called narcotics, and they are highly addictive. In this national survey, 9 percent of adolescents said they had abused cough medications to intentionally get high. Adolescents cite the medicine cabinets of their parents or of friends' parents as the main source for their prescription painkillers (Johnston & others, 2008).

The Roles of Development, Education, Parents, and Peers A special concern involves adolescents who begin to use drugs early in adolescence or even in childhood (Chassin, Hussong, & Beltran, 2009; Hoffman, 2009). A recent study revealed that individuals who began drinking alcohol before 14 years of age were more likely to become alcohol dependent than their counterparts who began drinking alcohol at 21 years of age or older (Hingson, Heeren, & Winter, 2006). A longitudinal study of individuals from 8 to 42 years of age also found that early onset of drinking was linked to increased risk of heavy drinking in middle age (Pitkanen, Lyyra, & Pulkkinen, 2005).

Educational success is also a strong buffer for the emergence of drug problems in adolescence. A recent analysis by Jerald Bachman and his colleagues (2008) revealed that early educational achievement considerably reduced the likelihood that adolescents would develop drug problems, including those involving alcohol abuse, smoking, and abuse of various illicit drugs.

Parents, peers, and social support can also play important roles in preventing adolescent drug abuse. Positive relationships with parents and others can reduce adolescents' drug use (Chassin, Hussong, & Beltran, 2009). In one study, parental control and monitoring were linked with a lower incidence of problem behavior by adolescents, including substance abuse (Fletcher, Steinberg, & Williams-Wheeler, 2004). A recent study also revealed that adolescents who averaged having less than two family dinners a week were more likely to drink alcohol, smoke cigarettes, and abuse prescription drugs than their adolescent counterparts who averaged five or more family dinners a week (National Center on Addiction and Substance Abuse [CASA], 2007). Another recent study of more than 5,000 middle school students revealed that having friends in their school's social network and having fewer friends who use substances were related to a lower level of substance use (Ennett & others, 2006). To read about a program created to reduce adolescent drinking and smoking, see the *Research in Children's Development* interlude.

What are ways that parents have been found to influence whether their adolescents take drugs?

How would You...?
As a human development and family studies professional, how would you explain to parents the importance of parental monitoring in preventing adolescent substance abuse?

Research in Children's Development

EVALUATION OF A FAMILY PROGRAM DESIGNED TO REDUCE DRINKING AND SMOKING IN YOUNG ADOLESCENTS

Few experimental studies have been conducted to determine if family programs can reduce drinking and smoking in young adolescents. In one recent experimental study, 1,326 families with 12- to 14-year-old adolescents living throughout the United States

(continued on next page)

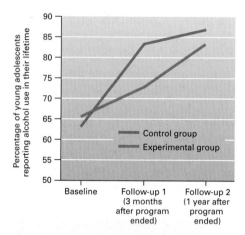

FIGURE 14.13 Young Adolescents' Reports of Alcohol Use in the Family Matters Program Note that at baseline (before the program started) the young adolescents in the Family Matters program (experimental group) and their counterparts who did not go through the program (control group) reported approximately the same lifetime use of alcohol (slightly higher use by the experimental group). However, three months after the program ended, the experimental group reported lower alcohol use, and this reduction was still present one year after the program ended, although at a reduced level.

were interviewed (Bauman & others, 2002). After the baseline interviews, participants were randomly assigned either to go through the Family Matters program (experimental group) or not to experience the program (control group) (Bauman & others, 2002).

The families assigned to the Family Matters program received four mailings of booklets. Each mailing was followed by a telephone call from a health educator to "encourage participation by all family members, answer any questions, and record information" (Bauman & others, 2002, pp. 36–37). The first booklet focused on the negative consequences of adolescent substance abuse to the family. The second booklet emphasized "supervision, support, communication skills, attachment, time spent together, educational achievement, conflict reduction, and how well adolescence is understood." The third booklet asked parents to "list things that they do that might inadvertently encourage their child's use of tobacco or alcohol, identify rules that might influence the child's use, and consider ways to monitor use. Then adult family members and the child meet to agree upon rules and sanctions related to adolescent use." Booklet four deals with what "the child can do to resist peer and media pressures for use."

Two follow-up interviews with the parents and adolescents were conducted three months and one year after the experimental group completed the program. Adolescents in the Family Matters program reported lower alcohol and cigarette use both at three months and again one year after the program had been completed. Figure 14.13 shows the results for alcohol.

Eating Problems and Disorders

Eating disorders have become increasingly common among adolescents (Frisco, 2009; Napierski-Pranci, 2009). Here are some research findings involving adolescent eating disorders:

- *Body image.* In general, adolescents were dissatisfied with their bodies, with males desiring to increase their upper body and females wanting to decrease the overall size of their body (Ata, Ludden, & Lally, 2007). In this study, low self-esteem and social support, weight-related teasing, and pressure to lose weight were linked to adolescents' negative body image. In another study, girls who felt negatively about their bodies in early adolescence were more likely to develop eating disorders, two years later, than their counterparts who did not feel negatively about their bodies (Attie & Brooks-Gunn, 1989).

- *Parenting.* Adolescents who reported observing more healthy eating patterns and exercise by their parents had more healthy eating patterns and exercised more themselves (Pakpreo & others, 2005). Negative parent-adolescent relationships were linked with increased dieting by girls over a one-year period (Archibald, Graber, & Brooks-Gunn, 1999).

- *Sexual activity.* Girls who were both sexually active with their boyfriends and in pubertal transition were the most likely to be dieting or engaging in disordered eating patterns (Cauffman, 1994).

- *Role models and the media.* Girls who were highly motivated to look like same-sex figures in the media were more likely than their peers to become very concerned about their weight (Field & others, 2001). Watching commercials with idealized thin female images increased adolescent girls' dissatisfaction with their bodies (Hargreaves & Tiggemann, 2004). A recent study of adolescent girls revealed that frequent reading of magazine articles about dieting and weight loss was linked with unhealthy weight-control behaviors such as fasting, skipping meals, and smoking more cigarettes five years later (van den berg & others, 2007).

What types of interventions have been successful in reducing overweight in adolescents? One research review indicated that clinical approaches that focus on the individual adolescent and include a combination of caloric restriction, exercise (walking or biking to school, participation in a regular exercise program), reduction of sedentary activity (watching TV, playing video games), and behavioral therapy (such as keeping weight-loss diaries and receiving rewards for meeting goals) have been moderately effective in helping overweight adolescents lose weight (Fowler-Brown & Kahwati, 2004). In general, school-based approaches (such as instituting a school-wide program to improve eating habits) have been less effective than the clinically based individual approaches (Lytle & others, 2004). A recent research review concluded that school-based approaches for reducing adolescents' weight have modest results, with TV watching the easiest behavior to change, followed by physical activity and then nutrition (Sharma, 2006).

These adolescent girls are attending a weight-management camp. *What types of interventions have been most successful in helping overweight adolescents lose weight?*

A concern is that as schools are under increasing pressure to spend more time on academic topics, health-oriented programs are likely to be shortchanged (Paxson & others, 2006). When this is an impediment, one possibility is to include obesity prevention in after-school programs, which conflict less with schools' academic mandates (Story, Kaphingst, & French, 2006). Another promising strategy is to provide students with healthier foods to eat at school. In 2005, several states began enacting laws that require more healthy foods and fewer nonhealthy foods be sold in vending machines at schools (Story, Kaphingst, & French, 2006). In one intervention, reducing soft drink consumption at schools was linked with a subsequent reduction in the number of 7- to 11-year-old children who were overweight or obese (James & others, 2004). Schools also can play an important role by implementing programs that increase the amount of time children exercise (Datar & Sturm, 2004; Paxson & others, 2006).

Let's now examine two eating problems—anorexia nervosa and bulimia nervosa. Researchers consistently have discovered that the onset of anorexia nervosa and bulimia nervosa occurs in adolescence and that their onset in adulthood is rare (Striegel-Moore & Bulik, 2007). They also have found that eating disorders, including anorexia nervosa and bulimia nervosa, are far more likely to characterize females than males (Hoek, 2006).

Anorexia Nervosa   **Anorexia nervosa** is an eating disorder that involves the relentless pursuit of thinness through starvation. It is a serious disorder that can lead to death. Anorexia nervosa is about 10 times more likely to occur in females than males. Although most U.S. girls have been on a diet at some point, slightly less than 1 percent ever develop anorexia nervosa.

Three main characteristics of anorexia nervosa are (1) weighing less than 85 percent of what is considered normal for a person's age and height, (2) having an intense fear of gaining weight—the fear does not decrease with weight loss, and (3) having a distorted image of body shape (Rigaud & others, 2007). Even when they are extremely thin, anorexics see themselves as too fat. They never think they are thin enough, especially in the abdomen, buttocks, and thighs. They usually weigh themselves frequently, often take their body measurements, and gaze critically at themselves in mirrors.

Anorexia nervosa typically begins in the early to middle teenage years, often following an episode of dieting and some type of life stress. When anorexia nervosa does occur in males, the symptoms and other characteristics (such as a distorted body image and family conflict) are usually similar to those reported by females who have the disorder (Ariceli & others, 2005).

Most anorexics are non-Latino White adolescent or emerging adult females from well-educated, middle- and upper-income families, and they are competitive and high-achieving (Schmidt, 2003). They become stressed about not being able to reach the high expectations and turn to something they can control: their weight. Offspring of mothers with anorexia nervosa are at risk for becoming anorexic themselves (Striegel-Moore & Bulik, 2007). Problems in family functioning are increasingly

Anorexia nervosa has become an increasing problem for adolescent girls and emerging adult women. *What are some possible causes of anorexia nervosa?*

anorexia nervosa An eating disorder that involves the relentless pursuit of thinness through starvation.

being found to be linked to the appearance of anorexia nervosa in adolescent girls (Benninghoven & others, 2007), and a recent research review indicated that family therapy is often the most effective treatment (Bulik & others, 2007).

The fashion image in U.S. culture contributes to the incidence of anorexia nervosa (Striegel-Moore & Bulik, 2007). The media portray thin as beautiful in their choice of fashion models, and many adolescent girls strive to emulate them. And many adolescent girls who want to be thin hang out together. A recent study of adolescent girls revealed that friends often share similar body image and eating problems (Hutchinson & Rapee, 2007). In this study, an individual girl's dieting and extreme weight-loss behavior could be predicted from her friends' dieting and extreme weight-loss behavior.

How Would You...?
As a health-care professional, how would you educate parents to identify the signs and symptoms that may signal an eating disorder?

Bulimia Nervosa   Whereas anorexics control their eating by restricting it, most bulimics do not. **Bulimia nervosa** is an eating disorder in which the individual consistently follows a binge-and-purge pattern. The bulimic goes on an eating binge and then purges by self-inducing vomiting or using a laxative. Although many people binge and purge occasionally and some experiment with it, a person is considered to have a serious bulimic disorder only if the episodes occur at least twice a week for three months.

As with anorexics, most bulimics are preoccupied with food, have a strong fear of becoming overweight, are depressed or anxious, and have a distorted body image. A recent study revealed that bulimics overvalued their body weight and shape, and this overvaluation was linked to higher depression and lower self-esteem (Hrabosky & others, 2007). Unlike anorexics, people who binge-and-purge typically fall within a normal weight range, which makes bulimia more difficult to detect.

About 90 percent of bulimics are females, and approximately 1 to 2 percent of U.S. females are estimated to develop bulimia nervosa. Bulimia nervosa typically begins in late adolescence or early adulthood. Many women who develop bulimia nervosa were somewhat overweight before the onset of the disorder, and the binge eating often began during an episode of dieting. As with anorexia nervosa, about 70 percent of individuals who develop bulimia nervosa eventually recover from the disorder (Agras & others, 2004).

Risk Factors, Developmental Assets, and Social Capital

Now that we have discussed many aspects of adolescent risk taking and several major problems that can develop in adolescence, we further explore the nature of risk factors and the developmental assets that can protect adolescents from experiencing problems. Many studies have shown that factors such as poverty, ineffective parenting, and mental disorders in parents *predict* adolescent problems (Mash & Wolfe, 2007). Predictors of problems are called *risk factors*. Risk factor means that there is an elevated probability of a problem outcome in groups of people who have that factor. Children with many risk factors are said to have a "high risk" for problems in childhood and adolescence, but not every one of these children will develop problems.

The Search Institute in Minneapolis has described 40 developmental assets that they believe adolescents need to achieve positive outcomes in their lives (Benson, 2006; Benson & others, 2006). Half of these assets are external; half are internal. The 20 *external* assets include the following:

- *Support*—such as family and neighborhood
- *Empowerment*—such as adults in the community valuing youth, and youth being given useful community roles
- *Boundaries and expectations*—such as the family setting clear rules and consequences and monitoring the adolescent's whereabouts, as well as positive peer influence

bulimia nervosa An eating disorder in which the individual consistently follows a binge-and-purge eating pattern.

- *Constructive use of time*—such as engaging in creative activities three or more times a week and participating three or more hours a week in organized youth programs

The 20 *internal* assets include the following:

- *Commitment to learning*—such as motivation to achieve in school and to do at least one hour of homework on school days
- *Positive values*—such as helping others and demonstrating integrity
- *Social competencies*—such as knowing how to plan and make decisions and having interpersonal competencies like empathy and friendship skills
- *Positive identity*—such as having a sense of control over life and high self-esteem

In research conducted by the Search Institute, adolescents with more assets reported engaging in fewer risk-taking behaviors, such as alcohol and tobacco use, sexual intercourse, and violence. For example, in one survey of more than 12,000 ninth- to twelfth-graders, 53 percent of the students with 0 to 10 assets reported using alcohol three or more times in the past month or getting drunk more than once in the past two weeks, compared with only 16 percent of the students with 21 to 30 assets or 4 percent of the students with 31 to 40 assets.

Related to the concept of developmental assets, a recent study found that these activities, resources, and relationships promoted adolescents' health-enhancing behaviors (Youngblade & Curry, 2006): (1) participation in school-related organized activities, such as sports; (2) availability of positive community resources, such as boys and girls clubs, and volunteering; and (3) secure attachment to parents. In this study, health-enhancing behavior was assessed by asking adolescents the extent to which they engaged in such behaviors as wearing a seat belt and engaging in physical activities in and out of school. Another recent study found that a higher level of what was labeled *social capital* (in this study, number of schools, number of churches/temples/synagogues, number of adults with high school diplomas, and number of high school diplomas) was linked with lower levels of adolescent risky behavior (in this study, gunshot wounds, pregnancy, alcohol and drug treatment, and sexually transmitted infections) (Youngblade & others, 2006).

These adolescents are participating in Girls Club and Boys Club activities. Such community resources can provide important support for adolescents' health-enhancing behavior.

Review and Reflect: Learning Goal 4

 Summarize adolescents' health and eating disorders

REVIEW

- What are key concerns about the health of adolescents?
- What are the leading causes of death in adolescence and emerging adulthood?
- What are some characteristics of adolescents' substance use and abuse?
- What are the characteristics of the major eating disorders?
- What characterizes risk taking, developmental assets, and social capital in adolescence?

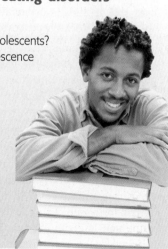

REFLECT

- What do you think should be done to reduce the use of drugs by adolescents?

Reach Your Learning Goals

Physical Development in Adolescence

1 WHAT IS THE NATURE OF ADOLESCENCE? DISCUSS VIEWS AND DEVELOPMENTAL TRANSITIONS THAT INVOLVE ADOLESCENCE

Positive and Negative Views of Adolescence

- Many stereotypes about adolescents are negative. Today, however, the majority of adolescents successfully negotiate the path from childhood to adulthood, although too many are not provided with adequate support and opportunities. It is important to view adolescents as a heterogeneous group. Acting out and boundary testing by adolescents move them toward accepting, rather than rejecting, parental values. In Damon's view, many U.S. adults instill shortsighted thinking and a desire for immediate gratification in their adolescents and children. Parents can help guide their adolescents by talking about their own setbacks and dilemmas and purpose in life.

Developmental Transitions

- Two important transitions in development are those from childhood to adolescence and from adolescence to adulthood. In the transition from childhood to adolescence, pubertal change is prominent, although cognitive and socioemotional changes occur as well. Emerging adulthood recently has been proposed to describe the transition from adolescence to adulthood. Five key characteristics of emerging adulthood are identity exploration (especially in love and work), instability, being self-focused, feeling in-between, and experiencing possibilities to transform one's life.

2 WHAT ARE THE PHYSICAL AND PSYCHOLOGICAL ASPECTS OF PUBERTY? DESCRIBE PUBERTY'S CHARACTERISTICS, DEVELOPMENTAL CHANGES, PSYCHOLOGICAL DIMENSIONS, AND THE DEVELOPMENT OF THE BRAIN

Sexual Maturation, Height, and Weight

- Puberty is a rapid physical maturation involving hormonal and bodily changes that take place primarily in early adolescence. A number of changes occur in sexual maturation including increased size of the penis and testicles in boys and breast growth and menarche in girls. The growth spurt involves height and weight and occurs about two years earlier for girls than for boys.

Hormonal Changes

- Extensive hormonal changes characterize puberty. The pituitary gland plays an important role in these hormonal changes. During puberty, testosterone concentrations increase considerably in boys, and estradiol increases considerably in girls.

Timing and Variations in Puberty

- In the United States, the age of menarche (a girl's first menstrual period) has declined since the mid-1800s. The basic genetic program for puberty is wired into the nature of the species, but nutrition, health, and other environmental factors affect puberty's timing and makeup. Menarche typically appears between 9 and 15 years of age. Boys can start the pubertal sequence as early as 10 years of age or as late as 17.

Psychological Dimensions of Puberty

- Adolescents show heightened interest in their bodies and body images. Younger adolescents are more preoccupied with these images than are older adolescents. Adolescent girls often have a more negative body image than do adolescent boys. Early maturation often favors boys, at least during early adolescence, but as adults, late-maturing boys have a more positive identity than early-maturing boys. Early-maturing girls are at risk for a number of developmental problems. They are more likely to smoke and drink and have an eating disorder and are likely to have earlier sexual experiences than will later-maturing girls.

| The Brain | • The thickening of the corpus callosum in adolescence is linked to improved processing of information. The amygdala, which is involved in emotions such as anger, matures earlier than the prefrontal cortex, which functions in reasoning and self-regulation. This gap in development may help to explain the increase in risk-taking behavior that often characterizes adolescence. |

3 WHAT ARE THE DIMENSIONS OF ADOLESCENT SEXUALITY? CHARACTERIZE ADOLESCENT SEXUALITY

| Developing a Sexual Identity | • Adolescence is a time of sexual exploration and sexual experimentation. Mastering emerging sexual feelings and forming a sense of sexual identity are multifaceted. An adolescent's sexual identity includes sexual orientation, activities, interests, and styles of behavior. |

| Timing and Trends in Adolescent Sexual Behavior | • The timing of sexual initiation in adolescence varies by country, gender, and socioeconomic characteristics. A recent U.S. survey revealed that 63 percent of twelfth-graders (64 percent males, 62 percent females) reported having had sexual intercourse compared with 34 percent of ninth-graders (39 percent males, 29 percent females). There has been a dramatic increase in oral sex among U.S. adolescents. |

| Sexual Risk Taking in Adolescence | • Having sexual intercourse in early adolescence, as well as various contextual and family factors, is associated with sexual problems and negative developmental outcomes. Adolescents are increasing their use of contraceptives, but large numbers still do not use them. Sexually transmitted infections (STIs) are contracted primarily through sexual contact. Approximately one in four sexually active adolescents have an STI. Among the STIs are bacterial infections such as gonorrhea, syphilis, and chlamydia, and viral infections such as genital herpes, genital warts, and AIDS. Although the U.S. adolescent pregnancy rate is still among the highest in the developed world, the rate declined considerably in the 1990s; however, the U.S. adolescent birth rate increased in 2006. Adolescent pregnancy often increases health risks for the mother and the offspring, although it often is not pregnancy alone that places adolescents at risk. Easy access to family-planning services and sex education programs in schools can help reduce the U.S. adolescent pregnancy rate. |

4 HOW CAN ADOLESCENTS' HEALTH AND HEALTH-ENHANCING ASSETS BE CHARACTERIZED? SUMMARIZE ADOLESCENTS' HEALTH AND EATING DISORDERS

| Adolescent Health | • Adolescence is a critical juncture in health because many of the factors related to poor health habits and early death in the adult years begin during adolescence. Poor nutrition, lack of exercise, and inadequate sleep are concerns. |

| Leading Causes of Death in Adolescence | • The three leading causes of death in adolescence and emerging adulthood are accidents, homicide, and suicide. |

| Substance Use and Abuse | • Despite recent declines in use, the United States has one of the highest rate of adolescent drug use of any industrialized nation. Alcohol abuse is a major adolescent problem, although its rate has been dropping in recent years, as has cigarette smoking. A recent concern is the increased use of prescription painkillers by adolescents. Drug use in childhood or early adolescence has more negative outcomes than drug use that begins in late adolescence. Parents and peers play important roles in whether adolescents take drugs. |

Eating Problems and Disorders	• Eating disorders have increased in adolescence, with a substantial increase in the percentage of adolescents who are overweight. Three eating disorders that may occur in adolescence are obesity, anorexia nervosa, and bulimia nervosa. A combination of behavioral therapy, calorie restriction, exercise, and reduction of sedentary activities such as TV watching has been more effective for overweight adolescents than school-based approaches. Anorexia nervosa is an eating disorder that involves the relentless pursuit of thinness through starvation. Anorexics are intensely afraid of weight gain, have a distorted body image, and weigh less than 85 percent of weight considered to be normal. Bulimia nervosa is an eating disorder in which a binge-and-purge pattern is consistently followed. Most bulimics are depressed or anxious, fear becoming overweight, and their weight typically falls within a normal range. About 70 percent of bulimics and anorexics eventually recover.
Risk Factors, Developmental Assets, and Social Capital	• The of number of risk factors are linked to adolescent problems. A number of developmental assets (support, commitment to learning, positive identity, for example) and various aspects of social capital (number of schools, number of churches/temples/synagogues, for example) help to protect adolescents from developing problems.

KEY TERMS

emerging adulthood 467
puberty 468
menarche 468
hormones 468
hypothalamus 468

pituitary gland 468
gonads 470
gonadotropins 470
testosterone 470
estradiol 470

precocious puberty 471
corpus callosum 473
amygdala 473
sexually transmitted
  infections (STIs) 477

AIDS 477
melatonin 485
anorexia nervosa 489
bulimia nervosa 490

KEY PEOPLE

G. Stanley Hall 465
Daniel Offer 465
Jacqueline Lerner 465

William Damon 466
Jeffrey Arnett 467
Judith Blakemore 471

Charles Nelson 472
Mary Carskadon 485

Lloyd Johnston 486

MAKING A DIFFERENCE

Supporting Adolescent Physical Development and Health

What are some strategies for supporting and guiding adolescent physical development and health?

• *Develop positive expectations for adolescents.* Adolescents often are negatively stereotyped. These negative expectations have a way of becoming self-fulfilling prophecies and harming adult-adolescent communication. Don't view adolescence as a time of crisis and rebellion. View it as a time of evaluation, decision making, commitment, and the carving out of a place in the world.

• *Understand the many physical changes adolescents are going through.* The physical changes adolescents go through can be very perplexing to them. They are not quite sure what they are going to change into, and this can create considerable uncertainty for them.

• *Be a good health role model for adolescents.* Adolescents benefit from being around adults who are good health role models: individuals who exercise regularly, eat healthily, and don't take drugs or smoke.

• *Communicate effectively with adolescents about sexuality.* Emphasize that young adolescents should abstain from sex. If adolescents are going to be sexually active, they need to take contraceptive precautions. Adolescents also need to learn about sexuality and human reproduction before they become sexually active.

RESOURCES FOR IMPROVING CHILDREN'S LIVES

Search Institute
www.search-institute.org

The Search Institute has available a large number of resources for improving the lives of adolescents. In 1995, the Institute began distributing the excellent publications of the Center for Early Adolescence, University of North Carolina, which had just closed. The brochures and books include resource lists and address school improvement, adolescent literacy, parent education, program planning, and adolescent health. A free quarterly newsletter is also available.

The Society for Adolescent Medicine (SAM)
www.adolescenthealth.org

SAM is a valuable source of information about competent physicians who specialize in treating adolescents. It maintains a list of recommended adolescence specialists across the United States.

The Path to Purpose
by William Damon (2008)
New York: Free Press

A provocative new book by leading expert William Damon on helping adolescents find their calling in life.

E-LEARNING TOOLS

Connect to **www.mhhe.com/santrockc11e** to research the answers and complete these exercises. In addition, you'll find a number of other resources and valuable study tools for Chapter 14, "Physical Development in Adolescence," on this Web site.

Taking It to the Net

1. Allison hangs out with a group of high school seniors who like to party and drink alcohol on the weekends. Even though she has heard all of the slogans and seen films about the hazards of drinking and driving, she continues to drink. "It's not as bad as doing hard drugs," she rationalizes. "Besides, practically everyone drinks in high school." However, Allison is not aware of the physiological effects drinking has on teenagers. How, specifically, might drinking affect brain development in adolescents?

2. Peter, a high school junior, has known since he was about 6 years old that he is gay. However, he has not told anyone at school, because he is worried that the other kids would reject and harass him. He also has not told his parents. What kinds of issues do gay youth face in high school? What is the high school environment like for most gay and lesbian youth? Are gay and lesbian youth more at risk for disorders such as depression and anxiety? What interventions might ease the coming-out process?

3. Marguerite is very concerned about her sister, Rosalina. Rosalina has lost a significant amount of weight recently, and she now refuses to eat dinner with her family. This behavior is causing Rosalina's parents to become very upset, as food is an important part of their traditional Mexican American household. Marguerite thinks Rosalina might have an eating disorder. How might Marguerite approach Rosalina? What are the signs and symptoms of the various eating disorders? How

might Rosalina's cultural background complicate the issues around her disordered eating?

Health and Well-Being, Parenting, and Education

Build your decision-making skills by trying your hand at the health and well-being, parenting, and education exercises.

Video Clips

The Online Learning Center includes the following videos for this chapter:

- *Girls and Body Image—1241*
  Two mature 14-year-olds talk about the social pressure for physical appearance. Brekke says that magazines greatly influence girls to look a certain way. She also describes how some girls look a certain way to be popular.

- *15-Year-Old Girls' Relationships with Boys—1161*
  In this clip, you can hear three high school students talk about how their relationships with boys have changed since middle school. They discuss how boys are more mature in high school and are often easier to talk to than girls.

- *Talking About Teen Sex at 14—1243*
  Two mature 14-year-old girls give their opinions about teen sex. They point out that teens do not consider the long-term consequences of having sexual intercourse. They both agree that if teens are going to engage in sex, they need to be sure, think ahead, and "use precautions."

- *Talking About Drugs at Age 14—1245*
  Two adolescent girls express their views about drug use among teens. One girl says frankly that smoking a joint is no worse than drinking a glass of wine.

15

> *The thoughts of youth are long, long thoughts.*
>
> —HENRY WADSWORTH LONGFELLOW
> *American Poet, 19th Century*

LEARNING GOALS

- ◆ Discuss different approaches to adolescent cognition

- ◆ Describe adolescents' values, moral education, and religion

- ◆ Characterize schools for adolescents

- ◆ Summarize career development in adolescence

COGNITIVE DEVELOPMENT IN ADOLESCENCE

CHAPTER OUTLINE

1 HOW DO ADOLESCENTS THINK AND PROCESS INFORMATION?

Piaget's Theory

Adolescent Egocentrism

Information Processing

2 WHAT CHARACTERIZES ADOLESCENTS' VALUES, MORAL EDUCATION, AND RELIGION?

Values

Moral Education

Religion

3 WHAT IS THE NATURE OF SCHOOLS FOR ADOLESCENTS?

The American Middle School

The American High School

High School Dropouts

4 HOW DO ADOLESCENTS EXPERIENCE CAREER DEVELOPMENT?

Views of Career Development

Exploration, Decision Making, and Planning

Sociocultural Influences

Images of Children's Development
Kim-Chi and Thuy

Kim-Chi Trinh was only 9 years old in Vietnam when her father used his savings to buy passage for her on a fishing boat. It was a costly and risky sacrifice for the family, who placed Kim-Chi on the small boat, among strangers, in the hope that she eventually would reach the United States, where she would get a good education and enjoy a better life.

Kim-Chi made it to the United States and coped with a succession of three foster families. When she graduated from high school in San Diego in 1988, she had a straight A average and a number of college scholarship offers. When asked why she excels in school, Kim-Chi says that she has to do well because she owes it to her parents, who are still in Vietnam.

Kim-Chi is one of a wave of bright, highly motivated Asians who are immigrating to America. Percentage-wise, Asian Americans are the fastest-growing ethnic minority group in the United States—two out of five immigrants are now Asian. Although Asian Americans make up only 4 percent of the U.S. population, they constituted 18.5 percent of the 2008 freshman class at Harvard and a staggering 49 percent at the University of California at Irvine.

Not all Asian American youth do this well, however. Poorly educated Vietnamese, Cambodian, and Hmong refugee youth are especially at risk for school-related problems. Many refugee children's histories are replete with losses and trauma. Thuy, a 12-year-old Vietnamese girl, has been in the United States for two years and resides with her father in a small apartment with a cousin's family of five in the inner city of a West Coast metropolitan area (Huang, 1989). While trying to escape from Saigon, "the family became separated, and the wife and two younger children remained in Vietnam. . . . Thuy's father has had an especially difficult time adjusting to the United States. He struggles with English classes and has been unable to maintain several jobs as a waiter" (Huang, 1989, p. 307). When Thuy received a letter from her mother saying that her 5-year-old brother had died, Thuy's schoolwork began to deteriorate, and she showed marked signs of depression—lack of energy, loss of appetite, withdrawal from peer relations, and a general feeling of hopelessness. At the insistence of the school, she and her father went to the child and adolescent unit of a community mental health center. It took the therapist a long time to establish credibility with Thuy and her father, but eventually they began to trust the therapist, who was a good listener and gave them competent advice about how to handle different experiences in the new country. The therapist also contacted Thuy's teacher, who said that Thuy had been involved in several interethnic skirmishes at school. With the assistance of the mental health clinic, the school initiated interethnic student panels to address cultural differences and discuss reasons for ethnic hostility. Thuy was selected to participate in these panels. Her father became involved in the community mutual assistance association, and Thuy's academic performance began to improve.

PREVIEW

When people think of the changes that characterize adolescents, they often focus on puberty and adolescent problems. However, some impressive cognitive changes occur during adolescence. We begin this chapter by focusing on these cognitive changes and then turn our attention to adolescents' values, moral education, and religion. Next, we study the characteristics of schools for adolescents and conclude the chapter by examining career development in adolescence.

1 HOW DO ADOLESCENTS THINK AND PROCESS INFORMATION?

Piaget's Theory   **Adolescent Egocentrism**   **Information Processing**

Adolescents' developing power of thought opens up new cognitive and social horizons. Let's examine the characteristics of this developing power of thought, beginning with Piaget's theory (1952).

Piaget's Theory

As we discussed in Chapter 12, "Cognitive Development in Middle and Late Childhood," Jean Piaget proposed that at about 7 years of age children enter the *concrete operational stage* of cognitive development. They can reason logically about concrete events and objects, and they make gains in the ability to classify objects and to reason about the relationships between classes of objects. According to Piaget, the concrete operational stage lasts until the child is about 11 years old, when the fourth and final stage of cognitive development begins, the formal operational stage.

The Formal Operational Stage   What are the characteristics of the formal operational stage? Formal operational thought is more abstract than concrete operational thought. Adolescents are no longer limited to actual experiences as anchors for thought. They can conjure up make-believe situations, events that are purely hypothetical possibilities or abstract propositions and can try to reason logically about them.

The abstract quality of thinking during the formal operational stage is evident in the adolescent's verbal problem-solving ability. Whereas the concrete operational thinker needs to see the concrete elements A, B, and C to be able to make the logical inference that, if A = B and B = C, then A = C, the formal operational thinker can solve this problem merely through verbal presentation.

Another indication of the abstract quality of adolescents' thought is their increased tendency to think about thought itself. One adolescent commented, "I began thinking about why I was thinking what I was. Then I began thinking about why I was thinking about what I was thinking about what I was." If this sounds abstract, it is, and it characterizes the adolescent's enhanced focus on thought and its abstract qualities.

Accompanying the abstract nature of formal operational thought is thought full of idealism and possibilities, especially during the beginning of the formal operational stage, when assimilation dominates. Adolescents engage in extended speculation about ideal characteristics—qualities they desire in themselves and in others. Such thoughts often lead adolescents to compare themselves with others in regard to such ideal standards. And their thoughts are often fantasy flights into future possibilities. It is not unusual for the adolescent to become impatient with these newfound ideal standards and to become perplexed over which of many ideal standards to adopt.

At the same time that adolescents think more abstractly and idealistically, they also think more logically about abstract concepts. Children are likely to solve problems through trial-and-error; adolescents begin to think more as a scientist thinks, devising plans to solve problems and systematically testing solutions. This type of problem solving requires **hypothetical-deductive reasoning.** Such reasoning involves creating a hypothesis and deducing its implications, which provide ways to test the hypothesis. Thus, formal operational thinkers develop hypotheses about ways to solve problems and then systematically deduce the best path to follow to solve the problem.

Might adolescents' ability to reason hypothetically and to evaluate what is ideal versus what is real lead them to engage in demonstrations, such as this protest related to better ethnic relations? What other causes might be attractive to adolescents' newfound cognitive abilities of hypothetical-deductive reasoning and idealistic thinking?

hypothetical-deductive reasoning Piaget's formal operational concept that adolescents have the cognitive ability to develop hypotheses, or best guesses, about ways to solve problems.

One example of hypothetical-deductive reasoning involves a modification of the familiar game Twenty Questions. Individuals are shown a set of 42 color pictures, displayed in a rectangular array (six rows of seven pictures each) and then are asked to determine which picture the experimenter has in mind (that is, which is "correct"). The individuals are allowed to ask only questions to which the experimenter can answer yes or no. The object of the game is to select the correct picture by asking as few questions as possible. Adolescents who are deductive hypothesis testers formulate a plan and test a series of hypotheses, steps that considerably narrow the field of choices. The most effective plan is a "halving" strategy (Q: Is the picture in the right half of the array? A: No. Q: Okay. Is it in the top half? And so on.). A correct halving strategy guarantees the answer in seven questions or less. By contrast, concrete operational thinkers may persist with questions that continue to test some of the same possibilities that previous questions could have eliminated. For example, they may ask whether the correct picture is in row 1 and are told that it is not. Later, they may ask whether the picture is X, which is in row 1.

Thus, formal operational thinkers test their hypotheses with judiciously chosen questions and tests. By contrast, concrete operational thinkers often fail to understand the relation between a hypothesis and a well-chosen test of it, stubbornly clinging to ideas that already have been discounted.

Evaluating Piaget's Theory   Some of Piaget's ideas on the formal operational stage have been challenged (Diamond, Casey, & Munakata, 2010; Kuhn, 2008, 2009). The stage includes much more individual variation than Piaget envisioned. Only about one in three young adolescents is a formal operational thinker. Many American adults never become formal operational thinkers, and neither do many adults in other cultures.

Furthermore, education in the logic of science and mathematics promotes the development of formal operational thinking. This point recalls a criticism of Piaget's theory that we discussed in Chapter 12, "Cognitive Development in Middle and Late Childhood,": Culture and education exert stronger influences on cognitive development than Piaget maintained (Holzman, 2009; Sternberg & Williams, 2010).

Piaget's theory of cognitive development has been challenged on other points as well (Bauer, 2009; Spelke & Kinster, 2009). As we noted in Chapter 9, "Cognitive Development in Early Childhood," Piaget conceived of stages as unitary structures of thought, with various aspects of a stage emerging at the same time. However, most contemporary developmentalists agree that cognitive development is not as stage-like as Piaget thought (Kuhn, 2009; Mayer, 2008; Sternberg & Williams, 2010). Furthermore, children can be trained to reason at a higher cognitive stage, and some cognitive abilities emerge earlier than Piaget thought (Aslin, 2009). For example, even 2-year-olds are nonegocentric in some contexts. When they realize that another person will not see an object, they investigate whether the person is blindfolded or looking in a different direction. Some understanding of the conservation of number has been demonstrated as early as age 3, although Piaget did not think it emerged until 7. Other cognitive abilities can emerge later than Piaget thought (Kuhn, 2009). As we have discussed, many adolescents still think in concrete operational ways or are just beginning to master formal operations. Even many adults are not formal operational thinkers.

Despite these challenges to Piaget's ideas, we owe him a tremendous debt. Piaget was the founder of the present field of cognitive development, and he established a long list of masterful concepts of enduring power and fascination: assimilation, accommodation, object permanence, egocentrism, conservation, and others (Carpendale, Muller, & Bibok, 2008). Psychologists also owe him the current vision of children as active, constructive thinkers. And they have a debt to him for creating a theory that generated a huge volume of research on children's cognitive development.

Piaget was a genius when it came to observing children. His careful observations demonstrated inventive ways to discover how children act on and adapt to their world. He also showed us how children need to make their experiences fit their schemes yet simultaneously adapt their schemes to experience. Piaget revealed how cognitive change is likely to occur if the context is structured to allow gradual movement to the next higher level. Concepts do not emerge suddenly, full-blown, but instead develop through a series of partial accomplishments that lead to increasingly comprehensive understanding (Johnson, 2009a, b, c; Quinn & Bhatt, 2009).

Adolescent Egocentrism

Adolescent egocentrism is the heightened self-consciousness of adolescents. David Elkind (1976) argues that adolescent egocentrism has two key components—the imaginary audience and personal fable. The **imaginary audience** is adolescents' belief that others are as interested in them as they themselves are, as well as attention-getting behavior. An adolescent might think that others are as aware of a small spot on his trousers as he is, possibly knowing that he has masturbated. Another adolescent, an eighth-grade girl, walks into her classroom and thinks that all eyes are riveted on her complexion.

According to Elkind, the **personal fable** is the part of adolescent egocentrism involving a sense of uniqueness and invincibility. This sense of invincibility may also lead adolescents to believe that they themselves are invulnerable to dangers and catastrophes (such as deadly car wrecks) that happen to other people. As a result, some adolescents engage in risky behaviors such as drag racing, using drugs, and having sexual intercourse without using contraceptives or barriers against STIs (Alberts, Elkind, & Ginsberg, 2007). However, some research studies suggest that rather than perceiving themselves to be invulnerable, adolescents tend to portray themselves as vulnerable to experiencing a premature death (Bruine de Bruin, Parker, & Fischhoff, 2007; Reyna & Rivers, 2008). For example, during a conversation between two 14-year-old girls, one named Margaret says, "Are you kidding, I won't get pregnant."

Adolescents' sense of personal uniqueness makes them believe that no one can understand how they really feel. Thirteen-year-old Adam describes himself: "No one understands me, particularly my parents. They have no idea of what I am feeling." As part of their effort to retain a sense of personal uniqueness, adolescents might craft a story about the self that is filled with fantasy, immersing themselves in a world that is far removed from reality. Personal fables frequently show up in adolescent diaries.

Many adolescent girls spend long hours in front of the mirror, depleting cans of hairspray, tubes of lipstick, and jars of cosmetics. *How might this behavior be related to changes in adolescent cognitive and physical development?*

Information Processing

Deanna Kuhn (2009) recently discussed some important characteristics of adolescents' information processing and thinking. In her view, in the later years of childhood and continuing in adolescence, individuals approach cognitive levels that may or may not be achieved, in contrast to the largely universal cognitive levels that young children attain. By adolescence, considerable variation in cognitive functioning is present across individuals. This variability supports the argument that adolescents are producers of their own development to a greater extent than are children.

Kuhn (2009) further argues that the most important cognitive change in adolescence is improvement in *executive functioning,* which involves higher-order cognitive activities such as reasoning, making decisions, monitoring thinking critically, and monitoring one's cognitive progress. Improvements in executive functioning permit more effective learning and an improved ability to determine how attention will be allocated, to make decisions, and to engage in critical thinking. We begin our discussion of information processing in adolescence by focusing on memory, then turn our attention to executive functioning.

adolescent egocentrism The heightened self-consciousness of adolescents that is reflected in their belief that others are as interested in them as they are in themselves, and in their sense of personal uniqueness and invincibility.

imaginary audience Adolescents' belief that others are as interested in them as they themselves are, as well as attention-getting behavior.

personal fable The part of adolescent egocentrism that involves an adolescent's sense of uniqueness and invincibility.

Memory What are some aspects of memory that change during adolescence? They include short-term memory, working memory, and long-term memory.

Short-Term Memory How might short-term memory be used in problem solving? In a series of experiments, Robert Sternberg (1977) and his colleagues (Sternberg & Nigro, 1980; Sternberg & Rifkin, 1979) attempted to answer this question by giving third-grade, sixth-grade, ninth-grade, and college students analogies to solve. The main differences occurred between the younger (third- and sixth-grade) and older (ninth-grade and college) students. The older students were more likely to complete the information processing required to solve the analogy task. The children, by contrast, often stopped their processing of information before they had considered all of the necessary steps required to solve the problems. Sternberg maintains that incomplete information processing occurred because the children's short-term memory was overloaded. Solving problems, such as analogies, requires individuals to make continued comparisons between newly encoded information and previously encoded information. Sternberg argues that adolescents probably have more storage space in short-term memory, which results in fewer errors on such problems as analogies.

In addition to more storage space, are there other reasons adolescents perform better on memory span tasks and in solving analogies than do children? Although many other factors may be involved, information-processing psychologists believe that changes in the speed and efficiency of information processing are important, especially the speed with which information can be identified.

Working Memory An increasing number of psychologists point out that the way short-term memory has been historically described is too passive and does not do justice to the amount of cognitive work that is done over the short term in memory (Yen, 2008). They prefer the concept of working memory to describe how memory works on a short-term basis (Cowan, 2008). British psychologist Alan Baddeley (1992, 2000, 2007) proposed the concept of *working memory*, which is a kind of "mental workbench" where information is manipulated and assembled to help make decisions, solve problems, and comprehend written and spoken language.

In one study, the performances of individuals from 6 to 57 years of age were examined on both verbal and visuospatial working memory tasks (Swanson, 1999). The two verbal tasks were auditory digit sequence (the ability to remember numerical information embedded in a short sentence, such as "Now suppose somebody wanted to go to the supermarket at 8651 Elm Street") and semantic association (the ability to organize words into abstract categories) (Swanson, 1999, p. 988).

In the semantic association task, the participant was presented with a series of words (such as shirt, saw, pants, hammer, shoes, and nails) and then asked to remember how they go together. The two visuospatial tasks involved mapping/directions and a visual matrix. In the mapping/directions task, the participant was shown a street map indicating the route a bicycle (child/young adolescent) or car (adult) would take through a city. After briefly looking at the map, participants were asked to redraw the route on a blank map. In the visual matrix task, participants were asked to study a matrix showing a series of dots. After looking at the matrix for five seconds, they were asked to answer questions about the location of the dots. As shown in Figure 15.1, working memory increased substantially from 8 through 24 years of age—that is, through the transition to adulthood and beyond—no matter what the task. Thus, the adolescent years are likely to be an important developmental period for improvement in working memory (Swanson, 2005).

Task

	Verbal		Visuospatial	
Age	Semantic Association	Digit/ Sentence	Mapping/ Directions	Visual Matrix
8	1.33	1.75	3.13	1.67
10	1.70	2.34	3.60	2.06
13	1.86	2.94	4.09	2.51
16	2.24	2.98	3.92	2.68
24	2.60	3.71	4.64	3.47

Highest Working Memory Performance

3.02 (age 45)	3.97 (age 35)	4.90 (age 35)	3.47 (age 24)

FIGURE 15.1 Developmental Changes in Working Memory *Note:* The scores shown here are the means for each age group and the age also represents a mean age. Higher scores reflect superior working memory performance.

Long-Term Memory Long-term memory increases substantially in the middle and late childhood years and likely continues to improve during adolescence, although this has not been well documented by researchers. If anything at all is known about long-term memory, it is that it depends on the learning activities children and adolescents engage in when learning and remembering information (Pressley & Hilden, 2006).

Executive Functioning
Attention and memory are important dimensions of information processing, but other dimensions also are important. Once adolescents attend to information and retain it, they can use the information to engage in a number of higher-order cognitive activities, such as making decisions and thinking critically. These types of higher-order, complex cognitive processes are often called *executive functioning*. Alan Baddeley (2007) recognizes the importance of these higher-order cognitive processes and actually calls this aspect of his cognitive model the *executive*.

It is increasingly thought that executive functioning strengthens during adolescence (Kuhn, 2008). This executive functioning "assumes a role of monitoring and managing the deployment of cognitive resources as a function of a task demands. As a result, cognitive development and learning itself become more effective. . . . Emergence and strengthening of this executive (functioning) is arguably the single most important and consequential intellectual development to occur in the second decade of life" (Kuhn & Franklin, 2006, p. 987). An example of how executive functioning increases in adolescence is its role in determining how attention will be allocated. These improvements in executive functioning during adolescence are likely linked with advances in the prefrontal cortex that we discussed in Chapter 14, "Physical Development in Adolescence," We begin our examination of executive functioning by focusing on decision making.

Decision Making Adolescence is a time of increased decision making—which friends to choose, which person to date, whether to have sex, buy a car, go to college, and so on (Reyna & Rivers, 2008). How competent are adolescents at making decisions? In some reviews, older adolescents are described as more competent than younger adolescents, who in turn are more competent than children (Keating, 2004). Compared with children, young adolescents are more likely to generate different options, examine a situation from a variety of perspectives, anticipate the consequences of decisions, and consider the credibility of sources.

One study documented that older adolescents are better at decision making than younger adolescents are (Lewis, 1981). Eighth-, tenth-, and twelfth-grade students were presented with dilemmas involving the choice of a medical procedure. The oldest students were most likely to spontaneously mention a variety of risks, to recommend consultation with an outside specialist, and to anticipate future consequences. For example, when asked a question about whether to have cosmetic surgery, a twelfth-grader said that different aspects of the situation need to be examined along with its effects on the individual's future, especially relationships with other people. By contrast, an eighth-grader presented a more limited view, commenting on the surgery's effects on getting turned down for a date, on the money involved, and on being teased by peers.

In sum, the ability to regulate one's emotions during decision making, to remember prior decisions and their consequences, and to adapt subsequent decision making on the basis of those consequences appear to improve with age at least through the early adulthood years (Byrnes, 2008).

Older adolescents' (as well as adults') decision-making skills are far from perfect and

> *The error of youth is to believe that intelligence is a substitute for experience, while the error of age is to believe that experience is a substitute for intelligence.*
>
> —Lyman Bryson
> *American Author, 20th Century*

What are some of the decisions adolescents have to make? What characterizes their decision making?

having the capacity to make competent decisions does not guarantee they will be made in everyday life, where breadth of experience often comes into play (Gerrard & others, 2008; Sunstein, 2008). As an example, driver-training courses improve adolescents' cognitive and motor skills to levels equal to, or sometimes superior to, those of adults. However, driver training has not been effective in reducing adolescents' high rate of traffic accidents, although recently researchers have found that implementing a graduated driver licensing (GDR) program can reduce crash and fatality rates for adolescent drivers (Keating, 2007). GDR components include a learner's holding period, practice-driving certification, night-driving restriction, and passenger restriction.

Most people make better decisions when they are calm rather than emotionally aroused, which often is especially true for adolescents (Rivers, Reyna, & Mills, 2008; Steinberg & others, 2009). Recall from our discussion of brain development in Chapter 14, "Physical Development in Adolescence," that adolescents have a tendency to be emotionally intense. Thus, the same adolescent who makes a wise decision when calm may make an unwise decision when emotionally aroused (Paus, 2009; Steinberg, 2009). In the heat of the moment, then, adolescents' emotions may especially overwhelm their decision-making ability.

The social context plays a key role in adolescent decision making. For example, adolescents' willingness to make risky decisions is more likely to occur in contexts where alcohol, drugs, and other temptations are readily available (Gerrard & others, 2008; Reyna & Rivers, 2008). Recent research reveals that the presence of peers in risk-taking situations increases the likelihood that adolescents will make risky decisions (Steinberg, 2008). In one study of risk taking involving a simulated driving task, the presence of peers increased an adolescent's decision to engage in risky driving by 50 percent but had no effect on adults (Gardner & Steinberg, 2005). One view is that the presence of peers activates the brain's reward system, especially its dopamine pathways (Steinberg, 2008).

Adolescents need more opportunities to practice and discuss realistic decision making. Many real-world decisions on matters such as sex, drugs, and daredevil driving occur in an atmosphere of stress that includes time constraints and emotional involvement. One strategy for improving adolescent decision making in such circumstances is to provide more opportunities for them to engage in role playing and group problem solving. Another strategy is for parents to involve adolescents in appropriate decision-making activities.

One proposal to explain effective adolescent decision making is the **dual-process model,** which states that decision making is influenced by two cognitive systems—one analytical and one experiential, which compete with each other (Klaczynski, 2001; Reyna & Farley, 2006).

dual-process model States that decision making is influenced by two systems—one analytical and one experiential, which compete with each other; in this model, it is the experiential system—monitoring and managing actual experiences—that benefits adolescent decision making.

How do emotions and social contexts influence adolescents' decision making?

The dual-process model emphasizes that it is the experiential system—monitoring and managing actual experiences—that benefits adolescents' decision making, not the analytical system. In this view, adolescents don't benefit from engaging in reflective, detailed, higher-level cognitive analysis about a decision, especially in high-risk, real-world contexts. In such contexts, adolescents just need to know that there are some circumstances that are so dangerous that they need to be avoided at all costs (Mills, Reyna, & Estrada, 2008). However, some experts on adolescent cognition argue that in many cases adolescents benefit from both analytical and experiential systems (Kuhn, 2009).

Critical Thinking   In Chapter 12, "Cognitive Development in Middle and Late Childhood," we defined *critical thinking* as thinking reflectively and productively and evaluating evidence. Here we discuss how critical thinking changes in adolescence. In one study of fifth-, eighth-, and eleventh-graders, critical thinking increased with age, but still occurred only in 43 percent of eleventh-graders (Klaczynski & Narasimham, 1998). Among the factors that provide a basis for improvement in critical thinking during adolescence are (Keating, 1990):

- Increased speed, automaticity, and capacity of information processing, which free cognitive resources for other purposes.

- Greater breadth of content knowledge in a variety of domains

- Increased ability to construct new combinations of knowledge

- A greater range and more spontaneous use of strategies and procedures for obtaining and applying knowledge, such as planning, considering the alternatives, and cognitive monitoring

Although adolescence is an important period in the development of critical-thinking skills, if an individual has not developed a solid basis of fundamental skills (such as literacy and math skills) during childhood, critical-thinking skills are unlikely to mature in adolescence. For the subset of adolescents who lack such fundamental skills, potential gains in adolescent thinking are not likely. Laura Bickford is a secondary school teacher who encourages her students to think critically. To read about her work, see the *Careers in Children's Development* profile.

Careers in Children's Development

Laura Bickford, Secondary School Teacher

Laura Bickford teaches English and journalism in grades 9 to 12 and she is chair of the English Department at Nordhoff High School in Ojai, California.

Bickford especially believes it is important to encourage students to think. Indeed, she says that "the call to teach is the call to teach students how to think." She believes teachers need to show students the value in asking their own questions, in having discussions, and in engaging in stimulating intellectual conversations. Bickford says that she also encourages students to engage in metacognitive strategies (knowing about knowing). For example, she asks students to comment on their learning after particular pieces of projects have been completed. She requires students to keep reading logs so they can observe their own thinking as it happens.

Laura Bickord, working with students writing papers.

Review and Reflect: Learning Goal 1

1 **Discuss different approaches to adolescent cognition**

REVIEW

- What is Piaget's view of adolescent cognitive development?
- What is adolescent egocentrism?
- How does information processing change during adolescence?

REFLECT

- Suppose an 8-year-old and a 16-year-old are watching a political convention on television. In view of where they are likely to be in terms of Piaget's stages of cognitive development, how would their perceptions of the proceedings likely differ?

2 WHAT CHARACTERIZES ADOLESCENTS' VALUES, MORAL EDUCATION, AND RELIGION?

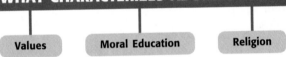

Values   Moral Education   Religion

What are adolescents' values like today? How can moral education be characterized? How powerful is religion in adolescents' lives?

Values

Adolescents carry with them a set of values that influences their thoughts, feelings, and actions (Pratt & others, 2008). **Values** are beliefs and attitudes about the way things should be. They involve what is important to us. We attach values to all sorts of things: politics, religion, money, sex, education, helping others, family, friends, career, cheating, self-respect, and so on.

Changing Values   One way of measuring what people value is to ask them what their goals are. Over the past three decades, traditional-aged college students have shown an increased concern for personal well-being and a decreased concern for the well-being of others, especially for the disadvantaged (Pryor & others, 2008). As shown in Figure 15.2, today's college freshmen are more strongly motivated to be well off financially and less motivated to develop a meaningful philosophy of life than were their counterparts of 20 or even 10 years ago. In 2008, 76.8 percent of students viewed becoming well off financially as an "essential" or "very important" objective compared with only 42 percent in 1971.

There are some signs that U.S. college students are shifting toward a stronger interest in the welfare of society. In the survey just described, interest in developing a

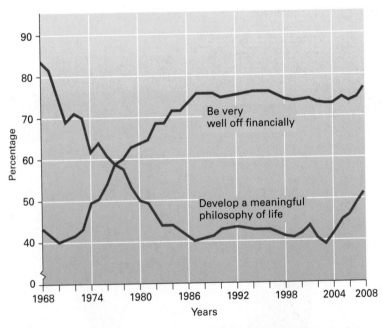

FIGURE 15.2 Changing Freshmen Life Goals, 1968 to 2008 In the last three decades, a significant change has occurred in freshmen students' life goals. A far greater percentage of today's college freshmen state that an "essential" or "very important" life goal is to be well off financially, and far fewer state that developing a meaningful philosophy of life is an "essential" or "very important" life goal.

meaningful philosophy of life increased from 39 percent to 51.4 percent of U.S. freshman from 2001 through 2008 (Pryor & others, 2008) (see Figure 15.2). Also in this survey, the percentage of college freshman who said the chances are very good that they will participate in volunteer or community service programs increased from 18 percent in 1990 to 28.3 percent in 2008 (Pryor & others, 2008). For successful adjustment in life, it is important to seek self-fulfillment *and* have a strong commitment to others.

Our discussion of values relates to William Damon's (2008) view in *The Path to Purpose,* which we described in Chapter 14, "Physical Development in Adolescence." Damon concluded that a major difficulty confronting today's youth is their lack of a clear sense of what they want to do with their lives—that too many youth are essentially "rudderless." Damon (2008, p. 8) found that only about 20 percent of 12- to 22-year-olds in the United States expressed "a clear vision of where they want to go, what they want to accomplish in life, and why." He argues that their goals and values too often focus on the short-term, such as getting a good grade on a test this week and finding a date for a dance, rather than developing a plan for the future based on positive values. As we indicated in Chapter 14, the types of questions that adults can pose to youth to guide them in the direction of developing more purposeful values include: "What's most important in your life? Why do you care about those things? . . . What does it mean to be a good person?" (Damon, 2008, p. 135).

How Would You...?
As an educator, how would you devise a program to increase adolescents' motivation to participate in service learning?

Service Learning

Service learning is a form of education that promotes social responsibility and service to the community. In service learning, adolescents engage in activities such as tutoring, helping older adults, working in a hospital, assisting at a child-care center, or cleaning up a vacant lot to make a play area. An important goal of service learning is for adolescents to become less self-centered and more strongly motivated to help others (Catalano, Hawkins, & Toumbourou, 2008). Service learning is often more effective when two conditions are met (Nucci, 2006): (1) giving students some degree of choice in the service activities in which they participate, and (2) providing students opportunities to reflect about their participation.

Service learning takes education out into the community (Enfield & Collins, 2008; Nelson & Eckstein, 2008). Adolescent volunteers tend to extraverted, committed to others, and have a high level of self-understanding (Eisenberg & Morris, 2004). Also, a recent study revealed that adolescent girls participated in service learning more than adolescent boys (Webster & Worrell, 2008).

Researchers have found that service learning benefits adolescents in a number of ways (Hart, Matsuba, & Atkins, 2008). These improvements in adolescent development related to service learning include higher grades in school, increased goal setting, higher self-esteem, an improved sense of being able to make a difference for others, and an increased likelihood that they will serve as volunteers in the future. A recent study of more than 4,000 high school students revealed that those who worked directly with individuals in need were better adjusted academically, whereas those who worked for organizations had better civic outcomes (Schmidt, Shumow, & Kackar, 2007).

One analysis revealed that 26 percent of U.S. public high schools require students to participate in service learning (Metz & Youniss, 2005). The benefits of service learning, both for the volunteer and the recipient, suggest that more adolescents should be required to participate in such programs (Enfield & Collins, 2008; Nelson & Eckstein, 2008). To read further about the positive outcomes of participating in service learning, see the *Research in Children's Development* interlude.

What are some of the positive effects of service learning?

values Beliefs and attitudes about the way things should be.

service learning A form of education that promotes social responsibility and service to the community.

Research in Children's Development

EVALUATING A SERVICE-LEARNING PROGRAM DESIGNED TO INCREASE CIVIC ENGAGEMENT

In one study, the possible benefits of a service-learning requirement for high school students were explored (Metz & Youniss, 2005). One group of students had a service-learning requirement, the other did not. Each group of students was also divided according to whether or not they were motivated to serve voluntarily. The participants in the study were 174 students (class of 2000) who were not required to engage in service learning, and 312 students (classes of 2001 and 2002) who were required to accumulate 40 hours of community service. The school was located in a middle- to upper-middle-SES suburban community outside Boston, Massachusetts. The focus of the study was to compare the 2001 and 2002 classes, which were the first ones to have a 40-hour community service requirement, to the class of 2000, the last year in which the school did not have this requirement. For purposes of comparison, the 2001 and 2002 classes were combined into one group to be compared with the 2000 class.

The service-learning requirement for the 2001 and 2002 classes was designed to give students a sense of participating in the community in positive ways. Among the most common service-learning activities that students engaged in were "tutoring, coaching, assisting at shelters or nursing homes, organizing food or clothing drives, and assisting value-centered service organizations or churches" (p. 420). To obtain credit for the activities, students were required to write reflectively about the activities and describe how the activities benefited both the recipients and themselves. Students also had to obtain an adult's or supervisor's signature to document their participation.

Detailed self-reported records of students' service in grades 10 through 12 were obtained. In addition to describing the number of service hours they accumulated toward their requirement, they also were asked to indicate any voluntary services they provided in addition to the required 40 hours. Since students in the 2000 class had no required service participation, all of their service was voluntary.

The students rated themselves on four 5-point scales of civic engagement: (1) the likelihood of voting when reaching 18; (2) the likelihood they would "volunteer" or "join a civic organization" after they graduate from high school; (3) their future unconventional civic involvement (such as boycotting a product, demonstrating for a cause, or participating in a political campaign); and (4) their political interest and understanding (how much they discuss politics with parents and friends, read about politics in magazines and newspapers, or watch the news on TV).

The results indicated that students who were already inclined to engage in service learning scored high on the four scales of civic engagement throughout high school and showed no increase in service after it was required. However, students who were less motivated to engage in service learning increased their civic engagement on three of the four scales (future voting, join a civic organization after graduating from high school, and interest and understanding) after they were required to participate. In sum, this research documented that a required service-learning program can especially benefit the civic engagement of students who are inclined not to engage in service learning.

Moral Education

Moral education is hotly debated in educational circles (Nucci & Narváez, 2008). We study one of the earliest analyses of moral education and then turn to some contemporary views.

The Hidden Curriculum   More than 70 years ago, educator John Dewey (1933) recognized that, even when schools do not have specific programs in moral education, they provide moral education through a "hidden curriculum." The **hidden curriculum** is conveyed by the moral atmosphere that is a part of every school. The moral atmosphere is created by school and classroom rules, the moral orientation of teachers and school administrators, and text materials. Teachers serve as models of ethical or unethical behavior (Mayhew & King, 2008; Sanger, 2008). Classroom rules and peer relations at school transmit attitudes about cheating, lying, stealing, and consideration of others. And, through its rules and regulations, the school administration infuses the school with a value system.

Character Education   Currently 40 of 50 states have mandates regarding **character education,** a direct education approach that involves teaching students a basic moral literacy to prevent them from engaging in immoral behavior and doing harm to themselves or others (Nucci & Narváez, 2008). The argument is that such behaviors as lying, stealing, and cheating are wrong, and students should be taught this throughout their education (Berkowitz, Battistich, & Bier, 2008; Davidson, Lickona, & Khmelkov, 2008).

In the character education approach, every school should have an explicit moral code that is clearly communicated to students. Any violations of the code should be met with sanctions. Instruction in specified moral concepts, such as cheating, can take the form of example and definition, class discussions and role playing, or rewarding students for proper behavior. More recently, an emphasis on the importance of encouraging students to develop a care perspective has been accepted as a relevant aspect of character education (Noddings, 2008; Sherblom, 2008). Rather than just instructing adolescents in refraining from engaging in morally deviant behavior, a care perspective advocates educating students in the importance of engaging in prosocial behaviors, such as considering others feelings, being sensitive to others, and helping others.

Values Clarification   **Values clarification** means helping people to make clear what is important to them, what is worth working for, and what purpose their lives are to serve. In this approach, students are encouraged to define their own values and understand the values of others. Values clarification differs from character education in that it does not tell students what their values should be. In our chapter-opening story, we saw that Kim-Chi had clear values about doing well in school out of respect for her parents.

In values clarification exercises, there are no right or wrong answers. The clarification of values is left up to the individual student. Advocates of values clarification say it is value-free. However, critics argue that its controversial content offends community standards. They also say that because of its relativistic nature, values clarification undermines accepted values and fails to stress distinctions between right and wrong behavior.

Cognitive Moral Education   **Cognitive moral education** is a concept based on the belief that students should learn to value such aspects of life as democracy and justice as their moral reasoning develops. Lawrence Kohlberg's theory, which we discussed in Chapter 13, "Socioemotional Development in Middle and Late Childhood," has been the basis for a number of cognitive moral education programs. In a typical program, high school students meet in a semester-long course to discuss a number of moral issues. The instructor acts as a facilitator, rather than as a director, of the class. The hope is that students will develop more advanced notions of concepts such as cooperation, trust, responsibility, and community (Enright & others, 2008). Toward the end of his career, Kohlberg (1986) recognized that the moral atmosphere of the school is more important than he initially envisioned. For example, in one study, a semester-long moral education class based on Kohlberg's theory

hidden curriculum Dewey's concept that every school has a pervasive moral atmosphere, even if it doesn't have a program of moral education.

character education A direct education approach that involves teaching students a basic moral literacy to prevent them from engaging in immoral behavior and doing harm to themselves and others.

values clarification An approach to moral education that emphasizes helping people clarify what their lives are for and what's worth working for. Students are encouraged to define their own values and to understand the values of others.

cognitive moral education A concept based on the belief that students should develop such values as democracy and justice as their moral reasoning develops; Kohlberg's theory has been the basis of a number of cognitive moral education programs.

Why do students cheat? What are some strategies teachers can adopt to prevent cheating?

How Would You...?
As an educator, how would you try to reduce the incidence of cheating in schools?

was successful in advancing moral thinking in three democratic schools, but not in three authoritarian schools (Higgins, Power, & Kohlberg, 1983).

Recall from Chapter 13, "Socioemotional Development in Middle and Late Childhood," that Carol Gilligan (1982, 1996) argues that moral development should focus on social relationships more than Kohlberg does. Thus, if we apply Gilligan's view to moral education, emphasis should be placed on such topics as caring, sensitivity to others' feelings, and relationships. In her view, schools should better recognize the importance of relationships in the development of adolescent girls.

Cheating   A moral education concern is whether students cheat and how to handle the cheating if they discover it (Anderman & Murdock, 2007; Narváez & others, 2008). Academic cheating can take many forms including plagiarism, using "cheat sheets" during an exam, copying from a neighbor during a test, purchasing papers, and falsifying lab results. A 2006 survey revealed that 60 percent of secondary school students said they had cheated on a test in school during the past year, and one-third of the students reported that they had plagiarized information from the Internet in the past year (Josephson Institute of Ethics, 2006).

Why do students cheat? Among the reasons students give for cheating include the pressure for getting high grades, time pressures, poor teaching, and lack of interest (Stephens, 2008). In terms of poor teaching, "students are more likely to cheat when they perceive their teacher to be incompetent, unfair, and uncaring" (Stephens, 2008, p. 140).

A long history of research also implicates the power of the situation in determining whether students cheat or not (Hartshorne & May, 1928–1930; Murdock, Miller, & Kohlbhardt, 2004; Vandehey, Diekhoff, & LaBeff, 2007). For example, students are more likely to cheat when they are not being closely monitored during a test, when they know their peers are cheating, whether they know whether another student has been caught cheating, and when student scores are made public (Anderman & Murdock, 2007; Carrell, Malmstrom, & West, 2008; Harmon, Lambrinos, & Kennedy, 2008).

Among the strategies for decreasing academic cheating are preventive measures such as making sure students are aware of what constitutes cheating, what the consequences will be if they cheat, closely monitoring students' behavior while they are taking tests, and the importance of being a moral, responsible individual who engages in academic integrity. In promoting academic integrity, many colleges have instituted an honor code policy that emphasizes self-responsibility, fairness, trust, and scholarship. However, few secondary schools have developed honor code policies. The Center for Academic Integrity (www.academicintegrity.org/) has extensive materials available to help schools develop academic integrity policies.

An Integrative Approach   Darcia Narváez (2006, 2008) emphasizes an *integrative approach* to moral education that encompasses both the reflective moral thinking and commitment to justice advocated in Kohlberg's approach, and developing a particular moral character as advocated in the character education approach. She highlights the Child Development Project as an excellent example of an integrative moral education approach. In the Child Development Project, students are given multiple opportunities to discuss other students' experiences, which encourages empathy and perspective taking, and they participate in exercises that encourage them to reflect on their own behaviors in terms of such values as fairness and social responsibility (Battistich, 2008; Solomon & others, 2002). Adults coach students in ethical decision making and guide them in becoming more caring individuals. Students experience a caring community, not only in the classroom, but also in after-school activities and through parental involvement in the program. Research evaluations of the Child Development Project indicate that it is related to an improved sense of community, an increase in prosocial behavior, better interpersonal understanding, and an increase in social problem solving (Battistich, 2008; Solomon & others, 1990).

Religion

Religious issues are important to adolescents. In one survey, 95 percent of 13- to 18-year-olds said that they believe in God or a universal spirit (Gallup & Bezilla, 1992). Almost three-fourths of adolescents said that they pray, and about one-half indicated that they had attended religious services within the past week. Almost half of the youth said that it is very important for a young person to learn religious faith.

A recent developmental study revealed that religiousness declined from 14 to 20 years of age in the United States (Koenig, McGue, & Iacono, 2008) (see Figure 15.3). In this study, religiousness was assessed with items such as frequency of prayer, frequency of discussing religious teachings, frequency of deciding moral actions for religious reasons, and the overall importance of religion in everyday life. As indicated in Figure 15.3, more change in religiousness occurred from 14 to 18 years of age than from 20 to 25 years of age. Also, attending religious services was highest at 14 years of age, declined from 14 to 18 years of age, and increased at 20 years of age. More change occurred in attending religious services than in religiousness.

The Positive Role of Religion in Adolescents' Lives
Researchers have found that various aspects of religion are linked with positive outcomes for adolescents (Benson & Roehlkepartain, 2008; Lerner, Roeser, & Phelps, 2009). In one study, adolescents who viewed religion as a meaningful part of their life and a way to cope with problems were half as likely to use drugs than were adolescents who did not view religion as important (Wills, Yaeger, & Sandy, 2003). A recent study of Indonesian Muslim 13-year-olds revealed that their religious involvement was linked to their social competence, including positive peer relations, academic achievement, emotional regulation, prosocial behavior, and self-esteem (French & others, 2008).

Religion also plays a role in adolescents' health and whether they engage in problem behaviors (King & Benson, 2005). Researchers have found that religious affiliation is linked to lower rates of delinquent behavior and drug use (Piko & Fitzpatrick, 2004). Also, in one study, adolescents with higher levels of spiritual well-being had fewer depressive symptoms and were less likely to engage in risk-taking behaviors than their counterparts with lower levels of spiritual well-being (Cotton & others, 2005). And in a recent national random sample of more than 2,000 11- to 18-year-olds, those who were higher in religiosity were less likely to smoke, drink alcohol, or use marijuana—and were more likely not be truant from school, not to engage in delinquent activities, and not to be depressed than their low-religiosity counterparts (Sinha, Cnaan, & Gelles, 2007).

Many religious adolescents also internalize their religion's message about caring and concern for people (Ream & Savin-Williams, 2003). For example, in one survey, religious youth were almost three times as likely to engage in community service as nonreligious youth (Youniss, McLellan, & Yates, 1999).

Developmental Changes
Adolescence can be an important juncture in religious development (Koenig, McGue, & Iacono, 2008; Lerner, Roeser, & Phelps, 2009). Even if children have been indoctrinated into a religion by their parents, because of advances in their cognitive development they may begin to question what their own religious beliefs truly are.

Cognitive Changes Many of the cognitive changes thought to influence religious development involve Piaget's cognitive developmental theory, which we discussed earlier in this chapter. More so than in childhood, adolescents think more abstractly, idealistically, and logically. The increase in abstract thinking lets adolescents consider various ideas

> *R*eligion enlightens, terrifies, subdues; it gives faith, inflicts remorse, inspires resolutions, and inflames devotion.
>
> —HENRY NEWMAN
> *English Churchman and Writer, 19th Century*

FIGURE 15.3 Developmental Changes in Religiousness from 14 to 25 Years of Age *Note:* The religiousness scale ranged from 0 to 32 with higher scores indicating stronger religiousness.

Many children and adolescents show an interest in religion, and many religious institutions created by adults (such as this Muslim school in Malaysia) are designed to introduce them to religious benefits and ensure that they will carry on a religious tradition.

Adolescents participating in a religious youth group. *What are some cognitive changes that influence religious development?*

about religious and spiritual concepts. For example, an adolescent might ask how a loving God can possibly exist given the extensive suffering of many people in the world (Good & Willoughby, 2008). Adolescents' increased idealistic thinking provides a foundation for thinking about whether religion provides the best route to a better, more ideal world than the present. And adolescents' increased logical reasoning gives them the ability to develop hypotheses and systematically sort through different answers to spiritual questions (Good & Willoughby, 2008).

Erikson's Theory and Identity During adolescence, especially in late adolescence and the college years, identity development becomes a central focus. In Erik Erikson's (1968) theory, adolescents want to know answers to questions like these: "Who am I?" "What am I all about as a person?" "What kind of life do I want to lead?" As part of their search for identity, adolescents begin to grapple in more sophisticated, logical ways with such questions as "Why am I on this planet?" "Is there really a God or higher spiritual being, or have I just been believing what my parents and the church imprinted in my mind?" "What really are my religious views?" A recent analysis of the link between identity and spirituality concluded that adolescence and emerging adulthood can serve as gateways to a spiritual identity that "transcends, but not necessarily excludes, the assigned religious identity in childhood" (Templeton & Eccles, 2005, p. 261).

Religious Beliefs and Parenting Religious institutions created by adults are designed to introduce certain beliefs to children and thereby ensure that they will carry on a religious tradition. Various societies utilize Sunday schools, parochial education, tribal transmission of religious traditions, and parental teaching of children at home to further this aim.

Does this socialization work? In many cases it does (Paloutzian, 2000). In general, adults tend to adopt the religious teachings of their upbringing. However, when examining religious beliefs and adolescence, it is important to consider the quality of the parent-adolescent relationship (Brelsford & Mahoney, 2008). Adolescents who have a positive relationship with their parents, or are securely attached to them, are likely to adopt their parents' religious affiliation. But when conflict or insecure attachment characterizes parent-adolescent relationships, adolescents may seek religious affiliation that is different from their parents' (Streib, 1999).

Religiousness and Sexuality in Adolescence One area of religion's influence on adolescent development involves sexual activity. Although variability and change in teachings make it difficult to generalize about religious doctrines, most religions discourage premarital sex. Thus, the degree of adolescent participation in religious organizations may be more important than affiliation with a particular religion as a determinant of premarital sexual attitudes and behavior. Adolescents who frequently attend religious services are likely to hear messages about abstaining from sex. Involvement of adolescents in religious organizations also enhances the probability that they will become friends with adolescents who have restrictive attitudes toward premarital sex.

A national study of 3,356 adolescent girls revealed a link between engaging in personal devotion and having fewer sexual partners outside a romantic relationship (Miller & Gur, 2002). In this study, frequent attendance at religious events was related to fear of contracting HIV or pregnancy from unprotected intercourse and planned use of birth control. Also, having a personal conservative orientation was associated with not engaging in unprotected sex. Another study similarly found links between religion and sexuality (Fehring & others, 1998). In college students, guilt, prayer, organized religious activity, and religious well-being were associated with fewer sexual encounters.

Review and Reflect: Learning Goal 2

 2 **Describe adolescents' values, moral education, and religion**

REVIEW

- What characterizes adolescents' values? What is service learning?
- What are some variations in moral education?
- What are adolescents' religious views and experiences?

REFLECT

- What are your values? What is really important to you in life? Does the way you spend your time reflect the values that are most important to you?

---

3 WHAT IS THE NATURE OF SCHOOLS FOR ADOLESCENTS?

| The American Middle School | The American High School | High School Dropouts |

The impressive changes in adolescents' cognition lead us to examine the nature of schools for adolescents. In Chapter 13, "Socioemotional Development in Middle and Late Childhood," we discussed different ideas about the effects of schools on children's development. Here, we focus more exclusively on the nature of secondary schools.

The American Middle School

One worry of educators and psychologists is that middle schools (most often consisting of grades 6 through 8) are simply watered-down versions of high schools, mimicking their curricular and extracurricular schedules. The critics argue that the unique curricular and extracurricular activities reflecting a wide range of individual differences in biological and psychological development in early adolescence should be incorporated into our junior high and middle schools. The critics also stress that many high schools foster passivity rather than autonomy, and that schools should create a variety of pathways for students to achieve an identity.

The transition from elementary to middle or junior high school occurs at the same time as a number of other developmental changes. *What are some of these other developmental changes?*

The Transition to Middle or Junior High School   The transition to middle school from elementary school interests developmentalists because, even though it is a normative experience for virtually all children, the transition can be stressful (Anderman & Mueller, 2010; Eccles & Roeser, 2009). Why? The transition takes place at a time when many changes—in the individual, in the family, and in school—are occurring simultaneously. These changes include puberty and related concerns about body image; the emergence of at least some aspects of formal operational thought, including accompanying changes in social cognition; increased responsibility and independence in association with decreased dependence on parents; change from a small, contained classroom structure to a larger, more impersonal school structure; change from one teacher to many teachers and from a small, homogeneous set of peers to a larger, more heterogeneous set of peers; and an increased focus on achievement and performance and their assessment.

This list includes a number of negative, stressful features, but there can be positive aspects to the transition. Students are more likely to feel grown up, to have more subjects from which to select, to have more opportunities to spend time with peers and to locate compatible friends, to enjoy increased independence from direct parental monitoring—and they may be more challenged intellectually by academic work.

When students make the transition from elementary school to middle or junior high school, they experience the **top-dog phenomenon,** the circumstance of moving from the top position (in elementary school, being the oldest, biggest, and most powerful students in the school) to the lowest position (in middle or junior high school, being the youngest, smallest, and least powerful students in the school). Researchers who have charted the transition from elementary to middle school find that the first year of middle school can be difficult for many students (Hawkins & Berndt, 1985). A recent study in North Carolina schools revealed that sixth-grade students attending middle schools were far more likely to be cited for discipline problems than their counterparts who were attending elementary schools (Cook & others, 2008).

Effective Middle Schools

Effective Middle Schools   How effective are the middle schools U.S. students attend? The Carnegie Council on Adolescent Development (1989) issued an extremely negative evaluation of U.S. middle schools. In the report—*Turning Points: Preparing American Youth for the Twenty-First Century*—the conclusion was reached that most young adolescents attend massive, impersonal schools; learn from seemingly irrelevant curricula; trust few adults in school; and lack access to health care and counseling. The Carnegie report recommended:

- Developing smaller "communities" or "houses" to lessen the impersonal nature of large middle schools
- Lowering student-to-counselor ratios from several hundred-to-1 to 10-to-1
- Involving parents and community leaders in schools
- Developing curricula that produce students who are literate, understand the sciences, and have a sense of health, ethics, and citizenship
- Having teachers team-teach in more flexibly designed curriculum blocks that integrate several disciplines, instead of presenting students with disconnected, rigidly separated 50-minute segments
- Boosting students' health and fitness with more in-school programs and helping students who need public health care to get it

Turning Points 2000 (Jackson & Davis, 2000) continued to endorse the recommendations set forth in *Turning Points 1989*. One new recommendation in the 2000 report stated that it is important to teach a curriculum grounded in rigorous academic standards for what students should, and should be able, to know. A second new recommendation was to engage in instruction to achieve higher standards and become lifelong learners. These new recommendations reflect the increasing emphasis on challenging students to meet higher standards (Manzo, 2008).

Extracurricular Activities

Extracurricular Activities   Adolescents in U.S. schools usually have a wide array of extracurricular activities they can participate in beyond their academic courses.

How Would You...?
As an educator, how would you improve middle schools?

top-dog phenomenon The circumstance of moving from the top position (in elementary school, the oldest, biggest, and most powerful students) to the lowest position (in middle or junior high school, the youngest, smallest, and least powerful students).

These adult-sanctioned activities typically occur in the after-school hours and can be sponsored either by the school or the community. They include such diverse activities as sports, academic clubs, band, drama, and math clubs.

Researchers have found that participation in extracurricular activities is linked to higher grades, school engagement, less likelihood of dropping out of school, improved probability of going to college, higher self-esteem, and lower rates of depression, delinquency, and substance abuse (Fredricks, 2008; Parente & Mahoney, 2009; Peck & others, 2008). Adolescents benefit from a breadth of extracurricular activities more than focusing on a single extracurricular activity (Mahoney & others, 2009). Also, the more years adolescents spend in extracurricular activities, the stronger the link is with positive developmental outcomes (Mahoney & others, 2009). For example, a longitudinal study revealed that youths who participated in organized school-sponsored activities (sports, cheerleading, music groups, plays, student government, honor societies, and service clubs, for example) and community-sponsored activities (religious activities, community youth groups, music/art/dance lessons, sports lessons, and community service, for example) for two years during adolescence had better educational and occupational outcomes in early adulthood than those who participated for one year (Gardner, Roth, & Brooks-Gunn, 2008). In this study, more intensive participation was linked to more positive educational, occupational, and civic success in early adulthood.

Of course, the quality of the extracurricular activities matters (Fredricks, 2008; Mahoney & others, 2009; Parente & Mahoney, 2009). High-quality extracurricular activities that are likely to promote positive adolescent development include competent, supportive adult mentors, opportunities for increasing school connectedness, challenging and meaningful activities, and opportunities for improving skills (Fredricks & Eccles, 2006). A recent study identified educationally vulnerable youth at the end of the eighth grade and found that their participation in particular patterns of positive extracurricular activities in the eleventh grade were linked to subsequent educational success (Peck & others, 2008). In the study, vulnerable youth were much more likely to go to college if they participated in both school clubs and organized sports, both organized sports and volunteering, and multiple positive activities. The highest rate of college attendance by vulnerable youth was predicted by participation in a combination of sports and school clubs. By contrast, vulnerable youth who mainly engaged in paid work or spent little time in positive organized extracurricular activities were less likely to go to college.

The American High School

Many high school graduates not only are poorly prepared for college, they also are poorly prepared for the demands of the modern, high-performance workplace (Elmore, 2009; Smith, 2009). In a review of hiring practices at major companies, it was concluded that many companies now have sets of basic skills they want their employees to have. These include the ability to read at relatively high levels, do at least elementary algebra, use personal computers for straightforward tasks such as word processing, solve semistructured problems in which hypotheses must be formed and tested, communicate effectively (orally and in writing), and work effectively in groups with persons of various backgrounds (Murnane & Levy, 1996).

The National Research Council (2004) made a number of recommendations for improving U.S. high schools. They especially emphasized the importance of finding ways to get students more engaged in learning. The council concluded that the best way to get students engaged in learning is to focus on the psychological factors involved in motivation. For increasing students' engagement in learning, this consists of promoting a sense of belonging "by personalizing instruction, showing an interest in students' lives, and creating a supportive, caring social environment"

(National Research Council, 2004, p. 3). The council said that this description of engaging students applies to very few urban high schools that too often are characterized by low expectations, alienation, and low achievement. A recent study examined school transition of multiethnic urban adolescents from the seventh to tenth grade (Benner & Graham, 2009). The transition to high school was especially challenging for African American and Latino youth when the number of students in their own ethnic groups declined from middle to high school.

A special concern regarding secondary schools—middle and high schools—involves adolescents who are growing up in economically disadvantaged contexts (Jimerson, 2009; Taylor & Graham, 2007). Although the studies are few in number, those that have been conducted indicate that living in economically disadvantaged families during adolescence may have more negative achievement outcomes than corresponding circumstances in childhood (McLoyd & others, 2009). The possible timing difference in poverty effects might be due to adolescents' awareness of barriers to their success and the difficulties they will encounter in becoming successful.

Some innovative programs indicate that improving certain characteristics of schools improves the achievement of adolescents from economically disadvantaged backgrounds (McLoyd & others, 2009). For example, a recent study at the Center for Collaborative Education (Tung & Ouimette, 2007) of a series of pilot schools in Boston revealed that the following changes were linked with higher levels of achievement in high school: having smaller class sizes and longer classes, creating more advisory sessions, and allotting more time for teachers to explore teaching methods.

Are American secondary schools different from those in other countries? To explore this question, see the *Diversity in Children's Development* interlude.

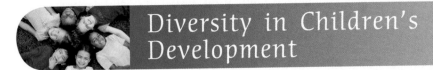

Diversity in Children's Development

CROSS-CULTURAL COMPARISONS OF SECONDARY SCHOOLS

Secondary schools in different countries share a number of features, but differ on others. Let's explore the similarities and differences in secondary schools in seven countries: Australia, Brazil, Germany, Japan, China, Russia and the United States.

Most countries mandate that children begin school at 6 to 7 years of age and stay in school until they are 14 to 17 years of age. Brazil requires students to go to school only until they are 14 years old, whereas Russia mandates that students stay in school until they are 17. Germany, Japan, Australia, and the United States require school attendance until at least 15 to 16 years of age, with some states, such as California, recently raising the mandatory age to 18.

Most secondary schools around the world are divided into two or more levels, such as middle school (or junior high school) and high school. However, Germany's schools are divided according to three educational ability tracks: (1) the main school provides a basic level of education, (2) the middle school gives students a more advanced education, and (3) the academic school prepares students for entrance to a university. German schools, like most European schools, offer a classical education, which includes courses in Latin and Greek. Japanese secondary schools have an entrance exam, but secondary schools in the other five countries do not. Only Australia and Germany have comprehensive exit exams.

The United States and Australia are among the few countries in the world in which sports are an integral part of the public school system. Only a few private schools in other countries have their own sports teams, sports facilities, and highly organized sports events.

In Brazil, students are required to take Portuguese (the native language) and four foreign languages (Latin, French, English, and Spanish). Brazil requires these languages because of the country's international character and emphasis on trade and commerce. Seventh-grade students in Australia take courses in sheep husbandry and weaving, two areas of economic and cultural interest in the country. In Japan, students take a number of Western courses in addition to their basic Japanese courses; these courses include Western literature and languages (in addition to Japanese literature and language), Western physical education (in addition to Japanese martial arts classes), and Western sculpture and handicrafts (in addition to Japanese calligraphy). The Japanese school year is also much longer than that of other countries (225 days versus 180 days in the United States, for example).

I recently visited China and interviewed parents about their adolescents' education. Several aspects of education in China are noteworthy, especially in comparison to the United States. Being motivated to provide adolescents with the best possible education and ensuring that they work extremely hard in school and on homework were clearly evident in parents' comments. Also, when I asked parents if there are disciplinary problems in Chinese schools, they responded that if an adolescent acts up in school, the school immediately sends the adolescent home. In China, it is considered parents' responsibility to orient their adolescents to behave in school and focus on schoolwork. These observations coincide with the description in Chapter 10, "Socioemotional Development in Early Childhood," of Asian American parents as training parents. When Chinese adolescents are sent home because of discipline problems, they are not allowed to return until parents work with the adolescent to ensure that the discipline problems don't recur. In China, classroom sizes are often large, in some cases having 50 to 70 students, yet observers describe such classes as orderly and disciplined (Cavanagh, 2008).

The juku, or "cramming school," is available to Japanese children and adolescents in the summertime and after school. It provides coaching to help them improve their grades and their entrance exam scores for high schools and universities. The Japanese practice of requiring an entrance exam for high school is a rarity among the nations of the world.

High School Dropouts

Dropping out of high school has been viewed as a serious educational and societal problem for many decades (Jimerson, 2009). By leaving high school before graduating, adolescents approach adult life with educational deficiencies that severely curtail their economic and social well-being (Steinberg & Almeida, 2008). In this section, we study the scope of the problem, the causes of dropping out, and ways to reduce dropout rates.

High School Dropout Rates   In the last half of the twentieth century and the first several years of the twenty-first century, U.S. high school dropout rates declined (National Center for Education Statistics, 2008) (see Figure 15.4). In the 1940s, more than half of U.S. 16- to 24-year-olds had dropped out of school; by 2006, this figure had decreased to 9.3 percent. The dropout rate of Latino adolescents remains high, although it has been decreasing in the twenty-first century (from 28 percent in 2000 to 22 percent in 2006). The highest dropout rate in the United States, though, occurs for Native American youth—less than 50 percent finish their high school education.

Gender differences characterize U.S. dropout rates, with males more likely to drop out than females (12 percent male, 9 percent female). The gender gap in dropout rates is especially large for Latino adolescents (32 percent male, 22 percent female) and African American adolescents (13 percent male, 9 percent female) (data for 2001).

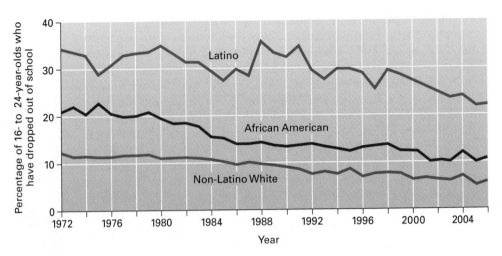

FIGURE 15.4 Trends in High School Dropout Rates From 1972 through 2006, the school dropout rate for Latinos remained very high (22 percent of 16- to 24-year-olds in 2006). The African American dropout rate was still higher (10 percent) than the White non-Latino rate (6 percent) in 2006. (*Source:* National Center for Education Statistics, 2008.)

Students in the technology training center at Wellpoint Elementary/High School located on the Spokane Indian Reservation in Washington State. An important educational goal is to increase the high school graduation rate of Native American adolescents.

How Would You...?
As an educator, how would you reduce the school dropout rate of high-risk adolescents?

The Causes of Dropping Out of School   Students drop out of school for school-related, economic, family-related, peer-related, and personal reasons. School-related problems are consistently associated with dropping out of school (Christensen & Thurlow, 2004; Jimerson, 2009). In one investigation, almost 50 percent of the dropouts cited school-related reasons for leaving school, such as not liking school, being suspended, or being expelled (Rumberger, 1995). Twenty percent of the dropouts (but 40 percent of the Latino students) cited economic reasons for dropping out. Many of these students quit school and go to work to help support their families. A recent study revealed that when children's parents were involved in their school in middle and late childhood, and when parents and adolescents had good relationships in early adolescence, a positive trajectory toward academic success was the likely outcome (Englund, Egeland, & Collins, 2008). By contrast, those who had poor relationships with their parents were more likely to drop out of high school despite doing well academically and behaviorally. Many school dropouts have friends who also are school dropouts. Approximately one-third of the girls who drop out of school do so for personal reasons, such as pregnancy or marriage.

Reducing the Dropout Rate   A review of school-based dropout programs found that the most effective programs provided early reading programs, tutoring, counseling, and mentoring (Lehr & others, 2003). They also emphasized the importance of creating caring environments and relationships and offered community-service opportunities.

Clearly, then, early detection of children's school-related difficulties, and getting children engaged with school in positive ways, are important strategies for reducing the dropout rate (Jimerson, 2009). Also, recently the Bill and Melinda Gates Foundation (2008) has funded efforts to reduce the dropout rate in schools where dropout rates are high. One strategy that is being emphasized in the Gates' funding is keeping students at risk for dropping out of school with the same teachers through their high school years. The hope is that the teachers will get to know these students much better, their relationship with the students will improve, and they will be able to monitor and guide the students toward graduating from high school. One program that has been very effective in reducing school dropout rates is described in the following *Caring for Children* interlude.

Caring for Children

THE "I HAVE A DREAM" PROGRAM

"I Have a Dream" (IHAD) is an innovative comprehensive, long-term dropout prevention program administered by the National "I Have a Dream" Foundation in New York. Since the National IHAD Foundation was created in 1986, it has grown to number over 180 projects in 64 cities and 27 states serving more than 15,000 children ("I Have a Dream" Foundation, 2009). Local IHAD projects around the country "adopt" entire grades (usually the third or fourth) from public elementary schools, or corresponding age cohorts from public housing developments. These children—"Dreamers"—are then provided with a program of academic, social, cultural, and recreational activities throughout their elementary, middle school, and high school years. An important part of this program is that it is personal rather than institutional: IHAD sponsors and staff develop close long-term relationships with the children. When participants complete high school, IHAD provides the tuition assistance necessary for them to attend a state or local college or vocational school.

The IHAD program was created in 1981, when philanthropist Eugene Lang made an impromptu offer of college tuition to a class of graduating sixth-graders at P.S. 121 in East Harlem. Statistically, 75 percent of the students should have dropped out of school; instead, 90 percent graduated and 60 percent went on to college. Other evaluations of IHAD programs have found dramatic improvements in grades, test scores, and school attendance, as well as a reduction of behavioral problems of Dreamers. For example, in Portland, Oregon, twice as many Dreamers as control-group students had reached a math standard, and the Dreamers were less likely to be referred to the juvenile justice system (Davis, Hyatt, & Arrasmith, 1998). And in a recent analysis of the I Have A Dream program in Houston, 91 percent of the participants received passing grades in reading/English, 83 percent said they liked school, 98 percent said getting good grades is important to them, 100 percent said they plan to graduate from high school, and 94 percent reported they plan to go to college ("I Have a Dream" Foundation, 2009).

These adolescents participate in the "I Have a Dream" (IHAD) program, a comprehensive, long-term dropout prevention program that has been very successful. *What are some other strategies for reducing high school dropout rates?*

Review and Reflect: Learning Goal 3

3 **Characterize schools for adolescents**

REVIEW

- What is the transition from elementary to middle school like? What are some criticisms of, and recommendations for, improving U.S. middle schools?
- How can the American high school be improved so that students are better prepared for the demands of the modern workplace?
- What are some of the reasons why adolescents drop out of school?

REFLECT

- What was your own middle school like? How did it measure up to the Turning Points recommendations?

4 HOW DO ADOLESCENTS EXPERIENCE CAREER DEVELOPMENT?

| Views of Career Development | Exploration, Decision Making, and Planning | Sociocultural Influences |

What views of career development have been proposed? What are some important cognitive processes in career development? How do sociocultural contexts influence career development?

Views of Career Development

What are some developmental changes that characterize adolescents' career choices? How might personality types influence career development?

Developmental Changes   Many children have idealistic fantasies about what they want to be when they grow up. For example, many young children want to be superheroes, sports stars, or movie stars. In the high school years, they often have begun to think about careers on a somewhat less idealistic basis. In their late teens and early twenties, their career decision making has usually turned more serious as they explore different career possibilities and zero in on the career they want to enter. In college, this often means choosing a major or specialization that is designed to lead to work in a particular field. By their early and mid-twenties, many individuals have completed their education or training and started to enter a full-time occupation. From the mid-twenties through the remainder of early adulthood, individuals often seek to establish their emerging career in a particular field. They may work hard to move up the career ladder and improve their financial standing.

William Damon (2008) recently described how it is not only children who have idealistic fantasies about careers but that too many of today's adolescents also dream about fantasy careers that may have no connection to reality. Too often the adolescents have no idea about what it takes to become such a career star, and it usually is the case that there is no one in their lives who can help them to reach this pinnacle in a career. Consider adolescents playing basketball who dream of becoming the next Kobe Bryant and adolescents participating in theater who want to become the next Angelina Jolie, for example.

"Your son has made a career choice, Mildred. He's going to win the lottery and travel a lot."
Copyright © 1985. Reprinted courtesy of Bunny Hoest and Parade Magazine.

Holland's Personality–Type Theory   **Personality-type theory** is John Holland's theory that an effort should be made to match an individual's career choice with the individual's personality (Holland, 1987). Once individuals find a career that fits with their personality, they are more likely to enjoy that career and stay in a job for a longer period of time than are individuals who work at jobs unsuitable for their personality. Holland believes that counselors should consider six basic personality types when matching the individual's psychological makeup with a career (see Figure 15.5):

FIGURE 15.5 Holland's Model of Personality Types and Career Choices

personality-type theory Holland's theory that an effort should be made to match an individual's career choice with the individual's personality.

- *Realistic.* These individuals show characteristically "masculine" traits. They are physically strong, deal in practical ways with problems, and may not excel in social communication. They are best oriented toward practical careers, such as labor, farming, truck driving, and construction.

- *Intellectual.* These individuals are conceptually and theoretically oriented. They are thinkers, rather than doers. Often, they avoid interpersonal relations and are best suited to careers in math and science.

- *Social.* These individuals often show characteristically "feminine" traits, especially those associated with verbal skills and interpersonal relations. They are likely to be best equipped to enter "people" professions, such as teaching, social work, and counseling.

- *Conventional.* These youth show a distaste for unstructured activities. They are best suited for jobs as subordinates, such as bank tellers, secretaries, and file clerks.

- *Enterprising.* These individuals energize their verbal abilities toward leading others, dominating individuals, and selling people on issues or products. They are best counseled to enter careers such as sales, politics, and management.

- *Artistic.* These youth prefer to interact with their world through artistic expression, avoiding conventional and interpersonal situations in many instances. They should be oriented toward careers such as art and writing.

If all individuals were to fall conveniently into Holland's personality types, career counselors would have an easy job. But individuals are more varied and complex than Holland's theory suggests. Even Holland now admits that most individuals are not pure types. Still, the basic idea of matching individuals' abilities to particular careers is an important contribution to the career field (Brown, 1987; Lent & others, 2003). Holland's personality types are incorporated into the Strong-Campbell Vocational Interest Inventory, a widely used measure in career guidance.

Exploration, Decision Making, and Planning

Exploration, decision making, and planning play important roles in adolescents' career choices (Hager, 2008). In countries where equal employment opportunities have emerged—such as the United States, Canada, Great Britain, and France—the exploration of various career paths is critical in the adolescent's career development. Adolescents often approach career exploration and decision making with considerable ambiguity, uncertainty, and stress. Their career decisions often involve floundering and unplanned changes. Many adolescents not only do not know *what* information to seek about careers but also do not know *how* to seek it.

Sociocultural Influences

Not every individual born into the world can grow up to become a nuclear physicist or a doctor—a genetic limitation keeps some adolescents from performing at the high intellectual levels necessary to enter such careers. Similarly, genetic limitations restrict some adolescents from becoming professional football players or professional golfers. But usually many careers are available to each of us, careers that provide a reasonable match with our abilities. Our sociocultural experiences exert strong influences on our career choices from among the wide available range (Bennett, 2008; Messersmith & others, 2008). Among the important sociocultural factors that influence career development are parents and peers, schools, and socioeconomic status.

Parents can play an important role in the adolescent's achievement and career development. It is important for parents to neither pressure the adolescent too much nor challenge the adolescent too little.

Parents and Peers   Parents and peers are strong influences on adolescents' career choices. From an early age, children see and hear about what jobs their parents have. Many factors influence the parent's role in the adolescent's career development (Messersmith & others, 2008). For one, mothers who work regularly outside the home and show effort and pride in their work probably have strong influences on their adolescents' career development. A reasonable conclusion is that, when both parents work and enjoy their work, adolescents learn work values from both parents. Peers also can influence the adolescent's career development. A recent study of Vietnamese adolescents in the Washington, D.C., area revealed that peer support and English-language acculturation were the most important factors in career decision-making self-efficacy (Patel, Salahuddin, & O'Brien, 2008).

How Would You...?
As a human development and family studies professional, how would you advise parents to talk with their adolescents about their future career?

School Influences Schools, teachers, and counselors can exert a powerful influence on adolescents' career development (Diemer & Hsieh, 2008; Metheny, McWhirter, & O'Neil, 2008). School is the primary setting where individuals first encounter the world of work. School provides an atmosphere for continuing self-development in relation to achievement and work. And school is the only institution in society that is presently capable of providing the delivery systems necessary for career education—instruction, guidance, placement, and community connections.

Counselors' consultation with students about careers may change from middle school to high school (Baggerly, 2008). In middle schools, counselors often focus on students' career exploration, guiding students to examine work options in terms of their own strengths, weaknesses, interests, and skills. Middle school students are often taught how to use career exploration computer programs to assess their career talents and engage in occupation searches. High school counselors link students' interests and skills with occupational and education options. They also advise students to engage in career planning and be realistic about their career possibilities. High school counselors may guide students to attend career fairs, visit college campuses, and participate in a career internship.

However, too many adolescents receive little direction from school guidance counselors and do not adequately explore careers on their own. On the average, high school students spend less than three hours per year with guidance counselors, and in some schools the average is even less. School counseling has been criticized both inside and outside the educational establishment. Insiders complain about the large number of students per school counselor and the weight of noncounseling administrative duties. Outsiders complain that school counseling is ineffective, biased, and a waste of money. Clearly, major improvements can be made in the area of school counseling.

Armando Ronquillo is one high school counselor who has made a difference in the lives of many students. To read about his work helping youth to plot the course to college, see the *Careers in Children's Development* profile.

How Would You...?
As a psychologist, how would you discuss career development with adolescents?

Careers in Children's Development

Armando Ronquillo, High School Counselor/College Advisor

Armando Ronquillo is a high school counselor and college advisor at Pueblo High School, which is in a low-socioeconomic-status area in Tucson, Arizona. More than 85 percent of the students have a Latino background. Ronquillo was named top high school counselor in the state of Arizona for the year 2000. He has especially helped to increase the number of Pueblo High School students who go to college.

Ronquillo has an undergraduate degree in elementary and special education, and a master's degree in counseling. He counsels the students on the merits of staying in school and on the lifelong opportunities provided by a college education. Ronquillo guides students in obtaining the academic preparation that will enable them to go to college, including how to apply for financial aid and scholarships. He also works with parents to help them understand that "their child going to college is not only doable but also affordable."

Ronquillo works with students on setting goals and planning. He has students plan for the future in terms of 1-year (short-term),

5-year (midrange), and 10-plus-year (long-term) time periods. Ronquillo says he does this "to help students visualize how the educational plans and decisions they make today will affect them in the future." He also organizes a number of college campus visitations for students from Pueblo High School each year.

Armando Ronquillo, counseling a Latina high school student about college.

Socioeconomic Status   The channels of upward mobility open to lower-SES youth are largely educational in nature. The school hierarchy from grade school through high school, as well as through college and graduate school, is programmed to orient individuals toward some type of career. Less than 100 years ago, it was believed that only eight years of education were necessary for vocational competence, and anything beyond that qualified the individual for advanced placement in higher-status occupations. By the middle of the twentieth century, the high school diploma had already lost ground as a ticket to career success, and in today's workplace college is a prerequisite for entering a higher-status occupation.

Many of the ideas that have guided career development theory were based on experiences in middle-income and well-educated contexts. Underlying this theory is the concept that individuals have a wide range of career choices from which they can select and pursue. However, youth in low-income circumstances may have more limited career choices. Barriers such as low-quality schools, violence, and lack of access to jobs can restrict low-income inner-city youths' access to desirable careers (Foskett, Dyke, & Maringe, 2008).

Review and Reflect: Learning Goal 4

 Summarize career development in adolescence

REVIEW

- What characterizes views of career development?
- What are some key cognitive processes in career development in adolescence?
- How do sociocultural contexts influence career development?

REFLECT

- What careers were you interested in during adolescence? How have your career interests changed since high school? What have been some key influences on your career decision making?

Reach Your Learning Goals

Cognitive Development in Adolescence

---

1 HOW DO ADOLESCENTS THINK AND PROCESS INFORMATION? DISCUSS DIFFERENT APPROACHES TO ADOLESCENT COGNITION

Piaget's Theory

- During the formal operational stage, Piaget's fourth stage of cognitive development, thought is more abstract, idealistic, and logical than during the concrete operational stage. Adolescents become capable of hypothetical-deductive reasoning. However, many adolescents are not formal operational thinkers but are consolidating their concrete operational thought. Piaget made a number of important contributions to understanding children's development, but his theory has undergone considerable criticism.

Adolescent Egocentrism

- Elkind proposed that adolescents, especially young adolescents, develop an egocentrism that includes both an imaginary audience (the belief that others are as interested in the adolescent as the adolescent is) and a personal fable (a sense of uniqueness and invincibility).

Information Processing

- Three aspects of memory that improve during adolescence are short-term memory, working memory, and long-term memory. Higher-order cognitive processes such as making decisions and thinking critically are often called executive functioning. It is increasingly thought that executive functioning strengthens during adolescence. Adolescence is a time of increased decision making. Older adolescents make better decisions than younger adolescents, who in turn are better at this skill than children are. Being able to make competent decisions, however, does not mean they actually will make these in everyday life, where breadth of experience comes into play. One proposal to explain effective adolescent decision making is the dual-process model. Adolescence is an important transitional period in critical thinking because of such cognitive changes as increased speed, automaticity, and capacity of information processing; more breadth of content knowledge; increased ability to construct new combinations of knowledge; and increased use of spontaneous strategies.

---

2 WHAT CHARACTERIZES ADOLESCENTS' VALUES, MORAL EDUCATION, AND RELIGION? DESCRIBE ADOLESCENTS' VALUES, MORAL EDUCATION, AND RELIGION

Values

- Values are the beliefs and attitudes about the way things should be. Over the past three decades, traditional-aged college students have shown an increased concern for personal well-being and a decreased interest in the welfare of others. Recently, U.S. college freshmen have shown an increased interest in developing a meaningful philosophy of life. Service learning is a form of education that promotes social responsibility and service to the community. Service learning is increasingly required by schools and has positive effects on adolescent development.

Moral Education

- The hidden curriculum is a term used by Dewey to describe his belief that even when schools do not have specific moral education programs, every school does provide a moral education. Character education is a direct education approach that advocates teaching adolescents a basic moral literacy. Values clarification emphasizes helping students to clarify what purposes their lives are to serve and what goals are worth working for. Cognitive moral education (often based on Kohlberg's theory) states that students should develop such values as democracy and justice as their moral reasoning develops. Cheating is a moral education concern and can take many forms. Various aspects of the situation influence whether students will cheat or not. Recently, an integrative moral education approach has been advocated.

| Religion | • Religious issues are important to adolescents. Adolescence may be a special juncture in religious development for many individuals. Various aspects of religion are linked with positive outcomes in adolescent development. Religious affiliation is linked to lower drug use and delinquency rates, less school truancy, and lower rates of depression. Erikson's ideas on identity can be applied to understanding the increased interest in religion during adolescence. Piaget's theory provides a theoretical foundation for understanding developmental changes in religion. When adolescents have a positive relationship with parents, and/or are securely attached to them, they often adopt their parents' religious beliefs. Links have been found between adolescent sexuality and religiousness. |

3 WHAT IS THE NATURE OF SCHOOLS FOR ADOLESCENTS? CHARACTERIZE SCHOOLS FOR ADOLESCENTS

The American Middle School

• The transition to middle or junior high school coincides with many physical, cognitive, and socioemotional changes. The transition involves moving from the top-dog position to the lowest position, and this transition is often difficult for many children. Criticisms of U.S. middle schools indicate they are too massive and impersonal, and that curricula are often irrelevant. Recommendations for improving U.S. middle schools include developing small communities of students within the schools, having lower student-counselor ratios, and raising academic standards. Participation in extracurricular activities is associated with positive academic and psychological outcomes.

The American High School

• The American high school needs to prepare students for today's workplace by providing them with an education that gives them skills in computers, effective written and oral communication, high-level reading comprehension, and working in groups with diverse others.

High School Dropouts

• Many school dropouts have educational deficiencies that limit their economic and social well-being for much of their adult lives. Progress has been made in lowering the dropout rate for African American youth, but the dropout rate for Native American and Latino youth remains very high. Native American youth have the highest dropout rate. Males are more likely to drop out than females. Dropping out of school is associated with demographic, family-related, peer-related, school-related, economic, and personal factors.

4 HOW DO ADOLESCENTS EXPERIENCE CAREER DEVELOPMENT? SUMMARIZE CAREER DEVELOPMENT IN ADOLESCENCE

Views of Career Development

• Many children have fantasies about what careers they want to enter when they grow up. In high school, these fantasies have decreased for many individuals, although still too many adolescents have a fantasy career they want to reach but don't have an adequate plan for how to reach their aspirations. In the late teens and early twenties, career decision making usually has turned more serious. Holland stresses that an individual's career choice should fit with his or her personality type: realistic, intellectual, social, conventional, enterprising, or artistic.

Exploration, Decision Making, and Planning

• Exploration, decision making, and planning of career options are important aspects of adolescents' career development. Too many youth flounder and make unplanned career choices.

Sociocultural Influences

• Sociocultural influences include parents and peers, schools, and socioeconomic status. The channels of opportunity for adolescents from low-income families are primarily educational.

KEY TERMS

hypothetical-deductive
   reasoning 499
adolescent egocentrism 501
imaginary audience 501

personal fable 501
dual-process
   model 504
values 507

service learning 507
hidden curriculum 509
character education 509
values clarification 509

cognitive moral
   education 509
top-dog phenomenon 514
personality-type theory 520

KEY PEOPLE

Jean Piaget 499
David Elkind 501

Robert Sternberg 502
Alan Baddeley 502

John Dewey 509
Lawrence Kohlberg 509

Erik Erikson 512
John Holland 520

MAKING A DIFFERENCE

Supporting Adolescents' Cognitive Development

What are some good strategies for nourishing adolescents' cognitive development?

- *Provide support for adolescents' information processing.* Provide opportunities and guide adolescents in making good decisions, especially in real-world settings; stimulate adolescents to think critically; and encourage them to engage in self-regulatory learning.

- *Give adolescents opportunities to discuss moral dilemmas.* Provide adolescents with group opportunities to discuss the importance of cooperation, trust, and caring.

- *Create better schools for adolescents.* Schools for adolescents need to emphasize socioemotional development as well as cognitive development.

- *Take individual variation in adolescents seriously.*

- *Develop curricula that involve high expectations for success and the support to attain that success.*

- *Develop smaller communities.*

- *Involve parents and community leaders more.*

- *Break down the barriers between school and work to reduce the high school dropout rate.*

- *Provide adolescents with information about careers.* Adolescents do not get adequate information about careers. Career decision making needs to be given a higher priority in schools.

RESOURCES FOR IMPROVING CHILDREN'S LIVES

Turning Points 2000
by Gayle Davis and Anthony Jackson (2000)

This follow-up to earlier Turning Points' recommendations includes a number of strategies for meeting the educational needs of adolescents, especially young adolescents.

E-LEARNING TOOLS

Connect to **www.mhhe.com/santrockc11e** to research the answers and complete these exercises. In addition, you'll find a number of other resources and valuable study tools for Chapter 15, "Cognitive Development in Adolescence," on this Web site.

Taking It to the Net

1. Roger has two daughters: Ellen, who is a senior in high school; and Lisa, who is in the eighth grade. Roger remembers that Ellen had a very difficult time when she transitioned from middle school to high school, and he wants to make the process easier

for Lisa. What kinds of things would help Lisa ease the transition? What makes this process so stressful for young teenagers?

2. LaTricia is an excellent student. She is on the debate team, and she makes extremely convincing arguments for the issues she is debating. However, when it comes to picking an outfit to wear in the morning, LaTricia has much more difficulty. She often stands in front of the closet, seemingly overwhelmed with the choices. Why might LaTricia be so skilled at challenging academic tasks, yet still have trouble with daily choices?

3. Steven is a high school junior. He was always a C student throughout elementary school and middle school. Now he is in danger of failing two of his classes. Steven is tired of school and wants to drop out. What might help Steven improve his grades and stay in school? What academic, social, and emotional factors might be contributing to Steven's school failure?

Health and Well-Being, Parenting, and Education

Build your decision-making skills by trying your hand at the health and well-being, parenting, and education exercises.

Video Clips

The Online Learning Center includes the following videos for this chapter:

- *Thoughts on School—1991*
  Three adolescent friends describe experiences with school and what they like and dislike about school.

- *Non-College-Bound Adolescents—923*
  A discussion of the unique problems faced by non-college-bound adolescents.

16

In case you're worried about what's going to become of the younger generation, it's going to grow up and start worrying about the younger generation.

—ROGER ALLEN
Contemporary American Writer

LEARNING GOALS

- ◆ Discuss changes in the self and emotional development during adolescence

- ◆ Describe changes that take place in adolescents' relationships with their parents

- ◆ Characterize the changes that occur in peer relations during adolescence

- ◆ Explain how culture influences adolescent development

- ◆ Identify adolescent problems in socioemotional development and strategies for helping adolescents with problems

SOCIOEMOTIONAL DEVELOPMENT IN ADOLESCENCE

CHAPTER OUTLINE

Images of Children's Development
Jewel Cash, Teen Dynamo

Jewel Cash, seated next to her mother, participating in a crime watch meeting at a community center.

The mayor of the city says that she is "everywhere." She recently persuaded the city's school committee to consider ending the practice of locking tardy students out of their classrooms. She also swayed a neighborhood group to support her proposal for a winter jobs program. According to one city councilman, "People are just impressed with the power of her arguments and the sophistication of the argument" (Silva, 2005, pp. B1, B4). She is Jewel E. Cash, and she is just 16 years old.

A junior at the prestigious Boston Latin Academy, Jewel was raised in one of Boston's housing projects by her mother, a single parent. Today she is a member of the Boston Student Advisory Council, mentors children, volunteers at a women's shelter, manages and dances in two troupes, and is a member of a neighborhood watch group—among other activities. Jewel is far from typical, but her activities illustrate that cognitive and socioemotional development allows adolescents—including adolescents from disadvantaged backgrounds—to be capable, effective individuals.

> ## PREVIEW
>
> **Significant changes characterize socioemotional development in adolescence. These changes include increased efforts to understand oneself, a search for identity, and emotional fluctuations. Changes also occur in the social contexts of adolescents' lives with transformations occurring in relationships with families and peers. Adolescents are also at risk for developing socioemotional problems, such as delinquency and depression.**

1 WHAT CHARACTERIZES EMOTIONAL AND PERSONALITY DEVELOPMENT IN ADOLESCENCE?

Self-Esteem   **Identity**   **Emotional Development**

Jewel Cash told an interviewer from the *Boston Globe*, "I see a problem and I say, 'How can I make a difference?' . . . I can't take on the world, even though I can try. . . . I'm moving forward but I want to make sure I'm bringing people with me" (Silva, 2005, pp. B1, B4). Jewel's confidence, sense of self, and emotional maturity sound at least as impressive as her activities. In this section, we examine how adolescents develop characteristics like these. How much did you understand yourself during adolescence, and how did you acquire the stamp of your identity? The section examines self-esteem, identity, and emotional development during adolescence.

Self-Esteem

Recall from Chapter 13, "Socioemotional Development in Middle and Late Childhood," that *self-esteem* is the overall way we evaluate ourselves. Controversy characterizes the extent to which self-esteem changes during adolescence and whether there are gender differences in adolescents' self-esteem (Harter, 2006). In one study, both boys and girls had particularly high self-esteem in childhood, but their self-esteem dropped considerably during adolescence (Robins & others, 2002) (see Figure 16.1). The self-esteem of girls declined more than the self-esteem of boys during adolescence in this study.

Does self-esteem in adolescence foreshadow adjustment and competence in adulthood? A New Zealand longitudinal study assessed self-esteem at 11, 13, and 15 years of age and adjustment and competence of the same individuals when they were 26 years old (Trzesniewski & others, 2006). The results revealed that adults characterized by poorer mental and physical health, worse economic prospects, and higher levels of criminal behavior were more likely to have low self-esteem in adolescence than were their better-adjusted, more competent adult counterparts.

Some critics argue that developmental changes and gender differences in self-esteem during adolescence have been exaggerated (Harter, 2002). For example, in one analysis of research studies on self-esteem in adolescence, it was concluded that girls have only slightly more negative self-esteem than do boys (Kling & others, 1999). Despite the differing results and interpretations, the self-esteem of girls is likely to decline at least somewhat during early adolescence.

One explanation for the decline in the self-esteem among females during early adolescence focuses on girls' more negative body images during pubertal change compared with boys (Harter, 2006). Another explanation involves the greater interest young adolescent girls take in social relationships and society's failure to reward that interest. A recent study examined why some adolescent girls recover and develop healthy self-esteem but others don't (Impett & others, 2008). In this study, both self-esteem and relationship authenticity (a consistency between what one thinks and feels, and what one says and does in relational contexts) increased from the eighth through the twelfth grade. Also, the self-esteem of girls who scored high on relationship authenticity in the eighth grade increased over the course of adolescence more than girls who scored low on this measure in the eighth grade.

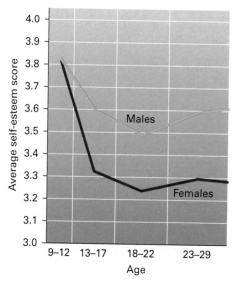

FIGURE 16.1 Developmental Changes in Self-Esteem A large-scale study asked individuals to rate the extent to which they have high self-esteem on a 5-point scale from 5 = "strongly agree" to 1 = "strongly disagree" (Robins & others, 2002). Self-esteem dropped in adolescence, more for girls than boys, then increased in emerging adulthood. Even though self-esteem decreased during adolescence, it still was in the positive range (between approximately 3.3 and 3.6 on the 5-point scale).

Identity

"Who am I? What am I all about? What am I going to do with my life? What is different about me? How can I make it on my own?" These questions reflect the search for an identity. By far the most comprehensive and provocative theory of identity development is Erik Erikson's. In this section, we examine his views on identity. We also discuss contemporary research on how identity develops and how social contexts influence that development.

What Is Identity?   Identity is a self-portrait composed of many pieces, including these:

- The career and work path the person wants to follow (vocational/career identity)
- Whether the person is conservative, liberal, or middle-of-the-road (political identity)
- The person's spiritual beliefs (religious identity)
- Whether the person is single, married, divorced, and so on (relationship identity)
- The extent to which the person is motivated to achieve and is intellectual (achievement, intellectual identity)
- Whether the person is heterosexual, homosexual, or bisexual (sexual identity)
- Which part of the world or country a person is from and how intensely the person identifies with his or her cultural heritage (cultural/ethnic identity)

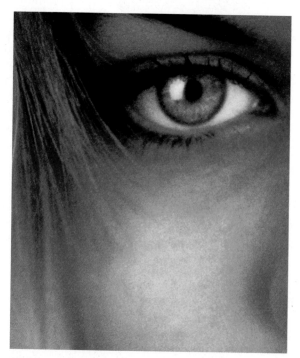

What are some important dimensions of identity?

- The kinds of things a person likes to do, which can include sports, music, hobbies, and so on (interests)
- The individual's personality characteristics (such as being introverted or extraverted, anxious or calm, friendly or hostile, and so on) (personality)
- The individual's body image (physical identity)

Synthesizing the identity components can be a long and drawn-out process, with many negations and affirmations of various roles and faces (Azmitia, Syed, & Radmacher, 2008). Decisions are not made once and for all, but have to be made again and again. Identity development does not happen neatly, and it does not happen cataclysmically (Cote, 2009; Kroger, 2007).

Erikson's View Questions about identity surface as common, virtually universal, concerns during adolescence. Some decisions made during adolescence might seem trivial: whether to study or play, which major to study, whom to date, whether or not to break up, whether or not to be politically active, and so on. Over the years of adolescence, however, such decisions begin to form the core of what the individual is all about as a human being—what is called his or her identity.

It was Erik Erikson (1950, 1968) who first understood how central questions about identity are to understanding adolescent development. That identity is now believed to be a key aspect of adolescent development is a result of Erikson's masterful thinking and analysis.

We discussed Erikson's theory in Chapter 1, "Introduction." Recall that his fifth developmental stage, which individuals experience during adolescence, is **identity versus identity confusion.** During this time, said Erikson, adolescents are faced with deciding who they are, what they are all about, and where they are going in life.

The search for an identity during adolescence is aided by a **psychosocial moratorium,** which is Erikson's term for the gap between childhood security and adult autonomy. During this period, society leaves adolescents relatively free of responsibilities and free to try out different identities. Adolescents in effect search their culture's identity files, experimenting with different roles and personalities. They may want to pursue one career one month (lawyer, for example) and another career the next month (doctor, actor, teacher, social worker, or astronaut, for example). They may dress neatly one day, sloppily the next. This experimentation is a deliberate effort on the part of adolescents to find out where they fit in the world. Most adolescents eventually discard undesirable roles.

Youth who successfully cope with conflicting identities emerge with a new sense of self that is both refreshing and acceptable. Adolescents who do not successfully resolve this identity crisis suffer what Erikson calls *identity confusion.* The confusion takes one of two courses: Individuals withdraw, isolating themselves from peers and family, or they immerse themselves in the world of peers and lose their identity in the crowd.

A current concern about the development of identity in adolescence and emerging adulthood was voiced in William Damon's (2008) book, *The Path to Purpose,* which we described in Chapters 14, "Physical Development in Adolescence," and 15, "Cognitive Development in Adolescence." Damon acknowledges that successful identity development is a long-term process of extended exploration and reflection, and in some instances can involve postponing decisions for a number of years. However, what concerns Damon is that too many of today's youth aren't moving toward any identity resolution. In Damon's (2008, pp. 5, 7) words,

> Their delay is characterized more by indecision than by motivated reflection, more by confusion than by pursuit of clear goals, more by ambivalence than by determination. Directionless shift is not a constructive moratorium in either a developmental or a societal sense. Without a sense of direction, opportunities are lost, and doubt and self-absorption can set in. Maladaptive habits are established and adaptive ones not built. . . . What is too often missing is . . . the kind of wholehearted

"Who are you?" said the Caterpillar. Alice replied, rather shyly, "I—I hardly know, Sir, just at present—at least I know who I was when I got up this morning, but I must have changed several times since then."

—LEWIS CARROLL
English Writer, 19th Century

Erik Erikson.

identity versus identity confusion Erikson's fifth developmental stage, which occurs about the time of adolescence. At this time, adolescents are faced with deciding who they are, what they are all about, and where they are going in life.

psychosocial moratorium Erikson's term for the gap between childhood security and adult autonomy.

Position on Occupation and Ideology	Identity Status			
	Identity diffusion	Identity foreclosure	Identity moratorium	Identity achievement
Crisis	Absent	Absent	Present	Present
Commitment	Absent	Present	Absent	Present

FIGURE 16.2 Marcia's Four Statuses of Identity According to Marcia, an individual's status in developing an identity can be described as identity diffusion, identity foreclosure, identity moratorium, or identity achievement. The status depends on the presence or absence of (1) a crisis or exploration of alternatives and (2) a commitment to an identity. *What is the identity status of most young adolescents?*

dedication to an activity or interest that stems from serious purpose, a purpose that can give meaning and direction to life.

In Damon's (2008, p. 47) view, too many youth are left to their own devices in dealing with some of life's biggest questions: "What is my calling? What do I have to contribute to the world? What am I here for?" Damon acknowledges that adults can't make youths' decisions for them, but he emphasizes that it is very important for parents, teachers, mentors, and other adults to provide guidance, feedback, and contexts that will improve the likelihood youth will develop a positive identity. Youth need a cultural climate that inspires rather than demoralizes them and supports their chances of reaching their aspirations.

Developmental Changes Although questions about identity may be especially important during adolescence, identity formation neither begins nor ends during these years. It begins with the appearance of attachment, the development of the sense of self, and the emergence of independence in infancy; the process reaches its final phase with a life review and integration in old age. What is important about identity development in adolescence, especially late adolescence, is that for the first time, physical development, cognitive development, and socioemotional development advance to the point at which the individual can sort through and synthesize childhood identities and identifications to construct a viable path toward adult maturity.

What concerns about today's adolescents' identity development did William Damon (2008) voice in The Path to Purpose?

How do individual adolescents go about the process of forming an identity? Eriksonian researcher James Marcia (1980, 1994) argues that Erikson's theory of identity development contains four *statuses* of identity, or ways of resolving the identity crisis: identity diffusion, identity foreclosure, identity moratorium, and identity achievement. What determines an individual's identity status? Marcia classifies individuals based on the existence or extent of their crisis or commitment (see Figure 16.2). **Crisis** is defined as a period of identity development during which the individual is exploring alternatives. Most researchers use the term *exploration* rather than crisis. **Commitment** is personal investment in identity.

The four statuses of identity are as follows:

- **Identity diffusion,** the status of individuals who have not yet experienced a crisis or made any commitments. Not only are they undecided about occupational and ideological choices, they are also likely to show little interest in such matters.

- **Identity foreclosure** is the status of individuals who have made a commitment but have not experienced a crisis. This occurs most often when parents hand down commitments to their adolescents, usually in an authoritarian way, before adolescents have had a chance to explore different approaches, ideologies, and vocations on their own.

How Would You...?
As a psychologist, how would you apply Marcia's theory of identity formation to describe your current identity status or the identity status of adolescents you know?

crisis Marcia's term for a period of identity development during which the individual is exploring alternatives.

commitment Marcia's term for the part of identity development in which individuals show a personal investment in identity.

identity diffusion Marcia's term for the status of individuals who have not yet experienced a crisis (explored alternatives) or made any commitments.

identity foreclosure Marcia's term for the status of individuals who have made a commitment but have not experienced a crisis.

How does identity change in emerging adulthood?

> *Once formed, an identity furnishes individuals with a historical sense of who they have been, a meaningful sense of who they are now, and a sense of who they might become in the future.*
>
> —JAMES MARCIA
> *Contemporary Psychologist, Simon Fraser University*

identity moratorium Marcia's term for the status of individuals who are in the midst of a crisis, but their commitments are either absent or vaguely defined.

identity achievement Marcia's term for the status of individuals who have undergone a crisis and have made a commitment.

individuality Characteristic consisting of two dimensions: self-assertion (the ability to have and communicate a point of view) and separateness (the use of communication patterns to express how one is different from others).

- **Identity moratorium** is the status of individuals who are in the midst of a crisis but whose commitments are either absent or only vaguely defined.

- **Identity achievement** is the status of individuals who have undergone a crisis and have made a commitment.

Emerging Adulthood and Beyond   A consensus is developing that the key changes in identity are more likely to take place in emerging adulthood (18 to 25 years of age) or later than in adolescence (Luyckx & others, 2008; Orbe, 2008). For example, Alan Waterman (1985, 1999) has found that from the years preceding high school through the last few years of college, the number of individuals who are identity achieved increases, while the number who are identity diffused decreases. College upperclassmen are more likely to be identity achieved than college freshmen or high school students. Many young adolescents, on the other hand, are identity diffused. These developmental changes are especially true for vocational choice. In terms of religious beliefs and political ideology, fewer college students reach the identity-achieved status; a substantial number are characterized by foreclosure and diffusion. Thus, the timing of identity development may depend on the particular dimension (Arehart & Smith, 1990).

Why might college produce some key changes in identity? Increased complexity in the reasoning skills of college students combined with a wide range of new experiences that highlight contrasts between home and college and between themselves and others stimulates them to reach a higher level of integrating various dimensions of their identity (Phinney, 2008).

One of emerging adulthood's themes is not having many social commitments, which gives individuals considerable independence in developing a life path. James Cote (2006, 2009) argues that because of this freedom, developing a positive identity in emerging adulthood requires considerable self-discipline and planning. Without this self-discipline and planning, emerging adults are likely to drift and not follow any particular direction. Cote also stresses that emerging adults who obtain a higher education are more likely to be on a positive identity path. Those who don't obtain a higher education, he says, tend to experience frequent job changes, not because they are searching for an identity but rather because they are just trying to eke out a living in a society that rewards higher education.

Resolution of the identity issue during adolescence and emerging adulthood does not mean that identity will be stable through the remainder of life. Many individuals who develop positive identities follow what are called "MAMA" cycles—that is, their identity status changes from *moratorium* to *achievement* to *moratorium* to *achievement* (Marcia, 1994). These cycles may be repeated throughout life (Francis, Fraser, & Marcia, 1989). Marcia (2002) argues that the first identity is just that—it is not, and should not be expected to be, the final product.

In short, questions about identity come up throughout life. An individual who develops a healthy identity is flexible and adaptive, open to changes in society, in relationships, and in careers. This openness assures numerous reorganizations of identity throughout the individual's life.

Family Influences   Parents are important figures in the adolescent's development of identity (Beyers & Goossens, 2008; Schachter & Ventura, 2008). Researchers have found that a family atmosphere that promotes both individuality and connectedness is important in the adolescent's identity development (Cooper & Grotevant, 1989):

- **Individuality** consists of two dimensions: self-assertion (the ability to have and communicate a point of view) and separateness (the use of communication patterns to express how one is different from others).

• **Connectedness** also consists of two dimensions: mutuality, which involves sensitivity to and respect for others' views, and permeability, which involves openness to others' views.

In general, then, research indicates that identity formation is enhanced by family relationships that sustain both individuation, which encourages adolescents to develop their own point of view, and connectedness, which provides a secure base from which adolescents can explore their widening social worlds (Cooper, Behrens, & Trinh, 2008). When connectedness is strong and individuation weak, adolescents often have an identity foreclosure status. When connectedness is weak, adolescents often reveal identity confusion.

How might parents influence the adolescent's identity development?

Ethnic Identity   Throughout the world, ethnic minority groups have struggled to maintain their ethnic identities while blending in with the dominant culture (Erikson, 1968). **Ethnic identity** is an enduring aspect of the self that includes a sense of membership in an ethnic group, along with the attitudes and feelings related to that membership. Thus, for adolescents from ethnic minority groups, the process of identity formation has an added dimension: the choice between two or more sources of identification—their own ethnic group and the mainstream, or dominant culture (Phinney, 2008). Many adolescents resolve this choice by developing a *bicultural identity*. That is, they identify in some ways with their ethnic group and in other ways with the majority culture (Phinney, 2006). One recent study of Mexican American and Asian American college students found that they identified with both the American mainstream culture and their culture of origin (Devos, 2006).

For ethnic minority individuals, adolescence and emerging adulthood are often special junctures in their development (Fuligni, Hughes, & Way, 2009; Syed & Azmitia, 2008; Way & others, 2008). Although children are aware of some ethnic and cultural differences, individuals consciously confront their ethnicity for the first time in adolescence or emerging adulthood. Unlike children, adolescents and emerging adults have the ability to interpret ethnic and cultural information, to reflect on the past, and to speculate about the future.

The indicators of identity change often differ for each succeeding generation (Phinney & Ong, 2007). First-generation immigrants are likely to be secure in their identities and unlikely to change much; they may or may not develop a new identity. The degree to which they begin to feel "American" appears to be related to whether or not they learn English, develop social networks beyond their ethnic group, and become culturally competent in their new country. Second-generation immigrants are more likely to think of themselves as "American," possibly because citizenship is granted at birth. Their ethnic identity is likely to be linked to retention of their ethnic language and social networks. In the third and later generations, the issues become more complex. Historical, contextual, and political factors that are unrelated to acculturation may affect the extent to which members of this generation retain their ethnic identities.

Michelle Chin, age 16: "Parents do not understand that teenagers need to find out who they are, which means a lot of experimenting, a lot of mood swings, a lot of emotions and awkwardness. Like any teenager, I am facing an identity crisis. I am still trying to figure out whether I am a Chinese American or an American with Asian eyes."

How Would You...?
As a human development and family studies professional, how would you design a community program that assists ethnic minority adolescents to develop a healthy bicultural identity?

Researchers are increasingly finding that a positive ethnic identity is linked to positive outcomes for ethnic minority adolescents (Umana-Taylor, 2006; Umana-Taylor, Gonzales-Backen, & Guimond, 2009). For example, in one study ethnic identity was related to higher school engagement and lower aggression (Van Buren & Graham, 2003). And in a recent study, Navajo adolescents' affirmation and belonging to their ethnic heritage were linked to higher self-esteem, school connectedness, and social functioning (Jones & Galliher, 2007). And a recent longitudinal study of Latino adolescents found that ethnic identity resolution predicted proactive coping with discrimination over time (Umana-Taylor & others, 2008). Further, another recent study found that exploration was an important aspect of establishing a secure sense of one's ethnic identity, which in turn

connectedness Characteristic consisting of two dimensions: mutuality (sensitivity to and respect for others' views) and permeability (openness to others' views).

ethnic identity An enduring, basic aspect of the self that includes a sense of membership in an ethnic group and the attitudes and feelings related to that membership.

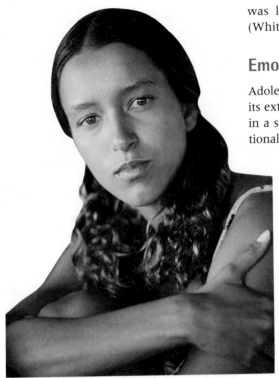

What characterizes ethnic identity development in adolescence?

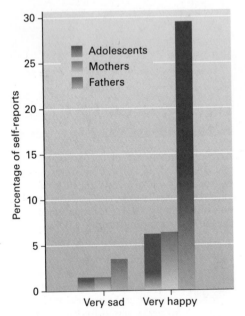

FIGURE 16.3 Self-Reported Extremes of Emotion by Adolescents, Mothers, and Fathers Using the Experience Sampling Method In the study by Reed Larson and Maryse Richards (1994), adolescents and their mothers and fathers were beeped at random times by researchers using the experience sampling method. The researchers found that adolescents were more likely to report more emotional extremes than their parents.

was linked to a positive attitude toward one's own group and other groups (Whitehead & others, 2009).

Emotional Development

Adolescence has long been described as a time of emotional turmoil (Hall, 1904). In its extreme form, this view is too stereotypical because adolescents are not constantly in a state of "storm and stress." Nonetheless, early adolescence is a time when emotional highs and lows increase (Rosenblum & Lewis, 2003). Young adolescents can be on top of the world one moment and down in the dumps the next. In many instances, the intensity of their emotions seems out of proportion to the events that elicit them. Young adolescents might sulk a lot, not knowing how to adequately express their feelings. With little or no provocation, they might blow up at their parents or siblings, or use the defense mechanism to displace their feelings onto another person.

Reed Larson and Maryse Richards (1994) found that adolescents reported more extreme emotions and more fleeting emotions than their parents did. For example, adolescents were five times more likely to report being "very happy" and three times more likely to report being "very sad" than their parents (see Figure 16.3). These findings lend support to the perception of adolescents as moody and changeable (Rosenblum & Lewis, 2003).

Researchers have also found that from the fifth through the ninth grades, both boys and girls experience a 50 percent decrease in being "very happy" (Larson & Lampman-Petraitis, 1989). In this same study, adolescents were more likely than preadolescents to report mildly negative mood states.

It is important for adults to recognize that moodiness is a *normal* aspect of early adolescence, and most adolescents make it through these moody times to become competent adults. Nonetheless, for some adolescents, such emotions can reflect serious problems. For example, rates of depressed moods become more elevated for girls during adolescence (Zahn-Waxler, Shirtcliff, & Marceau, 2008). We will have more to say about depression later in the chapter.

What causes the emotional swings of early adolescence? As we saw in Chapter 14, "Physical Development in Adolescence," significant hormonal changes characterize puberty. Emotional fluctuations in early adolescence may be related to the variability of hormones during this time period. Moods become less extreme as adolescents move into adulthood, and this decrease in emotional fluctuation may be due to adaptation to hormone levels over time (Rosenbaum & Lewis, 2003).

Researchers have discovered that pubertal change is associated with an increase in negative emotions (Archibald, Graber, & Brooks-Gunn, 2003). However, most researchers conclude that hormonal influences are small, and that when they occur they usually are associated with other factors, such as stress, eating patterns, sexual activity, and social relationships (Susman & Rogol, 2004).

Indeed, environmental experiences may contribute more to the emotions of adolescence than hormonal changes. Recall from Chapter 14, "Physical Development in Adolescence," that in one study, social factors accounted for two to four times as much variance as hormonal factors in young adolescent girls' depression and anger (Brooks-Gunn & Warren, 1989). In sum, both hormonal changes and environmental experiences are involved in the changing emotional landscape of adolescence.

Being able to control one's emotions is an important aspect of adolescent development (Giedd, 2008). For example, one study revealed the importance of emotion regulation and mood in academic success (Gumora & Arsenio, 2002). Even when their level of cognitive ability was controlled, young adolescents who said they experienced more negative emotion regarding academic routines had lower grade-point averages.

Review and Reflect: Learning Goal 1

 Discuss changes in the self and emotional development during adolescence

REVIEW

- What are some changes in self-esteem that take place in adolescence?
- How does identity develop in adolescence?
- What factors affect emotional development in adolescence?

REFLECT

- Where are you in your identity development? Get out a sheet of paper and list each of the pieces of identity (vocational, political, religious, relationship, achievement/intellectual, sexual, cultural/ethnic, interests, personality, and physical) in a column on the left side of the paper. Then write the four identity statuses (diffused, foreclosed, moratorium, and achieved) across the top of the page. Next to each dimension of identity, place a check mark in the appropriate space that reflects your identity status for the particular aspect of identity. If you checked diffused or foreclosed for any of the dimensions, think about what you need to do to move on to a moratorium status in those areas.

2 WHAT IS THE NATURE OF PARENT-ADOLESCENT RELATIONSHIPS?

| Autonomy and Attachment | Parent-Adolescent Conflict |

Adolescence typically alters the relationship between parents and their children. Among the most important aspects of family relationships in adolescence are those that involve autonomy, attachment, and parent-adolescent conflict.

Autonomy and Attachment

With most adolescents, parents are likely to find themselves engaged in a delicate balancing act, weighing competing needs for autonomy and control, for independence and connection.

The Push for Autonomy   The typical adolescent's push for autonomy and responsibility puzzles and angers many parents. As parents see their teenager slipping from their grasp, they may have an urge to take stronger control. Heated emotional exchanges may ensue, with either side calling names, making threats, and doing whatever seems necessary to gain control. Parents may seem frustrated because they *expect* their teenager to heed their advice, to want to spend time with the family, and to grow up to do what is right. Most parents anticipate that their teenager will have some difficulty adjusting to the changes that adolescence brings, but few parents imagine and predict just how strong an adolescent's desires will be to spend time with peers or how intensely adolescents will want to show that it is they—not their parents—who are responsible for their successes and failures.

> *When I was a boy of 14, my father was so ignorant I could hardly stand to have the man around. But when I got to be 21, I was astonished at how much he had learnt in 7 years.*
>
> —**MARK TWAIN**
> **American Writer and Humorist, 20th Century**

How Would You...?
As a social worker, how would you counsel parents who are experiencing stress about anticipated family conflicts as their child enters adolescence?

What are strategies parents can use to guide adolescents in effectively handling their increased motivation for autonomy?

Stacey Christensen, age 16: "I am lucky enough to have open communication with my parents. Whenever I am in need or just need to talk, my parents are there for me. My advice to parents is to let your teens grow at their own pace, be open with them so that you can be there for them. We need guidance; our parents need to help but not be too overwhelming."

Adolescents' ability to attain autonomy and gain control over their behavior is acquired through appropriate adult reactions to their desire for control (McElhaney & others, 2009). At the onset of adolescence, the average individual does not have the knowledge to make appropriate or mature decisions in all areas of life. As the adolescent pushes for autonomy, the wise adult relinquishes control in those areas where the adolescent can make reasonable decisions, but continues to guide the adolescent to make reasonable decisions in areas in which the adolescent's knowledge is more limited. Gradually, adolescents acquire the ability to make mature decisions on their own (Harold, Colarossi, & Mercier, 2007).

Gender differences characterize autonomy-granting in adolescence. Boys are given more independence than girls. In one study, this tendency was especially true in U.S. families with a traditional gender-role orientation (Bumpus, Crouter, & McHale, 2001). Also, Latino parents protect and monitor their daughters more closely than is the case for non-Latino White parents (Allen & others, 2008).

The Role of Attachment Recall from Chapter 7, "Socioemotional Development in Infancy," that one of the most widely discussed aspects of socioemotional development in infancy is secure attachment to caregivers (Woodhouse, Dykas, & Cassidy, 2009). In the past decade, researchers have explored whether secure attachment also might be an important concept in adolescents' relationships with their parents. For example, Joseph Allen and his colleagues (Allen, 2007, 2008; Allen & others, 2007, 2009) found that securely attached adolescents were less likely than those who were insecurely attached to engage in problem behaviors such as juvenile delinquency and drug abuse. In a recent longitudinal study, Allen and colleagues (2009) found that secure attachment at 14 years of age was linked to a number of positive outcomes at 21 years of age, including relationship competence, financial/career competence, and fewer problematic behaviors.

Other research has examined possible links between secure attachment to parents and good relations with peers. Researchers have found that securely attached adolescents have better peer relations than their insecurely attached counterparts (Laible, Carlo, & Raffaeli, 2000). However, the correlations between adolescent-parent attachments and adolescent outcomes are moderate, an indication that the success or failure of parent-adolescent attachments does not necessarily guarantee success or failure in peer relationships.

Balancing Freedom and Control We have seen that parents play very important roles in adolescent development (Allen, 2008). Although adolescents are moving toward independence, they still need to stay connected with families (Hair & others, 2008). For example, the National Longitudinal Study on Adolescent Health of more than 12,000 adolescents, those who did not eat dinner with a parent five or more days a week had dramatically higher rates of smoking, drinking, marijuana use, getting into fights, and initiation of sexual activity (Council of Economic Advisors, 2000). In another study, parents who played an active role in monitoring and guiding their adolescents' development were more likely to have adolescents with positive peer relations and lower drug use than parents who had a less active role (Mounts, 2002).

Parent-Adolescent Conflict

Although parent-adolescent conflict increases in early adolescence, it does not reach the tumultuous proportions G. Stanley Hall envisioned at the beginning of the twentieth century (Eisenberg & others, 2008). Rather, much of the conflict involves the everyday events of family life, such as keeping a bedroom clean, dressing neatly, getting home by a certain time, and not talking forever on the phone. The conflicts rarely involve major dilemmas such as drugs or delinquency.

Conflict with parents often escalates during early adolescence, remains somewhat stable during the high school years, and then lessens in emerging adulthood. Parent-adolescent relationships become more positive if adolescents go away to college than if they attend college while living at home (Sullivan & Sullivan, 1980).

The everyday conflicts that characterize parent-adolescent relationships may actually serve a positive developmental function. These minor disputes and negotiations facilitate the adolescent's transition from being dependent on parents to becoming an autonomous individual. For example, in one study, adolescents who expressed disagreement with their parents explored identity development more actively than did adolescents who did not express disagreement with their parents (Cooper & others, 1982). Recognizing that conflict and negotiation can serve a positive developmental function can tone down parental hostility.

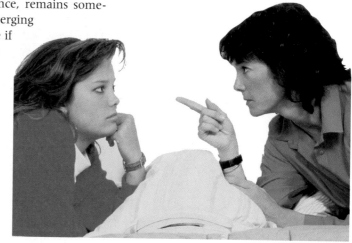

Conflict with parents increases in early adolescence. *What is the nature of this conflict in a majority of American families?*

The old model of parent-adolescent relationships suggested that as adolescents mature they detach themselves from parents and move into a world of autonomy apart from parents. The old model also suggested that parent-adolescent conflict is intense and stressful throughout adolescence. The new model emphasizes that parents serve as important attachment figures and support systems while adolescents explore a wider, more complex social world. The new model also emphasizes that, in most families, parent-adolescent conflict is moderate rather than severe and that the everyday negotiations and minor disputes not only are normal but also can serve the positive developmental function of helping the adolescent make the transition from childhood dependency to adult independence (see Figure 16.4).

Still, a high degree of conflict characterizes some parent-adolescent relationships. One estimate of the proportion of parents and adolescents who engage in prolonged, intense, repeated, unhealthy conflict is about one in five families (Montemayor, 1982). While this figure represents a minority of adolescents, it indicates that 4 to 5 million American families encounter serious, highly stressful parent-adolescent conflict. And this prolonged, intense conflict is associated with various adolescent problems: movement out of the home, juvenile delinquency, school dropout, pregnancy and early marriage, membership in religious cults, and drug abuse. In a recent study of Latino families, higher levels of conflict with either the mother or the father were linked to higher levels of adolescent boys' and girls' internalizing (depression, for example) and externalizing (delinquency, for example) problems (Crean, 2008). To read about some strategies for parenting adolescents, see the *Caring for Children* interlude.

> *It is not enough for parents to understand children. They must accord children the privilege of understanding them.*
>
> —**Milton Sapirstein**
> *American Psychiatrist, 20th Century*

Old Model		New Model
Autonomy, detachment from parents; parent and peer worlds are isolated		Attachment and autonomy; parents are important support systems and attachment figures; adolescent-parent and adolescent-peer worlds have some important connections
Intense, stressful conflict throughout adolescence; parent-adolescent relationships are filled with storm and stress on virtually a daily basis		Moderate parent-adolescent conflict is common and can serve a positive developmental function; conflict is greater in early adolescence

FIGURE 16.4 Old and New Models of Parent-Adolescent Relationships

Caring for Children

STRATEGIES FOR PARENTING ADOLESCENTS

Competent adolescent development is most likely when adolescents have parents who:

- *Show them warmth and respect, and avoid the tendency to be too controlling or too permissive.*
- *Serve as positive role models for adolescents.*
- *Demonstrate sustained interest in their lives.* Parents need to spend time with their adolescents and monitor their lives.
- *Understand and adapt to their cognitive and socioemotional development.*
- *Communicate expectations for high standards of conduct and achievement.*
- *Display constructive ways of dealing with problems and conflict.* Moderate conflict is a normal part of the adolescent's desire for independence and search for an identity.
- *Understand that adolescents don't become adults overnight.* Adolescence is a long journey.

Review and Reflect: Learning Goal 2

 Describe changes that take place in adolescents' relationships with their parents

REVIEW

- How do needs for autonomy and attachment develop in adolescence?
- What characterizes parent-adolescent conflict?

REFLECT

- How much autonomy did your parents give you in adolescence? Too much? Too little? How intense was your conflict with your parents during adolescence? What kinds of conflicts did you have? Would you behave differently toward your own adolescents from the way your parents did with you? If so, how?

---

3 WHAT ASPECTS OF PEER RELATIONSHIPS ARE IMPORTANT IN ADOLESCENCE?

| Friendship | Peer Groups | Dating and Romantic Relationships |

Peers play powerful roles in the lives of adolescents (Brown & Dietz, 2009; Bukowski, Motzoi, & Meyer, 2009). When you think back to your own adolescent years, you probably recall many of your most enjoyable moments as experiences shared with peers. Peer relations undergo important changes in adolescence, including changes in friendships and in peer groups and the beginning of romantic relationships. In middle and late childhood, as we discussed in Chapter 13, "Socioemotional Development in Middle and Late Childhood," the focus of peer relations is on being liked by classmates and on being included in games or lunchroom conversations. Being overlooked or, worse yet, being rejected can have damaging effects on children's development that sometimes are carried forward to adolescence (Dishion, Piehler, & Myers, 2008).

Friendship

For most children, being popular with their peers is a strong motivator. Beginning in early adolescence, however, teenagers typically prefer to have a smaller number of friendships that are more intense and intimate than those of young children.

Harry Stack Sullivan (1953) was the most influential theorist to discuss the importance of adolescent friendships. In contrast to other psychoanalytic theorists who focused almost exclusively on parent-child relationships, Sullivan argued that friends are also important in shaping the development of children and adolescents. Everyone, said Sullivan, has basic social needs, such as the need for tenderness (secure attachment), playful companionship, social acceptance, intimacy, and sexual relations. Whether or not these needs are fulfilled largely determines our emotional well-being. For example, if the need for playful companionship goes unmet, then we become bored and depressed; if the need for social acceptance is not met, we suffer a lowered sense of self-worth.

During adolescence, said Sullivan, friends become increasingly important in meeting social needs. In particular, Sullivan argued that the need for intimacy intensifies during early adolescence, motivating teenagers to seek out close friends. If adolescents fail to forge such close friendships, they experience loneliness and a reduced sense of self-worth.

Many of Sullivan's ideas have withstood the test of time (Buhrmester, 2005). For example, adolescents report disclosing intimate and personal information to their friends more often than do younger children (Buhrmester, 1998) (see Figure 16.5). Adolescents also say they depend more on friends than on parents to satisfy their needs for companionship, reassurance of worth, and intimacy. The ups and downs of experiences with friends shape adolescents' well-being (Vitaro, Boivin, & Bukowski, 2009).

Gossip about peers often dominates the conversation of friends in adolescence (Buhrmester & Chong, 2009). Much of the gossip is characterized by negative comments about others, such as talking about how someone got drunk last weekend, how unattractive someone looked at school yesterday, and how someone could have the nerve to say what they did. In some cases, the negative gossip takes the form of *relational aggression*, which involves spreading disparaging rumors to harm someone (discussed in Chapter 13, "Socioemotional Development in Middle and Late Childhood."). However, not all gossip among friends is negative. Some gossip can involve collaborative construction that contributes to developing perspectives on intimacy and close relationships. Friends also can show their trust by disclosing risky opinions. The talk-featured, gossip aspect of friendship is more common in girls than boys.

Although having friends can be a developmental advantage, not all friendships are alike and the quality of friendship is also important to consider (Laursen & Pursell, 2009; Rubin, Fredstrom, & Bowker, 2008). People differ in the company they keep—that is, who their friends are. It is a developmental disadvantage to have coercive, conflict-ridden, and poor-quality friendships (Snyder & others, 2008; Waldrip, Malcolm, & Jensen-Campbell, 2008). Developmental advantages occur when adolescents have friends who are socially skilled, supportive, and oriented toward academic achievement (Crosnoe & others, 2008). A recent study found that friends' grade-point average consistently predicted positive school achievement

What changes take place in friendship during the adolescent years?

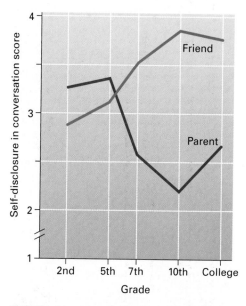

FIGURE 16.5 Developmental Changes in Self-Disclosing Conversations In this study children and youth completed a 5-point rating scale, with a higher score representing greater self-disclosure (Buhrmester, 1998). The data shown here represent the means for each age group. Self-disclosing conversations with friends increased dramatically in adolescence while declining in an equally dramatic fashion with parents. However, self-disclosing conversations with parents began to pick up somewhat during the college years.

(Cook, Deng, & Morgano, 2007). Another recent study revealed that the achievement of adolescent girls' best friends was linked to whether the adolescent girls took math classes in high school (Crosnoe & others, 2008).

Although most adolescents develop friendships with individuals who are close to their own age, some adolescents become best friends with younger or older individuals. Do older friends encourage adolescents to engage in delinquent behavior or early sexual behavior? Adolescents who interact with older youth do engage in these behaviors more frequently, but it is not known whether the older youth guide younger adolescents toward deviant behavior or whether the younger adolescents were already prone to deviant behavior before they developed the friendship with the older youth (Billy, Rodgers, & Udry, 1984). A recent study also revealed that over time from the sixth through tenth grades girls were more likely to have older male friends, which places some girls on a developmental trajectory for engaging in problem behavior (Poulin & Pedersen, 2007).

Peer Groups

How extensive is peer pressure in adolescence? What roles do cliques and crowds play in adolescents' lives? As we see next, researchers have found that the standards of peer groups and the influence of crowds and cliques become increasingly important during adolescence.

Peer Pressure Young adolescents conform more to peer standards than children do. Around the eighth and ninth grades, conformity to peers—especially to their antisocial standards—peaks (Brown & Larson, 2009; Brown & others, 2008). At this point, adolescents are most likely to go along with a peer to steal hubcaps off a car, draw graffiti on a wall, or steal cosmetics from a store counter. A recent study revealed that 14 to 18 years of age is an especially important time for developing the ability to stand up for what one believes and resist peer pressure to do otherwise (Steinberg & Monahan , 2007). One study also found that U.S. adolescents are more likely than Japanese adolescents to put pressure on their peers to resist parental influence (Rothbaum & others, 2000).

Which adolescents are most likely to conform to peers? Mitchell Prinstein and his colleagues (Cohen & Prinstein, 2006; Prinstein, 2007; Prinstein & Dodge, 2008; Prinstein & others, 2009) have recently conducted research and analysis that address this question. They conclude that adolescents who are uncertain about their social identity, which can appear in the form of low self-esteem and high social anxiety, are most likely to conform to peers. This uncertainty often increases during times of change, such as school and family transitions. Also peers are more likely to conform when they are in the presence of someone they perceive to have higher status than themselves.

Cliques and Crowds Cliques and crowds assume more important roles in the lives of adolescents than they do of children (Brown & Dietz, 2009; Brown & Larson, 2009). **Cliques** are small groups that range from two to about twelve individuals and average about five to six individuals. The clique members are usually of the same sex and about the same age.

Cliques can form because adolescents engage in similar activities, such as being in a club or on a sports team. Several adolescents may form a clique because they have spent time with each other, share mutual interests, and enjoy each other's company. Not necessarily friends, they often develop a friendship if they stay in the clique. What do adolescents do in cliques? They share ideas and hang out together. Often they develop an in-group identity in which they believe that their clique is better than other cliques.

Some cliques also form because of friendship. In the high school years, friendship cliques become more heterosexual with many high school seniors averaging

What characterizes peer pressure in adolescence?

clique A small group that ranges from two to about twelve individuals, averaging about five to six individuals, and one can that can form because adolescents engage in similar activities.

two opposite-sex and four same-sex friendships (Buhrmester & Chong, 2009). High school seniors average two opposite-sex and four same-sex friendships compared with none or one opposite-sex and five or more same-sex friendships in sixth-graders. These mixed-sex friendships can provide adolescents with access to potential romantic partners.

Crowds are larger than cliques and less personal. Adolescents are usually members of a crowd based on reputation, and they may or may not spend much time together. Many crowds are defined by the activities adolescents engage in (such as "jocks" who are good at sports or "druggies" who take drugs) (Brown, 2004). Reputation-based crowds often appear for the first time in early adolescence and usually become less prominent in late adolescence (Collins & Steinberg, 2006).

In one study, crowd membership was associated with adolescent self-esteem (Brown & Lohr, 1987). The crowds included jocks (athletically oriented), populars (well-known students who led social activities), normals (middle-of-the-road students who made up the masses), druggies or toughs (known for illicit drug use or other delinquent activities), and nobodies (low in social skills or intellectual abilities). The self-esteem of the jocks and the populars was highest, whereas that of the nobodies was lowest. One group of adolescents not in a crowd had self-esteem equivalent to that of the jocks and the populars; this group was the independents, who indicated that crowd membership was not important to them. Keep in mind that these data are correlational; self-esteem could increase an adolescent's probability of becoming a crowd member, just as crowd membership could increase the adolescent's self-esteem.

What characterizes adolescents' cliques and crowds?

Dating and Romantic Relationships

Adolescents spend considerable time either dating or thinking about dating (Connolly & McIsaac, 2009). Dating can be a form of recreation, a source of status, and a setting for learning about close relationships, as well as a way of finding a mate.

Types of Dating and Developmental Changes   A number of dating variations and developmental changes characterize dating and romantic relationships. First, we examine heterosexual romantic relationships and then turn to romantic relationships in sexual minority youth (gay male and lesbian adolescents).

Heterosexual Romantic Relationships   Three stages characterize the development of romantic relationships in adolescence (Connolly & McIsaac, 2009):

What are dating relationships like in adolescence?

- *Entering into romantic attractions and affiliations at about 11 to 13 years of age.* This initial stage is triggered by puberty. From 11 to 13, adolescents become intensely interested in romance, and it dominates many conversations with same-sex friends. Developing a crush on someone is common, and the crush often is shared with a same-sex friend. Young adolescents may or may not interact with the individual who is the object of their infatuation. When dating occurs, it usually occurs in a group setting.

- *Exploring romantic relationships at approximately 14 to 16 years of age.* At this point in adolescence, two types of romantic involvement occur: casual dating and group dating. *Casual dating* emerges between individuals who are mutually

crowd A larger group than a clique, one that is usually formed based on reputation; members may or may not spend much time together.

attracted. These dating experiences are often short-lived, last a few months at best, and usually endure for only a few weeks. *Dating in groups* is common and reflects embeddedness in the peer context. Friends often act as a third-party facilitator of a potential dating relationship by communicating their friend's romantic interest and confirming whether this attraction is reciprocated.

- *Consolidating dyadic romantic bonds at about 17 to 19 years of age.* At the end of the high school years, more serious romantic relationships develop. This is characterized by strong emotional bonds more closely resembling those in adult romantic relationships. These bonds often are more stable and enduring than earlier bonds, typically lasting one year or more.

Two variations on these stages in the development of romantic relationships in adolescence involve early and late bloomers (Connolly & McIssac, 2009). *Early bloomers* include 15 to 20 percent of 11- to 13-year-olds who say that they currently are in a romantic relationship and 35 percent who indicate that they have had some prior experience in romantic relationships. *Late bloomers* comprise approximately 10 percent of 17- to 19-years-olds who say that they have had no experience with romantic relationships and another 15 percent who report that they have not engaged in any romantic relationships that lasted more than four months.

In their early romantic relationships, today's adolescents are not motivated to fulfill attachment or even sexual needs. Rather, early romantic relationships serve as a context for adolescents to explore how attractive they are, how to interact romantically, and how all of these aspects look to the peer group. Only after adolescents acquire some basic competencies in interacting with romantic partners does the fulfillment of attachment and sexual needs become a central function of these relationships (Furman & Wehner, 1997).

Adolescents often find comfort in numbers in their early exploration of romantic relationships (Connolly & McIsaac, 2009). They may begin hanging out together in heterosexual groups. Sometimes they just hang out at someone's house or get organized enough to ask an adult to drive them to a mall or a movie. A special concern in early dating and "going with" someone is the associated risk for adolescent pregnancy and problems at home and school.

Romantic Relationships in Sexual Minority Youth

Recently, researchers have begun to study romantic relationships in gay male and lesbian youth (Diamond & Savin-Williams, 2009; Savin-Williams, 2007, 2008). Many sexual minority youth date other-sex peers, a practice that can help them to clarify their sexual orientation or disguise it from others (Savin-Williams & Ream, 2007). Most gay male and lesbian youth have had some same-sex sexual experience, often with peers who are "experimenting" and then go on to a primarily heterosexual orientation (Diamond & Savin-Williams, 2009; Savin-Williams & Cohen, 2007); however, relatively few gay male and lesbian youth have had same-sex romantic relationships. In one study, gay male and lesbian youth rated the breakup of a current romance as their second most stressful problem, second only to disclosure of their sexual orientation to their parents (D'Augelli, 1991).

Sociocultural Contexts and Dating

The sociocultural context exerts a powerful influence on adolescents' dating patterns. This influence may be seen in differences in dating patterns among ethnic groups within the United States. For example, one recent study found that Asian American adolescents were less likely to have been involved in a romantic relationship in the past 18 months than were African American or Latino adolescents (Carver, Joyner, & Udry, 2003).

Values, religious beliefs, and traditions often dictate at what age dating begins, how much freedom in dating is allowed, whether dates must be chaperoned by adults or parents, and the roles of males and females in dating. For example, Latino and Asian American cultures have more conservative standards regarding adolescent dating than does the Anglo-American culture. Dating may become a source of conflict within a family if the parents have immigrated from cultures in which dating begins

How Would You...?
As a human development and family studies professional, how would you explain to parents the developmental challenges faced by a gay male or lesbian adolescent?

at a late age, little freedom in dating is allowed, dates are chaperoned, and adolescent girl dating is especially restricted. When immigrant adolescents choose to adopt the ways of the dominant U.S. culture (such as unchaperoned dating), they often clash with parents and extended-family members who have more traditional values.

In one study, Latina young adults in the midwestern United States reflected on their experiences in dating during adolescence (Raffaelli & Ontai, 2004). They said that their parents placed strict boundaries on their romantic involvement. As a result, the young women said that their adolescent dating experiences were filled with tension and conflict. Over half of the Latinas engaged in "sneak dating" without their parents' knowledge.

What are some ethnic variations in dating during adolescence?

Dating and Adjustment   Researchers have linked dating and romantic relationships with various measures of how well adjusted adolescents are (Crissey, 2009; Connolly & McIsaac, 2009; Furman & Simon, 2008). For example, a recent study of 200 tenth-graders revealed that the more romantic experiences they had, the more they reported higher levels of social acceptance, friendship competence, and romantic competence—however, having more romantic experience also was linked to a higher level of substance use, delinquency, and sexual behavior (Furman, Low, & Ho, 2009). Another study found that 14- to 19-year old adolescents who were not involved in a romantic relationship had more social anxiety than did their counterparts who were dating or romantically involved (La Greca & Harrison, 2005). A recent study of adolescent girls revealed that a higher frequency of dating was linked to having depressive symptoms and emotionally unavailable parents (Steinberg & Davila, 2008). Another recent study of adolescent girls found that those who engaged in co-rumination (excessive discussion of problems with friends) were more likely to be involved in a romantic relationship, and together co-rumination and romantic involvement predicted an increase in depressive symptoms (Starr & Davila, 2009).

How are romantic relationships linked to adolescents' adjustment?

Dating and romantic relationships at an unusually early age also have been linked with several problems (Connolly & McIsaac, 2009). For example, early dating and "going with" someone are associated with adolescent pregnancy and problems at home and school (Furman & Collins, 2009). In one study, girls' early romantic involvement was linked with lower grades, less active participation in class discussion, and other school-related problems (Buhrmester, 2001).

Review and Reflect: Learning Goal 3

 3   **Characterize the changes that occur in peer relations during adolescence**

REVIEW

- What changes take place in friendship during adolescence?
- What are adolescents' peer groups like?
- What is the nature of adolescent dating and romantic relationships?

REFLECT

- What were your peer relationships like during adolescence? What peer groups were you involved in? How did they influence your development? What were your dating and romantic relationships like in adolescence? If you could change anything about the way you experienced peer relations in adolescence, what would it be?

4 WHY IS CULTURE AN IMPORTANT CONTEXT FOR ADOLESCENT DEVELOPMENT?

| Cross-Cultural Comparisons | Ethnicity | Media and Technology |

Boys-only Muslim school in Middle East.

We live in an increasingly diverse world, one in which there is increasing contact between adolescents from different cultures and ethnic groups. In this section, we explore these differences as they relate to adolescents. We explore how adolescents in various cultures spend their time and some of the rites of passage they undergo. We also examine how ethnicity affects U.S. adolescents and their development, as well as the dramatic increase in the use of media and technology by adolescents.

Cross-Cultural Comparisons

What traditions remain for adolescents around the globe? What circumstances are changing adolescents' lives?

Traditions and Changes in Adolescence Around the Globe Consider some of the variations of adolescence around the world (Brown & Larson, 2002):

- Two-thirds of Asian Indian adolescents accept their parents' choice of a marital partner for them.
- In the Philippines, many female adolescents sacrifice their own futures by migrating to the city to earn money that they can send home to their families.
- In the Middle East, many adolescents are not allowed to interact with the other sex, even in school.
- Street youth in Kenya and other parts of the world learn to survive under highly stressful circumstances (Nsamenang, 2002). In some cases abandoned by their parents, they may engage in delinquency or prostitution to provide for their economic needs.
- Whereas individuals in the United States are marrying later than in past generations, youth in Russia are marrying earlier to legitimize sexual activity (Stetsenko, 2002).

Thus, depending on the culture being observed, adolescence may involve many different experiences (Larson & Wilson, 2004).

Some cultures have retained their traditions regarding adolescence, but rapid global change is altering the experience of adolescence in many places, presenting new opportunities and challenges to young people's health and well-being. Around the world, adolescents' experiences may differ.

Street youth in Rio De Janeiro. *What are some cultural variations in adolescent peer relations?*

Health In recent years, adolescent health and well-being have improved in some respects but not in others. Overall, fewer adolescents around the world die from infectious diseases and malnutrition now than in the past (UNICEF, 2010). However, a number of adolescent health-compromising behaviors (especially illicit drug use and unprotected sex) are increasing in frequency (Blum & Nelson-Mmari, 2004). Extensive increases in the rates of HIV in adolescents have occurred in many sub-Saharan countries (UNICEF, 2010).

Gender Around the world, the experiences of male and female adolescents continue to be quite different (Brown & Larson, 2002). Except in a few regions, such as Japan, the Philippines, and Western countries, males have far greater access to educational opportunities than females (UNICEF, 2010). In many countries, adolescent females have less freedom than males to pursue a variety of careers and engage in various leisure activities. Gender differences in sexual expression are widespread, especially in India, Southeast Asia, Latin America, and Arab countries, where there are far more restrictions on the sexual activity of adolescent females than on males. These gender differences do appear to be narrowing over time, however. In some countries, educational and career opportunities for women are expanding, and control over adolescent girls' romantic and sexual relationships is weakening.

How Would You...?
As a health-care professional, how would you explain to policy makers and insurance providers the importance of cultural context when creating guidelines for adolescent health coverage?

Family In some countries, adolescents grow up in closely knit families with extensive extended-kin networks that retain a traditional way of life. For example, in Arab countries, "adolescents are taught strict codes of conduct and loyalty" (Brown & Larson, 2002, p. 6). However, in Western countries such as the United States, parenting is less authoritarian than in the past, and much larger numbers of adolescents are growing up in divorced families and stepfamilies.

In many countries around the world, current trends "include greater family mobility, migration to urban areas, family members working in distant cities or countries, smaller families, fewer extended-family households, and increases in mothers' employment" (Brown & Larson, 2002, p. 7). Unfortunately, many of these changes may reduce the ability of families to spend time with their adolescents.

Peers Some cultures give peers a stronger role in adolescence than others (Brown & Larson, 2002). In most Western nations, peers figure prominently in adolescents' lives, in some cases taking on roles that are otherwise assumed by parents. Among street youth in South America, the peer network serves as a surrogate family that supports survival in dangerous and stressful settings. In other regions of the world, such as in Arab countries, peer relations are restricted, especially for girls (Booth, 2002).

In sum, adolescents' lives are characterized by a combination of change and tradition. Researchers have found both similarities and differences in the experiences of adolescents in different countries (Larson & Wilson, 2004). To read about how adolescents around the world spend their time, see the *Diversity in Children's Development* interlude.

How strong is the role that peers play in the development of U.S. adolescents?

Diversity in Children's Development

HOW ADOLESCENTS AROUND THE WORLD SPEND THEIR TIME

Reed Larson, Suman Verma, and their colleagues (Larson, 2001; Larson & Verma, 1999; Watkins, Larson, & Sullivan, 2007) have examined how adolescents spend their time in work, play, and developmental activities such as school. U.S. adolescents spend about 60 percent as much time on schoolwork as East Asian adolescents do, mainly because U.S. adolescents do less homework than East Asians do (Larson & Varma, 1999).

What U.S. adolescents have in greater quantities than do adolescents in other industrialized countries is discretionary time (Larson & Wilson, 2004). About 40 to 50 percent of U.S. adolescents' waking hours (not counting summer vacations) is spent in discretionary activities, compared with 25 to 35 percent in East Asia and 35 to 45 percent in Europe. Whether this additional discretionary time is a liability or an asset for U.S. adolescents, of course, depends on how they use it.

According to Larson (2001), for optimal development, U.S. adolescents may have too much unstructured time. Indeed, when adolescents are allowed to choose what they do with their time, they typically engage in unchallenging activities such as hanging out and watching TV. Although relaxation and social interaction are important aspects of adolescence, it seems unlikely that spending large numbers of hours per week in unchallenging activities fosters development. Structured voluntary activities may provide more

How do East Asian and U.S. adolescents spend their time differently?

(continued on next page)

promise for adolescent development than unstructured time, especially if adults give responsibility to adolescents, challenge them, and provide competent guidance in these activities (Larson & others, 2007; Watkins, Larson, & Sullivan, 2007).

Rites of Passage   Another variation in the experiences of adolescents in different cultures is whether the adolescents go through a rite of passage. Some societies have elaborate ceremonies that signal the adolescent's move to maturity and achievement of adult status (Kottak, 2004). A **rite of passage** is a ceremony or ritual that marks an individual's transition from one status to another. Most rites of passage focus on the transition to adult status. In some traditional cultures, rites of passage are the avenue through which adolescents gain access to sacred adult practices, to knowledge, and to sexuality. These rites often involve dramatic practices intended to facilitate the adolescent's separation from the immediate family, especially the mother. The transformation is usually characterized by some form of ritual death and rebirth, or by means of contact with the spiritual world. Bonds are forged between the adolescent and the adult instructors through shared rituals, hazards, and secrets to allow the adolescent to enter the adult world. This kind of ritual provides a forceful and discontinuous entry into the adult world at a time when the adolescent is perceived to be ready for the change.

An especially rich tradition of rites of passage for adolescents has prevailed in African cultures, especially sub-Saharan Africa. Under the influence of Western industrialized culture, many of these rites are disappearing today, although they are still prevalent in locations where formal education is not readily available.

Do we have such rites of passage for American adolescents? We certainly do not have universal formal ceremonies that mark the passage from adolescence to adulthood. Certain religious and social groups do, however, have initiation ceremonies that indicate that an advance in maturity has been reached: the Jewish bar and bat mitzvah, the Catholic confirmation, and social debuts, for example. School graduation ceremonies come the closest to being culture-wide rites of passage in the United States. The high school graduation ceremony has become nearly universal for middle-class adolescents and increasing numbers of adolescents from low-income backgrounds.

Ethnicity

Earlier in this chapter, we explored the identity development of ethnic minority adolescents. Here we further examine immigration and the relationship between ethnicity and socioeconomic status.

Immigration   Relatively high rates of immigration are contributing to the growth of ethnic minorities in the United States (Grigorenko, 2010; Liu & others, 2009; Tewari & Alvarez, 2009). Immigrants often experience stressors uncommon to, or less prominent among, longtime residents such as language barriers, dislocations and separations from support networks, changes in SES status, and the dual struggle to preserve identity and to acculturate (Fuligni, Hughes, & Way, 2009; Kim & others, 2009).

The adjustment of immigrants to their new country is complicated by the fact that both native-born Americans and immigrants may be torn between two values related to ethnic issues: assimilation and pluralism.

- **Assimilation** is the absorption of ethnic minority groups into the dominant group, which often means the loss of some or virtually all of the behavior and values of the ethnic group. Individuals who endorse assimilation usually advocate that ethnic minority groups become more American.

- **Pluralism** is the coexistence of distinct ethnic and cultural groups in the same society, each of which maintains its cultural differences.

These Congolese Kota boys painted their faces as part of a rite of passage to adulthood. *What rites of passage do American adolescents have?*

How Would You...?
As an educator, how would you modify high school graduation to be a more meaningful rite of passage for adolescents in the United States?

rite of passage A ceremony or ritual that marks an individual's transition from one status to another. Most rites of passage focus on the transition to adult status.

assimilation The absorption of ethnic minority groups into the dominant group, which often involves the loss of some or virtually all of the behavior and values of the ethnic group.

pluralism The coexistence of distinct ethnic and cultural groups in the same society, each of which maintains its cultural differences.

Many of the families that have immigrated in recent decades to the United States, such as Mexican Americans and Asian Americans, come from collectivist cultures in which family obligation is strong (Hayashino & Chopra, 2009). For adolescents, this family obligation may take the form of assisting parents in their occupations and contributing to the family's welfare (Fuligni, Hughes, & Way, 2009; Parke & Buriel, 2006). This often means helping out in jobs in construction, gardening, cleaning, or restaurants. In some cases, the long hours that immigrant youth work in such jobs can be detrimental to their academic achievement.

Ethnicity and Socioeconomic Status   Much of the research on ethnic minority adolescents has failed to tease apart the influences of ethnicity and socioeconomic status. Ethnicity and socioeconomic status can interact in ways that exaggerate the influence of ethnicity because ethnic minority individuals are overrepresented in the lower socioeconomic levels of American society (Healey, 2009; Rowley, Kurtz-Costes, & Cooper, 2009). Consequently, researchers too often have given ethnic explanations for aspects of adolescent development that were largely due instead to socioeconomic status.

A recent longitudinal study illustrated the importance of teasing apart SES and ethnicity in determining the educational and occupational aspirations of individuals from 14 to 26 years of age (Mello, 2009). SES successfully predicted educational and occupational expectations across ethnic groups. In this study, after controlling for SES, African American youth reported the highest educational expectations followed by Latino and Asian American/Pacific Islander, non-Latino White, and Native American/ Alaska Native youth. African American and Asian American/Pacific Islander youth had the highest occupational expectations, followed by Latino, Native American/Alaskan Native, and non-Latino White youth. The ethnic group patterns were consistent across the adolescent and emerging adult years.

Not all ethnic minority families are poor. However, poverty contributes to the stressful life experiences of many ethnic minority adolescents (Leon-Guerrero, 2009). Thus, many ethnic minority adolescents experience a double disadvantage: (1) prejudice, discrimination, and bias because of their ethnic minority status; and (2) the stressful effects of poverty.

Although some ethnic minority youth have middle-income backgrounds, economic advantage does not entirely enable them to escape the prejudice, discrimination, and bias associated with being a member of an ethnic minority group (Harris & Graham, 2007). Even Japanese Americans, who are often characterized as a "model minority" because of their strong achievement orientation and family cohesiveness, still experience stress associated with ethnic minority status.

Recent studies provide insight into the discrimination experienced by ethnic minority adolescents (Paluck & Green, 2009; Rivas-Drake, Hughes, & Way, 2009; Seaton & others, 2008). One such study revealed that adolescents' perceived racial discrimination is linked to negative views that the broader society has about African Americans (Seaton, Yip, & Sellers, 2009). In another study, discrimination against seventh- to tenth-grade African American students was related to their lower level of psychological functioning, including perceived stress, symptoms of depression, and lower perceived well-being; more positive attitudes toward African American students by others were associated with more positive psychological functioning in the African American adolescents (Sellers & others, 2006). The most frequent type of racial hassles reported by the African American adolescents were being accused of something or treated suspiciously and being treated as if you were "stupid, being talked down to" (see Figure 16.6). Also, in a study of

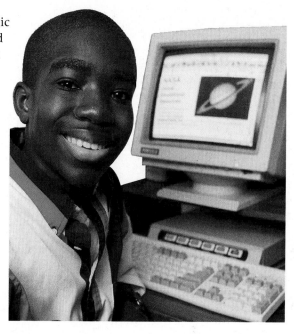

Jason Leonard, age 15: "I want America to know that most of us black teens are not troubled people from broken homes and headed to jail. . . . In my relationships with my parents, we show respect for each other and we have values in our house. We have traditions we celebrate together, including Christmas and Kwanzaa."

Type of Racial Hassle	Percent of African American Adolescents Who Reported the Racial Hassle in the Past Year
Being accused of something or treated suspiciously	71.0
Being treated as if you were "stupid", being "talked down to"	70.7
Others reacting to you as if they were afraid or intimidated	70.1
Being observed or followed while in public places	69.1
Being treated rudely or disrespectfully	56.4
Being ignored, overlooked, not given service	56.4
Others expecting your work to be inferior	54.1
Being insulted, called a name, or harassed	52.2

FIGURE 16.6 Adolescents' Reports of Racial Hassles in the Past Year

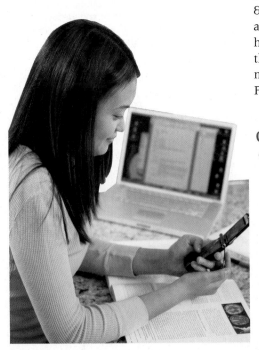

What characterizes adolescents' media multitasking?

Latino youth, discrimination was negatively linked and social and parental support was positively related to their academic success (DeGarmo & Martinez, 2006).

Media and Technology

In Chapter 10, "Socioemotional Development in Early Childhood," we discussed the role of television in children's development. Here we focus on a major change in children's and adolescents' lives: the dramatic increase in the use of media and technology by children and adolescents (Roberts, Henriksen, & Foehr, 2009; Strasberger, 2009; Uhls & Greenfield, 2009). As one commentator described the change: "Unlike their parents, they have never known anything but a world dominated by technology. Even their social lives revolve around the Web, iPods, and cell phones" (Jayson, 2006, p. ID).

A major trend in the use of technology is the dramatic increase in media multitasking (Roberts & Foehr, 2008; Roberts, Henriksen, & Foehr, 2009). It is not unusual for children and youth to simultaneously watch TV while text messaging their friends, for example. In some cases, media multitasking—such as text messaging, listening to an iPod, and updating a YouTube site—is engaged in at the same time as doing homework. It is hard to imagine how that can be a good thing for doing homework efficiently, although there is little research on such media multitasking.

Media Use If the amount of time spent in an activity is any indication of its importance, then there is no doubt that the mass media play important roles in the lives of U.S. children and adolescents (Robers, Henriksen, & Foehr, 2009). A national study that surveyed more than 2,000 children and adolescents from 8 through 18 years of age confirmed that they use media heavily (Rideout, Roberts, & Foehr, 2005). The average child and adolescent in the study spent almost 6 hours a day using media compared with approximately 2¼ hours with parents, about 1¼ hours in physical activity, and 50 minutes in homework. A recent estimate indicates that when media multitasking is taken into account, 8- through 18-year-olds use media an average of 8 hours per day rather than just 6 hours per day (Roberts & Foehr, 2008).

Computers and the Internet Culture involves change, and nowhere is that change greater than in the technological revolution today's children and adolescents are experiencing with increased use of computers and the Internet. Today's children and adolescents are using computers to communicate the way their parents used pens, postage stamps, and telephones.

The digitally mediated social environment of adolescents and emerging adults includes e-mail, chat rooms, instant messaging, blogs, social networking sites such as Facebook MySpace, and Twitter, videosharing and photosharing, multiplayer online computer games, and virtual worlds (Subrahmanyam & Greenfield, 2008; Uhls & Greenfield, 2009). Most of these digitally mediated social interactions began on computers but more recently have also shifted to cell phones, especially smartphones (Robertson, Henriksen, & Foehr, 2009).

The Internet continues to serve as the main focus of digitally mediated social interaction. Chat-room conversations are mainly public and often involve multiple participants and simultaneous conversations; in many cases, the participants are strangers (Subrahmanyam & Greenfield). Adolescents and emerging adults usually use instant messaging on their computers and cell phones to communicate with friends from school. Gossip is a frequent component of such communication.

One recent study examined the content of 583 participants in online teen chat rooms (Subrahmanyam, Smahel, & Greenfield, 2006). More than 50 percent of the participants provided identity information, usually their gender. Younger participants (self-described as 10 to 13 years of age) were the most self-disclosing about their identity, older ones the least (self-described as 18 to 24 years of age). Sexual themes comprised 5 percent of the utterances (one sexual comment per minute) and bad/obscene language occurred in 3 percent of the utterances. Females discussed sex in more implicit ways, males in a more explicit manner. Older participants discussed sex more explicitly than younger participants.

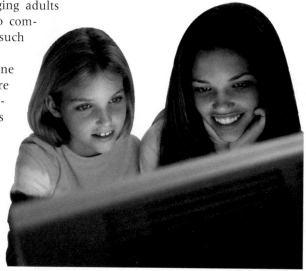

What characterizes the online social environment of adolescents?

Special concerns have emerged about children's and adolescents' access to information on the Internet, which has been largely unregulated. Youth can access adult sexual material, instructions for making bombs, and other information that is inappropriate for them. Another concern is peer bullying and harassment on the Internet (called *cyberbullying*). A recent survey found that peer bullying and harassment both online and offline were the most frequent threats that minors encounter (Palfrey & others, 2009).

A recent study examined the sequence of using electronic communication technologies that college students in a midwestern university used in managing their social networks (Yang & Brown, 2009). In this study, female college students followed a consistent sequence as their relationships developed, typically beginning by contacting new acquaintances on Facebook, then moving on to instant messaging, after which they may "exchange cell phone numbers, text each other, talk over their cell phone, and finally schedule a time to meet, if everything went well" (Yang & Brown, 2009, p. 2). Male college students were less likely to follow this sequence as consistently, although they did follow it more when communicating with females than males, suggesting that females may maintain more control over communication patterns.

Recent research has found that approximately one of three adolescents self-disclose better online than in person; in this research, boys report that they feel more comfortable self-disclosing online than do girls (Schouten, Valkenburg, & Peter, 2007; Valkenburg & Peter, 2009). Offline, girls are more likely to feel comfortable self-disclosing in person than are boys. Thus, boys' self-disclosure may benefit from online communication with friends (Valkenburg & Peter, 2009).

Clearly, the Internet is a technology that needs parents to monitor and regulate adolescents' use of it (Willoughby, 2008; Uhls & Greenfield, 2009). Consider Bonita Williams, who began to worry about how obsessed her 15-year-old daughter, Jade, had become with MySpace (Kornblum, 2006). She became even more concerned when she discovered that Jade was posting suggestive photos of herself and gave her cell phone number out to people in different parts of the United States. She grounded her daughter, blocked MySpace at home, and moved Jade's computer out of her bedroom and into the family room. A recent study revealed that parents' high estimates of online dangers were not matched by their low rates of setting limits and monitoring their adolescents' online activities (Rosen, Cheever, & Carrier, 2008). Also in this study, adolescents who perceived their parents as having an indulgent parenting style (high in warmth and involvement but low in strictness and supervision) reported engaging in the most risky online behavior, such as meeting someone in person they initially had communicated with online.

Review and Reflect: Learning Goal 4

4 **Explain how culture influences adolescent development**

REVIEW

- What are some comparisons of adolescents in different cultures? How do adolescents around the world spend their time? What are rites of passage?
- How does ethnicity influence adolescent development?
- What characterizes adolescents' use of media and technology?

REFLECT

- What is your ethnicity? Have you ever been stereotyped because of your ethnicity? How different is your identity from the mainstream culture?

---

5 WHAT ARE SOME SOCIOEMOTIONAL PROBLEMS IN ADOLESCENCE?

| Juvenile Delinquency | Depression and Suicide | The Interrelation of Problems and Successful Prevention/Intervention Programs |

In Chapter 14, "Physical Development in Adolescence," we described several adolescent problems: substance abuse, sexually transmitted infections, and eating disorders. In this chapter, we examine the problems of juvenile delinquency, depression, and suicide. We also explore interrelationships among adolescent problems and how such problems can be prevented or remedied.

Juvenile Delinquency

The label **juvenile delinquent** is applied to an adolescent who breaks the law or engages in behavior that is considered illegal. Like other categories of disorders, juvenile delinquency is a broad concept; legal infractions range from littering to murder. Because the adolescent technically becomes a juvenile delinquent only after being judged guilty of a crime by a court of law, official records do not accurately reflect the number of illegal acts juvenile delinquents commit. Estimates of the number of juvenile delinquents in the United States are sketchy, but FBI statistics indicate that at least 2 percent of all youth are involved in juvenile court cases.

U.S. government statistics reveal that juvenile court caseloads for males were three times higher than for females in 2002 (National Center for Juvenile Justice, 2006). In the last two decades, however, there has been a greater increase in female delinquency than in male delinquency (National Center for Juvenile Justice, 2006). For both male and female delinquents, rates for property offenses are higher than rates for other offenses (such as offenses against persons, drug offenses, and public order offenses). Arrests of adolescent males for delinquency continue to be much higher than arrests of adolescent females.

Delinquency rates among minority groups and lower-socioeconomic-status youth are especially high in proportion to the overall population of these groups (Thio, 2010). However, such groups have less influence over the judicial decision-making process in the United States and, therefore, may be judged delinquent more readily than their non-Latino White, middle-socioeconomic-status counterparts.

juvenile delinquent An adolescent who breaks the law or engages in behavior that is considered illegal.

One issue in juvenile justice is whether an adolescent who commits a crime should be tried as an adult (Steinberg, 2009). In one study, trying adolescent offenders as adults increased rather than reduced their crime rate (Myers, 1999). The study evaluated more than 500 violent youth in Pennsylvania, which has adopted a "get tough" policy. Although these 500 offenders had been given harsher punishment than a comparison group retained in juvenile court, they were more likely to be rearrested—and rearrested more quickly—for new offenses once they were returned to the community. This pattern suggests that the price of short-term public safety attained by prosecuting juveniles as adults might increase the number of criminal offenses over the long run.

A distinction is made between early-onset—before age 11—and late-onset—after 11—antisocial behavior of minors. Early-onset antisocial behavior is associated with more negative developmental outcomes than late-onset antisocial behavior (Schulenberg & Zarrett, 2006). Early-onset antisocial behavior is more likely to persist into emerging adulthood and is more frequently associated with mental health and relationship problems than is late-onset antisocial behavior (Loeber, Burke, & Pardini, 2009; Loeber & others, 2007).

Causes of Delinquency   What causes delinquency? Many causes have been proposed, including heredity, identity problems, community influences, and family experiences. Erik Erikson (1968), for example, argues that adolescents whose development has restricted them from acceptable social roles or made them feel that they cannot measure up to the demands placed on them may choose a negative identity. Adolescents with a negative identity may find support for their delinquent image among peers, reinforcing the negative identity. For Erikson, delinquency is an attempt to establish an identity, although a negative one.

Although delinquency is less exclusively a phenomenon of lower socioeconomic status (SES) than it was in the past, some characteristics of lower-SES culture might promote delinquency. The norms of many lower-SES peer groups and gangs are antisocial, or counterproductive, to the goals and norms of society at large (Thio, 2010). Getting into and staying out of trouble are prominent features of life for some adolescents in low-income neighborhoods (Flannery & others, 2003). Being "tough" and "masculine" are high-status traits for lower-SES boys, and these traits are often measured by the adolescent's success in performing and getting away with delinquent acts. Furthermore, adolescents in communities with high crime rates observe many models who engage in criminal activities (Loeber, Burke, & Pardini, 2009). These communities may be characterized by poverty, unemployment, and feelings of alienation toward the middle class (Farrington, 2009). Quality schooling, educational funding, and organized neighborhood activities may be lacking in these communities (Molnar & others, 2008).

Certain characteristics of family support systems are also associated with delinquency (Cavell & others, 2007; Farrington, Ttofi, & Coid, 2009). Parents of delinquents are less skilled in discouraging antisocial behavior and in encouraging skilled behavior than are parents of nondelinquents. Parental monitoring of adolescents is especially important in determining whether an adolescent becomes a delinquent (Laird & others, 2008). A study of families living in high-risk neighborhoods revealed that parents' lack of knowledge of their young adolescents' whereabouts was linked to whether the adolescents engaged in delinquency later in adolescence (Lahey & others, 2008). Another study revealed that maternal monitoring was linked to a lower incidence of delinquency in Latino girls (Loukas, Suizzo, & Prelow, 2007). Family discord and inconsistent and inappropriate discipline are also associated with delinquency (Bor, McGee, & Fagan, 2004). A recent study indicated that being physically abused in the first five years of life was linked to a greater risk of delinquency in adolescence (Lansford & others, 2007). And another recent study revealed that harsh discipline at 8 to 10 years of age was linked to which adolescents would persist in criminal activity after age 21 (Farrington, Ttofi, & Coid, 2009).

What are some factors that are linked to whether adolescents engage in delinquent acts?

Rare are the studies that actually demonstrate in an experimental design that changing parenting practices in childhood is related to a lower incidence of juvenile delinquency in adolescence. However, one recent study by Marion Forgatch and her colleagues (2009) randomly assigned divorced mothers with sons to an experimental group (mothers received extensive parenting training) and a control group (mothers received no parenting training) when their sons were in the first to third grades. The parenting training consisted of 14 parent group meetings that especially focused on improving parenting practices with their sons (skill encouragement, limit setting, monitoring, problem solving, and positive involvement). Best practices for emotion regulation, managing interparental conflict, and talking with children about divorce also were included in the sessions. Improved parenting practices and reduced contact with deviant peers were linked with lower rates of delinquency in the experimental group than in the control group at a nine-year follow-up assessment.

An increasing number of studies have found that siblings can have a strong influence on delinquency (Bank, Burraston, & Snyder, 2004). In one study, high levels of hostile sibling relationships and older sibling delinquency were linked with younger sibling delinquency in both brother and sister pairs (Slomkowski & others, 2001).

Having delinquent peers greatly increases the risk of becoming delinquent (Dishion, Piehler, & Myers, 2008; Loeber, Burke, & Pardini, 2009). For example, a recent study found that being rejected by peers and having deviant friends at 7 to 13 years of age were linked with increased delinquency at 14 to 15 years of age (Vitaro, Pedersen, & Brendgen, 2007). Also, another study revealed that associating with deviant peers was linked to a higher incidence of delinquency in male African American adolescents (Bowman, Prelow, & Weaver, 2007).

Cognitive factors, such as low self-control, low intelligence, and lack of sustained attention, are also implicated in delinquency. For example, a recent study revealed that low-IQ serious delinquents were characterized by low self-control (Koolhof & others, 2007). Another study found that at age 16 nondelinquents were more likely to have a higher verbal IQ and engage in sustained attention than delinquents (Loeber & others, 2007). And in a longitudinal study, one of the strongest predictors of reduced likelihood of engaging in serious theft was high school academic achievement (Loeber & others, 2008).

One individual whose goal is to help at-risk adolescents, such as juvenile delinquents, cope more effectively with their lives is Rodney Hammond. Read about his work in the *Careers in Children's Development* profile.

How Would You...?

As a psychologist, how would you seek to lower the risk of juvenile delinquency?

Depression and Suicide

What is the nature of depression in adolescence? What causes an adolescent to commit suicide?

Depression   Depression is more likely to occur in adolescence than in childhood and more likely to occur in adulthood than adolescence. Researchers have found a linear increase in major depressive disorder from 15 to 22 years of age (Kessler & Waters, 1998). However, an early onset of a mood disorder, such as major depressive disorder in adolescence, is linked with more negative outcomes than late onset of a mood disorder (Schulenberg & Zarrett, 2006). For example, the early onset is associated with further recurrences of depression and with an increased risk of being diagnosed with an anxiety disorder, substance abuse, eating disorder, suicide attempt, and unemployment at a future point in development (Graber, 2004).

How serious a problem is depression in adolescence? Rates of ever experiencing a major depressive disorder range from 1.5 to 2.5 percent in school-age children and 15 to 20 percent for adolescents (Graber & Sontag, 2009). By about age 15, adolescent females have a rate of depression that is twice that of adolescent males. Among the reasons for this gender difference are that females tend to ruminate in their depressed mood and amplify it; females' self-images, especially their body images, are more negative than males'; females face more discrimination than males do; and

Careers in Children's Development

Rodney Hammond, Health Psychologist

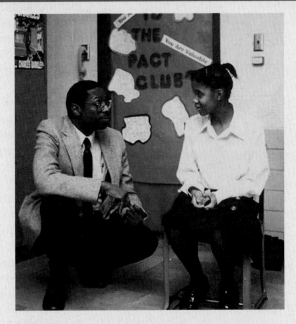

Rodney Hammond described his college experiences: "When I started as an undergraduate at the University of Illinois, Champaign-Urbana, I hadn't decided on my major. But to help finance my education, I took a part-time job in a child development research program sponsored by the psychology department. There, I observed inner-city children in settings designed to enhance their learning. I saw first-hand the contribution psychology can make, and I knew I wanted to be a psychologist" (American Psychological Association, 2003, p. 26).

Rodney Hammond went on to obtain a doctorate in school and community psychology with a focus on children's development. For a number of years, he trained clinical psychologists at Wright State University in Ohio and directed a program to reduce violence in ethnic minority youth. There, he and his associates taught at-risk youth how to use social skills to effectively manage conflict and to recognize situations that could lead to violence. Today, Hammond is director of Violence Prevention at the Centers for Disease Control and Prevention in Atlanta. Hammond says that if you are interested in people and problem solving, psychology is a wonderful way to put these together.

Rodney Hammond, counseling an adolescent girl about the risks of adolescence and how to effectively cope with them.

(Source: American Psychological Association, 2003, pp. 26–27)

puberty occurs earlier for girls than for boys. As a result, girls experience a piling up of changes and life experiences in the middle school years that can increase depression (Nolen-Hoeksema, 2010).

Certain family factors place adolescents at risk for developing depression. These include having a depressed parent, emotionally unavailable parents, parents who have high marital conflict, and parents with financial problems. For example, a recent study revealed that parent-adolescent conflict and low parental support were linked to adolescent depression (Sheeber & others, 2007). Another recent study found that being in a two-parent family structure and feeling connected to parents, peers, and school were protective factors associated with a lower incidence of depressed mood during adolescence (Costello & others, 2008).

Poor peer relationships also are associated with adolescent depression (Kistner & others, 2006). Not having a close relationship with a best friend, having little contact with friends, and experiencing peer rejection all increase depressive tendencies in adolescents. Problems in adolescent romantic relationships can also trigger depression, especially for girls (Steinberg & Davila, 2008).

Friendship often provides social support. However, a recent study of third- through ninth-graders revealed that one aspect of social support in friendship may have costs as well as benefits (Rose, Carlson, & Waller, 2007). In the study, girls' co-rumination (as reflected in excessively discussing problems) predicted not only an increase in positive friendship quality but also an increase in further co-rumination as well as an increase in depressive and anxiety symptoms. However, for boys, co-rumination predicted only an increase in positive friendship quality—not an increase in depressive and anxiety symptoms. One implication of the research is that some girls who are vulnerable to developing internalized problems may go undetected because they have supportive friendships (Rose & Smith, 2009).

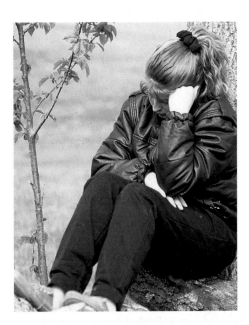

Depression is more likely to occur in adolescence than in childhood, and female adolescents are more likely than male adolescents to be depressed. *What are some factors that contribute to adolescent depression?*

The presence of rumination in girls' depression was reflected in a recent study (Chaplin, Gillham, & Seligman, 2009). In this study of 11- to 14-year-olds, initial assessment of worry, anxiety, and oversensitivity were more strongly linked to an increase in girls' than boys' depressive symptoms one year later.

In Chapter 14, "Physical Development in Adolescence," we indicated that hormonal changes associated with puberty may contribute to the development of depression in adolescent girls. A recent study revealed that depression was more likely to occur when girls were at a more mature pubertal status and had matured early (Conley & Rudolph, 2009). For the more mature, early-maturation girls, depression increased when they were involved in stressful peer relations.

What type of treatment is most likely to reduce depression in adolescence? According to the Treatment for Adolescents with Depression Study (TADS), depressed adolescents recovered faster when they took an antidepressant and received cognitive behavior therapy that involved improving their coping skills than when they took only an antidepressant or received only cognitive behavior therapy (TADS, 2007). However, a safety concern has emerged with regard to taking antidepressants such as Prozac (fluoxetine), and in 2004 the U.S. Food and Drug Administration assigned warnings to such drugs stating that they slightly increase the risk of suicidal behavior in adolescents. In the study just described, 15 percent of depressed adolescents who took only Prozac had suicidal thoughts or attempted suicide compared with 6 percent receiving cognitive behavior therapy alone and 8 percent receiving the combined Prozac and cognitive behavior therapy.

Suicide Suicidal behavior is rare in childhood but escalates in adolescence and then increases further in emerging adulthood (Park & others, 2006). Suicide is the third leading cause of death in 10- to 19-year-olds today in the United States (National Center for Health Statistics, 2007). After increasing to high levels in the 1990s, suicide rates in adolescents have declined in recent years (Gould & others, 2003). In 2004, 4,214 U.S. individuals from 15 to 24 years of age committed suicide (Minino, Heron, & Smith, 2006). Emerging adults have triple the rate of suicide of adolescents (Park & others, 2006).

Although a suicide threat should always be taken seriously, far more adolescents contemplate or attempt it unsuccessfully than actually commit it (Miranda & others, 2008). In a national study, in 2005, 17 percent of U.S. high school students said that they had seriously considered or attempted suicide in the last 12 months (Eaton & others, 2006). As shown in Figure 16.7, this percentage has declined since 1991. In the 2005 survey, 2.3 percent reported a suicide attempt that had resulted in an injury, poisoning, or drug overdose that was treated by a doctor. Females were more likely to attempt suicide than males, but males were more likely to succeed in committing suicide. Males use more lethal means, such as guns, in their suicide attempts, whereas adolescent females are more likely to cut their wrists or take an overdose of sleeping pills—methods less likely to result in death.

One issue focuses on whether lesbian and gay male adolescents are especially vulnerable to suicide. In one study of 12,000 adolescents, approximately 15 percent of lesbian and gay male youth said that they had attempted suicide compared with 7 percent of heterosexual youth (Russell & Joyner, 2001). However, Ritch Savin-Williams (2001) found that lesbian and gay male adolescents were only slightly more likely than heterosexual adolescents to attempt suicide. He argues that most studies have exaggerated the suicide rates for lesbian and gay male adolescents because they survey only the most disturbed youth who are attending support groups or spend time at shelters for lesbian and gay male youth.

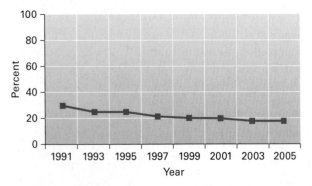

FIGURE 16.7 Percentage of U.S. Ninth- to Twelfth-Grade Students Who Seriously Considered Attempting Suicide in the Previous 12 Months from 1991 to 2005

Distal, or earlier, experiences often are involved in suicide attempts as well. The adolescent may have a long-standing history of family instability and unhappiness. Just as a lack of affection and emotional support, high control, and pressure for achievement by parents during childhood are related to adolescent depression, such combinations of family experiences also are likely to show up as distal factors in adolescents' suicide attempts.

Adolescents' peer relations also are linked to suicide attempts. A recent research review revealed that prior suicide attempts by members of an adolescent's social groups was linked to the probability the adolescent also would attempt suicide (de Leo & Heller, 2008). Adolescents who attempt suicide may lack supportive friendships. One study found that social isolation was linked with suicide attempts in adolescent girls (Bearman & Moody, 2004). A recent study revealed that peer victimization was linked to suicide thoughts and attempts (Klomek & others, 2008). Yet another recent study revealed that early conduct problems and school failures in adolescence placed adolescent girls at risk for developing a major depressive episode in emerging adulthood (McCarty & others, 2008).

Cultural contexts also are linked to suicide attempts, and adolescent suicide attempts vary across ethnic groups in the United States. As indicated in Figure 16.8, more than 20 percent of Native American/Alaska Native (NA/AN) female adolescents reported that they had attempted suicide in the previous year, and suicide accounts for almost 20 percent of NA/AN deaths in 15- to 19-year-olds (Goldston & others, 2008). African-American and non-Latino White males reported the lowest incidence of suicide attempts. A major risk factor in the high rate of suicide attempts by NA/AN adolescents is their elevated rate of alcohol abuse.

Just as genetic factors are associated with depression, they also are associated with suicide (Kapornai & Vetro, 2008). The closer a person's genetic relationship is to someone who has committed suicide, the more likely will that person commit suicide.

What is the psychological profile of the suicidal adolescent? Suicidal adolescents often have depressive symptoms (Ash, 2008). Although not all depressed adolescents are suicidal, depression is the most frequently cited factor associated with adolescent suicide (Bethell & Rhodes, 2008). A sense of hopelessness, low self-esteem, and high self-blame are also associated with adolescent suicide (O'Donnell & others, 2004). A recent study found that perception of being a burden on others and thwarted belongingness were linked to suicidal thoughts (Van Orden & others, 2008). A recent study also revealed that overweight middle school students were more likely to think about, plan, and attempt suicide than their counterparts who were not overweight (Whetstone, Morrissey, & Cummings, 2007). And another study found that preteen alcohol use was linked to suicide attempts in adolescence (Swahn, Bossarte, & Sullivent, 2008). Further, yet another recent study indicated that adolescents who used alcohol while they were sad or depressed were linked with risk for making a suicide attempt (Schilling & others, 2009). And a recent analysis using data from the National Longitudinal Study of Adolescent Health found that the following were indicators of suicide risk: depressive symptoms, a sense of hopelessness, engaging in suicidal ideation, having a family background of suicidal behavior, and having friends with a history of suicidal behavior (Thompson, Kuruwita, & Foster, 2009).

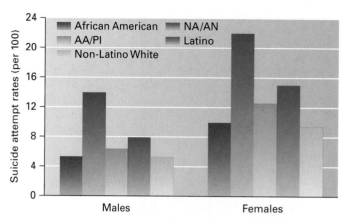

FIGURE 16.8 Suicide Attempts by U.S. Adolescents from Different Ethnic Groups *Note*: Data shown are for one-year rates of self-reported suicide attempts. NA/AN = Native American/Alaska Native; AA/PI = Asian/American/Pacific Islander.

How Would You...?
As a psychologist, how would you talk with an adolescent who has just threatened suicide?

The Interrelation of Problems and Successful Prevention/ Intervention Programs

We have discussed some of the major adolescent problems in this chapter and in Chapter 15, "Cognitive Development in Adolescence": substance abuse; juvenile delinquency; school-related problems, such as dropping out of school; adolescent pregnancy and sexually transmitted infections; eating disorders; depression; and suicide.

The four problems that affect the most adolescents are (1) drug abuse, (2) juvenile delinquency, (3) sexual problems, and (4) school-related problems (Dryfoos, 1990; Dryfoos & Barkin, 2006). The adolescents most at risk have more than one of

How are problems interrelated in adolescence?

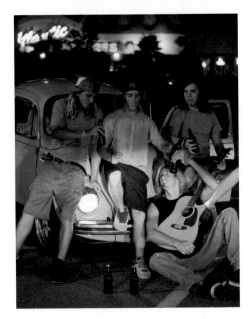

What are some strategies for preventing and intervening in adolescent problems?

these problems. Researchers are increasingly finding that problem behaviors in adolescence are interrelated (Costello & others, 2008; Thompson, Ho, & Kingree, 2007). For example, heavy substance abuse is related to early sexual activity, lower grades, dropping out of school, and delinquency (D'Amico & others, 2008). Early initiation of sexual activity is associated with the use of cigarettes and alcohol, the use of marijuana and other illicit drugs, lower grades, dropping out of school, and delinquency. Delinquency is related to early sexual activity, early pregnancy, substance abuse, and dropping out of school (Doherty, Green, & Ensminger, 2008). As many as 10 percent of adolescents in the United States have been estimated to engage in all four of these problem behaviors (for example, adolescents who have dropped out of school, are behind in their grade level, are users of heavy drugs, regularly use cigarettes and marijuana, and are sexually active but do not use contraception). In 1990, it was estimated that another 15 percent of high-risk youth engage in two or three of the four main problem behaviors (Dryfoos, 1990). Recently, this figure was increased to 20 percent of all U.S. adolescents (Dryfoos & Barkin, 2006).

A review of the programs that have been successful in preventing or reducing adolescent problems, found the following common components (Dryfoos, 1990; Dryfoos & Barkin, 2006):

1. *Intensive individualized attention.* In successful programs, high-risk adolescents are attached to a responsible adult, who gives the adolescent attention and deals with the adolescent's specific needs. This theme occurs in a number of programs. In a successful substance-abuse program, a student assistance counselor is available full-time for individual counseling and referral for treatment.

2. *Community-wide multiagency collaborative approaches.* The basic philosophy of community-wide programs is that a number of different programs and services have to be in place. In one successful substance-abuse program, a community-wide health promotion campaign has been implemented that uses local media and community education, in concert with a substance-abuse curriculum in the schools.

3. *Early identification and intervention.* Reaching younger children and their families before children develop problems, or at the beginning of their problems, is a successful strategy (Aber & others, 2006). One preschool program serves as an excellent model for the prevention of delinquency, pregnancy, substance abuse, and dropping out of school. Operated by the High/Scope Foundation in Ypsilanti, Michigan, the Perry Preschool has had a long-term positive impact on its students. This enrichment program, directed by David Weikart, serves disadvantaged African American children. They attend a high-quality two-year preschool program and receive weekly home visits from program personnel. Based on official police records, by age 19, individuals who had attended the Perry Preschool program were less likely to have been arrested and reported fewer adult offenses than a control group did. The Perry Preschool students also were less likely to drop out of school, and teachers rated their social behavior as more competent than that of a control group who had not received the enriched preschool experience (High/Scope Resource, 2005). To read further about an extensive intervention program, see the *Research in Children's Development* interlude.

Research in Children's Development

FAST TRACK

Fast Track is an intervention that attempts to lower the risk of juvenile delinquency and other problems (Conduct Problems Prevention Research Group, 2007; Dodge, 2009; Dodge & the Conduct Problems Prevention Research Group, 2007; Lochman & the

Conduct Problems Prevention Research Group, 2007; Slough, McMahon, & the Conduct Problems Prevention Group, 2008; Thomas & others, 2009). Schools in four areas (Durham, North Carolina; Nashville, Tennessee; Seattle, Washington; and rural central Pennsylvania) were identified as high risk based on neighborhood crime and poverty data. Researchers screened more than 9,000 kindergarten children in the four schools and randomly assigned 891 of the highest-risk and moderate-risk children to intervention or control conditions. The average age of the children when the intervention began was 6.5 years of age.

The 10-year intervention consisted of parent behavior management training, child social cognitive skills training, reading tutoring, home visitations, mentoring, and a revised classroom curriculum that was designed to increase socioemotional competence and decrease aggression. Outcomes were assessed in the third, sixth, and ninth grades for conduct disorder (multiple instances of behaviors such as truancy, running away, fire setting, cruelty to animals, breaking and entering, and excessive fighting across a six-month period); oppositional defiant disorder (an ongoing pattern of disobedient, hostile, and defiant behavior toward authority figures); attention deficit hyperactivity disorder (as described in Chapter 11, "Physical Development in Middle and Late Childhood," being characterized by one or more of these characteristics over a period of time: inattention, hyperactivity, and impulsivity); any externalizing disorder (presence of any of the three disorders previously described); and self-reported antisocial behavior (a list of 34 behaviors, such as skipping school, stealing, and attacking someone with an intent to hurt them).

The extensive intervention was successful only for children and adolescents who were identified as the highest risk in kindergarten, lowering their incidence of conduct disorder, attention deficit hyperactivity disorder, any externalized disorder, and antisocial behavior. Positive outcomes for the intervention occurred as early as the third grade and continued through the ninth grade. For example, in the ninth grade the intervention reduced the likelihood that the highest-risk kindergarten children would develop conduct disorder by 75 percent, attention deficit hyperactivity disorder by 53 percent, and any externalized disorder by 43 percent.

Review and Reflect: Learning Goal 5

 5 **Identify adolescent problems in socioemotional development and strategies for helping adolescents with problems**

REVIEW

- What is juvenile delinquency? What causes it?
- What is the nature of depression and suicide in adolescence?
- How are adolescent problems interrelated? What are some components of successful prevention/intervention programs for adolescents?

REFLECT

- Are the consequences of risk taking in adolescence today more serious than in the past? If so, why?

Reach Your Learning Goals

Socioemotional Development in Adolescence

1 WHAT CHARACTERIZES EMOTIONAL AND PERSONALITY DEVELOPMENT IN ADOLESCENCE? DISCUSS CHANGES IN THE SELF AND EMOTIONAL DEVELOPMENT DURING ADOLESCENCE

Self-Esteem

- Some researchers have found that self-esteem declines in early adolescence for both boys and girls, but the drop for girls is greater. Other researchers caution that these declines are often exaggerated and actually are small.

Identity

- Identity development is complex and is done in bits and pieces. Erikson argues that identity versus identity confusion is the fifth stage of the human life span, which individuals experience during adolescence. A psychosocial moratorium during adolescence allows the personality and role experimentation that are important aspects of identity development. James Marcia proposed four identity statuses—identity diffusion, foreclosure, moratorium, and achievement—that are based on crisis (exploration) and commitment. Increasingly, experts argue that the main changes in identity occur in emerging adulthood rather than adolescence. Individuals often follow *moratorium-achievement-moratorium-achievement* ("MAMA") cycles in their lives. Parents are important figures in adolescents' identity development. Identity development is facilitated by family relations that promote both individuality and connectedness. Throughout the world ethnic minority groups have struggled to maintain their identities while blending into the majority culture.

Emotional Development

- Adolescents report more extreme and fleeting emotions than their parents, and as individuals go through early adolescence they are less likely to report being very happy. However, it is important to view moodiness as a normal aspect of early adolescence. Although pubertal change is associated with an increase in negative emotions, hormonal influences are often small, and environmental experiences may contribute more to the emotions of adolescence than hormonal changes.

2 WHAT IS THE NATURE OF PARENT-ADOLESCENT RELATIONSHIPS? DESCRIBE CHANGES THAT TAKE PLACE IN ADOLESCENTS' RELATIONSHIPS WITH THEIR PARENTS

Autonomy and Attachment

- Many parents have a difficult time handling the adolescent's push for autonomy, even though the push is one of the hallmarks of adolescence. Adolescents do not simply move into a world isolated from parents; attachment to parents increases the probability that an adolescent will be socially competent.

Parent-Adolescent Conflict

- Parent-adolescent conflict increases in early adolescence. The conflict is usually moderate rather than severe, and the increased conflict may serve the positive developmental function of promoting autonomy and identity. A subset of adolescents experiences high parent-adolescent conflict, which is linked with negative outcomes.

3 WHAT ASPECTS OF PEER RELATIONSHIPS ARE IMPORTANT IN ADOLESCENCE? CHARACTERIZE THE CHANGES THAT OCCUR IN PEER RELATIONS DURING ADOLESCENCE

Friendship

- Harry Stack Sullivan was the most influential theorist to discuss the importance of adolescent friendships. He argued that there is a dramatic increase in the psychological importance and intimacy of close friends in early adolescence.

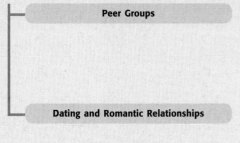

Peer Groups

- Children groups are less formal and less heterogeneous than adolescent groups. The pressure to conform to peers is strong during adolescence, especially during the eighth and ninth grades. Cliques and crowds assume more importance in the lives of adolescents than in the lives of children. Membership in certain crowds—especially jocks and populars—is associated with increased self-esteem. Independents also show high self-esteem.

Dating and Romantic Relationships

- Three stages characterize the development of romantic relationships in adolescence: (1) entry into romantic attractions and affiliations at about 11 to 13 years of age, (2) exploring romantic relationships at approximately 14 to 16 years of age, and (3) consolidating dyadic romantic bonds at about 17 to 19 years of age. A special concern is early dating, which is associated with a number of problems. Most sexual minority youth have had some same-sex sexual experience, but relatively few have had same-sex romantic relationships. Many sexual minority youth date other-sex peers, which can help them to clarify their sexual orientation or disguise it from others. Adolescents who date have more problems, such as substance abuse, than those who do not date, but they also have more acceptance with peers. Culture can exert a powerful influence on dating. Many adolescents from immigrant families face conflicts with their parents about dating.

4 WHY IS CULTURE AN IMPORTANT CONTEXT FOR ADOLESCENT DEVELOPMENT? EXPLAIN HOW CULTURE INFLUENCES ADOLESCENT DEVELOPMENT

Cross-Cultural Comparisons

- There are both similarities and differences in adolescents across different countries. In some countries, traditions are being continued in the socialization of adolescents, whereas in others, substantial changes in the experiences of adolescents are taking place. Adolescents often fill their time with different activities, depending on the culture in which they live. Rites of passage are ceremonies that mark an individual's transition from one status to another, especially into adulthood. In primitive cultures, rites of passage are often well defined. In contemporary America, universal, formal rites of passage to adulthood are ill-defined, but certain religious groups have initiation ceremonies, such as the Jewish bat and bar mitzvah and the Catholic confirmation. The high school graduation ceremony has become a nearly universal rite of passage for U.S. adolescents.

Ethnicity

- Many of the families that have immigrated in recent decades to the United States come from collectivist cultures in which there is a strong sense of family obligation. Much of the research on ethnic minority adolescents has not teased apart the influences of ethnicity and socioeconomic status. Because of this failure, too often researchers have given ethnic explanations for characteristics that were largely due to socioeconomic factors. Although not all ethnic minority families are poor, poverty contributes to the stress of many ethnic minority adolescents.

Media and Technology

- In terms of exposure, the average U.S. 8- to 18-year-old spends almost 6 hours a day using electronic media, with the most time spent watching television (if media multitasking is taken into account, they use electronic media 8 hours per day). Today's children and adolescents are experiencing a technology revolution through computers, the Internet, and sophisticated cell phones. The social environment of adolescents has increasingly become digitally mediated. The Internet continues to serve as the main focus of digitally mediated social interaction for adolescents but increasingly involves a variety of digital devices, including cell phones (especially smartphones). Adolescents' online time can have positive or negative outcomes. Large numbers of adolescents and college students engage in social networking on Facebook. A special concern is the difficulty parents have monitoring the information their children are accessing.

---

5 WHAT ARE SOME SOCIOEMOTIONAL PROBLEMS IN ADOLESCENCE? IDENTIFY ADOLESCENT PROBLEMS IN SOCIOEMOTIONAL DEVELOPMENT AND STRATEGIES FOR HELPING ADOLESCENTS WITH PROBLEMS

Juvenile Delinquency	• A juvenile delinquent is an adolescent who breaks the law or engages in conduct that is considered illegal. Heredity, identity problems, community influences, and family experiences have been proposed as causes of juvenile delinquency.
Depression and Suicide	• Adolescents and emerging adults have a rate of depression higher than that for children. Female adolescents and emerging adult women are more likely to have mood and depressive disorders than their male counterparts. Adolescent suicide is the third leading cause of death in U.S. 10- to 19-year-olds. Both proximal (recent) and distal (earlier) factors are likely involved in suicide's causes.
The Interrelation of Problems and Successful Prevention/Intervention Programs	• Researchers are increasingly finding that problem behaviors in adolescence are interrelated. A number of common components in successful programs are designed to prevent or reduce adolescent problems: providing individual attention to high-risk adolescents, developing community-wide intervention, and including early identification and intervention.

KEY TERMS

identity versus identity confusion 532
psychosocial moratorium 532
crisis 533

commitment 533
identity diffusion 533
identity foreclosure 533
identity moratorium 534
identity achievement 534

individuality 534
connectedness 535
ethnic identity 535
clique 542
crowd 543

rite of passage 548
assimilation 548
pluralism 548
juvenile delinquent 552

KEY PEOPLE

Erik Erikson 531
William Damon 532
James Marcia 533

Alan Waterman 534
Reed Larson and Maryse Richards 536

G. Stanley Hall 538
Harry Stack Sullivan 541

Marion Forgatch 554
Ritch Savin-Williams 556

MAKING A DIFFERENCE

Supporting Adolescents' Socioemotional Development

What are some good strategies for helping adolescents improve their socioemotional competencies?

• *Let adolescents explore their identity.* Adolescence is a time of identity exploration. Adults should encourage adolescents to try out different options as they seek to find what type of life they want to pursue.

• *Understand the importance of autonomy and attachment.* A common stereotype is that parents are less important in adolescent development than in child development. However, parents continue to play a crucial role in adolescents' development. They need their parents as a resource and support system, especially in stressful times. Value the adolescent's motivation for independence. However, continue to monitor the adolescent's whereabouts, although less intrusively and directly than in childhood.

• *Keep parent-adolescent conflict from being turbulent, and use good communication skills with the adolescent.* Adolescents' socioemotional development benefits when conflict with parents is either low or moderate. Keep communication channels open with the adolescent. Be an active listener and show respect for the adolescent's advancing developmental status. As with childhood, authoritative parenting is the best choice in most situations. Communicate expectations for high standards of achievement and conduct.

• *Recognize the importance of peers, youth organizations, and mentors.* Respected peers need to be used more frequently in programs that promote health and education. Adolescents need greater access to youth organizations staffed by caring peers and adults. Mentors can play a strong role in supporting adolescents' socioemotional development.

- *Help adolescents better understand the nature of differences, diversity, and value conflicts.* Adolescents need to be encouraged to take the perspective of adolescents from diverse ethnic backgrounds.

- *Give adolescents individualized attention.* One of the reasons that adolescents develop problems is that they have not been given adequate attention.

- *Provide better community-wide collaboration for helping youth.* In successful programs, a number of different services and programs cooperate to help adolescents.

- *Prevent adolescent problems through early identification and intervention.* The seeds of many adolescent problems are already in place in childhood.

RESOURCES FOR IMPROVING CHILDREN'S LIVES

Adolescence: Growing Up in America Today
by Joy Dryfoos and Carol Barkin (2006)
New York: Oxford University Press.

Dryfoos' recent update of her 1990 book on at-risk adolescents contains extensive information about programs and strategies for improving adolescents' lives.

You and Your Adolescent
by Laurence Steinberg and Ann Levine (1997, 2nd ed.)
New York: HarperCollins

You and Your Adolescent provides a broad, developmental overview of adolescence, with parental advice mixed in along the way.

E-LEARNING TOOLS

Connect to **www.mhhe.com/santrockc11e** to research the answers and complete these exercises. In addition, you'll find a number of other resources and valuable study tools for Chapter 16, "Socioemotional Development in Adolescence," on this Web site.

Taking It to the Net

1. Marissa is 12 years old, and she has already begun puberty. She is much taller than her classmates, and she has well-developed breasts and other secondary sex characteristics. Marissa is embarrassed about the sudden physical changes in her body, and she feels very insecure. Moreover, Marissa, who has always done very well in school, is learning very quickly that the "brains" in school are not very popular. What factors may be contributing to Marissa's struggles? What can family members and teachers do to support adolescent girls during the early stages of development?

2. Shawn just learned that a classmate of his, Glenn, was hospitalized for depression and suicidality. Shawn was very surprised when he heard this; he saw Glenn as very popular and never would have guessed that he was depressed. How common is it for adolescents to be depressed? How common is adolescent suicide? How can friends, family members, and teachers determine whether someone is depressed and/or suicidal? What can they do to support the depressed/suicidal adolescent?

3. Shelley's mother is Euro-American, and her father is Japanese. Many people who do not know her have a hard time identifying her ethnic background, and she is constantly asked, "What are you?" There are a couple of other students from diverse ethnic backgrounds at her school, although few of them openly identify as biracial or multiracial. Shelley is now in the process of figuring out who she is. What are some of the challenges biracial or multiracial adolescents face? How might the process of identity development progress?

Health and Well-Being, Parenting, and Education

Build your decision-making skills by trying your hand at the health and well-being, parenting, and education exercises.

Video Clips

The Online Learning Center includes the following videos for this chapter:

- *Relationships with Parents at Age 16—1982*
  In this clip, three adolescent friends describe their relationships with their parents. They describe "normal" fights, and they discuss differences between their relationships with their mothers versus fathers.

- *Ethnic and Racial Identity in Adolescence—2259*
  Two African American girls discuss candidly their feelings about being Black. One describes being Black as being a mixture of many cultures. The other says it's hard to be African American because there is no distinct culture for Blacks.

- *Talking About Ethnic Identity in Adolescence—1994*
  Students view the diversity among them, as well as among their peers, very positively. They admit that they are different from one another, because of their ethnic backgrounds, but they each benefit from one another because of these differences.

GLOSSARY

A

A-not-B error Also called AB̄ error, this occurs when infants make the mistake of selecting the familiar hiding place (A) rather than the new hiding place (B̄) as they progress into substage 4 in Piaget's sensorimotor stage. 189

accommodation Piagetian concept of adjusting schemes to fit new information and experiences. 184

active (niche-picking) genotype-environment correlations Correlations that exist when children seek out environments they find compatible and stimulating. 79

adolescence The developmental period of transition from childhood to early adulthood, entered at approximately 10 to 12 years of age and ending at 18 to 22 years of age. 18

adolescent egocentrism The heightened self-consciousness of adolescents that is reflected in their belief that others are as interested in them as they are in themselves, and in their sense of personal uniqueness and invincibility. 501

adoption study A study in which investigators seek to discover whether, in behavior and psychological characteristics, adopted children are more like their adoptive parents, who provided a home environment, or more like their biological parents, who contributed their heredity. Another form of the adoption study is to compare adopted and biological siblings. 78

affordances Opportunities for interaction offered by objects that fit within our capabilities to perform functional activities. 166

afterbirth The third stage of birth, when the placenta, umbilical cord, and other membranes are detached and expelled. 119

AIDS AIDS, or acquired immune deficiency syndrome, is caused by a virus, the human immunodeficiency virus (HIV), which destroys the body's immune system. 477

amnion The life-support system that is a thin bag or envelope that contains a clear fluid in which the developing embryo floats. 90

amygdala The seat of emotions, such as anger. 473

analgesics Drugs used to alleviate pain, such as tranquilizers, barbiturates, and narcotics. 121

androgyny The presence of positive masculine and feminine characteristics in the same individual. 439

anesthesia Drugs used in late first-stage labor and during expulsion of the baby to block sensation in an area of the body or to block consciousness. 121

anger cry A cry similar to the basic cry, with more excess air forced through the vocal cords. 223

animism The belief that inanimate objects have lifelike qualities and are capable of action. 283

anorexia nervosa An eating disorder that involves the relentless pursuit of thinness through starvation. 489

Apgar Scale A widely used method to assess the health of newborns at one and five minutes after birth. The Apgar Scale evaluates infants' heart rate, respiratory effort, muscle tone, body color, and reflex irritability. 125

aphasia A loss or impairment of language processing caused by brain damage in Broca's area or Wernicke's area. 206

articulation disorders Problems in pronouncing sounds correctly. 371

Asperger syndrome A relatively mild autism spectrum disorder in which the child has relatively good verbal language, milder nonverbal language problems, and a restricted range of interests and relationships. 374

assimilation (1) Piagetian concept of the incorporation of new information into existing schemes. (2) The absorption of ethnic minority groups into the dominant group, which often involves the loss of some or virtually all of the behavior and values of the ethnic group. 182, 548

asthma A chronic lung disease that involves episodes of airflow obstruction. 365

attachment A close emotional bond between two people. 233

attention The focusing of mental resources on select information. 192

attention deficit hyperactivity disorder (ADHD) A disability in which children consistently show one or more of the following characteristics: (1) inattention, (2) hyperactivity, and (3) impulsivity. 370

authoritarian parenting A restrictive punitive style in which parents exhort the child to follow their directions and to respect work and effort. The authoritarian parent places firm limits and controls on the child and allows little verbal exchange. Authoritarian parenting is associated with children's social incompetence. 325

authoritative parenting A parenting style in which parents encourage their children to be independent but still place limits and controls on their actions. Extensive verbal give-and-take is allowed, and parents are warm and nurturant toward the child. Authoritative parenting is associated with children's social competence. 325

autism spectrum disorders (ASDs) Also called pervasive developmental disorders; disorders that range from the severe disorder labeled autistic disorder to the milder disorder called Asperger syndrome. Children with these disorders are characterized by problems with social interaction, with verbal and nonverbal communication, and with repetitive behaviors. 372

autistic disorder A severe autism spectrum disorder that has its onset in the first three years of life and includes deficiencies in social relationships, abnormalities in communication, and restricted, repetitive, and stereotyped patterns of behavior. 374

autonomous morality The second stage of moral development in Piaget's theory, displayed by older children (about 10 years of age and older). The child becomes aware that rules and laws are created by people and that, in judging an action, one should consider the actor's intentions as well as the consequences. 319

average children Children who receive an average number of both positive and negative nominations from peers. 444

B

Babinski reflex A reflex in which infants fan out their toes and twist their foot inward when the sole of their foot is stroked. 161

basic cry A rhythmic pattern usually consisting of a cry, a briefer silence, a shorter inspiratory whistle that is higher pitched than the main cry, and then a brief rest before the next cry. 222

Bayley Scales of Infant Development Scales developed by Nancy Bayley that are widely used in the assessment of infant development. The current version, the Bayley Scales of Infant and Toddler Development—Third Edition (Bayley-III), has five components: a cognitive scale, a language scale, a motor scale, a socio-emotional scale, and an adaptive scale. 198

behavior genetics The field that seeks to discover the influence of heredity and environment on individual differences in human traits and development. 78

biological processes Changes in an individual's body. 17

blastocyst The inner mass of cells that develops during the germinal period. These cells later develop into the embryo. 89

bonding A close connection, especially a physical bond between parents and their newborn in the period shortly after birth. 134

brainstorming A technique in which individuals are encouraged to come up with creative ideas in a group, play off each other's ideas, and say practically whatever comes to mind. 391

Brazelton Neonatal Behavioral Assessment Scale (NBAS) A test performed within 24 to 36 hours after birth to assess newborns' neurological development, reflexes, and reactions to People. 125

breech position The baby's position in the uterus that causes the buttocks to be the first part to emerge from the vagina. 123

Broca's area An area in the brain's left frontal lobe involved in speech production. 206

Bronfenbrenner's ecological theory An environmental systems theory that focuses on five environmental systems: microsystem, mesosystem, exosystem, macrosystem, and chronosystem. 32

bulimia nervosa An eating disorder in which the individual consistently follows a binge-and-purge eating pattern. 490

C

care perspective The moral perspective of Carol Gilligan, which views people in terms of their connectedness with others and emphasizes interpersonal communication, relationships with others, and concern for others. 434

case study An in-depth look at a single individual. 36

centration The focusing of attention on one characteristic to the exclusion of all others. 285

cephalocaudal pattern The sequence in which the earliest growth always occurs at the top—the head—with physical growth and feature differentiation gradually working from top to bottom. 145

cerebral palsy A disorder that involves a lack of muscular coordination, shaking, and unclear speech. 372

cesarean delivery Delivery in which the baby is removed from the mother's uterus through an incision made in her abdomen. This also is sometimes referred to as a cesarean section. 123

character education A direct education approach that involves teaching students a basic moral literacy to prevent them from engaging in immoral behavior and doing harm to themselves and others. 509

child-centered kindergarten Education that involves the whole child by considering both the child's physical, cognitive, and socioemotional development and the child's needs, interests, and learning styles. 301

child-directed speech Language spoken in a higher pitch than normal with simple words and sentences. 209

chromosomes Threadlike structures made up of deoxyribonucleic acid, or DNA. 64

clique A small group that ranges from two to about twelve individuals, averaging about five to six individuals, and one that can form because adolescents engage in similar activities. 542

cognitive moral education A concept based on the belief that students should develop such values as democracy and justice as their moral reasoning develops; Kohlberg's theory has been the basis of a number of cognitive moral education programs. 509

cognitive processes Changes in an individual's thought, intelligence, and language. 17

commitment Marcia's term for the part of identity development in which individuals show a personal investment in identity. 533

connectedness Characteristic consisting of two dimensions: mutuality (sensitivity to and respect for others' views) and permeability (openness to others' views). 535

conscience An internal regulation of standards of right and wrong that involves an integration of moral thought, feeling, and behavior. 319

conservation The concept that an object's or substance's basic properties stay the same even though its appearance has been altered. 285

constructive play Play that combines sensorimotor/practice play with symbolic representation. Constructive play occurs when children engage in self-regulated creation or construction of a product or a solution. 343

constructivist approach A learner-centered approach that emphasizes the importance of individuals actively constructing their knowledge and understanding with guidance from the teacher. 451

context The settings, influenced by historical, economic, social, and cultural factors, in which development occurs. 9

continuity-discontinuity issue The issue regarding whether development involves gradual, cumulative change (continuity) or distinct stages (discontinuity). 20

controversial children Children who are frequently nominated both as someone's best friend and as being disliked. 444

conventional reasoning The second, or intermediate, level in Kohlberg's theory of moral development. At this level, individuals abide by certain standards, but they are the standards of others such as parents or the government. 431

convergent thinking Thinking that produces one correct answer and is characteristic of the kind of thinking tested by standardized intelligence tests. 390

coordination of secondary circular reactions Piaget's fourth sensorimotor substage, which develops between 8 and 12 months of age. Actions become more outwardly directed, and infants coordinate schemes and act with intentionality. 186

core knowledge approach View that infants are born with domain-specific innate knowledge systems. 190

corpus callosum The location where fibers connect the brain's left and right hemispheres. 473

correlation coefficient A number based on statistical analysis that is used to describe the degree of association between two variables. 37

correlational research A research design whose goal is to describe the strength of the relationship between two or more events or characteristics. 37

creative thinking The ability to think in novel and unusual ways and to come up with unique solutions to problems. 390

crisis Marcia's term for a period of identity development during which the individual is exploring alternatives. 533

critical thinking The ability to think reflectively and productively, as well as to evaluate the evidence. 390

cross-cultural studies Comparisons of one culture with one or more other cultures. These comparisons provide information about the degree to which children's development is similar, or universal, across cultures, and the degree to which it is culture-specific. 10

cross-sectional approach A research strategy in which individuals of different ages are compared at one time. 39

crowd A larger group than a clique, one that is usually formed based on reputation; members may or may not spend much time together. 543

culture The behavior patterns, beliefs, and all other products of a group that are passed on from generation to generation. 9

cultural-familial retardation Retardation that is characterized by no evidence of organic brain damage, but the individual's IQ generally is between 50 and 70. 402

culture-fair tests Tests of intelligence that are designed to be free of cultural bias. 401

D

deferred imitation Imitation that occurs after a delay of hours or days. 194

Denver Development Screening Test II A test used to diagnose developmental delay in children from birth to 6 years of age; includes separate assessments of gross and fine motor skills, language, and personal-social ability. 261

descriptive research A research design that has the purpose of observing and recording behavior. 37

design stage Kellogg's term for 3- to 4-year-olds' drawings that mix two basic shapes into more complex designs. 262

development The pattern of movement or change that begins at conception and continues through the human life span. 7

developmental quotient (DQ) An overall score that combines subscores in motor, language, adaptive, and personal-social domains in the Gesell assessment of infants. 198

developmentally appropriate practice Education that focuses on the typical developmental patterns of children (age appropriateness) as well as the uniqueness of each child (individual appropriateness). Such practice contrasts with *developmentally inappropriate practice*, which ignores the concrete, hands-on approach to learning. Direct teaching largely through abstract paper-and-pencil activities presented to large groups of young children is believed to be developmentally inappropriate. 302

difficult child A child who tends to react negatively and cry frequently, who engages in irregular daily routines, and who is slow to accept new experiences. 225

direct instruction approach A structured, teacher-centered approach that is characterized by teacher direction and control, mastery of academic skills, high expectations for students' progress, maximum time spent on learning tasks, and efforts to keep negative affect to a minimum. 451

dishabituation Recovery of a habituated response after a change in stimulation. 167

divergent thinking Thinking that produces many different answers to the same question and is characteristic of creativity. 390

DNA A complex molecule with a double helix shape; contains genetic information. 64

doula A caregiver who provides continuous physical, emotional, and educational support to the mother before, during, and after childbirth. 120

Down syndrome A chromosomally transmitted form of mental retardation, caused by the presence of an extra copy of chromosome 21. 68

dual-process model States that decision making is influenced by two systems—one analytical and one experiential, which compete with each other; in this model, it is the experiential system—monitoring and managing actual experiences—that benefits adolescent decision making. 504

dynamic systems theory The perspective on motor development that seeks to explain how motor skills are assembled for perceiving and acting. 159

dyscalculia Also known as developmental arithmetic disorder; a learning disability that involves difficulty in math computation. 369

dysgraphia A learning disability that involves difficulty in handwriting. 369

dyslexia A category of learning disabilities involving a severe impairment in the ability to read and spell. 369

E

early childhood The developmental period that extends from the end of infancy to about 5 to 6 years of age; sometimes called the preschool years. 18

early-later experience issue The issue of the degree to which early experiences (especially infancy) or later experiences are the key determinants of the child's development. 20

easy child A child who is generally in a positive mood, who quickly establishes regular routines in infancy, and who adapts easily to new experiences. 225

eclectic theoretical orientation An orientation that does not follow any one theoretical approach but rather selects from each theory whatever is considered the best in it. 32

ecological view The view that perception functions to bring organisms in contact with the environment and to increase adaptation. 166

ectoderm The outermost layer of cells, which becomes the nervous system and brain, sensory receptors (ears, nose, and eyes, for example), and skin parts (hair and nails, for example). 90

educationally blind Unable to use one's vision in learning and must use their hearing and touch to learn. 372

egocentrism Piaget's concept that describes the inability to distinguish between one's own perspective and someone else's perspective. 283

elaboration An important strategy that involves engaging in more extensive processing of information. 388

embryonic period The period of prenatal development that occurs two to eight weeks after conception. During the embryonic period, the rate of cell differentiation intensifies, support systems for the cells form, and organs appear. 89

emerging adulthood Occurring from approximately 18 to 25 years of age, this transitional period between adolescence and adulthood is characterized by experimentation and exploration. 467

emotion Feeling, or affect, that occurs when a person is in a state or interaction that is important to him or her. Emotion can be characterized as positive (enthusiasm, joy, love, for example) or negative (anxiety, guilt, or sadness, for example). 221

emotional and behavioral disorders Serious, persistent problems that involve relationships, aggression, depression, fears associated with personal or school matters, as well as other inappropriate socioemotional characteristics. 372

endoderm The inner layer of cells, which develops into digestive and respiratory systems. 90

epigenetic view Emphasizes that development is the result of an ongoing, bidirectional interchange between heredity and environment. 80

equilibration A mechanism that Piaget proposed to explain how children shift from one stage of thought to the next. 184

Erikson's theory Includes eight stages of human development. Each stage consists of a unique developmental task that confronts individuals with a crisis that must be resolved. 24

estradiol A hormone associated in girls with breast, uterine, and skeletal development. 470

ethnic gloss The use of an ethnic label such as African American or Latino in a superficial way that portrays an ethnic group as being more homogeneous than it really is. 42

ethnic identity An enduring, basic aspect of the self that includes a sense of membership in an ethnic group and the attitudes and feelings related to that membership. 535

ethnicity A characteristic based on cultural heritage, nationality, race, religion, and language. 10

ethology Stresses that behavior is strongly influenced by biology, is tied to evolution, and is characterized by critical or sensitive periods. 31

evocative genotype-environment correlations Correlations that exist when the child's characteristics elicit certain types of physical and social environments. 79

evolutionary psychology Branch of psychology that emphasizes the importance of adaptation, reproduction, and "survival of the fittest" in shaping behavior. 62

executive attention Involves action planning, allocating attention to goals, error detection and compensation, monitoring progress on tasks, and dealing with novel or difficult circumstances. 291

experiment A carefully regulated procedure in which one or more of the factors believed to influence the behavior being studied are manipulated, while all other factors are held constant. 38

explicit memory Conscious memory of facts and experiences. 194

extrinsic motivation Involves external incentives such as rewards and punishments. 410

F

fertilization A stage in reproduction whereby an egg and a sperm fuse to create a single cell, called a zygote. 65

fetal alcohol spectrum disorders (FASD) A cluster of abnormalities and problems that appears in the offspring of mothers who drink alcohol heavily during pregnancy. 103

fetal period The prenatal period of development that begins two months after conception and lasts for seven months, on the average. 91

fine motor skills Motor skills that involve finely tuned movements, such as finger dexterity. 164

first habits and primary circular reactions Piaget's second sensorimotor substage, which develops between 1 and 4 months of age. In this substage, the infant coordinates sensation and two types of schemes: habits and primary circular reactions. 185

fluency disorders Various disorders that involve what is commonly called "stuttering." 371

fragile X syndrome A genetic disorder involving an abnormality in the X chromosome, which becomes constricted and often breaks. 68

fuzzy trace theory A theory stating that memory is best understood by considering two types of memory representations: (1) verbatim memory trace and (2) gist. In this theory, older children's better memory is attributed to the fuzzy traces created by extracting the gist of information. 388

G

games Activities engaged in for pleasure that include rules and often competition with one or more individuals. 343

gender The characteristics of people as females or males. 10

gender identity The sense of one's own gender, including knowledge, understanding, and acceptance of being male or female. 321

gender role A set of expectations that prescribes how females or males should think, act, and feel. 321

gender schema theory The theory gender typing emerges as children gradually develop gender schemas of what is considered gender-appropriate and gender-inappropriate in their culture. 324

gender stereotypes Broad categories that reflect our impressions and beliefs about females and males. 435

gender typing Acquisition of a traditional masculine or feminine role. 321

gene × environment (G × E) interaction The interaction of a specific measured variation in the DNA and a specific measured aspect of the environment. 81

genes Units of hereditary information composed of DNA. Genes direct cells to reproduce themselves and manufacture the proteins that maintain life. 64

genetic epistemology The study of how children's knowledge changes over the course of their development. 16

genotype A person's genetic heritage; the actual genetic material. 66

germinal period The period of prenatal development that takes place in the first two weeks after conception. It includes the creation of the zygote, continued cell division, and the attachment of the zygote to the uterine wall. 89

gifted Having above-average intelligence (an IQ of 130 or higher) and/or superior talent for something. 402

gonadotropins Hormones that stimulate the testes or ovaries. 470

gonads The sex glands—the testes in males, the ovaries in females. 470

goodness of fit Refers to the match between a child's temperament and the environmental demands with which the child must cope. 227

grasping reflex A neonatal reflex that occurs when something touches the infant's palms. The infant responds by grasping tightly. 161

gross motor skills Motor skills that involve large-muscle activities, such as walking. 161

growth hormone deficiency The absence or deficiency of growth hormone produced by the pituitary gland to stimulate the body to grow. 254

H

habituation Decreased responsiveness to a stimulus after repeated presentations of the stimulus. 167

helpless orientation An orientation in which one seems trapped by the experience of difficulty and attributes one's difficulty to a lack of ability. 411

heritability The fraction of variance in a population that is attributed to genetics and is computed using correlational techniques. 399

heteronomous morality (1) Kohlberg's first stage in preconventional reasoning in which moral thinking is tied to punishment. (2) The first stage of moral development in Piaget's theory, occurring from approximately 4 to 7 years of age. Justice and rules are conceived of as unchangeable properties of the world, removed from the control of people. 319, 430

hidden curriculum Dewey's concept that every school has a pervasive moral atmosphere, even if it doesn't have a program of moral education. 509

hormones Powerful chemical substances secreted by the endocrine glands and carried through the body by the bloodstream. 468

hypothalamus A structure in the brain that monitors eating and sex. 468

hypothesis A specific assumption or prediction that can be tested to determine its accuracy. 22

hypothetical-deductive reasoning Piaget's formal operational concept that adolescents have the cognitive ability to develop hypotheses, or best guesses, about ways to solve problems. 499

I

identity achievement Marcia's term for the status of individuals who have undergone a crisis and have made a commitment. 534

identity diffusion Marcia's term for the status of individuals who have not yet experienced a crisis (explored alternatives) or made any commitments. 533

identity foreclosure Marcia's term for the status of individuals who have made a commitment but have not experienced a crisis. 533

identity moratorium Marcia's term for the status of individuals who are in the midst of a crisis, but their commitments are either absent or vaguely defined. 534

identity versus identity confusion Erikson's fifth developmental stage, which occurs about the time of adolescence. At this time, adolescents are faced with deciding who they are, what they are all about, and where they are going in life. 532

imaginary audience Adolescents' belief that others are as interested in them as they themselves are, as well as attention-getting behavior. 501

immanent justice The concept that, if a rule is broken, punishment will be meted out immediately. 319

implicit memory Memory without conscious recollection; involves skills and routine procedures that are automatically performed. 194

inclusion Educating a child with special education needs full-time in the regular classroom. 376

individual differences The stable, consistent ways in which people are different from each other. 395

individualism, instrumental purpose, and exchange The second Kohlberg stage in preconventional reasoning. At this stage, individuals pursue their own interests but also let others do the same. 430

individuality Characteristic consisting of two dimensions: self-assertion (the ability to have and communicate a point of view) and separateness (the use of communication patterns to express how one is different from others). 534

individualized education plan (IEP) A written statement that spells out a program tailored to a child with a disability. The plan should be (1) related to the child's learning capacity, (2) specially constructed to meet the child's individual needs and not merely a copy of what is offered to other children, and (3) designed to provide educational benefits. 375

Individuals with Disabilities Education Act (IDEA) The IDEA spells out broad mandates for services to all children with disabilities (IDEA is a renaming of Public Law 94-142); these include evaluation and eligibility determination, appropriate education and the individualized education plan (IEP), and education in the least restrictive environment (LRE). 375

indulgent parenting A style of parenting in which parents are highly involved with their children but place few demands or controls on them. Indulgent parenting is associated with children's social incompetence, especially a lack of self-control. 326

infancy The developmental period that extends from birth to 18 to 24 months of age. 18

infinite generativity The ability to produce an endless number of meaningful sentences using a finite set of words and rules. 202

information-processing theory Emphasizes that individuals manipulate information, monitor it, and strategize about it. Central to this theory are the processes of memory and thinking. 28

innate goodness view The idea, presented by Swiss-born French philosopher Jean-Jacques Rousseau, that children are inherently good. 14

insecure avoidant babies Babies that show insecurity by avoiding the caregiver. 235

insecure disorganized babies Babies that show insecurity by being disorganized and disoriented. 235

insecure resistant babies Babies that often cling to the caregiver, then resist her by fighting against the closeness, perhaps by kicking or pushing away. 235

intelligence Problem-solving skills and the ability to learn from and adapt to the experiences of everyday life. 3

intelligence quotient (IQ) A person's mental age divided by chronological age, multiplied by 100. 395

intermodal perception The ability to relate and integrate information from two or more sensory modalities, such as vision and hearing. 173

internalization of schemes Piaget's sixth and final sensorimotor substage, which develops between 18 and 24 months of age. In this substage, the infant develops the ability to use primitive symbols. 186

intimacy in friendships Self-disclosure and the sharing of private thoughts. 449

intrinsic motivation Involves internal factors such as self-determination, curiosity, challenge, and effort. 410

intuitive thought substage Piaget's second substage of preoperational thought, in which children begin to use primitive reasoning and want to know the answers to all sorts of questions (occurs between about 4 and 7 years of age). 285

involution The process by which the uterus returns to its prepregnant size. 132

J

joint attention Occurs when individuals focus on the same object or event, and an ability to track another's behavior is present; one individual directs another's attention, and reciprocal interaction is present. 193

justice perspective A moral perspective that focuses on the rights of the individual; individuals independently make moral decisions. 434

juvenile delinquent An adolescent who breaks the law or engages in behavior that is considered illegal. 552

K

kangaroo care A way of holding a preterm infant so that there is skin-to-skin contact. 129

Klinefelter syndrome A genetic disorder in which males have an extra X chromosome, making them XXY instead of XY. 68

kwashiorkor A condition caused by a severe deficiency in protein in which the child's abdomen and feet become swollen with water; usually appears between 1 to 3 years of age. 155

L

laboratory A controlled setting in which many of the complex factors of the "real world" are removed. 34

language A form of communication, whether spoken, written, or signed, that is based on a system of symbols. 202

language acquisition device (LAD) Chomsky's term that describes a biological endowment that enables the child to detect the features and rules of language, including phonology, syntax, and semantics. 206

lateralization Specialization of function in one hemisphere of the cerebral cortex or the other. 147

learning disability Disability in which a child has difficulty in learning that involves understanding or using spoken or written language, and the difficulty can appear in listening, thinking, reading, writing, or spelling. A learning disability also may involve difficulty in doing mathematics. To be classified as a learning disability, the learning problem is not primarily the result of visual, hearing, or motor disabilities; mental retardation; emotional disorders; or due to environmental, cultural, or economic disadvantage. 368

least restrictive environment (LRE) The concept that a child with a disability must be educated in a setting that is as similar as possible to the one in which children who do not have a disability are educated. 375

long-term memory A relatively permanent type of memory that holds huge amounts of information for a long period of time. 388

longitudinal approach A research strategy in which the same individuals are studied over a period of time, usually several years or more. 39

low birth weight infants Babies that weigh less than 5½ pounds at birth. 126

low vision Visual acuity between 20/70 and 20/2000. 372

M

manual approaches Educational approaches to help hearing-impaired children; they include sign language and finger spelling. 372

marasmus A wasting away of body tissues in the infant's first year, caused by severe protein-calorie deficiency. 155

mastery motivation An orientation in which one is task-oriented; instead of focusing on one's ability, the person is concerned with learning strategies and the achievement process. 411

meiosis A specialized form of cell division that occurs to form eggs and sperm (or gametes). 65

melatonin A sleep-inducing hormone that is produced in the brain's pineal gland. 485

memory A central feature of cognitive development, involving the retention of information over time. 194

menarche A girl's first menstrual period. 468

mental age (MA) Binet's measure of an individual's level of mental development, compared with that of others. 395

mental retardation A condition of limited mental ability in which an individual has a low IQ, usually below 70 on a traditional test of intelligence, and has difficulty adapting to everyday life. 402

mesoderm The middle layer of cells, which becomes the circulatory system, bones, muscles, excretory system, and reproductive system. 90

metacognition Cognition about cognition, or knowing about knowing. 393

metalinguistic awareness Refers to knowledge about language, such as knowing what a preposition is or the ability to discuss the sounds of a language. 406

middle and late childhood The developmental period that extends from about 6 to 11 years of age; sometimes called the elementary school years. 18

mindfulness Being alert, mentally present, and cognitively flexible while going through life's everyday activities and tasks. 390

mindset The cognitive view, either fixed or growth, that individuals develop for themselves. 411

mitosis Cellular reproduction in which the cell's nucleus duplicates itself with two new cells being formed, each containing the same DNA as the parent cell, arranged in the same 23 pairs of chromosomes. 65

Montessori approach An educational philosophy in which children are given considerable freedom and spontaneity in choosing activities and specially designed curriculum materials. 301

moral development Development that involves thoughts, feelings, and behaviors regarding rules and conventions about what people should do in their interactions with other people. 319

Moro reflex A neonatal startle response that occurs in reaction to a sudden, intense noise or movement. When startled, the newborn arches its back, throws its head back, and flings out its arms and legs. Then the newborn rapidly closes its arms and legs to the center of the body. 161

morphology Units of meaning involved in word formation. 202

mutual interpersonal expectations, relationships, and interpersonal conformity Kohlberg's third stage of moral development. At this stage, individuals value trust, caring, and loyalty to others as a basis of moral judgments. 431

myelination The process in which the nerve cells are covered and insulated with a layer of fat cells, which increases the speed at which information travels through the nervous system. 256

N

natural childbirth Method developed in 1914 by English obstetrician Grantley Dick-Read; it attempts to reduce the mother's pain by decreasing her fear through education about childbirth and breathing methods and relaxation techniques during delivery. 121

naturalistic observation Observing behavior in real-world settings. 34

nature-nurture issue The issue regarding whether development is primarily influenced by nature or nurture. The "nature" proponents claim biological inheritance is the most important influence on development; the "nurture" proponents claim that environmental experiences are the most important. 19

neglected children Children who are infrequently nominated as a best friend but are not disliked by their peers. 444

neglectful parenting A style of parenting in which the parent is very uninvolved in the child's life; it is associated with children's social incompetence, especially a lack of self-control. 326

Neonatal Intensive Care Unit Network Neurobehavioral Scale (NNNS) An "offspring" of the NBAS, the NNNS provides a more comprehensive analysis of the newborn's behavior, neurological and stress responses, and regulatory capacities. 125

neo-Piagetians Developmentalists who have elaborated on Piaget's theory, giving more emphasis to information processing, strategies, and precise cognitive steps. 386

neurogenesis The formation of new neurons. 93

neurons The term for nerve cells, which handle information processing at the cellular level. 92

night terrors Characterized by sudden arousal from sleep, intense fear, and usually physiological reactions such as rapid heart rate and breathing, loud screams, heavy perspiration, and physical movement. 265

nightmares Frightening dreams that awaken the sleeper. 265

nonshared environment experiences The child's own unique experiences, both within the family and outside the family, that are not shared by another sibling. Thus, experiences occurring within the family can be part of the "nonshared environment." 80

normal distribution A symmetrical distribution with most scores falling in the middle of the possible range of scores and few scores appearing toward the extremes of the range. 395

O

object permanence Piagetian term for understanding that objects continue to exist, even when they cannot directly be seen, heard, or touched. 186

operations In Piaget's theory, reversible mental actions that allow children to do mentally what they formerly did physically. 283

oral approaches Educational approaches to help hearing-impaired children; they include lip reading, speech reading, and whatever hearing the child has. 372

organic retardation Mental retardation that involves some physical damage and is caused by a genetic disorder or brain damage. 402

organization Piaget's concept of grouping isolated behaviors and thoughts into a higher-order, more smoothly functioning cognitive system. 184

organogenesis Process of organ formation that takes place during the first two months of prenatal development. 91

original sin view Advocated during the Middle Ages, the belief that children were born into the world as evil beings and were basically bad. 14

orthopedic impairments Restrictions in movement abilities due to muscle, bone, or joint problems. 372

oxytocin A synthetic hormone that is used to stimulate contractions. 121

P

pain cry A sudden appearance of a long, initial loud cry without preliminary moaning, followed by breath holding. 223

passive genotype-environment correlations Correlations that exist when the biological parents, who are genetically related to the child, provide a rearing environment for the child. 78

perception The interpretation of what is sensed. 166

performance orientation An orientation in which one focuses on achievement outcomes; winning is what matters most, and happiness is thought to result from winning. 411

personal fable The part of adolescent egocentrism that involves an adolescent's sense of uniqueness and invincibility. 501

personality-type theory Holland's theory that an effort should be made to match an individual's career choice with the individual's personality. 520

perspective taking The ability to assume other people's perspectives and understand their thoughts and feelings. 425

phenotype The way an individual's genotype is expressed in observed and measurable characteristics. 66

phenylketonuria (PKU) A genetic disorder in which an individual cannot properly metabolize phenylalanine, an amino acid. PKU is now easily detected—but if left untreated, results in mental retardation and hyperactivity. 69

phonics approach The idea that reading instruction should teach basic rules for translating written symbols into sounds. 407

phonology The sound system of the language, including the sounds that are used and how they may be combined. 202

Piaget's theory States that children actively construct their understanding of the world and go through four stages of cognitive development. 27

pictorial stage Kellogg's term for 4- to 5-year-olds' drawings depicting objects that adults can recognize. 262

pituitary gland An important endocrine gland that controls growth and regulates other glands. 468

placement stage Kellogg's term for 2- to 3-year-olds' drawings that are drawn on a page in placement patterns. 262

placenta Consists of a disk-shaped group of tissues in which small blood vessels from the mother and the offspring intertwine but don't join. 90

pluralism The coexistence of distinct ethnic and cultural groups in the same society, each of which maintains its cultural differences. 548

popular children Children who are frequently nominated as a best friend and are rarely disliked by their peers. 444

postconventional reasoning The highest level in Kohlberg's theory of moral development. At this level, the individual recognizes alternative moral courses, explores the options, and then decides on a personal moral code. 431

postpartum depression Involves a major depressive episode characterized by strong feelings of sadness, anxiety, or despair in new mothers, making it difficult for them to carry out daily tasks. 132

postpartum period The period after childbirth when the mother adjusts, both physically and psychologically, to the process of childbearing. This period lasts for about six weeks, or until her body has completed its adjustment and has returned to a near-prepregnant state. 131

practice play Play that involves repetition of behavior when new skills are being learned or when physical or mental mastery and coordination of skills are required for games or sports. 341

pragmatics The appropriate use of language in different contexts. 203

precocious puberty The very early onset and rapid progression of puberty. 471

preconventional reasoning The lowest level in Kohlberg's theory of moral development. The individual's concept of good and bad is interpreted primarily by external rewards and punishment. 430

prenatal period The time from conception to birth. 18

preoperational stage Piaget's second stage, lasting from 2 to 7 years of age, during which time children begin to represent the world with words, images, and drawings. In this stage, they also form stable concepts and begin to reason. At the same time, their cognitive world is dominated by egocentrism and magical beliefs. 283

prepared childbirth Method developed by French obstetrician Ferdinand Lamaze; this childbirth strategy is similar to natural childbirth but includes a special breathing technique to control pushing in the final stages of labor, and also a more detailed anatomy and physiology course. 121

pretense/symbolic play Play in which the child transforms the physical environment into a symbol. 342

preterm infants Babies born three weeks or more before the pregnancy has reached its full term. 126

primary circular reaction A scheme based on the attempt to reproduce an event that initially occurred by chance. 185

primary emotions Emotions that are present in humans and other animals, and emerge early in life; examples are joy, anger, sadness, fear, and disgust. 221

Project Head Start Compensatory education designed to provide children from low-income families the opportunity to acquire the skills and experiences important for school success. 302

proximodistal pattern The sequence in which growth starts at the center of the body and moves toward the extremities. 146

psychoanalytic theories Describe development as primarily unconscious and heavily colored by emotion. Behavior is merely a surface characteristic, and the symbolic workings of the mind have to be analyzed to understand behavior. Early experiences with parents are emphasized. 23

psychoanalytic theory of gender A theory deriving from Freud's view that the preschool child develops a sexual attraction to the opposite-sex parent, by approximately 5 or 6 years of age renounces this attraction because of anxious feelings, and subsequently identifies with the same-sex parent, unconsciously adopting the same-sex parent's characteristics. 322

psychosocial moratorium Erikson's term for the gap between childhood security and adult autonomy. 532

puberty A period of rapid physical maturation involving hormonal and bodily changes that occur primarily in early adolescence. 468

Public Law 94-142 The Education for All Handicapped Children Act, created in 1975, which requires that all children with disabilities be given a free, appropriate public education and which provides the funding to help with the costs of implementing this education. 374

R

rapport talk The language of conversation and a way of establishing connections and negotiating relationships; more characteristic of females than of males. 438

reciprocal socialization Socialization that is bidirectional; children socialize parents, just as parents socialize children. 239

reflexes Built-in reactions to stimuli that govern the newborn's movements, which are automatic and beyond the newborn's control. 161

reflexive smile A smile that does not occur in response to external stimuli. It happens during the month after birth, usually during sleep. 223

rejected children Children who are infrequently nominated as a best friend and are actively disliked by their peers. 444

report talk Talk that conveys information; more characteristic of males than females. 438

rite of passage A ceremony or ritual that marks an individual's transition from one status to another. Most rites of passage focus on the transition to adult status. 548

rooting reflex A newborn's built-in reaction that occurs when the infant's cheek is stroked or the side of the mouth is touched. In response, the infant turns its head toward the side that was touched in an apparent effort to find something to suck. 161

S

scaffolding In cognitive development, Vygotsky used this term to describe the changing level of support over the course of a teaching session, with the more-skilled person adjusting guidance to fit the child's current performance level. 240

scaffolding Parents time interactions so that infants experience turn-taking with the parents. 286

schemes In Piaget's theory, actions or mental representations that organize knowledge. 182, 186

scientific method An approach that can be used to obtain accurate information. It includes these steps: (1) conceptualize the problem, (2) collect data, (3) draw conclusions, and (4) revise research conclusions and theory. 22

secondary circular reactions Piaget's third sensorimotor substage, which develops between 4 and 8 months of age. In this substage, the infant becomes more object-oriented, moving beyond preoccupation with the self. 186

securely attached babies Babies that use the caregiver as a secure base from which to explore the environment. 234

self-concept Domain-specific evaluations of the self. 426

self-conscious emotions Emotions that require self-awareness, especially consciousness and a sense of "me"; examples include jealousy, empathy, and embarrassment. 222

self-efficacy The belief that one can master a situation and produce favorable outcomes. 412

self-esteem The global evaluative dimension of the self. Self-esteem is also referred to as self-worth or self-image. 426

self-understanding The child's cognitive representation of self, the substance and content of the child's self-conceptions. 315

semantics The meaning of words and sentences. 203

sensation The product of the interaction between information and the sensory receptors—the eyes, ears, tongue, nostrils, and skin. 166

sensorimotor play Behavior engaged in by infants to derive pleasure from exercising their existing sensorimotor schemas. 341

sensorimotor stage The first of Piaget's stages, which lasts from birth to about 2 years of age; infants construct an understanding of the world by coordinating sensory experiences with motoric actions. 184

separation protest An infant's distressed reaction when the caregiver leaves. 224

seriation The concrete operation that involves ordering stimuli along a quantitative dimension (such as length). 385

service learning A form of education that promotes social responsibility and service to the community. 507

sexually transmitted infections (STIs) Diseases that are contracted primarily through sexual contact. This contact is not limited to vaginal intercourse but includes oral-genital contact and anal-genital contact as well. 477

shape constancy The recognition that an object's shape remains the same even though its orientation to us changes. 170

shape stage Kellogg's term for 3-year-olds' drawings consisting of diagrams in different shapes. 262

shared environment experiences Siblings' common experiences, such as their parents' personalities and intellectual orientation, the family's socioeconomic status, and the neighborhood in which they live. 80

short-term memory The memory component in which individuals retain information for up to 30 seconds, assuming there is no rehearsal. 292

sickle-cell anemia A genetic disorder that affects the red blood cells and occurs most often in people of African descent. 69

simple reflexes Piaget's first sensorimotor substage, which corresponds to the first month after birth. In this substage, sensation and action are coordinated primarily through reflexive behaviors. 185

size constancy The recognition that an object remains the same even though the retinal image of the object changes as you move toward or away from the object. 170

slow-to-warm-up child A child who has a low activity level, is somewhat negative, and displays a low intensity of mood. 225

small for date (small for gestational age) infants Babies whose birth weight is below normal when the length of pregnancy is considered. 126

social cognitive theory The view of psychologists who emphasize behavior, environment, and cognition as the key factors in development. 30

social cognitive theory of gender A theory that emphasizes that children's gender development occurs through the observation and imitation of gender behavior and through the rewards and punishments children experience for gender-appropriate and gender-inappropriate behavior. 322

social constructivist approach An approach that emphasizes the social contexts of learning and the fact that knowledge is mutually built and constructed; Vygotsky's theory is a social constructivist approach. 289

social contract or utility and individual rights The fifth Kohlberg stage. At this stage, individuals reason that values, rights, and principles undergird or transcend the law. 431

social conventional reasoning Thoughts about social consensus and convention in order to control behavior and maintain the social system. 434

social play Play that involves social interactions with peers. 342

social policy A government's course of action designed to promote the welfare of its citizens. 12

social referencing "Reading" emotional cues in others to help determine how to act in a particular situation. 232

social role theory A theory that gender differences result from the contrasting roles of men and women. 322

social smile A smile in response to an external stimulus, which, early in development, typically is a face. 223

social systems morality The fourth stage in Kohlberg's theory of moral development. Moral judgments are based on understanding the social order, law, justice, and duty. 431

socioeconomic status (SES) An individual's position within society based on occupational, educational, and economic characteristics. 10

socioemotional processes Changes in an individual's relationships with other people, changes in emotions, and changes in personality. 17

somnambulism Sleep walking; occurs in the deepest stage of sleep. 266

standardized test A test with uniform procedures for administration and scoring. Many standardized tests allow a person's performance to be compared with the performance of other individuals. 36

Strange Situation An observational measure of infant attachment that requires the infant to move through a series of introductions, separations, and reunions with the caregiver and an adult stranger in a prescribed order. 234

stranger anxiety An infant's fear and wariness of strangers; it tends to appear in the second half of the first year of life. 223

strategies Deliberate mental activities to improve the processing of information. 294

sucking reflex A newborn's built-in reaction to automatically suck an object placed in its mouth. The sucking reflex enables the infant to get nourishment before he or she has associated a nipple with food and also serves as a self-soothing or self-regulating mechanism. 161

sudden infant death syndrome (SIDS) A condition that occurs when an infant stops breathing, usually during the night, and suddenly dies without an apparent cause. 151

sustained attention Focused and extended engagement with an object, task, event, or other aspect of the environment. 291

symbolic function substage Piaget's first substage of preoperational thought, in which the child gains the ability to mentally represent an object that is not present (occurs roughly between 2 and 4 years of age). 283

syntax The ways words are combined to form acceptable phrases and sentences. 203

T

tabula rasa view The idea, proposed by John Locke, that children are not innately bad but are like a "blank tablet." 14

telegraphic speech The use of content words without grammatical markers such as articles, auxiliary verbs, and other connectives. 206

temperament An individual's behavioral style and characteristic way of emotionally responding. 225

teratogen From the Greek word *tera*, meaning "monster," any agent that can potentially cause a physical birth defect. The field of study that investigates the causes of birth defects is called teratology. 101

tertiary circular reactions, novelty, and curiosity Piaget's fifth sensorimotor substage, which develops between 12 and 18 months of age. In this substage, infants become intrigued by the many properties of objects and by the many things that they can make happen to objects. 186

testosterone A hormone associated in boys with the development of genitals, an increase in height, and a change in voice. 470

theory An interrelated, coherent set of ideas that helps to explain and make predictions. 22

theory of mind A concept that refers to awareness of one's own mental processes and the mental processes of others. 294

top-dog phenomenon The circumstance of moving from the top position (in elementary school, the oldest, biggest, and most powerful students) to the lowest position (in middle or junior high school, the youngest, smallest, and least powerful students). 514

transitional objects Objects that children repeatedly use as bedtime companions. These usually are soft and cuddly and probably mark the child's transition from being dependent to being more independent. 264

transitivity The ability to logically combine relations to understand certain conclusions. 385

triarchic theory of intelligence Sternberg's theory that intelligence consists of analytical intelligence, creative intelligence, and practical intelligence. 396

trophoblast The outer layer of cells that develops in the germinal period. These cells later provide nutrition and support for the embryo. 89

Turner syndrome A chromosomal disorder in females in which either an X chromosome is missing, making the person XO instead of XX, or the second X chromosome is partially deleted. 69

twin study A study in which the behavioral similarity of identical twins is compared with the behavioral similarity of fraternal twins. 78

type 1 diabetes An autoimmune disease, in which the body's immune system destroys insulin-producing cells. 364

type 2 diabetes The most common type of diabetes, in which the body is able to produce insulin, but it may not be enough or the body cells may be unable to use it. 364

U

umbilical cord Contains two arteries and one vein, and connects the baby to the placenta. 90

universal ethical principles The sixth and highest stage in Kohlberg's theory of moral development. Individuals develop a moral standard based on universal human rights. 431

V

values Beliefs and attitudes about the way things should be. 507

values clarification An approach to moral education that emphasizes helping people clarify what their lives are for and what's worth working for. Students are encouraged to define their own values and to understand the values of others. 509

visual preference method A method used to determine whether infants can distinguish one stimulus from another by measuring the length of time they attend to different stimuli. 167

voice disorders Disorders reflected in speech that is hoarse, harsh, too loud, too high-pitched, or too low-pitched. 371

Vygotsky's theory A sociocultural cognitive theory that emphasizes how culture and social interaction guide cognitive development. 28

W

Wernicke's area An area of the brain's left hemisphere that is involved in language comprehension. 206

whole-language approach An approach to reading instruction based on the idea that instruction should parallel children's natural language learning. Reading materials should be whole and meaningful. 407

X

XYY syndrome A chromosomal disorder in which males have an extra Y chromosome. 69

Z

zone of proximal development (ZPD) Vygotsky's term for the range of tasks that are too difficult for children to achieve alone and what they can achieve with the guidance and assistance of adults or more-skilled children. 286

zygote A single cell formed through fertilization. 65

REFERENCES

A

ABC News. (2005, December 12). Larry Page and Sergey Brim. Retrieved February 15, 2006, from http://abcnews.go.com?Entertainment/12/8/05

Aber, J. L., Bishop-Josef, S. J., Jones, S. M., McLern, T., & Phillips, D. A. (2006). *Child development and social policy.* Washington, DC: American Psychological Association.

Abruscato, J. A., & DeRosa, D. A. (2010). *Teaching children science: A discovery approach* (7th ed.). Boston: Allyn & Bacon.

Accornero, V. H., Amado, A. J., Morrow, C. E., Xue, L., Anthony, J. C., & Bandstra, E. S. (2007). Impact of prenatal cocaine exposure on attention and response inhibition as assessed by continuous performance tests. *Journal of Developmental and Behavioral Pediatrics, 28,* 195–205.

Adamson, L., & Frick, J. (2003). The still face: A history of a shared experimental paradigm. *Infancy, 4,* 451–473.

Adi-Japha, E., Landau, Y. E., Frenkel, L., Ticher, M., Gross-Tsur, V., & Shalev, R. S. (2007). ADHD and dysgraphia: underlying mechanisms. *Cortex, 43,* 700–709.

Administration for Children and Families. (2008). *Statistical fact sheet fiscal year 2008.* Washington, DC: Author.

Adolph, K. E. (1997). Learning in the development of infant locomotion. *Monographs of the Society for Research in Child Development, 62* (3, Serial No. 251).

Adolph, K. E. (2008). Motor and physical development: Locomotion. In M. M. Haith & J. B. Benson (Eds.), *Encyclopedia of infant and early childhood development.* Oxford, UK: Elsevier.

Adolph, K. E. (2009). Perceptual learning. Retrieved May 10, 2009, from http://www.psych.nyu.edu/adolph/research1.php

Adolph, K. E., & Berger, S. E. (2005). Physical and motor development. In M. H. Bornstein & M. E. Lamb (Eds.), *Developmental psychology* (5th ed.). Mahwah, NJ: Erlbaum.

Adolph, K. E., & Joh, A. S. (2009). Multiple learning mechanisms in the development of action. In A. Needham & A. Woodward (Eds.), *Learning and the infant mind.* New York: Oxford University Press.

Adolph, K. E., Karasik, L. B., & Tamis-LeMonda, C. S. (2010). Moving between cultures: Cross-cultural research on motor development. In M. Bornstein & L. R. Cote (Eds.), *Handbook of cross-cultural developmental science: Vol. 1, Domains of development across, cultures.* Clifton, NJ: Psychology Press.

Adolph, K. E., Vereijken, B., & Shrout, P. E. (2003). What changes in infant walking and why. *Child Development, 74,* 475–497.

Agency for Healthcare Research and Quality. (2007). *Evidence report/technology assessment number 153: Breastfeeding and maternal and health outcomes in developed countries.* Rockville, MD: U.S. Department of Health and Human Services.

Agras, W. S., Hammer, L. D., McNicholas, F., & Kraemer, H. C. (2004). Risk factors for childhood overweight: A prospective study from birth to 9.5 years. *Journal of Pediatrics, 145,* 20–25.

Agras, W. S., & others. (2004). Report of the National Institutes of Health workshop on overcoming barriers to treatment research in anorexia nervosa. *International Journal of Editing Disorders, 35,* 509–521.

Ahamed, M., Verma, S., Kumar, A., & Siddiqui, M. K. (2005). Environmental exposure to lead and its correlation with biochemical indices in children. *Science of the Total Environment, 346,* 48–55.

Ahluwalia, I. B., Tessaro, I., Grumer-Strawn, L. M., MacGowan, C., & Benton-Davis, S. (2000). Georgia's breastfeeding promotion program for low-income women. *Pediatrics, 105,* E85–E87.

Ahrens, B., Beyer, K., Wahn, U., & Niggemann, B. (2008). Differential diagnosis of food-induced symptoms. *Pediatric Allergy and Immunology, 19,* 92–96.

Ahrons, C. (2004). *We're still family.* New York: HarperCollins.

Ahrons, C. R. (2007). Family ties after divorce: Long-term implications for children. *Family Process, 46,* 53–65.

Ainsworth, M. D. S. (1979). Infant-mother attachment. *American Psychologist, 34,* 932–937.

Akcan, E., Yigit, R., & Atici, A. (2009). The effect of kangaroo care on pain in premature infants during invasive procedures. *Turkish Journal of Pediatrics, 51,* 14–18.

Akhtar, N., & Herold, K. (2008). Pragmatic development. In M. M. Haith & J. B. Benson (Eds.), *Encyclopedia of infant and early childhood development.* Oxford, UK: Elsevier.

Alan Guttmacher Institute. (1998). *Teen sex and pregnancy.* New York: Author.

Alario, A., & Birnkrant, J. (2008). *Practical guide to the care of the pediatric patient* (2nd ed.). Oxford, UK: Elsevier.

Alberts, A., Elkind, D., & Ginsberg, S. (2007). The personal fable and risk-taking in early adolescence. *Journal of Youth and Adolescence, 36,* 71–76.

Allen, E. G., Freeman, S. B., Druschel, C., Hobbs, C. A., O'Leary, L. A., Romitti, P. A., Royle, M. H., Torfs, C. P., & Sherman, S. L. (2009, in press). Maternal age and risk for trisomy 21 assessed by the origin of chromosome nondisjunction: A report from the Atlanta and National Down Syndrome Projects. *Human Genetics.*

Allen, J. P. (2007, March). *A transformational perspective on the attachment system in adolescence.* Paper presented at the meeting of the Society for Research in Child Development, Boston.

Allen, J. P. (2008). The attachment system in adolescence. In J. Cassidy & P. R. Shaver (Eds.), *Handbook of attachment* (2nd ed.). New York: Guilford.

Allen, J. P., & others. (2009, April). *Portrait of the secure teen as an adult: Predictions from attachment to family, peer, and romantic relationship functioning.* Paper presented at the meeting of the Society for Research in Child Development, Denver.

Allen, J. P., Philliber, S., Herring, S., & Kuperminc, G. P. (1997). Preventing teen pregnancy and academic failure: Experimental evaluation of a developmentally-based approach. *Child Development, 68,* 729–742.

Allen, J. P., Porter, M., McFarland, C., McElhaney, K., & Marsh, P. (2007). The relation of attachment security to adolescents' paternal and peer relationships, depression, and externalizing behavior. *Child Development, 78,* 1222–12239.

Allen, K. L., Byrne, S. M., McLean, N. J., & Davis, E. A. (2008). Overconcern with weight and shape is not the same as body dissatisfaction: Evidence from a prospective study of pre-adolescent boys and girls. *Body Image, 5,* 261–270.

Allen, M., Svetaz, M. V., Hardeman, R., & Resnick, M. D. (2008, February). *What research tells us about parenting practices and their relationship to youth sexual behavior.* Campaign to Prevent Teen and Unplanned Pregnancy. Retrieved December 2, 2008, from *www.TheNationalCampaign.org*

Alm, B., Lagercrantz, H., & Wennergren, G. (2006). Stop SIDS—sleeping solitary supine, sucking soother, stopping smoking substitutes. *Acta Paediatrica, 95,* 260–262.

Als, H., & Butler, S. C. (2008). Screening, newborn, and maternal well-being. In M. M. Haith & J. B. Benson (Eds.), *Encyclopedia of infant and early childhood development.* Oxford, UK: Elsevier.

Altarac, M., & Saroha, E. (2007). Lifetime prevalence of learning disability among U.S. children. *Pediatrics, 119,* (Suppl 1), S77–S83.

Altimer, L. (2008). Shaken baby syndrome. *Journal of Perinatal and Neonatal Nursing, 22,* 68–76.

Alvarez, A., & del Rio, P. (2007). Inside and outside the zone of proximal development. In H. Daniels, J. Wertsch, & M. Cole (Eds.), *The Cambridge companion to Vygotsky.* New York: Cambridge University Press.

Amabile, T. (1993). Commentary. In D. Goleman, P. Kaufman, & M. Ray (Eds.), *The creative spirit.* New York: Plume.

Amabile, T. M., & Hennessey, B. A. (1992). The motivation for creativity in children. In A. K. Boggiano & T. S. Pittman (Eds.), *Achievement and motivation.* New York: Cambridge University Press.

Amato, P. R. (2006). Marital discord, divorce, and children's well-being: Results from a 20-year longitudinal study of two generations. In A. Clarke-Stewart & J. Dunn (Eds.), *Families count.* New York: Cambridge University Press.

Amato, P. R., & Booth, A. (1996). A prospective study of divorce and parent-child relationships. *Journal of Marriage and the Family, 58,* 356–365.

Amato, P. R., & Irving, S. (2006). Historical trends in divorce and dissolution. In M. A. Fine & J. H. Harvey (Eds.), *Handbook of divorce and relationship dissolution.* Mahwah, NJ: Erlbaum.

American Academy of Pediatrics. (2001). Falls from heights: Windows, roofs, and balconies. *Pediatrics, 107,* 1188–1191.

American Academy of Pediatrics Task Force on Infant Positioning and SIDS (AAPTFIPS). (2000). Changing concepts of sudden infant death syndrome. *Pediatrics, 105,* 650–656.

American Academy of Pediatrics Work Group on Breastfeeding (AAPWGB). (1997). Breastfeeding and the use of human milk. *Pediatrics, 100,* 1035–1039.

American College of Obstetricians and Gynecologists. (2008). *Exercise during pregnancy.* Retrieved October 13, 2008, from www.acog.org/publications/patienteducation/bp119.cfm

American Psychological Association. (2003). *Psychology: Scientific problem solvers.* Washington. DC: Author.

American Public Health Association. (2006). *Understanding the health culture of recent immigrants to the United States.* Retrieved July 28, 2006, from www.apha.org/ppp/red/Intro.htm.

Amsterdam, B. K. (1968). *Mirror behavior in children under two years of age.* Unpublished doctoral dissertation. University of North Carolina, Chapel Hill.

Amuna, P., & Zotor, F. B. (2008). Epidemiological and nutrition transition in developing countries: Impact on human health and development. *Proceedings of the Nutrition Society, 67,* 82–90.

Anastasi, A., & Urbina, S. (1997). *Psychological testing* (11th ed.). Upper Saddle River, NJ: Prentice Hall.

Anderman, E. M., & Mueller, C. E. (2010). Middle school transitions and adolescent development: Disentangling psychological, social, and biological effects. In J. Meece & J. Eccles (Eds.), *Handbook of research on schools, schooling, and human development.* Clifton, NJ: Psychology Press.

Anderman, E. M., & Murdock, T. B. (Eds.). (2007). *Psychology of academic cheating.* San Diego: Academic Press.

Anderson, B. L., & Cu-Uvin, S. (2009, in press). Pregnancy and optimal care of HIV-infected infants. *Clinical Infectious Diseases.*

Anderson, B. M., & others. (2009). Examination of associations of genes in the serotonin system to autism. *Neurogenetics, 10,* 209–216.

Anderson, D. R., Huston, A. C., Schmitt, K., Linebarger, D. L., & Wright, J. C. (2001). Early childhood viewing and adolescent behavior: The recontact study. *Monographs of the Society for Research in Child Development, 66* (1, Serial No. 264).

Anderson, D. R., Lorch, E. P., Field, D. E., Collins, P. A., & Nathan, J. G. (1985, April). *Television viewing at home: Age trends in visual attention and time with TV.* Paper presented at the biennial meeting of the Society for Research in Child Development, Toronto.

Anderson, E., Greene, S. M., Hetherington, E. M., & Clingempeel, W. G. (1999). The dynamics of parental remarriage. In E. M. Hetherington (Ed.), *Coping with divorce, single parenting, and remarriage.* Mahwah, NJ: Erlbaum.

Anderson, J. L., Waller, D. K., Canfield, M. A., Shaw, G. M., Watkins, M. L., & Werler, M. M. (2005). Maternal obesity, gestational diabetes, and central nervous system birth defects. *Epidemiology, 16,* 87–92.

Andrews, K. M., Brouilette, D. B., & Brouilette, R. T. (2008). Mortality, infant. In M. M. Haith & J. B. Benson (Eds.), *Encyclopedia of infant and early childhood development.* Oxford, UK: Elsevier.

Antonarakis, S. E. (2009). Whole genome association studies: What have we learned and where do we go from here? *Annual Review of Genomics and Human Genetics* (Vol. 10). Palo Alto, CA: Annual Reviews.

Appleton, J. V., & Stanley, N. (2009). Editorial: Childhood outcomes. *Child Abuse Review, 18,* 1–5.

Ara, I., Vicente-Rodriguez, G., Jimenez-Ramirez, J., Dorado, C., Serrano-Sanchez, J. A., & Calbet, J. A. (2004). Regular participation in sports is associated with enhanced physical fitness and lower body mass in prepubertal boys. *International Journal of Obesity and Related Metabolic Disorders. 28,* 1585–1593.

Archibald, A. B., Graber, J. A., & Brooks-Gunn, J. (2003). Pubertal processes and physical growth in adolescence. In G. R. Adams & M. Berzonsky (Eds.), *Blackwell Handbook of adolescence.* Malden, MA: Blackwell.

Archibald, A. B., Graeber, J. A., & Brooks-Gunn, J. (1999). Associations among parent-adolescent relationships, pubertal growth, dieting, and body image in young adolescent girls: A short-term longitudinal study. *Journal of Research on Adolescence, 9,* 395–415.

Arditi, H., Feldman, R., Hammerman, C., & Eidelman, A. I. (2008). Cerebral blood flow velocity asymmetry, neurobehavioral maturation, and the cognitive development of premature infants across the first two years. *Journal of Developmental and Behavioral Pediatrics, 28,* 362–368.

Arehart, D. M., & Smith, P. H. (1990). Identity in adolescence: Influences on dysfunction and psychosocial task issues. *Journal of Youth and Adolescence, 19,* 63–72.

Ariceli, G., Castro, J., Cesena, J., & Toro, J. (2005). Anorexia nervosa in male adolescents: Body image, eating attitudes, and psychological traits. *Journal of Adolescent Health, 36,* 221–226.

Ariès, P. (1962). *Centuries of childhood* (R. Baldric, Trans.). New York: Knopf.

Armstrong, D. G., Henson, K. T., & Savage, T. V. (2009). *Teaching today* (8th ed.). Boston: Allyn & Bacon.

Arnett, J. J. (2000). Emerging adulthood. *American Psychologist, 55,* 469–480.

Arnett, J. J. (2006). Emerging adulthood: Understanding the new way of coming of age. In J. J. Arnett & J. L. Tanner (Eds.), *Emerging adults in America.* Washington, DC: American Psychological Association.

Arnett, J. J. (2007). Socialization in emerging adulthood. In J. E. Grusec & P. D. Hastings (Eds.), *Handbook of socialization.* New York: Guilford.

Aronowitz, T., Rennels, R. E., & Todd, E. (2006). Ecological influences of sexuality on early adolescent African American females. *Journal of Community Mental Health, 23,* 113–122.

Aronson, E. (1986, August). *Teaching students things they think they already know about: The case of prejudice and desegregation.* Paper presented at the meeting of the American Psychological Association, Washington, DC.

Arora, S. (2009). Kangaroo mother care. *Nursing Journal of India, 99,* 248–250.

Arredondo, E. M., Elder, J. P., Ayala, G. X., Campbell, N., Baquero, B., & Duerksen, S.

(2006). Is parenting style related to children's healthy eating and physical activity in Latino families? *Health Education Research, 21,* 862–871.

Arria, A. M., & others. (2006). Methamphetamine and other substance use during pregnancy: Preliminary estimates from the Infant Development, Environment, and Lifestyle (IDEAL) Study. *Maternal and Child Health Journal, 5,* 1–10.

Arseneault, L., Milne, B. J., Taylor, A., Adams, F., Delgado, K., Caspi, A., & Moffit, T. E. (2008). Being bullied as an environmentally mediated contributing factor to children's internalizing problems: A study of twins discordant for victimization. *Archives of Pediatric and Adolescent Medicine, 162,* 145–150.

Arterberry, M. E. (2008). Perceptual development. In M. M. Haith & J. B. Benson (Eds.), *Encyclopedia of infant and early childhood development.* Oxford, UK: Elsevier.

Artiles, A. J., Rueda, R., Salazar, J. J., & Higareda, I. (2005). Within-group diversity in minority disproportionate representation: English Language Learners in urban school districts. *Exceptional Children, 71,* 283–300.

Asendorph, J. B. (2008). Shyness. In M. M. Haith & J. B. Benson (Eds.), *Encyclopedia of infant and early childhood development.* Oxford, UK: Elsevier.

Ash, P. (2006). Adolescents in adult court: Does the punishment fit the criminal? *The Journal of the American Academy of Psychiatry and the Law, 34,* 145–149.

Ash, P. (2008). Suicidal behavior in children and adolescents. *Journal of Psychosocial Nursing and Mental Health Services, 46,* 26–30.

Asher, S. R., & McDonald, K. L. (2009). The behavioral basis of acceptance, rejection, and perceived popularity. In K. H. Rubin, W. M., Bukowski, & B. Laursen (Eds.), *Handbook of peer interactions, relationships, and groups.* New York: Guilford.

Aslin, R. N. (2009). The role of learning in cognitive development. In A. Woodward & A. Needham (Eds.), *Learning and the infant mind.* New York: Oxford University Press.

Aslin, R. N., Jusczyk, P. W., & Pisoni, D. B. (1998). Speech and auditory processing during infancy: Constraints on and precursors to language. In W. Damon (Ed.), *Handbook of child psychology* (5th ed., Vol. 2). New York: Wiley.

Aslin, R. N., & Lathrop, A. L. (2008). Visual perception. In M. M. Haith & J. B. Benson (Eds.), *Encyclopedia of infant and early childhood development.* Oxford, UK: Elsevier.

Assanand, S., Dias, M., Richardson, E., & Waxler-Morrison, N. (1990). The South Asians. In N. Waxler-Morrison, J. M. Anderson, & E. Richardson (Eds.), *Cross-cultural caring.* Vancouver, BC: UBC Press.

Astington, J. W., & Dack, L. A. (2008). Theory of mind. In M. M. Haith & J. B. Benson (Eds.), *Encyclopedia of infant and early childhood development.* Oxford, UK: Elsevier.

Astrom, R. L., Wadsworth, S. J., & DeFries, J. C. (2007). Etiology of the stability of reading difficulties: The longitudinal twin study of reading disabilities. *Twin Research and Human Genetics, 10,* 434–439.

Ata, R. N., Ludden, A. B., & Lally, M. M. (2007). The effect of gender and family, friend, and media influences on eating behaviors and body image during adolescence. *Journal of Youth and Adolescence, 36,* 1024–1037.

Attie, I., Brooks-Gunn, J. (1989). Development of eating problems in adolescent girls: A longitudinal study. *Developmental Psychology, 25,* 70–79.

Aucoin, K. J., Frick, P. J., & Bodin, S. D. (2006). Corporal punishment and child adjustment. *Journal of Applied Developmental Psychology, 27,* 527–541.

Auyeung, B., Baron-Cohen, S., Ashwin, E., Knikmeyer, R., Taylor, K., Hackett, G., & Hines, M. (2009). Fetal testosterone predicts sexually differentiated childhood behavior in girls and in boys. *Psychological Science, 20,* 144–148.

Avent, N. D., Plummer, Z. E., Madgett, T. E., Maddocks, D. G., & Soothill, P. W. (2008). Post-genomic studies and their application to non-invasive prenatal diagnosis. *Seminars in Fetal and Neonatal Medicine, 13,* 19–98.

Axelrad, D. A., Bellinger, D. C., Ryan, L. M., Woodruff, T. J. (2007). Dose-response relationship of prenatal mercury exposure and IQ: An integrative analysis of epidemiologic data. *Environmental Health Perspectives, 115,* 609–615.

Azmitia, M., Syed, M., & Radmacher, K. (2008). On the intersection of personal and social identities: Introduction and evidence from a longitudinal study of emerging adults. *New Directions for Child and Adolescent Development, 120,* 1–16.

B

Bachman, J. G., O'Malley, P. M., Schulenberg, J. E., Johnston, L. D., Freedman-Doan, P., & Messersmith, E. E. (2008). *The education-drug connection.* New York: Psychology Press.

Badaly, D., & Adolph, K. E. (2008). Beyond the average: Walking infants take steps longer than their leg length. *Infant Behavior and Development, 31,* 554–558.

Baddeley, A. (1992). Working memory. *Science, 255,* 556–560.

Baddeley, A. (2000). Short-term and working memory. In E. Tulving & F. I. M. Craik (Eds.), *The Oxford handbook of memory.* New York: Oxford University Press.

Baddeley, A. D. (2007). Working memory. In H. Roediger, Y. Dudai, & S. M. Fitzgerald (Eds.), *Science of memory.* New York: Oxford University Press.

Baddock, S. A., Galland, B. C., Taylor, B. J., & Bolton, D. P. (2007). Sleep arrangements and behavior of bed-sharing families in the home setting. *Pediatrics, 119,* e200–e2007.

Baggerly, J. (2008). School counseling. In N. J. Salkind (Ed.), *Encyclopedia of educational psychology.* Thousand Oaks, CA: Sage.

Bahrick, L. E., & Hollich, G. (2008). Intermodal perception. In M. M. Haith & J. B. Benson (Eds.), *Encyclopedia of infant and early childhood development.* Oxford, UK: Elsevier.

Baillargeon, R. (1995). The object concept revisited: New directions in the investigation of infants' physical knowledge. In C. E. Granrud (Ed.), *Visual perception and cognition in infancy.* Hillsdale, NJ: Erlbaum.

Baillargeon, R. (2004). The acquisition of physical knowledge in infancy: A summary in eight lessons. In U. Goswami (Ed.), *Blackwell handbook of childhood cognitive development.* Malden, MA: Blackwell.

Baillargeon, R. (2008). Innate ideas revisited: For a principle of persistence in infants' physical reasoning. *Perspectives on Psychological Science, 3,* 2–13.

Baillargeon, R., & DeVos, J. (1991). Object permanence in young children: Further evidence. *Child Development, 62,* 1227–1246.

Baillargeon, R., Li, J., Ng, W., & Yuan, S. (2009). A new account of infants' physical reasoning. In A. Woodward & A. Needham (Eds.), *Learning and the infant mind.* New York: Oxford University Press.

Baillargeon, R. H., Zoccolillo, M., Keenna, K., Cote, S., Perusse, D., Wu, H-X., Boivin, M., & Tremblay, R. E. (2007). Gender differences in physical aggression: A prospective population-based survey of children before and after two years of age. *Developmental Psychology, 43,* 13–26.

Bajanowski, T., Brinkmann, B, Mitchell, E. A., Vennemann, M. M., Leukel, H. W., Larsch, K. P., Beike, J., & the GeSID Group. (2007). Nicotine and cotinine in infants dying from sudden infant death syndrome. *International Journal of Legal Medicine, 122,* 23–28

Bakeman, R., & Brown, J. V. (1980). Early interaction: Consequences for social and mental development at three years. *Child Development, 51,* 437–447.

Bakermans-Kranenburg, M. J., Breddels-Van Bardewijk, F., Juffer, M. K., Velderman, M. H., & van IJzendoorn, M. H. (2007). Insecure mothers with temperamentally reactive infants. In F. Juffer, M. J. Bakermans-Kranenburg, & M. H. van IJzendoorn (Eds.), *Promoting positive parenting.* Mahwah, NJ: Erlbaum.

Balasubramanian, A., Koontz, J., & Reynolds, C. A. (2008). Genetics and inheritance. In M. M. Haith & J. B. Benson (Eds.), *Encyclopedia of infant and early childhood development.* Oxford, UK: Elsevier.

Balchin, I., & Steer, P. J. (2007). Race, prematurity, and immaturity. *Early Human Development, 83,* 749–754.

Bales, K. L., & Carter, C. S. (2009). Neuroendocrine mechanisms of social bonds and child-parent attachment, from the child's perspective. In M. de Haan & M. R. Gunnar (Eds.), *Handbook* *of developmental social neuroscience.* New York: Guilford.

Ballentine, J. H., & Hammock, F. H. (2009). *The sociology of education* (6th ed.). Upper Saddle River, NJ: Prentice Hall.

Balsano, A. B., Theokas, C., & Bobek, D. L. (2009). A shared commitment to youth: The integration of theory, research, and policy. In R. M. Lerner & L. Steinberg (Eds.), *Handbook of adolescent psychology* (3rd ed.). New York: Wiley.

Baltes, P. B. (2009). Aging and wisdom. In D. C. Park & N. Schwarz (Eds.), *Cognitive aging* (2nd ed.). Clifton, NJ: Psychology Press.

Bandura, A. (1997). *Self-efficacy: The exercise of control.* New York: W. H. Freeman.

Bandura, A. (1998, August). *Swimming against the mainstream: Accentuating the positive aspects of humanity.* Paper presented at the meeting of the American Psychological Association, San Francisco.

Bandura, A. (1999). Moral disengagement in the perpetuation of inhumanities. *Personality and Social Psychology Review, 3,* 193–209.

Bandura, A. (2001). Social cognitive theory. *Annual Review of Psychology* (Vol. 52). Palo Alto, CA: Annual Reviews.

Bandura, A. (2002). Selective moral disengagement in the exercise of moral agency. *Journal of Moral Education, 31,* 101–119.

Bandura, A. (2004, May). *Toward a psychology of human agency.* Paper presented at the meeting of the American Psychological Society, Chicago.

Bandura, A. (2007). Social cognitive theory. In W. Donsbach (Ed.), *International encyclopedia of communication.* Thousand Oaks, CA: Sage.

Bandura, A. (2008). Reconstrual of "free will" from the agentic perspective of social cognitive theory. In J. Baer, J. C. Kaufman & R. F. Baumeister (Eds.), *Are we free?: Psychology and free will.* Oxford, UK: Oxford University Press.

Bandura, A. (2009, in press). Social and policy impact of social cognitive theory. In M. Mark, S. Donaldson & B. Campell (Eds.), *Social psychology and program/policy evaluation.* New York: Guilford.

Bandura, A. (2010). Self-efficacy. In D. Matsumoto (ed.). *Cambridge dictionary of psychology.* New York: Cambridge University Press.

Bank, L., Burraston, B., & Snyder, J. (2004). Sibling conflict and ineffective parenting as predictors of adolescent boys' antisocial behavior and peer difficulties: Additive and interactive effects. *Journal of Research on Adolescence, 14,* 99–125.

Banks, J. A. (2008). *Introduction to multicultural education* (4th ed.). Boston: Allyn & Bacon.

Banks, J. A. (ed.) (2010). *Routledge international companion to multicultural eduction.* New York: Routledge.

Banks, M. S. (2005). The benefits and costs of combining information between and within the senses. In J. J. Reiser, J. J. Lockman, & C. A.

Nelson (Eds.), *The role of action in learning and development.* Mahwah, NJ: Erlbaum.

Barabasaz, A., & Perez, N. (2007). Salient findings: Hypnotizability as core construct and the clinical utility of hypnosis. *International Journal of Clinical Hypnosis, 55,* 372–379.

Barajas, R. G., Philipsen, N., & Brooks-Gunn, J. (2008). Cognitive and emotional outcomes for children living in poverty. In D. R. Crane & T. B. Heaton (Eds.), *Handbook of families and poverty.* Thousand Oaks, CA: Sage.

Barakat, R., Ruiz, J. R., & Lucia, A. (2009, in press). Exercise during pregnancy and risk of maternal anemia: A randomized controlled trial. *British Journal of Sports Medicine.*

Baren, J., Rothrock, S., Brennan, J., & Brown, L. (2008). *Pediatric emergency medicine.* Oxford, UK: Elsevier.

Barker, R., & Wright, H. F. (1951), *One boy's day.* New York: Harper & Row.

Baron-Cohen, S. (1995). *Mindblindness: An essay on autism and theory of mind.* Cambridge, MA: MIT Press.

Baron-Cohen, S. (2008). Autism, hypersystemizing, and truth. *Quarterly Journal of Experimental Psychology, 61,* 64–75.

Baron-Cohen, S., Golan, O., Chapman, E., & Granader, Y. (2007). Transported to a world of emotion. *The Psychologist, 20,* 76–77.

Baron, N. S. (1992). *Growing up with language.* Reading, MA: Addison-Wesley.

Barrett, D. E., Radke-Yarrow, M., & Klein, R. E. (1982). Chronic malnutrition and child behavior: Effects of calorie supplementation on social and emotional functioning at school age. *Developmental Psychology, 18,* 541–556.

Barrett, L. F., Mesquita, B., Ochsner, K. N., & Gross, J. J. (2007). The experience of emotion. *Annual Review of Psychology* (Vol. 58). Palo Alto, CA: Annual Reviews.

Barrett, T. M., Davis, E. F., & Needham, A. (2007). Learning about tools in infancy. *Developmental Psychology, 43,* 352–368.

Barrett, T. M., & Needham, A. (2008). Developmental differences in infants' use of an object's shape to grasp it securely. *Developmental Psychobiology, 50,* 97–106.

Barrett, T. M., Traupman, E., & Needham, A. (2008). Infant's visual anticipation of object structure in grasp planning. *Infant Behavior and Development, 31,* 1–9.

Barron, J., Petrilli, F., Strath, L., & McCaffrey, R. (2007). Successful interventions for smoking cessation in pregnancy. *MCN American Journal of Maternal Child Nursing, 32,* 42–47.

Barry, R. A., Kochanska, G., & Philibert, R. A. (2008). G × E interaction in the organization of attachment: Mothers' responsiveness as a moderator of children's genotypes. *Journal of Child Psychology and Psychiatry, 49,* 1313–1320.

Bartle, C. (2007). Developing a service for children with iron deficiency anemia. *Nursing Standard, 21,* 44–49.

Bartsch, K., & Wellman, H. M. (1995). *Children talk about the mind.* Oxford University Press.

Bart, W. M., & Peterson, D. P. (2008). Standford-Binet test. In N. J. Salkind (Ed.), *Encyclopedia of educational psychology.* Thousand Oaks, CA: Sage.

Basaran, S., Guler-Uysal, F., Ergen, N., Seydaoglu, G., Bingol-Karakoe, G., & Ufuk Altintas, D. (2006). Effects of physical exercise on quality of life, exercise capacity, and pulmonary function in children with asthma. *Journal of Rehabilitation Medicine and Science, 38,* 130–135.

Basatemur, E., & Sutcliffe, A. (2008). Follow-up of children born after ART. *Placenta, 29* (Suppl. B), 135–140.

Bass, J. E., Contant, T. L., & Carin, A. A. (2009). *Activities for teaching science as inquiry* (7th ed.). Boston: Allyn & Bacon.

Bateman, B. T., & Simpson, L. L. (2006). Higher rate of stillbirth at the extremes of reproductive age: A large nationwide sample of deliveries in the United States. *American Journal of Obstetrics and Gynecology, 194,* 840–845.

Bates, E. (1990). Language about me and you: Pronomial reference and the emerging concept of self. In D. Cicchetti & M. Beeghly (Eds.), *The self in transition: Infancy to childhood.* Chicago: University of Chicago Press.

Bates, J. E. (2008). Unpublished review of J. W. Santrock's *Children,* 11th ed. (New York: McGraw-Hill).

Bates, J. E., & Pettit, G. S. (2007). Temperament, parenting, and socialization. In J. E. Grusec & P. D. Hastings (Eds.), *Handbook of socialization.* New York: Guilford.

Bates, J. E., Viken, R. J., Alexander, D. B., Beyers, J., & Stockton, L. (2002). Sleep and adjustment in preschool children: Sleep diary reports by mothers relate to behavior reports by teachers. *Child Development, 73,* 62–74.

Battistich, V. A. (2008). The Child Development Project: Creating caring school communities. In L. Nucci & D. Narváez (Eds.), *Handbook of moral and character education.* Clifton. NJ: Psychology Press.

Bauer. P. J. (2007). *Remembering the times of our lives.* Mahwah, NJ: Erlbaum.

Bauer, P. J. (2009). Learning and memory: Like a horse and carriage. In A. Netdham & A. Woodward (Eds.), *Learning and the infant mind.* New York: Oxford University Press.

Bauer, P. J., Wenner, J. A., Dropik, P. I., & Wewerka, S. S. (2000). Parameters of remembering and forgetting in the transition from infancy to early childhood. *Monographs of the Society for Research in Child Development, 65* (4, Serial No. 263).

Bauer, P. J., Wiebe, S. A., Carver, L. J., Waters, J. M., & Nelson, C. A. (2003). Developments in long-term explicit memory late in the first year of life: Behavioral and electrophysiological indices. *Psychological Science, 14,* 629–635.

Bauman, K. E., Ennett, S. T., Foshee, V. A., Pemberton, M., King. T. S., & Koch, G. G.

(2002). Influence of a family program on adolescent smoking and drinking prevalence. *Prevention Science, 3,* 35–42.

Baumeister, R. F., Campbell, J. D., Krueger, J. I., & Vohs, K. D. (2003). Does high self-esteem cause better performance, interpersonal success, happiness, or healthier lifestyles? *Psychological Science in the Public Interest, 4* (1), 1–44.

Baumrind, D. (1971). Current patterns of parental authority. *Developmental Psychology Monographs, 4* (1, Pt. 2).

Bauserman, R. (2002). Child adjustment in joint-custody versus sole-custody arrangements: A meta-analytic review. *Journal of Family Psychology, 16,* 91–102.

Baxley, F., & Miller, M. (2006). Parental misperceptions about children and firearms. *Archives of Pediatric and Adolescent Medicine, 160,* 542–547.

Bayley, N. (1969). *Manual for the Bayley Scales of Infant Development.* New York: Psychological Corporation.

Bayley, N. (1970). Development of mental abilities. In P. H. Mussen (Ed.), *Manual of child psychology* (3rd ed., Vol. 1). New York: Wiley.

Bayley, N. (2005). *Bayley Scales of Infant and Toddler Development—Third Edition (Bayley-III).* Upper Saddle River, NJ: Pearson.

Bear, D. R., Invemizzi, M., Johnston, F., & Templeton, S. (2010). *Words their way* (2nd ed.). Boston: Allyn & Bacon.

Bearman, P. S., & Moody, J. (2004). Suicide and friendships among American adolescents. *American Journal of Public Health, 94,* 89–95.

Bearman, S. K., Presnall, K., Martinez, E., & Stice, E. (2006). The skinny on body dissatisfaction: A longitudinal study of adolescent girls and boys. *Journal of Youth and Adolescence, 35,* 217–229.

Beaty, L. A., & Alexeyev, E. B. (2008, Spring). The problem of school bullies: What the research tells us. *Adolescence, 43,* 1–11.

Bechtold, A. G., Busnell, E. W., & Salapatek, P. (1979, April). *Infants' visual localization of visual and auditory targets.* Paper presented at the meeting of the Society for Research in Child Development, San Francisco.

Beck, C. T. (2002). Theoretical perspectives of postpartum depression and their treatment implications. *American Journal of Maternal/Child Nursing, 27,* 282–287.

Beck, C. T. (2006). Postpartum depression: It isn't just the blues. *American Journal of Nursing, 106,* 40–50.

Beckmann, M. M., & Garrett, A. J. (2006). Antenatal perineal massage for reducing perineal trauma. *Cochrane Database of Systematic Reviews, 1,* CD005123.

Bednar, R. L., Wells, M. G., & Peterson, S. R. (1995). *Self-esteem* (2nd ed.). Washington, DC: American Psychological Association.

Beeghly, M., Martin, B., Rose-Jacobs, R., Cahral, H., Heeren, T., Augustyn, M.,

Bellinger, D., & Frank, D. A. (2006). Prenatal cocaine exposure and children's language functioning at 6 and 9.5 years: Moderating effects of child age, birthweight, and gender. *Journal of Pediatric Psychology, 31,* 98–115.

Beets, M. W., & Foley, J. T. (2008). Association of father involvement and neighborhood quality with kindergartners' physical activity: A multilevel structural equation model. *American Journal of Health Promotion, 22,* 195–203.

Begum, E. A., Bonno, M., Ohtani, N., Yamashita, S., Tanaka, S., Yamamoto, H., Kawai, M., & Komada, Y. (2008). Cerebral oxygenation responses during kangaroo care in low birth weight infants. *BMC Pediatrics, 8,* 51.

Beilin, L., & Huang, R. C. (2008). Childhood obesity, hypertension, the metabolic syndrome, and adult cardiovascular disease. *Clinical and Experimental Pharmacology and Physiology, 35,* 409–411.

Beins, B. C. (2009). *Research methods.* Boston: Allyn & Bacon.

Bellinger, D. C. (2008). Very low lead exposures and children's neurodevelopment. *Current Opinion in Pediatrics, 20,* 172–177.

Bell, K. N., & Oakley, G. P. (2009). Update on prevention of folic acid–preventable spina bifida and anencephaly. *Birth Defects Research Part A: Clinical and Molecular Teratology, 85,* 102–107.

Bell, M. A., & Fox, N. A. (1992). The relations between frontal brain electrical activity and cognitive development during infancy. *Child Development, 63,* 1142–1163.

Bell, M. A., & Morasch, K. C. (2007). Individual differences in the development of working memory during infancy. In L. M. Oakes & P. J. Bauer (Eds.), *Short- and long-term memory in early childhood: Taking the first steps toward remembering.* New York: Guilford.

Bell, M. A., & Wolfe, C. D. (2007). The cognitive neuroscience of early socioemotional development. In C. A. Brownell & C. B. Kopp (Eds.), *Socioemotional development in the toddler years.* New York: Guilford.

Bell, M. A., & Wolfe, C. D. (2007). The use of the electroencephalogram in research on cognitive development. In L. A. Schmidt & S. J. Segalowitz (Eds.), *Developmental psychophysiology: Theory, systems, and methods.* New York: Cambridge.

Bell, S. M., & Ainsworth, M. D. S. (1972). Infant crying and maternal responsiveness. *Child Development, 43,* 1171–1190.

Belsky, J. (1981). Early human experience: A family perspective. *Developmental Psychology, 17,* 3–23.

Belsky, J. (2009). Classroom composition, childcare history, and social development: Are children effects disappearing or spreading? *Social Development, 18,* 230–238.

Belsky, J., & Pasco Fearon, R. (2002). Early attachment security, subsequent maternal sensitivity, and later child development: Does continuity in development depend upon continuity

of caregiving? *Attachment and Human Development, 4,* 361–387.

Belsky, J., Vandell, D. L., Burchinal, M., Clarke-Stewart, A., McCartney, K., Owen, M. T., & the NICHD Early Child Care Research Network. (2007). Are there long-term effects of early child care? *Child Development, 78,* 681–701.

Belson, W. (1978). *Television violence and the adolescent boy.* London: Saxon House.

Bem, S. L. (1977). On the utility of alternative procedures for assessing psychological androgyny. *Journal of Consulting and Clinical Psychology, 45,* 196–205.

Bender, H. L., Allen, J. P., McElhaney, K. B., Antonishak, J., Moore, C. M., Kello, H. O., & Davis, S. M. (2007). Use of harsh physical discipline and developmental outcomes in adolescence. *Development and Psychopathology, 19,* 227–242.

Bendersky, M., & Sullivan, M. W. (2007). Basic methods in infant research. In A. Slater & M. Lewis (Eds.), *Introduction to infant development* (2nd ed.). New York: Oxford University Press.

Bender, W. N. (2008). *Learning disabilities* (6th ed.) Boston: Allyn & Bacon.

Benenson, J. F., Apostolaris, N. H., & Parnass, J. (1997). Age and sex differences in dyadic and group interaction. *Developmental Psychology, 33,* 538–543.

Benner, A. D., & Graham, S. (2009). The transition to high school as a developmental process among multiethnic urban youth. *Child Development, 80,* 356–376.

Benner, A. D., & Mistry, R. S. (2007). Congruence of mother and teacher educational expectations and low-income youth's academic competence. *Journal of Educational Psychology, 99,* 140–153.

Bennett, S. L. R. (2008). Contextual affordances of rural Appalachian individuals. *Journal of Career Development, 34,* 241–262.

Bennett, T., Szatmari, P., Bryson, S., Volden, J., Zwaigenbaum, L., Vaccarella, L., Duku, E., & Boyle, M. (2007). Differentiating autism and Asperger syndrome on the basis of language delay or impairment. *Journal of Autism and Developmental Disorders, 38,* 616–625.

Benninghoven, D., Tetsch, N., Kunzendorf, S., & Jantschek, G. (2007). Body image in patients with eating disorders and their mothers, and the role of family functioning. *Comprehensive Psychiatry, 48,* 118–123.

Benoit, D., Coolbear, J., & Crawford, A. (2008). Abuse, neglect, and maltreatment of infants. In M. M. Haith & J. B. Benson (Eds.), *Encyclopedia of infant and early childhood development.* Oxford, UK: Elsevier.

Benson, A. C., Torode, M. E., & Fiatarone Singh, M. A. (2008). The effect of high-intensity progressive resistance training on adiposity in children: A randomized controlled trial. *International Journal of Obesity, 32,* 1016–1027.

Benson, L., Baer, H. J., & Kaelber, D. C. (2009). Trends in the diagnosis of overweight and obesity in children and adolescents: 1999–2007. *Pediatrics, 123,* e153–e158.

Benson, P. L. (2006). *All kids are our kids.* San Francisco: Jossey-Bass.

Benson, P. L., & Roehlkepartain, E. C. (2008). Spiritual development: A missing priority in youth development. *New Directions for Youth Development, 118,* 13–28.

Benson, P. L., Scales, P. C., Hamilton, S. F., & Sesma, A. (2006). Positive youth development. In W. Damon & R. Lerner (Eds.), *Handbook of child psychology* (6th ed.). New York: Wiley.

Benzies, K., Keown, L. A., & Magill-Evans, J. (2009). Immediate and sustained effects of parenting on physical aggression in Canadian children aged 6 years and younger. *Canadian Journal of Psychiatry, 54,* 55–64.

Berenson, G. S. (2005). Obesity—A critical issue in preventive cardiology: The Bogalusa Heart Study. *Preventive Cardiology, 8,* 234–241.

Bergen, D. (1988). Stages of play development. In D. Bergen (Ed.), *Play as a medium for learning and development.* Portsmouth, NH: Heinemann.

Berghella, V., Baxter, J. K., & Chauhan, S. P. (2008). Evidence-based labor and delivery management. *American Journal of Obstetrics and Gynecology, 199,* 445–454.

Berk, L. E. (1994). Why children talk to themselves. *Scientific American, 271* (5), 78–83.

Berk, L. E., & Spuhl, S. T. (1995). Maternal interaction, private speech, and task performance in preschool children. *Early Childhood Research Quarterly, 10,* 145–169.

Berko, J. (1958). The child's learning of English morphology. *Word, 14,* 150–177.

Berko Gleason, J. (2003). Unpublished review of J. W. Santrock's *Life-span development,* 9th ed. (New York: McGraw-Hill).

Berko Gleason, J. (2005). The development of language. In J. Berko Gleason (Ed.), *The development of language* (6th ed.). Boston: Allyn & Bacon.

Berko Gleason, J. (2009). The development of language: An overview and a preview. In J. Berko Gleason & N. Ratner (Eds.), *The development of language* (7th ed.). Boston: Allyn & Bacon.

Berkowitz, M. W., Battistich, V. A., & Bier, M. (2008). What works in character education: What is known and what needs to be known. In L. Nucci & D Narváez (Eds.), *Handbook of moral and character education.* Clifton, NJ: Psychology Press.

Berlin, C. M., Paul, I. M., & Vesell, E. S. (2009). Safety issues of maternal drug therapy during breastfeeding. *Clinical Pharmacology and Therapeutics, 85,* 20–22.

Berlyne, D. E. (1960). *Conflict, arousal, and curiosity.* New York: McGraw-Hill.

Bernard, K., & Dozier, M. (2008). Adoption and foster placement. In M. M. Haith & J. B. Benson (Eds.). *Encyclopedia of infant and early childhood development.* Oxford. UK: Elsevier.

Berndt, T. J., & Perry, T. B. (1990). Distinctive features and effects of early adolescent friendships. In R. Montemayor (Ed.), *Advances in adolescent research.* Greenwich, CT: JAI Press.

Berninger, V. W. (2006). Learning disabilities. In W. Damon & R. Lerner (Eds.), *Handbook of child psychology* (6th ed.). New York: Wiley.

Berninger, V. W., & Abbott, R. (2005, April). *Paths leading to reading comprehension in at-risk and normally developing second-grade readers.* Paper presented at the meeting of the Society for Research in Child Development, Atlanta.

Bersamin, M. M., Walker, S., Fisher, D. A., & Grube, J. W. (2006). Correlates of oral sex and vaginal intercourse in early and middle adolescence. *Journal of Research on Adolescence, 16,* 59–68.

Bertenthal, B. I. (2008). Perception and action. In M. M. Haith & J. B. Benson (Eds.), *Encyclopedia of infant and early childhood development.* Oxford, UK: Elsevier.

Bertenthal, B. I., Longo, M. R., & Kenny, S. (2007). Phenomenal permanence and the development of predictive tracking. *Child Development, 78,* 354.

Bessey, P. Q., Arons, R. R., Dimaggio, C. J., & Yurt, R. W. (2006). The vulnerabilities of age: Burns in children and older adults. *Surgery, 140,* 705–715.

Best, D. L. (2010). Gender. In M. H. Bornstein (Ed.), *Handbook of cultural developmental science.* New York: Psychology Press.

Bethell, J., & Rhodes, A. E. (2008). Adolescent depression and emergency department use: The roles of suicidality and deliberate self-harm. *Current Psychiatry Reports, 10,* 53–59.

Betz, C. L., & Snowden, L. A. (2008). *Mosby's pediatric nursing reference* (6th ed.). Oxford, UK: Elsevier.

Beyers, W., & Goossens, L. (2008). Dynamics of perceived parenting and identity formation in late adolescence. *Journal of Adolescence, 31,* 165–184.

Bhagwat, J., & Casasola, M. (2008). Semantic development. In M. M. Haith & J. B. Benson (Eds.), *Encyclopedia of infant and early childhood development.* Oxford, UK: Elsevier.

Bhutta, Z. A., & others. (2008). What works? Interventions for maternal and child undernutrition and survival. *Lancet, 371,* 471–440.

Bialystok, E. (1993). Metalinguistic awareness: The development of children's representations in language. In C. Pratt & A. Garton (Eds.), *Systems of representation in children.* London: Wiley.

Bialystok, E. (1997). Effects of bilingualism and biliteracy on children's emerging concepts of print. *Developmental Psychology, 33,* 429–440.

Bialystok, E. (1999). Cognitive complexity and attentional control in the bilingual mind. *Child Development, 70,* 537–804.

Bialystok, E. (2001). *Bilingualism in development: Language, literacy, and cognition.* New York: Cambridge University Press.

Bialystok, E. (2007). Acquisition of literacy in preschool children: A framework for research. *Language Learning, 57,* 45–77.

Bibok, M. B., Carpendale, J. I. M., & Lewis, C. (2008). Social knowledge and social skill: An action-based view of social understanding. In U. Mueller, J. I. M. Carpendale, N. Budwig, & B. W. Sokol (Eds.), *Social life and social knowledge.* Philadelphia: Psychology Press.

Bickham, D. S. (2009). Media and technology use, childhood and adolescence. In D. Carr (Ed.), *Encyclopedia of the life course and human development.* Gale Cengage.

Biehil, M. C., Natsuaki, M. N., & Ge, X. (2007). The influence of pubertal timing on alcohol use and heavy drinking trajectories. *Journal of Youth and Adolescence, 36,* 153–167.

Bierman, K. L. (2004). *Peer rejection.* New York: Guilford.

Bill and Melinda Gates Foundation. (2008). *Report gives voice to dropouts.* Retrieved July 5, 2008, from www.gatesfoundation.org/UnitedStates/Education/TransformingHighSchools/Relatd...

Billy, J. O. G., Rodgers, J. L., & Udry, J. F. (1984). Adolescent sexual behavior and friendship choice. *Social Forces, 62,* 653–678.

Binder, T., & Vavrinkova, B. (2008). Prospective randomized comparative study of the effect of buprenorphine, methadone, and heroin on the course of pregnancy, birthweight of newborns, early postpartum adaptation, and the course of neonatal abstinence syndrome (NAS). *Neuroendocrinology Letters, 29,* 80–86.

Birnbach, D. J., & Ranasinghe, J. S. (2008). Anesthesia complications in the birthplace: Is the neuraxial block always to blame? *Clinical Perinatology, 35,* 35–52.

Bjorklund, D. F. (2006). Mother knows best: Epigenetic inheritance, maternal effects, and the evolution of human intelligence. *Developmental Review, 26,* 213–242.

Bjorklund, D. F. (2007). *Why youth is not wasted on the young.* Malden, MA: Blackwell.

Bjorklund, D. F., & Pellegrini, A. D. (2002). *The origins of human nature.* New York: Oxford University Press.

Black, M. M., & Hurley, K. M. (2007). Helping children develop healthy eating habits. In R. E. Tremblay, R. G. Barr, R. Peters, & M. Boivin (Eds.), *Encyclopedia on early childhood development* (rev. ed.). Retrieved March 11, 2008, from www.child-encyclopedia.com/documents/Black-HurleyANGxp_rev-Earing.pdf

Black, M. M., Hurley, K. M., Oberlander, S. E., Hager, E. R., McGill, A. E., White, N. T., & Quigg, A. M. (2009). Participants' comments on changes in the revised special supplemental nutrition program for women, infants, and children food packages: The Maryland food preference study. *Journal of the American Dietetic Association, 109,* 116–123.

Black, M. M., & Lozoff, B. (2008). Nutrition and diet. In M. M. Haith & J. B. Benson (Eds.),

Encyclopedia of infant and early childhood development. Oxford, UK: Elsevier.

Black, R. E., Allen, L. H., Bhutta, Z. A., Caulfield, L. E., de Onis, M., Ezzati, M., Mathers, C., Rivera, J., & the Child Undernutrition Study Group. (2008). Maternal and child undernutrition: Global and regional exposures and health consequences. *Lancet, 371,* 243–260.

Blaine, S. M., & others (2008, in press). Interactive genetic counseling role-play: A novel educational strategy for family physicians. *Journal of Genetic Counseling.*

Blakemore, J. E. O., Berenbaum, S. A., & Liben, L. S. (2009). *Gender development.* Clifton, NJ: Psychology Press.

Blass, E. (2008). Suckling. In M. M. Haith & J. B. Benson (Eds.), *Encyclopedia of infant and early childhood development.* Oxford, UK: Elsevier.

Block, C. C., & Pressley, M. (2007). Best practices in teaching comprehension. In L. B. Gambrell, L. M. Morrow, & M. Pressley (Eds.), *Best practices in literacy instruction.* New York: Guilford.

Bloom, B. (1985). *Developing talent in young people.* New York: Ballentine.

Bloom, B., & Dey, A. N. (2006). Summary health statistics for U.S. children: National Health Interview Survey, 2004. *Vital Health Statistics, 227,* 1–85.

Bloom, L., Lifter, K., & Broughton, J. (1985). The convergence of early cognition and language in the second year of life: Problems in conceptualization and measurement. In M. Barrett (Ed.), *Single word speech.* London: Wiley.

Blum, J. W., Beaudoin, C. M., & Caton-Lemos, L. (2005). Physical activity patterns and maternal well-being in postpartum women. *Maternal and Child Health Journal, 8,* 163–169.

Blum, R., & Nelson-Mmari, K. (2004). Adolescent health from an international perspective. In R. Lerner & L. Steinberg (Eds.), *Handbook of adolescent psychology.* New York: Wiley.

Bodrova, E., & Leong, D. J. (2007). *Tools of the mind* (2nd ed.). Geneva: International Bureau of Education, UNESCO.

Boeving, C. A., & Forsyth, B. (2008). AIDS and HIV. In M. M. Haith & J. B. Benson (Eds.), *Encyclopedia of infant and early childhood development.* Oxford, UK: Elsevier.

Bohannon, J. N., & Bonvillian, J. D. (2009). Theoretical approaches to language acquisition. In J. Berko Gleason & N. B. Ratner (Eds.), *The development of language* (7th ed.). Boston: Allyn & Bacon.

Bojesen, A., & Gravholt, C. H. (2007). Klinefelter syndrome in clinical practice. *Nature Clinical Practice: Urology, 4,* 192–204.

Boles, R. E., & Roberts, M. C. (2008). Supervising children during parental distractions. *Journal of Pediatric Psychology, 33,* 833–841.

Bolling, C. F., & Daniel, S. R. (2008). Obesity. In M. M. Haith & J. B. Benson (Eds.), *Encyclopedia of infant and early childhood development.* Oxford, UK: Elsevier.

Bolte, G., Fromme, H., & the GME Study Group. (2009). Socioeconomic determinants of children's environmental tobacco smoke exposure and family's home smoking policy. *European Journal of Public Health, 19,* 52–58.

Boonstra, H. (2002, February). Teen pregnancy: Trends and lessons learned. *The Guttmacher Report on Public Policy,* pp. 7–10.

Booth, A. (2006). Object function and categorization in infancy: Two mechanisms of facilitation. *Infancy, 10,* 145–169.

Booth, A., & Crouter, A. C. (Eds.). (2007). *Disparities in school readiness: How families contribute to transitions into school.* Clifton, NJ: Psychology Press.

Booth, M. (2002). Arab adolescents facing the future: Enduring ideals and pressures to change. In B. B. Brown, R. W. Larson, & T. S. Saraswathi (Eds.), *The world's youth.* New York: Cambridge University Press.

Booth-Laforce, C., & Kerns, K. A. (2009). Child-parent attachment relationships, peer relationships, and peer-group functioning. In K. H. Rubin, W. M., Bukowski, & B. Laursen (Eds.), *Handbook of peer interactions, relationships, and groups.* New York: Guilford.

Bornstein, M. H. (1975). Qualities of color vision in infancy. *Journal of Experimental Child Psychology, 19,* 401–409.

Bornstein, M. H., & Cote, L. R. (2010). Immigration and acculturation. In M. H. Bornstein (Ed.), *Handbook of cultural developmental science.* New York: Psychology Press.

Bornstein, M. H., & Zlotnik, D. (2008). Parenting styles and their effects. In M. M. Haith & J. B. Benson (Eds.), *Encyclopedia of infant and early childhood development.* Oxford, UK: Elsevier.

Bor, W., McGee, T. R., & Fagan, A. A. (2004). Early risk factors for adolescent antisocial behavior: An Australian longitudinal study. *Australian and New Zealand Journal of Psychiatry, 38,* 365–372.

Borowski, K., & Niebyl, J. R. (2008). Drugs in pregnancy. In J. Studd, S. L. Tan, & F. A. Cherenak (Eds.), *Progress in obstetrics and gynecology.* London: Elsevier.

Bortfeld, H., Fava, E., & Boas, D. A. (2009). Identifying cortical lateralization of speech processing in infants using near-infared spectroscopy. *Developmental Neuropsychology, 34,* 52–65.

Borup, L., Wurlitzer, W., Hedegaard, M., Kesmodel, U. S., & Hvidman, L. (2009). Acupuncture as pain relief during delivery: A randomized controlled trial. *Birth, 36,* 5–12.

Bouchard, T. J. (1995, August). *Heritability of intelligence.* Paper presented at the meeting of the American Psychological Association, New York.

Bouchard, T. J. (2008). Genes and human psychological traits. In P. Carruthers, S. Laurence & S. Stich (Eds.), *The innate mind: Foundations for the future (Vol. 3).* Oxford, UK: Oxford University Press.

Boukydis, C. F., & Lester, B. M. (2008). Mother-infant consultation during drug treatment: Research and innovative clinical practice. *Harm Reduction Journal, 5,* 6.

Bower, B. (1985). The left hand of math and verbal talent. *Science News, 127,* 263.

Bower, J. K., Hales, D. P., Tate, D. F., Rubin, D. A., Benjamin, S. E., & Ward, D. S. (2008). The childcare environment and children's physical activity. *American Journal of Preventive Medicine, 34,* 23–29.

Bower, T. G. R. (1966). Slant perception and shape constancy in infants. *Science, 151,* 832–834.

Bowes, D., Marquis, M., Young, W., Holowaty, P., & Issac, W. (2008, in press). Process evaluation of a school-based intervention to increase physical activity and reduce bullying. *Health Promotion Practice.*

Bowlby, J. (1969). *Attachment and loss* (Vol. 1). London: Hogarth Press.

Bowlby, J. (1989). *Secure and insecure attachment.* New York: Basic Books.

Bowman, M. A., Prelow, H. M., & Weaver, S. R. (2007). Parenting behaviors, association with deviant peers, and delinquency in African American adolescents: A mediated-moderation model. *Journal of Youth and Adolescence, 36,* 517–527

Boyer, K., & Diamond, A. (1992). Development of memory for temporal order in infants and young children. In A. Diamond (Ed.), *Development and neural bases of higher cognitive function.* New York: New York Academy of Sciences.

Boyle, J., & Cropley, M. (2004). Children's sleep: Problems and solutions. *Journal of Family Health Care, 14,* 61–63.

Bracken, M. B., Eskenazi, B., Sachse, K., McSharry, J., Hellenbrand, K., & Leo-Summers, L. (1990). Association of cocaine use with sperm concentration, motility, and morphology. *Fertility and Sterility, 53,* 315–322.

Bradley, R. H., & Corwyn, R. F. (2008). Infant temperament, parenting, and externalizing behavior in first grade: A test of the differential susceptibility hypothesis. *Journal of Child Psychology and Psychiatry, 49,* 124–131.

Bradley, R. H., & McKelvey, L. (2007). Managing the differences within: Immigration and early childhood education in the United States. In J. E. Lansford, K. Deater-Deckhard, & M. H. Bornstein (Eds.), *Immigrant families in contemporary society.* New York: Guilford.

Brady, S. S., Tschann, J. M., Ellen, J. K., & Flores, E. (2009). Infidelity, trust, and condom use among Latino youth in dating relationships *Sexually Transmitted Diseases, 36,* 227–231.

Brainerd, C. J., & Reyna, V. E. (1993). Domains of fuzzy-trace theory. In M. L. Howe & R. Pasnak

(Eds.), *Emerging themes in cognitive development.* New York: Springer.

Brams, H., Mao, A. R., & Doyle, R. L. (2009). Onset of efficacy of long-lasting psychostimulants in pediatric attention-deficit/hyperactivity disorder. *Postgraduate Medicine, 120,* 69–88.

Brandon, P. D. (2009). Poverty, childhood, and adolescence. In D. Carr (Ed.), *Encyclopedia of the life course and human development.* Boston: Gale Cengage.

Bransford, J., & others. (2006). Learning theories in education. In P. A. Alexander & P. H. Winne (Eds.), *Handbook of educational psychology* (2nd ed.). Mahwah, NJ: Erlbaum.

Brazelton, T. B. (1956). Sucking in infancy. *Pediatrics, 17,* 400–404.

Breakstone, S., Dreiblatt, S. & Dreiblatt, M. (2009). *How to stop bullying and social aggression.* Thousand Oaks, CA: Corwin.

Brelsford, G. M., & Mahoney, A. (2008). Spiritual disclosure between older adolescents and their mothers. *Journal of Family Psychology, 22,* 62–70.

Bremner, G. (2007). Perception and knowledge of the world. In A. Slater & M. Lewis (Eds.), *Introduction to infant development* (2nd ed.). Malden, MA: Blackwell.

Brendgen, R. M. (2009). Aggression, childhood and adolescence. In D. Carr (Ed.), *Encyclopedia of the life course and human development.* Boston: Gale Cengage.

Brent, R. L. (2008). Environmental causes of human congenital malformations. In J. Studd, S. L. Tan, & F. A. Cherenak (Eds.), *Progess in obstetrics and gynecology.* London: Elsevier.

Brent, R. L. (2009). Saving lives and changing family histories: Appropriate counseling of pregnant women and men and women of reproductive age concerning the risk of diagnostic radiation exposure during and before pregnancy. *American Journal of Obstetrics and Gynecology, 200,* 4–24.

Breslau, N., Paneth, N. S., & Lucia, V. C. (2004). The lingering academic deficits of low birth weight children. *Pediatrics, 114,* 1035–1040.

Bretherton, I., & Munholland, K. A. (2008). Internal working models in attachment relationships: Elaborating a central construct in attachment theory. In J. Cassidy & P. R. Shaver (Eds.), *Handbook of attachment* (2nd ed.). New York: Guilford.

Bretherton, I., Stolberg, U., & Kreye, M. (1981). Engaging stragngers in proximal interaction: Infants' social initiative. *Developmental Psychology, 17,* 746–755.

Brewster, K. L., & Tillman, K. H. (2008). Who's doing it? Patterns and predictors of youths' oral sexual experiences. *Journal of Adolescent Health, 42,* 73–80.

Bridgett, D. J., Gartstein, M. A., Putnam, S. P., McKay, T., Iddins, E., Robertson, C., Ramsay, K., & Rittmueller, A. (2009). Maternal and contextual influences and the effect of temperament development during infancy on parenting in toddlerhood. *Infant Behavior and development, 32,,* 103–116.

Briefel, R. R., Redy, K., Karwe, V., Jankowski, L., & Hendricks, K. (2004). Toddler's transition to table foods: Impact on nutrient intakes and food patterns. *Journal of the American Dietetic Association, 104,* 38–44.

Briem, V., Radeborg, K., Salo, I., & Bengtsson, H. (2004). Developmental aspects of children's behavior and safety while cycling. *Journal of Pediatric Psychology, 29,* 369–377.

Bril, B. (1999). Dires sur l'enfant selon les cultures. Etat des lieux et perspectives. In B. Brill, P. R. Dasen, C. Sabatier, & B. Krewer (Eds.), *Propos sur l'enfant et l'adolescent. Quels enfants, pour quelles cultures?* Paris: L'Harmattan.

Brodsky, J. L., Viner-Brown, S., & Handler, A. S. (2009, in press). Changes in maternal cigarette smoking among pregnant WIC participants in Rhode Island. *Maternal and Child Health Journal.*

Brody, N. (2000). Intelligence. In A. Kazdin (Ed.), *Encyclopedia of psychology.* Washington, DC, & New York: American Psychological Association and Oxford University Press.

Brody, N. (2007). Does education influence intelligence? In P. C. Kyllonen, R. D. Roberts, & L. Stankov (Eds.), *Extending intelligence.* Mahwah, NJ: Erlbaum.

Brodzinsky, D. M., & Pinderhughes, E. (2002). Parenting and child development in adoptive families. In M. H. Bornstein (Ed.), *Handbook of parenting* (Vol. 1). Mahwah. NJ: Erlbaum.

Bronfenbrenner, U. (1986). Ecology of the family as a context for human development: Research perspectives. *Developmental Psychology, 22,* 723–742.

Bronfenbrenner, U. (2000). Ecological theory. In A. Kazdin (Ed.), *Encyclopedia of psychology.* Washington, DC, & New York: American Psychological Association and Oxford University Press.

Bronfenbrenner, U., & Morris, P. A. (2006). The ecology of developmental processes. In W. Damon & R. Lerner (Eds.), *Handbook of child psychology* (6th ed.). New York: Wiley.

Bronstein, P. (2006). The family environment: Where gender role socialization begins. In J. Worell & C. D. Goodheart (Eds.), *Handbook of girls' and women's psychological health.* New York: Oxford University Press.

Brooker, R. J. (2009). *Genetics* (3rd ed.). New York: McGraw-Hill.

Brooks, J. G., & Brooks, M. G. (2001). *The case for constructivist classrooms* (2nd ed.). Upper Saddle River, NJ: Erlbaum.

Brooks, R., & Meltzoff, A. N. (2005). The development of gaze in relation to language. *Development Science, 8,* 535–543.

Brooks, R., & Meltzoff, A. N. (2008). Infant gaze following and pointing predict accelerated vocabulary growth through two years of age: A longitudinal, growth curve modeling study. *Journal of Child Language, 35,* 207–220.

Brooks-Gunn, J. (2003). Do you believe in magic?: What we can expect from early childhood programs. *Social Policy Report, Society for Research in Child Development, XVII* (No. 1), 1–13.

Brooks-Gunn, J., & Warren, M. P. (1989). The psychological significance of secondary sexual characteristics in 9- to 11-year-old girls. *Child Development, 59,* 161–169.

Brown, B. B. (2004). Adolescents-relationships with peers. In R. Lerner & L. Steinberg (Eds.), *Handbook of adolescent Psychology* (2nd ed.). New York: Wiley.

Brown, B. B., Bakken, J. P., Ameringer, S. W., & Mahon, S. D. (2008). A comprehensive conceptualization of the peer influence process in adolescence. In M. J. Prinstein & K. A. Dodge (Eds.), *Understanding peer influence in children and adolescents.* New York: Guilford.

Brown, B. B., & Dietz, E. L. (2009). Informal peer groups in middle childhood and adolescence. In K. H. Rubin, W. M. Bukowski, & B. Laursen (Eds.), *Handbook of peer interaction, relationships, and groups.* New York: Guilford.

Brown, B. B., & Larson, J. (2009). Peer relationships in adolescence. In R. M. Lerner & L. Steinberg (Eds.), *Handbook of adolescent psychology* (3rd ed.). New York: Wiley.

Brown, B. B., & Larson, R. W. (2002). The kaleidoscope of adolescence: Experiences of the world's youth at the beginning of the 21st century. In B. B. Brown, R. W. Larson, & T. S. Saraswathi (Eds.), *The world's youth.* New York: Cambridge University Press.

Brown, B. B., & Lohr, M. J. (1987). Peer-group affiliation and adolescent self-esteem: An integration, of ego-identity and symbolic-interaction theories. *Journal of Personality and Social Psychology, 52,* 47–55.

Brown, D. (1987). The status of Holland's theory of vocational choice. *Career Development Quarterly, 36,* 13–24.

Browne, G. J., & Lam, L. T. (2006). Concussive head injury in children and adolescents related to sports and other leisure physical activities. *British Journal of Sports Medicine, 40,* 163–168.

Brownell, C. A., & Kopp, C. B. (Eds.). (2007). *Socioemotional development in the toddler years.* New York: Guilford.

Brownell, C. A., Ramani, G. B., & Zerwas, S. (2006). Becoming a social partner with peers: Cooperation and social understanding in one- and two-year-olds. *Child Development, 77,* 803–821.

Brown, R. (1958). *Words and things.* Glencoe, IL: Free Press.

Brown, R. (1973). *A first language: The early stages.* Cambridge, MA: Harvard University Press.

Brown, T. N., & Lesane-Brown, C. L. (2009). Socialization, race. In D. Carr (Ed.), *Encyclopedia of the life course and human development.* Boston: Gale Cengage.

Brown, W. H., Pfeiffer, K. A., Mclver, K. L., Dowda, M., Addy, C. L., & Pate, R. R.

(2009). Social and environmental factors associated with preschoolers' nonsedentary physical activity. *Child Development, 80,* 45–58.

Bruck, M., & Ceci, S. J. (1999). The suggestibility of children's memory, *Annual Review of Psychology, 50,* 419–439.

Bruck, M., Ceci, S. J., & Hembrooke, H. (1998). Reliability and credibility of young children's reports: From research to policy and practice. *American Psychologist, 53* (2), 136–151.

Bruck, M., Ceci, S. J., & Principe, G. F. (2006). The child and the law. In W. Damon & R. Lerner (Eds.), *Handbook of child psychology* (6th ed.). New York: Wiley.

Bruine de Bruin, W., Parker, A., & Fischhoff, B. (2007) Individual Differences in Adult Decision-Making Competence (A-DMC). *Journal of Personality and Social Psychology, 92,* 938–956.

Brune, C. W., & Woodward, A. L. (2007). Social cognition and social responsiveness in 10-month-old infants. *Journal of Cognition and Development, 2,* 3–27.

Bruni, O., Ferri, R., Novelli, L., Finotti, E., Miano, S., & Guilleminault, C. (2008). NREM sleep instability in children with sleep terrors: The role of slow wave activity interruptions. *Clinical Neurophysiology, 119,* 985–992.

Brunstein Klomek, A., Marrocco, F., Kleinman, M., Schofeld, I. S., & Gould, M. S. (2007). Bullying, depression, and suicidality in adolescents. *Journal of the American Academy of Child and Adolescent Psychiatry, 46,* 40–49.

Bryant, J. A. (Ed.). (2007). *The children's television community.* Mahwah, NJ: Erlbaum.

Bryant, J. B. (2009). Language in social contexts: Communicative competence in the preschool years. In J. Berko Gleason & N. Ratner (Eds.), *The development of language* (7th ed.). Boston: Allyn & Bacon.

Bugental, D., & Grusec, J. (2006). Socialization processes. In W. Damon & R. Lerner (Eds.), *Handbook of child psychology* (6th ed.). New York: Wiley.

Buhimschi, C. S., & Weiner, C. P. (2009). Medications in pregnancy and lactation: Part. l. Teratology. *Obstetrics and Gynecology, 113,* 166–188.

Buhrmester, D. (1998). Need fulfillment. Interpersonal competence, and the developmental contexts of early adolescent friendship In W. M. Bukowski & A. F. Newcomb (Eds.), *The company they keep: Friendship in childhood and adolescence.* New York: Cambridge University Press.

Buhrmester, D. (2005, April). *The antecedents of adolescents' competence in close relationships: A six-year-study.* Paper presented at the meeting of the Society for Research in Child Development, Atlanta.

Buhrmester, D., & Chong, C. M. (2009). Friendship in adolescence. In H. Reis & S. Sprecher (Eds.), *Encyclopedia of human relationships.* Thousand Oaks, CA: Sage.

Buhs, E. S., & Ladd, G. W. (2001). Peer rejection as an antecedent of young children's school

adjustment: An examination of mediating processes. *Developmental Psychology, 37,* 550–560.

Bukowski, R., & others. (2008, January). *Folic acid and preterm birth.* Paper presented at the meeting of the Society for Maternal-Fetal Medicine, Dallas.

Bukowski, W. M., Brendgen, M., & Vitaro, F. (2007). Peers and socialization: Effects on externalizing and internalizing problems. In J. E. Grusec & P. D. Hastings (Eds.), *Handbook of socialization.* New York: Guilford.

Bukowski, W. M., Motzoi, C., & Meyer, F. (2009). Friendship process, function, and outcome. In K. H. Rubin, W. M. Bukowksi, & B. Laursen (Eds.), *Handbook of peer interaction, relationships, and groups.* New York: Guilford.

Bulik, C. M., Berkman, N. D., Brownley, K. A., Sedway, J. A., & Lohr, K. N. (2007). Anorexia nervosa treatment: A systematic review of randomized controlled trials. *International Journal of Eating Disorders, 40,* 310–320.

Bumpus, M. F., Crouter, A. C., & McHale, M. (2001). Parental autonomy granting during adolescence: Exploring gender differences in context. *Developmental Psychology, 37,* 163–173.

Burgess-Champoux , T. L., Larson, N., Neumark-Sztain, D., Hannan, P. J., & Story, M. (2009). Are family meal patterns associated with overall diet quality during the transition from early to middle adolescence. *Journal of Nutrition Education and Behavior, 41,* 79–86.

Burke, R. V., Kuhn, B. R., & Peterson, J. L. (2004). Brief report: A "storybook" ending to children's bedtime problems—the use of a rewarding social story to reduce bedtime resistance and frequent nighttime waking. *Journal of Pediatric Psychology, 29,* 389–396.

Burke-Adams, A. (2007). The benefits of equalizing standards and creativity: Discovering a balance in instruction. *Gifted Child Quarterly, 30,* 58–63.

Burnette, J. (1998). Reducing the disproportionate representation of minority students in special education. *ERIC/OSEP Digest, No. E566.*

Burns, C., Dunn, A., Brady, M., Starr, N. B., & Blosser, C. (2009). *Pediatric primary care.* Oxford, UK: Elsevier.

Burns, L., Mattick, R. P., Lim, K., & Wallace, C. (2007). Methadone in pregnancy: Treatment retention and neonatal outcomes. *Addiction, 102,* 264–270.

Burrington, L. A., & Browning, C. R. (2009). Neighborhood context, childhood and adolescence. In D. Carr (Ed.), *Encyclopedia of the life course and human development.* Boston: Gale Cengage.

Bursuck, W. D., & Damer, M. (2007). *Reading instruction for students who are at risk or have disabilities.* Boston: Allyn & Bacon.

Bushnell, I. W. R. (2003). Newborn face recognition. In O. Pascalis & A. Slater (Eds.), *The development of face processing in infancy and early childhood.* New York: NOVA Science.

Buss, D. M. (1995). Psychological sex differences: Origins through sexual selection. *American Psychologist, 50,* 164–168.

Buss, D. M. (2000). Evolutionary psychology. In A. Kazdin (Ed.), *Encyclopedia of psychology.* Washington, DC, & New York: American Psychological Association and Oxford University Press.

Buss, D. M. (2004). *Evolutionary psychology* (2nd ed.). Boston: Allyn & Bacon.

Buss, D. M. (2008). *Evolutionary psychology* (3rd ed.). Boston: Allyn & Bacon.

Bussey, K., & Bandura A. (1999). Social cognitive theory of gender development and differentiation. *Psychological Review, 106,* 676–713.

Buss, K. A., & Goldsmith, H. H. (2007). Biobehavioral approaches to early socioemotional development. In C. A. Brownell & C. B. Kopp (Eds.), *Socioemotional development in the toddler years.* New York: Guilford.

Butcher, K., Sallis, J. F., Mayer, J. A., & Woodruff, S. (2008). Correlates of physical activity guideline compliance for adolescents in 100 cities. *Journal of Adolescent Health, 42,* 360–368.

Butte, N. F. (2006). Energy requirements of infants and children. *Nestle Nutrition Workshop Series: Pediatric Program, 58,* 19–32.

Butterworth, G. (2004). Joint visual attention in infancy. In G. Bremner & A. Slater (Eds.), *Theories of infant development.* Malden, MA: Blackwell.

Buzwell, S., & Rosenthal, D. (1996). Constructing a sexual self: Adolescents' sexual self-perceptions and sexual risk-taking. *Journal of Research on Adolescence, 6,* 489–513.

Byrd-Williams, C. E., Shaibi, G. Q., Sun, P., Lane, C. J., Ventura, E. E., Davis, J. N., Kelly, L. A., & Goran, M. I. (2008). Cardiorespiratory fitness predicts change in adiposity in overweight Hispanic boys. *Obesity, 16,* 1072–1077.

Byrnes, J. P. (2008). Piaget's cognitive developmental theory. In M. M. Haith & J. B. Benson (Eds.), *Encyclopedia of infant and early childhood development.* Oxford, UK: Elsevier.

C

Cabezon, C., Vigil, P., Rojas, I., Leiva, M. E., Riquelme, R., Aranda, W., & Garcia, C. (2005). Adolescent pregnancy prevention: An abstinence-centered randomized controlled intervention in a Chilean public high school. *Journal of Adolescent Health, 36,* 64–69.

Cabrera, N., Hutchens, R., & Peters, H. E. (Eds.). (2006). *From welfare to childcare.* Mahwah, NJ: Erlbaum.

Cairns, R. B., & Cairns, B. D. (2006). The making of developmental psychology. In W. Damon & R. Lerner (Eds.), *Handbook of child psychology* (6th ed.). New York: Wiley.

Caley, L., Syms, C., Robinson, L., Cederbaum, J., Henry, M., & Shipkey, N. (2008). What human service professionals know and want to know about fetal alcohol syndrome. *Canadian Journal of Clinical Pharmacology, 15,* e117–e123.

Calkins, S. D. (2007). The emergence of self-regulation: Biological and behavioral control mechanisms supporting toddler competencies. In C. A. Brownell & C. B. Kopp (Eds.), *Socioemotional development in the toddler years.* New York: Guilford.

Callaway, L. K., Lust, K., & McIntyre, H. D. (2005). Pregnancy outcomes in women of very advanced maternal age. *Obstetrics and Gynecology Survey, 60,* 562–563.

Cameron, J., & Pierce, D. (2008). Intrinsic versus extrinsic motivation. In N. J. Salkind (Ed.), *Encyclopedia of educational psychology.* Thousand Oaks, CA: Sage.

Campbell, D. A., Lake, M. F., Falk, M., & Backstrand, J. R. (2006). A randomized controlled trial of continuous support by a lay doula. *Journal of Obstetrics and Gynecology: Neonatal Nursing, 35,* 456–464.

Campbell, F. A. (2007). The malleability of the cognitive development of children of low-income African American families: Intellectual test performance over twenty-one years. In P. C. Kyllonen, R. D. Roberts, & L. Stankov (Eds.), *Extending intelligence.* Mahwah, NJ: Erlbaum.

Campbell, L., Campbell, B., & Dickinson, D. (2004). *Teaching and learning through multiple intelligences* (3rd ed.). Boston: Allyn & Bacon.

Campbell, M. K., & Mottols, M. F. (2001). Recreational exercise and occupational safety during pregnancy and birth weight: A case control study. *American Journal of Obstetrics and Gynecology, 184,* 403–408.

Campos, J. J. (2005). Unpublished review of J. W. Santrock's *Life-span development,* 10th ed. (New York: McGraw-Hill).

Campos, J. J., Langer, A., & Krowitz, A. (1970). Cardiac responses on the visual cliff in prelocomotor human infants. *Science, 170,* 196–197.

Camras, L. A., & others. (1998). Production of emotional facial expressions in European American, Japanese, and Chinese infants. *Developmental Psychology, 34,* 616–628.

Canfield, R. L., Gendle, M. H., Cory-Slechta, D. A. (2004). Impaired neuropsychological functioning in lead-exposed children. *Developmental Neuropsychology, 26,* 513–540.

Canfield, R. L., & Haith, M. M. (1991). Young infants' visual expectations for symmetric and asymmetric stimulus sequences. *Developmental Psychology, 27,* 198–208.

Canfield, R. L., & Jusko, T. A. (2008). Lead poisoning. In M. M. Haith & J. B. Benson (Eds.), *Encyclopedia of infant and early childhood development.* Oxford, UK: Elsevier.

Canfield, R. L., & Jusko, T. A. (2008). Lead poisoning. In M. M. Haith & J. B. Benson (Eds.), *Encyclopedia of infant and early childhood development.* Oxford, UK: Elsevier.

Canterino, J. C., Ananth, C. V., Smulian, J., Harrigan, J. T., & Vintzileos, A. M. (2004). Maternal age and risk of fetal death in singleton

question: United States, 1995–2000. *Obstetrics and Gynecology Survey, 59,* 649–650.

Carey, D. P. (2007). Is bigger really better? The search for brain size and intelligence in the twenty-first century. In S. Della Sala (Ed.), *Tall tales about the mind and brain: Separating fact from fiction.* Oxford, UK: University Press.

Carlo, G. (2006). Care-based and altruistically based morality. In M. Killen & J. Smetana (Eds.), *Handbook of moral development.* Mahwah, NJ: Erlbaum.

Carlson, S. M., & Zelazo, P. D. (2008). Symbolic thought. In M. M. Haith & J. B. Benson (Eds.), *Encyclopedia of infant and early childhood development.* Oxford, UK: Elsevier.

Carlton, M. P., & Winsler, A. (1999). School readiness: The need for a paradigm shift. *School Psychology Review, 28,* 338–352.

Carnegie Council on Adolescent Development. (1989). *Turning points: Preparing youth for the 21st century.* New York: Carnegie Foundation.

Carpendale, J. I., & Chandler, M. J. (1996). On the distinction between false belief understanding and subscribing to an interpretive theory of mind. *Child Development, 67,* 1686–1706.

Carpendale, J. I. M., Muller, U., & Bibok, M. B. (2008). Piaget's theory of cognitive development. In N. J. Salkind (Ed.), *Encyclopedia of educational psychology.* Thousand Oaks, CA: Sage.

Carpenter, J., Nagell, K., & Tomasello, M. (1998). Social cognition, joint attention, and communicative competence from 9 to 15 months of age. *Monographs of the Society for Research in Child Development, 70* (1, Serial No. 279).

Carrell, S. E., Malmstrom, F. V., & West, J. E. (2008). Peer effects in academic cheating. *Journal of Human Resources, 43,* 173–207.

Carskadon, M. A. (Ed.). (2002). *Adolescent sleep patterns.* New York: Cambridge University Press.

Carskadon, M. A. (2004). Sleep difficulties in young people. *Archives of Pediatric and Adolescent Medicine, 158,* 597–598.

Carskadon, M. A. (2006, March). *Too little, too late: Sleep bioregulatory processes across adolescence.* Paper presented at the meeting of the Society for Research on Adolescence, San Francisco.

Carter, N., Prater, M. A., & Dyches, T. T. (2009). *What every teacher should know about: Adaptations and accommodations for students with mild to moderate disabilities.* Upper Saddle River, NJ: Prentice Hall.

Carter-Saltzman, L. (1980). Biological and sociocultural effects on handedness: Comparison between biological and adaptive families. *Science, 209,* 1263–1265.

Cartwright, R., Agargun, M. Y., Kirkby, J., & Friedman, J. K. (2006). Relation of dreams to waking concerns. *Psychiatry Research, 141,* 261–270.

Carvalho Bos, S., & others. (2009). Sleep and behavioral/emotional problems in children: A population-based study. *Sleep Medicine, 10,* 66–74.

Carver, K., Joyner, K., & Udry, J. R. (2003). National estimates of romantic relationships. In P. Florsheim (Ed.), *Adolescent romantic relations and sexual behavior.* Mahwah, NJ: Erlbaum.

Carver, L. J., & Bauer, P. J. (2001). The dawning of a past: The emergence of long-term explicit memory in infancy. *Journal of Experimental Psychology: General, 130* (4), 726–745.

Case, R., & Mueller, M. P. (2001). Differentiation, integration, and covariance mapping as fundamental processes in cognitive and neurological growth. In J. L. McClelland & R. S. Siegler (Eds.), *Mechanisms of cognitive development.* Mahwah, NJ: Erlbaum.

Caspers, K. M., Paraiso, S., Yucuis, R., Troutman, B., Arndt, S., & Philibert, R. (2009). Association between the serotonin transporter polymorphism (*5-HTTLPR*) and adult unresolved attachment. *Developmental Psychology, 45,* 64–76.

Caspi, A., Sugden, K., Moffitt, T. E., Taylor, A., Craig, I., Harrington, H., McClay, J., Mill, J., Martin, J., Braithwaite, A., & Poulton, R. (2003). Influence of life stress on depression: Moderation by a polymorphism in the *5-HTT* gene. *Science, 301,* 386–389.

Cassidy, J. (2008). The nature of the child's ties. In J. Cassidy & P. R. Shaver (Eds.), *Handbook of attachment* (2nd ed.). New York: Guilford.

Catalano, R. F., Hawkins, J. D., & Toumbourou, J. W. (2008). Positive youth development in the United States: History, efficacy, and links to moral and character education. In L. Nucci & D. Narváez (Eds.), *Handbook of moral and character education.* Clifton, NJ: Psychology Press.

Cauffman, B. E. (1994, February). *The effects of puberty, dating, and sexual involvement on dieting and disordered eating in young adolescent girls.* Paper presented at the meeting of the Society for Research on Adolescence, San Diego.

Caughey, A. B., Hopkins, L. M., & Norton, M. E. (2006). Chorionic villus sampling compared with amniocentesis and the difference in the rate of pregnancy loss. *Obstetrics and Gynecology, 108,* 612–616.

Cavalcante, S. R., Cecatti, J. G., Pereira, R. I., Baciuk, E. P., Bernardo, A. L., & Silveira, C. (2009). Water aerobics II: Maternal body composition and perinatal outcomes after a program for low risk pregnant women. *Reproductive Health, 6,* 1.

Cavanagh, S. E. (2009). Puberty. In D. Carr (Ed.), *Encyclopedia of the life course and human development.* Boston: Gale Cengage.

Cavanaugh, S. (2008). *Asian equation.* Retrieved April 9, 2008, from www.edweek.org/login.html?source=http%3A%2F%2Fpeabody.vanderbilt.edu2Fx

Cavell, T. A., Hymel, S., Malcolm, K. T., & Seay, A. (2007). Socialization and interventions for antisocial youth. In J. E: Grusec & P. D. Hastings (Eds.), *Handbook of socialization.* New York: Gulford.

Ceci, S. J., & Gilstrap, L. L. (2000). Determinants of intelligence: Schooling and intelligence. In A. Kazdin (Ed.), *Encyclopedia of psychology*. Washington, DC, & New York: American Psychological Association and Oxford University Press.

Ceci, S. J., Kulkofsky, S., Klemfuss, J. Z., Sweeney, C. D., & Bruck, M. (2007). Unwarranted assumptions about children's testimonial accuracy. *Annual Review of Clinical Psychology, 3*, 311–328.

Center for Science in the Public Interest. (2008). *Obesity on the kid's menu at top chains*. Retrieved October 24, 2008, from www.cspinet.org/new/200808041.html

Centers for Disease Control and Prevention. (2000). *CDC growth charts: United States*. Atlanta: Author.

Centers for Disease Control and Prevention. (2007). *Autism and developmental disabilities monitoring (ADDM) network*. Atlanta: Author.

Centers for Disease Control and Prevention. (2008a, June 5). *Teen sexual activity increases, condom use decreases*. Atlanta: Author.

Centers for Disease Control and Prevention. (2008b). *HIV/AIDS in the United States*. Atlanta: Author.

Centers for Disease Control and Prevention. (2009). *Body mass index for children and teens*. Atlanta: Author.

Centers for Disease Control and Prevention. (2009). *Obesity and overweight*. Atlanta: Author.

Cepeda, M. S., Carr, D. B., Lau, J., & Alvarez, H. (2006). Music for pain relief. *Cochrane Database of Systematic Reviews, 2*, CD004843.

Cetin, I., & Alvino, G. (2009, in press). Intrauterine growth restriction: Implications for placental metabolism and transport: A review. *Placenta*.

Chaillet, N., & Dumont, A. (2007). Evidence-based strategies for reducing cesarean section rates: A meta-analysis. *Birth, 34*, 53–64.

Chan, C. (2008). Childhood obesity and adverse health effects in Hong Kong. *Obesity Reviews, 9* (Suppl. 1), S87–S90.

Chance, P. (2008). *Learning and behavior* (6th ed.). Belmont, CA: Cengage.

Chandra, A., Martino, S. C., Collins, R. L., Elliott, M. N., Berry, S. H., Kanouse, D. E., & Miu, A. (2008). Does watching sex on television predict teen pregnancy? Findings from a national longitudinal survey of youth. *Pediatrics, 122*, 1047–1054.

Chang, F., Dell, G. S., & Bock, K. (2006). Becoming syntactic. *Psychological Review, 113*, 234–272.

Chang, J. S. (2009). Parental smoking and childhood leukemia. *Methods in Molecular Biology, 472*, 103–337.

Chang, M. Y., Chen, C. H., & Huang, K. F. (2006). A comparison of massage effects on labor pain using the McGill Pain Questionnaire. *Journal of Nursing Research, 14*, 190–197.

Chao, R. K. (2005, April). *The importance of Guan in describing control of immigrant Chinese*. Paper presented at the meeting of the Society for Research in Child Development, Atlanta.

Chao, R. K. (2007, March). *Research with Asian Americans: Looking back and moving forward*. Paper presented at the meeting of the Society for Research in Child Development, Boston.

Chao, R., & Tseng, V. (2002). Parenting of Asians. In M. H. Bornstein *Handbook of parenting* (2nd ed., Vol. 4). Mahwah, NJ: Erlbaum.

Chaplin, T. M., Gillham, J. E., & Seligman, M. E. P. (2009). Gender, anxiety, and depressive symptoms. *Journal of Early Adolescence, 29*, 307–327.

Chassin, L., Hussong, A., & Beltran, I. (2009). Adolescent substance use In R. M. Lerner & L. Steinberg (Eds.), *Handbook of adolescent psychology* (3rd ed.). New York: Wiley.

Chattin-McNichols, J. (1992). *The Montessori controversy*. Albany, NY: Delmar.

Chaudhuri, J. H., & Williams, P. H. (1999, April). *The contribution of infant temperament and parent emotional availability to toddler attachment*. Paper presented at the meeting of the Society for Research in Child Development, Albuquerque.

Chedraui, P. (2008). Pregnancy among young adolescents: Trends, risk factors, and maternal-perinatal outcome. *Journal of Perinatal Medicine, 36*, 256–259.

Chen, C., & Stevenson, H. W. (1989). Homework: A cross cultural comparison. *Child Development, 60*, 551–561.

Chen, M. Y., Wang, E. K., & Jeng. Y. J. (2006). Adequate sleep among adolescents is positively associated with health status and health-related behaviors. *BMC Public Health, 6*, 59.

Chen, W., Srinivasan, S. R., & Berenson, G. S. (2008). Path analysis of metabolic syndrome components in black versus white children, adolescents, and adults: The Bogalusa Heart Study. *Annals of Epidemiology, 18*, 85–91.

Chen, X., Hastings, P. D., Rubin, K. H., Chen, H., Cen, G., & Stewart, S. L. (1998). Childrearing attitudes and behavioral inhibition in Chinese and Canadian toddlers: A cross-cultural study. *Developmental Psychology, 34*, 677–686.

Chen, X., & others. (2009). Interactions of IL-12A and IL-12B polymorphisms on the risk of cervical cancer in Chinese women. *Clinical Cancer Research, 15*, 400–405.

Chen, X. K., Wen, S. W., Fleming, N., Demissie, K., Rhoads, G. G., & Walker, M. C. (2007). Teenage pregnancy and adverse birth outcomes: A large population based retrospective cohort study. *International Journal of Epidemiology, 36*, 368–373.

Chen, X. K., Wen, S. W., Yang, Q., & Walker, M. C. (2007). Adequacy of prenatal care and neonatal mortality in infants born to mothers with and without antenatal high-risk conditions. *Australian and New Zealand Journal of Obstetrics and Gynecology, 47*, 122–127.

Chen, Z.-Y. (2009a). Parenting style. In D. Carr (Ed.), *Encyclopedia of the life course and human development*. Boston: Gale Cengage.

Chen, Z.-Y. (2009b). Parent-child relationships, childhood, and adolescence. In D. Carr (Ed.), *Encyclopedia of the life course and human development*. Boston: Gale Cengage.

Cheok, M. H., Pottier, N., Kager, L., & Evans, W. E. (2009). Pharmacogenetics in acute lymphoblastic leukemia. *Seminars in Hematology, 46*, 39–51.

Cherlin, A. J., & Furstenberg, F. F. (1994). Stepfamilies in the United States: A reconsideration. *Annual Review of Sociology* (Vol. 20). Palo Alto, CA: Annual Reviews.

Chess, S., & Thomas, A. (1977). Temperamental individuality from childhood to adolescence. *Journal of Child Psychiatry, 16*, 218–226.

Cheung, A. P. (2006). Assisted reproductive technology: Both sides now. *Journal of Reproductive Medicine, 51*, 283–292.

Chia, P., Sellick, K., & Gan, S. (2006). The attitudes and practices of neonatal nurses in the use of kangaroo care. *Australian Journal of Advanced Nursing, 23*, 20–27.

Children's Defense Fund. (2009). *Policy initiatives*. Retrieved January 13, 2009, from *www.childrensdefense.org*.

Child Trends. (2006, April). *Fast facts at a glance*. Washington, DC: Author.

Child Trends. (2008, July). *Facts at a glance*. Washington, DC: Author.

Chi, M. T. (1978). Knowledge structures and memory development. In R. S. Siegler (Ed.), *Children's thinking: What develops?* Hillsdale, NJ: Erlbaum.

Ching, T. Y., van Wanrooy, E., Hill, M., & Incerti, P. (2006). Performance in children with hearing aids or cochlear implants: Bilateral stimulation and binaural hearing. *International Journal of Audiology, 45,*(Suppl.), S108–S112.

Chiu, M. M. (2007). Families, economies, cultures, and science achievement in 41 countries: Country-, school-, and student-level analyses. *Journal of Family Psychology, 21*, 510–519.

Chomsky, N. (1957). *Syntactic structures*. The Hague: Mouton.

Chouinard, R., Karsenti, T., & Roy, N. (2007). Relations among competence beliefs, utility value, achievement goals, and effort in mathematics. *British Journal of Educational Psychology, 77*, 501–517.

Christenson, S. L., & Thurlow, M. L. (2004). School dropouts: Prevention considerations, interventions, and challenges. *Current Directions in Psychological Science, 13*, 36–39.

Christian, P. (2009). Prenatal origins of undernutrition. *Nestle Nutrition Workshop Series: Pediatric Program, 63*, 59–73.

Chuang, S. S., & Tamis-Lemonda, C. (2009). Gender roles in immigrant families: Parenting views, practices, and child development. *Sex Roles, 60*, 451–455.

584   References

Chu, S. Y., Callaghan, W. M., Bish, C. L., & D'Angelo, D. (2009, in press). Gestational weight gain by body mass index among U.S. women delivering live births, 2004–2005: Fueling future obesity. *American Journal of Obstetrics and Gynecology*.

Cicchetti, D., & Toth, S. L. (2006). Developmental psychopathology and preventive intervention. In W. Damon & R. Lerner (Eds.), *Handbook of child psychology* (6th ed.). New York: Wiley.

Cicchetti, D., Toth, S. L., Nilsen, W. J., & Manly, J. T. (2009, in press). What do we know and why does it matter? The dissemination of evidence-based interventions for child maltreatment. In H. R. Schaffer & K. Durkin (Eds.), *Blackwell handbook of developmental psychology in action*. Oxford: Blackwell.

Cicchetti, D., Toth, S. L., & Rogosch, F. A. (2005). *A prevention program for child maltreatment*. Unpublished manuscript, University of Rochester, Rochester, NY.

Cillessen, A. H. N. (2009). Sociometric methods. In K. H. Rubin, W. M. Bukowski, & B. Laursen (Eds.), *Handbook of peer interactions, relationships, and groups*. New York: Guilford.

Cipriano, L. E., Rupar, C. A., & Zaric, G. S. (2007). The cost effectiveness of expanding newborn screening for up to 21 inherited metabolic disorders using tandem mass spectrometry: Results from a decision-analytic model. *Value Health, 10*, 83–97.

Cisneros-Cohernour, E. J., Moreno, R. P., & Cisneros, A. A. (2000). Curriculum reform in Mexico: Kindergarten teachers' challenges and dilemmas. Proceedings of the Lilian Katz Symposium. In D. Rothenberg (Ed.), *Issues in early childhood education: Curriculum reform, teacher education, and dissemination of information*. Urbana-Champaign: University of Illinois.

Citkovitz, C., Klimenko, E., Bolyai, M., Applewhite, L., Julliard, K., & Weiner, Z. (2009, in press). Effects of acupuncture during labor and delivery in a U.S. hospital setting: A case-control panel. *Journal of Alternative and Complementary Medicine*.

Clark, B. (2008). *Growing up gifted* (7th ed.). Upper Saddle River, NJ: Prentice Hall.

Clark, E. (1993). *The lexicon in acquisition*. New York: Cambridge University Press.

Clark, E. V. (2009). What shapes children's language? Child-directed speech and the process of acquisition. In V. C. M. Gathercole (Ed.), *Routes to Language, Essays in honor of Melissa Bowerman*. New York: Psychology Press.

Clarke-Stewart, K. A., & Miner, J. L. (2008). Child and day care, effects of. In M. M. Haith & J. B. Benson (Eds.), *Encyclopedia of infant and early childhood development*. Oxford, UK: Elsevier.

Clarke-Stewart, K. A. (2006). What have we learned: Proof that families matter, policies for families and children, prospects for future research. In A. Clarke-Stewart & J. Dunn (Eds.), *Families count*. New York: Cambridge University Press.

Clay, R. (2001, February). Fulfilling an unmet need. *Monitor on Psychology*, No. 2.

Clearfield, M. W., Diedrich, F. J., Smith, L. B., & Thelen, E. (2006). Young infants teach correctly in A-not-B tasks: On the development of stability and perseveration. *Infant Behavior and Development, 29*, 435–444.

Clearfield, M. W., Dineva, E., Smith, L. B., Diedrich, F. J., & Thelen, E. (2009). Cue salience and infant perseverative reaching: Tests of the dynamic field theory. *Developmental Science, 12*, 26–40.

Clifton, R. K., Morrongiello, B. A., Kulig, J. W., & Dowd, J. M. (1981). Developmental changes in auditory localization in infancy. In R. N. Aslin, J. R. Alberts, & M. R. Petersen (Eds.), *Development of perception* (Vol. 1). Orlando, FL: Academic Press.

Clifton, R. K., Muir, D. W., Ashmead, D. H., & Clarkson, M. G. (1993). Is visually guided reaching in early infancy a myth? *Child Development, 64*, 1099–1110.

Cloud, J. (2007, August 27). Failing our geniuses. *Time*, pp. 40–47.

Cluett, E. R., & Burns, E. (2009). Immersion in water in labor and birth. *Cochrane Database of Systematic Reviews, 2*, CD000111.

Cohen, D. (2009). *What every man should know about being a dad*. New York: Psychology Press.

Cohen, G. L., & Prinstein, M. J. (2006). Peer contagion of aggression and health-risk behavior among adolescent males: An experimental investigation of effects of public conduct and private attitudes. *Child Development, 77*, 967–983.

Cohen, L. B. (1995). *Violent video games: Aggression, arousal, and desensitization in young adolescent boys*. Doctoral dissertation, University of Southern California. *Dissertation Abstracts International, 57* (2-B), 1463. University Microfilms No. 9616947.

Cohen, L. B. (2002, April). *Can infants really add and subtract?* Paper presented at the meeting of the International Conference on Infant Studies, Toronto.

Cohen, L. B. (2009). Commentary on Part I: Unresolved issues in infant categorization. In D. H. Rakison & L. M. Oakes (Eds.), *Early category and concept development*. New York: Oxford University Press.

Cohen, N. J., Lojkasek, M., Zadeh, Z. Y., Pugliese, M., & Kiefer, H. (2008). Children adopted in China: A prospective study of their growth and development. *Journal of Child Psychology and Psychiatry, 49*, 458–468.

Coie, J. (2004). The impact of negative social experiences on the development of antisocial behavior. In J. B. Kupersmidt & K. A. Dodge (Eds.), *Children's peer relations: From development to intervention*. Washington, DC: American Psychological Association.

Colby, A., Kohlberg, L., Gibbs, J., & Lieberman, M. (1983). A longitudinal study of moral judgment. *Monographs of the Society for Research in Child Development* (Serial No. 201).

Cole, M. (2006). Culture and cognitive development in phylogenetic, historical, and ontogenetic perspective. In W. Damon & R. Lerner (Eds.), *Handbook of child psychology* (6th ed.). New York: Wiley.

Cole, P. M., Dennis, T. A., Smith-Simon, K. E., & Cohen, L. H. (2009, in press). Preschoolers' emotion regulation strategy understanding: Relations with emotion socialization and child self-regulation. *Social Development*.

Cole, P. M., & Tan, P. Z. (2007). Emotion socialization from a cultural perspective. In J. E. Grusec & P. D. Hastings (Eds.), *Handbook of socialization*. New York: Guilford.

Coleman, M., Ganong, L., & Fine, M. (2004). Communication in stepfamilies. In A. L. Vangelisti (Ed.), *Handbook of family communication*. Mahwah, NJ: Erlbaum.

Coleman-Phox, K., Odouli, R., & Li, D.-K. (2008). Use of a fan during sleep and the risk of sudden infant death syndrome. *Archives of Pediatric and Adolescent Medicine, 162*, 963–968.

Coleman, V. H., Erickson, K., Schulkin, J., Zinberg, S., & Sachs, B. P. (2005). Vaginal birth after cesarean delivery: Practice patterns of obstetricians-gynecologists. *Journal of Reproductive Medicine, 50*, 261–266.

Collins, W. A., & Steinberg, L. (2006). Adolescent development in interpersonal context. In W. Damon & R. Lerner (Eds.), *Handbook of child psychology* (6th ed.). New York: Wiley.

Collins, W. A., & van Dulmen, M (2006). The significance of middle childhood peer competence for work and relationships in early childhood. In A. C. Huston & M. N. Ripke (Eds.), *Developmental contexts in middle childhood*. New York: Cambridge University Press.

Colom, R., Jung, R. E., & Haier, R. J. (2007). General intelligence and memory span: Evidence for a common neuro-anatomic framework. *Cognitive Neuropsychology, 24* (8), 867–878.

Colom, R., & others. (2009). Gray matter correlates of fluid, crystallized, and spatial intelligence. *Intelligence, 37*, 124–135.

Colombo, J., & Mitchell, D. W. (2009). Infant visual habituation. *Neurobiology of Learning and Memory, 92*, 225–234.

Colombo, J., Shaddy, D. J., Blaga, O. M., Anderson, C. J., & Kannass, K. N. (2009). High cognitive ability in infancy and early childhood. In F. D. Horowitz, R. F. Subotnik, & D. J. Matthews (Eds.), *The development of giftedness and talent across the life span*. Washington, DC: American Psychological Association.

Colombo, J., Shaddy, D. J., Richman, W. A., Maikranz, J. M., & Blaga, O. M. (2004). The developmental course of attention in infancy and preschool cognitive outcome. *Infancy, 4*, 1–38.

Coltrane, S. L., Parke, R. D., Schofield, T. J., Tsuha, S. J., Chavez, M., & Lio, S. (2008). Mexican American families and poverty. In D. R. Crane & T. B. Heaton (Eds.), *Handbook of families and poverty*. Thousand Oaks, CA: Sage.

Combs, M. (2010). *Readers and writers in the primary grades* (4th ed.). Boston: Allyn & Bacon.

Comer, J. (2004). *Leave no child behind.* New Haven, CT: Yale University Press.

Comer, J. (2006). Child development: The under-weighted aspect of intelligence. In P. C. Kyllonen, R. D. Roberts, & L. Stankov (Eds.), *Extending intelligence.* Mahwah, NJ: Erlbaum.

Comer, J. P. (1988). Educating poor minority children. *Scientific American, 259,* 42–48.

Commoner, B. (2002). Unraveling the DNA myth: The spurious foundation of genetic engineering. *Harper's Magazine, 304,* 39–47.

Comstock, G., & Scharrer, E. (2006). Media and popular culture. In W. Damon & R. Lerner (Eds.), *Handbook of child psychology* (6th ed.). New York: Wiley.

Conduct Problems Prevention Research Group. (2007). The Fast Track randomized controlled trial to prevent externalizing psychiatric disorders: Findings from grades 3 to 9. *Journal of the American Academy of Child and Adolescent Psychiatry, 46,* 1250–1262.

Conger, R. D., & Chao, W. (1996). Adolescent depressed mood. In R. L. Simons (Ed.), *Understanding differences between divorced and intact families: Stress, interaction, and child outcome.* Thousand Oaks, CA: Sage.

Conley, C. S., & Rudolph, K. D. (2009). The emerging sex difference in adolescent depression: Interacting contributions of puberty and peer stress. *Developmental Psychopathology, 21,* 593–620.

Connolly. J. A., & McIsaac, C. (2009). Romantic relationships in adolescence. In R. M. Lerner & L. Steinberg (Eds.), *Handbook of adolescent psychology* (3rd ed.). New York: Wiley.

Connors, J. (2007). Casualities of reform. *Phi Delta Kappan, 88,* 518–522.

Constantine. N. A. (2008). Editorial: Converging evidence leaves policy behind: Sex education in the United States. *Journal of Adolescent Health, 42,* 324–326.

Cook, M., & Birch, R. (1984). Infant perception of the shapes of tilted plane forms. *Infant Behavior and Development, 7,* 389–402.

Cook, P. J., MacCoun, R., Muschkin, C., & Vigdor, J. (2008). The negative impacts of starting middle school in the sixth grade. *Journal of Policy Analysis and Management, 27,* 104–121.

Cooksey, E. C. (2009). Sexual activity, adolescent. In D. Carr (Ed.), *Encyclopedia of the lift and human development.* Boston: Gale Cengage.

Cook, T. D., Deng, Y., & Morgano, E. (2007). Friendship influences during early adolescence: The special role of friends' grade point average. *Journal of Research on Adolescence, 17,* 325–356.

Cooper, A. R., & Moley, K. H. (2008). Maternal tobacco use and its preimplantation effects on fertility: More reasons to stop smoking. *Seminars in Reproductive Medicine, 26,* 204–212.

Cooper, C., Harvey, N., Javaid, K., Hanson, M., & Dennison, E. (2008). Growth and bone development. *Nestle Nutrition Workshop Series, 61,* 53–68.

Cooper, C. R., Behrens, R., & Trinh, N. (2008, in press). Identity development. In R. A. Shweder, T. R. Bidell, A. C. Daily, S. D. Dixon, P. J. Miller, & J. Model (Eds.), *The Chicago companion to the child.* Chicago: University of Chicago Press.

Cooper, C. R., & Grotevant, H. D. (1989, April). *Individuality and connectedness in the family and adolescent's self and relational competence.* Paper presented at the meeting of the Society for Research in Child Development, Kansas City.

Cooper, C. R., Grotevant, H. D., Moore, M. S., & Condon, S. M. (1982, August). *Family support and conflict: Both foster adolescent identity and role taking.* Paper presented at the meeting of the American Psychological Association, Washington, DC.

Coplan, R. J. & Arbeau, K. A. (2008). The stresses of a brave new world: Shyness and adjustment in kindergarten. *Journal of Research in Childhood Education, 22,* 377–389.

Coplan, R. J., & Arbeau, K. A. (2009). Peer interactions and play in early childhood. In K. H. Rubin, W. M. Bukowski, & B. Laursen (Eds.), *Handbook of peer interactions, relationships, and groups.* New York: Guilford.

Corbetta, D., & Snapp-Childs, W. (2009). Seeing and touching: The role of sensory-motor experience on the development of reaching. *Infant Behavior and Development, 32,* 44–58.

Corbin, C. B., Welk, G. J., Corbin, W. R., & Welk, K. A. (2008). *Concepts of fitness and wellness* (7th ed.). New York: McGraw-Hill.

Cordier, S. (2008). Evidence for a role of paternal exposure in developmental toxicity. *Basic and Clinical Pharmacology and Toxicology, 102,* 176–181.

Cornelius, J. R., Clark, D. B., Reynolds, M., Kirisci, L., & Tarter, R. (2006). Early age of first sexual intercourse and affiliation with deviant peers predict development of SUD: A prospective longitudinal study. *Addictive Behavior, 32,* 850–854.

Costello, D. M., Swendsen, J., Rose, J. S., & Dierker, L. C. (2008). Risk and protective factors associated with trajectories of depressed mood from adolescent to early adulthood. *Journal of Consulting and Clinical Psychology, 766,* 173–183.

Costello, E. J., Sung, M., Worthman, C., & Angold, A. (2007). Pubertal maturation and the development of alcohol use and abuse. *Drug and Alcohol Dependence, 88* (Suppl. 1), S50–S59.

Coté, J. E. (2006). Emerging adulthood as an institutionalized moratorium: Risks and benefits to identity formation. In J. J. Arnett & J. L. Tanner (Eds.), *Emerging adults in America.* Washington, DC: American Psychological Association.

Cote, J. E. (2009). Identity formation and self-development. In R. M. Lerner & L. Steinberg (Eds.), *Handbook of adolescent psychology* (3rd ed.). New York: Wiley.

Cotton, S., Larkin, E., Hoopes, A., Comer, B. A., & Rosenthal, S. L. (2005). The impact of adolescent spirituality on depressive symptoms and health risk behaviors. *Journal of Adolescent Health, 36,* 529.

Council of Economic Advisors. (2000). *Teens and their parents in the 21st century: An examination of trends in teen behavior and the role of parent involvement.* Washington, DC: Author.

Courage, M. L., Howe, M. L., & Squires, S. E. (2004). Individual differences in 3.5-month-olds' visual attention: What do they predict at 1 year? *Infant Behavior and Development, 127,* 19–30.

Courage, M. L., & Richards, J. E. (2008). Attention. In M. M. Haith & J. B. Benson (Eds.), *Encyclopedia of infant and early childhood development.* Oxford, UK: Elsevier.

Courtin, C. (2000). The impact of sign language on the cognitive development of deaf children: The case of theories of mind. *Journal of Deaf Studies and Deaf Education, 5,* 201–219.

Cowan, C. P., & Cowan, P. A. (2000). *When partners become parents.* Mahwah, NJ: Erlbaum.

Cowan, M. K., & Talaro, K. P. (2009). *Microbiology* (2nd ed.). New York: McGraw-Hill.

Cowan, N. (2008). Working memory. In N. J. Salkind (Ed.), *Encyclopedia of educational psychology.* Thousand Oaks, CA: Sage.

Cowan, P., Cowan, C., Ablow, J., Johnson, V. K., & Measelle, J. (2005) *The family context of parenting in children's adaptation to elementary school.* Mahwah, NJ: Erlbaum.

Cox, J. (2006). Postnatal depression fathers. *Lancet, 366,* 982.

Cox, M. J., Neilbron, N., Mills-Koonce, W. R., Pressel, A., Oppenheimer, C. W., & Szwedo, D. E. (2008). Marital relationship. In M. M. Haith & J. B. Benson (Eds.), *Encyclopedia of infant and early childhood development.* Oxford, UK: Elsevier.

Craik, F. I. M. (2006). Brain-behavior relations across the lifespan: A commentary. *Neuroscience and Biobehavioral Reviews, 30,* 885–892.

Crean, H. F. (2008). Conflict in the Latino parent-youth dyad: The role of emotional support from the opposite parent. *Journal of Family Psychology, 22,* 484–493.

Crick, N., Murray-Close, D., Marks, P. E. L., & Moharjeri-Nelson, N. (2009). Agression and peer relationships in school-age children: Relational and physical aggression in group and dyadic contexts. In K. H. Rubin, W. M. Bukowski, & B. Laursen (Eds.), *Handbook of peer interactions, relationships, and groups.* New York: Guilford.

Crissey, S. R. (2009). Dating and romantic relationships, childhood and adolescence. In D. Carr (Ed.), *Encyclopedia, of the life course and human development.* Boston: Gale Cengage.

Crockenberg, S. B. (1986). Are temperamental differences in babies associated with predictable differences in caregiving? In J. V. Lerner & R. M. Lerner (Eds.), *Temperament and social interaction during infancy and childhood.* San Francisco: Jossey-Bass.

Crockett, L. J., Raffaeli, M., & Shen, Y-L. (2006). Linking self-regulation and risk proneness to risky sexual behavior: Pathways through peer pressure and early substance use. *Journal of Research on Adolescence, 16,* 503–525.

Crone, E. A., Windelken, C., van Leijenhorst, L., Honomichi, R. D., Christoff, K., & Bunge, S. A. (2009). Neurocognitive development of relational reasoning. *Developmental Science, 12,* 55–66.

Crosby, R. A., & Holtgrave, D. R. (2006). The protective value of social capital against teen pregnancy: A state-level analysis. *Journal of Adolescent Health, 38,* 556–559.

Crosnoe, R., Riegle-Crumb, C., Field, S., Frank, K., & Muller, C. (2008). Peer group contexts of girls' and boys' academic experiences. *Child Development, 79,* 139–155.

Crosnoe, R., & Trinitapoli, J. (2008). Shared family activities and the transition from childhood into adolescence. *Journal of Research on Adolescence, 18,* 23–48.

Crossman, A. M., Scullin, M. H., & Melnyk, L. (2004). Individual and developmental differences in suggestibility. *Applied Cognitive Psychology, 18,* 941–945.

Crouter, A. C. (2006). Mothers and fathers at work. In A. Clarke-Stewart & J. Dunn (Eds.), *Families count.* New York: Cambridge University Press.

Crowley, K., Callahan, M. A., Tenenbaum, H. R., & Allen, E. (2001). Parents explain more to boys than to girls during shared scientific thinking. *Psychological Science, 12,* 258–261.

Csaba, A., Bush, M. C., & Saphier, C. (2006). How painful are amnioncentesis and chorionic villus sampling? *Prenatal Diagnosis, 26,* 35–38.

Cullen, K. (2001). *Context and eating behavior in children.* Unpublished research, Children's Nutrition Research Center, Baylor School of Medicine, Houston.

Cummings, E. M., & Merrilees, C. E. (2009, in press). Identifying the dynamic processes underlying links between marital conflict and child adjustment. In M. S. Schulz, P. K. Kerig, M. K. Pruett, & R. D. Parke (Eds.), *Feathering the nest.* Washington, DC: American Psychological Association.

Cummings, M. (2009). *Human heredity* (8th ed.). Boston: Cengage.

Curran, K., DuCette, J., Eisenstein, J., & Hyman, I. A. (2001, August). *Statistical analysis of the cross-cultural data: The third year.* Paper presented at the meeting of the American Psychological Association, San Francisco.

Cushner, K. H., McClelland, A., & Stafford, P. (2009). *Human diversity in education* (6th ed.). New York: McGraw-Hill.

Cuzon, V. C., Yeh, P. W., Yanagawa, Y., Obata, K., & Yeh, H. H. (2008). Ethanol consumption during early pregnancy alters the disposition of tangentially migrating GABAergic interneurons in the fetal cortex. *Journal of Neuroscience, 28,* 1854–1864.

Czeizel, A. E., & Puho, E. (2005). Maternal use of nutritional supplements during the first month of pregnancy and decreased risk of Down syndrome: Case-control study. *Nutrition, 21,* 698–704.

D

Dahl, R. E. (2004). Adolescent brain development: A period of vulnerabilities and opportunities. *Annals of the New York Academy of Sciences, 1021,* 1–22.

Dahl, R. E. (2006). Sleeplessness and aggression in youth. *Journal of Adolescent Health, 38,* 641–642.

Daley, A. J., Macarthur, C., & Winter, H. (2007). The role of exercise in treating postpartum depression: A review of the literature. *Journal of Midwifery and Women's Health, 52,* 56–62.

Daley, D. (2006). Attention deficit hyperactivity disorder: A review of the essential facts. *Child: Care, Health, and Development, 32,* 193–204.

Dalton, T. C., & Bergenn, V. W. (2007). *Early experience, the brain, and consciousness.* Mahwah, NJ: Erlbaum.

D'Amico, E. J., Edelen, M. O., Miles, J. N., & Morral, A. R. (2008). The longitudinal association between substance abuse and delinquency among high-risk youth. *Drug and Alcohol Dependence, 93,* 85–92.

Damon, W. (1988). *The moral child.* New York: Free Press.

Damon, W. (2008). *The path to purpose.* New York: Free Press.

Damon, W., & Lerner, R. (Eds.) (2006). *Handbook of child psychology* (6th eds.). New York: Wiley.

Daniels, H. (2007). Pedagogy. In H. Daniels, J. Wertsch, & M. Cole (Eds.), *The Cambridge companion to Vygotsky.* New York: Cambridge University Press.

Darling-Hammond, L. (2007). Race, inequality, and educational accountability: The irony of "No Child Left Behind." *Race, Ethnicity, and Education, 10,* 245–260.

Darrah, J., Senthilselvan, A., & Magill-Evans, J. (2009). Trajectories of serial motor scores of typically developing children: Implications for clinical decision making. *Infant Behavior and Development, 32,* 72–78.

Darwin, C. (1859). *On the origin of species.* London: John Murray.

Dasen, P. R. (1977). Are cognitive processes universal? A contribution to cross-cultural Piagetian psychology. In N. Warran (Ed.), *Studies in cross-cultural psychology* (Vol. 1). London: Academic Press.

Datar, A., & Jacknowitz, A. (2009, in press). Birth weight effects on children's mental, motor, and physical development: Evidence from twins data. *Maternal and Child Health Journal.*

Datar, A., & Sturm, R. (2004). Childhood overweight and parent- and teacher-reported behavior problems: Evidence from a prospective study of kindergartners. *Archives of Pediatric and Adolescent Medicine, 158,* 804–810.

D'Augelli, A. R. (1991). Gay men in college: Identity processes and adaptations. *Journal of College Student Development, 32,* 140–146.

Davidson, J. (2000). Giftedness. In A. Kazdin (Ed.), *Encyclopedia of psychology.* Washington, DC, & New York: American Psychological Association and Oxford University Press.

Davidson, M., Lickona, T., & Khmelkov, V. (2008). A new paradigm for high school character education. In L. Nucci & D. Narváez (Eds.), *Handbook of moral and character education.* Clifton, NJ: Psychology Press.

Davidson, M. R., London, M. L., & Ladewig, P. A. (2008). *Olds' maternal-newborn nursing and women's health across the lifespan* (8th ed.). Upper Saddle River, NJ: Prentice Hall.

Davies, J., & Brember, I. (1999). Reading and mathematics attainments and self-esteem in years 2 and 6—an eight-year cross-sectional study. *Educational Studies, 25,* 145–157.

Davis, A. E., Hyatt, G., & Arrasmith, D. (1998, February). "I Have a Dream" program. *Class One Evaluation Report,* Portland, OR: North-West Regional Education Laboratory.

Davis, B. E., Moon, R. Y., Sachs, M. C., & Ottolini, M. C. (1998). Effects of sleep position on infant motor development. *Pediatrics, 102,* 1135–1140.

Davis, C. L., Tomporowski, P. D., Boyle, C. A., Waller, J. L., Miller, P. H., Nagieri, J. A., & Gregoski, M. (2007). Effects of aerobic exercise on overweight children's cognitive functioning: A randomized controlled trial. *Research Quarterly for Exercise and Sport, 78,* 510–519.

Davis, D. K. (2005). Leading the midwifery renaissance. *RCM Midwives, 8,* 264–268.

Davis, E. P., Glynn, L. M. Schetter, C. D., Hobel, C., Chicz-Demet, A., & Sandman, C. A. (2007). Prenatal exposure to maternal depression and cortisol influences infant development. *Journal of the American Academy of Child and Adolescent Psychiatry, 46,* 737–746.

Davis, K. F., Parker, K. P., & Montgomery, G. L. (2004). Sleep in infants and young children: Part one: Normal sleep. *Journal of Pediatric Health Care, 18,* 65–71.

Davison, K. K., & Birth, L. L. (2001). Weight status, parent reaction, and self-concept in five-year-old girls. *Pediatrics, 107,* 46–53.

Day, N. L., Goldschmidt, L., & Thomas, C. A. (2006). Prenatal marijuana exposure contributes to the prediction of marijuana use at age 14. *Addiction, 101,* 1313–1322.

Day, R. H., & McKenzie, B. E. (1973). Perceptual shape constancy in early infancy. *Perception, 2,* 315–320.

Deater-Deckard, K., & Dodge K. (1997). Externalizing behavior problems and discipline revisited: Non-linear effects and variation by culture, context and gender, *Psychological Inquiry, 8,* 161–75.

DeCasper, A. J., & Spence, M. J. (1986). Prenatal maternal speech influences newborn's perception of speech sounds. *Infant Behavior and Development, 9,* 133–150.

Declerck, D., & others. (2008). Factors associated with prevalence and severity of caries experience in preschool children. *Community Dentistry and Oral Epidemiology, 36,* 168–178

DeGarmo, D. S., & Martinez, C. R. (2006). A culturally informed model of academic well-being for Latino youth: The importance discriminatory experiences and social support. *Family Relations, 55,* 267–278.

de Haan, M., & Gunnar, M. R. (Eds.). (2009). *Developmental social neuroscience.* New York: Guilford.

de Haan, M., & Gunnar, M. R. (Eds.). (2009). *Handbook of social developmental neuroscience.* New York: Guilford.

de Haan, M., Martinos, M. (2008). Brain function. In M. M. Haith & J. B. Benson (Eds.), *Encyclopedia of infant and early childhood development.* Oxford, UK: Elsevier.

de Haan, M., & Matheson, A. (2009). The development and neural bases of processing emotion in faces and voices. In M. de Haan & M. R. Gunnar (Eds.), *Handbook of developmental social neuroscience.* New York: Guilford.

de la Rocheborchard, E., & Thonneau, F. (2002). Paternal age and maternal age are risk factors for miscarriage: Results of a multicentre European study. *Human Reproduction, 17,* 1649–1656.

de Leo, D., & Heller, T. (2008). Social modeling in the transmission of suicidality. *Crisis, 29,* 11–19.

DeLeon, C. W., & Karraker, K. H. (2007). Intrinsic and extrinsic factors associated with night waking in 9-month-old infants. *Infant Behavior and Development, 30,* 596–605.

DeLoache, J. S., Ganea, P. A. (2009). Symbol-based learning in infancy. In A. Woodward & A. Needham (Eds.), *Learning and the infant mind.* New York: Oxford University Press.

DeLoache, J. S., Simcock, G., & Macari, S. (2007). Planes, trains, automobiles and tea-sets: Extremely intense interests in very young children. *Developmental Psychology, 43,* 1579–1586.

de Moraes Barros, M. C., Guinsburg, R., Mitsuhiro, S. S., Chalem, E., & Larenjeira, R. R. (2008). Neurobehavior of full-term for gestational age newborn infants of adolescent mothers. *Journal of Pediatrics, 84,* 217–223.

Dempster, F. N. (1981). Memory span: Sources of individual and developmental differences. *Psychological Bulletin, 80,* 63–100.

Denham, S. A., Bassett, H. H., & Wyatt, T. (2007). The socialization of emotional competence. In J. E. Grusec & P. D. Hastings (Eds.), *Handbook of socialization.* New York: Guilford.

Denmark, F. L., Russo, N. F., Frieze, I. H., & Eschuzur, J. (1988). Guidelines for avoiding sexism in psychological research: A report of the ad hoc committee on nonsexist research. *American Psychologist, 43,* 582–585.

Dennis, C. L., Hodnett, E., Kenton, L., Weston, J., Zupancic, J., Stewart, D. E., & Kiss, A. (2009). Effect of peer support on prevention of postnatal depression among high risk women: Multisite randomized controlled trial. *British Medical Journal, 338,* 3064.

DeRose, L., & Brooks-Gunn, J. (2008). Pubertal development in early adolescence: Implications for affective processes. In N. B. Allen & L. Sheeber (Eds.), *Adolescent emotional development and the emergence of depressive disorders.* New York, NY: Cambridge University Press.

DeRosier, M. E., & Marcus, S. R. (2005). Building friendships and combating bullying: Effectiveness of S. S. Grin at one-year follow-up. *Journal of Clinical Child and Adolescent Psychology, 34,* 140–150.

de Rosnay, M., Cooper, P. J., Tsigaras, N., & Murray, L. (2006). Transmission of social anxiety from mother to infant: An experimental study using a social referencing paradigm. *Behavior Research and Therapy, 44,* 1165–1175.

DeSantis, L. (1998). Building healthy communities with immigrants and refugees. *Journal of Transcultural Nursing, 9,* 20–31.

Deutsch, R. & Pruett, M. K. (2009). Child adjustment and high conflict divorce. In R. M. Galatzer-Levy and L. Kraus (Eds.), *The scientific basis of custody decisions* (2nd ed.). New York: Wiley.

Devos, T. (2006). Implicit bicultural identity among Mexican American and Asian American college students. *Cultural Diversity and Ethnic Minority Psychology, 12,* 1381–1402.

Dewey, J. (1933). *How we think.* Lexington, MA: D. C. Heath.

Diamond, A. D. (1985). Development of the ability to use recall to guide action, as indicated by infants' performance on AB. *Child Development, 56,* 866–883.

Diamond, A. D. (2001). A model system for studying the role of dopamine in the prefrontal cortex during early development in humans: Early and continuously treated phenylketonuria. In C. Nelson & M. Luciana (Eds.), *Handbook of developmental cognitive neuroscience.* Cambridge, MA: MIT Press.

Diamond, A. D. (2009). The interplay of biology and the environment broadly defined. *Developmental Psychology, 45,* 1–8.

Diamond, A. D., Casey, B. J., & Munakata, Y. (2010). *Developmental cognitive neuroscience.* New York: Oxford University Press.

Diamond, L. M. (2008). Female bisexuality from adolescence to adulthood: Results from a 10-year longitudinal study. *Developmental Psychology, 44,* 5–14.

Diamond, L. M., & Savin-Williams, R. C. (2009). Adolescent sexuality. In R. M. Lerner & L. Steinberg (Eds.), *Handbook of adolescent psychology* (3rd ed.). New York: Wiley.

Diaz-Rico, L. T. (2008). *A course for teaching English learners.* Boston: Allyn & Bacon.

Diego, M. A., Field, T., Hernandez-Reif, M. Schanberg, S., Kuh, C., & Gonzales-Quinterto, V. H. (2009). Prenatal depression restricts fetal growth. *Early Human Development, 85,* 65–70.

Diemer, M. A., & Hsieh, C. (2008). Sociopolitical development and vocational expectations among lower socioeconomic status adolescents of color. *Career Development Quarterly, 56,* 257–267.

Dietz, L. J., Jennings, K. D., Kelley, S. A., & Marshal, M. (2009). Maternal depression, paternal psychopathology, and toddlers' behavior problems. *Journal of Clinical Child and Adolescent Psychology, 38,* 48–61.

DiPietro, J. (2008). Unpublished review of J. W. Santrock's *Children,* 11th ed. (New York: McGraw-Hill).

Dishion, T. J., & Piehler, T. F. (2009). Deviant by design: Peer contagion in development, interventions, and schools. In K. H. Rubin, W. M. Bukowski, & B. Laursen (Eds.), *Handbook of peer interactions, relationships, and groups.* New York: Guilford.

Dishion, T. J., Piehler, T. F., & Myers, M. W. (2008) Dynamics and ecology of adolescent peer influence. In M. J. Prinstein & K. A. Dodge (Eds.), *Understanding peer influence in children and adolescents.* New York: Guilford.

Dixit, A., & Girling, J. C. (2008). Obesity and pregnancy. *Journal of Obstetrics and Gynecology, 28,* 14–23.

Dixon, L., Browne, K., & Hamilton-Giachritsis, C. (2005). Risk factors of parents abused as children: A mediational analysis of the intergenerational continuity of child maltreatment (Part I). *Journal of Child Psychology and Psychiatry and Allied Disciplines, 46,* 47–57.

Dodge, K. A. (1983). Behavioral antecedents of peer social status. *Child Development, 54,* 1386–1399.

Dodge, K. A. (2009). Community intervention and public policy in the prevention of antisocial behavior. *Journal of Child Psychology and Psychiatry, 50,* 194–200.

Dodge, K. A., Coie, J. D., & Lynam, D. R. (2006). Aggression and antisocial behavior in youth. In W. Damon & R. Lerner (Eds.), *Handbook of child psychology* (6th ed.). New York: Wiley.

Dodge, K. A., & the Conduct Problems Prevention Research Group. (2007, March). *The impact of Fast Track on adolescent conduct disorder.* Paper presented at the meeting of the Society for Research in Child Development, Boston.

Doherty, E. E., Green, K. M., & Ensminger, M. E. (2008). Investigating the long-term influence of adolescent delinquency on drug use initiation. *Drug and Alcohol Dependence, 93,* 72–84.

Doherty, M. (2008). *Theory of mind.* Philadelphia: Psychology Press.

Domsch, H., Lohaus, A., & Thomas, H. (2009). Prediction of childhood cognitive abilities from a set of early indicators of information processing capabilities. *Infant Behavior and Development, 32,* 91–102.

D'Onofrio, B. M. (2008). Nature vs. nurture. In M. M. Haith & J. B. Benson (Eds.), *Encyclopedia of infant and early childhood development.* Oxford, UK: Elsevier.

Dontigny, L., & others. (2008). Rubella in pregnancy. *Journal of Obstetrics and Gynecology Canada, 30,* 152–168.

Dorn, C. M., Madeja, S. S., & Sabot, P. R. (2004). *Assessing expressive learning.* Mahwah. NJ: Erlhaum.

Doty, R. L., & Shah, M. (2008). Taste and smell. In M. M. Haith & J. B. Benson (Eds.), *Encyclopedia of infant and early childhood development.* Oxford, UK: Elsevier.

Dovey, T. M., Staples, P. A., Gibson, E. L., & Halford, J. C. (2008). Food neophobia and "picky/fussy" eating in children: A review. *Appetite, 50,* 181–193.

Dowda, M., Brown, W. H., McIver, K. L., Pfeiffer, K. A., O'Neill, J. R., Addy, C. L., & Pate, R. R. (2009). Policies and characteristics of the preschool environment and physical activity of young children. *Pediatrics, 123,* e261–e266.

Downe, S. (Ed.). (2008). *Normal childbirth* (2nd ed.). Oxford, UK: Elsevier.

Doyen, A. L., Dufour, T., Caroff, X., Cherfouh, A., & Carlier, M. (2008). Hand preference and hand performance: Cross-sectional developmental trends and family resemblance in degree of laterality. *Laterality, 13,* 179–197.

Dozier, M., Stovall-McClough, K. C., & Albus, K. E. (2009). Attachment and psychopathy in adulthood. In J. Cassidy & P. R. Shaver (Eds.), *Handbook of attachment* (2nd ed.). New York: Guilford.

Draghi-Lorenz (2007, July). *Self-conscious emotions in young infants and the direct perception of self and others in interaction.* Paper presented at the meeting of the International Society for Research on Emotions, Sunshine Coast, Australia.

Drake, M. (2008). Developing resilient children: After 100 years of Montessori education. *Montessori Life, 20,* 2, 28–31.

Dryfoos, J., & Barkin, C. (2006). *Growing up in America today.* New York: Oxford University Press.

Dryfoos, J. G. (1990). *Adolescents at risk: Prevalence or prevention.* New York: Oxford University Press.

Dubay, I., Joyce, T., Kaestner, R., & Kenney, G. M. (2001). Changes in prenatal care timing and low birth weight by race and socioeconomic status: Implications for the Medicaid expansions for pregnant women. *Health Services Research, 36,* 373–398.

Dubois, J., & others (2008). Microstructural correlates of infant functional development: Example of the visual pathways. *Journal of Neuroscience, 28,* 1943–1948.

Dubow, E. F., Huesmann, L. R., & Greenwood, D. (2007). Media and youth socialization. In J. E. Grusec & P. D. Hastings (Eds.), *Handbook of socialization.* New York: Guilford.

Dugan, S. A. (2008). Exercise for preventing childhood obesity. *Physical Medicine and Rehabilitation Clinics of North America, 19,* 205–216.

Duncan, G. J., & others. (2007). School readiness and later achievement. *Developmental Psychology, 43,* 1428–1446.

Duncan, S. C., Duncan, T. E., Strycker, L. A., & Chaumeton, N. R. (2007). A cohort-sequential latent growth model of physical activity from 12 to 17 years. *Annals of Behavioral Medicine, 33,* 80–89.

Dundek, L. H. (2006). Establishment of a Somali doula program at a large metropolitan hospital. *Journal of Perinatal and Neonatal Nursing, 20,* 128–137.

Dunkel, L. (2006). Management of children with idiopathic short stature. *European Journal of Endocrinology, 155* (Suppl. 1), S35–S38.

Dunn, J. (2007). Siblings and socialization. In J. E. Grusec & P. D. Hastings (Eds.), *Handbook of socialization.* New York: Guilford.

Dunn, J., & Kendrick, C. (1982). *Siblings.* Cambridge, MA: Harvard University Press.

Dunn, N. F., Miller, R., Griffioen, A., & Lee, C. A. (2008, in press). Carrier testing in haeophilia A and B: Adult carriers' and their partners' experiences and their views on the testing of young females. *Haemophilia.*

Dunson, D. B., Baird, D. D., & Columbo, B. (2004). Increased fertility with age in men and women. *Obstetrics and Gynecology, 103,* 51–56.

Durrant, J. E. (2008). Physical punishment, culture, and rights: Current issues for professionals. *Journal of Developmental and Behavioral Pediatrics, 29,* 55–66.

Durston, S., & Casey, B. J. (2006). What have we learned about cognitive development from neuroimaging? *Neuropsychologia, 44,* 2149–2157.

Durston, S., Davidson, M. C., Tottenham, N. T., Galvan, A., Spicer, J., Fossella, J. A., & Casey, B. J. (2006). A shift from diffuse to focal cortical activity with development. *Developmental Science, 9,* 1–8.

Dweck, C. S. (2006). *Mindset.* New York: Random House.

Dworkin, S. L., & Santelli, J. (2007). Do abstinence-plus interventions reduce sexual risk behavior among youth? *PLoS Medicine, 4,* 1437–1439.

Dwyer, T., & Ponsonby, A. L. (2009). Sudden infant death syndrome and prone sleeping position. *Annals of Epiemiology, 19,* 245–249.

E

Eagly, A. H. (2001). Social role theory of sex differences and similarities. In J. Worell (Ed.), *Encyclopedia of women and gender.* San Diego: Academic Press.

Eagly, A. H. (2009, in press). Gender roles. In J. Levine & M. Hogg (Eds.), *Encyclopedia of group processes and intergroup relations.* Thousand Oaks, CA: Sage

Eagly, A. H., & Crowley, M. (1986). Gender and helping: A meta-analytic review of the social psychological literature. *Psychological Bulletin, 108,* 233–256.

Eagly, A. H., & Steffen, V. J. (1986). Gender and aggressive behavior: A meta-analytic review of the social psychological literature. *Psychological Bulletin, 100,* 309–330.

Eaton, D. K., & others. (2006, June 9). Youth risk behavior surveillance—United States, 2005. *MMWR, 55,* 1–108.

Eaton, D. K., & others. (2008). Youth risk behavior surveillance—United States, 2007. *MMWR Surveillance Summaries, 57,* 1–131.

Eaton, W. O. (2008). Milestones: Physical. In M. M. Haith & J. B. Benson (Eds.), *Encyclopedia of infant and early childhood development.* Oxford, UK: Elsevier.

Ebbeling, C. A., & Ludwig, D. S. (2008). Tracking pediatric obesity. *Journal of the American Medical Association, 299,* 2442–2443.

Eby, J. W., Herrell, A. L., & Jordan, M. L. (2009). *Teaching in elementary school: A reflective approach* (5th ed.). Boston: Allyn & Bacon.

Eccles, J. S. (2007). Families, schools, and developing achievement-related motivations and engagement. In J. E. Grusec & P. D. Hastings (Eds.), *Handbook of socialization.* New York: Guilford.

Eccles, J. S., & Roeser, R. W. (2009). Schools, academic motivation, and stage-environment fit. In R. M. Lerner & L. Steinberg (Eds.), *Handbook of adolescent psychology* (3rd ed.). New York: Wiley.

Echevarria, J., Vogt, M. J., & Short, D. J. (2010). *Making content comprehensible for elementary English learners: The SIOP Model.* Boston: Allyn & Bacon.

Eckerman, C., & Whitehead, H. (1999). How toddler peers generate coordinated action: A cross-cultural exploration. *Early Education and Development, 10,* 241–266.

Eckstein, K. C., Mikhail, L. M., Ariza, A. J., Thompson, J. S., Millard, S. C., Binns, H. J., & the Pediatric Practice Research Group (2006). Parents' perceptions of their child's weight and health. *Pediatrics, 117,* 681–690.

Edelman, M. W. (1992). *The measure of our success.* Boston: Beacon Press.

Edmond, K. M., Kirkwood, B. R., Tawaih, C. A., & Agyei, S. O. (2008). Impact of early infant feeding practices on mortality in low birth weight infants from rural Ghana. *Journal of Perinatology, 28,* 438–444.

Edwards, R., & Hamilton, M. A. (2004). You need to understand my gender role: An empirical test of Tannen's model of gender and communication. *Sex Roles, 50,* 491–504.

Edwards, S. L., & Sarwark, J. F. (2005). Infant and child motor development. *Clinical and Orthopedic Related Research, 434,* 33–39.

Egan, S. K., & Perry, D. G. (2001). Gender identity: A multidimensional analysis with implications for psychosocial adjustment. *Developmental Psychology, 37,* 451–463.

Egeland, B., Jacobvitz, D., & Sroufe, L. A. (1988). Breaking the cycle of abuse. *New Directions for Child Development, 11,* 77–92.

Einarson, A., & Ito, S. (2007). Re: Use of contemporary antidepressants during breastfeeding: A proposal for a specific safety index. *Drug Safety, 30,* 643.

Eisenberg, M. E., Bernat, D. H., Bearinger, L. H., & Resnick, M. D. (2008). Support for comprehensive sexuality education: Perspectives from parents of school-aged youth. *Journal of Adolescent Research, 42,* 352–359.

Eisenberg, N. (Ed.). (1982). *The development of prosocial behavior.* New York: Wiley.

Eisenberg, N., Fabes, R. A., & Spinrad, T. L. (2006). Prosocial development. In W. Damon & R. Lerner (Eds.), *Handbook of child psychology* (6th ed.). New York: Wiley.

Eisenberg, N., & Morris, A. S. (2004). Moral cognitions and social responding in adolescence. In R. Lerner & L. Steinberg (Eds.), *Handbook of adolescent psychology.* New York: Wiley.

Eisenberg, N., Morris, A. S., McDaniel, B,. & Spinrad, T. L. (2009) Moral cognitions and prosocial responding in adolescence. In R. M. Lerner & L. Steinberg (Eds.), *Handbook of adolescent psychology* (3rd ed.). New York: Wiley.

Eisenberg, N., & others. (2008). Understanding mother-adolescent conflict discussions: Concurrent and across-time prediction from youths' dispositions and parenting. *Monographs of the Society for Research in Child Development, 73* (2), 1–160.

Eisenberg, N., Spinrad, T. L., & Smith, C. L. (2004). Emotion-related regulation: Its conceptualization, relations to social functioning, and socialization. In P. Philippot & R. S. Feldman (Eds.), *The regulation of emotion.* Mahwah, NJ: Erlbaum.

Elkind, D. (1970, April 5). Erik Erikson's eight ages of man. *New York Times Magazine.*

Elkind, D. (1976). *Child development and education: A Piagetian perspective.* New York: Oxford University Press.

Elkind, D. (1988, January). Educating the very young: A call for clear thinking. *NEA Today,* pp. 22–27.

Elliott, M. R., Kallan, M. J., Durbin, D. R., & Winston, F. K. (2006). Effectiveness of child safety seats versus seat belts in reducing risk for death in children in passenger vehicle crashes. *Archives of Pediatric and Adolescent Medicine, 160,* 617–621.

Elliott, V. S. (2004). Methamphetamine use increasing. Retrieved January 16, 2005, from www.amaasson.org/amednews/2004/07/26/hlsc0726.htm.?

Elmore, R. F. (2009). Schooling adolescents. In R. M. Lerner & L. Steinberg (Eds.), *Handbook of adolescent psychology* (3rd ed.). New York: Wiley.

Emery, R. E. (1994). *Renegotiating family relationships.* New York: Guilford.

Enfield, A., & Collins, D. (2008). The relationship of service-learning, social justice, multicultural competence, and civic engagement. *Journal of College Student Development. 49,* 95–109.

Enger, E., Ross, F. C., & Bailey, D. (2009). *Concepts in biology* (13th ed.). New York: McGraw-Hill.

Engler, A. J., Ludington-Hoe, S. M., Cusson, R. M., Adams, R., Bahnsen, M., Brumbaugh, E., Coates, P., Grief, J., McHargue, L., Ryan, D. L., Settle, M., & Williams, D. (2002). Kangaroo care: National survey of practice, knowledge, barriers, and perceptions. *American Journal of Maternal/Child Nursing, 27,* 146–153.

Englund, M. M., Egeland, B., & Collins, W. A. (2008). Exceptions to high school dropout predictions in a low-income sample: Do adults make a difference? *Journal of Social Issues, 64, 1,* 77–93.

Ennett, S. T., Bauman, K. E., Hussong, A., Faris, R., Foshee, V. A., & Cai, L. (2006). The peer context of adolescent substance use: Findings from social network analysis. *Journal of Research on Adolescence, 16,* 159–186.

Enright, M. S., Schaefer, L. V., Schaefer, P., & Schaefer, K. A. (2008). Building a just adolescent community *Montessori Life, 20,* 36–42.

Ensembl Human (2008). *Explore the* Homo sapiens *genome.* Retrieved October 10, 2008, from the Internet at www.ensembl.org/Homo_sapiens/index.html

Entringer, S., Kumsta, R., Hellhammer, D. H., Wadhwa, P. D., & Wust, S. (2009, in press). Prenatal exposure to maternal psychosocial stress and HPA axis regulation in young adults. *Hormones and Behavior.*

Epstein, M., & Ward, L. M. (2008). "Always use protection": Communication boys receive about sex education from parents, peers, and the media. *Journal of Youth and Adolescence, 37,* 113–126.

Ercikan, K. (2006). Developments in assessment of student learning. In P. A. Alexander & P. H. Winne (Eds.), *Handbook of educational psychology* (2nd ed.). Mahwah, NJ: Erlbaum.

ERIC/EECE. (2002). Academic redshirting. *ERIC Clearinghouse on Elementary and Early Childhood Education,* pp. 1–15.

Ericson, N. (2001, June). *Addressing the problem of juvenile bullying.* Washington, DC: Office of Juvenile Justice and Delinquency Prevention, Office of Justice Programs, U.S. Department of Justice.

Ericsson, K. A., Charness, N., Feltovich, P. J., & Hoffman, R. R. (Eds.). (2006). *The Cambridge handbook of expertise and expert performance.* New York: Cambridge University Press.

Erikson, E. H. (1950). *Childhood and society.* New York: W. W. Norton.

Erikson, E. H. (1968). *Identity: Youth and crisis.* New York: W. W. Norton.

Eriksson, U. J. (2009, in press). Congenital malformations in diabetic pregnancy. *Seminars in Fetal and Neonatal Medicine.*

Escobar-Chaves, S. L., & Anderson, C. A. (2008). Media and risky behavior. *The Future of Children, 18* (1), 147–180.

Etzel, R. (1988, October). *Children of smokers.* Paper presented at the American Academy of Pediatrics meeting, New Orleans.

Evans, G. W., & English, K. (2002). The environment of poverty. *Child Development, 73,* 1238–1248.

Evans, G. W., & Kim, P. (2007). Childhood poverty and health: Cumulative risk exposure and stress dysregulation. *Psychological Science, 18,* 953–957.

F

Fabiano, G. A., Pelham, W. E., Coles, E. K., Gnagy, E. M., Chronis-Tuscano, A., & O'Connor, B. C. (2009). A meta-analysis of behavioral treatments for attention deficit/hyperactivity disorder. *Clinical Psychology Review, 29,* 129–140.

Fadnes, L. T., Engebretsen, I. M., Wamani, H., Wangisi, J., Tumwine, J. K., & Tylleskar, T. (2009). Need to optimize infant feeding counseling: A cross-sectional survey among HIV-positive mothers in Eastern Uganda. *BMC Pediatricsk, 9* (1), 2.

Fagan, J. F. (1992). Intelligence: A theoretical viewpoint. *Current Directions in Psychological Science, 1,* 82–86.

Fagan, J. F., Holland, C. R., & Wheeler, K. (2009). Prediction of childhood cognitive abilities from a set of early indicators of information processing capabilities. *Infant Behavior and Development, 32,* 91–102.

Fagot, B. I., Rodgers, C. S., & Leinbach, M. D. (2000). Theories of gender socialization. In T. Eckes & H. M. Trautner (Eds.), *The developmental social psychology of gender.* Mahwah, NJ: Erlbaum.

Fahey, T. D., Insel, P. M., & Roth, W. T. (2009). *Fit and well, Brief* (8th ed.). New York: McGraw-Hill.

Fair, D., & Schlaggar, B. L. (2008). Brain development. In M. M. Haith & J. B. Benson (Eds.), *Encyclopedia of infant and early childhood development.* Oxford, UK: Elsevier.

Falbo, T., & Poston, D. L. (1993). The academic, personality, and physical outcomes of only children in China. *Child Development, 64,* 18–35.

Fallon, A., Engel, C., & Boyle, N. (2009). Midwifery basics: Caring for women with medical conditions: Infections in pregnancy. *Practicing Midwife, 12,* 27–33.

Fan, F., Zou, Y., Ma, A., Yue, Y., Mao, W., & Ma, X. (2009). Hormonal changes and somatopsychologic manifestations in the first trimester of pregnancy and postpartum. *International Journal of Gynecology and Obstetrics, 105,* 46–49.

Fanjiang, G., & Kleinman, R. E. (2007). Nutrition and performance in children. *Current Opinion in Clinical Nutrition and Metabolic Care, 10,* 342–347.

Fantasia. H. C. (2008). Concept analysis: Sexual decision-making in adolescence. *Nursing Forum, 43,* 80–90.

Fantz, R. L. (1963). Pattern vision in newborn infants. *Science, 140,* 286–297.

Faraone, S. V. (2007). Stimulant therapy in the management of ADHD: Mixed amphetamine salts (extended release). *Expert Opinion on Pharmacotherapy, 8,* 2127–2134.

Faris, R. (2009). Bullying and peer victimization. In D. Carr (Ed.), *Encyclopedia of the life course and human development.* Boston: Gale Cengage.

Farrington, D. P. (2009). Conduct disorder, aggression, and delinquency. In R. M. Lerner & L. Steinberg (Eds.), *Handbook of adolescent psychology* (3rd ed.), New York: Wiley.

Farrington, D. P., Ttofi, M. M., & Coid, J. W. (2009). Development of adolescence-limited, late-onset, and persistent offenders from 8 to age 48. *Aggressive Behavior, 35,* 150–163.

Fasig, L. (2000). Toddlers' understanding of ownership: Implications for self-concept development. *Social Development, 9,* 370–382.

Fear, N. T., Hey, K., Vincent, T., & Murphy, M. (2007). Paternal occupation and neural tube defects: A case-control study based on the Oxford Record Linkage Study register. *Pediatric and Perinatal Epidemiology, 21,* 163–168.

Federal Interagency Forum on Child and Family Statistics (2008). *America's children: Key indicators of well-being.* Washington, DC: U.S. Government Printing Office.

Feeney, S., Moravcik, E., Nolte, S., & Christensen, D. (2010). *California version of who am I in the lives of children?* (8th ed.) Upper Saddle River, NJ: Prentice Hall.

Feeney, S., Moravcik, E., Nolte, S., & Christensen, D. (2010). *Colifornio version of who am I in the lives of children* (8th ed.). Upper Saddle River, NJ: Prentice Hall.

Fein, G. G. (1986). Pretend play. In D. Görlitz & J. F. Wohlwin (Eds.), *Curiosity, imagination, and play.* Hillsdale, NJ: Erlbaum.

Feldman, R. (2007). Parent-infant synchrony. *Current Directions in Psychological Science, 16,* 340–345.

Feldman, R., & Eidelman, A. I. (2007). Maternal postpartum behavior and the emergence of infant-mother and infant-father synchrony in preterm and full-term infants: The role of neonatal vagal tone. *Developmental Psychobiology, 49,* 290–302.

Feldman, R., Weiler, A., Sirota, L., & Eidelman, A. I. (2002). Skin-to-skin contact (kangaroo care) promotes self-regulation in premature infants: Sleep-wake cyclicity, arousal modulation, and sustained exploration. *Developmental Psychology, 38,* 194–207.

Feldman, S. S., Turner, R., & Aruajo, K. (1999). Interpersonal context as an influence on sexual timetables of youths: Gender and ethnic effects. *Journal of Research on Adolescence, 9,* 25–52.

Feleszko, W., & others. (2006). Parental tobacco smoking is associated with IL-13 secretion in children with allergic asthma. *Journal of Allergy and Clinical Immunology, 117,* 97–102.

Fenson, L., Marchman, V. A., Thal, D., Dale, P. S., Bates, E., & Reznick, J. S. (2007). *The MacArthur-Bates communicative development inventories user's guide and technical manual* (2nd ed.). Baltimore: Brookes.

Ferber, S. G., & Makhoul, I. R. (2008). Neurobehavioral assessment of skin-to-skin effects on reaction to pain in preterm infants: A randomized, controlled within-subject trial. *Acta Pediatrica, 97,* 171–176.

Ferguson, D. M., Harwood, L. J., & Shannon, F. T. (1987). Breastfeeding and subsequent social adjustment in 6- to 8-year-old children. *Journal of Child Psychology and Psychiatry, 28,* 378–386.

Fernandes, O., Sabharwal, M., Smiley, T., Pastuszak, A., Koren, G., & Einarson, T. (1998). Moderate to heavy caffeine consumption during pregnancy and relationship to spontaneous abortion and abnormal fetal growth: A meta-analysis. *Reproductive Toxicology, 12,* 435–444.

Fertig, A. R. (2009, in press). Selection and the effect of prenatal smoking. *Health Economics.*

Fidler, D. J. (2008). Down syndrome. In M. M. Haith & J. B. Benson (Eds.), *Encyclopedia of infant and early childhood development.* Oxford, UK: Elsevier.

Field, A. E., Cambargo, C. A., Taylor, C. B., Berkey, C. S., Roberts, S. B., & Colditz, G. A. (2001). Peer, parent, and media influences on the development of weight concerns and frequent dieting among preadolescent and adolescent girls and boys. *Pediatrics, 107,* 54–60.

Field, T. (2007). *The amazing infant.* Malden, MA: Blackwell.

Field, T. (2008). Breastfeeding and antidepressants. *Infant Behavior and Development, 31,* 481–487.

Field, T., & Diego, M. (2008). Vagal activity, early growth, and emotional development. *Infant Behavior and Development, 31,* 361–373.

Field, T., Diego, M., & Hernandez-Reif, M. (2007). Massage therapy research. *Developmental Review, 27,* 75–89.

Field, T., Diego, M., & Hernandez-Reif, M. (2008). Prematurity and potential predictors. *International Journal of Neuroscience, 118,* 277–289.

Field, T., Diego, M., Hernandez-Reif, M., Deeds, O., Holder, V., Schanberg, S., & Kuhn, C. (2009). Depressed pregnant black women have a greater incidence of prematurity and low birthweight outcomes. *Infant Behavior and Development, 32,* 10–16.

Field, T., Diego, M., & Sanders, C. E. (2001). Exercise is positively related to adolescents' relationships and academics. *Adolescence, 36,* 105–110.

Field, T., & Hernandez-Reif, M. (2008). Touch and pain. In M. M. Haith & J. B. Benson (Eds.), *Encyclopedia of infant and early childhood development.* Oxford, UK: Elsevier.

Field, T. M. (2001). Massage therapy facilitates weight gain in preterm infants. *Current Directions in Psychological Science, 10,* 51–55.

Field, T. M. (2003). Stimulation of preterm infants. *Pediatrics Review, 24,* 4–11.

Field, T. M. (2007). *The amazing infant.* Malden, MA: Blackwell.

Field, T. M., Grizzle, N., Scafidi, F., & Schanberg, S. (1996). Massage and relaxation therapies effects on depressed adolescent mothers. *Adolescence, 31,* 903–911.

Field, T. M., Henteleff, T., Hernandez-Reif, M., Martines, E., Mavunda, K., Kuhn, C., & Schanberg, S. (1998). Children with asthma have improved pulmonary functions after massage therapy. *Journal of Pediatrics, 132,* 854–858.

Field, T. M., Hernandez-Reif, M., Feije, L., & Freedman, J. (2006). Prenatal, perinatal, and neonatal stimulation, *Infant Behavior and Development, 29,* 24–31.

Field, T. M., Hernandez-Reif, M., Freedman, J. (2004, Fall). Stimulation programs for preterm infants. *SRCD Social Policy Reports, XVIII* (No. 1), 1–20.

Field, T. M., Hernandez-Reif, M., Taylor, S., Quinitino, O., & Burnman, I. (1997). Labor pain is reduced by massage therapy. *Journal of Psychosomatic Obstetrics and Gynecology, 18,* 286–291.

Field, T. M., Lasko, D., Mundy, P., Henteleff, T., Kabat, S., Talpins, S., & Dowling, M. (1997). Brief report: Autistic children's attentiveness and responsivity improve after touch therapy. *Journal of Autism and Developmental Disorders, 27,* 333–338.

Field, T. M., Quintino, O., Hernandez-Reif, M., & Koslosky, G. (1998). Adolescents with attention deficit hyperactivity disorder benefit from massage therapy. *Adolescence, 33,* 103–108.

Fiese, B. H., & Winter, M. A. (2008). Family influence. In M. M. Haith & J. B. Benson (Eds.), *Encyclopedia of infant and early childhood development.* Oxford, UK: Elsevier.

Figueiredo, B., & Costa, R. (2009). Mother's stress, mood, and emotional involvement with the infant: 3 months before and 3 months after childbirth. *Archives of Women's Mental Health, 12,* 143–153.

Findlay, L. C., Coplan, R. J., & Bowker, A. (2009, in press). Keeping it all inside: Shyness, internalizing coping strategies and socio-emotional adjustment in middle childhood. *International Journal of Behavioural Development.*

Finger, B., Hans, S. L., Bernstein, V. J. & Cox, S. M. (2009). Parent relationship quality and infant-mother attachment. *Attachment and Human Development, 11,* 285–306.

Finning, K. M., & Chitty, L. S. (2008). Noninvasive fetal sex determination: Impact on clinical practice. *Seminars in Fetal and Neonatal Medicine, 13,* 69–75.

Fiscella, K., & Kitzman, H. (2009). Disparities in academic achievement and health: The intersection of child education and health policy. *Pediatrics, 123,* 1073–1080.

Fisher, P. A. (2005, April). *Translational research on underlying mechanisms of risk among foster children: Implications for prevention science.* Paper presented at the meeting of the Society for Research in Child Development, Washington, DC.

Fivush, R. (1993). Developmental perspectives on autobiographical recall. In G. S. Goodman, & B. Bottoms (Eds.), *Child victims and child witnesses: Understanding and improving testimony.* New York: Guilford.

Flannery, D. J., Hussey, D., Biebelhausen, L., & Wester, K. (2003). Crime, delinquency, and youth gangs. In G. Adams & M. Berzonsky (Eds.), *Blackwell handbook of adolescence.* Maiden, MA: Blackwell.

Flavell, J. H. (2004). Theory-of-mind development: Retrospect and prospect. *Merrill-Palmer Quarterly, 50,* 274–290.

Flavell, J. H., Friedrichs, A., & Hoyt, J. (1970). Developmental changes in memorization processes. *Cognitive Psychology, 1,* 324–340.

Flavell, J. H., Green, F. L., & Flavell, E. R. (1998). The mind has a mind of its own: Developing knowledge about mental uncontrollability. *Cognitive Development, 13,* 127–138.

Flavell, J., Mumme, D., Green, F., & Flavell E. (1992). Young children's understanding of different types of beliefs. *Child Development, 63,* 960–977.

Flegal, W. A. (2007). Blood group genotyping in Germany. *Transfusion, 47* (Suppl. 1), S47–S53.

Fletcher, A. C., Steinberg, L., & Williams-Wheeler, M. (2004). Parental influences on adolescent problem behavior: Revisiting Stattin and Kerr. *Child Development, 75,* 781–796.

Flint, M. S., Baum, A., Chambers, W. H., & Jenkins, F. J. (2007, in press). Induction of DNA damage, alteration of DNA repair, and transcriptional activation by stress hormones. *Psychoneuroendocrinology, 32,* 470–479.

Flom, R., & Pick, A. D. (2003). Verbal encouragement and joint attention in 18-month-old infants. *Infant Behavior and Development, 26,* 121–134.

Florence, N. (2010). *Multiculturalism 101.* New York: McGraw-Hill.

Flores, G., Abreu, M., & Tomany-Korman, S. C. (2005). Limited English proficiency, primary language at home, and disparities in children's health care: How language barriers are measured matters. *Public Health Reports, 120,* 418–420.

Floriani, V., & Kennedy, C. (2008). Promotion of physical activity in children. *Current Opinion in Pediatrics, 20,* 90–95.

Floyd, P. A., Mimms, S. E., & Yelding, C. (2008). *Personal health* (4th ed.). Belmont, CA: Wadsworth.

Flynn, J. R. (1999). Searching for justice: The discovery of IQ gains over time. *American Psychologist. 54,* 5–20.

Flynn, J. R. (2007). The history of the American mind in the 20th century: A scenario to explain IQ gains over time and a case for the relevance of *g.* In P. C. Kyllonen, R. D. Roberts, & L. Stankov (Eds.), *Extending intelligence.* Mahwah, NJ: Erlbaum.

Flynn, L., Budd, M., & Modelski, J. (2008). Enhancing resource utilization among pregnant adolescents. *Public Health Nursing, 25,* 140–148.

Fogelholm, M. (2008). How physical activity can work? *International Journal of Pediatric Obesity, 3* (Suppl. 1), S10–S14.

Fonseca, E. B., Celik, E., Parra, M., Singh, M., Nicolaides, K. H., & the Fetal Medicine Foundation Second Trimester Screening Group. (2007). Progesterone and the risk of preterm birth among women with a short cervix. *New England Journal of Medicine, 357,* 462–469.

Fontenot, H. B. (2007). Transition and adaption to adoptive motherhood. *Journal of Obsterics. Gynecologic, and Neonatal Nursing, 36,* 175–182.

Food & Nutrition Service. (2009). *The new look of the women, infants, and children (WIC) program.* Retrieved January 21, 2009, from www.health.state.ny.us/prevention/nutrition/wic/the_new_look_of_wic.htm

Forgatch, M. S., Patterson, G. R., Degarmo, D. S., & Beldavs, Z. G. (2009). Testing the Oregon delinquency model with 9-year follow-up of the Oregon Divorce Study. *Development and Psychopathology, 21,* 637–660.

Forget-Dubois, N., Dionne, G., Lemelin, J.-P., Perusse, D., Tremblay, R. E., & Boivin, M. (2009). Early child language mediates the relation between home environment and school readiness. *Child Development, 80,* 736–749.

Fornari, E., Knyazeva, M. G., Meuli, R., & Maeder, P. (2007). Myelination shapes functional activity in the developing brain. *Neuroimage, 38,* 511–518.

Forrester, M. B. (2007). Oxycodone abuse in Texas, 1998–2004. *Journal of Toxicology and Environmental Health A, 70,* 534–538.

Forrester, M. B., & Merz, R. D. (2007). Risk of selected birth defects with prenatal illicit drug use, Hawaii, 1986–2002. *Journal of Toxicology and Environmental Health A, 70,* 7–18.

Foskett, N., Dyke, M., & Maringe, F. (2008). The influence of the school in the decision to participate in learning post-16. *British Educational Research Journal, 34,* 37–61.

Foster-Cohen, S., Edgin, J. O., Champion, P. R., & Woodward, L. J. (2007). Early delayed language development in very preterm infants. Evidence from the MacArthur-Bates. CDI. *Journal of Child Language, 34,* 655–675.

Fowden, A. L., Forhead, A. J., Coan, P. M., & Burton, G. J. (2008). The placenta and intrauterine programming. *Journal of Neuroendcrinology, 20,* 439–450.

Fowler-Brown, A., & Kahwati, L. C. (2004). Prevention and treatment of overweight in children and adolescents. *American Family Physician, 69,* 2591–2598.

Fox, B. J. (2010). *Phonics and structural analysis for the teacher of reading* (10th ed.). Boston: Allyn & Bacon.

Fox, M. K., Pac, S., Devaney, B., & Jankowski, L. (2004). Feeding infants and toddlers study: What foods are infants and toddlers eating? *American Dietetic Association Journal 104* (Suppl.), S22–S30.

Fraga, C. G., Motchnik, P. A., Shigenaga, M. K., Helbock, H. J., Jacob, R. A., & Ames, B. N. (1991). Ascorbic acid protects against endogenous oxidative DNA damage in human sperm. *Proceedings of the National Academy of Sciences USA, 88,* 11003–11006.

Francis, J., Fraser, G., & Marcia, J. E. (1989). *Cognitive and experimental factors in moratorium-achievement (MAMA) cycles.* Unpublished manuscript. Department of Psychology, Simon Fraser University, Burnaby, British Columbia.

Fraser, S. (Ed.). (1995). *The bell curve wars: Race, intelligence, and the future of America.* New York: Basic Books.

Fratelli, N., Papageorghiou, A. T., Prefumo, F., Bakalis, S., Homfray, T., & Thilaganathan, B. (2007, in press). Outcome of prenatally diagnosed agenesis of the corpus callosum. *Prenatal Diagnosis, 512–517.*

Frederick, I. O., Williams, M. A., Sales, A. E., Martin, D. P., & Killien, M. (2008). Pre-pregnancy body mass index, gestational weight gain, and other maternal characteristics in relation to infant birth weight. *Maternal Child Health Journal, 12,* 557–567.

Frederikse, M., Lu, A., Aylward, E., Barta, P., Sharma, T., & Pearlson, G. (2000). Sex differences in inferior lobule volume in schizophrenia. *American Journal of Psychiatry, 157,* 422–427.

Fredricks, J. A. (2008). Extracurricular activities. In N. J. Salkind (Ed.), *Encyclopedia of educational psychology.* Thousand Oaks, CA: Sage.

Fredricks, J. A., & Eccles, J. S. (2006). Extracurricular involvement and adolescent adjustment: Impact of duration, number of activities, and breadth of participation. *Applied Developmental Science, 10,* 132–146.

Freedman, D. S., Khan, L. K., Serdula, M. K., Dietz, W. H., Srinivasan, S. R., & Berenson, G. S. (2005). The relation of childhood BMI to adult adiposity: The Bogalusa Heart Study. *Pediatrics, 115,* 22–27.

Freedman, D. S., Patel, D. A., Srinivasan, S. R., Chen, W., Tang, R., Bond, M. G., & Berenson, G. S. (2008). The contribution of childhood obesity to adult carotid intima-media thickness: The Bogalusa Heart Study. *International Journal of Obesity, 32,* 749–756.

French, D. C., Eisenberg, N., Vaughan, J., Purwono, U., & Suryanti, T. A. (2008). Religious involvement and the social competence and adjustment of Indonesian Muslim adolescents. *Developmental Psychology, 44*, 597–611.

Fretts, R. C., Zera, C., & Heffner, C. Z. (2008). Maternal age and pregnancy. In M. M. Haith & J. B. Benson (Eds.), *Encyclopedia infant and early childhood development*. London, UK: Elsevier.

Freud, S. (1917). *A general introduction to psychoanalysis*. New York: Washington Square Press.

Frey, K. S., Hirschstein, M. K., Snell, J. L., Edstrom, L. V. S., & Broderick, C. J. (2005). Reducing playground bullying and supporting beliefs: An experimental trial of the Steps to Respect program. *Developmental Psychology, 41*, 479–490.

Fridriksson, J., Baker, J. M., Whiteside, J., Eoute, D., Moser, D., Vesselinov, R., & Rorden, C. (2009). Treating visual speech perception to improve speech production in nonfluent aphasia. *Stroke, 40*, 853–858.

Friedman, S. L., Melhuish, E. & Hill, C. (2009, in press). Childcare research at the dawn of a new millennium: An update. In G. Bremner & T. Wachs, *Wiley-Blackwell handbook of infant development*. Oxford, UK: Wiley-Blackwell.

Friend, M. (2008). *Special education* (2nd ed.). Boston: Allyn & Bacon.

Frisco, M. L. (2009). Obesity, childhood and adolescence. in D. Carr (Ed.), *Encyclopedia of the life course and human development*. Boston: Gale Cengage.

Fritschmann, N. S., & Solari, E. J. (2008). Learning disabilities. In N. J. Salkind (Ed.), *Encyclopedia of educational psychology*. Thousand Oaks, CA: Sage.

Frontini, M. G., Srinivasan, S. R., Xu, J., Tang, R., Bond, M. G., & Berenson, G. S. (2008). Usefulness of childhood non–high density lipoprotein cholesterol levels versus other lipoprotein measures in predicting adult subclinical atherosclerosis: The Bogalusa Heart Study. *Pediatrics, 121*, 924–929.

Fry, B. G. (2009). Mining genomes to identify toxins. *Annual Review of Genomics and Human Genetics* (Vol. 10). Palo Alto, CA: Annual Reviews.

Frye, D. (1999). Development of intention: The relation of executive function to theory of mind. In P. D. Zelazo, J. W. Astington, & D. R. Olson (Eds.), *Developing theories of intention: Social understanding and self-control*. Mahwah, NJ: Erlbaum.

Fuligni, A. J., & Hardway, C. (2006). Daily variation in adolescents' sleep, activities, and psychological well-being. *Journal of Research on Adolescence, 16*, 353–378.

Fuligni, A. J., Hughes, D. L., & Way. N. (2009). Ethnicity and immigration. In R. M. Lerner & L. Steinberg (Eds.), *Handbook of adolescent psychology* (3rd ed.). New York: Wiley.

Fu, L. Y., Colson, E. R., Corwin, M. J., & Moon, R. Y. (2008). Infant sleep location: Associated maternal and infant characteristics with sudden infant death syndrome prevention recommendations. *Journal of Pediatrics, 153*, 503–508.

Funai, E. F., Evans, M., & Lockwood, C. J. (2008). *High risk obstetrics*. Oxford, UK: Elsevier.

Furman, W., & Collins, W. A. (2009). Adolescent romantic relationships and experiences. In K. H. Rubin, W. M. Bukowksi, & B. Laursen (Eds.), *Handbook of peer interactions, relationships, and groups*. New York: Wiley.

Furman, W., Low, S., & Ho, M. J. (2009). Romantic experience and psychosocial adjustment in middle adolescence. *Journal of Clinical Child and Adolescent Psychology, 38*, 75–90.

Furman, W., & Wehner, E. A. (1997). Adolescent romantic relationships: A developmental perspective. In S. Shulman & W. A. Collins (Eds.), *New directions for child development: Adolescent romantic relationships*. San Francisco: Jossey-Bass.

Furman, W. & Simon, V. (2008). Homophily in adolescent romantic relationships. In M. J. Prinstein & K. A. Dodge (Eds.), *Understanding peer influence in children and adolescents*. New York: Guilford.

Furth, H. G., & Wachs, H. (1975). *Thinking goes to school*. New York: Oxford University Press.

G

Gaff, C. L., Williams, J. K., & McInerney, J. D. (2008, in press). Genetics in health practice and education special issue. *Journal of Genetic Counseling*.

Gajados, Z. K., Hirschhorn, J. N., & Palmert, M. R. (2009). What controls the timing of puberty? An update on progress from genetic investigations. *Current Opinion in Endocrinology, Diabetes, and Obesity, 16*, 16–24.

Galambos, N. L., Berenbaum, S. A., & McHale, S. M. (2009). Gender development in adolescence. In R. M. Lerner & L. Steinberg (Eds.), *Handbook of adolescent psychology* (3rd ed.). New York: Wiley.

Galindo, C, & Durham, R. E. (2009). Immigration, childhood, and adolescence. In D. Carr (Ed.), *Encyclopedia of the life course and human development*. Boston: Gale Cengage.

Galinsky, E., & David, J. (1988). *The preschool years: Family strategies that work—from experts and parents*. New York: Times Books.

Gallagher, J. J. (2007). *Teaching science for understanding*. Upper Saddle River, NJ: Prentice Hall.

Galloway, J. C., & Thelen, E. (2004). Feet first: Object exploration in young infants. *Infant Behavior and Development, 27*, 107–112.

Gallup, G. W., & Bezilla, R. (1992). *The religious life of young Americans*, Princeton, NJ: Gallup Institute.

Galtier, F., Raingeard, I., Renards, E., Boulot, P., & Bringer, J. (2008). Optimizing the outcome of pregnancy in obese women: From pregestational to long-term management. *Diabetes and Metabolism, 34*, 19–25.

Gao, L. L., Chan, S. W., & Mao, Q. (2009). Depression, perceived stress, and social support among first-time Chinese mothers and fathers in the postpartum period. *Research in Nursing and Health, 32*, 50–58.

Garcia-Bournissen, F., & others. (2008). Fetal exposure to isotretinoin—an international problem. *Reproductive Toxicology, 25*, 124–128.

Garcia Coll, C., & Pachter, L. M. (2002). Ethnic and minority parenting. In M. H. Bornstein (Ed.), *Handbook of parenting* (2nd ed., Vol. 4). Mahwah, NJ: Erlbaum.

Garcia Coll, C. T., Szalacha, L. A., & Palacios, N. (2005). Children of Dominican, Portuguese, and Cambodian immigrant families: Academic attitudes and pathways during middle childhood. In C. R. Cooper, C. T. Gacia Coll, W. T. Bartko, H. M. Davis, & C. Chatman (Eds.), *Developmental pathways through middle childhood*. Mahwah, NJ: Erlbaum.

Gardner, D. S., Hosking, J., Metcalf, B. S., An, J., Voss, L. D., & Wilkin, T. J. (2009). Contribution of early weight gain to childhood overweight and metabolic health: A longitudinal study (EarlyBird 36). *Pediatrics, 123*, e67–e73.

Gardner, H. (1983). *Frames of mind*. New York: Basic Books.

Gardner, H. (1993). *Multiple intelligences*. New York: Basic Books.

Gardner, H. (2002). The pursuit of excellence through education. In M. Ferrari (Ed.), *Learning from extraordinary minds*. Mahwah, NJ: Erlbaum.

Gardner, M., Roth, J., & Brooks-Gunn, J. (2008). Adolescents' participation in organized activities and developmental success 2 and 8 years after high school: Do sponsorship, duration, and intensity matter? *Developmental Psychology, 44*, 814–830.

Gardner, M., & Steinberg, L. (2005). Peer influence on risk taking, risk preference, and risky decision making in adolescence and adulthood. *Developmental Psychology, 41*, 625–635.

Garel, C. (2008). Fetal MRI: What is the future? *Ultrasound in Obstetrics and Gynecology, 31*, 123–128.

Gargiulo, R. M. (2009). *Special education in contemporary society*. Thousand Oaks, CA: Sage.

Gartstein M. A., Peleg, Y., Young, B. N., & Slobodskaya, H. R. (2009). Infant temperament in Russia, United States of America, and Israel: Differences and similarities between Russian-speaking families. *Child Psychiatry and Human Development, 40*, 241–256.

Garvey, C. (2000). *Play* (enlarged ed.). Cambridge, MA: Harvard University Press.

Garwick, A. W., Rhodes, K. L., Peterson-Hickey, M., & Hellerstedt, W. L. (2008). Native teen voices: Adolescent pregnancy prevention recommendations. *Journal of Adolescent Health, 42*, 81–88.

Gasser, L. & Keller, M. (2009, in press). Are the competent the morally good? Perspective taking and moral motivation of children involved in bullying. *Social Development*.

Gates, W. (1998, July 20). Charity begins when I'm ready (interview). *Fortune* (www.pathfinder.com/fortune/1998/980720/bil7.html), (p. 409).

Gathwala, G., Singh, B., & Balhara, B. (2008). KMG facilitates mother baby attachment in low birth weight infants. *Indian Journal of Pediatrics, 75,* 43–47.

Gaudet, L. M., Dyzak, R., Aung, S. K., & Smith, G. N. (2008). Effectiveness of acupuncture for the initiation of labor at term: A randomized controlled trial. *Journal of Obstetrics and Gynecology Canada, 30,* 1118–1123.

Gauvain, M. (2008). Vygotsky's sociocultural theory. In M. M. Haith & J. B. Benson (Eds.), *Encyclopedia of infant and early childhood development.* Oxford, UK: Elsevier.

Gauvain, M., & Parke, R. D. (2010). Socialization. In M. H. Bornstein (Ed.), *Handbook of cultural developmental science.* New York: Psychology Press.

Gauvain, M., & Perez, S. M. (2007). The socialization of cognition. In J. E. Grusec & P. D. Hastings (Eds.), *Handbook of socialization.* New York: Guilford.

Gay, L. R., Mills, G., & Airasian, P. W. (2009). *Educational research* (9th ed.). Upper Saddle River, NJ: Prentice Hall.

Gee, C. L., & Heyman, G. D. (2007). Children's evaluations of other people's self-descriptions. *Social Development, 16,* 800–818.

Geher, G., & Miller, G. (Eds.) (2007). *Mating intelligence.* Mahwah, NJ: Erlbaum.

Geissbuehler, V., Stein, S., & Eberhard, J. (2004). Waterbirths compared to landbirths: An observational study of nine years. *Journal of Perinatal Medicine, 32,* 308–314.

Gelman, R. (1969). Conservation acquisition: A problem of learning to attend to relevant attributes. *Journal of Experimental Child Psychology, 7,* 67–87.

Gelman, S. A. (2009). Learning from others: Children's construction of concepts. *Annual Review of Psychology* (Vol. 60). Palo Alto, CA: Annual Reviews.

Gelman, S. A., & Kalish, C. W. (2006). Conceptual development. In W. Damon & R. Lerner (Eds.), *Handbook of child psychology* (6th ed.). New York: Wiley.

Gennetian, L. A., & Miller, C. (2002). Children and welfare reform: A view from an experimental welfare reform program in Minnesota. *Child Development, 73,* 601–620.

Gerards, F. A., Twisk, J. W., Fetter, W. P., Wijnaendts, L. C., & van Vugt, J. M. (2008). Predicting pulmonary hypoplasia with 2- or 3-dimensional ultrasonography in complicated pregnancies. *American Journal of Gynecology and Obstetrics, 198,* e1–e6.

Gerrard, M., Gibbons, F. X., Houlihan, A. E., Stock, M. L., & Pomery, E. A. (2008). A dual-process approach to health risk decision-making. *Developmental Review, 28,* 29–61.

Gershoff, E. T. (2002). Corporal punishment by parents and associated child behaviors and experiences: A meta-analysis and theoretical review. *Psychological Bulletin, 128,* 539–579.

Geschwind, N., & Behan, P. O. (1984). Laterality, hormones, and immunity. In N. Geschwind & A. M. Galaburda (Eds.), *Cerebral dominance: The biological foundations.* Cambridge, MA: Harvard University Press.

Gesell, A. L. (1928). *Infancy and human growth.* New York: Macmillan.

Gesell, A. L. (1934). *Infancy and human growth.* New York: Macmillan.

Gewirtz, J. (1977). Maternal responding and the conditioning of infant crying: Directions of influence within the attachment-acquisition process. In B. C. Etzel, J. M. LeBlanc & D. M. Baer (Eds.), *New developments in behavioral research.* Hillsdale, NJ: Erlbaum.

Ghetti, S., & Alexander, K. W. (2004). "If it happened, I would remember it": Strategic use of event memorability in the rejection of false autobiographical events. *Child Development, 75,* 542–561.

Gibbons, F. X., Pomery, E. A., & Gerrard, M. (2008). Cognitive social influence: Moderation, mediation, and modification, and . . . the media. In M. J. Prinstein & K. A. Dodge (Eds.), *Understanding peer influence in children and adolescents.* New York: Guilford.

Gibbons, J., & Ng, S. H. (2004). Acting bilingual and thinking bilingual. *Journal of Language and Social Psychology, 23,* 4–6.

Gibbs, J. C. (2009). *Moral development and reality* (2nd ed.). Boston: Allyn & Bacon.

Gibbs, J. C., Basinger, K. S., Grime, R. L., & Snarey, J. R. (2007). Moral judgment development across cultures: Revisiting Kohlberg's universality claims, *Developmental Review, 27,* 443–500.

Gibson, E. J. (1969). *Principles of perceptual learning and development.* New York: Appleton-Century-Crofts.

Gibson, E. J. (1989). Exploratory behavior in the development of perceiving, acting, and the acquiring of knowledge. *Annual Review of Psychology* (vol. 39). Palo Alto, CA: Annual Reviews.

Gibson, E. J. (2001). *Perceiving the affordances.* Mahwah, NJ: Erlbaum.

Gibson, E. J., & Walk, R. D. (1960). The "visual cliff." *Scientific American, 202,* 64–71.

Gibson, J. J. (1966). *The senses considered as perceptual systems.* Boston: Houghton Mifflin.

Gibson, J. J. (1979). *The ecological approach to visual perception.* Boston: Houghton Mifflin.

Gibson, L. Y., Bryne, S. M., Blair, E., Davis, E. A., Jacoby, P., & Zubrick, S. R. (2008). Clustering of psychological symptoms in overweight children. *Australian and New Zealand Journal of Psychiatry, 42,* 118–125.

Giedd, J. N. (2007, September 27). Commentary in S. Jayson "Teens driven to distraction." *USA Today,* pp. D1–2.

Giedd, J. N. (2008). The teen brain: Insights from neuroimaging. *Journal of Adolescent Medicine, 42,* 335–343.

Gilbert, S. J., Meusese, J. D., Towgood, K. J., Frith, C. D., & Burgess, P. W. (2009). Abnormal functional specialization within prefrontal cortex in high-function autism: A multi-voxel similarity analysis. *Brain, 132,* 869–878.

Gilligan, C. (1982). *In a different voice.* Cambridge, MA: Harvard University Press.

Gilligan, C. (1992, May). *Joining the resistance: Girls' development in adolescence.* Paper presented at the symposium on development and vulnerability in close relationships, Montreal, Quebec.

Gilligan, C. (1996). The centrality of relationships in psychological development: A puzzle, some evidence, and a theory. In G. G. Noam & K. W. Fischer (Eds.), *Development and vulnerability in close relationships.* Hillsdale, NJ: Erlbaum.

Gilligan, C., Spencer, R., Weinberg, M. K., & Bertsch, T. (2003). On the listening guide: A voice-centered relational model. In P. M. Carnic & J. E. Rhodes (Eds.), *Qualitative research in psychology* Washington, DC: American Psychological Association.

Gill, S. V., Adolph, K. E., & Vereijken, B. (2009, in press). Change in action: How infants learn to walk down slopes. *Developmental Science.*

Ginder, G. D., Gnanapragasam, M. N., & Mian, O. Y. (2008). The role of the epigenetic signal, DNA methylation, in gene regulation during erythroid development. *Current Topics in Developmental Biology, 82,* 85–116.

Girling, A. (2006). The benefits of using the Neonatal Behavioral Assessment Scale in health visiting practice. *Community Practice, 79,* 118–120.

Girls, Inc. (1991). *Truth, trusting, and technology: New research on preventing adolescent pregnancy.* Indianapolis: Author.

Glascher, J., & others. (2009). Lesion mapping of cognitive abilities linked to intelligence. *Neuron, 61,* 681–691.

Gluck, M. E., Venti, C. A., Lindsay, R. S., Knowler, W. C., Salbe, A. D., & Krakoff, J. (2009, in press). Maternal influence, not diabetic intraturine environment, predicts children's energy intake. *Obesity.*

Glynn, L. M., Schetter, C. D., Hobel, C. J., & Sandman, C. A. (2008). Pattern of perceived stress and anxiety in pregnancy predicts preterm birth. *Health Psychology, 27,* 43–51.

Godding, V., Bonnier, C., Fiasse, L., Michel, M., Longueville, E., Lebecque, P., Robert, A., & Galanti, L. (2004). Does in utero exposure to heavy maternal smoking induce nicotine withdrawal symptoms in neonates? *Pediatric Research, 55,* 645–651.

Goetghebuer, T., & others. (2009, in press). Effects of early antiretroviral therapy on the risk of AIDS/death in HIV-infected infants. *AIDS.*

Goffin, S. G., & Wilson, C. S. (2001). *Curriculum models and early childhood education. Appraising* *the relationship* (2nd ed.). Upper Saddle River, NJ: Prentice Hall.

Goh, V. I., & Koren, G. (2008). Folic acid in pregnancy and fetal outcomes. *Journal of Obstetrics and Gynecology, 28,* 3–13.

Goldberg, W. A., & Lucas-Thompson, R. (2008). Maternal and paternal employment, effects of. In M. M. Haith & J. B. Benson (Eds.), *Encyclopedia of infant and early childhood development.* Oxford, UK: Elsevier.

Goldenberg, R. L., & Culhane, J. F. (2007). Low birth weight in the United States. *American Journal of Clinical Nutrition, 85* (Suppl.), S584–S590.

Goldfield, B. A., & Snow, C. A. (2009). Individual difference in language development. In J. Berko Gleason & N. Ratner (Eds.), *The development of language* (7th ed.). Boston: Allyn & Bacon.

Goldin-Meadow, S. (2008). Language acquisition theories. In M. M. Haith & J. B. Benson (Eds.), *Encyclopedia of infant and early childhood development.* Oxford, UK: Elsevier.

Goldman, S., Wang, C., Salgado, M. W., Greene, P. E., Kim, M., & Rapin, I. (2009). Motor stereotypies in children with autism and other developmental disorders. *Developmental Medicine and Child Neurology, 51,* 30–38.

Goldschmidt, L., Richardson, G. A., Willford, J., & Day, N. L. (2008). Prenatal marijuana exposure and intelligence test performance at age 6. *Journal of the American Academy of Child and Adolescent Psychiatry, 47,* 254–263.

Goldsmith, H. H. (2008). Behavior genetics. In M. M. Haith & J. B. Benson (Eds.) *Encyclopedia of infancy and early childhood development.* Oxford, UK: Elsevier.

Goldsmith, H. H. (2010). Human development: Biological and genetic processes in development. *Annual Review of Psychology (Vol. 61).* Palo Alto, CA: Annual Reviews.

Goldstein, M. H., King, A. P., & West, M. J. (2003). Social interaction shapes babbling: Testing parallels between birdsong and speech. *Proceedings of the National Academy of Sciences USA, 100* (13), 8030–8035.

Goldstein, M. H., & Schwade, J. A. (2008). Social feedback to infants' babbling facilitates rapid phonological learning. *Psychological Science, 19,* 515–523.

Goldston, D. B., Molock, S. D., Whitbeck, L. B., Murakami, J. L., Zayas, L. H., & Hall, G. C. (2008). Cultural considerations in adolescent suicide prevention and psychosocial treatment. *American Psychologist, 63,* 14–31.

Goleman, D., Kaufman, P., & Ray, M. (1993). *The creative spirit.* New York: Plume.

Golianu, B., Krane, E., Seybold, J., Almgren, C., & Anand, K. J. (2007). Nonpharmacological techniques for pain management in neonates. *Seminars in Perinatology, 31,* 318–322.

Gollnick, D. M., & Chinn, P. C. (2009). *Multicultural education in a pluralistic society* (8th ed.). Boston: Allyn & Bacon.

Golomb, C. (2008). Artistic development. In M. M. Haith & J. B. Benson (Eds.), *Encyclopedia of infant and early childhood development.* Oxford, UK: Elsevier.

Golombok, S., MacCallum, F., & Goodman, E. (2001). The "test-tube" generation: Parent-child relationships and the psychological well-being of in vitro fertilization children at adolescence. *Child Development, 72,* 599–608.

Golombok, S., Rust, J., Zervoulis, K., Croudace, T., Golding, J., & Hines, M. (2008). Developmental trajectories of sex-typed behavior in boys and girls: A longitudinal general population study of children aged 2.5–8 years. *Child Development, 79,* 1583–1593.

Gong, X., & others. (2009). An investigation of ribosomal protein L10 gene in autism spectrum disorders. *BMC Medical Genetics, 10,* 7.

Gonzalez, A., Atkinson, L., & Fleming, A. S. (2009). Attachment and the comparative psychobiology of mothering. In M. de Haan & M. R. Gunnar (Eds.), *Handbook of developmental social neuroscience.* New York: Guilford.

Good, M., & Willoughby, T. (2008). Adolescence as a sensitive period for spiritual development. *Child Development Perspectives, 2,* 32–37.

Gopnik, A., & Schulz, L. (Eds.). (2007). *Causal learning.* New York: Oxford University Press.

Gore, K. (2009). Socialization, gender. In D. Carr (Ed.), *Encyclopedia of the life course and human development.* Boston: Gale Cengage.

Gottlieb, G. (2007). Probabalistic epigenesis. *Developmental Science, 10,* 1–11.

Gottlieb, G., Wahlsten, D., & Lickliter, R. (2006). The significance of biology for human development: A development psychobiological systems view. In W. Damon & R. Lerner (Eds.). *Handbook of child psychology* (6th ed.). New York: Wiley.

Gottman, J. M. (2009). *Research on parenting.* Retrieved January 30, 2009, from www.gottman.com/parenting/research

Gottman, J. M., & DeClaire, J. (1997). *The heart of parenting: Raising an emotionally intelligent child.* New York: Simon & Schuster.

Gottman, J. M., & Parker, J. G. (Eds.).(1987). *Conversations of friends.* New York: Cambridge University Press.

Gottman, J. M., Shapiro, A. F., & Parthemer, J. (2004). Bringing baby home: A preventative intervention program for expectant couples. *International Journal of Childbirth Education, 19,* 28–30.

Gould, M. S., Greenberg, T., Velting, D. M., & Shaffer, D. (2003). Youth suicide risk and preventive interventions: A review of the past 10 years. *Journal of the American Academy of Child and Adolescent Psychiatry, 42,* 386–405.

Gould, S. J. (1981). *The mismeasure of man.* New York: W. W. Norton.

Graber, J. A. (2004). Internalizing problems during adolescence. In R. Lerner & L. Steinberg (Eds.), *Handbook of adolescent psychology.* New York: Wiley.

Graber, J. A. (2008). Pubertal and neuroendocrine development and risk for depressive disorders. In N. B. Allen & L. Sheeber (Eds.), *Adolescent emotional development and the emergence of depressive disorders.* New York: Cambridge University Press.

Graber, J. A., & Brooks-Gunn, J. (2002). Adolescent girls' sexual development. In G. M. Wingood & R. J. DiClemente (Eds.), *Handbook of women's sexual and reproductive health.* New York: Kluwer Academic/Plenum.

Graber, J. A., Brooks-Gunn, J., & Warren, M. P. (2006). Pubertal effects on adjustment in girls: Moving from demonstrating effects to identifying pathways. *Journal of Youth and Adolescence, 35,* 391–401.

Graber, J. A., & Sontag, L. (2009). Internalizing problems during adolescence. In R. M. Lerner & L. Steinberg (Eds.), *Handbook of adolescent psychology* (3rd ed.). New York: Wiley.

Graham, S. (1986, August). *Can attribution theory tell us something about motivation in blacks?* Paper presented at the meeting of the American Psychological Association, Washington, DC.

Graham, S. (1990). Motivation in Afro-Americans. In G. L. Berry & I. K. Asamen (Eds.), *Black students: Psychosocial issues and academic achievement.* Newbury Park, CA: Sage.

Graham, S. (2005, February 16). Commentary in *USA Today,* p. 2D.

Graham, S. (Ed.) (2006). Our children too: A history of the first 25 years of the Society for Research in Child Development. *Monographs of the Society for Research in Child Development, (Vol. 71. No. 1),* 1–227.

Grantham-McGregor, C., Ani, C., & Fernald, L. (2001). The role of nutrition in intellectual development. In R. J. Stemberg & E. I. Girogorenko (Eds.), *Environmental effects on cognitive abilities.* Mahwah, NJ: Erlbaum.

Grant, J. (1997). *The state of the world's children.* New York: UNICEF and Oxford University Press.

Graue, M. E., & DiPerna, J. (2000). Redshirting and early retention: Who gets the "gift of time" and what are its outcomes? *American Educational Research Journal, 37,* 509–534.

Graven, S. (2006). Sleep and brain development. *Clinical Perinatology, 33,* 693–706.

Gray, K. A., Day, N. L., Leech, S., & Richardson, G. A. (2005). Prenatal marijuana exposure: Effect on child depressive symptoms at ten years of age. *Neurtoxicology and Teratology, 27,* 439–448.

Graziano, A. M., & Raulin, M. L. (2010). *Research methods* (7th ed.). Boston: Allyn & Bacon.

Gredler, M. E. (2008). Vygotsky's cultural historical theory of development. In N. J. Salkind (Ed.),

Encyclopedia of educational psychology. Thousand Oaks, CA: Sage.

Greene, M. F. (2009). Making small risks even smaller. *New England Journal of Medicine, 360,* 183–184.

Greenfield, P. M. (1966). On culture and conservation. In J. S. Bruner, R. P. Oliver, & P. M. Greenfield (Eds.), *Studies in cognitive growth.* New York: Wiley.

Greenfield, P. M., Suzuki, L. K., & Rothstein-Fisch, C. (2006). Cultural pathways through human development. In W. Damon & R. Lerner (Eds.), *Handbook of child psychology* (6th ed.). New York: Wiley.

Greenough, A. (2007). Late respiratory outcomes after preterm birth. *Early Human Development, 83,* 785–788.

Greer, F. R., Sicherer, S. H., Burks, A. W., & the Committee on Nutrition and Section on Allergy and Immunology. (2008). Effects of early nutritional interventions on the development of atopic disease in infants and children: The role of maternal dietary restriction, breast feeding, timing of introduction of complementary foods, and hydrolyzed formulas. *Pediatrics, 121,* 183–191.

Grigorenko, E. (2000). Heritability and intelligence. In R. J. Sternberg (Ed.), *Handbook of intelligence.* New York: Cambridge University Press.

Grigorenko, E. L., & Takanishi, R. (2010, in press). *Handbook of U. S. immigration and education.* New York: Springer.

Grigoriadis, S., & Kennedy, S. H. (2002). Role of estrogen in the treatment of depression. *American Journal of Therapy, 9,* 503–509.

Gronlund, N. E., & Waugh, C. K. (2009). *Assessment of student achievement* (9th ed.). Upper Saddle River, NJ: Prentice Hall.

Gropman, A. L., & Adams, D. R. (2007). Atypical patterns of inheritance. *Seminars in pediatric Neurology, 14,* 34–45.

Gross, D., Garvey, C., Julion, W., Fogg, L., Tucker, S., & Mokros, H. (2009, in press). Efficacy of the Chicago Parent Program with low-income African American and Latino parents of young children. *Prevention Science.*

Grossmann, K., Grossmann, K. E., Spangler, G., Suess, G., & Unzner, L. (1985). Maternal sensitivity and newborn's orientation responses as related to quality of attachment in northern Germany. In I. Bretherton & E. Waters (Eds.), Growing points of attachment theory and research. *Monographs of the Society for Research in Child Development, 50* (1–2, Serial No. 209).

Grotevant, H. D., van Dulmen, M. H. M. Dunbar, N., Nelson Christinedaughter, J., Christensen, M., Fan, X., & Miller, B. C. (2006). Antisocial behavior of adoptees and nonadoptees: Prediction from early history and adolescent relationships. Journal of Research on Adolescence, 16, 105–130.

Grusec, J. E., Almas, A., & Willoughby, K. (2008). Discipline and compliance. In

M. M. Haith & J. B. Benson (Eds.), *Encyclopedia of infant and early childhood development.* Oxford, UK: Elsevier.

Grusec, J. E., & Davidov, M. (2007). Socialization in the family: The role of parents. In J. E. Grusec & P. D. Hastings (Eds.), *Handbook of socialization.* New York: Guilford.

Guelinckx, I., Devlieger, R., Beckers, K., & Vansant, G. (2008). Maternal obesity: Pregnancy complications, gestational weight gain, and nutrition. *Obesity Review, 9,* 140–150.

Guidozzi, F., & Black, V. (2009). The obstetric face and challenge of HIV/AIDS. *Clinical Obstetrics and Gynecology, 52,* 270–284.

Guilford, J. P. (1967). *The structure of intellect.* New York: McGraw-Hill.

Gumora, G., & Arsenio, W. (2002). Emotionality, emotion regulation, and school performance in middle school children. *Journal of School Psychology, 40,* 395–413.

Gunderson, E. P., Rifas-Shiman, S. L., Oken, E., Rich-Edwards, J. W., Kleinman, K. P., Taveras, E. M., & Gilman, M. W. (2008). Association of fewer hours of sleep at 6 months postpartum with substantial weight retention at 1 year postpartum. *American Journal of Epidemiology, 167,* 178–187.

Gunnar, M. R., Fisher, P. A., & the Early Experience, Stress, and Prevention Network. (2006). Bringing basic research on early experience and stress neurobiology to bear on preventive interventions for neglected and maltreated children. *Development and Psychopathology, 18,* 651–677.

Gunnar, M. R., Malone, S., & Fisch, R. O. (1987). The psychobiology of stress and coping in the human neonate: Studies of the adrenocortical activity in response to stress in the first week of life. In T. Field, P. McCabe, & N. Scheiderman (Eds.), *Stress and coping.* Hillsdale, NJ: Erlbaum.

Gunnar, M. R., & Quevedo, K. (2007). The neurobiology of stress and development. *Annual Review of Psychology* (Vol. 58). Palo Alto, CA: Annual Reviews.

Guo, G., & Tillman, K. H. (2009). Trajectories of depressive symptoms, dopamine D2 and D4 receptors, family socioeconomic status, and social, support in adolescence and young adulthood. *Psychiatric Genetics, 19,* 14–26.

Gupta, A., Thornton, J. W., & Huston, A. C. (2008). Working families should be poor—the New Hope program. In D. R. Crane & T. B. Heaton (Eds.), *Handbook of families and poverty.* Thousand Oaks, CA: Sage.

Guralnick, S. (2007). Firearms. *Pediatric Review, 28,* 396–397.

Gurgan, T., & Demirol, A. (2007). Unresolved issues regarding assisted reproduction technology. *Reproductive Biomedicine Online, 14,* (Suppl 1), S40–S43.

Gur, R. C., Mozley, L. H., Mozley, P. D., Resnick, S. M., Karp, J. S., Alavl, A., Arnold,

S. E., & Gur, R. E. (1995). Sex differences in regional cerebral glucose metabolism during a resting state. *Science, 267,* 528–531.

Gurwitch, R. H., Silovksy, J. F., Schultz, S., Kees, M., & Burlingame, S. (2001). *Reactions and guidelines for children following trauma/disaster.* Norman, OK: Department of Pediatrics, University of Oklahoma Health Sciences Center.

Gustafsson, J.-E. (2007). Schooling and intelligence: Effects of track of study on level and profile of cognitive abilities. In P. C. Kyllonen, R. D. Roberts, & L. Stankov (Eds.), *Extending intelligence.* Mahwah, NJ: Erlbaum.

Gutherie, G. M., Masangkay, Z., & Gutheric, H. A. (1976). Behavior, malnutrition, and mental development. *Journal of Cross-Cultural Psychology, 7,* 169–180.

Gutman, L. M. (2008). Risk and resilience. In M. M. Haith & J. B. Benson (Eds.), *Encyclopedia of infant and early childhood development.* Oxford, UK: Elsevier.

H

Hack, M., Taylor, H. G., Schulchter, M., Andreias, L., Drotar, D., & Klein, N. (2009). Behavioral outcomes of extremely low birth weight children at age 8 years. *Journal of Developemental and Behavioral Pediatrics, 30,* 122–130.

Hagen, J. W., & Lamb-Parker, F. G. (2008). Head Start. In M. M. Haith & J. B. Benson (Eds.), *Encyclopedia of infant and early childhood development.* Oxford, UK: Elsevier.

Hager, P. J. (2008). Vocational education. In N. J. Salkind (Ed.), *Encyclopedia of educational psychology.* Thousand Oaks, CA: Sage.

Hahn, C. S., & DiPietro, J. A. (2001). In vitro fertilization and the family: Quality of parenting, family functioning, and child psychosocial adjustment. *Developmental Psychology, 37,* 37–48.

Hahn, D. B., Payne, W. A., & Lucas, E. B. (2009). *Focus on health* (9th ed.). New York: McGraw-Hill.

Hahn, S., Zhong, X. Y., & Holzgreve, W. (2008). Recent progress in non-invasive prenatal diagnosis. *Seminars in Fetal and Neonatal Medicine, 13,* 57–62.

Hahn, W. K. (1987). Cerebral lateralization of function: From infancy through childhood. *Psychological Bulletin, 101,* 376–392.

Haier, R. J. (2009). Neuro-intelligence, neuro-metrics, and the next phase of brain imaging studies. *Intelligence, 37,* 121–123.

Haier, R. J., & others. (2009). Gray matter and intelligence factors: Is there a neuro-*g*? *Intelligence, 37,* 136–144.

Hair, E. C., Moore, K. A., Garrett, S. B., Ling, T., & Cleveland, K. (2008). The continued importance of quality parent-adolescent relationships during late adolescence. *Journal of Research on Adolescence, 18,* 187–200.

Haith, M. M., Hazen, C., & Goodman, G. S. (1988). Expectation and anticipation of dynamic visual events by 3.5-month-old babies. *Child Development, 59,* 467–479.

Hakuta, K. (2000). Bilingualism. In A. Kazdin (Ed.), *Encyclopedia of psychology.* Washington, DC, & New York: American Psychological Association and Oxford University Press.

Hakuta, K. (2001, April). *Key policy milestones and directions in the education of English language leyeners.* Paper prepared for the Rockefeller Foundation Symposium, Leveraging change: An Emerging framework for educational equity, Washington, DC.

Hakuta, K. (2005, April). *Bilingualism at the intersection of research and public policy.* Paper presented at the meeting of the Society for Research in Child Development, Atlanta.

Hakuta, K., Butler, Y. G., & Witt, D. (2001). *How long does it take English learners to attain proficiency?* Berkeley, CA: The University of California Linguistic Minority Research Institute Policy Report 2000–1.

Halford, G. S. (2008). Cognitive developmental theories. In M. M. Haith & J. B. Benson (Eds.), *Encyclopedia of infant and early childhood development.* Oxford, UK: Elsevier.

Hall, G. N. (2010). *Multicultural psychology* (2nd ed.). Upper Saddle River, NJ: Prentice Hall.

Hall, G. S. (1904). *Adolescence* (Vols. 1 & 2). Englewood Cliffs, NJ: Prentice Hall.

Hall, L. (2009). *Autism spectrum disorders: From therapy to practice.* Boston: Allyn & Bacon.

Hallahan, D. P., & Kauffman, J. M. (2006). *Exceptional learners* (10th ed.). Boston: Allyn & Bacon.

Hallahan, D. P., Kauffman, J. M., & Pullen, P. C. (2009). *Exceptional learners* (11th ed.). Boston: Allyn & Bacon.

Halle, T., Reidy, M., Moorehouse, M., Zaslow, M., Walsh, C., Margie, N. G., & Dent, A. (2007). Progress in the development of school readiness. In B. Brown (Ed.), *Key indicators of child and youth well-being.* Mahwah, NJ: Erlbaum.

Halpern, D. (2006). Assessing gender gaps in learning and academic achievement. In P. A. Alexander & P. H. Wynne (Eds.), *Handbook of educational psychology* (2nd ed.). Mahwah, NJ: Erlbaum.

Halpern, D. F., Benbow, C. P., Geary, D. C., Gur, R. C., Hyde, J. S., & Gernsbacher, M. A. (2007). The science of sex differences in science and mathematics. *Psychological Science in the Public Interest, 8,* 1–51.

Hamilton, S. F., & Hamilton, M. A. (2006). School, work, and emerging adulthood. In J. J. Arnett & J. L. Tanner (Eds.), *Emerging adults in America.* Washington, DC: American Psychological Association.

Hamlin, J. K., Hallinan, E. V., & Woodward, A. L. (2008). Do as I do: 7-month-old infants

selectively reproduce others' goals. *Developmental Science, 11,* 487–494.

Hampton, T. (2008). Scientists build map of imprinted genes. *Journal of the American Medical Association, 299,* 161.

Han, W.-J. (2009). Maternal employment. In D. Carr (Ed.), *Encyclopedia of the life course and human development.* Boston: Gale Cengage.

Hancox, R. J., Milne, B. J., & Poulton, R. (2004). Association between child and adolescent television viewing and adult health: A longitudinal birth cohort study. *Lancet, 364,* 257–262.

Hanish, L. D., & Guerra, N. G. (2004). Aggressive victims, passive victims, and bullies: Developmental continuity or developmental change? *Merrill-Palmer Quarterly, 50,* 17–38.

Hannan, M. A., Faraji, B., Tanguma, J., Longoria, N., & Rodriguez, R. C. (2009). Maternal milk concentration of zinc, iron, selenium, and iodine and its relationship to dietary intake. *Biological Trace Element Research, 127,* 6–15.

Hansen, M. L., Gunn, P. W., & Kaelber, D. C. (2007). Underdiagnosis of hypertension in children and adolescents. *Journal of the American Medical Association, 298,* 874–879.

Hargreaves, D. A., & Tiggemann, M. (2004). Idealized media images and adolescent body image: "Comparing" boys and girls. *Body Image, 1,* 351–361.

Harkness, S., & Super, E. M. (1995). Culture and parenting. In M. H. Bornstein (Ed.), *Handbook of parenting* (Vol. 3). Hillsdale, NJ: Erlbaum.

Harlow, H. F. (1958). The nature of love. *American Psychologist, 13,* 673–685.

Harmon, O. R., Lambrinos, J., & Kennedy, P. (2008). Are online exams an invitation to cheat? *Journal of Economic Education, 39,* 116–125.

Harold, R. D., Colarossi, L. G., & Mercier, L. R. (2007). *Smooth sailing or stormy waters: Family transitions through adolescence and their implications for practice and policy.* Mahwah, NJ: Erlbaum.

Harris, J. B. (1998). *The nurture assumption: Why children turn out the way they do: Parents matter less than you think and peers matter more.* New York: Free Press.

Harrison-Hale, A. O., McLoyd, V. C., & Smedley, B. (2004). Racial and ethnic status: Risk and protective processes among African-American families. In K. L. Maton, C. J. Schellenbach, B. J. Leadbetter, & A. L. Solarz (Eds.), *Investing in children, families, and communities.* Washington, DC: American Psychological Association.

Harris, P. L. (2000). *The work of the imagination.* Oxford University Press.

Harris, P. L. (2006). Social cognition. In W. Damon & R. Lerner (Eds.), *Handbook of child psychology* (6th ed.). New York: Wiley.

Harris, Y. R., & Graham, J. A. (2007). *The African American child.* New York: Springer.

Hart, B., & Risley, T. R. (1995). *Meaningful differences in the everyday experience of young Americans.* Baltimore: Paul H. Brookes.

Hart, C. H., Yang, C., Charlesworth, R., & Burts, D. C. (2003, April). *Early childhood teachers' curriculum beliefs, classroom practices, and children's outcomes: What are the connections?* Paper presented at the biennial meeting of the Society for Research in Child Development, Tampa, FL.

Hart, D., Burock, D., London, B., & Atkins, R. (2003). Prosocial development, antisocial development, and moral development. In A. M. Slater & G. Bremner (Eds.), *An introduction to developmental psychology.* Malden, MA: Blackwell.

Hart, D., & Karmel, M. P. (1996). Self-awareness and self-knowledge in humans, great apes, and monkeys. In A. Russori, K. Bard, & S. Parker (Eds.), *Reaching into thought.* New York: Cambridge University Press.

Hart, D., Matsuba, M. K., & Atkins, R. (2008). The moral and civic effects of learning to serve. In L. Nucci & D. Narváez (Eds.), *Handbook of moral and character education.* Clifton, NJ: Psychology Press.

Harter, S. (2002). Unpublished review of J. W. Santrock's *Child development,* 10th ed. (New York: McGraw-Hill).

Harter, S. (2006). The self. In W. Damon & R. Lerner (Eds.), *Handbook of child psychology* (6th ed.). New York: Wiley.

Hart, S., & Carrington, H. (2002). Jealousy in 6-month-old infants. *Infancy, 3,* 395–402.

Hartshorne, H., & May, M. S. (1928–1930). *Moral Studies in the nature of character: Studies in deceit* (Vol. 1); *Studies in self-control* (Vol. 2); *Studies in the organization of character* (Vol. 3). New York: Macmillan.

Hartup, W. W. (1983). The peer system. In P. H. Mussen (Ed.), *Handbook of child psychology* (4th ed., Vol. 4). New York: Wiley.

Hartup, W. W. (1996). The company they keep: Friendships and their development significance. *Child Development, 67,* 1–13.

Hartup, W. W. (2009). Critical issues and theoretical viewpoints. In K. H. Rubin, W. M. Bukowski, & B. Laursen (Eds.), *Handbook of peer interactions, relationships, and groups.* New York: Guilford.

Hartup, W. W., & Abecassis, M. (2004). Friends and enemies. In P. K. Smith & C. H. Hart (Eds.), *Blackwell handbook of childhood social development.* Malden, MA: Blackwell.

Hartwell, L. (2008). *Genetics* (3rd ed.). New York: McGraw-Hill.

Harwood, R., Leyendecker, B., Carlson, V., Asencio, M., & Miller, A. (2002). Parenting among Latino families in the U.S. In M. H. Bornstein (Ed.), *Handbook of parenting* (2nd ed.). Mahwah, NJ: Erlbaum.

Hasirci, D., & Demirkan, H. (2003). Creativity in learning environments: The case of two sixth grade art rooms. *Journal of Creative Behavior, 37,* 17–41.

Hastings, P. D., Utendale, W. T., & Sullivan, C. (2007). In J. E. Grusec & P. D. Hastings (Eds.),

The socialization of prosocial behavior. *Handbook of socialization.* New York: Guilford.

Hattery, A. J., & Smith, E. (2007). *African American families.* Thousand Oaks: Sage.

Hauck, F. R., Signore, C., Fein, S. B., & Raju, T. N. (2008). Infant sleeping arrangements and practices during the first year of life. *Pediatrics, 122* (suppl. 2), S113–S120.

Hausenblas, H. A., Brewer, B. W., Van Raalte, J. L., Cook, B., Down, D. S., Weis, C. A., Nigg, C., & Cruz, A. (2008). Development and evaluation of a multimedia CD-ROM for exercise during pregnancy and postpartum. *Patient Education and Counseling, 70,* 215–219.

Hausman, B. L. (2005). Risky business: Framing childbirth in hospital settings. *Journal of Medical Ethics, 26,* 23–38.

Hawkins, J. A., & Berndt, T. J. (1985, April). *Adjustment following the transition to junior high school.* Paper presented at the biennial meeting of the Society for Research in Child Development, Toronto.

Hayashino, D., & Chopra, S. B. (2009). Parenting and raising families. In N. Tewari & A. Alvarez (Eds.). *Asian American psychology.* New York: Psychology Press.

Haynes, R. L., Folkerth, R. D., Szweda, L. I., Volpe, J. J., & Kinney, H. C. (2006). Lipid peroxidation during cerebral myelination. *Journal of Neuropathology and Experimental Neurology, 65,* 894–904.

Healey, J. F. (2009). *Race, ethnicity, and class* (5th ed.). Thousand Oaks, CA: Sage.

Health Management Resources. (2001). *Child health and fitness* Boston: Author.

Hegaard, H. K., Hedegaard, M., Damm, P., Ottesen, B., Petersson, K., & Henriksen, T. B. (2008). Leisure time physical activity is associated with a reduced risk of preterm delivery. *American Journal of Obstetrics and Gynecology, 198,* e1–e5.

Heguy, L., Garneau, M., Goldberg, M. S., Raphoz, M., Guay, F., & Valois, M. F. (2008). Associations between grass and weed pollen and emergency department visits for asthma among children in Montreal. *Environmental Research, 106,* 203–211.

Heimann, M., Strid, K., Smith, L., Tjus, T., Ulvund, S. E., & Meltzoff, A. N. (2006). Exploring the relation between memory, gestural communication, and the emergence of language in infancy: A longitudinal study. *Infant and Child Development, 15,* 233–249.

Heinig, M. J., Ishii, K. D., Banuelos, J. L., Campbell, E., O'Laughlin, C., & Becerra, L. E. (2009, in press). Sources and acceptance of infant-feeding advice among low-income women. *Journal of Human Lactation.*

Heitzler, C. D., Martin, S. L., Duke, J., & Huhman, M. (2006). Correlates of physical activity in a national sample of children aged 9–13 years. *Preventive Medicine, 42,* 254–260.

Helgeson, V. (2009). *Psychology of gender* (3rd ed.). Upper Saddle River, NJ: Prentice Hall.

Hellstrom-Lindahl, D., & Nordberg, A. (2002). Smoking during pregnancy: A way to transfer the addiction to the next generation? *Respiration, 69,* 289–293.

Henderson, A. J. (2008). The effects of tobacco smoke exposure on respiratory health in school-aged children. *Pediatric Respiratory Reviews 9,* 21–28.

Henderson, V. L., & Dweck, C. S. (1990). Motivation and achievement. In S. S. Feldman & G. R. Elliott (Eds.), *At the threshold: The developing adolescent.* Cambridge, MA: Harvard University Press.

Hendrick, J., & Weissman, P. (2010). *The whole child: Developmental education for the early years* (9th ed.). Upper Saddle River, NJ: Prentice Hall.

Hendry, J. (1995). *Understanding Japanese society.* London: Routledge.

Henniger, M. L. (2009). *Teaching young children* (4th ed.). Upper Saddle River, NJ: Prentice Hall.

Henriksen, T. B., Hjollund, N. H., Jensen, T. K., Bonde, J. P., Andersson, A. M., Kolstad, H., Ernst, E., Giwereman, A., Skakkebaek, N. E., & Olsen, J. (2004). Alcohol consumption at the time of conception and spontaneous abortion. *American Journal of Epidemiology, 160,* 661–667.

Henry, D. B., Schoeny, M. E., Deptula, D. P., & Slavick, J. T. (2007). Peer selection and socialization effects on adolescent intercourse without a condom and attitudes about the costs of sex. *Child Development, 78,* 825–838.

Hentz, K., & Fields, J. (2009). Sex education/abstinence education. In D. Carr (Ed.), *Encyclopedia of the life course and human development.* Boston: Gale Cengage.

Hepper, P. (2007). The foundations of development. In A. Slater & M. Lewis, *Introduction to infant development* (2nd ed.). New York: Oxford University Press.

Hepper, P. G., Shahidullah, S., & White, R. (1990). Origins of fetal handedness. *Nature, 347,* 431.

Herbison, A. E., Porteus, R., Paper, J. R., Mora, J. M., & Hurst, P. R. (2008). Gonadotropin-releasing hormone neuron requirements for puberty, ovulation, and fertility. *Endocrinology, 149,* 597–604.

Herbst, M. A., Mercer, B. M., Beasley, D., Meyer, N., & Carr, T. (2003). Relationship of prenatal care and perinatal morbidity in low-birth-weight infants. *American Journal of Obstetrics and Gynecology, 189,* 930–933.

Herman, D. R., Harrison, G. G., Afifi, A. A., & Jenks, E. (2008). Effect of a target subsidy on intake of fruits and vegetables among low-income women in the Special Supplemental Nutrition Program for Women, Infants, and Children. *American Journal of Public Health, 98,* 98–105.

Hermann-Giddens, M. E. (2007). The decline in the age of menarche in the United States: Should we be concerned? *Journal of Adolescent Health, 40,* 201–203.

Hernandez-Reif, M., Diego, M., & Field, T. (2007). Preterm infants show reduced stress behaviors and activity after 5 days of massage therapy. *Infant Behavior and Development, 30,* 557–561.

Herrera, S., Perez, D. R., & Escamilla, K. (2010). *Teaching reading to English language learners.* Boston: Allyn & Bacon.

Herrmann, M., King, K., & Weitzman, M. (2008). Prenatal tobacco smoke and postnatal secondhand smoke exposure and child neurodevelopment. *Current Opinion in Pediatrics, 20,* 184–190.

Hesmet, S., & Lo, K. C. (2006). Evaluation and treatment of ejaculatory duct obstruction in infertile men. *Canadian Journal of Urology, 13,* (Suppl 1), 18–21.

Hetherington, E. M. (1989). Coping with family transitions: Winners, losers, and survivors. *Child Development, 60,* 1–14.

Hetherington, E. M. (2000). Divorce. In A. Kazdin (Ed.), *Encyclopedia of psychology.* Washington, DC, & New York: American Psychological Association and Oxford University Press.

Hetherington, E. M. (2006). The influence of conflict, marital problem solving, and parenting on children's adjustment in nondivorced, divorced, and remarried families. In A. Clarke-Stewart & J. Dunn (Eds.), *Families count.* New York: Oxford University Press.

Hetherington, E. M., & Kelly, J. (2002). *For better or for worse: Divorce reconsidered.* New York: Norton.

Hetherington, E. M., Reiss, D., & Plomin, R. (Eds.). (1994). *Separate social worlds of siblings: The impact of nonshared environment on development.* Hillsdale, NJ: Erlbaum.

Hetherington, E. M., & Stanley-Hagan, M. (2002). Parenting in divorced and remarried families. In M. H. Bornstein (Ed.), *Handbook of parenting* (2nd ed., Vol. 3). Mahwah, NJ: Erlbaum.

Heuwinkel, M. K. (1996). New ways of learning = new ways of teaching. *Childhood Education, 72,* 27–31.

Hewitt-Taylor, J. (2009, in press). Children who have complex health needs: Parents' experiences of their child's education. *Child Care, Health, and Development.*

Hewlett, B. S. (1991). *Intimate fathers: The nature and context of Aka pygmy.* Ann Arbor: University of Michigan Press.

Hewlett, B. S. (2000). Culture, history and sex: Anthropological perspectives on father involvement. *Marriage and Family Review, 29,* 324–340.

Heyman, G. D., Fu, G., & Lee, K. (2007). Evaluating claims people make about themselves: The development of skepticism. *Child Development, 78,* 367–375.

Heyman, G. D., & Legare, C. H. (2005). Children's evaluation of sources of information about traits. *Developmental Psychology, 41,* 636–647.

Hibell, B., Andersson, B., Bjarnasson, T., & others. (2004), *The ESPAD report 2003: Alcohol* *and other drug use among students in 35 European Countries.* The Swedish Council for Information on Alcohol and Other Drugs (CAN) and Council of Europe Pompidou Group.

Hick, P., & Thomas, G. (Eds.). (2009). *Inclusion and diversity in education.* Thousand Oaks, CA: Sage.

Hickson, G. B., & Clayton, E. W. (2002). Parents and children's doctors. In M. H. Bornstein (Ed.), *Handbook of parenting* (Vol. 5). Mahwah, NJ: Erlbaum.

Higgins, A., Power, C., & Kohlberg, L. (1983, April). *Moral atmosphere and moral judgment.* Paper presented at the biennial meeting of the Society for Research in Child Development, Detroit.

Highfield, R. (2008, April 30). *Harvard's baby brain research lab.* Retrieved January 24, 2009, from http://www.telegraph.co.uk/science-andtechnology/science/sciencenews/3341166/Harvards-baby-brain-research-lab.html

High/Scope Resource. (2005, Spring). The High/Scope Perry Preschool Study and the man who began it. *High/Scope Resource,* p. 9. Ypsilanti, MI: High/Scope Press.

Hijiya, N., & others. (2007). Cumulative incidence of secondary neoplasms as a first event after childhood acute lymphoblastic leukemia. *Journal of the American Medical Association, 297,* 1207–1215.

Hildebrandt, E., & Stevens, P. (2009, in press). Impoverished women with children and no welfare benefits: The urgency of researching failures of the temporary assistance for needy families program. *American Journal of Public Health.*

Hill, C. R., & Stafford, F. P. (1980). Parental care of children: Time diary estimate of quantity, predictability, and variety. *Journal of Human Resources, 15,* 219–239.

Hill, M. A. (2007). Early human development. *Clinical Obstetrics and Gynecology, 50,* 2–9.

Hillman, C. H., Buck, S. M., Themanson, J. R., Pontifex, M. B., & Castelli, D. M. (2009). Aerobic fitness and cognitive development: Event-related brain potential and task performance indices of executive control in preadolescent children. *Developmental Psychology, 45,* 114–129.

Hills, A. P., King, N. A., & Armstrong, T. P. (2007). The contribution of physical activity and sedentary behaviors to the growth and development of children and adolescents: Implications for overweight and obesity. *Sports Medicine, 37,* 533–545.

Hindmarsh, P. C., & Dattani, M. T. (2006). Use of hormone in children. *Nature Clinical Practice: Endocrinology and Metabolism, 2,* 260–268.

Hinduja, S., & Patchin, S. (2009). *Bullying beyond the schoolyard.* Thousand Oaks, CA: Corwin.

Hingson, R. W., Heeren, T., & Winter, M. R. (2006). Age at drinking onset and alcohol dependence: Age at onset, duration, and severity.

Archives of Pediatric and Adolescent Medicine, 160, 739–746.

Hoban, T. F. (2004). Sleep and its disorders in children. *Seminars in Neurology 24,* 327–340.

Hockenberry, M., & Wilson, D. (2009). *Wong's essentials of pediatric nursing.* Oxford, UK: Elsevier.

Hocutt, A. M. (1996). Effectiveness of special education: Is placement the critical factor? *Future of Children, 6* (1), 77–102.

Hoefnagels, M. (2009). *Biology.* New York: McGraw-Hill.

Hoek, H. W. (2006). Incidence, prevalence and mortality of anorexia nervosa and other eating disorders. *Current Opinion in Psychiatry, 19,* 389–394.

Hofer, A., Siedentopf, C. M., Ischebeck, A., Rettenbacher, M. A., Verius, M., Felber, S., & Fleischhacker, W. (2007a). Sex differences in brain activation patterns during processing of positively and negatively balanced emotional stimuli. *Psychological Medicine, 37,* 109–119.

Hofer, A., Siedentopf, C. M., Ischebeck, A., Rettenbacher, M. A., Verius, M., Felber, S., & Fleischhacker, W. (2007b). Gender differences in regional cerebral activity during the perception of emotion: A functional MRI study. *Neuroimage, 132,* 854–862.

Hoff, E., Laursen, B., & Tardif, T. (2002). Socioeconomic status and parenting. In M. H. Bornstein (Ed.), *Handbook of parenting* (2nd ed.). Mahwah, NJ: Erlbaum.

Hoff, E., & Shatz, M. (Eds.). (2007). *Blackwell handbook of language development.* Malden, MA: Blackwell.

Hofferth, S. L., & Reid, L. (2002). Early childbearing and children's achievement behavior over time. *Perspectives on sexual and reproductive health, 34,* 41–49.

Hoffman, E., & Ewen, D. (2007). Supporting families, nurturing young children. *CLASP Policy Brief 9,* 1–11.

Hoffman, J. P. (2009). Drug use, adolescent. In D. Carr (Ed.), *Encyclopedia of the life course and human development.* Boston: Gage Cengage.

Hoffman, J. R., Kang, J., Faigenbaum, A. D., & Ratamess, N. A. (2005). Recreational sports participation is associated with enhanced physical fitness in children. *Research in Sports Medicine, 13,* 149–161.

Hoffman, M. L. (1970). Moral development. In P. H. Mussen (Ed.), *Manual of child psychology* (3rd ed., Vol. 2). New York: Wiley.

Hofheimer, J. A., & Lester, B. M. (2008). Neuropsychological assessment. In M. M. Haith & J. B. Benson (Eds.), *Encyclopedia of infant and early childhood development.* Oxford, UK: Elsevier.

Hogan, M. A., Glazebrook, R., Brancato, V., & Rogers, J. (2007). *Maternal-newborn nursing: Review and rationales* (2nd ed.). Upper Saddle River, NJ: Prentice Hall.

Holcombe, E., Carrier, D., Manlove, J., & Ryan, S. (2008, February). Contraceptive use patterns across teens' sexual relationships. *Child Fact Sheet.* Washington, DC: Child Trends.

Holland, J. L. (1987). Current status of Holland's theory of careers: Another perspective. *Career Development Quarterly, 36,* 24–30.

Hollich, G., Newman, R. S., & Jusczyk, P. W. (2005). Infants' use of synchronized visual information to separate streams of speech. *Child Development, 76,* 598–613.

Hollier, L., & Wendel, G. (2008). Third trimester antiviral prophylaxis for preventing maternal genital herpes simplex virus (HSV) recurrences and neonatal infection. *Cochrane Database of Systematic Reviews, 1,* CD004946.

Holtzen, D. W. (2000). Handedness and professional tennis. *International Journal of Neuroscience, 105,* 101–119.

Holzman, L. (2009). *Vygotsky at work and play.* Oxford, UK: Routledge.

Hong, G., & Raudenbush, S. W. (2005). Effects of kindergarten retention policy on children's cognitive growth in reading and mathematics. *Educational Evaluation and Policy Analysis, 27,* 205–224.

Hooper, S. R., & others (2008). Executive functions in young males with fragile X syndrome in comparison to mental age-matched controls: Baseline findings from a longitudinal study. *Neuropsychology, 22,* 36–47.

Hopkins, B. (1991). Facilitating early motor development: An intracultural study of West Indian mothers and their infants living in Britain. In J. K. Nugent, B. M. Lester, & T. B. Brazelton (Eds.), *The cultural context of infancy: Vol. 2. Multi-cultural and interdisciplinary approaches to parent-infant relations.* Norwood, NJ: Ablex.

Hopkins, B., & Westra, T. (1988). Maternal handling and motor development: An intracultural study. *Genetic Psychology Monographs, 14,* 377–420.

Hopkins, B., & Westra, T. (1990). Motor development, maternal expectations, and the role of handling. *Infant Behavior and Development, 13,* 117–122.

Horner, C. C., & Bacharier, L. B. (2009). Diagnosis and management of asthma in preschool and school age children: Focus on the 2007 NAEPP guidelines. *Current Opinion in Pulmonary Medicine, 15,* 52–56.

Horne, R. S., Franco, P., Adamson, T. M., Groswasser, J., & Kahn, A. (2002). Effects of body position on sleep and arousal characteristics in infants. *Early Human Development, 69,* 25–33.

Horowitz, F. D. (2009). Introduction: A developmental understanding of giftedness and talent. In F. D. Horowitz, R. F. Subotnik, & D. J. Matthews (Eds.), *The development of giftedness and talent across the life span.* Washington, DC: American Psychological Association.

Horsthemke, B., & Buiting, K. (2008). Genomic imprinting and imprinting defects in humans. *Advances in Genetics, 61,* 225–246.

Hoskin, J., & Herman, R. (2001). The communication, speech, and gesture of a group of hearing impaired children. *International Journal of Language and Communication Disorders, 36* (Suppl.), 206–209.

Hotelling, B. A. (2009). Teaching normal birth, normally. *Journal of Perinatal Education, 18,* 51–55.

Howe, L. D., Huttly, S. R., & Abramsky, T. (2006). Risk factors for injuries in young children in four developing countries: The Young Lives Study. *Tropic Medicine and International Health, 11,* 1557–1566.

Howell, D. C. (2010). *Statistical methods for psychology* (7th ed.). Boston: Cengage.

Howe, M. J. A., Davidson, J. W., Moore, D. G., & Sloboda, J. A. (1995). Are there early childhood signs of musical ability? *Psychology of Music, 23,* 162–176.

Howe, N., & Recchia, H. E. (2008). Siblings and sibling rivalry. In M. M. Haith & J. B. Benson (Eds.), *Encyclopedia of infant and early childhood development.* Oxford, UK: Elsevier.

Howes, C. (2009). Friendship in early childhood. In K. H. Rubin, W. M., Bukowski, & B. Laursen (Eds.), *Handbook of peer interactions, relationships, and groups.* New York: Guilford.

Howlin, P., Magiati, I., & Charman, T. (2009). Systematic review of early intensive behavioral interventions with autism. *American Journal on Intellectual and Developmental Disabilities, 114,* 23–41.

Hoyert, D. L., Mathews, T. J., Menacker, F., Strobino, D. M., & Guyer, B. (2006). Annual summary of vital statistics: 2004. *Pediatrics, 117,* 168–183.

Hrabosky, J. I., Masheb, R. M., White, M. A., & Grilo, C. M. (2007). Overvaluation of shape and weight in binge eating disorder. *Journal of Consulting and Clinical Psychology, 75,* 175–180.

Hsu, H.-C. (2004). Antecedents and consequences of separation anxiety in first-time mothers: Infant, mother, and social-contextual characteristics. *Infant Behavior and Development, 27,* 113–133.

Huang, L. N. (1989). Southeast Asian refugee children and adolescents. In J. T. Gibbs & L. N. Huang (Eds.), *Children of color.* San Francisco: Jossey-Bass.

Hudley, C. (2009). Academic motivation and achievement of African American youth. In H. A. Neville, B. M. Tynes, & S. O. Utley (Eds.), *Handbook of African American psychology.* Thousand Oaks, CA: Sage.

Huebner, A. M., & Garrod, A. C. (1993). Moral reasoning among Tibetan monks: A study of Buddhist adolescents and young adults in Nepal. *Journal of Cross-Cultural Psychology, 24,* 167–185.

Huesmann, L. R., Dubow, E. F., Eron, L. D., & Boxer, P. (2006). Middle childhood family-contextual and personal factors as predictors of adult outcomes. In A. C. Huston & M. N. Ripke (Eds.), *Developmental contexts in middle childhood: Bridges to adolescence and Adulthood.* New York: Cambridge University Press.

Huesman, M. L. R., Moise-Titus, J., Podolski, C., & Eron, L. D. (2003). Longitudinal Relations between children's exposure to TV violence and their aggressive and violent behavior in young adulthood 1977–1992. *Developmental Psychology, 39,* 201–221.

Hueston, W. J., Geesey, M. E., & Diaz, V. (2008). Prenatal care initiation among pregnant teens in the United States: An analysis over 25 years. *Journal of Adolescent Health, 42,* 243–248.

Hu, H., & others. (2007). Fetal lead exposure at each stage of pregnancy as a predictor of infant mental development. *Environmental Health Perspectives, 114,* 1730–1735.

Huisman, T. A., & Kellenberger, C. J. (2008). MRI. imaging characteristics of the normal fetal gastrointestinal tract and abdomen. *European Journal of Radiology, 65,* 170–181.

Huizink, A. C., & Mulder, E. J. (2006). Maternal smoking, drinking, or cannibis use during pregnancy and neurobehavioral and cognitive functioning in human offspring. *Neuroscience and Biobehavioral Research, 30,* 24–41.

Hunter, L. P. (2009). A descriptive study of "being with woman" during labor and birth. *Journal of Midwifery and Women's Health, 54,* 111–118.

Hunter, L. P., Rychnovsky, J. D., & Yount, S. M. (2009). A selective review of maternal sleep characteristics in the postpartum period. *Journal of Obstetric, Gynecologic, and Neonatal Nursing.*

Hurt, H., Brodsky, N. L., Roth, H., Malmud, F., & Giannetta. J. M. (2005). School performance of children with gestational cocaine exposure. *Neurotoxicology and Teratology, 27,* 203–211.

Huston, A. C., & Bentley, A. C. (2010). Human development in societal context. *Annual Review of Psychology* (Vol. 61). Palo Alto, CA: Annual Reviews.

Huston, A. C., Epps, S. R., Shim, M. S., Duncan, G. J., Crobsy, D. A., & Ripke, M. N. (2006). Effects of a poverty intervention program lasting from middle childhood to adolescence. In A. C. Huston & M. N. Ripke (Eds.), *Developmental contexts of middle childhood: Bridges to adolescence and adulthood.* New York: Cambridge University Press.

Huston, A. C., & Ripke, N. N. (2006). Experiences in middle and late childhood and children's development. In A. C. Huston & M. N. Ripke (Eds.), *Developmental contexts in middle childhood.* New York: Cambridge University Press.

Hutchinson, D. M., & Rapee, R. M. (2007). Do friends share similar body image and eating problems? The role of social networks and peer influences in early adolescence. *Behavior Research and Therapy, 45,* 1557–1577.

Hutson, R. A. (2008). Poverty. In N. J. Salkind (Ed.), *Encyclopedia of educational psychology.* Thousand Oaks, CA: Sage.

Huttenlocher, J., Haight, W., Bruk, A., Seltzer, M., & Lynos, T. (1991). Early vocabulary growth: Relation to language input and gender. *Developmental Psychology, 27,* 236–248.

Huttenlocher, P. R., & Dabholkar, A. S. (1997). Regional differences in synaptogenesis in human cerebral cortex. *Journal of Comparative Neurology, 37* (2), 167–178.

Hyde, D. C., & Spelke, E. S. (2009, in press). All numbers are not equal: An electrophysiological investigation of small and large number representations. *Journal of Cognitive Neuroscience.*

Hyde, D. R. (2009). *Introduction to genetic principles.* New York: McGraw-Hill.

Hyde, J. S. (2007a). *Half the human experience* (7th ed.). Boston: Houghton Mifflin.

Hyde, J. S. (2007b). New directions in the study of gender similarities and differences. *Current Directions in Psychological Science, 16,* 259–263.

Hyde, J. S., & DeLamater, J. D. (2008). *Understanding human sexuality* (10th ed.). New York: McGraw-Hill.

Hyde, J. S., Lindberg, S. M., Linn, M. C., Ellis, A. B., & Williams, C. C. (2008). Gender similarities characterize math performance. *Science, 321,* 494–495.

Hyde, J. S., & Price, M. (2007, November). *When two isn't better than one: Predictors of early sexual activity in adolescence using a cumulative risk model.* Paper presented at the meeting of the Society for the Scientific Study of Sexuality, Indianapolis.

Hyson, M. (2007). Curriculum. In R. New & M. Cochran (Eds.), *Early childhood education: An international encyclopedia of early childhood education.* New York: Greenwood.

Hyson, M. C., Copple, C., & Jones, J. (2006). Early childhood development and education. In W. Damon & R. Lerner (Eds.), *Handbook of child psychologh* (6th ed.). New York: Wiley.

I

Iacoboni, M., & Dapretto, M. (2006). The mirror neuron system and the consequences of its dysfunction. *Nature Reviews: Neuroscience, 7,* 942–951.

Ige, F., & Shelton, D. (2004). Reducing the risk of sudden infant death syndrome (SIDS) in African-American communities. *Journal of Pediatric Nursing, 19,* 290–292.

"I Have a Dream Foundation." (2009). *About us.* Retrieved July 5, 2009, from www.ihaveadreamfoundation.org/html/

Imada, T., Zhang, Y., Cheour, M., Taulu, S., Ahonen, A., & Kuhl, P. K. (2007). Infant speech perception activates Broca's area: A developmental magnetoencephalography study. *Neuroreport, 17,* 957–962.

Impett, E. A., Schoolder, D., Tolman, L., Sorsoli, L., & Henson, J. M. (2008). Girls' relationship authenticity and self-esteem across adolescence. *Developmental Psychology, 44,* 722–733.

Insel, P. M., & Roth, W. T. (2010). *Core concepts in health* (11th ed.). New York: McGraw-Hill.

International Montessori Council. (2006). Much of their success on prime-time television. Retrieved March 16, 2007, from www.Montessori.org/enews/barbara_walters.html

Ip, S., Chung, M., Raman, G., Chew, P., Magula, N., Devine, D., Trikalinos, T., & Lau, J. (2007). Breastfeeding and maternal and infant health outcomes in developed countries. *Evidence Report/Technology Assessment, 153,* 1–86.

Irwin, C. E. (2004). Eating and physical activity during adolescence: Does it make a difference in adult health status? *Journal of Adolescent Health, 34,* 459–460.

Isen, J., & Baker, L. A. (2008). Genetic disorders: Sex-linked. In M. M. Haith & J. B. Benson (Eds.), *Encyclopedia of infant and early childhood development.* Oxford, UK: Elsevier.

Isen, J. D., Bakeer, L. A., Raine, A., & Bezdjian, S. (2009). Genetic and environmental influences on the Junior Temperament and Character Inventory in a preadolescent twin sample. *Behavior Genetics, 39,* 36–47.

Ishii-Kuntz, M. (2004). Asian American families. In M. Coleman & L. Ganong (Eds.), *Handbook of contemporary families.* Thousand Oaks, CA: Sage.

Izard C. E. (2009). Emotion theory and research: Highlights, unanswered questions, and emerging issues. *Annual Review of Psychology* (Vol. 60). Palo Alto, CA: Annual Reviews.

Izard, V., Dehaene-Lambertz, G., & Dehaene, S. (2008). Distinct cerebral pathways for object identity and number in human infants. *PLoS Biology, 6,* e11.

J

Jabr, Z. (2010). *Student orientation series: English language learners.* Upper Saddle River, NJ: Prentice Hall.

Jackson, A., & Davis, G. (2000). *Turning points 2000.* New York: Teachers College Press.

Jackson, S. L. (2008). *Research methods.* Belmont, CA: Wadsworth.

Jacobson, J. L., & Jacobson, S. W. (2002). Association of prenatal exposure to an environmental contaminant with intellectual function in childhood. *Journal of Toxicology—Clinical Toxocology, 40,* 467–475.

Jacobson, J. L, & Jacobson, S. W. (2003). Prenatal exposure to polychlorinated biphenyls and attention at school age. *Journal of Pediatrics, 143,* 780–788.

Jacobson, J. L., & Jacobson, S. W., Fein, G. G., Schwartz, P. M., & Dowler, J. (1984). Prenatal exposure to an environmental toxin: A test of the multiple-effects model. *Developmental Psychology, 20,* 523–532.

Jaddoe, V. W., Troe, E. J., Hofman, A., Mackenbach, J. P., Moll, H. A., Steegeers, E. A., & Witteman, J. C. (2008). Active and passive smoking during pregnancy and the risks of low birthweight and preterm birth: The Generation R Study. *Pediatric and Perinatal Epidemiology, 22,* 162–171.

Jafar, T. H. (2009). Children, obesity, and high blood pressure: Asian populations at high risk. *American Journal of Hypertension, 22,* 6–7.

Jaffee, S., & Hyde, J. S. (2000). Gender differences in moral orientation: A meta-analysis. *Psychological Bulletin, 126,* 703–726.

James, A. H., Brancazio, L. R., & Price, T. (2008). Aspirin and reproductive outcomes. *Obstetrical and Gynecological Survey, 63,* 49–57.

James, D. C. & Dobson, B. (2005). Position of the American Dietetic Association: Promoting and supporting breastfeeding. *Journal of the American Dietetic Association, 105,* 810–818.

James, J., Thomas, P., Cavan, D., & Kerr, D. (2004). Preventing childhood obesity by reducing consumption of carbonated drinks: Cluster randomized trial. *British Medical Journal, 328,* 1237.

James, S. R., & Ashwill, J. (2007). *Nursing care of children* (3rd ed.). London: Elsevier.

James, W. (1890/1950). *The principle of psychology.* New York: Dover.

Janssen, I., Katzmarzyk, P. T., Boyce, W. F., Vereecken, C., Mulvihill, C., Roberts, C., Currie, C., & Picket, W. (2005). Comparison of overweight and obesity prevalence in school-aged youth from 34 countries and their relationships with physical activity and dietary patterns. *Obesity Reviews, 6,* 123–132.

Jaswal, V. K., & Fernald, A. (2007). Learning to communicate. In A. Slater & M. Lewis (Eds.), *Introduction infant development* (2nd ed.). New York: Oxford University Press.

Jayson, S. (2006, June 29). The "millenials" come of age. *USA Today,* pp. 1–2D.

Jenkins, J. M., & Astington, J. W. (1996). Cognitive factors and family structure associated with theory of mind development in young children. *Developmental Psychology, 32,* 70–78.

Jenni, O. G. & Carskadon, M. A. (2007). Sleep behavior and sleep regulation from infancy through adolescence: Normative aspects. In O. G. Jenni & M. A. Carskadon (Eds.), *Sleep medicine clinics: Sleep in children and adolescents.* Philadelphia: W. B. Saunders.

Jensen, A. R. (2008). Book review. *Intelligence, 36,* 96–97.

Ji, B. T., Shu, X. O., Linet, M. S., Zheng, W., Wacholde, S., Gao, Y. T., Ying, D. M., & Jin, F. (1997). Paternal cigarette smoking and the risk of childhood cancer among offspring of nonsmoking mothers. *Journal of the National Cancer Institute, 89,* 235–244.

Ji, C. Y., & Chen, T. J. (2008). Secular changes in stature and body mass index for Chinese youth in sixteen major cities, 1950s–2005. *American Journal of Human Biology, 20,* 530–537.

Jimerson, S. R. (2009). High school dropout. In D. Carr (Ed.), *Encyclopedia of the life course and human development.* Boston: Gale Cengage.

Johannsson, A., Ludvigsson, J., & Hermansson, G. (2008). Adverse health effects related to tobacco smoke exposure in a cohort of three-year olds. *Acta Pediatrica, 97,* 354–357.

Johnson, A. D., Tarrant, K., & Brooks-Gunn, J. (2008). Early childhood education and care: An opportunity to enhance the lives of poor children. In D. R. Crane & T. B. Heaton (Eds.), *Handbook of families and poverty.* Thousand Oaks, CA: Sage.

Johnson, A. N. (2007). Factors influencing implementation of kangaroo holding in a special care nursery. *MCN American Journal of Maternal Child Nursing, 32,* 25–29.

Johnson, G. B., & Losos, J. (2010). *The living world* (6th ed.). New York: McGraw-Hill.

Johnson, H. L., Erbelding, E. J., & Ghanem, K. G. (2007). Sexually transmitted infections during pregnancy. *Current Infectious Disease Reports, 9,* 125–133.

Johnson, J. S., & Newport, E. L. (1991). Critical period effects on universal properties of language: The status of subjacency in the acquisition of a second language. *Cognition, 39,* 215–258.

Johnson, M. H. (2008, April 30). Commentary In R. Highfield, "Harvard's baby brain research lab." Retrieved January 24, 2008, from http://www.telegraph.co.uk/scienceandtechnology/science/sciencenews/3341166/Harvards-baby-brain-research-lab.html

Johnson, M. H., Grossmann, T. and Cohen-Kadosh, K. (2009) Mapping functional brain development: Building a social brain through interactive specialization. *Developmental Psychology, 45,* 151–159.

Johnson, R. J. (2008). Advances in understanding and treating childhood sexual abuse: Implications for research and policy. *Family and Community Health, 31* (Suppl. 1), S24–S31.

Johnson, S. (2007). Cognitive and behavioral outcomes following very preterm birth. *Seminars in Fetal and Neonatal Medicine, 12,* 363–373.

Johnson, S. P. (2004). Development of perceptual completion in infancy. *Psychological Science, 15,* 769–775.

Johnson, S. P. (2009a, in press). Perceptual completion in infancy. To appear in S. P. Johnson (Ed.), *Neoconstructivism: The new science of cognitive development.* New York: Oxford University Press.

Johnson, S. P. (2009b, in press). A constructivist view of object perception in infancy. In

L. M. Oakes, C. H. Cashon, M. Casasola, & D. H. Rakison (Eds.), *Early perceptual and cognitive development*. New York: Oxford University Press.

Johnson, S. P. (2009c). Developmental origins of object perception. In A. Woodward & A. Needham (Eds.), *Learning and the infant mind*. New York: Oxford University Press.

Johnson, S. P., Bremner, J. G., Slater, A., & Mason, U. (2000). The role of good form in young infants' perception of partly occluded objects. *Journal of Experimental Child Psychology, 76*, 1–25.

Johnson, W., Bouchard, T. J. Jr., McGue, M., Segal, N. L., Tellegen, A., Keyes, M. & Gottesman, I. I. (2007). Genetic and environmental influences on the verbal-perceptual-image rotation (VPR) model of the structure of mental abilities in the Minnesota study of twins reared apart. *Intelligence, 35*, 542–562.

Johnson, W., Bouchard, T. J., Krueger, R. F., McGue, M., & Gottesman, I. I. (2004). Just one *g:* consistent results from three test batteries. *Intelligence, 32*, 95–107.

John-Steiner, V. (2007). Vygotsky on thinking and speaking. In H. Daniels, J. Wertsch, & M. Cole (Eds.), *The Cambridge companion to Vygotsky*. New York: Cambridge University Press.

Johnston, C. C., Filion, F., Campbell-Yeo, M., Goulet, C., Bell, L., McNaughton, K., & Bryon, J. (2009). Enhanced kangaroo care for heel lance in preterm neonates: A crossover trial. *Journal of Perinatology, 29*, 51–56.

Johnston, L. D., O'Malley, P. M., Bachman, J. G., & Schulenberg, J. E. (2009). *Monitoring the future national results on adolescent drug use: Overview of key findings, 2008*. Bethesda, MD: National Institute on Drug Abuse.

Jones, H. W. (2007). Iatrogenic multiple births: A 2003 checkup. *Fertility and Sterility, 87*, 453–455.

Jones, J. M. (1994). The African American: A duality dilemma? In W. J. Lonner & R. Malpass (Eds.), *Psychology and culture*. Needham Heights, MA: Allyn & Bacon.

Jones, K. L. (2008). Role of obesity in complicating and confusing diagnosis and treatment of diabetes in children. *Pediatrics, 121*, 361–368.

Jones, M. C. (1965). Psychological correlates of somatic development. *Child Development, 36*, 899–911.

Jones, M. D., & Galliher, R. V. (2007). Ethnic identity and psychosocial functioning in Navajo adolescents. *Journal of Research on Adolescence, 17*, 683–696.

Jonsdottir, G., Smarason, A. K., Geirsson, R. T., & Bjaradottir, R. I. (2009). No correlation between cesarean section rates and perinatal mortality of singleton infants over 2,500 g. *Acta Obstetricia et Gynecologica Scandinavica, 88*, 621–623.

Jordan, S. J., & others. (2008). Serious ovarian, fallopian tube and primary peritoneal cancers: A comparative epidemiological analysis. *International Journal of Cancer, 122*, 1598–1603.

Joseph, J. (2006). *The missing gene*. New York: Algora.

Josephson Institute of Ethics. (2006). *2006 Josephson Institute report card on the ethics of American youth. Part one—integrity*. Los Angeles: Josephson Institute.

Joyner, K. (2009). Transition to parenthood. In D. Carr (Ed.), *Encyclopedia of the life course and human development*. Boston: Gale Cengage.

Juffer, F., Bakermans-Kranenburg M. J., & van IJzendoorn, M. H. (2007). *Promoting positive parenting*. Mahwah, NJ: Erlbaum.

Juffer, F., & van IJzendoorn, M. H. (2005). Behavior problems and mental health referrals of international adoptees: A meta-analysis. *Journal of the American Medical Association, 293*, 2501–2513.

Juffer, F., & van IJzendoorn, M. H. (2007). Adoptees do not lack self-esteem: A meta-analysis of studies on self-esteem of transracial. international, and domestic adoptees. *Psychological Bulletin, 133*, 1067–1083.

Juhl, M., Andersen, P. K., Olsen, J., Madsen, M., Jorgensen, T., Nohr, E. A., & Andersen, A. M. (2008). Physical exercise during pregnancy and the risk of preterm birth: A study within the Danish National Birth Cohort. *American Journal of Epidemiology, 167*, 859–866.

Jumping-Eagle, S., Sheeder, J., Kelly, L. S., & Stevens-Simon, C. (2008). Association of conventional goals and perceptions of pregnancy with female teenagers' pregnancy avoidance behavior and attitudes. *Perspectives on Sexual and Reproductive Health, 40*, 74–80.

Jung, R. E., & Haier, R. J. (2007). The Parieto-Frontal Integration Theory (P-FIT) of intelligence: Converging neuroimaging evidence. *Behovioral and Brain Sciences, 30*, 135–187.

Jusczyk, P. W. (2000). *The discovery of spoken language*. Cambridge, MA: MIT Press.

Jusczyk, P. W., & Hohne, E. A. (1997). Infants' memory for spoken words. *Science, 277*, 1984–1986.

Jylhava, J., & others. (2009). Genetics of C-reactive protein and complement factor H have an epistatic effect on carotid artery compliance: The Cardiovascular Risk in Young Finns Study. *Clinical and Experimental Immunology, 155*, 53–58.

K

Kagan, J. (1987). Perspectives on infancy. In J. D. Osofsky (Ed.), *Handbook on infant development* (2nd ed.). New York: Wiley.

Kagan, J. (1992). Yesterday's promises, tomorrow's promises. *Developmental Psychology, 28*, 990–997.

Kagan, J. (2000). Temperament. In A. Kazdin (Ed.), *Encyclopedia of psychology*. Washington. DC, & New York: American Psychological Association and Oxford University Press.

Kagan, J. (2002). Behavioral inhibition as a temperamental category. In R. J. Davidson, K. R. Scherer, & H. H. Goldsmith (Eds.), *Handbook of affective science*. New York: Oxford University Press.

Kagan, J. (2008). Fear and wariness. In M. M. Haith & J. B. Benson (Eds.), *Encyclopedia of infant and early childhood development*. Oxford, UK: Elsevier.

Kagan, J. (2010). Emotions and temperament. In M. H. Bornstein (ed.), *Handbook of cultural developmental science*. New York: Psychology Press.

Kagan, J. J., Kearsley, R. B., & Zelazo, P. R. (1978). *Infancy: Its place in human development*. Cambridge, MA: Harvard University Press.

Kagan, J., & Snidman, N. (1991). Infant predictors of inhibited and uninhibited behavioral profiles. *Psychological Science, 2*, 40–44.

Kagitcibasi, C. (2007). *Family, self, and human development across cultures*. Mahwah, NJ: Erlbaum.

Kahn, J. A., Huang, B., Gillman, M. W., Field, A. E., Austin, S. B., Colditz, G. A., & Frazier, A. L. (2008). Patterns and determinants of physical activity in U.S. adolescents. *Journal of Adolescent Health, 42*, 369–377.

Kail, R. V. (2007). Longitudinal evidence that increases in processing speed and working memory enhance children's reasoning. *Psychological Science, 18*, 312–313.

Kaiser, B., & Rasminsky, J. (2009). *Challenging behavior in elementary and middle school*. Upper Saddle River, NJ: Prentice Hall.

Kaiser Family Foundation. (2006). *The media family: Electronic media in the lives of infants, toddlers, preschoolers, and their parents*. Menlo Park, CA: Author.

Kajantie, E., & others. (2008). Young adults with very low birth weight: Leaving the parental home and sexual relationships—Helsinki study of very low birth weight adults. *Pediatrics, 122*, e62–e72.

Kalant, H. (2004). Adverse effects of cannabis on health: An update of the literature since 1996. *Progress in Neuropsychopharmacology and Biological Psychiatry, 28*, 849–863.

Kamerman, S. B. (1989). Child care, women, work, and the family: An international overview of child-care services and related policies. In J. S. Lande, S. Scarr, & N. Gunzenhauser (Eds.), *Caring for children: Challenge to America*. Hillsdale, NJ: Erlbaum.

Kamerman, S. B. (2000a). Parental leave policies. *Social Policy Report of the Society for Research in Child Development, XIV* (No. 2), 1–15.

Kamerman, S. B. (2000b). From maternity to paternity leave policies. *Journal of the Medical Women's Association, 55*, 98–99.

Kamii, C. (1985). *Young children reinvent arithmetic: Implications of Piaget's theory*. New York: Teachers College Press.

Kamii, C. (1989). *Young children continue to reinvent arithmetic*. New York: Teachers College Press.

Kandler, C., Riemann, R., & Kampfe, N. (2009). Genetic and personality mediation between measures of personality and family environment in twins reared together. *Behavior Genetics, 39,* 24–35.

Kanoy, K., Ulku-Steiner, B., Cox, M., & Burchinal, M. (2003). Marital relationship and individual psychological characteristics that predict physical punishment of children. *Journal of Family Psychology, 17,* 20–28.

Kaplan, H. B. (2009). Self-esteem. In D. Carr (Ed.), *Encyclopedia of the life course and human development.* Boston: Gale Cengage.

Kapornai, K., & Vetro, A. (2008). Depression in children. *Current Opinion in Psychiatry, 21,* 1–7.

Karama, S., & others. (2009). Positive association between cognitive ability and cortical thickness in a representative sample of healthy 6 to 18 year olds. *Intelligence, 37,* 145–155.

Kar, B. R., Rao, S. L., & Chandramouli, B. A. (2008). Cognitive development in children with chronic energy malnutrition. *Behavioral and Brain Functions, 4,* 31.

Kar, N. (2009). Psychological impact of disasters on children: Review of assessment and interventions. *World Journal of Pediatrics, 5,* 5–11.

Karnes, F. A., & Stephens, K. R. (2008). *Achieving excellence: Educating the gifted and talented.* Upper Saddle River, NJ: Prentice Hall.

Karniol, R., Grosz, E., & Schorr, I. (2003). Caring, gender-role orientation, and volunteering. *Sex Roles, 49,* 11–19.

Karoly, L. A., & Bigelow, J. H. (2005). *The Economics of investing in universal preschool education in California.* Santa Monica, CA: RAND Corporation.

Karpov, Y. V. (2006). *The neo-Vygotskian approach to child development.* New York: Cambridge University Press.

Karreman, A., van Tuijil, C., van Aken, M. A., & Dekovic, M. (2008). Parenting, coparenting, and effortful control in preschoolers. *Journal of Family Psychology, 22,* 30–40.

Katz, L. (1999). Curriculum disputes in early childhood education. *ERIC Clearinghouse on Elementary and Early Childhood Education,* Document EDO-PS-99-13.

Katz, P. A. (1987, August). *Children and social issues.* Paper presented at the meeting of the American Psychological Association, New York.

Kauffman Early Education Exchange. (2002). *Set for success: Building a strong foundation for school readiness based on the social-emotional development of young children. 1* (No. 1). Kansas City: The Ewing Marion Kauffman Foundation.

Kauffman, J. M., & Hallahan, D. P. (2005). *Special education.* Boston: Allyn & Bacon.

Kauffman, J. M., & Landrum, T. J. (2009). *Characteristics of emotional and behavioral disorders of children and youth* (9th ed.). Boston: Allyn & Bacon.

Kauffman, J. M., McGee, K., & Brigham, M. (2004). Enabling or disabling? Observations on changes in special education. *Phi Delta Kappan, 85,* 613–620.

Kaufman, J. C., & Sternberg, R. J. (2007). Resource review: Creativity. *Change, 39,* 55–58.

Kavanaugh, R. D. (2006). Pretend play. In B. Spodek & O. N. Saracho (Eds.), *Handbook of research on the education of young children* (2nd ed.). Mahwah, NJ: Erlbaum.

Kavsek, M. (2004). Predicting IQ from infant visual habituation and dishabituation: a meta-analysis. *Journal of Applied Developmental Psychology, 25,* 369–393.

Kazdin, A. E., & Benjet, C. (2003). Spanking children: Evidence and issues. *Current Directions in Psychological Science, 12,* 99–103.

Keating, D. P. (1990). Adolescent thinking. In S. S. Feldman & G. R. Elliott (Eds.), *At the threshold: The developing adolescent,* Cambridge, MA: Harvard University Press.

Keating, D. P. (2004). Cognitive and brain development. In R. Lerner & L. Steinberg (Eds.), *Handbook of adolescence* (2nd ed.). New York: Wiley.

Keating, D. P. (2007). Understanding adolescent development: Implications for driving safety. *Journal of Safety Research, 38,* 147–157.

Keating, D. P. (2009). Developmental science and giftedness: An integrated life-span framework. In F. D. Horowitz, R. F. Subotnik, & D. J. Matthews (Eds.), *The development of giftedness and talent across the life span.* Washington, DC: American Psychological Association.

Keens, T. G., & Gemmill, D. R. (2008). SIDS. In M. M. Haith & J. B. Benson (Eds.), *Encyclopedia of infant and early childhood development.* Oxford, UK: Elsevier.

Keller, A., Ford, L., & Meacham, J. (1978). Dimensions of self-concept in preschool children. *Developmental Psychology, 14,* 483–489

Keller, H. (2007). *Cultures of infancy.* Mahwah, NJ: Erlbaum.

Kellman, P. J., & Arterberry, M. E. (2006). Infant visual perception. In W. Damon & R. Lerner (Eds.), *Handbook of child psychology* (6th ed.). New York: Wiley.

Kellman, P. J., & Banks, M. S. (1998). Infant visual perception. In W. Damon (Ed.), *Handbook of child psychology* (5th ed., Vol. 2). New York: Wiley.

Kellogg, R. (1970). *Understanding children's art: Readings in developmental psychology today.* Del Mar, CA: CRM.

Kelly, D. J., Liu, S., Lee, K., Quinn, P. C., Pascalis, O., Slater, A. M., & Ge, L. (2009, in press). Development of the other-race effect in infancy: Evidence toward universality? *Journal of Experimental Child Psychology.*

Kelly, D. J., & others (2005). Three-month-olds, but not newborns, prefer own-race faces. *Developmental Science, 8,* F31–F36.

Kelly, D. J., & others (2007). Cross-race preferences for same-race faces extend beyond the African versus Caucasian contrast in 3-month-old infants. *Infancy, 11,* 87–95.

Kelly, G. F. (2008). *Sexuality today* (9th ed.). New York: McGraw-Hill.

Kelly, J. P., Borchert, J., & Teller, D. Y. (1997). The development of chromatic and achromatic sensitivity in infancy as tested with the sweep VEP. *Vision Research, 37,* 2057–2072.

Kennedy, M. A. (2009). Child abuse. In D. Carr (Ed.), *Encyclopedia of the life course and human development.* Boston: Gale Cengage.

Kennedy, R. D., & D'Andrea, A. D. (2006). DNA repair pathways in clinical practice: Lessons from pediatric cancer susceptibility syndromes. *Journal of Clinical Oncology, 24,* 3799–3808.

Kennell, J. H. (2006). Randomized controlled trial of skin-to-skin contact from birth versus conventional incubator for physiological stabilization in 1200 g to 2199 g newborns. *Acta Paediatrica (Sweden), 95,* 15–16.

Kennell, J. H., & McGrath, S. K. (1999). Commentary: Practical and humanistic lessons from the third world for perinatal caregivers everywhere. *Birth, 26,* 9–10.

Kenner, C., Sugrue, N. M., & Finkelman, A. (2007). How nurses around the world can make a difference. *Nursing for Women's Health, 11,* 468–473.

Kenny-Benson, G. A., Pomerantz, E. M., Ryan, & Patrick, H. (2006). Sex differences in math performance: The role of children's approach to schoolwork. *Developmental Psychology, 42,* 11–26.

Kent, A. (2008). Non-invasive prenatal diagnosis: public and patient perceptions. *Seminars in Fetal and Neonatal Medicine, 13,* 109–112.

Kessen, W., Haith, M. M., & Salapatek, P. (1970). Human infancy. In P. H. Mussen (Eds.), *Manual of child psychology* (3rd ed., Vol. 1). New York: Wiley.

Kessler, R. C., & Waters, E. E. (1988). Epidemiology of *DSM-III-R* major depression and minor depression among adolescents and young adults in the National Comorbidity Survey. *Depression and Anxiety, 7,* 3–14.

Key, J. D., Gebregziabher, M. G., Marsh, L. D., & O'Rourke, K. M. (2008). Effectiveness of an intensive, school-based intervention for teen mothers. *Journal of Adolescent Health, 42,* 394–400.

Kiess, H. O., & Green, B. A. (2010). *Statistical concepts for the behavioral sciences* (4th ed.). Boston: Allyn & Bacon.

Kimber, L., McNabb, M., McCourt, C., Haines, A., & Brocklehurst, P. (2008). Massage or music for pain relief in labour: A pilot randomised placebo controlled trial. *European Journal of Pain, 12,* 961–969.

Kimbro, R. T., Brooks-Gunn, J., & McClanahan, S. (2006). Racial and ethnic differences in overweight and obesity among 3-year-old children. *American Journal of Public Health, 97,* 298–305.

Kim, J., Peterson, K. E., Scanlon, K. S., Fitzmaurice, G. M., Must, A., Oken, E.,

Rifas-Shiman, S. L., Rich-Edwards, J. W., & Gillman, M. W. (2006). Trends in overweight from 1980 through 2001 among preschool-aged children enrolled in a health maintenance organization. *Obesity, 14,* 1107–1112.

Kim, S. Y., Su, J., Yancura, L., & Yee, B. (2009). Asian American and Pacific Islander families. In N. Tewari & A. Alvarez (Eds.), *Asian American psychology.* Clifton, NJ: Psychology Press.

Kim, Y.-K. (2009). The relationship between home literacy practices and developmental trajectories of emergent literacy and conventional literacy skills for Korean children. *Reading and Writing, 22,* 57–84.

King, A. A., DeBraun, M. R., & White, D. A. (2008). Need for cognitive rehabilitation for children with sickle-cell disease and strokes. *Expert Review of Neurotherapeutics, 8,* 291–296.

King, L., & Kepner, A. (2008). *States getting serious about pre-K programs.* Retrieved October 24, 2008, from www.delawareonline.com/apps/pbcs.dll/article?Date=20080103&Category=NEWS…

King, P. E., & Benson, P. L. (2005). Spiritual development and adolescent well-being and thriving. In E. C. Roehlkepartain, P. E. King, L. Wagner, & P. L. Benson (Eds.), *Handbook of spiritual development in childhood and adolescence.* Thousand Oaks, CA: Sage.

Kingston, N. (2008). Standardized tests. In N. J. Salkind (Ed.), *Encyclopedia of educational psychology.* Thousand Oaks, CA: Sage.

Kinney, H. C., Richerson, G. B., Dymecki, S. M., Darnall, R. A., & Nattie, E. E. (2009). The brainstem and serotonin in sudden infant death syndrome. *Annual Review of Pathology, 4,* 517–550.

Kinzler, K. D., & Spelke, E. S. (2007). Core systems in human cognition. *Progress in Brain Research, 164,* 257–264.

Kirby, D., Laris, B. A., & Rolleri, L. A. (2007). Sex and HIV education programs: Their impact on sexual behaviors of young people throughout the world. *Journal of Adolescent Health, 40,* 206–217.

Kisilevsky, B. S., Hains, S. M., Lee, K., Xic, X., Huang, H., Ye, H. H., Zhang, K., & Wang, Z. (2003). Effects of experience on fetal voice recognition. *Psychological Science, 14,* 220–224.

Kisilevsky, B. S., & others. (2009). Fetal sensitivity to properties of maternal speech and language. *Infant Behavior and Development, 32,* 59–71.

Kistner, J., A., David-Ferdon, C. F., Repper, K. K., & Joiner, T. E. (2006). Bias and accuracy of childrens' perceptions of peer acceptance: Prospective associations with depressive symptoms. *Journal of Abnormal Child Psychology, 34,* 349–361.

Klaczynski, P. (2001). The influence of analytic and heuristic processing on adolescent reasoning and decision making. *Child Development, 72,* 844–861.

Klaczynski, P. A., & Narasimham, G. (1998). Development of scientific reasoning biases: Cognitive versus ego-protective explanations. *Developmental Psychology, 34,* 175–187.

Klaus, M., & Kennell, H. H. (1976). *Materanl-infant bonding.* St. Louis: Mosby.

Klein, S. B. (2009). *Learning.* Thousand Oaks, CA: Sage.

Kliegman, R. M., Behrman, R. E., Jenson, H. B., & Stanton, B. F. (2007). *Nelson textbook of pediatrics* (18th ed.). London: Elsevier.

Klima, C., Norr, K., Conderheld, S., & Handler, A. (2009). Introduction of CenteringPregnancy in a public health clinic. *Journal of Midwifery and Women's Health, 54,* 27–34.

Kling, K. C., Hyde, J. S., Showers, C. J., & Buswell, B. N. (1999). Gender differences in self-esteem: A meta-analysis. *Psychological Bulletin, 125,* 470–500.

Klingman, A. (2006). Children and war trauma. In W. Damon & R. Lerner (Eds.), *Handbook of child psychology* (6th ed.). New York: Wiley.

Klomek, A. B., Marrocco, F., Kleinman, M., Schonfeld, I. S., & Gould, M. S. (2008). Peer victimization, depression, and suicidality in adolescents. *Suicide and Life Threatening Behavior, 38,* 166–180.

Knecht, S., Drager, B., Deppe, M., Bobe, I., Lohmann, H., Floel, A., Ringelstein, E. B., & Henningsen, H. (2000). Handedness and hemispheric language dominance in healthy humans. *Brain, 135,* 2512–2518.

Knopfli, B. H., Radtke, T., Lehmann, M., Schatzle, B., Eisenblatter, J., Gachang, A., Wiederkehr, P., Hammer, J., & Brooks-Wildhaber, J. (2008). Effect of a inpatient intervention on body composition, aerobic fitness, and quality of life in severely obese girls and boys. *Journal of Adolescent Health, 42,* 119–127.

Knopik, V. S. (2009). Maternal smoking during pregnancy and child outcomes: Real or spurious effect? *Developmental Neuropsychology, 34,* 1–36.

Kobayashi, K., Tajima, M., Toishi, S., Fujimori, K. Suzuki, Y., & Udagama, H. (2005). Fetal growth restriction associated with measles virus infection during pregnancy. *Journal of Perinatal Medicine, 33,* 67–68.

Kochanska, G., & Aksan, N. (2007). Conscience in childhood: Past, present, and future. *Merrill-Palmer Quarterly, 50,* 299–310.

Kochanska, G., Aksan, N., Knaack, A., & Rhines, H. M. (2004). Maternal parenting and children's conscience: Early security as a moderator. *Child Development, 75,* 1229–1242.

Kochanska, G., Aksan, N., Prisco, T. R., & Adams, E. E. (2008). Mother-child and father-child mutually responsive orientation in the first two years and children's outcomes at preschool age: Mechanisms of influence. *Child Development, 79,* 30–44.

Kochi, C., Longui, C. A., Lemos-Marini, S. H., Guerra-Junior, G., Melo, M. B., Calliari, L. E., & Monte, O. (2007). The influence of parental origin of X chromosome genes on the stature of patients with 45 X Turner syndrome. *Genetics and Molecular Research, 18,* 1–7.

Koenig, L. B., McGue, M., & Iacono, W. G. (2008). Stability and change in religousness during emerging adulthood. *Developmental Psychology, 44,* 523–543.

Kohen, D. E., Leventhal, T., Dahinten, V. S., & McIntosh, C. N. (2008). Neighborhood disadvantage: Pathways of effects for young children. *Child Development, 79,* 156–169.

Kohlberg, L. (1958). *The development on modes of moral thinking and choice in the years 10 to 16.* Unpublished doctoral dissertation, University of Chicago.

Kohlberg, L. (1969). Stage and sequence: The cognitive-developmental approach to socialization. In D. A. Goslin (Ed.), *Handbook of socialization theory and research.* Chicago: Rand McNally.

Kohlberg, L. (1986). A current statement of some theoretical issues. In S. Modgil & C. Modgil (Eds.), *Lawrence Kohlberg.* Philadelphia: Falmer.

Kohler, P. K., Manhart, L. E., & Lafferty, W. E. (2008). Abstinence-only and comprehensive sex education and the initiation of sexual activity and teen pregnancy. *Journal of Adolescent Health, 42,* 344–351.

Koolhof, R., Loeber, R., Wei, E. H., Pardini, D., & D'Escury, A. C. (2007). Inhibition deficits of serious delinquent boys of low intelligence. *Criminal Behavior and Mental Health, 17,* 274–292.

Kopp, C. B. (2008). Self-regulatory processes. In M. M. Haith & J. B. Benson (Eds.), *Encyclopedia of infant and early childhood development.* Oxford, UK: Elsevier.

Korat, O. (2009). The effect of maternal teaching talk on children's emergent literacy as a function of type of activity and maternal education level. *Journal of Applied Developmental Psychology, 30,* 34–42.

Kornblum, J. (2006, March 9). How to monitor the kids? *USA Today,* 1D, p. 1.

Kotovsky, L., & Baillargeon, R. (1994). Calibration-based reasoning about collision events in 11-month-old infants. *Cognition, 51,* 107–129.

Kottak, C. P. (2004). *Cultural anthropology* (10th ed.). New York: McGraw-Hill.

Koulouglioti, C., Cole, R., & Kitzman, H. (2008). Inadequate sleep and unintentional injuries in young children. *Public Health Nursing, 25,* 106–104.

Kovar, S. K., Combs, C. A., Campbell, K., Napper-Owen, G., & Worrell, V. J. (2007). *Elementary classroom teachers as movement educators* (2nd ed.). New York: McGraw-Hill.

Kozol, J. (2005). *The shame of the nation.* New York: Crown.

Kramer, L. (2006, July 10). Commentary in "How your siblings make you who you are," by J. Kluger. *Time*, pp. 46–55.

Kramer, L., & Perozynski, L. (1999). Parental beliefs about managing sibling conflict. *Developmental Psychology, 35*, 489–499.

Kramer, L., & Radey, C. (1997). Improving sibling relationships among young children: A social skills training model. *Family Relations, 46*, 237–246.

Kramer, L. S., & Goldman-Rakic, P. S. (2001). Prefrontal microcircuits. *Journal of Neuroscience, 21*, 3788–3796.

Kramer, M. (2003). Commentary: Breastfeeding and child health, growth, and survival. *International Journal of Epidemiology, 32*, 96–98.

Kranz, S., Lin, P. J., & Wagstaff, D. A. (2007). Children's dairy intake in the United States: Too little, too fat? *Journal of Pediatrics, 151*, 642–646.

Kranz, S., & Siega-Riz, A. M. (2002). Sociodemographic determinants of added sugar intake in preschoolers 2 to 5 years old. *Journal of Pediatrics, 140*, 667–672.

Kreutzer, M., Leonard, C., & Flavell, J. H. (1975). An interview study of children's knowledge about memory. *Monographs of the Society for Research in Child Development, 40* (1, Serial No. 159).

Kroger, J. (2007). *Identity development: Adolescence through adulthood*. Thousand Oaks, CA: Sage.

Krueger, J. I., Vohs, K. D., & Baumeister, R. F. (2008). Is the allure of self-esteem a mirage after all? *American Psychologist, 63*, p. 64.

Kuczynski, L., & Parkin, C. N. (2007). Agency and bidirectionality in socialization: Interactions, transactions, and relational dialectics. In J. E. Grusec & P. D. Hastings (Eds.), *Handbook of socialization*. New York: Guilford.

Kuebli, J. (1994, March). Young children's understanding of everyday emotions. *Young Children*, pp. 36–48.

Kuhl, P. K. (1993). Infant speech perception: A window on psycholinguistic development. *International Journal of Psycholinguistics, 9*, 33–56.

Kuhl, P. K. (2000). A new view of language acquisition. *Proceedings of the National Academy of Sciences USA, 97* (22), 11850–11857.

Kuhl, P. K. (2007). Is speech learning "gated" by the social brain? *Developmental Science, 10*, 110–120.

Kuhl, P. K. (2009). Linking infant speech perception in language acquisition: Phonetic learning predicts languages growth. In J. Colombo, P. McCardle, & L. Freund (Eds.), *Infant pathways to language*. Clifton, NJ: Psychology Press.

Kuhn, D. (1998). Afterword to Volume 2: Cognition, perception, and language. In W. Damon (Ed.), *Handbook of child psychology* (5th ed., Vol. 2). New York: Wiley.

Kuhn, D. (1999). Metacognitive development. In L. Balter & S. Tamis-Lemonda (Eds.), *Child psychology: A handbook of contemporary issues*. Philadelphia: Psychology Press.

Kuhn, D. (2008). Formal operations from a twenty-first century perspective. *Human Development, 51*, 48–55.

Kuhn, D. (2009). Adolescent thinking. In R. M. Lerner & L. Steinberg (Eds.), *Handbook of adolescent psychology* (3rd ed.). New York: Wiley.

Kuhn, D., Cheney, R., & Weinstock, M. (2000). The development of epistemological understanding. *Cognitive Development, 15*, 309–328.

Kuhn, D., & Franklin, S. (2006). The second decade: What develops (and how)? In W. Damon & R. Lerner (Eds.), *Handbook of child psychology* (6th ed.). New York: Wiley.

Kuhn, D., Schauble, L., & Garcia-Mila, M. (1992). Cross-domain development of scientific reasoning. *Cognition and Instruction, 9*, 285–327.

Kukulu, K., & Demirok H. (2008). Effects of epidural anesthesia on labor progress. *Pain Management Nursing, 9*, 10–16.

Kulkofsky, S., & Klemfuss, J. Z. (2008). What the stories children tell can tell about their memory: Narrative skill and young children's suggestibility. *Developmental Psychology, 44*, 1442–1456.

Kupersmidt, J. B., & Coie, J. D. (1990). Preadolescent peer status, aggression, and school adjustment as predictors of externalizing problems in adolescence. *Child Development, 61*, 1350–1363.

Kuppens, S., Grietens, H., Onghena, P., & Michiels, D. (2009). Relations between parental psychological control and childhood relational aggression: Reciprocal in nature? *Journal of Clinical Child and Adolescent Psychology, 38*, 117–131.

Kwak, H. K., Kim, M., Cho, B. H., & Ham, Y. M. (1999, April). *The relationship between children's temperament, maternal control strategies, and children's compliance*. Paper presented at the meeting of the Society for Research in Child Development, Albuquerque.

L

Laberge, L., Tremblay, R. E., Vitarao. F., & Montplaiser, J. (2000). Development of parasomnias from childhood to early adolescence. *Pediatrics, 106*, 67–74.

Ladd, G. W. (2009). Trends, travails, and turning points in early research on children's peer relationships: Legacies and lessons for our time? In K. H. Rubin, W. M. Bukowski, & B. Laursen (Eds.), *Handbook of peer interactions, relationships, and groups*. New York: Guilford.

Ladd, G. W., Buhs, E., & Troop, W. (2004). School adjustment and social skills training. In P. K. Smith & C. H. Hart (Eds.), *Blackwell handbook of childhood social development*. Malden, MA: Blackwell.

Ladd, G. W., Herald-Brown, S. L., & Reiser, M. (2008). Does chronic peer rejection predict the development of children's classroom participation during the grade school years? *Child Development, 79*, 1001–1015.

Laflin, M. T., Wang, J., & Barry, M. (2008). A longitudinal study of adolescent transition from virgin to nonvirgin status. *Journal of Adolescent Health, 42*, 228–236.

LaFontana, K. M., & Cillessen, A. H. N. (2009, in press). Developmental changes in the priority of perceived status in childhood and adolescence. *Social Development*.

La Greca, A. M., & Harrison, H. M. (2005). Adolescent peer relations, friendships, and romantic relationships: Do they predict social anxiety and depression? *Journal of Clinical Child and Adolescent Psychology, 34*, 49–61.

Lahey, B. B., Van Hulle, C. A., D'Onofrio, B. M., Rodgers, J. L., & Waldman, I. D. (2008). Is parental knowledge of their adolescent offspring's whereabouts and peer associations spuriously associated with offspring delinquency? *Journal of Abnormal Child Psychology, 36*, 807–823.

Laible, D. J., Carlo, G., & Raffaelli, M. (2000). The differential relations of parent and peer attachment to adolescent adjustment. *Journal of Youth and Adolescence, 29*, 45–53.

Laible, D., & Thompson, R. A. (2007). Early socialization: A relationship perspective. In J. E. Grusec & P. D. Hastings (Eds.), *Handbook of socialization*. New York: Guilford.

Laird, R. D., Criss, M. M., Pettit, G. S., Dodge, K. A., & Bates, J. A. (2008). Parents' monitoring knowledge attenuates the link between antisocial friends and adolescent delinquent behavior. *Journal of Abnormal Psychology, 36*, 299–310.

Lajunen, H. R., Keski-Rahkonen, A., Pulkkinen, L., Rose, R. J., Rissanen, A., & Kaprio, J. (2007). Are computer and cell phone use associated with body mass index and overweight? A population study among twin adolescents. *BMC Public Health, 26*, 24.

Lamb, M. E. (1994). Infant care practices and the application of knowledge. In C. B. Fisher & R. M. Lerner (Eds.), *Applied developmental psychology*. New York: McGraw-Hill.

Lamb, M. E. (2000). The history of research on father involvement: An overview. *Marriage and Family Review, 29*, 23–42.

Lamb, M. E. (2005). Attachments, social networks, and developmental contexts. *Human Development, 48*, 108–112.

Lamb, M. E., Bornstein, M. H., & Teti, D. M. (2002). *Development in infancy* (4th ed.). Mahwah, NJ: Erlbaum.

Lamb, M. E., & Bougher, L. D. (2009). How does migration affect mothers' and fathers' roles within their families? Reflections on some general research. *Sex Roles, 60*, 611–614.

Lamb, M. E., & Lewis, C. (2005). The role of parent-child relationships in child development. In M. H. Bornsetin & M. E. Lamb (Eds.), *Developmental psychology* (5th ed.). Mahwah, NJ: Erlbaum.

Lamb, M. E., & Sternberg, K. J. (1992). Sociocultural perspectives in nonparental childcare. In M. E. Lamb, K. J. Sternberg, C. Hwang, &

A. G. Broberg (Eds.), *Child care in context.* Hills-dale, NJ: Erlbaum.

Lam, J. C., & Mason, T. B. (2007). Treatment of sleep disorders in children. *Current Treatment Options in Neurology, 9,* 404–413.

Lamont, R. F., & Jaggat, A. N. (2007). Emerging drug therapies for preventing spontaneous labor and preterm birth. *Expert Opinion on Investigational Drugs, 16,* 337–345.

Lamont, R. F., & Jayasooriya, G. S. (2009). Progestational agents for the prevention of preterm birth. *Journal of Perinatal Medicine, 37,* 12–14.

Lampl, M. (2008). Physical growth. In M. M. Haith & J. B. Benson (Eds.), *Encyclopedia of infant and early childhood development.* Oxford, UK: Elsevier.

Landau, B., Smith, L., & Jones, S. (1998). Object perception and object naming in early development. *Trends in Cognitive Science, 2,* 19–24.

Landau, L. I. (2008). Tobacco smoke exposure and tracking of lung function into adult life. *Pediatric Respiratory Reviews, 9,* 39–44.

Lane, H. (1976). *The wild boy of Aveyron.* Cambridge, MA: Harvard Univeristy Press.

Langer, E. J. (2005). *On becoming an artist.* New York: Ballentine.

Langer, O. (2008a). Management of obesity in GDM: Old habits die hard. *Journal of Maternal-Fetal and Neonatal Medicine, 21,* 165–171.

Lansford, J. E. (2009). Parental divorce and children's adjustment. *Perspectives on Psychological Science, 4,* 140–152.

Lansford, J. E., Miller-Johnson, S., Berlin, L. J., Dodge, K. A., Bates, J. E., & Pettit, G. S. (2007). Early physical abuse and later violent delinquency: A prospective longitudinal study. *Child Maltreatment, 12,* 233–245.

Larson, K., Russ, S. A., Crall, J. J., & Halfon, N. (2008). Influence of multiple social risks on children's health. *Pediatrics, 121,* 337–344.

Larson, R., & Lampman-Petraitis, C. (1989). Daily emotional states as reported by children and adolescents. *Child Development, 60,* 1250–1260.

Larson, R., Pearce, N., Sullivan, P. & Jarrett, R. L. (2007). Participation in youth programs as a catalyst for negotiation of family autonomy with connection. *Journal of Youth and Adolescence, 36* (1), 31–45.

Larson, R. & Richards, M. H. (1994). *Divergent realities.* New York: Basic Books.

Larson, R. W. (2001). How U. S. children and adolescents spend their time: What it does (and doesn't) tell us about their development. *Current Directions in Psychological Science, 10,* 160–164.

Larson, R. W., & Verma, S. (1999). How children and adolescents spend time across the world: Work, play, and developmental opportunities. *Psychological Bulletin, 125,* 701–736.

Larson, R. W. & Wilson, S. (2004). Adolescence across place and time: Globalization and the changing pathways to adulthood. In R. Lerner & L. Steinberg (Eds.), *Handbook of adolescent psychology.* New York: Wiley.

Latendresse, G. (2009). The interaction between chronic stress and pregnancy: Preterm birth from biobehavioral perspective. *Journal of Midwifery and Women's Health, 54,* 8–17.

Latimer, J. (2007). Becoming informed: Genetic counseling, ambiguity, and choice. *Health Care Analysis, 15,* 13–23.

Laursen, B., & Collins, W. A. (2009). Parent-child relationships in adolescence. In R. M. Lerner & L. Steinberg (Eds.), *Handbook of adolescent psychology* (3rd ed.). New York: Wiley.

Laursen, B., & Pursell, G. (2009). Conflict in peer relationships. In K. H. Rubin, W. M. Bukowski, & B. Laursen (Eds.), *Handbook of peer interaction, relationships, and groups.* New York: Guilford.

Lawrence, J. M., Contreras, R., Chen, W., & Sacks, D. A. (2008). Trends in the prevalence of preexisting diabetes and gestational diabetes mellitus among a racially/ethnically diverse population of pregnant women, 1999–2005. *Diabetes Care, 31,* 899–904.

Lawrence, R. A. (2008). Breastfeeding. In M. M. Haith & J. B. Benson (Eds.), *Encyclopedia of infant and early childhood development.* Oxford, UK: Elsevier.

Leadbeater, B. J. R., & Way, N. (2001). *Growing up fast.* Mahwah, NJ: Erlbaum.

Leaper, C., & Friedman, C. K. (2007). The socialization of gender. In J. E. Grusec & P. D. Hastings (Eds.), *Handbook of socialization.* New York: Guilford.

Leaper, C., & Smith, T. E. (2004). A meta-analytic review of gender variations in children's language use: Talkativeness, affiliative speech, and assertive speech. *Developmental Psychology, 40,* 993–1027.

Leedy, P. D., & Ormrod, J. E. (2010). *Practical research* (9th ed.). Upper Saddle River, NJ: Prentice Hall.

Lee, E., Mitchell-Herzfeld, S. D., Lowenfels, A. A., Greene, R., Dorabawila, V., & DuMont, K. A. (2009). Reducing low birth weight through home visitation: A randomized controlled trial. *American Journal of Preventive Medicine, 36,* 154–160.

Lee, H. C., El-Sayed, Y. Y., & Gould, J. B. (2008). Population trends in cesarean delivery for breech presentation in the United States, 1997–2003. *American Journal of Obstetrics and Gynecology, 199,* e1–e8.

Lee, J. M., & Howell, J. D. (2006). Tall girls: The social shaping of a medical therapy. *Archives of Pediatric and Adolescent Medicine, 160,* 1035–1059.

Lee, K., Cameron, C. A., Doucette, J., & Talwar, V. (2002). Phantoms and fabrications: Young children's detection of implausible lies. *Child Development, 73,* 1688–1702.

Lee, K. C., Shults, R. A., Greenspan, A. I., Haileyesus, T., & Dellinger, A. M. (2008). Child passenger restraint use and emergency department-reported injuries: A special study using the National Electronic Injury Surveillance System–All Injury Program, 2004. *Journal of Safety Research, 39,* 25–31.

Lee, S. J., & Wong, A. N. (2009). The model minority and the perceptual foreigner: Stereotypes of Asian Americans. In N. Tewari & A. Alvarez (Eds.), *Asian American psychology.* Clifton, NJ: Psychology Press.

Legerstee, M. (1997). Contingency effects of people and objects on subsequent cognitive functioning in 3-month-old infants. *Social Development, 6,* 307–321.

Lehr, C. A., Hanson, A., Sinclair, M. F., & Christensen, S. I. (2003). Moving beyond dropout prevention towards school completion. *School Psychology Review, 32,* 342–364.

Lehrer, R., & Schauble, L. (2006). Scientific thinking and science literacy: Supporting developmental change in learning contexts. In W. Damon & R. Lerner (Eds.), *Handbook of child psychology* (6th ed.). New York: Wiley.

Leifer, A. D. (1973). *Television and the development of social behavior.* Paper presented at the meeting of the International Society for the Study of Behavioral Development, Ann Arbor, MI.

Leis, J. A., Mendelson, T., Tandon, S. D., & Perry, D. F. (2009, in press). A systematic review of home-based interventions to prevent and treat postpartum depression. *Archives of Women's Mental Health.*

Lempers, J. D., Flavell, E. R., & Flavell, J. H. (1977). The development in very young children of tacit knowledge concerning visual perception. *Genetic Psychology Monographs, 95,* 3–53.

Lennon, E. M., Gardner, J. M., Karmel, B. Z., & Flory, M. J. (2008). Bayley Scales of Infant Development. In M. M. Haith & J. B. Benson (Eds.), *Encyclopedia of infant and early childhood development.* Oxford, UK: Elsevier.

Lenoir, C. P., Mallet, E, & Calenda, E. (2000). Siblings of sudden infant death syndrome and near miss in about 30 families: Is there a genetic link? *Medical Hypotheses, 54,* 408–411.

Lenroot, R. K., & Giedd, J. N. (2006). Brain development in children and adolescents: Insights from anatomical magnetic resonance imaging. *Neuroscience and Biobehavioral Reviews, 30,* 718–729.

Lenroot, R. K., Schmitt, J. E., Ordaz, S. J., Wallace, G. L., Neale, M. C., Lerch, J. P., Kendler, K. S., Evans, A. C., & Giedd, J. N. (2009). Differences in genetic and environmental influences on the human cerebral cortex associated with development during childhood and adolescence. *Human Brain Mapping, 30,* 163–174.

Lent, R. W., Brown, S. D., Nota, L., & Sorest, S. (2003). Testing social cognitive interest and choice hypotheses across Holland types in Italian high school students. *Journal of Vocational Behavior, 62,* 101–118.

Lenzi, T. A., & Johnson, T. R. B. (2008). Screening, prenatal. In M. M. Haith & J. B. Benson

(Eds.), *Encyclopedia of infant and early childhood development*. Oxford, UK: Elsevier.

Leonardi-Bee, J. A., Smyth, A. R., Britton, J., & Coleman, T. (2008). Environmental tobacco smoke and fetal health: Systematic review and analysis. *Archives of Disease in Childhood: Fetal and Neonatal Edition, 93*, F351–F361.

Leon-Guerrero, A. (2009). *Social problems* (2nd ed). Thousand Oaks: CA: Sage.

Leppanen, J. M., Moulson, M., Vogel-Farley, V. K., & Nelson, C. A. (2007). An ERP study of emotional face processing in the adult and infant brain. *Child Development, 78*, 232–245.

Lerner, J. V., Phelps, E., Forman, Y. E., & Bowers, E. (2009) Positive youth development. In R. M. Lerner & L. Steinberg (Eds.), *Handbook of adolescent psychology* (3rd ed.), New York: Wiley.

Lerner, R. M., Boyd, M., & Du, D. (2008). Adolescent development. In I. B. Weiner & C. B. Craighead (Eds.). *Encyclopedia of psychology* (4th ed.). Hoboken, NJ: Wiley.

Lerner, R. M., Roeser, R. W., & Phelps, E. (Eds.). (2009, in press). *Positive youth development and spirituality: From theory to research*. West Conshohocken, PA: Templeton Foundation Press.

Lesaux, N. K., & Siegel, L. S. (2003). The development of reading in children who speak English as a second language. *Developmental Psychology, 39*, 1005–1019.

Lesley, C. (2005). *Burning fence: A western memoir of fatherhood*. New York: St Martin's Press.

Lester, B. M., Tronick, E. Z., & Brazelton, T. B. (2004). The Neonatal Intensive Care Unit Network Neurobehavioral Scale procedures. *Pediatrics, 113* (Suppl.), S641–S667.

Lester, B. M., Tronick, E. Z., LaGasse, L., Seifer, R., Bauer, C. R., Shankaran, S., Bada, H. S., Wright, L. L., Smeriglio, V. L., Lu, J., Finnegan, L. P., & Maza, P. L. (2002). The maternal lifestyle study: Effects of substance exposure during pregnancy on neurodevelopmental outcome in 1-month-old infants. *Pediatrics, 110*, 1182–1192.

Levene, M. I., & Chervenak, F. A. (2009). *Fetal and neonatal neurology and neurosurgery* (4th ed.). London: Elsevier.

Leventhal, T., Dupere, V., & Brooks-Gunn, J. (2009). Neighborhood influences on adolescent development. In R. M. Lerner & L. Steinberg (Eds.), *Handbook of adolescent psychology* (3rd ed.). New York: Wiley.

Levine, T. P., Ku, J., Das, A., Lester, B., Lagasse, L., Shankaran, S., Bada, H., Bauer, C. R., & Higgins, R. (2008). Effects of prenatal cocaine exposure on special education in school-aged children. *Pediatrics, 122*, e83–e91.

Levy, F. (2009). Dopamine vs noradrenaline: Inverted-U effects and ADHD theories. *Australian and New Zealand Journal of Psychiatry, 43*, 101–108.

Lewis, A. C. (2007). Looking beyond NCLB. *Phi Delta Kappan, 88*, 483–484.

Lewis, B. A., Kirchner, H. L., Short, E. J., Minnes, S., Weishampel, P., Satayathum, S., & Singer, L. T. (2007). Prenatal cocaine and tobacco effects on children's language trajectories. *Pediatrics, 120*, e78–e85.

Lewis, C. G. (1981). How adolescents approach decisions: Changes over grades seven to twelve and policy implications. *Child Development, 52*, 538–554.

Lewis, M. (2005). Selfhood. In B. Hopkins (Ed.), *The Cambridge encyclopedia of child development*. Cambridge, UK: Cambridge University Press.

Lewis, M. (2007). Early emotional development. In A. Slater & M. Lewis (Eds.), *Introduction to infant development*. Malden, MA: Blackwell.

Lewis, M. (2008). The emergence of human emotions. In M. Lewis, J. M. Haviland Jones, & L. Feldman Barrett (Eds.), *Handbook of emotions* (3rd ed.). New York: Guilford.

Lewis, M., & Brooks-Gunn, J. (1979). *Social cognition and the acquisition of the self*. New York: Plenum.

Lewis, M., Feiring, C., & Rosenthal, S. (2000). Attachment over time. *Child Development, 71*, 707–720.

Lewis, M., & Ramsay, D. S. (1999). Effect of maternal soothing and infant stress response. *Child Development, 70*, 11–20.

Lewis, R. B., & Doorlag, D. (2006). *Teaching special students in general education classrooms* (7th ed.). Upper Saddle River, NJ: Prentice Hall.

Li, C., Goran, M. I., Kaur, H., Nollen, N., & Ahluwalia, J. S. (2007). Development trajectories of overweight during childhood: Role of early life factors. *Obesity, 15*, 760–761.

Li, D. K., Willinger, M., Petitti, D. B., Odulil, R. K., Liu, L., & Hoffman, H. J. (2006). Use of a dummy (pacifier) during sleep and risk of sudden infant death syndrome (SIDS): Population based case-control study. *British Medical Journal, 332*, 18–22.

Li, L., Law, C., Lo Conte, R., & Power, C. (2009). Intergenerational influences on childhood body mass index: The effect of parental body mass index trajectories. *American Journal of Clinical Nutrition, 89*, 551–557.

Li, M. D., Lou, X. Y., Chen, G., Ma, J. Z., & Elston, R. C. (2008). Gene-gene interactions among *CHRNA4, CHRNB2, BDNF*, and *NTRK2* in nicotine dependence. *Biological Psychiatry, 64*, 951–957.

Li, P. (2009). What's in a lexical system? Discovering meaning through an interactive eye. In V. C. M. Gathercole (Ed.), *Routes to language: Essays in honor of Melissa Bowerman*. New York: Psychology Press.

Li, X., Li, S., Ulusovy, E., Chen, W., Srinivasan, S. R., & Berensen, G. S. (2004). Childhood adiposity as a predictor of cardiac mass in adulthood: The Bogalusa Heart Study. *Circulation, 110*, 3488–3492.

Li, Y., Yang, X., Zhai, F., Piao, J., Zhao, W. Zhang, J., & Ma, G. (2008). Childhood obesity and its health consequence in China. *Obesity Reviews, 9* (Suppl. 1), S82–S86.

Liben, L. S. (1995). Psychology meets geography: Exploring the gender gap on the national geography bee. *Psychological Science Agenda, 8*, 8–9.

Liben, L. S. (2009). Giftedness during childhood: The spatial-graphic domain. In F. D. Horowitz, R. F. Subotnik, & D. J. Matthews (Eds.), *The development of giftedness and talent across the life span*. Washington, DC: American Psychological Association.

Lieberman, E., Davidson, K., Lee-Parritz, A., & Shearer, E. (2005). Changes in fetal position during labor and their association with epidural analgesia. *Obstetrics and Gynecology, 105*, 974–982.

Liederman, J., Kantrowitz, L., & Flannery, K. (2005). Male vulnerability to reading disability is not likely to be a myth: A call for new data. *Journal of Learning Disabilities, 38*, 109–129.

Lie, E., & Newcombe, N. (1999) Elementary school children's explicit and implicit memory for faces of preschool classmates. *Developmental Psychology, 35*, 102–112.

Liegeois, F., Connelly, A., Baldeweg, T., & Vargha-Khadem, F. (2008). Speaking with a single cerebral hemisphere: FMRI language organization after hemispherectomy in childhood. *Brain and Language, 106*, 195–203.

Lieven, E. (2008). Language development: Overview. In M. M. Haith & J. B. Benson (Eds.), *Encyclopedia of infant and early childhood development*. Oxford, UK: Elsevier.

Lieven, E., & Stoll, S. (2010). Language. In M. H. Bornstein (Ed.), *Handbook of cultural developmental science*. New York: Psychology Press.

Lillard, A. (2006). Pretend play in toddlers. In C. A. Brownell & C. B. Kopp (Eds.), *Socioemotional development in the toddler years*. New York: Oxford University Press.

Lillard, A. (2008). How important are the Montessori materials? *Montessori Life, 20*, 4, 20–25.

Lima, J. J., Blake, K. V., Tantisira, K. G., & Weiss, S. T. (2009). Pharmacogenetics of asthma. *Current Opinion of Pulmonary Medicine, 15*, 57–62.

Lindsay, A. C., Sussner, K. M., Kim, J., & Gortmaker, S. (2006). The role of parents in preventing childhood obesity. *The Future of Children, 16*, (1), 169–186.

Lin, M., Johnson, J. E., & Johnson, K. M. (2003). *Dramatic play in Montessori kindergartens in Taiwan and mainland China*. Unpublished manuscript, Department of Curriculum and Instruction, Pennsylvania State University, University Park, PA.

Lippa, R. A. (2005). *Gender, nurture, an nature* (2nd ed.). Mahwah, NJ: Erlbaum.

Lipton, J., & Spelke, E. (2004). Discrimination of large and small numerosities by human infants. *Infancy, 5*, 271–290.

Litt, J., Taylor, H. G., Klein, N., & Hack, M. (2005). Learning disabilities in children with very low birthweight: Prevalence, neuropsychological correlates, and educational interventions. *Journal of Learning Disabilities, 38,* 130–141.

Liu, A. H. (2002). Early intervention for asthma prevention in children. *Allergy and Asthma Processes, 23,* 289–293.

Liu, A., Hu, X, Ma, G., Cui, Z., Pan, Y., Chang, S. Zhao, W., & Chen, C. (2008). Evaluations of a classroom-based physical activity promoting program. *Obesity Reviews, 9* (Suppl. 1), S130–S134.

Liu, C. H., Murakami, J., Eap, S., & Nagayama Hall, G. C. (2009). Who are Asian Americans? An overview of history, immigration, and communities. In N. Tewari & A. Alvarez (Eds.), *Asian American psychology* Clifton, NJ: Psychology Press.

Liu, D., Wellman, H. M., Tardif, T., & Sabbagh, M. A. (2008). Theory of mind development in Chinese children: A meta-analysis of false-belief understanding across cultures and languages. *Developmental Psychology, 44,* 523–531.

Liu, J., Raine, A., Venables, P. H., Dalais, C., & Mednick, S. A. (2003). Malnutrition at age 3 years and lower cognitive ability at age 11 years: Independence from psychosocial adversity. *Archives of Pediatric and Adolescent Medicine, 157,* 593–600.

Liu, J., Raine, A., Venables, P. H., & Mednick, S. A. (2004). Malnutrition at 3 years and externalizing behavior problems at age 8, 11, and 17 years. *American Journal of Psychiatry, 161,* 2005–2013.

Liu, T., Shi, J., Zhang, Q., Zhao, D., & Yang, J. (2007). Neural mechanisms of auditory sensory processing in children with high intelligence. *Neuroreport, 18* (15), 1571–1575.

Liu, X., Zhao, Z., Jia, C., & Buysse, D. J. (2008). Sleep patterns and problems among Chinese adolescents. *Pediatrics, 121,* 1165–1173.

Lively, W., & Bromley, D. (1973). *Person perception in childhood and adolescence.* New York: Wiley.

Lochman, J., & the Conduct Problems Prevention Research Group. (2007, March). *Fast Track intervention outcomes in the middle school years.* Paper presented at the meeting of the Society for Research in Child Development, Boston.

Lockl, K., & Schneider, W. (2007). Knowledge about the mind: Links between theory of mind and later metamemory. *Child Development, 78,* 147–167.

Loebel, M., & Yali, A. M. (1999, August). *Effects of positive expectancies on adjustments to pregnancy.* Paper presented at the meeting of the American Psychological Association, Boston.

Loeber, R., Burke, J., & Pardini, D. (2009, in press). The etiology and development of antisocial and delinquent behavior. *Annual Review of Psychology* (Vol. 60). Palo Alto, CA: Annual Reviews.

Loeber, R., Farrington, D. P., Stouthamer-Loeber, M., & White, H. R. (2008). *Violence and secious theft: Development and prediction from childhood to adulthood.* New York: Routledge.

Loeber, R., Pardini, D. A. Stouthamer-Loeber, M., & Raine, A. (2007). Do cognitive, physiological, and psychosocial risk and promotive factors predict desistance from delinquency in males? *Development and Psychopathology, 19,* 867–887.

Loehlin, J. C., Horn, J. M., & Ernst, J. L. (2007). Genetic and environmental influences on adult life outcomes: Evidence from the Texas adoption project. *Behavior Genetics, 37,* 463–476.

Loessl, B., Valerius, G., Kopasz, M., Hornyak, M., Riemann, D., & Voderholzer, U. (2008). Are adolescents chronically sleep-deprived? An investigation of sleep habits of adolescents in the southwest of Germany. *Child Care, Health, and Development, 34,* 549–556.

Logsdon, M. C., Wisner, K., & Hanusa, B. H. (2009). Does maternal role functioning improve with antidepressant treatment in women with postpartum depression? *Journal of Women's Health, 18,* 85–90.

Longo-Mbenza, B., Lukoki, L. E, & M'Buyambia-Kabangu, J. R. (2007). Nutritional status, socioeconomic status, heart rate, and blood pressure in African school children and adolescents. *International Journal of Cardiology, 121,* 229–238.

Lonnerdal, B., & Kelleher, S. L. (2007). Iron metabolism in infants and children. *Food and Nutrition Bulletin, 28* (Suppl. 4), S491–S499.

Lorenz, K. Z. (1965). *Evolution and the modification of behavior.* Chicago: University of Chicago Press.

Lou, J. E., Ganley, T. J., & Flynn, A. J. (2002). Exercise and children's health. *Current Sports Medicine Reports, 1,* 349–353.

Loukas, A., Suizzo, M. A., & Prelow, H. M. (2007). Examining resource and protective factors in the adjustment of Latino youth in low income families: What role does maternal acculturation play? *Journal of Youth and Adolescence, 36,* 489–501.

Lovell, M. R., & Fazio, V. (2008). Concussion management in the child and adolescent athlete. *Current Sports Medicine Reports, 7,* 12–15.

Lozoff, B., Corapci, F., Burden, M. J., Kaciroti, N., Angulo-Baaroso, R., Sazawal, S., & Black, M. (2007). Preschool-aged children with iron deficiency anemia show altered affect and behavior. *Journal of Nutrition, 137,* 683–689.

Luders, E., Narr, K. L., Thompson, P. M., Rex, D. E., Jancke, L., Steinmetz, H., & Toga, A. W. (2004). Gender differences in cortical complexity. *Nature Neuroscience, 1,* 799–800.

Lu, M. C., & Lu, J. S. (2008). Prenatal care. In M. M. Haith & J. B. Benson (Eds.), *Encyclopedia of infant and early childhood development.* Oxford, UK: Elsevier.

Luders, E., Narr, K. L., Thompson, P. M., & Toga, A. W. (2009). Neuroanatomical correlates of intelligence. *Intelligence, 37,* 156–163.

Ludington-Hoe, S. M., Lewis, T., Morgan, K., Cong, X., Anderson, L., & Reese, S. (2006). Breast and infant temperatures with twins during kangaroo care. *Journal of Obstetric, Gynecologic, and Neonatal Nursing, 35,* 223–231.

Lumpkin, A. (2008). *Introduction to physical education exercise science, and sport studies* (7th ed.). New York: McGraw-Hill.

Lunkenheimer, E. S., Shields, A. M., & Cortina, K. S. (2007). Parental emotion coaching and dismissing in family interaction. *Social Development, 16,* 232–248.

Lunney, K. M., & others. (2008). HIV-positive poor women may stop breast-feeding early to protect their infants from HIV infection although available replacement diets are grossly inadequate. *Journal of Nutrition, 138,* 351–357.

Luo, Y., Kaufman, L., & Baillargeon, R. (2009). Young infants' reasoning about events involving inert and self-propelled objects. *Cognitive Psychology, 58,* 441–486.

Luria, A., & Herzog, E. (1985, April). *Gender segregation across and within settings.* Paper presented at the biennial meeting of the Society for Research in Child Development, Toronto.

Lust, R. (2007). *Child language.* New York: Cambridge University Press.

Luyckx, K., Schwartz, S. J., Goossens, L., Soenens, B., & Beyers, W. (2008). Developmental typologies of identity formation and adjustment in emerging adulthood: A latent class growth analysis approach. *Journal of Research on Adolescence, 18,* 595–619.

Lyon, T. D., & Flavell, J. H. (1993). Young children's understanding of forgetting over time. *Child Development, 64,* 789–800.

Lytle, L. A., Murray, D. M., Perry, C. L., Story, M., Birnbaum, A. S., Kubik, M. Y., & Varnell, S. (2004). School-based approaches to affect adolescents' diets: Results from the TEENS study. *Health Education and Behavior, 31,* 270–287.

M

Maas, C., Herrenkohl, T. I., & Sousa, C. (2008). Review of research on child maltreatment and violence in youth. *Trauma, Violence, and Abuse, 9,* 56–67.

Maas, J. (2008, March 4). Commentary in L. Szabo, "Parents with babies need time to reset inner clock." *USA Today,* p. 4D.

Maccoby, E. E. (1998). *The two sexes: Growing up apart, coming together.* Cambridge, MA: Harvard University Press.

Maccoby, E. E. (2002). Gender and group processes. *Current Directions in Psychological Science, 11,* 54–58.

Maccoby, E. E. (2007). Historical overview of socialization research and theory. In J. E. Grusec &

P. D. Hastings (Eds.), *Handbook of socialization*. New York: Guilford.

Maccoby, E. E., & Martin, J. A. (1983). Socialization in the context of the family: Parent-child interaction. In P. H. Mussen (Ed.), *Handbook of child psychology* (4th ed., Vol. 4). New York: Wiley.

Maccoby, E. E., & Mnookin, R. H. (1992). *Dividing the child: Social and legal dilemmas of custody*. Cambridge, MA: Harvard University Press.

MacDorman, M. F., Declercq, E., Menacker, F., & Malloy M. H. (2008). Neonatal mortality for primary cesarean and vaginal births to low-risk women: Application of a "intention-to-treat" model. *Birth, 35,* 3–8.

MacFarlane, J. A. (1975). Olfaction in the development of social preferences in the human neonate. In *Parent-infant interaction*. Ciba Foundation Symposium No. 33. Amsterdam: Elsevier.

MacGeorge, E. L. (2003). Gender differences in attributions and emotions in helping contexts. *Sex Roles, 48,* 175–182.

MacGeorge, E. L. (2004). The myth of gender cultures: Similarities outweigh differences in men's and women's provisions of and responses to supportive communication. *Sex Roles, 50,* 143–175.

Macmillan, H. L., Wathen, C. N., Barlow, J., Fergusson, D. M., Leventhal, J. M., & Taussig, H. N. (2009). Interventions to prevent child maltreatment and associated impairment. *Lancet, 373,* 250–266.

Maconochie N., Doyle, P., Prior, S., & Simmons, R. (2007). Risk factors for first trimester miscarriage—results from a UK-population-based case control study. *British Journal of Obstetrics and Gynecology, 114,* 170–176.

Mader, S. S. (2010). *Biology* (10th ed.). New York: McGraw-Hill.

Magnusson, S. J., & Palinscar, A. S. (2005). Teaching to promote the development of scientific knowledge and reasoning about light at the elementary school level. In *How people learn*. Washington, DC: National Academies Press.

Magriples, U., Kershaw, T. S., Rising, S. S., Massey, Z., & Ickovics, J. R. (2008). Prenatal health care beyond the obstetrics service: Utilization and predictors of unscheduled care. *American Journal of Obstetrics and Gynecology, 198,* e1–e7.

Mahler, M. (1979). *Separation-individuation* (Vol. 2). London: Jason Aronson.

Mahoney, J. L., Vandell, D. L., Simpkins, S., & Zarrett, N. (2009). Adolescent out-of-school activities. In R. M. Lerner & L. Steinberg (Eds.), *Handbook of adolescent psychology* (3rd ed.). New York: Wiley.

Malamitsi Puchner, A., & Boutsikou, T. (2006). Adolescent pregnancy and perinatal outcome. *Pediatric Endocrinology Reviews, 3* (Suppl. 1), 170–171.

Malchiodi, C. A. (2008). A group art and play therapy program for children from violent homes.

In C. A. Malchiodi (Ed.), *Creative interventions with traumatized children*. New York: Guilford.

Malizia, B. A., Hacker, M. R., & Penzias, A. S. (2009). Cumulative live-birth rates after in vitro fertilization. *New England Journal of Medicine, 360,* 236–243.

Mamtani, M., Patel, A., & Kulkarni, H. (2008). Association of the pattern of transition between arousal states in neonates with the cord blood lead level. *Early Human Development, 84,* 231–235.

Mandara, J. (2006). The impact of family functioning on African American males' academic achievement: A review and clarification of the empirical literature. *Teachers College Record, 108,* 206–233.

Mandler, J. M. (2004). *The foundations of the mind: Origins of conceptual thought*. New York: Oxford University Press.

Mandler, J. M. (2006). *Jean Mandler*. Retrieved January 15, 2006, from http://cogsci.ucsd.edu/-jean/

Mandler, J. M. (2009). Conceptual categorization. In D. H. Rakison & L. M. Oakes (Eds.), *Early category and concept development*. New York: Oxford University Press.

Mandler, J. M., & McDonough, L. (1993). Concept formation in infancy. *Cognitive Development, 8,* 291–318.

Mangelsdorf, S. C., & Wong, M. S. (2008). Independence/dependence. In M. M. Haith & J. B. Benson (Eds.), *Encyclopedia of infant and early childhood development*. Oxford, UK: Elsevier.

Manios, Y., & others. (2008). Nutrient intakes of toddlers and preschoolers in Greece: The GENESIS study. *Journal of the American Dietetic Association, 108,* 357–361.

Manzo, K. K. (2008). Motivating students in the middle years. *Education Week, 27,* 22–25.

Marcia, J. E. (1980). Ego identity development. In J. Adelson (Ed.), *Handbook of adolescent psychology*. New York: Wiley.

Marcia, J. E. (1994). The empirical study of ego identity. In H. A. Bosma, T. L. G. Graafsma, H. D. Grotevant, & D. J. De Levita (Eds.), *Identity and development*. Newbury Park, CA: Sage.

Marcia, J. E. (2002). Identity and psychosocial development in adulthood. *Identity: An International Journal of Theory and Research, 2,* 7–28.

Marcon, R. A. (2003). The physical side of development. *Young Children, 58,* 80–87.

Marcovitch, H. (2004). Use of stimulants for attention deficit hyperactivity disorder: AGAINST. *British Medical Journal, 329,* 908–909.

Marcus, D. L., Mulrine, A., & Wong, K. (1999, September 13). How kids learn. *U.S. News & World Report*, pp. 44–50.

Marinucci, L., Balloni, S., Bodo, M., Carinci, F., Pezzetti, F., Stabellini, G., Carmela, C., & Lumare, E. (2009, in press). Patterns of some extracellular matrix gene expres-

sion are similar in cells from cleft lip–palate patients and in human palatal fibroblasts to diazepam in culture. *Toxicology*.

Marion, M. C. (2010). *Introduction to early childhood education*. Upper Saddle River, NJ: Prentice Hall.

Marsh, H., Ellis, L., & Craven, R. (2002). How do preschool children feel about themselves? Unraveling measurement and multidimensional self-concept structure. *Developmental Psychology, 38,* 376–393.

Marsh, R., Zhu, H., Schultz, R. T., Quackenbush, G., Royal, J., Skudlarksi, P., & Peterson, B. S. (2006). A developmental fMRI study of self-regulatory control. *Human Brain Mapping, 27,* 848–863.

Martin, C. L., & Ruble, D. (2004). Children's search for gender cues. *Current Directions in Psychological Science, 13,* 67–70.

Martin, D. W. (2008). *Doing psychology experiments* (7th ed.). Belmont, CA: Wadsworth.

Martin, E., Mazzucco, M., Nasciben, E., Martinuzzi, A., & Longatti, P. (2007). Severe head injury in early infancy: Analysis of causes and possible predictive factors for outcome. *Child's Nervous System, 23,* 873–880.

Martin, J. A., Hamilton, B. E., Sutton, P. D., Ventura, S. J., Menacker, F., & Munson, M. L. (2005, September). Births: Final data for 2003. *National Vital Statistics Reports, 54* (No. 2), 1–116.

Martin, J. A., Kochanek, K. D., Strobino, D. M., Guyer, B., & MacDorman, M. F. (2005). Annual summary of vital statistics—2003. *Pediatrics, 115,* 619–634.

Mashburn, A. J., Justice, L. M., Downer, J. T., & Pianta, R. C. (2009). Peer effects on children's language achievement during pre-kindergarten. *Child Development, 80,* 686–702.

Mash, E. J., & Wolfe, D. A. (2007). *Abnormal child psychology* (3rd ed.). Belmont, CA: Wadsworth.

Mason, T. B., & Pack, A. I. (2006). Sleep terrors in childhood. *Journal of Pediatrics, 147,* 388–392.

Massaro, A. N., Hammad, T. A., Jazzo, B., & Aly, H. (2009). Massage with kinesthetic stimulation improves weight gain in preterm infants. *Journal of Perinatology, 29,* 352–357.

Massey, Z., Rising, S. S., & Ickovics, J. (2006). CenteringPregnancy group prenatal care: Promoting relationship-centered care. *Journal of Obstetric, Gynecologic, and Neonatal Nursing, 35,* 286–294.

Masten, A. S. (2001). Ordinary magic: Resilience processes in development. *American Psychologist, 56,* 227–238.

Masten, A. S. (2006). Developmental psychopathology: Pathways to the future. *International Journal of Behavioral Development, 31,* 46–53.

Masten, A. S. (2007). Resilience in developing systems: Progress and promise as the fourth wave rises. *Developmental Psychopathology, 19,* 921–930.

Masten, A. S., Burt, K., & Coatsworth, J. D. (2006). Competence and psychopathology in development. In D. Cicchetti & D. Cohen (Eds.), *Developmental psychopathology, Vol 3, Risk, disorder and psychopathology (2nd ed.)* New York: Wiley.

Masten, A. S., Obradovic, J., & Burt, K. B. (2006). Resilience in emerging adulthood. In J. J. Arnett & J. L. Tanner (Eds.), *Emerging adults in America.* Washington, DC: American Psychological Association.

Mathes, P. G., & Fletcher, J. M. (2008). Dyslexia. In N. J. Salkind (Ed.), *Encyclopedia of educational psychology.* Thousand Oaks, CA: Sage.

Matlin, M. W. (2008). *The psychology of women* (6th ed.). Belmont, CA: Wadsworth.

Matsumoto, D., & Juang, L. (2008). *Culture and psychology* (4th ed.). CA: Wadsworth.

Matthews, D. J. (2009). Developmental transitions in giftedness and talent: Childhood into adolescence. In F. D. Horowitz, R. F. Subotnik, & D. J. Matthews (Eds.), *The development of giftedness and talent across the life span.* Washington, DC: American Psychological Association.

Matthews, D. J., Subotnik, R. F., & Horowitz, F. D. (2009). A developmental perspective on giftedness and talent: Implications for research, policy, and practice. In F. D. Horowitz, R. F. Subotnik, & D. J. Matthews (Eds.), *The development of giftedness and talent across the life span.* Washington, DC: American Psychological Association.

Matthews, J. D., & Cramer, E. P. (2006). Envisioning the adoption process to strengthen gay- and lesbian-headed families: Recommendations for adoption professionals. *Child Welfare, 85,* 317–340.

Maurer, D., & Salapatek, P. (1976). Developmental changes in the scanning of faces by young infants. *Child Development, 47,* 523–527.

Maxim, G. W. (2010). *Dynamic social studies for constructive classrooms* (9th ed.). Boston: Allyn & Bacon.

Mayer, K. D., & Zhang, L. (2009). Short- and long-term effects of cocaine abuse during pregnancy on heart development. *Therapeutic Advances in Cardiovascular Disease, 3,* 7–16.

Mayer, R. E. (2008). *Learning and instruction* (2nd ed.). Upper Saddle River, NJ: Prentice Hall.

Mayhew, M. J., & King, P. (2008). How curricular content and pedagogical strategies affect moral reasoning development in college students. *Journal of Moral Education, 37,* 17–40.

Mbonye, A. K., Neema, S., & Magnussen, P. (2006). Treatment-seeking practices for malaria in pregnancy among rural women in Mukono district, Uganda. *Journal of Biosocial Science, 38,* 221–237.

Mbugua Gitau, G., Liversedge, H., Goffey, D., Hawton, A., Liversedge, N., & Taylor, M. (2009). The influence of maternal age on the outcomes of pregnancy complicated by bleeding at less than 12 weeks. *Acta Obstetricia et Gynecologica Scandinavica, 88,* 116–118.

McAlister, A., & Peterson, C. (2007). A longitudinal study of child siblings and theory of mind development. *Cognitive Development, 22,* 258–270.

McAnarney, E. R. (2008). Editorial: Adolescent brain development: Forging new links? *Journal of Adolescent Health, 42,* 321–323.

McCarthy, J. (2007). Children with autism spectrum disorders and intellectual disability. *Current Opinion in Psychiatry, 20,* 472–476.

McCartney, K. (2003, July 16). Interview with Kathleen McCartney in A. Bucuvalas, "Child care and behavior." *HGSE News,* pp. 1–4. Cambridge, MA: Harvard Graduate School of Education.

McCartney, K., Dearing, E., Taylor, B. A., & Bub, K. L. (2007). Quality child care supports the achievement of low-income children: Direct and indirect pathways through caregiving and the home environment. *Journal of Applied Developmental Psychology, 28,* 411–426.

McCarty, C. A., Mason, W. A., Kosterman, R., Hawkins, J. D., Lengua, L. J., & McCauley, E. (2008). Adolescent school failure predicts later depression among girls. *Journal of Adolescent Health, 43,* 180–187.

McComish, J. F., & Visger, J. M. (2009). Domains of postpartum doula care and maternal responsiveness and competence. *Journal of Obstetric, Gynecologic, and Neonatal Nursing, 38,* 148–156.

McDonald, J. A., Manlove, J., & Ikamullah, E. N. (2009). Immigration measures and reproductive health among Hispanic youth: Findings from the National Longitudinal Survey of Youth, 1997–2003. *Journal of Adolescent Health, 44,* 14–24.

McDowell, D. J., & Parke, R. D. (2009). Parental correlates of children's peer relations: An empirical test of a tripartite model. *Developmental Psychology, 45,* 224–235.

McElhaney, K. B., Allen, J. P., Stephenson, J. C., & Hare, A. L. (2009). Attachment and autonomy during adolescence. In R. M. Lerner & L. Steinberg (Eds.), *Handbook of adolescent psychology* (3rd ed.). New York: Wiley.

McFarlin, B. L. (2009). Solving the puzzle of prematurity. *American Journal of Nursing, 109,* 60–63.

McGarry, J., Kim, H., Sheng, X., Egger, M., & Baksh, L. (2009). Postpartum depression and help-seeking behavior. *Journal of Midwifery and Women's Health, 54,* 50–56.

McGarvey, C., McDonnell, M., Hamilton, K., O'Regan, M., & Matthews, T. (2006). An 8-year study of risk factors for SIDS: Bed-sharing versus non-bed-sharing. *Archives of Disease in Childhood, 91,* 318–323.

McHale, J. (2007) *Charting the bumpy road of coparenthood.* Washington: Zero to Three Press.

McHale, J., & Sullivan, M. (2008). Family systems. In M. Hersen & A. Gross (Eds.), *Handbook of clinical psychology, Volume II: Children and adolescents.* New York: Wiley.

McLoyd, V. C. (1998). Children in poverty: Development, public policy, and practice. In W. Damon (Ed.), *Handbook of child psychology* (5th ed., Vol. 4). New York: Wiley.

McLoyd, V. C., Kaplan, R., Purtell, K. M., Bagley, E., Hardaway, C. R., & Smalls, C. (2009). Poverty and socioeconomic disadvantage in adolescence. In R. M. Lerner & L. Steinberg (Eds.), *Handbook of adolescent psychology* (3rd ed). New York: Wiley.

McLoyd, V. C., Purtell, I. M., Bagley, E., Hardaway, C. R., Smalls, C. (2009). Poverty and socioeconomic disadvantage in adolescence. In R. M. Lerner & L. Steinberg (Eds.), *Handbook of adolescent psychology* (3rd ed.). New York: Wiley.

McMillen, I. C., MacLaughlin, S. M., Muhlhausler, B. S., Gentili, S., Duffield, J. L., & Morrison, J. L. (2008). Developmental origins of adult health and disease: The role of periconceptional and fetal nutrition. *Basic and Clinical Pharmacology and Toxicology 102,* 82–89.

McMullen, S. L., Lipke, B., & LeMura, C. (2009). Sudden infant death syndrome prevention: A model program for NICUs. *Neonatal Network, 28,* 7–12.

McMurray, R. G., Harrell, J. S., Creighton, D., Wang, Z., & Bangdiwala, S. I. (2008). Influence of physical activity on change in weight status as children become adolescents. *International Journal of Pediatric Obesity, 3,* 69–77.

McNally, D. (1990). *Even eagles need a push.* New York: Dell.

McNamara, F., & Sullivan, C. E. (2000). Obstructive sleep apnea in infants. *Journal of Pediatrics, 136,* 318–323.

Meade, C., Kershaw, T. S., & Ickovics, J. R. (2008). The intergenerational cycle of teenage motherhood: An ecological approach. *Health Psychology, 27,* 419–429.

Meece, J., & Eccles, J. (Eds.). (2009). *Handbook of research on schools, schooling and human development.* Clifton, NJ: Psychology Press.

Meerlo, P., Sgoifo, A., & Suchecki, D. (2008). Restricted and disrupted sleep: Effects on autonomic function, neuroendocrine stress systems, and stress responsivity. *Sleep Medicine Review, 12,* 197–210.

Mehl, R. C., O'Brien, L. M., Jones, J. H., Dreisbach, J. K., Mervis, C. B., & Gozal, D. (2006). Correlates of sleep and pediatric bipolar disorder. *Sleep, 29,* 193–197.

Meis, P. J., & Peaceman, A. M. (2003). Prevention of recurrent preterm delivery by 17-alpha-hydroxyprogesterone caproate. *New England Journal of Medicine, 348,* 2379–2385.

Melamed, B. G. (2002). Parenting the ill child. In M. H. Bornstein (Ed.), *Handbook of parenting* (Vol. 5). Mahwah, NJ: Erlbaum.

Melamed, B. G., Roth, B., & Fogel, J. (2001). Childhood health issues across the life span. In A. Baum, A. Revenson, & J. E. Singer (Eds.), *Handbook of health psychology.* Mahwah, NJ: Erlbaum.

Melgar-Quinonez, H. R., & Kaiser, L. L. (2004). Relationship of child-feeding practices to overweight in low-income Mexican-American preschool-aged children. *Journal of the American Dietetic Association, 104,* 1110–1119.

Mello, Z. R. (2009). Racial/ethnic group and socioeconomic status variation in educational and occupational expectations from adolescence to adulthood. *Journal of Applied Developmental Psychology, 30,* 494–504.

Melnyk, B. M., & Feinstein, N. F. (2009). Reducing hospital expenditures with the COPE (Creating Opportunities for Parent Empowerment) program for parents and premature infants: An analysis of direct healthcare neonatal intensive care unit costs and savings. *Nursing Administration Quarterly, 33,* 32–37.

Meltzi, G., & Ely, R. (2009). Language development in the school years. In J. B. Gleason & N. Ratner (Eds.), *The development of language* (7th ed.). Boston: Allyn & Bacon.

Meltzoff, A. N. (1988). Infant imitation and memory: Nine-month-old infants in immediate and deferred tests. *Child Development, 59,* 217–225.

Meltzoff, A. N. (2004). Imitation as a mechanism of social cognition: Origins of empathy, theory of mind, and the representation of action. In U. Goswami (Ed.), *Blackwell handbook of childhood cognitive development.* Malden, MA: Blackwell.

Meltzoff, A. N. (2005). Imitation. In B. Hopkins (Ed.), *Cambridge encyclopedia of child development.* Cambridge; UK: Cambridge University Press.

Meltzoff, A. N. (2007). Infants' causal learning. In A. Gopnik & L. Schulz (Eds.), *Casual learning.* New York: Oxford University Press.

Meltzoff, A. N. (2007). "Like me": A foundation for social cognition. *Developmental Sciences, 40,* 126–134.

Meltzoff, A. N. (2008). Unpublished review of J. W. Santrocks, *Life-span development,* 12th ed. (New York: McGraw-Hill).

Meltzoff, A. N., & Brooks, R. (2006). Eyes wide shut: The importance of eyes in infant gaze following and understanding of other minds. In R. Flom, K. Lee, & D. Muir (Eds.), *Gaze following: Its development and significance.* Mahwah. NJ: Erlbaum.

Meltzoff, A. N., & Brooks, R. (2009). Social cognition and language: The role of gaze following in early word learning. In J. Colombo, P. McCardle, & L. Freund (Eds.), *Infant pathways to language.* Clifton, NJ: Psychology Press.

Meltzoff, A. N., & Moore, M. K. (1999). A new foundation for cognitive development in infancy: The birth of the representational infant. In E. K. Skolnick, K. Nelson, S. A. Gelman, & P. H. Miller (Eds.), *Conceptual development.* Mahwah, NJ: Erlbaum.

Meltzoff, A. N., & Williamson, R. A. (2008). Imitation and modeling. In M. M. Haith & J. B. Benson (Eds.), *Encyclopedia of infant and early childhood development.* Oxford, UK: Elsevier.

Mendelson, C. R. (2009, in press). Minireview: Fetal-maternal hormonal signaling in pregnancy and labor. *Molecular Endocrinology.*

Mendle, J., Turkheimer, E., & Emery, R. E. (2007). Detrimental psychological outcomes associated with early pubertal timing in adolescent girls. *Developmental Review, 27,* 151–171.

Mendoza, J. A., Drewnowski, A., Cheadle, A., & Christakis, D. A. (2006). Dietary energy density is associated with selected predictors of obesity in U.S. children. *Journal of Nutrition, 136,* 1318–1322.

Menias, C. O., Elsayes, K. M., Peterson, C. M., Huete, A., Gratz, B. I., & Bhalla, S. (2007). CT of pregnancy-related complications. *Emergency Radiology, 13,* 299–306.

Menn, L., & Stoel-Gammon, C. (2009). Phonological development: Learning sounds and sound patterns. In J. Berko Gleason & N. Ratner (Eds.), *The development of language* (7th ed.). Boston: Allyn & Bacon.

Mennuti, M. T. (2008). Genetic screening in reproductive health care. *Clinical Obstetrics and Gynecology, 51,* 3–23.

Menon, M., Tobin, D. D., Corby, B. C., Menon, M., Hodges, E. V. E., & Perry, D. G. (2007). The developmental costs of high self-esteem in aggressive children. *Child Development, 78,* 1627–1639.

Menyuk, P., Liebergott, J., & Schultz, M. (1995). *Early language development in full-term and premature infants.* Hillsdale, NJ: Erlbaum.

Meredith, N. V. (1978). Research between 1960 and 1970 on the standing height of young children in different parts of the world. In H. W. Reece & L. P. Lipsitt (Eds.), *Advances in child development and behavior* (Vol. 12). New York: Academic Press.

Merewood, A., Patel, B., Newton, K. N., MacAuley, L. P., Chamberlin, L. B., Francisco, P., & Mehta, S. D. (2007). Breastfeeding duration rates and factors affecting continued breastfeeding among infants born at an inner-city U.S. baby-friendly hospital. *Journal of Human Lactation, 23,* 157–164.

Mesman, J., van IJzendoom, M. H., & Bakersman-Kranenburg, M. J. (2009). The many faces of the still-face paradigm: A review and meta-analysis. *Developmental Review, 29,* 120–162.

Messermith, E. E., Garrett, J. L., Davis-Kean, P. E., Malanchuk, O., & Eccles, J. S. (2008). Career development from adolescence through emerging adulthood: Insights from information technology occupations. *Journal of Adolescent Research, 23,* 206–227.

Messinger, D. (2008). Smiling. In M. M. Haith & J. B. Benson (Eds.), *Encyclopedia of infant and early childhood development.* Oxford, UK: Elsevier.

Metheny, J., McWhirter, E. W., & O'Neil, M. E. (2008). Measuring perceived teacher support and its influence on adolescent career development. *Journal of Career Assessment, 16,* 218–237.

Metz, E. C., & Youniss, J. (2005). Longitudinal gains in civic development through school-based required service. *Political Psychology, 26,* 413–437.

Metzl, J. D. (2008). Managing sports injuries in the pediatric office. *Pediatrics in Review, 29,* 75–84.

Meyers, A. F., Sampson, A. E., Weitzman, M., Rogers, B. L., & Kayne, H. (1989). School breakfast program and school performance. *American Journal of Diseases of Children, 143,* 1234–1239.

Miano, S., & others. (2009). Development of NREM sleep instability-continuity (cyclic alternating pattern) in healthy term infants aged 1 to 4 months. *Sleep, 32,* 83–90.

Michel, G. L., (1981). Right-handedness: A consequence of infant supine head-orientation preference? *Science, 212,* 685–687.

Mikkelsson, L., Kaprio, J., Kautiainen, H., Kujala, U., Mikkelsson, M., & Nupponen, H. (2006). School fitness tests as predictors of adult health-related fitness. *American Journal of Human Biology, 18,* 342–349.

Miller, B. C., Benson, B., & Galbraith, K. A. (2001). Family relationships and adolescent pregnancy risk: A research synthesis. *Developmental Review, 21,* 1–38.

Miller, B. C., Fan, X., Christensen, M., Grotevant, H. D., & von Dulmen, M. (2000). Comparisons of adopted and nonadopted adolescents in a large, nationally representative sample. *Child Development, 71,* 1458–1473.

Miller, C. F., Lurye, L. E., Zosuls, K. M., & Ruble, D. N. (2008). *Content and accessibility of children's gender stereotypes: Girls are what they look like and boys are what they do.* Unpublished manuscript, Department of Psychology, Princeton University.

Miller, C. F., Lurye, L. E., Zusuls, K, M., & Ruble, D. N. (2009). Accessibility of gender stereotype domains: Developmental and gender differences in children. *Sex Roles, 60,* 870–881.

Miller, J. (2007). Cultural psychology of moral development. In S. Kitayama & D. Cohen (Eds.), *Handbook of cultural psychology.* New York: Guilford.

Miller, J. W., Javadev, S., Dodrill, C. B., & Ojemann, G. A. (2006). Gender differences in handedness and speech lateralization related to early neurological results. *Neurology, 65,* 1974–1975.

Miller, L., & Gur, M. (2002). Religiousness and sexual responsibility in adolescent girls. *Journal of Adolescent Health, 31,* 401–406.

Miller-Perrin, C. L., Perrin, R. D., & Kocur, J. L. (2009). Parental physical and psychological aggression: Psychological symptoms in young adults. *Child Abuse and Neglect, 33,* 1–11.

Miller, T. W., Nigg, J. T., & Faraone, S. V. (2007). Axis I and II comorbidity in adults with ADHD. *Journal of Abnormal Psychology, 116,* 519–528.

Mills, B., Reyna, V., & Estrada, S. (2008). Explaining contradictory relations between risk perception and risk taking. *Psychological Science, 19*, 429–433.

Mills, D., & Mills, C. (2000). *Hungarian kindergarten curriculum translation*. London: Mills Production.

Minde, K., & Zelkowitz, P. (2008). Premature babies. In M. M. Haith & J. B. Benson (Eds.), *Encyclopedia of infant and early childhood development*. Oxford, UK: Elsevier.

Mindell, J. A., & Barrett, K. M. (2002), Nightmares and anxiety in elementary-aged children: Is there a relationship? *Child Care: Health and Development, 28*, 317–322.

Minino, A. M., Heron, M. P., & Smith, B. L. (2006). Deaths: Preliminary data 2004. *National Vital Statistics Reports, 54*, 1–49.

Minnesota Family Investment Program. (2009). *Longitudinal study of early MFIP recipients*. Retrieved January 12, 2009, from www.dhs.state.mn.us/main/idcplg?IdcService=GET_DYNAMIC_CONVERSION&...

Miranda, R., Scott, M., Hicks, R., Wilcox, H. C., Harris Munfakh, J. L., & Shaffer, D. (2008). Suicide attempt characteristics, diagnoses, and future attempts: Comparing multiple attempters to single attempters and ideators. *Journal of the American Academy of Child and Adolescent Psychiatry, 47*, 32–40.

Mischel, W. (2004). Toward an integrative science of the person. *Annual Review of Psychology* (Vol. 55). Palo Alto, CA: Annual Reviews.

Mitchell, E. A. (2007). Recommendations for sudden infant death syndrome prevention: A discussion document. *Archives of Disease in Childhood, 92*, 155–159.

Mitchell, E. A. (2009). What is the mechanism of SIDS? Clues from epidemiology. *Developmental Psychobiology, 51*, 215–222.

Mitchell, E. A., Stewart, A. W., Crampton, P., & Salmond, C. (2000). Deprivation and sudden infant death syndrome. *Social Science and Medicine, 51*, 147–150.

Miyake, K., Chen, S., & Campos, J. (1985). Infants' temperament, mothers' mode of interaction and attachment in Japan: An interim report. In I. Bretherton & F. Waters (Eds.), Growing points of attachment theory and research, *Monographs of the Society for Research in Child Development, 50* (1–2, Serial No. 109), 276–297.

MMWR. (2006, June 9). Youth risk behavior surveillance—United States, 2005 (Vol. 255). Atlanta: Centers for Disease Control and Prevention.

Moffitt, T. E., Caspi, A., & Rutter, M. (2006). Measured gene-environment interactions in psychopathology. *Perspectives on Psychological Science, 1*, 5–27.

Moise, K. J. (2005). Fetal RhD typing with free DNA I maternal plasma. *American Journal of Obstetrics and Gynecology, 192*, 663–665.

Moleti, C. A. (2009). Trends and controversies in labor induction. *MCN: American Journal of Maternal Child Nursing, 34*, 40–47.

Moll, H., Richter, N., Carpenter, M., & Tomasello, M. (2008). 14-month-olds know what "we" have shared in a special way. *Infancy, 13*, 90–101.

Molnar, B. E., Cerda, M., Roberts, A. L., & Buka, S. L. (2008). Effects of neighborhood resources on aggressive and delinquent behaviors among urban youths. *American Journal of Public Health, 98*, 1086–1093.

Monge, P., & others. (2007). Parental occupation exposure to pesticides and the risk of childhood leukemia in Costa Rica. *Scandinavian Journal of Work, Environment, and Health, 33*, 293–303.

Montan, S. (2007). Increased risk in the elderly parturient. *Current Opinion in Obstetrics and Gynecology, 19*, 110–112.

Montemayor, R. (1982). The relationship between parent-adolescent conflict and the amount of time adolescents spend with parents, peers, and alone. *Child Development, 53*, 1512–1519.

Mood, D. P., Musker, F. F., & Rink, J. E. (2007). *Sports and recreational activities* (14th ed.). New York: McGraw-Hill.

Moore, D. (2001). *The dependent gene*. New York: W. H. Freeman.

Moore, G. A., Hill-Soderlund, A. L., Propper, C. B., Calkins, S. D., Mills-Koonce, W. R., & Cox, M. J. (2009). Mother-infant vagal regulation in the face-to-face still-face paradigm is moderated by maternal sensitivity. *Child Development, 80*, 209–223.

Moore, M. K., & Meltzoff, A. N. (2008). Factors affecting infants' manual search for occluded objects and the genesis of object permanence. *Infant Behavior and Development, 31*, 168–180.

Moore, M., & Meltzer, L. J. (2008). The sleepy adolescent: Causes and consequences of sleepiness in teens. *Pediatric Respiratory Reviews, 9*, 114–120.

Moorthy, A., & others. (2009). Nevirapine resistance and breast-milk HIV transmission: Effects of single and extended-dose nevirapine prophylaxis in sub-type C HIV-infected infants. *PLoS ONE, 4*, e4096.

Moralez, L. S., Gutierrez, P., & Escarce, J. J. (2005). Demographic and socioeconomic factors associated with blood levels among Mexican-American children and adolescents in the United States. *Public Health Reports, 120*, 448–454.

Moran, S., & Gardner, H. (2006). Extraordinary achievements. In W. Damon & R. Lerner (Eds.), *Handbook of child psychology* (6th ed.). New York: Wiley.

Moran, S., & Gardner, H. (2007). Hill, skill, and will: Executive function from a multiple intelligences perspective. In L. Meltzer (Ed.), *Executive function in education*. New York: Guilford.

Morawaska, A., Winter, L., & Sanders, M. R. (2009). Parenting knowledge and its role in the prediction of parenting and disruptive child behavior. *Child Care, Health, and Development, 35*, 217–226.

Moreno, A., Posada, G. E., & Goldyn, D. T. (2006). Presence and quality of touch influence coregulation in mother-infant dyads: *Infancy, 9*, 1–20.

Morokuma, S., & others (2008). Developmental change in fetal response to repeated low-intensity sound. *Development Science, 11*, 47–52.

Morra, S., Gobbo, C., Marini, Z., & Sheese, R. (2007). *Cognitive development: Neo-Piagetian perspectives*. Mahwah, NJ: Erlbaum.

Morris, D. S., Tenkku, L. E., Salas, J., Xaverius, P. K., & Mengel, M. B. (2008). Exploring pregnancy-related changes in alcohol consumption between Black and White women. *Alcoholism: Clinical and Experimental Research, 32*, 505–512.

Morrison, F. J., & Hindman, A. H. (2008). School readiness. In M. M. Haith & J. B. Benson (Eds.), *Encyclopedia of infant and early childhood development*. Oxford, UK: Elsevier.

Morrison, G. S. (2009). *Early childhood education today* (11th ed.). Upper Saddle River, NJ: Prentice Hall.

Morrissey-Ross, M. (2000). Lead poisoning and its elimination. *Public Health Nursing, 17*, 229–230.

Morrissey, T. W. (2009). Multiple child-care arrangements and young children's behavioral outcomes. *Child Development, 80*, 59–76.

Morrongiello, B. A., & Mathesis, S. (2007). Addressing the issue of falls off playground equipment: An empirically based intervention to reduce fall-risk behaviors on playgrounds. *Journal of Pediatric Psychology, 32*, 819–830.

Morrow, C. E., Culbertson, J. L., Accornero, V. H., Xue, L., Anthony, J. C., & Bandstra, E. S. (2006). Learning disabilities and intellectual functioning in school-aged children with prenatal cocaine exposure. *Developmental Neuropsychology, 30*, 905–931.

Morrow, L. (2009). *Literacy development in the early years*. Boston: Allyn & Bacon.

Morse, S. B., Zheng, H., Tang, Y., & Roth, J. (2009). Early school-age outcomes of late preterm infants. *Pediatrics, 123*, e622–e629.

Mortensen, L. H., Diderichsen, F., Davery-Smith, G., & Andersen, A. M. (2009, in press). Time is on whose side? Time trends in the association between social disadvantage and offspring fetal growth. A study of 1,409,339 births in Denmark 1981–2004. *Journal of Epidemiology and Community Health*.

Moschonis, G., Grammatikaki, E., & Manios, Y. (2008). Perinatal predictors of overweight at infancy and preschool childhood: The GENESIS study. *International Journal of Obesity, 32*, 39–47.

Most, O. L., Kim, J. H., Arsian, A. A., & Klauser, C. (2009, in press). Maternal and neonatal outcomes in early glucose tolerance testing in an obstetric population in New York City. *Journal of Perinatal Medicine*.

Moster, D., Lie, T. L., & Markestad, T. (2008). Long-term medical and social consequences of preterm birth. *New England Journal of Medicine, 359,* 262–273.

Mottershead, N. (2006). Hypnosis: Removing labor from birth. *Practicing Midwife, 9,* 26–27, 29.

Moulson, M. C., & Nelson, C. A. (2008). Neurological development. In M. M. Haith & J. B. Benson (Eds.), *Encyclopedia of infant and early childhood development.* Oxford, UK: Elsevier.

Mounts, N. S. (2002). Parental management of adolescent peer relationships in context: The role of parenting style. *Journal of Family Psychology, 16,* 58–69.

Moyer, R. H., Hackett, J. K., & Everett, S. A. (2007). *Teaching science as investigations.* Upper Saddle River, NJ: Prentice Hall.

Mueller, A. S. (2009). Body image, childhood and adolescence. In D. Carr (Ed.), *Encyclopedia of the life course and human development.* Boston: Gale Cengage.

Mueller, U., Carpendale, J. I. M., Budwig, N., & Sokol, B. W. (Eds.). (2008). *Social life and social knowledge.* Philadelphia: Psychology Press.

Mullis, P. E., & Tonella, P. (2008). Regulation of fetal growth: Consequences and impact of being born small. *Best Practice Research: Clinical Endocrinology and Metabolism, 22,* 173–190.

Mulvaney, M. K., & Mebert, C. J. (2007). Parental corporal punishment predicts behavior problems in early childhood. *Journal of Family Psychology, 21,* 389–397.

Munakata, Y. (2006). Information processing: Approaches to development. In W. Damon & R. Lerner (Eds.), *Handbook of educational psychology.* New York: Wiley.

Mundy, P., Block, J., Delgado, C., Pomares, Y., Van Hecke, A. V., & Parlade, M. V. (2007). Individual differences and the development of joint attention in infancy. *Child Development, 78,* 938–954.

Murdock. T. B., Miller. A., & Kohlhardt, J., (2004). Effects of classroom context variables on high school students' judgments of the acceptability and likelihood of cheating. *Journal of Educational Psychology, 96,* 765–777.

Murnane, R. J., & Levy, F. (1996). *Teaching the new basic skills.* New York: Free Press.

Murphy, M. M., & Mazzocco, M. M. (2008). Mathematics learning disabilities in girls with fragile X or Turner syndrome during late elementary school. *Journal of Learning Disabilities, 41,* 29–46.

Murray, E. A. (2007). Visual memory. *Annual Review of Neuroscience* (Vol. 29). Palo Alto, CA: Annual Reviews.

Murray, J. P. (2007). TV violence: Research and controversy. In N. Pecora, J. P. Murray, & E. A. Wartella (Eds.), *Children and television.* Mahwah, NJ: Erlbaum.

Myers, D. G. (2010). *Psychology* (9th ed.). New York: Worth.

Myers, D. L. (1999). *Excluding violent youths from juvenile court: The effectiveness of legislative waiver.*

Doctoral dissertation, University of Maryland, College Park, MD.

Myerson, J., Rank, M. R., Raines, F. Q., & Schnitzler, M. A. (1998). Race and general cognitive ability: The myth of diminishing returns in education. *Psychological Science, 9,* 139–142.

N

Nabet, C., Lelong, N., Ancel, P. Y., Saurel-Cubizolles, M. J., & Kaminski, M. (2007). Smoking during pregnancy according to obstetric complications and parity: Results of the EUROPOP study. *European Journal of Epidemiology, 22,* 715–721.

Nadar P. R., Bradley, R. H., Houts, R. M., McRitchie, S. L., & O'Brain, M. (2008). Moderate-to-vigorous physical activity from 9 to 15 years. *Journal of the American Medical Association, 300,* 295–305.

Nader, K. (2001). Treatment methods for childhood trauma. In J. P. Wilson, M. J. Friedman, & J. Lindy (Eds.), *Treating psychological trauma and PTSD.* New York: Guilford.

Nader, P., O'Brien, M., Houts, R., Bradley, R., Belsky, J., Corsnoe, R., Friedman, S., Mei, Z., & Susman, E. J. (2006). Identifying risk for obesity in early childhood. *Pediatrics, 118,* e594–e601.

NAEYC. (1990). NAEYC position statement on school readiness. *Young Children, 46,* 21–28.

NAEYC. (2002). *Early learning standards: Creating the conditions for success.* Washington, DC: Author.

NAEYC. (2009). Developmentally appropriate practice in early childhood programs serving children from birth through age 8. Washington, DC: Author.

Nagahawatte, N. T., & Goldenberg, R. (2008). Poverty, maternal health, and adverse pregnancy outcomes. *Annals of the New York Academy of Sciences, 1136,* 80–85.

Nagel, H. T., Kneght, A. C., Kloosterman, M. D., Wildschut, H. I., Leschot, N. J., & Vandenbussche, F. P. (2007). Prenatal diagnosis in the Netherlands, 1991–2000: Number of invasive procedures, indications, abnormal results, and terminations of pregnancies. *Prenatal Diagnosis, 27,* 251–257.

Nahar, B., Hamadani, J. D., Ahmed, T., Tofail, F., Rahman, A., Huda, S. N., & Grantham-McGregor, S. M. (2008). Effects of psychosocial stimulation on growth and development of severely malnourished children in a nutrition unit in Bangladesh. *European Journal of Clinical Nutrition, 63,* 725–731.

Naigles, L. R., & Swensen, L. D. (2007). Syntactic supports for word learning. In E. Hoff & M. Shatz (Eds.), *Blackwell handbook of language development.* Malden, MA: Blackwell.

Najman, J. M., Hayatbakhsh, M. R., Heron, M. A., Bor, W., O'Callaghan, M. J., & Williams, G. M. (2009). The impact of episodic and chronic poverty of child cognitive development. *Journal of Pediatrics, 154,* 284–289.

Nanovskaya, T. N., Nekhayeva, I. A., Hankins, G. D., & Ahmed, M. S. (2008). Transfer of methadone across the dually perfused preterm human placental lobule. *American Journal of Obsterics and Gynecology, 198,* e1–e4.

Nansel, T. R., Overpeck, M., Pilla, R., Ruan, W., Simons-Morton, B., & Scheidt, P. (2001). Bullying behaviors among U.S. youth. *Journal of the American Medical Association, 285,* 2094–2100.

Napierski-Prancl, M. (2009). Eating disorders. In D. Carr (Ed.), *Encyclopedia of the life course and human development.* Boston: Gale Cengage.

Narberhaus, A., Segarra, D., Caldu, X., Gimenez, M., Pueyo, R., Botet, F., & Junque, C. (2008). Corpus callosum and prefrontal functions in adolescents with history of very preterm birth. *Neuropsychologia, 46,* 111–116.

Narr, K. L., & others. (2007). Relationships between IQ and regional cortical gray matter thickness in healthy adults. *Cerebral Cortex, 17,* 2163–2171.

Narváez, D. (2006). Integrative moral education. In M. Killen & J. Smetana (Eds.), *Handbook of moral development.* Mahwah, NJ: Erlbaum.

Narváez, D. (2008). Four component model. In F. C. Power, R. J. Nuzzi, D, Narváez, D. K. Lapsley, & T. C. Hunt (Eds.), *Moral education: A handbook.* Westport, CT: Greenwood.

Narváez, D., & Lapsley, D. (Eds.). (2009, in press). *Moral personality, identity, and character: An interdisciplinary future.* New York: Cambridge University Press.

Narváez, D., Lynchard, N., Vaydich, J., & Mattan. B. (2008, March). *Cheating: Explicit recognition, implicit evaluation, moral judgment and honor code training.* Annual Meeting of the Society for Research in Adolescence, Chicago.

National Assessment of Educational Progress. (2005). *The nation's report card.* Washington, DC: National Center for Education Statistics.

National Assessment of Educational Progress. (2007). *The nation's report card.* Washington, DC: U.S. Department of Education.

National Association for Sport and Physical Education. (2002). *Active start: A statement of physical activity guidelines for children birth to five years.* Reston, VA: Author.

National Autism Association. (2008). *All about autism.* Retrieved October 24, 2008, from www. nationalautismassociation.org/definitions.php

National Cancer Institute. (2008a). *Cancer trends progress report.* Retrieved January 15, 2008, from http://progressreport.cancer.gov/highlights.asp

National Cancer Institute. (2008b). *Acute lymphoblastic leukemia in children.* Retrieved January 15, 2008, from www.cancer.gov/cancertopics/factsheet/ALLinchildren

National Center for Education Statistics. (2007). *Children with disabilities in public schools.* Washington, DC. U.S. Department of Education.

National Center for Education Statistics. (2008). *School dropouts.* Washington, DC: U.S. Department of Education.

National Center for Education Statistics. (2008). *The condition of education, 2008.* Washington, DC: US Department of Education.

National Center for Health Statistics. (2002). *Sexual behavior and selected health measures: Men and women 15–44 years of age, United States, 2002,* PHS 2003–1250. Atlanta: Centers for Disease Control and Prevention.

National Center for Health Statistics. (2007). *Death rates.* Atlanta: Centers for Disease Control and Prevention.

National Center for Health Statistics. (2007). *Health, United States, 2007.* Hyattsville, MD: Author.

National Center for Health Statistics. (2008). *Health United States, 2008.* Atlanta: Centers for Disease Control and Prevention.

National Center for Health Statistics. (2009, January 7). *Public Release Statement: Preterm births rise 36 percent since early 1980s.* Atlanta: Centers for Disease Control and Prevention.

National Center for Juvenile Justice. (2006). *Juvenile offenders and victims: 2006 national report.* Pittsburgh: Author.

National Center for Learning Disabilities. (2006). *Learning disabilities.* Retrieve March 6, 2006, from http://www.ncld.org/

National Center on Addiction and Substance Abuse (CASA). (2007). *The importance of family dinners IV.* New York: Author.

National Center on Shaken Baby Syndrome. (2008). *Shaken baby syndrome.* Retrieved October 16, 2008, from www.dontshake.org/

National Clearinghouse on Child Abuse and Neglect. (2004). *What is child abuse and neglect?* Washington, DC: U. S. Department of Health and Human Services.

National Institute of Mental Health. (2004). *Austism spectrum disorders.* Bethesda, MD: Author.

National Institute of Mental Health. (2008) *Autism spectrum disorders (pervasive developmental disorders).* Retrieved January 6, 2008, from http://www.nimh.nih.gov/Publicat/autism.cfm.

National Institutes of Health. (1993). *Learning disabilities* (NIH publication No. 93–3611). Bethesda, MD: Author.

National Institutes of Health. (2007). *Night terror.* Retrieved January 19, 2007, from *http://www.nlm.nih.gov/medlineplus/ency/article/000809.htm.*

National Institutes of Health. (2008). *Clinical trial.gov* Retrieved on April 22, 2008, from http://clinicaltrials.gov/ct2/show/NCT00059293?cond=%22Intracranial1Embolism%22&r...

National Research Council. (1999). *How people learn.* Washington, DC: National Academy Press.

National Research Council. (2004). *Engaging schools: Fostering high school students' motivation to learn.* Washington, DC: National Academies Press.

National Sleep Foundation. (2006). *2006 Sleep in America poll.* Washington, DC: National Sleep Foundation.

National Sleep Foundation. (2007). *Sleep in America poll 2007.* Washington, DC: Author.

National Sleep Foundation. (2009). *Children's sleep habits.* Retrieved on January 29, 2009, from *www.sleepfoundation.org*

National Vital Statistics Report. (2004, March 7). *Deaths: Leading causes for 2002.* Atlanta: Centers for Disease Control and Prevention.

National Vital Statistics Reports. (2008, June 11). Table 7. Deaths and death rates for the 10 leading causes of death in specified age groups: United States, preliminary 2006. *National Vital Statistics Reports, 56* (No. 16), p. 30.

Natsopoulos, D., Kiosseoglou, G., Xeroxmeritou, A., & Alevriadou, A. (1998). Do the hands talk on the mind's behalf? Differences in language between left- and right-handed children. *Brain and Language, 64,* 182–214.

Naude, H., Pretorius, E., & Vijoen, J. (2003). The impact of impoverished language development on preschoolers' readiness-to-learn during the foundation phase. *Early Child Development and Care, 173,* 271–291.

Nava-Ocampo, A. A., & Koren, G. (2007). Human teratogens and evidence-based teratogen risk counseling: The Motherisk approach. *Clinical Obstetrics and Gynecology, 50,* 123–131.

Neal, A. R. (2009). Autism. In D. Carr (Ed.), *Encyclopedia of the life course and human development.* Boston: Gale Cengage.

Needham, A. (2009). Learning in infants' object perception, object-directed action, and tool use. In A. Needham & A. Woodward (Eds.), *Learning and the infant mind.* New York: Oxford University Press.

Needham, A., Barrett, T., & Peterman, K. (2002). A pick-me-up for infants' exploratory skills: Early simulated experiences reaching for objects using "sticky mittens" enhances young infants' object exploration skills. *Infant Behavior and Development, 25,* 279–295.

Neisser, U., Boodoo, G., Bouchard, T. J., Boykin, A. W., Brody, N., Ceci, S. J., Halpern, D. F., Loehlin, J. C., Perloff, R. J., Sternberg, R., & Urbins, S. (1996). Intelligence: Knowns and unknowns. *American psychologist, 51,* 77–101.

Nelson, C. A. (2003). Neural development and lifelong plasticity. In R. M. Lerner, F. Jacobs, & D. Wertlieb (Eds.), *Handbook of applied developmental science* (Vol. 1). Thousand Oaks, CA: Sage.

Nelson, C. A. (2009, in press). Brain development and behavior. In A. M. Rudolph, C. Rudoloph, L. First, G. Lister, & A. A. Gershon (Eds.), *Rudolph's pediatrics* (22nd ed.). New York: McGraw-Hill.

Nelson, C. A., Thomas, K. M., & De Haan, M. (2006). Neural bases of cognitive development. In W. Damon & R. Lerner (Eds.), *Handbook of child psychology* (6th ed.). New York: Wiley.

Nelson, C. A., Zeanah, C., & Fox, N. A. (2007). The effects of early deprivation on brain-behavioral development: The Bucharest Early Intervention Project. In D. Romer & E. Walker (Eds.), *Adolescent psychopathology and the developing brain: Integrating brain and prevention science.* New York: Oxford University Press.

Nelson, J. A., & Eckstein, D. (2008). A service-learning model for at-risk adolescents. *Education and Treatment of Children, 31,* 223–237.

Nelson, K. (1999). Levels and modes of representation: Issues for the theory of conceptual change and development. In E. K. Skolnick., K. Nelson, S. A. Gelman, & P. H. Miller (Eds.), *Conceptual development.* Mahwah, NJ: Erlbaum.

Nelson, S. L., & Lee, J. C. (2009). Socioeconomic inequality in education. In D. Carr (Ed.), *Encyclopedia of the life course and human development.* Boston: Gale Cengage.

Ness, A., Dias, T., Damus, K., Burd, I., & Berghella, V. (2006). Impact of recent randomized trials on the use of progesterone to prevent preterm birth: A 2005 follow-up survey. *American Journal of Obstetrics and Gynecology, 195,* 1174–1179.

Neubauer, A. C., & Fink, A. (2009). Intelligence and neural efficiency: Measures of brain activation versus measures of functional connectivity in the brain. *Intelligence, 37,* 223–229.

Neumann, C. G., Gewa, C., & Bwibo, N. B. (2004). Child nutrition in developing countries. *Pediatric Annals 33,* 658–674.

Neville, H. J. (2006). Different profiles of plasticity within human cognition. In Y. Munakata & M. H. Johnson (Eds.), *Attention and performance XXI: Processes of change in brain and cognitive development.* Oxford, UK: Oxford University Press.

Nevsimalova, S. (2009). Narcolespy in childhood. *Sleep Medicine Reviews, 13,* 169–180.

New, R. (2007). Reggio Emilia as cultural activity. *Theory into Practice, 46,* 5–13.

Newburg, D. S., & Walker, W. A. (2007). Protection of the neonate by the innate immune system of developing gut and of human milk. *Pediatric Research, 61,* 2–8.

Newcombe, N. (2008). The development of implicit and explicit memory. In N. Cowan & M. Courage (Eds.), *The development of memory in childhood.* Philadelphia: Psychology Press.

Newcombe, N. S. (2007). Developmental psychology meets the mommy wars. *Journal of Applied Developmental Psychology, 28,* 553–555.

Newell, K., Scully, D. M., McDonald, P. V., & Baillargeon, R. (1989). Task constraints and infant grip configurations. *Developmental Psychobiology, 22,* 817–832.

Newman, R. S. (2008). The level of detail in infants' word learning. *Current Directions in Psychological Science, 17,* 229–232.

Newnham, C. A., Milgrom, J., & Skouteris, H. (2009). Effectiveness of a modified Mother-Infant Transaction program on outcomes for preterm infants from 3 to 24 months of age. *Infant Behavior and Development, 32,* 17–26.

Newson, A. J. (2008). Ethical aspects arising from non-invasive fetal diagnosis. *Seminars in Fetal and Neonatal Medicine, 13,* 103–108.

Newson, J., Newson, E., & Mahalski, P. A. (1982). Persistent infant comfort habits and their sequelae at 11 and 16 years. *Journal of Child Psychology and Psychiatry, 23,* 421–436.

Ney, D. M., Hull, A. K., van Calcar, S. C., Liu, X., & Etzel, M. R. (2008). Dietary glyco-macropeptide supports growth and reduces the concentrations of phenylalanine in plasma and brain in a murine model of phenylketonuria. *Journal of Nutrition, 138,* 316–322.

NICHD. (2008). *SIDS facts.* Retrieved January 18, 2008, from www.nichd.nih.gov/sids

NICHD Early Child Care Research Network. (2000). Factors associated with fathers' caregiving activities and sensitivity with young children. *Developmental Psychology, 14,* 200–219.

NICHD Early Child Care Research Network. (2001). Nonmaternal care and family factors in early development: An overview of the NICHD study of early child care. *Journal of Applied Developmental Psychology, 22,* 457–492.

NICHD Early Child Care Research Network. (2002). Structure → Process → Outcome: Direct and indirect effects of child care quality on young children's development. *Psychological Science, 13,* 199–206.

NICHD Early Child Care Research Network. (2003). Does amount of time spent in child care predict socioemotional adjustment during the transition to kindergarten? *Child Development, 74,* 976–1005.

NICHD Early Child Care Research Network. (2004). Type of child care and children's development at 54 months. *Early Childhood Research Quarterly, 19,* 203–230.

NICHD Early Child Care Research Network. (2005). Duration and developmental timing of poverty and children's cognitive and social development from birth through third grade. *Child Development, 76,* 795–810.

NICHD Early Child Care Research Network (2005). Predicting individual differences in attention, memory, and planning in first graders from experiences at home, child care, and school. *Developmental Psychology, 41,* 99–114.

NICHD Early Child Care Research Network (2006). Infant-mother attachment classification: Risk and protection in relation to changing maternal caregiving quality. *Developmental Psychology, 42,* 38–58.

NICHD Early Child Care Research Network. (2009, in press). Family-peer linkages: The meditational role of attentional processes. *Social Development.*

Nicklas, T. A., Webber, L. S., Jonson, C. S., Srinivasan, S. R., & Berenson, G. S. (1995). Foundations for health promotion with youth: A review of observations from the Bogalusa Heart Study. *Journal of Health Education, 26,* S18–S26.

Nicklas, T. A., Yang, S. J., Baranowski, T., Zakeri, I., & Berenson, G. (2003). Eating patterns and obesity in children. The Bogalusa Heart Study. *American Journal of Preventive Medicine, 25,* 9–16.

Nielsen, S. J., Siega-Riz, A. M., & Popkin, B. M. (2002). Trends in energy intake in U.S. between 1977 and 1996: Similar shifts seen across age-groups. *Obesity Research, 10,* 370–378.

Nieto, S., & Bode, P. (2008). *Affirming diversity* (5th ed.). Boston: Allyn & Bacon.

Nisbett, R. (2003). *The geography of thought.* New York: Free Press.

Nishiyama, T., Tanial, H., Miyachi, T., Ozaki, K., Tomita, M., & Sumi, S. (2009). Genetic correlation between autistic traits and IQ in a population-based sample of twins with autism spectrum disorders (ASDs). *Journal of Human Genetics, 54,* 56–61.

Nixon, G. M., & others. (2008). Short sleep duration in middle childhood: Risk factors and consequences. *Sleep, 31,* 71–78.

Noddings, N. (2007). *When school reform goes wrong.* New York: Teachers College Press.

Noddings, N. (2008). Caring and moral education. In L. Nucci & D. Narváez (Ed.), *Handbook of moral and character education.* Clifton, NJ: Psychology Press.

Nohr, E. A., Bech, B. H., Davies, M. J., Fryenberg, M., Henriksen, T. B., & Olsen, J. (2005). Prepregnancy obesity and fetal death: A study with the Danish National Birth Cohort. *Obstetrics and Gynecology, 106,* 250–259.

Noland, J. S., Singer, L. T., Short, E. J., Minnes, S., Arendt, R. E., Kirchner, H. L., & Bearer, C. (2005). Prenatal drug exposure and selective attention in preschoolers. *Neurotoxicology and Teratology, 27,* 429–438.

Nolen-Hoeksema, S. (2010, in press). *Abnormal psychology* (5th ed.). New York: McGraw-Hill.

Nommsen-Rivers, L. A., Mastergeorge, A. M., Hansen, R. L., Cullum, A. S., & Dewey, K. G. (2009). Doula care, early breastfeeding outcomes, and breastfeeding status at 6 weeks postpartum among low-income primiparae. *Journal of Obstetric, Gynecologic, and Neonatal Nursing, 38,* 157–173.

Norbury, G., & Norbury, C. J. (2008). Non-invasive prenatal diagnosis of single gene disorders: How close are we? *Seminars in Fetal and Neonatal Medicine, 13,* 76–83.

Norgard, B., Puho, E., Czeizel, A. E., Skriver, M. V., & Sorensen, H. T. (2005). Aspirin use during early pregnancy and the risk of congenital abnormalities. *American Journal of Obstetrics and Gynecology, 192,* 922–923.

Nottelmann, E. D., Susman, E. J., Blue, J. H., Inoff-Germain, G., Dorn, L. D., Lorlaux, D. I., Cutler, G. B., & Chrousos, G. P. (1987). Gonadal and adrenal hormone correlates of adjustment in early adolescence. In R. M. Lerner & T. T. Foch (Eds.), *Biological-psychological interactions in early adolescence.* Hillsdale, NJ: Erlbaum.

Nowicka, P., & Flodmark, C. E. (2008). Family in pediatric obesity management: A literature review. *International Journal of Pediatric Obesity, 3* (Suppl. 1), S44–S50.

Nsamenang, A. B. (2002). Adolescence in sub-Saharan Africa: An image constructed from Africa's triple heritage. In B. B. Brown, R. W. Larson, & T. S. Saraswathi (Eds.), *The world's youth.* New York: Cambridge University Press.

Nucci, L. (2006). Education for moral development. In M. Killen & J. Smetana (Eds.), *Handbook of moral development.* Mahwah, NJ: Erlbaum.

Nucci, L., & Narváez, D. (Eds.). (2008). *Handbook of moral and character education.* Clifton, NJ: Psychology Press.

Nyaronga, D., & Wickrama, K. A. S. (2009). Health behaviors, childhood and adolescence. In D. Carr (Ed.), *Encyclopedia of the life course and human development.* Boston: Gale Cengage.

Nylund, K., Bellmore, A., Nishina, A., & Graham, S. (2007). Subtypes, severity, and structural stability of peer victimization: What does latent class analysis say? *Child Development, 78,* 1706–1722.

O

Oakes, L. M. (2008). Categorization skills and concepts. In M. M. Haith & J. B. Benson (Eds.), *Encyclopedia of infant and early childhood development.* Oxford, UK: Elsevier.

Oakes, L. M., Horst, J. S., Kovack-Lesh, K. A., & Perone, S. (2009). How infants learn categories. In A. Woodward & A. Needham (Eds.), *Learning and the infant mind.* New York: Oxford University Press.

Oakes, L. M., Kannass, K. N., & Shaddy, D. J. (2002). Developmental changes in endogenous control of attention: The role of target familiarity on infants' distraction latency. *Child Development, 73,* 1644–1655.

Oakes, L. M., & Rakison, D. H. (2009). Issues in the early development of concepts and categories: An introduction. In D. H. Rakison & L. M. Oakes (Eds.), *Early category and concept development.* New York: Oxford University Press.

Obel, C., & others. (2009). Smoking during pregnancy and hyperactivity-inattention in the offspring—comparing results from three Nordic cohorts. *International Journal of Epidemiology, 38,* 698–705.

Obenauer, S., & Maestre, L. A. (2008). Fetal MRI of lung hypoplasia: imaging findings. *Clinical Imaging, 32,* 48–50.

Oberlander, T. F., Bonaguro, R. J., Misri, S., Papsdorf, M., Ross, C. J., & Simpson, E. M.

(2008). Infant serotonin transporter (SLC6A4) promoter genotype is associated with adverse neonatal outcomes after prenatal exposure to serotonin reuptake inhibitor medications. *Molecular Psychiatry, 13,* 65–73.

O'Connor, A. B., & Roy, C. (2008). Electric power plant emissions and public health. *American Journal of Nursing, 108,* 62–70.

O'Donnell, L., O'Donnell, C., Wardlaw, D. M., & Stueve, A. (2004). Risk and resiliency factors influencing suicidality among urban African American and Latino youth. *American Journal of Community Psychology, 33,* 37–49.

Offer, D., Ostrov E., Howard, K. I., & Atkinson, R. (1988). *The teenage world: Adolescents' self-image in ten countries.* New York: Plenum.

Ogbu, J., & Stern, P. (2001). Caste status and intellectual development. In R. J. Sternberg & E. L. Grigorenko (Eds.), *Environmental effects on cognitive abilities.* Mahwah, NJ: Erlbaum.

Ogden, C. L., Carroll, M. D., & Flegal, K. M. (2008). High body mass index for age among U.S. children and adolescents, 2003–2006. *Journal of the American Medical Association, 299,* 2401–2405.

Ohgi, S., Fukuda, M., Moriuchi, H., Kusumoto, T., Akiyama, T., Nugetn, J. K., Brazelton, T. B., Arisawa, K., Takahashi, T., & Saitoh, H. (2002). Comparison of kangaroo care and standard care: Behavioral organization, development, and temperament in healthy, low birth weight infants through 1 year. *Journal of Perinatology, 22,* 374–379.

Olds, D. L., & others. (2004). Effects of home visits by paraprofessionals and nurses: Age 4 follow-up of a randomized trial. *Pediatrics, 114,* 1560–1568.

Olds, D. L., & others. (2007). Effects of nurse home visiting on maternal and child functioning: Age-9 follow-up of a randomized trial. *Pediatrics, 120,* e832–e845.

Olson, B. H., Haider, S. J., Vangjel, L., Bolton, T. A., & Gold, J. G. (2009b, in press). A quasi-experimental evaluation of a breastfeeding support program for low income women in Michigan. *Maternal and Child Health Journal.*

Olson, B. H., Horodynski, M. A., Brophy-Herb, H., & Iwanski, K. C. (2009a, in press). Health professionals' perspectives on the infant feeding practices of low income mothers. *Maternal and Child Health Journal.*

Olson, D., Sikka, R. S., Hayman, J., Novak, M., & Stavig, C. (2009). Exercise in pregnancy. *Current Sports Medicine Reports, 8,* 147–153.

Olson, H. C., King, S., & Jirikowic, T. (2008). Fetal alcohol spectrum disorders. In M. M. Haith & J. B. Benson (Eds.), *Encyclopedia of infant and early childhood development.* Thousand Oaks, CA: Sage.

Olson, L. M., Tang, S. F., & Newacheck, P. W. (2005). Children in the United States with discontinuous health insurance coverage. *New England Journal of Medicine, 353,* 418–419.

Olweus, D. (2003). Prevalence estimation of school bullying with the Olweus bully/victim questionnaire. *Aggressive Behavior, 29* (3), 239–269.

Ong, A. D. & Fuller-Rowell, T. Longitudinal methods. In S. J. Lopez & A. Beauchamp (Eds.). *The Encyclopedia of positive psychology.* Malden, MA: Blackwell.

Ono, M. Y., Farzin, F., & Hagerman, R. J. (2008). Fragile X syndrome. In M. M. Haith & J. B. Benson (Eds.), *Encyclopedia of infant and early childhood development.* Oxford, UK: Elsevier.

Oostdam, N., van Poppel, M. N., Eekohff, E. M., Wouters, M. G., & van Mechelen, W. (2009, in press). Design of FitFor2 study: The effects of an exercise program on insulin sensitivity and plasma glucose levels in pregnant women at high risk for gestational diabetes. *BMC Pregnancy and Childbirth, 9.*

Orbe, M. P. (2008). Theorizing multidimensional identity negotiation: Reflections on the lived experiences of first-generation college students. *New Directions for Child and Adolescent Development, 120,* 81–95.

Orecchia, R., Lucignani, G., & Tosi, G. (2008). Prenatal irradiation and pregnancy: The effects of diagnostic imaging and radiation therapy. *Recent Results in Cancer Research, 178,* 3–20.

Oscarsson, M. E., Amer-Wahlin, I., Rydhstroem, H., & Kallen, K. (2006). Outcome in obstetric care related to oxytocin use: A population-based study. *Acta Obstetricia et Gynecologica Scandinavica, 85,* 1094–1098.

Osofsky, J. D. (Ed.). (2007). *Young children and trauma.* New York: Guilford.

Ostchega, Y., Carroll, M., Prineas, R. J., McDowell, M. A., Louis, T., & Tilert, T. (2009). Trends of elevated blood pressure among children and adolescents: Data from the National Health and Nutrition Examination Survey, l988–2006. *American Journal of Hypertension, 22,* 59–67.

Oswiecimska, J. M., & others. (2008). Growth hormone therapy in boy with panhypopituitarism may induce pilomatricoma recurrence: Case report. *Neuroendocrinology Letters, 29,* 51–54.

Otto, B. W. (2010). *Language development in early childhood* (3rd ed.). Upper Saddle River, NJ: Prentice Hall.

Oude, L. H., Baur, L., Jansen, H., Shrewsbury, V. A., O'Malley, C., Stolk, R. P., & Summerbell, C. D. (2009). Interventions for treating obesity in children. *Cochrane Database of Systematic Reviews, 1,* CD001872.

Oxford, M. L., Gilchrist, L. D., Gillmore, M. R., & Lohr, M. J. (2006). Predicting variation in the life course of adolescent mothers as they enter adulthood. *Journal of Adolescent Health, 39,* 20–36.

Ozer, E. M., & Irwin, C. (2009). Adolescent and youth adult health: From basic health status to clinical interventions. In R. M. Lerner & L. Steinberg (Eds.), *Handbook of adolescent psychology* (3rd ed.). New York: Wiley.

P

Pakpreo, P., Ryan, S., Auinger, P., & Aten, M. (2005). The association between parental lifestyle behaviors and adolescent knowledge, attitudes, intentions, and nutritional and physical activity behaviors. *Journal of Adolescent Health, 34,* 129–130.

Palfrey, J., Sacco, D., Boyd, D., & DeBonis, L. (2009). *Enhancing child safety and online technologies.* Cambridge, MA: Berkman Center for Internet & Society.

Palmer, S. E. (2004). Custody and access issues with children whose parents are separated or divorced. *Canadian Journal of Community Mental Health, 4* (Suppl.), 25–38.

Palomaki, G. E., Steinort, K., Knight, G. J., & Haddow, J. E. (2006). Comparing three screening strategies for combining first- and second-trimester Down syndrome markers. *Obstetrics and Gynecology, 107,* 1170.

Paloutzian, R. F. (2000). *Invitation to the psychology of religion* (3rd ed.). Needham Heights, MA: Allyn & Bacon.

Paluck, E. L., & Green, D. P. (2009). Prejudice reduction: What works? A review and assessment of research and practice. *Annual Review of Psychology* (Vol. 60). Palo Alto, CA: Annual Reviews.

Pan, B. A. (2008). Unpublished review of J. W. Santrock's *Life-span development,* 12th ed. (New York: McGraw-Hill).

Pan, B. A., Rowe, M. L., Singer, J. D., & Snow, C. E. (2005). Maternal correlates of growth in toddler vocabulary production in low-income families. *Child Development, 76,* 763–782.

Pan, B. A., & Uccelli, P. (2009). Semantic development. In J. Berko Gleason & N. Ratner (Eds.), *The development of language* (7th ed.). Boston: Allyn & Bacon.

Pang, V. O. (2005). *Multicultural education* (3rd ed.). New York: McGraw-Hill.

Panneton, R., McIlreavy, M., & Bhullar, N. (2008). Preverbal development and speech production. In M. M. Haith & J. B. Benson (Eds.), *Encyclopedia of infant and early childhood development.* Oxford, UK: Elsevier

Parens, E., & Johnston, J. (2009). Fact, values, and attention-deficit hyperactivity disorder (ADHD): An update on the controversies. *Child and Adolescent Psychiatry and Mental Health, 3,* 1.

Parente, M. E., & Mahoney, J. L. (2009). Activity participation in childhood and adolescence. Invited chapter to appear in D. Carr (Ed.), *Encyclopedia of the life course and human development.* Farmington Hills, MI: Gale Research.

Park, M. J., Brindis, C. D., Chang, F., & Irwin, C. E. (2008). A midcourse review of the healthy people 2010: 21 critical health objectives for adolescents and young adults. *Journal of Adolescent Health, 42,* 329–334.

Park, M. J., Mulye, T. P., Adams, S. H., Brindis, C. D., & Irwin, C. E. (2006). The health status of young adults in the United States. *Journal of Adolescent Health, 39*, 305–317.

Parkay, F. W., & Stanford, B. H. (2010). *Becoming a teacher* (8th ed.). Upper Saddle River, NJ: Prentice Hall.

Parke, R. D. (2004). Development in the family. *Annual Review of Psychology* (Vol. 55). Palo Alto, CA: Annual Reviews.

Parke, R. D., & Buriel, R. (2006). Socialization in the family: Ethnic and ecological perspectives. In W. Damon & R. Lerner (Eds.), *Handbook of child psychology* (6th ed.). New York: Wiley.

Parke, R. D., Leidy, M. S., Schofield, T. J., Miller, M. A., & Morris, K. L. (2008). Socialization. In M. M. Haith & J. B. Benson (Eds.), *Encyclopedia of infant and early childhood development.* Oxford, UK: Elsevier.

Parkes, A., Wight, D., Henderson, M., Stephenson, J., & Strange, V. (2009). Contraceptive method at first intercourse and subsequent pregnancy risk: Findings from a secondary analysis of 16-year-old girls from the RIPPLE and SHARE studies. *Journal of Adolescent Health, 44*, 55–63.

Parlade, M. V., Messinger, D. S., Delgado, C. D., Kaiser, M. Y., Van Hecke, A. V., Mundy, P. C. (2009). Anticipatory smiling: Linking early affective communication and social outcome. *Infant Behavior and Development, 32*, 33–43.

Parten, M. (1932). Social play among preschool children. *Journal of Abnormal Social Psychology, 27*, 243–269.

Partnership for a Drug-Free America. (2005). *Partnership Attitude Tracking Study.* New York: Author.

Pascalls, O., & Kelly, D. J. (2008). Face processing. In M. M. Haith & J. B. Benson (Eds.), *Encyclopedia of infant and early childhood development.* Oxford, UK: Elsevier.

Pasch, K. E., Nelson, M. C., Lytle, L. A., Moe, S. G., & Perry, C. L. (2008). Adoption of risk-related factors through early adolescence: Associations with weight gain status and implications of causal mechanisms. *Journal of Adolescent Health, 43*, 387–393.

Pasley, K., & Moorefield, B. S. (2004). Stepfamilies. In M. Coleman & L. Ganong (Eds.), *Handbook of contemporary families.* Thousand Oaks, CA: Sage.

Pasquini, E. S., Corriveau, K. H., Koenig, M., & Harris, P. L. (2007). Preschoolers monitor the relative accuracy of informants. *Developmental Psychology, 43*, 1216–1226.

Pate, R. R., Pfeiffer, K. A., Trost, S. G., Ziegler, P., & Dowda, M. (2004). Physical activity among children attending preschools. *Pediatrics, 114*, 1258–1263.

Patel, E. A., Cooper, H., & Robinson, J. C. (2008). The effects of choice on intrinsic motivation and related outcomes: A meta-analysis of research findings. *Psychological Bulletin, 134*, 270–300.

Patel, S. G., Salahuddin, N. M., & O'Brien, M. (2008). Career decision-making self-efficacy of Vietnamese adolescents: The role of acculturation, social support, socioeconomic status, and racism. *Journal of Career Development, 34*, 218–240.

Patel, S. R. & Hu, F. B. (2008). Short sleep duration and weight gain: A systematic review. *Obesity, 16*, 643–653.

Patrick, H., Ryan, A. M., & Kaplan, A. (2007). Early adolescents' perceptions of the classroom social environment, motivational beliefs, and engagement. *Journal of Educational Psychology, 99*, 83–98.

Patrick, M. E., Abar, C., & Maggs, J. L. (2009). Drinking, adolescent. In D. Carr (Ed.), *Encyclopedia of the life course and human development.* Boston: Gale Cengage.

Patterson, C. J. (2009). Lesbian and gay parents and their children: A social science perspective. *Nebraska Symposium on Motivation, 54*, 142–182.

Patterson, K., & Wright, A. E. (1990, Winter). The speech, language, or hearing-impaired child: At-risk academically. *Childhood Education, 67*, 91–95.

Paulhus, D. L. (2008). Birth order. In M. M. Haith & J. B. Benson (Eds.), *Encyclopedia of infant and early childhood development.* Oxford, UK: Elsevier.

Pauli-Pott, U., Friedl, S., Hinney, A., & Hebebrand, J. (2009). Serotonin transporter gene polymorphism (*5-HTTLPR*), environmental conditions, and developing negative emotionality and fear in early childhood. *Journal of Neural Transmission, 116*, 503–512.

Paulson, J. F., Dauber, S., & Leiferman, J. A. (2006). Individual and combined effects of postpartum depression in mothers and fathers on parenting behavior. *Pediatrics, 118*, 659–668.

Paus, T. (2009). Brain development. In R. M. Lerner & L. Steinberg (Eds.), *Handbook of adolescent psychology* (3rd ed.). New York: Wiley.

Paus, T., Toro, R., Leonard, G., Lerner, J. V., Lerner, R. M., Perron, M., Pike, G. B., Richer, L., Steinberg, L., Veillete, S., & Pausova, Z. (2008). Morphological properties of the action-observation cortical network in adolescents with low and high resistance to peer influence. *Social Neuroscience, 3*, 303–316.

Pavlov, I. P. (1927). In G. V. Anrep (Trans.), *Conditioned reflexes.* London: Oxford University Press.

Paxson, C., Donahue, E., Orleans, C. T., & Grisso, J. A. (2006). Introducing the issue. *The Future of Children, 16*, 3–17.

Payne, C., & Bachevalier, J. (2009). Neuroanatomy and the developing brain. In M. de Haan & M. R. Gunnar (Eds.), *Handbook of developmental social neuroscience.* New York: Guilford.

Paz, M. S., & others. (2009). Maternal depression and neurobehavior in newborns prenatally exposed to methamphetamine. *Neurotoxicology and Teratology, 31*, 177–182.

Pearlstein, T., Howard, M., Salisbury, A., & Zlotnick, C. (2009). Postpartum depression. *American Journal of Obstetrics and Gynecology, 200*, 357–364.

Pearson, N., Biddle, S. J., & Gorely, T. (2008). Family correlates of fruit and vegetable consumption in children and adolescents: A systematic review. *Public Health Nutrition, 12*, 267–283.

Peck, S. C., Roeser, R. W., Zarrett, N., & Eccles, J. S. (2008). Exploring the roles of extracurricular activity quantity and quality in the educational resilience of vulnerable adolescents: Variable- and pattern-centered approaches. *Journal of Social Issues, 64, 1*, 135–155.

Pederson, D. R., & Moran, G. (1996). Expressions of the attachment relationship outside of the Strange Situation. *Child Development, 67*, 915–927.

Pedroso, F. S. (2008). Reflexes. In M. M. Haith & J. B. Benson (Eds.), *Encyclopedia of infant and early childhood development.* Oxford, UK: Elsevier.

Pei, J. R., Rinaldi, C. M., Rasmussen, C., Massey, V., & Massey, D. (2008). Memory patterns of acquisition and retention of verbal and nonverbal information in children with fetal alcohol spectrum disorders. *Canadian Journal of Clinical Pharmacology, 15*, e44–e56.

Pelayo, R., Owens, J., Mindell, J., & Sheldon, S. (2006). Bed sharing with unimpaired parents is not an important risk for sudden infant death syndrome: To the editor, *Pediatrics, 117*, 993–994.

Pena, E., & Bedore, J. A. (2009). Bilingualism. In R. G. Schwartz (Ed.), *Handbook of child language disorders.* Clifton, NJ: Psychology Press.

Penagarikano, O., Mulle, J. G., & Warren, S. T. (2007, in press). The pathophysiology of fragile X syndrome. *Annual Review of Genomics and Human Genetics, 8*, 109–129.

Pennington, B. F., & others. (2009). Gene × environment interactions in reading disability and attention-deficit/hyperactivity disorder. *Developmental Psychology, 45*, 77–89.

Perez-Febles, A. M. (1992). *Acculturation and interactional styles of Latina mothers and their infants.* Unpublished honors thesis, Brown University, Providence, RI.

Perner, J., Stummer, S., Sprung, M., & Doherty, M. (2002). Theory of mind finds its Piagetian perspective: Why alternative naming comes with understanding belief. *Cognitive Development, 17*, 1451–1472.

Peskin, H. (1967). Pubertal onset and ego functioning. *Journal of Abnormal Psychology, 72*, 1–15.

Peterson, C. C. (2005). Mind and body: Concepts of human cognition, physiology and false belief in children with autism or typical development. *Journal of Autism and Developmental Disorders, 35*, 487–497.

Peterson, C. C., Garnett, M., Kelly, A., & Attwood, T. (2009). Everyday social and conversation applications of theory-of-mind understanding by children with autism-spectrum disorders or typical development. *European Child and Adolescent Psychiatry, 18,* 105–115.

Peterson, M. B., Wang, Q., & Willems, P. J. (2008). Sex-linked deafness. *Clinical Genetics, 73,* 14–23.

Petrini, J. R., Dias, T., McCormick, M. C., Massolo, M. L, Green, N. S., & Escobar, G. J. (2009). Increased risk of adverse neurological development for later preterm infants. *Journal of Pediatrics, 154,* 169–176.

Pfeifer, M., Goldsmith, H. H., Davidson, R. J., & Rickman, M. (2002). Continuity and change in inhibited and uninhibited children. *Child Development, 73,* 1474–1485.

Philipsen, N. M., Johnson, A. D., & Brooks-Gunn, J. (2009, in press). Poverty, effects on social and emotional development. *International encyclopedia of education* (3rd ed.). St. Louis, MO: Elsevier.

Phillips, J., Sharpe, L., Matthey, S., & Charles, M. (2009, in press). Subtypes of postnatal depression? A comparison of women with recurrent and de novo postnatal depression. *Journal of Affective Disorders.*

Phinney, J. S. (2006). Ethnic identity exploration in emerging adulthood. In J. J. Arnett & J. L. Tanner (Eds.), *Emerging adults in America.* Washington, DC: American Psychological Association.

Phinney, J. S. (2008). Bridging identities and disciplines: Advances and challenges in undemanding multiple identities. *New Directions for Child and Adolescent Development, 120,* 97–109.

Phinney, J. S., & Ong, A. D. (2007). Conceptualization and measurement of ethnic identity. Current status and future directions. *Journal of Counseling Psychology, 54,* 271–281.

Piaget, J. (1932). *The moral judgment of the child.* New York: Harcourt Brace Jovanovich.

Piaget, J. (1952). *The origins of intelligence in children.* (M. Cook, Trans.). New York: International Universities Press.

Piaget, J. (1954). *The construction of reality in the child.* New York: Basic Books.

Piaget, J. (1962). *Play, dreams, and imitation.* New York: W. W. Norton.

Piaget, J., & Inhelder, B. (1969). *The child's conception of space* (F. J. Langdon & J. L. Lunger, Trans.). New York: W. W. Norton.

Piko, B. F., & Fitzpatrick, K. M. (2004). Substance use, religiosity, and other protective factors among Hungarian adolescents. *Addictive Behavior, 29,* 1095–1107.

Pinette, M., Wax, J., & Wilson, E. (2004). The risks of underwater birth. *American Journal of Obstetrics and Gynecology, 190,* 1211–15.

Ping, H., & Hagopian, W. (2006). Environmental factor in the development of type 1 diabetes. *Reviews in Endocrine and Metabolic Disorders, 7,* 149–162.

Pinkhardt, E. H., Kassubek, J., Brummer, D., Koeich, M., Ludolph, A. C., Fegert, J. M.,

& Ludolph, A. G. (2009, in press). Intensified testing for attention deficit hyperactivity disorder (ADHD) in girls should reduce depression and smoking in adult females and the prevalence of ADHD in the longterm. *Medical Hypotheses.*

Pinto, K. M., & Coltrane, S. (2009). Divisions of labor in Mexican origin and Anglo families: Structure and culture. *Sex roles, 60,* 482–495.

Pipe, M. (2008). Children as eye witnesses: Memory in the forensic context. In M. Courage & N. Cowan (Eds.), *The development of memory in infancy and childhood.* Philadelphia: Psychology Press.

Pitkanen, T., Lyyra, A. L., & Pulkkinen, L. (2005). Age of onset of drinking and the use of alcohol in adulthood: A follow-up study from age 8–42 for females and males. *Addiction, 100,* 652–661.

Pliszka, S. R. (2007). Pharmacologic treatment of attention deficit hyperactivity disorder: Efficacy, safety, and mechanisms of action. *Neuropsychology Review, 17,* 61–72.

Plomin, R. (2004). Genetics and developmental psychology. *Merrill-Palmer Quarterly, 50,* 341–352.

Plomin, R., DeFries, J. C., & Fulker, D. W. (2007). *Nature and nurture during infancy and early childhood.* New York: Cambridge University Press.

Plomin, R., DeFries, J. C., McClearn, G. E., & McGuffin, P. (2009). *Behavioral genetics* (5th ed.). New York: W.H. Freeman.

Plomin, R., DeFries, J. C., McClearn, G. E., & McGuffin. P. (2009). *Biological psychology and neuroscience* (5th ed.) New York: Worth.

Pluess, M., & Belsky, J. (2009). Differential susceptibility to rearing experience: The case of childcare. *Journal of Child Psychology and Psychiatry, 50,* 396–404.

Pollack, W. (1999). *Real boys.* New York: Owl Books.

Pollard, I. (2007). Neuropharmacology of drugs and alcohol in mother and fetus. *Seminars in Fetal and Neonatal Medicine, 12,* 106–113.

Pollitt, E. P., Gorman, K. S., Engle, P. L., Martorell, R., & Rivera, J. (1993). Early supplementary feeding and cognition. *Monographs of the Society for Research in Child Development, 58* (7, Serial No. 235).

Poole, D. A., & Lindsay, D. S. (1995). Interviewing preschoolers: Effects of nonsuggestive techniques, parental coaching, and leading questions on reports of nonexperienced events. *Journal of Experimental Child Psychology. 60,* 129–154.

Porath, A. J., & Fried, P. A. (2005). Effects of prenatal cigarette and marijuana exposure on drug use among offspring. *Neurotoxicology and Teratology, 27,* 267–277.

Posada, G. (2008). Attachment. In M. M. & Haith & J. B. Benson (Eds.), *Encyclopedia of infant and early childhood development.* Oxford, UK: Elsevier.

Posner, M. I. (2003). Imaging a science of mind. *Trends in Cognitive Science, 7,* 450–453.

Posner, M. I., & Rothbart, M. K. (2007). Research on attention networks as a model for

the integration of psychological sciences. *Annual Review of Psychology, 58,* 1–23.

Potard, C., Courtois, R., & Rusch, E. (2008). The influence of peers on risky behavior during adolescence. *European Journal of Contraception and Reproductive Health Care, 13,* 264–270.

Pott, W., Albayrak, O., Hebebrand, J., & Pauli-Pott, U. (2009). Treating childhood obesity: Family background variables and the child's success in a weight-controlled intervention. *International Journal of Eating Disorders, 42,* 284–289.

Poulin-Dobois, D., & Graham, S. A. (2007). Cognitive processes in early word learning. In E. Hoff & M. Shatz (eds.), *Blackwell of language development.* Malden, MA: Blackwell.

Poulin, F., & Pedersen, S. (2007). Developmental changes in gender composition of friendship networks in adolescent girls and boys. *Developmental Psychology, 43,* 1484–1496.

Powell, D. R. (2006). Families and early childhood interventions. In W. Damon & R. Lerner (Eds.), *Handbook of child psychology* (6th ed.). New York: Wiley.

Pratt, C., & Bryant, P. E. (1990). Young children understand that looking leads to knowing (so long as they are looking in a single barrel). *Child Development, 61,* 973–982.

Pratt, M. W., Norris, J. E., Hebblethwaite, S., & Arnold, M. O. (2008). Intergenerational transmission of values: Family generativity and adolescents' narratives of parent and grandparent value teaching. *Journal of Personality, 76,* 171–198.

Pressley, M. (2003). Psychology of literacy and literacy instruction. In I. B. Weiner (Ed.), *Handbook of psychology* (Vol. 7). New York: Wiley.

Pressley, M. (2007). An interview with Michael Pressley by Terri Flowerday and Michael Shaughnessy. *Educational Psychology Review, 19,* 1–12.

Pressley, M., Allington, R., Wharton-McDonald, R., Block, C. C., & Morrow, L. M. (2001). *Learning to read: Lessons from exemplary first grades.* New York: Guilford.

Pressley, M., Cariligia-Bull, T., Deane, S., & Schneider, W. (1987). Short-term memory, verbal competence, and age as predictors of imagery instructional effectiveness. *Journal of Experimental Child Psychology, 43,* 194–211.

Pressley, M., Dolezal, S. E., Raphael, L. M., Welsh, L. M., Bongner, K., & Roehring, A. D. (2003). *Motivating primary-grades teachers.* New York: Guilford.

Pressley, M., & Harris, K. R. (2006). Cognitive strategies instruction. In P. A. Alexander & P. H. Winne (Eds.), *Handbook of educational psychology* (2nd ed.). Mahwah, NJ: Erlbaum.

Pressley, M., & Hilden, K. (2006). Cognitive strategies. In W. Damon & R. Lerner (Eds.), *Handbook of child psychology* (6th ed.). New York: Wiley.

Pressley, M., & McCormick, C. B. (2007). *Child and adolescent development for educators.* New York: Guilford.

Pressley, M., Mohan, L., Raphael, L. M., & Fingeret, L. (2007). How does Bennett Woods Elementary School produce such high reading and writing achievement? *Journal of Educational Psychology, 99*, 221–240.

Pressley, M., Raphael, L. Gallagher, D., & DiBella, J. (2004). Providence–St. Mel School: How a school that works for African-American students works. *Journal of Educational Psychology, 96*, 216–235.

Presson, J. C. & Jenner, J. C. (2008) *Biology*. New York: McGraw-Hill.

Preston, A. M., Rodriguez, C., Rivera, C. E., & Sahai, H. (2003). Influence of environmental tobacco smoke on vitamin C status in children. *American Journal of Clinical Nutrition, 77*, 167–172.

Prinstein, M. J. (2007). Moderators of peer contagion: A longitudinal examination of depression socialization between adolescents and their best friends. *Journal of Clinical Child and Adolescent Psychology, 36*, 159–170.

Prinstein, M. J., Boivan, M., & Bukowski, W. M. (2009). Peer reputations and psychological adjustment. In K. H. Rubin, W. M. Bukowski, & B. Laursen (Eds.), *Handbook of peer interactions, relationships, and groups*. New York: Guilford.

Prinstein, M. J., & Dodge, K. A. (2008). Current issues in peer influence. In M. J. Prinstein & K. A. Dodge (Eds.), *Understanding peer influence in children and adolescents*. New York: Guilford.

Prinstein, M. J., Rancourt, D., Guerry, J. D., & Browne, C. B. (2009). Peer reputations and psychological adjustment. In K. H. Rubin, W. M. Bukowksi, & B. Laursen (Eds.), *Handbook of peer interactions, relationships, and groups*. New York: Guilford.

Prinz, R. J., Sanders, M. R., Shapiro, C. J., Witaker, D. J., Lutzker, J. R. (2009). Population-based prevention of child maltreatment: The U.S. Triple P System Population Trial. *Prevention Science, 10*, 1–12.

Pruett, M. K., & Barker, R. (2009a, in press). Children of divorce: New trends and ongoing dilemmas. In J. Bray (Ed.), *Family handbook of psychology*. Washington DC: American Psychological Association.

Pruett, M. K., & Barker, R. (2009b, in press). Influencing co-parenting effectiveness after divorce: What works and how it works. In M. Schulz, P. Kerig, M. K. Pruett, & R. Parke (Eds.), *Feathering the nest: Couple relationships, couples interventions and children's development*. Washington DC: American Psychological Association.

Pryor, J. H. Y., Hurtado, S., DeAngelo, L., Sharkness, J., Romero, L. C., & Korn, W. S., & Tran, S. (2008). *The American freshman: National norms for fall, 2008*. Los Angeles: Higher Education Research Institute, UCLA.

Pueschel, S. M., Scola, P. S., Weidenman, L. E., & Bernier, J. C. (1995). *The special child*. Baltimore: Paul H. Brookes.

Pujol, J., Lopez-Sala, A., Sebastian-Galles, N., Deus, J., Cardoner, N., Soriano-Mas, C.,

Moreno, A., & Sans, A. (2004). Delayed myelination in children with developmental delay detected by volumetric MRI. *Neuroimage, 22*, 897–903.

Pungello, E. P., Iruka, I. U., Dotterer, A. M., Mills-Koonce, R., & Reznick, J. S. (2009). The effects of socioeconomic status, race, and parenting on language development in early childhood. *Developmental Psychology, 45*, 544–557.

Putallaz, M., Grimes, C. L., Foster, K. J., Kupersmidt, J. B., Clie, J. D., & Dearing, K. (2007). Overt and relational aggression and victimization: Multiple perspectives within the school setting. *Journal of School Psychology, 45*, 523–547.

Putnam, S. P., Sanson, A. V., & Rothbart, M. K. (2002). Child temperament and parenting. In M. H. Bornstein (Ed.), *Handbook of parenting* (2nd ed.). Mahwah, NJ: Erlbaum.

Q

Quadrelli, R., Quadrelli, A., Mechoso, B., Laufer, M., Jaumandreu, C., & Vaglio, A. (2007). Parental decisions to abort or continue a pregnancy following prenatal diagnosis of chromosomal abnormalities in a setting where termination of pregnancy is not legally available. *Prenatal Diagnosis, 27*, 228–232.

Quinn, P. C. (2009). Concepts are not just for objects: Categorization of spatial relation information by infants. In D. H. Rakison & L. M. Oakes (Eds.), *Early category and concept development*. New York: Oxford University Press.

Quinn, P. C., & Bhatt, R. S. (2009, in press). Transfer and scaffolding of perceptual grouping occurs across organizing principles in 3- to 7-month-old infants. *Psychological Science*.

Quinn, P. C., Doran, M. M., Reiss, J. E., & Hoffman, J. E. (2009). Time course of visual attention in infant categorization of cats versus dogs: Evidence for a head bias as revealed through eye tracking. *Child Development, 80*, 151–161.

Quinn, P. C., & Eimas, P. D. (1996). Perceptual cues that permit categorical differentiation of animal species by infants. *Journal of Experimental Child Psychology, 63*, 189–211.

Quinn, P. C., Lee, K., Pascalis, O., & Slater, A. M. (2009, in press). Perceptual development: Face perception. In E. B. Goldstein (Ed.), *Encyclopedia of perception*. Thousand Oaks, CA: Sage.

R

Raabe, A., & Muller, W. U. (2008). Radiation exposure during pregnancy. *Neurosurgery Review, 31*, 351–352.

Raffaelli, M., & Ontai, L. L. (2004). Gender socialization in Latino/a families: Results from two retrospective studies. *Sex Roles, 50*, 287–299.

Rafla, N., Nair, M. S., & Kumar, S. (2008). Exercise in pregnancy. In J. Studd, S. L. Tan, &

F. A. Cherenak (Eds.), *Progress in obstetrics and gynecology*. Oxford, UK: Elsevier.

Raikes, H. Pan, B. A., Luze, G., Tamis-LeMonda, C. S., Brooks-Gunn, J., Constantine, J., Tarullo, L. B., Raikes, H. A., & Rodriquez, E. T. (2006). Mother-child bookreading in low-income families: Correlates and outcomes during the first three years of life. *Child Development, 77*, 924–953.

Raizada, R. S., Richards, T. L., McItzoff, A. N., & Kuhl, P. K. (2008). Socioeconomic status predicts hemispheric specialisation of the left inferior frontal gyrus in young children. *Neuroimage, 40*, 1392–1401.

Rajendran, G., & Mitchell, P. (2007). Cognitive theories of autism. *Developmental Review, 27*, 224–260.

Ram, K. T., Bobby, P., Hailpern, S. M., Lo, J. C., Schocken, M., Skurnick, J., & Santoro, N. (2008). Duration of lactation is associated with lower prevalence of the metabolic syndrome in midlife—SWAN, the study of women's health across the nation. *American Journal of Obstetrics and Gynecology, 198*, el–e6.

Ramchandani, P. G., Sein, A., O'Connor, T. G., Heron, J., Murray, L., & Evans, J. (2008). Depression in men in the postnatal period and later psychopathology: A population cohort study. *Journal of the American Academy of Child and Adolescent Psychiatry, 47*, 390–398.

Ramey, C. T., & Campbell, P. A. (1984). Preventive education for high-risk children: Cognitive consequences of the Carolina Abecedarian Project. *American Journal of Mental Deficiency, 88*, 515–523.

Ramey, C. T., & Ramey, S. L. (2004). Early learning and school readiness. Can early intervention make a difference? *Merrill-Palmer Quarterly, 50*, 471–491.

Ramey, C. T., Ramey, S. L., & Lanzi, R. G. (1998). Early prevention and early experience. *American Psychologist, 53*, 109–120.

Ramey, C. T., Ramey, S. L., & Lanzi, R. G. (2001). Intelligence and experience. In R. J. Sternberg & E. L. Grigorenko (Eds.), *Environmental effects on cognitive abilities*. Mahwah, NJ: Erlbaum.

Ramey, C. T., Ramey, S. L., & Lanzi, R. G. (2006) Children's health and education. In W. Damon & R. Lerner (Eds.), *Handbook of child psychology* (6th ed.). New York: Wiley.

Ramey, S. L. (2005). Human developmental science serving children and families: Contributions of the NICHD study of early child care. In NICHD Early Child Care Network (Eds.), *Child care and development*. New York: Guilford.

Ramey, S. L., & Ramey, C. T. (1999). *Going to school: How to help your child succeed*. New York: Goddard.

Ramsay, D. S. (1980). Onset of unimanual handedness in infants. *Infant Behavior and Development, 3*, 377–385.

Ramsey-Rennels, J. L., & Langlois, J. H. (2007). How infants perceive and process faces. In A. Slater & M. Lewis (Eds.), *Introduction to infant development* (2nd ed.). Malden, MA: Blackwell.

Ratcliffe, S. D. (2008). *Family medicine obstetrics* (3rd ed.). Oxford, UK: Elsevier.

Ratner, N. B. (2009). A typical language development. In J. Berko Gleason & N. B. Ratner (Eds.), *The development of language* (7th ed.). Boston: Allyn & Bacon.

Ream, G. L., & Savin-William S. R. (2003). Religious development in adolescence. In G. Adams & M. Berzonsky (Eds.), *Blackwell handbook of adolescence*. Malden, MA: Blackwell.

Reddy, U. M., Wapner, R. J., Rebar, R. W., & Tasca, R. J. (2007). Infertility, assisted reproductive technology, and adverse pregnancy outcomes: executive summary of a National Institute of Child Health and Human Development workshop. *Obstetrics and Gynecology, 109*, 967–977.

Reeb, B. C., Fox, N. A., Nelson, C. A., & Zeanah, C. H. (2009). The effects of early institutionalization on social behavior and underlying neural correlates. In M. de Haan & M. Gunnar (Eds.), *Handbook of developmental social neuroscience*. Maldon, MA: Blackwell.

Regalado, M., Sareen, H., Inkelas, M., Wissow L. S., & Halfon, N. (2004). Parents' discipline of young children: Results from the National Survey of Early Childhood Health. *Pediatrics, 113*, 1952–1958.

Regev, R. H., Lusky, A., Dolfin, T., Litmanovitz, I., Arnon, S., Reichman, B., & the Israel Neonatal Network. (2003). Excess mortality and morbidity among small-for-gestational-age premature infants: A population based study. *Journal of Pediatrics, 143*, 186–191.

Reid, G., Fawcett, A., Manis, F., & Siegel, L. (2009). *The SAGE handbook of dyslexia*. Thousand Oaks, CA: Sage.

Reid, P. T., & Zalk, S. R. (2001). Academic environments: Gender and ethnicity in U.S. higher education. In J. Worrell (Ed.), *Encyclopedia of women and gender*. San Diego: Academic Press.

Remulla, A., & Guilleminault, C. (2004). Somnambulism (sleepwalking). *Expert Opinions in Pharmacotherapy, 5*, 2069–2074.

Renner, P., Grofer Klinger, L., & Klinger, M. R. (2006). Exogenous and endogenous attention orienting in autism spectrum disorders. *Child Neuropsychology, 12*, 361–382.

Repacholi, B. M., & Gopnik, A. (1997). Early reasoning about desires: Evidence from 14- and 18-month-olds. *Developmental Psychology, 33*, 12–21.

Reutzel, D. R., & Cooter, R. B. (2008). *Teaching children to read* (5th ed.). Upper Saddle River, NJ: Prentice Hall.

Reyna, V. F. (2004). How people make decisions that involve risk: A dual-process approach. *Current Directions in Psychological Science, 13*, 60–66.

Reyna, V. F., & Brainerd, C. J. (1995). Fuzzy-trace theory: An interim analysis. *Learning and Individual Differences, 7*, 1–75.

Reyna, V. F., & Farley, F. (2006). Risk and rationality in adolescent decision-making: Implications for theory, practice, and public policy. *Psychological Science in the Public Interest, 7*, 1–44.

Reyna, V. F., & Rivers, S. E. (2008). Current theories and rational decision making. *Developmental Review, 28*, 1–11.

Richardson, G. A., Goldschmidt, L., & Larkby, C. (2008). Effects of prenatal cocaine exposure on growth: A longitudinal analysis. *Pediatrics, 120*, e1017–e1027.

Richardson, G. A., Goldschmidt, L., & Willford, J. (2008). The effects of prenatal cocaine use on infant development. *Neurotoxicology and Teratology, 30*, 96–106.

Richardson, G. A., Ryan, C., Willford, J., Day, N. L., & Goldschmidt, L. (2002). Prenatal alcohol and marijuana exposure: Effects on neuropsychological outcomes at 10 years. *Neurotoxicology and Teratology, 24*, 309–320.

Richmond, E. J., & Rogal., A. D. (2007). Male pubertal development and the role of androgen therapy. *Nature Clinical Practice: Endocrinology and Metabolism, 3*, 338–344.

Rickards, T., Moger, S., & Runco, M. (Eds.). (2009). *The Routledge companion to creativity*. Milton Park, UK: Routledge.

Riddle, D. B., & Prinz, R. (1984, August). *Sugar consumption in young children*. Paper presented at the meeting of the American Psychological Association, Toronto.

Rideout, V., Roberts, D. F., & Foehr, U. G. (2005). *Generation M: Media in the lives of 8–18-year-old*. San Francisco: Kaiser Family Foundation.

Rigaud, D., Verges, B., Colas-Linhart, N., Petiet, A., Moukkaddem, M., Van Wymelbeke, V., & Brondel, L. (2007). Hormonal and psychological factors linked to the increased thermic effect of food in malnourished fasting anorexia nervosa. *Journal of Clinical Endocrinology and Metabolism, 92*, 1623–1629.

Rink, J. E. (2009). *Designing the physical education curriculum*. New York: McGraw-Hill.

Rittenberg, C., Newman, R. B., Istwn, N. B., Rhea, D. J., & Stanziano, G. J. (2009). Preterm birth prevention by 7-alpha-hydroxyprogesterone caproate vs. daily nursing surveillance. *Journal of Reproductive Medicine, 54*, 47–52.

Rivas-Drake, D., Hughes, D., & Way, N. (2009). Public ethnic regard and perceived socioeconomic stratification: Associations with well-being among Dominican and Black American youth. *Journal of Early Adolescence, 29*, 122–141.

Rivers, S. E., Reyna, V. F., & Mills, B. (2008). Risk taking under the influence: A fuzzy-trace theory of emotion in adolescence. *Developmental Review, 28*, 107–144.

Rizzo, M. S. (1999, May 8). Genetic counseling combines science with a human touch. *Kansas City Star*, p. 3.

Robbins, G., Powers, D., & Burgess, S. (2008). *A fit way of life*. New York: McGraw-Hill.

Roberts, D. F., & Foehr, U. G. (2008). Trends in media use. *The Future of Children, 18* (1), 11–37.

Roberts, D. F., Henriksen, L., & Foehr, U. G. (2004). Adolescents and the media. In R. Lerner & L. Steinberg (Eds.), *Handbook of adolescent psychology* (2nd ed.), New York: Wiley.

Roberts, D. F., Henriksen, L., & Foehr, U. G. (2009). Adolescence, adolescents, and the media. In R. M. Lerner & L Steinberg (Eds.), *Handbook of adolescent psychology* (3rd ed.). New York: Wiley.

Robinson, P. D., & Van Asperen, P. (2009). Asthma in childhood. *Pediatric Clinics of North America, 56*, 191–226.

Robins, R. W., Trzesniewski, K. H., Tracey, J. L. Potter, J., & Gosling, S. D. (2002). Age differences in self-esteem from age 9 to 90. *Psychology and Aging, 17*, 423–434.

Rochlen, A. B., McKelley, R. A., Suizzo, M.-A., & Scaringi, V. (2008). Predictors of relationship satisfaction, psychological well-being, and life-satisfaction among stay-at-home fathers. *Psychology of Men and Masculinity, 9*, 17–28.

Rode, S. S., Chang, P., Fisch, R. O., & Sroufe, L. A. (1981). Attachment patterns of infants separated at birth. *Developmental Psychology, 17*, 188–191.

Rodriguez, B. L., Hines, R., & Montiel, M. (2008, in press). Mexican-American mothers of low and middle socioeconomic status: Communication behaviors and interactive strategies during shared book reading. *Language, Speech, and Hearing Services in Schools*.

Rodriguez, E. T., Tamis-LeMonda, C. S., Spellman, M. E., Pan, B. A., Riakes, H., Lugo-Gil, J., & Luze, G. (2009, in press). The formative role of home literacy experiences across the first three years of life in children from low-income families. *Journal of Applied Developmental Psychology*.

Roessner, V., Manzke, T., Becker, A., Rothenberger, A., & Bock, N. (2009). Development of 5-HT transporter density and long-term effects of methylphenidate in an animal model of ADHD. *World journal of Biological Psychiatry, 26*, 1–5.

Rogoff, B., Moore, L., Najafi, B., Dexter, A., Correa-Chavez, M., & Solis, J. (2007). Children's development of cultural repertoires through participation in everyday routines and practices. In J. E. Grusec & P. D. Hastings (Eds.), *Handbook of socialization*. New York: Guilford.

Romano, A. M., & Lothian, J. A. (2008). Promoting, protecting, and supporting normal birth: A look at the evidence. *Journal of Obstetric, Gynecological, and Neonatal Nursing, 37*, 94–104.

Romo, A., Carceller, R., & Tobajas, J. (2009). Intrauterine growth retardation (IGUR): Epidemiology and etiology. *Pediatric Endocrinology Reviews, 6* (Suppl. 3), S332–S336.

Roopnarine, J. L., & Metingdogan, A. (2006). Early childhood education research in cross-national perspective. In B. Spodek & O. N. Saracho (Eds.), *Handbook of research on the education of young children.* Mahwah, NJ: Erlbaum.

Rose, A. J., Carlson, W., & Waller, E. M. (2007). Prospective associations of co-rumination with friendship and emotional adjustment: Considering the socioemotional trade-offs of co-rumination. *Developmental Psychology, 43,* 1019–1031.

Rose, A. J., & Smith, R. L. (2009). Sex differences in peer relationships. In K. H. Rubin, W. M. Bukowski, & B. Laursen (Eds.), *Handbook of peer interactions, relationships, and groups.* New York: Guilford.

Rose, S. A. (1990). Cross-module transfer in human infants: What is being transferred? *Annals of the New York Academy of Sciences, 608,* 38–47.

Rose, S. A., Feldman, J. F., & Wallace, I. F. (1992). Infant information processing in relation to six-year cognitive outcomes. *Child Development, 63,* 1126–1141.

Rosen, L. D., Cheever, N. A., & Carrier, L. M. (2008). The association of parenting style and child age with parental limit setting and adolescent MySpace behavior. *Journal of Applied Developmental Psychology, 29,* 459–471.

Rosenblith, J. F. (1992). *In the beginning* (2nd ed.). Newbury Park, CA: Sage.

Rosenblum, G. D., & Lewis, M. (2003). Emotional development in adolescence. In G. R. Adams & M. Berzonsky (Eds.), *Blackwell handbook of adolescence.* Malden MA: Blackwell.

Rosenfeld, R. G., & Bakker, B. (2008). Compliance and persistence in pediatric and adult patients receiving growth hormone therapy. *Endocrine Practice, 14,* 143–154.

Rosengard, C. (2009). Confronting the intendedness of adolescent rapid repeat pregnancy. *Journal of Adolescent Health, 44,* 5–6.

Rosenheck, R. (2008). Fast food consumption and increased caloric intake: A systematic review of a trajectory towards weight gain and obesity risk. *Obesity Reviews, 9,* 537–547.

Rosenstein, D., & Oster, H. (1988). Differential facial responses to four basic tastes in newborns. *Child Development, 59,* 1555–1568.

Rosnati, R., Montirosso, R., & Barni, D. (2008). Behavioral and emotional problems among Italian international adoptees and non-adopted children: Father's and mother's reports. *Journal of Family Psychology, 22,* 541–549.

Ross, H., & Howe, N. (2009). Family influences on children's peer relationships. In K. H. Rubin, W. M. Bukowski, & B. Laursen (Eds.), *Handbook of peer interactions, relationships, and groups.* New York: Guilford.

Ross, J. L., & others (2008, in press). Cognitive and motor development during childhood in boys with Klinefelter syndrome. *American Journal of Medical Genetics A, 146A,* 708–719.

Roth, J. L., Brooks-Gunn, J., Murray, L., & Foster, W. (1998). Promoting healthy adolescents: Synthesis of youth development program evaluations. *Journal of Research on Adolescence, 8,* 423–459.

Rothbart, M. K. (2004). Temperament and the pursuit of an integrated developmental psychology. *Merrill-Palmer Quarterly, 50,* 492–505.

Rothbart, M. K. (2007). Temperament, development, and personality. *Current Directions in Psychological Science, 16,* 207–212.

Rothbart, M. K., & Bates, J. E. (2006). Temperament. In W. Damon & R. Lerner (Eds.), *Handbook of child psychology* (6th ed.). New York: Wiley.

Rothbart, M. K., & Gartstein, M. A. (2008). Temperament. In M. M. Haith & J. B. Benson (Eds.), *Encyclopedia of infant and early childhood development.* Oxford, UK: Elsevier.

Rothbart, M. K., & Putnam, S. P. (2002). Temperament and socialization. In L. Pulkkinen & A. Caspi (Eds.), *Paths to successful development.* New York: Cambridge University Press.

Rothbaum, E., Poll, M., Azuma, H., Miyake, K., & Weisz, J. (2000). The development of close relationships in Japan and the United States: Paths of symbiotic harmony and generative tension. *Child Development, 71,* 1121–1142.

Rothbaum, F., & Trommsdorff, G. (2007). Do roots and wings complement or oppose one another? The socialization of relatedness and competence in cultural context. In J. E. Grusec & P. D. Hastings (Eds.), *Handbook of socialization.* New York: Guilford.

Rouse, D. J., & others. (2007). A trial of 17 alpha-hydroxyprogesterone caproate to prevent prematurity in twins. *New England Journal of Medicine, 357,* 454–461.

Rovee-Collier, C. (1987). Learning and memory in children. In J. D. Osofsky (Ed.), *Handbook of infant development* (2nd ed.). New York: Wiley.

Rovee-Collier, C. (2004). Infant learning and memory. In U. Goswami (Ed.), *Blackwell handbook of childhood cognitive development.* Malden, MA: Blackwell.

Rovee-Collier, C. (2008). The development of infant memory. In N. Cowan & M. Courage (Eds.), *The development of memory in childhood.* Philadelphia: Psychology Press.

Rovers, M. M., de Kok, I. M., & Schilder, A. G. (2006). Risk factors for otitis media: An international perspective. *International Journal of Otorhinoloaryngology, 70,* 1251–1256.

Rowley, S. R., Kurtz-Costas, B., & Cooper, S. M. (2010). The role of schooling in ethnic minority achievement and attainment. In J. Meece & J. Eccles (Eds.), *Handbook of research on schools, schooling, and human development.* New York: Psychology Press.

Rubie-Davies, C. M. (2007). Classroom interactions: Exploring the practices of high- and low-expectation teachers. *British Journal of Educational Psychology, 77,* 289–306.

Rubin, D. H., Krasilnikoff, P. A., Leventhal, J. M., Weile, B., & Berget, A. (1986, August 23). Effect of passive smoking on birthweight. *The Lancet,* 415–417.

Rubin, K. H., Bowker, J. C., & Kennedy, A. E. (2009). Avoiding and withdrawing from the peer group. In K. H. Rubin, W. M. Bukowski, & B. Laursen (Eds.), *Handbook of peer interactions, relationships, and groups.* New York: Guilford.

Rubin, K. H., Bukowski, W., & Parker, J. G. (1998). Peer interactions, relationships, and groups. In N. Eisenberg (Ed.), *Handbook of child psychology* (5th ed., Vol. 3). New York: Wiley.

Rubin, K. H., Bukowski, W., & Parker, J. G. (2006). Peer interactions, relationships, and groups. In W. Damon & R. Lerner (Eds.), *Handbook of child psychology* (6th ed.). New York: Wiley.

Rubin, K. H., Fredstrom, B., & Bowker, J. (2008, in press). Future directions in friendship in childhood and early adolescence. *Social Development.*

Rubinsten, O., & Henik, A. (2009). Developmental dyscalculia: Heterogeneity might not mean different mechanisms. *Trends in Cognitive-Science, 13,* 92–99.

Ruble, D. M. (1983). The development of social comparison processes and their role in achievement-related self-socialization. In E. Higgins, D. Ruble, & W. Hartup (Eds.), *Social cognitive development: A social-cultural perspective.* New York: Cambridge University Press.

Ruble, D. N., Martin, C. L., & Berenbaum, S. (2006). Gender development. In W. Damon & R. Lerner (Eds.), *Handbook of child psychology* (6th ed.). New York: Wiley.

Ruel, M. T., & others. (2008). Age-based preventive targeting of food assistance and behavior change and communication for reduction of childhood undernutrition in Haiti: A cluster randomized trial. *Lancet, 371,* 588–595.

Ruff, H. A., & Capozzoli, M. C. (2003). Development of attention and distractibility in the first 4 years of life. *Developmental Psychology, 39,* 877–890.

Ruffman, T., Slade, L., & Crowe, E. (2002). The relation between children's and mothers' mental state language and theory-of-mind understanding. *Child Development, 73,* 734–751.

Rumberger, R. W. (1983). Dropping out of high school: The influence of race, sex, and family background. *American Educational Research Journal, 20,* 199–220.

Runquist, J. (2007). Persevering through postpartum fatigue. *Journal of Obstetric, Gynecologic, and Neonatal Nursing, 36,* 28–37.

Russell, S. T. & Joyner, K. (2001). Adolescent sexual orientation and suicide risk: Evidence from a national study. *American Journal of Public Health, 91,* 1276–1281.

Russ, S., Regalado, M., & Halfon, N. (2008). Healthcare. In M. M. Haith & J. B. Benson (Eds.), *Encyclopedia of infant and early childhood development.* Oxford, UK: Elsevier.

Rutter, M. (2007). Gene-environment interdependence. *Developmental Science, 10,* 12–18.

Rutter, M., & Schopler, E. (1987). Autism and pervasive developmental disorders: Concepts and diagnostic issues. *Journal of Autism and Pervasive Developmental Disorders, 17,* 159–186.

Ryan, R. M., & Deci, E. L. (2001). When rewards compete with nature. In C. Sansone & J. M. Harackiewicz (Eds.), *Intrinsic and extrinsic motivation.* San Diego: Academic Press.

Ryan, R. M., Fauth, R. C., & Brooks-Gunn, J. (2006). Childhood poverty: Implications for school readiness and early childhood education. In B. Spodek & O. N. Saracho (Eds.), *Handbook of research on the education of young children.* Mahwah, NJ: Erlbaum.

Ryan, S. D., Pearlmutter, S., & Groza, V. (2004). Coming out of the closet: Opening agencies to gay and lesbian adoptive parents. *Social Work 49,* 85–95.

S

Saarni, C. (1999). *The development of emotional competence.* New York: Guilford.

Saarni, C. (2002). Unpublished review of J. W. Santrock's *Life-span development,* 10th ed. (New York: McGraw-Hill).

Saarni, C., Campos, J., Camras, L. A., & Witherington, D. (2006). Emotional development. In W. Damon & R. Lerner (Eds.), *Handbook of child psychology (6th ed.).* New York: Wiley.

Sabbagh, M. A., Xu, F., Carlson, S. M., Moses, L. J., & Lee, K. (2006). The development of executive functioning and theory of mind: A comparison of Chinese and U.S. preschoolers. *Psychological Science, 17,* 74–81.

Sabiston, C. M., & Crocker, P. R. E. (2008). Examining an integrative model of physical activity and healthy eating self-perceptions and behaviors among adolescents. *Journal of Adolescent Health, 42,* 64–72.

Sachs, J. (2009). Communication development in infancy. In J. Berko Gleason & N. B. Batner (Eds.), *The development of language* (7th ed.). Boston: Allyn & Bacon.

Sadeh, A. (2008). Sleep. In M. M. Haith & J. B. Benson (Eds.), *Encyclopedia of infant and early childhood development.* Oxford, UK: Elsevier.

Saffran, J. R., Werker, J. F., & Werner, L. A. (2006). The infant's auditory world: Hearing, speech, and the beginnings of language. In W. Damon & R. Lerner (Eds.), *Handbook of child psychology (6th ed.).* New York: Wiley.

Salkind, N. J. (2009). *Exploring research* (7th ed.). Upper Saddle River, NJ: Prentice Hall.

Salmivalli, C., & Peets, K. (2009). Bullies, victims, and bully-victim relationships in middle childhood and adolescence. In K. H. Rubin, W. M. Bukowski, & B. Laursen (Eds.), *Handbook of peer interactions, relationships, and groups.* New York: Guilford.

Salmon, J., Campbell, K. J., & Crawford, D. A. (2006). Television viewing habits associated with obesity risk factors: A survey of Melbourne schoolchildren. *Medical Journal of Australia, 184,* 64–67.

Sandberg, D. E., & Colsman, M. (2005). Growth hormone treatment of short stature: Status of quality of life rationale. *Hormone Research, 63,* 275–283.

Sanders, E. (2008). Medial art and play therapy with accident survivors. In C. A. Malchiodi (Ed.), *Creative interventions with traumatized children.* New York: Guilford.

Sanger, M. N. (2008). What we need to prepare teachers for the moral nature of their work. *Journal of Curriculum Studies, 40,* 169–185.

Sann, C., & Streri, A. (2007). Perception of object shape and texture in human newborns: Evidence from cross-modal tasks. *Developmental Science, 10,* 399–410.

Sanson, A., & Rothbart, M. K. (1995). Child temperament and parenting. In M. H. Bornstein (Ed.), *Handbook of parenting* (Vol. 4). Hillsdale, NJ: Erlbaum.

Santelli, J. S., Abraido-Lanza, A. F., & Melnikas, A. J. (2009). Migration, acculturation, and sexual and reproductive health of Latino adolescents. *Journal of Adolescent Health, 44,* 3–4.

Santelli, J. S., Kaiser, J., Hirsch, L., Radosh, A., Simkin, L., & Middlestadt, S. (2004). Initiation of intercourse among middle school adolescents: The influence of social factors. *Journal of Adolescent Health, 34,* 200–208.

Santo, J. L., Portuguez, M. W., & Nunes, M. L. (2009, in press). Cognitive and behavioral status of low birth weight preterm children raised in a developing country at preschool age. *Journal of Pediatrics, 85.*

Santrock, J. W., Sitterle, K. A., & Warshak, R. A. (1988). Parent-child relationships in stepfather families. In P. Bronstein & C. P. Cowan (Eds.), *Fatherhood today: Men's changing roles in the family.* New York: Wiley.

Santrock, J. W., & Warshak, R. A. (1979). Father custody and social development in boys and girls. *Journal of Social Issues, 35,* 112–125.

Sartor, C. E., Agrawal, A., Lynskey, M. T., Bucholz, K. K., Maden, P. A., & Health, A. C., (2009, in press). Common genetic influences on the timing of first use for alcohol, cigarettes, and cannabis in young African-American women. *Drug and Alcohol Dependence.*

Sausenthaler, S., Kompauer, I., Mielck, A., Borte, M., Herbarth, O., Schaaf, B., von Berg, A., & Heinrich, J. (2007). Impact of parental education and income equality on children's food intake. *Public Health Nutrition, 10,* 24–33.

Savin-Williams, R. C. (2001). *Mom, dad, I'm gay.* Washington, DC: American Psychological Association.

Savin-Williams, R. C. (2006). *The new gay teenager.* Cambridge, MA: Harvard University Press.

Savin-Williams, R. C. (2007). Girl-on-girl sexuality. In B. J. R. Leadbeater & N. Way (Eds.), *Urban girls revisited: Building strengths* (pp. 301–318). New York: New York University Press.

Savin-Williams, R. C. (2008). Who's gay? It depends on how you measure it. In D. A. Hope (Ed.), *Nebraska Symposium on Motivation: Contemporary perspectives on lesbian, gay, and bisexual identities.* Lincoln, NE: University of Nebraska Press.

Savin-Williams, R. C., & Cohen, K. M. (2007). Development of same-sex attracted youth. In I. H. Meyer & M. E. Northridge (Eds.), *The health of sexual minorities: Public health perspectives on lesbian, gay, bisexual and transgender populations* (pp. 27–47). New York: Springer.

Savin-Williams, R. C., & Diamond, L. (2004). Sex. In R. Lerner & L. Steinberg (Eds.), *Handbook of adolescent psychology.* New York: Wiley.

Savin-Williams, R. C., & Ream, G. L. (2007). Prevalence and stability of sexual orientation components during adolescence and young adulthood. *Archives of Sexual Behavior, 36,* 385–394.

Sayal, K., Heron, J., Golding, J., & Emond, A. (2007). Prenatal alcohol exposure and gender differences in childhood mental health problems: A longitudinal population-based study. *Pediatrics, 119,* e426–e434.

Sayer, L. C. (2006). Economic aspects of divorce and relationship dissolution. In M. A. Fine & J. H. Harvey (Eds.), *Handbook of divorce and relationship dissolution.* Mahwah. NJ: Erlbaum.

Scarr, S. (1993). Biological and cultural diversity: The legacy of Darwin for development. *Child Development, 64,* 1333–1353.

Scarr, S., & Weinberg, R. A. (1983). The Minnesota adoption studies: Genetic differences and malleability. *Child Development, 54,* 182–259.

Schachter, E. P., & Ventura, J. J. (2008). Identity agents: Parents as active and reflective participants in their children's identity formation. *Journal of Research on Adolescence, 18,* 449–476.

Schachter, S. C., & Ransil, B. J. (1996). Handedness distributions in nine professional groups. *Perceptual and Motor Skills, 82,* 51–63.

Schaefer, C., Meister, R., & Weber-Schoendorfer, C. (2009, in press). Isoretrion exposure and pregnancy outcome: An observational study of the Berlin Institute for Clinical Teratology and Drug Risk Assessment in Pregnancy. *Archives of Gynecology and Obstetrics.*

Schaffer, H. R. (1996). *Social development.* Cambridge, MA: Blackwell.

Scharrer, E., & Demers, L. (2009). Media effects. In D. Carr (Ed.), *Encyclopedia of the life course and human development.* Boston: Gale Cengage.

Schattschneider, C., Fletcher, J. M., Francis, D. J., Carlson, C. D., & Foorman, B. R. (2004). Kindergarten prediction of reading skills: A longitudinal comparative analysis. *Journal of Educational Psychology, 96,* 265–282.

Schatz, J., McCellan, C. B., Puffer, E. S., Johnson, K., & Roberts, C. W. (2008).

Neurodevelopmental screening in toddlers and early preschoolers with sickle cell disease. *Journal of Child Neurology, 23,* 44–50.

Schauble, L., Beane, D. B., Coates, G. D., Martin, L. M. W., & Sterling, P. V. (1996). Outside classroom walls: Learning in informal environments. In L. Schauble & R. Glaser (Eds.), *Innovations in learning.* Mahwah, NJ: Erlbaum.

Scher, A., & Harel, J. (2008). Separation and stranger anxiety. In M. M. Haith & J. B. Benson (Eds.), *Encyclopedia of infant and early childhood development.* Oxford, UK: Elsevier.

Schiff, W. J. (2009). *Nutrition for healthy living.* New York: McGraw-Hill.

Schilling, E. A., Aseltine, R. H., Glanovsky, J. L., James, A., & Jacobs, D. (2009). Adolescent alcohol use, suicidal ideation, and suicide attempts. *Journal of Adolescent Health, 44,* 335–341.

Schlegel, M. (2000). All work and play. *Monitor on Psychology, 31* (No. 11), 50–51.

Schmalz, D. L., Deane, G. D., Birch, L. L., & Davison, K. D. (2007). A longitudinal assessment of the links between physical activity and self-esteem in early adolescent non-Hispanic females. *Journal of Adolescent Health, 41,* 559–565.

Schmidt, J., Shumow, L., & Kackar, H. (2007). Adolescents' participation in service activities and its impact on academic, behavioral, and civic outcomes. *Journal of Youth and Adolescence, 36,* 127–140.

Schmidt, L. A., & Jetha, M. K. (2009). Temperament and affect vulnerability: Behavioral, electrocortical, and neuroimaging perspectives. In M. de Haan & M. R. Gunnar (Eds.), *Handbook of developmental social neuroscience.* New York: Guilford.

Schmidt, L. A., Miskovic, V., Boyle, M. H., & Saigal, S. (2008). Shyness and timidity in young adults who were born at extremely low birth weight. *Pediatrics, 122,* e181–e187.

Schmidt, U. (2003). Aetiology of eating disorders in the 21st century: New answers to old questions. *European Child and Adolescent Psychiatry, 12* (Suppl. 1), 1130–1137.

Schmitt, D. P., & Pilcher, J. J. (2004). Evaluating evidence of psychological adaptation: How do we know one when we see one? *Psychological Science, 15,* 643–649.

Schneider, M., Dunton, G. F., & Cooper, D. M. (2008). Physical activity and physical self-concept among sedentary adolescent females: An intervention study. *Psychology of Sport and Exercise, 9,* 1–14.

Schneider, W. (2004). Memory development in childhood. In P. Smith & C. Hart (Eds.), *Blackwell handbook of childhood cognitive development.* Malden, MA: Blackwell.

Schneider, W., & Pressley, M. (1997). *Memory development between 2 and 20* (2nd ed.). Mahwah, NJ: Eribaum.

Schofield, H. L., Bierman, K. L., Heinrichs, B., Nix, R. L., & the Conduct Problems Prevention Research Group. (2008). Predict-

ing early sexual activity with behavior problems exhibited at school entry and in early adolescence. *Journal of Abnormal Child Psychology, 36,* 1175–1188.

Schoppe-Sullivan, S. J., Mangelsdorf, S. C., Brown, G. L., & Sokolowski, M. S. (2007). Goodness-of-fit in family context: Infant temperament, marital quality, and early coparenting behavior. *Infant Behavior and Development, 30,* 82–96.

Schouten, A. P., Valkenburg, P. M., & Peter, J. (2007). Precursors and underlying processes of adolescents' online self-disclosure: Developing and testing an "Internet-attribute-perception" model. *Media Psychology, 10,* 292–314.

Schrag, S. G., & Dixon, R. L. (1985). Occupational exposure associated with male reproductive dysfunction. *Annual Review of Pharmacology and Toxicology, 25,* 467–592.

Schraw, G. (2006). Knowledge structures and processes. In P. A. Alexander & P. H. Winne (Eds.), *Handbook of educational psychology* (2nd ed.). Mahwah, NJ: Erlbaum.

Schreiber, L. R. (1990). *The parents guide to kids' sports.* Boston: Little, Brown.

Schroeder-Yu, G. (2008). Documentation: Ideas and applications from the Reggio Emilia approach. *Teaching Artist Journal, 6,* 126–134.

Schulenberg, J. E., & Zarrett, N. R. (2006). Mental health during emerging adulthood: Continuities and discontinuities in course, content, and meaning. In J. J. Amen & J. Tanner (Eds.), *Advances in emerging adulthood.* Washington, DC: American Psychological Association.

Schultz, M. S., Kerig, P. K., Pruett, M. K., & Parke, R. D. (Eds.). (2009). *Feathering the nest.* Washington, DC: American Psychological Association.

Schumacher, M., Zubaran, C., & White, G. (2008). Bringing birth-related paternal depression to the fore. *Women and Birth, 21,* 65–70.

Schunk, D. H. (2008). *Learning theories: An educational perspective* (5th ed.). Upper Saddle River, NJ: Prentice Hall.

Schunk, D. H., Pintrich, P. R., & Meece, J. (2008). *Motivation in education: Theory, research, and applications* (3rd ed.). Upper Saddle River, NJ: Prentice Hall.

Schwebel, D. C. (2008). Safety and childproofing. In M. M. Haith & J. B. Benson (Eds.), *Encyclopedia of infant and early childhood development.* Oxford, UK: Elsevier.

Schweinhart, L. J., Montie, J., Xiang, Z., Barnett, W. S., Belfield, C. R., & Nores, M. (2005). *Lifetime effects: The High/Scope Perry Preschool Study Through Age 40.* Ypsilanti, MI: High/Scope Press.

Sciutto, M. J., & Eisenberg, M. (2007). Evaluating the evidence for and against an overdiagnosis of ADHD. *Journal of Attention Disorders, 11,* 106–113.

Scourfield, J., Van den Bree, M., Martin, N., & McGuffin, P. (2004). Conduct problems in children and adolescents: A twin study. *Archives of General Psychiatry, 61,* 489–496.

Seaton, E. K., Caldwell, C. H., Sellers, R. M., & Jackson, J. S. (2008). The prevalence of perceived discrimination among African American and Caribbean Black youth. *Developmental Psychology, 44,* 1288–1297.

Seaton, E. K., Yip, T., & Sellers, R. M. (2009). A longitudinal examination of racial identity and racial discrimination among African American adolescents. *Child Development, 80,* 406–417.

Sellers, R. M., Copeland-Linder, N., Martin, P. P., & Lewis, R. L. (2006). Racial identity matters: The relationship between racial discrimination and psychological functioning in African American adolescents. *Journal of Research on Adolescence, 16,* 187–216.

Sellner, J., Buonomano, R., Nedeltchev, K., Findling, O., Schroth, G., Surbek, D. V., & Leib, S. L. (2009). A case of maternal herpes simplex virus encephalitis during pregnancy. *Nature Clinical Practice: Neurology, 5,* 51–56.

Selman, R. L. (1980). *The growth of interpersonal understanding.* New York: Academic Press.

Semmler, C., Ashcroft, J., van Jaarsveld, C. H., Carnell, S., & Wardle, J. (2009). Development of overweight in children in relation to parental weight and socioeconomic status. *Obesity, 17,* 814–820.

Shalev, R. S. (2004). Developmental dyscalculia. *Journal of Child Neurology, 19,* 765–771.

Shapiro. A. F., & Gottman, J. M. (2005). Effects on marriage of a psycho-education intervention with couples undergoing the transition to parenthood, evaluation at 1-year post-intervention. *Journal of Family Communication, 5,* 1–24.

Shapiro-Mendoza, C. K., & others. (2008). Effect of late-term birth and maternal medical conditions on newborn morbidity risk. *Pediatrics, 121,* e223–e232.

Sharma, A. R., McGue, M. K., & Benson, P. L. (1996). The emotional and behavioral adjustment of adopted adolescents: Part I: Age at adoption. *Children and Youth Services Review, 18,* 101–114.

Sharma, M. (2006). School-based interventions for childhood and adolescent obesity. *Obesity Review, 7,* 261–269.

Shatz, M., & Gelman, R. (1973). The development of communication skills: Modifications in the speech of young children as a function of the listener. *Monographs of the Society for Research in Child Development, 38* (Serial No. 152).

Shaw, P., Eckstrand, K., Sharp, W. Blumenthal, J., Lerch, J. P., Greenstein, D., Clasen, L., Evans, A., Giedd, J., & Rapport, J. L. (2007). Attention-deficit/hyperactivity disorder is characterized by a delay in cortical maturation. *Proceedings of the National Academy of Sciences USA, 104,* 19649–19654.

Shaya, F. T., Flores, D., Gbarayor, C. M., & Wang, J. (2008). School-based obesity interventions: A literature review. *Journal of School Health, 78,* 189–196.

Shaywitz, S. E., Gruen, J. R., & Shaywitz, B. A. (2007). Management of dyslexia, its rationale, and underlying neurobiology. *Pediatric Clinics of North America, 54,* 609–623.

Shaywitz, S. E., Morris, R., & Shaywitz, B. A. (2008). The education of dyslexic children from childhood to young adulthood. *Annual Review of Psychology* (Vol. 59). Palo Alto, CA: Annual Reviews.

Shea, A. K., & Steiner, M. (2008). Cigarette smoking during pregnancy. *Nicotine and Tobacco Research, 10,* 267–278.

Sheeber, L. B., Davis, B., Leve, C., Hops, H., & Tildesley, E. (2007). Adolescents' relationships with their mothers and fathers: Associations with depressive disorder and subdiagnostic symptomatology. *Journal of Abnormal Psychology, 116,* 144–154.

Shema, L, Ore, L., Ben-Shachar, M., Haj, M., & Linn, S. (2007). The association between breastfeeding and breast cancer occurrence among Jewish women: A case control study. *Journal of Cancer Research and Clinical Oncology, 133,* 903.

Shen, J. (2009). Evaluation of environmental and personal susceptibility characteristics that modify genetic risks. *Methods in Molecular Biology, 471,* 163–177.

Shenkin, S. D., Rivers, C. S., Deary, I. J., Starr, J. M., & Wardlaw, J. M. (2009). Maximum (prior) brain size, not atrophy, correlates with cognition in community-dwelling older people: A cross-sectional study. *BMC Geriatrics, 9,* 12.

Sherblom, S. (2008). The legacy of the "care challenge": Re-envisioning the outcome of the justice-care debate. *Journal of Moral Education, 37,* 81–98.

Shi, L., & Stevens, G. D. (2005). Disparities in access to care and satisfaction among U.S. children: The roles of race/ethnicity and poverty status. *Public Health Report, 120,* 431–441.

Shields, S. A. (1991). Gender in the psychology of emotion. In K. T. Strongman (Ed.), *International review of studies of emotion* (Vol. 1). New York: Wiley.

Shiraev, E., & Levy, D. (2007). *Cross-cultural psychology: Critical thinking and critical applications* (3rd ed.). Belmont, CA: Wadsworth.

Shiraev, E., & Levy, D. (2010). *Cross-cultural psychology* (4th ed.). Boston: Allyn & Bacon.

Shiva, F., Nasiri, M., Sadeghi, B., & Padyab, M. (2004). Effects of passive smoking on common respiratory symptoms in young children. *Acta Pediatrics, 92,* 1394–1397.

Shoup, J. A., Gattshall, M., Dandamudi, P., & Estabrooks, P. (2008). Physical activity, quality of life, and weight status in overweight children. *Quality of Life Research, 17,* 407–412.

Siega-Riz, A. M., Siega-Riz, A. M., & Laiaira, B. (2006). The implications of maternal overweight and obesity on the course of pregnancy and birth outcomes. *Maternal and Child Health, 10* (Suppl. 7), S153–S156.

Siegel, L. S. (2003). Learning disabilities. In I. B. Weiner (Ed.), *Handbook of psychology* (Vol. VI). New York: Wiley.

Siegler, R. S. (2006). Microgenetic analysis of learning. In W. Damon & R. Lerner (Eds.), *Handbook of child psychology* (6th ed.). New York: Wiley.

Signore, R. J. (2004). Bradley method offers option for natural childbirth. *American Family Physician, 70,* 650.

Silva, C. (2005, October 31). When teen dynamo talks, city listens. *Boston Globe,* pp. B1, B4.

Silver, E. J., & Bauman, L. J. (2006). The association of sexual experience with attitudes, beliefs, and risk behaviors of inner-city adolescents. *Journal of Research on Adolescence, 16,* 29–45.

Simard, V., Nielsen, T. A., Tremblay, R. E., Boivan, M., & Montplaisir, J. Y. (2008). Longitudinal study of bad dreams in preschool-aged children: Prevalence, demographic correlates, risk, and protective factors. *Sleep, 31,* 62–70.

Simeoni, U., & Barker, D. J. (2009). Offspring of diabetic pregnancy: Long-term outcomes. *Seminars in Fetal and Neonatal Medicine, 14,* 119–124.

Simmons, R. G., & Blyth, D. A. (1987). *Moving into adolescence.* Hawthorne, NY: Aldine.

Simos, P. G., Fletcher, J. M., Sarkari, S., Billingsley, R. L., Denton, C., & Papanicolaou, A. C. (2007). Altering the brain circuits for reading through intervention: A magnetic source imaging study. *Neuropsychology, 21,* 485–496.

Simpkin, P., & Bolding, A. (2004). Update on nonpharmacological approaches to relieve labor pain and prevent suffering. *Journal of Midwifery and Women's Health, 49,* 489–504.

Simpkins, S. D., Fredricks, J. A., Davis-Kean, P. E., & Eccles, J. S. (2006). Healthy mind, healthy habits: The influence of activity involvement in middle childhood. In A. C. Huston & M. N. Ripke (Eds.), *Developmental contexts in middle childhood.* New York: Cambridge University Press.

Sim, T. N., & Ong, L. P. (2005). Parent punishment and child aggression in a Singapore Chinese preschool sample. *Journal of Marriage and the Family, 67,* 85–99.

Singh, S., Darroch, J. E., Vlasoff, M., & Nadeau, J. (2004). *Adding it up: The benefits of investing in sexual and reproductive health care.* New York: The Alan Guttmacher Institute.

Singh, S., Wulf, D., Samara, R., & Cuca, Y. P. (2000). Gender differences in the timing of first intercourse. Data from 14 countries. *International Family Planning Perspectives, 26,* 21–28, 43.

Sinha, J. W., Cnaan, R. A., & Gelles, R. J. (2007). Adolescent risk behaviors and religion: Findings from a national study. *Journal of Adolescence, 30,* 231–249.

Sivell, S. & others (2008). How risk is perceived, constructed, and interpreted by clients in clinical genetics, and the effects on decision making: A review. *Journal of Genetic Counseling, 17,* 30–63.

Skinner, B. F. (1938). *The behavior of organisms: An experimental analysis.* New York: Appelton-Century-Crofts.

Skinner, B. F. (1957). *Verbal behavior.* New York: Appleton-Century-Crofts.

Skinner, J. D., Ziegler, P., Pac, S., & Devaney, B. (2004). Meal and snack patterns of infants and toddlers. *Journal of the American Dietetic Association, 104,* 65–70.

Slater, A., Field, T., & Hernandez-Reif, M. (2007). The development of the senses. In A. Slater & M. Lewis (Eds.), *Introduction to infant development* (2nd ed.). New York: Oxford University Press.

Slater, A., Morison, V., & Somers, M. (1988). Orientation discrimination and cortical function in the human newborn. *Perception, 17,* 597–602.

Slater, A. M., Riddell, P., Quinn, P. C., Pascalis, O., Lee, K., & Kelly, D. J. (2009, in press). Visual perception. In G. Bremner & T. Wachs (Eds.), *Blackwell handbook of infant development,* (2nd ed.). Oxford, UK: Blackwell.

Slawta, J. N., & Deneui, D. (2009, in press). Be a fit kid: Nutrition and physical activity for the fourth grade. *Health Promotion Practice.*

Sleet, D. A., & Mercy, J. A. (2003). Promotion of safety, security, and well-being. In M. H. Bornstein, L. Davidson, C. L. M., Keyes, & K. A. Moore (Eds.), *Well-being.* Mahwah, NJ: Erlbaum.

Slobin, D. (1972, July). Children and language: They learn the same way around the world. *Psychology Today,* 71–76.

Slomkowski, C., Rende, R., Conger, K. J., Simons, R. L., & Conger, R. D. (2001). Sisters, brothers, and delinquency: Social influence during early and middle adolescence. *Child Development, 72,* 271–283.

Slough, N. M., McMahon, R. J., & the Conduct Problems Prevention Research Group. (2008). Preventing serious conduct problems in school-aged youth: The Fast Track program. *Cognitive and Behavioral Practice, 15,* 3–17.

Smedje, H., Broman, J. E., & Hetta, J. (2001). Associations between disturbed sleep and behavioral difficulties in 635 children aged six to eight years: A study based on parents' perceptions. *European Journal of Child and Adolescent Psychiatry, 10,* 1–9.

Smetana, J. (2006). Social domain theory. In M. Killen & J. G. Smetana (Eds.), *Handbook of moral development.* Mahwah, NJ: Erlbaum.

Smithbattle, L. (2007). Legacies of advantage and disadvantage: The case of teen mothers. *Public Health Nursing, 24,* 409–420.

Smith, D. L. (2008). Birth complications and outcomes. In M. M. Haith & J. B. Benson (Eds.),

Encyclopedia of infant and early childhood development. Oxford, UK: Elsevier.

Smith, J. B. (2009). High school organization. In D. Carr (Ed.), *Encyclopedia of the life course and human development.* Boston: Gale Cengage.

Smith, J., & Ross, H. (2007). Training parents to mediate sibling disputes affects children's negotiation and conflict understanding. *Child Development, 78,* 790–805.

Smith, L. B. (1999). Do infants possess innate knowledge structures? The con side. *Developmental Science, 2,* 133–144.

Smith, L. E., & Howard, K. S. (2008). Continuity of paternal social support and depressive symptoms among new mothers. *Journal of Family Psychology, 22,* 763–773.

Smith, L. M., Chang, L., Yonekura, M. L., Gilbride, K., Kuo, J., Poland, R. E., Walot, I., & Ernst, T. (2001). Brain proton magnetic resonance spectroscopy and imaging in children exposed to cocaine in utero. *Pediatrics, 107,* 227.

Smith, L. M., & others. (2008). The infant development, environment, and lifestyle study: Effects of prenatal methamphetamine exposure, polydrug exposure, and poverty on intrauterine growth. *Pediatrics, 118,* 1149–1156.

Smith, P. K., Mahdavi, J., Carvalho, M., Fisher, S., Russell, S., & Tippett, N. (2008). Cyberbullying: Its nature and impact in secondary school pupils. *Journal of Child Psychology and Psychiatry, 49,* 376–385.

Smith, R. A., & Davis, S. F. (2010). *Psychologist as detective, the* (5th ed.). Upper Saddle River, NJ: Prentice Hall.

Smith, R. P. (2009). *Netter's obstetrics and gynecology* (2nd ed.). London: Elsevier.

Smith, T. E. C., Polloway, E. A., Patton, J. R., & Dowdy, C. A. (2008). *Teaching students with special needs in inclusive settings* (5th ed.). Boston: Allyn & Bacon.

Snarey, J. (1987, June). A question of morality. *Psychology Today,* pp. 6–8.

Snijders, B. E., & others (2007). Breast-feeding duration and infant atopic manifestations, by maternal allergic status, in the first two years of life (KOALA study). *Journal of Pediatrics, 151,* 347–351.

Snow, C. E., & Yang, J. Y. (2006). Becoming bilingual, biliterate, and bicultural. In W. Damon & R. Lerner (Eds.), *Handbook of child psychology* (6th ed.). New York: Wiley.

Snowdon, A. W., Hussein, A., High, L., Millar-Polgar, J., Patrick, L., & Ahmed, E. (2008). The effectiveness of a multimedia intervention on parents' knowledge and use of vehicle safety systems for children. *Journal of Pediatric Nursing, 23,* 126–139.

Snyder, J., Schrepferman, L., McDachern, A., Barner, S., Johnson, K., & Provines, J. (2008). Peer deviancy training and peer coercion: Dual processes associated with early-onset conduct problems. *Child Development, 79,* 252–268.

Snyder, K. A., & Torrence, C. M. (2008). Habituation and novelty. In M. M. Haith & J. B. Benson (Eds.), *Encyclopedia of infant and early childhood development.* Oxford, UK: Elsevier.

Solomon, D., Watson, M. S., & Battistich, V. A. (2002). Teaching and school effects on moral/prosocial development. In V. Richardson (Ed.), *Handbook for research on teaching.* Washington, DC: American Educational Research Association.

Solomon, D., Watson, M., Schapes, E., Battistich, V., & Solomon, J. (1990). Cooperative learning as part of a comprehensive program designed to promote prosocial development. In S. Sharan (Ed.), *Cooperative learning: Theory and research.* New York: Praeger.

Sonek, J. (2007). First trimester ultrasonography in screening and detection of fetal abnormalities. *American Journal of Genetics C, 145,* 45–61.

Song, S. H., & Hardisty, C. A. (2008). Early-onset type 2 diabetes mellitus: An increasing phenomenon of elevated cardiovascular risk. *Expert Review of Cardiovascular Therapy, 6,* 315–322.

Sontag, L. M., Graber, J., Brooks-Gunn, J., & Warren, M. P. (2008). Coping with social stress: Implications for psychopathology in young adolescent girls. *Journal of Abnormal Child Psychology, 36,* 1159–1174.

Sophian, C. (1985). Perseveration and infants' search: A comparison of two- and three-location tasks. *Developmental Psychology, 21,* 187–194.

Sorof, J. M., Lai, D., Turner, J., Poffenberger, T., & Portman, R. J. (2004). Overweight, ethnicity, and the prevalence of hypertension in school-aged children. *Pediatrics, 113,* 475–482.

Sotir, M., Yeatts, K., Miller, W., & Shy, C. (2006). Comparison of asthma-related functional consequences and health care utilization among children with and without upper respiratory infection–triggered wheezing. *Journal of Asthma, 43,* 629–632.

South, M., Ozonoff, S., & McMahon, W. M. (2005). Repetitive behavior profiles in Asperger syndrome and high-functioning autism. *Journal of Autism and Developmental Disorders, 35,* 145–158.

Sowell, E. R. (2004, July). Commentary in M. Beckman, "Crime, culpability, and the adolescent brain." *Science Magazine, 305,* 599.

Sowell, E. R., Thompson, P. M., Leonard, C. M., Welcome, S. E., Kan, E., & Toga, A. W. (2004). Longitudinal mapping of cortical thickness and brain growth in children. *Journal of Neuroscience, 24,* 8223–8231.

Spangler, G., Johann, M., Ronai, Z., & Zimmerman, P. (2009, in press) Genetic and environmental influences on attachment disorganization. *Journal of Child Psychology and Psychiatry.*

Sparks, P. J. (2009). Do biological, demographic, and behavioral characteristics explain racial/ethnic disparities in preterm births? *Social Science and Medicine, 68,* 1667–1675.

Spelke, E. S. (1979). Perceiving bimodally specified events in infancy. *Developmental Psychology, 5,* 626–636.

Spelke, E. S. (1991). Physical knowledge in infancy: Reflections on Piaget's theory. In S. Carey & R. Gelman (Eds.), *The epigenesis of mind: Essays on biology and cognition.* Hillsdale, NJ: Erlbaum.

Spelke, E. S. (2000). Core knowledge. *American Psychologist, 55,* 1233–1243.

Spelke, E. S., Breinlinger, K., Macomber, J., & Jacobson, K. (1992). Origins of knowledge. *Psychological Review, 99,* 605–632.

Spelke, E. S., & Hespos, S. J. (2001). Continuity, competence, and the object concept. In E. Dupoux (Ed.), *Language, brain, and behavior.* Combridge, MA: Bradford/MIT Press.

Spelke, E. S., & Kinzler, K. D. (2007). Core knowledge. *Developmental Science, 10,* 89–96.

Spelke, E. S. & Kinzler, K. D. (2009, in press). Innateness, learning and rationality. *Cognitive Development Perspectives.*

Spelke, E. S., & Owsley, C. J. (1979). Intermodal exploration and knowledge in infancy. *Infant Behavior and Development, 2,* 13–28.

Spence, J. T., & Helmreich, R. (1978). *Masculinity and feminity: Their psychological dimensions.* Austin: University of Texas Press.

Spencer, J. P., Blumberg, M. S., McMurray, B., Robinson, S. R., Samuelson, L. K., & Tomlin, J. B. (2009, in press). Short arms and talking eggs: Why we should no longer abide by the nativist-empiricist debate. *Child Development Perpectives.*

Spohr, H. L, Willms, J., & Steinhausen, H. C. (2007). Fetal alcohol spectrum disorders in young adulthood. *Journal of Pediatrics, 150,* 175–179.

Springer, S. P., & Deutsch, G. (1985). *Left brain, right brain.* San Francisco: Freeman.

Spring, J. (2008). *American education* (13th ed.). New York: McGraw-Hill.

Spring, J. (2010). *Deculturalization and the struggle for equality* (6th ed.). New York: McGraw-Hill.

Squire, W. (2008). Shaken baby syndrome: The quest for evidence. *Developmental Medicine and Child Neurology, 50,* 10–14.

Srabstein, J. C., McCarter, R. J., Shao, C., & Huang, Z. J. (2006). Morbidities associated with bullying behaviors in adolescents: School based study of American adolescents. *International Journal of Adolescent Medicine and Health, 18,* 587–596.

Sroufe, L. A. (2000, Spring). The inside scoop on child development: Interview, *Cutting through the hype.* Minneapolis: College of Education and Human Development. University of Minnesota.

Sroufe, L. A. (2007). Commentary: the place of development in developmental psychology. In A. Masten (ed.), *Multilevel dynamics in developmental psychology.* Mahwah, NJ: Erlbaum.

Sroufe, L. A., Egeland, B., Carlson, E., & Collins, W. A. (2005). Placing early experiences in developmental context. In K. E. Grossmann, K. Grossmann, & E. Waters (Eds.), *Attachment from infancy and adulthood: The Major Longitudinal Studies.* New York: Guilford.

Sroufe, L. A., Waters, E., & Matas, L. (1974). Contextual determinants of infant affectional response. In M. Lewis & L. Rosenblum (Eds.), *Origins of fear.* New York: Wiley.

Stanford University Medical Center. (2008). *Growth hormone deficiency.* Palo Alto, CA: Author.

Stanulla, M., & Schrappe, M. (2009). Treatment of childhood acute lymphoblastic leukemia. *Seminars in Hematology, 46,* 52–63.

Starr, C., Evers, C. E., & Starr, L. (2010). *Biology today and tomorrow with physiology* (3rd ed.). Boston: Cengage.

Starr, L. R., & Davila, J. (2009). Clarifying co-rumination: Associations with internalizing symptoms and romantic involvement among adolescent girls. *Journal of Adolescence, 32,* 19–37.

Steelman, L. C., & Koch, P. R. (2009). Sibling relationships, childhood, and adolescence. In D. Carr (Ed.), *Encyclopedia of the life course and human development.* Boston: Gale Cengage.

Steer, A. J., & Lehman, E. B. (2000). Attachment to transitional objects. *American Journal of Orthopsychiatry, 70,* 340–350.

Steinberg, A., & Almeida, C. A. (2008). *Raising graduation rates in an era of high standards: Five commitments for state action.* Boston: Jobs for the Future Available at Education Resources Information: ERIC document # ED500541.

Steinberg, L. (2008). A social neuroscience perspective on adolescent risk-taking *Developmental Review, 28,* 78–106.

Steinberg, L. (2009). Adolescent development and juvenile justice. *Annual review of Clinical Psychology* (Vol. 5). Palo Alto, CA: Annual Reviews.

Steinberg, L., Cauffman, E., Woolard, J., Graham, S., & Banich, M. (2009, in press). Are adolescents less mature than adults? Minors' access to abortion, the juvenile death penalty, and the alleged APA "flip-flop." *American Psychologist.*

Steinberg, L., & Monahan, K. C. (2007). Age differences in resistance to peer influence. *Developmental Psychology, 43,* 1531–1543.

Steinberg, S. J., & Davila, J. (2008). Romantic functioning and depressive symptoms among early adolescent girls: The moderating role of parental emotional availability. *Journal of Clinical Child and Adolescent Psychology, 37,* 350–362.

Steiner, J. E. (1979). Human facial expressions in response to taste and smell stimulation. In H. Reese & L. Lipsitt (Eds.), *Advances in child development* (Vol. 13). New York: Academic Press.

Steinhausen, H. C., & Blattmann, B., & Pfund, F. (2007). Developmental outcome in children with intrauterine exposure to substances. *European Addiction Research, 13,* 94–100.

Stein, M. T. (2004). ADHD: The diagnostic process from different perspectives. *Journal of Developmental and Behavioral Pediatrics, 25* (Suppl. 5), S54–S58.

Stephens, B. K., Barkey, M. E., & Hall, H. R. (1999). Techniques to comfort children during stressful procedures. *Advances in Mind-Body Medicine, 15,* 49–60.

Stephens, J. M. (2008). Cheating. In N. J. Salkind (Ed.), *Encyclopedia of educational psychology.* Thousand Oaks, CA: Sage.

Sterling, S. P., Sadler, L. S. (2009). Contraceptive use among Latinas living in the United States: The Impact of culture and acculturation. *Journal of Pediatric Health Care, 23,* 19–28.

Stern, D. N., Beebe, B., Jaffe, J., & Bennett, S. L. (1977). The infant's stimulus world during social interaction: A study of caregiver behaviors with particular reference to repetition and timing. In H. R. Schaffer (Ed.), *Studies in mother-infant interaction.* London: Academic Press.

Sternberg, R. J. (1977). *Intelligence, information processing, and analogical reasoning: The componential analysis of human abilities.* Hillsdale, NJ: Erlbaum.

Sternberg, R. J. (1986). *Intelligence applied.* San Diego: Harcourt Brace Jovanovich.

Sternberg, R. J. (2002). Intelligence: The triarchic theory of intelligence. In J. W. Gutherie (Ed.), *Encyclopedia of education* (2nd ed.). New York: Macmillan.

Sternberg, R. J. (2004). Individual differences in cognitive development. In U. Goswami (Ed.), *Blackwell handbook of childhood cognitive development.* Malden, MA: Blackwell.

Sternberg, R. J. (2007). *g, g's, or Jeez:* Which is the best model for developing abilities, competencies, and expertise? In P. C. Kyllonen, R. D. Roberts, & L. Stankov (Eds.), *Extending intelligence: Enhancement and new constructs* Mahwah, NJ: Erlbaum.

Sternberg, R. J. (2008). The triarchic theory of successful intelligence. In N. Salkind (Ed.), *Encyclopedia of educational psychology.* Thousand Oaks, CA: Sage.

Sternberg, R. J. (2009a, in press). Teaching for creativity. In R. A. Beghetto & J. C. Kaufman (Eds.), *Nurturing creativity in the classroom.* New York: Cambridge University Press.

Sternberg, R. J. (2009b, in press). Intelligence. In M. E. Laur (Ed.), *Chicago companion to the child.* Chicago: University of Chicago Press.

Sternberg, R. J. (2009c, in press). The triarchic theory of successful intelligence. In B. Kerr (Ed.), *Encyclopedia of giftedness, creativity, and talent.* Thousand Oaks, CA: Sage.

Sternberg, R. J. (2009d, in press). Wisdom. In S. J. Lopez (Ed.), *Encyclopedia of positive psychology.* Blackwell.

Sternberg, R. J. (2009e, in press). Wisdom, intelligence, creativity, synthesized: A model of giftedness. In T. Balchin, B. Hymer, & D. Matthews (Eds.), *International companion to gifted education.* London: RoutledgeFalmer.

Sternberg, R. J. (2009f, in press). Leadership and giftedness. In B. MacFarlane & T. Stambaugh (Eds.), *Leading change in gifted education.* Waco, TX: Prufrock.

Sternberg, R. J., & Grigorenko, E. L. (2008). Ability testing across cultures. In L. Suzuki (Ed.), *Handbook of multicultural assessment* (3rd ed.). New York: Jossey-Bass.

Sternberg, R. J., Jarvin, L., & Grigorenko, E. L. (2009, in press). *Teaching for intelligence, creativity, and wisdom.* Thousand Oaks, CA: Corwin.

Sternberg, R. J., Jarvin, L., & Reznitskaya, A. (2009, in press). Teaching for wisdom through history: Infusing wise thinking skills in the school curriculum. In M. Ferrari (Ed.), *Teaching for wisdom.* Amsterdam: Springer.

Sternberg, R. J., Kaufman, J., & Grigorenko, E. L. (2008). *Applied intelligence.* New York: Cambridge University Press.

Sternberg, R. J., & Nigro, C. (1980). Developmental patterns in the solution of verbal analogies. *Child Development, 51,* 27–38.

Sternberg, R. J., & Rifkin, B. (1979). The development of analogical reasoning processes, *Journal of Experimental Child Psychology, 27,* 195–232.

Sternberg, R. J., Roediger, H., & Halpern, D. (Eds.). (2007). *Critical thinking in psychology.* Mahwah, NJ: Erlbaum.

Sternberg, R. J., & Williams, W. M. (1996). *How to develop student creativity.* Alexandria, VA: ASCD.

Sternberg, R. J., & Williams, W. M. (2010). *Educational psychology* (2nd ed.). Upper Saddle River, NJ: Prentice Hall.

Stetsenko, A. (2002). Adolescents in Russia: Surviving the turmoil and creating a brighter future. B. B. Brown, R. W. Larson, & T. S. Saraswathi (Eds.), *The world's youth.* New York: Cambridge University Press.

Steur, F. B., Applefield, J. M., & Smith, R. (1971). Televised aggression and interpersonal aggression of preshool children. *Journal of Experimental Child Psychology, 11,* 442–447.

Stevenson, H. W. (1995). Mathematics achievement of American students: First in the world by the year 2000? In C. A. Nelson (Ed.), *Basic and applied perspectives on learning, cognition, and development.* Minneapolis: University of Minnesota Press.

Stevenson, H. W. (2000). Middle childhood: Education and schooling. In A. Kazdin (Ed.), *Encyclopedia of psychology.* Washington, DC, & New York: American Psychological Association and Oxford University Press.

Stevenson, H. W., Hofer, B. K., & Randel, B. (1999). *Middle childhood: Education and schooling.* Unpublished manuscript, Department of Psychology, University of Michigan, Ann Arbor.

Stevenson, H. W., Lee, S., Chen, C., Stigler, J. W., Hsu, C., & Kitamure, S. (1990). Contexts of achievement. *Monograph of the Society for Research in Child Development, 55* (Serial No. 221).

Stevenson, H. W., Lee, S., & Stigler, J. W. (1986). Mathematics achievement of Chinese, Japanese, and American children. *Science, 231,* 693–699.

Stevenson, H. W., & Newman, R. S. (1986). Long-term prediction of achievement and attitudes in mathematics and reading. *Child Development, 57,* 646–659.

Stevenson, H. W., & Zusho, A. (2002). Adolescence in China and Japan: Adapting to a changing environment. In B. B. Brown, R. W. Larson, & T. S. Saraswathi (Eds.), *The world's youth.* New York: Cambridge University Press.

Stipek, D. J. (2002). *Motivation to learn* (4th ed.). Boston: Allyn & Bacon.

Stipek, D. J. (2005, February 16). Commentary in *USA Today*, p. 1D.

Stocker, C., & Dunn, J. (1990). Sibling relationships in adolescence: Links with friendships and peer relationships. *British Journal of Developmental Psychology, 8,* 227–244.

Stolzer, J. M. (2009). Attention deficit/hyperactivity disorder. In D. Carr (Ed.), *Encyclopedia of the life course and human development.* Boston: Gale Cengage.

Story, M., Kaphingst, K. M., & French, S. (2006). The role of schools in obesity prevention. *The Future of Children, 16,* 109–142.

Strasberger, V. C. (2009). Why do adolescent health researchers ignore the impact of the media? *Journal of Adolescent Health, 44,* 203–205.

Strathearn, L. (2007). Exploring the neurobiology of attachment. In L. C. Mayes, P. Fonagy, & M. Target (Eds.), *Developmental science and psychoanalysis.* London: Karnac Press.

Strauss, M. A., Sugarman, D. B., & Giles-Sims, J. (1997). Spanking by parents and subsequent anti-social behavior in children. *Archives of Pediatrics and Adolescent Medicine, 151,* 761–767.

Strauss, R. S. (2001). Environmental tobacco smoke and serum vitamin C levels in children. *Pediatrics, 107,* 540–542.

Streib, H. (1999). Off-road religion? A narrative approach to fundamentalist and occult orientation of adolescents. *Journal of Adolescence, 22,* 255–267.

Streri, A. (1987) Tactile discrimination of shape and intermodal transfer in two- to three-month-old infants. *British Journal Developmental Psychology, 5,* 213–220.

Streubel, A. H, Donohue, P. K., & Aucott, S. W. (2008). The epidemiology of atypical chronic lung disease in extremely low birth weight infants. *Journal of Perinatology, 28,* 141–148.

Striano, T., Reid, V. M., & Hoehl, S. (2006). Neural mechanisms of joint attention in infancy. *European Journal of Neuroscience, 23,* 2819–2823.

Striegel-Moore, R. H., & Bulik, C. M. (2007). Risk factors for eating disorders. *American Psychologist, 62,* 181–198.

Stringer, M., Ratcliffe, S. J., Evans, E. C., & Brown, L. P. (2005). The cost of prenatal care attendance and pregnancy outcomes in low-income working women. *Journal of Obstetrical, Gynecologic, and Neonatal Nursing, 34,* 551–560.

Stroganova, T. A., Pushina, N. P., Orekhova, E. V., Posikera, I. N., & Tsetlin, M. M. (2004). Functional brain asymmetry and individual differences in hand preference in early ontogeny. *Human Physiology, 30,* 20–30.

Strong, B., Yarber, W., Sayad, B., & De Vault, C. (2008). *Human sexuality* (6th ed.). New York: McGraw-Hill.

Strong-Wilson, T., & Ellis, J. (2007). Children and place: Reggio Emilia's environment as a third teacher. *Theory into Practice, 46,* 40–47.

Stroobant, N., Buijs, D., & Vingerhoets, G. (2009, in press). Variation in brain lateralization during various language tasks: A functional transcranial Doppler study. *Behavioral Brain Research.*

Suarez-Orozco, M., & Suarez-Orozco, C. (2010). Globalization, immigration, and schooling. In J. A. Banks (Ed.), *The Routledge international companion to multicultural education.* New York: Routledge.

Subrahmanyan, K., & Greenfield, P. (2008). Online communication and adolescent relationships. *The Future of Children, 18* (1), 119–146.

Subrahmanyam, K., Smahel, D., & Greenfield, P. (2006). Connecting developmental constructions on the internet: Identity presentation and sexual exploration in online chat rooms. *Developmental Psychology, 42,* 395–406.

Sugita, Y. (2004). Experience in early infancy is indispensable for color perception. *Current Biology, 14,* 1267–1271.

Sullivan, H. S. (1953). *The interpersonal theory of psychiatry.* New York: W. W. Norton.

Sullivan, K., & Sullivan, A. (1980). Adolescent-parent separation. *Developmental Psychology, 16,* 93–99.

Suman, R. P., Udani, R., & Nanavati, R. (2008). Kangaroo mother care for low birth weight infants: A randomized controlled trial. *Indian Pediatrics, 45,* 17–23.

Sumaroka, M., & Bornstein, M. H. (2008). Play. In M. M. Haith & J. B. Benson (Eds.), *Encyclopedia of infant and early childhood development.* Oxford, UK: Elsevier.

Sun, S. S., Liang, R., Huang, T. T., Daniels, S. R., Arsianian, S., Liu, K., Grave, G. D., & Siervogel, R. M. (2008). Childhood obesity predicts adult metabolic syndrome: The Fels Longitudinal Study. *Journal of Pediatrics, 152,* 191–200.

Sunstein, C. R. (2008). Adolescent risk-taking and social meaning: A commentary. *Developmental Review, 28,* 145–152.

Super, C., & Harkness, S. (1997). The cultural structuring of child development. In J. W. Berry, Y. H. Poortinga, & J. Pandey (Eds.), *Handbook of cross-cultural psychology: Theory and method* (Vol. 2). Boston: Allyn & Bacon.

Susman, E. J., & Dorn, L. D. (2009). Puberty: Its role in development. In R. M. Lerner & L. Steinberg (Eds.), *Handbook of adolescent psychology* (3rd ed.). New York: Wiley.

Susman, E. J., & Rogol, A. (2004). Puberty and psychological development. In R. Lerner & L. Steinberg, (Eds.), *Handbook of adolescence.* New York: Wiley.

Sutterby, J. A., & Frost, J. (2006). Creating play environments for early childhood: Indoors and out. In B. Spodek & O. N. Saracho (Eds.), *Handbook of research on the education of young children* (2nd ed.). Mahwah, NJ: Erlbaum.

Svanborg, P., Therlund, G., Gustafsson, P. A., Hagglof, B., Poole, L., & Kadesjo, B. (2009). Efficacy and safety of atomoxetine as add-on to psychoeducation in the treatment of attention deficit/hyperactivity disorder: A randomized, double-blind, placebo-controlled study in stimulant-naïve Swedish children and adolescents. *European Child and Adolescent Psychiatry, 18,* 240–249.

Swaab, D. F., Chung, W. C., Kruijver, F. P., Hofman, M. A., & Ishunina, T. A. (2001). Structural and functional sex differences in the human hypothalamus. *Hormones and Behavior, 40,* 93–98.

Swahn, M., Bossarte, R. M., & Sullivent, E. E. (2008). Age of alcohol use initiation, suicidal behavior, and peer and dating violence victimization and perpetration among high-risk, seventh-grade adolescents. *Pediatrics, 121,* 297–305.

Swamy, G. K., Ostbye, T., & Skjaerven, R. (2008). Association of preterm birth with long-term survival, reproduction, and next-generation preterm birth. *Journal of the American Medical Association, 299,* 1429–1436.

Swanson, B. J., Roman-Shriver, C. R., Shriver, B. J., & Goodell, L. S. (2007). A comparison between improvers and non-improvers among children with anemia enrolled in the WIC program. *Maternal and Child Health Journal, 11,* 447–459.

Swanson, H. L. (1999). What develops in working memory? A life-span perspective. *Developmental Psychology, 35,* 986–1000.

Swanson, H. L. (2005). Memory. In S. W. Lee (Ed.), *Encyclopedia of school psychology.* Thousand Oaks, CA: Sage.

Swearer, S. M., Espelage, D. L., & Napolitano, S. A. (2009). *Bullying prevention and intervention.* New York: Guilford.

Sweeting, H. N. (2008). Gendered dimensions of obesity in childhood and adolescence. *Nutrition Journal, 7,* 1.

Syed, M., & Azmitia, M. (2008). A native approach to ethnic identity in emerging adulthood: Bringing life to the identity status model. *Developmental Psychology, 44,* 1012–1027.

Sykes, C. J. (1995). *Dumbing down our kids: Why American children feel good about themselves but can't read, write, or add.* New York: St. Martin's Press.

T

Taddio, A. (2008). Circumcision. In M. M. Haith & J. B. Benson (Eds.), *Encyclopedia of infant and early childhood development.* Oxford, UK: Elsevier.

TADS. (2007). The Treatment for Adolescents with Depression Study: Long-term effectiveness and safety outcomes. *Archives of General Psychiatry, 64,* 1132–1143.

Tager-Flusberg, H., & Zukowski, A. (2009). Putting words together: Morphology and syntax in the preschool years. In J. Berko Gleason &

N. Ratner (Eds.), *The development of language* (7th ed.). Boston: Allyn & Bacon.

Tagore, T. (2009). Why music matters in childbirth. *Midwifery Today with International. Midwife, 89,* 33–34, 67–68.

Talaro, K. P. (2008). *Foundations of microbiology* (6th ed.). New York: McGraw-Hill.

Talge, N. M., Neal, C., Glover, V., and the Early Stress, Translational Research and Prevention Science Network: Fetal and Neonatal Experience on Child and Adolescent Mental Health. (2007). Antenatal maternal stress and long-term effects on neurodevelopment: How and why? *Journal of Child Psychology and Psychiatry, 48,* 245–261.

Tannen, D. (1990). *You just don't understand!* New York: Ballantine.

Tarokh, L., & Carskadon, M. A. (2008). Sleep in adolescents. In L. R. Squire (Ed.), *New encyclopedia of neuroscience.* Oxford, UK, Elsevier.

Tasker, F. L., & Golombok, S. (1997). *Growing up in a lesbian family: Effects an child development.* New York: Guilford.

Tauman, R., & Gozal, D. (2006). Obesity and obstructive sleep apnea in children. *Pediatric Respiratory Reviews, 7,* 247–259.

Taylor, A., Glover, V., Marks, M., & Kammerer, M. (2009, in press). Diurnal pattern of cortisol output in postnatal depression. *Psychoneuroendocrinology.*

Taylor, A. Z., & Graham, S. (2007). A examination of the relationship between achievement values and perceptions of barriers among low-SES American and Latino students. *Journal of Educational Psychology, 99,* 52–64.

Taylor, F. M. A., Ko, R., & Pan, M. (1999). Prenatal and reproductive heath care. In E. J. Kramer, S. L. Ivey, & Y.-W. Ying (Eds.), *Immigrant women's health.* San Francisco: Jossey-Bass.

Taylor, L. S., & Whittaker, C. R. (2009). *Bridging multiple worlds* (2nd ed.). Boston: Allyn & Bacon.

Taylor, R. D., & Lopez, E. I. (2005). Family management practice, school achievement, and problem behavior in African American adolescents: Mediating processes. *Applied Developmental Psychology, 26,* 39–49.

Taylor, R. L., Smiley, L., & Richards, S. B. (2009). *Exceptional students.* New York: McGraw-Hill.

Teate, A., Leap, N., Rising, S. S., & Homer, C. S. (2009, in press). Women's experiences of group antenatal care in Australia—the CenteringPregnancy pilot study. *Midwifery.*

Templeton, J. L., & Eccles, J. S. (2005). The relation between spiritual development and identity processes. In E. Roehlkepartain, P. E. King, L. Wagener, & P. L. Benson (Eds.), *The handbook of spirituality in childhood and adolescence.* Thousand Oaks, CA: Sage.

Tenenbaum, H. R., Callahan, M., Alba-Speyer, C., & Sandoval, L. (2002). Parent-child science conversations in Mexican descent families: Educational background, activity, and past experience as moderators. *Hispanic Journal of Behavioral Science, 24,* 225–248.

Terman, L. (1925). *Genetic studies of genius. Vol. 1: Mental and physical traits of a thousand gifted children.* Stanford, CA: Stanford University Press.

Teti, D. M. (2001). Retrospect and prospect in the psychological study of sibling relationships. In J. P. McHale & W. S. Grolnick (Eds.), *Retrospect and prospect in the psychological study of families.* Mahwah, NJ: Erlbaum.

Teti, D. M., & Towe-Goodman, N. (2008). Postpartum depression, effects on infant. In M. M. Haith & J. B. Benson (Eds.), *Encyclopedia of infant and early childhood development.* Oxford, UK: Elsevier.

Tewari, N., & Alvarez, A. (Eds.). (2009). *Asian American psychology.* Clifton, NJ: Psychology Press.

Thapar, A., Fowler, T., Rice, F., Scourfield, J., Van Den Bree, M., Thomas, S., Harold, G., & Hay, D. (2003). Maternal smoking during pregnancy and attention deficit hyperactivity disorder symptoms in offspring. *American Journal of Psychiatry, 160,* 1985–1989.

Tharp, R. G. (1994). Intergroup differences among Native Americans in socialization and child cognition: An erthogenetic analysis. In P. M. Greenfield & R. Cocking (Eds.), *Cross-cultural roots of minority child development.* Mahwah, NJ: Erlbaum.

Tharp, R. G., & Gallimore, R. (1988). *Rousing minds to life: Teaching, learning, and schooling in social context.* New York: Cambridge University Press.

The Hospital for Sick Children, Dipchard, A., Friedman, J., Gupta, S., Bismilla, Z., & Lam, C. (2010). *The Hospital for Sick Children's handbook of pediatrics* (11th ed.). London: Elsevier.

Thelen, E. (2000). Perception and motor development. In A. Kazdin (Ed.), *Encyclopedia of psychology.* Washington, DC, & New York: American Psychological Association and Oxford University Press.

Thelen, E., Corbetta, D., Kamm, K., Spencer, J. P., Schneider, K., & Zernicke, R. F. (1993). The transition to reaching: Mapping intention and intrinsic dynamics. *Child Development, 64,* 1058–1098.

Thelen, E., & Smith, L. B. (1998). Dynamic systems theory. In W. Damon (Ed.), *Handbook of child psychology* (5th ed., Vol. 1.). New York: Wiley.

Thelen, E., & Smith, L. B. (2006). Dynamic development of action and thought. In W. Damon & R. Lerner (Eds.), *Handbook of child psychology* (6th ed.). New York: Wiley.

Thio, A. (2010). *Deviant behavior* (10th ed.). Boston: Allyn & Bacon.

Thomann, C. R., & Carter, A. S. (2008). Social and emotional development theories. In M. M. Haith & J. B. Benson (Eds.), *Encyclopedia of infant and early childhood development.* Oxford, UK: Elsevier.

Thomas, A., & Chess, S. (1991). Temperament in adolescence and its functional significance. In R. M. Lerner, A. C. Petersen, & J. Brooks-Gunn (Eds.), *Encyclopedia of adolescence* (Vol. 2). New York: Garland.

Thomas, D. E., Bierman, K. L., Thompson, C., & the Conduct Problems Prevention Research Group. (2009, in press). Double jeopardy: Child and school characteristics that undermine school readiness and predict disruptive behavior at school entry. *School Psychology Review.*

Thomas, M. S. C., & Johnson, M. H. (2008). New advances in understanding sensitive periods in brain development. *Current Directions in Psychological Science, 17,* 1–5.

Thompson, C. M. (2006). Repositioning the visual arts in early childhood education: A decade of reconsideration. In B. Spodek & O. N. Saracho (Eds.), *Handbook of research on the education of young children* (2nd ed.). Mahwah, NJ: Erlbaum.

Thompson, D. R., Obarzanek, E., Franko, D. L., Barton, B. A., Morrison, J., Biro, F. M., Daniels, S. R., & Striegel-Moore, R. H. (2007). Childhood overweight and cardiovascular disease risk factors: The National Heart, Lung, and Blood Institute Growth and Health Study. *Journal of Pediatrics, 150,* 18–25.

Thompson, M., Kuruwita, C., & Foster, E. M. (2009). Transitions in suicide risk in a nationally representative sample of adolescents. *Journal of Adolescent Health, 44,* 458–463.

Thompson, M. P., Ho, C. H., & Kingree, J. B. (2007). Prospective associations between delinquency and suicidal behaviors in a nationally representative sample. *Journal of Adolescent Health, 40,* 232–237.

Thompson, P. M., Giedd, J. N., Woods, R. P., MacDonald, D., Evans, A. C., & Toga, A. W. (2000). Growth patterns in the developing brain detected by using continuum mechanical tensor maps. *Nature, 404,* 190–193.

Thompson, R. A. (2006). The development of the person. In W. Damon & R. Lerner (Eds.), *Hand-book of child psychology* (6th ed.). New York: Wiley.

Thompson, R. A. (2007). Unpublished review of J. W. Snatrock's *Children,* 10th ed. (New York: McGraw-Hill).

Thompson, R. A. (2008a). Early attachment and later development: Familiar questions, new answers. In J. Cassidy & P. R. Shaver (Eds.), *Handbook of attachment* (2nd ed.). New York: Guilford.

Thompson, R. A. (2008b). Unpublished review of J. W. Santrock's *Life-span development,* 12th ed. (New York: McGraw-Hill).

Thompson, R. A. (2009a, in press). Emotional development. In R. A. Schweder (Ed.), *The Chicago companion to the child.* Chicago: University of Chicago Press.

Thompson, R. A. (2009b, in press). Feeling and understanding through the prism of relationships. In S. D. Calkins & M. A. Bell (Eds.), *Child development at the intersection of emotion and cognition.* Washington, DC: American Psychological Association.

Thompson, R. A. (2009c, in press). Early foundations: Conscience and the development of moral character. In D. Narváez & D. Lapsley (Eds.), *Moral self, identity and character: Prospects for a new field of study.* New York: Cambridge University Press.

Thompson, R. A. (2009d). Making the most of small effects. *Social Development, 18,* 247–251.

Thompson, R. A., & Goodvin, R. (2005). The individual child: Temperament, emotion, self and personality. In M. J. Bornstein & M. E. Lamb (Eds.) *Developmental psychology* (5th ed.). Mahwah, NJ: Erlbaum.

Thompson, R. A., Meyer, S., & Jochem, R. (2008). Emotion regulation. In M. M. Haith & J. B. Benson (Eds.), *Encyclopedia of infant and early childhood development.* Oxford, UK: Elsevier.

Thompson, R. A., Meyer, S., & McGinley, M. (2006). Understanding values in relationships: The development of conscience. In M. Killen & J. Smetana (Eds.), *Handbook of moral development.* Mahwah, NJ: Erlbaum.

Thompson, R. A., & Newton, E. (2009, in press). Infant-caregiver communication. In H. T. Reis & S. Sprecher (Eds.), *Encyclopedia of human relationships.* Thousand Oaks, CA: Sage.

Thompson, R. A., & Virmani, E. A. (2010). Self and personality. In M. H. Bornstein (Ed.), *Handbook of cultural developmental science.* New York: Psychology Press.

Thompson, T., Moore, T., & Symons, F. (2007). Psychotherapeutic medications and positive behavior support. In S. L. Odom, R. H. Horner, M. E. Snell, & J. Blacher (Eds.), *Handbook of developmental disabilities.* New York: Guilford.

Thoni, A., & Moroder, L. (2004). Waterbirth: A safe and natural delivery method. Experience after 1355 waterbirths in Italy. *Midwifery Today, 70,* 44–48.

Thorley, V. (2009, in press). Guidelines to improve maternity practices and support breast feeding are readily available. *Southern Medical Journal.*

Timmons, B. W., Naylor, P. J., & Pfeiffer, K. A. (2007). Physical activity for preschool children: How much and how? *Canadian Journal of Public Health, 98* (Suppl. 2), S122–S134.

TIMMS. (2008). *Trends in international mathematics and science study.* Washington, DC: National Center for Education Statistics.

Tinsley, B. J. (2003). *How children learn to be healthy.* New York: Cambridge University Press.

Tinsley, B. J., Markey, C. N., Ericksen, A. J., Kwasman, A., & Ortiz, R. V. (2002). Health promotion for parents. In M. H. Bornstein (Ed.), *Handbook of parenting* (Vol. 5). Mahwah, NJ: Erlbaum.

Tiran, D. (2008). *Bailliere's midwives' dictionary* (11th ed.). Oxford, UK: Elsevier.

Tita, A. T., & others. (2009). Timing of elective repeat cesarean delivery at term and neonatal outcomes. *New England Journal of Medicine, 360,* 111–1120.

Tita, A. T., & Rouse, D. J. (2009). Progesterone for preterm birth prevention: An evolving intervention. *American Journal of Obstetrics and Gynecology, 200,* 219–224.

Tobin, J. J., Wu, D. Y. H., & Davidson, D. H. (1989). *Preschool in three cultures.* New Haven, CT: Yale University Press.

Toga, A. W., Thompson, P. M., & Sowell, E. R. (2006). Mapping brain maturation. *Trends in Neurosciences, 29,* 148–159.

Tolani, N., & Brooks-Gunn, J. (2008). Family support, international trends. In M. M. Haith & J. B. Benson (Eds.), *Encyclopedia of infant and early childhood development.* Oxford, UK: Elsevier.

Tomasello, M. (2003). *Constructing a language: A usage-based theory of language acquisition.* Cambridge, MA: Harvard University Press.

Tomasello, M. (2006). Acquiring linguistic constructions. In W. Damon & R. Lerner (Eds.), *Handbook of child psychology* (6th ed.). New York: Wiley.

Tomasello, M., & Carpenter, M. (2007). Shared intentionality. *Development Science, 10,* 121–125.

Tomasello, M., Carpenter, M., & Liszkowski, U. (2007). A new look at infant pointing. *Child Development, 78,* 705–722.

Tompkins, G. E. (2010). *Literacy for the 21st century* (5th ed.). Boston: Allyn & Bacon.

Torloni, M. R., & others. (2009). Safety of ultrasonography in pregnancy: WHO systematic review of the literature and meta-analysis. *Ultrasound in Obstetrics and Gynecology, 33,* 599–608.

Tough, S. C., Newburn-Cook, C., Johnston, D. W., Svenson, L. W., Rose, S., & Belik, J. (2002). Delayed childbearing and its impact on population rate changes in lower birth weight, multiple birth, and preterm delivery. *Pediatrics, 109,* 399–403.

Treffers, P. E., Eskes, M., Kleiverda, G., & van Alten, D. (1990). Home births and minimal medical interventions. *Journal of the American Medical Association, 246,* 2207–2208.

Trehub, S. E., Schneider, B. A., Thorpe, L. A., & Judge, P. (1991). Observational measures of auditory sensitivity in early infancy. *Developmental Psychology, 27,* 40–49.

Trejos-Castillo, E., & Vazonyi, A. T. (2009, in press). Risky sexual behavior in first and second generation Hispanic immigrant youth. *Journal of Youth and Adolescence.*

Trimble, J. E. (1988, August). *The enculturation of contemporary psychology.* Paper presented at the meeting of the American Psychological Association, New Orleans.

Trost, S. G., Fees, B., & Dzewaltowski, D. (2008). Feasibility and efficacy of "move and learn" physical activity curriculum in preschool children. *Journal of Physical Activity and Health, 5,* 88–103.

Trzesniewski, K. H., Donnellan, M. B., Caspi, A., Moffitt, T. E., Robins, R. W., & Poultin, R. (2006). Adolescent low self-esteem is a risk factor for adult poor health, criminal behavior, and limited economic prospects. *Developmental Psychology, 42,* 381–390.

Tsal, Y., Shalev, L., & Mevorach, C. (2005). The diversity of attention deficits in ADHD. *Journal of Learning Disabilities, 38,* 142–157.

Tucker, J. S., Ellickson, P. L., & Klein, M. S. (2003). Predictors of the transition to regular smoking during adolescence and young adulthood. *Journal of Adolescent Health, 32,* 314–324.

Tung, R., & Ouimette, M. (2007, November). *Strong results, high demand: A four-year study of Boston's pilot high schools.* Cambridge, MA: Center for Collaborative Education, Harvard University.

Turiel, E. (2006). The development of morality. In W. Damon & R. Lerner (Eds.), *Handbook of child psychology* (6th ed.). New York: Wiley.

Turnbull, A., Turnbull, H. R., & Tompkins, J. R. (2007). *Exceptional lives* (5th ed.). Upper Saddle River, NJ: Prentice Hall.

Turnbull, H. R., Huerta, N., & Stowe, M. (2009). *What every teacher should know about: The Individuals with Disabilities Education Act as amended in 2004* (2nd ed.). Upper Saddle River, NJ: Prentice Hall.

U

Uba, L. (1992). Cultural barriers to health care for Southeast Asian refugees. *Public Health Reports, 107,* 544–549.

Uhls, Y. T., & Greenfield, P. M. (2009, in press). Adolescents and electronic communication: Risks, benefits, and ideas for parenting. To appear at *www.education.com*

Umana-Taylor, A. J. (2006, March). *Ethnic identity, acculturation, and enculturation: Considerations in methodology and theory.* Paper presented at the meeting of the Society for Research on Adolescence, San Francisco.

Umana-Taylor, A. J., Gonzales-Baken, M. A., & Guimond, A. B. (2009). Latino adolescents' ethnic identity: Is there a developmental progression and does growth in ethnic identity predict growth in self-esteem. *Child Development, 80,* 391–405.

Umana-Taylor, A. J., Vargas-Changes, D., Garcia, C. D., & Gonzales-Backen, M. (2008). A longitudinal examination of Latino adolescents' ethnic identity, coping with discrimination, and self-esteem. *Journal of Early Adolescence, 28,* 16–50.

Underhill, K., Montgomery, P., & Operario, D. (2007). Sexual abstinence programs to prevent HIV infection in high-income countries. *British Medical Journal, 335,* 248.

Underwood, M. (2004). Sticks and stones and social exclusion: Aggression among boys and girls. In P. K. Smith & C. H. Hart (Eds.), *Blackwell handbook of childhood social development.* Malden, MA: Blackwell.

UNICEF. (2004). *State of the world's children, 2004.* Geneva: Author.

UNICEF (2007). *The state of the world's children: 2007.* Geneva, SW: UNICEF.

UNICEF. (2008). *The state of the world's children, 2008.* Geneva: Author.

UNICEF. (2009). *The state of the world's children, 2009.* Geneva: Author.

UNICEF. (2010). *The state of the world's children, 2010.* Geneva: Author.

Urbano, M. T., & Tait, D. M. (2004). Can the irradiated uterus sustain a pregnancy? *Clinical Oncology, 16,* 24–28.

Urbina, E. M. (2008). Removing the mask: The danger of hidden hypertension. *Journal of Pediatrics, 152,* 455–456.

U.S. Census Bureau (2007). *Population statistics: People.* Washington, DC: Author.

U.S. Department of Energy. (2001). *The human genome project.* Washington, DC: Author.

U.S. Department of Health and Human Services. (2008). Child maltreatment, 2006. Washington, DC: Government Printing Office. Retrieved April 1, 2008, from *www.acf.hhs.gov/programs/cb/pubs/cm06/index.htm*

U.S. Food and Drug Administration. (2004, March 19). An important message for pregnant woman and women of childbearing age who may become pregnant about the risk of mercury in fish. Washington, DC: Author.

U.S. Office of Education. (2000). *To assure a free and appropriate public education of all children with disabilities.* Washington, DC: Author.

V

Vahratian, A., Siega-Riz, A. M., Savitz, D. A., & Throp, J. M. (2004). Multivitamin use and risk of preterm birth. *American Journal Epidemiology, 160,* 886–892.

Valkenburg, P. M., & Peter, J. (2009). Social consequences of the Internet for adolescents. *Current Directions in Psychological Science, 18,* 1–5.

Vallotton, C. D., & Fischer, K. W. (2008). Cognitive development. In M. M. Haith & J. B. Benson (Eds.), *Encyclopedia of infant and early childhood development.* Oxford, UK: Elsevier.

van Beijsterveldt, T. C., & Boomsma, D. I. (2008). An exploration of gene-environment interaction and asthma in a large sample of 5-year-old Dutch twins. *Twin Research and Human Genetics, 11,* 143–149.

Van Beveren, T. T. (2008, January). *Personal conversation.* Richardson, TX: Department of Psychology, University of Texas at Dallas.

Van Buren, E., & Graham, S. (2003). *Redefining ethnic identity: Its relationship to positive and negative school adjustment outcomes for minority youth.* Paper presented at the meeting of the Society for Research in Child Development, Tampa.

Vandehey, M., Diekhoff, G., & LaBeff, E. (2007). College cheating: A 20-year follow-up and the addition of an honor code. *Journal of College Development, 48,* 468–480.

Vandell, D. L. (2004). Early child care: The known and unknown. *Merrill-Palmer Quarterly, 50,* 387–414.

van den berg, P., Neumark-Sztainer, D., Hannan, P. J., & Haines, J. (2007). Is dieting advice from magazines helpful or harmful? Five-year associations with weight-control behaviors

and psychological outcomes in adolescents. *Pediatrics, 119,* e30–e37.

van den Boom, D. C. (1989). Neonatal irritability and the development of attachment. In G. A. Kohnstamm, J. E. Bates, & M. K. Rothbart (Eds.), *Temperament in childhood.* New York: Wiley.

van den Heuvel, A., & Marteau, T. M. (2008). Cultural variation in values attached to informed choice in the context of prenatal diagnosis. *Seminars in Fetal and Neonatal Medicine, 13,* 99–102.

van der Schoot, C. E., Hahn, S., & Chitty, L. S. (2008). Non-invasive prenatal diagnosis and determination of fetal RH status. *Seminars in Fetal and Neonatal Medicine, 13,* 63–68.

Vande Vusse, L., Irland, J., Healthcare, W. F., Berner, M. A., Fuller, S., & Adams, D. (2007). Hypnosis for childbirth: A retrospective comparative analysis of outcomes in one obstetrician's practice. *American Journal of Clinical Hypnosis, 50,* 109–119.

van Hof, P., van der Kamp, J., & Savelsbergh, G. J. (2008). The relation between infants' perception of catchableness and the control of catching. *Developmental Psychology, 44,* 182–194.

van IJzendoorn, M. H., & Kroonenberg, P. M. (1988). Cross-cultural patterns of attachment: A meta-analysis of the Strange Situation. *Child Development, 59,* 147–156.

van IJzendoorn, M. H., & Sagi-Schwartz, A. (2008). Cross-cultural patterns of attachment: Universal and contextual dimensions. In J. Cassidy & P. R. Shaver (Eds.), *Handbook of attachment* (2nd ed.). New York: Guilford.

Van Orden, K. A., Witte, T. K., Gordon, K. H., Bender, T. W., & Joiner, T. E. (2008). Suicidal desire and the capability for suicide: Tests of the interpersonal-psychological theory of suicidal behavior among adults. *Journal of Consulting and Clinical Psychology, 76,* 72–83.

Vargas, L., & Koss-Chiono, J. (1999). *Working with Latino youth.* San Francisco. Jossey-Bass.

Vaughan Van Hecke, A., Mundy, P. C., Acra, C. F., Block, J. J., Delgado, E. F., Parlade, M. V., Meyer, J. A., Neal, A. R., & Pomares, Y. B. (2007). Infant joint attention, temperament, and social competence in preschool children. *Child Development, 78,* 53–69.

Vaughn, S. S., Bos, C. S., & Schumm, J. S. (2007). *Teaching students who are exceptional, diverse, and at risk in the general education classroom.* (4th ed.). Boston: Allyn & Bacon.

Venners, S. A., Wang, X., Chen, C., Wang, L., Chen, D., Guang, W., Huang, A., Ryan, L., O'Conner, J., Lasley, B., Overstreet, J., Wilcox, A., & Xu, X. (2004). Paternal smoking and pregnancy loss: A prospective study using a biomarker of pregnancy. *American Journal of Epidemiology, 159,* 993–1001.

Victor, E., Kellough, R. D., & Tai, R. H. (2008). *Science K–8* (11th ed.). Upper Saddle River, NJ: Prentice Hall.

Viikari, J., Niinikoski, H., Raitakari, O. T., & Simell, O. (2009). The initiatives and outcomes

for cardiovascular risks that can be achieved through pediatric counseling. *Current Opinion in Lipidology, 20,* 17–23.

Vik, T., & others. (2009, in press). Infantile colic, prolonged crying, and maternal postnatal depression. *Acta Pediatrica.*

Villegas, R., Gao, Y. T., Yang, G., Li, H. L., Elasy, T., Zheng, W., & Shu, X. O. (2008). Duration of breast-feeding and the incidence of type 2 diabetes mellitus in the Shanghai Women's Health Study. *Diabetologia, 51,* 258–266.

Vitaro, F., Boivin, M., & Bukowski, W. M. (2009). The role of friendship in child and adolescent psychosocial development. In K. H. Rubin, W. M. Bukowski, & B. Laursen (Eds.), *Handbook of peer interaction, relationships, and groups.* New York: Guilford.

Vitaro, F., Pedersen, S., & Brendgen, M. (2007). Children's disruptiveness, peer rejection, friends' deviancy, and delinquent behaviors: A process-oriented approach. *Development and Psychopathology, 19,* 433–453.

Vogler, G. P. (2006). Behavior genetics and aging. In J. E. Birren & K. W. Schaie (Eds.), *Handbook of the psychology of aging* (6th ed.). San Diego: Academic Press.

Von Hofsten, C. (2008). Motor and physical development manual. In M. M. Haith & J. B. Benson (Eds.), *Encyclopedia of infant and early childhood development.* Oxford, UK: Elsevier.

Vonk, J. M., Postma, D. S., Boezen, H. M., Grol, M. H., Schouten, J. P., Koeter, G. H., & Gerristen, J. (2004). Childhood factors associated with asthma remission after year follow up. *Thorax, 59,* 925–929.

Votruba-Drzal, E., Coley, R. L., & Chase-Lansdale, P. L. (2004). Child care and low-income children's development: Direct and moderated effects. *Child Development, 75,* 296–312.

Vreeman, R. C., & Carroll, A. E. (2007). A systematic review of school-based interventions to prevent bullying. *Archives of Pediatric and Adolescent Medicine, 161,* 78–88.

Vurpillot, E. (1968). The development of scanning strategies and their relation to visual differentiation. *Journal of Experimental Child Psychology, 6,* 632–650.

Vyas, S., Ghani, L., Khazaezadeh, N., & Oteng-Ntim, E. (2008). Pregnancy and obesity. In J. Studd, S. L. Tan, & F. A. Cherenak (Eds.), *Progress in obstetrics and gynecology.* Oxford, UK: Elsevier.

Vygotsky, L. S. (1962). *Thought and language.* Cambridge, MA: MIT Press.

W

Wagenaar, K., Ceelen, M., van Weissenbruch, M. M., Knol, D. L., Delemarre-van de Waal, H. A., & Huisman, J. (2008a). School functioning in 8- to 18-year-old children born after in vitro fertilization. *European Journal of Pediatrics, 167,* 1289–1295.

Wagenaar, K., Huisman, J., Cohen-Kettenis, P. T., & Adelemarre-van Waal, H. (2008b). An overview of studies on early development, cognition, and psychosocial well-being in children born after in vitro fertilization. *Journal of Developmental and Behavioral Pediatrics, 29,* 219–230.

Wainright, J. L., & Patterson, C. J. (2008). Peer relations among adolescents with same-sex parents. *Developmental Psychology, 44,* 117–126.

Waiter, G. D., & others. (2009). Exploring possible neural mechanisms of intelligence differences using processing speed and working memory tasks. *Intelligence, 37,* 199–206.

Wakschlag, L. S., & others. (2009, in press). Interaction of prenatal exposure to cigarettes and MAOA genotype in pathways to youth antisocial behavior. *Molecular Psychiatry.*

Walden, T. (1991). Infant social referencing. In J. Garber & K. Dodge (Eds.), *The development of emotional regulation and dysregulation.* New York: Cambridge University Press.

Waldrip, A. M., Malcolm, K. T., & Jensen-Campbell, L. A. (2008). With a little help from your friends: The importance of high-quality friendships on early adolescent adjustment. *Social Development, 17,* 832–852.

Walker, D. S., & Worrell, R. (2008). Promoting healthy pregnancies through perinatal groups: A comparison of CenteringPregnancy® group prenatal care and childbirth education classes. *Journal of Perinatal Education, 17,* 27–34.

Walker, L. J. (1982). The sequentiality of Kohlberg's stages of moral development. *Child Development, 93,* 1130–1136.

Walker, L. J. (2002). In W. Damon (Ed.), *Bringing in a new era of character education.* Stanford, CA: Hoover Press.

Walker, L. J. (2004). Progress and prospects in the psychology of moral development. *Merrill-Palmer Quarterly, 50,* 546–557.

Walker, L. J., & Frimer, J. A. (2009a, in press). Being good for goodness' sake: Transcendence in the lives of moral heroes. In F. K. Oser & W. M. M. H. Veugelers (Eds.), *Getting involved: Global citizenship development and sources of moral values.* Rotterdam, the Netherlands: Sense.

Walker, L. J., & Frimer, J. A. (2009b, in press). Moral personality exemplified. In D. Narváez & D. K. Lapsley (Eds.), *Moral personality, identity, and character: Prospects for new field of study.* New York: Cambridge University Press.

Walker, S. (2006). Unpublished review of J. W. Santrock's *Topical life-span development,* 3rd ed. (New York: McGraw-Hill).

Wallerstien, J. S. (2008). Divorce. In M. M. Haith & J. B. Benson (Eds.), *Encyclopedia of infant and early childhood development.* Oxford, UK: Elsevier.

Walley, A. J., Blakemore, A. I., & Froguel, P. (2006). Genetics of obesity and the prediction of risk for health. *Human Molecular Genetics, 15* (Suppl. 2), R124–R130.

Walshaw, C. A., & Owens, J. M. (2006). Low breastfeeding rates and milk insufficiency. *British Journal of General Practice, 56,* 379.

Walsh, C. A., & Walsh, S. R. (2009, in press). Extraabdominal vs. intraabdominal uterine repair at cesarean delivery: A metaanalysis. *American Journal of Obstetrics and Gynecology.*

Walsh, J. (2008). Self-efficacy. In N. J. Salkind (Ed.), *Encyclopedia of educational psychology.* Thousand Oaks, CA: Sage.

Walsh, L. A. (2000, Spring). The inside scoop on child development: Interview, *Cutting through the hype.* Minneapolis: College of Education and Human Development, University of Minnesota.

Walsh, L. V. (2006). Beliefs and rituals in traditional birth attendant practice in Guatemala. *Journal of Transcultural Nursing, 17,* 148–154.

Wan, L. B., & Bartolomei, M. S. (2008). Regulation of imprinting in clusters: Noncoding RNAs versus insulators. *Advances in genetics, 61,* 207–223.

Wang, B., Zhou, T. G., Zhuo, Y., & Chen, L. (2007). Global topological dominance in the left hemisphere. *Proceedings of the National Academy of Sciences USA, 104,* 21014–21019.

Wang, L. Y., Chyen, D., Lee. L., & Lowry, R. (2008). The association between body mass index in adolescence and obesity in adulthood. *Journal of Adolescent Health, 42,* 512–518.

Wardlaw, G. M., & Hampl, J. (2007). *Perspectives in nutrition* (7th ed.). New York: McGraw-Hill.

Wardlaw, G. M., & Smith, A. M. (2009). *Contemporary nutrition* (9th ed.). New York: McGraw-Hill.

Wardle, J., Carnell, S., Haworth, C. M., & Plomin, R. (2008). Evidence for a strong genetic influence on childhood adiposity despite the force of the obesogenic environment. *American Journal of Clinical Nutrition, 87,* 398–404.

Warrick, P. (1992, March 1). The fantastic voyage of Tanner Roberts. *Los Angeles Times,* pp. E1, E11, E12.

Warshak, R. A. (2008, January). Personal communication, Department of Psychology, University of Texas at Dallas, Richardson.

Wasserman, M., Bender, D., & Lee, S. Y. (2007). Use of preventive maternal and child health services by Latina women: A review of published intervention studies. *Medical Care Research and Review, 64,* 4–45.

Watanabe, H., & Taga, G. (2006). General to specific development of movement patterns and memory for contingency between actions and events in young infants. *Infant Behavior and Development, 29,* 402–422.

Waterman, A. S. (1985). Identity in the context of adolescent psychology. In A. S. Waterman (Ed.), *Identity in adolescence: Processes and contents.* San Francisco: Jossey-Bass.

Waterman, A. S. (1999). Identity, the identity statuses, and identity status development: A contemporary statement. *Developmental Review, 19,* 591–621.

Watkins, N., Larson, R., & Sullivan, P. (2007). Learning to bridge difference: Community youth programs as contexts for developing multicultural competencies. *American Behavioral Scientist, 51,* 380–402.

Watson, J. B. (1928). *Psychological care of infant and child.* New York: W. W. Norton.

Watson, J. B., & Rayner, R. (1920). Conditioned emotional reactions. *Journal of Experimental Psychology, 3,* 1–14.

Way, N., Santos, C, Niwa, E. Y., & Kim-Gervey, C. (2008). To be or not to be: An exploration of ethnic identity development in context. *New Directions for Child and Adolescent Development, 120,* 61–79.

Webb, J. T., Gore, J. L., Mend, E. R., & DeVries, A. R. (2007). *A parent's guide to gifted children.* Scottsdale, AZ: Great Potential Press.

Webb, L. D., Metha, A., & Jordan, K. F. (2010). *Foundations of American education* (6th ed.). Upper Saddle River, NJ: Prentice Hall.

Webster, N. S., & Worrell, F. C. (2008). Academically-talented adolescents' attitudes toward service in the community. *Gifted Child Quarterly, 52,* 170–179.

Wegman, M. E. (1987). Annual summary of vital statistics—1986. *Pediatrics, 80,* 817–827.

Weihong, Y., Holland, S. K., Cecil, K. M., Dietrich, K. N., Wessel, S. D., Altaye, M., Hornung, R. W., Ris, M. D., Egelhoff, J. C., & Lanphear, B. P. (2006). The impact of early childhood lead exposure on brain organization: A functional magnetic resonance imaging study of language function. *Pediatrics, 188,* 971–977.

Weikert, D. P. (1993). [Long-term positive effects in the Perry Preschool Head Start Program.] Unpublished data, High Scope Foundation, Ypsilanti, MI.

Weiner, C. P., & Buhimschi, C. (2009). *Drugs for pregnant and lactating women* (2nd ed.). London: Elsevier.

Weiner, C. P., & Buhimschi, C. S. (2009). Medications in pregnancy and lactation: Part 2. Drugs with minimal or unknown human teratogenic effect. *Obstetrics and Gynecology, 113,* 417–432.

Weiss, L. A., & others. (2008). Association between microdeletion and microduplication at 16p 11.2 and autism. *New England Journal of Medicine, 358,* 667–675.

Wei, S., Wo, B. L., Xu, H., Luo, Z. C., Roy, C., & Fraser, W. D. (2009). Early amniotomy and early oxytocin for prevention of, or therapy for, delay in first stage spontaneous labor compared with routine care. *Cochrane Database of Systematic Reviews, 2,* CD006794.

Wekerle, C., Leung, E., Wall, A. M., Macmillan, H., Boyle, M., Trocme, N., & Waechter, R. (2009). The contribution of childhood emotional abuse to teen dating violence among child protective services-involved youth. *Child Abuse and Neglect, 33,* 45–58.

Wellman, H. M., Cross, D., & Watson, J. (2001). Meta-analysis of theory-of-mind development: The truth about false belief. *Child Development, 72,* 655–684.

Wellman, H. M., Lopez-Duran, S., Labounty, J., & Hamilton, B. (2008). Infant attention to intentional action predicts preschool theory of mind. *Developmental Psychology, 44,* 618–623.

Wellman, H. M. & Wooley, J. D. (1990). From simple desires to ordinary beliefs: The early development of everyday psychology. *Cognition, 35,* 245–275.

Wells, J. C., Hallal, P. C., Reichert, F. F., Menezes, A. M., Araujo, C. L., & Victora, C. G. (2008). Sleep patterns and television viewing in relation to obesity and blood pressure: Evidence from an adolescent Brazilian cohort. *International Journal of Obesity, 32,* 1042–1049.

Weng, X., Odouli, R., & Li, D. K. (2008). Maternal caffeine consumption during pregnancy and the risk of miscarriage: A prospective cohort study. *American Journal of Obstetrics and Gynecology, 198,* e1–e8.

Wentzel, K. R., & Asher, S. R. (1995). The academic lives of neglected, rejected, popular, and controversial children. *Child Development, 66,* 754–763.

Wentzel, K. R, Barry, C. M., & Caldwell, K. A. (2004). Friendships in middle school: Influences on motivation and school adjustment. *Journal of Educational Psychology, 96,* 195–203.

Wentzel, K. R., & Looney, L. (2007). Socialization in school settings. In J. E. Grusec & P. D. Hastings (Eds.), *Handbook of socialization.* New York: Guilford.

Wenze, G. T., & Wenze, N. (2004). Helping left-handed children adapt to school expectations. *Childhood Education, 81,* 25–31.

Werker, J. F., Maurer, D. M., & Yoshida, K. A. (2010). Perception. In M. H. Bornstein (Ed.), *Handbook of cultural developmental science.* New York: Psychology Press.

Werker, J. F., & Tees, R. C. (2005). Speech perception as a window for understanding plasticity and commitment in language systems of the brain. *Developmental Psychobiology, 46,* 233–251.

Werts, M. G., Culatta, R. A., & Tompkins, J. R. (2007). *Fundamentals of special education* (3rd ed.). Upper Saddle River, NJ: Prentice Hall.

Wertsch, J. V. (2007). Mediation. In H. Daniels, J. Wertsch, & M. Cole (Eds.), *The Cambridge companion to Vygotsky.* New York: Cambridge University Press.

Westerlund, M., & Lagerberg, D. (2008). Expressive vocabulary in 18-month-old children in relation to demographic factors, mother and child characteristics, communication style, and shared reading. *Child: Care, Health, and Development, 34,* 257–266.

West, J., Denton, K., & Germino-Hausken, E. (2000). *America's kindergartners.* Washington, DC: National Center for Education Statistics.

Westling, E., Andrews, J. A., Hampson, S. E., & Peterson, M. (2008). Pubertal timing and substance use: The effects of gender, parental monitoring, and deviant peers. *Journal of Adolescent Health, 42,* 555–563.

Wheeden, A., Scafidi, F. A., Field, T., Ironson, G., Valdeon, C. & Bandstra, E. (1993). Massage effects on cocaine-exposed preterm neonates. *Journal of Developmental and Behavioral Pediatrics, 14,* 318–322.

Whetstone, L. M., Morrissey, S. L., & Cummings, D. M. (2007). Children at risk: The association between perceived weight status and suicidal thoughts and attempts in middle school youth. *Journal of School Health, 77,* 59–66.

Whitehead, K. A., Ainsworth, A. T., Wittig, M. A., & Gadino, B. (2009). Implications of ethnic identity exploration and ethnic identity affirmation and belonging for intergroup attitudes among adolescents. *Journal of Research on Adolescence, 19,* 123–135.

White, J. W. (2001). Aggression and gender. In J. Worell (Ed.), *Encyclopedia of women and gender.* San Diego: Academic Press.

Whitescarver, K. (2006, April). *Montessori rising: Montessori education in the United States, 1955–present.* Paper presented at the meeting of the American Education Research Association, San Francisco.

Wickham, S. (2009). *Midwifery: Best practice.* London: Elsevier.

WIC New York. (2009). *The new look of the women, infants, and children (WIC) program.* Retrieved January 21, 2009, from www.health.state.ny.us/prevention/nutrition/wic/the_new_look_of_wic.htm

Wiebe, S. A., Espy, K. A., Stopp, C., Respass, J., Stewart, P., Jameson, T. R., Gilbert, D. G., & Huggenvik, J. I. (2009). Gene-environment interactions across development: Exploring DRD2 genotype and prenatal smoking effects on self-regulation. *Developmental Psychology, 45,* 31–44.

Wiesner, M., & Ittel, A. (2002). Relations of pubertal timing and depressive symptoms to substance use in early adolescence. *Journal of Early Adolescence, 22,* 5–23.

Wigfield, A., & Asher, S. R. (1984). Social and motivational influences on reading. In P. D. Pearson, R. Barr, M. L. Kamil, & P. Mosenthal (Eds.), *Handbook of reading research.* New York: Longman.

Wigle, D. T., Arbuckle, T. E., Walker, M., Wade, M. G., Liu, S., & Krewski, D. (2007). Environmental hazards: Evidence for effects on child health. *Journal of Toxicology and Environmental Health, 10,* 3–39.

Williams, C. L., & Strobino, B. A. (2008). Childhood diet, overweight, and CVD risk factors: The Healthy Start project. *Preventive Cardiology, 11,* 11–20.

Williams, J. H., & Ross, L. (2007). Consequences of prenatal toxin exposure for mental health in children and adolescents: A systematic review. *European Child and Adolescent Psychiatry, 16,* 243–253.

Willoughby, T. (2008). A short-term longitudinal study of internet and computer game use by adolescent boys and girls: Prevalence, frequency of use, and psychosocial predictors. *Developmental Psychology, 44,* 195–204.

Wills, T. A., Yaeger, A. M., & Sandy, J. M. (2003). Buffering effect of religiosity for adolescent substance use. *Psychology of Addictive Behaviors, 17,* 24–31.

Wilson, B. J. (2008). Media and children's aggression, fear, and altruism. *The Future of Children, 18* (1), 87–118.

Wilson, D., & Hockenberry, M. J. (2008). *Wong's clinical manual of pediatric nursing* (7th ed.). Oxford, UK: Elsevier

Wilson, M. N. (2008). Poor fathers', involvement in the lives of their children. In D. R. Crane & T. B. Heaton (Eds.), *Handbook of families and poverty.* Thousand Oaks, CA: Sage.

Windle, W. F. (1940). *Physiology of the human fetus.* Philadelphia: W. B. Saunders.

Winner, E. (1986, August.). Where pelicans kiss seals. *Psychology Today,* pp. 24–35.

Winner, E. (1996). *Gifted children: Myths and realities.* New York: Basic Books.

Winner, E. (2000). The origins and ends of giftedness. *American Psychologist, 55,* 159–169.

Winner, E. (2006). Development in the arts. In W. Damon & R. Lerner (Eds.), *Handbook of child psychology (6th ed.).* New York: Wiley.

Winner, E. (2009). Toward broadening our understanding of giftedness: The spatial domain. In F. D. Horowitz, R. F. Subotnik, & D. J. Matthews (Eds.), *The development of giftedness and talent across the life span.* Washington, DC: American Psychological.

Winsler, A., Carlton, M. P., & Barry, M. J. (2000). Age-related changes in preschool children's systematic use of private speech in a natural setting. *Journal of Child Language, 27,* 665–687.

Winslow, E. B., Bonds, D., Wolchik S., Sandler, I., & Braver, S. (2009). Predictors of enrollment and retention in a preventive parenting intervention for divorced families. *Journal of Primary Prevention, 30,* 151–172.

Witelson, S. F., Beresh, H., & Kigar, D. L. (2006). Intelligence and brain size in 100 postmortem brains: Sex, laterlization and age factors. *Brain, 129,* 386–398.

Witelson, S. F., Kigar, D. L., & Harvey, T. (1999). The exceptional brain of Albert Einstein. *The Lancet, 353,* 2149–2153.

Witkin, H. A., Mednick, S. A., Schulsinger, R., Bakkestrom, E., Christiansen, K. O., Goodenbough, D. R., Hirchhorn, K., Lunsteen, C., Owen, D. R., Philip, J., Ruben, D. B., & Stocking, M. (1976). Criminality in XYY and XXY men. *Science, 193,* 547–555.

Wittmeier, K. D., Mollar, R. C., & Kriellaars, D. J. (2008). Physical activity intensity and risk of overweight and adiposity in children. *Obesity, 16,* 415–420.

Wofford, L. G. (2008). Systematic review of childhood obesity prevention. *Journal of Pediatric Nursing, 23,* 5–19.

Wolraich, M., Dworkin, P., Drotar, D., & Perrin, E. (2008). *Developmental-behavioral pediatrics.* Oxford, UK: Elsevier.

Wong, E. C., Kinzie, J. D., & Kinzie, M. (2009). Stress, refugees, and trauma. In N. Tewari & A Alvarez (Eds.), *Asian American psychology.* Clifton. NJ: Psychology Press.

Wong, M. M., Brower, K. J., & Zucker, R. A. (2009, in press). Childhood sleep problems, early onset of substance use, and behavioral problems in adolescence. *Sleep Medicine.*

Wong, Y. J., & Rochlen, A. B. (2008). *The new psychology of men: The emotional side.* Greenwood.

Wong Briggs, T. W. (2004, October 14). *USA Today's* 2004 all-USA teacher team. *USA Today,* p. 6D.

Wood, A. C., Rijsdijk, F., Saudino, K. J., Asherson, P., & Kuntsi, J. (2008). High heritability for a composite index of children's activity level Measures. *Behavior Genetics, 38,* 266–276.

Wood, D., Kaplan, R., & McLoyd, V. C. (2007). Gender differences in educational expectations of urban, low-income African American youth: The role of parents and school. *Journal of Youth and Adolescence, 36,* 417–427.

Woodhouse, S. S., Dykas, M. J., & Cassidy, J. (2009). Perceptions of secure base provision within the family. *Attachment and Human Development, 11,* 47–67.

Woodward, A. L., & Markman, E. M. (1998). Early word learning. In D. Kuhn & R. S. Siegler (Eds.), *Handbook of child psychology* (5th ed., Vol. 2). New York: Wiley.

Woodward, A., & Needham, A. (Eds.). (2009). *Learning and the infant mind.* New York: Oxford University.

Woodward, L. J., & others. (2009, in press). Very preterm children show impairments across multiple neurodevelopmental domains by age 4 years. *Archives of Disease in Childhood: Fetal and Neonatal Edition.*

World Health Organization. (2000, February 2). *Adolescent health behavior in 28 countries.* Geneva: Author.

Wright, C. S., Rifas-Shiman, S. L., Rich-Edwards, J. W., Taveras, E. M., Gillman, M. W., & Oken, E. (2009). Intrauterine exposure to gestational diabetes, child adiposity, and blood pressure. *American Journal of Hypertension, 22,* 215–220.

Wynn, K. (1992). Addition and subtraction by human infants. *Nature, 358,* 749–570.

X

Xu, F., Spelke, E., & Goddard, S. (2005). Number sense in human infants. *Developmental Science, 8,* 88–101.

Xue, F., Holzman, C., Rahbar, M. H., Trosko, K., & Fischer, L. (2007). Maternal fish consumption, mercury levels, and risk of preterm delivery. *Environmental Health Perspectives, 115,* 42–47.

Y

Yang, C., & Brown, B. (2009, April). *From Facebook to cell calls: Layers of electronic intimacy in college students' peer relations.* Paper presented at the meeting of the Society for Research in Child Development, Denver.

Yang, Q., Wen, S. W., Leader, A., Chen, X. K., Lipson, J. & Walker, M. (2007). Paternal age and birth defects: How strong is the association. *Human Reproduction, 22,* 696–701.

Yang, S., & Sternberg, R. J. (1997). Taiwanese Chinese people's conceptions of intelligence. *Intelligence, 25,* 21–36.

Yell, M. L., & Drasgow, E. (2009). *What every teacher should know about No Child Left Behind* (2nd ed.). Upper Saddle River, NJ: Prentice Hall.

Yen, S.-C. (2008). Short-term memory. In N. J. Salkind (Ed.), *Encyclopedia of educational psychology.* Thousand Oaks, CA: Sage.

Youngblade, L. M., & Curry, L. A. (2006). The people they know: Links between interpersonal contexts and adolescent risky and health promoting behavior. *Developmental Science, 10,* 96–106.

Youngblade, L. M., Curry, L., Vogel, W. B., Novak, M. A., & Shenkman, E. A. (2006). The impact of community risks and resources on adolescents' risky behavior and health-care expenditures. *Journal of Adolescent Health, 38,* 486–494.

Young, D. (2001). The nature and management of pain: What is the evidence? *Birth, 28,* 149–151.

Young, E. L., Boye, A. E., & Nelson, D. A. (2006). Relational aggression: Understanding, identifying, and responding in schools. *Psychology in the Schools, 43,* 297–312.

Young, K. T. (1990). American conceptions of infant development from 1955 to 1984: What the experts are telling parents. *Child Development, 61,* 17–28.

Youniss, J., McLellan, J. A., & Yates, M. (1999). Religion, community service, and identity in American youth. *Journal of Adolescence, 22,* 243–253.

Yu, C. W., Sung, R. Y., So, R., Lam, K., Nelson, E. A., Li, A. M., Yuan, Y., & Lam, P. K. (2002). Energy expenditure and physical activity of obese children: Cross-sectional study. *Hong Kong Medical Journal, 8,* 313–317.

Z

Zahn-Waxler, C., Shirtcliff, E. A., & Marceau, K. (2008). Disorders of childhood and adolescence: Gender and psychopathology. *Annual Review of Clinical Psychology, 27,* 275–303.

Zeller, M. H., Reiter-Purtill, J., & Ramey, C. (2008). Negative peer perceptions of obese children in the classroom environment. *Obesity, 16,* 755–762.

Zentall, S. S. (2006). *ADHD and education.* Upper Saddle River, NJ: Prentice Hall.

Zhang, L.-F., & Sternberg, R. J. (2009). Learning in a cross-cultural perspective. In T. Husen & T. N. Postlethwaite (Eds.), *International encyclopedia of education learning and cognition* (3rd ed.). Oxford, UK: Elsevier.

Zhao, Z., Zhang, Z., Wang, Z., Ferm, M., Liang, Y., & Norback, D. (2008). Asthmatic symptoms among pupils in relation to winter indoor and outdoor air pollution in Taiyuan, China. *Environmental Health Perspectives, 116,* 90–97.

Zielinski, D. S., Eckenrode, J., & Olds, D. L. (2009). Nurse home visitation and the prevention of child maltreatment: Impact on the timing of official reports. *Development and Psychopathology, 21,* 441–453.

Zigler, E. F., & Styfco, S. J. (1994). Head Start: Criticisms in a constructive context. *American Psychologist, 49,* 127–132.

Zigler, E., Gilliam, W. S., & Jones, S. M. (2006). *A vision for universal preschool education.* New York: Cambridge University Press.

Zimmer-Gembeck, M. J., & Helfand, M. (2008). Ten years of longitudinal research on U.S. adolescent sexual behavior: Developmental correlates of sexual intercourse, and the importance of age, gender, and ethnic background. *Developmental Review, 28,* 153–224.

Zinn, M. B., & Wells, B. (2000). Diversity within Latino families: New lessons for family social science. In D. H. Demo, K. R. Allen, & M. A. Fine (Eds.), *Handbook of family diversity.* New York: Oxford University Press.

Ziol-Guest, K. M. (2009). Child custody and support. In D. Carr (Ed.), *Encyclopedia of the life course and and human development.* Boston: Gale Cengage.

Zosuls, K. M., Lurye, L. E., & Ruble, D. N. (2008). Gender: Awareness, identity, and stereotyping. In M. M. Haith & J. B. Benson (Eds.), *Encyclopedia of infant and early childhood development.* Oxford, UK: Elsevier.

Zuidgeest, M. G., & others. (2009). What drives prescribing asthma medication to children? A multilevel population-based study. *Annals of Family Medicine, 7,* 32–40.

Zverev, Y. P. (2006). Cultural and environmental pressure against left-hand preference in urban and semi-urban Malawi. *Brain and Cognition, 60,* 295–303.

CREDITS

Photo Credits

Title Page: © Ariel Skelley/Blend Images/Corbis RF
Prologue: © Bachmann/Photo Network/Grant Heilman

Section Openers

1: © Ariel Skelley/Corbis; 2: © Brand X Pictures/PunchStock RF; 3: © Elizabeth Hathon/Corbis; 4 & 5: © Ariel Skelley/Corbis; 6: © Paul Barton/Corbis

Chapter 1

Opener: © Ariel Skelley/The Stock Market/Corbis; p. 6 (top left): © Evergreen High School Yearbook/AP Photo; p. 6 (bottom left): © Rogers and Clark Co/AFP/Getty; p. 6 (top right): Photograph of Alice Walker from Manuscript, Archives, and Rare Book Library, Emory University, Alice Walker papers #1061 Box 180 folder 1. Reprinted by permission of Alice Walker; p. 6 (bottom right): © AP/Wide World Photos; p. 8: Courtesy of Luis Vargas; p. 9: © National Association for the Education of Young Children/photo © Robert Maust/Photo Agora; p. 10: © Nancy Agostini; p. 11: © Naser Siddique/UNICEF Bangladesh; p. 12: Courtesy Marian Wright Edelman, Children's Defense Fund; p. 13: © Nathan Benn/Corbis; p. 14: Photo © Erich Lessing/Art Resource, NY/Painting by Diego Velazquez, *Infanta Margarita Teresa in white garb*, Kunsthistorisches Museum, Vienna, Austria; p. 15 (top): © wolfgang Flamisch/zefa/Corbis; 1.3: © Archives of the History of American Psychology/Louise Bates Ames Gift; 1.5 (Prenatal): © Dr. Landrum B. Shettles; 1.5 (Infancy): Courtesy of John Santrock; 1.5 (Early childhood): © Dynamic Graphics Group/PunchStock RF; 1.5 (middle childhood): © Corbis RF; 1.5 (Adolescence): © Comstock PictureQuest RF; p. 21: © PhotoDisc RF; p. 23: © Bettmann/Corbis; p. 25: © Sarah Putnam/Index Stock; p. 26 (baby): © Corbis RF; p. 26 (toddler): © Punchstock/Image Source RF; p.26 (child): © Veer RF; p. 26 (teen): © BanaStock/PunchStock RF; p. 28 (top): © Yves DeBraine/Stock Photo; p. 28 (bottom): © Courtesy of A.R. Lauria/Dr. Michael Cole/Laboratory of Human Cognition; p. 29: © Creatas Images/Jupiter Images RF; p. 30: © AP/Wide World Photos; p. 31: Courtesy Albert Bandura; p. 32 (top): © Nina Leen/Time/Life Magazine/Getty News; p. 32 (bottom): © Corbis RF; p. 33: Courtesy of Urie Bronfenbrenner; 1.12 (Freud): © Bettmann/Corbis; 1.12 (Pavlov): © Corbis; 1.12 (Piaget): © Yves deBraine/Stock Photo; 1.12 (Vygotsky): © A.R. Lauria/Dr. Michael Cole, Laboratory of Human Cognition, University of California, San Diego; 1.12 (Skinner): © Harvard University News Office; 1.12 (Erikson): © UPI/Bettmann/Corbis; 1.12 (Bandura): Courtesy Albert Bandura; 1.12 (Bronfenbrenner): Courtesy of Urie Bronfenbrenner; p. 35: © Ray Stott/The Image Works; p. 37 (top): © Bettmann/Corbis; p. 37 (bottom): © Sovereign/Phototake; p. 41: © McGraw-Hill Companies, John Thoeming, photographer; p. 43: Courtesy of Pamela Trotman Reid; p. 44 (left): © Kevin Fleming/Corbis; p. 44 (right): © Ed Honowitz/Stone/Getty; p. 51: Courtesy of Valerie Pang; p. 54: Courtesy of Katherine Duchen Smith, Certified Pediatric Nurse Practicioner, Ft. Collins, Colorado

Chapter 2

Opener: © Design Pics/Corbis RF; p. 60 © Enrico Ferorelli; p. 61: © Frans Lemmens/zefa/Corbis; p. 62:

© Alan and Sandy Carey/Getty RF; p. 63: © David Wilkie; p. 64: © Rick Rickman; 2.3: © Science Source/Photo Researchers; 2.4a&b: © Custom Medical Stock Photo; p. 68: © Joel Gordon 1989; p. 69: From R. Simensen and R. Curtis Rogers, "Fragile X Syndrome," *American Family Physician,* 39 (5): 186, May 1989. © American Academy of Family Physicians.; p. 70: © Andrew Eccles/JBGPHOTO.COM; p. 71: Courtesy of Holly Ishmael; p. 72 (top): © Jacques Pavlosky/sygma/Corbis; 2.8: © Larry Berman; p. 73 (top): © Science Source/Photo Researchers; p. 73 (bottom): © Reuters/Corbis; p. 75: © James Devaney/WireImage/Getty; p. 76: © Sonda Dawes/The Image Works; p. 78: © Myrleen Ferguson Cate/Photo Edit; p. 80: © Duomo/Corbis

Chapter 3

Opener: © Lennart Nilsson; p. 88: © Dr. Santrock; 3.3a: © Lennart Nilsson; 3.3b&c: © Petit Format/Nestle/Photo Researchers; 3.4: © Lennart Nilsson/Albert Bonniers Forlag AB; p. 93 (bottom): © Spina Bifida Association of Greater New Orleans; p. 94 (top): © Vol. 15/PhotoDisc RF; p. 94 (bottom): © Photographer's Choice/Getty RF; p. 95: © Tracy Frankel/The Image Bank/Getty; p. 96: © Stockbyte/Getty RF; p. 97: © Roger Tully/Stone/Getty; p. 98: Courtesy of Rachel Thompson; p. 99 (top): © Sharon Schindler Rising, Centering Pregnancy Program; p. 99 (bottom): © Vivianne Moos/Corbis; p. 103: Courtesy of Ann Streissguth; p. 104: © Will & Deni McIntyre/Photo Researchers; p. 105: © John Chiasson; p. 106: © R.I.A. Novosti/Gamma/H.P.P./Eyedea; p. 108 (top): © Betty Press/Woodfin Camp & Associates; p. 108 (bottom): © iStock Photos; p. 109: © Karen Kasmauski/Corbis; p. 110 (top): © David Glick/Getty; p. 110 (bottom): © David Butow/Corbis

Chapter 4

Opener: © SIU/Peter Arnold; p. 120 (top): Marjorie Shostak/Anthro-Photo; p. 120 (bottom): © Brand X/Corbis RF; p. 122: Courtesy of Linda Pugh; p. 123 (top): © Dr. Holly Beckwith; p. 123 (bottom): © Nova Development RF; p. 124: © Tom Galliher/Corbis; 4.2: © Stephen Marks, Inc./The Image Bank/Getty; p. 126: © Charles Grupton/Stock Boston; p. 129: Courtesy of Dr. Susan M. Ludington; p. 130: © Dr. Tiffany Field; p. 134 (top): © Tony Schanuel; p. 134 (bottom): © Ariel Skelley/Corbis; p. 135: © Kaz Mori/The Image Bank/Getty

Chapter 5

Opener: © George Disario/The Stock Market/Corbis; p. 144 (top): © Wendy Stone/Corbis; p. 144 (bottom): © Dave Bartruff/Corbis; 5.2: © 1990 Kenneth Jarecke/Contact Press Images; 5.3: © A. Glauberman/Photo Researchers; 5.8a&b: Courtesy of Dr. Harry T. Chugani, Children's Hospital of Michigan; 5.9a: © David Grubin Productions Inc. Reprinted by permission; 5.9b: Courtesy of Dana Boatman, Ph.D., Department of Neurology, John Hopkins University. Reprinted with permission from *The Secret Life of the Brain,* © 2001 by the National Academy of Sciences, the National Academies Press, Washington, D.C.; p. 151: © C Squared Studios/Getty RF; p. 152 (top): © Tom Rosenthal/SuperStock; p. 152 (bottom): © McGraw-Hill Companies, photographer Jill Braaten; p. 154: © Vol. DV251 Digital Vision/Getty RF; p. 155:

© Bob Dammrich/The Image Works; p. 157: Courtesy of Dr. T. Berry Brazelton; p. 157: Courtesy of The Hawaii Family Support/Healthy Start Program; p. 159: Courtesy of Esther Thelen; 5.14a: © Elizabeth Crews/The Image Works; 5.14b: © James G. White; 5.14c: © Petit Format/Photo Researchers; p. 161: © BigStock Photos; p. 162: © Fabio Caardosa/zefa/Corbis; 5.15a & b: © Karen Adolph, New York University; p. 164 (top): Michael Greenlar/The Image Works; p. 164 (bottom): © Frank Bailey Studio; p. 165 (top): © Newstockimages/SuperStock RF; 5.17: Courtesy Amy Needham; p. 166: © Mika/zefa/Corbis; 5.18: Adapted from "The Origin of Form and Perception" by R.L. Fantz © 1961 by *Scientific American.* Photo © by David Linton; 5.20 (all) Courtesy of Dr. Charles Nelson; 5.23: © Enrico Ferorelli; 5.24 (top): © Michael Siluk; 5.24 (bottom): © Dr. Melanie J. Spence, University of Texas at Dallas; 5.25: © Jean Guichard/Sygma/Corbis; 5.26 (all): D. Rosenstein and R. Oster, "Differential Facial Response to Four Basic Tastes in Newborns" in *Child Development,* Volume 59, pp. 1561–1563. Reprinted with permission of the Society for Research in Child Development; p. 175: © Philip Kaake/Corbis

Chapter 6

Opener: © altrendo images/Getty; p. 183: © Laura Dwight/Corbis; p. 184: © Elyse Lewin/Brand X/Corbis RF; p. 186: © PunchStock RF; 6.2a&b: © Doug Goodman/Photo Researchers; p. 189: © Joe McNally; p. 191: © Don Mason/Corbis; 6.5: Courtesy of Carolyn Rovee-Collier; p. 193: © Myrleen Ferguson Cate/Photo Edit; 6.6a&b: Photos from: Meltzoff, A. N., & Brooks, R. (2007). Intersubjectivity before language: Three windows on preverbal sharing. In S. Bråten (Ed.), On being moved: From mirror neurons to empathy (pp. 149–174). Philadelphia, PA: John Benjamins.; p. 194: © Tom Stewart/Corbis; 6.9: © Andrew Meltzoff; 6.10: From Jean Mandler, University of California, San Diego. Reprinted by permission of Oxford University Press; p. 197: © John Santrock; p. 198 (top): Courtesy of John Santrock; p. 198 (bottom): Bayley Scales of Infant and Toddler Development—Third Edition (Bayley-III). Copyright © 2006 by NCS Pearson, Inc. Reproduced with permission. All rights reserved.; p. 200: © Time & Life Pictures/Getty; p. 201: © Peter Byron/Photo Researchers; 6.14a&b: © 2003 University of Washington, Institute for Learning and Brain Sciences (I-LABS).; p. 205: © Niki Mareschal/Photographers Choice/Getty; p. 206: © Anthony Bannister/Animals Animals/Earth Scenes; 6.18: © Michael Goldstein, Cornell University; p. 211: © John Carter/Photo Researchers

Chapter 7

Opener: © Jamie Marcial/SuperStock; p. 220: © Rick Gomez/Corbis; p. 221: © Zen Sekizawa/Getty; 7.1 (all): © Michael Lewis, Institute for the Study of Child Development, Robert Wood Johnson Medical School; 7.2: © Sybil L. Hart, Texas Tech University; p. 222 (bottom): © Andy Cox/Stone/Getty; p. 223: © Dr. Daniel Messinger, University of Miami, FL; p. 224: © Romilly Lockyer/The Image Bank/Getty; p. 226: © Michael Tcherevkoff/The Image Bank/Getty; p. 227: © Judith Oddie/Photo Edit; 7.5: © Digital Vision/Getty RF; p. 230: © Vol. 63 PhotoDisc/Getty RF; p. 231: © Britt Erlanson/Image Bank/Getty; 7.6: Courtesy Celia A. Brownell, University of Pittsburgh; p. 232: © Dan

Lepp/Corbis; 7.7: © Martin Rogers/Stock Boston; p. 234 (top): © Corbis RF; p. 234 (bottom): © David Young-Wolff/Photo Edit; p. 236: © Penny Tweedie/Stone/Getty; 7.10: © BrandXPictures/Getty RF; p. 239 (top): © Corbis RF; p. 239 (left): © National Geographic/Getty RF; p. 239 (bottom rt.): © Stephanie Rausser/Taxi/Getty RF; p. 240: © John Henley/Corbis; p. 241: © Schwartzwald Lawrence/Corbis; p. 242: Courtesy of Rashmi Nakhre, the Hattie Daniels Day Care Center; p. 243: © Lawrence Migdale/Stone/Getty

Chapter 8

Opener: © Larry Williams/Getty; p. 256: © Bob Daemmrich/The Image Works; 8.3: © SPL/Photo Researchers; 8.4: © Sam Gilbert, Institute of Cognitive Neuroscience, UK; p. 258: © C Squared Studios/Getty RF; p. 260: © Nestor Bachmann/dpa/Corbis; p. 263: © Eyewire Vol. EP078/Getty RF; p. 265: © Big Stock Photo; p. 267: © Ariel Skelley/Corbis; p. 268: © L. Perez/zefa/Corbis; p. 269 (top): © istock; p. 269 (bottom): © Michael Newman/Photo Edit; p. 273: Courtesy of Barbara Deloian; p. 275: © AP/Wide World Photos

Chapter 9

Opener: © Ariel Skelley/The Stock Market/Corbis; p. 282: From 'Open Window' © 1994 Municipality of Reggio Emilia Infant-toddler Centers and Preschools Published by Reggio Children; 9.3: © Paul Fusco/Magnum Photos; 9.5: © Bob Daemmrich/The Image Works; p. 287 (top): © James Wertsch/Washington University at St. Louis; p. 287 (bottom): © Gabe Palmer/Corbis; 9.6: Images courtesy of E. Bodrova and D.J. Leong, from *Tools of the Mind*, 2007; 9.7 (left): © A.R. Lauria/Dr. Michael Cole, Laboratory of Human Cognition, University of California, San Diego; 9.7 (right): © Bettmann/Corbis; p. 290 (bottom): © Ariel Skelley/Corbis; p. 293: © 2007 JamesKamp.com; p. 295: © Nita Winter; p. 297 (top): © Joe Baker, Images.com/Corbis; p. 297 (bottom): © AP/Wide World Photos; p. 299: © Ellen Senisi/The Image Works; p. 300: © Comstock/Punchstock RF; p. 301: © image100/Corbis RF; p. 302 (top): © AP/Wide World Photos; p. 302 (bottom): © Ariel Skelley/Corbis; p. 304: Courtesy of Yolanda Garcia; p. 305: © Ronnie Kaufman/The Stock Market/Corbis; p. 306: © image 100/SuperStock RF; p. 307 (top): © Karen Kasmauski/Corbis; p. 397 (bottom): © SOS Children's Villages (www.sos-usa.org)

Chapter 10

Opener: © Corbis RF; p. 315: © David Young-Wolff/Photo Edit; p. 316: © Corbis RF; p. 317 (top): © Imagestate Media/John Foxx/Imagestate RF; p. 317 (bottom): © LWA-Dann Tardif/zefa/Corbis; p. 318: © Yves De Braine/Black Star/Stock Photo; p. 319: © Randy Faris/Corbis; p. 320: © Corbis RF; p. 321: © Big Stock Photos; p. 323: © Digital Stock RF; 10.2: © Ariel Skelley/Corbis; p. 327: © Jose Luis Pelaez/Corbis; p. 328: © PunchStock RF; p. 329: D. Botkin (2000). Family play therapy: A creative approach to involving young children in family therapy. *Journal of Systematic Therapies*, 19, 30–41; p. 330: © David M. Wells/Corbis; p. 332 (top): © Don Hammond/Design Pics/Corbis RF; p. 332 (bottom): © Ariel Skelley/Corbis; p. 333 (top): © Ariel Skelley/Corbis; p. 333 (bottom): © Keith Brofsky/Getty RF; p. 334: © PunchStock RF; p. 336: © S. Gazin/The Image Works; p. 337: © Karen Kasmauski/Woodfin Camp & Associates; p. 338: © Spencer Grant/Photo Edit; p. 340: © Ariel Skelley/Corbis; p. 340: © Big Stock Photos; p. 342: © Bryan F. Peterson; p. 343: © Richard Hutchings/Photo Edit; p. 344: © Franco Vogt/Corbis

Chapter 11

Opener: © Michael Pole/The Stock Market/Corbis; p. 357: Â© Image Source/Corbis RF; p. 359 (top): © Aerial Skelley/Corbis; p. 359 (bottom): © PhotoDisc/Getty RF; p. 360: © Paul Barton/Corbis; p. 361: © Jules Frazier/Getty RF; p. 363: © Corbis/RF; p. 364: © Felicia Martinez/Photo Edit; p. 366: Courtesy of Sharon McLeod; 11.6: © AP/Wide World Photos; p. 370: © David Young-Wolff/Photo Edit; p. 372: Courtesy of

Charla Peltier; p. 373 (top): Used by permission of Don Johnston Inc.; p. 373 (bottom): © PunchStock RF; p. 374: © Michael Macor/San Francisco Chronicles/Corbis; p. 375: © Richard Hutchings/Photo Researchers

Chapter 12

Opener © Gabe Palmer/Corbis; p. 384: © Milwaukee Journal Sentinel, photographer Elizabeth Flores, © 2007 Journal Sentinel Inc., reproduced with permission; p. 386: © M & E Bernheim/Woodfin Camp & Associates; p. 387: © Gabe Palmer/Corbis; p. 389: © Brand X Pictures/PunchStock RF; p. 391: © Francisco Cruz/SuperStock; p. 392: © Stan Godlewski Photography; p. 393: © John Flavell; p. 394: © Ellen Senis/The Image Works; p. 396: © Robert J. Sternberg; p. 397: © Jay Gardner, 1998; p. 402: © Jill Cannefax/EKM-Nepenthe; p. 403: Courtesy of Sterling Jones; p. 404: © Doug Wilson/Corbis; p. 406: © Richard Howard; p. 407: © Gideon Mendel/Corbis; p. 409: © Elizabeth Crews; p. 410: © Elizabeth Crews/The Image Works; p. 412: © Ariel Skelley/Blend Images/Corbis RF; p. 413: © Ralf-Finn Hestoft/Corbis; p. 414: Courtesy of Sandra Graham; p. 415: © Eiji Miyazawa/Stock Photo

Chapter 13

Opener: © Stockbyte/Getty RF; p. 424: © Joseph Sohm/Visions of America/Corbis; p. 426: © Paul Edmondson/Corbis; p. 427 (top): © Jim Cummins/Corbis; p. 427 (bottom): © Jose Luis Pelaez/Corbis; p. 428 (top): © Jim Craigmyle/Corbis; p. 428 (bottom): © Christopher Thomas/Getty; p. 429 (top): © Reutuers/NewMedia Inc./Corbis; p. 429 (bottom): © AP/Wide World Photos; p. 433: © Raghu-Rai/Magnum Photos; p. 434: © Keith Carter; p. 435: © Norbert Schaefer/Corbis; p. 437: © Roy McMahon/Corbis RF; p. 438: Courtesy Deborah Tannen, Georgetown University; p. 440: © Catherine Gehm; p. 442: © Ariel Skelley/Corbis; p. 443: © Michael Newman/Photo Edit; p. 444: © Corbis RF; p. 447: © Catherine Ledner/Stone/Getty; p. 449: © Jiang Jin/SuperStock RF; p. 450 (top): © Martin Poole/Getty; p. 450 (bottom): © Elizabeth Crews; p. 451: © Bob Daemmrich/The Image Works; p. 452: © 2004, USA Today. Reprinted with permission; p. 453: © Michael Conroy/AP Wide World Photos; p. 454 (top): © Jose Luis Pelaez/Corbis; p. 454 (bottom): © John S. Abbott

Chapter 14

Opener: © Gabriela Medina/SuperStock; p. 464: © Ronald Cortes; p. 465: © M. Regine/The Image Bank/Getty; p. 467 (top): © Marleen Ferguson/Photo Edit; p. 467 (bottom): © Chuck Savage/The Stock Market/Corbis; p. 470: © VSS 22/Getty RF; p. 471 (top): © Jon Feingersh; p. 471 (bottom): © Value RF/Corbis RF; p. 473: © Davis Turner-Pool/Getty; p. 474: © Joel Gordon 1995; p. 475: © Marilyn Humphries; p. 476 (top): © Lawrence Migdale/Stock Boston; p. 476 (bottom): © Michael Ray; p. 478: © Louise Gubb/Corbis SABA; p. 480 (top): Courtesy Lynn Blankinship; p. 480 (bottom): © Dana Fineman; p. 481: © 1998 Frank Fournier; p. 482: © Stockbyte/Getty RF; p. 485: © Jim LoScalzo; p. 486: © Daniel Allan/Taxi/Getty; p. 487: © Charles Gullung/zefa/Corbis; p. 489 (top): © Karen Kasmausk/Corbis; p. 489 (bottom): © Ian Thraves/Alamy; p. 491: Courtesy of Boys and Girls Clubs of America

Chapter 15

Opener: © Vol. RFCD697/Corbis RF; p. 499: © David Young-Wolff/Photo Edit; p. 501: © Stewart Cohen/Stone/Getty; p. 503: © Big Cheese Photo/SuperStock RF; p. 504: © Scott Houston/Corbis; p. 505: Courtesy of Laura Bickford; p. 507: © David Young-Wolff/Photo Edit; p. 510: © Thinkstock/Corbis RF; p. 511: © Stone/Getty; p. 512: © SW Productions/Brand X Corbis RF; p. 513: © SuperStock RF; p. 515 (top): © Photo Spin/Getty RF; p. 515 (bottom): © D. Hurst/Alamy Images RF; p. 517: © Fujifots/The Image Works; p. 518: © Ed Kashi/Corbis; p. 519: Courtesy of I Have a Dream-Houston, Houston, TX; p. 521: © Comstock Select/Corbis RF; p. 522: Courtesy of Dr. Armando Ronquillo

Chapter 16

Opener: © George Disario/The Stock Market/Corbis; p. 530: © 2005, Globe Newspaper Company, Republished by permission. Matthew J. Lee, photographer; p. 531: © Dominic Rouse/The Image Bank/Getty; p. 532: © Bettmann/Corbis; p. 533: © A. Huber/U. Starke/zefa/Corbis; p. 534: © John Henley/Corbis; p. 535 (top): © Mike Watson Images/Corbis RF; p. 535 (bottom): © 1997 USA Today Library, photo by Robert Deutsch; p. 536: © ThinkStock/SuperStock RF; p. 538 (top): © Myrleen Ferguson Cate/Photo Edit; p. 538 (bottom): © Pat Vasquez-Cunningham 1999; p. 539: © Jeffry W. Myers/Stock Boston; 16.4: © Spencer Grant/Photo Edit; p. 541: © Tony Freeman/Photo Edit; p. 542: © Bob Jacobson/Corbis RF; p. 543 (top): © Rolf Bruderer/Corbis; 543 (bottom): © Tessa Codrington/Stone/Getty; p. 545 (top): © Tom & Dee Ann McCarthy/Corbis; p. 545 (bottom): © David De Lossy/The Image Bank/Getty p. 546: (top): © AFP/Getty; p. 546 (bottom): © AP/Wide World Photos; p. 547: © Getty RF; p. 548: © Daniel Laine; p. 549: © 1997 USA Today Library, photo by H. Darr Beiser; p. 550: © Yellow Dog Productions/Getty; p. 551: © L. Clarke/Corbis; p. 552: © Corbis RF; p. 553: © Chuck Savage/Corbis; p. 555 (top): Courtesy of Rodney Hammond, National Center for Injury Prevention and Control, CDCP; p. 555 (bottom): © Jim Smith/Photo Researchers; p. 558 (top): © David Young-Wolff/Stone/Getty; p. 558 (bottom): © Getty

Text/Line Art Credits

Chapter 1

p. 1: From the book *100 Ways to Build Self-Esteem and Teach Values* (formerly *Full Esteem Ahead*). Copyright © 1994, 2003, by Diana Loomans. Reprinted with permission of H.J. Kramer/New World Library, Novato, CA. www.newworldlibrary.com. **Fig. 1.2:** From Santrock, *Life-Span Development*, 12th ed., Fig. 1.4. Copyright © 2009. Reprinted by permission of The McGraw-Hill Companies, Inc. **Fig. 1.11:** "Bronfenbrenner's Ecological Theory of Development," from C.B. Kopp & J.B. Krakow, 1982, *Child Development in the Social Context*, p. 648. Copyright © 1982. Reprinted by permission of Pearson Education, Inc., Upper Saddle River, NJ. **Fig. 1.14:** From Crowley, et al., 2001, "Parents Explain More to Boys Than Girls During Shared Scientific Thinking," *Psychological Science*, 12, 258–261. Reprinted by permission of Wiley-Blackwell.

Chapter 2

Fig. 2.1: From Bonner, John, T.; The *Evolution of Culture in Animals*. Copyright © 1980 Princeton University Press. Reprinted by permission of Princeton University Press. **Fig. 2.9:** From Santrock, *Life-Span Development*, 12th ed., Fig. 2.9. Copyright © 2009. Reprinted by permission of The McGraw-Hill Companies, Inc. **Fig. 2.10:** From Center for Disease Control & Prevention, 2000, *Reproductive Technology Success Rates.* **Fig. 2.12:** From Santrock, *Life-Span Development*, 12th ed., Fig. 2.12. Copyright © 2009. Reprinted by permission of The McGraw-Hill Companies, Inc. **pp. 76–77:** From D. Brodzinsky & E. Pinderhughes, 2002, "Parenting and Child Development in Adoptive Families," in M. Bornstein (ed.) *Handbook of Parenting*, Vol. I, pp. 280–282. Reprinted by permission of Taylor & Francis Group LLC.

Chapter 3

Fig. 3.1: From Charles Carroll and Dean Miller, *Health: The Science of Human Adaptation*, 5th ed., Fig. 1.2. Copyright © 1991 The McGraw-Hill Companies. Reproduced with permission of The McGraw-Hill Companies. **Fig. 3.3:** Excerpted from *Pregnancy, Childbirth and the Newborn.* Copyright © 1984 by Childbirth Education Association of Seattle. Reprinted with permission from Meadowbrook Press, www.meadowbrookpress.com. **Fig. 3.5:** Data from Food and Nutrition Board, "Recommended Nutrient Increases for Adult Pregnancy," National Academy of Sciences, Washington, DC. **p. 96:** Exercise Guidelines for

Expectant Mothers, from S. B. Olds, M.L. London, & P.W. Ladewig, *Maternal Newborn Nursing: A Family-Centered Approach*, 3rd ed., p. 387–388. Copyright © 1988. Reproduced by permission of Pearson Education, Inc., Upper Saddle River, NJ. **Fig. 3.6:** From data presented by MacDorman, et al., 2002, "Annual Summary of Vital Statistics-2001," *Pediatrics*, 10, 1037–1052.

Chapter 4

p. 118: From P. Warrick, March 1, 1992, "The Fantastic Voyage of Tanner Roberts," *Los Angeles Times*, pp. E1, E12, E13. Reprinted by permission of the Los Angeles Times. **Fig. 4.2:** From Virginia A. Apgar, 1975, "A Proposal for a New Method of Evaluation of a Newborn Infant," in *Anesthesia and Analgesia*, Vol. 32, pp. 260–267. Reprinted by permission of Wolters Kluwer Health/Lippincott, Williams and Wilkins. **Fig. 4.4:** From Santrock, *Child Development*, 12th ed., Figure 3.9. Copyright © 2009 The McGraw-Hill Companies. Reproduced with permission of The McGraw-Hill Companies. **Fig. 4.5:** From Santrock, *Child Development*, 12th ed., Figure 3.10. Copyright © 2009 The McGraw-Hill Companies. Reproduced with permission of The McGraw-Hill Companies. **Fig. 4.6:** From Santrock, *Child Development*, 12th ed., Figure 3.11. Copyright © 2009 The McGraw-Hill Companies. Reproduced with permission of The McGraw-Hill Companies. **Fig. 4.7:** American College of Obstetricians and Gynecologists, 2002, *Postpartum Depression*. Obtained from the World Wide Web Medem Medical Library: www.medem.com/medlb

Chapter 5

Fig. 5.1: From Santrock, *Life-Span Development*, 12th ed., Fig. 4.1. Copyright © 2009. Reprinted by permission of The McGraw-Hill Companies, Inc. **Fig. 5.4:** From Santrock, *Life-Span Development*, 12th ed., Fig. 4.4. Copyright © 2009. Reprinted by permission of The McGraw-Hill Companies, Inc. **Fig. 5.6:** Reprinted by permission of the publisher from *The Postnatal Development of the Human Cerebral Cortex, Vol. I–VIII*, by Jesse LeRoy Conel. Cambridge, MA: Harvard University Press, Copyright © 1939, 1975 by the President and Fellows of Harvard College. **Fig. 5.7:** From Huttenlocher and Dabholkar, 1997, "Regional Differences in Synaptogenesis in Human Cerebral Cortex," *Journal of Comparative Neurology*, 387(2), 167–168, Figure 2. Reprinted with permission of Wiley-Blackwell. **Fig. 5.16:** From W.K. Frankenburg & J.B. Dodds, "The Denver Development Screening Test," *Journal of Pediatrics*, 71, 181–191. Copyright © 1967. Used by permission of Elsevier. **Fig. 5.18 (art):** Fantz' Experiment on Infants' Visual Perception, adapted from "The Origin of Form Perception," by R. L. Fantz, *Scientific American*, 1961. **Fig. 5.19:** From Slater, A., Morison, V. & Somers, M., 1988, "Orientation Discrimination and Cortical Functions in the Human Newborn," *Perception*, Vol. 17, pp. 597–602, Fig. 1 and Table 1. Reprinted by permission of Pion, London.

Chapter 6

p. 182 From "The Stories of Laurent, Lucienne, and Jacqueline," from J. Piaget, 1952, *The Origins of Intelligence in Children*, pp. 27, 159, 225, 273, 339, Routledge. Reprinted with permission of International Universities Press. **Fig. 6.1:** "Piaget's Six Substages of Sensorimotor Development," from Santrock, *Life-Span Development*, 10th ed., Fig. 6.1. Copyright © 2006 The McGraw-Hill Companies. Reproduced with permission of The McGraw-Hill Companies. **Fig. 6.3:** Raillargeon, R. & DeVoe, J., "Using the Violation of Expectations Method to Study Object Permanence in Infants," 1991, "Object Permanence in Young Children: Further Evidence," *Child Development*, 62, pp. 1227–1246. Reprinted with permission Wiley-Blackwell. **Fig. 6.8:** From Santrock, *Life-Span Development*, 12th ed., Fig. 5.6. Copyright © 2009. Reprinted by permission of The McGraw-Hill Companies, Inc. **Fig. 6.11:** From Santrock, *Life-Span Development*, 12th ed., Fig. 5.9. Copyright © 2009. Reprinted by permission of The McGraw-Hill Companies, Inc. **Fig. 6.12:** From Ramey, Craig T., Frances A. Campbell, and Clancy Blair.

"Retained in Grade by Age Fifteen, Abcedarian Project," in *Social Programs That Work*, Figure 6.7. Copyright © 1998 Russell Sage Foundation, 112 East 64th Street, New York, NY 10021. Reprinted with permission. **Fig. 6.13:** "The Rule Systems of Language," from Sherrel Lee Haight, *Language Overview*. Reprinted by permission. **Fig. 6.15:** From L. Bloom, "Language Acquisition in Development Context," in *Handbook of Child Psychology*, by W. Damon, ed. John Wiley & Sons, 1998. Reprinted with permission of John Wiley & Sons, Inc. **Fig. 6.16:** From Santrock, *Life-Span Development*, 12th ed., Fig. 5.13. Copyright © 2009. Reprinted by permission of The McGraw-Hill Companies, Inc. **Fig. 6.17:** From *Brain, Mind, and Behavior*, 3rd ed., by Floyd E. Bloom and Arlyne Lazerson. Copyright © 1985 by Educational Broadcasting Corporation. Used with permission of Worth Publishers. **Fig. 6.19:** From Hart & Risley, 1995, *Meaningful Differences in the Everyday Experiences of Young American Children*, Baltimore: Paul H. Brookes Publishing Co. Reprinted by permission of the publisher and the author.

Chapter 7

Fig. 7.4: Reprinted by permission of the publisher from *Infancy: Its Place in Human Development*, by Jerome Kagan, R.B. Kearsley and P.R. Zelazo, p. 107, Cambridge, Mass.: Harvard University Press, Copyright © 1978 by the President and Fellows of Harvard College. **Fig. 7.5:** From Santrock, *Life-Span Development*, 12th ed., p. 189. Copyright © 2009. Reprinted by permission of The McGraw-Hill Companies, Inc. **Fig. 7.7:** "Contact Time with Wire and Cloth Surrogate Mothers," from Santrock, *Life-Span Development*, 11th ed., Fig. 7.5. Copyright © 2008 The McGraw-Hill Companies. Reproduced with permission of The McGraw-Hill Companies. **Fig. 7.8:** From van Ijzendoorn & Kroonenberg, 1988, "Cross Cultural Patterns of Attachment," *Child Development*, 59, 147–156, Table 2. Used by permission of Wiley-Blackwell. **Fig. 7.11:** From Santrock, *Life-Span Development*, 12th ed., Fig. 6.10. Copyright © 2009. Reproduced with permission of The McGraw-Hill Companies. **Fig. 7.12:** From Santrock, *Life-Span Development*, 12th ed., Figure 6.11. Copyright © 2009. Reproduced with permission of The McGraw-Hill Companies.

Chapter 8

Fig. 8.1: "Height and Weight Changes From Two Through Six Years of Age," *CDC Growth Charts, 2000*. Center for Disease Control and Prevention, Atlanta, GA. **Fig. 8.2:** From *Human Biology and Ecology*, Second Edition, by Albert Damon. Copyright © 1977 by W.W. Norton & Company, Inc. Used by permission of W.W. Norton & Company, Inc. **Fig. 8.5:** "The Development of Gross Motor Skills in Early Childhood," data from *Performance Objectives for Preschool Children*, C.J. Schiner, ed. Sioux Falls, SD: Adapt Press, 1974. **Fig. 8.7:** Based on "The Stages of Young Children's Artistic Drawings," from Rhoda Kellogg, 1970, "Understanding Children's Art," in Readings in Developmental Psychology Today, P. Cramer, ed. Del Mar, CA: CRM. **Fig. 8.8:** From the Food and Nutrition Board. **Fig. 8.10:** From "Contexts and Young Children's Safety," from Sleet & Mercy, 2003, "Promotion of Safety, Security, and Well-Being," in M.H. Bornstein, et al. (eds.), *Well-Being*, Table 7.2. Reprinted by permission of Taylor & Francis Group LLP.

Chapter 9

Fig. 9.1: From Santrock, *Psychology: Essentials*, 2nd ed. Copyright © 2005 The McGraw-Hill Companies. Reproduced with permission of The McGraw-Hill Companies. **Fig. 9.2:** "The Symbolic Drawings of Young Children," reprinted courtesy of D.Wolf and J. Nove. Reprinted by permission of Dennie Palmer Wolf, Annenberg Institute, Brown University. **Fig. 9.3 (art):** From Santrock, *Life-Span Development*, 9th ed., Figure 8.8. Copyright © 2004 The McGraw-Hill Companies. Reproduced with permission of The McGraw-Hill Companies. **Fig. 9.5:** From Santrock, *Life-Span Development*, 9th ed., Figure 8.10. Copyright © 2004 The McGraw-Hill Companies. Reproduced with permission of The McGraw-Hill Companies. **Fig. 9.6:**

"Writing Progress of a 5-Month-Old Boy Over Two Months," From Bodrova, E. & Leong, D. J. (2001, 2007). *Tools of the Mind*. Geneva, Switzerland: International Bureau of Education, UNESCO. Reprinted with permission. **Fig. 9.7:** From Santrock, *Life-Span Development*, 9th ed., Figure 8.11. Copyright © 2004 The McGraw-Hill Companies. Reproduced with permission of The McGraw-Hill Companies. **Fig. 9.8:** Reprinted from E. Vorpillot, 1968, "The Development of Scanning Strategies," *Journal of Experimental Child Psychology*, 6(4), 632–650 Figure 1. Copyright © 1968 Elsevier. **Fig. 9.9:** "Developmental Changes in Memory Span," from Dempster, 1981, Memory Span," *Psychological Bulletin*, 80, 63–100. Copyright © 1981 by the American Psychological Association. Reprinted by permission. **Fig. 9.10:** From Santrock, *Life-Span Development*, 9th ed., Figure 8.15. Copyright © 2004 The McGraw-Hill Companies. Reproduced with permission of The McGraw-Hill Companies. **Fig. 9.11:** From Santrock, *Child Development*, 12th ed., Figure 7.14. Copyright © 2009 The McGraw-Hill Companies. Reproduced with permission of The McGraw-Hill Companies. **Fig. 9.13:** From Jean Berko, 1958, "The Child's Learning of English Morphology," in *Word*, Vol. 14, p. 154. Reprinted courtesy of Jean Berko Gleason. **Fig. 9.14:** Excerpted from the NAEYC Position Statement on Developmentally Appropriate Practice in Early Childhood Programs Serving Children from Birth through Age 8. Reprinted with permission from the National Association for the Education of Young Children. www.naeyc.org. **Fig. 9.15:** From Santrock, *Life-Span Development*, 9th ed., Figure 8.18. Copyright © 2004 The McGraw-Hill Companies. Reproduced with permission of The McGraw-Hill Companies.

Chapter 10

p. 314: From Craig Lesley, 2005, *Burning Fence: A Western Memoir of Fatherhood*, pp. 8–10. Copyright © 2005 by the author. Reprinted by permission of St. Martin's Press, LLC. **Fig. 10.1:** From Santrock, *Life-Span Development*, 12th ed., Fig. 8.1. Copyright © 2009. Reproduced with permission of The McGraw-Hill Companies. **Fig. 10.4:** From Santrock, *Life-Span Development*, 12th ed., Fig. 8.4. Copyright © 2009. Reproduced with permission of The McGraw-Hill Companies. **Fig. 10.5:** From the U.S. Census Bureau. **Fig. 10.7:** From D.F. Robitaille and R.A. Gardner, *The IEA Study of Mathematics II: Contexts and Outcomes of School Mathematics*. Reprinted by permission.

Chapter 11

Fig. 11.1: From *Nelson Textbook of Pediatrics*, R.E. Behman & V.C. Vaughan, eds. W.B. Saunders, 1987. Copyright © 1987 Elsevier. **Fig. 11.2:** From B.J. Cratty, *Perceptual and Motor Development in Infants and Children*. Prentice-Hall, 1979. Reprinted by permission of Pearson Education, Inc., Upper Saddle River, NJ. **Fig. 11.3:** Data presented by Health Management Resources, 2001. *Child Health and Times*. Boston: Health Management Resources. p. 358 Reprinted with permission from the Women's Sports Foundation's Parents' Guide to Girls' Sports, www.womenssportsfoundation.org. **Fig.11.5:** From Santrock, Educational Psychology, 4th ed., Fig. 6.1. Copyright © 2009 The McGraw-Hill Companies. Reproduced with permission of The McGraw-Hill Companies. **Fig. 11.7:** From Santrock, Educational Psychology, 4th ed., Fig. 6.3, Copyright © 2009 The McGraw-Hill Companies. Reproduced with permission of The McGraw-Hill Companies. **Fig. 11.9:** From Santrock, *Life-Span Development*, 12th ed., Fig. 9.7. Copyright © 2009. Reproduced with permission of The McGraw-Hill Companies.

Chapter 12

Fig. 12.1: From John Santrock, *Life Span Development*, 12th ed., Figure 10.4. Copyright © 2009. Reproduced with permission of The McGraw-Hill Companies. **Fig. 12.2:** Based on M. Pressley, et al., "Short-Term Memory, Verbal Competence, and Age as Predictors of Imagery Instructional Effectiveness," *Journal of Experimental*

Child Psychology, 43, 194–211. **Fig. 12.3:** From Santrock, *Psychology: Essentials*, 2nd ed., Figure 10.1. Copyright © 2005 The McGraw-Hill Companies. Reproduced with permission of The McGraw-Hill Companies. **Fig. 12.7:** From The Increase in IQ Scores from 1932 to 1997," by Dr. Ulric Neisser. Reprinted by permission.

Chapter 13

Fig. 13.2: Reprinted with permission from the Society for Research in Child Development. **Fig. 13.3:** Reproduced by special permission of the Publisher, Mind Garden, Inc., www.mindgarden.com from the *Bem Sex Role Inventory*, by Sandra Bem. Copyright © 1978, 1981 by Consulting Psychologists Press, Inc. Further reproduction is prohibited without the Publisher's written consent. **Fig. 13.4:** From Nansel, et al., 2001, "Bullying Behaviors Among U.S. Youth," *Journal of the American Medical Association*, Vol. 285, pp. 2094–2100.

Chapter 14

Fig. 14.1: From J.M. Tanner, et al., "Standards from Birth to Maturity for Height, Weight, Height Velocity: British Children," *Archives of Diseases in Childhood*, 41. Copyright © 1966. Used by permission of BMJ Publishing Group. **Fig. 14.4:** Based on "The Prefrontal Cortex," from *U.S. News & World Report*, Special Issue, "Mysteries of the Teen Years," May 1, 2005. **Fig. 14.5:** MMWR, 2006. **Fig. 14.7:** From John W. Santrock, *Life-Span Development*, 11e, Fig. 12.10, p. 413. Copyright © 2008 The McGraw-Hill Companies, Inc. Used with permission. **Fig. 14.8:** "Percentage of U.S. High School Students Who Ate Fruits and Vegetables ≥ Five Times a Day, 1999 to 2005," after data presented by the MMWR, 9 June 2006. *Youth Risk Behavior Surveillance-United States, 2005*, Vol. 255. Atlanta: Center for Disease

Control & Prevention. **Fig. 14.9:** From Figure 3 in Nader, P.R., Bradley, R.H., Houts, R.M., McRitichie, S.L., and O'Brian, M. (2008). "Moderate to vigorous physical activity from 9 to 15 years," JAMA 300, 295–305. Reprinted with permission. **Fig. 14.11:** "Developmental Changes in U.S. Adolescents' Sleep Patterns on an Average School Night," after data presented by the MMWR, *Youth Risk Behavior Surveillance-United States, 2007*, Vol. 57, Table 95. Atlanta: Center for Disease Control & Prevention. **Fig. 14.12:** "Trends in Drug Use by U.S. Eighth-, Tenth-, and Twelfth-Grade Students," from L.D. Johnston, P.M. O'Malley, & J.G. Bachman, 2001, *The Monitoring of the Future: National Results on Adolescent Drug Use*. Washington, DC: National Institute on Drug Abuse. **Fig. 14.13:** "Young Adolescents' Reports of Alcohol Use in the Family Matters Program," from K.E. Bauman, S.T. Ennett, et al., 2002, "Influence of a Family Program on Adolescent Smoking and Drinking Prevalence," *Prevention Science*, 3. pp. 35–42. With kind permission of the author and Springer Science and Business Media.

Chapter 15

Fig. 15.1: From H. Lee Swanson, "What Develops in Working Memory? A Life-Span Perspective," *Developmental Psychology*, 34(4), 986–1000. Copyright © 1998 by the American Psychological Association. Reprinted by permission. **Fig. 15.2:** Graph from L. J. Sax, A. W. Astin, J. A. Lindholm, W. S. Korn, V. B. Saenz, and K. M. Mahoney (2003). The American Freshman: National Norms for Fall 2003 Los Angeles: Higher Education Research Institute, UCLA. Data from L. J. Sax, S. Hurtado, J. A. Lindholm, A. W. Astin, W. S. Korn, and K. M. Mahoney (2004) The American Freshman: Norms for Fall 2004 Los Angeles: Higher Education Research Institute, UCLA. **Fig. 15.3:** From

Koenig, L.A. et al., "Stability and change in religiousness during emerging adulthood," *Developmental Psychology*, 44, 523–543, Table 1, p. 535.Copyright © American Psychological Association. Reprinted by permission. **Fig. 15.4:** From Santrock, *Adolescence*, 12th ed., Figure 10.2. Copyright © 2008 The McGraw-Hill Companies. Reproduced with permission of The McGraw-Hill Companies. **Fig. 15.5:** Reproduced by special permission of the publisher, Psychological Assessment Resources, Inc., 16204 North Florida Avenue, Lutz, FL 33549, from *Making Vocational Choices*, Third Edition. Copyright © 1973, 1985, 1992, 1997 by Psychological Assessment Resources, Inc. All rights reserved.

Chapter 16

Fig. 16.1: From Santrock, *Adolescence*, 12th ed., Figure 4.2. Copyright © 2008 The McGraw-Hill Companies. Reproduced with permission of The McGraw-Hill Companies. **Fig. 16.3:** From *Divergent Realities* by Reed Larson. Cambridge, MA: Perseus Books. Reprinted by permission of Basic Books, a member of Perseus Books Group. **Fig. 16.5:** From Santrock, *Topical Life Span Development*, 4th ed., Figure 15.3. Copyright © 2008 The McGraw-Hill Companies. Reproduced with permission of The McGraw-Hill Companies. **Fig. 16.6:** After Sellers, et al., 2006, "Racial Identity Matters," *Journal of Research on Adolescence*, 16(2), 187–216, Table 1. Reprinted by permission of Wiley-Blackwell. **Fig. 16.7:** "Percentage of U.S. 9th- to 12th-Grade Students Who Seriously Considered Attempting Suicide in the Previous 12 Months from 1991 to 2005," *National Risk Behavior Survey 1991–2005: Trends in the Prevalance of Suicide Ideating and Attempts*. Centers for Disease Control & Prevention.

NAME INDEX

SUBJECT INDEX

C

Caffeine as teratogen, 103
Cancer
　breast versus bottle feeding and, 154
　in middle and late childhood,
　　363–364
Cardiovascular disease in middle and
　late childhood, 364–365
Career counselor, career as, 53
Career development
　in adolescence, 520–523
　developmental changes and, 520
　exploration, decision making, and
　　planning and, 521
　Holland's personality-type theory of,
　　520–521
　sociocultural influences on, 521–522
Careers in child development, 50–55
　in clinical and counseling fields, 8,
　　52–53, 55, 71, 135, 198, 372,
　　522, 555
　in education and research, 43, 50–52,
　　242, 304, 366, 403, 480, 505, 522
　families and relationships and,
　　55, 329
　in medical, nursing, and physical
　　development fields, 53–54, 122,
　　135, 157, 454, 555
Caregiving. *See also* Child care; Parenting
　styles of, attachment and, 236–237
Care perspective, 434
Caring, positive youth development
　and, 466
Case studies as data collection
　method, 36–37
Categorization in infancy, 196–197
Celera Corporation, 64
CenteringPregnancy, 98
Centration in early childhood,
　284–286
Cephalocaudal pattern, 145
Cerebral cortex, 146
Cerebral palsy, 373
Cesarean delivery, 123–124
Character
　moral, 435
　positive youth development and, 466
Character education, 509
Childbirth. *See also* Birth process
　methods of, 120–124
Child care, 240–244
　longitudinal study of, 243–244
　variations in, 242–243
Child-care director, career as, 242
Child-care health consultant, career
　as, 54
Child-centered kindergartens, 301
Child development
　importance of studying, 7
　modern study of, 14–16
Child development theories,
　23–34
　behavioral, 29–30, 35
　cognitive, 27–29, 35
　eclectic orientation to, 34, 35
　ecological, 32–34, 35
　ethological, 31–32, 35
　psychoanalytic, 23–27, 35
　social cognitive, 30–31, 35
Child-directed speech, 209
Childhood, early views of, 14
Childhood amnesia, 195
Child life specialist, career as, 55

Child maltreatment, 329–331
　context of, 330
　developmental consequences of,
　　330–331
　types of, 330
Child neglect, 330
Child psychiatrist, career as, 454
Child-rearing leave, 241
Children, improving lives of, 8–13
Child welfare worker, career as, 55
Chlamydia, 477
Chorionic villus sampling (CVS), 72, 73
Chromosomal abnormalities, 68–69
Chromosomes, 64–66
　gender and, 321
　sex, 65, 321
Chronosystem in Bronfenbrenner's
　ecological theory, 33
Cigarette smoking
　in adolescence, 486–487, 487–488
　environmental tobacco smoke and, in
　　early childhood, 273
　during pregnancy, 103–104
Classical conditioning, 30
Clinical child psychologist, career as, 8
Clinical psychologist, career as, 52, 135
Cliques, 542–543
Cocaine as teratogen, 104–105
Cognition, social, in middle and late
　childhood, 446
Cognitive development. *See also*
　　Intelligence; Language; Memory
　in adolescence, 496–526
　brain and, 257–258
　in early childhood, 257–258, 280–310
　in infancy, 180–216
　infant measures of, 125, 198–199
　information processing and. *See*
　　Attention; Information processing
　　entries; Memory
　language and. *See* Language
　in middle and late childhood,
　　382–419, 437
　nutrition and, 200
　Piaget's theory of. *See* Piaget's theory
　poverty and, 200–201
　religion and, 511–512
　television and, 345
Cognitive influences on gender
　development, 324
Cognitive moral education, 509–510
Cognitive neuroscience
　developmental, 17
　social, 18
Cognitive processes, 17, 19
Cognitive theories, 27–29
　evaluation of, 29
　information-processing. *See*
　　Information processing *entries*
　of Piaget. *See* Piaget's theory
　of Vygotsky. *See* Vygotsky's theory
College advisor, career as, 522
College/university professor, career as,
　50, 51
Color vision in infancy, 170
Commitment, identity and, 533
Communication
　about divorce, 335–336
　gender differences in, 438–439
Companionship, friendship and, 449
Compassion, positive youth
　development and, 466
Competence, positive youth
　development and, 465

Computers, adolescent use of, 550–551
Concept formation in infancy, 196
Conclusions, drawing in research, 23
Concrete operational stage, 27, 28,
　385–386
Conditioning in infancy, 192
Confidentiality in research, 42
Connectedness, 535
Connection, positive youth
　development and, 466
Conscience in early childhood, 319–320
Consent, informed, 42
Conservation in Piaget's theory, 284–285
Constructive play, 343
Constructivist approach, 450–451
Consumer science educator, career as,
　52, 480
Contexts, 9
　of abuse, 330
　child are in, 266
　emotional regulation and, 224
　gender in, 440
　social, socioemotional development in
　　infancy and, 238–244
　sociocultural. *See* Culture; Sociocultural
　　entries
Continuity-discontinuity issue, 20
Contraceptives, use in adolescence,
　476–477
Control groups, 39
Control processes, 389
Controversial children, 444, 445
Conventional reasoning, 431, 432
　social, 434
Convergent thinking, 390
Cooing in infancy, 205
Cooperative play, 342–343
Coordination of secondary circular
　reactions, 186
Coparenting, 329
Coping in infancy, 224
Corpus callosum, puberty and, 472
Correlational research, 37–38
Correlation coefficient, 38
Co-sleeping, 151
Counseling psychiatrist, career as, 52
Counselors
　career, career as, 53
　drug, career as, 53
　genetic, career as, 54, 71
　high school, career as, 522
　school, career as, 52–53
Creative thinking
　in middle and late childhood, 390–392
　strategies for increasing, 391–392
Crisis, identity and, 533
Critical thinking
　in adolescence, 505
　in middle and late childhood, 390
Cross-cultural studies, 10
Cross-sectional research, 39–40
Crowds, 543
Crying in infancy, 205, 222–223
Cultural bias
　intelligence testing and, 401
　in research, 43–44
Cultural-familial retardation, 402
Culture, 9–10. *See also* Sociocultural
　　entries
　achievement and, 414
　adolescence and, 546–548
　adolescent suicide and, 557
　beliefs about pregnancy and, 99–100
　intelligence and, 398

　moral reasoning and, 433
　secondary schools and, 516–517
　Strange Situation and, 235
　temperament and, 227
Culture-fair tests, 401
Culture-reduced tests, 401
Curriculum for early childhood
　education, 304–305
Cyberbullying, 448, 551
Cystic fibrosis, 70

D

Data collection in research, 23, 34–37
　case studies for, 36–37
　observation for, 35–36
　physiological measures for, 37
　standardized tests for, 36
　surveys and interview for, 36
Dating in adolescence, 543–545
Death
　accidental, 271
　in adolescence, leading causes of, 485
　global mortality rates and, 274–275
　sudden infant death syndrome and,
　　151–152
Debriefing in research, 42
Deception in research, 42
Decision making in adolescence,
　503–505
Deferred imitation, 195–196
Delivery. *See* Birth process; Childbirth
Dendrites, 148
Denver Developmental Screening
　Test II, 261
Dependent variables, 39
Depression
　in adolescence, 554–556
　postpartum, 132–133
Depth perception in infancy, 171
Dermatitis, atopic, breast versus bottle
　feeding and, 154
Descriptive research, 37
Design stage, 262
Development. *See also specific areas
　of development, e.g.* Emotional
　development
　definition of, 7
　importance of studying, 7
　issues in, 19–21
　periods of, 18, 19
　processes of, 17–18, 19
　stages of. *See* Erikson's theory; Piaget's
　　theory; Stages of development
Developmental arithmetic disorder, 369
Developmental assets in adolescence,
　490–491
Developmental cognitive
　neuroscience, 17
Developmentally appropriate
　practice, 302
Developmental psychologist, career
　as, 43
Developmental quotient (DQ), 198
Developmental social neuroscience, 472
　attachment and, 237
Diabetes, 70
　breast versus bottle feeding and, 154
　in middle and late childhood, 362
　teratogenic effects of, 107
　type 1, 364
　type 2, 364
Diagnostic tests, prenatal, 72–73
Diarrhea, childhood death due to, 274